NATIONAL
MONUMENTS
of the
U.S.A.

WIDE EYED EDITIONS

CON

TENTS

CENTRAL
24-39

EAST
6-23

WELCOME TO THE
NATIONAL MONUMENTS OF THE U.S.A.

You're on the way to some amazing places! On your journey through the national monuments, you'll find quarries rich with dinosaur fossils, prairies bursting with flowers, and caves that shelter sparkling crystals. You'll paddle past majestic moose, dive to the ocean's deepest canyons, and get swept up in important events that shaped the U.S.A. Historic places, extraordinary landscapes, special plants, and awesome animals—the monuments have them all!

The first national monument was created in 1906, when President Theodore Roosevelt used the Antiquities Act to protect (or "designate") a spectacular rock formation in Wyoming called Devils Tower. Now, there are close to 130 national monuments! As this book went to print, the newest one was Camp Hale-Continental Divide National Monument, a 53,804-acre area in Colorado's Rocky Mountains, protected in October 2022.

The National Park Service preserves many of these incredible sites. Others are managed by agencies that focus on land, forests, wildlife, or oceans. National monuments are protected because they are historically, culturally, or scientifically important—which means they can hold everything from the homes where important leaders once lived to coastal rainforests and vast expanses of ocean.

The national monuments tell stories of how this land, and this country, came to be how they are today. Start with the landscape itself: some monuments explain how it was formed by enormous earthquakes, immense eruptions, and mountain-carving glaciers. Learn about animals that lived millions of years ago, and wildlife you can see right now.

Monuments tell people's stories across time, too. From the beginning, these stories include Indigenous peoples. National monuments protect places that remain sacred to Indigenous peoples today. Some monuments recount tales of the faces and places of the U.S.A.'s early days, from the American Revolution to railroads. And don't miss monuments honoring people who've helped this country become a more equal place for everyone.

Whatever you're interested in, you'll find a national monument for you.
So, turn the page, and let the stories begin!

EAST

The eastern United States is packed with historical monuments. Some of these monuments commemorate a time before the U.S.A. became a country, and some commemorate events so recent that your family may even have stories about them. In the east, you can imagine being a soldier during the American Revolution, or an immigrant greeted by the Statue of Liberty. Soak up the sights and sounds on the streets of New York City and Washington, D.C., where people have worked for equality for many years. Find out about the people who have shaped this land, from the first peoples here to presidents, activists, artists, scientists, and more. Along with history, this region is filled with places where you can learn more about the natural world. Listen to the rush of Maine's rivers and look for the tracks of lynx and moose in the snow. On the coast of Florida, feel the salt air on your face from atop a tower made of fossilized seashells as dolphins leap and play in the waters below.

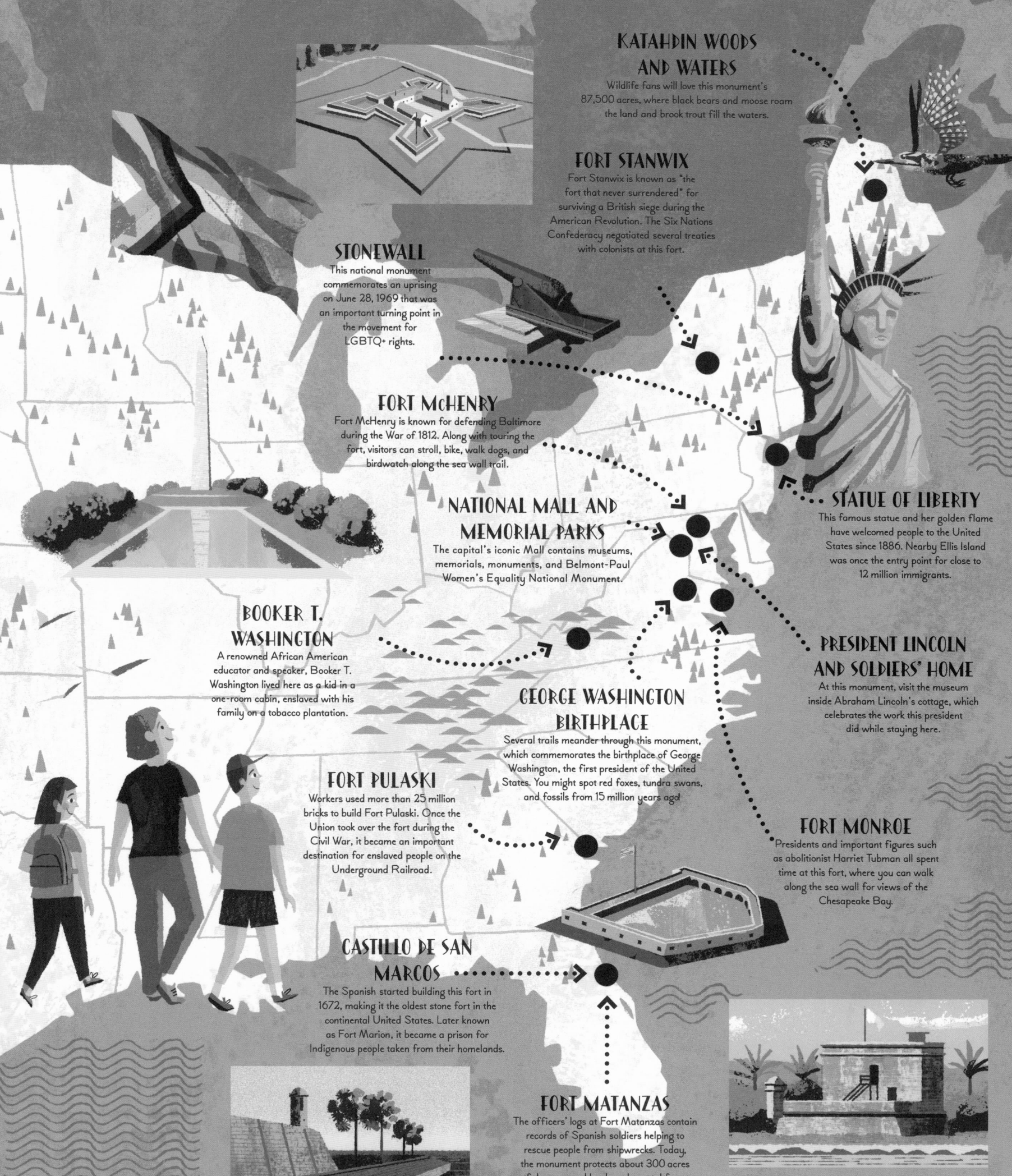

KATAHDIN WOODS AND WATERS

Wildlife fans will love this monument's 87,500 acres, where black bears and moose roam the land and brook trout fill the waters.

FORT STANWIX

Fort Stanwix is known as "the fort that never surrendered" for surviving a British siege during the American Revolution. The Six Nations Confederacy negotiated several treaties with colonists at this fort.

STONEWALL

This national monument commemorates an uprising on June 28, 1969 that was an important turning point in the movement for LGBTQ+ rights.

FORT MCHENRY

Fort McHenry is known for defending Baltimore during the War of 1812. Along with touring the fort, visitors can stroll, bike, walk dogs, and birdwatch along the sea wall trail.

NATIONAL MALL AND MEMORIAL PARKS

The capital's iconic Mall contains museums, memorials, monuments, and Belmont-Paul Women's Equality National Monument.

STATUE OF LIBERTY

This famous statue and her golden flame have welcomed people to the United States since 1886. Nearby Ellis Island was once the entry point for close to 12 million immigrants.

BOOKER T. WASHINGTON

A renowned African American educator and speaker, Booker T. Washington lived here as a kid in a one-room cabin, enslaved with his family on a tobacco plantation.

PRESIDENT LINCOLN AND SOLDIERS' HOME

At this monument, visit the museum inside Abraham Lincoln's cottage, which celebrates the work this president did while staying here.

GEORGE WASHINGTON BIRTHPLACE

Several trails meander through this monument, which commemorates the birthplace of George Washington, the first president of the United States. You might spot red foxes, tundra swans, and fossils from 15 million years ago!

FORT PULASKI

Workers used more than 25 million bricks to build Fort Pulaski. Once the Union took over the fort during the Civil War, it became an important destination for enslaved people on the Underground Railroad.

FORT MONROE

Presidents and important figures such as abolitionist Harriet Tubman all spent time at this fort, where you can walk along the sea wall for views of the Chesapeake Bay.

CASTILLO DE SAN MARCOS

The Spanish started building this fort in 1672, making it the oldest stone fort in the continental United States. Later known as Fort Marion, it became a prison for Indigenous people taken from their homelands.

FORT MATANZAS

The officers' logs at Fort Matanzas contain records of Spanish soldiers helping to rescue people from shipwrecks. Today, the monument protects about 300 acres of dunes, marshland, and coastal forest around the fort.

STATUE OF LIBERTY

Imagine it's 1892, and you're arriving to the United States after a long boat ride from Europe. Your family tells you that you're here to start a new life, far from the problems of home. But you're exhausted, seasick, and definitely unsure about what lies ahead. Then you see her: the Statue of Liberty, holding up her torch to light your way into New York Harbor. Since 1886, Lady Liberty has greeted immigrants and travelers alike—and for many, she symbolizes the freedom and equality that people hope to find in the U.S.A. Today, visit her by boarding a ferry to Liberty Island, where you can climb up 377 steps to look through the windows in her seven-pointed crown. Then ride the ferry to Ellis Island and learn more about the dreams and struggles of some of the people who came here to make this country their new home.

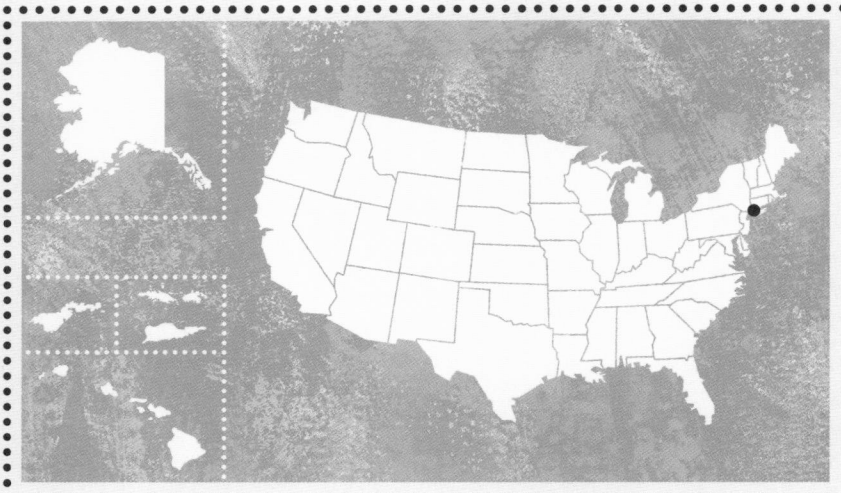

STATUE OF LIBERTY

STATES:
New York and New Jersey

DESIGNATED:
1924

THE STATUE TAKES SHAPE
French sculptor Auguste Bartholdi designed the outside of the statue. An architect and engineer named Gustave Eiffel, who later designed the Eiffel Tower in France, created the plan for the iron structure that held the statue up from the inside.

A LONG JOURNEY
People coming to the United States often traveled from far away. So did the statue. She was built in France, then taken apart and packed into 214 crates. These crates went onto a French navy ship, which traveled for 27 days to get to the statue's new island home.

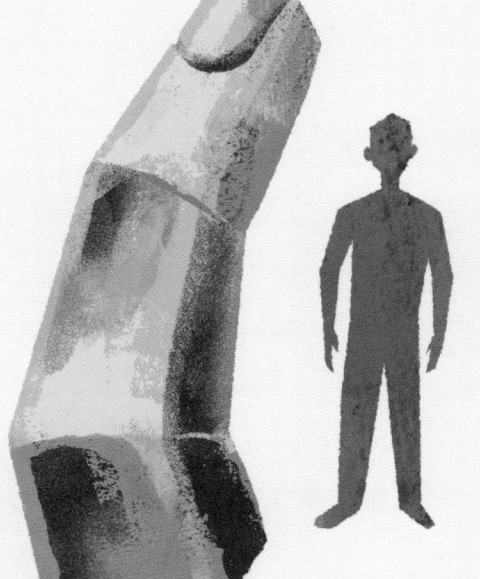

MEASURING UP
The Statue of Liberty stretches 305 feet, 1 inch from the ground below the pedestal to the tip of her torch. Her index finger is eight feet long. That's a lot taller than most grown-ups!

SKIN DEEP
Lady Liberty's skin is made from copper and is as thick as two pennies pressed together. At first, her skin was the color of pennies, too. But chemical reactions between the copper and the harbor's air and moisture turned her skin the beautiful blue-green it is today.

BEST FOOT FORWARD
Rangers think that if the statue needed new shoes, she'd ask for size 659. Her substantial feet are stepping over a broken shackle and chain, a symbol of the end of slavery in the U.S.

A STATUE'S NEW LOOK

In the 1980s, the Statue of Liberty got a makeover for her 100th birthday. Workers replaced every iron support bar with stainless steel and patched up her copper skin. More than $6 million of the money needed to fix her up came from schoolkids across the country.

WEATHERING THE WEATHER

During big storms, the Statue of Liberty can sway as much as three inches. Her torch can move six inches. She also gets struck by lightning many times each year.

OYSTER COMEBACK

Long before this area welcomed immigrants from overseas, the first people—the Lenape—gathered oysters from the enormous oyster beds surrounding these islands. Later, pollution and overharvesting wiped out oysters. But they're making a comeback: New Yorkers are working to restore a billion oysters to the harbor by 2035.

IMMIGRATION STATION

Most of the people who immigrated to the United States through Ellis Island came from all over Europe. People think about 40 percent of Americans have at least one ancestor who came to Ellis Island. Your friends or family may even tell stories about relatives arriving here—or you might have your own story about coming to this country!

AN ENORMOUS PRESENT

The Statue of Liberty was a gift from France to the people of the United States to celebrate the country's 100th birthday in 1876 and the friendship between the two countries. Workers in France made the statue. In the U.S., grown-ups and kids raised money to build its pedestal.

THE TORCH

When the statue was repaired, construction teams gave her a brand-new torch with a flame covered in 24-karat gold. In the Statue of Liberty Museum, you can stand next to the original torch, which is 16 feet high and weighs 3,600 pounds.

NEW LIFE, NEW CHALLENGES

Moving to a new country was very difficult for many of the immigrants arriving both at Ellis Island and elsewhere in the U.S.A. Many challenges face those coming to this country today, too—and moving here can be even harder for people from some countries and backgrounds. Imagine what it would be like to live in an unfamiliar place, far from the life you know. What would you do to feel at home?

11

STONEWALL

From where you're standing on Christopher Street in New York City, you might see rainbow flags waving in the breeze and wonder what makes this place special. To find out, imagine you've traveled back to 1969. You're here on a June night in Greenwich Village, a diverse neighborhood filled with artists, musicians, and people who want a place to express themselves. But you've time-traveled to a moment when not everyone can be themselves. In 1969, many laws discriminate against people who are LGBTQ+ (lesbian, gay, bisexual, transgender, or queer). They can't meet up, dance, or wear certain kinds of clothes— and they can go to jail for breaking these rules. Tonight, the police show up at the Stonewall Inn to arrest people inside. Outside on Christopher Street, everyone gets frustrated and angry. Eventually, the people start an uprising. What happened at Stonewall played a big part in the movement to make the country a better, safer place for LGBTQ+ people. The movement continues today—and in 2016, Stonewall became the first national monument dedicated to LGBTQ+ history.

STONEWALL

STATE: *New York*

DESIGNATED: *2016*

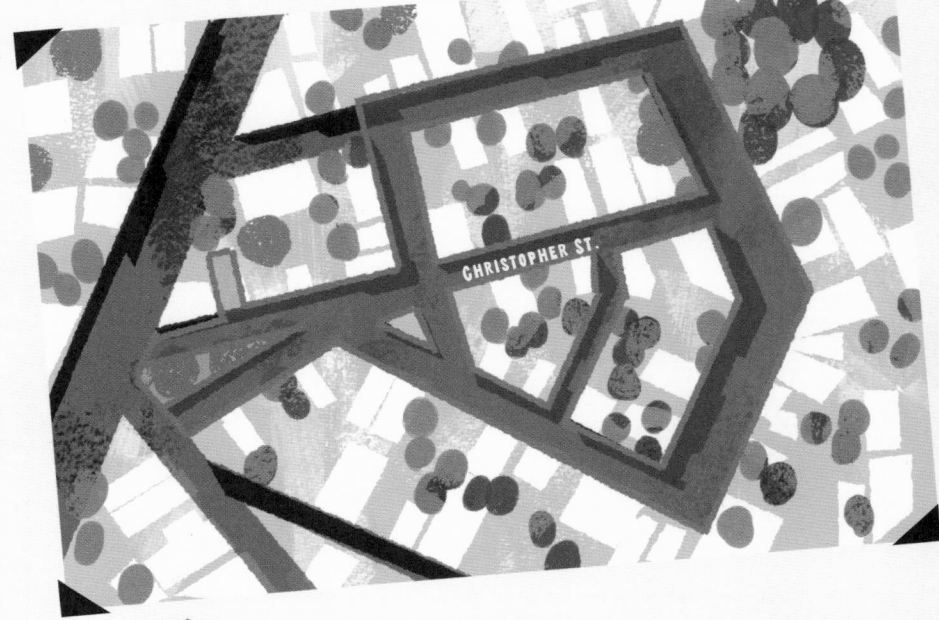

SMALL MONUMENT, BIG IMPACT

The Stonewall National Monument includes the buildings at 51 and 53 Christopher Street, which was the location of the original Stonewall Inn, as well as Christopher Park and the surrounding streets. At 7.7 acres, it's one of the smallest national monuments, but it has a big role in LGBTQ+ history.

RAINBOW FLAG

The rainbow flag is a symbol of the LGBTQ+ civil rights movement and of pride in the community. Over the years, people have created new versions of the flag to include more people in the LGBTQ+ community.

CHRISTOPHER PARK

This triangle-shaped park was an important place for LGBTQ+ youth to meet up during the 1960s, and it's still important today. Now you'll also find statues of two men standing and two women sitting on a bench. This sculpture, called *Gay Liberation*, was made by artist George Segal to honor the events at Stonewall.

CHRISTOPHER STREET LIBERATION DAY

A year after the uprising at Stonewall, thousands of people marched from Christopher Street up to Central Park to protest how police and society treated LGBTQ+ people. While people had been working for LGBTQ+ rights for many years, Stonewall sparked new events, organizations, and big protests like this one.

LGBTQ+ DIVERSITY

Black, white, brown, from a big city, from a small town—LGBTQ+ people come from everywhere and have a range of different backgrounds and experiences.

PRIDE MONTH

The uprising at Stonewall began on June 28, 1969. People now celebrate the month of June as Pride Month to honor this anniversary and the importance of the LGBTQ+ community. There is a huge parade in New York City, as well as parades and events across the country and around the world.

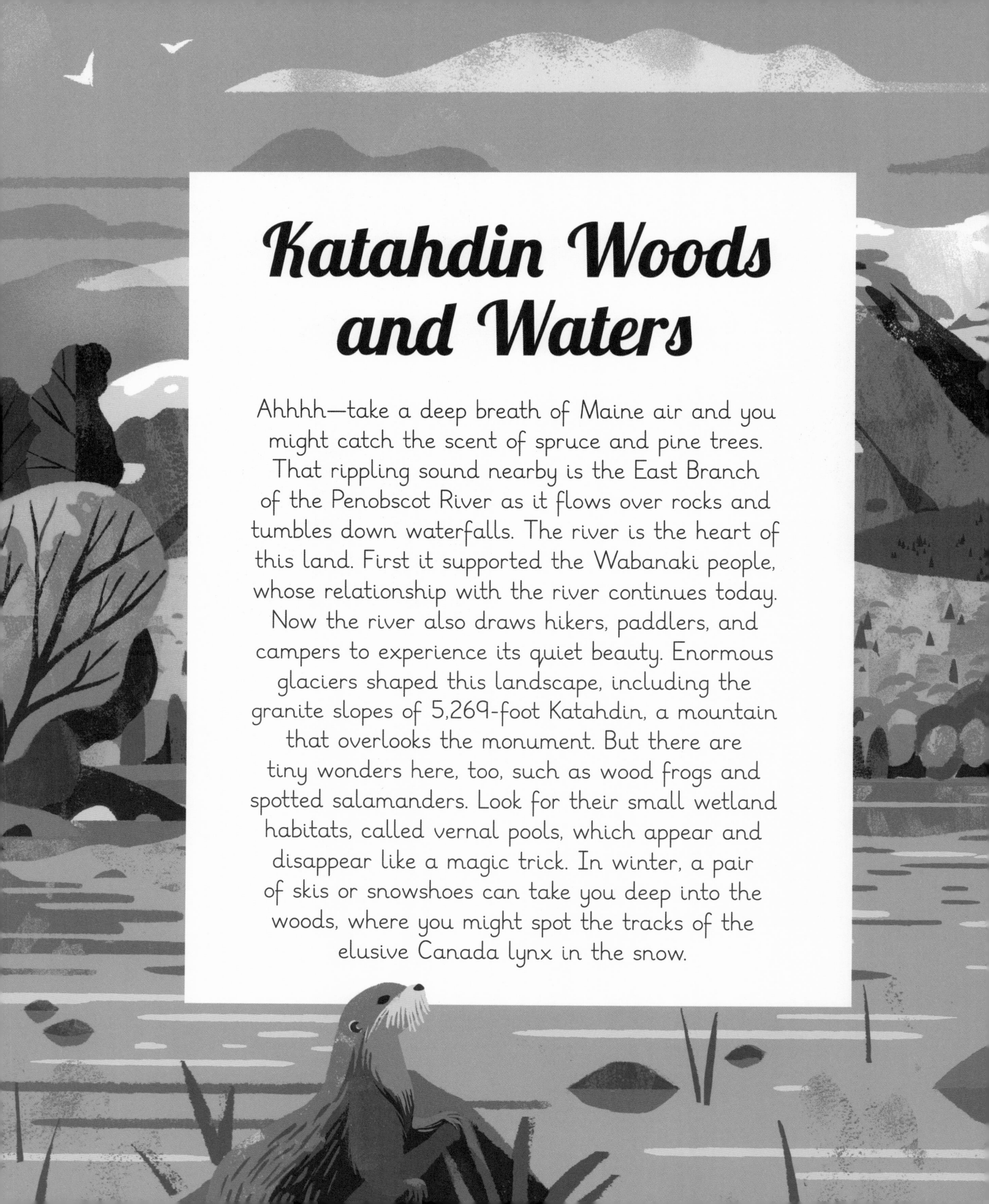

Katahdin Woods and Waters

Ahhhh—take a deep breath of Maine air and you might catch the scent of spruce and pine trees. That rippling sound nearby is the East Branch of the Penobscot River as it flows over rocks and tumbles down waterfalls. The river is the heart of this land. First it supported the Wabanaki people, whose relationship with the river continues today. Now the river also draws hikers, paddlers, and campers to experience its quiet beauty. Enormous glaciers shaped this landscape, including the granite slopes of 5,269-foot Katahdin, a mountain that overlooks the monument. But there are tiny wonders here, too, such as wood frogs and spotted salamanders. Look for their small wetland habitats, called vernal pools, which appear and disappear like a magic trick. In winter, a pair of skis or snowshoes can take you deep into the woods, where you might spot the tracks of the elusive Canada lynx in the snow.

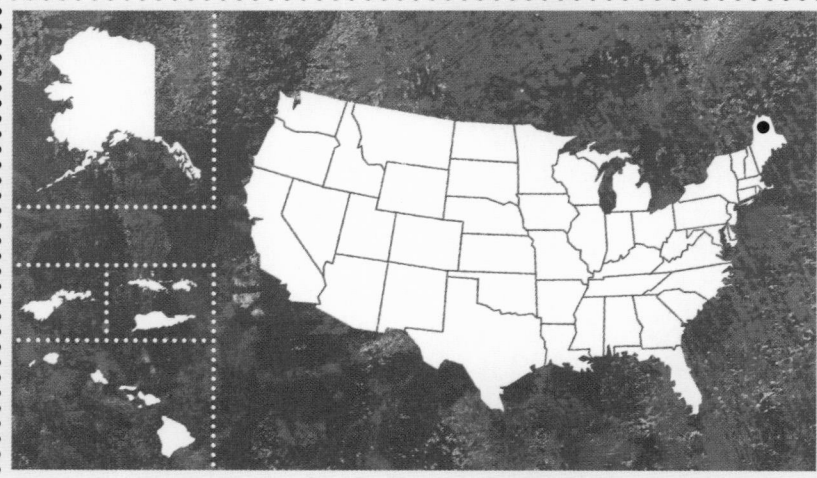

KATAHDIN WOODS AND WATERS

STATE:
Maine

DESIGNATED:
2016

GLACIER HITCHHIKERS
What's that huge rock doing in the forest? During the Ice Age, enormous sheets of ice covered much of northern North America, including this part of Maine. Giant rocks hitched rides on glaciers as they moved. When the glaciers melted, the rocks got dropped far away from their original homes.

A SPECIAL START
Roxanne Quimby, an entrepreneur and conservationist, bought land in Maine for many years to protect it. In August 2016, the 100th birthday of the National Park Service, she donated the land to the government to create the monument.

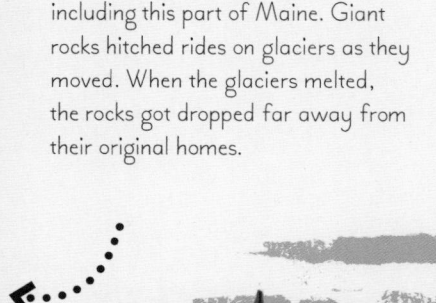

UPSIDE-DOWN RIVERS
A glacier can have a unique type of river called an esker running underneath it. Eskers carry sand, rocks, and gravel as they flow. When the glacier melts, the banks of this river disappear, too, leaving behind a raised, flat "river" made of the sediment the esker carried. People say eskers look like upside-down rivers!

LIFE ON THE RIVER
The Penobscot people and other Indigenous nations of the Wabanaki have lived here for more than 10,000 years, traveling the river and its tributaries by birchbark canoe. In the 1800s, loggers floated pine and spruce logs down the river to larger towns. Today, the Penobscot continue to paddle and connect to these waters and this land.

GREATEST MOUNTAIN
Katahdin, the highest mountain in Maine, means "greatest mountain" in the Penobscot language. The mountain itself is in nearby Baxter State Park, but you can get an amazing view of it from many places within the monument. The top of the mountain marks the end of the Appalachian Trail. At nearly 2,200 miles, it's one of the longest trails in the world!

SPRUCE GROUSE
Sometimes these proud-looking birds are called fool hens, because even in the wild, they'll let you get close up to take a look. Even from a distance, you might see the male grouse's red eyebrows and hear the *whoosh* of its tailfeathers.

YELLOW BIRCH
Long before there were pharmacies, the Wabanaki people used the bark of the yellow birch as medicine. This bark has a natural compound similar to what is in aspirin. Bend a twig beneath your fingers, and then take a sniff. Does yellow birch smell like minty chewing gum to you?

DARK SKY
Far away from bright city lights, this monument is a perfect place to look for stars, planets, and sometimes even the swirling colors of the aurora borealis. In 2020, the International Dark-Sky Association—an organization that works to reduce light pollution—designated Katahdin Woods and Waters an International Dark Sky Sanctuary.

MANY WAYS TO ENJOY
For many years, people have used this area for hunting and snowmobiling. You can still do these things east of the East Branch of the Penobscot River. Other spots in the monument are reserved for activities such as cross-country skiing, snowshoeing, hiking, and birdwatching.

MOOSE CENTRAL
Maine has the most moose of anywhere in the lower 48 states. The male moose's enormous antlers can grow to more than six feet wide. See that saggy flap of skin under its chin? That's called a dewlap or a bell.

WILDFLOWER WATCH
Lady slipper orchids (they look like tiny shoes!) can be found in rare wetlands called fens. The white petals of starflowers shine at the forest's edge. Take photos or draw pictures of the wildflowers you see in a nature journal. Then leave the flowers growing for other kids to enjoy!

CANADA LYNX
Canada lynx have large, furry paws that let these rare cats travel over the snow. Their favorite meal? Snowshoe hare. Sometimes a lynx can eat one or two hares a day.

National Mall and Memorial Parks

In Washington, D.C., the nation's capital, take in a sweeping view of the National Mall's memorials and museums. They stretch for more than a mile from the Lincoln Memorial, near the Potomac River, to the U.S. Capitol Building. While the Mall itself is not designated as a national monument, it contains more than 100 monuments and memorials that celebrate national leaders, military veterans, and U.S. history—and has one designated national monument, the Belmont-Paul Women's Equality National Monument. See these special spots on foot, by bike, or from a boat on the Tidal Basin. The National Mall is a place where the country gathers in good times and bad to celebrate, to protest injustice, and to enjoy the outdoors, too. You might even get the shivers knowing that presidents, leaders, and kids from around the world have walked these same paths.

NATIONAL MALL AND MEMORIAL PARKS

CITY:
Washington, D.C.

WASHINGTON MONUMENT

This towering monument rises over the National Mall to commemorate George Washington, who led the Continental Army during the American Revolution, and later led the United States as its first president. At 555 feet, $5\frac{1}{8}$ inches, the Washington Monument was the tallest structure in the world when it was completed in 1884. Even more amazing, its marble blocks are stacked on top of each other without any mortar—gravity and friction hold this pillar together.

LINCOLN MEMORIAL

In this impressive memorial, which was built to look like a Greek temple, there's a 19-foot-tall statue of the 16th president, Abraham Lincoln. He is sitting and looking out over the National Mall. Lincoln is especially known for the Emancipation Proclamation, which declared that all enslaved people in states and areas rebelling during the Civil War should be freed. The steps below the statue have been the site of many famous speeches and performances.

MARTIN LUTHER KING, JR. MEMORIAL

Civil rights leader Martin Luther King, Jr. gave his famous "I Have a Dream" speech nearby on the Lincoln Memorial steps. This memorial honoring King is engraved with inspiring quotes from his speeches and writing. The memorial's address is 1964 Independence Avenue, SW—a nod to the Civil Rights Act of 1964.

CAPITOL BUILDING

The Capitol Building is where the laws of the land get made. The Capitol Dome is substantial, too: it's made of 8,909,200 pounds of cast iron! Inside the building, stand in the Rotunda and look up at the dome—there's a beautiful painting called a fresco 180 feet above your head.

BELMONT-PAUL WOMEN'S EQUALITY NATIONAL MONUMENT

Women haven't always had the right to vote in the U.S. In 1916, a woman named Alice Paul founded the National Women's Party to change this. Women protested, marched, and were even arrested as they worked for suffrage, the right to vote. A historic house right behind the U.S. Capitol became the home of the NWP. Today, this 200-year-old house is a national monument celebrating the women who made history here.

MUSEUMS OF THE MALL

Along with memorials, the National Mall is surrounded by other keepers of history—museums! Start at the Smithsonian Castle for an overview of this area's many museums and galleries. Learn important stories at the National Museum of African American History and Culture, and the National Museum of the American Indian. See rocks from the Moon at the National Air and Space Museum, and find dinosaur fossils at the National Museum of Natural History.

VIETNAM VETERANS MEMORIAL

A 21-year-old college student named Maya Lin came up with the design of this monument—a reflective granite wall etched with the names of more than 58,000 American men and women who died or went missing during the Vietnam War. It's a quiet place: you might find yourself touching the name of a family member who was in Vietnam, or gazing at the flowers, letters, and mementos that loved ones have left to remember those they lost.

CHERRY BLOSSOMS

If you visit the National Mall at just the right time in the spring, you might catch the peak bloom of about 3,800 cherry trees. Japan gave the U.S. the first of these trees in the early 1900s. Some people say the clusters of pink and white blossoms look like clouds. Others say they look like popcorn!

TIDAL BASIN

People have lived along the Potomac River for thousands of years and seen its water rise and fall each day with the tide. The Tidal Basin, built more than 100 years ago, uses these ups and downs to form a lake—you can stroll along its banks or even ride a paddleboat! Today, people are working to make the Tidal Basin stronger for the future, when climate change might make the Potomac's tides more extreme.

FORTS

You're standing on the ramparts with the sea air blowing in your face. Look—there's a ship on the horizon. Is it a friend, a foe—or could it be a pirate? The monumental forts along the East Coast are an American version of castles—some have drawbridges and moats, too. Each fort also provides a small glimpse into the history of conflicts that shaped this land. At some forts, history comes to life with the help of rangers and volunteers dressed like the people who once worked and lived there. Watch soldiers loading cannons, hear the drums of military bands, or chat with colonial townspeople as they make candles and scrub linens on a washboard— they might even ask for your help!

FORT STANWIX
STATE: *New York*
DESIGNATED: *1985*

In 1758, the British built Fort Stanwix at an important place on the trading route between the Atlantic Ocean and Lake Ontario. The Six Nations Confederacy, a government of six allied Indigenous nations, negotiated treaties with both Great Britain and the United States at this site. During the American Revolution, a group of American soldiers survived for three weeks inside the fort under British attack. Today, explore the reconstructed fort and try out games like those colonial kids played.

FORT MONROE
STATE: *Virginia*
DESIGNATED: *2011*

Fort Monroe was a powerful Union stronghold during the Civil War. This place is also important because of what happened years before the fort was built: people were taken from Africa, enslaved, and sent by ship across the Atlantic Ocean. Some of them landed here at Old Point Comfort in 1619. This marked the beginning of what would become slavery in this country. Slavery continued for 246 years, and it still has ripple effects on life in the U.S. today.

FORT McHENRY
STATE: *Maryland*
DESIGNATED: *1939*

In 1814, British troops captured and burned the country's capital, Washington, D.C., and the city of Baltimore was next on their list. On September 13, the British Navy fired bombs and artillery rockets at Fort McHenry, which guarded the entrance to Baltimore's harbor. When the dust cleared the next morning, the fort was still standing with its American flag waving. This inspired a man named Francis Scott Key to write a song that became the country's national anthem: "The Star-Spangled Banner."

FORT MATANZAS
STATE: *Florida*
DESIGNATED: *1924*

Take a boat out to Rattlesnake Island and visit the fort's 30-foot watchtower. You'll pass through soldiers' and officers' rooms on your way up to the observation deck. Some loggerhead, green, and leatherback sea turtles travel for thousands of miles to lay their eggs on this monument's beaches. See the roseate spoonbill's hot-pink feathers? These birds get their color by eating crabs, shrimp, and other small crustaceans.

CASTILLO DE SAN MARCOS
STATE: *Florida* **DESIGNATED:** *1924*

FORT PULASKI
STATE: *Georgia* **DESIGNATED:** *1924*

Built after the War of 1812, this fort is so well preserved that you can see fingerprints of the free and enslaved masons who laid the fort's bricks. Later, Union soldiers stationed here during the Civil War played one of the first games of baseball ever photographed. Some rules were a little different than they are today—you could get the batter (called a striker) out by catching the ball after one bounce. Give it a try yourself, then walk the monument's trails and look for crabs, fish, and turtles in the moat. The tidal marshes and waterways around the fort are home to bald eagles and, sometimes, alligators!

Climb up to the gun deck of the oldest stone fort in the continental U.S. and keep your eye out for pirates, like Spanish soldiers did in the 1700s. The fort was built from coquina, a stone found only in Florida that's made of fossilized seashells. It's strong stuff, too: Castillo de San Marcos weathered attacks from buccaneers, British forces, and hurricanes. Once, the entire town of St. Augustine had to hide inside the star-shaped fort. But this fort was not a safe haven for everyone. Later, Indigenous people were imprisoned here in crowded conditions where sickness spread quickly. The fort also played a role in the creation of a system of boarding schools which separated Indigenous kids from their families and forced them to give up their languages, cultures, and traditions.

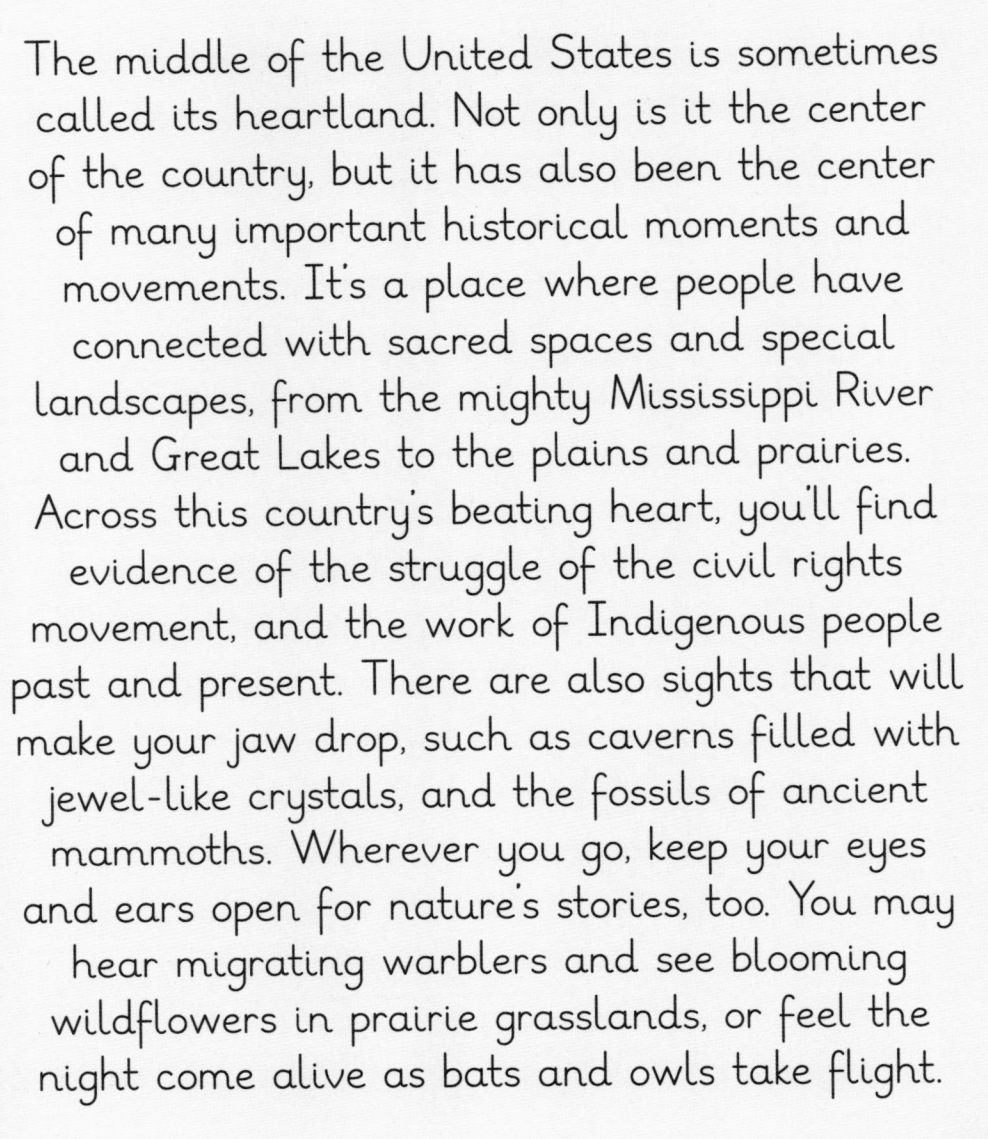

The middle of the United States is sometimes called its heartland. Not only is it the center of the country, but it has also been the center of many important historical moments and movements. It's a place where people have connected with sacred spaces and special landscapes, from the mighty Mississippi River and Great Lakes to the plains and prairies. Across this country's beating heart, you'll find evidence of the struggle of the civil rights movement, and the work of Indigenous people past and present. There are also sights that will make your jaw drop, such as caverns filled with jewel-like crystals, and the fossils of ancient mammoths. Wherever you go, keep your eyes and ears open for nature's stories, too. You may hear migrating warblers and see blooming wildflowers in prairie grasslands, or feel the night come alive as bats and owls take flight.

JEWEL CAVE

The gleaming "jewels" shining from the walls of the third-longest cave in the world are made of a mineral called calcite.

CENTRAL

PIPESTONE

The soft red stone of the quarries here has been used by Indigenous people to make sacred pipes—a tradition that continues today.

PULLMAN

The town of Pullman, Illinois, was designed to house workers who built fancy railroad sleeping cars. Pullman employees later became part of a movement for more rights for workers.

CHARLES YOUNG BUFFALO SOLDIERS

Brigadier General Charles Young was the first African American superintendent of a national park. He was also a diplomat who traveled to Liberia, Haiti, and the Dominican Republic.

GEORGE WASHINGTON CARVER

At the birthplace of this renowned African American scientist, visit a re-created classroom and see what school was like for kids in the 19th century.

BIRMINGHAM CIVIL RIGHTS

This national monument commemorates people, places, and events that were critical to the civil rights movement in Alabama and beyond.

FREEDOM RIDERS

At the former Greyhound bus station in Anniston, Alabama, look for the mural of a bus like the ones the Freedom Riders took to challenge segregation.

END SEGREGATION

MEDGAR AND MYRLIE EVERS HOME

These two important civil rights leaders worked to end segregation and to improve voting rights for African Americans. Their home became a national monument in 2020.

JEWEL CAVE

Sparkling crystals and otherworldly cave formations shine like buried treasure in Jewel Cave. And there's plenty to admire: at more than 210 miles long, it's the third-longest cave in the whole world. Travel into its depths by elevator, or follow a ranger through its caverns with an old-fashioned lantern in your hand to see fascinating features such as stalactites and stalagmites. Some people say being in the cave is like walking through a gorgeous geode! The air is humid down here, but it's a chilly 49 degrees Fahrenheit even in the summer. Whoosh—was that a bat flying past? One amazing thing about Jewel Cave is that there are many parts that still haven't been explored. Perhaps you'll be the first?

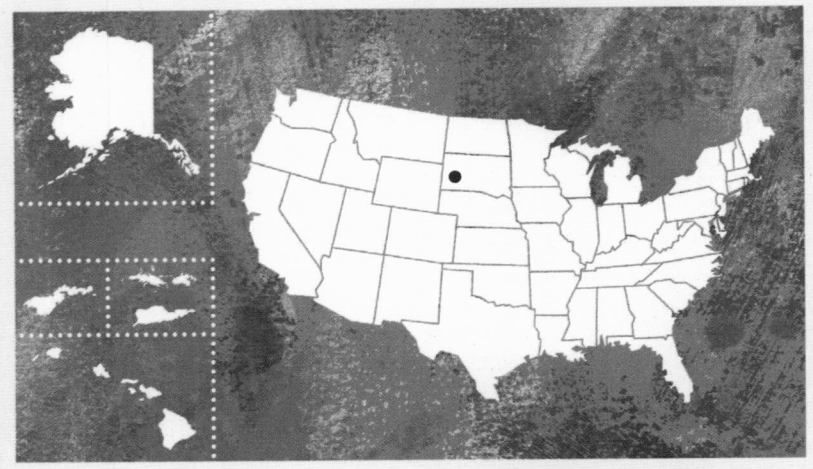

JEWEL CAVE

STATE:
South Dakota

DESIGNATED:
1908

CAVE FORMATIONS

Water drips and flows in the cave, depositing minerals that, over time, turn into cave formations called speleothems. There are speleothems called cave popcorn, soda straws—even cave bacon. Can you guess what these formations look like from their names?

STALACTITES AND STALAGMITES

Stalactites hang from the ceiling, while stalagmites sprout up from the cave floor. Some people remember the difference by saying that stalactites have to hold "tight" to the ceiling, while you "might" trip over a stalagmite on the floor.

COOL CRYSTALS

A mineral called calcite forms crystals that come in all sorts of shapes. Dogtooth spar is sharp and pointy, while blunt-tipped crystal is called nailhead spar.

CAVE EXPLORATION

Caves are extremely dark, so rangers take visitors in to see Jewel Cave's underground marvels. Depending on your tour, you could visit the Dungeon Room, Spooky Hollow, or the Heavenly Room. You might climb steps and wooden ladders, or even carry a 1930s-style lantern! However you go, wear sturdy shoes and bring a jacket to stay warm underground.

HISTORY AND HIKES

The blue-purple petals of American pasque, South Dakota's state flower, are one of the first signs of spring along the quarter-mile Roof Trail. The longer Canyons Trail visits a 1930s log cabin and the original entrance that the first known cavers used in 1900.

TOWNSEND'S BIG-EARED BATS

Bats have amazing ears, but the Townsend's big-eared bat has ears that are extra special. Its ears stretch out and point forward as the bat flies, which helps the bat hear better and might even give it some extra lift. When this bat's not flying, it sometimes curls its ears up like cinnamon rolls!

WINTER NEST

Some species of bat use the caves just inside the historic entrance of Jewel Cave as hibernacula—the places where they hibernate in the winter. Tours of this part of the cave take place only in the summer, when the bats aren't there. Hoary bats and silver-haired bats roost outside in the ponderosa pines. They tuck themselves in hollows and crevices during the summer, then fly south to find warmer winter homes.

BATS IN DANGER

There is a disease called white-nose syndrome that is infecting—and often killing—bats all over North America. White-nose syndrome is caused by a fungus that changes how well bats can hibernate. Visitors touring the caves can help stop the spread by wearing fresh clothes and shoes and sanitizing caving gear.

FIRES ON TOP

In 2000, the devastating Jasper Fire burned 90 percent of the monument's surface. (Firefighters protected all of the monument's buildings, and rangers put important documents into the cave for safekeeping.) But this land is resilient: plants and trees are growing back, and people have planted more than 150,000 ponderosa pines to help the forest recover.

UNIQUE BEAK

Even with more than 120 bird species flying aboveground at Jewel Cave, the red crossbill's beak stands out: when the crossbill closes its beak, the top crosses over the bottom. This unique beak helps the crossbill pry open pine cones to get the seeds inside.

LIFE UNDERGROUND

Animals that live in caves are called troglofauna. Some, called troglobites, spend their whole lives in caves. Others, called troglophiles or "cave lovers," can live both underground and on the surface. Tiger salamanders often live aboveground, but they love Jewel Cave's humid air, too. Like other amphibians, they need damp homes because otherwise they'd dry out—they breathe oxygen right through their skin!

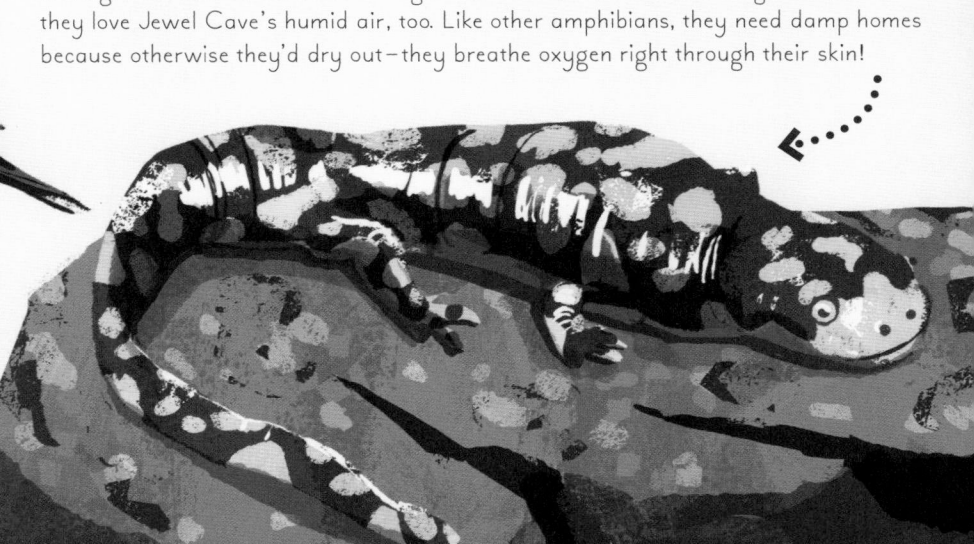

Birmingham Civil Rights and Freedom Riders

When you visit these two national monuments dedicated to civil rights, think about what it was like in Alabama in the early 1960s. Back then, Black people had to follow a whole series of laws and rules that white people didn't. Black people weren't allowed to have certain jobs or live in some neighborhoods. In some places, Black kids couldn't play at the same playgrounds, go to the same schools, or even swim at the pool with white kids. Adults and kids who wanted to change this were part of the civil rights movement to give everyone equal rights. At Birmingham Civil Rights National Monument and Freedom Riders National Monument, you'll learn the stories of some of the people and events that helped lead to the Civil Rights Act of 1964, which made discriminating against people based on their race, color, religion, sex, or national origin against the law. These monuments might inspire you to work for equality in your community and your world!

BIRMINGHAM CIVIL RIGHTS
STATE: *Alabama*
DESIGNATED: *2017*

A.G. GASTON MOTEL
The historic A.G. Gaston Motel catered to African American travelers when it was tricky to find safe, comfortable places to stay. The motel later became the headquarters of civil rights leaders as they put together marches, boycotts, and other actions to end segregation. The restored motel will be a centerpiece of the Birmingham Civil Rights National Monument.

SEGREGATION
Segregation is a word that means separating, and it was legal in many parts of the country. Segregation meant that some restaurants and movie theaters didn't let Black people in, or had separate areas for Black and white people to sit. In some places, Black kids and white kids couldn't even use the same drinking fountains.

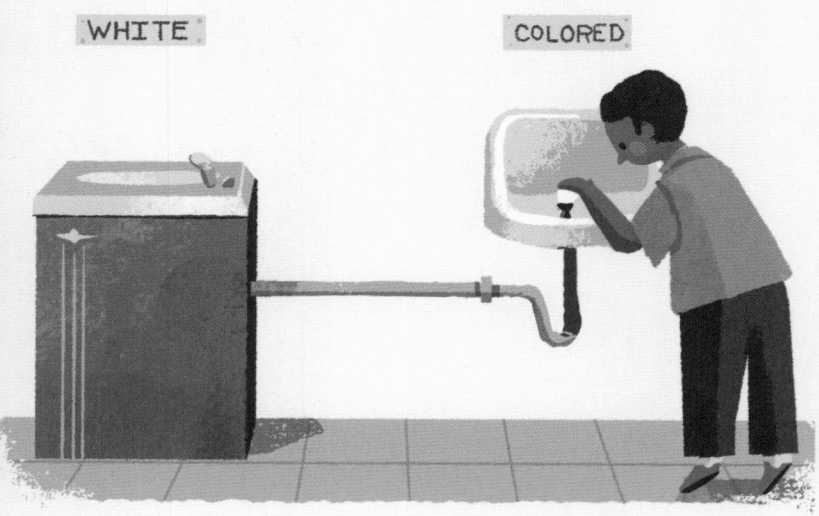

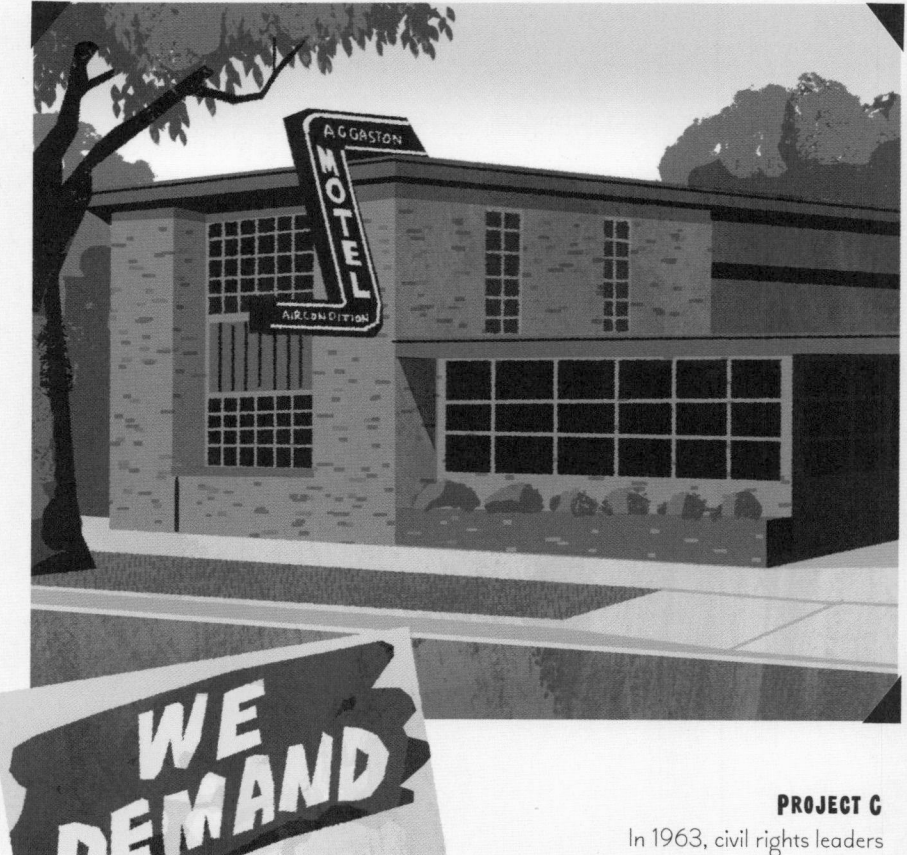

THE BIRMINGHAM CHILDREN'S CRUSADE
On a spring morning in 1963, more than a thousand kids marched through the streets of Birmingham to demand equal rights. Instead of protecting these marchers, the Birmingham police deliberately used high-pressure fire hoses, clubs, and police dogs against them. Some kids were arrested and put in jail. When people around the country learned about the violence in Birmingham and the young marchers' bravery, they were motivated to work harder for civil rights.

PROJECT C
In 1963, civil rights leaders started working on Project C in Birmingham, Alabama, one of the most segregated places in the country. The "C" stood for confrontation. The non-violent confrontations they planned included sit-ins, boycotts, and marches to protest segregation in the city.

BIRMINGHAM'S CIVIL RIGHTS LANDMARKS
This national monument includes many sites where you can learn more about the movement. At the Birmingham Civil Rights Institute, see what it was like to have segregated classrooms and visit a replica of the jail cell of Martin Luther King, Jr. Across the street, statues in Kelly Ingram Park honor important events and people, including the children who were jailed and the four young girls who were killed when the 16th Street Baptist Church, a meeting place for the civil rights movement, was bombed.

<table>
<tr><td>

FREEDOM RIDERS
STATE: *Alabama*
DESIGNATED: *2017*

</td></tr>
</table>

WHO WERE THE FREEDOM RIDERS?

In 1960, the U.S. Supreme Court decided that it was unconstitutional for bus stations serving interstate travelers to be segregated. Black and white travelers known as the Freedom Riders set out on a series of bus rides to test whether the Supreme Court's decision was really being followed. The first group of Freedom Riders started their journey in Washington, D.C. in May 1961. They arrived in Anniston, about 60 miles east of Birmingham, on May 14. The monument protects several sites in and around Anniston.

TROUBLE IN ANNISTON

An angry mob was waiting at the bus station when the Freedom Riders arrived. They smashed the bus with pipes and bats and damaged its tires. When the bus started to drive off, the mob began to chase it.

STATE ROUTE 202

After about six miles, the bus had to pull over on State Route 202. The mob threw bombs at the bus that set it on fire. When the Freedom Riders tried to get off the bus and escape, they were attacked. The stories of these Freedom Riders inspired others to participate in more Freedom Rides.

SIT-INS AND BOYCOTTS

The civil rights movement tried to use peaceful methods to protest segregation. During a sit-in, protestors would go to a restaurant that had segregated seating, and sit there to make their point. Boycotts happened when people protested by not buying things or using services. Civil rights activist Rosa Parks was arrested after refusing to give up her seat on a Montgomery bus. This led to a city-wide bus boycott. For more than a year, Black people walked, carpooled, and took taxis to put pressure on state and national leaders to end bus segregation.

MARCHING FOR JUSTICE

Marches were an important part of the civil rights movement. One well-known march for voting rights for African Americans took place in March 1965. Hundreds of people began walking from Selma to Montgomery, Alabama's capital. The marchers were turned back two times on their 54-mile route, but on the third attempt they reached Montgomery. The Voting Rights Act of 1965 was passed later that year.

PIPESTONE

Tink! Tink! Tink! That's the sound of people working in the quarries at Pipestone National Monument. For thousands of years, Indigenous people have come to this sacred site to quarry and carve this soft red stone into hand-held pipes that are used in ceremonies and prayer. Today, Indigenous people from nations across the country come to this special spot to continue this tradition. Many quarriers are part of families who have come here for generations to make pipes and other important objects by hand. Walk quietly as you pass by prayer ties and tobacco offerings attached to trees and bushes near the quarry. Listen to the wind blow through the tallgrass prairie, and to water rushing over Winnewissa Falls. Grab your binoculars—is that bird in the distance a turkey vulture or a bald eagle?

PIPESTONE

STATE: *Minnesota*
DESIGNATED: *1937*

PIPE TRADITION

Indigenous peoples, including the Dakota and Lakota, have carved, used, and traded pipes for thousands of years. People fill these sacred pipes with tobacco and traditional plant mixtures, then smoke them at significant occasions such as when celebrating someone being given a new name, when remembering someone who has died, or in prayer. The pipes themselves are so special that they are often passed down through families for many generations.

PRAIRIE WATERFALL

Did you know that there could be waterfalls right in the middle of the prairie? Follow the Circle Trail from the visitor center to the spot where Pipestone Creek flows over red and pink rocks to form beautiful Winnewissa Falls. In the winter, you can use snowshoes to visit the frozen falls.

PIPESTONE

Pipestone is about as soft as your fingernail, and can be red, pink, or somewhere in between. Quarriers use tools such as chisels and sledgehammers to remove this stone from the surrounding hard rock, called Sioux quartzite. If you're lucky, you may be able to watch a quarrier at work, or see an Indigenous artist carving a pipe in the shape of a powerful animal, like a raven, bear, or bison.

QUARTZITE

The hard quartzite makes unique rock formations throughout the monument. On the Circle Trail, look for two formations called the Oracle and Old Stone Face. You may see quartzite shaped like human faces or animals, too. What will you see in the rocks?

NICE PLACE TO NEST

Birds flock to the tallgrass prairie, which is full of seeds to eat and cozy spots to build a nest. See that striking bird with a yellowish patch on the back of its head? That's a male bobolink. Look for it perched on the tips of shrubs and grasses, and listen to its bubbly song. Some people say this bird sounds like R2-D2 from the *Star Wars* movies!

TALLGRASS PRAIRIE

In many places, native prairie grasses have been cleared for farms and cities. This is one of the few places in the Midwest that protects native tallgrass prairie. Pipestone has more than 70 types of grasses—some, like big bluestem, can grow as tall as eight feet!

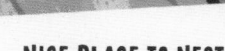
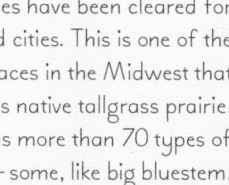
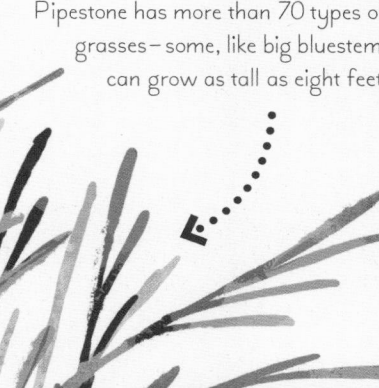

FLOWER POWER

Indigenous people use many of the prairie's flowers, such as prairie clover and coneflower, for medicine. Flowers also attract bees and butterflies: in late spring, migrating orange and black monarch butterflies arrive at the monument to feed on milkweed. Help protect the prairie's hundreds of wildflowers by staying on the trail to admire them.

PULLMAN

Choo choo! Railroads ruled the U.S. in the late 1800s. Here, at 203-acre Pullman National Monument, you'll see a place that had a huge effect on the nation's trains and how workers were treated, too. In the 1880s, industrialist George M. Pullman founded the town of Pullman to attract workers to build Pullman sleeping cars, which took passengers on overnight train trips in style. People still live in some of Pullman's beautiful brick homes today. Imagine living here around 140 years ago and building fancy train cars at the Pullman factory, or working as a Pullman porter, traveling across the country by train. But what if your job started to be unfair—would you do what Pullman's workers did in 1894 and walk out of the factory in protest? This was one of the events that helped turn Labor Day into a national holiday.

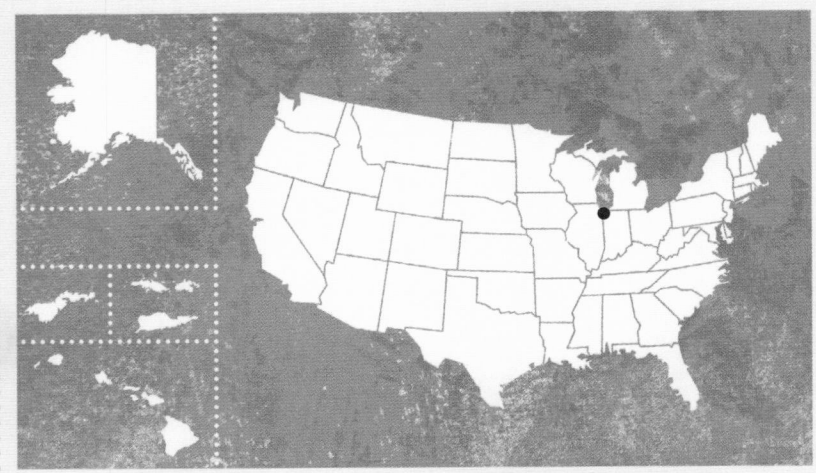

PULLMAN

STATE:

Illinois

DESIGNATED:

2015

TOWN RULES

George Pullman founded the Pullman Company, and the Pullman Company made the rules. Pullman's company decided what books would be in the library and what shows appeared in the theater. Town meetings, public speeches, and independent newspapers were not allowed.

COMPANY TOWN

George Pullman bought 4,000 acres about 14 miles south of downtown Chicago to build both a factory and a whole town for the people who would work there. Workers here had yards, indoor plumbing, and services like garbage pickup, which were unusual at the time.

PULLMAN SLEEPING CARS

Pullman palace cars were considered a luxurious way to travel. These sleeping cars were often painted a dark green, and had plush seats and fancy curtains. They could transform into rooms with sleeping berths once it was time to go to bed.

AMAZING ARCHITECTURE

Look around—the buildings in Pullman's town are gorgeous! George Pullman hired architects to design everything from the town's central clocktower to the row houses. Builders used bricks made from the red clay of nearby Lake Calumet for most buildings. All this red brick makes the Greenstone Church, made with green serpentine, really stand out!

STRIKE!

In 1893, there was a recession in the country—a time when people lost money and jobs. The Pullman Company began paying their workers less without lowering the rent on their homes. When workers tried to talk with the company's president, he fired them. So some workers decided to stop working and walk out of the factory on May 11, 1894. As the strike went on, other railroad workers joined in. This made a big impression—the strike stopped trains from running everywhere from Chicago to the West Coast!

FROM STRIKE TO FIGHT

Railroad workers on strike had large gatherings to support their cause. Toward the end of June, some of the gatherings outside Pullman turned violent. Some people destroyed train cars, and federal troops began shooting at workers. More than two dozen people were killed. The strike ended in July 1894 and raised people's awareness of the importance of workers' rights.

WOMEN OF PULLMAN

Women worked at Pullman during a time when women didn't usually have factory jobs. Here, they mainly made carpets, draperies, and bedding for the sleeper cars. African American women worked as maids on the railroad cars, taking care of female travelers and their children. Women were also a part of the Pullman strike and the creation of the Brotherhood of Sleeping Car Porters.

PULLMAN PORTERS

Pullman recruited African American men, some of whom were formerly enslaved, to become porters on the sleeping cars. Porters wore elegant uniforms with caps, suits, and black ties. They took care of everything from carrying passengers' suitcases to serving their food. These jobs offered travel experiences that weren't available to most African Americans at the time.

NATIONAL A. PHILIP RANDOLPH PULLMAN PORTER MUSEUM

Learn about the legacy of African American workers at this museum named for Randolph, the first president of the Brotherhood of Sleeping Car Porters. Randolph's influence led President Franklin D. Roosevelt to issue an executive order against racial discrimination in the defense industry in 1941.

BROTHERHOOD OF SLEEPING CAR PORTERS

Many things weren't fair for the Pullman Porters. African Americans often weren't allowed to join unions for railroad workers. On the train, some passengers still treated porters like servants. The porters asked a well-respected magazine publisher, Asa Philip Randolph, for help. In 1925, they founded a union called the Brotherhood of Sleeping Car Porters.

SOUTH

RAINBOW BRIDGE

At 290 feet, the natural sandstone bridge at this special site is almost as tall as the Statue of Liberty on her pedestal. Look for the single dinosaur footprint preserved at one of the viewing areas.

GRAND STAIRCASE-ESCALANTE

This rugged landscape's 1.87 million acres contain delights from slender slot canyons to dinosaur fossils. A hike to Lower Calf Creek Falls takes you past beaver dams and pictographs thought to be made by the Fremont culture.

BANDELIER

Canyons, cliff dwellings, and animals from coyotes to mule deer are all part of this monument's 33,000 acres. In fall, watch for tarantulas crossing one of Bandelier's backcountry trails, and for sandhill cranes migrating overhead.

MONTEZUMA CASTLE

An ancient 20-room apartment building tucked high in the limestone cliff is considered one of the best-preserved cliff dwellings in the country.

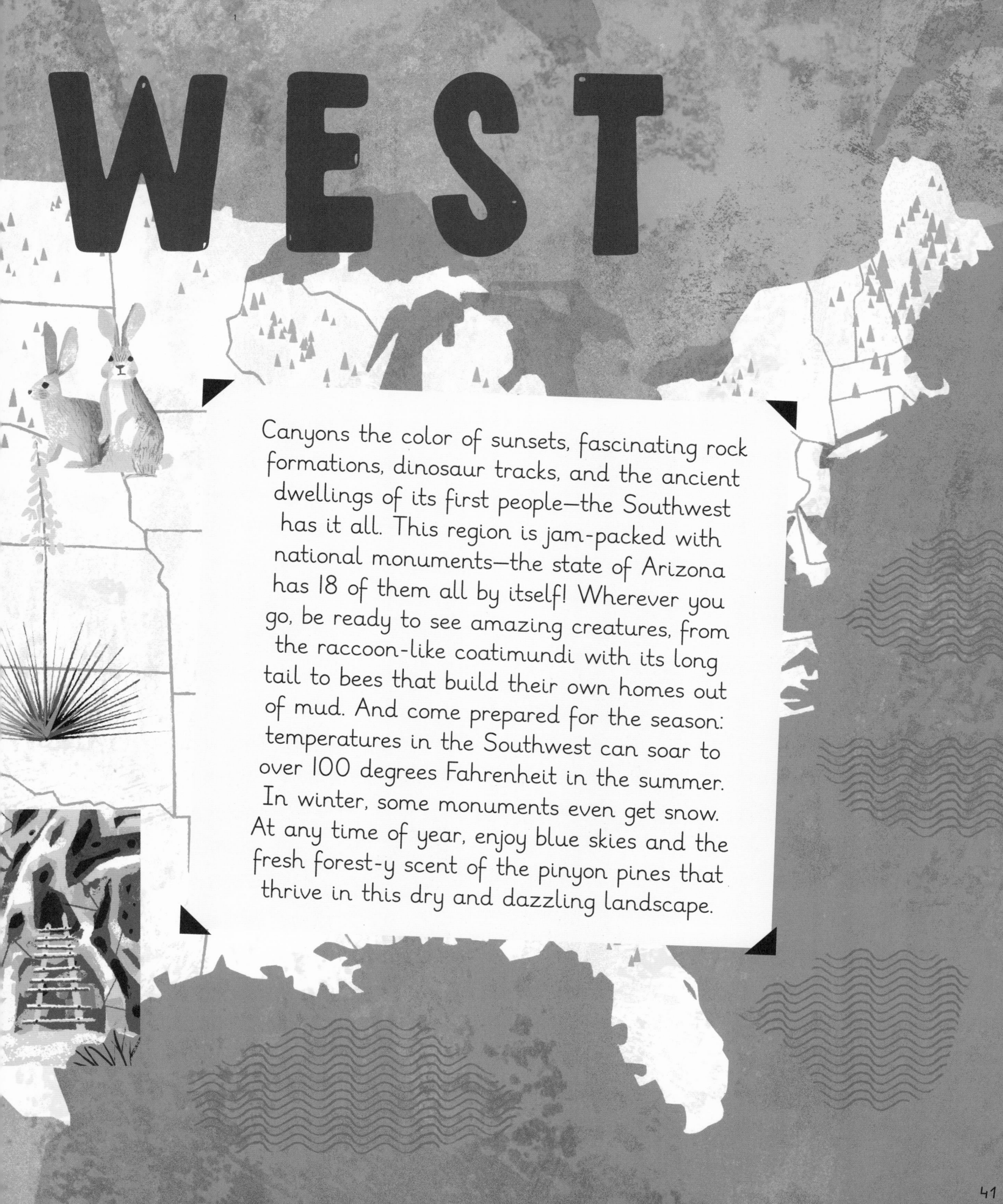

WEST

Canyons the color of sunsets, fascinating rock formations, dinosaur tracks, and the ancient dwellings of its first people—the Southwest has it all. This region is jam-packed with national monuments—the state of Arizona has 18 of them all by itself! Wherever you go, be ready to see amazing creatures, from the raccoon-like coatimundi with its long tail to bees that build their own homes out of mud. And come prepared for the season: temperatures in the Southwest can soar to over 100 degrees Fahrenheit in the summer. In winter, some monuments even get snow. At any time of year, enjoy blue skies and the fresh forest-y scent of the pinyon pines that thrive in this dry and dazzling landscape.

41

GRAND STAIRCASE-ESCALANTE

Wishing for miles and miles of wilderness? This is your place. At more than 1.8 million acres, this national monument is as big as the state of Delaware! This vast landscape has three main areas: Grand Staircase, Escalante Canyons, and Kaiparowits Plateau. The Grand Staircase's layers of colorful sandstone cliffs form a giant, rainbow staircase that ascends about 5,500 feet. Hikers head to Escalante Canyons to visit slot canyons. And on the remote Kaiparowits Plateau, paleontologists unearth fossils of never-before-seen dinosaurs. You'll be traveling through places where the Ancestral Puebloan and Fremont cultures once expertly farmed this rugged land. Many Indigenous nations, including the Hopi, Zuni, Paiute, Ute, and Navajo, maintain ties to this place today.

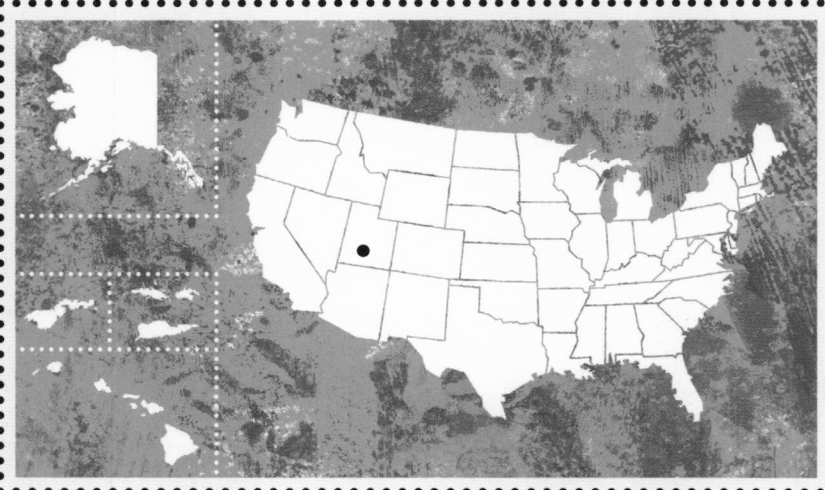

GRAND STAIRCASE-ESCALANTE

STATE:
Utah

DESIGNATED:
1996

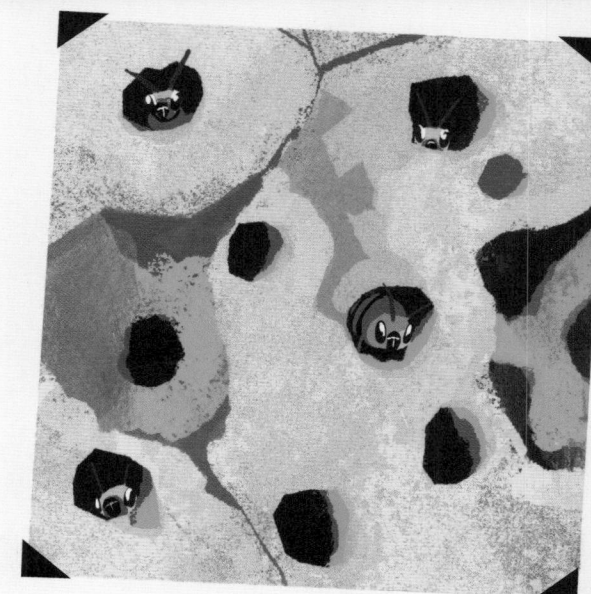

THE BUZZ ON BEES

Bees help plants thrive by carrying pollen from flower to flower. This lets plants reproduce by allowing them to make seeds. The monument is buzzing with at least 660 different bee species! Some bees are tiny, while others are as big as your thumb. These diverse bees support all of the monument's unique native plants.

HOMES FOR BEES

Utah's state insect is the honey bee. Honey bees live in big colonies inside hives—the state is even called the Beehive State! But most of Utah's bees live in the ground, in homes they excavate themselves. Some make small houses for themselves out of mud. One species of bee even carves its home out of the sandstone by using its mandibles, which are like jaws.

DINOSAUR DISCOVERIES

Imagine a *Triceratops*, but even fancier. That's the *Kosmoceratops*, a dinosaur first discovered here in 2006. Paleontologists found fossils of this dino's skull with 15 horn-like structures—the most of any dinosaur! Scientists can also see preserved insects, leaves, and even dinosaur skin, which means they can learn about the whole ecosystem in which *Kosmoceratops* and other dinosaurs lived.

KANGAROO RATS

They might weigh less than a medium-sized apple, but kangaroo rats can bound nine feet into the air to get away from predators. They're also pros when it comes to living in dry Southwestern deserts. Kangaroo rats don't even need to drink water. They get the moisture they need from the seeds they eat.

ANCIENT GRANARIES

The Fremont and Ancestral Puebloan peoples built granaries to store nuts, seeds, and other food. Granaries were in hard-to-reach places to protect them from hungry critters. Peer closely at the cliffsides to find one of these ancient structures. Imagine using ropes and ladders to bring food here—it makes putting the groceries into the fridge seem like a breeze!

BIRD HIGHWAY

The monument is an important stop on a migratory bird flyway, which is like a bird highway in the sky! Birds use this flyway to migrate between their summer and winter homes. One of these travelers is the rufous hummingbird. With red feathers at his throat and a bright orange back and belly, the male hummingbird glows in the Southwest's sunshine.

MIGHTY CRUST

The ground around you might look barren, but the soil's surface is actually packed with life. Lichen, moss, and organisms called cyanobacteria—one of the oldest kinds of life on Earth—create a layer on top of the dirt called biological soil crust. Organisms in these crusts can help slow down erosion, keep water in the soil, and make soil healthier. These crusts can get crushed, so hike on existing trails or find your way along rocks or sand, where soil crusts don't form.

DEEP ROOTS

The Utah juniper has several tricks to deal with the rugged desert landscape. This tree can send a taproot 25 feet down into the ground to reach underground water. The juniper can release chemicals into the soil to make it hard for other plants to grow, which means more water, nutrients, and sunshine for itself!

SLOT CANYONS

The inside of a narrow, steep-walled slot canyon is a magical place. The air is still, every sound echoes, and sometimes a stream of sunlight pours down through the opening high above your head. Some of these canyons are so slender that you can stand in the middle and touch the walls on either side. Sudden storms can flood a slot canyon, so make sure the weather is clear before you venture in.

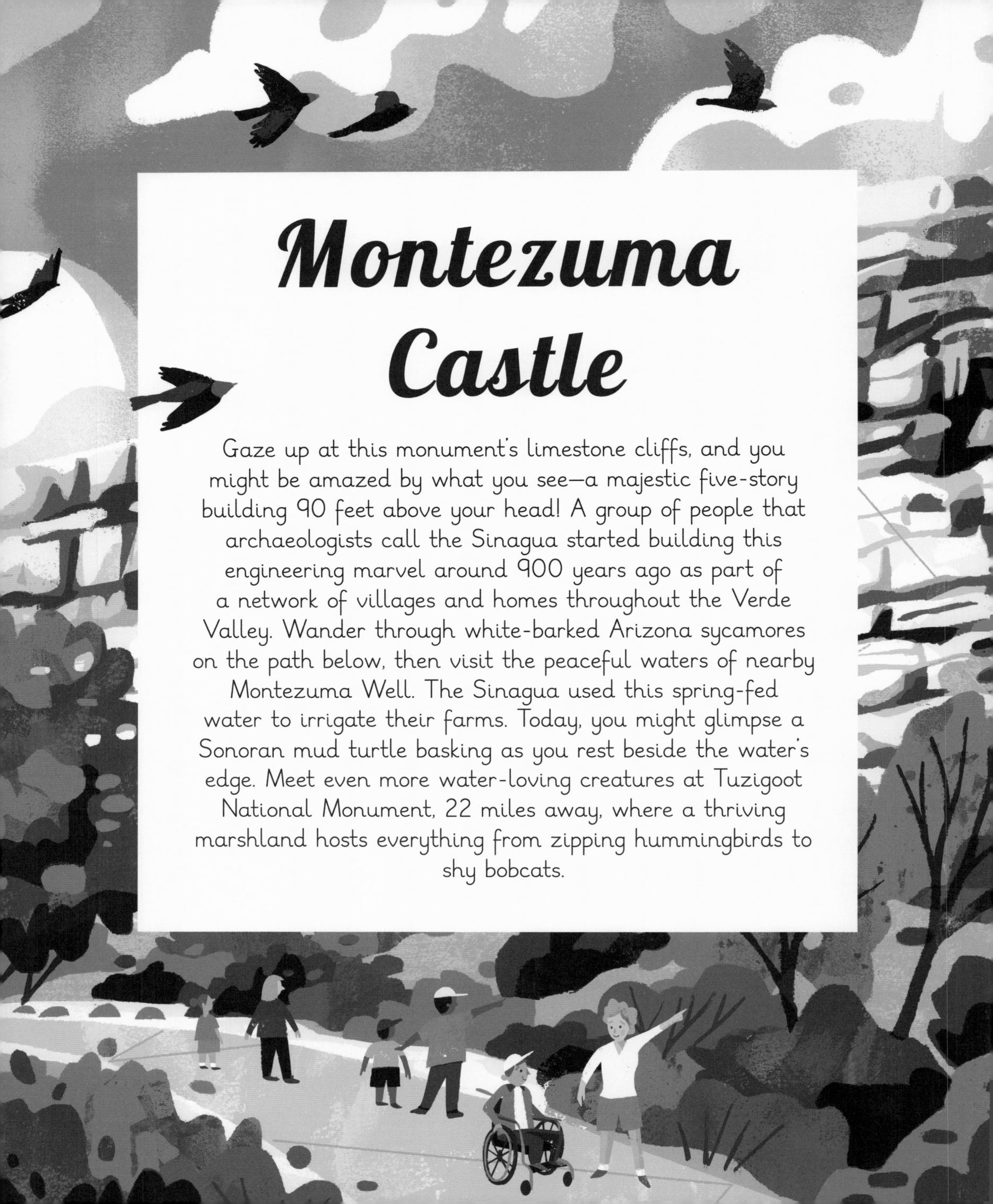

Montezuma Castle

Gaze up at this monument's limestone cliffs, and you might be amazed by what you see—a majestic five-story building 90 feet above your head! A group of people that archaeologists call the Sinagua started building this engineering marvel around 900 years ago as part of a network of villages and homes throughout the Verde Valley. Wander through white-barked Arizona sycamores on the path below, then visit the peaceful waters of nearby Montezuma Well. The Sinagua used this spring-fed water to irrigate their farms. Today, you might glimpse a Sonoran mud turtle basking as you rest beside the water's edge. Meet even more water-loving creatures at Tuzigoot National Monument, 22 miles away, where a thriving marshland hosts everything from zipping hummingbirds to shy bobcats.

MONTEZUMA CASTLE

STATE:

Arizona

DESIGNATED:

1906

NAME MIX-UP

Montezuma Castle got its name from settlers in the 1800s, who thought this place might have been built by the Mexica people and their famous emperor Montezuma, who ruled from what is now Mexico City. But Montezuma was born after the Sinagua migrated away from the Verde Valley. Rather than a castle, this 4,000-square-foot building was more like an ancient high-rise apartment block. As many as 35 people lived here at a time, climbing up ladders to get to their rooms.

MASTER BUILDERS

People have lived in lush Verde Valley for more than 10,000 years. The area became really busy around the year 650, when a group of master builders started building, farming, and trading goods. Hopi people call them Hisatsinom, which means "ancient people."

STORAGE SOLUTION

Like some modern peoples of the Southwest, the Sinagua stored food and water in large ceramic pots called ollas ("oy-yahs"). A museum at Tuzigoot National Monument has enormous ollas that were buried underground to keep their contents safe and cool. It was like having a pantry right below your feet! People today also use ollas to cook and to help irrigate their plants.

PROTECTING SPECIAL PLACES AND THINGS

In 1906, Montezuma Castle became one of the first national monuments established with the goal of preserving historical Indigenous sites. At this time, many important artifacts were looted, or stolen, every day. Looting is still a problem at many places across the Southwest. If you see something that looks like it's from another time, please leave it in place and let a ranger know!

MONTEZUMA WELL

This desert oasis was once an underground limestone cave filled with rainwater. Over the years, the cave collapsed, forming a 386-foot-wide lake that is still fed by an underground spring. Many of the Indigenous nations linked to the monument today consider the well a sacred place. Trails take you through shady trees, past irrigation canals and cliff dwellings, and to the well itself.

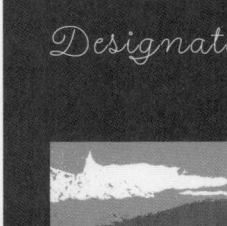

NIGHT LIFE

The days here are too hot for many creatures. Nighttime can be better for finding food and water. Animals living the night life (such as mountain lions, bats, and owls) are called nocturnal. Another word, crepuscular, covers wildlife such as coyotes and porcupines that are active around dawn and dusk. What time of the day is your favorite?

IT'S RAINING, IT'S POURING

The Verde Valley owes its life to the monsoon season, a period of hot weather, heavy rains, and afternoon thunderstorms between June and September. Find shelter during the downpour and feel the thunder boom in your chest. Once the storm passes, watch how the water creates life in the desert. You might even see a rainbow!

TUZIGOOT

Designated: 1939

If you're visiting Montezuma Castle, don't miss its neighbor: Tuzigoot National Monument. At Tuzigoot, you'll find a hilltop pueblo that once housed more than 200 people. This thriving community of farmers used the natural flooding of the Verde River to grow corn and other crops. Stand on the roof of the pueblo for a sweeping view of the valley after visiting a reconstructed pueblo room. Bird lovers can take the trails that wind through the cattails and cottonwoods of 96-acre Tavasci Marsh for glimpses of rare Yuma clapper rails and regal great blue herons.

DESERT FLOWERS

The hedgehog cactus might have spiky-looking spines, but it also produces gorgeous flowers that can be bright pink, magenta, or red. Find more blooms on the ocotillo—its name means "little torch," like its fiery red flowers. The stately soapstone yucca has clusters of white flowers that can only be pollinated by the yucca moth.

BANDELIER

STATE: *New Mexico*
DESIGNATED: *1916*

PUEBLO VIEW

The settlements of the Ancestral Puebloan people are also called pueblos. Tyuonyi (pronounced "Qu-weh-nee") is a circular pueblo where about 100 people once lived in one- and two-story homes. Today, take in the view of the 600-year-old pueblo's curving walls from the Tyuonyi Overlook trail.

HOMES IN THE ROCK

Climb up the ladders and explore the cavates, the cave rooms that people dug out of the pink rock. Four sets of ladders take visitors to Alcove House, which has a reconstructed kiva, or sacred room, and once held homes for 25 people.

KIVA

The kiva was the center of life in the village of Tyuonyi. Villagers would enter the kiva by climbing down a ladder into the circular, underground room. Inside the kiva, people participated in religious ceremonies and made important community decisions.

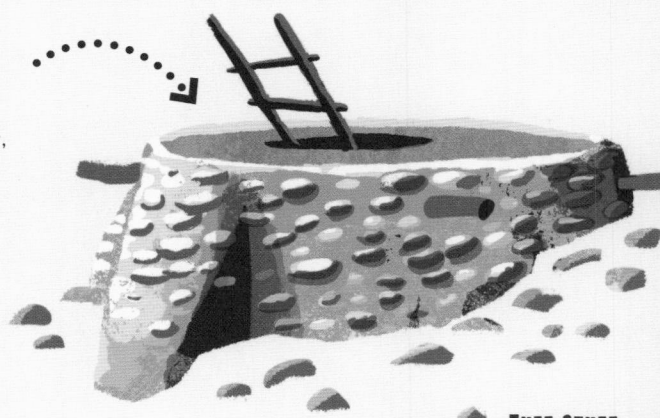

PICTURES ON THE ROCK

On the walls of Frijoles Canyon, the Ancestral Puebloan people carved petroglyphs of turkeys, a baby macaw, and even a dog that looks like it's wagging its tail. You may also find pictographs on the rocks along some of the monument's 70-plus miles of backcountry trails.

TUFF STUFF

Kaboom! A million years ago, two huge eruptions of the ancient Jemez volcano spewed volcanic ash everywhere. Over the years, the ash packed down and turned into a pinkish rock called tuff. Wind and rain can shape tuff—and so can people. The Ancestral Puebloan used tools to turn tuff into their homes.

ABERT'S SQUIRREL

See something fluffy in the trees? It's a good bet you've found an Abert's squirrel and its furry white tail. These squirrels have big, tassel-like tufts on their ears, too. Even with all the fur, they're great climbers. They use their back legs to grab onto a branch while gobbling ponderosa pine cones and twigs.

STINK BEETLES

Peee-yew! What's that smell? These odoriferous creatures, nicknamed "stink bugs," are part of the darkling beetle family. They squirt out a smelly liquid when they're trying to protect themselves from predators.

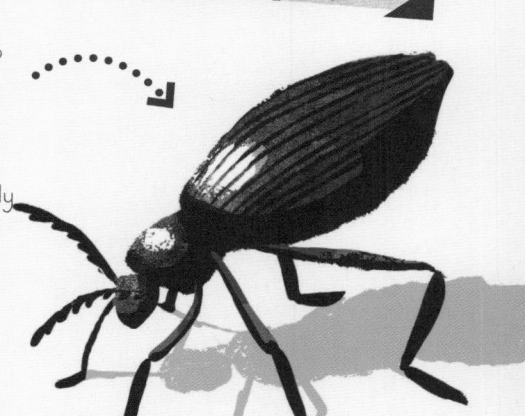

BANDELIER

Some homes are made of wood and bricks, others travel on wheels or even float on the water. Here, in Bandelier National Monument, you'll find homes made of volcanic rock, shaped by the Ancestral Puebloan people who lived here between about 1150 and 1550. They were expert farmers, growing corn, beans, and other crops in the desert by channeling rainfall. In Frijoles Canyon, they built their homes and sacred spaces into the pale-pink cliffsides. By the mid-16th century, the Ancestral Puebloans had migrated out of the canyon into communities along the Rio Grande, which are still there today. Pueblo people still carry stories of their ancestors who lived on this land. Climb the ladders up to the cliffside houses and feel the sunshine on your face. The winter sun makes the south-facing canyon wall and its ancient dwellings about 13 degrees Fahrenheit warmer than the canyon floor below.

RAINBOW BRIDGE

The trip to Rainbow Bridge National Monument, home to one of the world's largest natural bridges, always starts with an adventure. Take a boat ride across the waters of Lake Powell, a reservoir that's part of Glen Canyon National Recreation Area. You'll motor alongside the red rock walls of Forbidding Canyon before reaching the trailhead. From here, hike about a mile and there it is: a beautiful 290-foot-high archway of Navajo Sandstone, shaped by millions of years of flowing water. Take a deep breath and feel what it's like to be in this place, which several Indigenous nations hold sacred. With permission from the Navajo Nation, you can backpack around Navajo Mountain and into the monument. But come prepared: these rugged trails are 16 to 18 miles long!

RAINBOW BRIDGE
STATE: *Utah*
DESIGNATED: *1910*

NAVAJO SANDSTONE
The bridge is a feature made from Navajo Sandstone, a rock formation created from a prehistoric desert even larger than the Sahara. Sandstone is very porous, which means water can flow through it easily.

BRIDGE BUILDING
The rocks may seem dry here now, but water is what shaped Rainbow Bridge and the other beautiful rock formations in the area. Water flowing from nearby Navajo Mountain meandered around a bend in the rocks and, over time, created a rocky fin like you'd find on the back of a whale. Then the water started tunneling through the sandstone to form the bridge. If there's been enough rain, you might see Bridge Creek still running beneath the arch.

HANGING GARDENS
Along the hike to Rainbow Bridge, you'll find a surprise: lush green plants growing from the red rock walls. These hanging gardens are made by small springs, called seeps, that drip through sandstone and down the canyon walls. Water-loving plants including maidenhair ferns and desert orchids have trouble growing in most parts of the desert, but you'll find them here!

LAKE POWELL
When the Glen Canyon Dam was finished on the Colorado River in 1963, it formed this 186-mile-long lake. Today, people flock to Lake Powell for watersports and to visit its 96 major side canyons by motorboat, kayak, and stand-up paddleboard! Now, lower water levels are revealing hidden landscapes and ancient sites.

COLLARED LIZARD
This lizard gets its name from the pair of dark bands around its neck. Some collared lizards sport blues, greens, and yellows, making them look like little rainbows on the rocks. This speedy creature can leap, sprint, and rise up on its big, strong hind legs to scare off other lizards. It can even stand up on its back legs to run—it looks like a tiny *Tyrannosaurus rex* on the move!

GLEN CANYON NRA
Lake Powell is part of the Glen Canyon National Recreation Area, which covers more than a million acres in parts of both Arizona and Utah. Swim and fish along hundreds of miles of shoreline, and don't miss the iconic Horseshoe Bend, where the river curves around the red rocks in the shape of a giant horseshoe.

DEVILS TOWER
The first-ever national monument got its name from a mistranslation. A Lakota name for this amazing rock formation is Mato Tipila, or "Bear Lodge."

CRATERS OF THE MOON
This volcanic landscape looks like the Moon—astronauts have even trained here! Unlike the Moon, it's filled with animals, wildflowers, and plant-packed "islands" in the lava called kipuka.

DINOSAUR
Dinosaur fans love the Quarry Exhibit Hall, which holds close to 1,500 dinosaur bones right in the rock wall. You'll also find deep river canyons and hear a night-time orchestra of native toad calls and coyote howls.

COLORADO
Drive or bike 23-mile Rim Rock Drive for incredible views of red rock canyons and rocky towers. You might spot a bighorn sheep from a scenic overlook or hiking trail.

MOUNTAIN WEST

The spectacular Rocky Mountains run through this region, and they might be the first thing you think about when you imagine the Mountain West. On both sides of the Continental Divide, you'll also find unique landscapes shaped by wind, water, or lava! In this part of the country, you can visit weathered sandstone canyons carved by rivers flowing from the Rockies, and see the first-ever designated monument, an awe-inspiring rock formation that rises above the prairie. Dinosaurs once lived here—visit the land where they roamed and spot the fossils they left behind. Today, this region is home to bighorn sheep and pronghorn, which wander steep slopes and river valleys. Bring your skis and snowshoes for a snowy winter to remember—or pack a bathing suit for whitewater rafting in summer!

DINOSAUR

It's right there in the name: dinosaurs! At Dinosaur National Monument's Quarry Exhibit Hall, you'll get to look at more than 1,500 fossils right in the rock. Check out bones from *Stegosaurus*, the giant *Apatosaurus*, and the awesome *Allosaurus*. You can even touch some fossils, which means your fingers are feeling something that's almost 150 million years old! This monument is a great place to get outside, too, with more than 210,000 acres of wilderness in two states. On the Colorado side, raptors and endangered fish live in the deep river canyons that also attract thrill-seeking whitewater rafters. The canyon walls hold rock art made by people that archaeologists call the Fremont culture. They lived here more than a thousand years ago. Take a moment to listen to the flowing waters of the Green and Yampa Rivers, or the enthusiastic song of a mountain bluebird at dawn. What do you think this place sounded like when the dinosaurs were here?

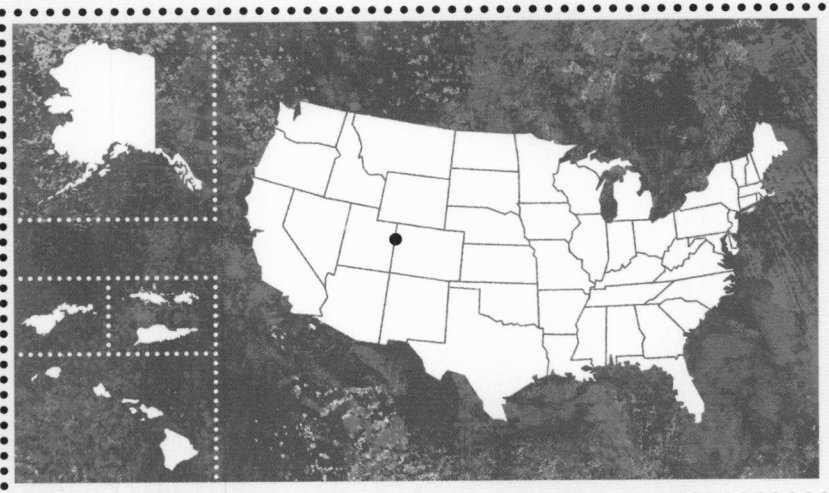

DINOSAUR

STATES: Colorado and Utah

DESIGNATED: 1915

DINOSAUR QUARRY

Step inside the Quarry Exhibit Hall and you'll be entering another time— the late Jurassic, when all kinds of plant- and meat-eating dinosaurs roamed this land. Paleontologists think these dinosaurs lived near ancient rivers. When they died, their bodies washed into the river beds. Then layers of mud and sand covered and protected the bones. Over time, the Earth's geological forces and erosion wore away at the protective rocks, revealing the fossils you can see today.

AWESOME ALLOSAURUS

At 30 feet long and more than 2,000 pounds, *Allosaurus* was a predator to watch out for during the Jurassic. It could open its enormous jaws extra wide and sink three-inch, serrated teeth into plant-eaters like *Stegosaurus*. Some research even suggests that *Allosaurus* might have hunted in packs like wolves!

ROCK ART

Along with being hunters and farmers, the Fremont culture also carved and painted images on the rocks around them. You might see thousand-year-old images of animals like lizards or bighorn sheep. Help protect this rock art by encouraging your friends and family to look at (but not touch) these sites.

DINOSAUR DISCOVERIES

Scientists are still finding dinosaurs at Dinosaur National Monument. In 2010, researchers announced that they had found a whole new species, called *Abydosaurus mcintoshi*, in a layer of rock called the Cedar Mountain Formation. *Abydosaurus* was a long-necked plant eater that lived about 100 million years ago, making it the youngest dinosaur found here—so far.

PLANTS HIGH AND LOW

Steep mountains, deep canyons, and stretches of desert mean Dinosaur National Monument has a huge range of trees and plants. Water-loving willows and cottonwoods grow down by the river. Up high, quaking aspens flutter their heart-shaped leaves, which turn a beautiful gold in the fall.

DINOSAUR MILK VETCH

One special plant grows only in and around the monument: dinosaur milk vetch. You'll recognize it in the spring because of its showstopping magenta flowers.

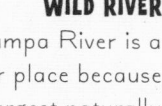

WILD RIVER

The Yampa River is a spectacular place because it's the largest naturally flowing river in the Colorado River system. This makes it a great spot for young fish, as well as other river lovers, such as beavers and otters. Did you know that beavers and otters have a set of transparent eyelids so they can see clearly underwater? It's like having built-in goggles!

QUIET PLACES

Far from city sounds like honking horns and roaring engines, this monument is a place where you can soak up the sounds of nature. Some people call it one of the quietest places in the West! There's a 3.2-mile hike on the Sound of Silence Trail, where you might hear things like wind whispering through cottonwood trees or the *kak-kak-kak* call of a peregrine falcon.

ENDANGERED FISH

The Colorado pikeminnow, one of the monument's three endangered fish, is the biggest minnow in North America. It once grew as long as six feet—as tall as some grown-ups—and weighed up to 80 pounds. These days, they're usually two to three feet long. These minnows migrate along the river for more than 200 miles.

CRATERS OF THE MOON

Surrounded by black lava and the cones of extinct volcanoes, this landscape can seem so strange that it might feel like you're on the Moon! These 750,000 acres were shaped by the same volcanic forces that carved out the Moon's dark seas. Here on Earth, lava flowed out of a huge crack called the Great Rift and formed weird and wonderful shapes, including tubes, coils, and a flow called the Blue Dragon, which looks like it has dragon scales! Unlike the Moon, though, there's plenty of life at this out-of-this-world monument, such as colorful islands of spring wildflowers and violet-green swallows that swoop and dive for insects. What's that cute, high squeak? It's the call of the pika, a furry creature the size of a guinea pig. Pikas store food each summer so that they can weather the snowy winters here. Take snowshoes or cross-country skis to experience this snow-covered "moon" for yourself.

CRATERS OF THE MOON
STATE: *Idaho*
DESIGNATED: *1924*

THE FLOOR IS LAVA!

The lava that covers most of the monument comes from a 52-mile-long series of cracks in the Earth's surface called the Great Rift. Lava first started flowing about 15,000 years ago. The most recent lava flow was 2,000 years ago. Lava can still get hot today, even though it's no longer flowing. In the summer, the surface of the hardened lava rock can reach 170 degrees Fahrenheit!

EARLIEST PEOPLE ON THE LAVA

The Shoshone and Bannock homelands include what's now Craters of the Moon. The first people on the lava stored meat from the animals they hunted in ice-filled lava tubes. At the monument, look for rings of lava rock that they might have used to set up their camps. Today, members of the Shoshone-Bannock Tribes still have traditional stories that describe past lava flows, which means their ancestors saw some of this area's volcanic activity in action!

SPACE SCIENCE ON EARTH

Craters of the Moon makes people think of the volcanic landscapes that future adventurers might find elsewhere in our solar system. Astronauts came here in 1969 to learn more about volcanic geology before they went to the Moon. Scientists still use the monument as a laboratory to prepare for missions to Mars.

CAVES AND TUBES

Many of the monument's 500-plus caves are actually tubes of lava. Underground rivers and streams of lava formed these lava tubes—when the flowing lava ran out, the empty tube was left behind. Now you can visit four of the monument's lava tubes, with names such as Dewdrop and Beauty. Check with the ranger station for a permit before you head out, then take a flashlight and wear sturdy shoes.

PRONGHORN

Pronghorn use the monument as part of their migration route each spring and fall, which takes them more than 100 miles across Idaho. They're the fastest land animal in the U.S., running at 60 miles per hour. A pronghorn could even beat a cheetah in a long-distance race! If you do spot a pronghorn in a lava field, it's probably stepping carefully, just like you.

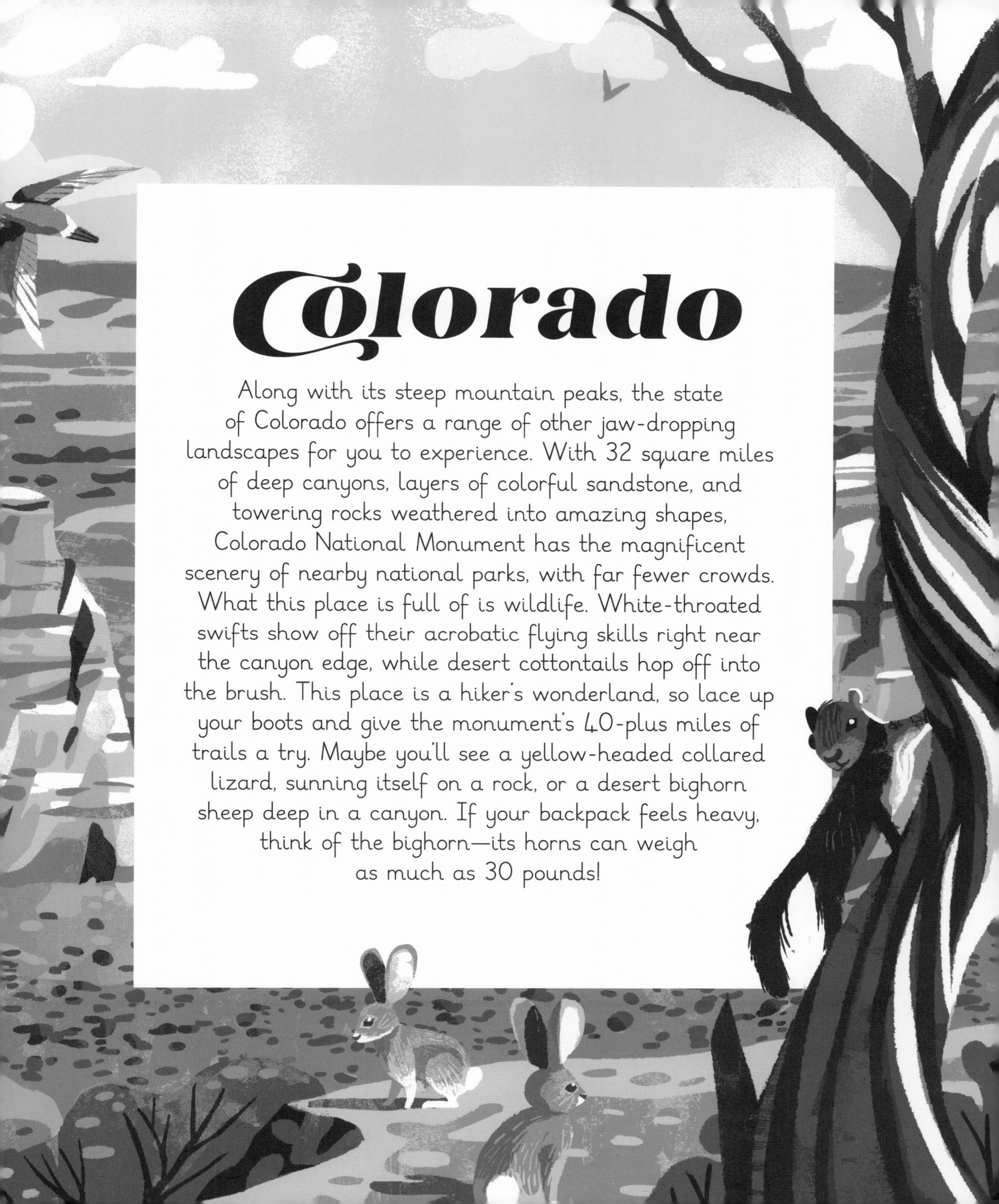

Colorado

Along with its steep mountain peaks, the state of Colorado offers a range of other jaw-dropping landscapes for you to experience. With 32 square miles of deep canyons, layers of colorful sandstone, and towering rocks weathered into amazing shapes, Colorado National Monument has the magnificent scenery of nearby national parks, with far fewer crowds. What this place is full of is wildlife. White-throated swifts show off their acrobatic flying skills right near the canyon edge, while desert cottontails hop off into the brush. This place is a hiker's wonderland, so lace up your boots and give the monument's 40-plus miles of trails a try. Maybe you'll see a yellow-headed collared lizard, sunning itself on a rock, or a desert bighorn sheep deep in a canyon. If your backpack feels heavy, think of the bighorn—its horns can weigh as much as 30 pounds!

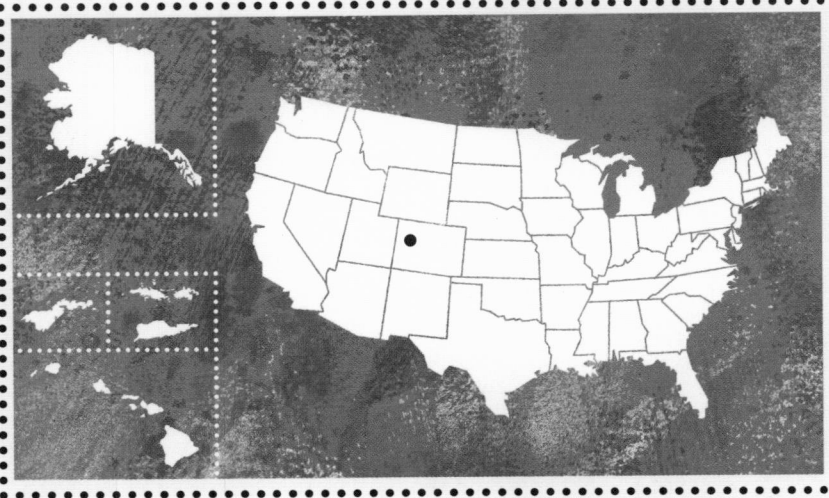

COLORADO

STATE:

Colorado

DESIGNATED:

1911

RIM ROCK DRIVE

Rim Rock Drive is one of the most beautiful winding roads in the West. The Civilian Conservation Corps, which worked on public lands in the 1930s, built this 23-mile-long road over and through these mountains almost entirely with hand tools! Look for three tunnels cut through the rock, and lots of trailheads and lookout points where you can start experiencing more of this monument.

DESERT BIGHORN SHEEP

Desert bighorn sheep lived here long ago, but then they disappeared. In 1979, scientists reintroduced this species to the monument. Desert bighorn sheep can go for days without drinking water, even during the hot summer. Then they can guzzle down several gallons of water in minutes to power back up. (People don't have the same superpower. If you're hiking, be sure to bring water along with you!)

THE CROOKEDEST TRAIL

One historic road in the monument has been called the crookedest road in the world! Part of it is now called Serpents Trail. Take 16 switchbacks up, up, up for 1.75 miles with plenty of views along the way. For a shorter hike, try Devils Kitchen, which has amazing sandstone features you can climb in and around. Wherever you are, watch out for steep drops as you check out the views.

WHICH BLACK BIRD?

Wheeling through the air, birds search for their next meal. But is that one with black feathers a turkey vulture or a raven? Look for the V shape of the vulture's big wings as it flies, and the long "fingers" of feathers at its wing tips. Ravens are smaller and fly more like gymnasts with wings, doing somersaults and even flying upside down!

SEASONS IN THE MONUMENT

Every season in the monument brings something new to see. Spring and summer burst with blooming wildflowers such as evening primrose and desert four o'clocks. Fall shows off the golden leaves of the cottonwood tree. And because the monument ranges between 4,700 and 7,000 feet in elevation, snow can form a sparkling frosting on the red rocks in the winter.

HIGH DESERT FOREST

The monument's trees can stand up to its dry climate and harsh winds. The Utah juniper makes what look like tiny blue berries, but they're actually the tree's cones. The pinyon pine, another hardy high-desert tree, makes energy-packed seeds that birds, animals, and people like to eat. The Ute people have harvested and eaten these pine nuts for hundreds of years. Maybe you've tried them, too!

THE RABBIT AND THE HARE

What's that hopping down the trail? The desert cottontail and the black-tailed jackrabbit both live in the monument, but the jackrabbit isn't a rabbit—it's a hare. Hares are usually larger and faster than rabbits. They can zigzag away from danger at speeds of up to 40 miles per hour!

Devils Tower

You're wandering through the rolling hills and prairies of Wyoming when—whoa!—a huge tower of rock seems to rise up out of nowhere. This enormous volcanic pillar has been a sacred place for Indigenous people for thousands of years. In 1906, President Theodore Roosevelt made this area the country's first national monument. Take one of the trails that goes around the tower, which rises 867 feet from its base. And be sure to look up—you might see rock climbers scaling the tower's sides or a peregrine falcon diving at record-breaking speed to snag its prey.

DEVILS TOWER
STATE: *Wyoming*
DESIGNATED: *1906*

HARD ROCK
This tremendous tower came from magma that bubbled up from beneath the Earth's surface. Some scientists think that Devils Tower was a volcano that never erupted. Over time, weather and wind have worn away the rock layers on the outside, leaving behind the cooled and hardened volcanic rock. The tower is made up of huge five- and six-sided columns that are hundreds of feet tall.

PEREGRINE FALCONS
When a peregrine falcon dives for its prey, it moves faster than any other animal in the whole world. The falcon's dive, called a stoop, can be more than 200 miles per hour! These birds nest on the rock, so certain parts of the tower are closed to climbers during nesting season.

UP, UP, UP
Rock climbers love to scale Devils Tower and its hundreds of cracks and columns. In the 1890s, climbers installed a ladder with log rungs up the south side of the tower. These days, climbers use ropes, but you can see some leftover parts of the ladder if you look through binoculars or one of the park's viewing tubes.

SACRED TOWER

This tower is a sacred place for more than 26 Indigenous nations, including the Arapahoe, Shoshone, Crow, and Kiowa. When you walk around the tower, you may see prayer ties and bundled offerings tied to trees. In June, the monument asks climbers to come back another time because some nations host ceremonies at the tower for the summer solstice, which is the longest day of the year.

PRAIRIE DOG TOWN
Right inside the monument's entrance, there's an enormous town—and the citizens are all black-tailed prairie dogs! About 300 of these small rodents live in a 60-acre network of underground burrows here in the prairie. Watch as they come out of their burrows and stand up on their hind legs. And listen, too—these prairie dogs communicate with at least 11 different types of calls.

MOUNT ST. HELENS
Learn about the eruption of the mighty volcano Mount St. Helens, then bring flashlights to visit dark, chilly Ape Cave, the third-longest lava tube in North America!

TULE LAKE
Before it became a stand-alone national monument, Tule Lake was grouped with sites in Alaska and Hawai'i as part of World War II Valor in the Pacific National Monument.

JOHN DAY FOSSIL BEDS
Get your fossil fix at this 14,000-acre national monument in the John Day River Basin, where scientists have found fossils from 44 million years ago.

MUIR WOODS
Walk among ancient giants at this 558-acre national monument. Coast redwoods are the tallest living things in the world—and some of the trees here are over 1,000 years old!

GOLDEN GATE
Home to Muir Woods National Monument, Golden Gate National Recreation Area covers nearly 81,000 acres on both sides of the Golden Gate Bridge. Watch for whales along the coast in winter, then look for spring wildflowers from the trails at Fort Funston.

CÉSAR E. CHÁVEZ
A leader who championed farmworkers, César E. Chávez was also an animal lover. At his home in Keene, California, he had two beloved dogs, Boycott and Huelga. They went almost everywhere with him.

WEST

If your vision of the western states only involves beaches and sunshine, get ready for your dreams to get even wilder. Here, you'll also find the tallest trees in the world and landscapes that hold evidence of fantastical creatures that lived long ago. Snowcapped mountain ranges harbor waterfalls and black bears, while orcas and porpoises swim the waters around remote islands. The national monuments here are also treasure troves for understanding more about this region's human history, from its Indigenous inhabitants to those who arrived more recently. At every turn, take in the West with all of your senses. The wind brushes your cheeks in the high desert, carrying with it the scent of sagebrush. Close to the coast, walking beneath majestic redwoods might make you feel like you're inside a cathedral, with a congregation of banana slugs and blue-feathered jays by your side. And there's that sound you were dreaming of: the gentle roar of the Pacific Ocean's waves.

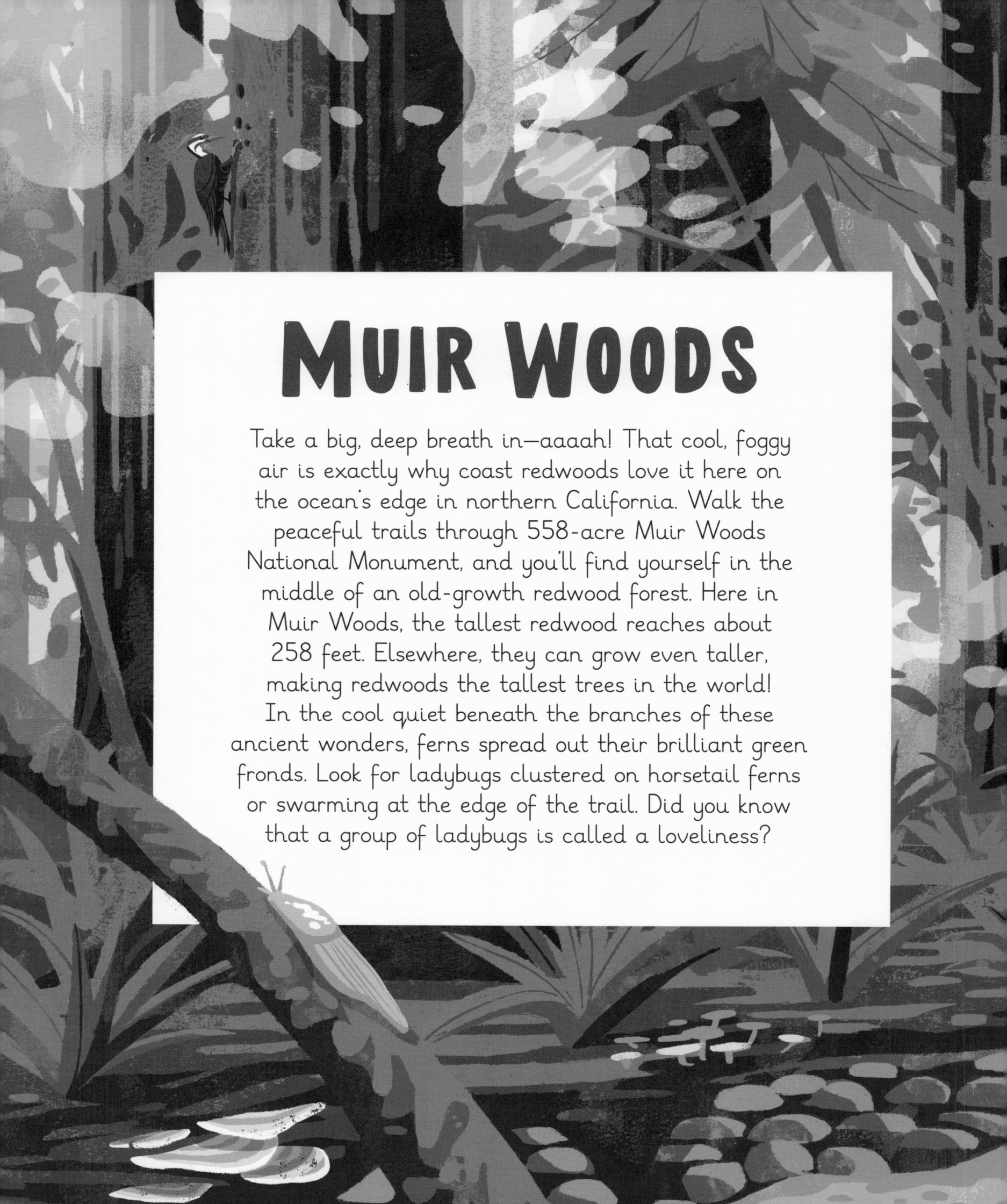

MUIR WOODS

Take a big, deep breath in—aaaah! That cool, foggy air is exactly why coast redwoods love it here on the ocean's edge in northern California. Walk the peaceful trails through 558-acre Muir Woods National Monument, and you'll find yourself in the middle of an old-growth redwood forest. Here in Muir Woods, the tallest redwood reaches about 258 feet. Elsewhere, they can grow even taller, making redwoods the tallest trees in the world!

In the cool quiet beneath the branches of these ancient wonders, ferns spread out their brilliant green fronds. Look for ladybugs clustered on horsetail ferns or swarming at the edge of the trail. Did you know that a group of ladybugs is called a loveliness?

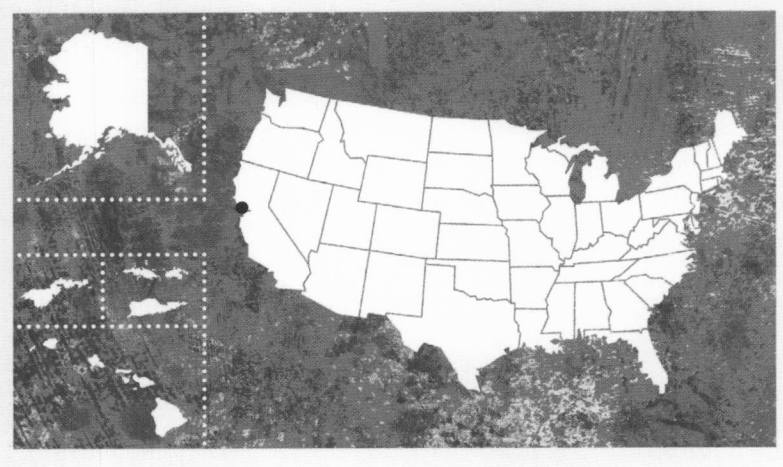

MUIR WOODS

STATE:
California

DESIGNATED:
1908

FOG-O-LICIOUS!

Redwood trees love fog! Tiny openings in their needles can soak up water from the fog as it rolls through. Fog can also drip down through the canopy, and redwoods and other plants on the forest floor can take in the moisture through their roots.

REDWOODS STICK TOGETHER

Even though redwoods are the tallest living things around, their roots only grow about 10 to 12 feet deep. How do they not tip over? Redwood trees weave their roots together with their neighbors'. This keeps the big trees stable, lets them share nutrients and maybe even communicate with each other!

REDWOODS AND FIRE

A little fire can be a good thing for redwoods! These trees have thick bark which protects them during fires. When a small fire burns through a redwood forest, it clears away dead plant material and brush on the forest floor. Fire adds nutrients to the soil and gives new redwoods room to sprout.

REDWOOD SORREL

Is that a lucky four-leaf clover you spy? It's actually a plant called redwood sorrel, a shade-loving species that looks just like a clover. When this plant gets too much sun, it folds up its leaves like a tiny umbrella.

BANANA SLUGS

Big, yellow, and slimy: if you see a banana slug on the forest floor, you won't forget it. They're the second-biggest land slug in the world. Some banana slugs can be nearly 10 inches long! At any size, they do great work for the redwood forest, eating everything from moss to animal poop and turning it into nutrients for the soil.

FABULOUS FERNS

Thirteen different kinds of fern thrive beneath the redwoods. They're actually even older than the redwoods—ferns have been around for more than 380 million years. Look for curled-up fiddleheads—the fern's new growth unfurls into feathery young fronds.

NORTHERN SPOTTED OWL

Northern spotted owls live in these woods, although they only appear at night. Try sitting quietly, right before sunset, when these owls begin swooping down on their favorite prey, the dusky-footed woodrat. These owls are considered an indicator species—how well they're doing indicates the health of the entire forest.

REDWOOD BURLS

Redwoods get bumps and scrapes, just like you. But these trees form a big lump on their trunks, called a burl, to cover up the injury. Other kinds of burls closer to the ground can grow new shoots and roots, making the beginnings of a whole new tree.

SALMON RUN

If you come upon coho salmon in Redwood Creek, you're witness to part of an amazing life cycle. Salmon are born here, then swim downstream to the ocean, where they live for up to two years. Then, as adults, the salmon swim back upstream to spawn, or lay their eggs. The Coast Miwok hold ceremonies each year to welcome the salmon back to their home waters.

FUNCTIONAL FUNGI

Fungi are a hard-working group of organisms that includes molds, mildews, yeasts, and mushrooms. Some fungi decompose, or break down, wood and other organic material to make nutrients for the soil. After a winter rain, check out the the colorful turkey tail mushroom. The artist's conk mushroom grows like a shelf on logs and dead trees. This shelf can get so big and strong that a grown-up could stand on it!

GOLDEN GATE

Muir Woods National Monument is part of a larger park called the Golden Gate National Recreation Area. Both north and south of the iconic Golden Gate Bridge, you can visit beaches and hike on trails where you can see migrating birds soaring overhead. This bigger recreation area also includes famous structures, such as the island prison of Alcatraz, and the former military forts of Fort Point, Fort Funston, and the Presidio. Wherever you go, uncover more about the history of this land, which has been shaped by earthquakes, tended to by the Ohlone and Coast Miwok, and now provides homes for everything from butterflies to harbor seals, which haul themselves out of the Pacific Ocean onto protected beaches.

GOLDEN GATE
STATE: *California*
DESIGNATED: *1972*

GOLDEN GATE BRIDGE

It's not a national monument, but it's a classic symbol of the West—so you don't want to miss it! The Golden Gate Bridge took more than four years to build. When it was finished in 1937, its 4,200-foot steel span made it the longest suspension bridge in the world. Today, you can drive across the 1.7-mile bridge or use protected sidewalks to walk or bike across. On wheels or on foot, enjoy an amazing view of the San Francisco Bay from about 245 feet above the water's surface.

HIDDEN IN THE FOG

European ships traveling along the coast hundreds of years ago sometimes didn't see the entrance to the San Francisco Bay. It might have been too foggy! Now, during the foggy summer months, the bridge's two sets of foghorns might send out their warning for more than five hours a day.

A SPECIAL ORANGE

The Golden Gate Bridge's unforgettable color has its very own name: International Orange. But did you know that this bridge could have looked like a bumblebee or a candy cane? The U.S. Navy wanted a black-and-yellow bridge so that ships could see it in the fog. The Army Air Corps wanted red and white to keep it visible for airplanes. Instead, the reddish color of the first coat of paint, or primer, got the nod, because it looked great against the sky, the hills, and the waters of the Bay. Plus, it was easy to see!

TOWER POWER

The Golden Gate Bridge has two main towers, each rising 746 feet above the water. If you stacked three tall redwood trees from Muir Woods on top of each other, they'd be about the same height as a bridge tower.

HAWK HILL

On the north side of the Golden Gate Bridge, the Marin Headlands are a perfect place to look for hawks and other raptors. During the fall migration, take your binoculars up to Hawk Hill to watch birds heading south to their winter homes.

ALCATRAZ

This former island prison held some of the country's most infamous prisoners. It's more than a mile away from shore across the cold waters of the San Francisco Bay. In November 1969, people from many Indigenous nations took boats to Alcatraz and started a protest that lasted for 19 months. This occupation led to more civil rights for Indigenous people.

RARE BUTTERFLIES

This area is home to several endangered butterflies with striking colors. Pale blue? That's the male Mission blue butterfly. Those eye-catching red or yellow caterpillars will turn into the San Bruno elfin butterfly. The bright colors of monarch butterflies are like a big warning sign to potential predators: watch out, I'm poisonous! But monarchs are in danger, too. More than a million monarchs once migrated to spend the winter on the California coast, but these populations have plummeted.

Tule Lake

Imagine it's 1941, and you're a kid whose family came to the United States from Japan. You go to school here, you play with your friends—this country is your home. But that December, Japanese planes attack a U.S. naval base in Hawai'i, and the U.S. joins World War II. Then, President Franklin D. Roosevelt issues orders to round up almost everyone with Japanese ancestry and take them to camps where they were imprisoned. The largest of these camps was at Tule Lake, near the California-Oregon border. Today, learn about life in the camps at the visitor's center and take a ranger-led tour. What would it have been like to live here, surrounded by an eight-foot-high fence?

TULE LAKE
STATE: *California*
DESIGNATED: *2019*

BARRACKS

As many as 18,000 people lived here all together, sleeping in crowded barracks. Most barracks had four to six units where people lived. Families would live in rooms that were about the size of a two-car garage.

SCHOOL AT TULE LAKE

Kids still went to school at these camps. Schools often didn't have enough books or desks. Kids and teachers worked to keep other school activities going, such as band, yearbook, and sports. At Tule Lake, kids got a "harvest vacation," but it wasn't relaxing. That's when kids worked on the camp's farm, doing everything from packing turnips to digging potatoes.

CAMP FOOD

People who lived in the camps ate in large, crowded mess halls. The food wasn't like home cooking, and was often made from cans and leftovers. So some people got creative. They bought supplies from the camp's canteen and made their own food in their rooms using a hot plate or wood stove. They even figured out how to make cupcakes and ice cream!

TULE

Tule is a marsh-loving plant that gives this area its name. The Modoc people used tule to make all sorts of things, from baskets to boats. They caught fish and birds with nets made from the tule plant, and crafted tule arrow shafts to hunt animals such as mule deer and pronghorn.

LAVA BEDS NATIONAL MONUMENT

Less than 10 miles from Tule Lake, Lava Beds National Monument showcases this area's turbulent past. Huge volcanic flows shaped stunning lava tube caves that you can visit today. The Modoc lived here until 1873, when they were forced onto reservations in Oklahoma after the Modoc War. More recently, the Caldwell Fire and the Antelope Fire together burned more than 97 percent of the monument's 46,000 acres. There's still plenty of beauty to experience, with mariposa lilies and blue-feathered scrub jays glowing against the monument's basalt rock.

GOING HOME?

World War II ended in September 1945, but Tule Lake stayed open until March 1946. Even after the camps closed, life was not easy for Japanese Americans. When some people returned home, their houses were attacked by racist vandals. Other people didn't even have homes to return to—they had been rented or sold while they were gone. It wasn't until 1988 that the U.S. government issued a formal apology and gave $20,000 to each person who had been in these camps.

MOUNT ST. HELENS

On May 18, 1980, a regular spring morning turned dramatic at 8:32 a.m., when an earthquake kicked off an enormous landslide from the north side of Mount St. Helens. This landslide uncorked the magma underneath, and—*BOOM!*—this volcano erupted in a huge sideways explosion that flattened forests for miles around. Fifty-seven people and much of the wildlife in the area lost their lives. So much was destroyed that it seemed like the mountain's plants and animals might never come back. Then something incredible started to happen. New life returned to the mountain much more quickly than people expected. Today, listen for the bugling call of elk and see the brilliant colors of wildflowers such as lupine and paintbrush on the 8,330-foot mountain. From the Johnston Ridge Observatory, right in the blast zone, gaze out at the mile-wide crater and marvel at this mountain's resilience after such an earth-shattering event.

MOUNT ST. HELENS
STATE: *Washington*
DESIGNATED: *1982*

EARLY RUMBLES
In March 1980, Mount St. Helens had been sleeping for more than 100 years. Then scientists began to notice a series of small earthquakes and mini-eruptions, so they knew that the mountain was starting to wake up. Still, the intensity of the sideways eruption on May 18 shocked everyone.

LARGEST LANDSLIDE
The landslide that triggered the eruption was as big as one million Olympic swimming pools—it still holds the record for the largest avalanche of rock on Earth. These tumbling rocks and dirt moved really fast. The landslide traveled between 110 and 155 miles per hour for 14 miles.

VOLCANIC ASH
Ash spewed 15 miles into the air during the eruption's peak. That's twice as high as most airplanes fly. In Spokane, 250 miles away, there was so much ash in the sky that it looked like night-time even when the sun was up.

MOUNTAIN GOATS
Before the 1980 eruption, only a handful of mountain goats lived on the mountain. But the blast actually created new habitat for them. Now more than 200 mountain goats live here. They've been spotted everywhere from the surrounding landscape to the rim of Mount St. Helens to inside the crater itself.

NEW PONDS BRING NEW LIFE
The huge chunks of mountain that broke off during the eruption turned out to be a good thing for some water-loving creatures. These rocks formed big lumps on the landscape called hummocks, and low spots that later became ponds and wetlands. Hear that chirping sound? That's the boreal toad, a species that is mostly endangered but thrives here. In the summer, its tiny black tadpoles dart and swim through water.

LAWETLAT'LA
In the Cowlitz language, this mountain's name is Lawetlat'la (pronounced "Lah-weight-LOT-lah"), which means "The Smoker." The Cowlitz and other nations have an oral tradition—which means the passing down of ideas by word of mouth—that includes stories from ancestors who saw Lawetlat'la erupt many times throughout its history.

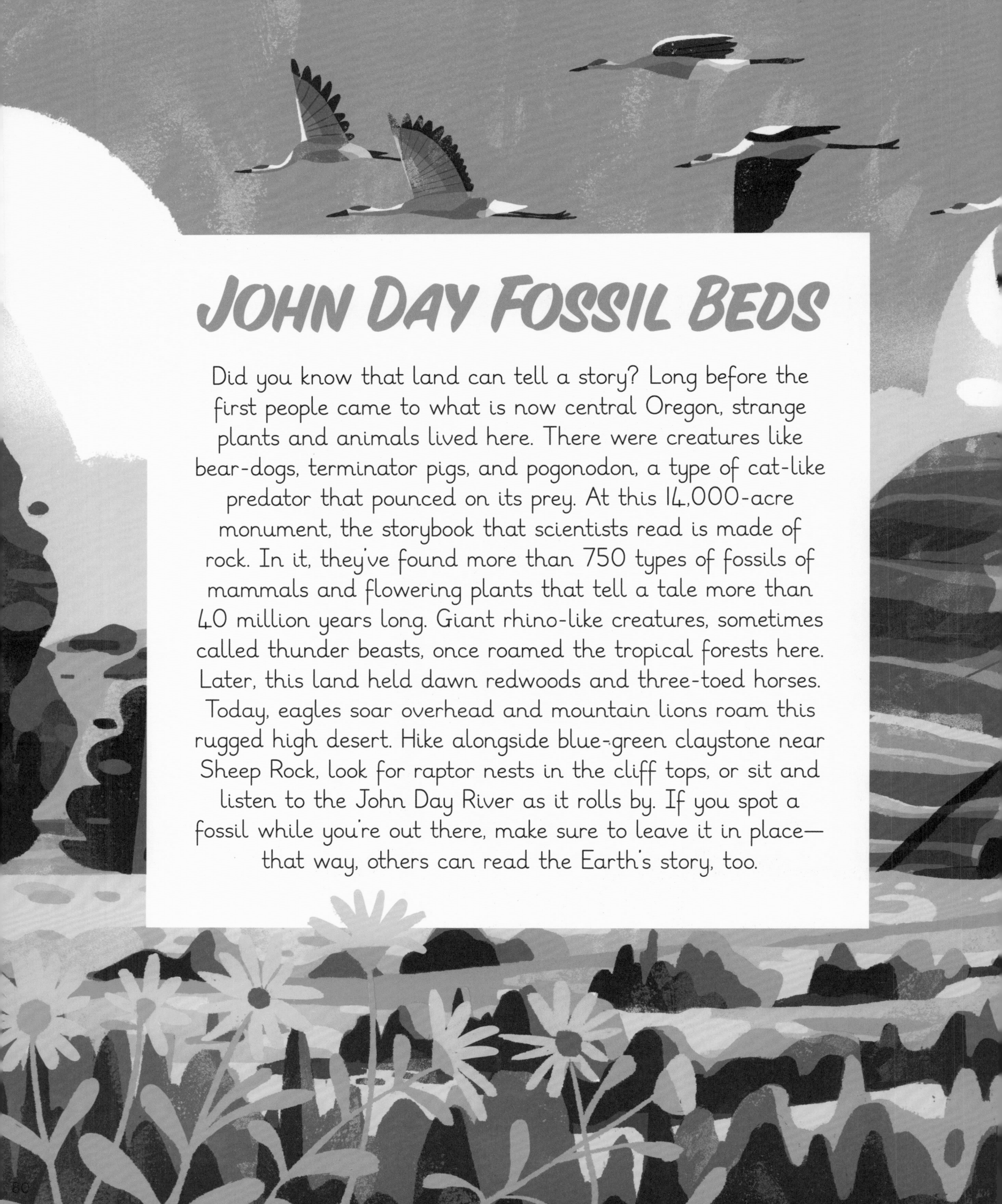

John Day Fossil Beds

Did you know that land can tell a story? Long before the first people came to what is now central Oregon, strange plants and animals lived here. There were creatures like bear-dogs, terminator pigs, and pogonodon, a type of cat-like predator that pounced on its prey. At this 14,000-acre monument, the storybook that scientists read is made of rock. In it, they've found more than 750 types of fossils of mammals and flowering plants that tell a tale more than 40 million years long. Giant rhino-like creatures, sometimes called thunder beasts, once roamed the tropical forests here. Later, this land held dawn redwoods and three-toed horses. Today, eagles soar overhead and mountain lions roam this rugged high desert. Hike alongside blue-green claystone near Sheep Rock, look for raptor nests in the cliff tops, or sit and listen to the John Day River as it rolls by. If you spot a fossil while you're out there, make sure to leave it in place—that way, others can read the Earth's story, too.

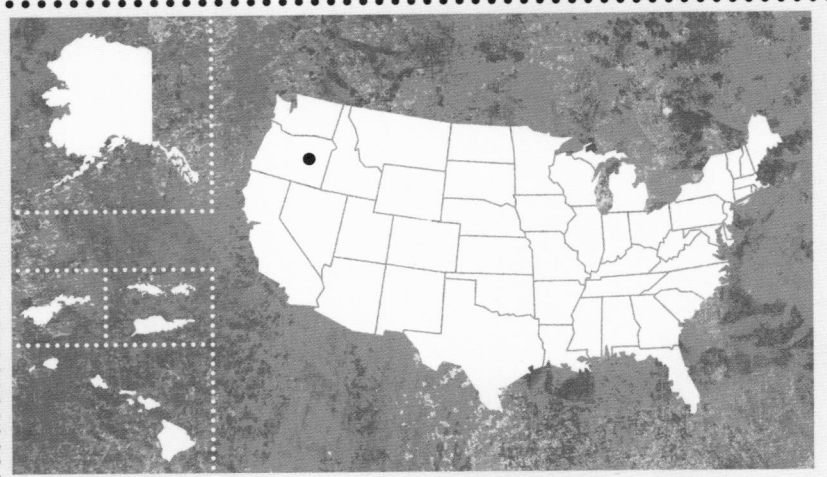

JOHN DAY FOSSIL BEDS

STATE:

Oregon

DESIGNATED:

1975

DAWN REDWOODS

Thirty-three million years ago, these trees were kings of the forest. People once thought they went extinct. Then in the 1940s, people discovered a group of dawn redwoods still growing in China. For tree lovers, it was like stumbling on a dinosaur still living today! Unlike most conifers, or trees with cones, they lose their needles after turning orange or red in the fall.

SCIENCE AT WORK

Researchers are still making discoveries at the monument. In the visitor's center, watch through the laboratory's observation window as scientists analyze newly found fossils. If you're hiking, you may even spot paleontologists at work in the field. Who knows what they'll find?

PRIMATE FIND

Scientists discovered the remains of an extinct species of primate here—that's a group that includes apes, monkeys, and us! This small, lemur-like animal only weighed about five pounds, but it has a big name: *Ekgmowechashala zancanellai*. It also played a big role in North American history: it's the last primate known to live on this continent before humans showed up.

PAINTED HILLS

The Painted Hills' stripes of red and yellow rock tell a story of what the climate was like in the past. The red layers get their color from iron-rich soils deposited during warm, wet times. Yellow layers come from drier periods. Rain, wind, and time helped uncover these colorful rocks.

REALLY MINIATURE HORSES

Imagine a horse the size of a border collie. (Would you want it to sleep on your bed with you?) If you were here 44 million years ago, you'd have seen the 12-inch-tall *Orohippus major* trotting through the thick, damp forest. It might have looked like a tiny deer!

PORCUPINE

Incredible creatures still live at the monument today. Take the porcupine and its 30,000 quills. While porcupines can't shoot their quills at predators, their quills detach easily and hook into anything that gets too close. Each quill has more than 700 tiny barbs near its tip, which makes them really stick!

RIVER NAMES

The John Day River runs through this land and gives the monument its name. It's named after a man who was part of an expedition to Oregon in the early 1800s. The Cayuse people call it the Mah-Hah River. The Cayuse and other nations, such as the Northern Paiute and Tenino, have long lived and traveled along its waters.

LAHARS

Massive mudflows called lahars once trapped everything from trees to nuts to wildlife. That's why we see so many fossils here today. Lahars also shaped a group of tall pinnacles called the Clarno Palisades. Look closely and you might find the images of ancient leaves and vines preserved in the rock.

SPOTTING SNAKES

The rattlesnake and the gophersnake look very similar with their dusky colors and dark spots. To tell them apart, look at the tail. The rattlesnake, which has venom, has its telltale rattles there. The nonvenomous gophersnake, which squeezes its prey, has none. Either way, admire any snakes you see from a safe distance!

ONE BIG PIG

Watch out, it's the terminator pig! Thirty million years ago, *Archaeotherium caninus* was the largest animal in Oregon, and an aggressive predator and scavenger. At over six feet tall at the shoulder, this big, pig-like entelodont might even intimidate your favorite basketball player.

WESTERN WILDFLOWERS

Spot the John Day pincushion and the golden bee plant in the cracks and crevices of the colorful Painted Hills. These and other wildflowers turn these hills into a sunset of color.

Everything is supersized in the biggest state in the country. Here, you'll find the tallest mountains, the coldest nights, and the longest days—because this far north, the summer sun stays up late! Use this extra helping of daylight to see Alaska's natural beauty, from coastal rainforests thick with towering spruces to sweeping views of the tundra. Listen for the far-off howl of a wolf, and reach out your arms to feel the spray of waterfalls that pour down the sides of granite cliffs. Glaciers and volcanoes have shaped a land whose first people were the ancestors of today's Alaska Natives. Much later, fur traders from Russia came in search of sea otters and other creatures, followed by prospectors seeking gold. You'll find something even more precious in this breathtaking region, where the swirling colors of the aurora borealis, the Northern Lights, brighten up a long winter's night.

ANIAKCHAK

In this rugged and remote place, you might see more caribou than people! Sockeye salmon swim up the Aniakchak River to reach Surprise Lake in the monument's six-mile-wide volcanic caldera.

ALASKA

ADMIRALTY ISLAND

Welcome to bear territory: this place has one of the highest concentrations of brown bears in the world! You can also visit tide pools and spot bald eagles flying overhead at this 955,000-acre monument.

MISTY FJORDS

Hear the distant howl of wolves from your kayak at this vast monument. This wilderness is part of the Tongass National Forest, home to the largest intact coastal rainforest in the U.S.

ADMIRALTY ISLAND

Look out the window of your floatplane: even before the pontoons touch down, you'll know you're flying somewhere special. Forty miles south of Juneau, this monument has almost a million acres of stunning beauty, from its old-growth rainforest to a coast full of bays, beaches, and bears. The Tlingit people call this island Kootznoowoo, or "fortress of the bear," for good reason. With about 1,600 brown bears, it has one of the highest concentrations of brown bears in the world.

Go with a ranger to the Pack Creek Bear Viewing Area, where you might see bears gathering to feast on migrating salmon. You can also glide in a kayak along the Seymour Canal, where bald eagles soar overhead. In the summer, sunset is after 9pm, but you'll know it's close to bedtime when you hear loons call across one of Admiralty Island's many lakes.

ADMIRALTY
ISLAND

STATE:
Alaska

DESIGNATED:
1978

BALD EAGLES

There are so many bald eagles along the Seymour Canal you might spot an eagle's nest for every mile you paddle. Bald eagles can hunt for their own fish and other prey. But what they really like to do is to snag food from other birds, mammals, and even people.

WHICH BEAR OVER THERE?

How can you tell a brown bear from a grizzly? Brown bears live close to the coast, while grizzlies live farther inland. Living by the coast gives brown bears access to rich food such as salmon and salmonberries, so they grow larger than grizzlies. Some male brown bears tip the scales at more than 1,000 pounds!

MOSSY MUSKEGS

A muskeg is a watery place on land that's full of soggy, boggy layers of moss. This incredible sphagnum moss can hold up to 30 times its weight in water. Muskegs can be surprisingly deep, so watch your step—you don't want to get your boots stuck!

SITKA BLACK-TAILED DEER

Do you wear different clothes during different times of year? The Sitka black-tailed deer's coat changes with the seasons, too—reddish-brown in the summer, and darker gray-brown in the winter. These deer are surprisingly good swimmers, and they don't even need to change into a bathing suit.

88

SITKA SPRUCE

They say everything is bigger in Alaska, and that's certainly true for trees. The Sitka spruce, the state tree, is the tallest spruce in the world. Spruces provide homes and food for many animals in the forest, including the Sitka deer, which shelters under this tree's branches in the winter.

SALMON, BIG AND SMALL

At around three to five pounds, pink salmon are the smallest salmon in the Pacific. Sometimes the males have a big bump on their backs, so they're also called humpback salmon. Chum salmon weigh in at the other end of the salmon scale—they can grow up to 35 pounds.

TEMPERATE RAINFOREST

Did you know there are rainforests in Alaska? Temperate rainforests are cool instead of balmy—but like tropical rainforests, they're really, really wet. Here on Admiralty Island, it can rain more than 100 inches a year.

LIKIN' LICHEN

Lichens are an amazing mashup of algae and fungi. Some lichens are bright orange or yellow, others have wispy tufts or scales. Way up in the mountains at Admiralty Island, people have found clumps of rare crab-eye lichen, which has little tips that look like crab eyes on their eyestalks.

KEEPING LANGUAGE ALIVE

The Tlingit residents of Angoon, the only village on Admiralty Island, helped to establish the monument to protect this area in 1978. Their language, Tlingit, is an official state language. About 500 people speak Tlingit today. Teachers and schools in Alaska are working to preserve this and other Alaska Native languages.

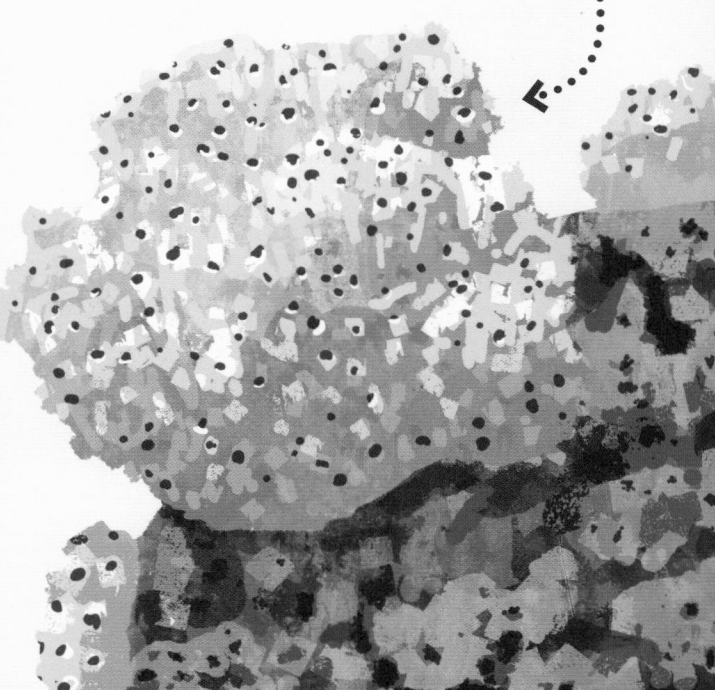

Misty Fjords

Dall's porpoises leap and play in front of the bow of your ship as you pass alongside jaw-dropping cliffs that rise straight up from the water. You're only 22 miles from Ketchikan, but you're already deep in Misty Fjords' glacier-carved wonderland. The Behm Canal runs for more than 100 miles through the monument, drawing humpback whales and orcas, harbor seals and Steller sea lions. If the mist lifts, catch a glimpse of a mountain goat perched high on the rocks or a waterfall tumbling off a cliff. Passing these majestic rock faces, you might find your heart beating faster and your smile getting bigger each time your boat glides around a watery bend. Look closely for pictographs made by the Tlingit, the first people of this land. Back in Ketchikan, experience more of the Tlingit, Haida, and Tsimshian cultures that are a vibrant part of this region today.

MISTY FJORDS
STATE: *Alaska*
DESIGNATED: *1978*

HOW TO MAKE A FJORD

As glaciers move, they carve out narrow channels with deep canyons and high cliffs. When seawater flows into these channels, they're called fjords. The cliffs at Misty Fjords are so tall they might seem like natural skyscrapers—they can soar up to 3,000 feet!

DALL'S PORPOISES

People sometimes confuse Dall's porpoises with orcas because of their black-and-white coloring. At about six feet long, these porpoises are smaller than orcas. They're also high-speed swimmers that can zoom through the water at 35 miles per hour.

WOLVES

Wolves can come in many colors, from white to gray to black. Here in southeast Alaska, they tend to be darker and smaller than wolves elsewhere in the state. A wolf pack usually has six or seven wolves in it. Some packs are even bigger, with 20 or 30 wolves working, hunting, and howling together.

RED-THROATED LOONS

The haunting evening call of a red-throated loon is something you'll always remember. It's also hard to miss this loon's striking colors. A breeding adult has red eyes and a rust-colored patch on its throat.

WHALE WATCHING

Humpback whales swim Misty Fjords' waters in search of krill and small fish. These whales take big gulps of seawater and filter their seafood meals through baleen, the brushy-looking structures they have instead of teeth. Baleen is made of keratin, the same stuff that's in your hair and fingernails.

BEAR JAMBOREE

Alaska's black and brown bears meet up at Misty Fjords! The black bear is the smallest bear in Alaska, weighing about 300 pounds. Both black and brown bears hibernate over winter. But bears don't sleep the whole time—they shift and move around like a snoozing dog to find the most comfortable spot.

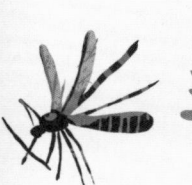

MOSQUITOES

People joke about mosquitoes being Alaska's state bird, because they're big and they're everywhere! Alaska has about 35 species of mosquito. Female mosquitoes are drawn to people's warm bodies, the scent of our skin, and the carbon dioxide we breathe out.

ANIAKCHAK
STATE: *Alaska*
DESIGNATED: *1978*

RING OF FIRE

It might sound like something a stunt double jumps through on a motorcycle, but this ring of fire is much bigger, and hotter! The "Ring of Fire" runs along both sides of the Pacific Ocean where several of the Earth's tectonic plates meet, slip, and slide. That means lots of earthquakes and more than 450 volcanoes, including the one that carved out Aniakchak's landscape.

SEA OTTERS

If you love sea otters, Alaska is the place to be—90 percent of the world's sea otters live along these coasts. Sea otters have two layers of thick fur that keeps them warm in chilly Pacific waters. They also have a flap of skin under each arm, which they use like pockets for saving food and the rocks they use to crack open shellfish.

MAKING TRACKS

You might not think about dinosaurs living so far north, but scientists have found dozens of dinosaur tracks preserved in the monument's rocks. A group of duck-billed dinosaurs called hadrosaurs left these footprints more than 66 million years ago. There were so many hadrosaurs back then that some researchers call them the caribou of the Cretaceous.

BERRY GOOD

You might have eaten blueberries, but have you tried crowberries, watermelon berries, or salmonberries? These and other berries ripen in late summer and early fall, and bears, caribou, birds, wolves, and people gobble them down. The Alutiiq people harvest berries at the monument today, just like their ancestors did thousands of years ago.

PUFFIN POWER

Sailors used to call puffins "sea parrots" because of their brightly colored beaks. Both tufted and horned puffins fish along the Alaska Peninsula, using a special swim stroke that looks like underwater flying. In the air, a puffin's wings can beat at a speedy 400 times a minute!

CARIBOU

Both male and female caribou have antlers that they grow and shed each year. They're also covered in hair from their noses to the bottoms of their hooves. Hairy hooves keep caribou from slipping and sliding on the frozen tundra while they look for their favorite winter meal: lichen.

aniakchak

You're standing in the middle of a gigantic crater at the edge of a turquoise lake. Look around: the vast stretches of tundra might contain caribou browsing on berries or the plate-sized tracks of a grizzly bear. But something's missing—other people. Only a few hundred people come each year to this remote, roadless, and spectacular national monument on the Alaska Peninsula, 450 miles from Anchorage. An enormous volcanic eruption about 3,500 years ago created the monument's caldera, which is more than six miles wide and 2,500 feet deep! From the caldera's glacier-fed Surprise Lake, river rafters ride the 27-mile-long Aniakchak River through a gorge called the Gates, and then on to the Pacific Ocean. Along the coast, puffins dive for fish while sea otters float on the water's surface. Sometimes these otters hold hands so they can stick together while they sleep.

MARIANAS TRENCH

Dive deep into this incredible place that is home to bubbling thermal vents, underwater mud volcanoes, and unique deep-sea creatures.

It might surprise you that there are monuments way out in the middle of the ocean and deep beneath its surface. But the oceans hold some of the world's most fascinating creatures, diverse coral reefs, and incredible geology, from underwater volcanoes to bubbling undersea vents. In the Pacific Ocean, several marine national monuments shelter these important—and increasingly threatened—places and species.

Imagine a warm breeze on an island beach, where seabirds circle overhead and sea turtles dig their nests. In the water, coral reefs teem with life in all colors of the rainbow, from orange and white clownfish to turquoise giant clams that are bigger than basketballs—the largest one ever found was more than four feet long! Or think about being a researcher who can use a submersible to see an unusual octopus glide along the ocean floor.

Because these marine national monuments often include islands, reefs, and the ocean itself, lots of groups work together to protect them, from government agencies such as the National Oceanic and Atmospheric Administration and the U.S. Fish & Wildlife Service to Indigenous peoples who have deep knowledge of their homelands and waters. Many of these national monuments are so remote that they're tricky to experience in person, but maybe someday you will help protect these special places as someone who studies the ocean and all the life it holds.

PAPAHĀNAUMOKUĀKEA
People are protecting monk seals, Hawaiian green sea turtles, and a wealth of wildlife from the marine debris that gathers around this monument's coral reefs and beaches.

TROPICS

ROSE ATOLL
Endangered green sea turtles come to Rose Atoll to make their nests. The little hatchlings migrate more than 1,000 miles away—and 25 to 30 years later, the grown-up females come back here to lay their own eggs!

Papahānaumokuākea

Sail north and west from the main islands of Hawai'i to encounter this 1,350-mile-long chain of ancient islands, a place where sea life thrives from beaches to the ocean floor. Papahānaumokuākea has half a million square miles of ocean, which makes it bigger than all the U.S. national parks put together. Honu, the iconic green sea turtles, come here to dig their nests, while deep under the surface, seawater flows through gigantic ocean sponges. Some of these sponges are thousands of years old! These islands have been woven into the lives of Native Hawaiians for a long time, too. One island, Mokumanamana, has the largest group of Hawaiian sacred sites in the world. Visit the Mokupāpapa Discovery Center in Hilo to get close to the stories of the monument's 10-plus islands and atolls. Maybe someday, you'll visit Midway Atoll as a researcher who protects the endangered Laysan duck, found nowhere else in the world. Or maybe you'll be a scientist piloting a submersible to learn more about the species that live along the ocean floor.

PAPAHĀNAUMOKUĀKEA
STATE: *Hawai'i*
DESIGNATED: *2006*

ISLANDS ON THE MOVE
Millions of years ago, lava from underwater volcanoes started to form the Hawaiian islands. Over time, erosion and eruptions whittled the islands' tops, while deep under the ocean, the islands' rocks settled and shifted. The islands are still in motion today, inching along about as fast as your fingernails grow.

CORAL AT ITS HEART
Coral polyps, or ko'a, are the tiny animals that build coral reefs. A traditional Hawaiian creation chant, the Kumulipo, says that the ko'a was the first life born from the lava, and the building block for everything from the Hawaiian people to the islands themselves. Midway Atoll is actually an old volcano covered in a 1,000-foot-thick coral cap!

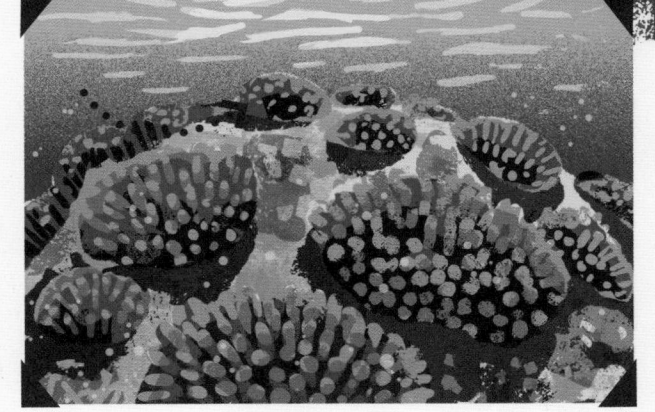

HAWAIIAN MONK SEALS
There are only about 1,570 endangered Hawaiian monk seals in the world, and most of them live in and around the monument. They can hold their breath for 20 minutes or more, and dive deeper than 1,800 feet.

VOYAGING
More than a thousand years ago, Hawaiians traveled long distances between Pacific islands. Instead of compasses and GPS, they used stars, currents, or the movement of seabirds to find their way. Today, people learning these traditional wayfinding skills practice by sailing from the main Hawaiian islands to the monument, which lies beyond the horizon.

LONG JOURNEYS, LONG LIVES
Three species of albatross travel thousands of miles across the open ocean to make their nests here. These excellent seafarers have extremely long lives. The oldest known wild bird is a Laysan albatross named Wisdom. In 2021, this 70-something bird hatched a new chick at Midway Atoll.

PACIFIC REMOTE ISLANDS
Designated: 2009

Want to get even more remote? The Pacific Remote Islands Marine National Monument is farther from a human town than any other group of islands in the Pacific. Instead, coral "cities" host incredible creatures, including the world's biggest parrotfish and graceful manta rays that glide through schools of bright-pink blenny fish. Melon-headed whales swim together in big groups. Sometimes there can be more than 1,000 whales in one spot! With seven islands and atolls, and nearly half a million square miles of land and water, you'll find everything from seabird colonies to underwater seamounts where Deepstaria jellyfish billow through the water like spooky-cool ghosts.

HONU HAVEN
More than 90 percent of all of Hawai'i's green sea turtles make their nests on an atoll called French Frigate Shoals. If a honu glides by as you're snorkeling in the main Hawaiian islands, it likely swam at least 500 miles from Papahānaumokuākea.

MARIANAS TRENCH

Are you fascinated by extreme habitats and unusual creatures? Then you'll fall deeply in love with this monument's plunging underwater landscape, which people call the Grand Canyon of the ocean. Here, underwater volcanoes bubble with blue mud and yawning canyons host some of the world's strangest marine species, from technicolored jellyfish to seldom-seen octopus species. Down in the seafloor ridges and deep rift basins, hydrothermal vents burp out gases. The most sunken spot in the whole monument—35,210-foot Sirena Deep—is even deeper than Mount Everest is tall! In shallower areas, colorful fish roam the coral reefs, and shark species from the whitetip to the whale shark feed on these waters' rich array of sea life.

DUMBO OCTOPUS
This charming deep-sea octopus has fins that look like elephant ears. It gets around by flapping these fins like a slow-moving bird (or flying elephant), and uses its eight "arms" to steer. A dumbo octopus can be as small as your forearm, or as tall as a grown-up.

SENSATIONAL SEAMOUNTS
Volcanoes can create underwater mountains called seamounts. Seamounts are like big parties for marine life, attracting creatures from tiny crustaceans to big fish such as jacks and sharks. More than 11 million square miles of the ocean floor might have seamounts, which means that there might be more seamounts than deserts, tundra, or any other habitat on land!

FAR-OUT JELLYFISH
On an underwater expedition in 2016, researchers spotted a jelly more than two miles under the ocean's surface. Its glowing red and yellow bell made it look like a creature from outer space!

UNDERWATER LABORATORY
SCUBA divers love exploring the Maug caldera, formed by an ancient volcano. Here, underwater vents bubble out carbon dioxide and heat—it feels like you're swimming in the middle of a glass of warm soda! The ocean's carbon dioxide levels are rising as the climate warms, so scientists use Maug as a living laboratory to see how carbon dioxide affects the ocean and its creatures.

DEEP-SEA EXPLORATION
To learn more about life deep underwater, scientists use high-tech underwater vehicles that can travel to these dark, cold waters. They've even used submersibles to visit Challenger Deep, a 35,876-foot-deep spot just outside the monument that is the deepest place on Earth.

Rose Atoll

Squawks, calls, twitters, and chirps create a bird symphony here at Rose Atoll, an important nesting site for thousands of seabirds. Birds are so big here that this area is called Nu'u O Manu ("village of seabirds") in the Samoan language. This southernmost island of American Samoa is home to other marvels, too, such as beautiful rose-colored coralline algae and nesting green and hawksbill sea turtles. The hundreds of fish species that swarm these rich waters come in many colors of the rainbow. They have colorful names, too, such as damselfish, parrotfish, and unicornfish! There are even giant clams that are green, teal, or electric blue. Humpback whales and pods of dolphins swim outside the monument's mile-wide lagoon. Deep in the ocean, creatures called sea lilies appear like feathery underwater flowers.

ROSE ATOLL
TERRITORY: *American Samoa*
DESIGNATED: *2009*

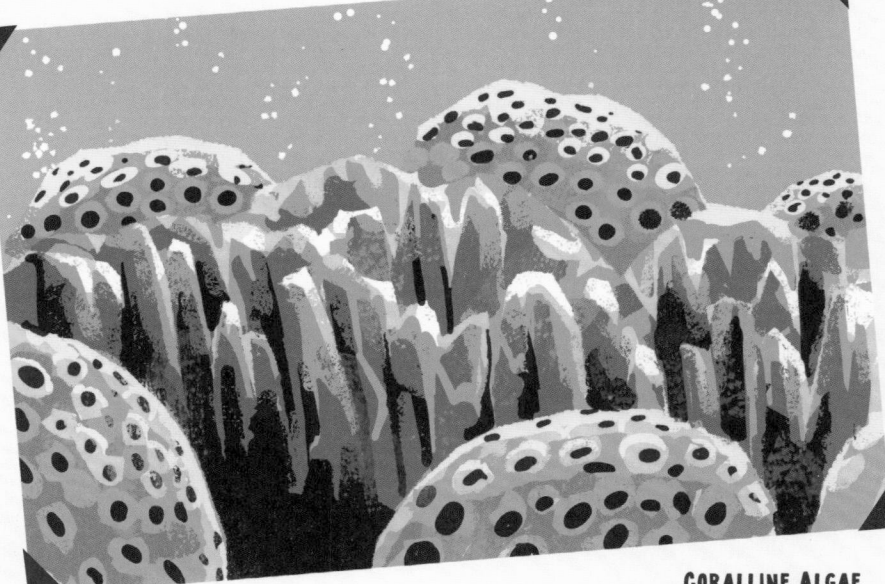

GREAT GUANO
The monument's many seabirds give the reefs a big (and stinky) boost! Guano, or bird poop, is high in nitrogen, which helps coral reefs to grow.

CORALLINE ALGAE
Coralline algae grows in and around coral reefs, and acts like a glue to hold reefs together. The coralline algae here is pink, which gives this atoll its rosy hue.

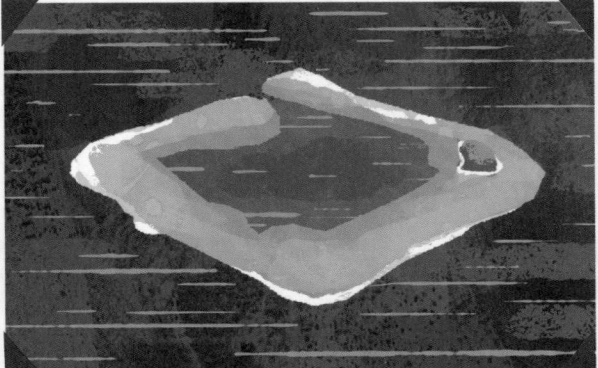

ATOLL IN ACTION
An atoll begins to form when coral grows around the edges of an island. The ring of coral expands while the island sinks lower and lower until it vanishes beneath the surface—a process that takes hundreds of thousands of years! The protected water in the center of an atoll is called a lagoon.

GIANT CLAMS
Along with being enormous, giant clams (also known by their Samoan name, faisua) have another superpower—they're actually part animal, part plant. Faisua can open their shells to let the sun shine on special plant cells called zooxanthellae (pronounced "zoh-uh-zan-THEL-lay"). These cells can then use sunlight to make energy for the clams—it's like having built-in solar panels and a restaurant in one!

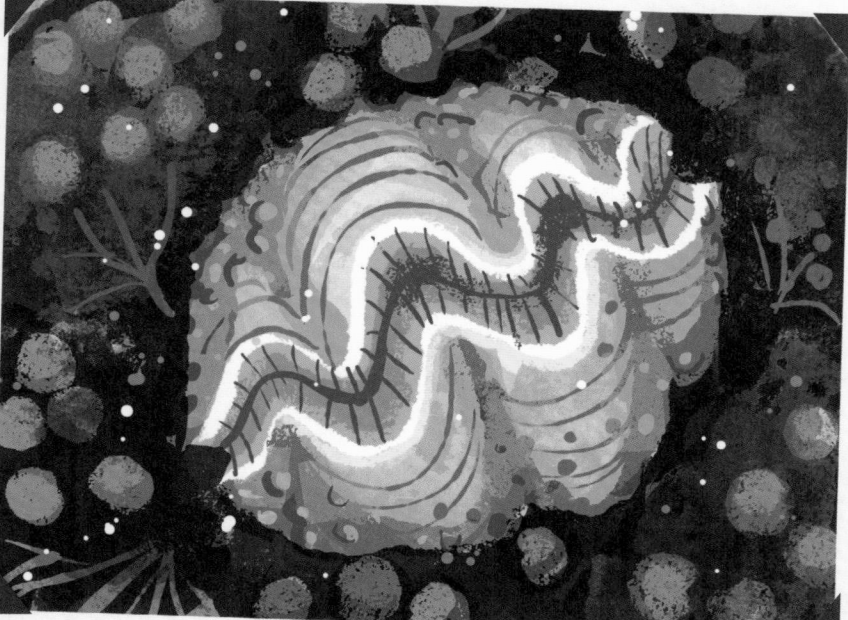

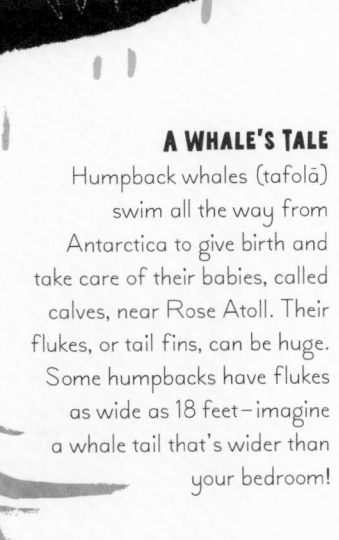

A WHALE'S TALE
Humpback whales (tafolā) swim all the way from Antarctica to give birth and take care of their babies, called calves, near Rose Atoll. Their flukes, or tail fins, can be huge. Some humpbacks have flukes as wide as 18 feet—imagine a whale tail that's wider than your bedroom!

Monumental Homes

Some national monuments celebrate important people at the places where they once lived. When you visit, picture them doing a lot of the same things you do at your own home, like sharing meals with family and spending time with friends. It might make you wonder what kids in the future might want to celebrate about YOU!

GEORGE WASHINGTON CARVER
STATE: *Missouri*
DESIGNATED: *1943*

George Washington Carver might be best known as a famous scientist who found 300 uses for the peanut. He also helped farmers grow new crops and keep the soil healthy. But did you know he knew so much about nature that people called him "the plant doctor" as a kid? At this monument, where Carver was born in a small cabin in the early 1860s, learn what his early days were like in the visitor center's re-created 19th-century schoolroom. Then take to the trails to see muskrats and turtles in the woods and visit the native tallgrass prairie. Who knows, maybe nature will inspire you to help others, too!

GEORGE WASHINGTON BIRTHPLACE
STATE: *Virginia*
DESIGNATED: *1930*

When a baby boy was born here in 1732, his parents had no idea he'd be the first president of a brand-new country. Today, George Washington's birthplace is a 551-acre national monument with a small museum and plenty of outdoors to explore. See red Devon cattle and Hog Island sheep, farm animals that are descended from and look like some of the animals that colonists brought to North America in the 1600s. Life here also goes back much further: along the water's edge, paleontologists have found fossils of shellfish, shark teeth, and small whales!

CHARLES YOUNG BUFFALO SOLDIERS
STATE: *Ohio*
DESIGNATED: *2013*

Brigadier General Charles Young was an Army officer and the first African American superintendent of a National Park. It wasn't always easy for Young. In 1884, he was one of the few Black students who attended the U.S. Military Academy at West Point. There, he was bullied and sometimes struggled with his schoolwork. He stuck with it and graduated in 1889. Young loved horses, and was in charge of all-Black cavalry regiments known as the Buffalo Soldiers. Buffalo Soldiers often served on the Plains and in the Southwest, which put them into conflict with Indigenous nations. In 1903, Young was appointed superintendent of Sequoia and General Grant national parks in California. His troops mapped landscapes, fought fires, and built sturdy roads that people still use today. At "Youngsholm," in Wilberforce, Ohio, he welcomed friends, family, and people he met as a diplomat in countries around the world.

BOOKER T. WASHINGTON
STATE: *Virginia*
DESIGNATED: *1956*

Dr. Booker T. Washington, born here to an enslaved family at what is now the monument in 1856, worked throughout his life to improve education for African Americans. Once his family was freed, he taught himself to read, went to school, and became the first principal of an Alabama college that's now Tuskegee University. The monument hosts special events during holidays such as Juneteenth, which commemorates the end of slavery in the United States. At any time of year, the Jack-O-Lantern Branch Trail is a place to wander through the woods. Spot the red feathers of the male cardinal—Washington might have seen this same species as he fished and gathered plants as a kid.

MEDGAR AND MYRLIE EVERS HOME
STATE: *Mississippi*
DESIGNATED: *2020*

The three-bedroom home of civil rights leaders Medgar and Myrlie Evers is one of the country's newest national monuments. Medgar Evers fought in Europe during World War II in the 1940s. When he returned to the U.S., he and his wife fought for civil rights as part of the NAACP, an important anti-racism organization. The couple worked to end segregation and help more Black people vote safely. But some people didn't agree with the work they were doing and tried to stop it with violence. In 1963, Medgar was shot and killed outside his home. After his death, people around the country rallied to work even harder for civil rights. Myrlie didn't stop working for civil rights, either. She became the national chair of the NAACP.

PRESIDENT LINCOLN AND SOLDIERS' HOME
CITY: *Washington, D.C.*
DESIGNATED: *2000*

Even presidents need to get away. This house, on a hill above Washington, D.C., was where President Abraham Lincoln and his family came during hot summers for a break from the capital's hustle and heat. At what's now called President Lincoln's Cottage, Lincoln had time to recharge and play checkers with his son Tad on the veranda. Once, the president rescued a group of peacocks that had gotten tangled up in the cedar trees! Lincoln also did some of his most important thinking in this peaceful landscape. Right here in the Cottage, he started writing the document that would lead to the end of slavery: the Emancipation Proclamation. Imagine what ideas you might have, too, if you took a break from your everyday life.

CÉSAR E. CHÁVEZ
STATE: *California*
DESIGNATED: *2012*

When César Chávez was a kid, he and his family worked on farms across California during the Great Depression. He left school after eighth grade to work, picking everything from avocados to peas. As a grown-up in 1962, he started a group for farmworkers that demanded better pay and safer jobs. Chávez and this union, called the United Farmworkers of America, used nonviolent strikes and marches to make their lives better. Chávez's home, also the union headquarters, is now a national monument honoring an important labor, civil rights, and environmental leader. The monument's 10.5-acre grounds are also a great place to see wildlife. Hear the *tap-tap-tap* of acorn woodpeckers and watch for red-shouldered hawks swooping overhead.

NATIONAL MONUMENTS OF THE U.S.A.

ALABAMA
Birmingham Civil Rights National Monument
Freedom Riders National Monument
Russell Cave National Monument

ALASKA
Admiralty Island National Monument
Aleutian Islands World War II National Monument
Aniakchak National Monument and Preserve
Cape Krusenstern National Monument
Misty Fjords National Monument

AMERICAN SAMOA
Rose Atoll Marine National Monument

ARIZONA
Agua Fria National Monument
Canyon de Chelly National Monument
Casa Grande Ruins National Monument
Chiricahua National Monument
Grand Canyon-Parashant National Monument
Hohokam Pima National Monument
Ironwood Forest National Monument
Montezuma Castle National Monument
Navajo National Monument
Organ Pipe Cactus National Monument
Pipe Spring National Monument
Sonoran Desert National Monument
Sunset Crater Volcano National Monument
Tonto National Monument
Tuzigoot National Monument
Vermilion Cliffs National Monument
Walnut Canyon National Monument
Wupatki National Monument

ATLANTIC OCEAN
Northeast Canyons and Seamounts Marine National Monument

CALIFORNIA
Berryessa Snow Mountain National Monument
Cabrillo National Monument
California Coastal National Monument
Carrizo Plain National Monument
Cascade-Siskiyou National Monument (shared with Oregon)
Castle Mountains National Monument
César E. Chávez National Monument
Devils Postpile National Monument
Fort Ord National Monument
Giant Sequoia National Monument
Lava Beds National Monument
Mojave Trails National Monument
Muir Woods National Monument
Saint Francis Dam Disaster National Memorial and National Monument
Sand to Snow National Monument
San Gabriel Mountains National Monument
Santa Rosa and San Jacinto Mountains National Monument
Tule Lake National Monument

COLORADO
Browns Canyon National Monument
Camp Hale-Continental Divide National Monument
Canyon of the Ancients National Monument
Chimney Rock National Monument
Colorado National Monument
Dinosaur National Monument (shared with Utah)
Florissant Fossil Beds National Monument
Hovenweep National Monument (shared with Utah)
Yucca House National Monument

D.C.
Belmont-Paul Women's Equality National Monument
President Lincoln and Soldiers' Home National Monument

FLORIDA
Castillo de San Marcos National Monument
Fort Matanzas National Monument

GEORGIA
Fort Frederica National Monument
Fort Pulaski National Monument

HAWAI'I
Papahānaumokuākea Marine National Monument

IDAHO
Craters of the Moon National Monument and Preserve
Hagerman Fossil Beds National Monument

ILLINOIS
Pullman National Monument

IOWA
Effigy Mounds National Monument

KENTUCKY
Camp Nelson National Monument
Mill Springs Battlefield National Monument

LOUISIANA
Poverty Point National Monument

MAINE
Katahdin Woods and Waters
National Monument

MARYLAND
Fort McHenry National Monument
and Historic Shrine

MINNESOTA
Grand Portage National Monument
Pipestone National Monument

MISSISSIPPI
Medgar and Myrlie Evers Home
National Monument

MISSOURI
George Washington Carver
National Monument

MONTANA
Little Bighorn Battlefield National
Monument
Pompeys Pillar National Monument
Upper Missouri River Breaks National
Monument

NEBRASKA
Agate Fossil Beds National Monument
Scotts Bluff National Monument

NEVADA
Basin and Range National Monument
Gold Butte National Monument
Tule Springs Fossil Beds National
Monument

NEW JERSEY
Statue of Liberty National Monument
(shared with New York)

NEW MEXICO
Aztec Ruins National Monument
Bandelier National Monument
Capulin Volcano National Monument
El Malpais National Monument
El Morro National Monument
Fort Union National Monument

Gila Cliff Dwellings National
Monument
Kasha-Katuwe Tent Rocks National
Monument
Organ Mountains-Desert Peaks
National Monument
Petroglyph National Monument
Prehistoric Trackways National
Monument
Rio Grande del Norte National
Monument
Salinas Pueblo Missions National
Monument

NEW YORK
African Burial Ground National
Monument
Castle Clinton National Monument
Fort Stanwix National Monument
Governors Island National Monument
Statue of Liberty National
Monument (shared with New Jersey)
Stonewall National Monument

NORTHERN MARIANA ISLANDS
Marianas Trench Marine National
Monument

OHIO
Charles Young Buffalo Soldiers
National Monument

OREGON
Cascade-Siskiyou National Monument
(shared with California)
John Day Fossil Beds National
Monument
Newberry National Volcanic
Monument
Oregon Caves National Monument
and Preserve

SOUTH DAKOTA
Jewel Cave National Monument

TEXAS
Alibates Flint Quarries National
Monument

U.S. Military Working Dog Teams
National Monument
Waco Mammoth National Monument

U.S. MINOR OUTLYING ISLANDS
Pacific Remote Islands Marine
National Monument

U.S. VIRGIN ISLANDS
Buck Island Reef National Monument
Virgin Islands Coral Reef National
Monument

UTAH
Bears Ears National Monument
Cedar Breaks National Monument
Dinosaur National Monument (shared
with Colorado)
Grand Staircase-Escalante National
Monument
Hovenweep National Monument
(shared with Colorado)
Jurassic National Monument
Natural Bridges National Monument
Rainbow Bridge National Monument
Timpanogos Cave National Monument

VIRGINIA
Booker T. Washington National
Monument
Fort Monroe National Monument
George Washington Birthplace
National Monument

WASHINGTON
Hanford Reach National Monument
Mount St. Helens National Volcanic
Monument
San Juan Islands National Monument

WYOMING
Devils Tower National Monument
Fossil Butte National Monument

CONCLUSION

You've come to the end of your tour, and by now you've learned a few stories about this amazing land! But did you know these stories are still being written? People like you are campaigning to protect important spots across the U.S.A. by making them national monuments, which could keep them safe for years to come. They're also maintaining the monuments that already exist—which is becoming even more important in the face of threats such as rising sea levels and wildfires caused by climate change.

You can help, too. When you visit a national monument, you can treat these places and everything you find there, such as amazing creatures and historic artifacts, with care and respect. Leave what you find in place, but definitely bring home great memories and cool photographs!

But you don't need to live near a national monument to pay attention to the world around you. It can even happen in your own backyard. Do you have a special spot in your neighborhood that you want to take care of? Maybe it's a place where something important happened in your life, or where there's a tree or animal you feel close to, or a person who really matters to you. These stories are important. They could be part of your own personal monument or one that you create with your family, your friends, or your community.

Not sure how to start? Use your senses. Stand next to a favorite tree and take a deep breath. What does it smell like? Cup your hands around your ears. Do you hear birdsong, people's voices, or the wind rustling through the leaves? Maybe there's a patch of dirt where you can kick off your shoes and feel the earth beneath your feet. You can also feel connected to the past by talking to the older people in your life. They might have even more stories of the places and historical events that you have read about here and elsewhere.

Now the story is up to you. What will be the next chapter?

INDEX

What is HOLT Science Spectrum?

TENNESSEE EDITION

A new science program for Integrated Physics and Chemistry (IPC) that keeps students on target!

Building on a core of high quality science instructional materials developed in the United Kingdom, **Holt Science Spectrum** was conceived to help solve the problems teachers and students face as they implement Texas' new Integrated Physics and Chemistry course. With that singular goal in mind, the development team focused on the following objectives:

✓ **Start students off on the right track with solid development of basic skills.**
Holt Science Spectrum helps students improve their skills in reading, writing and mathematics, while adding new critical thinking and life/work skills.

✓ **Show students that science can be engaging.**
Holt Science Spectrum includes a host of applications and cross-curricular connections to engage students in the learning process. *See pp. 34T through 37T for information on student features.*

correlated to

TENNESSEE Curriculum Standards

✓ **Make the program easy to teach.**
Though it can be exciting, starting with a new textbook program is never easy. **Holt Science Spectrum** includes many time-saving elements to make your first year go much smoother. *See p. 45T to learn about the exciting new HRW One-Stop Planner CD-ROM.*

✓ **Provide science content that is keyed to the IPC TEKS.**
Holt Science Spectrum emphasizes the inquiry, critical thinking, and problem-solving skills that students need for solid TEKS-based science instruction. *See pp. 22T through 28T for a conceptual overview.*

✓ **Integrate new technology that's easy to use into the instructional plan.**
It's the right mix of high quality instructional support, with NSTA's *sci*LINKS, Web site materials from the Smithsonian Institution, and videos from CNN, to name a few. *See pp. 42T through 44T for more details.*

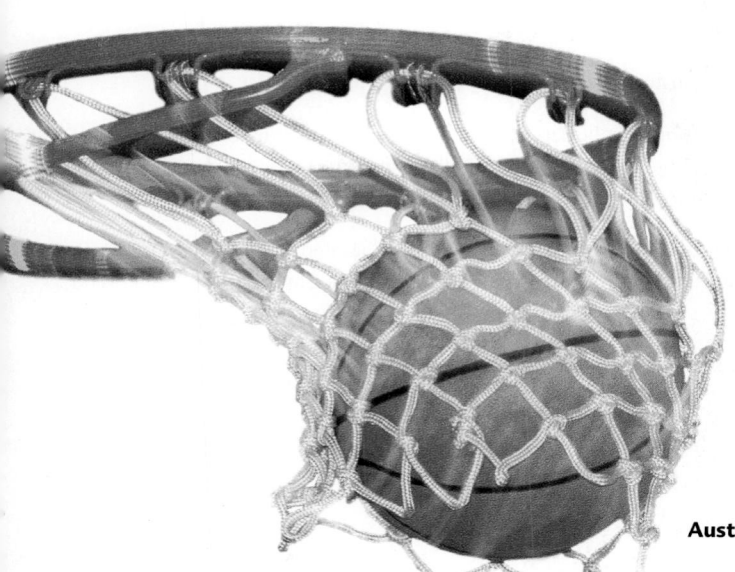

HOLT, RINEHART AND WINSTON

A Harcourt Education Company

Austin • New York • Orlando • Atlanta • San Francisco • Boston • Dallas • Toronto • London

Explanation of Correlation

The following document is a correlation of HOLT SCIENCE SPECTRUM: A Physical Approach to the Tennessee Science Curriculum Standards and End of Course Test. The format for this correlation follows the same basic format established by the Curriculum Standards, modified to accommodate the addition of page references. The correlation provides a cross-reference between the skills in the Curriculum Standards and representative page numbers where those skills are taught or assessed. Those references marked with an asterisk (*) represent pages which offer secondary support or where application of the required skill is implied.

The references contained in this correlation reflect Holt, Rinehart and Winston's interpretation of the Science objectives outlined in the Tennessee curriculum.

KEY TO REFERENCES

Prefix	Explanation
SE	*Student's Edition*
ATE	*Annotated Teacher's Edition*

Detailed Correlation of
Holt Science Spectrum: A Physical Approach to the
Tennessee Curriculum Standards

Physical Science
Component 1: Processes of Science

Processes of Science Goal: To enable students to apply the process of science by posing questions and investigating phenomena through the language, methods, and instruments of science.

Theme: 1.1 Observing

Senses are used to develop an awareness of events or objects and their properties.	**SE**	14, 48, 75, 113, 118, 133, 135, 166, 167, 172, 173, 189, 195, 204, 209, 226, 233, 269, 273, 292, 294, 309, 325, 333, 334, 335, 363, 371, 391, 392, 395, 434, 440, 449, 464, 466, 470, 475, 493, 532, 565, 650
	ATE	12–13, 38, 53, 54–55, 58, 70, 86, 93, 95, 108–109, 115, 123, 129, 148–149, 150–151, 154, 161, 169, 170, 186–187, 190, 192, 199, 203, 207, 229, 232, 236–237, 266–267, 284–285, 291, 308–309, 324, 330–331, 332–333, 336–337, 344, 357, 363, 372, 376, 394–395, 396–397, 406, 408–409, 414, 440, 462, 465, 468–469, 472, 479, 498–499, 500–501, 502, 536–537, 544, 549, 560–561, 567, 568, 572–573, 576–577, 579, 586, 599, 606, 607, 608–609, 610–611, 613, 630–631, 632–633, 635

Theme: 1.2 Questioning

Development of an inquisitive mind and the effective use of questioning techniques furthers the acquisition of information.	**SE**	57, 64–65, 104–105, 113, 135, 180–181, 204, 210, 311, 318–319, 329, 334, 350–351, 470, 484, 485, 518–519, 635, 660–661

Theme: 1.3 Collecting Data

Acquiring, recording, arranging and storing of information must be performed in a complete, accurate, concise, and user-friendly manner.	**SE**	30–31, 64–65, 104–105, 180–181, 216–217, 244–245, 318–319, 350–351, 384–385, 422–423, 456–457, 484–485, 518–519, 554–555, 592–593, 624–625, 660–661

Holt Science Spectrum: A Physical Approach:
Laboratory Experiments, Labs for Chapters 1–19

TENNESSEE EDITION

Theme: 1.4 Analyzing

Data should be examined to find patterns that may suggest cause and effect relationships or support inferences and hypotheses.	**SE** 57, 65, 105, 113, 180, 273, 311, 319, 351, 475, 484, 625, 635

Holt Science Spectrum: A Physical Approach:
Laboratory Experiments
Lab for Chapter 1, Designing a Pendulum Clock pp. 1–5
Lab for Chapter 13, Investigating How the Length of a conductor Affects Resistance, pp. 52–55
Lab for Chapter 16, Determining the Speed of an Orbiting Moon, pp. 64–67
Lab for Chapter 17, Relating Convection to the Movement of Tectonic Plates pp. 68–71

Theme: 1.5 Explaining

Phenomena and related information are made understandable through discussion that culminates in a higher level of learning.	**SE** 63, 103, 139, 179, 215, 243, 277, 349, 383, 454, 482, 517, 553, 623, 658

Theme: 1.6 Communicating

Essential to science is the act of accurately and effectively conveying oral, written, graphic, or electronic information.	**SE** 28, 103, 139, 179, 215, 243, 421, 454, 483, 553, 591, 623, 658

Component 2: Unifying Concepts of Science

Unifying Concepts of Science Goal: To enable students to acquire and integrate scientific knowledge by applying major concepts, theories, principles, and laws from the life, environmental, physical, and earth and space sciences.

Theme: 2.1 Scale and Models

Models provide a conceptual bridge between the concrete and the abstract, while the application of scale allows for understanding the difference in magnitude between the model and the target item.	**SE** 9–11, 45–48, 73–76, 110–114, 116–120, 194–197, 229–230, 332, 371, 431–432, 466–467, 526–534, 536–541, 542–543, 558–566, 567–568, 570, 572–575, 598–602, 606–607, 608–609, 611–612, 616

Theme: 2.2 Form and Function

Form is linked to the function of materials and systems, and function may alter form.	SE	70–71, 77–82, 86–94, 108–114, 115–120, 129–136, 291–296, 497, 502–503, 528–529, 540–541, 608–609, 613–614

Theme: 2.3 Organization

Everything is organized into related systems or subsystems.	SE	70–71, 77–82, 86–94, 108–119, 115–120, 129–136, 340–345, 526–530, 542–550, 560–566, 579–581, 598–602, 603–604, 606–607, 616, 631–637

Theme: 2.4 Interactions

Within all living and non-living systems, matter and energy interact.	SE	148–153, 154–160, 173–176, 192–198, 229–234, 331–338, 339–345, 572–575, 579–581, 583–588, 606–612, 617–620, 632–637, 638–645, 647–654

Theme: 2.5 Change

Interactions within and among systems result in changes in their properties, position, movement, form, or function.	SE	45–50, 58–60, 148–153, 154–160, 173–176, 192–198, 229–234, 331–338, 339–345, 572–575, 579–581, 583–588, 606–612, 617–620, 632–637, 638–645, 647–654

Theme: 2.6 Conservation

In any natural system, form may change but nothing is lost.	SE	50–52, 64–65, 161–168, 223–224, 306–311, 318–319, 576–581, 606–607, 638–645, 647–654

Component 3: Habits of Mind

Habits of Mind Goal: To enable students to think and act in a manner consistent with the practice and the nature of science; and exhibit an awareness of the historical and cultural contributions of science.

Theme: 3.1 Historical and Cultural Perspective

Scientific understanding evolves over time as an approximation of truth and within a cultural context.	**SE**	4–9, 12–14, 70–76, 531–534, 548, 560–566, 567–568

Theme: 3.2 Assumption

Establishing the validity of an argument through data and differentiating between fact and assumption are vital parts of the scientific process.	**SE**	4–9, 12–14, 64–65, 216–217, 318, 475

Theme: 3.3 Estimation and Computation

Scientists evaluate the level of precision needed to make a reasonable response and perform necessary calculations.	**SE**	15–19, 22–26, 27–28

Theme: 3.4 Methods

Scientists use a variety of techniques to describe and solve problems.	**SE**	8–9, 14–15, 20–22, 56, 98, 99, 100, 125, 165, 224, 227, 255, 257, 260, 270, 285, 286, 289, 299, 301, 313, 328, 337, 370, 443, 450, 672–678, 679–680, 681–683

Theme: 3.5 Science and Technology

Science and technology are separate but interdependent.	**SE**	7, 488–493, 493–496, 497–505, 506–541

Theme: 3.6 Creative Enterprise

Ideas and inventions contribute to the creative expression of science.	**SE**	4–6, 73–74, 222, 229, 268–270, 399–400, 468, 531, 560

Component 4: Science in Society

Science in Society Goal: To enable students to demonstrate positive attitudes toward science necessary for solving problems and making personal decisions about issues that affect individuals, society, and the environment.

TENNESSEE

Theme: 4.1 Attitudes

Scientific progress and the attitudes of society influence one another.	**SE**	4–6, 70, 229, 324–325, 399, 430–431, 462–463, 531, 630, 635–636, 647, 653–656
	ATE	5

Theme: 4.2 Personal Goals

Applications of science can affect the quality of life for individuals.	**SE**	43, 58, 66–67, 151, 164, 182–183, 238, 264, 280–281, 360, 403, 424–425, 440, 626–627, 646, 655
	ATE	66–67, 182–183, 280–281, 424–425, 626–627

Theme: 4.3 Career Goals

Development of scientific skills may lead to rewarding careers and productive contributions to society.	**SE**	142–143, 246–247, 320–321, 386–387, 458–459, 594–595
	ATE	143, 247, 320

Theme: 4.4 Societal Needs

Science and technology combine to meet the needs of a society.	**SE**	235–240, 488–513, 638–645, 647–655

Theme: 4.5 Economics

Scientific knowledge provides a basis for understanding the economic value of applied technology.	**SE**	66–67, 182–183, 235–240, 280–281, 424–425, 626–627, 643–645, 647–654
	ATE	66–67, 182–183, 280–281, 424–425, 626–627

Theme: 4.6 Politics

Sound scientific understanding should guide political decisions.	**SE**	66–67, 182–183, 235–240, 280–281, 424–425, 626–627, 643–645, 647–654
	ATE	66–67, 182–183, 280–281, 424–425, 626–627

Related Ancillaries: (The following ancillaries support the Component Themes.)
sciLINKS National Science Teachers Association On-Line Resources
go.hrw.com
Laboratory Experiments
Laboratory Manager's Professional Reference
One-Stop Planner CD-ROM supports all skills

TENNESSEE

Standard Number: 1.0 Force and Motion

Standard: The student will explore the concepts of force and motion.

Learning Expectations:

The student will		
1.1 investigate the relationship between speed, velocity, and acceleration.	**SE**	252–262
1.2 analyze and apply Newton's three laws of motion.	**SE**	268–274
	Holt Science Spectrum: A Physical Approach: *Laboratory Experiments, Lab 8, Forces pp. 29–33*	
1.3 relate gravitational force to mass and distance.	**SE**	266–267, 435
1.4 demonstrate the relationship between work, power, and machines.	**SE** **ATE**	284–290, 291–296 284–285, 288
	Holt Science Spectrum: A Physical Approach: *Laboratory Experiments, Lab 9, Work, pp. 34–38*	
1.5 examine the law of conservation of momentum in everyday situations.	**SE**	258

Performance Indicators State:

As documented through state assessment, at Level 1, the student is able to		
• distinguish between speed and velocity, given a scenario.	**SE** **ATE**	258, 275 255
	Holt Science Spectrum: A Physical Approach: *Study guide, Review, Section 8.1 Motion, p. 48*	
• relate inertia, force, or action–reaction forces to Newton's three laws of motion given an illustration or a diagram.	**SE** **ATE**	267, 269, 270, 273, 274 270, 272–273
• distinguish between mass and weight, given examples using SI units.	**SE**	274, 275, 276
• identify simple machines, given illustrations.	**SE**	296, 315

TN8 *TEACHER'S EDITION*

At Level 2, the student is able to

- interpret distance-time graphs for velocity or velocity-time graphs for acceleration.

SE 275
ATE 261

Holt Science Spectrum: A Physical Approach:
Study Guide, Chapter 8, Mixed Review p. 51

- calculate velocity, given distance and time; acceleration, given velocity and time; force, given mass and acceleration; work, given force and distance; or power, given work and time, using the provided formulas.

SE 255, 258, 260, 267, 270, 274, 276, 285, 287, 316

Holt Science Spectrum: A Physical Approach:
Study Guide, Chapter 8, Mixed Review, p. 51

- distinguish among the three laws of motion, given a scenario.

Holt Science Spectrum: A Physical Approach:
Study Guide, Review, Section 8.3, Newton's Laws of Motion, p. 50

- choose the correct illustration that relates the effects of gravity on the motion of falling bodies, tides or satellites.

SE 267, 275

Holt Science Spectrum: A Physical Approach: Study Guide, Chapter 8, Mixed Review, p. 275

At Level 3, the student is able to

- recognize the simple machines found in a compound machine, given an illustration.

  SE 315

- choose the correct scenario that illustrates the law of conservation of momentum.

  Holt Science Spectrum: A Physical Approach:
  Integration Enrichment Resources, Worksheet 8.7,
  Momentum of Line in Art, p. 55

Performance Indicators Teacher:

As documented through teacher observation, at Level 1, the student is able to

- create a situation that differentiates between speed and velocity.

  SE 258
  ATE 255

- model Newton's three laws of motion.

  ATE 269, 270, 272–273
  Holt Science Spectrum: A Physical Approach:
  Laboratory Experiments, Lab 8, Forces pp. 29–33

- research various definitions of mass and weight.

  SE 272, 274, 277

- design and construct simple machines.

  ATE 295
  Holt Science Spectrum: A Physical Approach:
  Integration Enrichment Resources, Enrichment
  Worksheet 9.2, The Pyramids, p. 59

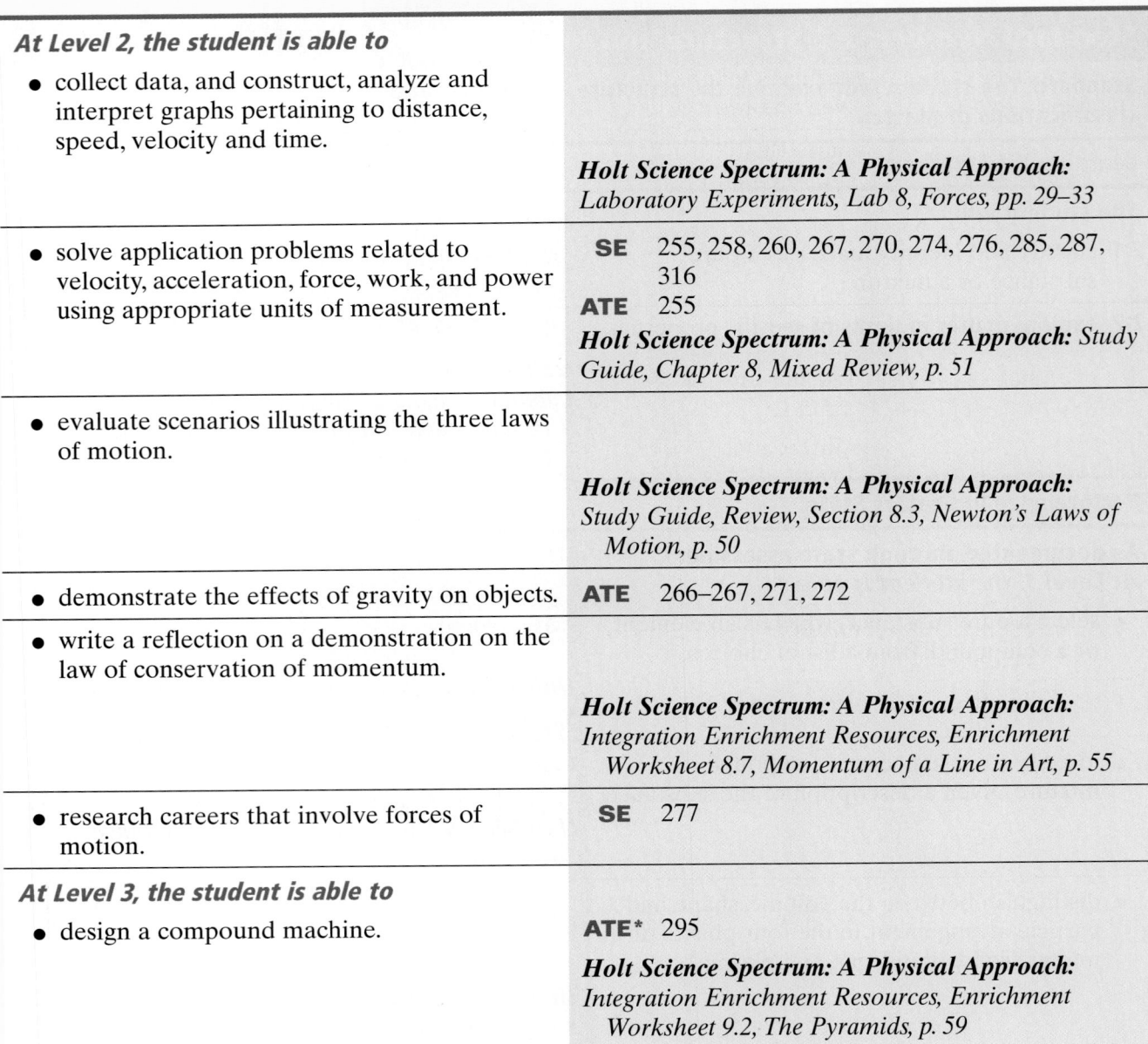

At Level 2, the student is able to

- collect data, and construct, analyze and interpret graphs pertaining to distance, speed, velocity and time.

    Holt Science Spectrum: A Physical Approach:
    Laboratory Experiments, Lab 8, Forces, pp. 29–33

- solve application problems related to velocity, acceleration, force, work, and power using appropriate units of measurement.

    SE 255, 258, 260, 267, 270, 274, 276, 285, 287, 316
    ATE 255
    Holt Science Spectrum: A Physical Approach: Study Guide, Chapter 8, Mixed Review, p. 51

- evaluate scenarios illustrating the three laws of motion.

    Holt Science Spectrum: A Physical Approach:
    Study Guide, Review, Section 8.3, Newton's Laws of Motion, p. 50

- demonstrate the effects of gravity on objects. **ATE** 266–267, 271, 272

- write a reflection on a demonstration on the law of conservation of momentum.

    Holt Science Spectrum: A Physical Approach:
    Integration Enrichment Resources, Enrichment Worksheet 8.7, Momentum of a Line in Art, p. 55

- research careers that involve forces of motion. **SE** 277

At Level 3, the student is able to

- design a compound machine. **ATE*** 295

    Holt Science Spectrum: A Physical Approach:
    Integration Enrichment Resources, Enrichment Worksheet 9.2, The Pyramids, p. 59

Related Ancillaries: (The following ancillaries support the Standard Number: 1.0 Force and Motion.)
sciLINKS National Science Teachers Association On-Line Resources
Integration Enrichment Resources
Math Skills Worksheet
Laboratory Experiment
Datasheets
Basic Skills Worksheet
Teaching Transparencies and Masters
Study Guide
CNN Presents Science in the News
Chapter Test
Guided Reading Audio CD Program
Test Generator Assessment Item Listing
One-Stop Planner CD-ROM supports all skills

Standard Number: 2.0 Structure and Properties of Matter

Standard: The student will examine the structure, properties, and classifications of matter.

Learning Expectations

The student will	
2.1 classify and identify matter as a pure substance or a mixture.	**SE** 41–44, 186–190
2.2 explore matter in terms of specific properties.	**SE** 53–57, 86–94
	Holt Science Spectrum: A Physical Approach: *Laboratory Experiments; Lab 3, Atoms and the Periodic Table, Predicting the Physical and Chemical Properties of Elements, pp. 10–12*

Performance Indicators State:

As documented through state assessment, At Level 1, the student is able to	
• select a pure substance, which is an element or a compound, from a list of choices.	**SE** 44, 61
	Holt Science Spectrum: A Physical Approach: *Study Guide, Review, Sec. 2.1, p. 8*
• identify a substance as a compound or mixture, given a description of the substance.	**SE** 61
	Holt Science Spectrum: A Physical Approach: *Study Guide, Review, Sec. 2.1, What is Matter, p. 8*
• distinguish between the volume, shape and particle arrangement in the four phases of matter (solid, liquid, gas, and plasma).	**SE** 52
	Holt Science Spectrum: A Physical Approach: *Study Guide Review, Sec. 2.2 Matter and Energy, p. 9*
• distinguish among elements, compounds, solutions, colloids, and suspensions, given an example.	**SE** 44, 61, 191, 213
	Holt Science Spectrum: A Physical Approach: *Study Guide, Review Sec. 6.1, Solutions and other Mixtures, p. 35*

At Level 2, the student is able to

- identify an element as a metal, nonmetal or metalloid using the periodic table.

  SE 94

  Holt Science Spectrum: A Physical Approach:
  Study Guide, Review, Sec. 3.3, Families of Elements

- identify the three major subatomic particles (protons, neutrons, and electrons) and their locations in the atom, given an illustration.

  SE 76, 85

  Holt Science Spectrum: A Physical Approach:
  Study Guide, Review Sec. 3.1, Atomic Structure, p. 14

- recognize the symbols for common elements (H2, He, Li,...) or formulas for common compounds (i.e. H2O, NaC1, CO2, HC1, Fe2O3, C6H12O6, NaOH), given a list.

  SE 128, 137, 138

  Holt Science Spectrum: A Physical Approach:
  Study Guide, Review Sec. 3.2, A Guided Tour of the
  Periodic Table, p. 15; Review Sec. 4.1, Compounds
  and Molecules, p. 21; Review Sec. 4.3, Compound
  Names and Formulas, p. 23

- calculate density, given mass and volume.

  SE 56, 62

  Holt Science Spectrum: A Physical Approach:
  Study Guide, Chapter 12, Mixed Review, p.12

- predict the behavior of an object when placed in water, given its density.

  SE 60

  Holt Science Spectrum: A Physical Approach:
  Laboratory Experiments, Chapter 2 Lab, Comparing
  the Buoyancy of Different
  Objects, pp. 6–9

At Level 3, the student is able to

- identify the atomic number, atomic mass, number of protons, number of neutrons, and number of electrons in an atom of a given element, using the periodic table.

  SE 85

  Holt Science Spectrum: A Physical Approach:
  Study Guide, Review Chapter 3, Mixed Review, p. 18

- determine the effects of pressure, temperature, or volume (related to Charles' and Boyle's law) on the behavior of gases, given a diagram.

  SE* 52

TENNESSEE

TENNESSEE EDITION

Performance Indicators Teacher:

As documented through teacher observation,
At Level 1, the student is able to

- identify matter as solid, liquid, gas, or plasma.

  SE 52
  ATE 52

  Holt Science Spectrum: A Physical Approach:
  Study Guide, Review, Sec. 2.2, Matter and Energy, p. 9

- illustrate the difference among solids, liquids, and gases based on volume, shape, and particle arrangement.

  SE 52
  ATE 52

  Holt Science Spectrum: A Physical Approach:
  Integration Enrichment Resources, Worksheet 2.7,
  Plasma, p. 12

- construct a chart of element, compound, and mixture examples, using pictures.

  Holt Science Spectrum: A Physical Approach:
  Study Guide, Review, Sec. 2.1, What is Matter, p. 8

- classify a given mixture as homogeneous or heterogeneous.

  SE 44

  Holt Science Spectrum: A Physical Approach:
  Study Guide, Review, Sec. 2.1 What is Matter, p. 8

- describe matter in terms of its atoms and molecules.

  SE 76

  Holt Science Spectrum: A Physical Approach:
  Study Guide, Pretest, Chap. 3, Atomas and The
  Periodic Table, p. 13, Review Sec. 3.1, Atomic
  Structure, p. 14, Review Sec. 3.2, A Guided Tour of
  the Periodic Table, p. 15

At Level 2, the student is able to

- construct a 3D model of the atom with its three subatomic particles in correct locations.

  Holt Science Spectrum: A Physical Approach:
  Study Guide, Review, Sec. 3.1, Atomic Structure, p. 14

- match symbols and formulas to element and compound examples or samples.

  SE 85
  ATE 85

  Holt Science Spectrum: A Physical Approach:
  Study Guide, Pretest, Chap. 3, Atoms and the Periodic Table, p. 13

- measure the mass and volume of a variety of items, using appropriate methods and units.

  SE 30–33, 57

- create an activity to determine if an object will float in water.

  Holt Science Spectrum: A Physical Approach:
  Laboratory Experiments, Lab 2, Comparing the Buoyancy of Different Objects, pp. 6–9

- classify substances as metals or nonmetals, based on physical properties.

  SE 94
  ATE 86

- explore chemistry-related occupations.

  SE 142–143

At Level 3, the student is able to

- create a density gradient for liquids of different densities.

  ATE 332, 560–561

- explore Archimedes principle or Bernoulli's principle through lab activities.

  Holt Science Spectrum: A Physical Approach:
  Laboratory Experiments, Lab 2, Comparing the Buoyancy of Different Objects, pp. 6–9

Related Ancillaries: (The following ancillaries support the Standard Number: 2.0 Structure and Properties of Matter.)
sciLINKS National Science Teachers Association On-Line Resources
Study Guide
Holt Science Skills Workshop, Reading in the Content Area
One-Stop Planner CD-ROM supports all skills

Standard Number: 3.0 Interactions of Matter

Standard: The student will investigate the interactions of matter.

Learning Expectations

The student will

3.1 investigate chemical and physical changes.	**SE** 58–60 **ATE** 58, 59, 60
3.2 analyze chemical equations.	**SE** 154–160, 161–168
3.3 compare and contrast acids and bases.	**SE** 199–206, 210–212
3.4 explore the laws of conservation of mass.	**SE** 51, 64–65, 162, 166

Performance Indicators State:

As documented through state assessment,
At Level 1, the student is able to

- determine whether a change in matter is physical or chemical, given examples.

  SE 60

  Holt Science Spectrum: A Physical Approach:
  Study Guide, Review Sec. 2.3, Properties of
      Matter, p. 10

- identify the reactants and products in a chemical reaction, given a chemical equation.

  ATE 154

  Holt Science Spectrum: A Physical Approach:
  Study Guide, Review Sec. 5.1, The Nature of Chemical
      Reactions, p. 28

- identify a substance as acidic, basic, or neutral, given its pH.

  SE 206

  Holt Science Spectrum: A Physical Approach:
  Study Guide, Review Sec. 6.3, Acids, Bases, and
      pHp. 37

At Level 2, the student is able to

- select the reaction that is endothermic or exothermic, given the temperature change during the reaction.

  SE 153

- identify a chemical reactions as either synthesis, decomposition, single-replacement or double-replacement reactions, given examples.

  SE 160

  Holt Science Spectrum: A Physical Approach:
  Study Guide, Review Sec. 5.2, Reaction Types, p. 29

- predict the effect of acid rain on people or the environment, given a scenario.

  SE 657

  Holt Science Spectrum: A Physical Approach:
  Study Guide, Review Sec. 19.3, Pollution and Recycling, p. 119

- demonstrate the law of conservation of mass in a chemical reaction by selecting the balanced equation.

  SE 168

At Level 3, the student is able to

- select the correct coefficients to balance a given chemical equation.

  SE 166, 168

  Holt Science Spectrum: A Physical Approach:
  Study Guide, Review Sec. 5.3, Balancing Chemical Equations, p. 30

- predict the products given the reactants of a chemical reaction.

  SE 153

  Holt Science Spectrum: A Physical Approach:
  Study Guide, Review Sec. 5.1, The Nature of Chemical Reactions, p. 28

Performance Indicators Teacher:

As documented through teacher observation, at Level 1, the student is able to

- describe how chemical symbols, formulas, and balanced chemical equations are used to explain a chemical reaction.

  SE   160, 166, 167, 168, 178
  ATE 166, 167

  Holt Science Spectrum: A Physical Approach:
  Study Guide, Review Sec. 5.2, Reaction Types, p. 29,
  Review Sec. 5.3 Balancing Chemical Equations, p. 30

- investigate processes of chemical reactions.

  SE   167, 172, 180–181
  ATE 148–149, 154, 167, 169, 172

  Holt Science Spectrum: A Physical Approach:
  Laboratory Experiments, Lab 5, Investigation the
  Effect of Temperature on the Rate of a Reaction,
  pp. 17–20

- describe synthesis, decomposition, single-replacement, and double-replacement reactions, using reaction equations.

  SE   160
  ATE 160

  Holt Science Spectrum: A Physical Approach:
  Study Guide, Review Sec. 5.1, The Nature of
  Chemical Reactions, p. 28, Review Sec. 5.2,
  Reaction Types, p. 29

- analyze how various indicators (litmus paper, red cabbage, universal indicator, or pH sensor) are used to determine the pH of a substance.

  SE   204
  ATE 199, 200, 204–205, 207

TENNESSEE

At Level 2, the student is able to		
● demonstrate exothermic and endothermic reactions.	**SE**	151
	ATE	151
	Holt Science Spectrum: A Physical Approach: *Study Guide, Review Sec. 5.1, The Nature of Chemical Reactions, p. 28*	
● research acid rain and its effect on the environment.	**SE**	650
	ATE	585, 650
● investigate the laws of conservation of mass through an experiment or teacher demonstration.	**SE**	64–65
● create a visual display detailing career options and the educational requirements for science careers.	**SE***	142–143, 246–247, 320–321, 386–387, 458–459, 517, 594–595

At Level 3, the student is able to		
● balance a simple chemical equation.	**SE**	163, 166, 167, 168
	Holt Science Spectrum: A Physical Approach: *Study Guide, Review Sec. 5.3, Balancing Chemical Reactions, p. 30*	
● develop a concept map for chemical bonding.	**SE**	139

Related Ancillaries: (The following ancillaries support the Standard Number: 3.0 Interactions of Matter.)
Study Guide
sciLINKS National Science Teachers Association On-Line Resources
www.si.edu/hrw Smithsonian Institution Web site
Math Skills Worksheet
Datasheets
Integrated Enrichment Worksheet
Holt Physical Science Interactive Tutor
One-Stop Planner CD-ROM supports all skills
CNNfyi.com

TENNESSEE

Standard Number: 4.0 Energy

Standard: The student will compare and contrast various forms of energy.

Learning Expectations:

The student will

4.1 investigate the properties and behaviors of waves.	**SE** 356–364, 365–373, 374–380, 384–385 **ATE** 357, 358–359, 363, 366, 372, 376, 378–379, 380
	Holt Science Spectrum: Laboratory Experiments, Chapter 11 Lab, Tuning a Musical Instrument, pp. 43–47
4.2 explore and explain the nature of sound and light energy.	**SE** 390–398, 399–402, 406–411, 412–418 **ATE** 390, 396–397, 406, 408–409, 414, 416–417
4.3 examine the applications and effects of heat energy.	**SE** 329–330, 331–338, 339–345, 350–351
	Holt Science Spectrum: A Physical Approach: Laboratory Experiments, Chapter 10 Lab, Determining the Better Insulator for Your Feet, pp. 39–42
4.4 probe the fundamental principles and applications of electrical energy.	**SE** 304, 430–436, 437–445, 446–452, 456–457, 462–467, 468–473, 474–480, 484–485
	Holt Science Spectrum: A Physical Approach: Laboratory Experiments, Chapter 14 Lab, Testing Magnets for an Electric Motor, pp. 56–59
4.5 distinguish between nuclear fission and nuclear fusion.	**SE** 229–234, 237–240, 304
4.6 investigate the law of conservation of energy.	**SE** 51–52, 310–311, 318–319, 475

Performance Indicators State:

As documented through state assessment, At Level 1, the student is able to

• classify waves as transverse or longitudinal, given an illustration.	**SE** 362, 364, 381, 384–385 **ATE** 362, 364, 366 *Holt Science Spectrum: A Physical Approach: Study Guide, Chapter 12 Pretest Sound and Light, p. 72*
• identify wavelength, frequency and amplitude, given an illustration.	**SE** 382 *Holt Science Spectrum: A Physical Approach: Study Guide, Review Sec. 11.3, Wave Interactions, p.69; Chapter 11 Mixed Review, p. 70*

• determine the temperature scale, given the boiling and/or freezing point of water.	**SE**	347
• identify a wave interaction as reflection, diffraction, refraction, and interference, given an example.	**ATE**	376, 380
	Holt Science Spectrum: A Physical Approach: Study Guide, Review Sec. 11.3, Wave Interactions, p. 69	
• select characteristics that best describe sound or light energy.	**SE**	398, 418, 419
	Holt Science Spectrum: A Physical Approach: Study Guide, Chapter 12, Pretest, Sound and Light, p. 72	
• determine whether the transfer of thermal energy is conduction, convection or radiation, given an illustration.	**SE**	335, 338, 350–351
	Holt Science Spectrum: A Physical Approach: Study Guide Review Sec. 10.2, Energy Transfer, p. 62	
• compare and contrast the four kinds of wave interactions (reflection, diffraction, refraction, and interference).	**ATE**	376, 380
	Holt Science Spectrum: A Physical Approach: Review Sec. 11.3, Wave Interactions, p. 69; Chapter 12 Pretest, Sound and Light, p. 72	
• calculate voltage, given resistance and current in a series circuit, given the formulas.	**SE**	443, 454
	Holt Science Spectrum: A Physical Approach: Study Guide, Review Sec. 13.3, Circuits, p. 82	
• distinguish between nuclear fission and nuclear fusion, given a scenario.	**SE**	234
	Holt Science Spectrum: A Physical Approach: Study Guide, Mixed Review Chapter 7, p. 46	
• select the statement that best describe the law of conservation of energy.	**SE***	52, 314

At Level 3, the student is able to

• calculate the amount of heat gained or lost by a substance during a chemical reaction, given the formula.	**SE***	153, 177
	Holt Science Spectrum: A Physical Approach: Study Guide, Review Sec. 5.1, The Nature of Chemical Reactions, p. 28	

TENNESSEE EDITION

T E N N E S S E E

Performance Indicators Teacher:

As documented through teacher observation, at Level 1, the student is able to

- create a situation that demonstrates how waves are produced and move.

  SE 362, 371, 384–385
  ATE 357, 358–359, 363, 364, 366, 371, 373, 378–379

- model or observe the relationship among kinetic, potential, and total energy within a closed system.

  SE 311, 318–319
  ATE 311

- describe the relationship between kinetic energy and temperature within a substance.

  SE 330
  ATE 308–309, 330

  Holt Science Spectrum: A Physical Approach:
  Study Guide, Review
  Sec. 10.1, Temperature, p. 61

- distinguish between heat and temperature, including units.

  SE 329, 330, 338, 348
  ATE 329

  Holt Science Spectrum: A Physical Approach:
  Study Guide, Pretest Chap. 10, Heat and
  Temperature, p. 60

- compare and contrast the efficiency of fluorescent and incandescent lights.

  SE* 645
  ATE 450

- create a progression of electricity from its source to the home.

  SE 483, 645, 658
  ATE 478

- identify sources of commercial/residential heat energy.

  SE 645, 658

- write an essay, supported by data, to emphasize the importance of energy conservation.

  SE* 645, 659

- research careers that relate to energy, heat, or electricity.

  SE* 455, 483

At Level 2, the student is able to

- calculate wave speed, given its frequency and wavelength.

  SE 370, 373, 382

- demonstrate how compressions and rarefactions of a sound wave change when they travel through different media.

  SE 391
  ATE 391

  Holt Science Spectrum: A Physical Approach:
  Study Guide, Review
  Sec. 12.1, Sound, p. 73

- differentiate between music and noise in terms of sound waves.

  SE 392, 398
  ATE 390, 392, 394–395, 396–397

- collect data, construct and interpret graphs pertaining to the frequency and wavelength of different sounds.

  Holt Science Spectrum: A Physical Approach:
  Laboratory Experiments, Lab 11, Tuning a Musical
  Instrument, pp. 43–47

- identify the medical and industrial uses of ultrasound.

  SE 398, 420, 421

- create an activity that demonstrates the conservation of heat energy.

  SE* 329
  ATE* 308–309, 329, 336–337

- construct a schematic of a simple electrical circuit.

  SE 449, 452
  ATE 449

- design an experiment to verify Ohm's law.

  SE* 456–457

  Holt Science Spectrum: A Physical Approach:
  Laboratory Experiments, Lab 13, Investigating How
  the Length of a Conductor Affects Resistance,
  pp. 52–55

- compare the types of energy and their impact on science and society.

  SE 645
  ATE 642, 643

  Holt Science Spectrum: A Physical Approach:
  Study Guide, Review
  Sec. 19.2, Energy and Resources, p. 118

TENNESSEE

At Level 3, the student is able to

- research the economies of various commercial heat sources, defending views about why they are or are not practical choices of energy.

SE* 645, 658

- analyze a series electrical circuit to show that the sum of the individual voltage drops across circuit resistors equals the total voltage source.

SE* 449
ATE* 449

Holt Science Spectrum: A Physical Approach:
Study Guide, Review
Sec. 13.3, Circuits, p. 82

At Level 3, the student is able to

- research and debate the relationship between current energy situations and the possibility of future energy crises.

SE* 645, 658, 659

Holt Science Spectrum: A Physical Approach:
Study Guide, Review Sec. 19.2, Energy and
Resources, p. 118

Related Ancillaries: (The following ancillaries support the Standard Number: 4.0 Energy.)
sciLINKS National Science Teachers Association On-Line Resources
www.si.edu/hrw Smithsonian Institution Web site
Study Guide
Laboratory Experiments
Datasheets
Integrated Enrichment Resources
Math Skills Worksheet
Transparencies
Chapter Test
One–Stop Planner CD–ROM supports all skills

Teaching Resources:

Laboratory Experiments blackline master worksheets provide teaching notes for technology–based labs that are not included in the Student's Edition.

Study Guide review worksheets are provided for each text section along with a chapter pretest and an end-of-chapter mixed review that includes concept mapping.

Math Skills Worksheets provide additional problem solving models and practice problems keyed to examples in the text.

Datasheets help students with their organizational skills and make reports easy to grade. Datasheets are included for all in-text labs and the labs in the Laboratory Experiments Manual.

Integration Enrichment Resources extend Real World Applications and Connection features in the student's text.

The **Basic Skills Worksheets** reteach and reinforce prerequisite skills.

The **Answer Key** booklet includes answer keys for the following resources: Study Guide, Integration Enrichment Resources, Basic Skills Worksheets, Math Skills Worksheets, and Lesson Focus Transparencies.

Chapter Tests with Answer Keys assess mastery of content objectives using multiple choice, short answer, essay, and problem solving formats.

Test Generator and Assessment Item Listing allows you to make custom tests. The Assessment Item listing shows you all available items at a glance.

The **Guided Reading Audio CD Program** provides audio instruction for each chapter.

The **Teaching Transparencies and Transparency Masters** include 165 color and 165 black line master transparencies include useful instructional illustrations from the text and warm-up activities for each lesson.

Holt Physical Science Interactive Tutor for Macintosh ® and Windows ® CD-ROM provides an interactive environment in which students can explore concepts and practice problem solving techniques. Each module presents a key concept using models and video animations. Frequent evaluation lets students know if they are on the right tract.

One-Stop Planner CD-ROM with Test Generator for Macintosh ® and Windows ® includes all of the program resources in printable format, as well as customizable lesson plans and an easy to use test generator with more than 2000 items.

The **Laboratory Manager's Professional Reference** provides information on risk management and how you can prevent or eliminate hazards in the classroom.

The **Teacher's Edition Holt Science Skills Workshop, Reading in the Content Area** workbook was designed to help students develop reading skills specific to the comprehension of science texts. Students learn to analyze text structure, recognize patterns, and organize information in ways that help them construct meaning. The exercises make excellent in class activities, remedial projects, and homework assignments.

Quick Concepts on the **Lesson Presentation CD-ROM** are organized to match the content coverage in each section of the text. These media based presentations can be projected for large group instruction or viewed individually by students using a computer. Quick Concepts provide more comprehensive coverage than transparencies or PowerPoint presentations because they combine audio and animation.

CNN Presents Science in the News includes 25 short video clips that show students the newsworthy nature of Science. The stories showcase useful applications of science concepts. Teacher's notes and student worksheets are included for each segment.

Holt, Rinehart and Winston **go.hrw.com** on-line resources provide articles, activities, teaching suggestions, and other resources that directly correlate to the textbook.

www.si.edu/hrw Smithsonian Institution is a Web site that includes interactive exhibits, scientist interviews, and a variety of other resources designed for use with the text.

www.scilinks.org is a Web site owned and maintained by the National Science Teachers Association and contains a collection of prescreened sites with up-to-date information and activities directly related to the text.

www.cnnfyi.com provides information on late breaking news and current event stories.

Assessment and Higher-Order Thinking Skills

What Are Higher-Order Thinking Skills?

Higher-order thinking skills, sometimes called critical thinking skills, are not a new phenomenon on the education scene. In 1956, Benjamin Bloom published a book that listed a taxonomy of education objectives in the form of a pyramid similar to the one in the following illustration:

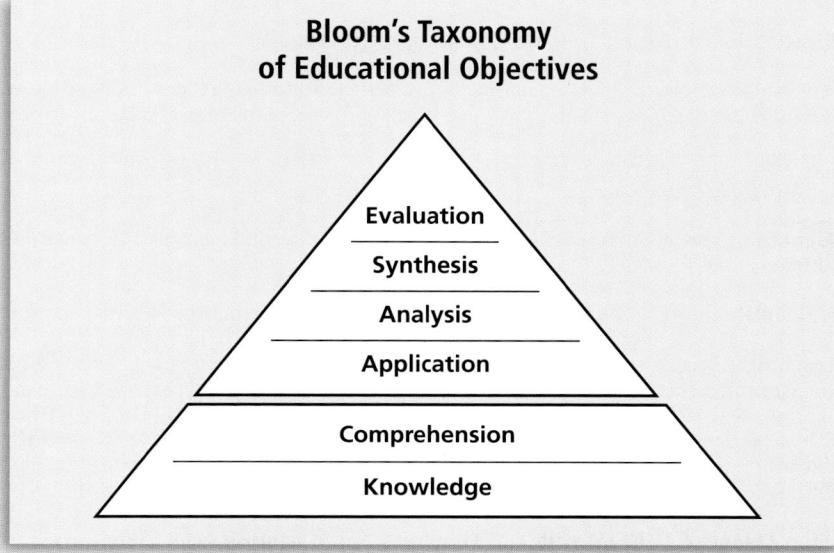

Bloom's Taxonomy of Educational Objectives

Evaluation
Synthesis
Analysis
Application
Comprehension
Knowledge

- **Knowledge** is the simplest level of education objectives and is not considered a higher-order thinking skill. It requires the learner to remember information without having to fully understand it. Tasks that students perform to demonstrate knowledge are recalling, identifying, recognizing, citing, labeling, listing, reciting, and stating.

  EXAMPLES

  1. *What is the capital of Minnesota?*

  2. *What is the French word for table?*

  3. *Label the parts of a plant.*

- **Comprehension** is not considered a higher-order thinking skill either. Learners demonstrate comprehension when they paraphrase, describe, summarize, illustrate, restate, or translate. Information isn't useful unless it's understood. Students can show they've understood by restating the information in their own words or by giving an example of the concept.

  EXAMPLES

  1. *Summarize the plot of the story in your own words.*

  2. *Interpret the information in the graph below.*

  3. *What were the underlying factors that contributed to the Revolutionary War?*

Many teachers tend to focus the most on knowledge and comprehension— and the tasks performed at these levels are important because they provide a solid foundation for the more complex tasks at the higher levels of Bloom's pyramid.

However, offering students the opportunity to perform at still higher cognitive levels provides them with more meaningful contexts in which to use the information and skills they have acquired, thus allowing them to more easily retain what they have learned.

When teachers incorporate **application, analysis, synthesis,** and **evaluation** as objectives, they allow students to utilize **higher-order thinking skills.**

- **Application** involves solving, transforming, determining, demonstrating, and preparing. Information becomes useful when students apply it to new situations—predicting outcomes, estimating answers—this is application.

  EXAMPLES

  1. *Organize the forms of pollution from most damaging to least damaging.*

  2. *Using the scale of 1 inch equals 200 miles, determine the point-to-point distance between Boston and Atlanta.*

  3. *Put the information below into graph form.*

- **Analysis** includes classifying, comparing, making associations, verifying, seeing cause-and-effect relationships, and determining sequences, patterns, and consequences. You can think of analysis as taking something apart in order to better understand it. Students must be able to think in categories in order to analyze.

  EXAMPLES

  1. *When it was written, how did the U. S. Constitution respond to the economic interests of certain classes of people?*

  2. *Using the vocabulary words from this unit, make a crossword puzzle.*

  3. *Analyze the literary elements in the following poem.*

- **Synthesis** requires generalizing, predicting, imagining, creating, making inferences, hypothesizing, making decisions, and drawing conclusions. Students create something which is new to them when they use synthesis. It's important to remember, though, that students can't create until they have the skills and information they have received in the comprehension through analysis levels.

  EXAMPLES

  1. *Create a newspaper using the details in this short story.*

  2. *Create a conversation that could have happened between General Grant and General Lee.*

  3. *Propose a plan for reorganizing your city's government.*

- **Evaluation** involves assessing, persuading, determining value, judging, validating, and solving problems. Evaluation is based on all the other levels. When students evaluate, they make judgments, but not judgments based on personal taste. These judgments must be based on criteria. It is important for students to evaluate because they learn to consider different points of view and to know how to validate their judgments.

  EXAMPLES

  1. *Justify the budget you created for your business.*

  2. *Explain and justify how this short story fulfills Edgar Allan Poe's requirements for a good story.*

  3. *Evaluate the methods used in your analysis of drinking water.*

Why is it Important for Students to Work with Higher-Order Thinking Skills?

For one thing, if students can determine the levels of questions that will appear on their tests, they will be able to study using appropriate strategies. Bloom's leveling of questions provides a useful structure in which to categorize test questions, since tests will characteristically ask questions within particular levels.

Also, thinking is a skill that can be taught. When you have students practice answering questions at all the levels of Bloom's taxonomy, you are helping to scaffold their learning. Information just becomes trivia unless that information is understood well enough to build more complicated concepts or generalizations. When students can comprehend—not just recall—the information, it becomes useful for future problem solving or creative thought. Think of information as a building material—like a board. It could be used to build something, but it is just useless litter unless you understand how to make use of it.

Below are some question stems you—or your students—could use to create questions for each of the levels of higher-order thinking:

Application

1. Make a timeline to show _____.

2. Use the key vocabulary words in this chapter to write a paragraph about _____.

3. Write a letter to (the main character, inventor, historical figure).

4. Explain how the (principle, theorem, concept) is evident in _____.

5. In what way is _____ a _____?

Analysis

1. Analyze the organizational structure of _____.

2. Evaluate the relevancy of the data in _____.

3. What other (stories, books, chapters, etc.) have similar messages/themes? Explain.

4. Compare and contrast the (main characters, theorems, classes, etc.).

5. On the basis of your observation of _____, which variables could you eliminate as _____ factors?

Synthesis

1. Change the setting and rewrite the (story, novel, chapter, etc.) based on the new setting and the changes it would cause.

2. Show how the fictional work _____ actually reflects the ideas in the nonfiction work _____.

3. Create a new way to classify _____.

4. Design your own _____ to show _____.

5. Create a new way to _____.

Evaluation

1. Which (poet, general, experiment, etc.) did you like more? Why?

2. What is _____'s most important contribution? Support your answer.

3. Is this _____ relevant for today's _____? Explain.

4. Justify your opinion of _____.

5. Were _____'s actions in this (battle, crisis, etc.) correct? Defend your answer.

Test-taking Tips For Students

Every school year, there are students who are asked to take one or more standardized tests to demonstrate the content and skills they have learned. You can share the following test-taking tips with your students to help them as they prepare for these assessments.

Remind students, though, that the best way to prepare for any standardized test is to pay close attention in class and to take every opportunity to improve their science, reading, writing, and mathematical skills.

Tips for Standardized Tests: Reading Sections

The main goal of the reading sections of standardized tests is to determine your understanding of different aspects of a reading passage. Basically, if you can grasp the main idea and the author's purpose, and then pay attention to the details and vocabulary so that you are able to draw inferences and conclusions, you will do well on a test.

Here are some suggestions for answering questions based on reading passages:

- First, **read the passage as if you were not even taking a test.** Do this to get a general overview of both the topic and the tone of a passage.

- **Look at the big picture.** In other words, examine the most obvious features of the passage. To do this, ask yourself the following questions as you read:

    What is the title?

    What do the illustrations or pictures tell me?

    What is the main idea?

    What is the author's purpose? To inform? To entertain? To show how to do something?

- Next, **read the questions.** This will help you to know what information to look for when you re-read.

- Re-read the passage. **Underline the information** that relates to the questions. This will help you when you begin answering the questions.

- **Go back to the questions.** Try to answer each one in your mind before looking at the answer choices.

- Finally, **read *all* the answer choices and eliminate those that are obviously incorrect.** After this process, mark the best answer.

Types of Multiple-Choice Questions Based on a Passage

Realize that many multiple-choice questions fall into categories. The following categories are the most common.

1. **Main idea:** The main idea of a reading passage is the most important point expressed in the passage. The main idea must relate to the entire passage, not just to a portion of a selection. After reading a passage, locate and underline the main idea.

2. **Significant details:** You will most probably be asked to recall specific details from a reading passage. You will know what details to look for if you read the questions before reading the passage. Underline these details as you read. *Remember that correct answers do not always use the precise phrases or words that appear in the passage.*

3. **Reading graphic information:** These kinds of items test your ability to interpret information presented in a visual form or a graphic, such as a map, schedule, time line, or chart. If the question involves a graphic, follow these steps:

   a) Look at the title and major labels to figure out the focus or purpose of the graphic;

   b) Read the other headings or labels to find out what data is given and how it is organized;

   c) If the item includes a map, look at the map's legend or key, which will explain symbols, lines, and shadings in the map;

   d) Analyze the data in the graphic to determine quantities, relationships, intervals of time, directions, sequences, or other patterns

4. **Vocabulary:** Standardized tests will often ask you to determine the meaning of a word within the context of the passage. In many instances, an answer choice will include an actual meaning of the word that does not fit the context in which the word appears. To avoid choosing such an incorrect answer, read the answer choices and then plug them into the sentence to determine which answer fits the context of the passage.

5. **Conclusion and inference:** Standardized tests often ask you to draw conclusions or make inferences. There is often some idea within a passage that the author is trying to convey but does not state directly. Consider various parts of the passage together in order to determine what the author is implying. *If an answer choice refers to only one or two sentences or details within the passage, this is probably not the correct answer.*

If you do not understand a passage at first, keep reading. Many times you will find that you know more answers than you first thought. Once you understand the main idea of a passage, you can go from there to figure out the specific information.

What is HOLT Science Spectrum?

A new science program for high school that keeps students on target!

Building on a core of high quality science instructional materials developed in the United Kingdom, **Holt Science Spectrum** was conceived to help solve the problems teachers and students face with introductory science courses at the high school level. With that singular goal in mind, the development team focused on the following objectives:

✓ **Start students off on the right track with solid development of basic skills.**
Holt Science Spectrum helps students improve their skills in reading and mathematics, while adding new critical thinking and life/work skills.

✓ **Show students that science can be engaging.**
Holt Science Spectrum includes a host of applications and cross-curricular connections to engage students in the learning process. *See pp. 26T through 29T for information on student features.*

✓ **Make the program easy to teach.**
Though it can be exciting, starting with a new textbook program is never easy. **Holt Science Spectrum** includes many time-saving elements to make your first year go much smoother. *See p. 37T to learn about the exciting new HRW One-Stop Planner CD-ROM.*

✓ **Provide science content that is developmentally appropriate for high school students.**
Holt Science Spectrum emphasizes the inquiry, critical thinking, and problem-solving skills that students need for solid science instruction. *See pp. 40T through 45T for a conceptual overview.*

✓ **Integrate new technology that's easy to use into the instructional plan.**
It's the right mix of high quality instructional support, with NSTA's *sci*LINKS, Web site materials from the Smithsonian Institution, and videos from CNN, to name a few. *See pp. 34T through 36T for more details.*

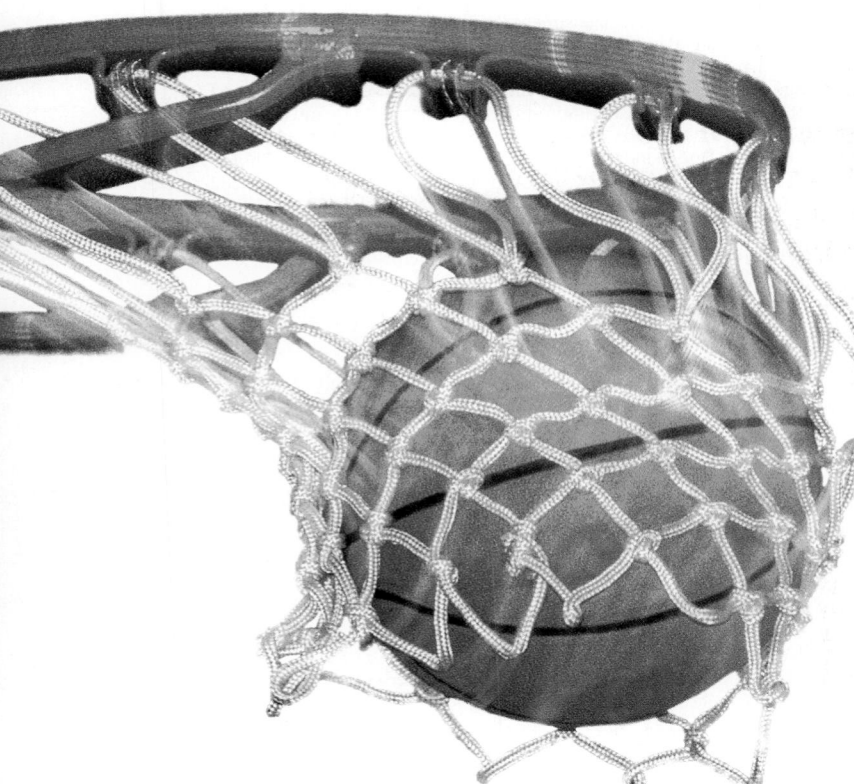

HOLT, RINEHART AND WINSTON

A Harcourt Classroom Education Company
Austin • New York • Orlando • Atlanta
San Francisco • Boston • Dallas • Toronto • London

KEN DOBSON   JOHN HOLMAN   MICHAEL ROBERTS

Contributing Writers

Jeffrey Bracken
Chemistry Teacher
Westerville North High School
Westerville, OH

Phillip G. Bunce
Science Writer
Austin, TX

Robert Davisson
Science Writer
Delaware, OH

Heather Flanagan, Ph.D.
Chemist
Austin, TX

Brook Ellen Hall
Instructor
California State University
  at Sacramento
Sacramento, CA

Doug Jenkins
*Physics and Physical
  Science Teacher*
Warren Central High School
Bowling Green, KY

Frances Jenkins
Science Writer and Editor
Croton, OH

Nanette Kalis
Science Writer
Albany, OH

Matt Lee, Ph.D.
Science Editor
Coos Bay, OR

Mitchell Leslie
Science Writer
Stanford University
Stanford, CA

Karen Ross
Science Writer
Georgetown, TX

Richard Olenick, Ph.D.
Professor of Physics
University of Dallas
Irving, TX

Alexis Wright
*Middle School Science
  Coordinator*
Rye Country Day School
Rye, NY

Cover: basketball image: David Madison/Tony Stone Images; celestial background image: Corbis Images   **Art Credits:** 3T, Kristy Sprott; 8T, Kristy Sprott; 9T, Kristy Sprott; 11T(t), Kristy Sprott; 11T(b), Uhl Studios Inc.; 12T, Stephen Durke/Washington-Artists' Represents; 15T, Uhl Studios Inc.; 16T, Uhl Studios Inc; 20T, Leslie Kell   **Photo Credits:** 1T, David Madison/Tony Stone Images; 3T, David Malin/Anglo-Australian Observatory; 5T, Glen M. Oliver/Visuals Unlimited; 6T (cl), Courtesy of TOGO International; 6T (cr), Tom Van Sant/The Geosphere Project/The Stock Market; 6T (br), Henry Groskinsky/Peter Arnold, Inc.; 8T (cl), Sam Dudgeon/HRW Photo; 8T (bl), Michael Keller/The Stock Market; 10T (tl), Sergio Purtell/Foca/HRW; 10T (bl, bc), Peter Van Steen/ HRW Photo; 12T (all), Courtesy Martha McCaslin/US Army; 13T (br), Rich Iwasaki/Allstock/PNI; 13T (tr), Peter Van Steen/HRW Photo; 14T (all), Peter Van Steen/HRW Photo; 15T, Celestial Image Picture Co./Science Photo Library/Photo Researchers, Inc.; 16T (cl), Richard Thom/Visuals Unlimited; 16T (bl), Mark Richards/Photo Edit; 16T (bc), Myrleen Ferguson/Photo Edit; 16T (br), Peter Dean/Grant Heilman Photography; 17T, Peter Van Steen/ HRW Photo; 18T, Peter Van Steen/HRW Photo; 19T, Nicholas Pinturas/Tony Stone Images; 46T, Sam Dudgeon/HRW Photo; 2A, Peter Van Steen/HRW Photo; 36A, Peter Van Steen/HRW Photo; 68A, Sam Dudgeon/HRW Photo; 106A, Sam Dudgeon/HRW Photo; 146A, Andy Christiansen/HRW Photo; 184A, Sam Dudgeon/HRW Photo; 218A, Sam Dudgeon/HRW photo; 250A, Andy Christiansen/HRW Photo; 282A, Peter Van Steen/HRW Photo; 322A, Sam Dudgeon/HRW Photo; 354A, Sam Dudgeon/HRW Photo; 388A, Peter Van Steen/HRW Photo; 428A, Michelle Bridwell/ HRW Photo; 460A, Peter Van Steen/HRW Photo; 486A, Peter Van Steen/HRW Photo; 524A, Sam Dudgeon/HRW Photo; 556A, Sam Dudgeon/ HRW Photo; 596A, Victoria Smith/HRW Photo; 628A, Victoria Smith/HRW Photo.

Printed in the United States of America

ISBN 0-03-055578-7

6 7 048 05 04 03 02

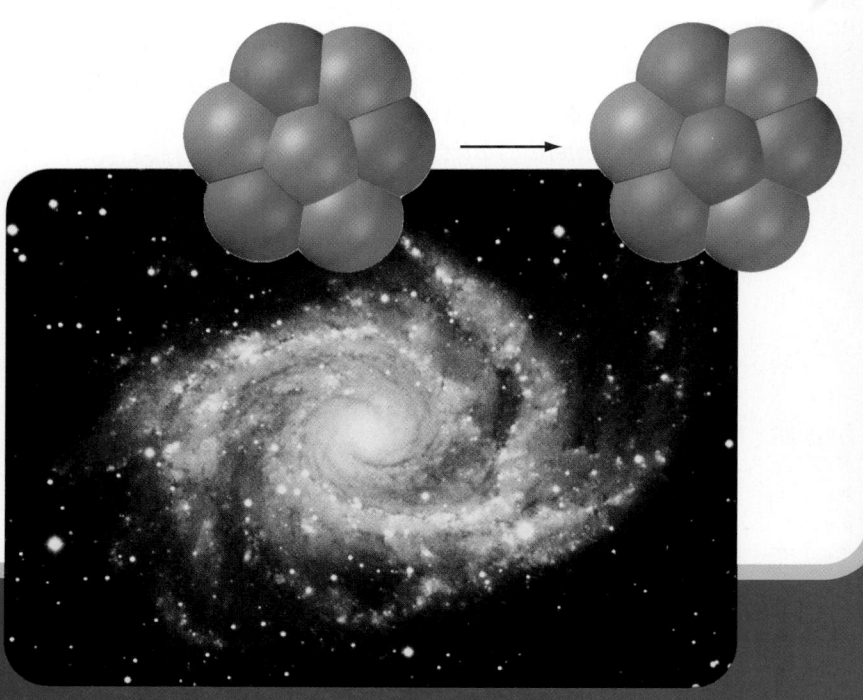

Acknowledgements

Lab Reviewers

Chris Crowell
Brockport High School
Brockport, NY

Bob Iveson
WARD'S Natural Science Est.

James Keefer
Brockport High School
Brockport, NY

Bryan Kommeth
WARD'S Natural Science Est.

Gregory Puskar
Laboratory Manager
Physics Department
West Virginia University
Morgantown, WV

Geof Smith
WARD'S Natural Science Est.

Sharon Wolsky
Rush Henrietta High School
Henrietta, NY

Text Reviewers

Tim Black
Albuquerque, NM

Larry Brown, Ph.D.
Science Department Chair
Morgan Park Academy
Chicago, IL

Jim Bryn
Physical Science Teacher
Sparks High School
Sparks, NV

Bonnie J. Buratti, Ph.D.
Research Scientist
Jet Propulsion Laboratory
CIT
Pasadena, CA

G. Lynn Carlson
University of Wisconsin-
    Parkside
Racine, WI

David S. Coco, Ph.D.
Research Physicist
University of Texas at Austin
Austin, TX

Bill Conway, Ph.D.
Physics Teacher
Northeastern Illinois
    University
Chicago, IL

Lillie M. Darke
*Integrated Physics and I.B.
    Chemistry Teacher*
Waltrip High School
Houston, TX

Martha M. Day, Ph.D.
Physical Science Teacher
Whites Creek High School
Whites Creek, TN

William Deutschman, Ph.D.
President
Oregon Laser Consultants
Klamath Falls, OR

Melody Law Ewey
Vice Principal
Holmes Junior High School
Davis, CA

Jean A. Fuller-Stanley, Ph.D.
Chemistry Professor
Wellesley College
Wellesley, MA

Michael Garcia, Ph.D.
Professor of Geology
University of Hawaii
Honolulu, HI

Bruce Gronich
Instructor
University of Texas
    at El Paso
El Paso, TX

David Hamilton, Ed.D.
Physics Teacher
Franklin High School
Portland, OR

John Hubisz, Ph.D.
Physics Professor
North Carolina State
    University
Raleigh, NC

Robert Hudson
Physics Professor Emeritus
Roanoke College
Salem, VA

William Ingham, Ph.D.
Physics Professor
James Madison University
Harrisonburg, VA

Doug Jenkins
Science Teacher
Warren Central High School
Bowling Green, KY

Jennifer Jordan
*Integrated Physics and
    Chemistry Teacher*
Fox Technical and Academic
    High School
San Antonio, TX

Karen Kwitter, Ph.D.
*Ebenezer Fitch Professor of
    Astronomy*
Williams College
Williamstown, MA

Joel S. Leventhal, Ph.D.
Research Chemist
USDI Geological Survey
Denver, CO

Timothy Lincoln, Ph.D
Professor of Geology
Albion College
Albion, MI

Jeff Lockwood
Secondary Science Specialist
Tucson Unified School District
Tucson, AZ

Crystal Long
Biology Teacher
Coral Springs High School
Coral Springs, FL

Julie Lutz, Ph.D.
Astronomy Program
Washington State University
Pullman, WA

Edgar McCullough, Jr., Ph.D.
Professor Emeritus Geosciences
University of Arizona
Tempe, AZ

George T. Ochs
Science Coordinator
Washoe County School District
Reno, NV

Keith Oldham, Ph.D.
Professor of Chemistry
Trent University
Peterborough, Ontario,
    Canada

Fred Redmore
Professor of Chemistry
Highland Community College
Freeport, IL

Walter Robinson, Ph.D.
*Department of Atmospheric
    Sciences*
University of Illinois
Urbana, IL

Melanie R. Stewart
Curriculum Consultant
Stow-Munroe Falls City
    Schools
Stow, OH

Richard S. Treptow
Professor of Chemistry
Chicago State University
Chicago, IL

Charles M. Wynn
Professor of Chemistry
Eastern Connecticut State
    University
Willimantic, CT

Carol Zimmerman, Ph.D.
Exploration Associate
Houston, TX

Teacher's Introduction

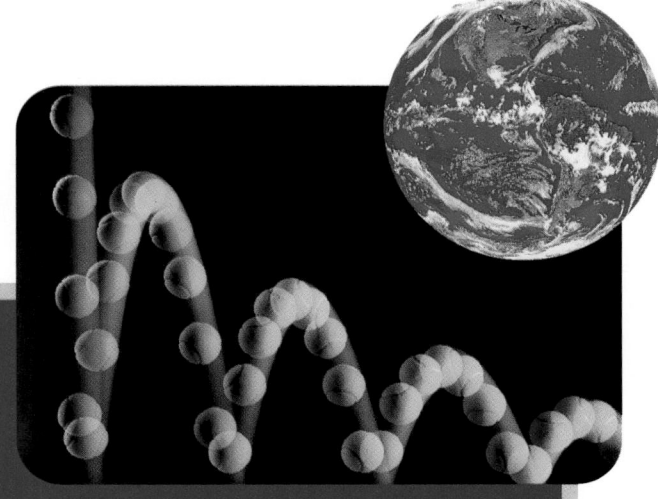

Table of Contents
in Brief

Table of CONTENTS

H_2O

3
Li
Lithium
6.941

11
Na
Sodium
22.989 768

19
K
Potassium
39.0983

37
Rb
Rubidium
85.4678

55
Cs
Cesium
132.905 43

87
Fr
Francium
(223.0197)

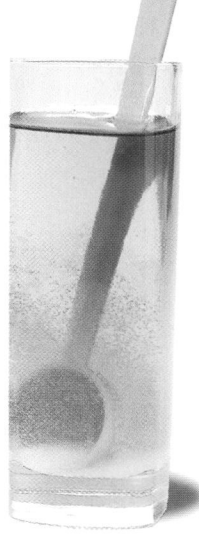

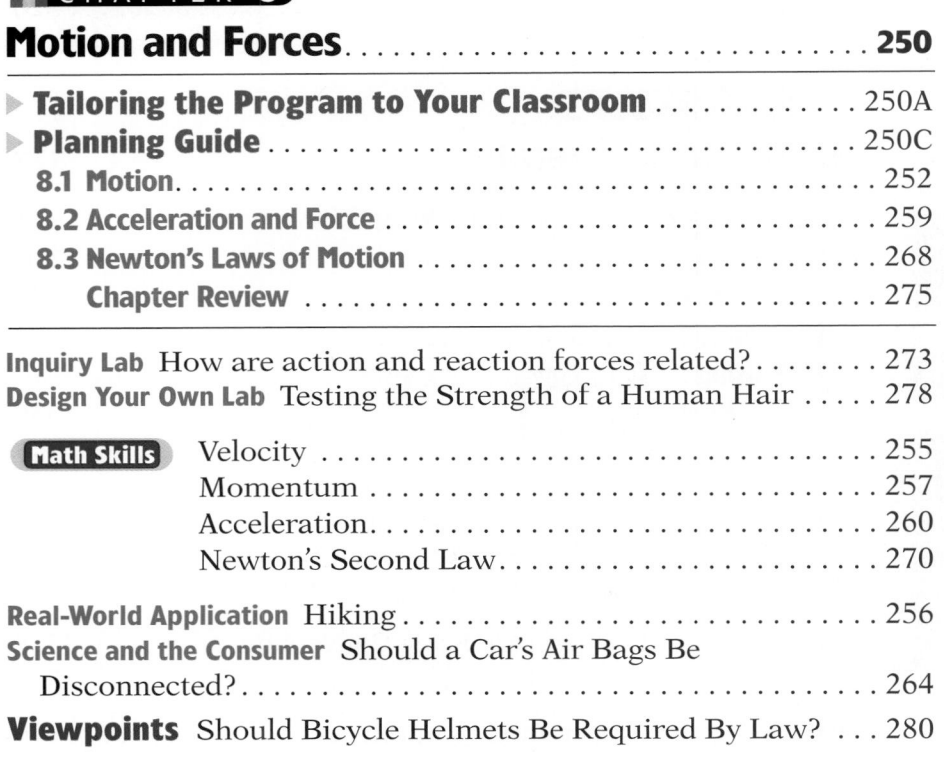

Unit 3 MOTION AND ENERGY ——————————— 248

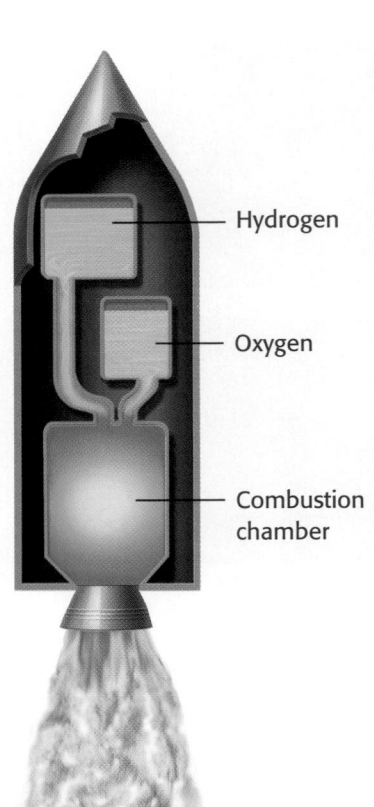

Hydrogen

Oxygen

Combustion chamber

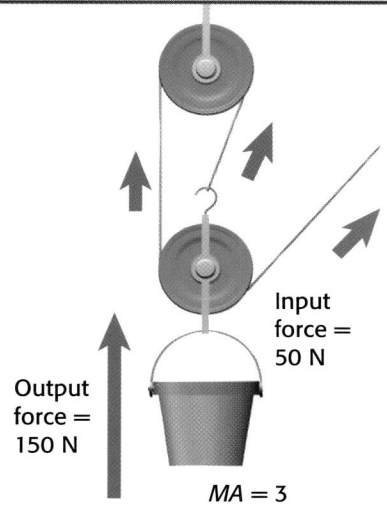

Output force = 150 N

Input force = 50 N

MA = 3

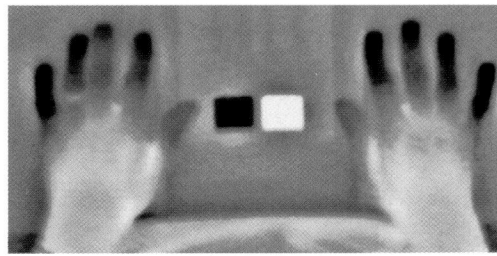

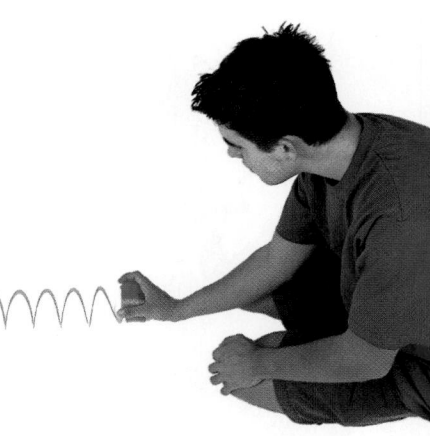

Unit 6 EXPLORING EARTH AND SPACE ————— 522

Crust

Mantle

Outer core

Inner core

REFERENCE SECTION

LABORATORY EXPERIMENTS

Inquiry Labs

Quick Activities

Math Skills

REAL WORLD APPLICATIONS

 internet connect

This textbook contains the following on-line resources to help you make the most of your science experience.

Visit **go.hrw.com** for extra help and study aids matched to your textbook. Just type in the keyword HK1 HOME.

Visit **www.scilinks.org** to find resources specific to topics in your textbook. Keywords appear through-out your book to take you further.

 Smithsonian Institution
Internet Connections

Visit **www.si.edu/hrw** for specifically chosen on-line materials from one of our nation's premier science museums.

Visit **www.cnnfyi.com** for late-breaking news and cur-rent events stories selected just for you.

Effective planning starts with all the resources you need in an easy-to-use package!

One-Stop Planner

CD-ROM

The heart of your program
All your program resources are integrated into suggested lesson plans. You can view and print any resource with a click of the mouse. You can easily customize the suggested lesson plans to match your daily or weekly calendar and your district's requirements. See page 37T for more information on this great new planning tool.

LABORATORY RESOURCES

Datasheets

Laboratory Experiments

MEDIA RESOURCES

Guided Reading Audio CD Program

Physical Science Interactive Tutor

Spanish Resources

CNN Presents: Science in the News

Teaching Transparencies

PRACTICE AND REINFORCEMENT

Study Guide

Math Skills Worksheets

Basic Skills Worksheets

TEACHER MANAGEMENT SYSTEM

One-Stop Planner

CD-ROM

Lesson Plans
For Traditional and Block Schedules

Resources
Worksheets
Media Resources
Assessments
Labs

TEACHING TIPS AND STRATEGIES

Annotated Teacher's Edition

Resource Teacher Guides and Answer Keys

ENRICHMENT AND ASSESSMENT

Integration Enrichment Resources

Chapter Tests

Test Generator

TEACHING TIPS AND STRATEGIES

Annotated Teacher's Edition
The ATE is loaded with great ideas including classroom management tips, demonstrations, group activities, and support for struggling students.

Resource Teacher Guides and Answer Keys

LABORATORY RESOURCES

Datasheets
Datasheets on the *One-Stop Planner CD-ROM* help students with their organizational skills and make reports easy to grade. Datasheets are included for all in-text labs, Quick Activities, and all of the labs in the Laboratory Experiments manual.

Laboratory Experiments
These 19 experiments use CBL™ probes for data collection and analysis.

PRACTICE AND REINFORCEMENT

Study Guide
Review worksheets are provided for each text section along with a chapter pretest and an end-of-chapter mixed review that includes concept mapping.

Basic Skills Worksheets
These worksheets reteach and reinforce prerequisite skills.

Math Skills Worksheets
These worksheets provide more problem-solving models and practice problems keyed to the examples in the text.

ENRICHMENT AND ASSESSMENT

Integration Enrichment Resources
These worksheets extend the Real World Applications, Integrating, and Connection to features in the student text.

Chapter Tests
Each chapter test assesses mastery of content objectives using items in multiple, short answer, essay, and problem formats.

Test Generator and Assessment Item Listing
Located on the One-Stop Planner CD-ROM, this simple-to-use software manager allows you to make custom tests quickly and easily. The Assessment Item Listing shows you all available items at a glance.

MEDIA RESOURCES

Guided Reading Audio CD Program
Audio instruction is available for each chapter. These CDs are the answer for struggling readers and ESL students.

Physical Science Interactive Tutor
This student interactive program provides thorough step-by-step instruction on key concepts using CD-ROM technology.

Spanish Resources
Guided Reading Audio CD Program provides Spanish translations of the Objectives, text concepts, Math Skills tutorials, and section summaries. These materials help integrate Spanish-speaking students into your classroom presentations. *Spanish Glossary* translates all definitions of Key Terms from the text.

CNN Presents: Science in the News
These video clips of newsworthy topics in science show students the relevance of science in everyday life. Package includes teacher's notes and a critical thinking worksheet for each news story.

Teaching Transparencies
You'll find 165 color transparencies along with 165 illustrations and tables in blackline master form, including Lesson Focus Transparencies and matching worksheets for the start of each lesson.

Preparing students to be strategic readers

Well-organized, readable text is the key to comprehension.

Reading level is monitored for sentence length, the rate at which new terms are introduced, and their frequency of use. Reading level data is available from your Holt sales representative.

Chapter Previews provide a framework for a chapter outline.

Objectives state clear performance goals for students.

Key Terms listing appears at the beginning of every section.

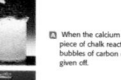

Short, single concept sections organize information and provide a cohesive flow of content.

Summaries for each section provide a capsule review of important concepts.

Reading Strategies include:

Anticipation Guides	Pattern Puzzles
Brainstorming	Power Notes
Discussion	Reader Response Logs
KWL (Know/Want to Know/Learned)	Reading Aloud/Discussion
	Reading Hints (specific to content)
L.I.N.K (List/Inquire/Notes/Know)	
	Reading Organizers
Paired Reading	Summarizing
Paired Summarizing	Two-Column Notes

Vocabulary Development

Each **Key Term** is highlighted and reinforced with a point-of-use definition in the margin so that the narrative flows without interruption. All key terms are also defined in the glossary.

Reading and Study Skills Appendix

This section provides in-depth instruction in proven strategies that students can employ while reading and studying for tests.

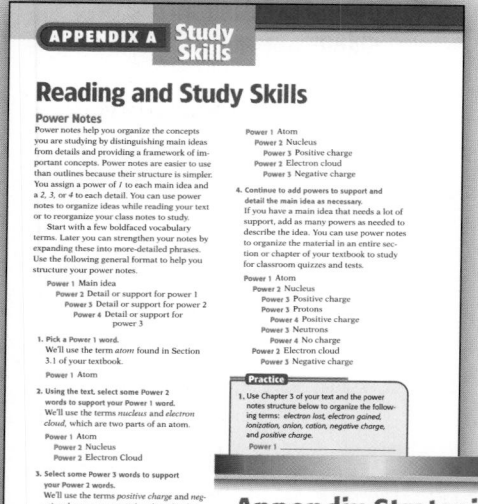

Appendix Strategies include:
Power Notes
Pattern Puzzles
KWL Notes
Two-Column Notes
Concept Mapping

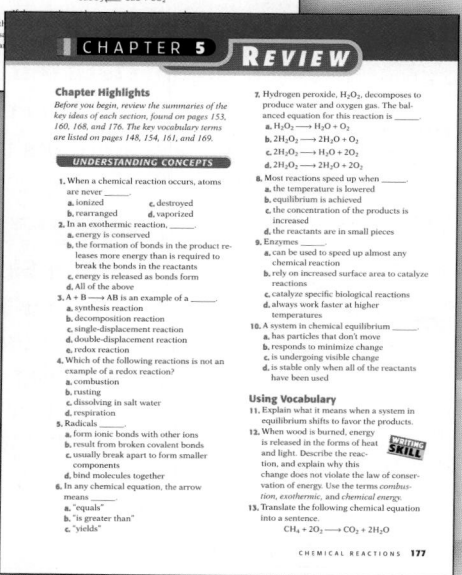

Vocabulary Skills Tips provide information on word origins and other strategies to derive meaning.

Using Vocabulary in the chapter review ensures comprehension of new terms.

Additional Emphasis on Reading Skills

ATE **Reading Skill Builders** throughout the Annotated Teacher's Edition give you reading and study strategies you can easily use.

Guided Reading Audio CD Program is an audio "guided tour" of each chapter. Auditory learners and struggling readers benefit greatly when they follow along with the text as they listen. Scripts for the audio program (in English and Spanish) are included on the *One-Stop Planner CD-ROM.*

WRITING SKILL **Writing skills practice** in the Section and Chapter Reviews helps students practice content-area writing skills.

Your Turn **Your Turn** items in the *Viewpoints* features give students practice with developing persuasive arguments on an issue.

In-depth skill development that gives every student the chance to succeed

The approach starts with a math refresher, followed by step-by-step problem solving models and problem-analysis strategies.

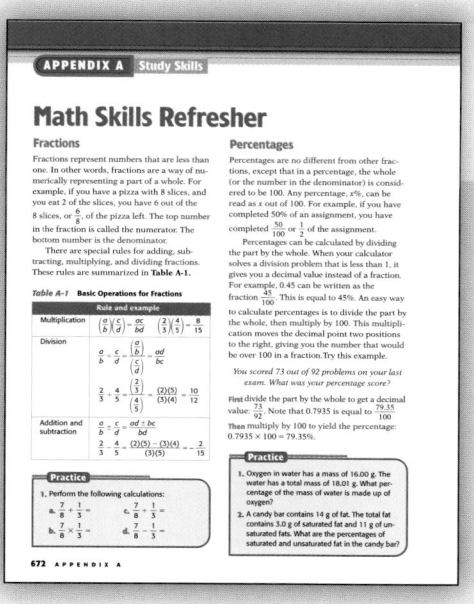

Math refresher topics in Chapter 1 and the Appendix include the background students need to start the year off right.

Math Skills Refresher includes:

Chapter 1	Appendix
SI Measurement	Algebraic Rearrangements
Graphing	Exponents
Exponential Notation	Fractions
Significant Figures	Geometry
	Order of Operations
	Percentages
	Scientific Notation
	Significant Figures
	SI Units

Equations are highlighted in the narrative portion of the text, making them easy to find and remember. Students see the connection between the quantities and the symbols used in the equation.

Math Skills provide the detailed models students need to understand how to solve problems. Problems are labeled so that students learn to recognize problem types.

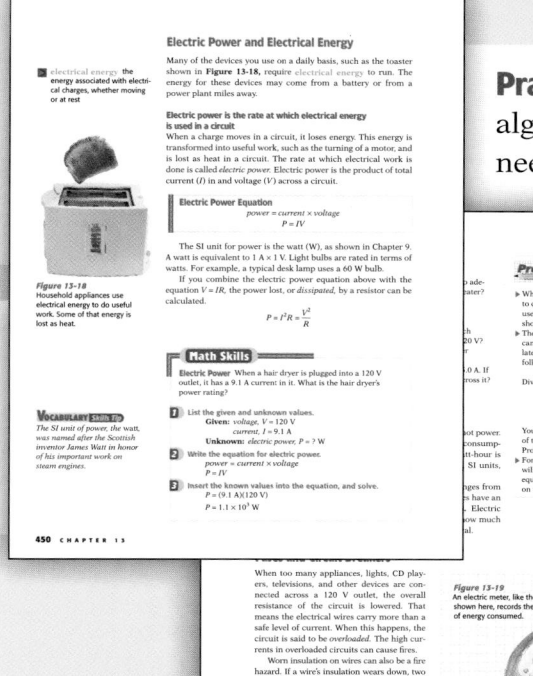

Practice Hints reinforce the algebraic manipulations needed to solve problems, and they guide students through the Practice that follows Math Skills.

There's Lots of Practice!

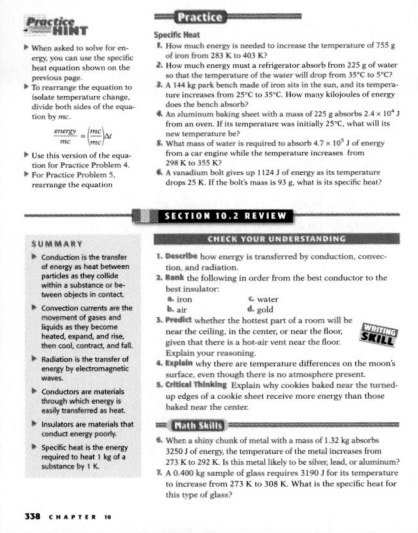

Practice gives students numerous problems to increase their skills.

Math Skills follow-ups in Section Reviews provide more practice problems.

Problem Solving items in the Chapter Review challenge students to apply their reasoning skills.

Building Math Skills in the Chapter Review provides more practice problems. All problems are labeled by type.

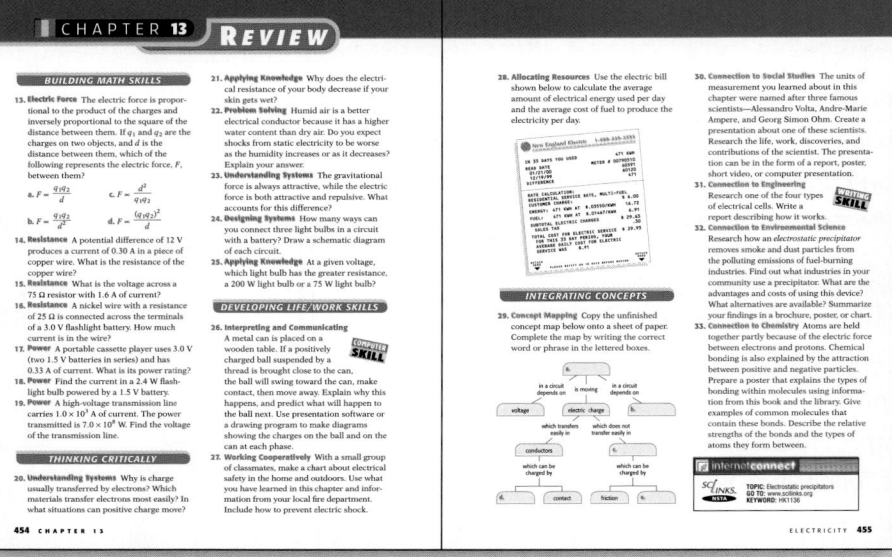

Problem Bank in the Appendix contains 135 more practice problems.

Additional Emphasis on Math Skills

 Additional Examples are provided with every Math Skill problem to use as chalkboard examples or quiz items.

 Skill Builders in the margins give you additional activities and strategies to develop math-related skills.

 **Computer Skills** practice in the Section and Chapter Reviews give students meaningful assignments using spreadsheets, presentation programs, and drawing programs.

One-Stop Planner CD-ROM

Math Skills Worksheets provide additional worked out examples and further practice with math related science concepts.

CROSS-DISCIPLINE OPTIONS

The tools you need for a diverse student population

Only *Holt Science Spectrum* provides the solid foundation in basic skills along with the rich set of curriculum integration options you see below. This range of text features helps you easily create a holistic learning environment where students not only master fundamental skills, but they are motivated by studying interesting topics that connect to science.

Architecture
- ▶ *Connection to . . . feature*
- ■ *Cross-Discipline Teaching*
- ● *Integration Enrichment Resources*

Engineering
- ▶ *Connection to . . . feature*
- ■ *Cross-Discipline Teaching*
- ● *Integration Enrichment Resources*

Fine Arts
- ▶ *Connection to . . . feature*
- ■ *Cross-Discipline Teaching*
- ● *Integration Enrichment Resources*

Technology and Computers
- ▶ *Integrating Technology and Society (ITS lessons)*
- ▶ *Integrating . . . feature*
- ■ *Cross-Discipline Teaching*
- ● *Integration Enrichment Resources*

Health
- ▶ *Integrating . . . feature*
- ■ *Cross-Discipline Teaching*
- ● *Integration Enrichment Resources*

Curriculum Integration

Social Studies
- ▶ *Connection to . . . feature*
- ■ *Cross-Discipline Teaching*
- ● *Integration Enrichment Resources*

Language Arts
- ▶ *Connection to . . . feature*
- ▶ *Reading Skill Builder*
- ▶ *Writing Skill Builder*
- ■ *Cross-Discipline Teaching*
- ● *Integration Enrichment Resources*

Science
(including biology, chemistry, earth science, environmental science, physics, and space science)
- ▶ *Integrating . . . feature*
- ■ *Cross-Discipline Teaching*

Physical Education
- ■ *Cross-Discipline Teaching*

Mathematics
- ▶ *Math Skills*
- ▶ *Practice Hints*
- ▶ *Math Skills Refresher*
- ▶ *Integrating . . . feature*
- ■ *Cross-Discipline Teaching*
- ● *Integration Enrichment Resources*

These options can be found in:
- ▶ Student Text   ■ Annotated Teacher's Edition   ● One-Stop Planner CD-ROM

Links within areas of *science* . . .

Integrating features show students how science concepts are applied in the different branches of science or mathematics.

. . . and links to other subject areas

Connections to features are activities for students that relate the concept just learned to another subject area.

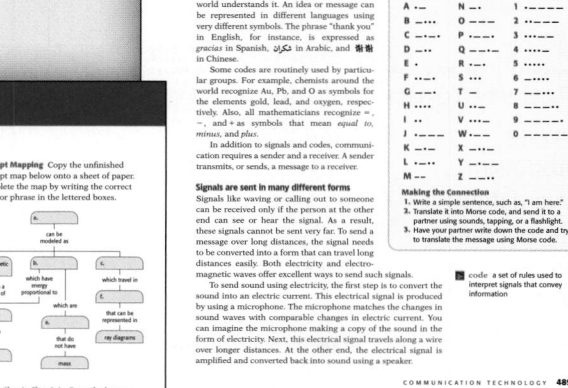

Integrating Concepts in the Chapter Reviews include concept mapping exercises and research projects related to other subject areas. *Includes Internet links!*

internet **connect**

Additional Emphasis on Integration

 Linking Chapters highlights the connections you can make between what student are learning now and what they learned in previous chapters.

 Cross-Discipline Teaching notes are suggestions you can use to show students how science relates to other fields they are studying.

One-Stop Planner CD-ROM

 Multicultural Connections highlight the scientific contributions of cultures throughout the world.

Integration Enrichment Resources give you worksheets related to the topic of each *Connection to, Integrating, Real World Applications,* and *Science and the Consumer* features.

STUDENT-CENTERED FEATURES

Bringing excitement and relevance to the classroom

High-interest features give you the foundation for an engaging learning environment.

Focus Activities

The chapter begins with activities that grab students' attention and set the tone for topics to come. *Includes Internet links!*

internet**connect**

Focus Activity Topics include:

Glass blowing	Infrared imaging
Rocket propulsion	Messaging systems
Radioactive dating and art forgeries	Crater Lake
Crash-test dummies	Rainbows
Kinetic sculpture	Solar-car racing

Real-World Applications

These interesting topics and activities show students how a concept is applied to everyday life.

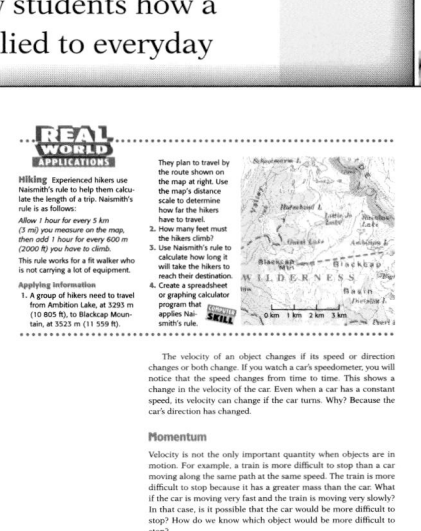

Science and the Consumer

These issues are subjects of on-going debate. Students use risk assessment models to analyze the issue. *Your Choice* items ask students to relate the issue to a science concept and then present suggestions for further research. *Includes Internet links!*

internet**connect**

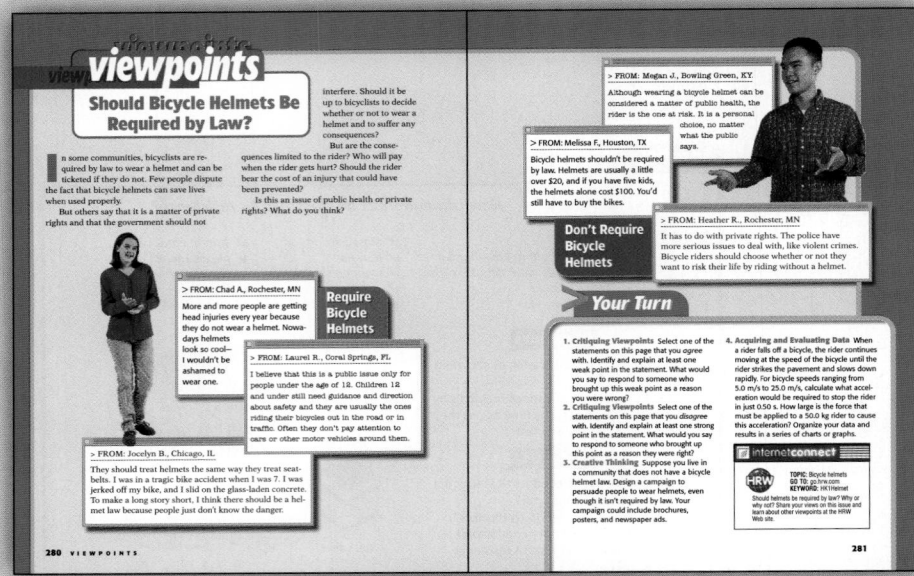

Viewpoints

Students throughout the nation share their opinions on interesting issues. *Your Turn* items help students learn to analyze arguments for bias and do additional research to formulate their own "informed" opinions which they can post on the HRW website. *Includes Internet links!*

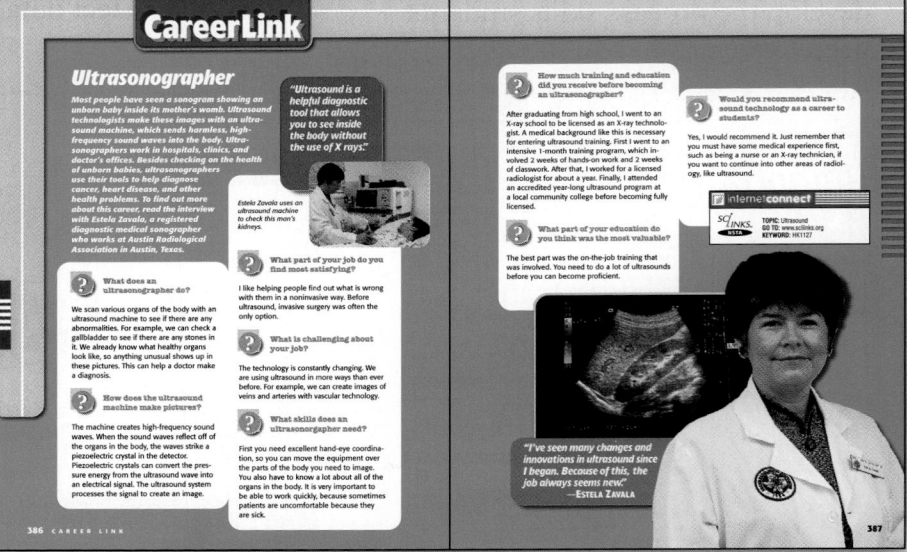

Career Links

Personal interviews give students a realistic view of the education and training required for some fascinating careers. *Includes Internet links!*

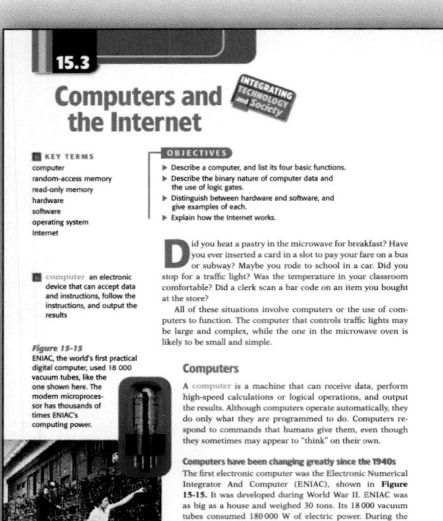

ITS Lessons—Integrating Technology and Society

These text sections probe science and technology topics that have environmental and societal implications.

LABS and ACTIVITIES

Providing options that save you time and money

Text Labs and Activities

Quick Activity

These 38 short activities require very little time and equipment, yet they provide the concrete experiences students need to thoroughly understand concepts.

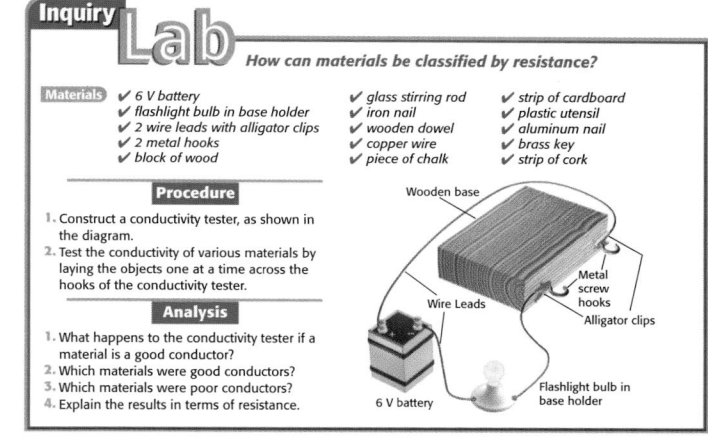

Skill Builder Lab

These 11 structured experiments develop the process skills students need to engage in real inquiry.

Inquiry Lab

These 22 experiments require students to collect data to resolve an inquiry-based question.

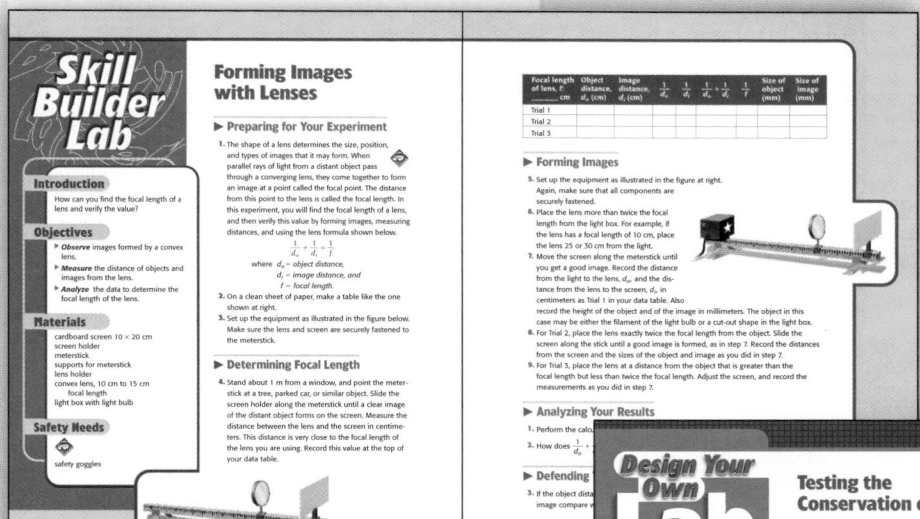

Design Your Own Lab

For these 8 experiments, students begin with a simple procedure and make observations that they will use in designing their own experiment to test a hypothesis.

Process skills are highlighted in the Objectives section. *Safety* is stressed in each procedure with thorough caution statements linked to pictorial icons. *Defending Your Conclusions* gives students practice in developing rational arguments.

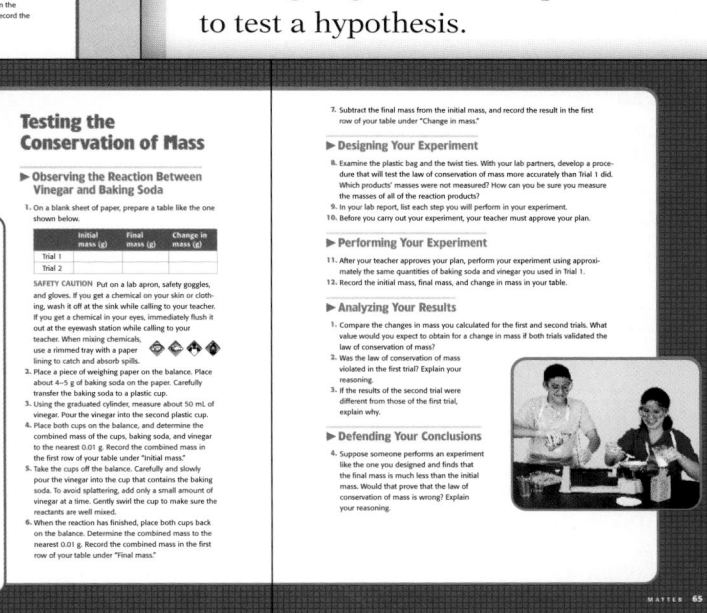

Lab Skills Appendix

Students get the necessary background in measurement techniques that ensure good lab results.

Lab Skills Appendix includes:

Making Measurements in the Laboratory
Reading a Balance
Measuring Temperature
Reading a Graduated Cylinder
How to Write a Laboratory Report

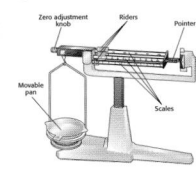

Lab Skills

Making Measurements in the Laboratory

Reading a balance for mass

When a balance is required for determining mass, you will probably use a centigram balance like the one shown in **Figure A-4.** The centigram balance is sensitive to 0.01 g. This means that your mass readings should all be recorded to the nearest 0.01 g.

Before using the balance, always check to see if the pointer is resting at zero. If the pointer is not at zero, check the riders. If all the riders are at zero, turn the zero adjust knob until the pointer rests at zero. The zero adjust knob is usually located at the far left end of the balance beam, as shown in **Figure A-4.** Note: The balance will not adjust to zero if the movable pan has been removed.

In many experiments, you will be asked to obtain a specified mass of a solid. When measuring the mass of a chemical, place a piece of weighing paper on the movable pan. **Never place chemicals or hot objects directly on the pan.** They can permanently damage the surface of the pan and affect the accuracy of later measurements.

Determine the mass of the paper by adjusting the riders on the various scales. Record the mass of the weighing paper to the nearest 0.01 g. Then add the mass you wish to obtain by sliding the appropriate riders on the scales. For example, if your weighing paper has a mass of 0.15 g, the balance reads 0.15 g. To measure 13 g of a solid, you then need to add 13 g to this mass. Do this by sliding the 10-gram rider to 10 and the 1-gram rider to 3. The balance is no longer balanced.

Slowly add the solid onto the weighing paper until the balance is once again balanced. Do not waste time trying to obtain *exactly* 13.00 g of a solid. Instead, read the mass when the pointer swings close to zero. Remember, you must read the final mass on the balance and subtract the mass of the weighing paper (0.15 g) from this final mass to determine the solid's mass to two decimal places, as is appropriate for measurements made using a centigram balance.

Figure A-4

Zero adjustment knob — Riders — Pointer

Movable pan — Scales

Laboratory Experiments

These 19 experiments start with a question and problem. Students are directed to collect the data necessary to answer the question and solve the problem. Student Datasheets are also available for these labs, so you can cut back on photocopies of the actual procedure and grade student reports easily.

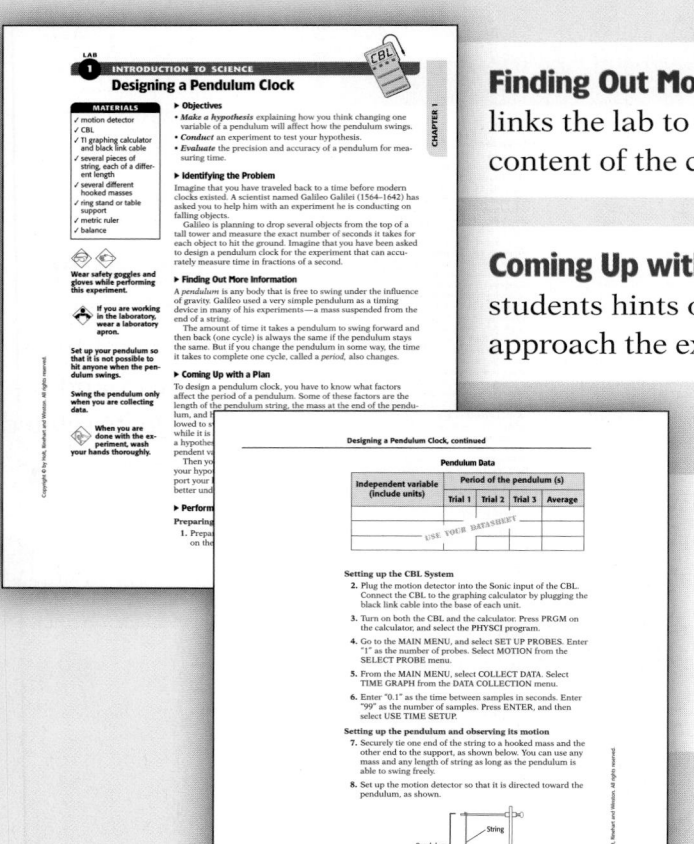

Finding Out More Information links the lab to the science content of the chapter.

Coming Up with a Plan gives students hints on how to approach the experiment.

Data Tables help students organize their work and make the task of grading less time consuming.

CBL Technology

Experiments in the laboratory manual use the Texas Instruments Calculator Based Laboratory™ system. CBL programs are written by Vernier Software for the use of their probes with TI graphing calculators. Instructions for the use of these probes is found in the Laboratory Experiments manual.

Vernier Probes/Sensors used:

CBL microphone
Conductivity probe
Current and voltage probes
Force sensor
Light sensor
Magnetic field sensor
Motion detector
pH probe
Temperature probe

Flexible tools allow you to monitor student performance quickly

There are lots of questions, including critical thinking!

Section Assessment

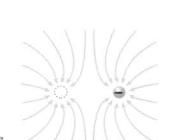

Check Your Understanding at the end of each section ties directly to the section objectives and measures students' understanding of those objectives.

Chapter Assessment

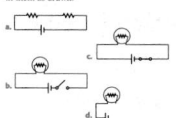

Understanding Concepts measures fundamental knowledge and re-inforces vocabulary development.

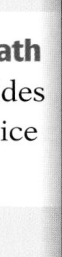

Building Math Skills provides more practice problems.

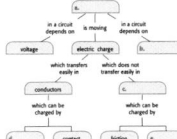

Integrating Concepts in Chapter Reviews include concept map-ping exercises and re-search projects related to other subject areas. *Includes Internet links!*

internet**connect**

Thinking Critically requires students to apply knowledge to new, related situations.

Life/Work Skills in Chapter Reviews help students acquire and practice useful behaviors and attitudes that they can use every day.

Study Guide

These blackline masters reinforce content, comprehension, and "thinking critically" skills developed in the student text.

Chapter Pretest allows you to assess students' prior knowledge and target weaknesses in instruction.

Section Review reinforces key concepts for the text section.

Mixed Review gives students the opportunity to assess their mastery before the Chapter Test.

These worksheets are also available on the *One-Stop Planner CD-ROM*.

Thinking Critically Categories

Acquiring and Evaluating Data
Applying Knowledge
Creative Thinking
Critical Thinking
Designing Systems
Evaluating Data
Improving Systems
Interpreting and Communicating
Interpreting Graphics
Making Comparisons
Problem Solving
Understanding Systems

Additional Assessment Support

ATE **Alternative Assessment** items in the margins provide class assessment strategies.

One-Stop Planner CD-ROM **Chapter Tests** include the following formats: multiple choice, short answer, essay, and problems to fully measure understanding. Each test item correlates with a chapter objective.

One-Stop Planner CD-ROM **Test Generator** contains a bank of over 2000 items, including 38 alternative assessment strategies from which you can construct your own custom tests. The software allows you to change any item in the bank and add your own items as well.

It's fully integrated!

PHYSICAL SCIENCE INTERACTIVE TUTOR

Holt Physical Science Interactive Tutor

The power of CD-ROM technology lets you help your students individually outside the classroom. Each module presents a key concept using concrete models and video animations. Students can work through the lessons at their own pace. Frequent evaluation lets students know if they are on the right track with diagnostic feedback. Modules include both concept tutorials and problem-solving tutorials following the structure of Math Skills within the textbook. The **interactive periodic table** makes the data needed for chemistry calculations readily available.

Available for both Macintosh®– and Windows®– compatible computers.

Module Titles

States of Matter/Classes of Matter
Models of the Atom
Periodic Properties
Chemical Bonding
Chemical Equations
Solutions
Heat
Batteries and Cells
Speed and Acceleration
Work
Conservation of Momentum
Frequency and Wavelength
Reflection
Refraction
Force Between Charges
Electrical Circuits
Electrical Field of a Wire

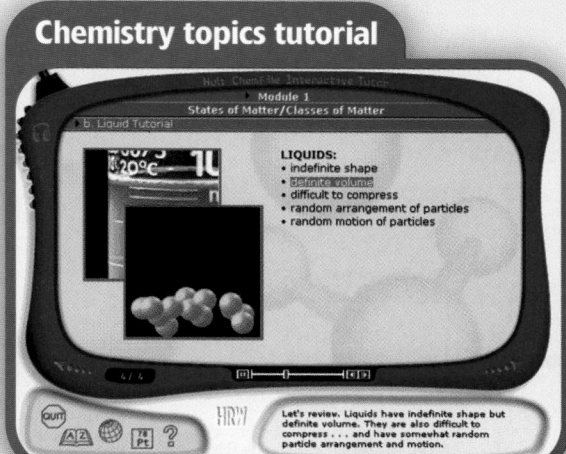

From States of Matter/Classes of Matter

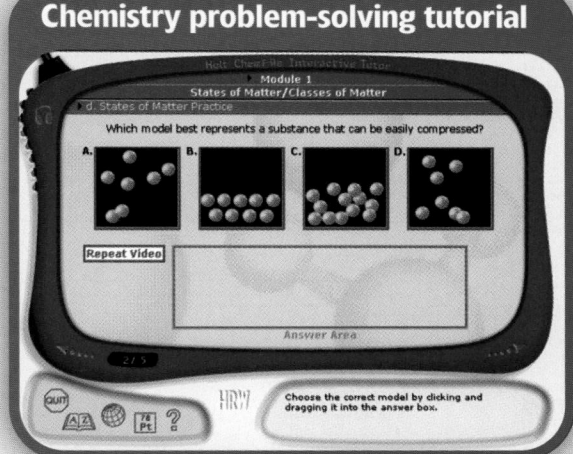

From States of Matter/Classes of Matter

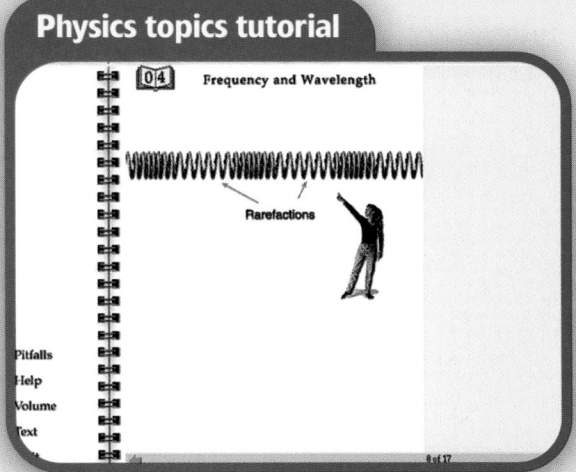

From Frequency and Wavelength

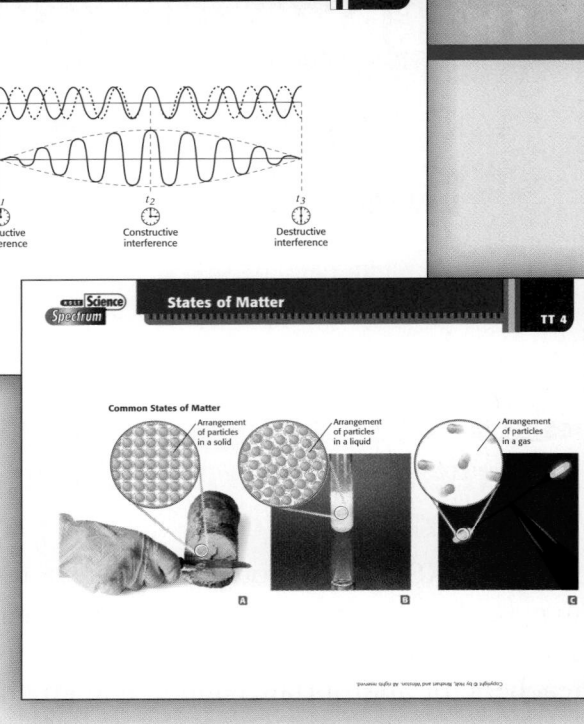

Tapping the Visual Learning Modality

Teaching Transparencies and Transparency Masters

The 165 color and 165 blackline masters include useful instructional illustrations from the text as well as warm-up activities for each lesson.

 Skill Builder Visual Strategies provide the tips for using these illustrations more effectively.

CNN PRESENTS Science in the News

This video package includes more than 25 short video clips that show students the newsworthy nature of science. The stories showcase useful applications of science concepts, often making cross-curricular connections to topics such as industry, careers, and economics. These clips make great warm-up activities to start lessons. Teacher's notes and student worksheets for each segment complete the package. Student worksheets focus on critical thinking and listening skills.

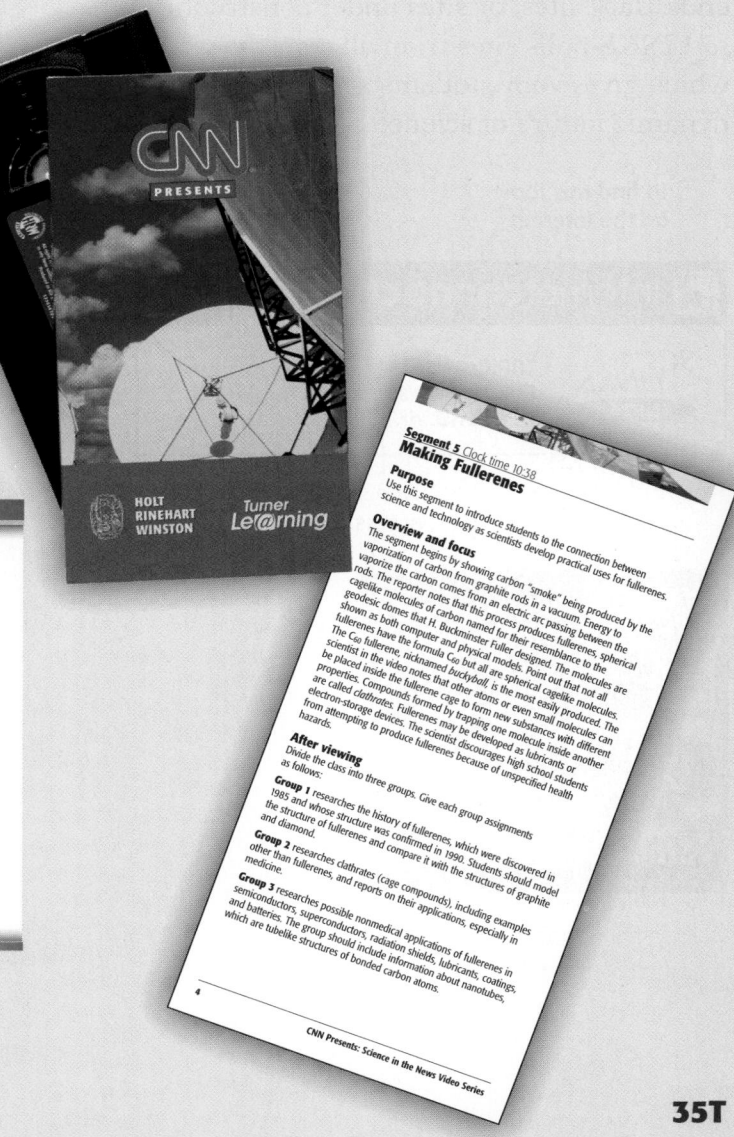

Video News Features include:

Multivitamins
Amusement Park Physics
Atom Builders
Making Fullerenes
Harvesting Salt
Acids in the Environment
Crash-Test Dummies
Egg Drop Contest
Trebuchet Catapult
Energy-Saving House

INTERNET SUPPORT

Online resources at your fingertips keep you up-to-date

SCi*LINKS* **NSTA** **does the legwork for you by screening the vast resources on the Internet.**

All *sci*LINKS topics throughout the text are managed and monitored by National Science Teachers Association staff. Sites are selected by teachers for appropriate content and grade level. Sites are continuously added and deleted from the system. Student don't end up at dead ends, dark sites, or sites under construction. *sci*LINKS pulls sites from all over the world, which gives your students a global view of the dynamic nature of science communication.

To find this topic on the Internet

Type in the *sci*LINKS Web address

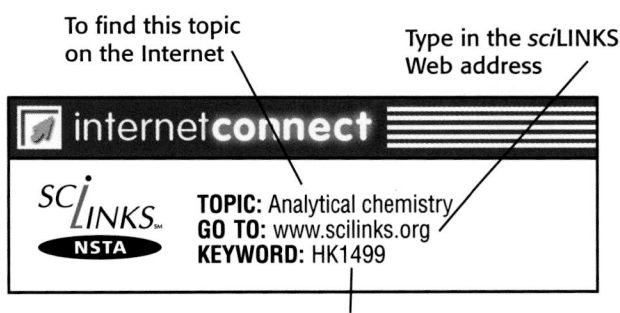

SCi*LINKS* **NSTA**
TOPIC: Analytical chemistry
GO TO: www.scilinks.org
KEYWORD: HK1499

Type in the keyword code to access the links to that topic

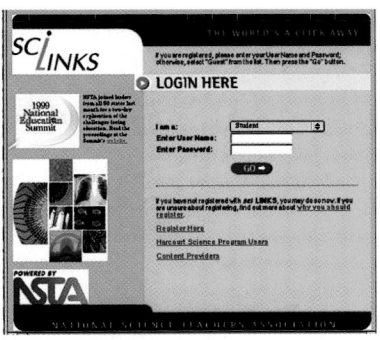

Holt, Rinehart and Winston Web Materials

 Visit **www.go.hrw.com** to stay up to date with additional resources developed for the ***Holt Science Spectrum*** program. Feedback from teachers helps determine the materials you'll find on the Web site. Look for content updates to keep you current, additional articles, activities, teaching suggestions, problem solutions, and lab tips.

Smithsonian Institution Web Materials

Smithsonian Institution®
The Smithsonian Institution maintains special Web sites for use with ***Holt Science Spectrum.*** Visit www.si.edu/hrw for a complete listing of these resources. You can find interactive exhibits, classroom activities, interviews with scientists, along with an interesting variety of application and extension topics.

LESSON PLANNING

It's simple, quick, and portable!

The *One-Stop Planner CD-ROM* is your high-tech roadmap to all resources in the program.

Finally, a new system that saves you time in reviewing, planning, and organizing all the resources in your science program. Starting with a suggested lesson plan for each text section, you can see how all resources are fully integrated into that lesson. You can print each resource right from the CD-ROM, so you no longer have to carry around multiple booklets when planning your lessons. Everything you need is on the disk!

Plan quickly with lesson plans that are easily changed to match your own objectives.

The suggested lesson plans are available as PDF files and as word-processing documents. You can change the word-processing lesson plans to reflect your style and schedule. These changes are easily saved as your own files for convenient storage.

Lesson Plan Formats
Microsoft Word
Microsoft Works
AppleWorks
ClarisWorks

Sort through resources quickly with a click of a mouse.

All resources are hot-linked at appropriate points in your lesson plan. You can also view resources by category, such as labs or worksheets. All worksheet resources can be printed from the CD-ROM and photocopied for classroom use.

One-Stop Planner

CD-ROM

Pacing suggestions consider block and traditional schedules.

Make your own custom lesson plan by selecting materials listed in the *Other Resource Options* section.

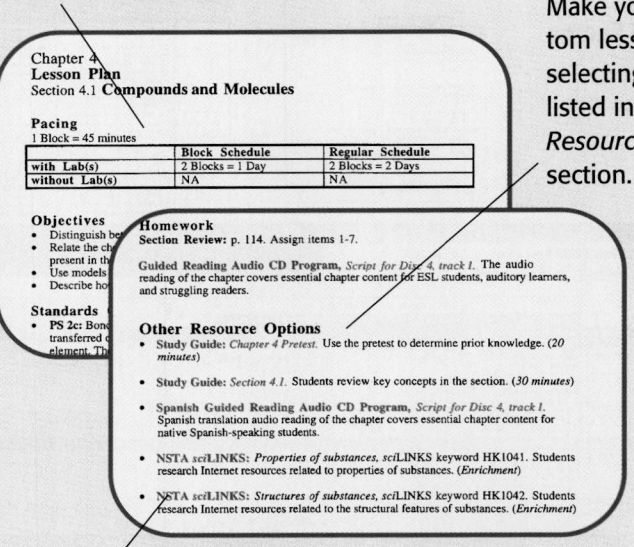

Titles that appear in blue are hot-linked to the actual resource. Click to view any resource or print any worksheet.

Resources include:

Lesson Plans	Laboratory Experiments
Basic Skills Worksheets	Lesson Focus Worksheets
Career Focus Worksheets	Limited English Proficiency
Chapter Tests and	Inclusion Strategies
Answer Key	Math Skills Worksheets
CNN Critical Thinking Work-	Occupational Applications
sheets/Teacher's Guide	Science Research Paper
Directed Reading Audio	Worksheets
Scripts (English and	Scoring Rubrics/Classroom
Spanish)	Management Checklists
Integration Enrichment	Study Guide
Resources	Teaching Transparencies
Internet Guide Portfolio	Transparency Blackline
Projects	Masters
Lab Datasheets	Test Generator Software with
Lab Safety Contract and Quiz	Test Item Files

ANNOTATED TEACHER'S EDITION

Tips for daily instruction right where you need them

Planning Support

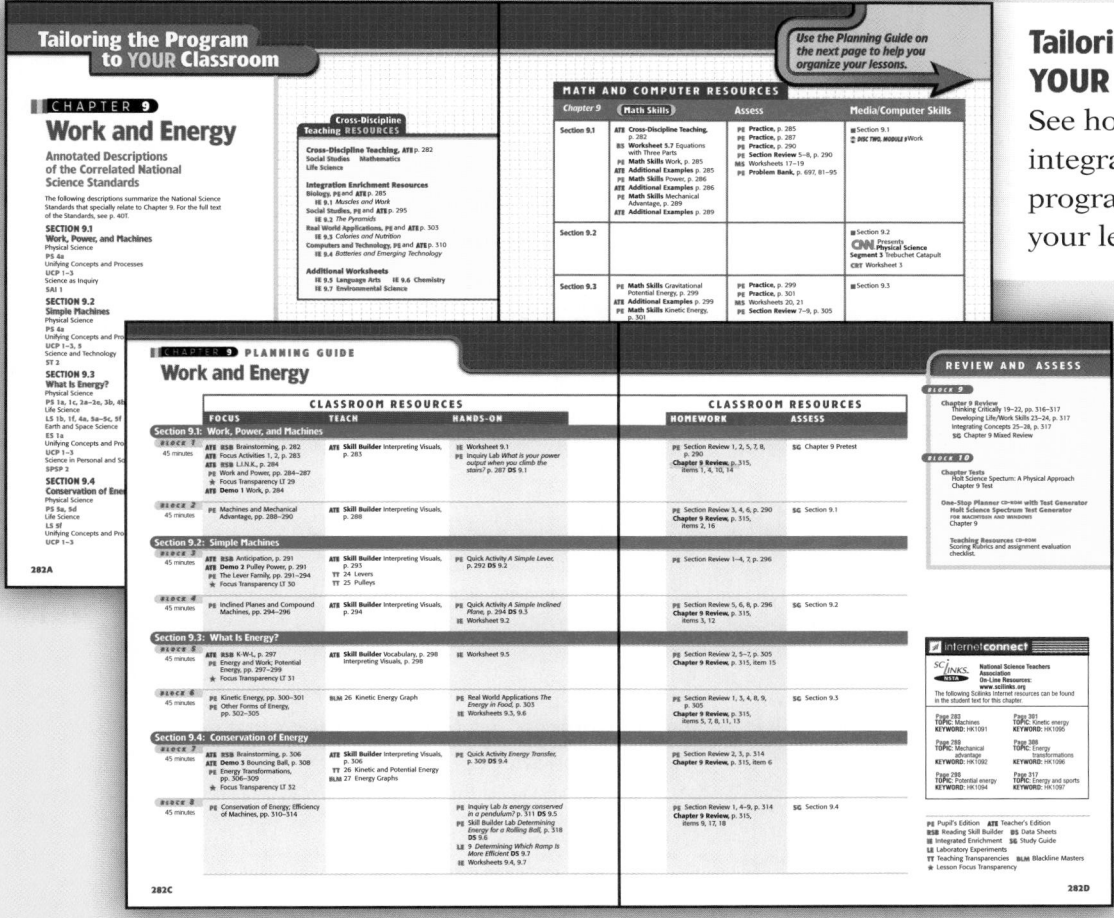

Tailoring the Program to YOUR Classroom

See how all of the subject integration built into this program can be used to enrich your lessons.

Planning Guide

Get a quick overview of how all the print and technology resources fit with the chapter content. Pacing suggestions are also included.

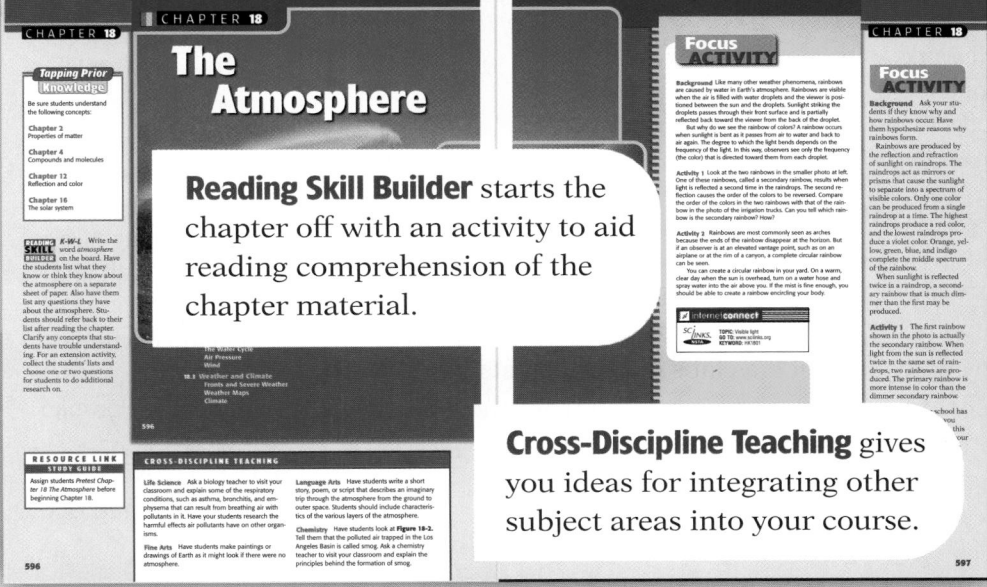

Tapping Prior Knowledge highlights essential prerequisite content to review with students at the start of a chapter to be sure they are ready.

Reading Skill Builder starts the chapter off with an activity to aid reading comprehension of the chapter material.

Cross-Discipline Teaching gives you ideas for integrating other subject areas into your course.

Daily Teaching Support

Scheduling suggests reviewing the available resources and selecting the **Lesson Focus Transparency** activity to start the lesson. These activities help prepare students for the lesson, which gives you time to get the lesson organized.

Resource Links are point-of-use reminders to use program supplements found in workbooks or on the One-Stop Planner CD-ROM.

Alternative Assessment provides suggestions for group and nontraditional individual assessment.

Linking Chapters helps you relate what students are learning now to previously learned material.

Misconception Alert describes common misconceptions students may have about a topic and provides tips on confronting and dispelling these misconceptions.

Skill Builder teaching tips provide suggestions to ensure skill mastery.

Multicultural Extension links science concepts to the advances and discoveries of people from different cultures.

Demonstration gives you great activities to stimulate class discussion. Tech Prep and Consumer topics are included.

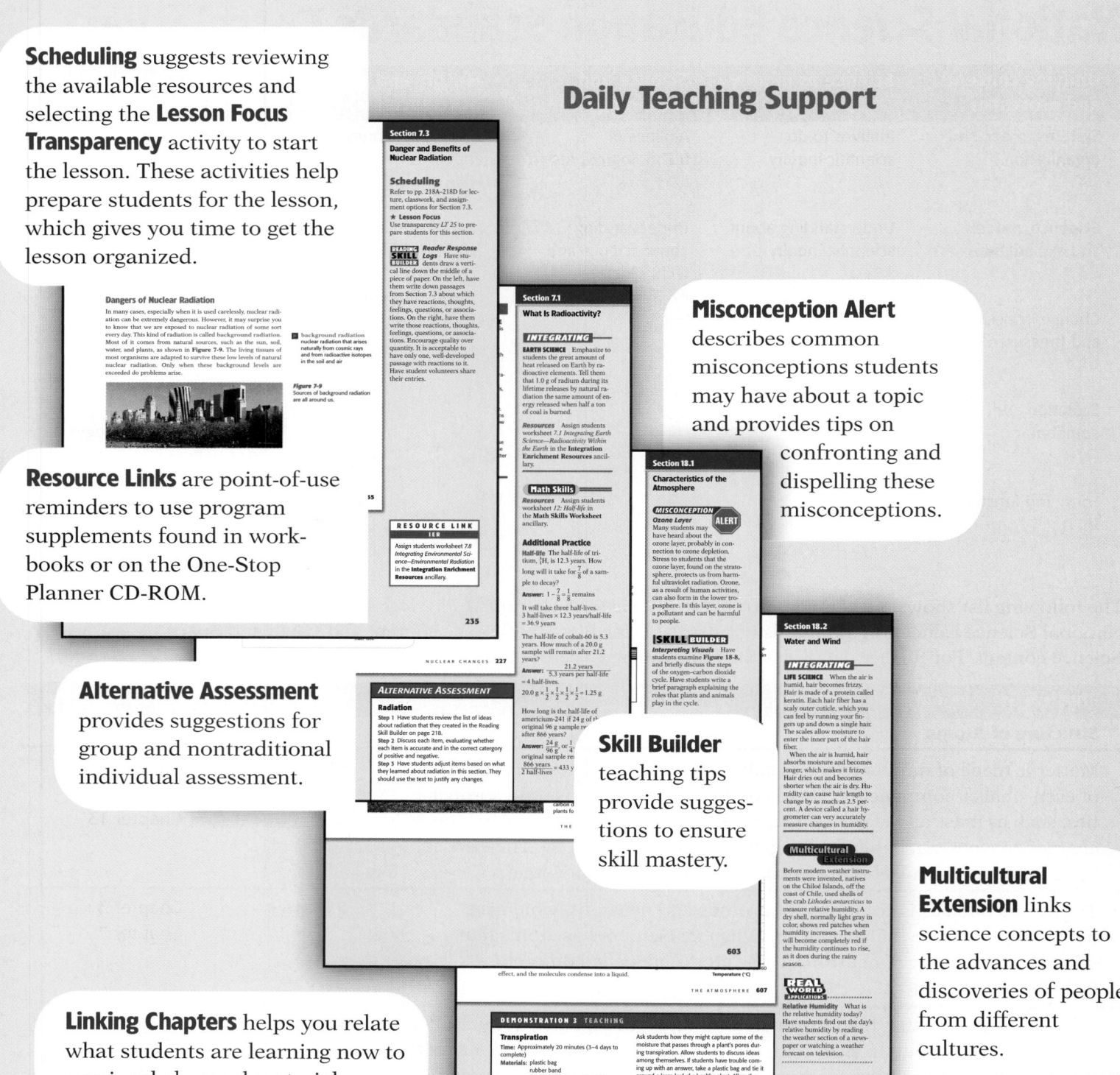

National Science Education Standards Correlation

Unifying concepts and processes	Science as inquiry	Science and technology	History and nature of science	Science in personal and social perspectives
Systems, order, and organization **UCP 1**	Abilities to do scientific inquiry **SAI 1**	Abilities of technological design **ST 1**	Science as a human endeavor **HNS 1**	Personal health **SPSP 1**
Evidence, models, and explanation **UCP 2**	Understanding about scientific inquiry **SAI 2**	Understanding about science and technology **ST 2**	Nature of science **HNS 2**	Populations, resources, and environments **SPSP 2**
Change, consistency, and measurements **UCP 3**			History of science **HNS 3**	Natural hazards **SPSP 3**
Evolution and equilibrium **UCP 4**				Risks and benefits **SPSP 4**
Form and function **UCP 5**				Science and technology in society **SPSP 5**

The following list shows the chapter correlation of *Science Spectrum: A Physical Approach* with the National Science Education Standards (grades 9-12) for Physical Science content and Earth and Space Science content. For further detail, see the interleaf pages before each chapter.

Physical Science Content Standards	Code	Chapter Correlation
Structure of Atoms		
Matter is made of minute particles called atoms, and atoms are composed of even smaller components. These components have measurable properties, such as mass and electrical charge. Each atom has a positively charged nucleus surrounded by negatively charged electrons. The electric force between the nucleus and electrons holds the atom together.	**PS 1a**	Chapter 3 Chapter 9 Chapter 13
The atom's nucleus is composed of protons and neutrons, which are much more massive than electrons. When an element has atoms that differ in the number of neutrons, these atoms are called different isotopes of the element.	**PS 1b**	Chapter 3 Chapter 7
The nuclear forces that hold the nucleus of an atom together, at nuclear distances, are usually stronger than the electric forces that would make it fly apart. Nuclear reactions convert a fraction of the mass of interacting particles into energy, and they can release much greater amounts of energy than atomic interactions. Fission is the splitting of a large nucleus into smaller pieces. Fusion is the joining of two nuclei at extremely high temperature and pressure, and is the process responsible for the energy of the sun and other stars.	**PS 1c**	Chapter 3 Chapter 7 Chapter 9

Physical Science Content Standards	Code	Chapter Correlation
Radioactive isotopes are unstable and undergo spontaneous nuclear reactions, emitting particles and/or wavelike radiation. The decay of any one nucleus cannot be predicted, but a large group of identical nuclei decay at a predictable rate. This predictability can be used to estimate the age of materials that contain radioactive isotopes.	PS 1d	Chapter 7
Structure and Properties of Matter		
Atoms interact with one another by transferring or sharing electrons that are furthest from the nucleus. These outer electrons govern the chemical properties of the element.	PS 2a	Chapter 3 Chapter 4 Chapter 9
An element is composed of a single type of atom. When elements are listed in order according to the number of protons (called the atomic number), repeating patterns of physical and chemical properties identify families of elements with similar properties. This "Periodic Table" is a consequence of the repeating pattern of outermost electrons and their permitted energies.	PS 2b	Chapter 3
Bonds between atoms are created when electrons are paired up by being transferred or shared. A substance composed of a single kind of atom is called an element. The atoms may be bonded together into molecules or crystalline solids. A compound is formed when two or more kinds of atoms bind together chemically.	PS 2c	Chapter 4 Chapter 9
The physical properties of compounds reflect the nature of the interactions among its molecules. These interactions are determined by the structure of the molecule, including the constituent atoms and the distances and angles between them.	PS 2d	Chapter 2 Chapter 4 Chapter 9
Solids, liquids, and gases differ in the distances and angles between molecules or atoms and therefore the energy that binds them together. In solids the structure is nearly rigid; in liquids molecules or atoms move around each other but do not move apart; and in gases molecules or atoms move almost independently of each other and are mostly far apart.	PS 2e	Chapter 2 Chapter 4 Chapter 9 Chapter 11 Chapter 12
Carbon atoms can bond to one another in chains, rings, and branching networks to form a variety of structures, including synthetic polymers, oils, and the large molecules essential to life.	PS 2f	Chapter 4
Chemical Reactions		
Chemical reactions occur all around us, for example in health care, cooking, cosmetics, and automobiles. Complex chemical reactions involving carbon-based molecules take place constantly in every cell in our bodies.	PS 3a	Chapter 5
Chemical reactions may release or consume energy. Some reactions such as the burning of fossil fuels release large amounts of energy by losing heat and by emitting light. Light can initiate many chemical reactions such as photosynthesis and the evolution of urban smog.	PS 3b	Chapter 5 Chapter 9 Chapter 19

Physical Science Content Standards	Code	Chapter Correlation
A large number of important reactions involve the transfer of either electrons (oxidation/reduction reactions) or hydrogen ions (acid/base reactions) between reacting ions, molecules, or atoms. In other reactions, chemical bonds are broken by heat or light to form very reactive radicals with electrons ready to form new bonds. Radical reactions control many processes such as the presence of ozone and greenhouse gases in the atmosphere, burning and processing of fossil fuels, the formation of polymers, and explosions.	**PS 3c**	Chapter 5
Chemical reactions can take place in time periods ranging from the few femtoseconds (10^{-15} seconds) required for an atom to move a fraction of a chemical bond distance to geologic time scales of billions of years. Reaction rates depend on how often the reacting atoms and molecules encounter one another, on the temperature, and on the properties—including shape—of the reacting species.	**PS 3d**	Chapter 5
Catalysts, such as metal surfaces, accelerate chemical reactions. Chemical reactions in living systems are catalyzed by protein molecules called enzymes.	**PS 3e**	Chapter 5
Motion and Forces		
Objects change their motion only when a net force is applied. Laws of motion are used to calculate precisely the effects of forces on the motion of objects. The magnitude of the change in motion can be calculated using the relationship $F = ma$, which is independent of the nature of the force. Whenever one object exerts force on another, a force equal in magnitude and opposite in direction is exerted on the first object.	**PS 4a**	Chapter 8 Chapter 9 Chapter 11
Gravitation is a universal force that each mass exerts on any other mass. The strength of the gravitational attractive force between two masses is proportional to the masses and inversely proportional to the square of the distance between them.	**PS 4b**	Chapter 1 Chapter 8 Chapter 9 Chapter 13 Chapter 16
The electric force is a universal force that exists between any two charged objects. Opposite charges attract while like charges repel. The strength of the force is proportional to the charges, and, as with gravitation, inversely proportional to the square of the distance between them.	**PS 4c**	Chapter 13
Between any two charged particles, electric force is vastly greater than the gravitational force. Most observable forces such as those exerted by a coiled spring or friction may be traced to electric forces acting between atoms and molecules.	**PS 4d**	Chapter 13
Electricity and magnetism are two aspects of a single electromagnetic force. Moving electric charges produce magnetic forces, and moving magnets produce electric forces. These effects help students to understand electric motors and generators.	**PS 4e**	Chapter 11 Chapter 12 Chapter 14

Physical Science Content Standards	Code	Chapter Correlation
Conservation of Energy and the Increase in Disorder		
The total energy of the universe is constant. Energy can be transferred by collisions in chemical and nuclear reactions, by light waves and other radiations, and in many other ways. However, it can never be destroyed. As these transfers occur, the matter involved becomes steadily less ordered.	**PS 5a**	Chapter 2 Chapter 9 Chapter 11 Chapter 12 Chapter 16
All energy can be considered to be either kinetic energy, which is the energy of motion; potential energy, which depends on relative position; or energy contained by a field, such as electromagnetic waves.	**PS 5b**	Chapter 9 Chapter 11 Chapter 13 Chapter 14
Heat consists of random motion and the vibrations of atoms, molecules, and ions. The higher the temperature, the greater the atomic or molecular motion.	**PS 5c**	Chapter 1 Chapter 2 Chapter 9 Chapter 12 Chapter 16
Everything tends to become less organized and less orderly over time. Thus, in all energy transfers, the overall effect is that the energy is spread out uniformly. Examples are the transfer of energy from hotter to cooler objects by conduction, radiation, or convection and the warming of our surroundings when we burn fuels.	**PS 5d**	Chapter 9 Chapter 10 Chapter 11 Chapter 12 Chapter 15 Chapter 16
Interactions of Energy and Matter		
Waves, including sound and seismic waves, waves on water, and light waves, have energy and can transfer energy when they interact with matter.	**PS 6a**	Chapter 9 Chapter 11 Chapter 12 Chapter 17
Electromagnetic waves result when a charged object is accelerated or decelerated. Electromagnetic waves include radio waves (the longest wavelength), microwaves, infrared radiation (radiant heat), visible light, ultraviolet radiation, x-rays, and gamma rays. The energy of electromagnetic waves is carried in packets whose magnitude is inversely proportional to the wavelength.	**PS 6b**	Chapter 9 Chapter 11 Chapter 12 Chapter 14 Chapter 15 Chapter 16
Each kind of atom or molecule can gain or lose energy only in particular discrete amounts and thus can absorb and emit light only at wavelengths corresponding to these amounts. These wavelengths can be used to identify the substance.	**PS 6c**	Chapter 13 Chapter 16
In some materials, such as metals, electrons flow easily, whereas in insulating materials such as glass they can hardly flow at all. Semiconducting materials have intermediate behavior. At low temperatures some materials become superconductors and offer no resistance to the flow of electrons.	**PS 6d**	Chapter 13

Earth and Space Science Content Standards	Code	Chapter Correlation
Energy in the Earth System		
Earth systems have internal and external sources of energy, both of which create heat. The sun is the major external source of energy. Two primary sources of internal energy are the decay of radioactive isotopes and the gravitational energy from the Earth's original formation.	**ES 1a**	Chapter 9 Chapter 17 Chapter 18 Chapter 19
The outward transfer of Earth's internal heat drives convection circulation in the mantle that propels the plates comprising Earth's surface across the face of the globe.	**ES 1b**	Chapter 17
Heating of Earth's surface and atmosphere by the sun drives convection within the atmosphere and oceans, producing winds and ocean currents.	**ES 1c**	Chapter 11 Chapter 18
Global climate is determined by energy transfer from the sun at and near the Earth's surface. This energy transfer is influenced by dynamic processes such as cloud cover and the Earth's rotation, and static conditions such as the position of mountain ranges and oceans.	**ES 1d**	Chapter 18
Geochemical Cycles		
The Earth is a system containing essentially a fixed amount of each stable chemical atom or element. Each element can exist in several different chemical reservoirs. Each element on Earth moves among reservoirs in the solid Earth, oceans, atmosphere, and organisms as part of geochemical cycles.	**ES 2a**	Chapter 18
Movement of matter between reservoirs is driven by the Earth's internal and external sources of energy. These movements are often accompanied by a change in the physical and chemical properties of the matter. Carbon, for example, occurs in carbonate rocks such as limestone, in the atmosphere as carbon dioxide gas, in water as dissolved carbon dioxide, and in all organisms as complex molecules that control the chemistry of life.	**ES 2b**	Chapter 17 Chapter 18
The Origin and Evolution of the Earth System		
The sun, the Earth, and the rest of the solar system formed from a nebular cloud of dust and gas 4.6 billion years ago. The early Earth was very different from the planet we live on today.	**ES 3a**	Chapter 16
Geologic time can be estimated by observing rock sequences and using fossils to correlate the sequences at various locations. Current methods include using the known decay rates of radioactive isotopes present in rocks to measure the time since the rock was formed.	**ES 3b**	Chapter 17
Interactions among the solid Earth, the oceans, the atmosphere, and organisms have resulted in the ongoing evolution of the Earth system. We can observe some changes such as earthquakes and volcanic eruptions on a human time scale, but many processes such as mountain building and plate movements take place over hundreds of millions of years.	**ES 3c**	Chapter 11 Chapter 17 Chapter 18

Earth and Space Science Content Standards	Code	Chapter Correlation
Evidence for one-celled forms of life—the bacteria—extends back more than 3.5 billion years. The evolution of life caused dramatic changes in the composition of the Earth's atmosphere, which did not originally contain oxygen.	**ES 3d**	Chapter 18
The Origin and Evolution of The Universe		
The origin of the universe remains one of the greatest questions in science. The "big bang" theory places the origin between 10 and 20 billion years ago, when the universe began in a hot dense state; according to this theory, the universe has been expanding ever since.	**ES 4a**	Chapter 16
Early in the history of the universe, matter, primarily the light atoms hydrogen and helium, clumped together by gravitational attraction to form countless trillions of stars. Billions of galaxies, each of which is a gravitationally bound cluster of billions of stars, now form most of the visible mass in the universe.	**ES 4b**	Chapter 16
Stars produce energy from nuclear reactions, primarily the fusion of hydrogen to form helium. These and other processes in stars have led to the formation of all the other elements.	**ES 4c**	Chapter 16

Safety in Your Laboratory

Risk Assessment

Making your laboratory a safe place to work and learn

Concern for safety must begin before any activity in the classroom and before students enter the lab. A careful review of the facilities should be a basic part of preparation for each school term. You should investigate the physical environment, identify any safety risks, and inspect your work areas for compliance with safety regulations.

The review of the lab should be thorough and all safety issues must be addressed immediately. Keep a file of your review, and add to the list each year. This will allow you to continue to raise the standard of safety in your lab and classroom.

Many classroom experiments, demonstrations, and other activities are classics that have been used for years. This familiarity may lead to a comfort that can obscure inherent safety concerns. Review all experiments, demonstrations, and activities for safety concerns before presenting them to the class. Identify and eliminate potential safety hazards.

1. Identify the Risks
Before introducing any activity, demonstration, or experiment to the class, analyze it and consider what could possibly go wrong. Carefully review the list of materials to make sure they are safe. Inspect the equipment in your lab or classroom to make sure it is in good working order. Read the procedures to make sure they are safe. Record any hazards or concerns you identify.

2. Evaluate the Risks
Minimize the risks you identified in the last step without sacrificing learning. Remember that no activity you can perform in the lab or classroom is worth risking injury. Thus, extremely hazardous activities, or those that violate your school's policies, must be eliminated. For activities that present smaller risks, analyze each risk carefully to determine its likelihood. If the pedagogical value of the activity does not outweigh the risks, the activity must be eliminated.

3. Select Controls to Address Risks
Even low-risk activities require controls to eliminate or minimize the risks. Make sure that in devising controls you do not substitute an equally or more hazardous alternative. Some control methods include the following:
- Explicit verbal and written warnings may be added or posted.
- Equipment may be rebuilt or relocated, have parts replaced, or be replaced entirely by safer alternatives.
- Risky procedures may be eliminated.
- Activities may be changed from student activities to teacher demonstrations.

4. Implement and Review Selected Controls
Controls do not help if they are forgotten or not enforced. The implementation and review of controls should be as systematic and thorough as the initial analysis of safety concerns in the lab and laboratory activities.

Some Safety Risks and Preventative Controls

The following list describes several possible safety hazards and controls that can be implemented to resolve them. This list is not complete, but it can be used as a starting point to identify hazards in your laboratory.

Identified risk	Preventative control
Facilities and equipment	
Lab tables are in disrepair, room is poorly lighted and ventilated, faucets and electrical outlets do not work or are difficult to use because of their location.	Work surfaces should be level and stable. There should be adequate lighting and ventilation. Water supplies, drains, and electrical outlets should be in good working order. Any equipment in a dangerous location should not be used; it should be relocated or rendered inoperable.
Wiring, plumbing, and air circulation systems do not work or do not meet current specifications.	Specifications should be kept on file. Conduct a periodic review of all equipment, and document compliance. Damaged fixtures must be labeled as such and repaired as soon as possible.
Eyewash fountains and safety showers are present but no one knows anything about their specifications.	Ensure that eyewash fountains and safety showers meet the requirements of the ANSI standard (Z358.1).
Eyewash fountains are checked and cleaned once at the beginning of each school year. No records are kept of routine checks and maintenance on the safety showers and eyewash fountains.	Flush eyewash fountains for 5 min every month to remove any bacteria or other organisms from pipes. Test safety showers (measure flow in gallons per min) and eyewash fountains every 6 months and keep records of the test results.
Labs are conducted in multipurpose rooms, and equipment from other courses remains accessible.	Only the items necessary for a given activity should be available to students. All equipment should be locked away when not in use.
Students are permitted to enter or work in the lab without teacher supervision.	Lock all laboratory rooms whenever a teacher is not present. Supervising teachers must be trained in lab safety and emergency procedures.
Safety equipment and emergency procedures	
Fire and other emergency drills are infrequent, and no records or measurements are made of the results of the drills.	Always carry out critical reviews of fire or other emergency drills. Be sure that plans include alternate routes. Don't wait until an emergency to find the flaws in your plans.
Emergency evacuation plans do not include instructions for securing the lab in the event of an evacuation during a lab activity.	Plan actions in case of emergency: establish what devices should be turned off, which escape route to use, where to meet outside the building.
Fire extinguishers are in out-of-the-way locations, not on the escape route.	Place fire extinguishers near escape routes so that they will be of use during an emergency.
Fire extinguishers are not maintained. Teachers are not trained to use them.	Document regular maintenance of fire extinguishers. Train supervisory personnel in the proper use of extinguishers. Instruct students not to use an extinguisher but to call for a teacher.

Safety in Your Laboratory

Identified risk	Preventative control
Teachers in labs and neighboring classrooms are not trained in CPR or first aid.	Teachers should receive training from the local chapter of the American Red Cross. Certifications should be kept current with frequent refresher courses.
Teachers are not aware of their legal responsibilities in case of an injury or accident.	Review your faculty handbook for your responsibilities regarding safety in the classroom and laboratory. Contact the legal counsel for your school district to find out the extent of their support and any rules, regulations, or procedures you must follow.
Emergency procedures are not posted. Emergency numbers are kept only at the switchboard or main office. Instructions are given verbally only at the beginning of the year.	Emergency procedures should be posted at all exits and near all safety equipment. Emergency numbers should be posted at all phones, and a script should be provided for the caller to use. Emergency procedures must be reviewed periodically, and students should be reminded of them at the beginning of each activity.
Spills are handled on a case-by-case basis and are cleaned up with whatever materials happen to be on hand.	Have the appropriate equipment and materials available for cleaning up; replace them before expiration dates. Make sure students know to alert you to spilled chemicals, blood, and broken glass.

Work habits and environment

Identified risk	Preventative control
Safety wear is only used for activities involving chemicals or hot plates.	Aprons and goggles should be worn in the lab at all times. Long hair, loose clothing, and loose jewelry should be secured.
There is no dress code established for the laboratory; students are allowed to wear sandals or open-toed shoes.	Open-toed shoes should never be worn in the laboratory. Do not allow any footwear in the lab that does not cover feet completely.
Students are required to wear safety gear but teachers and visitors are not.	Always wear safety gear in the lab. Keep extra equipment on hand for visitors.
Safety is emphasized at the beginning of the term but is not mentioned later in the year.	Safety must be the first priority in all lab work. Students should be warned of risks and instructed in emergency procedures for each activity.
There is no assessment of students' knowledge and attitudes regarding safety.	Conduct frequent safety quizzes. Only students with perfect scores should be allowed to work in the lab.
You work alone during your preparation period to organize the day's labs.	Never work alone in a science laboratory or a storage area.
Safety inspections are conducted irregularly and are not documented. Teachers and administrators are unaware of what documentation will be necessary in case of a lawsuit.	Safety reviews should be frequent and regular. All reviews should be documented, and improvements must be implemented immediately. Contact legal counsel for your district to make sure your procedures will protect you in case of a lawsuit.

Identified risk	Preventative control

Purchasing, storing, and using chemicals

The storeroom is too crowded, so you decide to keep some equipment on the lab benches.	Do not store reagents or equipment on lab benches. And keep shelves organized. Never place reactive chemicals (in bottles, beakers, flasks, wash bottles, etc.) near the edges of a lab bench.
You prepare solutions from concentrated stock to save money.	Reduce risks by ordering diluted instead of concentrated substances.
You purchase plenty of chemicals to be sure that you won't run out or to save money.	Purchase chemicals in class-size quantities. Do not purchase or have on hand more than one year's supply of each chemical.
You don't generally read labels on chemicals when preparing solutions for a lab, because you already know about a chemical.	Read each label to be sure it states the hazards and describes the precautions and first aid procedures (when appropriate) that apply to the contents in case someone else has to deal with that chemical in an emergency.
You never read the Material Safety Data Sheets (MSDSs) that come with your chemicals.	Always read the Material Safety Data Sheet (MSDS) for a chemical before using it. Follow the precautions described in that Material Safety Data Sheet. File and organize MSDSs for all chemicals where they can be found easily in case of an emergency.
The main stockroom contains chemicals that haven't been used for years.	Do not leave bottles of chemicals unused on the shelves of the lab for more than one week or unused in the main stockroom for more than one year. Dispose of or use up any chemicals leftover.
No extra precautions are taken when flammable liquids are dispensed from their containers.	When transferring flammable liquids from bulk containers, ground the container, and before transferring to a smaller metal container, ground both containers.
Students are told to put their broken glass and solid chemical wastes in the trash can.	Have separate containers for trash, for broken glass, and for different categories of hazardous chemical wastes.
You store chemicals alphabetically, instead of by hazard class. Chemicals are stored without consideration of possible emergencies (fire, earthquake, flood, etc.), which could compound the hazard.	Use MSDSs to determine which chemicals are incompatible. Store chemicals by the hazard class indicated on the MSDS. Store chemicals that are incompatible with common fire-fighting media like water (such as alkali metals) or carbon dioxide (such as alkali and alkaline-earth metals) under conditions that eliminate the possibility of a reaction with water or carbon dioxide if it is necessary to fight a fire in the storage area.
Corrosives are kept above eye level, out of reach from anyone who is not authorized to be in the storeroom.	Always store corrosive chemicals on shelves below eye level. Remember, fumes from many corrosives can destroy metal cabinets and shelving.
Chemicals are kept on the stockroom floor on the days that they will be used so that they are easy to find.	Never store chemicals or other materials on floors or in the aisles of the laboratory or storeroom, even for a few minutes.

Safety in Your Laboratory

Safety Symbols and Safety Guidelines for Students

EYE PROTECTION
- Wear safety goggles, and know where the eyewash station is located and how to use it.
- Swinging objects can cause serious injury.
- Avoid directly looking at a light source, as this may cause permanent eye damage.

HAND SAFETY
- Wear latex or nitrile gloves to protect yourself from chemicals in the lab.
- Use a hot mitt to handle resistors, light sources, and other equipment that may be hot. Allow equipment to cool before handling it and storing it.

CLOTHING PROTECTION
- Wear a laboratory apron to protect your clothing.
- Tie back long hair, secure loose clothing, and remove loose jewelry to prevent their getting caught in moving parts or coming in contact with chemicals.

HEATING SAFETY
- When using a Bunsen burner or a hot plate, always wear safety goggles and a laboratory apron to protect your eyes and clothing. Tie back long hair, secure loose clothing, and remove loose jewelry.
- Never leave a hot plate unattended while it is turned on.
- If your clothing catches on fire, walk to the emergency lab shower, and use the shower to put out the fire.
- Wire coils may heat up rapidly during experiments. If heating occurs, open the switch immediately, and handle the equipment with a hot mitt.
- Allow all equipment to cool before storing it.

CHEMICAL SAFETY
- Do not eat or drink anything in the lab. Never taste chemicals.
- If a chemical gets on your skin or clothing or in your eyes, rinse it immediately with lukewarm water, and alert your teacher.
- If a chemical is spilled, tell your teacher, but do not clean it up yourself unless your teacher says it is OK to do so.

ELECTRICAL SAFETY
- Never close a circuit until it has been approved by your teacher. Never rewire or adjust any element of a closed circuit.
- Never work with electricity near water; be sure the floor and all work surfaces are dry.
- If the pointer of any kind of meter moves off the scale, open the circuit immediately by opening the switch.
- Light bulbs or wires that are conducting electricity can become very hot.
- Do not work with any batteries, electrical devices, or magnets other than those provided by your teacher.

GLASSWARE SAFETY
- If a thermometer breaks, notify your teacher immediately.
- Do not heat glassware that is broken, chipped, or cracked. Always use tongs or a hot mitt to handle heated glassware and other equipment because it does not always look hot when it is hot. Allow the equipment to cool before storing it.
- If a piece of glassware breaks, do not pick it up with your bare hands. Place broken glass in a specially designated disposal container.
- If a light bulb breaks, notify your teacher immediately. Do not remove broken bulbs from sockets.

WASTE DISPOSAL
- Use a dustpan, brush, and heavy gloves to carefully pick up broken glass, and dispose of it in a container specifically provided for this purpose.
- Dispose of any chemical waste only as instructed by your teacher.

HYGIENIC CARE
- Keep your hands away from your face and mouth.
- Always wash your hands thoroughly when you are done with an experiment.

Master Materials List

The following list indicates the quantities needed for 10 lab groups to perform the labs and quick activities in the textbook. If you have a different number of lab groups to plan for, scale the quantities accordingly.

A number alone indicates an end-of-chapter Design Your Own Lab or a Skill-Builder Lab. IL indicates an Inquiry Lab and QA indicates a Quick Activity. These codes are followed by numbers for the chapter and section in which they occur.

WARD'S is the supplier for Holt Science Spectrum. Catalog numbers for WARD'S are provided.

WARD'S Natural Science Establishment
5100 W. Henrietta Road
P.O. Box 92912
Rochester, New York, 14692-9012
1-800-962-2660

Chemicals and Consumable Materials

Qty.	Description	Used in	WARD'S No.
2	Aluminum foil pan, round, pkg. of 10	IL4.4	15 R 9890
1	Aluminum foil roll, 12" × 25'	16	15 R 1009
1	Antacid tablets, pkg. of 75	IL6.4	37 R 1863
5	Apron, disposable polyethylene, box of 100	throughout	15 R 1050
1	Baking powder, 7 oz	IL6.3	37 R 2270
3	Balloons, pkg. of 12	QA13.1, QA16.1	15 R 0017
20	Battery, 6 V	IL13.2, QA13.3	15 R 3263
40	Battery, alkaline 1.5 V, size D	13, 14, QA14.2	15 R 3247
1	Bleach, 1 pint	IL6.3	37 R 5554
22	Box, corrugated, pkg. of 10	16, 9, IL 13.2	18 R 1395
1	Cellophane, blue sheet, 20" × 60"	IL15.2	15 R 9886
1	Cellophane, green sheet, 20" × 60"	IL15.2	15 R 9885
1	Cellophane, red sheet, 20" × 60"	IL15.2	15 R 9884

Qty.	Description	Used in	WARD'S No.
1	Chalk, white, box of 12	IL13.2	15 R 4637
20	Clay, red modeling, 1 lb	16, IL17.1	15 R 4640
10	Cloth, wool, 12" × 24"	QA13.1	15 R 2537
10	Copper foil, 100 g	IL5.4	37 R 2513
1	Copper metal, piece	3	37 R 2202
2	Corn starch, powder, 500 g	IL4.4	39 R 3271
1	Craft sticks, pkg. of 30	4	15 R 9893
1	Detergent, with phosphate, 50 g	IL6.3	15 R 1287
3	Distilled water, 1 gallon	4, QA5.4, QA6.4	88 R 7005
2	Dowel, wooden, 1" × 8", pkg. of 6	QA11.2	15 R 0082
1	Dowel, wooden, 1/4" × 5", pkg. of 12	IL13.2	15 R 0080
1	Electrode, aluminum, pkg. of 12	14	16 R 0081
1	Electrode, copper, pkg. of 12	QA13.2	16 R 0082
1	Electrode, iron pkg. of 12	14	16 R 0083
1	Electrode, nickel, pkg. of 12	14	16 R 0085
1	Electrode, zinc, pkg. of 12	14, QA13.2	16 R 0086
1	Ethyl alcohol, 95%, denatured, 500 mL	4	39 R 0277
1	Ethyl alcohol (ethanol), anhydrous	QA6.2	39 R 0273
1	Flat toothpicks, box of 750	QA5.3	15 R 9864
4	Gloves, latex disposable, medium, pkg. of 100	throughout	15 R 1071
30	Gloves, polyethylene disposable, medium	11	15 R 1073
1	Glycerol (glycerin), 500 mL	18	39 R 1438
2	Hydrochloric acid, 1.0 M	5	37 R 8605

Qty.	Description	Used in	WARD'S No.
1	Hydrogen peroxide, 3% solution	QA5.4	37 R 8450
1	Index cards, 3 × 5, lined, pkg. of 1000	16, QA8.3	15 R 9807
1	Iodine, tincture of	QA6.2	37 R 2383
1	Iron filings, fine	QA5.4	37 R 2312
1	Latex solution, red, 1 L	4	37 R 2571
1	Lead, sheet, 1/16" thick, 6.5" × 6.5"	3	37 R 2348
20	Light bulb, 150 W	16, IL10.2, IL19.1	36 R 4173
10	Light source for optical bench	12	16 R 0026
1	Limestone, gray, pkg. of 10	1	47 R 4602
1	Litmus paper, blue, pkg. of 12 vials	IL6.3, IL6.4	15 R 3105
1	Litmus paper, red, pkg. of 12 vials	IL6.3, IL6.4	15 R 3107
1	Magnesium, metal ribbon	IL5.4	37 R 2850
4	Masking tape, 3/4" × 60 yds, pkg. of 3	11, 13, 16, 7, 9, QA14.1a, QA19.3, QA3.1	15 R 9828
1	Matches, wooden safety, box of 300	10, IL5.4, QA1.2	15 R 9427
10	Metal coffee can	QA3.1	17 R 2111
1	Miniature lamp, GE 458 type, pkg. of 10	IL13.2, QA13.3	16 R 0538
1	Nail, (8d, Common), pkg. of 35	11, IL13.2, IL9.4, QA14.2	15 R 9478
1	Olive oil, 500 mL	IL19.3	39 R 2514
1	Paper cups, 5 oz, pkg. of 100	11, 4	15 R 9830
5	Paper towels, 2-ply, 90-sheet roll	4, 6	15 R 9844
1	Paraffin candles, pkg. of 12	10, QA1.2	15 R 0055
1	Paraffin, refined, white wax, 500 g	3	39 R 2860
5	Petroleum jelly, 1 oz	18	15 R 9832
2	Plastic cup with lid, 9 oz, pkg. of 25	2, 7	18 R 3676

Qty.	Description	Used in	WARD'S No.
1	Plastic foam cups, 8 oz, pkg. of 50	IL10.1	18 R 3677
1	Plastic spoons, pkg. of 100	IL13.2, IL6.4, QA12.1a	15 R 9800
1	Plastic stirrers, pkg. of 500	IL6.4	15 R 9894
1	Potassium bromide, 100 g	IL5.3	37 R 2734
1	Potassium iodide, granular	IL5.3	37 R 4770
1	Rubber bands, assorted, 1/4 lb	8, QA4.4	15 R 9824
1	Sand, black, 32 oz	11	45 R 1987
1	Sandpaper, 180 grit, pkg. of 10	IL5.4	15 R 3010
1	Silver nitrate	IL5.3	37 R 5150
5	Soap, liquid antibacterial, 8 oz	IL6.3, QA6.4	18 R 1533
1	Sodium bicarbonate (baking soda), 1 lb	1, 2, IL6.3	37 R 5467
1	Sodium chloride	1, IL4.1, IL5.3	37 R 5487
1	Sodium silicate	4	36 R 5671
1	Steel wool, medium, pkg. of 16 pads	IL5.4	15 R 8798
5	String, 1/2 lb spool	1, 11, IL10.1, IL9.4, QA12.1a, QA14.1a, QA9.2b	15 R 9863
1	Sugar cubes	IL5.4	87 R 2203
1	Sugar, granular, 5 lb	IL4.1, IL4.4	39 R 3180
1	Swab applicator, pkg. of 100	QA6.2	14 R 5502
10	Syringe, 60 cc, disposable	18	14 R 1620
1	Toothpicks, box of 800	19	15 R 4019
1	Twist ties, 1/4" × 200' roll	2, 6	14 R 0947
3	Vinegar, white, 1 pint	2, 4, IL5.4, IL6.3, IL6.4	39 R 0138
1	Wax paper, 12" × 75' roll	IL6.4, QA6.4	15 R 9857

Qty.	Description	Used in	WARD'S No.
1	Weighing papers, 3 1/8" circle	2	15 R 2000
1	Wire, annunciator (Bell), 1 lb spool	14, QA13.2	15 R 9425
1	Wire, bare copper magnet, 1 lb spool	10	15 R 9235
1	Wire, copper, PVC coated, 100'	13, 14, IL13.2, IL14.3, QA13.3, QA14.2	16 R 0549
1	Wire, nichrome, 18 gauge, 4 oz spool	10	15 R 9360
1	Wire, nichrome, 22 gauge, 4 oz spool	10	15 R 9370
1	Zinc, 100 pieces	3	37 R 6328
2	Zinc, sheet 30.48 cm × 30.48 cm	IL5.4	37 R 2347
4	Zipper resealable bags, pkg. of 10	2, 6	18 R 6921

Equipment and Reusable Materials

Qty.	Description	Used in	WARD'S No.
10	Alligator connector clip	IL13.2	15 R 9473
1	Aluminum metal sheet	16, 3	37 R 1883
5	Balance, triple-beam	1, 19, 2, 3, 9, QA3.1	15 R 6057
5	Bathroom scale, lb/kg	IL9.1	15 R 3800
20	Battery holder, double D cell	14	16 R 0603
10	Battery holder, single D cell	13	16 R 0602
10	Beaker, 1000 mL	6	17 R 4080
20	Beaker, 250 mL	1, IL2.3, IL4.4, IL6.4, QA5.4, QA8.3	17 R 4040
40	Beaker, 400 mL	18, 2, 3, IL10.1	17 R 4050
100	Beaker, 50 mL	5, IL6.3	17 R 4010
10	Bottle, HDPE, 125 mL	19	18 R 0081
10	Box, hinged clear plastic	1	18 R 6560

Qty.	Description	Used in	WARD'S No.
10	Bunsen burner, standard	19, IL4.1, IL5.4	15 R 0612
10	Calculator, TI-1706	17, QA15.3	27 R 3055
20	Clamp, vinyl, 3-finger	19	15 R 0699
1	Clock, 7" diameter wall	IL10.2	15 R 1492
10	Clothespin, large wooden, pkg. of 12	10	15 R 0018
10	Compass, ball-bearing, with pencil	17	15 R 4648
10	Compass, magnetic	QA14.1b, QA14.2	12 R 0602
1	Cork sheet	IL13.2	14 R 7602
10	Cutter	5	14 R 0945
20	Dissecting pin, nickel plated	16, QA6.4	14 R 0200
10	Dissection pan without wax	IL19.3, QA11.2	14 R 7010
20	Flasks, sidearm, 250 mL	5	17 R 3305
10	Fleshing knife, 7"	QA10.2, QA13.2	14 R 1190
10	Galvanometer	IL14.3, QA13.2	16 R 0537
2	Glass plate, 8" × 8", pkg. of 12	19	15 R 3821
1	Glass tubing, flint, 6 mm, 1 lb	19	17 R 0941
10	Globe, world relief	IL19.1	80 R 5630
10	Gloves, Heat-Defier	3	15 R 1095
30	Goggles, general purpose safety	throughout	15 R 3046
10	Graduated cylinder, glass, 500 mL	15	17 R 0580
10	Graduated cylinder, plastic, 10 mL	4, 5, IL5.4	18 R 1705
10	Graduated cylinder, plastic, 100 mL	2, 3, IL10.1, IL10.2, IL2.3	18 R 1730
20	Graduated cylinder, plastic, 25 mL	1, 4, 5, IL5.3	18 R 1710
10	Graduated cylinder, plastic, 250 mL	QA6.1	18 R 1740
10	Hammer, claw	IL4.4	12 R 0110
10	Hammer, rubber	15, IL12.1	16 R 0568

Qty.	Description	Used in	WARD'S No.
10	Hot plate, single burner	3, IL10.1, QA5.4	15 R 1799
10	Jar, clear polystyrene, 16 oz	QA6.1	18 R 1635
10	Jar, clear polystyrene, 8 oz	QA7.1	18 R 1634
10	Jar, glass, wide-mouth, 1/2 gal	4	17 R 2070
10	Jar, glass, wide-mouth, 240 mL	16	17 R 2040
10	Jar lid, 53 mm	QA7.1	17 R 2133
10	Jar lid, 70 mm	16	17 R 2145
10	Jar lid, 89 mm	QA6.1	17 R 2153
20	Knife, plastic	IL17.1, QA10.2	25 R 8128
2	Lamp receptacle, plastic, pkg. of 12	IL13.2, QA13.3	16 R 0064
10	Lamp with reflector and clamp	16, IL10.2, IL19.1	36 R 4168
10	Lens and mirror support	12	16 R 0021
10	Lens, double concave, 3.75 cm diam.	12	16 R 0061
10	Level, torpedo	IL9.4	12 R 0242
20	Magnet, steel bar	3, IL14.3, QA14.1a	13 R 0115
10	Map of U.S., raised relief	17	33 R 0460
1	Marbles, colored, pkg. of 25	QA6.1	15 R 3399
10	Marker, black lab	16, QA16.1	15 R 3083
10	Marking pen for glass, black wax	IL5.3	15 R 1155
10	Mass, hooked, 1000 g	IL8.3	15 R 3724
10	Mass set, hooked, 10 g–1000 g	8, IL8.3	15 R 3717
10	Meterstick, wood	1, 4, 9, 12, 15, 16, IL9.1, IL9.4, QA3.1	15 R 4065
10	Multimeter, economy analog	13	15 R 9426
10	Optical bench meter stick supports	12	16 R 0023
2	Optical bench screen, pkg. of 5	12	16 R 0027
10	Optical bench screen support	12	16 R 0028
1	Paper clips, #1, pkg. of 10 boxes	14, 8, IL5.4	15 R 9815
2	Pencils, no. 2, box of 12	8, IL9.4, QA9.2a	15 R 9816
10	Pendulum clamp	IL9.4	15 R 3124
40	Ping-pong balls, pkg. of 6	QA4.2	15 R 3636
1	Pipet bulbs, 1/4 oz, pkg. of 10	IL6.3, IL6.4	15 R 0511
1	Pipets, sterile plastic, 1 mL, pkg. of 200	IL6.4	18 R 7196
2	Pipets, sterile plastic, 10 mL, pkg. of 100	IL6.3	17 R 4853
6	Plastic bowl, 40 oz, pkg. of 5	QA10.1, QA10.2	18 R 7202
10	Pneumatic trough, polypropylene	5, 19	15 R 7565
2	Resistors, carbon, 10 ohm, pkg. of 10	13	16 R 0001
10	Resonance tube, 45 × 4 cm	15	17 R 0179
10	Ruler, 12 inch hardwood	QA9.2a, 11	15 R 4649
10	Ruler, plastic	3, 5, 8, 10, 17, IL17.1, QA12.1b, QA18.2	15 R 4655
10	Scissors, nickel-plated	11, 16, 5, 7, IL17.1	14 R 0525
10	Solenoid	IL14.3	20 R 1395
20	Spring scale, pull type, 3 kg/30 N	IL8.3	15 R 3774
10	Spring, wave demonstration	IL11.1	16 R 0513
10	Stapler	QA9.2b	15 R 1955
10	Stirring rods, glass, pkg. of 10	IL13.2	17 R 6005
10	Stopper, 1-hole black rubber, size 2	19	15 R 8482

Qty.	Description	Used in	WARD'S No.
10	Stopper, 2-hole black rubber, size 2	19	15 R 8512
20	Stoppers, black, size 6	5	15 R 8466
10	Stopwatch, digital	10, 11, 3, 5, 6, 9, IL10.1, IL4.1, IL9.1, QA10.2	15 R 0512
10	Support, rectangular, large, with base	8, 11, 19	15 R 0667
10	Support, rectangular, small, with base	QA14.1a	15 R 0719
10	Support ring, zinc plated	QA14.1a	15 R 0707
10	Switch, single pole, single throw	QA13.3	16 R 0547
10	Tape measure, metric/English	6	15 R 2541
10	Test-tube rack, 16 mm	IL5.3	18 R 4231
70	Test tube with rim, Pyrex®, 13 × 100 mm	1, IL4.1, IL5.3, IL5.4, QA5.4	17 R 0610
20	Test tube with rim, Pyrex®, 25 × 150 mm	19	17 R 0655
20	Thermometer −20°C to 110°C, red alcohol	5, 6, 16, 18, IL10.1, IL10.2	15 R 1416
1	Thermometer, wall model	1, 15	23 R 1400
10	Tongs	19, IL10.1, IL4.1, IL5.4	14 R 0960
10	Tray, polyethylene, with cover, 1 gallon	2	18 R 3650
1	Tubing, amber latex, 3/16" × 1/16"	5, 19	15 R 1133
10	Tuning fork, 128 Hz	15	16 R 0556
10	Tuning fork, 384 Hz	15	16 R 0561
10	Tuning forks, set of 4	IL12.1	16 R 0565
40	Washers, pkg. of 12	IL10.1	15 R 0030
10	Wire stripper, crimping tool	14, QA13.2, QA13.3	15 R 0749
10	Wood block, 3" × 5" × 1-3/4"	IL13.2, QA7.2	16 R 0606

Materials Obtained Locally

These common materials are not carried by WARD'S, but are easily obtained locally.

Qty.	Description	Used in
10	Basketball, volleyball, or soccer ball	1
10	Board, 6 ft	9, QA9.2B
30	Books	9, QA4.2, QA9.2a, QA9.2b
10	Brass key	IL13.2
10	Candle holder	10
10	Coat hanger, metal	QA9.4
10	Comb or hairbrush	8
100	Dice	7
210	Dominoes	QA7.2
10	Fiber-optic cable	QA15.1
30	Flashlights, adjustable	IL15.2
10	Golf ball	9
500	Gumdrops	QA5.3
	Ice	3, 5, 6, 18, QA10.2
10	Ice pick or awl	16
10	Lemon	QA13.2
	Liver, raw	QA5.4
	Mayonnaise	IL6.3
20	Metal hooks	IL13.2
	Milk	IL6.3
10	Nail, aluminum	IL13.2
	Paper ash	IL5.4
20	Paper, white	IL15.2, IL17.1
1000	Pennies	QA7.1, QA8.3
10	Plastic rings from 6-pack holders	QA4.4
	Ribbon	IL11.1
10	Rolling pin	IL17.1
10	Sock	QA3.1
40	Soft drinks	6, IL6.3
10	Soup can, empty	QA18.2,
	Water	3, QA10.1, IL4.4, IL6.3, IL19.3
	Water, mineral	IL6.3

CHAPTER 1

Introduction to Science

Annotated Descriptions of the Correlated National Science Standards

The following descriptions summarize the National Science Standards that specially relate to Chapter 1. For the full text of the Standards, see p. 40T.

SECTION 1.1
The Nature of Science

Physical Science
PS 4b, 5c

Unifying Concepts and Processes
UCP 1, 2

History and Nature of Science
HNS 1, 2, 3

Section 1.2
The Way Science Works

Science as Inquiry
SAI 2

Unifying Concepts and Processes
UCP 3

Science and Technology
ST 2

History and Nature of Science
HNS 2, 3

Section 1.3
Organizing Data

Unifying Concepts and Processes
UCP 2

History and Nature of Science
HNS 1

Cross-Discipline Teaching RESOURCES

Cross-Discipline Teaching, ATE p. 2
Life Science   Fine Arts
Social Studies

Integration Enrichment Resources
Biology, **PE** and **ATE** p. 5
    IE 1.1 *Serendipity and Science*
Language Arts, **PE** and **ATE** p. 15
    IE 1.2 *Medical Terminology*

Additional Integration Enrichment Worksheets
    IE 1.3 Chemistry   IE 1.4 Mathematics
    IE 1.5 Physics

Use the Planning Guide on the next page to help you organize your lessons.

MATH AND COMPUTER RESOURCES

Chapter 1	Math Skills	Assess	Media/Computer Skills
Section 1.1	**BS 1.3:** Concept Maps **BS 1.5:** Forming a Hypothesis **BS 1.6:** Testing a Hypothesis **BS 1.7:** Classifying Items		■ Section 1.1 **CNN** Presents **Physical Science** **Segment 1** Amusement Park Physics **CRT** Worksheet 1
Section 1.2	**BS 1.1:** Symbols **BS 1.2:** Basic Logic **BS 1.4:** Weighing Evidence **BS 1.8:** Reading to Evaluate and to Identify Bias **BS 1.9:** Evaluating Data **BS 2.3:** Dimensional Analysis and Conversions **PE Math Skills** Conversions, p. 17 **ATE Additional Examples,** p. 17	**PE Practice,** p. 17 **MS** Worksheet 1 **PE Problem Bank,** p. 693, 1–5	■ Section 1.2
Section 1.3	**BS 2.1:** Significant Figures **BS 2.2:** Scientific Notation **BS 2.4:** SI Units **BS 6.1:** Making Tables **BS 6.2:** Line Graphs **BS 6.3:** Bar and Pie Graphs **BS 6.4:** Choosing Graph Types **PE Math Skills** Writing Scientific Notation, p. 23 **PE Additional Examples,** p. 23 **PE Math Skills** Using Scientific Notation, p. 24 **ATE Additional Examples,** p. 24 **PE Math Skills** Significant Figures, p. 25 **ATE Additional Examples,** p. 25	**PE Practice,** pp. 23–25 **MS** Worksheets 2–4 **PE** Section Review 5–7, p. 26 **PE Problem Bank,** p. 693, 6–20	■ Section 1.3

PE Pupil's Edition   **ATE** Annotated Teacher's Edition   **MS** Math Skills   **BS** Basic Skills
IE Integration Enrichment   ■ Guided Reading Audio   **CRT** Critical Thinking

READING SKILL BUILDER

The following activities found in the Annotated Teacher's Edition provide techniques for developing useful reading strategies to increase your students' reading comprehension skills.

Section 1.1   **Brainstorming,** p. 2, 6
　　　　　　Discussion, p. 4
　　　　　　Paired Reading, p. 5

Section 1.3   **Paired Reading,** p. 21

Smithsonian Institution®
Visit www.si.edu/hrw for additional online resources.

Spanish Resources

The following resources are made available for students who speak Spanish as their first language.

Spanish Resources
Guided Reading Audio CD-ROM
Chapter 1

Spanish Glossary
Chapter 1

Introduction to Science

CLASSROOM RESOURCES

FOCUS	TEACH	HANDS-ON
Section 1.1: The Nature of Science		
BLOCK 1 45 minutes	**ATE RSB** Brainstorming, p. 2 **ATE** Focus Activities 1, 2, p. 3 **ATE RSB** Discussion, p. 4 **ATE RSB** Paired Reading, p. 5 **ATE RSB** Brainstorming, p. 6 **PE** How Does Science Happen? pp. 4–7 ★ Focus Transparency LT 1	**ATE Skill Builder** Interpreting Visuals, pp. 3, 4, 6, 7 Interpreting Diagrams, p. 6 **BLM** 1 Branches of Science	**IE** Worksheet 1.1 **IE** Worksheet 1.3
BLOCK 2 45 minutes	**PE** Scientific Theories and Laws, pp. 8–11	**ATE Skill Builder** Interpreting Visuals, p. 8	**IE** Worksheet 1.5
Section 1.2: The Way Science Works		
BLOCK 3 45 minutes	**ATE Demo** Are They the Same?, p. 12 **PE** Science Skills, pp. 12–15 ★ Focus Transparency LT 2	**ATE Skill Builder** Interpreting Visuals, pp. 12, 14 Interpreting Diagrams, p. 13 **BLM** 2 The Scientific Method	**LE 1** *Designing a Pendulum Clock* **DS** 1.3 **PE** Quick Activity *Making Observations*, p. 14 **DS** 1.1 **IE** Worksheet 1.2
BLOCK 4 45 minutes	**PE** Units of Measurement, pp. 15–19	**BLM** 3 SI Base Units **BLM** 4 SI Prefixes	
Section 1.3: Organizing Data		
BLOCK 5 45 minutes	**ATE RSB** Paired Reading, p. 21 **PE** Presenting Scientific Data, pp. 20–22 ★ Focus Transparency LT 3	**ATE Skill Builder** Graphing, pp. 20, 21 **TT** 1 Line Graph **TT** 2 Bar Graph	
BLOCK 6 45 minutes	**PE** Scientific Notation and Significant Figures, pp. 22–26	**TT** 3 Accuracy and Precision	**PE** Skill Builder Lab *Making Measurements,* p. 30 **DS** 1.2 **IE** Worksheet 1.4

CLASSROOM RESOURCES

HOMEWORK	ASSESS
PE Section Review 1, 2, 8, p. 11 **Chapter 1 Review,** p. 27, items 1–3, 10	**SG** Chapter 1 Pretest **ATE** *ALTERNATIVE ASSESSMENT,* Planning an Experiment, p. 6
PE Section Review 3–7, 9, p. 11 **Chapter 1 Review,** p. 27, item 11	**ATE** *ALTERNATIVE ASSESSMENT,* Scientific Theory and Law, p. 8 **SG** Section 1.1
PE Section Review 2–5, 7, p. 19 **Chapter 1 Review,** p. 27, items 4, 9	
PE Section Review 1, 6, p. 19 **Chapter 1 Review,** p. 27, item 5	**ATE** *ALTERNATIVE ASSESSMENT,* Evaluating Advertising Claims, p. 18 **SG** Section 1.2
PE Section Review 1–4, p. 26 **Chapter 1 Review,** p. 27, items 8, 13, 14	
PE Section Review 5–7, p. 26 **Chapter 1 Review,** p. 27, items 6, 7, 12, 15–17	**SG** Section 1.3

BLOCK 7

PE Chapter 1 Review
Thinking Critically 18–21, p. 28
Developing Life/Work Skills 22–24, p. 29
Integrating Concepts 25–26, p. 29
SG Chapter 1 Mixed Review

BLOCK 8

Chapter Tests
Holt Science Spectrum: A Physical Approach
Chapter 1 Test

One-Stop Planner CD–ROM with Test Generator
Holt Science Spectrum Test Generator
FOR MACINTOSH AND WINDOWS
Chapter 1

Teaching Resources
Scoring Rubrics and assignment evaluation
checklist.

internetconnect

SC*LINKS*
NSTA
National Science Teachers Association
Online Resources:
www.scilinks.org
The following *sci*LINKS Internet resources can be found
in the student text for this chapter.

Page 3 **TOPIC:** New discoveries in science **KEYWORD:** HK1011	**Page 22** **TOPIC:** Presenting scientific data **KEYWORD:** HK1014
Page 7 **TOPIC:** Leonardo da Vinci **KEYWORD:** HK1012	**Page 29** **TOPIC:** Studying the natural world **KEYWORD:** HK1015
Page 17 **TOPIC:** SI units **KEYWORD:** HK1013	

CNNfyi.com   **www.cnnfyi.com**

Visit this site for coverage of current events and related
classroom resources.

PE Pupil's Edition   **ATE** Annotated Teacher's Edition
RSB Reading Skill Builder   **DS** Datasheets
IE Integrated Enrichment   **SG** Study Guide
LE Laboratory Experiments
TT Teaching Transparencies   **BLM** Blackline Masters
★ Lesson Focus Transparency

Introduction to Science

Tapping Prior Knowledge

Students should be familiar with the basic skill of problem solving. Lead students in a discussion that allows them to explore the steps that a scientist might take to help solve a problem or to learn about a phenomenon.

READING SKILL BUILDER

Brainstorming Write the words *science* and *technology* on the chalkboard. Ask students to make a list with words or phrases that relate to the concepts of science and technology.

Teaching Tip

The Scientific Method Scientists follow a pattern of thinking called the scientific method. The scientific method is a way of thinking critically about a question and testing possible answers to that question by collecting data and making unbiased observations. The general steps in the scientific method include:

- making observations
- formulating questions
- collecting data
- forming a hypothesis
- testing the hypothesis through observation or experimentation
- drawing conclusions
- forming a modified hypothesis
- testing that hypothesis

Stress that the scientific method is a style of thinking that is learned; it is not a set of rigid steps. Encourage the students to regard the scientific method as a way of being open-minded about possible answers, not as a set of rules for solving problems.

Chapter Preview

1.1 The Nature of Science
How Does Science Happen?
Scientific Theories and Laws

1.2 The Way Science Works
Science Skills
Units of Measurement

1.3 Organizing Data
Presenting Scientific Data
Writing Numbers in Scientific Notation
Using Significant Figures

2

CROSS-DISCIPLINE TEACHING

Life Science Invite a biology teacher to be a guest lecturer in your classroom to explain the effect of X rays on the human body.

Social Studies The turn of the twentieth century was a time of changes in the United States. Ask a history teacher to lead a discussion of the impact of science and of technological changes on American culture between 1880 and 1920.

Fine Arts Although photographs were becoming more common by the turn of the twentieth century, photography was just beginning to emerge as an artistic medium. If your community has a museum that includes a photography collection, ask if the museum would give a survey lecture to the class, or ask an art teacher to show the class some images from this period.

Focus ACTIVITY

Background Imagine that it is 1895 and you are a scientist working in your laboratory. Outside, people move about on foot, on bicycles, or in horse-drawn carriages. A few brave and rich people have purchased the new invention called an automobile. When they can make it run, they ride along the street while the machine sputters, pops, puffs smoke, and frightens both horses and people.

Your laboratory is filled with coils of wire, oddly shaped glass tubes, magnets of all sorts, many heavy glass jars containing liquid and metal plates (batteries), and machines that generate high-voltages. Yellow light comes from a few electric bulbs strung along the ceiling. If more light is needed, it must be daylight coming through windows or light from the old gas lamps along the wall.

It's an exciting time in science because new discoveries about matter and energy are being made almost every day. A few European scientists are even beginning to pay attention to those upstart scientists from America. However, some people believe that humans have learned nearly everything that is worth knowing about the physical world.

Activity 1 Interview someone old enough to have witnessed a lot of technological changes, and ask them what scientific discoveries they think have made the biggest difference in their lifetime. Which changes do you think have been the most important?

Activity 2 A lot has changed since 1895. Research that time period, and find out the cost of a loaf of bread, a dozen eggs, a quart of milk, or a similar common item. How much did the average worker earn in a year? What forms of home entertainment did people have then?

TOPIC: New discoveries in science
GO TO: www.scilinks.org
KEYWORD: HK1011

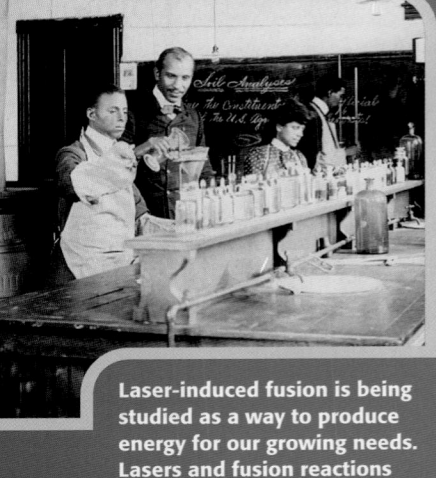

Laser-induced fusion is being studied as a way to produce energy for our growing needs. Lasers and fusion reactions would have been outlandish ideas in 1896 when Dr. George Washington Carver started teaching science at the Tuskegee Institute.

Focus ACTIVITY

Background Some of the advances that have made significant differences in the last 100 years will include those in the field of medicine, such as the discovery of antibiotics and many vaccines, understanding the roles that vitamins and minerals play in human health, and the development of more sophisticated diagnostic techniques. Students will also be interested in the changes in communications and transportation.

Activity 1 Encourage students to ask neighbors or grandparents about technological changes and scientific discoveries they have witnessed.

Activity 2 If your school has Internet access, encourage students to use an Internet search engine to perform this activity.

SKILL BUILDER

Interpreting Visuals Ask your students to try to imagine themselves in Dr. Carver's classroom and to describe how it would be different from their current classroom.

RESOURCE LINK
STUDY GUIDE

Assign students *Pretest Chapter 1 Introduction to Science* before beginning Section 1.1.

3

Scheduling

Refer to pp. 2A–2D for lecture, classwork, and assignment options for Section 1.1.

★ Lesson Focus

Use transparency *LT 1* to prepare students for this section.

READING SKILL BUILDER *Discussion* It is important for students to understand that science is a process, not just a set of facts. Inform students that information about the world around us is always changing. Lead students in a discussion that explores the idea that science always starts with a question. Ask students what they do when they have questions. Discuss their responses, and be sure students understand that every time they search for an answer to a question about the world, they are doing science.

SKILL BUILDER

Interpreting Visuals Have students examine **Figure 1-1.** Tell students that the illustration represents a technological advance. The television tube is a cathode-ray tube in which the direction of the rays is controlled by magnetic fields. Students will learn more about electricity and magnetism in Chapters 13 and 14.

The Nature of Science

▶ **KEY TERMS**

science
technology
scientific theory
scientific law

OBJECTIVES

▶ Describe the main branches of natural science and relate them to each other.
▶ Describe the relationship between science and technology.
▶ Distinguish among facts, theories, and laws.
▶ Explain the roles of models and mathematics in scientific theories and laws.

Generally, scientists believe that the universe can be described by basic rules and that these rules can be discovered by careful, methodical study. A scientist may perform experiments to find a new aspect of the natural world, to explain a known phenomenon, to check the results of other experiments, or to test the predictions of current theories.

How Does Science Happen?

Imagine that it is 1895 and you are experimenting with cathode rays. These mysterious rays were discovered almost 40 years before, but in 1895 no one knows what they are. To produce the rays, you create a vacuum by pumping the air out of a sealed glass tube that has two metal rods at a distance from each other, as shown in **Figure 1-1.** When the rods are connected to an electrical source, a current flows through the empty space between the rods, and the rays are produced.

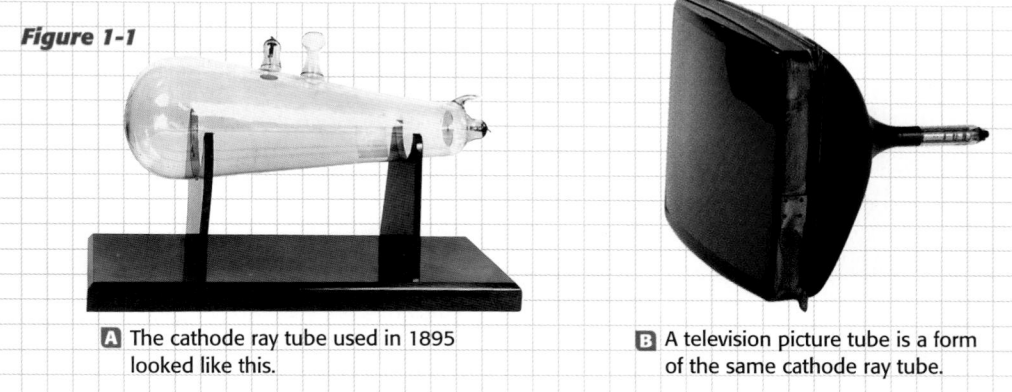

Figure 1-1

A The cathode ray tube used in 1895 looked like this.

B A television picture tube is a form of the same cathode ray tube.

Scientists investigate

You have learned from the work of other scientists and have conducted experiments of your own. From this, you know that when certain minerals are placed inside the tube, the cathode rays make them fluoresce (glow). Pieces of cardboard coated with powder made from these minerals are used to detect the rays. With a very high voltage, even the glass tube itself glows.

Other scientists have found that cathode rays can pass through thin metal foils, but they travel in our atmosphere for only 2 or 3 cm. You wonder if the rays could pass through the glass tube. Others have tried this experiment and have found that cathode rays don't go through glass. But you think that the glow from the glass tube might have outshined any weak glow from the mineral-coated cardboard. So, you decide to cover the glass tube with heavy black paper.

Scientists plan experiments

Before experimenting, you write your plan in your laboratory notebook and sketch the equipment you are using. You make a table in which you can write down the electric power used, the distance from the tube to the fluorescent detector, the air temperature, and anything you observe. You state the idea you are going to test: At a high voltage, cathode rays will be strong enough to be detected outside the tube by causing the mineral-coated cardboard to glow.

Scientists observe

Everything is ready. You want be sure that the black-paper cover doesn't have any gaps, so you darken the room and turn on the tube. The black cover blocks the light from the tube. Just before you switch off the tube, you glimpse a light nearby. When you turn on the tube again, the light reappears.

Then you realize that this light is coming from the mineral-coated cardboard you planned to use to detect cathode rays. The detector is already glowing, and it is on a table almost 1 m away from the tube. You know that 1 m is too far for cathode rays to travel in air. You decide that the tube must be giving off some new rays that no one has seen before. What do you do now?

This is the question Wilhelm Roentgen had to ponder in Würzburg, Germany, on November 8, 1895, when all this happened to him. Should he call the experiment a failure because it didn't give the results he expected? Should he ask reporters to cover this news story? Maybe he should send letters about his discovery to famous scientists and invite them to come and see it.

VOCABULARY *Skills Tip*

Cathode rays *got their name because they come from the* cathode, *the rod connected to the negative terminal of the electricity source. The positive terminal is called the* anode.

INTEGRATING

BIOLOGY

In 1928, the Scottish scientist Alexander Fleming was investigating disease-causing bacteria when he saw that one of his cultures contained an area where no bacteria were growing. Instead, an unknown organism was growing in that area. Rather than discarding the culture as a failure, Fleming investigated the unfamiliar organism and found that it was a type of mold. This mold produced a substance that prevented the growth of many disease bacteria. What he found by questioning the results of a "failed" experiment became the first modern antibiotic, penicillin.

READING SKILL BUILDER *Paired Reading* Have students silently read the section titled Scientists Observe. Instruct students to mark on self-adhesive notes those portions of the text that they do not understand.

Group students together in pairs, and have one student in each pair discuss with the other student those parts of the passage that he or she found difficult. The listener will either clarify the difficult passages or will help frame a common question for later explanation. Have each pair of students decide what they would have done in Roentgen's place. Survey the student responses, and summarize the results on the board.

Historical Perspective

Scientists at the turn of the twentieth century had to design and build most of their experimental equipment. Although scientists today still build prototypes of new instruments, they can get assistance from specialists in technologies that were not available in 1895. A scientist studying cathode-rays may have had to be a glass blower to make the tube, an electrician to build the batteries and connect the rods in the tube to the batteries, and a mechanic to build and maintain the vacuum pump used to evacuate the cathode-ray tube.

INTEGRATING

BIOLOGY Assign students worksheet *1.1: Integrating Biology—Serendipity and Science* in the **Integration Enrichment Resources** ancillary.

Interpreting Visuals Have students examine **Figure 1-2.** Group students in pairs, and have them create an explanation of why the bones are dark and the surrounding areas are bright. *(The bones block the X rays and create a shadow.)*

READING **SKILL** **BUILDER** *Brainstorming* Have students read the section titled Science Has Many Branches. As a group, brainstorm ideas for scientific study. Allow a student volunteer to create a list on the board of all the student contributions. Have the students create a diagram that summarizes the results of their brainstorming activity.

SKILL BUILDER

Interpreting Diagrams Have students look at **Figure 1-3** and consider where they would place astronomy, analytical chemistry, archeology, geophysics, organic chemistry, paleontology, nuclear physics, and biochemistry.

Resources Blackline Master 1 shows this visual.

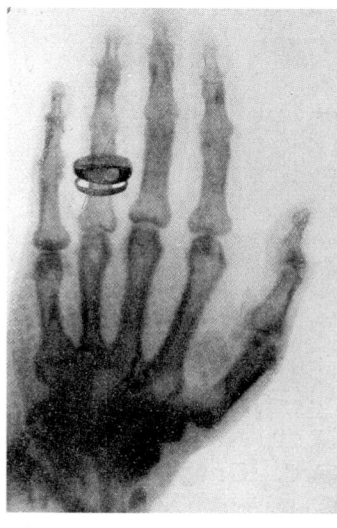

Figure 1-2
Roentgen included this X ray of his wife's hand in one of the first papers he wrote on X rays.

▶ **science** a system of knowledge based on facts or principles

Scientists always test results

Because Roentgen was a scientist, he first repeated his experiment to be sure of his observations. Then he began to think of new questions and to design more experiments to find the answers.

He found that the rays passed through almost everything, although dense materials absorbed them somewhat. If he held his hand in the path of the rays, the bones were visible as shadows on the fluorescent detector, as shown in **Figure 1-2.** When Roentgen published his findings in December, he still did not know what the rays were. He called them *X rays* because *x* represents an unknown in a mathematical equation.

Within 3 months of Roentgen's discovery, a doctor in Massachusetts used X rays to help set the broken bones in a boy's arm properly. After a year, more than a thousand scientific articles about X rays had been published. In 1901, Roentgen received the first Nobel Prize in physics for his discovery.

Science has many branches

Roentgen's work with X rays illustrates how scientists work, but what is **science** about? Science is observing, studying, and experimenting to find the nature of things. You can think of science as having two main branches: social science and natural science. Natural science tries to understand "nature," which really means "the whole universe." Natural science is usually divided into life science, physical science, and Earth science, as shown in **Figure 1-3.**

Life science is *biology*. Biology has many branches, such as *botany*, the science of plants; *zoology*, the science of animals; and *ecology*, the science of balance in nature. Medicine and agriculture are branches of biology too.

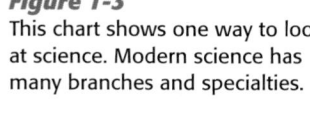

Figure 1-3
This chart shows one way to look at science. Modern science has many branches and specialties.

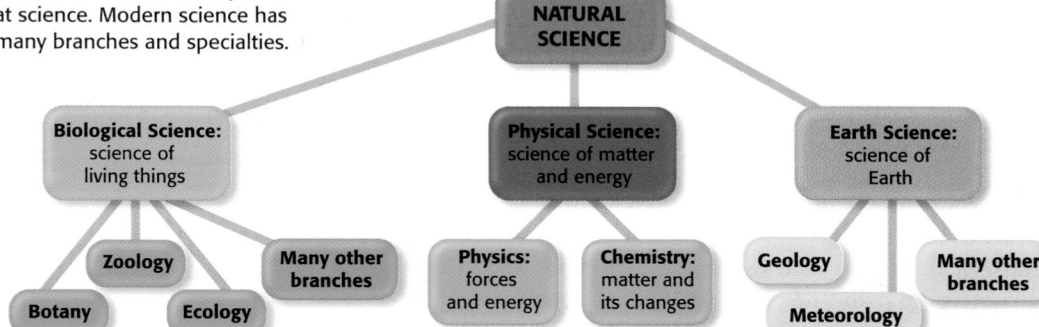

ALTERNATIVE ASSESSMENT

Planning an Experiment

Ask students to imagine that they are Wilhelm Roentgen. Have the students write their own plan for investigating cathode-rays. Students should include a diagram of their equipment setup and a data table for any information they plan to collect.

Some students may have trouble coming up with their own plan. Tell these students that Roentgen's plan was to see if the cathode-rays would pass through glass if the electric voltage applied to the rods was high enough.

Student diagrams should show a cathode-ray tube connected to a power source, a detector made from mineral-coated cardboard on a table (approximately 1 m away from the cathode-ray tube), and a cover for the cathode-ray tube made from heavy black paper. Students should set up

Physical science has two main branches—*chemistry* and *physics*. Chemistry is the science of matter and its changes, and physics is the science of forces and energy.

Some of the branches of Earth science are *geology*, the science of the physical nature and history of the Earth, and *meteorology*, the science of the atmosphere and weather.

This classification of science appears very tidy, like stacks of boxes in a shoe store, but there's a problem with it. As science has progressed, the branches of science have grown out of their little boxes. For example, chemists have begun to explain the workings of chemicals that make up living things, such as DNA, shown in **Figure 1-4.** This science is *biochemistry*, the study of the matter of living things. It is both a life science and a physical science. In the same way, the study of the forces that affect the Earth is *geophysics*, which is both an Earth science and a physical science.

Science and technology work together

Scientists who do experiments to learn more about the world are practicing *pure science*, also defined as the continuing search for scientific knowledge. Engineers look for ways to use this knowledge for practical applications. This application of science is called technology. For example, scientists who practice pure science want to know how certain kinds of materials, called superconductors, conduct electricity with almost no loss in energy. Engineers focus on how that technology can be used to build high-speed computers.

Technology and science depend on one another, as illustrated by **Figure 1-5.** For instance, scientists did not know that tiny organisms such as bacteria even existed until the technology to make precision magnifying lenses developed in the late 1600s.

Figure 1-4
Our DNA makes each of us unique.

▶ **technology** the application of science to meet human needs

internetconnect

SCI**LINKS**
NSTA

TOPIC: Leonardo da Vinci
GO TO: www.scilinks.org
KEYWORD: HK1012

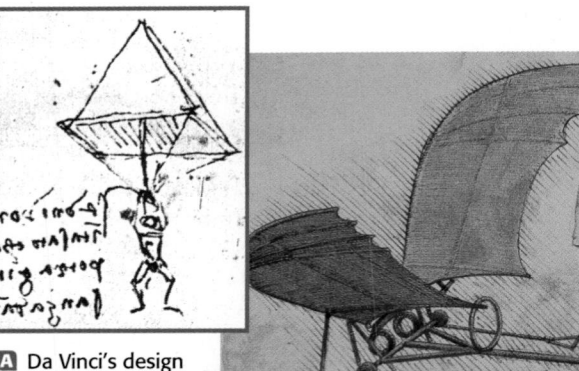

A Da Vinci's design for a parachute

B Da Vinci's design for a helicopter

Figure 1-5
Some of Leonardo da Vinci's ideas could not be built until twentieth-century technology was developed.

INTRODUCTION TO SCIENCE **7**

Additional Application

Leonardo da Vinci's Diagrams Have students look at Leonardo da Vinci's parachute and helicopter. Then discuss how his original ideas might have worked and how their modern counterparts do work. Ask students if they think Leonardo da Vinci's parachute was designed to fold up and be deployed similar to modern parachutes or if it was to be used more like a modern parasail. His helicopter was powered by the arm and leg motion of a human.

SKILL BUILDER

Interpreting Visuals Have students examine **Figure 1-5.** Allow students to brainstorm explanations for why the items shown could not be built until the twentieth century.

RESOURCE LINK
BASIC SKILLS

Assign students worksheet *1.6: Testing a Hypothesis* to help them understand how a scientist tests a hypothesis.

their data table to record the electric voltage used, the distance from the tube to the detector, the air temperature, and the type and quantity of mineral Roentgen used as a coating on the detector.

Interpreting Visuals Have students examine **Figure 1-6B.** Explain that some of the effort of sawing is used to overcome friction—the saw does not slide smoothly through the wood. Friction results in the higher temperatures of both the saw and the wood.

Additional Application

Theories and Laws Scientific theories and laws can be confusing to students. Stress that a scientific law is an observation about nature—a summary of a natural event. A law does not explain how or why something happens. A scientific theory is a possible explanation of an event. Theories are always open to challenges and testing.

▶ **scientific theory** a tested, possible explanation of a natural event

▶ **scientific law** a summary of an observed natural event

Figure 1-6
The kinetic theory explains many things that you can observe, such as why both the far end of the tube (A) and the saw blade (B) get hot.

Scientific Theories and Laws

People sometimes say things like, "My theory is that we'll see Jaime on the school bus," when they really mean, "I'm guessing that we'll find Jaime on the school bus." People use the word *theory* in everyday speech to refer to a guess about something. In science, a theory is much more than a guess.

Theories and laws are supported by observation

A **scientific theory** is an explanation that has been tested by repeated observations. Many theories can be tested by observations of experiments in a laboratory or under controlled conditions. Some scientific theories, such as how the continents move, are nearly impossible to test by laboratory experiments because the events occur slowly over long periods of time.

Scientific theories are always being questioned and examined. To be valid, a theory must continue to pass several tests.

▶ A theory must explain observations simply and clearly. The theory that heat is the energy of particles in motion explains how the far end of a metal tube gets hot when you hold the tip over a flame, as shown in **Figure 1-6A.**

▶ Experiments that illustrate the theory must be repeatable. The far end of the tube always gets hot when the tip is held over a flame, whether it is done for the first time or the thirty-first time.

▶ You must be able to predict from the theory. You might predict that anything that makes particles move faster will make the object hotter. Sawing a piece of wood will make the particles move faster. If, as shown in **Figure 1-6B,** you saw rapidly, the saw will get hot.

When you place a hot cooking pot in a cooler place, does the pot become hotter as it stands? No. It will always get cooler. This illustrates a law that states that warm objects always become cooler when they are placed in cooler surroundings. A **scientific law** states a repeated observation about nature. Notice that the law does not explain why warm objects become cooler.

Mathematics can describe physical events

How would you state the law of gravitation? You could say that something you hold will fall to Earth when you let go. This *qualitative* statement describes with words something you have seen many times. But many scientific laws and theories can be stated as mathematical equations, which are *quantitative* statements.

ALTERNATIVE ASSESSMENT

Scientific Theory and Law

Laws that are not correct under all circumstances are still used because these laws sometimes represent easy-to-understand models of many things that we observe in the natural world. Ask the students to write a paragraph explaining why the caloric theory was accepted. The caloric theory does not explain why rubbing rough surfaces together makes objects warmer, but the caloric theory does explain why fires keep people warm, how food cooks, and why the end of a tube gets hot if the tip is heated. The theory that heat was an invisible fluid that flows through objects explains observations about energy being transferred as heat from one object to another.

> **Rectangle Area Equation**
> $$A = l \times w$$

The rectangle area equation works for all rectangles, whether they are short, tall, wide, or thin.

> **Universal Gravitation Equation**
> $$F = G\frac{m_1 m_2}{d^2}$$

In the same way, the universal gravitation equation describes how big the force will be between two galaxies or between Earth and an apple dropped from your hand, as shown in **Figure 1-7.** Quantitative expressions of the laws of science make communicating about science easier. Scientists around the world speak and read many different languages, but mathematics, the language of science, is the same everywhere.

Theories and laws are not absolute

Sometimes theories have to be changed or replaced completely when new discoveries are made. Over 200 years ago, scientists used the *caloric theory* to explain how objects become hotter and cooler. Heat was thought to be an invisible fluid, called caloric, that could flow from a warm object to a cool one. People thought that fires were fountains of caloric that flowed into surrounding objects, making them warmer. The caloric theory could explain everything that people knew about heat.

But the caloric theory couldn't explain why rubbing two rough surfaces together made them warmer. Around 1800, after doing many experiments, some scientists suggested a new theory based on the idea that heat was a result of the motion of particles. The new theory was that heat is really a form of energy that is transferred when fast-moving particles hit others. Because this theory, the *kinetic theory*, explained the old observations as well as the new ones, it was kept and the caloric theory was discarded. You will learn about the kinetic theory in Chapter 2.

Models can represent physical events

When you see the word *model*, you may think of a small copy of an airplane or a person who shows off clothing. Scientists use models too. A scientific model is a representation of an object or event that can be studied to understand the real object or event. Sometimes, like a model airplane, models represent things that are too big, too complex, or too small to study easily.

What does this have to do with the force between two galaxies?

Figure 1-7
For a long time, people believed that gravity was part of the nature of things. Newton described gravitational attraction as a force that varies depending on the mass of the objects and the distance that separates them.

Teaching Tip

Theories and Laws When discussing the need for changing or revising theories and laws, be sure to point out that sometimes even laws that are not always correct are still used.

For example, Newton's laws of motion, discussed in Chapter 8, are learned and used by many people. But these laws do not apply for subatomic particles or moving particles approaching the speed of light.

Additional Application

Models Point out to students that they probably use models every day without even realizing that they are doing so. When they plan a route to their next class via their locker, they are using a mental map that is a model of the school. A paper map is also a model of the real world. Any set of instructions on how to build something or put something together is a model of that object. When students explain to their parents how to use the computer, they are using a mental model of the operating rules of the computer. Have students brainstorm as many commonly used models as they can.

The Nature of Science

Teaching Tip

Scientific Law Newton's first law of motion states that an object in motion will remain in motion unless an unbalanced force acts against it. Have your students describe what will happen if a dummy in a crash test simulation is wearing a seat belt, but the car does not have an air bag. Students should keep Newton's first law of motion in mind when responding to this question. *(When the car is stopped in a collision, the dummy's body continues in motion until it is stopped by the seat belt. But the dummy's head still stays in motion because there is not an unbalanced force—such as an air bag—to stop its motion.)*

See if students can pose any more hypothetical situations where a scientific law or theory may explain the outcome.

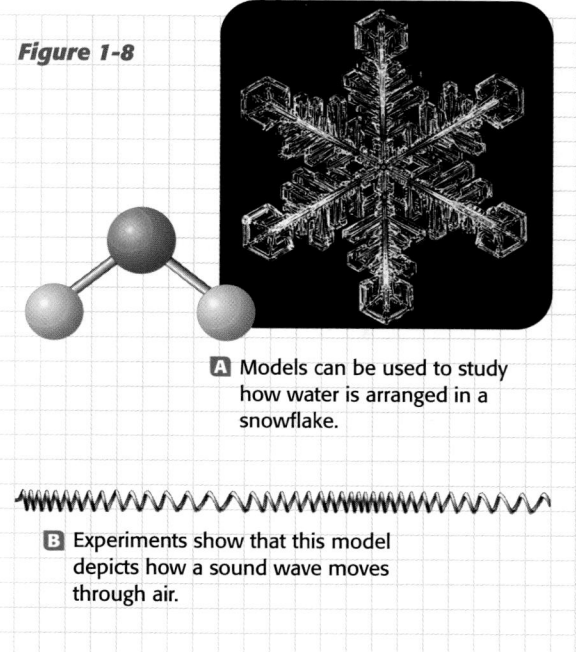

Figure 1-8

A Models can be used to study how water is arranged in a snowflake.

B Experiments show that this model depicts how a sound wave moves through air.

A model of water is shown in **Figure 1-8A.** Chemists use models to study how water forms an ice crystal, such as a snowflake. Models can be drawings on paper. The drawing in **Figure 1-8B** is a model of a sound wave moving through air. Also, a model can be a mental "picture" or a set of rules that describes what something does. After you have studied atoms in Chapter 3, you will be able to picture atoms in your mind and use models to predict what will happen in chemical reactions.

Scientists and engineers also use computer models. These can be drawings; more often, they are mathematical models of complex systems, such as those shown in **Figure 1-9.** Computer models can save time and money because long and complex calculations are done by a machine.

A

B

Figure 1-9
Crash tests give information that is used to make cars safer. Now, models (A) can replace some real-world crash tests. (B)

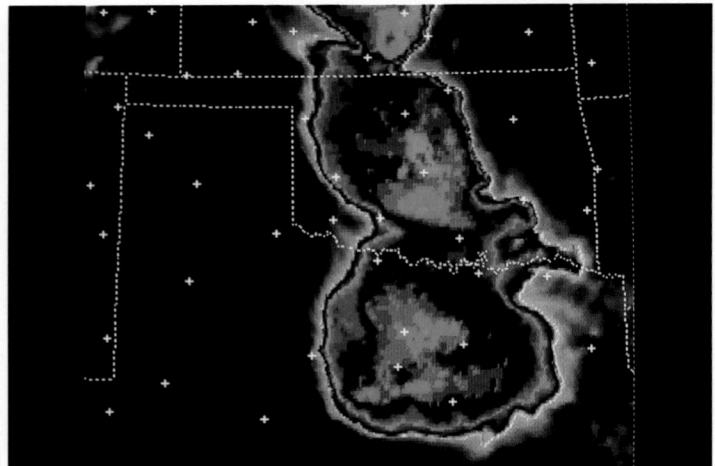

Computer models have a variety of applications. For example, they can be used instead of expensive crash tests to study the effects of motion and forces in car crashes. Engineers use the predictions from the models to improve the design of cars. *Meteorologists* have computer models such as the one shown in **Figure 1-10,** which uses information about wind speed and direction, air temperature, moisture levels, and ground shape to help forecast the weather.

SECTION 1.1 REVIEW

SUMMARY

▶ A scientist makes objective observations.

▶ A scientist confirms results by repeating experiments and learns more by designing and conducting new experiments.

▶ Scientific laws and theories are supported by repeated observation but may be changed when observations are made that are not consistent with predictions.

▶ Models are used to represent real situations and to make predictions.

CHECK YOUR UNDERSTANDING

1. **Compare and Contrast** the two main branches of physical science.
2. **Explain** how science and technology depend on each other.
3. **Explain** how a scientific theory differs from a guess or an opinion.
4. **Define** *scientific law* and give an example.
5. **Compare and Contrast** a scientific law and a scientific theory.
6. **Compare** quantitative and qualitative descriptions.
7. **Describe** how a scientific model is used, and give an example of a scientific model.
8. **Creative Thinking** How do you think Roentgen's training as a scientist affected the way he responded to his discovery?
9. **Creative Thinking** Pick a common happening, develop a theory about it, and describe an experiment you could perform to test your theory.

Section 1.1

The Nature of Science

SECTION 1.1 REVIEW

Check Your Understanding

1. Chemistry is the study of matter and its changes. Physics is the study of forces and energy and their interaction with matter.
2. Technology is the application of science. Improving technology involves someone finding a use for a scientific discovery. However, some scientific discoveries cannot be made until the technology for making the necessary observations exists.
3. A guess or opinion is usually an unsupported statement. A scientific theory is one that has been repeatedly tested through observations.
4. A scientific law states a repeated observation about nature. Examples may vary but could include the laws of gravitation and the conservation of matter.
5. A law does not attempt to explain why something happens; a theory does.
6. Quantitative descriptions use numbers. Qualitative descriptions do not.
7. A model is used to study or make predictions about the object or situation the model represents. Models are also used when an object or situation is too complex. A computer simulation of the launch of a new kind of rocket is an example of a model.
8. Instead of being disappointed he decided to experiment to find out more about his "failure."
9. Answers may vary.

RESOURCE LINK
STUDY GUIDE

Assign students *Review Section 1.1 The Nature of Science.*

11

Scheduling

Refer to pp. 2A–2D for lecture, classwork, and assignment options for Section 1.2.

★ **Lesson Focus**
Use transparency *LT 2* to prepare students for this section.

SKILL BUILDER

Interpreting Visuals Have students examine **Figure 1-11.** Have them brainstorm ideas about why the person is comparing peanut butter and why it might be important to do so. Be sure students consider differences other than price, such as ingredients (preservatives, fillers, sugar, salt), or size (how much is needed, will it go to waste).

For comparison, ask students to consider going to a book store. There are many books in the bargain rack, some for only $2 or $3. Have students brainstorm reasons why they would or would not want to buy the bargain books.

The Way Science Works

▶ **KEY TERMS**

critical thinking
scientific method
variable
length
mass
volume
weight

OBJECTIVES

▶ Understand how to use critical thinking skills to solve problems.
▶ Describe the steps of the scientific method.
▶ Know some of the tools scientists use to investigate nature.
▶ Explain the objective of a consistent system of units, and identify the SI units for length, mass, and time.
▶ Identify what each common SI prefix represents, and convert measurements.

If 16 ounces costs $3.59 and 8 ounces costs $2.19, then . . .

Figure 1-11
Making thoughtful decisions is important in scientific processes as well as in everyday life.

▶ **critical thinking** applying logic and reason to observations and conclusions

Throwing a spear accurately to kill animals for food or to ward off intruders was probably a survival skill people used for thousands of years. In our society, throwing a javelin is an athletic skill, and riding a bicycle or driving a car is considered almost a survival skill. The skills that we place importance on change over time.

Science Skills

Although pouring liquid into a test tube without spilling is a skill that is useful in science, other skills are more important. Planning experiments, recording observations, and reporting data are some of these more important skills. The most important skill is learning to think like a scientist.

Critical thinking

If you are doing your homework and the lights go out, what would you do? Would you call the electric company immediately? A person who thinks like a scientist would first ask questions and make observations. Are lights on anywhere in the house? If so, what would you conclude? Suppose everything electrical in the house is off. Can you see lights in the neighbors' windows? If their lights are on, what does that mean? What if everyone's lights are off?

If you approach the problem this way, you are thinking logically. This kind of thinking is very much like **critical thinking.** You do this kind of thinking when you consider if the giant economy-sized jar of peanut butter is really less expensive than the regular size, as shown in **Figure 1-11,** or consider if a specific brand of soap makes you more attractive.

12 CHAPTER 1

RESOURCE LINK
LABORATORY MANUAL

Have students perform *Lab 1 Introduction to Science: Designing a Pendulum Clock.*

DATASHEETS

Allow students to use *Datasheet 1.3* to record their results.

DEMONSTRATION TEACHING

Are They the Same?

Time: Approximately 15 minutes
Materials: isopropyl alcohol (70% solution), 200 mL beakers (2), distilled water

SAFETY CAUTION: *Be sure to wear gloves and safety goggles before lighting the isopropyl alcohol. Make sure that you perform this demonstration a safe distance away from the students.*

Before class, pour a small amount of isopropyl alcohol in a 200 mL beaker. Pour the same amount of distilled water in another beaker.

Review the steps of the scientific method with your students. Then show students the two beakers. Ask them if they can tell what the two liquids are. Write the following hypothesis on the chalkboard: "Although the two liquids look the same, you believe they are different."

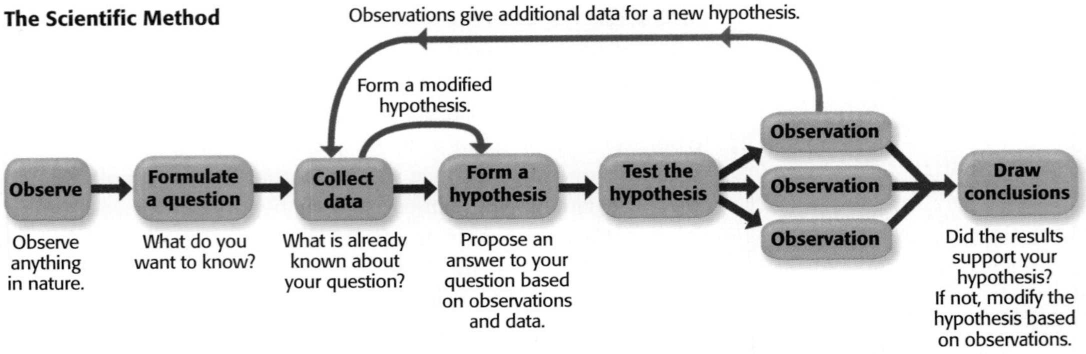

The Scientific Method

Observations give additional data for a new hypothesis.

Form a modified hypothesis.

Observe → Formulate a question → Collect data → Form a hypothesis → Test the hypothesis → Observation / Observation / Observation → Draw conclusions

Observe anything in nature.

What do you want to know?

What is already known about your question?

Propose an answer to your question based on observations and data.

Did the results support your hypothesis? If not, modify the hypothesis based on observations.

Figure 1-12
The scientific method is a general description of scientific thinking more than an exact path for scientists to follow.

When the lights go out, if you get more facts before you call the power company, you're thinking critically. You're not making a reasonable conclusion if you decide there is a citywide power failure when you observe that your lights are off. You don't have to be a scientist to make observations and use logic.

Using the scientific method

In the **scientific method,** critical thinking is used to solve scientific problems. The scientific method is a way to organize your thinking about everyday questions as well as about questions that you might think of as scientific. Using the scientific method helps you find and evaluate possible answers. The scientific method is often shown as a series of steps like those in **Figure 1-12.**

Most scientific questions begin with observations—simple things you notice. For example, you might notice that when you open a door, you hear a noise. You ask the question: Why does this door make noise? You may gather data by checking other doors and find that the other doors don't make noise. So you form a *hypothesis,* a possible answer that you can test in some way. If the door makes a noise, then the source of the noise is the doorknob.

Testing hypotheses

Scientists test a hypothesis by doing experiments. How can you design an experiment to test your hypothesis about the door? A good experiment tests only one **variable** at a time. You might remove the doorknob to see if that stops the squeak.

When you change more than one thing at a time, it's harder to make reasonable conclusions. If you remove the knob, sand the frame, and put oil on the hinges, you may stop the squeak, but you won't know what was causing the squeak. Even if you test one thing at a time, you may not find the answer on the first try. If you take the knob off the door and the door still makes noise, was your experiment a failure?

▶ **scientific method** a series of logical steps to follow in order to solve problems

▶ **variable** anything that can change in an experiment

Section 1.2

The Way Science Works

|SKILL BUILDER

Interpreting Diagrams
Have students examine **Figure 1-12.** Point out to students that scientists do not necessarily use all of these steps for each problem. Have students work in small groups to design a way to apply the scientific method to buying peanut butter, as shown in **Figure 1-11,** or to buying a CD or a book. Be sure to emphasize that thinking like a scientist is a valuable skill in any profession.

Resources Blackline Master 2 shows **Figure 1–12.**

MISCONCEPTION
Scientific Method **ALERT**
Emphasize that there is no single scientific method. Scientists approach problems from a variety of viewpoints. They conduct their research using available tools, data, time, and people. Research often leads to new problems and new hypotheses, which require further research and testing.

Encourage students to think of practical ways to test your hypothesis. Then dim the lights in the classroom. Place the beakers on a safe, flat surface. Using a stick lighter or a long match, try to set the water on fire. Students will see the liquid is not flammable. Then carefully set the alcohol on fire. Students will see that it burns with a blue flame.

Analysis
1. What conclusion can be drawn from this demonstration? *(Careful observation and testing was the only way to distinguish the two liquids.)*

Teaching Tip

Learning Through Success and Failure With experiments such as the discovery of X rays, it is easy to see that an unexpected result is not a failure. Point out to students that even experiments that do not work can be a learning experience and thus a success. For example, when a chemical reaction fails to occur and the student or scientist can determine why the reaction did not occur, he or she will have learned more about the reaction being tested. The experiment can also be repeated in order to avoid the factor that prevented the reaction the first time.

SKILL BUILDER

Interpreting Visuals The theory of plate tectonics was developed in the 1960s and has replaced the older theory of continental drift. The theory of plate tectonics provides a way to reconstruct Earth's past geography. Volcanic activity, areas prone to earthquakes, and mountain ranges mark some of the boundaries between plates. Seismic studies, changes in Earth's magnetic field over time, and trails of volcanic activity on the ocean floor have contributed to our understanding of the boundaries of the plates shown in **Figure 1-13.** Deep-sea drilling cores have been used to help determine the rate and direction of movement for the plates.

RESOURCE LINK
DATASHEETS

Allow students to use *Datasheet 1.1 Making Observations* to record their results.

Quick ACTIVITY

Making Observations
1. Get an ordinary candle of any shape and color.
2. Record all the observations you can make about the candle.
3. Light the candle, and watch it burn for 1 minute.
4. Record as many observations about the burning candle as you can.
5. Share your results with your class, and find out how many different things were observed.

Figure 1-13
Computer models of Earth's crust help geologists understand how the continental plates moved in the past and how they may move in the future.

Conducting experiments

In truth, no experiment is a failure. Experiments may not give the results you wanted, but they are all observations of real happenings in the world. A scientist uses the results to revise the hypothesis and to plan a new experiment that tests a different variable. For example, once you know that the doorknob did not cause the squeak, you can revise your hypothesis to see if oiling the door hinges stops the noise.

Scientists often do "what if" experiments to see what happens in a certain situation. These experiments are a form of data collection. Often, as with Roentgen's X rays, experimental results are surprising and lead in new directions.

Scientists always have the question being tested in mind. You can find out if ice is heavier than water without an experiment. Just think about which one floats. The thinking that led to the law of gravitation began in 1666 when Isaac Newton saw an apple fall from a tree. He wondered why objects fall toward the center of Earth rather than in another direction.

Some questions, such as how Earth's continents have moved over millions of years, cannot be answered with experimental data. Instead of getting data from experiments, geologists make observations all over Earth. They also use models based on the laws of physics, such as those shown in **Figure 1-13.**

Using scientific tools

Of course, logical thinking isn't the only skill used in science. Scientists must make careful observations. Sometimes only the senses are needed for observations, as in the case of field botanists using their eyes to identify plants. At other times, special tools are used. Scientists must know how to use these tools, what the limits of the tools are, and how to interpret data from them. Sometimes scientists use light *microscopes*. A light microscope uses lenses to magnify very small objects, such as bacteria, or the details of larger objects, such as the structure of leaves.

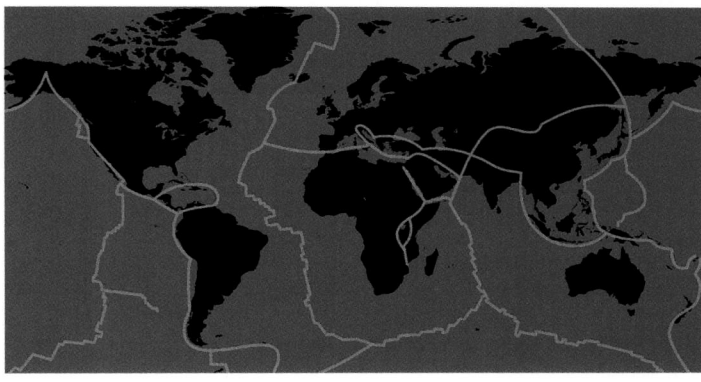

Quick ACTIVITY

Making Observations

SAFETY CAUTION: *Be sure to place the candles in a fireproof container, such as an aluminum pie plate, before lighting them. The container will also catch any wax that drips from the candles.*

In step 2, students should note the color of the wax and the wick. Students should also record the length and/or thickness of the candle.

Be sure to encourage students to observe the changes occurring, not just the end result in step 4. Observations of the burning candle may include relative assessments of the heat given off and the quantity of light, height of flame, color of flame, if the candle drips, condition or changes in the wick, rate of consumption of the wax, and any color change from the solid wax to the melted wax.

Figure 1-14

A The Gemini North observatory in Hawaii is a new tool for scientists. Its 8.1 m mirror is used to view distant galaxies.

B The Whirlpool galaxy (M51) and its companion NGC5195 are linked by a trail of gas and dust, which NGC5195 has pulled from M51 by gravitational attraction.

Astronomers use *telescopes* with lenses and mirrors to magnify objects that appear small because they are far away, such as the distant stars shown in **Figure 1-14.** Other kinds of telescopes do not form images from visible light. *Radio telescopes* detect the radio signals emitted by distant objects. Some of the oldest, most distant objects in the universe have been found with radio telescopes. Radio waves from those objects were emitted almost 15 billion years ago.

Several different types of *spectrophotometers* break light into a rainbowlike *spectrum*. A chemist can learn a great deal about a substance from the light it absorbs or emits. Physicists use *particle accelerators* to make fragments of atoms move extremely fast and then let them smash into atoms or parts of atoms. Data from these collisions give us information about the structure of atoms.

Units of Measurement

As you learned in Section 1.1, mathematics is the language of science, and mathematical models rely on accurate observations. But if your scientific measurements are in inches and gallons, many scientists will not understand because they do not use these units. For this reason scientists use the International System of Units, abbreviated SI, which stands for the French phrase *le Système Internationale d'Unités*.

**Connection to
LANGUAGE ARTS**

The word *scope* comes from the Greek word *skopein,* meaning "to see." Science and technology use many different scopes to see things that we can't see with unaided eyes. For example, the telescope gets its name from the Greek prefix *tele-* meaning "distant" or "far." So a telescope is a tool for seeing far.

Making the Connection

Use a dictionary to find out what is seen by a retinoscope, a kaleidoscope, a hygroscope, and a spectroscope.

INTRODUCTION TO SCIENCE **15**

MISCONCEPTION ALERT

Science and Technology Science and technology are not the same thing. The goal of science is to gain knowledge about the natural world. The goal of technology is to apply scientific understanding to solve problems.

LINKING CHAPTERS

Students will learn more about light and radio waves in Chapter 11.

Did You Know ?

Experiments do not always turn out as expected. In 1856, William Henry Perkin was experimenting to synthesize the antimalarial drug quinine from coal tar. He didn't succeed, but he accidentally made aniline purple (mauve), the first synthetic dye.

**Connection to
LANGUAGE ARTS**

Making the Connection
A retinoscope is an instrument used to see the retina of the eye. A kaleidoscope is a tube that contains bits of glass or plastic reflected by mirrors such that varied patterns are formed when the tube is held to the eye and rotated. A hygroscope is an instrument used to measure the changes in atmospheric humidity. A spectroscope measures the spectra of visible light, infrared light, and ultraviolet light.

Resources Assign students worksheet *1.2: Connection to Language Arts—Medical Terminology* in the **Integration Enrichment Resources** ancillary.

The Way Science Works

Teaching Tip

Units of Measurement Be sure students understand the need to use appropriate units when measuring. Many (but not all) scientists use the SI units. Pose a theoretical question to students, such as "How far is it to the nearest bathroom?" Help them realize there is a big difference between 15 m (about 50 ft) and 15 km (9 mi), especially for the person who needs the information. Another possibility, "How far is it to the sun?" The answer could be 8.5, but 8.5 what? meters? kilometers? Actually, it is 8.5 light-minutes. A light-minute is the distance that light travels in 1 min—18 000 000 000 m (about 11 million miles).

Additional Application

Standard Units of Measure Have students pick an object to use as a unit of measurement. Allow students to use anything including their hands, feet, or a pencil. Tell students to find out how many units wide their desk is, and have them compare their measurement with their classmates. Have a student volunteer write a list of all the units of measurements used on the chalkboard. Lead students into a discussion about why it is so important to use standard units of measure.

Table 1-1 **SI Base Units**

Quantity	Unit	Abbreviation
Length	meter	m
Mass	kilogram	kg
Time	second	s
Temperature	kelvin	K
Electric current	ampere	A
Amount of substance	mole	mol
Luminous intensity	candela	cd

Table 1-2 **Prefixes Used for Large Measurements**

Prefix	Symbol	Meaning	Multiple of base unit
kilo-	k	thousand	1000
mega-	M	million	1 000 000
giga-	G	billion	1 000 000 000

Table 1-3 **Prefixes Used for Small Measurements**

Prefix	Symbol	Meaning	Multiple of base unit
deci-	d	tenth	0.1
centi-	c	hundredth	0.01
milli-	m	thousandth	0.001
micro-	μ	millionth	0.000 001
nano-	n	billionth	0.000 000 001

Did You Know ?

SI started with the metric system in France in 1795. The meter was originally defined as 1/10 000 000 of the distance between the North Pole and the Equator.

SI units are used for consistency

When all scientists use the same system of measurement, sharing data and results is easier. SI is based on the metric system and uses the seven SI base units that you see in **Table 1-1.**

Perhaps you noticed that the base units do not include area, volume, pressure, weight, force, speed, and other familiar quantities. Combinations of the base units, called *derived units*, are used for these measurements.

Suppose you want to order carpet for a floor that measures 8.0 m long and 6.0 m wide. You know that the area of a rectangle is its length times its width.

$$A = l \times w$$

The area of the floor can be calculated as shown below.

$$A = 8.0 \text{ m} \times 6.0 \text{ m} = 48 \text{ m}^2$$
$$\text{(or 48 square meters)}$$

The SI unit of area, m^2, is a derived unit.

SI prefixes are for very large and very small measurements

Look at a meterstick. How would you express the length of a bird's egg in meters? How about the distance you traveled on a vacation trip? The bird's egg might be 1/100 m, or 0.01 m, long. Your trip could have been 800 000 m in distance. To avoid writing a lot of decimal places and zeros, SI uses prefixes to express very small or very large numbers. These prefixes, shown in **Table 1-2** and **Table 1-3,** are all *multiples* of 10.

Using the prefixes, you can now say that the bird's egg is 1 cm (1 *centi*meter is 0.01 m) long and your trip was 800 km (800 *kilo*meters are 800 000 m) long. Note that the base unit of mass is the *kilo*gram, which is already a multiple of the gram.

It is easy to convert SI units to smaller or larger units. Remember that to make a measurement, it takes more of a small unit or less of a large unit. A person's height could be 1.85 m, a fairly small number. In centimeters, the same height would be 185 cm, a larger number.

So, if you are converting to a smaller unit, multiply the measurement to get a bigger number. To write 1.85 m as *centi*meters, you multiply by 100, as shown below.

$$1.85 \text{ m} \times \frac{100 \text{ cm}}{1 \text{ m}} = 185 \text{ cm}$$

If you are converting to a larger unit, divide the measurement to get a smaller number. To change 185 cm to meters, divide by 100, as shown in the following.

$$185 \text{ cm} \times \frac{1 \text{ m}}{100 \text{ cm}} = 1.85 \text{ m}$$

Math Skills

Conversions A roll of copper wire contains 15 m of wire. What is the length of the wire in centimeters?

1 **List the given and unknown values.**
  Given: *length in meters*, $l = 15$ m
  Unknown: *length in centimeters* = ? cm

2 **Determine the relationship between units.**
  Looking at **Table 1-3**, you can find that 1 cm = 0.01 m. This also means that 1 m = 100 cm.
  You will multiply because you are converting from a larger unit (meters) to a smaller unit (centimeters).

3 **Write the equation for the conversion.**
  $$length \ in \ cm = \text{m} \times \frac{100 \text{ cm}}{1 \text{ m}}$$

4 **Insert the known values into the equation, and solve.**
  $$length \ in \ cm = 15 \text{ m} \times \frac{100 \text{ cm}}{1 \text{ m}}$$
  $$length \ in \ cm = 1500 \text{ cm}$$

Practice

Conversions
1. Write 550 *milli*meters as meters.
2. Write 3.5 seconds as *milli*seconds.
3. Convert 1.6 *kilo*grams to grams.
4. Convert 2500 *milli*grams to *kilo*grams.
5. Convert 4.00 *centi*meters to *micro*meters.
6. Change 2800 *milli*moles to moles.
7. Change 6.1 amperes to *milli*amperes.
8. Write 3 *micro*grams as *nano*grams.

INTRODUCTION TO SCIENCE **17**

Practice HINT

If you have done the conversions properly, all the units above and below the fraction will cancel except the units you need.

internet connect

SC*LINKS*
NSTA

TOPIC: SI units
GO TO: www.scilinks.org
KEYWORD: HK1013

The Way Science Works

Math Skills

Resources Assign students worksheet *1: Conversions* in the **Math Skills Resources** ancillary.

Additional Examples

Conversions Convert 15 m into: **a.** mm **b.** km

Answer: a. 15 000 mm
  b. 0.015 km

Convert 2.54 cm into: **a.** m **b.** mm

Answer: a. 0.0254 m **b.** 25.4 mm

Historical Perspective

A $125-million space probe, the Mars Climate Observer, crashed on Mars in 1999 because key numbers were calculated by one group in English units while another group used metric units. Because critical maneuvers necessary to place the spacecraft in a proper Mars orbit relied on calculations involving numbers from both incompatible groups, the probe crashed.

Did You Know?

The SI unit of temperature is called the kelvin and the unit of electric current is called the ampere. The kelvin was selected to honor William Thomson (later Lord Kelvin), a Scottish engineer, mathematician, and physicist. Lord Kelvin was a major contributor to the development of the second law of thermodynamics. The ampere was named to honor André-Marie Ampère, a French physicist, who by 1825 had laid the foundation of electromagnetic theory. Ampère's law states quantitatively the relation of a magnetic field to the electric current or changing electric field that produces it.

17

Solution Guide

1. $550 \text{ mm} \times \dfrac{1 \text{ m}}{1000 \text{ mm}} = 0.55 \text{ m}$

2. $3.5 \text{ s} \times \dfrac{1000 \text{ ms}}{1 \text{ s}} = 3500 \text{ ms}$

3. $1.6 \text{ kg} \times \dfrac{1000 \text{ g}}{1 \text{ kg}} = 1600 \text{ g}$

4. $2500 \text{ mg} \times \dfrac{1 \text{ g}}{1000 \text{ mg}} \times \dfrac{1 \text{ kg}}{1000 \text{ g}} = 0.0025 \text{ kg}$

5. $4.00 \text{ cm} \times \dfrac{1 \text{ m}}{100 \text{ cm}} \times \dfrac{1 \times 10^6 \text{ }\mu\text{m}}{1 \text{ m}} = 4.00 \times 10^4 \text{ }\mu\text{m}$

6. $2800 \text{ mmol} \times \dfrac{1 \text{ mol}}{1000 \text{ mmol}} = 2.8 \text{ moles}$

7. $6.1 \text{ A} \times \dfrac{1000 \text{ mA}}{1 \text{ A}} = 6100 \text{ mA}$

8. $3 \text{ }\mu\text{g} \times \dfrac{1 \text{ g}}{1 \times 10^6 \text{ }\mu\text{g}} \times \dfrac{1 \times 10^9 \text{ ng}}{1 \text{ g}} = 3000 \text{ ng}$

The Way Science Works

MISCONCEPTION ALERT
Weight and Mass

Be sure to reinforce the difference between weight and mass often. Emphasize that mass is how much matter an object has, while weight is how hard gravity is pulling on it.

When astronauts travel to the moon, they have the same mass, but they weigh less because the moon is smaller (both in size and mass) than the Earth. A change in weight is due to a change in gravitational attraction between the astronaut and the Earth and the astronaut and the moon.

LINKING CHAPTERS

Students will learn more about the difference between weight and mass in Chapter 8.

Teaching Tip

Tools Have the students consider some of the tools used for measuring time, length, mass, and volume and suggest other tools for those quantities. An hourglass, a sundial, and the atomic clock can be used for measuring time. Length can also be measured with a surveyor's wheel or a car odometer. A double-pan balance, a spring scale such as that used in a grocery produce department or for fishing, and a single-beam balance that students may have seen in medical offices are all used to measure mass. Volume can be measured with pipets and syringes.

RESOURCE LINK
BASIC SKILLS

Assign students worksheet *2.3: Dimensional Analysis and Conversions* to help them understand the conversion process.

Figure 1-15 Tools for Quantitative Measurements

Quantity	Time	Length
SI Unit	Second, s	Meter, m
Other units	Milliseconds, ms Minutes, min Hours, h	Millimeter, mm Centimeter, cm Kilometer, km
Examples		
Tools		

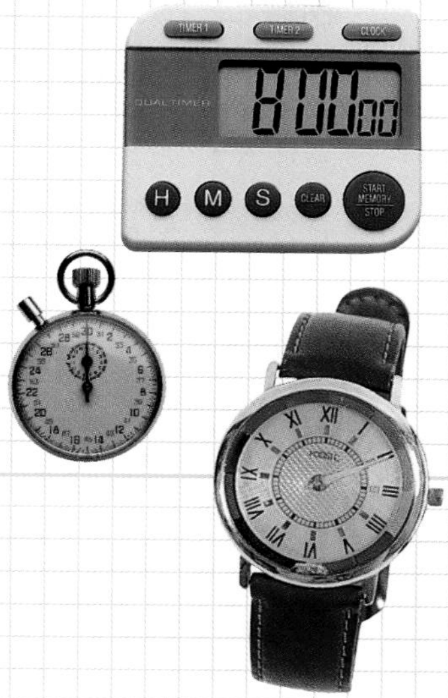

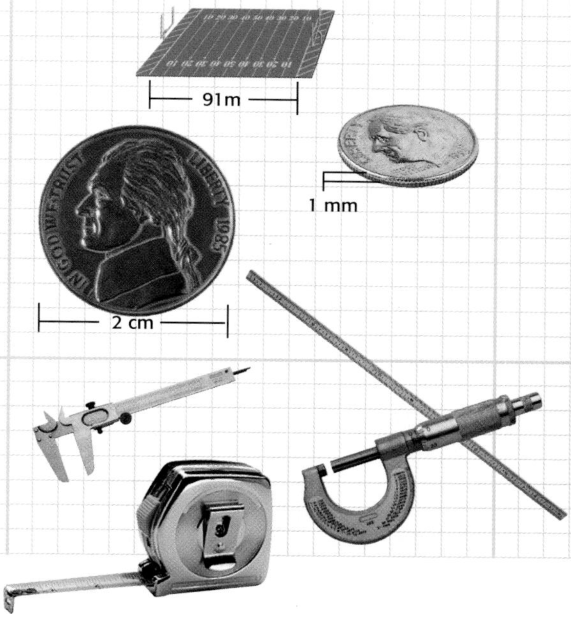

▶ **length** the straight-line distance between any two points

▶ **mass** a measure of the quantity of matter in an object

▶ **volume** a measure of space, such as the capacity of a container

▶ **weight** the force with which gravity pulls on a quantity of matter

Making measurements

Many observations rely on quantitative measurements. The most basic scientific measurements generally answer questions such as how much time did it take and how big is it?

Often, you will measure time, **length, mass,** and **volume.** The SI units for these quantities and the tools you may use to measure them are shown in **Figure 1-15.**

Although you may hear someone say that he or she is "weighing" an object with a balance, **weight** is not the same as mass. Mass is the quantity of matter and weight is the force with which Earth's gravity pulls on that quantity of matter.

In your lab activities, you will use a graduated cylinder to measure the volume of liquids. The volume of a solid that has a specific geometric shape, such as a rectangular block or a metal cylinder, can be calculated from the length of its surfaces. The volume of small solid objects is usually expressed in cubic centimeters, cm^3. One cubic centimeter is equal to 1 mL.

18 CHAPTER 1

ALTERNATIVE ASSESSMENT

Evaluating Advertising Claims

Have students bring in advertisements for products and services that contain claims that can be verified by measurement. Challenge students to identify the claim, describe the type of measurements that could verify or discredit the claim, and indicate which units they would use for the measurements. In addition, students should provide examples of sample data that would verify the claim and examples of sample data that would call the claim into question.

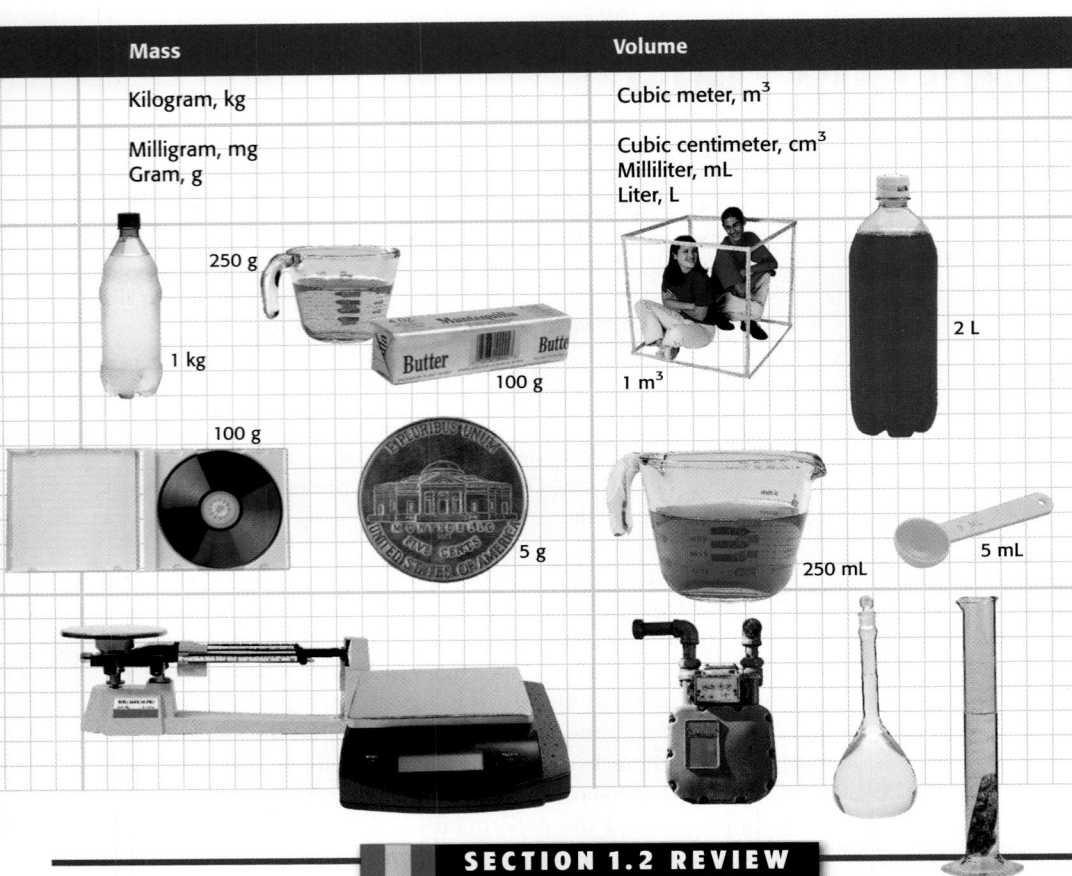

Mass	Volume
Kilogram, kg	Cubic meter, m^3
Milligram, mg Gram, g	Cubic centimeter, cm^3 Milliliter, mL Liter, L

250 g

1 kg

Butter

100 g

2 L

100 g

1 m^3

5 g

250 mL

5 mL

Check Your Understanding

1. Mass: solid food items, people, and mail; volume: liquid food items, gasoline, air flow (exhaust fans and a/c units); length: rope, distance, height.
2. Both involve thinking about a problem and checking details.
3. A hypothesis is a possible answer to a question that can be tested. An example would be, "I can pass the test if I study at least 5 hours."
4. No experiment should be called a failure because an experiment that has unexpected results provides a chance to learn something new.
5. Even now, there are scientific theories which have not been verified. In some cases these theories cannot be tested because the tools do not yet exist.
6. An SI base unit is a single unit while a derived unit is a combination of the base units. Base units include: seconds, meters, kilograms, kelvin, amperes, moles, and candelas. Examples of derived units are meters cubed (m^3) or the newton (N), which is a kg•m/s^2.
7. It is much easier to determine which factor your experiment depends on if you only check one factor at a time. If you change more than one thing and something unexpected happens, you will not know what caused the result.

SECTION 1.2 REVIEW

SUMMARY

▶ In the scientific method, a person asks a question, collects data about the question, forms a hypothesis, tests the hypothesis, draws conclusions, and if necessary, modifies the hypothesis based on results.

▶ In an ideal experiment, only one factor, the variable, is tested.

▶ SI has seven base units.

CHECK YOUR UNDERSTANDING

1. **List** three examples each of things that are commonly measured by mass, by volume, and by length.
2. **Explain** why the scientific method is said to be very similar to critical thinking.
3. **Describe** a hypothesis and how it is used. Give an example of a hypothesis.
4. **Explain** why no experiment should be called a failure.
5. **Relate** the discussion of scientists' tools to how science and technology depend on each other.
6. **Explain** the difference between SI base units and derived units. Give an example of each.
7. **Critical Thinking** Why do you think it is wise to limit an experiment to test only one factor at a time?

RESOURCE LINK
STUDY GUIDE

Assign students *Review Section 1.2 The Way Science Works.*

Scheduling

Refer to pp. 2A–2D for lecture, classwork, and assignment options for Section 1.3.

★ Lesson Focus

Use transparency *LT 3* to prepare students for this section.

|SKILL BUILDER|

Graphing Have students use a spreadsheet such as Microsoft Excel to create graphs for the data shown in **Table 1-4.** Print the graphs, and have students label important points on the graph.

Be sure that students can identify line graphs, pie charts, and bar graphs by type. Ask students if they have ever seen powers of ten, i.e., exponents, displayed in spreadsheet software or scientific calculators as E values.

Organizing Data

▶ **KEY TERMS**

scientific notation
precision
significant figures
accuracy

┌ OBJECTIVES

▶ Interpret line graphs, bar graphs, and pie graphs.
▶ Identify the significant figures in calculations.
▶ Use scientific notation and significant figures in problem solving.
▶ Understand the difference between precision and accuracy.

O ne thing that helped Roentgen discover X rays was that he could read about the experiments other scientists had performed with the cathode ray tube. He was able to learn from their data. Organizing and presenting data are important science skills.

Presenting Scientific Data

Suppose you are trying to determine the speed of a chemical reaction that produces a gas. You can let the gas displace water in a graduated cylinder, as shown in **Figure 1-16.** You read the volume of gas in the cylinder every 10 seconds from the start of the reaction until there is no change in volume for four successive readings. **Table 1-4** shows the data you collect in the experiment.

Because you did the experiment, you saw how the volume changed over time. But how can someone who reads your report see it? To show the results, you can make a graph.

Table 1-4 **Experimental Data**

Time (s)	Volume of gas (mL)	Time (s)	Volume of gas (mL)
0	0	90	116
10	3	100	140
20	6	110	147
30	12	120	152
40	25	130	154
50	43	140	156
60	58	150	156
70	72	160	156
80	100	170	156

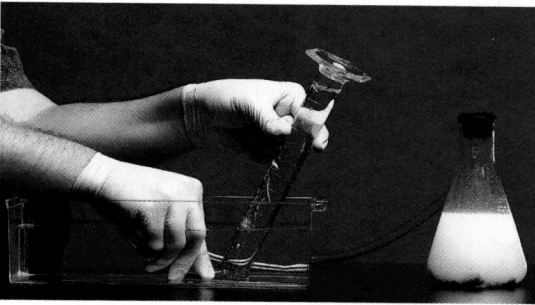

Figure 1-16
The volume of gas produced by a reaction can be determined by measuring the amount of water the gas displaces in a graduated cylinder.

RESOURCE LINK
BASIC SKILLS

Assign students worksheet *6.2: Making a Line Graph* and worksheet *6.3: Making and Interpreting Bar and Pie Graphs.*

Line graphs are best for continuous changes

Many types of graphs can be drawn, but which one should you use? A *line graph* is best for displaying data that change. Our example experiment has two variables, time and volume. Time is the *independent variable* because you chose the time intervals to take the measurements. The volume of gas is the *dependent variable* because its value depends on what happens in the experiment.

Line graphs are usually made with the *x*-axis showing the independent variable and the *y*-axis showing the dependent variable. **Figure 1-17** is a graph of the data that is in **Table 1-4.**

A person who never saw your experiment can look at this graph and know what took place. The graph shows that gas was produced slowly for the first 20 s and that the rate increased until it became constant from about 50 s to 100 s. The reaction slowed down and stopped after about 140 s.

Bar graphs compare items

A *bar graph* is useful when you want to compare data for several individual items or events. If you measured the melting temperatures of some metals, your data could be presented in a way similar to that in **Table 1-5. Figure 1-18** shows the same values as a bar graph. A bar graph often makes clearer how large or small the differences in individual values are.

Volumes Measured Over Time

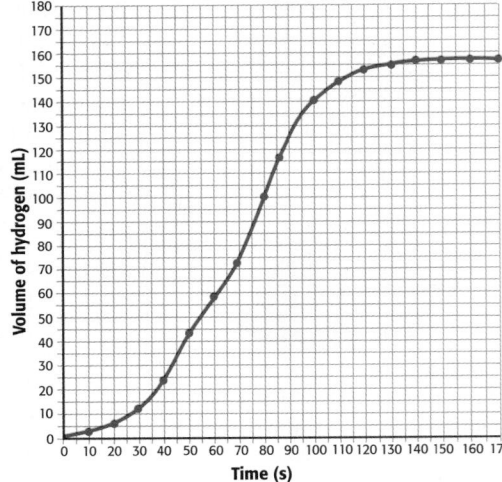

Figure 1-17
Data that change over a range are best represented by a line graph. Notice that many in-between volumes can be read.

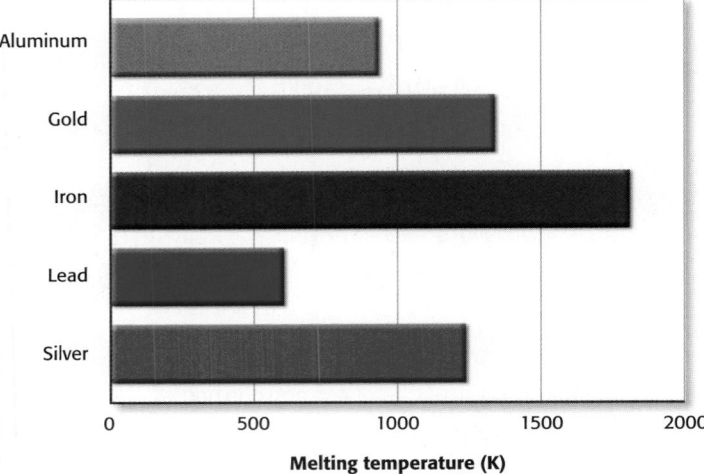

Table 1-5 Melting Points of Some Metals

Element	Melting temp. (K)
Aluminum	933
Gold	1337
Iron	1808
Lead	601
Silver	1235

Figure 1-18
A bar graph is best for data that have specific values for different events or things.

INTRODUCTION TO SCIENCE **21**

Organizing Data

READING SKILL BUILDER *Paired Reading*
Have students read the section on line graphs silently. Lead a discussion of the important features of the graph that are discussed in the paragraphs. Highlight these features on the overhead transparency as you discuss them. Have students make notes on their copies of the graphs.

‖SKILL BUILDER

Graphing Have students plot a line graph using the data given in the table. Ask students to guess what the graph might represent. Students should be able to identify that mass decreases rapidly as temperature goes from 40 °C to 80 °C. The graph might show how much of a solid material reacted as temperature increased or the distillation of a mixture.

Temperature (°C)	Mass (g)
0	100
20	100
40	100
60	60
80	20
100	5
120	3
140	2
160	1

Organizing Data

Teaching Tip

Scientific Notation Scientific notation is a shorthand way to represent where the decimal place is located in a measurement or value. Point out to students that a positive exponent, such as 10^4, means to move the decimal place to the right. So $5.4 \text{ m} \times 10^4$ is the same as $54\,000$ m (move the decimal four places to the right). A negative exponent means move the decimal place to the left, so 2.54×10^{-3} cm is the same as $0.002\,54$ cm (move the decimal three places to the left).

Historical Perspective

Numbers were expressed as powers during the Old Babylonian Empire almost 4000 years ago. Although the ancient Babylonians did not write numbers with exponents, they used squares and square roots to solve geometric problems. They expressed large numbers by positions with values of 60^0, 60^1, 60^2, and 60^3 just as we use 10^0, 10^1, 10^2, and 10^3 for ones, tens, hundreds, and thousands.

Composition of Calcite

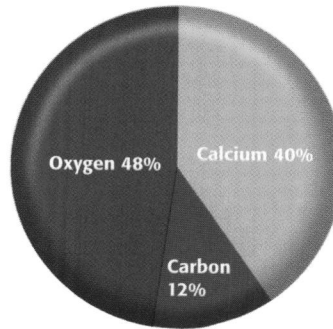

Figure 1-19
A pie chart is best for data that represent parts of a whole, such as the percentage of each element in the mineral calcite.

▶ **scientific notation** a value written as a simple number multiplied by a power of 10

internetconnect

SC*LINKS*
NSTA

TOPIC: Presenting scientific data
GO TO: www.scilinks.org
KEYWORD: HK1014

Pie charts show the parts of a whole

A *pie chart* is ideal for displaying data that are parts of a whole. Suppose you have analyzed a compound to find the percentage of each element it contains. Your analysis shows that the compound consists of 40 percent calcium, 12 percent carbon, and 48 percent oxygen. You can draw a pie chart that shows these percentages as a portion of the whole pie, the compound, as shown in **Figure 1-19.**

Writing Numbers in Scientific Notation

Scientists sometimes need to express measurements using numbers that are very large or very small. For example, the speed of light through space is about $300\,000\,000$ m/s. Suppose you want to calculate the time required for light to travel from Neptune to Earth when Earth and Neptune are $4\,600\,000\,000\,000$ m apart. To find out how long it takes, you would divide the distance between Earth and Neptune by the distance light travels in 1 s.

$$t = \frac{\text{distance from Earth to Neptune (m)}}{\text{distance light travels in 1 s (m/s)}}$$

$$t = \frac{4\,600\,000\,000\,000 \text{ m}}{300\,000\,000 \text{ m/s}}$$

This is a lot of zeros to keep track of when performing a calculation.

To reduce the number of zeros, you can express values as a simple number multiplied by a power of 10. This is called scientific notation. Some powers of 10 and their decimal equivalents are shown below.

$$10^4 = 10\,000$$
$$10^3 = 1000$$
$$10^2 = 100$$
$$10^1 = 10$$
$$10^0 = 1$$
$$10^{-1} = 0.1$$
$$10^{-2} = 0.01$$
$$10^{-3} = 0.001$$

When Earth and Neptune are $4\,600\,000\,000\,000$ m apart, the distance can be written in scientific notation as 4.6×10^{12} m. The speed of light in space is 3.0×10^8 m/s.

Math Skills

Writing Scientific Notation The adult human heart pumps about 18 000 L of blood each day. Write this value in scientific notation.

1 **List the given and unknown values.**
 Given: *volume, V* = 18 000 L
 Unknown: *volume, V* = ? × $10^?$ L

2 **Write the form for scientific notation.**
 $V = ? \times 10^? $ L

3 **Insert the known values into the form, and solve.**
 First find the largest power of 10 that will divide into the known value and leave one digit before the decimal point. You get 1.8 if you divide 10 000 into 18 000 L. So, 18 000 L can be written as (1.8 × 10 000) L.

 Then write 10 000 as a power of 10. Because 10 000 = 10^4, you can write 18 000 L as 1.8 × 10^4 L.
 $V = 1.8 \times 10^4$ L

Practice

Writing Scientific Notation
1. Write the following measurements in scientific notation:
 a. 800 000 000 m   **d.** 0.000 95 m
 b. 0.0015 kg   **e.** 8 002 000 km
 c. 60 200 L   **f.** 0.000 000 000 06 kg
2. Write the following measurements in long form:
 a. 4.5 × 10^3 g   **c.** 3.115 × 10^6 km
 b. 6.05 × 10^{-3} m   **d.** 1.99 × 10^{-8} cm

Using scientific notation
When you use scientific notation in calculations, you follow the rules of algebra for powers of 10. When you multiply two values in scientific notation, you add the powers of 10. When you divide, you subtract the powers of 10.

 So the problem about Earth and Neptune can be solved more easily as shown below.

$$t = \frac{4.6 \times 10^{12} \text{ m}}{3.0 \times 10^8 \text{ m/s}}$$

$$t = \left(\frac{4.6}{3.0} \times \frac{10^{12}}{10^8}\right) \frac{\text{m}}{\text{m/s}}$$

$$t = (1.5 \times 10^{(12-8)})\text{s}$$

$$t = 1.5 \times 10^4 \text{ s}$$

Practice HINT

▶ A shortcut for scientific notation involves moving the decimal point and counting the number of places it is moved. To change 18 000 to 1.8, the decimal point is moved four places to the left. The number of places the decimal is moved is the correct power of 10.

 18 000 L = 1.8 × 10^4 L

▶ When a quantity smaller than 1 is converted to scientific notation, the decimal moves to the right and the power of 10 is *negative*. For example, suppose an *E. coli* bacterium is measured to be 0.000 0021 m long. To express this measurement in scientific notation, move the decimal point to the right.

 0.000 0021 m = 2.1 × 10^{-6} m

INTRODUCTION TO SCIENCE **23**

Math Skills

Resources Assign students worksheet *2: Writing Scientific Notation* in the **Math Skills Worksheets** ancillary.

Additional Examples
Writing Scientific Notation
Write the following numbers in scientific notation and then convert them to the specified units.
a. 0.0254 m to cm
b. 6210 m to km

Answer: a. 2.54 × 10^{-2} m;
          2.54 cm
      b. 6.21 × 10^3 m;
          6.21 km

Convert the following numbers to the units specified and then write them in scientific notation.
a. 2.71 μg to kg
b. 62 800 km to m

Answer: a. 0.000 000 002 71 kg;
          2.71 × 10^{-9} kg
      b. 62 800 000 m;
          6.28 × 10^7 m

Solution Guide

1. a. 8 × 10^8 m
   b. 1.5 × 10^{-3} kg
   c. 6.02 × 10^4 L
   d. 9.5 × 10^{-4} m
   e. 8.002 × 10^6 km
   f. 6 × 10^{-11} kg

2. a. 4500 g
   b. 0.006 05 m
   c. 3 115 000 km
   d. 0.000 000 019 9 cm

Organizing Data

Math Skills

Resources Assign students worksheet *3: Using Scientific Notation* in the **Math Skills Worksheets** ancillary.

Additional Examples

Using Scientific Notation Perform the following calculations:

a.
$$\frac{(5.2 \times 10^3 \text{ kg})(4.3 \times 10^3 \text{ m})}{(3.5 \times 10^2 \text{ s})(3.5 \times 10^2 \text{ s})}$$

b. $\frac{(3.6 \times 10^3 \text{ kg})(6.5 \text{ m})}{(1.5 \times 10^2 \text{ m}^2)}$

Answer: *a.* 1.8×10^2 kg • m/s^2
   (or N)
b. 15.6×10^1 kg/m = 1.56×10^2 kg/m

Practice HINT

Because not all devices can display superscript numbers, scientific calculators and some math software for computers display numbers in scientific notation using E values. That is, 3.12×10^4 may be shown as 3.12 E4. Very small numbers are shown with negative values. For example, 2.637×10^{-5} may be shown as 2.637 E–5. The letter *E* signifies exponential notation. The E value is the exponent (power) of 10. The rules for using powers of 10 are the same whether the exponent is displayed as a superscript or as an E value.

▶ **precision** the degree of exactness of a measurement

▶ **significant figures** the digits in a measurement that are known with certainty

Math Skills

Using Scientific Notation Your state plans to buy a rectangular tract of land measuring 5.36×10^3 m by 1.38×10^4 m to establish a nature preserve. What is the area of this tract in square meters?

1 List the given and unknown values.
   Given: *length*, $l = 1.38 \times 10^4$ m
   width, $w = 5.36 \times 10^3$ m
   Unknown: *area*, $A = ?$ m^2

2 Write the equation for area.
   $A = l \times w$

3 Insert the known values into the equation, and solve.
   $A = (1.38 \times 10^4 \text{ m})(5.36 \times 10^3 \text{ m})$
   Regroup the values and units as follows.
   $A = (1.38 \times 5.36)(10^4 \times 10^3)(\text{m} \times \text{m})$
   When multiplying, add the powers of 10.
   $A = (1.38 \times 5.36)(10^{4+3})(\text{m} \times \text{m})$
   $A = 7.40 \times 10^7$ m^2

Practice

Using Scientific Notation
1. Perform the following calculations.
   a. $(5.5 \times 10^4 \text{ cm}) \times (1.4 \times 10^4 \text{ cm})$
   b. $(2.77 \times 10^{-5} \text{ m}) \times (3.29 \times 10^{-4} \text{ m})$
   c. $(4.34 \text{ g/mL}) \times (8.22 \times 10^6 \text{ mL})$
   d. $(3.8 \times 10^{-2} \text{ cm}) \times (4.4 \times 10^{-2} \text{ cm}) \times (7.5 \times 10^{-2} \text{ cm})$
2. Perform the following calculations.

   a. $\frac{3.0 \times 10^4 \text{ L}}{62 \text{ s}}$ *c.* $\frac{5.2 \times 10^8 \text{ cm}^3}{9.5 \times 10^2 \text{ cm}}$

   b. $\frac{6.05 \times 10^7 \text{ g}}{8.8 \times 10^6 \text{ cm}^3}$ *d.* $\frac{3.8 \times 10^{-5} \text{ kg}}{4.6 \times 10^{-5} \text{ kg/cm}^3}$

Using Significant Figures

Suppose you need to measure the length of a wire and you have two tape measures. One is marked every 0.001 m, and the other is marked every 0.1 m. Which tape should you use? The tape marked every 0.001 m gives you more **precision.** If you use this tape, you can report a length of 1.638 m. The other tape is only precise to 1.6 m.

Measured quantities are always reported in a way that shows the precision of the measurement. To do this, scientists use **significant figures.** The length of 1.638 m has four significant figures because the digits 1638 are known for sure. The measurement of 1.6 m has two significant figures.

Solution Guide

1. *a.* $(5.5 \times 10^4 \text{ cm}) \times (1.4 \times 10^4 \text{ cm}) = (5.5 \times 1.4)(10^{4+4})(\text{cm} \times \text{cm}) = 7.7 \times 10^8$ cm^2
   b. $(2.77 \times 10^{-5} \text{ m}) \times (3.29 \times 10^{-4} \text{ m}) = (2.77 \times 3.29)(10^{-5+-4})(\text{m} \times \text{m}) = 9.11 \times 10^{-9}$ m^2
   c. $\left(4.34 \frac{\text{g}}{\text{mL}}\right) \times (8.22 \times 10^6 \text{ mL}) = (4.34 \times 8.22)(10^6)\left(\frac{\text{g}}{\text{mL}} \times \text{mL}\right) = 3.57 \times 10^7$ g
   d. $(3.8 \times 10^{-2} \text{ cm}) \times (4.4 \times 10^{-2} \text{ cm}) \times (7.5 \times 10^{-2} \text{ cm}) = (3.8 \times 4.4 \times 7.5)(10^{-2+-2+-2})$
   $(\text{cm} \times \text{cm} \times \text{cm}) = 1.3 \times 10^{-4}$ cm^3
2. *a.* $\frac{3.0 \times 10^4 \text{ L}}{62 \text{ s}} = 4.8 \times 10^2$ L/s   *c.* $\frac{5.2 \times 10^8 \text{ cm}^3}{9.5 \times 10^2 \text{ cm}} = 5.5 \times 10^5$ cm^2
   b. $\frac{6.05 \times 10^7 \text{ g}}{8.8 \times 10^6 \text{ cm}^3} = 6.9$ g/cm^3 *d.* $\frac{3.8 \times 10^{-5} \text{ kg}}{4.6 \times 10^{-5} \text{ kg/cm}^3} = 8.3 \times 10^{-1}$ cm^3

A Good accuracy and good precision

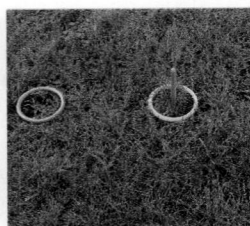
B Good accuracy and poor precision

C Poor accuracy and good precision

D Poor accuracy and poor precision

Figure 1-20
A ring toss is a game of skill, but it is also a good way to visualize accuracy and precision in measurements.

If a piece of your tape measure was broken off the tip, you can read 1.638 m precisely, but that number is not accurate. A measured quantity is only as accurate as the tool used to make the measurement. One way to think about the accuracy and precision of measurements is shown in **Figure 1-20.**

▶ **accuracy** the extent to which a measurement approaches the true value

Math Skills

Significant Figures Calculate the volume of a room that is 3.125 m high, 4.25 m wide, and 5.75 m long. Write the answer with the correct number of significant figures.

1 **List the given and unknown values.**
   Given: *length, l* = 5.75 m
   width, w = 4.25 m
   height, h = 3.125 m
   Unknown: *Volume, V* = ? m^3

2 **Write the equation for volume.**
   Volume, V = *l* × *w* × *h*

3 **Insert the known values into the equation, and solve.**
   V = 5.75 m × 4.25 m × 3.125 m
   V = 76.3671875 m^3
   The answer should have three significant figures because the value with the smallest number of significant figures has three significant figures.
   V = 76.4 m^3

Practice

Significant Figures
Perform the following calculations, and write the answer with the correct number of significant figures.
1. 12.65 m × 42.1 m
2. 3.02 cm × 6.3 cm × 8.225 cm
3. 3.7 g ÷ 1.083 cm^3
4. 3.244 m ÷ 1.4 s

▶ **Practice HINT**

When rounding to get the correct number of significant figures, do you round up or down if the last digit is a 5? Your teacher may have other ways to round, but one very common way is to round to get an even number. For example, 3.25 is rounded to 3.2, and 3.35 is rounded to 3.4. Using this simple rule, half the time you will round up and half the time you will round down. See the Math Skills Refresher in Appendix A for more about significant figures and rounding.

Solution Guide

1. 12.65 m × 42.1 m = 5.32 × 10^2 m^2
2. 3.02 cm × 6.3 cm × 8.225 cm = 1.6 × 10^2 cm^3
3. $\dfrac{3.7 \text{ g}}{1.083 \text{ cm}^3}$ = 3.4 g/cm^3
4. $\dfrac{3.244 \text{ m}}{1.4 \text{ s}}$ = 2.3 m/s

Section 1.3

Organizing Data

Math Skills

Resources Assign students worksheet *4: Significant Figures* in the **Math Skills Worksheets** ancillary.

Additional Examples

Significant Figures Perform the following calculations, and write the answer with the correct number of significant figures. Then write the answer in scientific notation.
a. 1550 m ÷ 1.2 s
b. 51 m × 45 m

Answer: *a.* 1300 m/s =
1.3 × 10^3 m/s
b. 2300 m^2 =
2.3 × 10^3 m^2

Teaching Tip

Accuracy Versus Precision
Students often have difficulty understanding the difference between accuracy and precision. In common speech, these terms are often used inaccurately or interchangeably, which makes it a greater burden for a student to understand the differences. Stress the differences with students using simple examples like a ring toss game or estimating the number of people in a crowd. When discussing accuracy, is 'about 2000' more accurate than '1383'? If the true value is 1826, then about 2000 is more accurate than 1383 even though 1383 is a more precise number. Have the students do the following problems:

Round the following numbers to two significant figures.
a. 13 589; **b.** 889;
c. 0.000 241 949; **d.** 0.725

Answer: a. 14 000; **b.** 890;
c. 0.000 24; **d.** 0.72

Organizing Data

When you use measurements in calculations, the answer is only as precise as the least precise measurement used in the calculation—the measurement with the fewest significant figures. Suppose, for example, that the floor of a rectangular room is measured to the nearest 0.01 m (1 cm). The measured dimensions are reported to be 5.871 m by 8.14 m.

If you use a calculator to multiply 5.871 by 8.14, the display may show 47.789 94 as an answer. But you don't really know the area of the room to the nearest 0.000 01 m^2, as the calculator showed. To have the correct number of significant figures, you must round off your results. In this case the correct rounded result is $A = 47.8$ m^2, because the least precise value in the calculation had three significant figures.

When adding or subtracting, use this rule: the answer cannot be more precise than the values in the calculation. A calculator will add 6.3421 s and 12.1 s to give 18.4421 as a result. But the least precise value was known to 0.1 s, so round to 18.4 s.

SECTION 1.3 REVIEW

SUMMARY

▶ Representing scientific data with graphs helps you and others understand experimental results.

▶ Scientific notation is useful for writing very large and very small measurements because it uses powers of 10 instead of strings of zeros.

▶ Accuracy is the extent to which a value approaches the true value.

▶ Precision is the degree of exactness of a measurement.

▶ Expressing data with significant figures tells others how precisely a measurement was made.

CHECK YOUR UNDERSTANDING

1. **Describe** the kind of data that is best displayed as a line graph.
2. **Describe** the kind of data that is best displayed as a pie chart. Give an example of data from everyday experiences that could be placed on a pie chart.
3. **Explain** in your own words the difference between accuracy and precision.
4. **Critical Thinking** An old riddle asks, Which weighs more, a pound of feathers or a pound of lead? Answer the question, and explain why you think people sometimes answer incorrectly.

WRITING SKILL

Math Skills

5. **Convert** the following measurements to scientific notation:
   a. 15 400 mm^3 c. 2050 mL
   b. 0.000 33 kg   d. 0.000 015 mol
6. **Calculate** the following:
   a. 3.16×10^3 m $\times$ 2.91×10^4 m
   b. 1.85×10^{-3} cm $\times$ 5.22×10^{-2} cm
   c. 9.04×10^5 g $\div$ 1.35×10^5 cm^3
7. **Calculate** the following, and round the answer to the correct number of significant figures.
   a. 54.2 cm^2 $\times$ 22 cm   b. 23 500 m $\div$ 89 s

Chapter Highlights

Before you begin, review the summaries of the key ideas of each section, found on pages 11, 19, and 26. The key vocabulary terms are listed on pages 4, 12, and 20.

UNDERSTANDING CONCEPTS

1. Which of the following is not included in physical science?
   a. physics
   b. chemistry
   c. astronomy
   d. zoology

2. What science deals most with energy and forces?
   a. biology
   b. physics
   c. botany
   d. agriculture

3. Using superconductors to build computers is an example of _____.
   a. technology
   b. applied biology
   c. pure science
   d. an experiment

4. A balance is a scientific tool used to measure _____.
   a. temperature
   b. time
   c. volume
   d. mass

5. Which of the following units is an SI base unit?
   a. liter
   b. cubic meter
   c. kilogram
   d. centimeter

6. The quantity 5.85×10^4 m is equivalent to _____.
   a. 5 850 000 m
   b. 58 500 m
   c. 5 840 m
   d. 0.000 585 m

7. Which of the following measurements has two significant figures?
   a. 0.003 55 g
   b. 500 mL
   c. 26.59 km
   d. 2.3 cm

8. The composition of the mixture of gases that makes up our air is best represented on what kind of graph?
   a. pie chart
   b. bar graph
   c. line graph
   d. variable graph

9. Making sure an experiment gives the results you expect is an example of _____.
   a. the scientific method
   b. critical thinking
   c. unscientific thinking
   d. objective observation

Using Vocabulary

10. Physical science was once defined as the science of the nonliving world. Write a paragraph explaining why that definition is no longer accepted. **WRITING SKILL**

11. Explain why the observation that the sun sets in the west could be called a scientific law.

12. The volume of a bottle has been measured to be 485 mL. Use the terms *significant figures, accuracy,* and *precision* to explain what this tells you about the way the volume was measured.

BUILDING MATH SKILLS

13. **Graphing**
    The graph at right shows the changes in temperature during a chemical reaction. Study the graph and answer the following questions:

    a. What was the highest temperature reached during the reaction?
    b. How many minutes passed before the highest temperature was reached?
    c. During what period of time was the temperature increasing at a steady rate?
    d. Which occurred more slowly, heating or cooling?

INTRODUCTION TO SCIENCE **27**

UNDERSTANDING CONCEPTS

1. d	6. b
2. b	7. d
3. a	8. a
4. d	9. c
5. c	

Using Vocabulary

10. Physical science is no longer the study of only the nonliving world. As knowledge has increased, scientists have learned that the discoveries in one area are applicable to another. For example, chemistry, a physical science, applies to living beings. This field of study is called biochemistry, which is partly life science and partly physical science.

11. It has been observed repeatedly, and it does not attempt to explain why the sun sets in the west.

12. Answers may vary. There are three significant figures, which means the volume was measured to the nearest milliliter. This is the precision of the measurement. The accuracy of the measurement is not known unless the measuring device has been compared to a standard, or has been calibrated.

BUILDING MATH SKILLS

13. a. 69 °C
    b. 3 minutes
    c. the first 3 minutes
    d. cooling

RESOURCE LINK
STUDY GUIDE

Assign students *Mixed Review Chapter 1.*

27

14. See pie chart below.

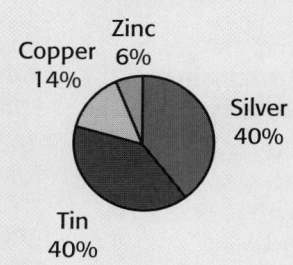

Zinc 6%
Copper 14%
Silver 40%
Tin 40%

15. a. 2.2×10^4 mg
   b. 5×10^{-3} km
   c. 6.59×10^7 m
   d. 3.7×10^{-6} kg
16. a. 2.6×10^{14}
   b. 6.42×10^{-7}
   c. 3.4×10^8 cm²
   d. 3.3×10^{-3} kg/cm³
17. a. 133 m²
   b. 210 L/min
   c. 0.0013 km²
   d. 105 m/s
   e. 7.4×10^7

THINKING CRITICALLY

18. On the back of the picture tube, there is a coating that lights up in different colors when the cathode rays hit it.
19. The law of gravitation states that objects fall to Earth; it even shows how to calculate the force. It does not explain why.
20. The type of fertilizer is the independent variable. Control factors are: the types of radishes, the amount of water, the amount of sunshine, etc. There are at least four things that could be used to determine the results: size, quantity, appearance, and taste.

14. Graphing Silver solder is a mixture of 40 percent silver, 40 percent tin, 14 percent copper, and 6 percent zinc. Draw a graph that shows the composition of silver solder.

15. Scientific Notation Write the following measurements in scientific notation:
   a. 22 000 mg   **c.** 65 900 000 m
   b. 0.005 km   **d.** 0.000 003 7 kg

16. Scientific Notation Do the following calculations, and write the answers in scientific notation:
   a. 37 000 000 × 7 100 000
   b. 0.000 312 ÷ 486
   c. 4.6×10^4 cm × 7.5 10^3 cm
   d. 8.3×10^6 kg ÷ 2.5×10^9 cm³

17. Significant Figures Do the following calculations, and write the answers with the correct number of significant figures:
   a. 15.75 m × 8.45 m
   b. 5650 L ÷ 27 min
   c. 0.0058 km × 0.228 km
   d. 6271 m ÷ 59.7 s
   e. $3.5 \times 10^3 \times 2.11 \times 10^4$

THINKING CRITICALLY

18. Applying Knowledge The picture tube in a television sends a beam of cathode rays to the screen. These are the same invisible rays that Roentgen was experimenting with when he discovered X rays. Use what you know about cathode rays to suggest what produces the light that forms the picture on the screen.

19. Creative Thinking At an air show, you are watching a group of skydivers when a friend says, "We learned in science class that things fall to Earth because of the law of gravitation." Tell what is wrong with your friend's statement, and explain your reasoning.

20. Applying Knowledge You have decided to test the effects of five different garden fertilizers by applying some of each to five separate rows of radishes. What is the independent variable? What factors should you control? How will you measure the results?

21. Interpreting and Communicating A person points to an empty, thick-walled glass bottle and says that the volume is 1200 cm³. Explain why the person's statement is not as clear as it should be.

DEVELOPING LIFE/WORK SKILLS

22. Interpreting Graphics A consumer magazine has tested several portable stereos and has rated them according to price and sound quality. The data is summarized in the bar graph shown below. Study the graph and answer the following questions:
   a. Which brand has the best sound?
   b. Which brand has the highest price?
   c. Which brand do you think has the best sound for the price?
   d. Do you think that sound quality corresponds to price?
   e. If you can spend as much as $150, which brand would you buy? Explain your answer.

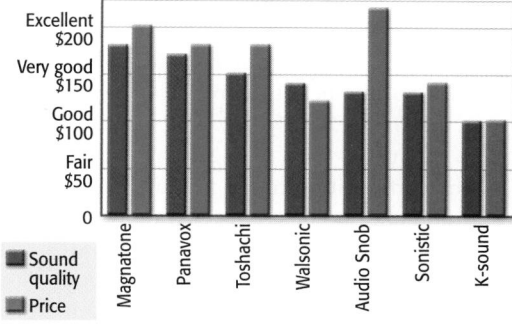

23. Making Decisions You have hired a painter to paint your room with a color that must be specially mixed. This color will be difficult to match if more has to be made. The painter tells you that the total length of your walls is 26 m and all walls are 2.5 m tall. You determine the area $(A = l \times w)$ to be painted is 65 m². The painter says that 1 gal of paint will cover about 30 m² and that you should order 2 gal of paint. List at least three questions you should ask the painter before you buy the paint.

24. Applying Technology Scientists discovered how to produce laser light in 1960. The substances in lasers emit an intense beam of light when electrical energy is applied. Find out what the word *laser* stands for, and list four examples of technologies that use lasers.

INTEGRATING CONCEPTS

25. Integrating Biology One of the most important discoveries involving X rays came in the early 1950s, when the work of Rosalind Franklin, a British scientist, provided evidence for the structure of a critical substance. Do library research to learn how Franklin used X rays and what her discovery was.

26. Concept Mapping Copy the unfinished concept map given below onto a sheet of paper. Complete the map by writing the correct word or phrase in the lettered box.

TOPIC: Studying the natural world
GO TO: www.scilinks.org
KEYWORD: HK1015

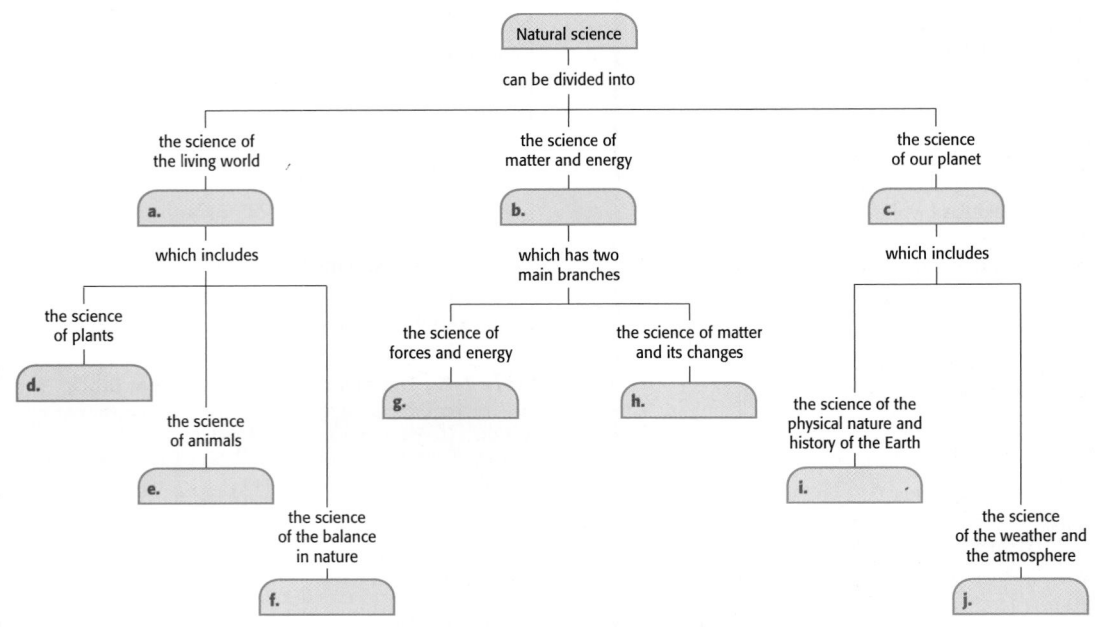

INTRODUCTION TO SCIENCE **29**

21. Is 1200 cm³ the volume of the glass used to make the container or the volume of the inside of the container or the volume that the container occupies? Is that 1200 with 4 significant figures or is that somewhere between 1100 and 1300 or between 1150 and 1250?

DEVELOPING LIFE/ WORK SKILLS

22. a. Magnatone
b. Audio Snob
c. Walsonic
d. No
e. Answers may vary. Walsonic costs about $125, and the sound quality is close to very good.

23. How precise is the measurement? How accurate is the measurement? What is he going to do if he runs out of paint?

24. LASER stands for **L**ight **A**mplification by **S**timulated **E**mission of **R**adiation. Some examples of laser technology are: CD players, eye surgery, fiber-optic communications, and laser-guided targeting (military, space exploration, surveying).

INTEGRATING CONCEPTS

25. Rosalind Franklin used X rays to try to determine the double-helical structure of DNA. Had she not died at 37, she would have probably shared the Nobel Prize with Watson and Crick, who used her data. Nobel Prize recipients must be living.

Answers continue on p. 33B.

Skill Builder Lab

Making Measurements

Introduction

The best way for students to become familiar with making measurements using laboratory tools and techniques is to handle the equipment while performing a lab. This lab can be used as an assessment of prior knowledge or as an introduction to the laboratory equipment used in making measurements.

Objectives

Students will:

▶ **Use** appropriate lab safety procedures.

▶ **Measure** mass, length, volume, and temperature.

▶ **Organize** data into tables and graphs.

Planning

Recommended Time: 1 lab period
Materials: *(for each lab group)*

▶ meterstick or metric ruler marked in centimeters and millimeters

▶ platform or triple-beam balance

▶ small beaker

▶ wall thermometer

▶ 25 mL graduated cylinder

▶ test tubes

▶ small block or box

▶ small rock or irregularly shaped object

▶ basketball, volleyball, or soccer ball

▶ string

▶ sodium chloride (table salt)

▶ sodium hydrogen carbonate (baking soda)
(**Note:** Some labs are equipped with test tubes having capacities of 35 mL or more. If the test tubes used are this size, a 50 mL graduated cylinder will be more appropriate than a 25 mL graduate.)

Skill Builder Lab

Introduction

How can you use laboratory tools to measure familiar objects?

Objectives

▶ **Measure** mass, length, volume, and temperature.

▶ **Organize** data into tables and graphs.

Materials

meterstick or metric ruler marked with centimeters and millimeters
platform or triple-beam balance
small beaker
wall thermometer
25 mL graduated cylinder
test tubes
small block or box
small rock or irregularly shaped object
basketball, volleyball, or soccer ball
string
sodium chloride (table salt)
sodium hydrogen carbonate (baking soda)

Safety Needs

safety goggles

Making Measurements

▶ Preparing for Your Experiment

1. In this laboratory exercise, you will use a meterstick to measure length, a graduated cylinder to measure volume, a balance to measure mass, and a thermometer to measure temperature. You will determine volume by liquid displacement.

▶ Measuring Temperature

2. At a convenient time during the lab, go to the wall thermometer and read the temperature. On the chalkboard, record your reading and the time at which you read the temperature. At the end of your lab measurements, you will make a graph of the temperature readings made by the class.

▶ Measuring Length

3. Measure the length, width, and height of a block or box in centimeters. Record the measurements in a table like **Table 1-6,** shown below. Using the equation below, calculate the volume of the block in cubic centimeters (cm^3), and write the volume in the table.

$$\text{Volume} = \text{length (cm)} \times \text{width (cm)} \times \text{height (cm)}$$
$$V = l \times w \times h$$
$$V = ? \ cm^3$$

4. Repeat the measurements twice more, recording the data in your table. Find the average of your measurements and the average of the volume you calculated.

Table 1-6 **Dimensions of a Rectangular Block**

	Length (cm)	Width (cm)	Height (cm)	Volume (cm³)
Trial 1				
Trial 2				
Trial 3				
Average				

SOLUTION/MATERIAL PREPARATION

1. Use salt and baking soda purchased through a supply company or a grocery store instead of reagent-grade sodium chloride and sodium hydrogen carbonate.

REQUIRED PRECAUTIONS

▶ Read all safety precautions, and discuss them with your students.

▶ Safety goggles and a lab apron must be worn at all times.

▶ Long hair and loose clothing must be tied back.

5. To measure the circumference of a ball, wrap a piece of string around the ball and mark the end point. Measure the length of the string using the meterstick or metric ruler. Record your measurements in a table like **Table 1-7,** shown below. Using a different piece of string each time, make two more measurements of the circumference of the ball, and record your data in the table.

6. Find the average of the three values and calculate the difference, if any, of each of your measurements from the average.

Table 1-7 **Circumference of a Ball**

	Circumference (cm)	Difference from average (cm)
Trial 1		
Trial 2		
Trial 3		
Average		—

▶ Measuring Mass

7. Place a small beaker on the balance, and measure the mass. Record the value in a table like **Table 1-8,** shown below. Measure to the nearest 0.01 g if you are using a triple-beam balance and to the nearest 0.1 g if you are using a platform balance.

8. Move the rider to a setting that will give a value 5 g more than the mass of the beaker. Add sodium chloride (table salt) to the beaker a little at a time until the balance just begins to swing. You now have about 5 g of salt in the beaker. Complete the measurement (to the nearest 0.01 or 0.1 g), and record the total mass of the beaker and the sodium chloride in your table. Subtract the mass of the beaker from the total mass to find the mass of the sodium chloride.

9. Repeat steps 7 and 8 two times, and record your data in your table. Find the averages of your measurements, as indicated in **Table 1-8.**

Table 1-8 **Mass of Sodium Chloride**

	Mass of beaker and sodium chloride (g)	Mass of beaker (g)	Mass of sodium chloride (g)
Trial 1			
Trial 2			
Trial 3			
Average			

Pre-lab
Teaching Tips

Use this lab as an opportunity to discuss significant figures and how they are estimated. Students are instructed to repeat the measuring process three times. This will help the students become familiar with the measuring process and it also allows students to better understand the concepts of accuracy, precision, bias, and reproducibility.

Show students how to measure volume properly by reading the bottom of the meniscus. The concept of parallax can also be introduced with a discussion or demonstration of how it affects measurement.

Procedure

▶Measuring Temperature

When students are ready to measure temperature, make sure they read the thermometer to the nearest 0.1°C or 0.5°C. Placing the thermometer near a window or a heating/cooling vent may produce greater variability.

Sample Data Table 1 Dimensions of a Rectangular Block			
	Length (cm)	Width (cm)	Height (cm)	Volume (cm³)
Trial 1	8.15	4.25	2.20	76.2
Trial 2	8.20	4.25	2.25	78.4
Trial 3	8.15	4.20	2.20	75.3
Average	8.17	4.23	2.22	76.7

Skill Builder Lab

Making Measurements

▶ Measuring Length

Students should be asked to vary the sequence of measurements of the block. The uncertainty or error in the measurement of each dimension of the block is multiplied when the volume of the block is calculated. The ball should be kept in a box or otherwise contained so that it is not a hazard. Remind students that while in the lab, everything used is a scientific tool, not a toy. Do not allow students to roll or throw the ball to each other.

▶ Measuring Mass

The differences in behavior between the granular salt and the powdery baking soda may cause differences in students' ability to measure 5 g of each solid.

▶ Measuring Volume

If the lab has large capacity test tubes, a 50 mL graduated cylinder will be appropriate instead of the 25 mL graduated cylinder. A demonstration or discussion of meniscus should be incorporated into this step.

▶ Measuring Volume by Liquid Displacement

Be sure to caution students to dry the cylinder so that it does not slip from their hands. If a small rock or mineral sample is used for liquid displacement, encourage students to tilt the cylinder and gently slide the object down the cylinder instead of dropping the rock in the cylinder.

10. Make a table like **Table 1-8,** substituting sodium hydrogen carbonate for sodium chloride. Repeat steps 7, 8, and 9 using sodium hydrogen carbonate (baking soda), and record your data.

▶ Measuring Volume

11. Fill one of the test tubes with tap water. Pour the water into a 25 mL graduated cylinder.
12. The top of the column of water in the graduated cylinder will have a downward curve. This curve is called a meniscus and is shown in the figure at right. Take your reading at the bottom of the meniscus. Record the capacity of the test tube in a table like **Table 1-9.** Measure the capacity of the other test tubes, and record their capacities. Find the average capacity of the three test tubes.

Table 1-9   **Liquid Volume**

	Volume (mL)
Test tube 1	
Test tube 2	
Test tube 3	
Average	

▶ Measuring Volume by Liquid Displacement

13. Pour about 10 mL of tap water into the 25 mL graduated cylinder. Record the volume as precisely as you can in a table like **Table 1-10,** shown below.

Table 1-10   **Volume of an Irregular Solid**

	Total volume (mL)	Volume of water only (mL)	Volume of object (mL)
Trial 1			
Trial 2			
Trial 3			
Average			

Sample Data Table 2 Circumference of a Ball		
	Circumference (cm)	Difference from average (cm)
Trial 1	34.7	−0.2
Trial 2	35.1	+0.2
Trial 3	34.9	0
Average	34.9	—

14. Gently drop a small object, such as a stone, into the graduated cylinder; be careful not to splash any water out of the cylinder. You may find it easier to tilt the cylinder slightly and let the object slide down the side. Measure the volume of the water and the object. Record the volume in your table. Determine the volume of the object by subtracting the volume of the water from the total volume.

▶ Analyzing Your Results

1. On a clean sheet of paper make a line graph of the temperatures that were measured with the wall thermometer over time. Did the temperature change during the class period? If it did, find the average temperature, and determine the largest rise and the largest drop.

▶ Defending Your Conclusions

2. On a clean sheet of paper make a bar graph using the data from the three calculations of the mass of sodium chloride. Indicate the average value of the three determinations by drawing a line that represents the average value across the individual bars. Do the same for the sodium hydrogen carbonate masses. Using the information in your graphs, determine whether you measured the sodium chloride or the sodium hydrogen carbonate more precisely.

3. Suppose one of your test tubes has a capacity of 23 mL. You need to use about 5 mL of a liquid. Describe how you could estimate 5 mL.

4. Why is it better to align the meterstick with the edge of the object at the 1 cm mark rather than at the end of the stick?

5. Why is it better to place the meterstick on edge with the scale resting on the surface being measured than on the flat side?

6. Why do you think it is better to measure the circumference of the ball using string than to use a flexible metal measuring tape?

Post-Lab

▶ Disposal

The salt and soda can be rinsed down the sink with water.

▶ Analyzing Your Results

1. See page 33B. Students' graphs should accurately represent their given data. It is unlikely that temperature changes over a few degrees will be experienced during the lab period.

▶ Defending Your Conclusions

2. See page 33B. The precision of the measurements for salt and baking soda may vary because of the behavior of the solids. This is an opportunity to reinforce the difference between precision and accuracy.

3. Answers may vary. Estimating the length of the test tube and dividing it into five equal parts, then filling it $\frac{1}{5}$ full is one way.

4. Metersticks may get damaged at the ends and not be accurate.

5. Placing the meterstick on edge minimizes error due to parallax.

6. The circumference is more easily measured with the string because it makes contact all around the ball. Most flexible metal tapes do not conform to the surface well enough to make contact and stay in place easily.

Continue on p. 33A.

RESOURCE LINK
DATASHEETS

Have students use *Datasheet 1.2: Skill Builder Lab—Making Measurements* to record their results.

Sample Data Table 3 Mass of Sodium Chloride			
	Mass of beaker and sodium chloride (g)	Mass of beaker (g)	Mass of sodium chloride (g)
Trial 1	60.10	55.20	4.90
Trial 2	59.90	55.20	4.70
Trial 3	60.45	55.20	5.25
Average	60.15	55.20	4.95

Skill Builder Lab from page 33
Making Measurements

Sample Data Table 4 Mass of Sodium Hydrogen Carbonate

	Mass of beaker and sodium hydrogen carbonate (g)	Mass of beaker (g)	Mass of sodium hydrogen carbonate (g)
Trial 1	60.35	55.20	5.15
Trial 2	60.20	55.20	5.00
Trial 3	59.90	55.20	4.70
Average	60.15	55.20	4.95

Sample Data Table 5 Liquid Volume

	Volume (mL)
Test Tube 1	16.5
Test Tube 2	15.8
Test Tube 3	16.0
Average	16.1

Sample Data Table 6 Volume of an Irregular Solid

	Total volume (mL)	Volume of water only (mL)	Volume of object (mL)
Trial 1	17.5	10.5	7.0
Trial 2	14.5	9.0	5.5
Trial 3	21.5	10.0	11.5
Average	17.8	9.8	8.0

Skill Builder Lab from page 33
Making Measurements

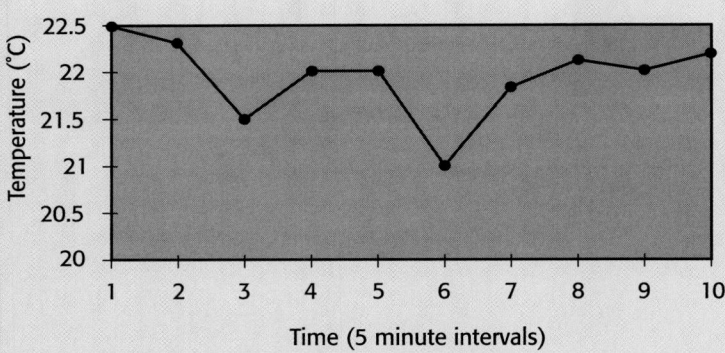

Temperature Readings

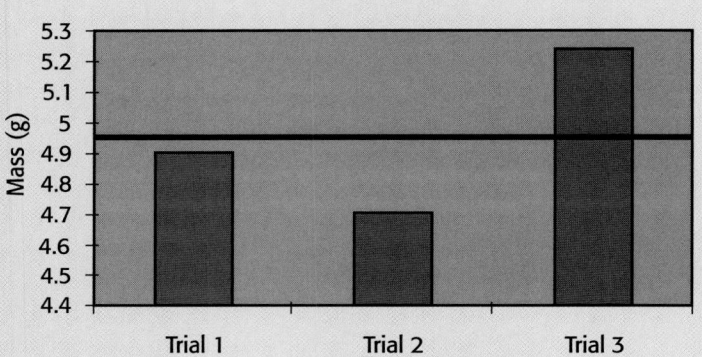

Mass of Sodium Chloride

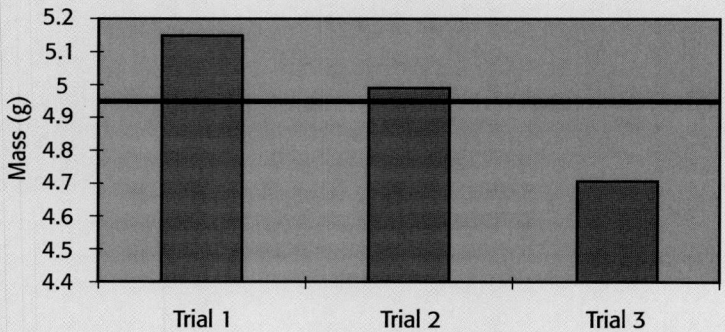

Mass of Sodium Hydrogen Carbonate

Answers from page 29

INTEGRATING CONCEPTS

26. a. life science (or biology)
  b. physical science
  c. Earth science
  d. botany
  e. zoology
  f. ecology
  g. physics
  h. chemistry
  i. geology
  j. meteorology

UNIT
1

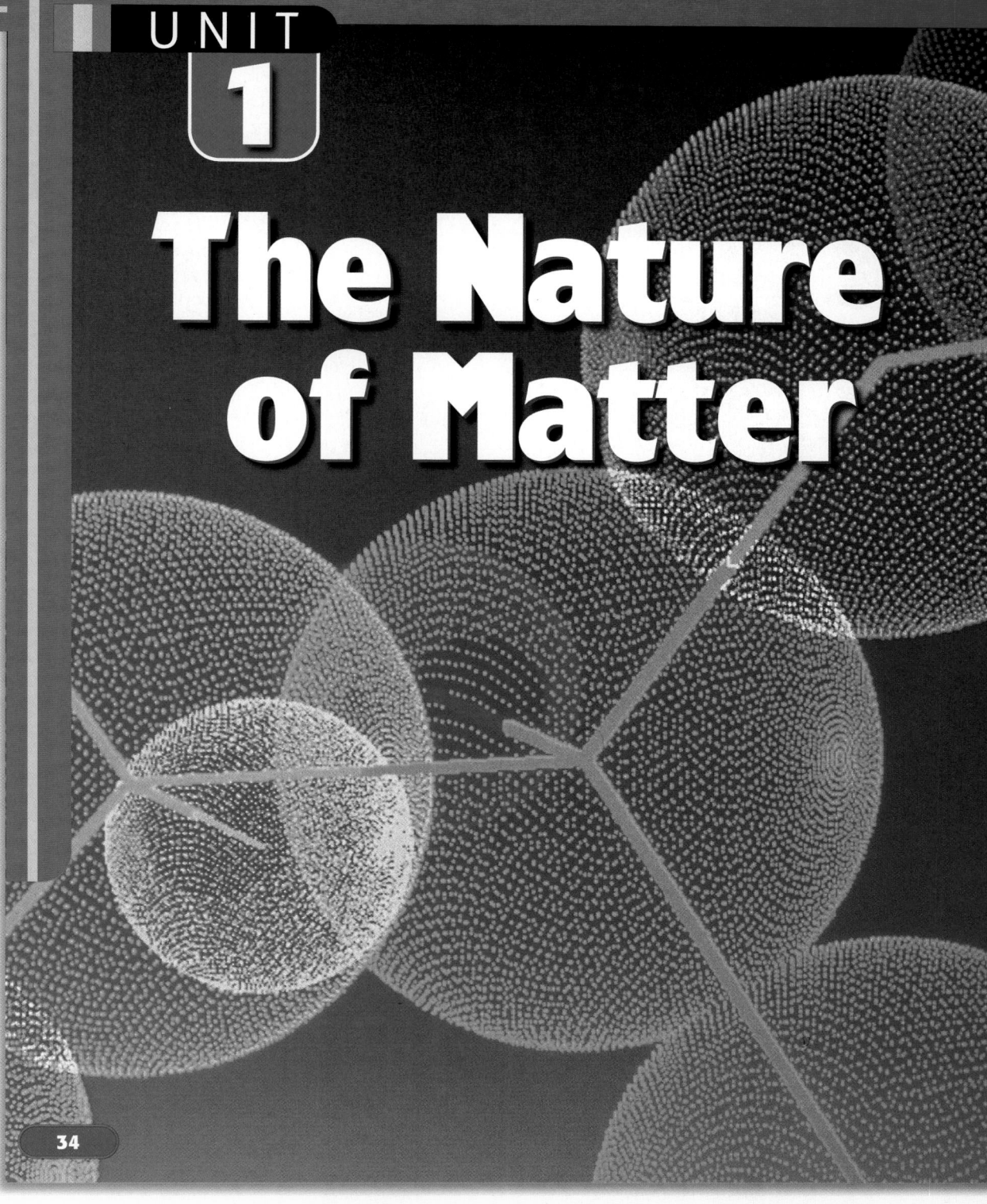

The Nature of Matter

READING **SKILL** BUILDER

Brainstorming
Write the words *matter* and *atom* on the chalkboard. Ask students to list words and phrases that apply to both terms or that are exclusive to one term or the other. Students should generally recognize that there are different terms involved, depending upon whether atomic or small-scale properties are at issue or whether large-scale properties of matter are being discussed.

MISCONCEPTION

Atomic Theory **ALERT**
Many students do not yet fully grasp the idea that all matter—whether solid, liquid, or gas—is made of atoms and that all atoms contain the same few particles. Another common misconception is that living things are not made of atoms.

SKILL BUILDER

Interpreting Visuals Ask students to describe what is portrayed in the picture. While a few may realize that the illustration shows atoms, they may not realize that this is actually a computer-generated model of a substance. The spherical shapes represent regions of electron density around atoms. The wirelike items indicate the connections and bonds between atoms.

Like all models, this one exaggerates or changes certain features of reality to help make it easier to understand. For example, representing different atoms with different colors can make the constituents of a substance easier to understand. Showing the atomic "spheres" as being transparent makes it easier to see different parts of the structure. Using wirelike images for bonds helps make structure and geometry easier to spot.

Be certain that students understand that real atoms are not colored, do not look like hollow spheres, and do not bond with wirelike links.

35

CHAPTER 2

Matter

Annotated Descriptions of the Correlated National Science Standards

The following descriptions summarize the National Science Standards that specially relate to Chapter 2. For the full text of the Standards, see p. 40T.

SECTION 2.1
What Is Matter?
Physical Science
PS 2d
Unifying Concepts and Processes
UCP 1
Science and Technology
ST 2

SECTION 2.2
Matter and Energy
Physical Science
PS 2d, 2e, 5a, 5c
Unifying Concepts and Processes
UCP 1, 2, 5

SECTION 2.3
Properties of Matter
Science as Inquiry
SAI 1

Cross-Discipline Teaching RESOURCES

Cross-Discipline Teaching, ATE p. 36
Fine Arts   Language Arts
Mathematics   Social Studies

Integration Enrichment Resources
Biology, PE and **ATE** p. 41
   IE 2.1 *What's Special About Indigo?*
Science and the Consumer, PE and **ATE** p. 43
   IE 2.2 *Is Dry Cleaning Dangerous?*
Earth Science, PE and **ATE** p. 44
   IE 2.3 *Uses of Pumice*
Space Science, PE and **ATE** p. 51
   IE 2.4 *Our Changing Universe*
Real World Applications, PE and **ATE** p. 58
   IE 2.5 *Choosing Materials for Bicycle Frames*

Additional Integration Enrichment Worksheets
   IE 2.6 Language Arts   **IE 2.7** Physics
   IE 2.8 Environmental Science

Use the Planning Guide on the next page to help you organize your lessons.

MATH AND COMPUTER RESOURCES

Chapter 2	Math Skills	Assess	Media/Computer Skills
Section 2.1	**ATE Cross-Discipline Teaching,** p. 36 **BS Worksheet 3.1:** Ratios and Proportions **BS Worksheet 6.3:** Making and Interpreting Bar and Pie Graphs		■ Section 2.1 💿 *DISC ONE, MODULE 1* States of Matter/Classes of Matter
Section 2.2	**BS Worksheet 5.5:** Rearranging Algebraic Equations		■ Section 2.2 **PE Section Review** 7, p. 52
Section 2.3	**PE Math Skills** Density, p. 56 **ATE Additional Examples** p. 56	**PE Practice,** p. 56 **PE Problem Bank,** p. 694, 21–25 **MS** Worksheet 5	■ Section 2.3 **PE Inquiry Lab,** p. 57 **CNN. Presents Chemistry Connections Segment 18** Chemical Separation Techniques for Plastics **CRT** Worksheet 18

PE Pupil's Edition   **ATE** Annotated Teacher's Edition   **MS** Math Skills   **BS** Basic Skills
IE Integration Enrichment   ■ Guided Reading Audio   **CRT** Critical Thinking

PHYSICAL SCIENCE INTERACTIVE TUTOR

READING SKILL BUILDER

The following activities found in the Annotated Teacher's Edition provide techniques for developing useful reading strategies to increase your students' reading comprehension skills.

Section 2.1   **Brainstorming,** p. 36
              K-W-L, p. 38

Section 2.2   **Reading Organizer,** p. 45

Section 2.3   **Discussion,** p. 53

Smithsonian Institution®
Visit www.si.edu/hrw for additional online resources.

Spanish Resources

The following resources are made available for students who speak Spanish as their first language.

**Spanish Resources
Guided Reading Audio** CD-ROM
Chapter 2

Spanish Glossary
Chapter 2

Matter

CLASSROOM RESOURCES		
FOCUS	**TEACH**	**HANDS-ON**

Section 2.1 What Is Matter?

BLOCK 1
45 minutes

ATE RSB Brainstorming, p. 36 **ATE** Focus Activities 1, 2, p. 37 **ATE RSB** K-W-L, p. 38 **PE** Matter, Atoms, and Elements, pp. 38–41 ★ Focus Transparency LT 4 **ATE Demo 1** Comparing Properties, p. 38	**ATE Skill Builder** Interpreting Visuals, pp. 37, 40, 41 Vocabulary, p. 39 Graphs, p. 39	

BLOCK 2
45 minutes

PE Pure Substances and Mixtures, pp. 41–44	**ATE Skill Builder** Vocabulary, p. 42 **ATE Graphic Organizer** Classifying Matter, p. 42	**IE** Worksheet 2.1 **PE** Science and the Consumer *Dry Cleaning: How Are Stains Dissolved?* p. 43 **IE** Worksheets 2.2, 2.3, 2.6

Section 2.2: Matter and Energy

BLOCK 3
45 minutes

ATE RSB Reading Organizer, p. 45 **ATE Demo 2** Moving Gas Particles, p. 45 **PE** Kinetic Theory, pp. 45–48 ★ Focus Transparency LT 5	**ATE Skill Builder** Interpreting Visuals, p. 46 **BLM** 5 Models of Water **BLM** 6 Chemical Formula **TT** 4 States of Matter **TT** 5 Gas Pressure	**PE** Quick Activity *Kinetic Theory,* p. 48 **DS** 2.1 **IE** Worksheet 2.7

BLOCK 4
45 minutes

PE Energy's Role, pp. 48–52	**ATE Skill Builder** Interpreting Visuals, p. 49 **BLM** 7 Changes of State **TT** 6 Conservation of Mass	**IE** Worksheet 2.4

Section 2.3: Properties of Matter

BLOCK 5
45 minutes

ATE RSB Discussion, p. 53 **ATE Demo 3** Properties of Iron, p. 53 **ATE Demo 4** Temperature and Density, p. 54 **ATE Demo 5** Soft Drink Densities, p. 57 **PE** Chemical and Physical Properties, pp. 53–57 ★ Focus Transparency LT 6	**ATE Skill Builder** Diagrams, p. 55	**PE** Inquiry Lab *How are the mass and volume of a substance related?* p. 57 **DS** 2.2 **LE 2** *Comparing the Buoyancy of Different Objects* **DS** 2.4

BLOCK 6
45 minutes

ATE Demo 6 Chemical Change, p. 58 **PE** Chemical and Physical Changes, pp. 58–60		**PE** Real World Applications *Choosing Materials,* p. 58 **IE** Worksheets 2.5, 2.8 **PE** Design Your Own Lab *Testing the Conservation of Mass,* p. 64 **DS** 2.3

CLASSROOM RESOURCES

HOMEWORK	ASSESS
PE Section Review 1–3, p. 44 **Chapter 2 Review,** p. 61, items 1–3	**SG** Chapter 2 Pretest
PE Section Review 4–8, p. 44 **Chapter 2 Review,** p. 61, items 4–5	**ATE** *ALTERNATIVE ASSESSMENT,* Making Models, p. 41 **SG** Section 2.1
PE Section Review 3, 5, 8, p. 52 **Chapter 2 Review,** p. 61, item 6	**ATE** *ALTERNATIVE ASSESSMENT,* Pressure, p. 47
PE Section Review 1–2, 4, 6–7, p. 52 **Chapter 2 Review,** p. 61, items 8, 11, 14–15	**SG** Section 2.2
PE Section Review 1–2, 6–7, p. 60 **Chapter 2 Review,** p. 61, items 7, 13, 16–21	
PE Section Review 3–5, p. 60 **Chapter 2 Review,** p. 61, items 9–10, 12	**ATE** *ALTERNATIVE ASSESSMENT,* Changes in Matter, p. 59 **ATE** *ALTERNATIVE ASSESSMENT,* Physical Change, p. 60 **SG** Section 2.3

BLOCK 7

Chapter 2 Review
Thinking Critically 22–24, p. 62
Developing Life/Work Skills 25–27, p. 63
Integrating Concepts 28–30, p. 63
SG Chapter 2 Mixed Review

BLOCK 8

Chapter Tests
Holt Science Spectrum: A Physical Approach
Chapter 2 Test

One-Stop Planner CD-ROM with Test Generator
Holt Science Spectrum Test Generator
FOR MACINTOSH AND WINDOWS
Chapter 2

Teaching Resources
Scoring Rubrics and assignment evaluation checklist.

---

internet connect

National Science Teachers Association
Online Resources:
www.scilinks.org
The following *sci*LINKS Internet resources can be found in the student text for this chapter.

Page 37
TOPIC: Glass
KEYWORD: HK1021

Page 43
TOPIC: Dry cleaning
KEYWORD: HK1022

Page 52
TOPIC: States of matter
KEYWORD: HK1023

Page 58
TOPIC: Chemical and physical changes
KEYWORD: HK1024

Page 63
TOPIC: Kinetic theory
KEYWORD: HK1025

CNN fyi.com   www.cnnfyi.com

Visit this site for coverage of current events and related classroom resources.

PE Pupil's Edition   **ATE** Teacher's Edition
RSB Reading Skill Builder   **DS** Datasheets
IE Integrated Enrichment   **SG** Study Guide
LE Laboratory Experiments
TT Teaching Transparencies   **BLM** Blackline Masters
★ Lesson Focus Transparency

CHAPTER 2

Matter

CHAPTER 2

Tapping Prior Knowledge

Be sure students understand the following concepts:

Chapter 1
Scientific laws, units of measurement, using significant figures

---

READING SKILL BUILDER

Brainstorming Have students read the definitions of *chemistry* and *matter*. Make two lists on the chalkboard, one labeled "matter" and one labeled "changes." Have students brainstorm to come up with a list of things they think are matter, and then have them list changes that they have observed each type of matter undergo.

Chapter Preview

2.1 What Is Matter?
Matter
Pure Substance or Mixture?

2.2 Matter and Energy
Kinetic Theory
Energy's Role

2.3 Properties of Matter
Chemical and Physical Properties
Chemical and Physical Changes

RESOURCE LINK

STUDY GUIDE

Assign students *Pretest Chapter 2 Matter* before beginning Section 2.1.

CROSS-DISCIPLINE TEACHING

Fine Arts Have students observe changes in state that occur as they work with various media.

Mathematics Review with students how to solve for a variable in a formula. Work through several examples for formulas, such as the area formula, $A = l \times w$, and show students how the same principles apply to the formula for density.

Language Arts Have students classify changes that occur in a story they are reading in their language arts class.

Social Studies Discuss how different elements have affected the materials in which they have been used throughout history.

Focus ACTIVITY

Background Ordinary sand is poured into pots with some finely ground limestone and a powder called soda ash. Then the mixture is heated to about 1500°C, and the sand begins to become transparent and flow like honey.

A glass blower dips a hollow iron blowpipe into the red-hot mixture. A gob of molten glass no larger than your hand sticks to the end of the blowpipe. Turning the sticky fluid mass on the pipe and blowing into the tube, the glass blower makes a hollow bulb.

The glass blower can pull, twist, and blow the soft bulb into many different shapes. The mass is reheated to stay soft until the glass blower achieves the desired final shape. Finally, the ball is broken off the tube. The original powder has become a fragile, clear glass object.

Activity 1 Visit a glass company that replaces automobile glass and window glass. Find out how many different types of glass the company has and what makes each type different.

Activity 2 Go to your local recycling center to find out how much glass and what kind of glass is recycled in your community. Why do you think glass is a popular material to recycle?

internetconnect

SC*i*LINKS.
NSTA

TOPIC: Glass
GO TO: www.scilinks.org
KEYWORD: HK1021

Glass changes from a solid to a liquid and back to a solid through heating and cooling.

Focus ACTIVITY

Background Students are probably aware that glass can be recycled. Pieces of glass that are to be recycled are known as cullet and are separated according to color and type of glass.

Activity 1 Glass used in automobiles or other windows is usually one of two types, based on its use. Some glass is laminated and consists of a layer of plastic between two layers of glass. This glass resists breaking and is used in windshields. Tempered glass goes through an additional firing process. Tempered glass breaks into chunks that have few sharp edges when broken. It is used in all car windows except for the windshield.

Activity 2 Although all glass is theoretically recyclable, students will probably discover that not all glass is accepted for recycling at most recycling centers. Often only clean bottles are accepted, and they must be separated by color. Recycling glass saves energy as well as raw materials.

|SKILL BUILDER

Interpreting Visuals Have students examine the glass sculpture shown in the photo. Ask them to describe other items that are made from glass but look different from the glass. Lead students to infer that even though the glass differs in appearance, all the items were formed by changing a solid to a liquid, shaping the liquid, and allowing the liquid to solidify.

Scheduling

Refer to pp. 36A–36D for lecture, classwork, and assignment options for Section 2.1.

★ Lesson Focus

Use transparency *LT 4* to prepare students for this section.

READING SKILL BUILDER *K-W-L* Students probably have preconceptions about what chemistry is. Have them list what they know about chemistry. Then have them list what they want to know about it. After they have completed Section 2.1, have them look at their list and write down what they have learned about chemistry. If they still have questions, have them research these questions using other sources.

What Is Matter?

▶ **KEY TERMS**

chemistry
matter
element
atom
compound
molecule
chemical formula
pure substance
mixture
miscible
immiscible

▶ **OBJECTIVES**

▶ Explain the relationship between matter, atoms, and elements.

▶ Distinguish between elements and compounds.

▶ Interpret and write some common chemical formulas.

▶ Categorize materials as pure substances or mixtures.

▶ **chemistry** the study of matter and how it changes

Making glass, as shown in **Figure 2-1,** involves changing the raw materials sand, limestone, and soda ash into a different substance. This is what **chemistry** is all about: what things are made of and how things change. Everything you use daily, from soap to food to glue, you choose because of chemistry—either because of what it is made of or how it changes.

Glass is used as a building material because its properties of being transparent, solid, and waterproof match the needs we have for windows. The properties of sand, on the other hand, do not match these needs. Chemistry keeps the choices among so many materials from being too confusing because it helps you recognize how the differences in material properties relate to what the materials are made of.

Matter

▶ **matter** anything that has mass and occupies space

You are made of **matter.** This book is also matter. All the materials you can hold or touch are matter. The air you are breathing is matter, even though you can't see it. Light, sound, and electricity are not matter. Unlike air, they have no mass or volume.

Figure 2-1
Glass blowers have been practicing their craft with few changes for more than 2000 years.

DEMONSTRATION 1 SCIENCE AND THE CONSUMER

Comparing Properties

Time: Approximately 5 minutes
Materials: charcoal; 2 vials with lids, one labeled "hydrogen" and one labeled "oxygen"; granulated sugar

Show students the four substances, then tell them that sugar is made from the other three substances.

Analysis

1. How is sugar like the substances that form it? *(Few similarities exist.)*

2. How is it different? *(Answers could include differences in appearance, state, and solubility.)*

3. Do you think sugar would form if you mixed charcoal, oxygen, and hydrogen together? *(No.)*

Atoms are matter

Wood is matter. Because it is fairly rigid and lightweight, wood is a good choice for furniture and buildings. When wood gets hot enough, it chars—its surface turns black. The wood surface breaks down to form another kind of material with different properties, carbon. No chemical reactions of the carbon in the charred residue will cause the carbon to decompose. Carbon is an **element,** and elements are made of **atoms.** An image of some specially arranged iron atoms is shown in **Figure 2-2.**

Diamonds are made of atoms of the element carbon. The shiny foil wrapped around a baked potato is made of atoms of the element aluminum. The elements that are most abundant on Earth and most abundant in the human body are shown in **Figure 2-3.** Each element also has a one- or two-letter symbol used worldwide to designate it. For example, carbon is C, iron is Fe, copper is Cu, and aluminum is Al. Each of the more than 110 elements that we now know is unique and behaves differently from the rest.

Two or more elements combine chemically to make a compound

Many familiar substances, such as aluminum and iron, are elements. Nylon is another familiar substance, but it is not an element. Nylon is a **compound.** The basic unit that makes up nylon contains carbon, hydrogen, nitrogen, and oxygen atoms, but each strand actually contains thousands of these units linked together.

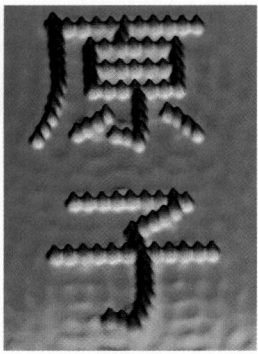

Figure 2-2
This scanning tunneling microscope image shows iron atoms (red) on copper atoms (blue).

▶ **element** a substance that cannot be broken down into simpler substances

▶ **atom** the smallest particle that has the properties of an element

▶ **compound** a substance made of atoms of more than one element bound together

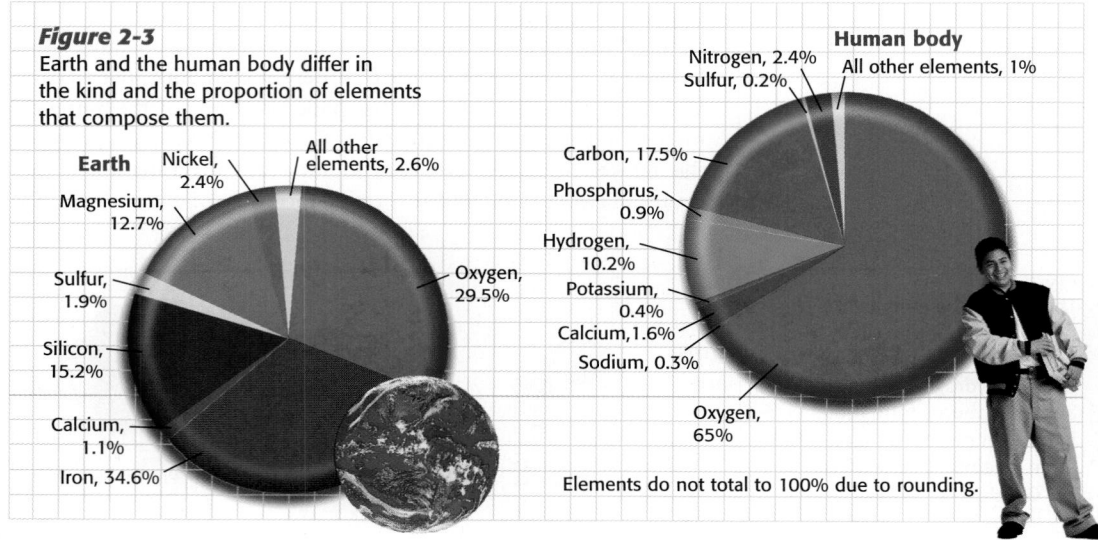

Figure 2-3
Earth and the human body differ in the kind and the proportion of elements that compose them.

Earth
Nickel, 2.4%
All other elements, 2.6%
Magnesium, 12.7%
Sulfur, 1.9%
Silicon, 15.2%
Calcium, 1.1%
Iron, 34.6%
Oxygen, 29.5%

Human body
Nitrogen, 2.4%
Sulfur, 0.2%
All other elements, 1%
Carbon, 17.5%
Phosphorus, 0.9%
Hydrogen, 10.2%
Potassium, 0.4%
Calcium, 1.6%
Sodium, 0.3%
Oxygen, 65%

Elements do not total to 100% due to rounding.

MATTER **39**

What Is Matter?

SKILL BUILDER

Interpreting Vocabulary
Show students the derivation of the word *atom* from its Greek roots, and ask them what idea about matter is conveyed by that meaning.

　　a-: not　　*tomos:* cutting

Literal meaning: *indivisible.* The idea, which also originated in ancient Greece, is that matter can be subdivided only as small as an elemental particle: the atom.

SKILL BUILDER

Interpreting Graphs Have students use the information from the graphs in **Figure 2-3** to make tables that show the relative percentages of the elements listed that are present on Earth and in the human body.

MISCONCEPTION　**ALERT**

Elements Students might think that the elements shown in **Figure 2-3** always occur as free elements. Explain that most of the elements listed exist on Earth or in the human body as parts of compounds.

Historical Perspective

In 1750, only 16 elements were known—antimony, arsenic, bismuth, carbon, cobalt, copper, gold, iron, lead, mercury, phosphorus, platinum, silver, sulfur, tin, and zinc. The next element to be identified was nickel, in 1751. Notice that none of the common gaseous elements, such as hydrogen, oxygen, and nitrogen, nor any of the halogens, had yet been identified, partly because scientists at that time were not clear about the nature of gases.

Writing formulas and naming compounds will be discussed in more detail in Chapter 4.

MISCONCEPTION ALERT

Compound Names
Students may misinterpret names of compounds when the names contain Roman numerals. They may think the numeral indicates the number of atoms of that element in the compound. Tell students that the Roman numeral indicates how many electrons from the associated atom are involved in forming the compound. For example, three electrons from each iron atom are involved in forming the compound iron(III) oxide.

Teaching Tip

Definite Ratios If students do not understand what is meant by "combine in the same proportions," illustrate this idea with substances whose formulas are already familiar to students. All water exists in a ratio represented by the formula H_2O, two atoms of hydrogen to every one atom of oxygen. It is a definite ratio because all water, regardless of its source, consists of these elements in the same ratio.

SKILL BUILDER

Interpreting Visuals A molecule may consist of two or more atoms of different elements or atoms of the same element. Molecular elements other than those mentioned in the student copy and **Figure 2-5** exist. Other examples include ozone, O_3, and several different molecules formed from carbon.

Figure 2-4
A water molecule can be represented as a formula, in physical models, or on a computer.

▶ **molecule** the smallest unit of a substance that exhibits all of the properties characteristic of that substance

Every compound is unique and is different from the elements it contains. For example, the elements hydrogen, oxygen, and nitrogen occur in nature as colorless gases. Yet when they combine with carbon to form nylon, the strands of nylon are a flexible solid.

Each unit of iron(III) oxide, which we see often as rust, is made of two atoms of iron and three atoms of oxygen. When elements combine to make a specific compound, the elements always combine in the same proportions. Iron(III) oxide always has two parts of iron for every three parts of oxygen.

A molecule acts as a unit

Atoms can join together to make millions of different **molecules** just as letters of the alphabet combine to form different words. A molecular substance you are familiar with is water. A water molecule is made of two hydrogen atoms and one oxygen atom, as shown in **Figure 2-4.**

When oxygen and hydrogen form a molecule of water, the atoms combine and act as a unit. That is what a molecule is—the smallest unit of a substance that behaves like the substance. Most molecules are made of atoms of different elements, just as water is. But a molecule also may be made of atoms of the same element, such as those in **Figure 2-5.** Besides the elements shown in the figure, fluorine, nitrogen, iodine, and bromine form molecules of two atoms. Sulfur forms a molecule of eight atoms, S_8.

Figure 2-5
The atoms of elements like neon, Ne, are found singly in nature. Other elements like oxygen, hydrogen, chlorine, and phosphorus form molecules with more than one atom. Their unit molecules are O_2, H_2, Cl_2, and P_4.

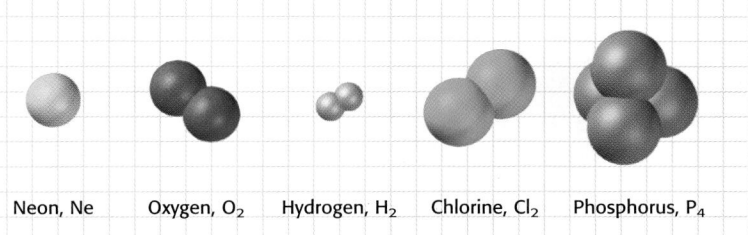

Neon, Ne   Oxygen, O_2 Hydrogen, H_2 Chlorine, Cl_2 Phosphorus, P_4

Chemical formulas represent compounds and molecules

Indigo is the dye originally used to turn jeans blue. The **chemical formula** for a molecule of indigo, $C_{16}H_{10}N_2O_2$, is shown in **Figure 2-6.** The chemical formula shows how many atoms of each element are in the basic unit of a substance. When the chemical formula is written, the number of atoms of each element in the basic unit is written after the element's symbol as a *subscript*. No subscript number is used if only one atom of an element is present, so the chemical formula for carbon dioxide is CO_2, not C_1O_2.

Numbers placed in front of the chemical formula show the number of molecules. For example, three molecules of table sugar are written as $3C_{12}H_{22}O_{11}$. Each molecule of the sugar contains 12 carbon atoms, 22 hydrogen atoms, and 11 oxygen atoms.

Pure Substance or Mixture?

When people use the word *pure*, they usually mean "not mixed with anything else." "Pure grape juice" contains only the juice of grapes, with nothing added or taken away. In chemistry, the word *pure* means more than this. A **pure substance** is matter with a fixed composition and definite properties.

Grape juice isn't a pure substance. It is a **mixture** of many different pure substances, such as water, sugars, acids, and vitamins. The composition of grape juice is not fixed; it can have different amounts of water or sugar or other compounds. Elements and compounds are pure substances, but mixtures are not. Practically all of the things we eat are mixtures. The air we breathe is mainly a mixture of nitrogen and oxygen.

A mixture like grape juice can be separated. The water in grape juice can evaporate, leaving the sugar, acids, and other compounds. Yet the water molecules are not changed by evaporation. A pure substance, like water, cannot be broken down by physical changes.

Pure substances blended together make mixtures

While a compound is different from the elements that make it, a mixture may have some properties similar to the pure substances that make it. Although you can't see the different substances in grape juice, the mixture has chemical and physical properties in common with its components. For example, grape juice is wet like the water and sweet like the sugar that is in it.

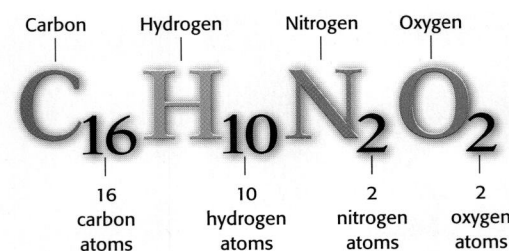

Carbon Hydrogen Nitrogen Oxygen

$$C_{16}H_{10}N_2O_2$$

| 16 carbon atoms | 10 hydrogen atoms | 2 nitrogen atoms | 2 oxygen atoms |

Figure 2-6
The chemical formula for a molecule of indigo shows that it is made of four elements and 30 atoms.

▶ **chemical formula** the chemical symbols and numbers indicating the atoms contained in the basic unit of a substance

▶ **pure substance** any matter that has a fixed composition and definite properties

▶ **mixture** a combination of more than one pure substance

INTEGRATING

BIOLOGY
Indigo is a natural plant dye made from members of the genus *Indigofera,* which is in the pea family. Before synthetic dyes were developed, indigo was widely grown in the East Indies, in India, and in the Americas. Most indigo species are shrubs 1 to 2 m in height. Leaves and branches of the plants are fermented to yield a paste, which is formed into blocks and then finely ground. The blue color develops as the material is exposed to air.

|SKILL| BUILDER

Interpreting Visuals As a class, use the formula in **Figure 2-6** to calculate the total number of atoms present. Provide students with other formulas, and have them calculate the total number of atoms in each. Examples of formulas might include that of caffeine, $C_8H_{10}N_4O_2$ *(24 atoms)* and that of rubbing alcohol, C_3H_8O *(12 atoms).*

Resources Blackline Master 6 shows this visual.

INTEGRATING

BIOLOGY The use of natural indigo dye decreased dramatically with its successful synthesis. The German chemist Adolf von Baeyer (1835–1917) analyzed indigo. While he was the first to accomplish the synthesis of indigo, others developed the methods used for its commercial production.

Resources Assign students worksheet *2.1: Integrating Biology—What's Special about Indigo?* in the **Integration Enrichment Resources** ancillary.

ALTERNATIVE ASSESSMENT

Making Models

Provide students with several ball-and-stick models of compounds. Model kits or gumdrops and toothpicks can be used. (Remind students to never taste anything in a laboratory.) Be sure that different-colored balls represent different elements. Have students use the models to write formulas for each of the compounds. Students probably will not list the elements in the proper order in the compound, but accept any formula that indicates the correct number of each type of atom present.

RESOURCE LINK
BASIC SKILLS

Assign students worksheet *3.1: Ratios and Proportions* to help them understand how these concepts apply to compounds.

Teaching Tip

Vocabulary *Solution* and *homogeneous mixture* are synonymous. Homogeneous mixtures are mixed intimately, which means they are mixed completely, all the way down to their most fundamental particles—atoms, molecules, or ions.

LINKING CHAPTERS

Solutions are studied in detail in Chapter 6.

MISCONCEPTION

Miscibility Be sure students understand that *miscible* and *immiscible* refer to liquids only. For example, flour and water don't mix, but they would not be considered immiscible because flour is not a liquid.

ALERT

SKILL BUILDER

Interpreting Vocabulary
The words *homogeneous* and *heterogeneous* have the following Greek prefixes:

> *homo-:* same
> *hetero-:* different

So a homogeneous mixture is one that appears the same throughout, and a heterogeneous mixture is one in which differences can be seen.

Figure 2-7

A Flour is suspended in water. | B Salt dissolves in water.

▶ **miscible** describes two or more liquids that are able to dissolve into each other in various proportions

▶ **immiscible** describes two or more liquids that do not mix into each other

Mixtures are classified by how thoroughly the substances mix

Some mixtures are made by putting solids and liquids together. In **Figure 2-7,** two white powdery solids, flour and salt, are each mixed with water. Despite the physical similarities of these solids, the mixtures they form with water are very different.

The flour doesn't mix well with the water, yielding a cloudy white mixture. You can see that flour does not dissolve in water. A mixture of flour and water is called a *heterogeneous mixture* because the substances aren't uniformly mixed.

The salt-and-water mixture looks very different from the flour-and-water mixture. You cannot see the salt, and the mixture is clear. That's because salt dissolves in water. Even if you leave the mixture for a long time, the salt will not settle out. Salt and water yield a *homogeneous mixture* because the mixing occurs between the individual units and is the same throughout.

Gasoline is a liquid mixture—a homogeneous mixture of at least 100 compounds in various quantities. Because the compounds are **miscible,** gasoline looks like a pure substance even though it isn't.

If you shake a mixture of oil and water, the water will settle out after a while. Oil and water form a heterogeneous mixture. Because oil and water are **immiscible,** you can see two layers in the mixture. **Figure 2-8** shows examples of liquid mixtures.

Figure 2-8 **Examples of Miscible and Immiscible Liquids**

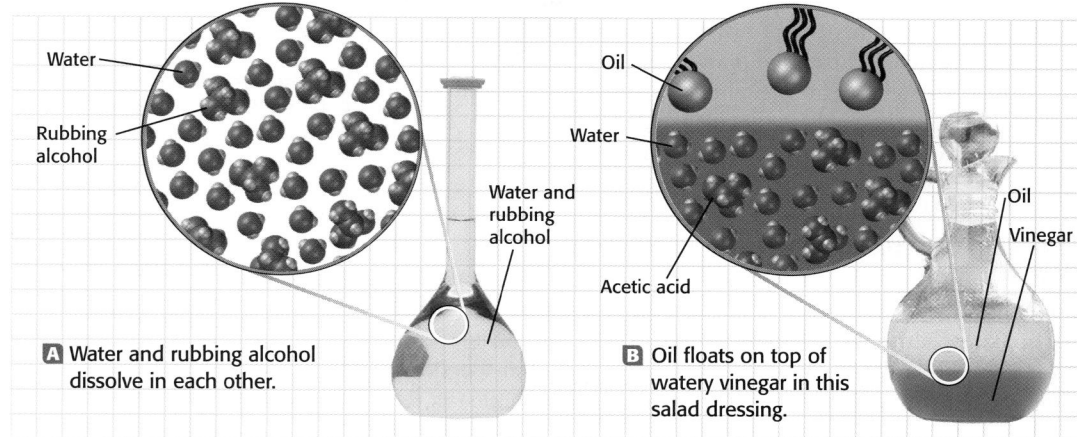

A Water and rubbing alcohol dissolve in each other.

B Oil floats on top of watery vinegar in this salad dressing.

Graphic Organizer
Classifying Matter

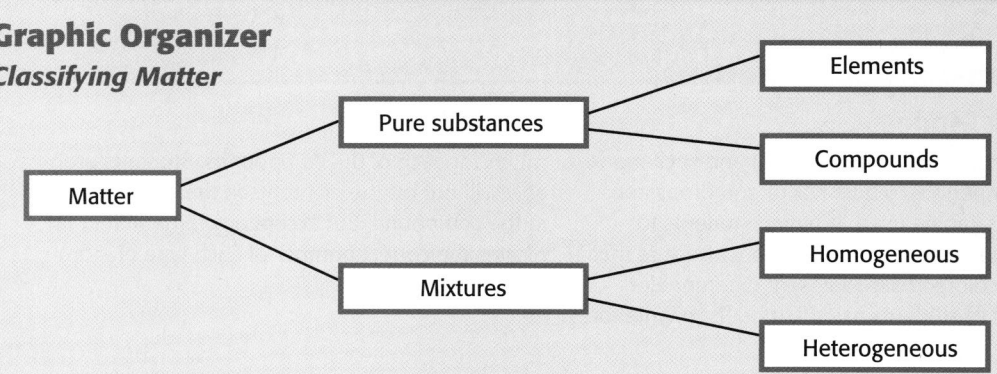

Science and the Consumer

Dry Cleaning: How Are Stains Dissolved?

Why do some clothes need to be dry cleaned, while others do not? Washing with water and detergents cleans most clothes. But if your clothes have a stubborn stain—such as ink or rust, if you have spilled something greasy on your clothes, or if the label on the clothing recommends dry cleaning, then dry cleaning may be necessary. Dry cleaning is recommended on a clothing label when the fabric does not respond well to water. Certain fabrics, like silk and wool, are usually cleaned without water because water causes them to shrink, take on stubborn wrinkles, or lose their shape.

Stain Removal

Knowing the composition of a stain helps dry cleaners decide how to treat it. Removing a stain that doesn't dissolve in water, such as oil or grease, involves two steps. First, the stain is treated with a substance that loosens the stain. Then the stain is removed when the garment is washed in a mechanical dry cleaner.

If a stain is water-soluble, it will dissolve in water. A water-soluble stain is first treated with a stain remover that is specific to that stain. The stain is then flushed away with a steam gun. After the garment is dry, it is cleaned in a dry-cleaning machine to remove any stains that do not dissolve in water.

Once the fabric has been treated for tough stains, the garment is washed in a dry-cleaning machine.

Dry Cleaning Isn't Really Dry

In spite of its name, dry cleaning does involve liquids. The process uses a liquid solvent instead of water. It is always difficult to remove fats, greases, and oils from fabrics with water-based washing.

A good dry-cleaning solvent must dissolve oil and grease, which trap the water-insoluble particles in the cloth fibers. The most commonly used dry-cleaning solvent is tetrachloroethylene, C_2Cl_4. Tetrachloroethylene is the preferred solvent because oil, grease, and alcohols dissolve in it. Also, tetrachloroethylene is not flammable, and it evaporates easily. This allows it to be recycled by distillation.

In distillation, the components of a mixture are separated based on their rates of evaporation. Upon heating, the component that evaporates most quickly is the first to vaporize and separate from the mixture. When the vapors are cooled, they condense to form a purified sample of that component.

Tetrachloroethylene is suspected of causing some kinds of cancer. To meet the standards of the United States Occupational Safety and Health Administration (OSHA) and other federal guidelines, dry-cleaning machines must be airtight so that no C_2Cl_4 escapes.

Your Choice

1. **Critical Thinking** Explain why it is difficult to remove fats, greases, and oils from fabrics with water-based washing alone.
2. **Critical Thinking** Tetrachloroethylene evaporates more quickly than the fats, grease, and oils it dissolves. Describe how C_2Cl_4 can be recycled by distillation.

📝 **internetconnect**

SCI**LINKS**™   **TOPIC:** Dry cleaning
NSTA   **GO TO:** www.scilinks.org
                          KEYWORD: HK1022

Dry Cleaning: How Are Stains Dissolved? Dry cleaning is said to have started in 1825, when a kerosene lamp was knocked over onto a greasy tablecloth at the house of a dye-factory owner, Jean-Baptiste Jolly. When the cloth dried, the area of the kerosene spill was noticeably cleaner. In the early decades of dry cleaning, some firms dipped items in kerosene and then in gasoline to clean them. While both substances are excellent degreasers, they are also dangerous to use because they are very flammable.

Your Choice

1. Fats, greases, and oils are insoluble in water, so it is difficult to remove them from fabrics with water-based washing alone.
2. Distillation is a separation technique based on the volatility of a substance. Since tetrachloroethylene evaporates more quickly than the fats, greases, and oils it dissolves, it is more volatile than they are and can be recycled by performing a distillation. When all the products of the dry-cleaning process are collected in a container and heated, C_2Cl_4 vaporizes first, separating from the fats, greases, and oils. The refined C_2Cl_4 vapor is then cooled, condensed, and collected in a different container.

Resources Assign students worksheet *2.2: Science and the Consumer—Is Dry Cleaning Dangerous?* in the **Integration Enrichment Resources** ancillary.

What Is Matter?

INTEGRATING

EARTH SCIENCE A finer-grained variety of pumice results when there is a large amount of gas in the lava. Coarser-grained pumice has fewer gas pockets. Some pumice has a very low density because of its gas pockets, which is why it can float on water and be carried by the wind.

Resources Assign students worksheet *2.3: Integrating Earth Science—Uses of Pumice* in the **Integration Enrichment Resources** ancillary.

SECTION 2.1 REVIEW

Check Your Understanding

1. Chemistry is the study of matter and how it changes.
2. elements, compounds
3. Light has neither mass nor volume.
4. miscible liquids
5. **a.** element
   b. compound
   c. compound
   d. element
6. Water contains two hydrogen atoms and one oxygen atom; H_2O.
7. A pure substance, such as table salt, has the same composition throughout and definite properties. A mixture, such as air, contains more than one pure substance.

Answers continue on p. 65B.

RESOURCE LINK
STUDY GUIDE

Assign students *Review Section 2.1 What Is Matter?*

INTEGRATING

EARTH SCIENCE
The molten rock in some types of volcanoes contains large quantities of gas. Pumice, a solid foam that occurs naturally on Earth, is a volcanic rock formed by the violent separation of these extremely hot gases from lava. As the exploding lava cools, it traps the gas bubbles. Some pumice is so soft that it is spongy, and some is so light that it floats on water. Often pumice occurs as small pea-size lumps, but it also occurs in deposits large enough to be mined and sold commercially as an abrasive.

Gases can mix with liquids

Air is a mixture of gases consisting mostly of nitrogen and oxygen. You get oxygen every time you breathe because the gases in air form a homogeneous mixture. Carbonated drinks are also homogeneous mixtures. They contain sugar, flavorings, and carbon dioxide gas, CO_2, dissolved in water. When carbonated drinks are manufactured, the carbon dioxide gas is mixed into the liquid under pressure and forms a solution.

Even a liquid that is not mixed with gas under pressure can contain dissolved gases. If you let a glass of cold water stand overnight, you may be able to see bubbles on the sides of the glass the next morning. The bubbles are some of the air that was dissolved in the cold water.

Carbonated drinks often have a foam on top. A foam is a different kind of gas-liquid mixture. The gas is not dissolved in the liquid but has formed tiny bubbles in it. Eventually, the tiny bubbles join together to form bigger bubbles that can escape from the foam, and the foam collapses.

Other foams are stable and last for a long time. If you whip egg white with enough air, you get a foam. If you heat that foam in an oven, the liquid egg white dries and hardens, and you have a solid foam—meringue.

SECTION 2.1 REVIEW

SUMMARY

▶ Matter has mass and occupies space.

▶ An element is a substance that cannot be broken down into a simpler substance.

▶ An atom is the smallest particle of matter that has the properties of a particular element.

▶ Atoms can join together to form molecules.

▶ A pure substance that contains two or more elements is a compound.

▶ A pure substance can be represented by a chemical formula.

CHECK YOUR UNDERSTANDING

1. **Define** *chemistry*.
2. **List** the two types of pure substances.
3. **Explain** why light is not matter.
4. **Complete** the following analogy:
   A heterogeneous mixture is to a homogeneous mixture as immiscible liquids are to _____.
5. **Classify** each of the following as an element or a compound:
   a. sulfur, S_8 **c.** carbon monoxide, CO
   b. methane, CH_4 **d.** cobalt, Co
6. **Describe** the makeup of pure water, and write its chemical formula.
7. **Compare and Contrast** mixtures and pure substances. Give an example of each.
8. **Critical Thinking** David and Susan are looking at a jar of honey labeled "Pure Honey." David says, "That means it's natural honey, with nothing else added." Susan says, "It isn't really pure. It's a mixture of lots of different substances." Who is right? Explain your answer.

WRITING SKILL

2.2

Matter and Energy

OBJECTIVES

▶ Use the kinetic theory to describe the properties and structures of the different states of matter.

▶ Describe the energy transfers involved in changes of state.

▶ Describe the laws of conservation of mass and conservation of energy, and explain how they apply to changes of state.

▶ KEY TERMS
pressure
viscosity
energy
evaporation
condensation
sublimation

Scheduling
Refer to pp. 36A–36D for lecture, classwork, and assignment options for Section 2.2.

★ **Lesson Focus**
Use transparency *LT 5* to prepare students for this section.

READING SKILL BUILDER *Reading Organizer* Have students read this section and create a concept map that shows what happens during the evaporation and condensation cycle. Concept maps should also include where energy is absorbed or released in the cycle.

If you go to a bakery, such as the one in **Figure 2-9,** you can smell the cookies baking even though you are a long way from the oven. One way to explain this phenomenon is to make some assumptions. First, assume that the particles (molecules and atoms) within substances can move. Second, assume that the molecules and atoms move faster as the temperature rises. A theory based on these assumptions, called the kinetic theory of matter, can be used to explain things like why you can smell cookies baking from far away.

When cookies are baking, energy is transferred from the oven to the cookies. As the temperature in the oven is increased, some molecules within the cookie dough move fast enough to become gases, which in turn spread through the air in the bakery.

Figure 2-9
The substances that make the fresh cookies smell so good may be vanillin, $C_8H_8O_3$, or cinnamaldehyde, C_9H_8O.

Kinetic Theory

Here are the main points of the kinetic theory of matter.

▶ All matter is made of atoms and molecules that act like tiny particles.

▶ These tiny particles are always in motion. The higher the temperature, the faster the particles move.

▶ At the same temperature, more massive (heavier) particles move slower than less massive (lighter) particles.

The kinetic theory is a useful tool for visualizing the differences between the three common states of matter: solids, liquids, and gases.

MATTER **45**

DEMONSTRATION 2 SCIENCE AND THE CONSUMER

Moving Gas Particles

Time: Approximately 5 minutes
Materials: balloon, dropper, vanilla extract

Before class, place five drops of vanilla extract into a balloon. Inflate the balloon, and tie it shut. Have students smell the balloon.

Analysis

1. What do you smell at the surface of the balloon? *(vanilla)*

2. What does this smell tell you about the particles that make up the vanilla extract? *(They are moving.)*

Teaching Tip

States of Matter Inform students that gas particles are approximately 10 times farther apart than the particles of a liquid or a solid. As a result, the volume of a substance as a gas is roughly 1000 ($10 \times 10 \times 10$) times the volume of the same amount of the substance as a liquid or a solid.

Did You Know ?

Although solids, liquids, and gases are the most common states of matter on Earth, plasmas are the most common state of matter in the universe. Stars are made from plasma. The space between bodies of matter in the universe contains a thin plasma. If scientists can find a way to contain a plasma without energy loss, the plasma could be a source for nuclear fusion, which produces great amounts of energy.

Common States of Matter

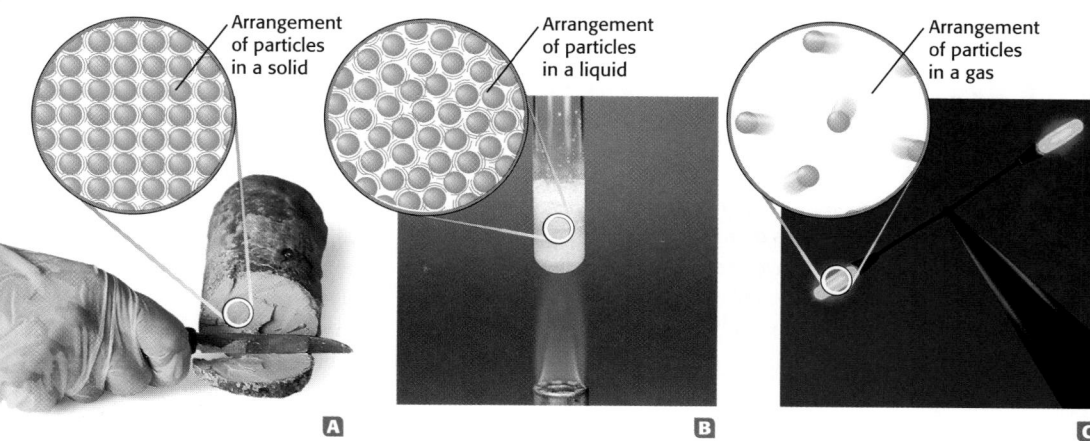

Arrangement of particles in a solid

Arrangement of particles in a liquid

Arrangement of particles in a gas

A **B** **C**

Figure 2-10
Gases, liquids, and solids are the most common states of matter on Earth. Here, the element sodium is shown as (A) the solid metal, (B) melted as a liquid, and (C) as a gas in a sodium-vapor lamp.

Did You Know ?

Very dense neutron stars and plasmas are examples of two other generally accepted states of matter. Our sun and most stars are plasmas made of fast-moving charged particles. In the Bose-Einstein condensate, atoms are at temperatures so close to absolute zero that they behave as one atom. This state of matter was first observed in 1995. Einstein predicted it in 1925 when he furthered the calculations of S. N. Bose, an Indian physicist.

The states of matter are physically different

The models for solids, liquids, and gases shown in **Figure 2-10** differ in the distances and angles between molecules or atoms and in how closely these particles are packed together. Gas particles, like those in helium, are in a constant state of motion and rarely stick together. In a liquid, like cooking oil, the particles are closely packed, but they can still slide past each other. Particles in a solid, like iron, are in fixed positions. Most matter found naturally on Earth is either a solid, a liquid, or a gas, but matter also exists in other states.

Gases are free to spread in all directions

Have you noticed that a balloon filled with a "light" gas such as helium goes flat more quickly than a balloon filled with air? You can use the kinetic theory to explain this. The wall of the balloon has tiny holes through which gas particles can escape. The helium particles are smaller and less massive than the nitrogen and oxygen particles found in air. The smaller and less massive particles move faster, so they get through the holes more quickly.

If you leave a jar of perfume open, you will soon smell it from across the room. This is one of the characteristics of a gas—it expands to fill the available space. Kinetic theory can be used to explain this property as well. Under standard conditions of temperature and pressure, particles of a gas move rapidly. Oxygen, O_2, averages almost 500 m/s, and helium, He, travels at more than 1200 m/s. At these speeds, gas particles collide billions of times a second. Like all particles of gas, helium atoms bounce off each other when they collide. As helium atoms bounce around and move freely, they spread to fill the available space.

Figure 2-11

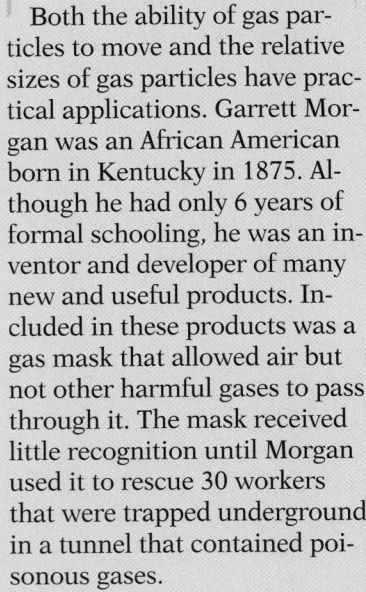

A Gas particles exert pressure by hitting the walls of a balloon.

B The balloon pops because the internal pressure is more than the balloon can hold.

Gases can exert pressure

You may know that a balloon filled with helium is under **pressure.** The gas in the balloon is pushing out against the balloon walls. The kinetic theory also helps to explain pressure. Helium atoms in the balloon are moving very quickly and are constantly hitting each other and the walls of the balloon, as shown in the model in **Figure 2-11.** Each particle's effect on the balloon wall is tiny, but the battering by millions of particles adds up to a steady force. The pressure inside the balloon is the measure of this steady force per unit area. If too many particles of gas are in the balloon, the battering overcomes the force of the balloon holding the gas in, and the balloon pops.

If you let go of a balloon that you've held pinched at the neck, most of the gas inside rushes out, causing the balloon to shoot through the air. Gases under pressure will escape their container if possible. If there is a lot of pressure in the container, the gas can escape with a lot of force. For this reason, gases in pressurized cylinders and similar containers, like propane tanks for gas grills, can be dangerous and must be handled carefully.

Solids have a rigid structure

If you take an ice cube out of the freezer and put it on a table, the ice will stay there as long as it remains solid. It has the same volume and shape that it had in the ice tray. Unlike gases, a solid does not need a container to have a shape. This is because the structure of a solid is very rigid, and the particles have almost no freedom to change position. The crystals of salt in **Figure 2-12** reflect the ordered arrangement of particles in most solids. The particles are held closely together by strong attractions, yet they can still vibrate around a fixed location.

▶ **pressure** the force exerted per unit area of a surface

PHYSICAL SCIENCE

Disc One, Module 1:
States of Matter/Classes of Matter
Use the Interactive Tutor to learn more about this topic.

Figure 2-12
The particles in these crystals of salt cannot move freely like the particles in a liquid or a gas can. These crystals of sodium chloride have been magnified 840 times.

MATTER **47**

Did You Know?

Both the ability of gas particles to move and the relative sizes of gas particles have practical applications. Garrett Morgan was an African American born in Kentucky in 1875. Although he had only 6 years of formal schooling, he was an inventor and developer of many new and useful products. Included in these products was a gas mask that allowed air but not other harmful gases to pass through it. The mask received little recognition until Morgan used it to rescue 30 workers that were trapped underground in a tunnel that contained poisonous gases.

Historical Perspective

The effects of air pressure on Earth are noticed only if air pressure differs from one area to another. In the 1600s, Otto von Guericke, a German scientist who invented an air pump, demonstrated the effect of differences in air pressure to the King of Prussia. He placed two hemispherical shells together and pumped the air out of the resulting sphere. The atmospheric pressure on the outside of the hollow sphere was so much greater than the pressure inside the sphere that teams of horses were unable to pull the two halves apart. When Von Guericke then opened a valve in the sphere to let in air and equalize the pressure, the hemispheres came apart easily.

ALTERNATIVE ASSESSMENT

Pressure

Have students write a paragraph that tells what happens to a nitrogen molecule from the time that it is pumped into a bicycle tire until the bicycle is parked after a ride. Encourage creativity. Students can write from either a first-person or a third-person perspective.

Matter and Energy

Quick ACTIVITY

Kinetic Theory

You will need water, vegetable oil, and rubbing alcohol.

SAFETY CAUTION The alcohol is flammable and toxic.

1. Dip one index finger into the water. Dip your other index finger into the oil. Wave each finger in the air. Do your fingers feel cool? How quickly does each liquid evaporate?
2. Repeat the experiment, using water and rubbing alcohol on different fingers.
3. Which of the three liquids evaporates the quickest? the slowest? Which liquid cools your skin the most? the least?
4. Use the kinetic theory to explain your observations.
5. Identify which liquid has the highest viscosity.

▶ **viscosity** the resistance of a fluid to flow

▶ **energy** the ability to change or move matter

Figure 2-13
Your body energy evaporates sweat.

Water vapor in air

Nitrogen molecule in air

Sweat droplet

Oxygen molecule in air

48

Liquids take the shape of their container

The particles of a liquid are close together, but they are not attracted to each other as strongly as they are in a solid. So the particles in a liquid have more freedom of movement. Because particles in a liquid can move randomly, liquids can spread out on their own. And because liquids and gases can spread, both are classified as *fluids*.

Liquids vary in the rate at which they spread. You know from experience that honey is thicker and flows more slowly than lemonade. This property, viscosity, is determined by the attraction between particles in a liquid. The stronger the attraction, the more slowly the liquid will flow, and the higher the viscosity will be.

Energy's Role

What sources of energy would you use if the electricity was off? You might use candles for light and batteries to power a clock. Electricity, candles, and batteries are sources of energy. So is the food you eat. Substances that release heat when they are mixed together are another source of energy. You can think of energy as the ability to change or move matter. In Chapter 9, you will learn how energy can be described as the ability to do work.

Energy must be added to cause melting or evaporation

The first major step in the process of recycling aluminum cans is to melt the aluminum. Heating solid aluminum transfers energy to the aluminum atoms. As the atoms gain energy, they vibrate faster. Eventually, they break away from their fixed positions, and the aluminum melts, becoming a liquid. Energy is required to melt aluminum or any solid because the particles must break away from their fixed positions.

You can feel the effects of an energy change when you feel a breeze after you have been perspiring. Energy from your body's molecules is transferred as heat to the water on your skin. When this transfer occurs, your body's molecules cool off and slow down, while the water molecules gain energy and move faster, as shown in **Figure 2-13**.

Quick ACTIVITY

Kinetic Theory

SAFETY CAUTION: *No open flames should be present anywhere in the classroom when alcohol is being used.*

1. Students' fingers should feel cool. The water evaporates more quickly.
2. Students' fingers should feel cool. The alcohol evaporates more quickly.
3. Alcohol, because it evaporates most quickly, cools skin the most. Oil, because it evaporates most slowly, cools skin the least.
4. The molecules present in each liquid absorb energy from their surroundings (skin), increasing the speed of the molecules. The alcohol molecules require the least energy to escape from the liquid. The oil molecules require the most.
5. The vegetable oil has the highest viscosity.

Figure 2-14
The Changes of State for Water

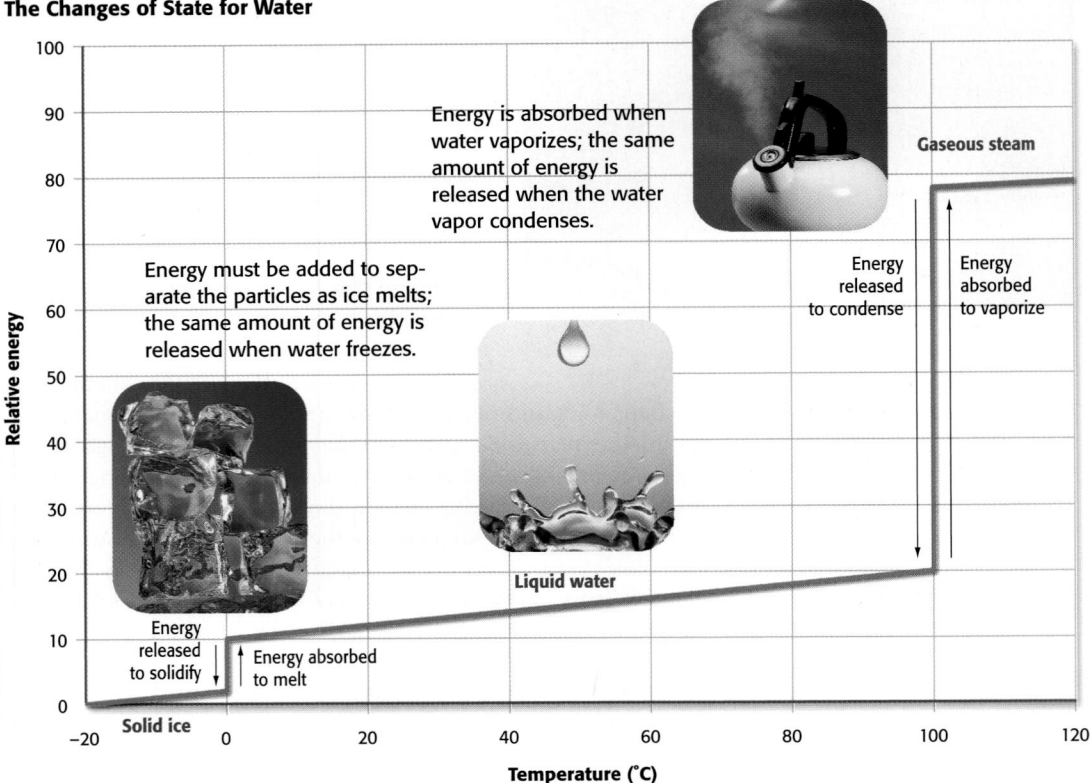

Energy is absorbed when water vaporizes; the same amount of energy is released when the water vapor condenses.

Energy must be added to separate the particles as ice melts; the same amount of energy is released when water freezes.

Gaseous steam

Energy released to condense

Energy absorbed to vaporize

Liquid water

Energy released to solidify

Energy absorbed to melt

Solid ice

Relative energy

Temperature (°C)

Eventually, the fastest moving molecules break away from the liquid surface to form a gas. The water is said to **evaporate.** It takes energy to separate the particles of a liquid to form a gas.

Evaporation occurs slowly when liquids are cool. But as the temperature of the liquid increases, more of the molecules gain enough energy to break away from the liquid surface and form a gas. If the liquid is heated enough, so many molecules become gas that bubbles form below the surface of the liquid and the liquid boils.

Energy is transferred in all changes of state

When water vapor **condenses** to become a liquid or liquid water freezes to form ice, energy is transferred from the water to its surroundings. The water molecules slow down during this energy transfer. The graph in **Figure 2-14** shows the energy transfers that occur as water changes among the three common states of matter.

▶ **evaporation** the change of a substance from a liquid to a gas

▶ **condensation** the change of a substance from a gas to a liquid

MATTER **49**

SKILL BUILDER

Interpreting Visuals Draw students' attention to the vertical segments of the graph in **Figure 2-14.** Ask students to speculate on what that energy is doing if it is not increasing the temperature. *(The energy is either used to do work on the molecules, moving them out of the crystal lattice at the melting point, or moving them farther from each other into the gaseous state at the boiling point.)*

Resources Blackline Master 7 shows this visual.

Multicultural Extension

Synthesizing glass by adding energy to sand and melting it is not the only way glass is made. Glass can also be formed in nature by volcanic action or by a lightning bolt striking sand. American Indian cultures frequently used this naturally made glass to build arrowheads and spear points.

Matter and Energy

Teaching Tip

Sublimation   Point out to students that many practical uses of sublimation exist. Dry ice (solid CO₂) is used when materials need to be kept cold but a liquid is undesirable. Wet clothes hung on a clothesline in below-freezing weather dry by sublimation. Certain foods and beverages, such as coffee, are "freeze-dried." But sublimation is not always a helpful process. If food is improperly wrapped or kept too long in a freezer, it becomes "freezer burned" as a result of sublimation.

MISCONCEPTION **ALERT**

Water Vapor
Students might think that when they see a cloud they see water vapor. Emphasize to them that water vapor cannot be seen. If they see clouds or steam, as shown in **Figure 2-16,** they are actually seeing small droplets of water that have condensed from the water vapor.

Figure 2-15
Dry ice (solid carbon dioxide) sublimes to form gaseous carbon dioxide but no liquid.

▷ **sublimation** the change of a substance from a solid to a gas

Figure 2-16
Whether it is ice, water, or steam, water in any form is always made of H₂O molecules.

Some substances do not have a liquid form at normal temperature and pressure. **Figure 2-15** shows solid carbon dioxide, CO_2, undergoing **sublimation**, that is, turning directly into a gas without becoming a liquid. Sometimes, ice made of water molecules sublimes, forming a gas. When left in the freezer for a couple of months, ice cubes get smaller as the ice sublimes.

Changing state does not change composition or mass

Heating or cooling can change the state of a substance. Look at the changes of state that are happening in **Figure 2-16.** Some of the steam is condensing. As this happens, heat is transferred to the surroundings, so the steam cools and turns back into liquid water. Changing the energy of a substance can change the state of the substance, but changing energy does not change the composition of a substance. Ice, water, and steam are all made of H_2O molecules. All that changes is the nature of the attractions between the molecules—strong in a solid and almost nonexistent in a gas.

When an ice cube melts, the mass of the liquid water is the same as the mass of the ice cube. Even though the ice underwent a physical change to produce the water, the mass was not increased or reduced. Similarly, when water boils, the number of water molecules stays the same even as the liquid water loses volume. The mass of the steam is the same as the mass of the liquid water that boiled off.

Graphic Organizer

Changes of State

Sublimation

| Solid | Melting → / ← Freezing | Liquid | Boiling or evaporation → / ← Condensation | Gas |

Properties of Matter

Section 2.3

Properties of Matter

Scheduling
Refer to pp. 36A–36D for lec-

Section 2.2

Matter and Energy

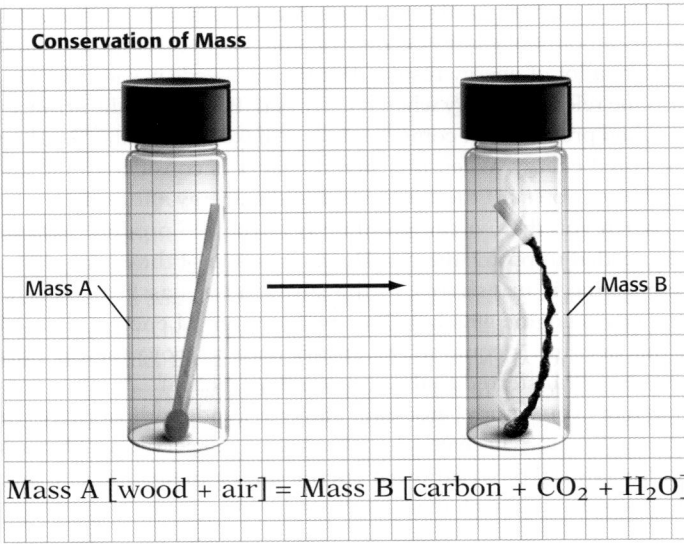

Conservation of Mass

Mass A

Mass B

$$\text{Mass A [wood + air]} = \text{Mass B [carbon + } CO_2 + H_2O]$$

Figure 2-17
The match is changed by burning, but the mass of the contents of the vial remains the same.

The law of conservation of mass

In chemical changes as well as in physical changes, the total mass of all matter stays the same before and after a change. Matter changes from one form to another, but the total mass stays the same. This is called the law of conservation of mass. The law of conservation of mass is stated as follows.

Mass cannot be created or destroyed.

When you burn a match, it seems to lose mass. The ash has less mass than the original match. But the burning reaction involves gases too, and gases have mass, even though they may be difficult to see or measure. There is also mass in the oxygen that reacts with the match, in the tiny particles that we see as smoke, and in the gases formed in the reaction. The total mass of the reactants (match and oxygen) is the same as the total mass of the products (ash, smoke, and gases), as you can see in **Figure 2-17.**

The law of conservation of energy

Although energy may be converted from one form to another during a physical or chemical change, the total amount of energy before and after the change is always the same. This is the law of conservation of energy, which can be stated as follows.

Energy cannot be created or destroyed.

The law of conservation of energy is described in more detail in Chapter 9.

INTEGRATING

SPACE SCIENCE
Studies of the chemical changes that stars and nebulae undergo are constantly adding to our knowledge. Present estimates are that hydrogen makes up more than 90 percent of the atoms in the universe and constitutes about 75 percent of the mass of the universe. Helium atoms make up most of the remainder. The total of all the other elements contributes very little to the total mass of the universe.

Teaching Tip
Conservation of Mass Emphasize to students that often it is difficult to show that mass is conserved before and after a change unless the change is done in a closed system. In a closed system, no materials enter or leave the system while the change is taking place.

INTEGRATING

SPACE SCIENCE In astronomy, the term *nucleosynthesis* refers to the process by which all of the chemical elements are produced from hydrogen, the simplest element, by thermonuclear reactions within stars. During these reactions, a star synthesizes the elements of the periodic table from its initial composition of hydrogen and a small amount of helium.

Resources Assign students worksheet *2.4: Integrating Space Science—Our Changing Universe* in the **Integration Enrichment Resources** ancillary.

LINKING CHAPTERS

During nuclear reactions, such as those discussed in Chapter 7, minute amounts of matter are changed to large quantities of energy according to the equation $E = mc^2$. E is the quantity of energy produced, m is the mass that is converted to energy, and c is the speed of light. Although the amount of mass is converted into an amount of energy, the total amount of mass and energy in the system remains constant. This law is known as the law of conservation of mass-energy.

MATTER **51**

Mercury is one of the oldest known elements and has been used extensively by many cultures throughout history. It was found in an Egyptian tomb dating back to 1500 B.C. One chemical property of mercury is that it is toxic. In the 1960s, residents of Minamata City, in Japan, suffered mercury poisoning because they ate fish that were contaminated by high levels of mercury in the water. As a result of this and other similar events, mercury contamination in the environment is closely monitored.

MISCONCEPTION ALERT

Vocabulary Be sure students understand the difference between boiling and evaporation. Evaporation occurs only at the surface of a liquid as individual molecules gain enough energy to escape the attraction of the particles of the liquid. When a liquid absorbs enough energy that it vaporizes throughout the liquid, it boils.

Figure 2-19
Rust is formed when oxygen in moist air reacts with iron to form iron(III) oxide, Fe_2O_3.

▶ **reactivity** the ability of a substance to combine chemically with another substance

▶ **physical property** a characteristic of a substance that can be observed or measured without changing the composition of the substance

▶ **melting point** the temperature at which a solid becomes a liquid

▶ **boiling point** the temperature at which a liquid becomes a gas below the surface

Chemical properties describe how a substance reacts

You can see rust on the bumper of a truck in **Figure 2-19.** The steel parts rust, but the rubber and plastic parts, such as those that surround the mirror, do not. The rust results when iron atoms in the steel react to form iron(III) oxide and other compounds. Rubber and plastic do not change in this way; they don't contain iron atoms. Steel, rubber, and plastic have different chemical properties. A chemical property describes how a substance acts when it changes, either by combining with other elements or by breaking apart into new substances. Chemical properties involve the **reactivity** of elements or compounds.

Chemical properties are related to the specific elements that make up substances. The carbon in charcoal will burn and is *flammable*. Flammability is a chemical property that describes whether substances will react in the presence of oxygen and burn when exposed to a flame.

Physical properties remain the same for a pure substance

Unlike chemical properties, **physical properties** can be observed or measured without a change in composition. You can use your senses to observe some of the basic physical properties of a substance: shape, color, odor, and texture. Other physical properties, such as **melting point, boiling point,** strength, hardness, and the ability to conduct electricity, magnetism, or heat, can be measured.

Physical properties remain constant for specific pure substances. At room temperature and atmospheric pressure, all samples of pure water are always colorless and liquid; pure water is never something like a powdery green solid.

54 CHAPTER 2

DEMONSTRATION 4 TEACHING

Temperature Effects on Density

Time: Approximately 15 minutes
Materials: aquarium, 2 glass jars with lids, 1000 mL beaker (2), red and blue food coloring, tap water, hot plate, ice, white paper

Step 1 Fill the aquarium with room-temperature tap water.

Step 2 Add water and ice to a beaker and allow the water to cool to almost 0°C. Remove any remaining ice once the water has cooled and add blue food coloring to the water. Fill one jar with the cold water.

Step 3 Add water to another beaker. Place this beaker on a hot plate and heat the water until it is at 80°C or higher. Once the water is heated, remove the beaker from the hot plate and add red food coloring to the water. Fill the second jar with

2.2 Matter and Energy.

Water boils at 100°C and freezes at 0°C. At atmospheric pressure, pure water always has the same boiling point and melting point. A characteristic of any pure substance is that its boiling point and its melting point are constant. It doesn't matter if you have a lot of water or a little water; the physical properties of the water are constant, regardless of the mass or volume involved. This is true for all pure substances.

Density is a physical property

A substance that has a low **density** is sometimes referred to as being "light." The balloons in **Figure 2-20** float because they are lighter than the air around them. A substance that has a high density is sometimes referred to as being "heavy." Earth's core is made of iron because it is heavier—more dense—than other substances that are abundant on our planet.

One way to compare the density of two objects of the same size is to hold one in each hand. The lighter one is less dense; the heavier one is more dense. If you held a brick in one hand and an equal-sized piece of sponge in the other hand, you would know instantly that the brick is more dense than the sponge. **Table 2-1** lists the densities of some common substances.

By knowing the density of a substance, you can know if the substance will float or sink. The density of an object is calculated by dividing the object's mass by its volume.

> **Density Equation**
> $$D = m/V$$
> $$density = mass/volume$$

Table 2-1 **Densities of Some Substances**

Substance	Chemical formula	Density in g/cm³
Air, dry	Mixture	0.00129
Brick, common	Mixture	1.9
Gasoline	Mixture	0.7
Helium	He	0.00018
Ice	H_2O	0.92
Iron	Fe	7.86
Lead	Pb	11.3
Nitrogen	N_2	0.00125
Steel	Mixture	7.8
Water	H_2O	1.00

> **density** the mass per unit volume of a substance

Figure 2-20
Helium-filled balloons float upward because helium is lighter—or less dense—than air. Similarly, hot-air balloons rise because hot air is less dense than cool air.

Did You Know ?

The elements osmium and iridium are the two densest substances on Earth. The density of osmium is 22.57 g/cm³. Iridium has a density of 22.42 g/cm³. A piece of either metal the size of a baseball has a mass of approximately 4700 g.

MATTER **55**

Historical Perspective

Blimps and dirigibles are types of airships. An airship consists of an engine, a large balloon that contains gas, and a gondola to carry passengers and crew. Airships float in air because the gases they contain are less dense than air. In the early 1900s, airships were commonly used for travel, including trans-Atlantic flights. Airships were less frequently used after the 1937 explosion and crash of the Hindenburg in New Jersey. The Hindenburg was filled with flammable hydrogen gas instead of helium gas, which is nonflammable.

SKILL BUILDER

Interpreting Diagrams The density of a liquid or a solid is affected little by a change in temperature or pressure. But an increase in temperature or a decrease in pressure does reduce the density of a gas. Similarly, a decrease in temperature or an increase in pressure increases the density of a gas. The densities of the substances listed in **Table 2-1** were measured at 20°C and 1 atm.

Teaching Tip

Volume Review the concept of volume with students. Display several items, and have students discuss how the volume of each item can be determined. Some items should be regular in shape so that dimensions can be measured and the volume calculated. Other items should be irregular in shape so that students must estimate or use displacement to find the volume.

---

the hot water. Both jars should be filled completely so that little, if any, air is present in the jars once the lids are on.

Step 4 Place each jar inside the aquarium and remove both lids. Tip the cold-water jar on its side so that the water spills onto the floor of the aquarium. White paper taped on the back of the aquarium will help make the demonstration more visible to students.

Analysis

1. Why does the hot water rise to the top of the aquarium? *(The hot water is less dense than the room-temperature water.)*
2. Why does the cold water remain in the jar until it is tipped on its side? *(The cold water is more dense than the room-temperature water.)*
3. How does temperature affect the density of water? *(Temperature affects the spacing between water molecules.)*

Properties of Matter

Math Skills

Resources Assign students worksheet *5: Density* in the **Math Skills Worksheets** ancillary.

RESOURCE LINK

BASIC SKILLS

Assign students worksheet *5.5: Rearranging Algebraic Equations* to help them understand the density equation.

LABORATORY MANUAL

Have students perform *Lab 2 Matter: Comparing the Buoyancy of Different Objects* in the lab ancillary.

DATASHEETS

Have students use *Datasheet 2.4* to record their results from the lab.

Practice HINT

▶ When a problem requires you to calculate density, you can use the density equation.

$$D = \frac{m}{V}$$

▶ You can solve for mass by multiplying both sides of the density equation by volume.

$$DV = \frac{m\cancel{V}}{\cancel{V}} \qquad m = DV$$

You will need to use this form of the equation in Practice Problems 6 and 7.

▶ You can solve for volume by dividing both sides of the equation shown above by density.

$$\frac{m}{D} = \frac{\cancel{D}V}{\cancel{D}} \qquad V = \frac{m}{D}$$

You will need to use this form of the equation in Practice Problems 8 and 9.

The density of a liquid or a solid is usually reported in units of grams per cubic centimeter (g/cm^3). For example, 10.0 cm^3 of water has a mass of 10.0 g. Its density is 10.0 g for every 10.0 cm^3, or 1.00 g/cm^3. As you learned in Section 1.2, a cubic centimeter contains the same volume as a milliliter. Therefore, in some cases, you may see the density of water expressed as 1 g/mL.

Math Skills

Density If we know that 10.0 cm^3 of ice has a mass of 9.17 g, what is the density of ice?

1 List the given and unknown values.

Given: *mass*, m = 9.17 g
volume, V = 10.0 cm^3
Unknown: *density*, D = ? g/cm^3

2 Write the equation for density.

$$D = \frac{m}{V} \qquad density = \frac{mass}{volume}$$

3 Insert the known values into the equation, and solve.

$$D = \frac{9.17 \text{ g}}{10.0 \text{ cm}^3}$$

$$D = 0.917 \text{ g/cm}^3$$

Practice

Density

1. A piece of tin has a mass of 16.52 g and a volume of 2.26 cm^3. What is the density of tin?

2. A man has a 50.0 cm^3 bottle completely filled with 163 g of a slimy green liquid. What is the density of the liquid?

3. A sealed 2500 cm^3 flask is full to capacity with 0.36 g of a substance. Determine the density of the substance. Guess if the substance is a gas, a liquid, or a solid.

4. A piece of metal has a volume of 6.7 cm^3 and a mass of 75.7 g. Find the metal's density. Using the data in **Table 2-1,** suggest what element the metal could be.

5. The mass of a 125 cm^3 piece of a material is 83.75 g. Determine the density of this material.

6. What is the mass of an object that has a density of 8 g/cm^3 and a volume of 64 cm^3?

7. Different kinds of wood have different densities. The density of pine is generally about 0.5 g/cm^3. What is the mass of a 800 cm^3 piece of pine?

8. What is the volume of 325 g of metal with a density of 9.0 g/cm^3?

9. Diamonds have a density of 3.5 g/cm^3. How big is a diamond that has a mass of 0.10 g ?

56 CHAPTER 2

Solution Guide

1. D = 16.52 g/2.26 cm^3
D = 7.31 g/cm^3

2. D = 163 g/50.0 cm^3
D = 3.26 g/cm^3

3. D = 0.36 g/2500 cm^3
D = 1.4×10^{-4} g/cm^3
Because the density is so low, the substance is a gas.

4. D = 75.7 g/6.7 cm^3 = 11 g/cm^3
The element is lead.

5. D = 83.75 g/125 cm^3 = 0.670 g/cm^3

6. m = 8 g/cm^3 × 64 cm^3 = 500 g

7. m = 0.5 g/cm^3 × 800 cm^3 = 400 g

8. V = 325 g/(9.0 g/cm^3) = 36 cm^3

9. V = 0.10 g/(3.5 g/cm^3) = 0.029 cm^3

The difference in the densities of cream and milk allows us to make skim milk. If whole milk, which has not been homogenized, is allowed to stand, the cream will rise to the top, leaving the more watery milk on the bottom. When the cream is skimmed off, what is left is called skim milk.

In **Figure 2-21,** ice is floating in water because of a difference in the densities of the two substances. Water pushes ice to the surface because ice is less dense than water. The tendency of a less dense substance, like ice, to rise and float in a more dense liquid, like water, is called **buoyancy.** A cork floats in water because it is less dense than water and the water pushes up against it.

Figure 2-21
Ice floats in water because ice is less dense than water.

 **buoyancy** the force with which a more dense fluid pushes a less dense substance upward

Properties help determine uses

We use physical properties to help us select a substance that may be useful to us. Copper is used in electrical power lines, telephone lines, and electric motors because of its good electrical conductivity. Antifreeze, which contains ethylene glycol (a poisonous liquid), remains a liquid at temperatures that would freeze or boil the water in a car radiator.

Inquiry Lab

How are the mass and volume of a substance related?

1. Predictions should be approximately 55 g and 100 g.
2. Predictions should be approximately 25 mL and 75 mL.
3. Divide the mass in the third column of the table by the corresponding volume from the first column. For any two points on the graph, divide the difference in the x values by the difference in the y values to determine density. Student answers will vary; accept any answer students can justify.

RESOURCE LINK
DATASHEETS

Have students use *Datasheet 2.2 Inquiry Lab: How are the mass and volume of a substance related?* to record their results.

Inquiry Lab

How are the mass and volume of a substance related?

Materials
- ✔ 100 mL graduated cylinder
- ✔ 250 mL beaker with 200 mL water
- ✔ balance
- ✔ graph paper

Procedure

1. Make a data table with 3 columns and 12 rows. In the first row, label the columns "Volume of H_2O (mL)," "Mass of cylinder (g) and H_2O (g)," and "Mass of H_2O (g)." In the remaining spaces of the first column, write: 0, 10, 20, 30, 40, 50, 60, 70, 80, 90, and 100. All of your data will be entered on this table.
2. Measure the mass of the empty graduated cylinder, and record it in your data table.
3. Pour the amounts of water listed in the first column of your table from the beaker into the graduated cylinder. Then use the balance to find the mass of the graduated cylinder with the water. Record each value in your data table.
4. On the graph paper, make a graph and label the horizontal x-axis "Mass of water (g)." Mark the x-axis in 10 equal increments for 10, 20, 30, 40, 50, 60, 70, 80, 90 and 100 g. Label the vertical y-axis "Volume of water (mL)." Mark the y-axis in 10 equal increments for 10, 20, 30, 40, 50, 60, 70, 80, 90 and 100 mL.
5. Plot a graph of your data either on paper, on a graphing calculator, or by using a graphing/spreadsheet computer program. **COMPUTER SKILL**

Analysis

1. Use your graph to predict the mass of 55 mL of water and 100 mL of water.
2. Use your graph to predict the volume of 25 g of water and 75 g of water.
3. How could you use your data table to calculate the density of water? How could you use your graph to calculate the density of water? Which method do you think gives better results? Why?

MATTER **57**

DEMONSTRATION 5 SCIENCE AND THE CONSUMER

Soft Drink Densities

Time: Approximately 10 minutes
Materials: 12 oz. can of regular soda, 12 oz. can of diet soda (same brand as regular), aquarium, tap water, balance

Measure the masses of the two cans of soda. Place the cans of soda in an aquarium filled with tap water. Remind students that the cans have the same volume.

Analysis

1. Which soda has the greater density? *(The volumes are identical, so the soda with the greater mass has the greater density. The regular soda has the greater mass due to the large amount of sugar required to sweeten it.)*
2. Which is sweeter, 1 g of artificial sweetener or 1 g of sugar? *(The lower mass of the diet soda shows that artificial sweetener is sweeter, gram for gram, than sugar.)*

Choosing Materials In addition to being made from a single material, false teeth are also made from composite materials. Composite materials are those in which one material is embedded in another. The resultant material is stronger than either material by itself.

Applying Information
1. Answers will vary but could include that gold is easily shaped and is unreactive. Bone is similar in composition to actual teeth and would have similar strength.
2. Answers will vary but could include that gold is a relatively soft metal and might become misshapen. Bone does not have the hard covering that teeth have, so bone might react with certain foods. If bone breaks, it could form splinters.

Resources Assign students worksheet *2.5: RWA—Choosing Materials for Bicycle Frames* in the **Integration Enrichment Resources** ancillary.

Choosing Materials When you choose materials, you have to make sure their properties are suitable. For example, white acrylic plastic can be used to make false teeth. Sometimes a kind of porcelain is used. Metals are less common, although gold teeth are made sometimes. Fillings usually are made of metal or a special kind of glass.

False teeth have a demanding job to do. They are constantly bathed in saliva, which is corrosive. They must withstand the forces from chewing hard objects, like popcorn or hard candy. The material chosen has to be nontoxic, hard, waterproof, unreactive, toothlike in appearance, and preferably reasonably priced. Acrylic plastic satisfies these requirements well.

George Washington wore false teeth, but contrary to the legend that they were wood, they were made of hippopotamus bone.

Applying Information
1. Identify some advantages of gold false teeth and Washington's bone teeth.
2. Identify some disadvantages of gold false teeth and Washington's bone teeth.

Chemical and Physical Changes

Some materials benefit us because they stay in the same state and do not change under normal conditions. Long surgical steel pins are used to reinforce broken bones because surgical steel stays the same even after many years in the human body. Concrete and glass are used as building materials because they change very little under most weather conditions.

Other materials are valued for their ability to change physical states easily. Water is turned into steam to heat homes and factories. Liquid gasoline is changed into a gas so it can burn in car engines.

Still other materials are useful because of their ability to change and combine to form new substances. The compounds in gasoline burn in oxygen to form carbon dioxide and water, releasing energy in the process. This is a **chemical change** because the substances after the change are different from the substances at the beginning.

You see chemical changes happening more often than you may think. When a battery "dies," the chemicals inside the battery have changed so that the battery can no longer supply energy. The oxygen you inhale is used in a series of chemical reactions in your body. You exhale oxygen in carbon dioxide after it has undergone a chemical change. Chemical changes occur when fruits and vegetables ripen and when the food you eat is digested.

internet connect

SciLINKS
NSTA

TOPIC: Chemical and physical changes
GO TO: www.scilinks.org
KEYWORD: HK1024

 **chemical change** a change that occurs when a substance changes composition by forming one or more new substances

58 CHAPTER 2

DEMONSTRATION 6 TEACHING

Chemical Change

Time: Approximately 15 minutes
Materials: $CuSO_4$ solution, beaker, large iron nail

Place the iron nail in a $CuSO_4$ solution for several minutes. If time allows, let the nail remain in the solution overnight, and observe the nail and solution the next day.

Analysis
1. What change in the nail indicates that a chemical change occurred? *(Copper from the solution appears on the nail as copper metal.)*
2. How do you know that this change was not physical? *(The copper was initially in a compound. It changed to a free element, which is a different substance.)*

Figure 2-22
Electrolysis is a method by which water can be broken down into hydrogen and oxygen gases.

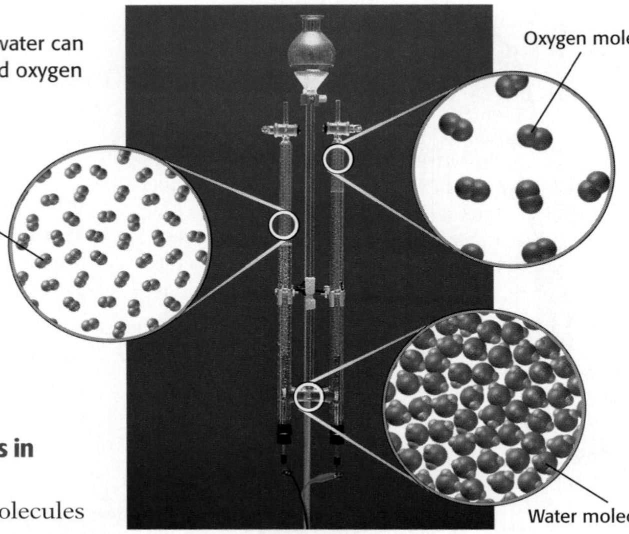

Oxygen molecule, O_2

Hydrogen molecule, H_2

Water molecule, H_2O

Chemical changes are changes in composition

When gasoline burns, the molecules involved combine with the oxygen molecules in air to produce new substances. A chemical change also occurs when a compound breaks apart to form at least two other pure substances. When water is broken down, the atoms of oxygen or hydrogen are not destroyed. Rather, these atoms rearrange to form hydrogen gas, H_2, and oxygen gas, O_2, as shown in **Figure 2-22.** The law of conservation of mass applies to all chemical changes. This is because new atoms are not created, and old atoms are not destroyed.

You can learn about the chemical properties of a substance by observing the chemical changes the substance undergoes. A change in odor or color is a good clue that a substance is changing chemically. When food burns, you can often smell the gases given off by the chemical changes that occur. When paint fades, you can see the effects of chemical changes in the paint.

Physical changes do not change composition

Both quartz crystals and sand are made of SiO_2, but they look very different. When quartz crystals are crushed into sand, a physical change takes place. During physical changes, energy always is absorbed or released. After a **physical change,** a substance may look different, but the atoms that make up the substance are not changed or rearranged.

Grinding peanuts into peanut butter or pounding a gold nugget into a ring result in physical changes. But physical changes do not change all the properties of a substance. For example, the color of the gold, its melting point, and its density do not change. Melting, freezing, and evaporating are physical changes, too.

▶ **physical change** a change in the physical form or properties of a substance that occurs without a change in composition

MATTER **59**

Teaching Tip

Physical and Chemical Changes Students may develop the idea that physical and chemical changes are mutually exclusive and that every observable change is easily classified as one or the other. In fact, it is not always easy to separate and classify changes. Many chemical changes also involve physical changes. An example is the change of liquid water to a vapor because of the heat released during a chemical change.

ALTERNATIVE ASSESSMENT

Changes in Matter

Ask students to evaluate the following four examples and decide whether the process is primarily a physical change or a chemical change. Students may not be able to give definitive answers, but their responses should provide evidence that they are thinking of pertinent factors in each change.
- Baking soda releases CO_2 and H_2O when heated strongly. *(chemical)*

- Melting antimony and tin together produces pewter. *(physical)*
- Rubbing alcohol cools your skin as it evaporates. *(physical)*
- A piece of zinc is placed into a solution of hydrochloric acid, and bubbles begin to rise to the surface. *(chemical)*

Properties of Matter

Check Your Understanding

1. a. physical
   b. physical
   c. chemical
   d. physical
   e. chemical
2. Answers will vary but could include use of strong, rigid plastic in cases for electronic devices, such as CD players, and use of flexible, transparent plastic as plastic food wrap.
3. a. physical
   b. physical
   c. chemical
   d. chemical
4. The composition of the substance does not change when it changes state.
5. a. absorbed
   b. absorbed
   c. released
   d. absorbed
6. $D = 454$ g/100 cm^3
   $D = 4.54$ g/cm^3
7. Answers will vary. Physical properties could include a density less than that of water, enough strength to not bend or break when a load is placed on it, and insolubility in water. Chemical properties could include not reacting with water or not burning.

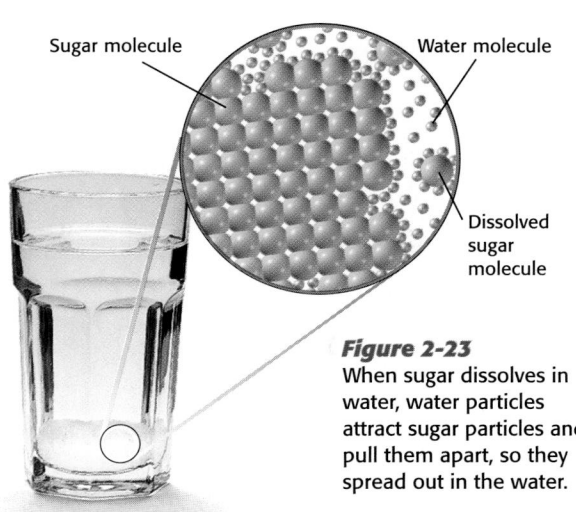

Sugar molecule

Water molecule

Dissolved sugar molecule

Figure 2-23
When sugar dissolves in water, water particles attract sugar particles and pull them apart, so they spread out in the water.

Dissolving is a physical change

When you stir sugar into water, the sugar dissolves and seems to disappear. But the sugar is still there; you can taste the sweetness when you drink the water. **Figure 2-23** shows how the kinetic theory describes this. When sugar dissolves, it seems to disappear because the sugar particles get spread out between the particles of the water. The molecules of the sugar haven't changed because dissolving is a physical change. Dissolving a solid in a liquid, a gas in a liquid, or a liquid in a liquid are all physical changes.

SECTION 2.3 REVIEW

SUMMARY

▶ Chemical properties can be observed when one substance reacts with another.

▶ Physical properties can be observed or measured without changing the composition of matter.

▶ The density of a substance is equal to its mass divided by its volume.

▶ New substances are formed in chemical changes.

▶ Physical changes do not affect all properties because physical changes do not change composition.

▶ Changes of state, including melting, subliming, evaporating, boiling, condensing, and freezing, are physical changes.

CHECK YOUR UNDERSTANDING

1. **Classify** the following as either chemical or physical properties:
   a. is shiny and silvery
   b. melts easily
   c. burns in air
   d. has a density of 2.3 g/cm^3
   e. tarnishes in moist air
2. **Describe** several uses for plastic, and explain why plastic is a good choice for these purposes.
3. **Classify** the following as either a chemical or a physical change:
   a. ice melting in a drink
   b. sugar added to lemonade
   c. mixing vinegar and baking soda to generate bubbles
   d. plants using CO_2 and H_2O to form O_2 and sugar
4. **Explain** why changes of state are physical changes.
5. **Categorize** the following as either absorbing or releasing energy:
   a. solid carbon dioxide going to CO_2 gas
   b. rubbing alcohol evaporating
   c. aluminum solidifying in a mold
   d. chocolate melting
6. **Calculate** the density of a rock that has a mass of 454 g and a volume of exactly 100 cm^3.
7. **Critical Thinking** You need to build a raft. Write a paragraph describing the physical and chemical properties of the raft that would be important to ensure your safety. You are not limited to the properties discussed in this chapter.

WRITING SKILL

Assign students *Review Section 2.3 Properties of Matter.*

ALTERNATIVE ASSESSMENT

Physical Change

Ask students to bring in different brands and types of sandwich bags, along with packaging, ads, and other promotional materials. Have students design and perform a simple experiment to test how much mass each bag can hold before breaking. Pool the data from the entire class and have students write their procedure, data, and conclusions in a simple lab report, answering the following questions.

• What inferences can be drawn from the data collected? *(Some claims of strength will be upheld, and others may not.)*
• Was this a test of physical or chemical changes? *(Tearing a bag is a physical change—the plastic hasn't changed its properties.)*

Chapter Highlights

Before you begin, review the summaries of the key ideas of each section, found on pages 44, 52, and 60. The key vocabulary terms are listed on pages 38, 45, and 53.

UNDERSTANDING CONCEPTS

1. "Anything that takes up space and has mass" is the definition of _____.
   a. a solid   c. matter
   b. a liquid   d. a gas

2. Which of the following is a compound?
   a. sodium   c. iodine
   b. chlorine   d. water

3. What is the chemical formula for iron(III) oxide?
   a. H_2O c. H_2O_2
   b. NaCl   d. Fe_2O_3

4. Which of the following is a mixture?
   a. air   c. water
   b. salt   d. sulfur

5. Most of the hot flavor in peppers comes from capsaicin, $C_{18}H_{27}NO_3$. Capsaicin is a(n) _____.
   a. element   c. pure substance
   b. mixture   d. atom

6. Which of the following assumptions is not part of the kinetic theory?
   a. All matter is made up of tiny, invisible particles.
   b. The particles are always moving.
   c. Particles move faster at higher temperatures.
   d. Particles are smaller at lower pressure.

7. The cube of metal shown below has a mass of 64 g. The density of the metal is _____.
   a. 2.0 g/cm³
   b. 4.0 g/cm³
   c. 8.0 g/cm³
   d. 21 g/cm³

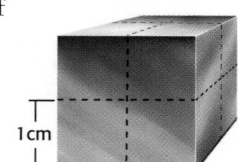
1cm

8. Three common states of matter are _____.
   a. solid, water, gas
   b. ice, water, gas
   c. solid, liquid, gas
   d. solid, liquid, air

9. Which of the following is a physical change?
   a. melting ice cubes
   b. burning paper
   c. rusting iron
   d. burning gasoline

10. In the figure below, the particles above the cup have _____.
    a. lost enough energy to sublime
    b. gained enough energy to sublime
    c. lost enough energy to evaporate
    d. gained enough energy to evaporate

Using Vocabulary

11. In an alcohol thermometer, the height of a constant amount of liquid alcohol in a thin glass tube increases or decreases as temperature changes. Using what you have learned about the kinetic theory, explain the behavior of the alcohol using the following terms: *lose energy, gain energy, volume (or space), movement, molecules (or particles).*

    WRITING SKILL

12. The figure at right shows magnesium burning in the presence of oxygen. Give some evidence that the figure shows signs that a chemical change is occurring.

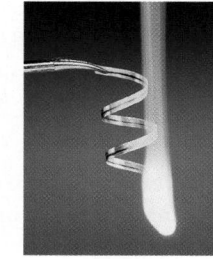

UNDERSTANDING CONCEPTS

1. c	**6.** d
2. d	**7.** c
3. d	**8.** c
4. a	**9.** a
5. c	**10.** d

Using Vocabulary

11. When the thermometer is placed in a warmer environment, the alcohol molecules gain energy, move more quickly and farther apart, and take up more space, so the column of alcohol moves higher in the tube. When placed in a cooler environment, the alcohol molecules lose energy, move more slowly, and take up less space, so the alcohol moves lower in the tube.

12. Energy is released; the properties of the magnesium change.

13. Physical properties include viscosity, density, buoyancy, melting point, dissolving, and conducting electricity. Chemical properties include reactivity, corrosion, flammability, and tarnishing.

14. The laws are not violated. The total missing mass of the wax, the burned wick, and the reacted oxygen equals the total mass of the gases and ash that result. The amount of energy released equals the amount of energy contained in the materials that were involved in the reaction.

RESOURCE LINK
STUDY GUIDE

Assign students *Mixed Review Chapter 2.*

15. The temperature is increasing. Ethylene glycol undergoes a change of state at 197°C; it is changing from a liquid to a gas. At 197°C, ethylene glycol molecules are absorbing energy to vaporize; there is no increase in temperature.

16. $D = 67.5 \text{ g}/15 \text{ cm}^3$
    $D = 4.5 \text{ g/cm}^3$

17. $D = 480 \text{ g}/620 \text{ cm}^3$
    $D = 0.77 \text{ g/cm}^3$

18. $D = 85 \text{ g}/110 \text{ cm}^3$
    $D = 0.77 \text{ g/cm}^3$
    It will float because its density is less than that of water (1.00 g/cm^3).

19. $V = 510 \text{ g}/(8.4 \text{ g/cm}^3)$
    $V = 61 \text{ cm}^3$

20. $m = 1 \text{ g/cm}^3 \times (100 \text{ cm} \times 50 \text{ cm} \times 30 \text{ cm})$
    $m = 1.5 \times 10^5 \text{ g}$

21. $V = 63.4 \text{ mL} - 40.0 \text{ mL}$
    $V = 23.4 \text{ mL} = 23.4 \text{ cm}^3$
    $m = 8.9 \text{ g/cm}^3 \times 23.4 \text{ cm}^3$
    $m = 210 \text{ g}$

THINKING CRITICALLY

22. Answers could include high melting point, hardness, and strength.

23. Both are insoluble in water and unreactive. The density of gold is greater than that of sand, so the gold sinks and the sand can be washed away.

24. nitrogen and oxygen; nitrogen; air

13. Make a table with two columns. Label one column "Physical properties" and the other "Chemical properties." Put each of the following terms in the proper column: *viscosity, density, reactivity, buoyancy, melting point, corrosion, flammability, dissolving, conducting electricity, tarnishing.*

14. When a candle is burned, the wax seems to disappear, and heat and light are given off. Does this violate the laws of conservation of mass and energy? Explain why or why not.

BUILDING MATH SKILLS

15. **Graphing** The graph below shows some effects of heating on ethylene glycol, the liquid commonly used as antifreeze. Until the temperature is 197°C, is the temperature increasing or decreasing? What physical change is taking place when the ethylene glycol is at 197°C? Describe what is happening to the ethylene glycol molecules at 197°C. How can you tell?

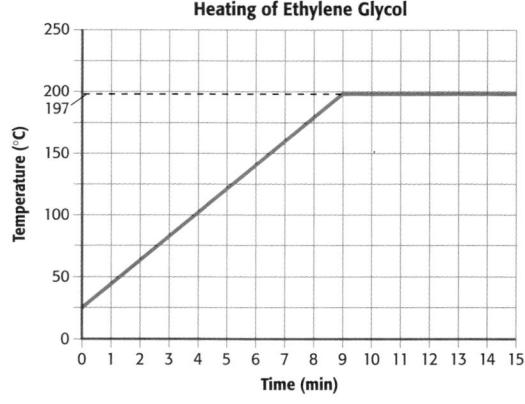

Heating of Ethylene Glycol

16. **Density** A piece of titanium metal has a mass of 67.5 g and a volume of 15 cm³. What is the density of titanium?

17. **Density** If a liquid has a volume of 620 cm³ and a mass of 480 g, what is its density?

18. **Density** A sample of a substance with a mass of 85 g occupies a volume of 110 cm³. What is the density of the substance? Will it float in water?

19. **Density** The density of a piece of brass is 8.4 g/cm³. If its mass is 510 g, find its volume.

20. **Density** What mass of water in grams will fill a tank 100 cm long, 50 cm wide, and 30 cm high?

21. **Density** A graduated cylinder is filled with water to a level of 40.0 mL. When a piece of copper is lowered into the cylinder, the water level rises to 63.4 mL. Find the volume of the copper sample. If the density of the copper is 8.9 g/cm³, what is its mass?

THINKING CRITICALLY

22. **Creative Thinking** Suppose you are planning a journey to the center of the Earth in a self-propelled tunneling machine. List properties of the special materials that would be needed to build the machine.

23. **Applying Knowledge** In the early history of the United States, people would search out sandy stream beds in which small particles of gold were mixed with the sand. The particles were separated by "panning." What properties of the two substances, gold and sand, made panning possible?

24. **Acquiring and Evaluating Data** The air in the Earth's atmosphere is a mixture. Research the atmosphere's contents. What are the main components of the Earth's atmosphere? What is the most abundant substance in the mixture? Is air or nitrogen more dense?

DEVELOPING LIFE/WORK SKILLS

25. **Applying Technology** Use a computer art program to illustrate a chemical change in which one atom and one molecule interact to form two molecules.

COMPUTER SKILL

26. **Working Cooperatively** Suppose you are given a piece of a material that is painted black so you cannot tell its normal appearance. Working in groups of three, plan tests you would do on the material to decide whether it is metal, glass, plastic, or wood.

27. **Making Decisions** The frame of a tennis racket needs to be strong and stiff, yet light. Tennis racket frames were once made of wood. But to be strong and stiff, the frame had to be thick and heavy. Now rackets can be made from different materials. Make a table of the advantages and disadvantages of each of the materials described in the graphs below.

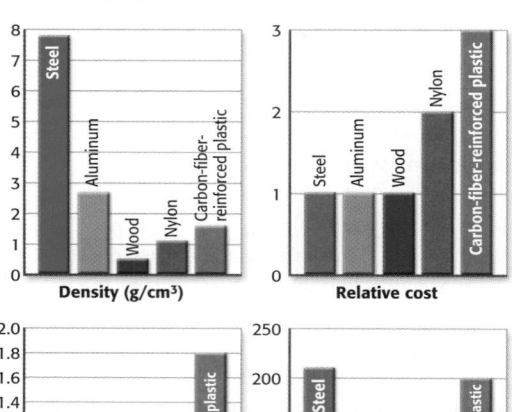

Density (g/cm³)

Relative cost

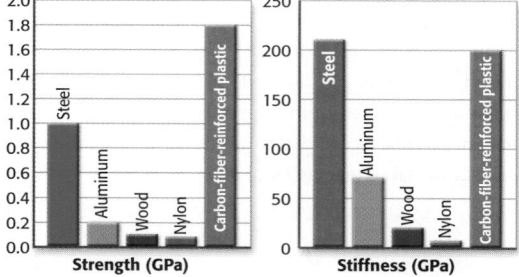

Strength (GPa)

Stiffness (GPa)

INTEGRATING CONCEPTS

28. **Concept Mapping** Copy the unfinished concept map below onto a sheet of paper. Complete the map by writing the correct word or phrase in the lettered boxes.

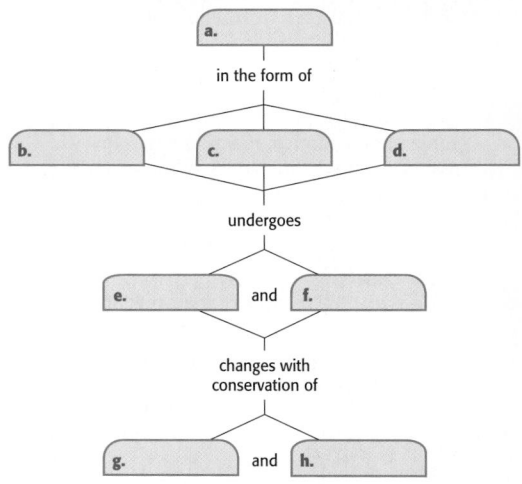

29. **Connection to Biology** Your body uses the food you eat to do work. However, some of the food energy is lost as heat. How does your body give off this heat?

30. **Connection to Language Arts** An element is sometimes named for one of its properties, an interesting fact about the element, or for the person who first discovered the element. Research the origin of the name of each of the following elements: promethium, oxygen, iridium, fermium, curium, tantalum, silver, polonium, ytterbium, and hafnium.

internetconnect

SCiLINKS
NSTA

TOPIC: Kinetic theory
GO TO: www.scilinks.org
KEYWORD: HK1025

MATTER **63**

DEVELOPING LIFE/ WORK SKILLS

25. Student art will vary but may include one atom and a three-atom molecule forming two two-atom molecules.
26. Student answers will vary but may include testing to see if the material conducts electricity (metal), burns (wood), or has a low melting point (plastic).
27. Tables should indicate that steel is strong, inexpensive, and stiff but too heavy; aluminum and wood are lightweight and inexpensive but not very strong or stiff; nylon is lightweight and somewhat inexpensive but not strong or stiff; and carbon-fiber is strong, lightweight, and stiff but expensive.

INTEGRATING CONCEPTS

28. **a.** matter
    b. solid
    c. liquid
    d. gas
    e. physical
    f. chemical
    g. mass
    h. energy
29. Answers could include heat given off during breathing and excretion and heat given off by the skin.

Answers continue on p. 65B.

RESOURCE LINK
IER

Assign students worksheet *2.6: Connection to Language Arts— Hidden Meanings.*

Design Your Own Lab

Testing the Conservation of Mass

Introduction

Students will probably be familiar with the concepts of chemical change and conservation of mass. This lab can be used as a discrepant event that challenges what the students already know about these topics.

Objectives

Students will:

▶ **Use** appropriate lab safety procedures.

▶ **Measure** the masses of reactants and products in a chemical reaction.

▶ **Design** an experiment to test the law of conservation of mass.

▶ **Relate** the observations of a chemical reaction to the law of conservation of mass.

Planning

Recommended Time: 1 lab period
Materials: *(for each lab group)*

▶ 15 g of baking soda, NaHCO₃

▶ 100 mL graduated cylinder

▶ 200 mL of vinegar

▶ 400 mL beaker

▶ 2 clear plastic cups (capable of holding at least 150 mL each)

▶ Balance

▶ 2 weighing papers

▶ Plastic sandwich bag with zipper-type closure

▶ 2 twist ties

RESOURCE LINK
DATASHEETS

Have students use *Datasheet 2.3 Design Your Own Lab: Testing the Conservation of Mass* to record their results.

Design Your Own Lab

Introduction

How can you show that mass is conserved in a chemical reaction between two household substances—vinegar and baking soda?

Objectives

▶ **Measure** the masses of reactants and products in a chemical reaction.

▶ **Design** an experiment to test the law of conservation of mass.

Materials

baking soda (sodium bicarbonate)
vinegar (acetic acid solution)
400 mL beaker (optional)
100 mL graduated cylinder
2 clear plastic cups (capable of holding at least 150 mL each)
balance (with standard masses, if necessary)
2 weighing papers
plastic sandwich bag with zipper-type closure
twist tie

Safety Needs

safety goggles
lab apron
polyethylene gloves
rimmed tray with paper lining

Testing the Conservation of Mass

▶ Observing the Reaction Between Vinegar and Baking Soda

1. On a blank sheet of paper, prepare a table like the one shown below.

	Initial mass (g)	Final mass (g)	Change in mass (g)
Trial 1			
Trial 2			

SAFETY CAUTION Put on a lab apron, safety goggles, and gloves. If you get a chemical on your skin or clothing, wash it off at the sink while calling to your teacher. If you get a chemical in your eyes, immediately flush it out at the eyewash station while calling to your teacher. When mixing chemicals, use a rimmed tray with a paper lining to catch and absorb spills.

2. Place a piece of weighing paper on the balance. Place about 4–5 g of baking soda on the paper. Carefully transfer the baking soda to a plastic cup.

3. Using the graduated cylinder, measure about 50 mL of vinegar. Pour the vinegar into the second plastic cup.

4. Place both cups on the balance, and determine the combined mass of the cups, baking soda, and vinegar to the nearest 0.01 g. Record the combined mass in the first row of your table under "Initial mass."

5. Take the cups off the balance. Carefully and slowly pour the vinegar into the cup that contains the baking soda. To avoid splattering, add only a small amount of vinegar at a time. Gently swirl the cup to make sure the reactants are well mixed.

6. When the reaction has finished, place both cups back on the balance. Determine the combined mass to the nearest 0.01 g. Record the combined mass in the first row of your table under "Final mass."

SOLUTION/MATERIAL PREPARATION

1. Use vinegar and baking soda purchased through a supply company or at a grocery store. Use white vinegar instead of diluted glacial acetic acid.

2. Provide fairly large plastic bags, such as the 1 qt size available at most stores.

3. Have students do the reaction over a rimmed tray lined with absorbent paper to catch spills.

4. The weighing paper you provide should be large enough to hold 4–5 g of baking soda. If plastic weighing boats are available, you might want to have students use them instead of weighing paper to minimize spills.

7. Subtract the final mass from the initial mass, and record the result in the first row of your table under "Change in mass."

▶ Designing Your Experiment

8. Examine the plastic bag and the twist ties. With your lab partners, develop a procedure that will test the law of conservation of mass more accurately than Trial 1 did. Which products' masses were not measured? How can you be sure you measure the masses of all of the reaction products?
9. In your lab report, list each step you will perform in your experiment.
10. Before you carry out your experiment, your teacher must approve your plan.

▶ Performing Your Experiment

11. After your teacher approves your plan, perform your experiment using approximately the same quantities of baking soda and vinegar you used in Trial 1.
12. Record the initial mass, final mass, and change in mass in your table.

▶ Analyzing Your Results

1. Compare the changes in mass you calculated for the first and second trials. What value would you expect to obtain for a change in mass if both trials validated the law of conservation of mass?
2. Was the law of conservation of mass violated in the first trial? Explain your reasoning.
3. If the results of the second trial were different from those of the first trial, explain why.

▶ Defending Your Conclusions

4. Suppose someone performs an experiment like the one you designed and finds that the final mass is much less than the initial mass. Would that prove that the law of conservation of mass is wrong? Explain your reasoning.

Pre-Lab

Teaching Tips

The less you demonstrate for the students and the more they figure out on their own, the better. To explain what has actually happened and come up with a procedure that truly tests conservation of mass, students will have to think about what they observed and imagine what is going on at the level of individual particles. You may need to show students the equation for the reaction. If students need hints, the following leading questions may help them understand why mass did not appear to be conserved in Trial 1.

▶ What evidence was there of a chemical reaction?
▶ Were the products of the reaction solids, liquids, or gases?
▶ How well do the containers you used hold liquids? How well do they hold gases?
▶ How can you use the plastic bag and twist ties to be certain that the reaction takes place in a container that holds liquids and gases?

Continue on p. 65A.

REQUIRED PRECAUTIONS

▶ Safety goggles and a lab apron must be worn at all times.
▶ Read all safety cautions, and discuss them with your students.
▶ In case of an acid spill, first dilute the spill with water. Then mop up the spill with wet cloths or a wet cloth mop while wearing disposable gloves. Designate separate cloths or mops for acid spills.

Design Your Own Lab from page 65
Testing the Conservation of Mass

Pre-Lab

Teaching Tips

It may be necessary to show students that you can use a twist tie to keep the baking soda isolated in one corner of the bag so the vinegar can be poured in without the two immediately reacting.

Procedure

▶ Designing Your Experiment

The second half of the lab is designed to be an open-ended inquiry. Students need to come up with a way to make sure that the reaction system is truly closed.

Measure out 4–5 g of baking soda. Pour it into the corner of the bag. Using a twist tie, separate the corner from the rest of the bag. Add about 50 mL of vinegar to the bag. Seal the top of the bag so that the vinegar cannot leak out and the bag is airtight. Place the bag in the 400 mL beaker. Measure the mass of the bag, the beaker, and the reactants. Remove the twist tie that kept the baking soda separate from the vinegar, and allow the two to mix. Replace the bag in the beaker. As the reaction occurs, the bag will inflate. After the reaction is complete, measure the mass of the bag, beaker, and products.

Note: *Because the bag inflates, a mass loss of as much as 0.5-0.7 g will be found even if the bag is perfectly sealed, due to the effect of the buoyant force of air displaced.* If you wish to avoid this error, one way of reducing it is to inflate the bag with air to the approximate volume it is expected to be filled by the CO_2 and seal it prior to measuring its mass the first time. Thus, the volume change and the effects of the buoyant force that it induces will be minimized. Then deflate the bag completely, re-seal it and allow the reactants to mix.

Post-Lab

▶ Disposal

All of the solutions and chemicals used in this investigation may be washed down the sink with an excess of water. Weighing papers, paper cups, and disposable gloves can be placed in the trash can.

▶ Analyzing Your Results

1. Most students will observe that the mass change was greater in the first trial than in the second trial. The expected change in mass would be 0 g.
2. No. One of the products of the reaction is a gas, carbon dioxide. Since it escapes from the cup, its mass is not measured in the first test. Although students may not know that the reaction produces carbon dioxide, they can infer that some gas is produced by watching the bubbles that are formed.
3. The second test should have retained the gas within the plastic bag, so that the masses of all of the products could be determined.

▶ Defending Your Conclusions

4. No. The plastic bag may not have been sealed tight, allowing much of the gas produced by the reaction to escape, or one of the masses may have been measured incorrectly.

Answers from page 44

8. David's statement reflects the common use of *pure*. Susan's use of *pure* is more correct scientifically because honey is a mixture of several different compounds.

Answers from page 52

8. Gas particles have enough energy to move freely in all directions. Every time a person touches something, traces that are characteristic of that person are left behind. As those traces absorb energy and vaporize, a dog that has a keen sense of smell can detect them.

Answers from page 63

30. Promethium—named after Prometheus in Greek mythology; oxygen—named for Greek words that mean "acid former"; iridium—from the Greek word *iris,* meaning "rainbow"; fermium—named after Enrico Fermi; curium—named after Pierre and Marie Curie; tantalum—from the Greek word *tantalos,* which means "father of Niobe," because tantalum is closely related to niobium; silver—from the Anglo-Saxon word *siolfur;* polonium—named after Poland, the birthplace of Marie Curie; ytterbium—named after Ytterby, Sweden; hafnium—from the Latin word *Hafnia,* meaning "Copenhagen," because the element was discovered in Denmark.

Paper or Plastic at the Grocery Store?

viewpoints

viewpoints

Paper or Plastic at the Grocery Store?

viewpoints

LINKING CHAPTERS

The debate described in these pages is centered around a simple idea from Chapter 2—the selection of materials for specific uses based on their properties.

Challenge students to list chemical and physical properties of paper and plastic grocery bags. The following are some possible responses:

Chemical Properties
Paper: biodegradable
Plastic: breaks down when exposed to sunlight

Physical Properties
Paper: tears easily when wet; does not stretch
Plastic: does not break when wet; stretches

> **Your Turn**

1. Critiquing Viewpoints
Students' analyses of a single argument's weak points may vary. Be sure that student responses clearly identify a weakness and respond in some way that provides support. Possible responses are listed below. (Note that students should analyze only *one of the following.*)
Jaclyn M.: Effective recycling requires that there is an effective use for the recycled materials. Not many businesses need reused bags.

But grocery stores might be better off without constantly reordering bags.
Eric S.: While paper is a renewable resource, the time it takes to grow a tree is very long.

But it is still better to use renewable resources.
Christy M.: Obtaining and refining petroleum for plastic bags can displace animals and plants from their habitats.

However, removal of trees can change an entire ecosystem, too.

As people focus more on the environment, there is a debate raging at the grocery store. It begins with a simple question asked at the checkout counter: "Paper or plastic?"

Some say that paper is a bad choice because making paper bags requires cutting down trees. Yet these bags are naturally biodegradable, and they recycle easily.

Others say that plastic is not a good choice because plastic bags are made from nonrenewable petroleum products. But recent advances have made plastic bags that can break down when exposed to sunlight. Many stores collect used plastic bags and recycle them to make new ones.

How should people decide which bags to use? What do you think?

> FROM: Jaclyn M., Chicago, IL

I think people should choose paper bags because they can be recycled and reused. There should be a mandatory law that makes sure each community has a weekly recycling service for paper bags.

PAPER!

> FROM: Eric S., Rochester, MN

When it comes down to it, both types of bags can be recycled. However, as we know, not everybody recycles bags. Therefore, paper is a better choice because it is a renewable resource.

PLASTIC!

> FROM: Christy M., Houston, TX.

I believe we should use more plastic bags in grocery stores. By using paper we are chopping down not only trees but also the homes of animals and plants.

> FROM: Ashley A., Dyer, IN

Plastic is not necessarily better, but is a lot more convenient. You can reuse plastic bags as garbage bags or bags to carry anything you need to take with you. Plastic is also easier to carry when you leave the store. Plastic bags don't get wet in the rain and break, causing you to drop your groceries on the ground.

66 VIEWPOINTS

Ashley A.: A plastic bag's handles can stretch and tear if it is too full.

But it's a simple matter to make sure you don't overload a plastic bag.
Andrew S.: People don't always make the right choices.

But if everyone were recycling their bags, fewer bags would get used in the first place.
Alice K: Bringing canvas bags may not work if you don't always buy the same amount of groceries.

However, even if you use an extra bag every now and then, you're still saving more bags.

2. Critiquing Viewpoints
Students' analyses of strong points in opposing arguments may vary. Be sure that student responses clearly identify the strong points and respond in some way that provides support for the opposite point of view. Possible responses are listed below. (Note that students should analyze only *one of the following.*)
Jaclyn M.: Mandatory recycling laws would greatly increase recycling.

Community size may make such services hard to manage.

> FROM: Andrew S., Bowling Green, KY
> ---
> People should be able to use the bags they want. People that use paper bags should try to recycle them. People that use plastic bags should reuse them. We should be able to choose, as long as we recycle the bags in some way.

> FROM: Alicia K., Coral Springs, FL
> ---
> Canvas bags would be a better choice than the paper or plastic bags used in stores. Canvas bags are made mostly of cotton, a very renewable resource, whereas paper bags are made from trees, and plastic bags are made from nonrenewable petroleum products.

BOTH or NEITHER!

Your Turn

1. **Critiquing Viewpoints** Select one of the statements on this page that you *agree* with. Identify and explain at least one weak point in the statement. What would you say to respond to someone who brought up this weak point as a reason you were wrong?

2. **Critiquing Viewpoints** Select one of the statements on this page that you *disagree* with. Identify and explain at least one strong point in the statement. What would you say to respond to someone who brought up this point as a reason they were right?

3. **Creative Thinking** Make a list of at least 12 additional ways for people to reuse their plastic or paper bags.

4. **Life/Work Skills** Imagine that you are trying to decrease the number of bags being sent to the local landfill. Develop a presentation or a brochure that you could use to convince others to reuse or recycle their bags.

internet connect

TOPIC: Paper vs. plastic
GO TO: go.hrw.com
KEYWORD: HK1Grocery bag

Which kind of bag do you think is best to use? Why? Share your views on this issue and learn about other viewpoints at the HRW Web site.

67

Creative Thinking continued

2. Use bags to line household trash cans.
3. Use bags to carry lunches.
4. Use bags to carry gym clothes.
5. Use plastic bags to keep books and papers dry.
6. Use bags to organize clothes placed in storage.

4. **Life/Work Skills**

Evaluate students' presentations or brochures using a scale of 1–5 points for each of the following: creativity, factuality, persuasiveness, attention to detail, and effort. (25 total possible points)

Eric S.: It's better to use renewable resources, because not everyone recycles bags.

Maybe people should change.
Christy M.: Logging can disrupt ecosystems.

However, paper bags are biodegradable.
Ashley A.: Plastic bags are sturdier than paper bags are when wet.

But should the environment be sacrificed for convenience's sake?
Andrew S.: Improve recycling of all bags instead of making laws.

But why continue to let people use a less effective kind of bag?
Alicia K: Canvas bags can be reused for years without wearing out.

Canvas bags are paid for by the consumer instead of the seller.

3. **Creative Thinking**
Evaluate students' lists based on how creative and practical they are. Sample lists are provided below.

Paper Bag Reuses

1. Bring bags back to the store and reuse them.
2. Use bags to line household trash cans.
3. Use bags to carry lunches.
4. Keep unripe fruit in paper bags to ripen.
5. Cut apart bags and place them on the garage floor to catch oil leaks from cars.
6. Cut apart bags and use them to make book covers for textbooks.

Plastic Bag Reuses

1. Bring bags back to the store and reuse them.

---

internet connect

The HRW Web site has more opinions from other students and also provides an opportunity for your students to contribute their points of view. Every few months, more opinions will be added from the ones submitted. Student opinions that are posted will be identified only by the student's first name, last initial, and city to protect his or her privacy.

Tailoring the Program to YOUR Classroom

CHAPTER 3

Atoms and the Periodic Table

Annotated Descriptions of the Correlated National Science Standards

The following descriptions summarize the National Science Standards that specially relate to Chapter 3. For the full text of the Standards, see p. 40T.

SECTION 3.1
Atomic Structure
Physical Science
PS 1a, 1c, 2b
Unifying Concepts and Processes
UCP 2
History and Nature of Science
HNS 1, 3

SECTION 3.2
A Guided Tour of the Periodic Table
Physical Science
PS 1c, 2a, 2b
Unifying Concepts and Processes
UCP 1, 5

SECTION 3.3
Families of Elements
Physical Science
PS 2a, 2b
Science as Inquiry
SAI 1
Science in Personal and Social Perspectives
SPSP 2, 5

SECTION 3.4
Using Moles to Count Atoms
Unifying Concepts and Processes
UCP 3
History and Nature of Science
HNS 3

Cross-Discipline Teaching RESOURCES

Cross-Discipline Teaching, ATE p. 68
Mathematics   Social Studies

Integration Enrichment Resources
Real World Applications, **PE** and **ATE** p. 74
  IE 3.1 *How Do Scientists Find Cures for Diseases?*
Architecture, **PE** and **ATE** p. 91
  IE 3.2 *Buckyball*
Earth Science, **PE** and **ATE** p. 92
  IE 3.3 *Magnesium: From Sea Water to Fireworks*

Additional Integration Enrichment Worksheets
  IE 3.4 Language Arts   IE 3.5 Fine Arts
  IE 3.6 Biology   IE 3.7 Technology
  IE 3.8 Physics

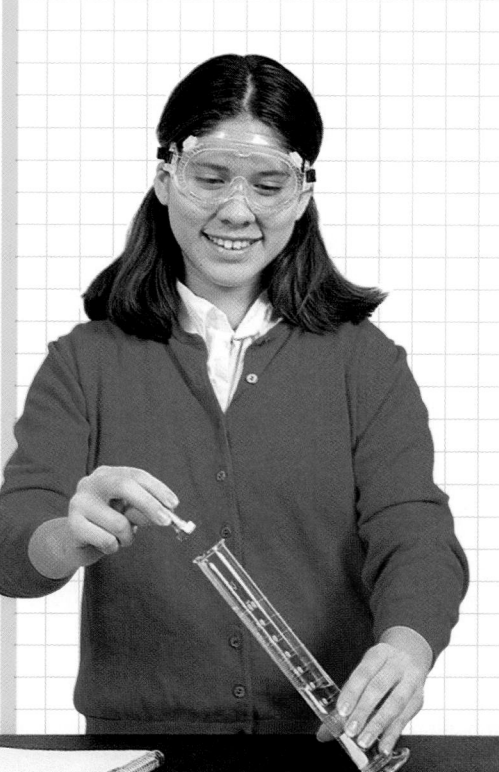

Use the Planning Guide on the next page to help you organize your lessons.

MATH AND COMPUTER RESOURCES

Chapter 3	Math Skills	Assess	Media/Computer Skills
Section 3.1	**ATE Cross-Discipline Teaching,** p. 68 **BS Worksheet 2.2:** Scientific Notation		■ Section 3.1 💿 **DISC ONE, MODULE 2** Models of the Atom **CNN Presents Chemistry Connections** Segment 13 Atom Builders **CRT** Worksheet 13
Section 3.2		**PE Building Math Skills,** p. 102, item 16	■ Section 3.2 💿 **DISC ONE, MODULE 3** Periodic Properties
Section 3.3			■ Section 3.3 **PE Inquiry Lab,** p. 90 **CNN Presents Chemistry Connections** Segment 5 Making Fullerenes **CRT** Worksheet 5
Section 3.4	**BS Worksheet 2.3:** Dimensional Analysis and Conversions **PE Math Skills** Conversion Factors, p. 98 **ATE Additional Examples** p. 98 **PE Math Skills** Converting Amount to Mass, p. 99 **ATE Additional Examples** p. 99 **PE Math Skills** Converting Mass to Amount, p. 100	**MS** Worksheets 6–8 **PE Practice,** p. 98 **PE Practice,** p. 99 **PE Section Review** 6–9, p. 100 **PE Building Math Skills,** p. 102, items 17–20 **PE Problem Bank,** p. 694, 26–40	■ Section 3.4

PE Pupil's Edition **ATE** Annotated Teacher's Edition **MS** Math Skills **BS** Basic Skills
IE Integration Enrichment ■ Guided Reading Audio **CRT** Critical Thinking

READING SKILL BUILDER

The following activities found in the Annotated Teacher's Edition provide techniques for developing useful reading strategies to increase your students' reading comprehension skills.

Section 3.1 **Brainstorming,** p. 68
Prediction Guide, p. 70, 75

Section 3.2 **Reading Hint,** p. 77

Section 3.3 **Summarizing,** p. 86

Section 3.4 **Reading Organizer,** p. 95

Smithsonian Institution®
Visit www.si.edu/hrw for additional online resources.

Spanish Resources

The following resources are made available for students who speak Spanish as their first language.

Spanish Resources Guided Reading Audio CD-ROM Chapter 3

Spanish Glossary Chapter 3

Atoms and the Periodic Table

CLASSROOM RESOURCES		
FOCUS	**TEACH**	**HANDS-ON**

Section 3.1: Atomic Structure

BLOCK 1
45 minutes

ATE **RSB** Brainstorming, p. 68
ATE Focus Activities 1, 2, p. 69
ATE **RSB** Prediction Guide, p. 70
  PE What Are Atoms? pp. 70–72
  ★ Focus Transparency LT 7
ATE **Demo 1** Charged Particles, p. 70
	ATE **Skill Builder** Interpreting Visuals,
	pp. 69, 72
		IE Worksheet 3.7

BLOCK 2
45 minutes

ATE **RSB** Prediction Guide, p. 75 **PE** Models of the Atom, pp. 73–76	**TT** 7 Building Model **BLM** 8 Subatomic Particles	**PE** Quick Activity *Convincing John Dalton,* p. 73 **DS** 3.1 **PE** Real World Applications *Designing Drugs,* p. 74 **IE** Worksheets 3.1, 3.8 **PE** Quick Activity *Constructing a Model,* p. 75 **DS** 3.2

Section 3.2: A Guided Tour of the Periodic Table

BLOCK 3
45 minutes

ATE **RSB** Reading Hint, p. 77
ATE **Demo 2** Periodicity, p. 77
  PE Organization of the Periodic Table, pp. 77–82
  ★ Focus Transparency LT 8
	ATE **Skill Builder** Vocabulary,
	pp. 77, 81
	Interpreting Visuals, p. 78
	BLM 9 Periodic Table
		LE **3** *Predicting the Physical and Chemical Properties of Elements* **DS** 3.7
		IE Worksheets 3.4, 3.6

BLOCK 4
45 minutes

PE How Do the Structures of Atoms Differ? pp. 82–85	**ATE** **Graphic Organizer** Mass Number, p. 82 **ATE** **Skill Builder** Diagrams, p. 84 **TT** 8 Nucleus **TT** 9 Isotopes	**PE** Quick Activity *Isotopes,* p. 84 **DS** 3.3 **IE** Worksheet 3.5

Section 3.3: Families of Elements

BLOCK 5
45 minutes

ATE **RSB** Summarizing, p. 86
ATE **Demo 3** Conductivity, p. 86
  PE Metals, pp. 86–90
  ★ Focus Transparency LT 9
	ATE **Skill Builder** Interpreting Visuals,
	p. 89
	Vocabulary, p. 90
		PE Quick Activity *Elements in Your Food,* p. 88 **DS** 3.4
		PE Inquiry Lab *Why do some metals cost more than others?* p. 90 **DS** 3.5

BLOCK 6
45 minutes

ATE **Demo 4** Greeting, p. 93 **PE** Nonmetals, pp. 91–94	**ATE** **Skill Builder** Interpreting Visuals, p. 91	**IE** Worksheets 3.2, 3.3

Section 3.4: Using Moles to Count Atoms

BLOCK 7
45 minutes

ATE **RSB** Reading Organizer, p. 95
ATE **Demo 5** Counting by Mass, p. 95
  PE Calculating with Moles, pp. 95–98
  ★ Focus Transparency LT 10
	BLM 10 Mole–Mass Graph
	BLM 11 Mole–Mass Conversion	

BLOCK 8
45 minutes

PE Relating Moles to Grams, pp. 98–100	**ATE** **Skill Builder** Graphs, p. 98 Interpreting Visuals, p. 99 **ATE** **Graphic Organizer** Conversion Factors, p. 100	**PE** Design Your Own Lab *Comparing the Physical Properties of Elements,* p. 104 **DS** 3.6

CLASSROOM RESOURCES

HOMEWORK	ASSESS
PE Section Review 3, 5, p. 76 **Chapter 3 Review,** p. 101, items 1, 11	**SG** Chapter 3 Pretest
PE Section Review 1, 2, 4, 6–8, p. 76 **Chapter 3 Review,** p. 101, items 2, 3	**SG** Section 3.1
PE Section Review 3–5, p. 85 **Chapter 3 Review,** p. 101, items 6, 13	**ATE** *ALTERNATIVE ASSESSMENT,* Chemical Symbols, p. 78 **ATE** *ALTERNATIVE ASSESSMENT,* Periodicity, p. 80
PE Section Review 1, 2, 6–8, p. 85 **Chapter 3 Review,** p. 101, items 4, 12, 16	**ATE** *ALTERNATIVE ASSESSMENT,* Weighted Average, p. 85 **SG** Section 3.2
PE Section Review 1, 2, 6–8, p. 94 **Chapter 3 Review,** p. 101, item 5	
PE Section Review 3–5, p. 94 **Chapter 3 Review,** p. 101, items 7–9, 14	**SG** Section 3.3
PE Section Review 1, 4, p. 100 **Chapter 3 Review,** p. 101, items 10, 15	**ATE** *ALTERNATIVE ASSESSMENT,* Conversion Factors, p. 97
PE Section Review 2, 3, 5–9, p. 100 **Chapter 3 Review,** p. 101, items 17–20	**SG** Section 3.4

BLOCK 9

Chapter 3 Review
Thinking Critically 21–25, p. 102
Developing Life/Work Skills 26–29, p. 102–103
Integrating Concepts 30–32, p. 103
SG Chapter 3 Mixed Review

BLOCK 10

Chapter Tests
Chapter 3 Test

One-Stop Planner CD-ROM with Test Generator
Chapter 3

Teaching Resources
Scoring Rubrics and assignment checklist.

---

internet**connect**

SC*i*LINKS
NSTA

National Science Teachers
Association
Online Resources:
www.scilinks.org
The following *sci*LINKS Internet resources can be found
in the student text for this chapter.

Page 69 **TOPIC:** Metals **KEYWORD:** HK1031	**Page 86** **TOPIC:** Element families **KEYWORD:** HK1035
Page 72 **TOPIC:** Parts of an atom **KEYWORD:** HK1032	**Page 97** **TOPIC:** Avogadro's constant **KEYWORD:** HK1036
Page 73 **TOPIC:** History of atomic models **KEYWORD:** HK1033	**Page 101** **TOPIC:** Silicon **KEYWORD:** HK1037
Page 80 **TOPIC:** Periodic table **KEYWORD:** HK1034	**Page 103** **TOPIC:** Origin of elements **KEYWORD:** HK1038

CNNfyi.com www.cnnfyi.com

Visit this site for coverage of current events and related
classroom resources.

PE Pupil's Edition **ATE** Teacher's Edition
RSB Reading Skill Builder **DS** Datasheets
IE Integrated Enrichment **SG** Study Guide
LE Laboratory Experiments
TT Teaching Transparencies **BLM** Blackline Masters
★ Lesson Focus Transparency

CHAPTER 3

Atoms and the Periodic Table

READING SKILL BUILDER *Brainstorming* Review with students the definition of an element. Have them brainstorm a list of substances that they think are elements. Have them use Sections 3.2 and 3.3 to confirm whether or not each of the substances on their list is an element. Have them use the properties of the elements to devise a classification system for elements.

Chapter Preview

68

CROSS-DISCIPLINE TEACHING

Mathematics Have students brainstorm counting units, such as gross, score, or those mentioned in Section 3.4. Give students certain quantities of items and have them calculate the number of each unit present.

Social Studies From the business section of a major newspaper, obtain current costs of precious metals. While studying moles in Section 3.4, have students find the current cost of 1 mol of each metal.

Social Studies Have students do research and then make a timeline that shows the development of the modern atomic theory, identifying on the timeline the contributions of key physicists and chemists.

Focus ACTIVITY

Background Have you ever wondered why coins shine? Coins shine because they are made of metals that reflect light. Another property of metals is that they do not shatter. Metals bend as they are pressed into thin, flat sheets during the coin-making process. All metals share some similarities, but each metal has its own unique chemical and physical properties.

Metals, like everything around us, are made of trillions of tiny units that are too small to see called atoms. Atoms determine the properties of all substances. For example, gold atoms make gold coins softer and shinier than silver coins, which are made of silver atoms. Pennies get their color from the copper atoms they are coated with. In this chapter, you will learn what determines an atom's properties, why atoms are considered the smallest units of elements, and how elements are classified.

Activity 1 What metals do you see during a typical day? Describe their uses and their properties.

Activity 2 Describe several different ways to classify the coins shown on the opposite page.

internetconnect

SCILINKS NSTA

TOPIC: Metals
GO TO: www.scilinks.org
KEYWORD: HK1031

Atoms determine the properties of objects. For example, metal atoms give these coins their shine and their ability to be pressed flat by this stamping press.

Focus ACTIVITY

Background Certain elements are classified as metals because of their properties. Two properties of all metals are malleability and ductility.

Malleability is the ability of a metal to be hammered or rolled into a sheet without breaking. Malleability enables metals to be shaped into useful objects, such as sheets.

Ductility is the ability to be drawn into a wire. Ductility and the ability to conduct electricity make metals good materials for electrical wiring.

Activity 1 Answers will vary but could include the steel that is used in vehicles, which is strong and durable, or the lightweight aluminum used in beverage cans.

Activity 2 Answers will vary but could include classification according to size, denomination, or composition.

SKILL BUILDER

Interpreting Visuals Have students look at the coins in the photos and list the metals that they think are used in the coins. Observe the edges of several clad coins. Discuss how a combination of value and properties determines what metals are used to make coins.

69

Scheduling

Refer to pp. 68A–68D for lecture, classwork, and assignment options for Section 3.1.

★ **Lesson Focus**
Use transparency *LT 7* to prepare students for this section.

READING SKILL BUILDER *Prediction Guide*
Write the following statements on the chalkboard:
- An atom cannot be broken down into smaller parts.
- An atom is the same throughout.
- An atom is made up of several different, smaller parts.

Ask students their opinions of the statements. Have them discuss the opinions and try to justify their own opinions. Save a list of the opinions for discussion after completing the section.

3.1

Atomic Structure

▶ **KEY TERMS**
nucleus
proton
neutron
electron
energy level
orbital
valence electron

PHYSICAL SCIENCE **INTERACTIVE TUTOR**

Disc One, Module 2:
Models of the Atom
Use the Interactive Tutor to learn more about this topic.

OBJECTIVES

▶ Explain Dalton's atomic theory, and describe why it was more successful than Democritus's theory.

▶ State the charge, mass, and location of each part of an atom according to the modern model of the atom.

▶ Compare and contrast Bohr's model with the modern model of the atom.

Atoms are all around you. They make up the air you are breathing, the chair you are sitting in, and the clothes you are wearing. This book, including this page you are reading, is also made of atoms.

What Are Atoms?

Atoms are tiny units that determine the properties of all matter. The aluminum cans shown in **Figure 3-1** are lightweight and easy to crush because of the properties of the atoms that make up the aluminum.

Aluminum Atoms

Our understanding of atoms required many centuries

In the fourth century B.C., the Greek philosopher Democritus suggested that the universe was made of invisible units called atoms. The word *atom* is derived from the Greek word meaning "unable to be divided." He believed movements of atoms caused the changes in matter that he observed.

Although Democritus's theory of atoms explained some observations, Democritus was unable to provide the evidence needed to convince people that atoms really existed. Throughout the centuries that followed, some people supported Democritus's theory. But other theories were also proposed. As the science of chemistry was developing in the 1700s, more emphasis was put on making careful and repeated measurements in scientific experiments. As a result, more-reliable data were collected that were used to favor one theory over another.

Figure 3-1
The atoms in aluminum, seen here as an image from a scanning tunneling electron microscope, give these aluminum cans their properties.

DEMONSTRATION 1 **TEACHING**

Charged Particles

Time: Approximately 10 minutes
Materials: glass rod, silk, rubber rod, fur, electroscope

Rub the glass rod with silk. Touch the rod to an electroscope. Then rub the rubber rod with fur. Touch this rod to the electroscope.

Analysis
1. What did you observe? *(The electroscope leaves repel each other when the glass rod is used and do not when the rubber rod is used.)*
2. Explain these observations. *(The glass rod became charged. The rubber rod acquired an opposite charge.)*
3. What do you think are the sources for the charges? *(charge transfers from silk and fur)*

Atoms are the building blocks of molecules

In 1808, an English schoolteacher named John Dalton proposed his own atomic theory. Dalton's theory was widely accepted because there was much evidence to support it. In his theory, Dalton proposed the following:

- Every element is made of tiny, unique particles called atoms that cannot be subdivided.
- Atoms of the same element are exactly alike.
- Atoms of different elements can join to form molecules.

An atom is the smallest part of an element that still has the element's properties. Imagine dividing a coin made of pure copper until the pieces were too small for you to see. If you were able to continue dividing these pieces, you would be left with the simplest units of the coin—copper atoms. All the copper atoms would be exactly alike. Each copper atom would have chemical properties mostly the same as the coin you started with.

You learned in Chapter 2 that atoms can join. **Figure 3-2** shows how atoms join to form molecules of water. The water we see is actually made of a very large number of water molecules. Whether it gushes downstream in a riverbed or is bottled for us to drink, water is always the same: each molecule is made of two hydrogen atoms and one oxygen atom.

Figure 3-2

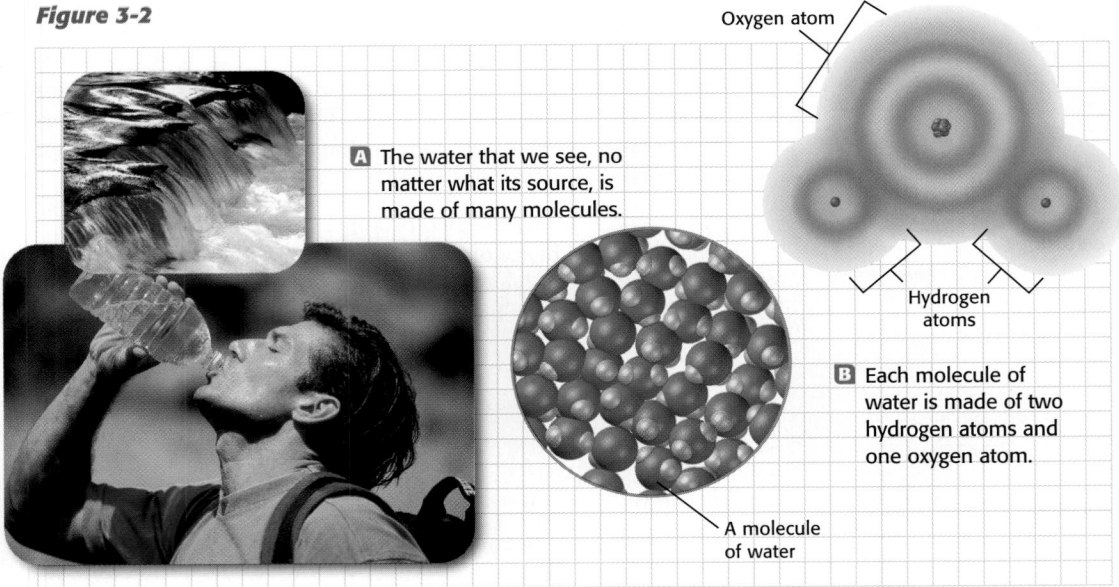

Oxygen atom

A The water that we see, no matter what its source, is made of many molecules.

Hydrogen atoms

B Each molecule of water is made of two hydrogen atoms and one oxygen atom.

A molecule of water

Multicultural Extension

The ancient Greeks accepted an atomic theory that attributed the properties of a substance to the properties of the atoms that made it up. For example, they thought gold was shiny because its atoms were shiny.

Islamic philosophers of the Middle Ages accepted an atomic theory that attributed properties to the arrangement of atoms, not to the atoms themselves.

MISCONCEPTION ALERT

Properties Be sure students understand that atoms are responsible for properties, but the atoms themselves do not possess them. For example, silver is shiny, but silver atoms are not shiny. Electron arrangement in atoms is the largest determining factor of properties.

Teaching Tip

Neutral Atoms On the chalkboard, write a number line that contains both positive and negative numbers. Use the number line to show students that adding equal numbers of positive and negative charges results in no charge—zero on the number line.

SKILL BUILDER

Interpreting Visuals Students might ask why the protons in the nucleus stay together since positive charges repel each other.

Tell students that even though the protons in the nucleus do electrically repel each other, they are held together by a force known simply as the *nuclear force*. This force is unique to the nucleus and exists only over very short distances.

Gravity also attracts nuclear particles to each other. But gravity is not the main force that holds the nucleus together, as in **Figure 3-3,** because it is not strong enough to overcome the electrical repulsion.

72

---

internet connect

SCLINKS
NSTA

TOPIC: Parts of an atom
GO TO: www.scilinks.org
KEYWORD: HK1032

▶ **nucleus** the center of an atom; made up of protons and neutrons

▶ **proton** a positively charged subatomic particle in the nucleus of an atom

▶ **neutron** a neutral subatomic particle in the nucleus of an atom

▶ **electron** a tiny negatively charged subatomic particle moving around outside the nucleus of an atom

VOCABULARY *Skills Tip*

Remember that **p**rotons *have a* **positive** *charge and* **neutr**ons *are* **neutral.**

Figure 3-3
A helium atom is made of two protons, two neutrons, and two electrons ($2e^-$).

Helium Atom

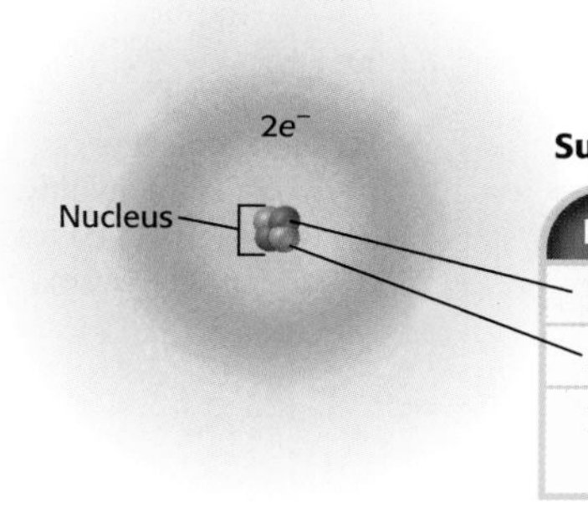

$2e^-$

Nucleus

72 CHAPTER 3

What's in an Atom?

Less than 100 years after Dalton published his atomic theory, scientists determined that atoms could be split, or broken down even further. While we now know that there are many different subatomic particles making up atoms, only three of these are involved in the everyday chemistry of most substances.

Atoms are made of protons, neutrons, and electrons

At the center of each atom is a small, dense **nucleus** with a positive electric charge. The nucleus is made of **protons** and **neutrons.** These two subatomic particles are almost identical in size and mass, but protons have a positive charge while neutrons have no charge at all. Moving around outside the nucleus and encircling it is a cloud of very tiny negatively charged subatomic particles with very little mass. These particles are called **electrons.** To get an idea of how far from the nucleus an electron can be, consider this: If the nucleus of a hydrogen atom were the size of a tennis ball, its one electron could be found up to 6.4 km (4 mi) away! A helium atom, shown in **Figure 3-3,** has one more proton and one more electron than a hydrogen atom has. That's because the number of protons and electrons an atom has is unique for each element.

Unreacted atoms have no overall charge

You might be surprised to learn that atoms are not charged even though they are made of charged protons and electrons. Atoms do not have a charge because they have an equal number of protons and electrons whose charges exactly cancel. A helium atom has two protons and two electrons. The atom is neutral because the positive charge of the two protons exactly cancels the negative charge of the two electrons.

Charge of two protons:	+2
Charge of two neutrons:	0
Charge of two electrons:	−2
Total charge of a helium atom:	0

Subatomic Particles

Particle	Charge	Mass (kg)	Location in the atom
Proton	+1	1.67×10^{-27}	In the nucleus
Neutron	0	1.67×10^{-27}	In the nucleus
Electron	−1	9.11×10^{-31}	Moving around outside the nucleus

Models of the Atom

Democritus in the fourth century B.C. and later Dalton, in the nineteenth century, thought that the atom could not be split. That theory had to be modified when it was discovered that atoms are made of protons, neutrons, and electrons. Like most scientific models and theories, the model of the atom has been revised many times to explain such new discoveries.

Bohr's model compares electrons to planets

In 1913, the Danish scientist Niels Bohr suggested that electrons in an atom move in set paths around the nucleus much like the planets orbit the sun in our solar system. In Bohr's model, each electron has a certain energy that is determined by its path around the nucleus. This path defines the electron's **energy level.** Electrons can only be in certain energy levels. They must gain energy to move to a higher energy level or lose energy to move to a lower energy level.

One way to imagine Bohr's model is to compare an atom to the stairless building shown in **Figure 3-4.** Imagine that the nucleus is in a very deep basement and that the electronic energy levels begin on the first floor. Electrons can be on any floor of the building but not between floors. Electrons gain energy by riding up in the elevator and lose energy by riding down in the elevator. Higher energy levels are closer together. (Ceiling height decreases toward the top of this modified building.)

According to modern theory, electrons behave more like waves

By 1925, Bohr's model of the atom no longer explained all observations. So a new model was proposed that no longer assumed that electrons orbited the nucleus along definite paths like planets orbiting the sun. In this modern model of the atom, it is believed that electrons behave more like waves on a vibrating string than like particles.

Quick ACTIVITY

Convincing John Dalton
If Dalton were still alive, he might argue: "Atoms are neutral, so they can't be made of charged particles."
Explain why this statement is not true.

---

internet connect

SCI*LINKS*
NSTA

TOPIC: History of atomic models
GO TO: www.scilinks.org
KEYWORD: HK1033

▶ **energy level** any of the possible energies an electron may have in an atom

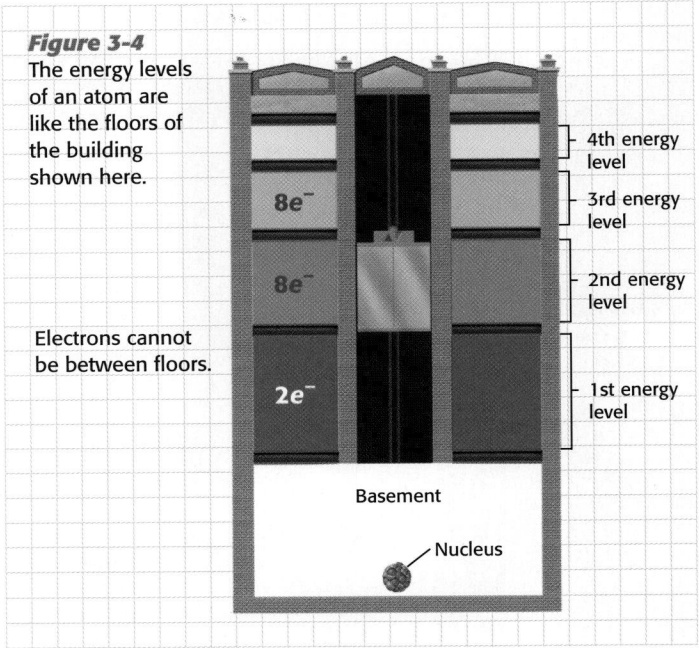

Figure 3-4
The energy levels of an atom are like the floors of the building shown here.

8e⁻

Electrons cannot be between floors.

8e⁻

2e⁻

4th energy level

3rd energy level

2nd energy level

1st energy level

Basement

Nucleus

ATOMS AND THE PERIODIC TABLE **73**

Teaching Tip

Waves and Particles Scientists discovered that particles act as waves, and waves act as particles. This concept is called the *wave-particle duality of nature.* The wave nature of most particles does not affect the particle much. However, the smaller the particle, the more the particle acts as both a wave and a particle.

Historical Perspective

In 1923, Louis de Broglie, a French physicist, made a hypothesis that led to a statement of the wave-particle duality of nature and the present theory of how atoms are structured. De Broglie used research done by Albert Einstein and Max Planck to develop a mathematical equation that relates the mass and velocity of a particle to its wavelength.

Quick ACTIVITY

Convincing John Dalton Student answers will vary but should include that because an atom consists of charged particles does not mean it has an overall charge. A charged atom is composed of unequal numbers of oppositely charged particles.

Dalton might also argue that, because atoms themselves are far too tiny to be seen, it is impossible for anything smaller to exist. As an extension, ask students to contradict this position. Give students examples of indirect evidence, such as footprints made in mud. Much information can be inferred from the footprint, such as the size of the shoe, the weight of the person, and an approximation of when the footprint was made. Similarly, evidence for atoms is indirect evidence. Atoms cannot be seen any more than subatomic particles can. Indirect evidence for smaller particles also exists.

RESOURCE LINK
DATASHEETS

Have students use *Datasheet 3.1 Quick Activity: Convincing John Dalton* to record their results.

IER

Assign students worksheet *3.8: Integrating Physics—Atomic Fingerprints.*

Atomic Structure

Designing Drugs Enzymes operate by forming a complex with reactant molecules called substrates. After the reaction, the enzyme is released unchanged from the product, which is a combination of the substrates used. Enzymes also catalyze the reverse reaction.

Applying Information

1. Student paragraphs will vary but might include that drugs mimic molecules that interact with enzymes and antibodies, controlling how they operate.

2. Computers can model the molecules of drugs, enzymes, and antibodies. The computer can then model the interactions of these molecules and determine the effect of a drug before humans use it on a living organism.

Resources Assign students worksheet *3.1: RWA—How Do Scientists Find Cures for Diseases?* in the **Integration Enrichment Resources** ancillary.

REAL WORLD APPLICATIONS

Designing Drugs In living things, enzymes (compounds that speed up biological reactions) and antibodies (chemical defense agents) use electron arrangements to recognize certain molecules. Because drugs for treating disease and infection are often similar in size and shape to molecules that occur naturally in the body, they can "trick" enzymes and antibodies into behaving in a desired way.

Scientists use computers, along with an equation that represents the wavelike behavior of electrons, to predict the properties of possible new drugs. Computers test how well the drug (shown in yellow in the figure at right) interacts with enzymes and antibodies. Promising compounds are then made. Several prescription medicines on the market today were developed by this process.

Applying Information

Write a paragraph that answers the following questions:

1. Describe how some drugs work.
2. Why are computers used to test certain drugs before they are made?

WRITING SKILL

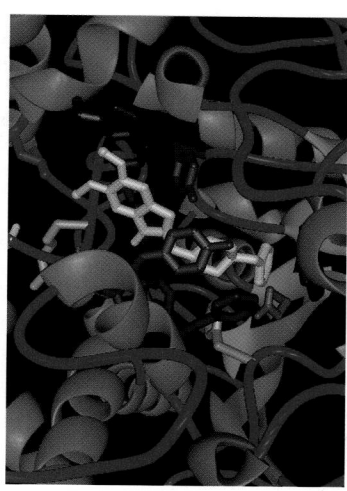

Imagine the moving blades of a fan, like the one shown in **Figure 3-5.** If you were asked where any one of the blades was located at a certain instant, you would not be able to give an exact answer. In fact, it's nearly impossible to know the exact location of any of the blades because they are moving so quickly. All you know for sure is that each blade could be anywhere within the blurred area you see as the blades turn.

It is also impossible to determine both the exact location of an electron in an atom and its speed and direction. The best scientists can do is calculate the chance of finding an electron in a certain place within an atom. One way to visually show the likelihood of finding an electron in a given location is by shading. The darker the shading, the better the chance of finding an electron at that location. The whole shaded region is called an electron cloud.

Figure 3-5
Just like these blades turning in this fan, the exact positions, speeds, and directions of electrons in an atom cannot be determined.

Quick ACTIVITY

Constructing a Model

A scientific model is a simplified representation based on limited knowledge that describes how an object looks or functions. In this activity, you will construct your own model.

1. Obtain from your teacher a can that is covered by a sock and sealed with tape. An unknown object is inside the can.

2. Without unsealing the container, try to determine the characteristics of the object inside by examining it through the sock. What is the object's mass?

What is its size, shape, and texture? Record all of your observations in a data table.

3. Remove the taped sock so that you can touch the object without looking at it. Record these observations as well.

4. Use the data you have collected to draw a model of the unknown object.

5. Finally remove the object to see what it is. Compare and contrast the model you made with the object it is meant to represent.

Electrons are found in orbitals within energy levels

The regions in an atom where electrons are found are called **orbitals.** Electrons may occupy four different kinds of orbitals within atoms. The simplest kind of orbital is an *s* orbital. An *s* orbital can have only one possible orientation in space because it is shaped like a sphere, as shown in **Figure 3-6.** An *s* orbital's spherical shape enables it to surround the nucleus of an atom.

A *p* orbital, on the other hand, is dumbbell-shaped and can be oriented three different ways in space, as shown in **Figure 3-7.** The axes on the graphs are drawn to help you picture how these orbitals look in three dimensions. Imagine the *z*-axis being flat on the page. Imagine the dotted lines on the *x*- and *y*-axes going into the page, and the darker lines coming out of the page.

The *d* and *f* orbitals are much more complex. There are five possible *d* orbitals and seven possible *f* orbitals. Although all these orbitals are very different in shape, each can hold a maximum of two electrons.

Electrons usually occupy the lowest energy levels available in an atom. And within each energy level, electrons occupy orbitals with the lowest energy. In any energy level, an *s* orbital has the lowest energy. A *p* orbital has slightly more energy, followed by a *d* orbital. An *f* orbital has the greatest energy.

▶ **orbital** a region in an atom where there is a high probability of finding electrons

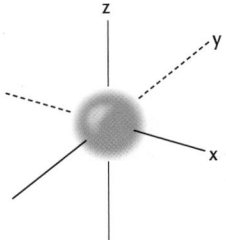

Figure 3-6
An *s* orbital is shaped like a sphere, so it has only one possible orientation in space. An *s* orbital can hold a maximum of two electrons.

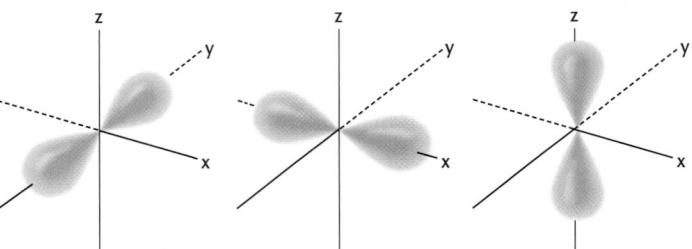

Figure 3-7
Each of these *p* orbitals can hold a maximum of two electrons, so all three together can hold a total of six electrons.

ATOMS AND THE PERIODIC TABLE **75**

READING SKILL BUILDER *Prediction Guide* Have students revisit their active reading opinions from the beginning of the section. Have them discuss whether their opinions have changed or remain the same. Have them cite passages in the text that account for the change in or reinforcement of their opinions.

Teaching Tip

Levels and Sublevels A sublevel consists of all the *s, p, d,* or *f* orbitals for an electron energy level. The first energy level—the one closest to the nucleus—contains only one sublevel, the *s.* Thus, this level contains only one orbital and can contain only two electrons.

The second energy level contains two sublevels, *s* and *p.* It contains one *s* orbital and three *p* orbitals, so it can hold up to eight electrons.

The third energy level contains *s, p,* and *d* sublevels for a maximum of 2 + 6 + 10, or 18, electrons.

The fourth energy level contains *s, p, d,* and *f* sublevels for a maximum of 2 + 6 + 10 + 14, or 32, electrons.

MISCONCEPTION ALERT

Orbitals Be sure students understand that an orbital exists as a physical entity only when it is occupied by an electron.

Quick ACTIVITY

Constructing a Model Be sure students are aware that a model is often used to represent an item or event that is too small, too large, or too dangerous to view directly. Models can include any representation of that event or item and include drawings, computer models, and three-dimensional physical models.

Tell students that they use models in daily life. A globe, a map, and a board used to

sketch plays by a coach are all examples of models. Have students list other models they commonly use.

Discuss with students how close their model is to the actual object. Have them explain why the model might not match the object exactly.

RESOURCE LINK
DATASHEETS

Have students use *Datasheet 3.2 Quick Activity: Constructing a Model* to record their results.

▶ **valence electron** an electron in the outermost energy level of an atom

Neon Atom

$2e^-$

$8e^-$
(Valence electrons)

Every atom has one or more valence electrons

An electron in the outermost energy level of an atom is called a **valence electron.** The single electron of a hydrogen atom is a valence electron because it is the only electron the atom has. The glowing red sign shown in **Figure 3-8** is made of neon atoms. In a neon atom, two electrons fill the lowest energy level. Its valence electrons, then, are the eight electrons that are farther away from the nucleus in the atom's second (and outermost) energy level.

Figure 3-8
The neon atoms of this sign have eight valence electrons. The sign lights up because atoms first gain energy and then release this energy in the form of light.

SECTION 3.1 REVIEW

SUMMARY

▶ Elements are made of very small units called atoms.

▶ The nucleus of an atom is made of positively charged protons and uncharged neutrons.

▶ Surrounding the nucleus are tiny negatively charged electrons.

▶ Atoms have an equal number of protons and electrons.

▶ In Bohr's model of the atom, electrons orbit the nucleus in set paths much like the planets orbit the sun in our solar system.

▶ In the modern atomic model, electrons are found in orbitals within each energy level.

▶ Electrons in the outermost energy level are called valence electrons.

CHECK YOUR UNDERSTANDING

1. **Summarize** the main ideas of Dalton's atomic theory.
2. **Explain** why Dalton's theory was more successful than Democritus's theory.
3. **List** the charge, mass, and location of each of the three subatomic particles found within atoms.
4. **Predict** how many valence electrons a nitrogen atom has. (Nitrogen has a total of seven electrons, two of which fill the lowest energy level.)
5. **Explain** why oxygen atoms are neutral. (Oxygen has eight positively charged protons.)
6. **Compare** an atom's structure to a ladder. What parts of the ladder correspond to the energy levels of the atom? Identify one way a real ladder is not a good model for the atom.
7. **Explain** how the path of an electron differs in Bohr's model and in the modern model of the atom.
8. **Critical Thinking** In the early 1900s, two associates of New Zealander Ernest Rutherford bombarded thin sheets of gold with positively charged subatomic particles. They found that most of the particles passed right through the sheets but some bounced back as if they had hit something solid. Based on their results, what do you think the majority of an atom is made of? What part of the atom caused the particles to bounce back? (**Hint:** Positive charges repel other positive charges.)

3.2

A Guided Tour of the Periodic Table

OBJECTIVES

▶ Relate the organization of the periodic table to the arrangement of electrons within an atom.

▶ Explain why some atoms gain or lose electrons to form ions.

▶ Determine how many protons, neutrons, and electrons an isotope has, given its symbol, atomic number, and mass number.

▶ Describe how the abundance of isotopes affects an element's average atomic mass.

▶ **KEY TERMS**

periodic law
period
group
ionization
ion
cation
anion
atomic number
mass number
isotopes
atomic mass unit (amu)
average atomic mass

When you are in a store, chances are you know where to look for your favorite items because they are not placed randomly on the shelves. Similar items are usually grouped together, as shown in **Figure 3-9,** so that you can find what you need quickly. The periodic table organizes all the elements in a similar way.

Organization of the Periodic Table

The periodic table groups similar elements together. This organization makes it easier to predict the properties of an element based on where it is in the periodic table. In the periodic table shown in **Figure 3-10,** on the following pages, elements are represented by their symbols. The elements are also arranged in a certain order. The order is based on the number of protons an atom of that element has in its nucleus.

A hydrogen atom has one proton, so hydrogen is the first element listed in the periodic table. A helium atom has two protons and is the second element listed, and so on. Elements are listed in this order in the periodic table because the **periodic law** states that when elements are arranged this way, similarities in their properties will occur in a regular pattern.

▶ **periodic law** properties of elements tend to change in a regular pattern when elements are arranged in order of increasing atomic number, or number of protons in their atoms

Figure 3-9
In many stores, similar items are grouped so that they are easier to find.

ATOMS AND THE PERIODIC TABLE **77**

SKILL BUILDER

Interpreting Visuals Inform students of the information available in the periodic table in **Figure 3-10,** including symbol, name, atomic number, average atomic mass, group number, period number, and whether the element is a metal or a nonmetal.

Resources Blackline Master 9 shows this visual.

Teaching Tip

Names and Symbols To familiarize students with the periodic table, have students make a flashcard for each element. Each card should contain the name of an element on one side and its symbol on the other side.

MISCONCEPTION

The Periodic Table ALERT

Students sometimes think that they have to memorize the information in the periodic table. Point out that the table exists as a scientific tool. The student's job is to learn to interpret the information on the table, not to memorize it.

Multicultural Extension

Elements have connections to many different cultures. Carbon, sulfur, tin, gold, and silver were isolated, named, and used by many ancient civilizations. Platinum was introduced to Europe in 1750 when it was taken there from pre-Colombian culture in South America. The name for zirconium comes from the Arabic word *zargun*, which means "gold color." Vanadium was discovered in Mexico and was named after a Scandinavian goddess.

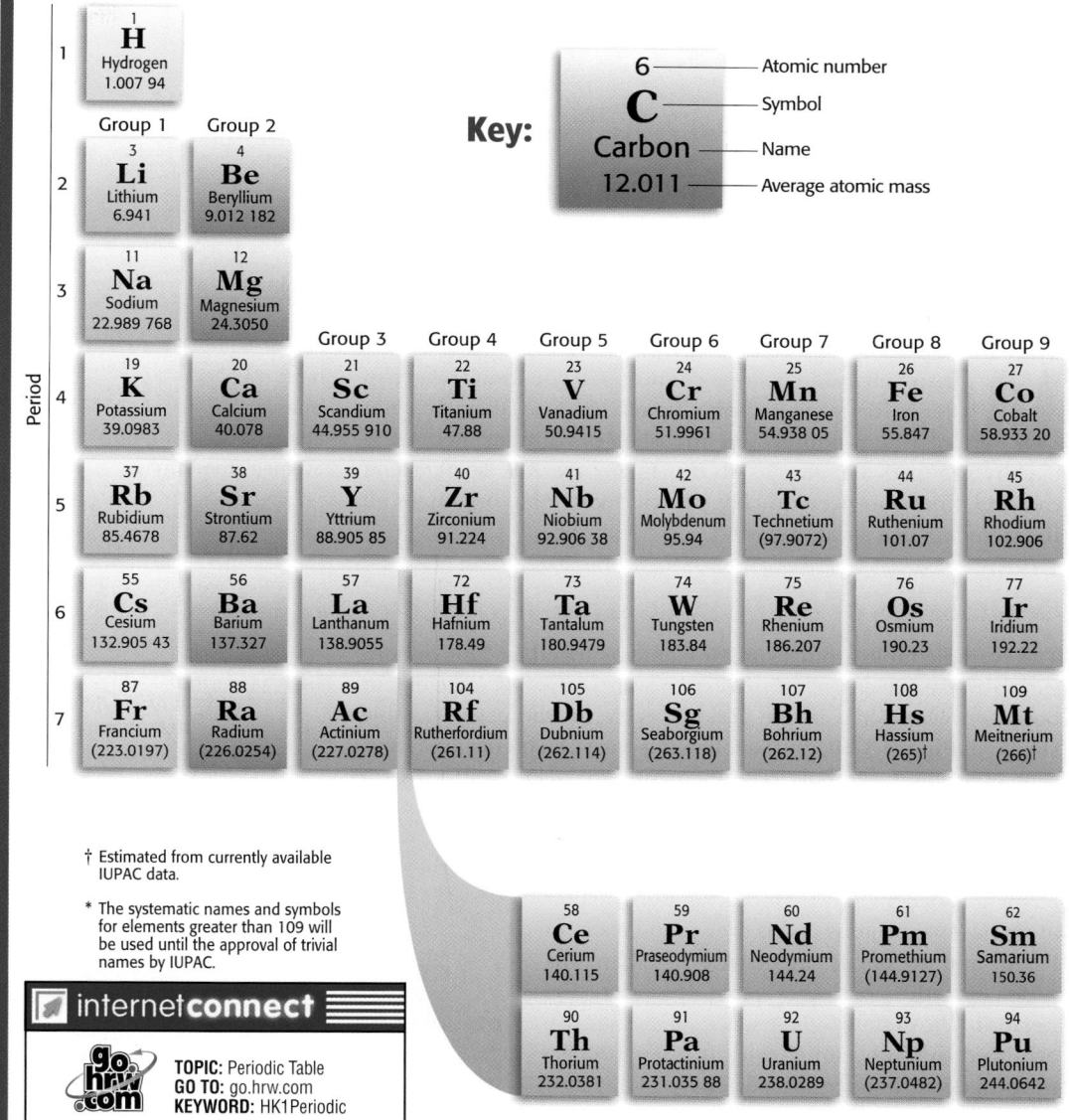

Figure 3-10

The Periodic Table of the Elements

† Estimated from currently available IUPAC data.

* The systematic names and symbols for elements greater than 109 will be used until the approval of trivial names by IUPAC.

internetconnect

TOPIC: Periodic Table
GO TO: go.hrw.com
KEYWORD: HK1Periodic

Visit the HRW Web site to see the most recent version of the periodic table.

78 CHAPTER 3

ALTERNATIVE ASSESSMENT

Chemical Symbols

Step 1 Give students the names of several of the most common elements. Emphasize that students should not try to memorize all symbols but that it is helpful to know common ones.

Step 2 Allow them to use the cards they made in the Teaching Tip above to learn the symbols. Then quiz students orally on the symbols.

A Guided Tour of the Periodic Table

Metals
- Alkali metals
- Alkaline-earth metals
- Transition metals
- Other metals

Nonmetals
- Hydrogen
- Semiconductors
- Halogens
- Noble gases
- Other nonmetals

Group 10	Group 11	Group 12	Group 13	Group 14	Group 15	Group 16	Group 17	Group 18
								2 **He** Helium 4.002 602
			5 **B** Boron 10.811	6 **C** Carbon 12.011	7 **N** Nitrogen 14.006 74	8 **O** Oxygen 15.9994	9 **F** Fluorine 18.998 4032	10 **Ne** Neon 20.1797
			13 **Al** Aluminum 26.981 539	14 **Si** Silicon 28.0855	15 **P** Phosphorus 30.9738	16 **S** Sulfur 32.066	17 **Cl** Chlorine 35.4527	18 **Ar** Argon 39.948
28 **Ni** Nickel 58.6934	29 **Cu** Copper 63.546	30 **Zn** Zinc 65.39	31 **Ga** Gallium 69.723	32 **Ge** Germanium 72.61	33 **As** Arsenic 74.921 59	34 **Se** Selenium 78.96	35 **Br** Bromine 79.904	36 **Kr** Krypton 83.80
46 **Pd** Palladium 106.42	47 **Ag** Silver 107.8682	48 **Cd** Cadmium 112.411	49 **In** Indium 114.818	50 **Sn** Tin 118.710	51 **Sb** Antimony 121.757	52 **Te** Tellurium 127.60	53 **I** Iodine 126.904	54 **Xe** Xenon 131.29
78 **Pt** Platinum 195.08	79 **Au** Gold 196.966 54	80 **Hg** Mercury 200.59	81 **Tl** Thallium 204.3833	82 **Pb** Lead 207.2	83 **Bi** Bismuth 208.980 37	84 **Po** Polonium (208.9824)	85 **At** Astatine (209.9871)	86 **Rn** Radon (222.0176)
110 **Uun*** Unununilium (269)†	111 **Uuu*** Unununium (272)†	112 **Uub*** Ununbium (277)†		114 **Uuq*** Ununquadium (285)†		116 **Uuh*** Ununhexium (289)†		118 **Uuo*** Ununoctium (293)†

63 **Eu** Europium 151.966	64 **Gd** Gadolinium 157.25	65 **Tb** Terbium 158.925 34	66 **Dy** Dysprosium 162.50	67 **Ho** Holmium 164.930	68 **Er** Erbium 167.26	69 **Tm** Thulium 168.934 21	70 **Yb** Ytterbium 173.04	71 **Lu** Lutetium 174.967
95 **Am** Americium (243.0614)	96 **Cm** Curium (247.0703)	97 **Bk** Berkelium (247.0703)	98 **Cf** Californium (251.0796)	99 **Es** Einsteinium (252.083)	100 **Fm** Fermium (257.0951)	101 **Md** Mendelevium (258.10)	102 **No** Nobelium (259.1009)	103 **Lr** Lawrencium (262.11)

The atomic masses listed in this table reflect the precision of current measurements. (Values listed in parentheses are those of the element's most stable or most common isotope.) In calculations throughout the text, however, atomic masses have been rounded to two places to the right of the decimal.

Did You Know?

Transuranium elements, which are those past uranium on the periodic table, have been difficult to study because they do not exist in nature. They must be created in a laboratory, and many exist for an extremely short period of time.

One particularly troublesome element is element 104. American scientists Albert Ghiorso and James Harris, an African American, finally created this elusive element at the Lawrence Radiation Laboratory at the University of California at Berkeley.

Historical Perspective

The modern periodic table is based on one developed and presented by Dmitri Mendeleev, a Russian chemist, in 1869. Mendeleev arranged elements in a table based on repeating properties.

He not only arranged known elements, but he left blank spaces in his table for elements that were at that time unknown but had properties that would place them in a certain family.

Most discrepancies involving properties were eliminated when the periodic table was modified to list elements according to atomic mass.

A Guided Tour of the Periodic Table

Teaching Tip

Energy Levels Be sure students do not attempt to show how electrons are arranged in atoms past calcium in the periodic table. As electron energy levels increase, the difference in their energies decreases.

Starting with the third energy level, the levels overlap and the order in which orbitals fill becomes irregular. The pattern of this overlap is beyond the scope of this course, but more information can be found in a high school chemistry textbook.

MISCONCEPTION ALERT

Groups Be sure students understand that physical properties may or may not be similar among elements in a group. Although groups of elements may share certain physical properties, chemical properties are more likely to be similar.

LINKING CHAPTERS

The importance of similar chemical properties will be emphasized in Chapter 5 when chemical reactions are discussed.

period a horizontal row of elements in the periodic table

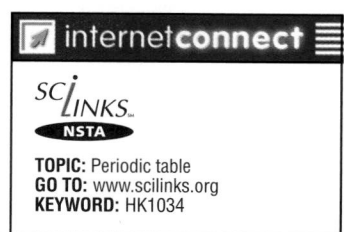
internet connect

SCLINKS
NSTA

TOPIC: Periodic table
GO TO: www.scilinks.org
KEYWORD: HK1034

group (family) a vertical column of elements in the periodic table

Figure 3-11
The electronic arrangement of atoms becomes increasingly more complex as you move further right across a period and further down a group of the periodic table.

Electron Locations

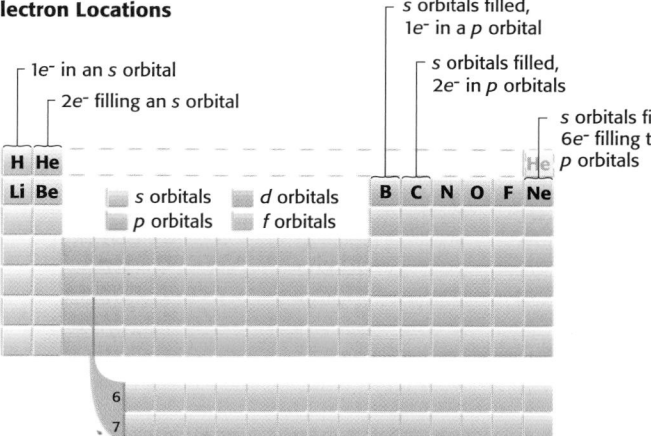

Using the periodic table to determine electronic arrangement

Horizontal rows in the periodic table are called **periods.** Just as the number of protons an atom has increases by one as you move from left to right across a period, so does its number of electrons. You can determine how an atom's electrons are arranged if you know where the corresponding element is located in the periodic table.

Hydrogen and helium are both located in Period 1 of the periodic table. **Figure 3-11** shows that a hydrogen atom has one electron in an s orbital, while a helium atom has one more electron, for a total of two. Lithium is located in Period 2. A lithium atom is just like a helium atom, except that it has a third electron in an s orbital in the second energy level, as follows:

Energy level	Orbital	Number of electrons
1	s	2
2	s	1

As you continue to move to the right in Period 2, you can see that a carbon atom has electrons in p orbitals and s orbitals. The locations of the six electrons in a carbon atom are as follows:

Energy level	Orbital	Number of electrons
1	s	2
2	s	2
2	p	2

A nitrogen atom has three electrons in p orbitals, an oxygen atom has four, and a fluorine atom has five. **Figure 3-11** shows that a neon atom has six electrons in p orbitals. Each orbital can hold two electrons, so all three p orbitals are filled.

Elements in the same group have similar properties

Valence electrons determine the chemical properties of atoms. Atoms of elements in the same **group,** or column, have the same number of valence electrons, so these elements have similar properties. Remember that these elements are not exactly alike, though, because atoms of these elements have different numbers of protons in their nuclei and different numbers of electrons in their filled inner energy levels.

80 CHAPTER 3

RESOURCE LINK
LABORATORY MANUAL

Have students perform *Lab 3 Atoms and the Periodic Table: Predicting the Physical and Chemical Properties of Elements* in the lab ancillary.

DATASHEETS

Have students use *Datasheet 3.7* to record their results from the lab.

ALTERNATIVE ASSESSMENT

Periodicity

Step 1 Divide the class into four groups. Assign each student group one of the following groups: Group 1, Group 2, Group 17, or Group 18 from the periodic table.

Step 2 Have students find out the properties and uses of the elements in their assigned group and determine what the elements have in common.

Step 3 Have each student group prepare a poster that shows what they learned so that they can present this information to the class.

Some Atoms Form Ions

Atoms of Group 1 elements are reactive because their outermost energy levels are only partially filled. Atoms that do not have filled outermost energy levels may undergo a process called **ionization.** That is, they may gain or lose valence electrons so that they have a full outermost energy level. If an atom gains or loses electrons, it no longer has the same number of electrons as it does protons. Because the charges do not cancel completely as they did before, the **ion** that forms has a net electric charge, as shown for the lithium ion in **Figure 3-12.**

A lithium atom loses one electron to form a 1+ charged ion

Lithium is located in Group 1 of the periodic table. It is so reactive that it even reacts with air. An electron is easily removed from a lithium atom, as shown in **Figure 3-12.** The model for the atomic structure of lithium explains its reactivity. A lithium atom has three electrons. Two of these electrons occupy the first energy level, but only one electron occupies the second energy level. This single valence electron makes lithium very reactive. Removing this electron forms a positive ion, or **cation.**

A lithium ion, written as Li$^+$, is much less reactive than a lithium atom because it has a full outermost energy level. Atoms of other Group 1 elements also have one valence electron. They are also reactive and behave similarly to lithium. You will learn more about Group 1 elements in Section 3.3.

A fluorine atom gains one electron to form a 1– charged ion

Like lithium, fluorine is also very reactive. However, instead of losing an electron to become less reactive, an atom of the element fluorine gains one electron to form an ion with a 1– charge. Fluorine is located in Group 17 of the periodic table, and each atom has nine electrons. Two of these electrons occupy the first energy level, and seven valence electrons occupy the second energy level. A fluorine atom needs only one more electron to have a full outermost energy level. An atom of fluorine easily gains this electron to form a negative ion, or **anion,** as shown in **Figure 3-13.**

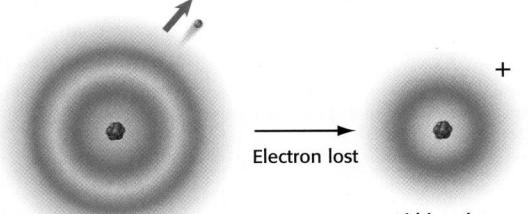

Lithium atom   Electron lost   Lithium ion

Figure 3-12
The valence electron of a reactive lithium atom may be removed to form a lithium ion, Li$^+$, with a 1+ charge.

▶ **ionization** the process of adding electrons to or removing electrons from an atom or group of atoms

▶ **ion** an atom or group of atoms that has lost or gained one or more electrons and therefore has a net electric charge

▶ **cation** an ion with a positive charge

▶ **anion** an ion with a negative charge

Figure 3-13
A fluorine atom easily gains one valence electron to form a fluoride ion, F$^-$, with a 1– charge.

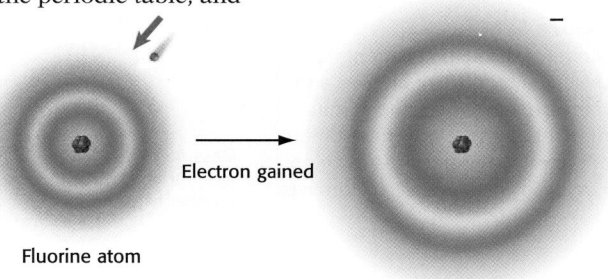

Fluorine atom   Electron gained   Fluoride ion

ATOMS AND THE PERIODIC TABLE **81**

MISCONCEPTION **ALERT**

Charge Students are sometimes confused by how the sign of an ion's charge is related to the loss and gain of electrons. Remind them that the *gain* of an electron means the gain of a negative charge, producing a negatively charged ion. Conversely, the *loss* of an electron means the loss of a negative charge, leaving a positively charged ion.

SKILL BUILDER

Interpreting Vocabulary Inform students that because anions and cations are types of ions, they are pronounced accordingly. Anion is pronounced "an-ion," and cation is pronounced "cat-ion." Students who are familiar with batteries might relate these terms to the negative pole of a battery, the cathode, which attracts cations, and the positive pole of a battery, the anode, which attracts anions.

Teaching Tip

Complete Levels The first electron energy level in an atom can contain only two electrons. If this level contains the valence electrons, it is full with two electrons. Energy levels two and higher are considered full when they have eight valence electrons, known as an octet. Atoms that ionize do so in a manner that will complete an octet.

A Guided Tour of the Periodic Table

Teaching Tip

Protons and Neutrons

Have students create a table of number of protons (atomic number) and number of neutrons (mass number – atomic number) for 20 different elements from various places in the periodic table. Then, ask them to summarize the information in their table. *(For light elements, the number of protons and the number of neutrons are approximately equal. For heavier elements, the number of neutrons increases faster than the number of protons in an atom.)*

Historical Perspective

The concept of atomic number was proposed by the British scientist Henry Moseley in 1915. Moseley found that the progression of the elements in the periodic table corresponded to an increase of one fundamental unit in the nucleus and that each element could be assigned an atomic number equal to the number of these units. In 1920, Rutherford announced the existence of the proton, Moseley's fundamental unit.

PHYSICAL SCIENCE

Disc One, Module 3:
Periodic Properties
Use the Interactive Tutor to learn more about this topic.

▶ **atomic number** the number of protons in the nucleus of an atom

▶ **mass number** the total number of protons and neutrons in the nucleus of an atom

Figure 3-14
Atoms of the same element have the same number of protons and therefore have the same atomic number. But they may have different mass numbers, depending on how many neutrons each atom has.

Ions of fluorine are called fluoride ions and are written as F⁻. Because atoms of other Group 17 elements also have seven valence electrons, they are also reactive and behave similarly to fluorine. You will learn more about Group 17 elements in Section 3.3.

How Do the Structures of Atoms Differ?

As you have seen with lithium and fluorine, atoms of different elements have their own unique structures. Because these atoms have different structures, they have different properties. An atom of hydrogen found in a molecule of swimming-pool water has properties very different from an atom of uranium in nuclear fuel.

Atomic number equals the number of protons

The **atomic number**, Z, tells you how many protons are in an atom. Remember that atoms are always neutral because they have an equal number of protons and electrons. Therefore, the atomic number also equals the number of electrons the atom has. Each element has a different atomic number. For example, the simplest atom, hydrogen, has just one proton and one electron, so for hydrogen, $Z = 1$. The largest naturally occurring atom, uranium, has 92 protons and 92 electrons, so $Z = 92$ for uranium. The atomic number for a given element never changes.

Mass number equals the total number of subatomic particles in the nucleus

The **mass number**, A, of an atom equals the number of protons plus the number of neutrons. A fluorine atom has 9 protons and 10 neutrons, so $A = 19$ for fluorine. This mass number includes only the number of protons and neutrons (and not electrons) because protons and neutrons provide most of the atom's mass. Although atoms of an element always have the same atomic number, they can have different mass numbers. **Figure 3-14** shows which subatomic particles in the nucleus of an atom contribute to the atomic number and which contribute to the mass number.

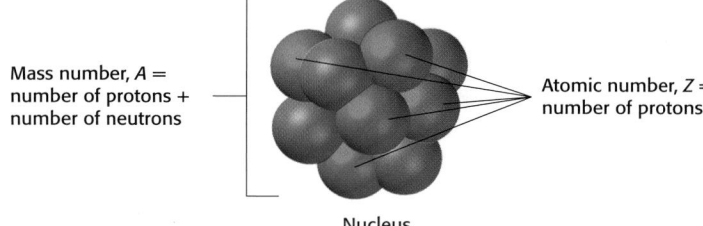

Mass number, A = number of protons + number of neutrons

Atomic number, Z = number of protons

Nucleus

Graphic Organizer
Mass Number

Number of protons in an atom (atomic number of the atom)	+	Number of neutrons in an atom	=	Mass number of an atom

Isotopes of Hydrogen

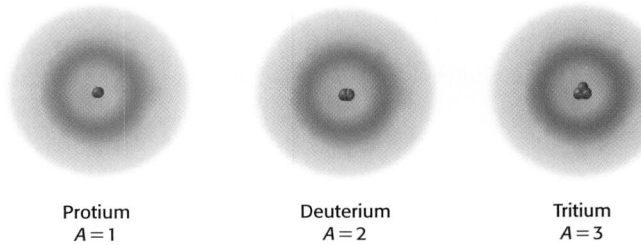

Protium
$A = 1$

Deuterium
$A = 2$

Tritium
$A = 3$

Figure 3-15
Protium has only a proton in its nucleus. Deuterium has both a proton and a neutron in its nucleus, while tritium has a proton and two neutrons.

Isotopes of an element have different numbers of neutrons

Neutrons can be added to an atom without affecting the number of protons and electrons the atom is made of. Many elements have only one stable form, while other elements have different "versions" of their atoms. Each version has the same number of protons and electrons as all other versions but a different number of neutrons. These different versions, or **isotopes,** vary in mass but are all atoms of the same element because they each have the same number of protons.

The three isotopes of hydrogen, shown in **Figure 3-15,** all share similar chemical properties because each is made of one proton and one electron. The most common hydrogen isotope, protium, has only a proton in its nucleus. A second isotope of hydrogen has a proton and a neutron. The mass number, *A*, of this second isotope is two, and the isotope is twice as massive. In fact, this isotope is sometimes called "heavy hydrogen." It is also known as deuterium, or hydrogen-2. A third isotope has a proton and two neutrons in its nucleus. This third isotope, tritium, has a mass number of three.

▶ **isotopes** any atoms having the same number of protons but different numbers of neutrons

Some isotopes are more common than others

Hydrogen is present on both the sun and on Earth. In both places, protium (the hydrogen isotope without neutrons in its nucleus) is found most often. Only a very small fraction of the less common isotope of hydrogen, deuterium, is found on the sun and on Earth, as shown in **Figure 3-16.** Tritium is an unstable isotope that decays over time, so it is found least often.

Figure 3-16

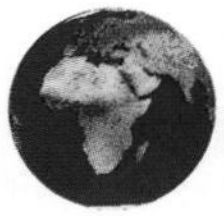

Ⓐ Hydrogen makes up less than 1 percent of Earth's crust. Only 1 out of every 6000 of these hydrogen atoms is a deuterium isotope.

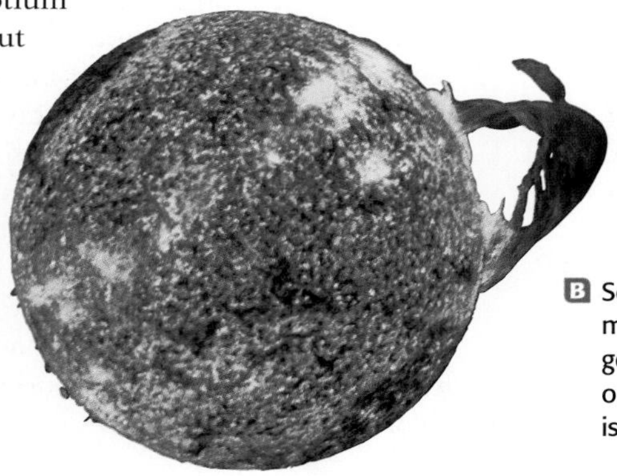

Ⓑ Seventy-five percent of the mass of the sun is hydrogen, with protium isotopes outnumbering deuterium isotopes 50 000 to 1.

ATOMS AND THE PERIODIC TABLE **83**

MISCONCEPTION

ALERT

Isotopes Make it clear to students that the identity of an atom is determined entirely by the number of protons in its nucleus. Atoms of the same element (same number of protons) may have varying numbers of neutrons. When an atom forms an ion, it may have more or fewer electrons than protons.

Students may also have the idea that all isotopes are radioactive and therefore dangerous. Point out that the water students drink every day contains two different isotopes of hydrogen (hydrogen-1 and hydrogen-2) and three isotopes of oxygen (oxygen-16, oxygen-17, and oxygen-18), none of which are radioactive or dangerous.

Teaching Tip

Deuterium Deuterium is the fuel required for a nuclear fusion reaction that is a potential energy source. The amount of energy released by fusing two deuterium atoms is about 10 times the amount of energy released by an equal mass of uranium during a nuclear fission reaction.

A Guided Tour of the Periodic Table

Figure 3-17
One isotope of chlorine has 18 neutrons, while the other isotope has 20 neutrons.

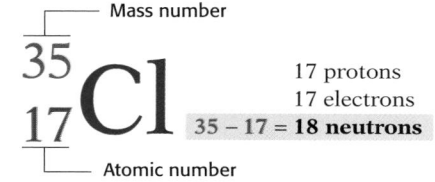
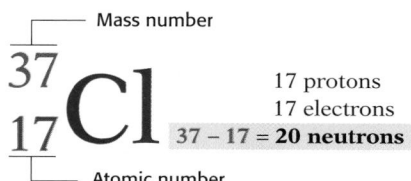

Quick ACTIVITY

Isotopes
Calculate the number of neutrons there are in the following isotopes. (Use the periodic table to find the atomic numbers.)
1. carbon-14
2. nitrogen-15
3. sulfur-35
4. calcium-45
5. iodine-131

▶ **atomic mass unit (amu)**
a quantity equal to one-twelfth of the mass of a carbon-12 atom

▶ **average atomic mass**
the weighted average of the masses of all naturally occurring isotopes of an element

Calculating the number of neutrons in an atom

Atomic numbers and mass numbers may be included along with the symbol of an element to represent different isotopes. The two isotopes of chlorine are represented this way in **Figure 3-17.** If you know the atomic number and mass number of an atom, you can calculate the number of neutrons it has.

Uranium has several isotopes. The isotope that is used in nuclear reactors is uranium-235, or $^{235}_{92}U$. Like all uranium atoms, it has an atomic number of 92, so it must have 92 protons and 92 electrons. It has a mass number of 235, which means its number of protons and neutrons together is 235. The number of neutrons must be 143.

Mass number (A):	235
Atomic number (Z):	$- \ 92$
Number of neutrons:	143

The mass of an atom

The mass of a single atom is very small. A single fluorine atom has a mass less than one trillionth of a billionth of a gram. Because it is very hard to work with such tiny masses, atomic masses are usually expressed in atomic mass units. An **atomic mass unit (amu)** is equal to one-twelfth of the mass of a carbon-12 atom. This isotope of carbon has six protons and six neutrons, so individual protons and neutrons must each have a mass of about 1.0 amu because electrons contribute very little mass.

Often, the atomic mass listed for an element in the periodic table is an **average atomic mass** for the element as it is found in nature. The average atomic mass for an element is a weighted average, so the more commonly found isotopes have a greater effect on the average than rare isotopes.

Figure 3-18 shows how the natural abundance of chlorine's two isotopes affects chlorine's average atomic mass. The average atomic mass of chlorine is 35.45 amu. This mass is much closer to 35 amu than to 37 amu. That's because the atoms of chlorine with masses of nearly 35 amu are found more often and therefore contribute more to chlorine's average atomic mass than chlorine atoms with masses of nearly 37 amu.

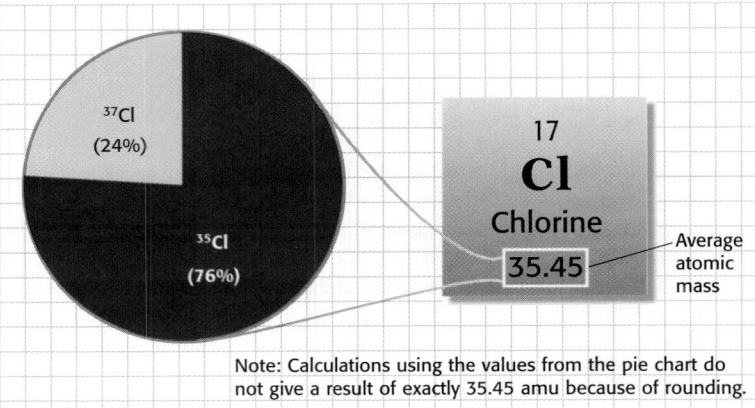

Figure 3-18
The average atomic mass of chlorine is closer to 35 amu than it is to 37 amu because ^{35}Cl isotopes are found more often than ^{37}Cl isotopes.

^{37}Cl (24%)

^{35}Cl (76%)

17
Cl
Chlorine
35.45 — Average atomic mass

Note: Calculations using the values from the pie chart do not give a result of exactly 35.45 amu because of rounding.

SECTION 3.2 REVIEW

SUMMARY

▸ Elements are arranged in order of increasing atomic number so that elements with similar properties are in the same column, or group.

▸ Elements in the same group have the same number of valence electrons.

▸ Reactive atoms may gain or lose valence electrons to form ions.

▸ An atom's atomic number is its number of protons.

▸ An atom's mass number is its total number of subatomic particles in the nucleus.

▸ Isotopes of an element have different numbers of neutrons, and therefore have different masses.

▸ An element's average atomic mass is a weighted average of the masses of its naturally occurring isotopes.

CHECK YOUR UNDERSTANDING

1. **Explain** how you can determine the number of neutrons an atom has from an atom's mass number and its atomic number.
2. **Calculate** how many neutrons a phosphorus-32 atom has.
3. **Name** the elements represented by the following symbols:
   a. Li   **d.** Br   **g.** Na
   b. Mg   **e.** He   **h.** Fe
   c. Cu   **f.** S   **i.** K
4. **Compare** the number of valence electrons an oxygen, O, atom has with the number of valence electrons a selenium, Se, atom has. Are oxygen and selenium in the same period or group?
5. **Describe** how a sodium ion differs from a sodium atom. (**Hint:** The behavior of sodium is similar to that of lithium.) Which form of sodium is more likely to be found in nature? Explain your reasoning.
6. **Predict** which isotope of nitrogen is more commonly found, nitrogen-14 or nitrogen-15. (**Hint:** What is the average atomic mass listed for nitrogen in the periodic table?)
7. **Describe** why the elements in the periodic table are arranged in order of increasing atomic number.
8. **Critical Thinking** Before 1937, all naturally occurring elements had been discovered, but no one had found any trace of element 43. Chemists were still able to predict the chemical properties of this element (now called technetium), which is widely used today for diagnosing medical problems. How were these predictions possible? Which elements would you expect to be similar to technetium?

ATOMS AND THE PERIODIC TABLE **85**

A Guided Tour of the Periodic Table

SECTION 3.2 REVIEW

Check Your Understanding

1. Atomic number is the number of protons only. Mass number is the total number of protons and neutrons. The number of neutrons is found by subtracting the atomic number from the mass number.
2. $A - Z = 32 - 15 = $ 17 neutrons
3. **a.** lithium
   b. magnesium
   c. copper
   d. bromine
   e. helium
   f. sulfur
   g. sodium
   h. iron
   i. potassium
4. Both elements have six valence electrons. They are in the same group.
5. A sodium atom is uncharged and has one valence electron. A sodium ion is a sodium atom that has lost this valence electron and become Na^+. The ion is more often found in nature because the atom easily loses the valence electron to achieve a complete outermost energy level.
6. Atomic mass is a weighted average of all the isotopes. The average atomic mass for nitrogen is 14.01 amu, so nitrogen-14 is more commonly found.

Answers continue on p. 105B.

RESOURCE LINK
STUDY GUIDE

Assign students *Review Section 3.2 A Guided Tour of the Periodic Table.*

ALTERNATIVE ASSESSMENT

Weighted Average

Tell students that a weighted average is based on both the number of items and the value of each.

Step 1 Provide students with the following example: a student received four As, 10 Bs, three Cs, and one F as grades. Using a 4-point grading scale, what is the student's average grade?
$\{(4 \times 4) + (10 \times 3) + (3 \times 2) + (1 \times 0)\} \div (4 + 10 + 3 + 1) = 52/18 = 2.9$

Step 2 Have students work the following problem, then write problems of their own and share them. Juan had four quarters, six dimes, nine nickels, and 15 pennies. What is the average value of the coins? $\{(4 \times 25) + (6 \times 10) + (9 \times 5) + (15 \times 1)$ cents$\} \div (4 + 6 + 9 + 15) = 220$ cents$/34 = $ 6.5 cents

85

Families of Elements

Scheduling

Refer to pp. 68A–68D for lecture, classwork, and assignment options for Section 3.3.

★ **Lesson Focus**

Use transparency *LT 9* to prepare students for this section.

 **READING SKILL BUILDER** **Summarizing** As students read each passage about a family of elements, ask for a volunteer to summarize the passage for the class. Then have the class, as listeners, ask for clarification of parts of the summary. All students may consult the text during the clarification process.

Teaching Tip

The Periodic Table Remind students of what they have already learned about the periodic table. They should know that it is an arrangement of elements in order of increasing atomic number, which also means that the elements are in order of increasing numbers of protons in the nuclei of their atoms. They should also know that the table gives the average atomic mass of an element, which is the weighted average of the element's stable isotopes. Ask if students have learned anything that helps account for the table's arrangement. Lead them to note the relationship between electron configurations and the arrangement of the elements in the table.

▶ **KEY TERMS**

metals
nonmetals
semiconductors
alkali metals
alkaline-earth metals
transition metals
halogens
noble gases

 **internetconnect**

SCI*LINKS*

NSTA

TOPIC: Element families
GO TO: www.scilinks.org
KEYWORD: HK1035

Figure 3-19
(A) Just like the members of this family, (B) elements in the periodic table share certain similarities.

OBJECTIVES

▶ Locate alkali metals, alkaline-earth metals, and transition metals in the periodic table.

▶ Locate semiconductors, halogens, and noble gases in the periodic table.

▶ Relate an element's chemical properties to the electron arrangement of its atoms.

You may have wondered why groups in the periodic table are sometimes called families. Consider your own family. Though each member is unique, you all share certain similarities. All members of the family shown in **Figure 3-19A,** for example, have a similar appearance. Members of a family in the periodic table have many chemical and physical properties in common because they have the same number of valence electrons.

How Are Elements Classified?

Think of each element as a member of a family that is also related to other elements nearby. Elements are classified as metals or nonmetals, as shown in **Figure 3-19B.** This classification groups elements that have similar physical and chemical properties. You will learn more about the chemical properties of elements in Chapter 5.

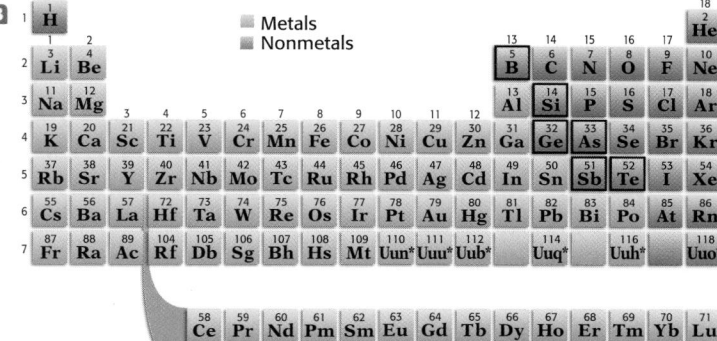

Note: Sometimes the boxed elements toward the right side of the periodic table are classified as a separate group and called semiconductors or metalloids.

86 CHAPTER 3

DEMONSTRATION 3 TEACHING

Conductivity

Time: Approximately 15 minutes
Materials: conductivity tester (one can be made from insulated wire, a battery, and a flashlight bulb); samples of elements, such as copper coin, iron nail, charcoal, and sulfur

Use the conductivity tester to see which elements conduct an electric current.

Analysis

1. Which elements were metals? How do you know? *(Any elements that conduct a current are metals.)*

2. Which elements were nonmetals? How do you know? *(Any elements that do not conduct a current are nonmetals.)*

As you can see in **Figure 3-19B,** most elements are **metals.** Most metals are shiny solids that can be stretched and shaped. They are also good conductors of heat and electricity. All **nonmetals,** except for hydrogen, are found on the right side of the periodic table. Nonmetals may be solids, liquids, or gases. Solid nonmetals are typically dull and brittle and are poor conductors of heat and electricity. But some elements that are classified as nonmetals can conduct under certain conditions. These elements are sometimes considered to be their own group and are called **semiconductors** or metalloids.

Metals

Many elements are classified as metals. To further classify metals, similar metals are grouped together. There are four different kinds of metals. Two groups of metals are located on the left side of the periodic table. Other metals, like aluminum, tin, and lead, are located toward the right side of the periodic table. Most metals, though, are located in the middle of the periodic table.

The alkali metal sodium is very reactive

Sodium is found in Group 1 of the periodic table, as shown in **Figure 3-20A.** Like other **alkali metals,** it is soft and shiny and reacts violently with water. For this reason, it must be stored in oil, as shown in **Figure 3-20B,** to prevent it from reacting with moisture in the air.

An atom of an alkali metal is very reactive because it has one valence electron that can easily be removed to form a positive ion. You have already seen in Section 3.2 how lithium, another alkali metal, forms positive ions with a 1+ charge. Similarly, the valence electron of a sodium atom can be removed to form the positive sodium ion Na^+.

Because alkali metals such as sodium are so reactive, they are not found in nature as elements. Instead, they combine with other elements to form compounds. For example, the salt you use to season your food is actually the compound sodium chloride, NaCl. Potassium is another common alkali metal.

Alkali Metals

Figure 3-20

A The alkali metals are located on the left edge of the periodic table.

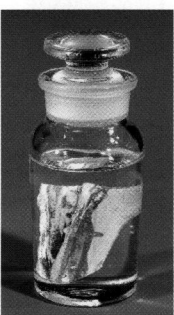 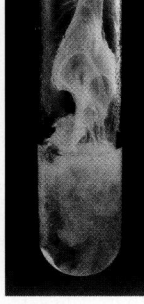

B The alkali metal sodium must be stored in oil. Otherwise, it will react violently with moisture and oxygen in the air.

Group 1		
	3 **Li** Lithium 6.941	
	11 **Na** Sodium 22.989 768	
	19 **K** Potassium 39.0983	
	37 **Rb** Rubidium 85.4678	
	55 **Cs** Cesium 132.905 43	
	87 **Fr** Francium (223.0197)	

▶ **metals** the elements that are good conductors of heat and electricity

▶ **nonmetals** the elements that are usually poor conductors of heat and electricity

▶ **semiconductors** the elements that are intermediate conductors of heat and electricity

▶ **alkali metals** the highly reactive metallic elements located in Group 1 of the periodic table

ATOMS AND THE PERIODIC TABLE **87**

Families of Elements

MISCONCEPTION ALERT

Metals Make sure students distinguish between the meaning of *metal* as applied to individual elements and as applied to metallic objects that we encounter every day, which are almost always alloys, homogeneous mixtures of metals with other metals and/or nonmetals.

Teaching Tip

Uses of Alkali Metals Compounds of alkali metals are used extensively, especially those of sodium and potassium. Sodium hydroxide is an important industrial compound that is used in the manufacture of paper, soap, and synthetic fabrics and in petroleum refining. Sodium chloride is common table salt, and potassium chloride is a table salt substitute. Potassium compounds are important components of chemical fertilizers.

Additional Application

Ions in the Human Body Too much sodium can be harmful, but sodium ions and potassium ions are important for the proper functioning of nerves in the human body. They allow electrical impulses to pass from one nerve to another.

Did You Know?

Because sodium is a lightweight electrical conductor, it has been incorporated into high-voltage power lines. Sodium's low density reduces the weight of the cables without impairing their conductivity, which reduces sag and permits longer cable spans.

Families of Elements

Teaching Tip

Reactivity Alkaline-earth metals are less reactive than al-kali metals because of ioniza-tion energy. Ionization energy is the amount of energy needed to remove an electron from an atom. The ionization energy for an alkali metal is low because one electron is easy to remove.

The first electron in an alkaline-earth atom is easy to remove also. However, the second electron requires more energy to remove. It must be removed from a positively charged particle, which does not lose an electron as easily as a neutral atom does.

Did You Know ?

Magnesium and magne-sium alloys are vital to the aero-space industry because of their low densities. But machining magnesium parts can be haz-ardous. Magnesium can catch fire and burn with an intensely hot, blinding white light. For this reason, magnesium is often machined in an inert atmos-phere.

Historical Perspective

Strontium-90 is a common ra-dioactive waste product in nu-clear reactors. Strontium-90 was released into the atmos-phere as a result of the melt-down of the nuclear reactor at Chernobyl, in Ukraine, in 1986.

RESOURCE LINK

DATASHEETS

Have students use *Datasheet 3.4 Quick Activity: Elements in Your Food* to record their results.

Alkaline-earth Metals   Group 2

Figure 3-21

A The alkaline-earth metals make up the second column of elements from the left edge of the periodic table.

| 4 |
| Be |
| Beryllium |
| 9.012 182 |

| 12 |
| Mg |
| Magnesium |
| 24.3050 |

| 20 |
| Ca |
| Calcium |
| 40.078 |

| 38 |
| Sr |
| Strontium |
| 87.62 |

| 56 |
| Ba |
| Barium |
| 137.327 |

| 88 |
| Ra |
| Radium |
| (226.0254) |

▶ **alkaline-earth metals** the reactive metallic elements located in Group 2 of the periodic table

B Fish can escape their predators by hiding among the hard projections of limestone coral reefs that are made of calcium compounds.

Compounds of the alkaline-earth metal calcium are found in limestone and marble

Calcium is in Group 2 of the periodic table, as shown in **Figure 3-21A,** and is an **alkaline-earth metal.** Atoms of alkaline-earth metals, such as calcium, have two valence electrons. Alkaline-earth metals are less reactive than al-kali metals, but they may still react to form positive ions with a 2+ charge. When the valence electrons of a calcium atom are re-moved, a calcium ion, Ca^{2+}, forms. Alkaline-earth metals like calcium also combine with other elements to form compounds.

Calcium compounds make up the hard shells of many sea animals. When the animals die, their shells settle to form large deposits that eventually become limestone or marble, both of which are very strong materials used in construc-tion. Coral is one example of a limestone structure. The "skele-tons" of millions of tiny animals combine to form sturdy coral reefs that many fish rely on for protection, as shown in **Figure 3-21B.** Your bones and teeth also get their strength from calcium compounds.

Magnesium is another alkaline-earth metal that has properties similar to calcium. Magnesium is the lightest of all structural met-als and is used to build some airplanes. Magnesium, as Mg^{2+}, acti-vates many of the enzymes that speed up processes in the human body. Magnesium also combines with other elements to form many useful compounds. Two magnesium compounds are com-monly used medicines—milk of magnesia and Epsom salt.

Quick ACTIVITY

Elements in Your Food

1. For 1 day, make a list of the ingredients in all the foods and drinks you consume.
2. Identify which ingredi-ents on your list are compounds.
3. For each compound on your list, try to figure out what elements it is made of.

88 CHAPTER 3

Quick ACTIVITY

Elements in Your Food Student lists will vary. If students need help performing this activity, give them the following hints. Ingre-dients that are not named as elements are probably compounds. Ingredients that are plant or animal products probably contain carbon, hydrogen, and oxygen. Commas sep-arate ingredients. For example, if an ingredi-ent is sodium citrate, it is a compound by that name, not the element sodium and then a compound.

Transition Metals

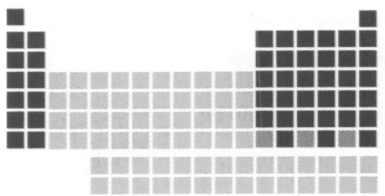

Figure 3-22

A The transition metals are located in the middle of the periodic table.

B The transition metals gold, silver, and platinum are often shaped to make jewelry.

The transition metal gold is mined

Gold is a valuable **transition metal**. **Figure 3-22A** shows that the transition metals are located in Groups 3–12 of the periodic table. Unlike most other transition metals, gold is not found combined with other elements as an ore but as the free metal.

Transition metals, like gold, are much less reactive than sodium or calcium, but they can lose electrons to form positive ions too. There are two possible cations that a gold atom can form. If an atom of gold loses only one electron, it forms Au^+. If the atom loses three electrons, it forms Au^{3+}. Some transition metals can form as many as four differently charged cations because of their complex arrangement of electrons.

All metals, including transition metals, conduct heat and electricity. Most metals can also be stretched and shaped into flat sheets, or pulled into wire. Because gold, silver, and platinum are the shiniest metals, they are often molded into different kinds of jewelry, as shown in **Figure 3-22B.**

There are many other useful transition metals. Copper is often used for electrical wiring or plumbing. Light bulb filaments are made of tungsten. Iron, cobalt, copper, and manganese play vital roles in your body chemistry. Mercury, shown in **Figure 3-23,** is the only metal that is a liquid at room temperature. It is often used in thermometers because it flows quickly and easily without sticking to glass.

▶ **transition metals** the metallic elements located in Groups 3–12 of the periodic table

VOCABULARY *Skills Tip*

The properties of transition metals gradually transition, or shift, from being more similar to Group 2 elements to being more similar to Group 13 elements as you move from left to right across a period.

Figure 3-23

Mercury is an unusual metal because it is a liquid at room temperature. Continued exposure to this volatile metal can harm you because if you breathe in the vapor, it accumulates in your body.

ATOMS AND THE PERIODIC TABLE **89**

Teaching Tip

Variable Charges Because they have different numbers of electrons they can gain or lose, many transition elements can form more than one ion. Common transition element ions include Cu^+, Cu^{2+}, Fe^{2+}, Fe^{3+}, Hg^+, Hg^{2+}, Sn^{2+}, Sn^{4+}, Pb^{2+}, and Pb^{4+}.

|SKILL BUILDER

Interpreting Visuals The metals in **Figure 3-22B** are grouped together because of a common use. Other groups of transition elements are also grouped by use. Copper, silver, and gold, which are in the same family, are called the coinage metals. Iron, cobalt, and nickel, which are in the same period, are called the iron triad and are the only elements that can be magnetized.

Did You Know ?

The transition elements frequently form colorful compounds. Traces of transition elements provide the color in many gems, such as rubies and emeralds.

Additional Application

Gold Although silver is the best conductor, gold is also a very good conductor and has the advantage of not corroding or tarnishing under ordinary conditions. For this reason, gold is widely used on connectors in computers and other electronic devices.

Radioactivity is further defined in Chapter 7.

Teaching Tip

Uses of Synthetic Elements

Although a few synthetic elements have practical uses, many do not. The most common reason for this is that many synthetic elements have extremely short half-lives, sometimes measured in seconds. The half-life of a radioactive element is the amount of time it takes for half of the amount of element present to break down into other elements.

SKILL BUILDER

Interpreting Vocabulary

Ask students what is meant by the common use of the term *decay*. Student descriptions will probably include how plant and animal materials break down into other materials. From this description, ask them to hypothesize what it means for an element to decay. Student answers should indicate that these elements break down, forming other elements.

Inquiry Lab

Why do some metals cost more than others?

Procedure

1. The table at right gives the abundance of some metals in Earth's crust. List the metals in order from most to least abundant.
2. List the metals in order of price, from the cheapest to the most expensive.

Analysis

3. If the price of a metal depends on its abundance, you would expect the order to be the same on both lists. How well do the two lists match? Mention any exceptions.
4. The order of reactivity of these metals, from most reactive to least reactive, is aluminum, zinc, chromium, iron, tin, copper, silver, and gold. Use this information to explain any exceptions you noticed in item 3.

5. Create a spreadsheet that can be used to calculate how many grams of each metal you could buy with $100.

Metal	Abundance in Earth's crust (%)	Price ($/kg)
Aluminum (Al)	8.2	1.55
Chromium (Cr)	0.01	0.06
Copper (Cu)	0.0060	2.44
Gold (Au)	0.000 0004	11 666.53
Iron (Fe)	5.6	0.03
Silver (Ag)	0.000 007	154.97
Tin (Sn)	0.0002	6.22
Zinc (Zn)	0.007	1.29

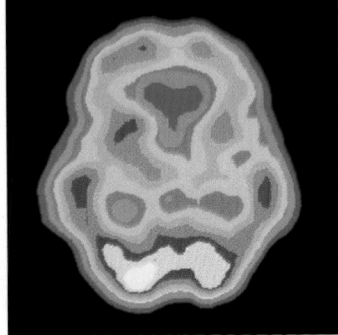

Figure 3-24
With the help of the radioactive isotope technetium-99, doctors are able to confirm that this patient has a healthy brain.

Technetium and promethium are synthetic elements

Technetium and promethium are both man-made elements. They are also both *radioactive*, which means the nuclei of their atoms are continually decaying to produce different elements. There are several different isotopes of technetium. The most stable isotope is technetium-99, which has 56 neutrons. Technetium-99 can be used to diagnose cancer as well as other medical problems in soft tissues of the body, as shown in **Figure 3-24.**

When looking at the periodic table, you might have wondered why part of the last two periods of the transition metals are placed toward the bottom. This keeps the periodic table narrow so that similar elements elsewhere in the table still line up. Promethium is one element located in this bottom-most section. Its most useful isotope is promethium-147, which has 86 neutrons. Promethium-147 is an ingredient in some "glow-in-the-dark" paints.

All elements with atomic numbers greater than 92 are also man-made and are similar to technetium and promethium. For example, americium, another element in the bottom-most section of the periodic table, is also radioactive. Tiny amounts of americium-241 are found in most household smoke detectors. Although it may seem scary to have a radioactive element inside your home, so little of the element is present that it does not affect you.

Inquiry Lab

Why do some metals cost more than others?

1. Al, Fe, Cr, Zn, Cu, Sn, Ag, Au
2. Fe, Cr, Zn, Al, Cu, Sn, Ag, Au
3. The lists match perfectly, except for the price of aluminum compared with its abundancy.
4. Aluminum is the most reactive metal on the list. While aluminum is also the most abundant, its extra cost is due to a necessary purification process.
5. Dividing $100 by the price per gram for each metal will give the number of grams of the metal. Because the prices listed in the table are given in dollars per kilogram, students should incorporate the conversion of kilograms to grams in their spreadsheets.

Nonmetals

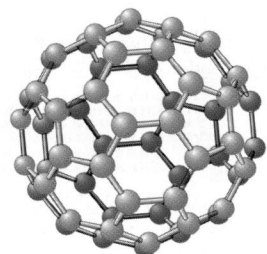

Figure 3-25

A Most nonmetals are located on the right side of the periodic table.

B The way carbon atoms are connected in the most recently discovered form of carbon resembles the familiar pattern of a soccer ball.

Nonmetals

Except for hydrogen, nonmetals are found on the right side of the periodic table. They include some elements in Groups 13–16 and all the elements in Groups 17 and 18.

Carbon is found in three different forms and can also form many compounds

Carbon and other nonmetals are found on the right side of the periodic table, as shown in **Figure 3-25A.** Although carbon in its pure state is usually found as graphite (pencil "lead") or diamond, the existence of fullerenes, a third form, was confirmed in 1990. The most famous fullerene consists of a cluster of 60 carbon atoms, as shown in **Figure 3-25B.**

Carbon can also combine with other elements to form millions of carbon-containing compounds. Carbon compounds are found in both living and nonliving things. Glucose, $C_6H_{12}O_6$, is a sugar in your blood. A type of chlorophyll, $C_{55}H_{72}O_5N_4Mg$, is found in all green plants. Many gasolines contain isooctane, C_8H_{18}, while rubber tires are made of large molecules with many repeating C_5H_8 units.

Nonmetals and their compounds are plentiful on Earth

Oxygen, nitrogen, and sulfur are other common nonmetals. Each may form compounds or gain electrons to form the negative ions oxide, O^{2-}, sulfide, S^{2-}, and nitride, N^{3-}. The most plentiful gases in the air are the nonmetals nitrogen and oxygen. Although sulfur itself is an odorless yellow solid, many sulfur compounds, like those in rotten eggs and skunk spray, are known for their terrible smell.

Connection to ARCHITECTURE

The discoverers of the first and most famous fullerene named the molecule *buckminster-fullerene.* Its structure resembles a geodesic dome, a kind of structure designed by American engineer and inventor R. Buckminster Fuller. A geodesic dome encloses the most space using the fewest materials. Any strains caused by the ground shifting or strong winds have little affect on a geodesic dome. That's because the strains are spread evenly throughout the entire structure. These sturdy structures have been used successfully as radar towers in Antarctica in winds as strong as 90 m/s (200 mi/h) for over 25 years. Geodesic domes provide the framework for some sports arenas, theaters, greenhouses, and even some homes.

Making the Connection

1. How does the shape of a geodesic dome differ from a more typical building?
2. Explain why energy savings are greater in this kind of structure than in a boxlike building that encloses the same amount of space.

SKILL BUILDER

Interpreting Visuals One reason carbon has so many forms and can form so many compounds is that it has the ability to bond to up to four other carbon atoms. This ability of carbon to bond to itself is called *catenation.*

One form of carbon is shown in **Figure 3-25B.** In addition to diamond and graphite, which are described in the text, carbon also exists as charcoal and amorphous carbon, which has no crystalline form.

Connection to ARCHITECTURE

Geodesic domes are commonly made from triangles because of their strength. Have students use plastic drinking straws and modeling clay to form a triangle and a square. By pressing on the side of each, the strength of the triangle can be seen.

Making the Connection

1. The shape is more of a sphere than a cube or a rectangular prism.
2. Answers might include that airflow is more natural.

Resources Assign students worksheet *3.2: Connection to Architecture—Buckyballs* in the **Integration Enrichment Resources** ancillary.

EARTH SCIENCE One common way that magnesium and bromine are recovered from sea water is by the use of electrolysis. Bromide ions release an electron to the anode of the electrolysis setup, and free bromine is formed. At the cathode, magnesium ions accept electrons and become metallic magnesium.

Resources Assign students worksheet *3.3: Integrating Earth Science—Magnesium: From Sea Water to Fireworks* in the **Integration Enrichment Resources** ancillary.

Teaching Tip

Halogen Elements Point out to students that halogen elements all have the same number of valence electrons, seven. This configuration is one electron short of the complete octet found in the noble gas atoms. As a result, halogen elements react by gaining one electron to form ions with a 1– charge.

Additional Application

Chlorine Inform students that the toxicity of chlorine gas is one reason certain cleaning agents should never be mixed. Liquid bleach, for example, frequently contains sodium hypochlorite. When mixed with certain other chemicals, chlorine gas is released from the bleach. This gas is quite hazardous to humans.

Halogens

Figure 3-26

A The halogens are in the second column from the right of the periodic table.

▶ **halogens** the highly reactive elements located in Group 17 of the periodic table

Group 17

9
F
Fluorine
18.998 4032

17
Cl
Chlorine
35.4527

35
Br
Bromine
79.904

53
I
Iodine
126.904

85
At
Astatine
(209.9871)

 EARTH SCIENCE No fewer than 81 elements have been detected in sea water. Magnesium (mostly as Mg^{2+} ions) and bromine (mostly as Br^- ions) are two such elements. To recover an element from a sample of sea water, you must evaporate some of the water from the sample. When you do this, sodium chloride crystallizes and the liquid that remains becomes more concentrated in bromide, magnesium, and other ions than the original sea water was, making their recovery easier.

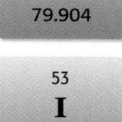

B Chlorine keeps pool water bacteria-free for swimmers to enjoy.

Chlorine is a halogen that protects you from harmful bacteria

Chlorine and other **halogens** are located in Group 17 of the periodic table, as shown in **Figure 3-26A.** You have probably noticed the strong smell of chlorine in swimming pools. Chlorine is widely used to kill bacteria in pools, like the one shown in **Figure 3-26B,** as well as in drinking-water supplies.

Like fluorine atoms, which you learned about in Section 3.2, chlorine atoms are very reactive. As a result, chlorine forms compounds. For example, the chlorine in most swimming pools is added in the form of the compound calcium hypochlorite, $Ca(OCl)_2$. Elemental chlorine is a poisonous yellowish green gas made of pairs of joined chlorine atoms. Chlorine gas has the chemical formula Cl_2. A chlorine atom may also gain an electron to form a negative chloride ion, Cl^-. The attractions between Na^+ ions and Cl^- ions form table salt, NaCl.

Fluorine, bromine, and iodine are other Group 17 elements. Fluorine is a poisonous yellowish gas, bromine is a dark red liquid, and iodine is a dark purple solid. Atoms of each of these elements can also form compounds by gaining an electron to become negative ions. A compound containing the negative ion fluoride, F^-, is used in some toothpastes and added to some water supplies to help prevent tooth decay. Adding a compound containing iodine as the negative ion iodide, I^-, to table salt makes "iodized" salt. You need this ion in your diet for your thyroid gland to function properly.

The noble gas neon is inert

Neon is one of the **noble gases** that make up Group 18 of the periodic table, as shown in **Figure 3-27A**. It is responsible for the bright reddish orange light of "neon" signs. **Figure 3-27B** shows how mixing neon with another substance, such as mercury, can change the color of a sign.

The noble gases are different from most elements that are gases because they exist as single atoms instead of as molecules. Like other members of Group 18, neon is inert, or unreactive, because its outer energy level is full of electrons. For this reason, neon and other noble gases do not gain or lose electrons to form ions. They also don't join with other atoms to form compounds under normal conditions.

Helium and argon are other common noble gases. Helium is less dense than air and is used to give lift to airships and balloons. Argon is used to fill light bulbs because its lack of reactivity prevents filaments from burning.

Semiconductors are intermediate conductors of heat and electricity

Figure 3-28 shows that the elements sometimes referred to as semiconductors or metalloids are clustered toward the right side of the periodic table. Only six elements—boron, silicon, germanium, arsenic, antimony, and tellurium—are semiconductors. Although these elements are classified as nonmetals, each one also has some properties of metals. And as their name implies, semiconductors are able to conduct heat and electricity under certain conditions.

Boron is an extremely hard element. It is often added to steel to increase steel's hardness and strength at high temperatures. Compounds of boron are often used to make heat-resistant glass. Arsenic is a shiny solid that tarnishes when exposed to air. Antimony is a bluish white, brittle solid that also shines like a metal. Some compounds of antimony are used as fire retardants. Tellurium is a silvery white solid whose ability to conduct increases slightly with exposure to light.

Noble Gases

Figure 3-27

A The noble gases are located on the right edge of the periodic table.

Group 18

2 **He** Helium 4.002 602
10 **Ne** Neon 20.1797
18 **Ar** Argon 39.948
36 **Kr** Krypton 83.80
54 **Xe** Xenon 131.29
86 **Rn** Radon (222.0176)

B A neon sign is usually reddish orange, but adding a few drops of mercury makes the light a bright blue.

▶ **noble gases** the unreactive gaseous elements located in Group 18 of the periodic table

Semiconductors

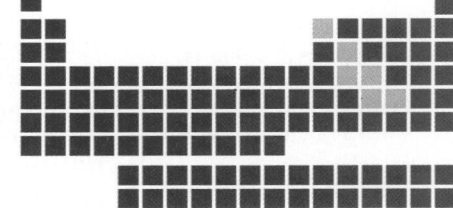

Figure 3-28
Semiconductors are located toward the right side of the periodic table.

Historical Perspective

Argon was the first noble gas to be identified. Its existence was proposed in 1785 because chemists could not account for all the major constituents of air. Argon makes up about 1 percent of air. It was not until 1894 that British chemist William Ramsay identified it. Because of its chemical inertness, it was given the name argon from the Greek *argos*, which means "lazy" or "inactive."

Did You Know ?

Group 18 gases were always considered to be completely inert. However, in 1962, the first Group 18 compound was formed from xenon. Currently, compounds of xenon, krypton, and radon exist.

In the heavier Group 18 gases, the outer electrons are farther away from the pull of the nucleus. Also, inner electrons shield the outer electrons from the pull of the nucleus. Thus, the valence electrons are more easily removed.

Helium, neon, and argon have more nuclear attraction for their electrons, and no compounds of these gases currently exist.

Teaching Tip

Doping The conductivity of semiconductors increases when certain impurities are added to them. This process is called *doping*.

The most common doping process is adding small amounts of arsenic or gallium to silicon. Because these elements contain different numbers of valence electrons, electrons flow more easily and conductivity increases.

Semiconductor Greeting

Time: Approximately 10 minutes
Materials: several musical greeting cards
hand lens

Play the greeting cards. Take the cards apart and let groups of students examine the mechanisms. Tell students that semiconductors play a part in the mechanisms.

Analysis
1. What parts of the mechanism can you recognize? *(Answers will vary, but students will probably locate the speaker.)*
2. What do you think a semiconductor is? *(Answers might include that it conducts electricity but not as well as a metal does.)*

Families of Elements

SECTION 3.3 REVIEW

Check Your Understanding

1. a. transition metal
   b. alkali metal
   c. alkaline-earth metal
   d. transition metal

2. Cesium is an alkali metal, so it has one valence electron that is removed to form a Cs^+ ion.

3. Reactive chemicals might react with oxygen or water vapor in the air. They will not react with argon because it is inert. Argon is a noble gas.

4. a. metal
   b. nonmetal
   c. nonmetal
   d. metal

5. Bromine, a halogen, is one electron short of having a complete outermost energy level. It will readily react with an element that can supply that electron.

6. Beryllium is an alkaline-earth metal. Therefore, it has two valence electrons that can be removed to form a Be^{2+} ion.

7. Lithium is an alkali metal and is more reactive than an alkaline-earth metal such as barium.

8. Answers will vary, but one method is to check the reactivity of the metal against the reactivities of other alkali, alkaline-earth, and transition metals. The element belongs to the family that is most similar to the element chemically.

RESOURCE LINK
STUDY GUIDE

Assign students *Review Section 3.3 Families of Elements.*

Figure 3-29
Silicon wafers are the basic building blocks of computer chips.

Silicon is the most familiar semiconductor

Silicon atoms, usually in the form of compounds, account for 28 percent of the mass of Earth's crust. Sand is made of the most common silicon compound, called silicon dioxide, SiO_2. Small chips made of silicon, like those shown in **Figure 3-29,** are used in the internal parts of computers.

Silicon is also an important component of other semiconductor devices such as transistors, LED display screens, and solar cells. Impurities such as boron, aluminum, phosphorus, and arsenic are added to the silicon to increase its ability to conduct electricity. These impurities are usually added only to the surface of the chip. This process can be used to make chips of different conductive abilities. This wide range of possible semiconductor devices has led to great advances in electronic technology.

SECTION 3.3 REVIEW

SUMMARY

▶ Metals are shiny solids that conduct heat and electricity.

▶ Alkali metals, located in Group 1 of the periodic table, are very reactive.

▶ Alkaline-earth metals, located in Group 2, are less reactive than alkali metals.

▶ Transition metals, located in Groups 3–12, are not very reactive.

▶ Nonmetals usually do not conduct heat or electricity well.

▶ Nonmetals include the inert noble gases in Group 18, the reactive halogens in Group 17, and some elements in Groups 13–16.

▶ Semiconductors are nonmetals that are intermediate conductors of heat and electricity.

CHECK YOUR UNDERSTANDING

1. Classify the following elements as alkali, alkaline-earth, or transition metals based on their positions in the periodic table:
   a. iron, Fe   **c.** strontium, Sr
   b. potassium, K   **d.** platinum, Pt

2. Predict whether cesium forms Cs^+ or Cs^{2+} ions.

3. Describe why chemists might sometimes store reactive chemicals in argon, Ar. To which family does argon belong?

4. Determine whether the following substances are likely to be metals or nonmetals:
   a. a shiny substance used to make flexible bed springs
   b. a yellow powder from underground mines
   c. a gas that does not react
   d. a conducting material used within flexible wires

5. Describe why atoms of bromine, Br, are so reactive. To which family does bromine belong?

6. Predict the charge of a beryllium ion.

7. Identify which element is more reactive: lithium, Li, or barium, Ba.

8. Creative Thinking Imagine you are a scientist who has just discovered a new element. You have confirmed that the element is a metal but are unsure whether it is an alkali metal, an alkaline-earth metal, or a transition metal. Write a paragraph describing the additional tests you can do to further classify this metal.

WRITING SKILL

3.4

Using Moles to Count Atoms

OBJECTIVES

▶ Explain the relationship between a mole of a substance and Avogadro's constant.

▶ Find the molar mass of an element by using the periodic table.

▶ Solve problems converting the amount of an element in moles to its mass in grams, and vice versa.

▶ **KEY TERMS**
mole
Avogadro's constant
molar mass
conversion factor

Counting objects is one of the very first things children learn to do. Counting is easy when the objects being counted are not too small and there are not too many of them. But can you imagine counting the grains of sand along a stretch of beach or the stars in the night-time sky? Counting these would be very difficult.

Counting Things

When people count out large numbers of small things, they often simplify the job by using counting units. For example, when you order popcorn at a movie theater, the salesperson does not count out the individual popcorn kernels to give you. Instead, you specify the size of container you want, and that determines how much popcorn you get. So the "counting unit" for popcorn is the size of the container: small, medium, or large.

There are many different counting units

The counting units for popcorn are only an approximation and are not exact. Everyone who orders a large popcorn will not get exactly the same number of popcorn kernels. Many other items, however, require more-exact counting units, as shown in **Figure 3-30.** For example, you usually cannot buy just one egg at the grocery store. Eggs are packaged by the dozen. Items that are needed in large quantities are packaged into groups as well. Grocers buy fruit from farmers in bushels, or 32 qt containers. Copy shops buy paper in reams, or 500-sheet bundles.

Figure 3-30
Eggs are counted by the dozen, peaches are counted by the bushel, and paper is counted by the ream.

ATOMS AND THE PERIODIC TABLE **95**

DEMONSTRATION 5 TEACHING

Counting by Mass

Time: Approximately 15 minutes
Materials: large container, such as a gallon jar; enough identical small items, such as pennies, candies, or beans, to fill the jar; balance

Find the mass of the following: the container; a small, known number of the items; and the container and items together.

Analysis

1. What is the purpose of this demonstration? *(to find out how many small items are present without actually counting them)*

2. How can you use your data to do this? {*(combined mass–mass of the container) ÷ (mass of the small, known number of items ÷ the small, known number of items)*}

Section 3.4

Using Moles to Count Atoms

Scheduling
Refer to pp. 68A–68D for lecture, classwork, and assignment options for Section 3.4.

★ **Lesson Focus**
Use transparency *LT 10* to prepare students for this section.

READING SKILL BUILDER *Reading Organizer* Have students read the section and then organize the ideas presented in the section in the form of a concept map. Concept maps might show how to convert from moles to grams or grams to moles. Have students share their maps after you have checked them for accuracy.

Teaching Tip
Scientific Notation Students may think that extremely large and small numbers do not apply to their daily lives. These concepts seem abstract because students cannot directly measure the quantities or count the numbers involved. Use the following example that applies to the human body to emphasize that extremely large and small numbers do affect students.

The average human body contains about 10^{14} cells. Each cell membrane has a thickness of 7×10^{-9} m. Of the cells in the human body, about 2.5×10^{12} are red blood cells. Each red blood cell has a diameter of about 7.5×10^{-6} m and a thickness of about 2×10^{-6} m. Each milliliter of blood contains about 5×10^9 red blood cells. Because some cells die every moment, the human body replenishes itself with red blood cells at a rate of about 3×10^6 each second.

Using Moles to Count Atoms

▶ **mole** the SI base unit that describes the amount of a substance

▶ **Avogadro's constant** the number of particles in 1 mol; equals 6.022×10^{23}/mol

▶ **molar mass** the mass in grams of 1 mol of a substance

Did You Know ?

Did you know that Avogadro never knew his own constant? Count Amedeo Avogadro (1776–1856) was a lawyer who became interested in mathematics and physics. Avogadro's constant was actually determined by Joseph Loschmidt, a German physicist in 1865, nine years after Avogadro's death.

Figure 3-31
One mole of magnesium (6.022×10^{23} Mg atoms) has a mass of 24.30 g. Note that the balance is only accurate to one-tenth of a gram, so it reads 24.3 g.

An object's mass may sometimes be used to "count" it. For example, if a candy shopkeeper knows that 10 gumballs have a mass of 21.4 g, then the shopkeeper can assume that there are 50 gumballs on the scale when the mass is 107 g (21.4 g × 5).

The mole is useful for counting small particles

Because chemists often deal with large numbers of small particles, they use a large counting unit—the **mole**, abbreviated *mol*. A mole is a collection of a very large number of particles.

602 213 670 000 000 000 000 000 to be exact!

This number is usually written as 6.022×10^{23}/mol and is referred to as **Avogadro's constant.** The constant is named in honor of the Italian scientist Amedeo Avogadro. Avogadro's constant is defined as the number of particles, 6.022×10^{23}, in exactly 1 mol of a pure substance.

One mole of gumballs is 6.022×10^{23} gumballs. One mole of popcorn is 6.022×10^{23} kernels of popcorn. This amount of popcorn would not only cover the United States but form a pile about 500 km (310 mi) high! It is highly unlikely that you will ever come in contact with this much gum or popcorn, so it does not make sense to use moles to count either of these items. The mole is very useful, however, for counting tiny atoms.

Moles and grams are related

The mass in grams of 1 mol of a substance is called its **molar mass.** For example, 1 mol of carbon-12 atoms has a molar mass of 12.00 g. But an entire mole of an element will usually include atoms of several isotopes. So the molar mass of an element in grams is the same as its average atomic mass in amu, which is listed in the periodic table. The average atomic mass listed for carbon in the periodic table is 12.01 amu. One mole of carbon, then, has a mass of 12.01 g. **Figure 3-31** demonstrates this idea for magnesium.

12
Mg
Magnesium
24.30

You might wonder why 6.022×10^{23} represents the number of particles in 1 mol. Experiments have shown that 6.022×10^{23} is the number of carbon-12 atoms in 1 mol of carbon-12. One mole of carbon consists of 6.022×10^{23} carbon atoms, with an average mass of 12.01 amu. So 6.022×10^{23} carbon atoms together have a mass of 12.01 g.

Calculating with Moles

Because the amount of a substance and its mass are related, it is often useful to convert moles to grams, and vice versa. You can use **conversion factors** to relate units.

Using conversion factors

How did the shopkeeper mentioned on page 96 know the mass of 50 gumballs? He multiplied by a conversion factor to determine the number of gumballs on the scale from their combined mass. Multiplying by a conversion factor is like multiplying by 1 because both parts of the conversion factor are always equal.

The shopkeeper knows that exactly 10 gumballs have a combined mass of 21.4 g. This relationship can be written as two equivalent conversion factors, both of which are shown below.

$$\frac{10 \text{ gumballs}}{21.4 \text{ g}} \qquad \frac{21.4 \text{ g}}{10 \text{ gumballs}}$$

The shopkeeper can use one of these conversion factors to determine the mass of 50 gumballs because mass increases in a predictable way as more gumballs are added to the scale, as you can see from **Figure 3-32.**

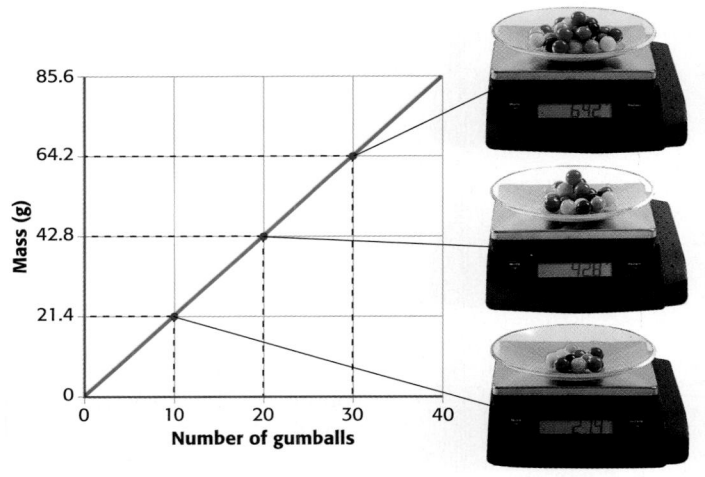

📝 **internet connect** ☰

SC*LINKS*.
NSTA

TOPIC: Avogadro's constant
GO TO: www.scilinks.org
KEYWORD: HK1036

▶ **conversion factor** a ratio equal to one that expresses the same quantity in two different ways

Figure 3-32
There is a direct relationship between the number of gumballs and their mass. Ten gumballs have a mass of 21.4 g, 20 gumballs have a mass of 42.8 g, and 30 gumballs have a mass of 64.2 g.

Teaching Tip

Avogadro's Constant Students might wonder how a number such as 6.02×10^{23} became Avogadro's constant. If the molar mass of an element is divided by the mass of one atom of that element, the answer is Avogadro's constant.

For example, carbon-12 has 12 particles in its nucleus, each of which has a mass of approximately 1.67×10^{-24} g. The total mass per atom is $12 \times 1.67 \times 10^{-24}$ g/atom, or 2.00×10^{-23} g/atom. The molar mass of carbon-12 is 12.00 g. 12.00 g divided by 2.00×10^{-23} g/atom equals 6.00×10^{23} atoms.

Similar calculations involving more accurate mass values result in the accepted value of Avogadro's constant.

ALTERNATIVE ASSESSMENT

Conversion Factors

Step 1 Have students choose one of the following properties: length, mass and weight, volume, or area. Have them then make two sets of cards of units that can be used to measure that property. For example, length cards can include inches, feet, meters, kilometers, and so on.

Step 2 Have them shuffle one set of cards then draw two of them. Have students place those cards side-by-side with space between.

Step 3 Have them use the other set of cards to create the units of the conversion factors needed to change from the unit on the left to the unit on the right. Tell students that sometimes more than one conversion factor is needed.

Using Moles to Count Atoms

Math Skills

Resources Assign students worksheet *6: Conversion Factors* in the **Math Skills Worksheets** ancillary.

Additional Examples

Conversion Factors The mileage for Maria's car is 21 mi/gal of gasoline. If she needs to drive 97 mi, how much gas will her car use?

Answer: 4.6 gal

A school bus seat can hold three students. How many seats must the bus have if it is to haul 52 students on a field trip?

Answer: 18 seats

A bicycle travels at a speed of 30.0 km/h. How fast does the bicycle travel in m/s? (More than one conversion factor must be used.)

Answer: 8.33 m/s

SKILL BUILDER

Graphing Have students study the graph in **Figure 3-33.** After they have completed this section, have them arbitrarily choose at least three different amounts, in moles, of an element other than iron. Then have them create a graph similar to that in **Figure 3-33** to confirm the direct relationship of mass and amount.

Resources Blackline Master 10 shows this visual.

RESOURCE LINK
BASIC SKILLS

Assign students worksheet *2.1: Significant Figures* for additional practice.

Math Skills

Conversion Factors What is the mass of exactly 50 gumballs?

1 List the given and unknown values.
Given: mass of 10 gumballs = 21.4 g
Unknown: mass of 50 gumballs = ? g

2 Write down the conversion factor that converts number of gumballs to mass.
The conversion factor you choose should have the unit you are solving for (g) in the numerator and the unit you want to cancel (number of gumballs) in the denominator.

$$\frac{21.4 \text{ g}}{10 \text{ gumballs}}$$

3 Multiply the number of gumballs by this conversion factor, and solve.

$$50 \text{ gumballs} \times \frac{21.4 \text{ g}}{10 \text{ gumballs}} = 107 \text{ g}$$

Practice

Conversion Factors

1. What is the mass of exactly 150 gumballs?
2. If you want 50 eggs, how many dozens must you buy? How many extra eggs do you have to take?
3. If a football player is tackled 1.7 ft short of the end zone, how many more yards does the team need to get a touchdown?

Figure 3-33
There is a direct relationship between the amount of an element and its mass.

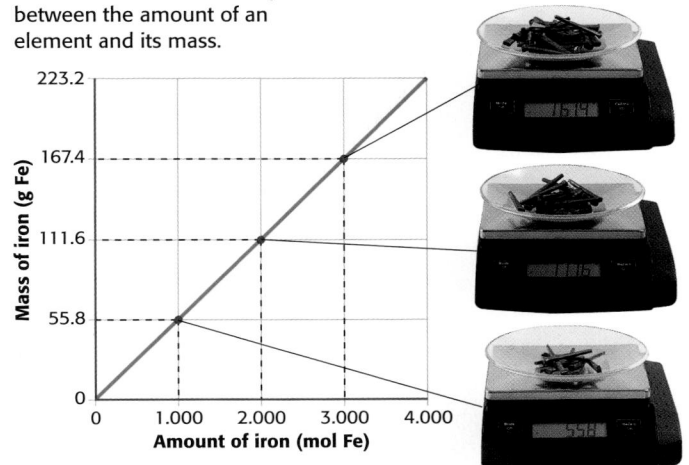

Relating moles to grams

Just as in the gumball example, there is also a relationship between the amount of an element in moles and its mass in grams. This relationship is graphed for iron nails in **Figure 3-33.** Because the amount of iron and the mass of iron are directly related, the graph is a straight line.

An element's molar mass can be used as if it were a conversion factor. Depending on which conversion factor you use, you can solve for either the amount of the element or its mass.

Solution Guide

1. 150 gumballs × 21.4 g/10 gumballs = 321 g
2. 50 eggs × 1 dozen/12 eggs = 4.2 dozen; 5 dozen eggs must be bought;
5 dozen × 12 eggs/1 dozen − 50 eggs = 10 extra eggs
3. 1.7 ft × 1 yd/3 ft = 0.57 yd

Converting between the amount of an element in moles and its mass in grams is outlined in **Figure 3-34.** For example, you can determine the mass of 5.50 mol of iron by using **Figure 3-34** as a guide. First you must find iron in the periodic table. Its average atomic mass is 55.85 amu. This means iron's molar mass is 55.85 g/mol Fe. Now you can set up the problem using the molar mass as if it were a conversion factor, as shown in the sample problem below.

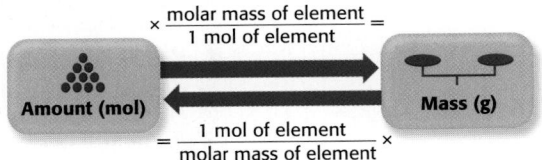

Figure 3-34
The molar mass of an element allows you to convert between the amount of the element and its mass.

Math Skills

Converting Amount to Mass Determine the mass in grams of 5.50 mol of iron.

1 **List the given and unknown values.**
  Given: amount of iron = 5.50 mol Fe
      molar mass of iron = 55.85 g/mol Fe
  Unknown: mass of iron = ? g Fe

2 **Write down the conversion factor that converts moles to grams.**
  The conversion factor you choose should have what you are trying to find (grams of Fe) in the numerator and what you want to cancel (moles of Fe) in the denominator.

$$\frac{55.85 \text{ g Fe}}{1 \text{ mol Fe}}$$

3 **Multiply the amount of iron by this conversion factor, and solve.**

$$5.50 \ \text{mol Fe} \times \frac{55.85 \text{ g Fe}}{1 \ \text{mol Fe}} = 307 \text{ g Fe}$$

Practice HINT

Notice how iron's molar mass, 55.85 g/mol Fe, includes units (g/mol) and a chemical symbol (Fe). The units specify that this mass applies to 1 mol of substance. The symbol for iron, Fe, clearly indicates the substance. Remember to always include units in your answers and make clear the substance to which these units apply. Otherwise, your answer has no meaning.

Practice

Converting Amount to Mass
What is the mass in grams of each of the following?
1. 2.50 mol of sulfur, S
2. 1.80 mol of calcium, Ca
3. 0.50 mol of carbon, C
4. 3.20 mol of copper, Cu

You can determine the amount of an element from its mass in much the same way, as the next sample problem on the next page shows.

MISCONCEPTION ALERT
Conversions Students will quickly associate moles with mass. Emphasize that moles are a measure of the number of particles, not the mass. For example, 16.00 g of oxygen is the mass of 1 mol of oxygen. It is not 1 mol of oxygen. One mole of oxygen is 6.022×10^{23} atoms of oxygen.

SKILL BUILDER
Interpreting Visuals Figure **3-34** illustrates how to convert between the amount of an element and its mass. Look at the periodic table to determine the average atomic mass of the element in question. Then arrange the conversion factor in the correct orientation based on what information is given.

Resources Blackline Master 11 shows this visual.

Math Skills

Resources Assign students worksheet *7: Converting Amount to Mass* in the **Math Skills Worksheets** ancillary.

Additional Example

Converting Amount to Mass
What is the mass in grams of 1.93 mol of cobalt, Co?
Answer: 114 g Co

Solution Guide

1. 2.50 mol S × 32.07 g S/1 mol S = 80.2 g S
2. 1.80 mol Ca × 40.08 g Ca/1 mol Ca = 72.1 g Ca
3. 0.50 mol C × 12.01 g C/1 mol C = 6.0 g C
4. 3.20 mol Cu × 63.55 g Cu/1 mol Cu = 203 g Cu

Using Moles to Count Atoms

Math Skills ═══════

Resources Assign students worksheet *8: Converting Mass to Amount* in the **Math Skills Worksheets** ancillary.

SECTION 3.4 REVIEW

Check Your Understanding

1. Avogadro's constant is 6.022×10^{23}/mol. It is the number of particles in one mole of anything.

2. **a.** 54.94 g/mol Mn
   b. 112.41 g/mol Cd
   c. 74.92 g/mol As
   d. 87.62 g/mol Sr

3. 1 mol Ag/107.87 g Ag; 107.87 g Ag/1 mol Ag

4. A direct relationship exists between the amount of an element in moles and the element's mass in grams.

5. 3.0 g Fe × 1 mol Fe/ 55.85 g Fe = 0.054 mol Fe; 2.0 g S × 1 mol S/32.07 g S = 0.062 mol S. Because the number of moles of sulfur is greater, the number of atoms of sulfur is greater.

Math Skills ═══════

6. 0.48 mol Pt × 195.08 g Pt/ 1 mol Pt = 94 g Pt

7. 620 g Hg × 1 mol Hg/ 200.59 g Hg = 3.1 mol Hg

8. 11 g Si × 1 mol Si/ 28.09 g Si = 0.39 mol Si

9. 205 g He × 1 mol He/ 4.00 g He = 51.3 mol He

RESOURCE LINK
STUDY GUIDE

Assign students *Review Section 3.4 Using Moles to Count Atoms.*

Math Skills ═══════

Converting Mass to Amount Determine the amount of iron present in 352 g of iron.

1 **List the given and unknown values.**
   Given: mass of iron = 352 g Fe
   molar mass of iron = 55.85 g/mol Fe
   Unknown: amount of iron = ? mol Fe

2 **Write down the conversion factor that converts grams to moles.**
   The conversion factor you choose should have what you are trying to find (moles of Fe) in the numerator and what you want to cancel (grams of Fe) in the denominator.

   $$\frac{1 \text{ mol Fe}}{55.85 \text{ g Fe}}$$

3 **Multiply the mass of iron by this conversion factor, and solve.**

   $$352 \text{ g Fe} \times \frac{1 \text{ mol Fe}}{55.85 \text{ g Fe}} = 6.30 \text{ mol Fe}$$

SECTION 3.4 REVIEW

SUMMARY

▶ One mole of a substance has as many particles as there are atoms in exactly 12 g of carbon-12.

▶ Avogadro's constant, 6.022×10^{23}/mol, is equal to the number of particles in 1 mol.

▶ Molar mass is the mass in grams of 1 mol of a substance.

▶ An element's molar mass in grams is equal to its average atomic mass in amu.

▶ An element's molar mass can be used to convert from amount to mass, and vice versa.

CHECK YOUR UNDERSTANDING

1. **Define** Avogadro's constant. Describe how Avogadro's constant relates to a mole of a substance.

2. **Determine** the molar mass of the following elements:
   a. manganese, Mn   **c.** arsenic, As
   b. cadmium, Cd   **d.** strontium, Sr

3. **List** the two equivalent conversion factors for the molar mass of silver, Ag.

4. **Explain** why a graph showing the relationship between the amount of a particular element and the element's mass is a straight line.

5. **Critical Thinking** Which has more atoms: 3.0 g of iron, Fe, or 2.0 g of sulfur, S?

Math Skills ═══════

6. What is the mass in grams of 0.48 mol of platinum, Pt?

7. How many moles are present in 620 g of mercury, Hg?

8. How many moles are present in 11 g of silicon, Si?

9. How many moles are present in 205 g of helium, He?

Graphic Organizer
Conversion factors

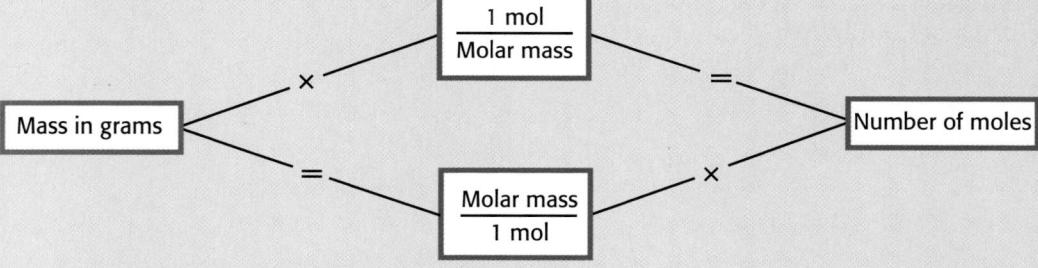

Chapter Highlights

Before you begin, review the summaries of the key ideas of each section, found on pages 76, 85, 94, and 100. The key vocabulary terms are listed on pages 70, 77, 86, and 95.

UNDERSTANDING CONCEPTS

1. Which of Dalton's statements about the atom was later proven false?
   a. Atoms cannot be subdivided.
   b. Atoms are tiny.
   c. Atoms of different elements are not identical.
   d. Atoms join to form molecules.
2. Which statement is not true of Bohr's model of the atom?
   a. The nucleus can be compared to the sun.
   b. Electrons orbit the nucleus.
   c. An electron's path is not known exactly.
   d. Electrons exist in energy levels.
3. According to the modern model of the atom, _____.
   a. moving electrons form an electron cloud
   b. electrons and protons circle neutrons
   c. neutrons have a positive charge
   d. the number of protons an atom has varies
4. If an atom has a mass of 11 amu and contains five electrons, its atomic number must be _____.
   a. 55   c. 6
   b. 16   d. 5
5. Which statement is true concerning atoms of elements in the same group of the periodic table?
   a. They have the same number of protons.
   b. They have the same mass number.
   c. They have similar chemical properties.
   d. They have the same number of total electrons.

6. The organization of the periodic table is based on _____.
   a. the number of protons in an atom
   b. the mass number of an atom
   c. the number of neutrons in an atom
   d. the average atomic mass of an element
7. Elements with some properties of metals and some properties of nonmetals are known as _____.
   a. alkali metals   c. halogens
   b. semiconductors   d. noble gases
8. An atom of which of the following elements is unlikely to form a positively charged ion?
   a. potassium, K   c. barium, Ba
   b. selenium, Se   d. silver, Ag
9. Atoms of Group 18 elements are inert because _____.
   a. they combine to form molecules
   b. they have no valence electrons
   c. they have filled inner energy levels
   d. they have filled outermost energy levels
10. Which of the following statements about krypton is not true?
    a. Its molar mass is 83.80 g/mol Kr.
    b. Its atomic number is 36.
    c. One mole of krypton atoms has a mass of 41.90 g.
    d. It is a noble gas.

Using Vocabulary

11. How many *protons* and *neutrons* does a silicon, Si, atom have, and where are each of these subatomic particles located? How many *electrons* does a silicon atom have?

internet**connect**

SCI**LINKS**
NSTA
TOPIC: Silicon
GO TO: www.scilinks.org
KEYWORD: HK1037

UNDERSTANDING CONCEPTS

1. a	**6.** a
2. c	**7.** b
3. a	**8.** b
4. d	**9.** d
5. c	**10.** c

Using Vocabulary

11. In the nucleus, a silicon atom has 14 protons, and it usually has 14 neutrons. A silicon atom has 14 electrons, four of which are valence electrons.

12. Atomic number tells the number of protons in the atom. All atoms of the same element have the same number of protons, so they have the same atomic number. The mass number is the total number of protons and neutrons in an atom. The number of neutrons can vary, so the mass number can vary among atoms of the same element. These different atoms are called isotopes.

13. **a.** An atom is the smallest unit of an element, and a molecule consists of two or more atoms.
    b. An atom has no charge. An ion is a charged atom or group of atoms.
    c. A cation has a positive charge, and an anion has a negative charge.

RESOURCE LINK
STUDY GUIDE

Assign students *Mixed Review Chapter 3.*

14. All halogens have the same number of valence electrons and similar chemical properties.
15. the mass of one mole, or 6.022×10^{23} particles, of the element

BUILDING MATH SKILLS

16. Graphs should show increasing atomic mass with increasing atomic number with one exception. The atomic number of Ni is higher than that of Co, but the atomic mass is less. Ni has more protons than Co does, but Co has more neutrons.
17. 1.5 g Fe × 1 mol Fe/ 55.85 g Fe = 0.027 mol Fe
18. 0.54 g He × 1 mol He/ 4.00 g He = 0.14 mol He
19. 19.55 mol Au × 196.97 g Au/ 1 mol Au = 3851 g Au
20. 15.1 mol Al × 26.98 g Al/ 1 mol Al = 407 g Al

THINKING CRITICALLY

21. Because like charges repel each other and unlike charges attract, protons repel each other and attract electrons. Electrons repel each other and attract protons.
22. Magnesium has two valence electrons. To achieve a full outermost energy level, it will lose both electrons, forming Mg^{2+}.

12. Explain why different atoms of the same element always have the same *atomic number* but can have different *mass numbers*. What are these different atoms called?
13. Distinguish between the following:
    a. an *atom* and a *molecule*
    b. an *atom* and an *ion*
    c. a *cation* and an *anion*
14. How is the *periodic law* demonstrated with the *halogens*?
15. What does an element's *molar mass* tell you about the element?

BUILDING MATH SKILLS

16. **Graphing** Use a graphing calculator, a computer spreadsheet, or a graphing program to plot the atomic number on the *x*-axis and the average atomic mass in amu on the *y*-axis for the transition metals in Period 4 of the periodic table (from scandium to zinc). Do you notice a break in the trend near cobalt? Explain why elements with larger atomic numbers do not necessarily have larger atomic masses.

    COMPUTER SKILL

17. **Converting Mass to Amount** For an experiment you have been asked to do, you need 1.5 g of iron. How many moles of iron do you need?
18. **Converting Mass to Amount** James is holding a balloon that contains 0.54 g of helium gas. What amount of helium is this?
19. **Converting Amount to Mass** A pure gold bar is made of 19.55 mol of gold. What is the mass of the bar in grams?
20. **Converting Amount to Mass** Robyn recycled 15.1 mol of aluminum last month. What mass of aluminum in grams did she recycle?

THINKING CRITICALLY

21. **Creative Thinking** Some forces push two atoms apart while other forces pull them together. Describe how the subatomic particles in each atom interact to produce these forces.
22. **Applying Knowledge** Explain why magnesium forms ions with the formula Mg^{2+}, not Mg^+ or Mg^-.
23. **Evaluating Data** The figure below shows relative ionic radii for positive and negative ions of elements in Period 2 of the periodic table. Explain the trend in ion size as you move from left to right across the periodic table. Why do the negative ions have larger radii than the positive ions?

0.60	0.31	1.71	1.40	1.36
Li^+	Be^{2+}	N^{3-}	O^{2-}	F^-

24. **Creative Thinking** Although carbon and lead are in the same group, some of their properties are very different. Propose a reason for this. (**Hint:** Look at the periodic table to locate each element and find out how each is classified.)
25. **Problem Solving** How does halving the amount of a sample of an element affect the sample's mass?

DEVELOPING LIFE/WORK SKILLS

26. **Locating Information** Some "neon" signs contain substances other than neon to produce different colors. Design your own lighted sign, and find out which substances you could use to produce the colors you want your sign to be.

27. Making Decisions Suppose you have only 1.9 g of sulfur for an experiment and you must do three trials using 0.030 mol of S each time. Do you have enough sulfur?

28. Communicating Effectively The study of the nucleus produced a new field of medicine called nuclear medicine. Pretend you are writing an article for a hospital newsletter. Describe how radioactive substances called tracers are sometimes used to detect and treat diseases.

WRITING
SKILL

29. Working Cooperatively With a group of your classmates, make a list of 10 elements and their average atomic masses. Calculate the amount in moles for 6.0 g of each element. Rank your elements from the element with the greatest amount to the element with the least amount in a 6.0 g sample. Do you notice a trend in the amounts as atomic number increases? Explain why or why not.

INTEGRATING CONCEPTS

30. Connection to Health You can keep your bones healthy by eating 1200–1500 mg of calcium a day. Use the table below to make a list of the foods you might eat in a day to satisfy your body's need for calcium. How does your typical diet compare with this?

Item, serving size	Calcium (mg)
Plain lowfat yogurt, 1 cup	415
Ricotta cheese, 1/2 cup	337
Skim milk, 1 cup	302
Cheddar cheese, 1 ounce	213
Cooked spinach, 1/2 cup	106
Vanilla ice cream, 1/2 cup	88

31. Concept Mapping Copy the unfinished concept map below onto a sheet of paper. Complete the map by writing the correct word or phrase in the lettered boxes.

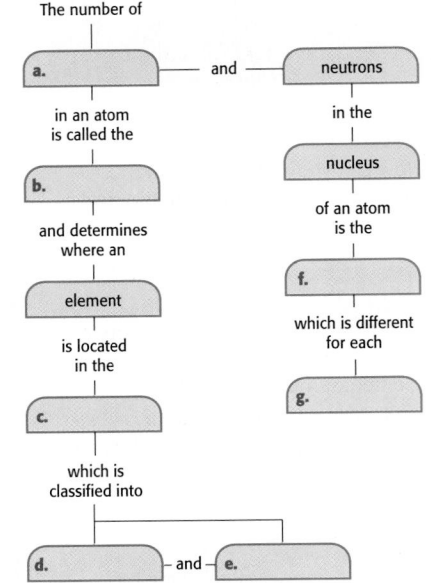

32. Connection to Physics The big bang theory suggests that the universe began with an enormous explosion. What was formed as a result of the big bang? Describe the matter that was present after the explosion. How much time passed before the elements as we know them were formed?

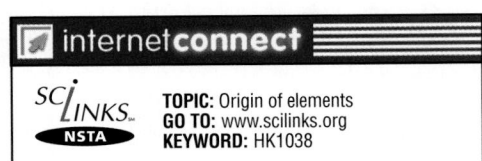

internet**connect**

SC**LINKS**
NSTA

TOPIC: Origin of elements
GO TO: www.scilinks.org
KEYWORD: HK1038

ATOMS AND THE PERIODIC TABLE **103**

23. All atoms in a period have the same number of electron energy levels. When an atom in that period becomes a positive ion, it loses that outer level and becomes smaller. An atom that becomes a negative ion keeps the outer level and becomes larger. Within their positive and negative groups, ions become smaller from left to right because the number of protons increases, increasing the attraction of the nucleus for the electrons.

24. Carbon is a nonmetal and lead is a metal.

25. The mass becomes halved also because only half the amount is present.

DEVELOPING LIFE/ WORK SKILLS

26. Answers may vary but could include that argon gives off a purple glow, and krypton gives off a pale violet glow.

27. 1.9 g S × 1 mol S/ 32.07 g S = 0.059 mol S. The experiment requires 3 × 0.030 mol, or 0.090 mol, so there is not enough sulfur.

28. Tracers are radioactive isotopes that can be detected by certain medical instruments but have low enough radioactivity that they do not hurt human cells in low concentrations. After entering the body, some tracers accumulate in certain body tissues. They can then be used to detect problems, such as tumors, or treat problems by accumulating and destroying undesirable tissues.

Answers continue on p. 105B.

Comparing the Physical Properties of Elements

Introduction

Russian chemist Dmitri Mendeleev is generally credited as being the first chemist to observe that patterns emerge when the elements are arranged according to their atomic numbers. Challenge your students to identify the unknown metals in this lab.

Objectives

Students will:

▶ **Use** appropriate lab safety procedures.

▶ **Determine** which physical properties can help distinguish between different metals.

▶ **Identify** unknown metals by comparing the data collected with reference information.

Planning

Recommended time: 1 lab period
Materials: *(for each lab group)*

▶ several unknown metal samples
▶ balance
▶ graduated cylinder
▶ water
▶ several beakers
▶ ice
▶ magnet
▶ stopwatch
▶ metric ruler
▶ wax
▶ hot plate

RESOURCE LINK
DATASHEETS

Have students use *Datasheet 3.6 Design Your Own Lab: Comparing the Physical Properties of Elements* to record their results.

Design Your Own Lab

Introduction

How can you distinguish metal elements by analyzing their physical properties?

Objectives

▶ **Determine** which physical properties can help you **distinguish** between different metals.

▶ **Identify** unknown metals by **comparing** the data you collect with reference information.

Materials

several unknown metal samples
balance
graduated cylinder
water
several beakers
ice
magnet
stopwatch
metric ruler
wax
hot plate

Safety Needs

safety goggles
gloves
laboratory apron

SOLUTIONS/MATERIAL PREPARATION

Depending on which method students use to determine heat conductivity, the wax is used in solid or liquid form. Students could choose to test heat conductivity by adding hot melted wax to room temperature metals. In this case, melt the wax by placing it in a beaker on the hot plate and heating it. Caution students not to touch the hot beaker.

Comparing the Physical Properties of Elements

▶ Identifying Metal Elements

1. In this lab, you will identify samples of unknown metals by comparing the data you collect with reference information listed in the table at right. Use at least two of the physical properties listed in the table to identify each metal.

▶ Deciding Which Physical Properties You Will Analyze

2. Density is the mass per unit volume of a substance. If the metal is box-shaped, you can measure its length, width, and height, and then use these measurements to calculate the metal's volume. If the shape of the metal is irregular, you can add the metal to a known volume of water and determine what volume of water is displaced.

3. Relative hardness indicates how easy it is to scratch a metal. A metal with a higher value can scratch a metal with a lower value, but not vice versa.

4. Relative heat conductivity indicates how quickly a metal heats or cools. A metal with a value of 100 will heat or cool twice as quickly as a metal with a value of 50.

5. If a magnet placed near a metal attracts the metal, then the metal has been magnetized by the magnet.

▶ Designing Your Experiment

6. With your lab partner(s), decide how you will use the materials provided to identify each metal you are given. There is more than one way to measure some of the physical properties that are listed, so you might not use all of the materials that are provided.

7. In your lab report, list each step you will perform in your experiment.

8. Have your teacher approve your plan before you carry out your experiment.

Physical Properties of Some Metals

Metal	Density (g/mL)	Relative hardness	Relative heat conductivity	Magnetized by magnet?
Aluminum (Al)	2.7	28	100	No
Iron (Fe)	7.9	50	34	Yes
Nickel (Ni)	8.9	67	38	Yes
Tin (Sn)	7.3	19	28	No
Tungsten (W)	19.3	100	73	No
Zinc (Zn)	7.1	28	49	No

▶ Performing Your Experiment

9. After your teacher approves your plan, carry out your experiment. Keep in mind that the more careful your measurements are, the easier it will be for you to identify the unknown metals.
10. Record all the data you collect and any observations you make in your lab report.

▶ Analyzing Your Results

1. Make a table listing the physical properties you compared and the data you collected for each of the unknown metals.
2. Which metals were you given? Explain the reasoning you used to identify each metal.
3. Which physical properties were the easiest for you to measure and compare? Which were the hardest? Explain why.
4. What would happen if you tried to scratch aluminum foil with zinc?
5. Explain why it would be difficult to distinguish between iron and nickel unless you calculate each metal's density.
6. Suppose you find a metal fastener and determine that its density is 7 g/mL. What are two ways you could determine whether the unknown metal is tin or zinc?

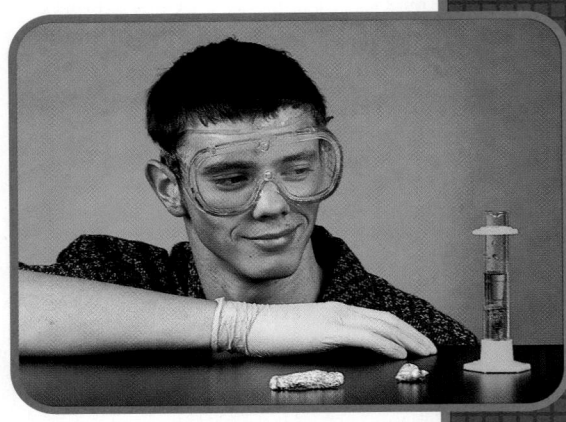

▶ Defending Your Conclusions

7. Suppose someone gives you an alloy that is made of both zinc and nickel. In general, how do you think the physical properties of the alloy would compare with those of each individual metal?

REQUIRED PRECAUTIONS

▶ Read all safety cautions, and discuss them with your students.

▶ Safety goggles and a lab apron must be worn at all times.

▶ Students should wash their hands immediately and avoid touching their eyes if they accidentally touch a tin sample. This element poses a health risk if it enters a student's body.

Pre-Lab
Teaching Tips

Discuss the work of Dmitri Mendeleev and the concept of periodicity with your students before starting this activity. In your discussion, emphasize the trends among groups of elements in the periodic table, but do not explain the chemical basis for these trends. Doing so might distract students from observing the various trends in the properties.

Minimize some of the initial frustration by directing students' attention to the trends in the properties among the alkali metals in the periodic table. Seeing the trends in the properties of lithium, sodium, and potassium should help students as they try to identify the unknown elements.

Procedure

▶ Designing Your Experiment

For each lab group, provide samples of several of the metals listed in the table **Physical Properties of Some Metals,** but do not reveal the identities of the metals. Emphasize to students that they may not use all the materials provided.

Students can measure heat conductivity in one of two ways. They could place the metal sample on a hot plate, add a drop of hardened wax, and then heat. (The wax on the metal with the greatest heat conductivity will melt first.) Or students could add hot melted wax to room temperature metals. (The wax on the metal with the greatest heat conductivity will harden first.)

Continue on p. 105A.

Answers from page 104
Comparing the Physical Properties of Elements

▶ Analyzing Your Results

1. Student tables will vary depending on which unknown metals were analyzed.
2. Student answers will vary. Make sure answers are consistent with the properties of the unknown elements the student identifies.
3. Student answers will vary but should include a discussion of the measurement and comparison of each property.
4. Nothing. Neither aluminum nor zinc should be able to scratch the other one since they have such similar measurements of relative hardness.

5. Unless the densities of iron and nickel are calculated, it is difficult to distinguish between the two metals because their other physical properties are too similar.
6. Measuring the relative hardness and the relative heat conductivity of the metal fastener are two ways to determine whether the metal is tin or zinc.

▶ Defending Your Conclusions

7. The physical properties of an alloy of zinc and nickel would have intermediate values compared with the values of the properties of the metals alone.

Answers from page 85

7. When arranged according to atomic number, the properties of elements repeat in a regular pattern.
8. Scientists would predict that technetium would have the same properties as other elements in the same group, such as manganese or rhenium.

Answers from page 103

DEVELOPING LIFE/ WORK SKILLS

29. Lists will vary. As atomic mass increases, the number of moles present decreases. In general, the number of moles decreases as the atomic number increases because atomic mass increases as atomic number increases.

INTEGRATING CONCEPTS

30. Answers will vary. Any combination of the listed foods that has a total of 1200–1500 mg Ca is acceptable.

31. a. protons
    b. atomic number
    c. periodic table
    d. metals
    e. nonmetals
    f. mass number
    g. isotope
32. The big bang theory proposes that all matter was originally found at one point in the universe. An immense explosion occurred approximately 15 billion years ago, breaking this matter up into a cloud of energy and subatomic particles that expanded at the speed of light. These particles fused to form hydrogen and helium. Eventually, clouds of these materials formed, with further fusion forming elements through iron. Heavier elements are formed during supernovas.

CHAPTER 4

The Structure of Matter

Annotated Descriptions of the Correlated National Science Standards

The following descriptions summarize the National Science Standards that specially relate to Chapter 4. For the full text of the Standards, see p. 40T.

SECTION 4.1
Compounds and Molecules
Physical Science
PS 2c–2e
Science as Inquiry
SAI 1
Science in Personal and Social Perspectives
SPSP 5

SECTION 4.2
Ionic and Covalent Bonding
Physical Science
PS 2a, 2c
Unifying Concepts and Processes
UCP 2
History and Nature of Science
HNS 3

SECTION 4.3
Compound Names and Formulas
Science as Inquiry
SAI 1

SECTION 4.4
Integrating Technology and Society—Organic and Biochemical Compounds
Physical Science
PS 2f
Science in Personal and Social Perspectives
SPSP 5

Cross-Discipline Teaching RESOURCES

Cross-Discipline Teaching, ATE p. 106
Biology   Language Arts
Mathematics

Integration Enrichment Resources
Fine Arts, **PE** and **ATE** p. 110
    IE 4.1 *What Happens in a Kiln?*
Social Studies, **PE** and **ATE** p. 116
    IE 4.2 *Linus Pauling: A Life Well Spent*
Space Science, **PE** and **ATE** p. 121
    IE 4.3 *Ions and Molecules in Space*

Additional Integration Enrichment Worksheets
    IE 4.4 Environmental Science
    IE 4.5 Math   IE 4.6 Engineering

Use the Planning Guide on the next page to help you organize your lessons.

MATH AND COMPUTER RESOURCES

Chapter 4	**Math Skills**	Assess	Media/Computer Skills
Section 4.1	**ATE** **Cross-Discipline Teaching,** p. 106		■ Section 4.1
Section 4.2		**PE** **Building Math Skills,** p. 138, items 16–17	■ Section 4.2 💿 *DISC ONE, MODULE 4* Chemical Bonding  **Presents** **Chemistry Connections** **Segment 12** Alloy Technology **CRT** Worksheet 12
Section 4.3	**PE** **Math Skills** Writing Ionic Formulas, p. 125 **ATE** **Additional Examples** p. 125	**PE** **Practice Problems,** p. 125 **MS** Worksheet 9 **PE** **Section Review** 5–7, p. 128 **PE** **Building Math Skills,** p. 138, item 18 **PE** **Problem Bank,** p. 695, 41–45	■ Section 4.3 **PE** **Chapter Review,** p. 139
Section 4.4			■ Section 4.4

PE Pupil's Edition   **ATE** Annotated Teacher's Edition   **MS** Math Skills   **BS** Basic Skills
IE Integration Enrichment   ■ Guided Reading Audio   **CRT** Critical Thinking   **PHYSICAL SCIENCE** *INTERACTIVE TUTOR*

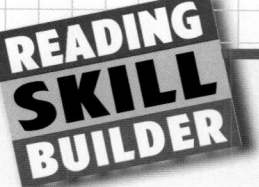

READING SKILL BUILDER

The following activities found in the Annotated Teacher's Edition provide techniques for developing useful reading strategies to increase your students' reading comprehension skills.

Section 4.1   **Brainstorming,** p. 106
             Discussion, p. 108

Section 4.2   **Reading Hint,** p. 115

Section 4.3   **Summarizing,** p. 123

Section 4.4   **Paired Reading,** p. 129

Smithsonian Institution®

Visit
www.si.edu/hrw
for additional
online resources.

Spanish Resources

The following resources are made available for students who speak Spanish as their first language.

Spanish Resources
Guided Reading Audio CD-ROM
Chapter 4

Spanish Glossary
Chapter 4

The Structure of Matter

CLASSROOM RESOURCES

	FOCUS	TEACH	HANDS-ON
Section 4.1 Compounds and Molecules			
BLOCK 1 45 minutes	ATE **RSB** Brainstorming, p. 106 ATE Focus Activities 1, 2, p. 107 ATE **RSB** Discussion, p. 108 PE Compounds, pp. 108–111 ★ Focus Transparency LT 11 ATE **Demo 1** Form a Bond, p. 108	ATE **Skill Builder** Interpreting Visuals, pp. 107, 109, 111	IE Worksheet 4.1
BLOCK 2 45 minutes	PE How Does Structure Affect Properties? pp. 111–114	ATE **Skill Builder** Vocabulary, pp. 111, 114 Interpreting Visuals, p. 113 TT 10 Water Bonding	PE Inquiry Lab *Which melts more easily, sugar or salt?* p. 113 **DS** 4.1
Section 4.2: Ionic and Covalent Bonding			
BLOCK 3 45 minutes	ATE **RSB** Reading Hint, p. 115 ATE **Demo 2** Springy Bonds, p. 115 PE Ionic and Metallic Bonds, pp. 115–118 ★ Focus Transparency LT 12	ATE **Graphic Organizer** p. 116 ATE **Skill Builder** Graphs, p. 117	IE Worksheet 4.2 PE Quick Activity *Building a Close-Packed Structure*, p. 118 **DS** 4.2
BLOCK 4 45 minutes	PE Covalent Bonds and Polyatomic Ions, pp. 119–122	ATE **Skill Builder** Vocabulary, pp. 119, 120 TT 11 Multiple Bonds BLM 12 Polyatomic Anions	IE Worksheet 4.3
Section 4.3: Compound Names and Formulas			
BLOCK 5 45 minutes	ATE **RSB** Summarizing, p. 123 ATE **Demo 3** Balancing Charge, p. 123 PE Ionic Compounds, pp. 123–125 ★ Focus Transparency LT 13	BLM 13 Common Cations BLM 14 Common Anions	LE 4 *Determining Which Household Solutions Conduct Electricity* **DS** 4.6
BLOCK 6 45 minutes	PE Covalent Compounds, pp. 126–128	ATE **Skill Builder** Vocabulary, p. 127 BLM 15 Naming Prefixes	
Section 4.4: Organic and Biochemical Compounds			
BLOCK 7 45 minutes	ATE **RSB** Paired Reading, p. 129 ATE **Demo 4** Substances, p. 129 PE Organic Compounds, pp. 129–132 ★ Focus Transparency LT 14	ATE **Skill Builder** Vocabulary, p. 130 Diagrams, p. 131 ATE **Graphic Organizer** p. 130 TT 12 Six-Carbon Alkanes	IE Worksheet 4.6
BLOCK 8 45 minutes	ATE **Demo 5** Model a Polymer, p. 134 PE Polymers and Biochemical Compounds, pp. 133–136	TT 13 DNA Model	PE Quick Activity *Polymer Memory*, p. 133 **DS** 4.3 PE Inquiry *Lab What properties does a polymer have?* p. 135 **DS** 4.4 PE Skill Builder Lab *Comparing Polymers*, p. 140 **DS** 4.5 IE Worksheets 4.4, 4.5

CLASSROOM RESOURCES

HOMEWORK	ASSESS
PE Section Review 1, p. 114	**ATE** *ALTERNATIVE ASSESSMENT,* Network Structures, p. 110 **SG** Chapter 4 Pretest
PE Section Review 2–7, p. 114	**SG** Section 4.1
Chapter 4 Review, p. 137, items 1–4, 14	**ATE** *ALTERNATIVE ASSESSMENT,* Polar Covalent Bond, p. 120
PE Section Review 1–8, p. 122 **Chapter 4 Review,** p. 137, items 5, 11, 16–17	**SG** Section 4.2
PE Section Review 1, 6, p. 128 **Chapter 4 Review,** p. 137, items 7, 18	**ATE** *ALTERNATIVE ASSESSMENT,* Transition Metals, p. 124
PE Section Review 2–5, 7, p. 128 **Chapter 4 Review,** p. 137, items 6, 8, 12–13	**ATE** *ALTERNATIVE ASSESSMENT,* Naming Covalent Compounds, p. 126 **SG** Section 4.3
PE Section Review 1–2, 5–6, p. 136 **Chapter 4 Review,** p. 137, items 9–10	
PE Section Review 3–4, p. 136 **Chapter 4 Review,** p. 137, item 15	**SG** Section 4.4

BLOCK 9

Chapter 4 Review
Thinking Critically 19–21, p. 138
Developing Life/Work Skills 22–25, p. 139
Integrating Concepts 26–27, p. 139
SG Chapter 4 Mixed Review

BLOCK 10

Chapter Tests
Holt Science Spectrum: A Physical Approach
Chapter 4 Test

One-Stop Planner CD-ROM with Test Generator
Holt Science Spectrum Test Generator
FOR MACINTOSH AND WINDOWS
Chapter 4

Teaching Resources
Scoring Rubrics and assignment evaluation checklist.

internetconnect

SCILINKS **NSTA**
National Science Teachers Association
Online Resources:
www.scilinks.org
The following *sci*LINKS Internet resources can be found in the student text for this chapter.

Page 107 **TOPIC:** Properties of substances **KEYWORD:** HK1041	**Page 123** **TOPIC:** Naming compounds **KEYWORD:** HK1044
Page 111 **TOPIC:** Structures of substances **KEYWORD:** HK1042	**Page 130** **TOPIC:** Carbon compounds **KEYWORD:** HK1045
Page 118 **TOPIC:** Chemical bonding **KEYWORD:** HK1043	**Page 139** **TOPIC:** Vitamin C **KEYWORD:** HK1046

CNNfyi.com www.cnnfyi.com

Visit this site for coverage of current events and related classsroom resources.

PE Pupil's Edition **ATE** Teacher's Edition
RSB Reading Skill Builder **DS** Datasheets
IE Integrated Enrichment **SG** Study Guide
LE Laboratory Experiments
TT Teaching Transparencies **BLM** Blackline Masters
★ Lesson Focus Transparency

The Structure of Matter

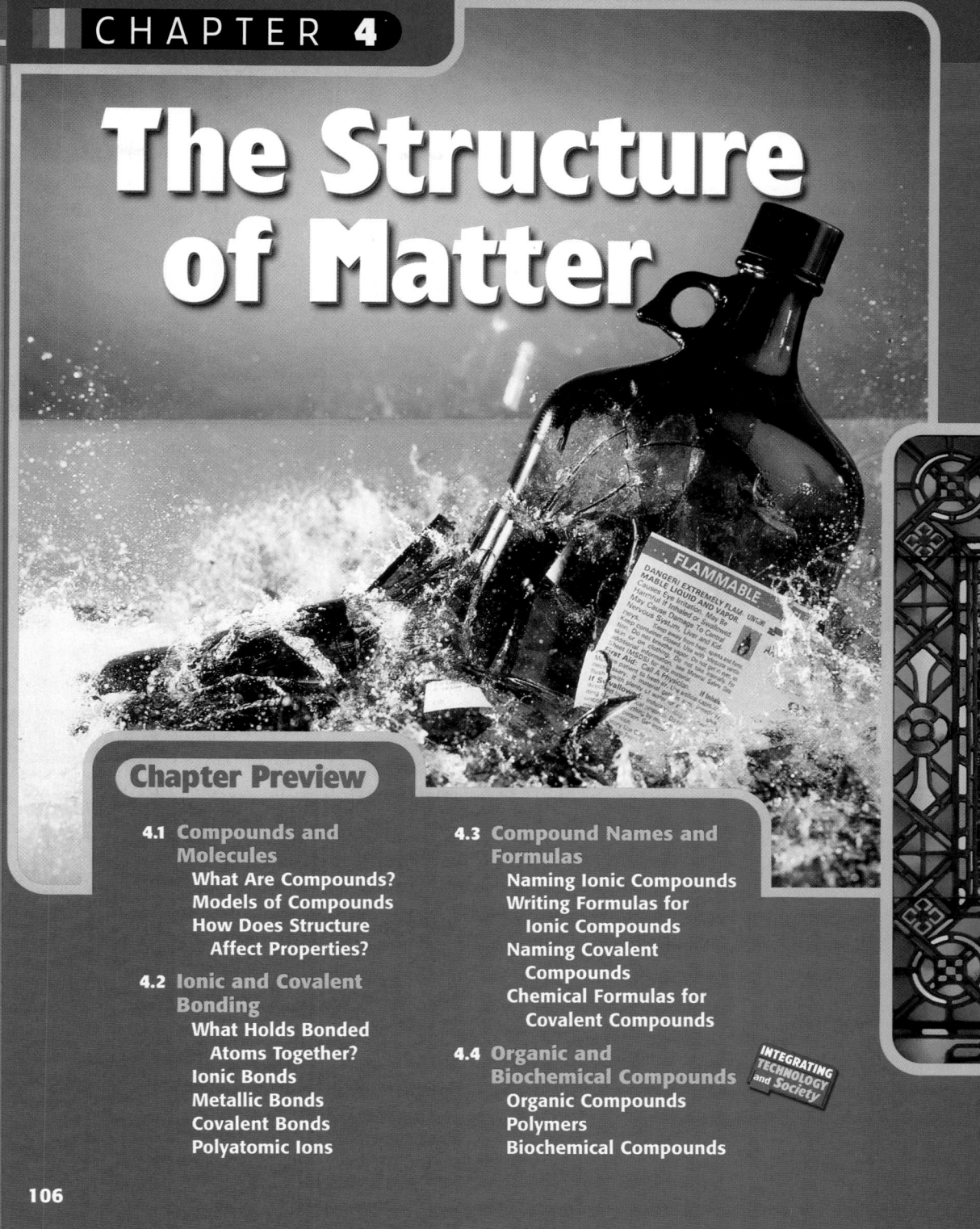

Tapping Prior Knowledge

Be sure students understand the following concepts:

Chapter 2
Elements and compounds, properties

Chapter 3
Atomic structure, the periodic table, families of elements, metals and nonmetals, ions, atomic mass, molar mass

READING SKILL BUILDER *Brainstorming*
Have students list as many uses of the term *compound* as they can. Lists might include compound sentences, chemical compounds, compound fracture, or compound interest rates. Ask them what the items on their lists have in common. Students should recognize that *compound* involves more than one thing.

Chapter Preview

4.1 Compounds and Molecules
What Are Compounds?
Models of Compounds
How Does Structure Affect Properties?

4.2 Ionic and Covalent Bonding
What Holds Bonded Atoms Together?
Ionic Bonds
Metallic Bonds
Covalent Bonds
Polyatomic Ions

4.3 Compound Names and Formulas
Naming Ionic Compounds
Writing Formulas for Ionic Compounds
Naming Covalent Compounds
Chemical Formulas for Covalent Compounds

4.4 Organic and Biochemical Compounds
Organic Compounds
Polymers
Biochemical Compounds

INTEGRATING TECHNOLOGY and Society

106

RESOURCE LINK
STUDY GUIDE

Assign students *Pretest Chapter 4 The Structure of Matter* before beginning Section 4.1.

CROSS-DISCIPLINE TEACHING

Biology   Have a biology teacher visit the classroom and explain the importance of different compounds to a healthy human body. Have them emphasize the importance of trace minerals and how to obtain needed substances by eating a balanced diet.

Mathematics   To help students determine the charge of an ion in a compound, review with them how to add positive and negative integers.

Provide a number line to students who have problems with this concept.

Language Arts   Ask students to list abbreviations for common terms. Lists might include abbreviations for units of measurement and abbreviations for phrases, such as *etc.* and *e.g.* Relate the use of abbreviations in daily life to the use of chemical formulas to represent the composition of substances.

Focus
ACTIVITY

Background Suddenly, a glass object slips from your hand and crashes to the ground. You watch it break into many tiny pieces as you hear it hit the floor. Glass is a brittle substance. When enough force is applied, it breaks into many sharp, jagged pieces. Glass behaves the way it does because of its composition.

A glass container and a stained glass window have some similar properties because both are made mainly from silicon dioxide. But other compounds are responsible for the window's beautiful colors. Adding a compound of nickel and oxygen to the glass produces a purple tint. Adding a compound of cobalt and oxygen makes the glass deep blue, while adding a compound of copper and oxygen makes the glass dark red.

Activity 1 There are many different kinds of glass, each with its own use. List several kinds of glass that you encounter daily. Describe the ways that each kind of glass differs from other kinds of glass.

Activity 2 Research other compounds that are sometimes added to glass. Describe how each of these compounds changes the properties of glass. Write a report on your findings.

internet connect

SCI LINKS
NSTA

TOPIC: Properties of substances
GO TO: www.scilinks.org
KEYWORD: HK1041

Glass is a brittle substance that is made from silicon dioxide, a compound with a very rigid structure. The addition of small amounts of other compounds changes the color of the glass, "staining" it.

107

Focus
ACTIVITY

Background Glass is made primarily of silicon dioxide, the main ingredient in quartz and some types of sand. Have students compare the strength of glass and the strength of quartz. Emphasize that when other materials are added to silicon dioxide, the structure of the compound might be affected. The resulting glass is usually more brittle than quartz or sand.

Activity 1 Answers will vary but might include glass used in drinking glasses and dishes, high-heat ceramics used in cooking, and safety (break-resistant) glass used in some types of windows and eyeglasses.

Activity 2 Answers will vary. For example, glass that is used for optical fibers often contains the elements arsenic, selenium, and tellurium. Other optical glass includes the compound arsenic sulfide. Be sure students understand that sometimes glass differs in properties because of the way the glass has been processed, not what has been added to it.

|SKILL BUILDER

Interpreting Visuals Ask students why recycling centers closely monitor the types of glass that are recycled. *(The glass being recycled must have the properties desired in the final product.)* Ask them to explain why all glass cannot be recycled to make stained glass. *(All glass cannot be recycled to make stained glass because, in addition to silicon dioxide, stained glass contains other compounds that give it color.)*

Compounds and Molecules

Scheduling

Refer to pp. 106A–106D for lecture, classwork, and assignment options for Section 4.1.

★ **Lesson Focus**
Use transparency *LT 11* to prepare students for this section.

READING SKILL BUILDER

Discussion Discuss with students the two principal differences between mixtures and compounds that they will learn as they read this section. The properties of a mixture reflect the properties of the substances it contains, but the properties of a compound often bear no resemblance to the properties of the elements that compose it. And compounds have a definite composition by mass of their combining elements, while the components of mixtures may be present in varying proportions. For example, water has a definite composition by mass. It is always 88.8% oxygen and 11.2% hydrogen. In contrast, substances in a mixture can have any mass ratio. The sand in a sand-and-gravel mixture may make up as much as 99% or as little as 1% of the overall mass.

▶ **KEY TERMS**
chemical bond
chemical structure
bond length
bond angle

OBJECTIVES

▶ Distinguish between compounds and mixtures.
▶ Relate the chemical formula of a compound to the relative numbers of atoms or ions present in the compound.
▶ Use models to visualize a compound's chemical structure.
▶ Describe how the chemical structure of a compound affects its properties.

If you step on a sharp rock with your bare foot, you feel pain. That's because rocks are hard substances; they don't bend. Many rocks are made of quartz. Table salt and sugar look similar; both are grainy, white solids. But they taste very different. In addition, salt is hard and brittle and breaks into uniform cube-like granules, while sugar does not. Quartz, salt, and sugar are all compounds. Their similarities and differences result from the way their atoms or ions are joined.

What Are Compounds?

Table salt is a compound made of two elements, sodium and chlorine. When elements combine to form a compound, the compound has properties very different from those of the elements that make it. **Figure 4-1** shows how the metal sodium combines with chlorine gas to form sodium chloride, NaCl, or table salt.

Figure 4-1

(A) The silvery metal sodium combines with (B) poisonous, yellowish green chlorine gas in a violent reaction (C) to form (D) white granules of table salt that you can eat.

DEMONSTRATION 1 TEACHING

Form a Bond

Time: Approximately 10 minutes

Materials: iodine crystals, powdered zinc, test tube, balance, stopper to fit test tube, ring stand, clamp, water, 10 mL graduated cylinder

SAFETY CAUTION: *The reaction gives off toxic fumes and heat. Do this demonstration outside or in a fume hood only. Wear safety goggles, protective gloves, and a lab apron while performing this demonstration. Students should stand at least 10 ft from the demonstration.*

Measure out 3 g of powdered zinc and 2 g of iodine crystals. Place them in a test tube. Stopper the tube and shake it to mix the elements. Attach the clamp to the ring stand, then clamp the test tube upright. Remove the stopper. Measure 1 mL of water and add it to the test tube. Have students observe the reaction between zinc and iodine.

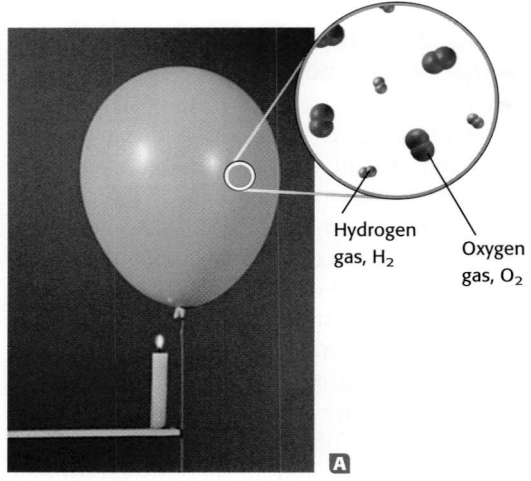

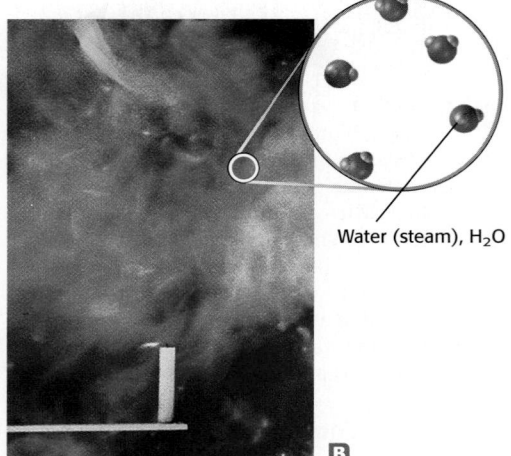

Hydrogen gas, H₂   Oxygen gas, O₂

Water (steam), H₂O

A   B

Chemical bonds distinguish compounds from mixtures

The attractive forces that hold different atoms or ions together in compounds are called **chemical bonds.** Recall from Chapter 2 how compounds and mixtures are different. Mixtures are made of different substances that are just placed together. Each substance in the mixture keeps its own properties.

For example, mixing blue paint and yellow paint makes green paint. Different shades of green can be made by mixing the paints in different proportions, but both original paints remain chemically unchanged.

Figure 4-2 shows that when a mixture of hydrogen gas and oxygen gas is heated, a violent reaction takes place and a compound forms. Chemical bonds are broken, and atoms are rearranged. New bonds form water, a compound with properties very different from those of the original gases.

A compound always has the same chemical formula

The chemical formula for water is H_2O, and that of table sugar is $C_{12}H_{22}O_{11}$. The salt you season your food with has the chemical formula NaCl. A chemical formula shows the types and numbers of atoms or ions making up the simplest unit of the compound.

There is another important way that compounds and mixtures are different. Compounds are always made of the same elements in the same proportion. A molecule of water, for example, is always made of two hydrogen atoms and one oxygen atom. This is true for all water, no matter how much water there is or where it is found. That means water frozen in a comet in outer space and water at 37°C (98.6°F) inside the cells of your body both have the same chemical formula—H_2O.

Figure 4-2
(A) Placing a lit candle under a balloon containing hydrogen gas and oxygen gas causes the balloon to melt, releasing the mixed gases. (B) The mixed gases are ignited by the candle flame, and water is produced.

▶ **chemical bond** the attractive force that holds atoms or ions together

Compounds and Molecules

THE STRUCTURE OF MATTER **109**

Compounds and Molecules

Be sure students realize the distinction between materials that bond for added strength when they dry and those materials that just dry. Have students think about each of their examples. Would the dried material return to its original consistency if the original solvent were added to it? If so, it probably just dried and did not change its bonding.

Making the Connection
1. Answers will vary but might include dental ceramics and some paints.
2. Paragraphs will vary. Each paragraph should refer to one substance and should include a discussion of how bonding changes in the substance.

Resources Assign students worksheet *4.1: Connection to Fine Arts—What Happens in a Kiln?* in the **Integration Enrichment Resources** ancillary.

Teaching Tip

Molecular Models Discuss with students other examples of how something can be represented in more than one way. One example is found in music. The desired sounds can be represented as single notes on a staff or as letters that represent groups of notes, or chords.

In math, the process of multiplication can be represented by several different symbols—a multiplication sign, a dot, parentheses, or just two symbols written side by side. Emphasize to students that molecules can be represented in many different ways as well.

110

Connection to
FINE ARTS

Clay has a layered structure of silicon, oxygen, aluminum, and hydrogen atoms. Artists can mold wet clay into any shape because water molecules let the layers slide over one another. When clay dries, water evaporates and the layers can no longer slide. To keep the dry, crumbly clay from breaking apart, artists change the structure of the clay by heating it. The atoms in one layer bond to atoms in the layers above and below. When this happens, the clay hardens, and the artist's work is permanently set.

Making the Connection
1. Think of other substances that can be shaped when they are wet and that "set" when they are dried or heated.
2. Write a paragraph about one of these substances, and explain why it has these properties. Report your findings to the class.

WRITING SKILL

▶ **chemical structure** the arrangement of bonded atoms or ions within a substance

▶ **bond length** the average distance between the nuclei of two bonded atoms

▶ **bond angle** the angle formed by two bonds to the same atom

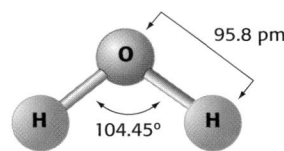
95.8 pm
O
H   H
104.45°

Figure 4-3
The ball-and-stick model in this figure is a giant representation of one molecule of water. A picometer (pm) is equal to 1×10^{-12} m.

110 CHAPTER 4

Chemical structure shows the bonding within a compound

Although water's chemical formula tells us what atoms it is made of, it doesn't reveal anything about the way these atoms are connected. You can see how a compound's atoms or ions are connected by its **chemical structure.** The structure of a compound can be compared to that of a rope. The kinds of fibers used to make a rope and the way the fibers are intertwined determine how strong the rope is. Similarly, the atoms in a compound and the way the atoms are arranged determine many of the compound's properties.

Two terms are used to specify the positions of atoms relative to one another in a compound. A **bond length** gives the distance between the nuclei of two bonded atoms. And when a compound has three or more atoms, **bond angles** tell how these atoms are oriented. **Figure 4-3** shows the chemical structure of a water molecule. You can see that the way hydrogen and oxygen atoms bond to form water looks more like a boomerang than a straight line.

Models of Compounds

Figure 4-3 is a ball-and-stick model of a water molecule. Ball-and-stick models, as well as other kinds of models, help you "see" a compound's structure by showing you how the atoms or ions are arranged in the compound.

Some models give you an idea of bond lengths and angles

In the ball-and-stick model of water shown in **Figure 4-3,** the atoms are represented by balls. The bonds that hold the atoms together are represented by sticks. Although bonds between atoms aren't really as rigid as sticks, this model makes it easy to see the bonds and the angles they form in a compound.

Structural formulas can also show the structures of compounds. Notice how water's structural formula, which is shown below, is a lot like its ball-and-stick model. The difference is that only chemical symbols are used to represent the atoms.

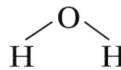
O
H   H

ALTERNATIVE ASSESSMENT

Network Structures

Students can work individually or in small groups. Provide students with gumdrops of two different colors and toothpicks. Ball-and-stick model kits can also be used. Have them model two network solids—quartz and a one-to-one ionic solid, such as potassium bromide. Start the quartz model by making a tetrahedron from four oxygen atoms with a silicon atom in the center. Then expand this basic unit until it shows the pattern of a network solid. The ionic solid should have alternating colors representing positive and negative ions in several layers. Challenge students to create a model of a network ionic solid in which the ions are in a 2:1 ratio. Caution students to never eat anything in a laboratory.

Space-filling models show the space occupied by atoms

Figure 4-4 shows another way chemists picture a water molecule. It is called a space-filling model because it shows the space that is occupied by the oxygen and hydrogen atoms. The problem with this model is that it is harder to "see" bond lengths and angles.

How Does Structure Affect Properties?

Some compounds, such as the quartz found in many rocks, exist as a large network of bonded atoms. Other compounds, such as table salt, are also large networks, but of bonded positive and negative ions. Still other compounds, such as water and sugar, are made of many separate molecules. Different structures give these compounds different properties.

Compounds with network structures are strong solids

Quartz is sometimes found in the form of beautiful crystals, as shown in **Figure 4-5.** Quartz has the chemical formula SiO_2, and so does the less pure form of quartz, sand. **Figure 4-5** shows that every silicon atom in quartz is bonded to four oxygen atoms. The bonds that hold these atoms together are very strong. All of the Si—O—Si and O—Si—O bond angles are the same. That is, each one is 109.5°. This arrangement continues throughout the substance, holding the silicon and oxygen atoms together in a very strong, rigid structure.

This is why rocks containing quartz are hard and inflexible solids. Silicon and oxygen atoms in sand have a similar arrangement. It takes a lot of energy to break the strong bonds between silicon and oxygen atoms in quartz and sand. That's why the melting point and boiling point of quartz and sand is so high, as shown in **Table 4-1.**

Table 4-1   **Some Compounds with Network Structures**

Compound	State (25°C)	Melting point (°C)	Boiling point (°C)
Silicon dioxide, SiO_2 (quartz, sand)	Solid	1700	2230
Magnesium fluoride, MgF_2	Solid	1261	2239
Sodium chloride, NaCl (table salt)	Solid	801	1413

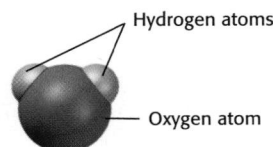

Figure 4-4
This space-filling model of water shows that the two hydrogen atoms take up much less space than the oxygen atom.

internetconnect

SCI*LINKS*
NSTA

TOPIC: Structures of substances
GO TO: www.scilinks.org
KEYWORD: HK1042

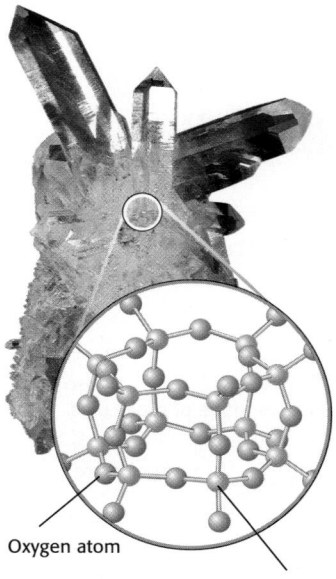

Oxygen atom

Silicon atom

Figure 4-5
Quartz and sand are made of silicon and oxygen atoms bonded in a strong, rigid structure.

SKILL BUILDER

Interpreting Visuals   Ask students to speculate why space-filling models, such as the one in **Figure 4-4,** look so different from structural formulas and from ball-and-stick models. Point out that the shape of the space-filling models represents the best estimation of the way the molecule would actually appear (but without the colors) if it could be seen. Students should not get the impression that atoms are balls at the ends of sticks.

SKILL BUILDER

Interpreting Vocabulary
Ask students what they think of when they hear the term *network*. Television networks or networked computers will probably be mentioned. Elicit from students that a network takes many individual parts and joins them as a unit. Another name for a network solid is a macromolecule.

Teaching Tip

Network Solids   Many network solids, such as diamond and many silicon compounds, are arranged in a tetrahedral pattern. Have students make tetrahedrons out of four equilateral triangles and tape. For SiO_4, for example, each of the four corners of the tetrahedron represents an oxygen atom. A silicon atom is located exactly in the center of the tetrahedron. Students can place their tetrahedrons together, showing how the network solid is formed.

Teaching Tip

Structure of Network Solids
Sometimes a crystal of a network solid reveals the pattern made by the ions in the solid. Have students use a hand lens to examine some granulated salt and compare what they see with the network structure shown in **Figure 4-6.** Students should see that the salt granules are cubic, as is the arrangement of its ions.

MISCONCEPTION ALERT

States of Matter
Students might think that a compound is, by nature, either a solid, a liquid, or a gas. Emphasize that most substances can be in any state, depending on temperature and sometimes, pressure. When a substance is classified as a solid, a liquid, or a gas, and no temperature is mentioned, the temperature is usually room temperature.

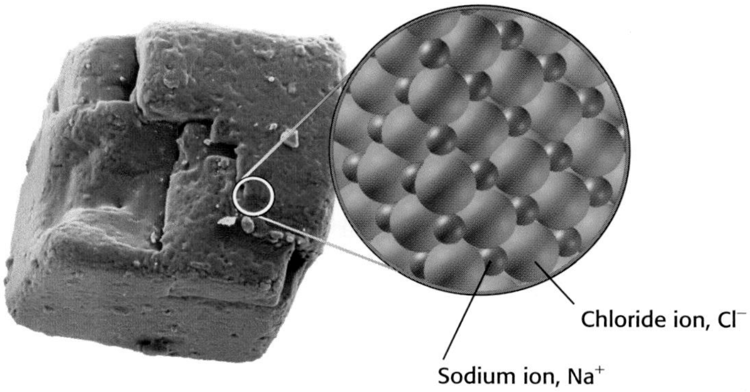

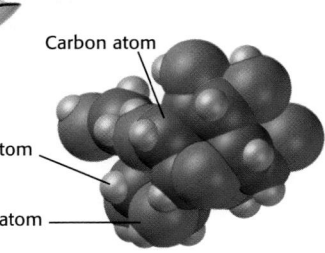

Chloride ion, Cl⁻

Sodium ion, Na⁺

Figure 4-6
Each grain of table salt, or sodium chloride, is composed of a tightly packed network of Na⁺ ions and Cl⁻ ions.

Some networks are made of bonded ions
Like some quartz, table salt—sodium chloride—is found in the form of regularly shaped crystals. Crystals of sodium chloride are cube shaped. Like quartz and sand, sodium chloride is made of a repeating network connected by strong bonds. But the network is not made of atoms. Instead, sodium chloride is made of a network of tightly packed, positively charged sodium ions and negatively charged chloride ions, as shown in **Figure 4-6.** The strong attractions between the oppositely charged ions causes table salt and other similar compounds to have high melting points and boiling points, as shown in **Table 4-1.**

Some compounds are made of molecules
Salt and sugar are both white solids you can eat, but their structures are very different. Unlike salt, sugar is made of molecules. A molecule of sugar, shown in **Figure 4-7,** is made of carbon, hydrogen, and oxygen atoms joined by bonds. Molecules of sugar do attract each other to form crystals. But these attractions are much weaker than those that hold bonded carbon, hydrogen, and oxygen atoms together to make a sugar molecule.

We breathe nitrogen, N_2, oxygen, O_2, and carbon dioxide, CO_2, every day. All three substances are colorless, odorless gases made of molecules. Within each molecule, the atoms are so strongly attracted to one another that they are bonded. But the molecules of each gas have very little attraction for one another. Because the molecules of these gases are not very attracted to one another, they spread out as much as they can. That is why gases can take up a lot of space.

Figure 4-7
Sugar is made of molecules.

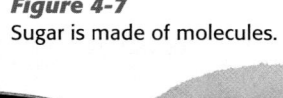

Carbon atom

Hydrogen atom

Oxygen atom

Table 4-2 **Comparing Compounds Made of Molecules**

Compound	State (25°C)	Melting point (°C)	Boiling point (°C)
Sugar, $C_{12}H_{22}O_{11}$	Solid	185–186	——
Water, H_2O	Liquid	0	100
Dihydrogen sulfide, H_2S	Gas	–85	–60

The strength of attractions between molecules

Compare sugar, water, and dihydrogen sulfide in **Table 4-2**. Although all three compounds are made of molecules, their properties are very different. Sugar is a solid, water is a liquid, and dihydrogen sulfide is a gas. That means that sugar molecules have the strongest attractions for each other, followed by water molecules. Dihydrogen sulfide molecules have the weakest attractions for each other. The fact that sugar and water have such different properties probably doesn't surprise you. Their chemical structures are not at all alike. But what about water and dihydrogen sulfide, which do have similar chemical structures?

 **Inquiry Lab**

Which melts more easily, sugar or salt?

Materials
- ✔ table salt
- ✔ 2 test tubes
- ✔ table sugar
- ✔ stopwatch
- ✔ Bunsen burner
- ✔ tongs

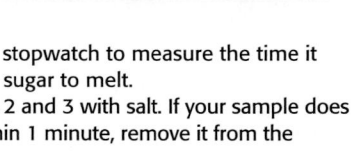

Procedure

SAFETY CAUTION Wear safety goggles and gloves. Tie back long hair, confine loose clothing, and use tongs to handle hot glassware. When heating a substance in a test tube, always point the open end of the test tube away from yourself and others.

1. Use your knowledge of structures to make a hypothesis about whether sugar or salt will melt more easily.
2. To test your hypothesis, place about 1 cm³ of sugar in a test tube.
3. Using tongs, position the test tube with sugar over the flame, as shown in the figure at right. Move the test tube back and forth slowly over the flame. Use a stopwatch to measure the time it takes for the sugar to melt.
4. Repeat steps 2 and 3 with salt. If your sample does not melt within 1 minute, remove it from the flame.

Analysis

1. Which compound is easier to melt? Was your hypothesis right?
2. How can you relate your results to the structure of each compound?

THE STRUCTURE OF MATTER **113**

Teaching Tip

Hydrogen Bonds Students might ask why water is a liquid at room temperature when most molecules of similar mass are gases. Water molecules exhibit what is known as hydrogen bonding. Hydrogen bonding occurs between molecules formed from hydrogen and a strongly electronegative element, such as oxygen. Because this element pulls the shared electrons away from the hydrogen atom, the proton of the hydrogen atom is exposed, and it attracts the negative parts of other polar molecules. This bonding results in greater attraction between water molecules than exists between most other molecules.

SKILL BUILDER

Interpreting Visuals Some students might have trouble interpreting the negative numbers found in **Table 4-2**. Provide students with a number line so that they can see that –85 is a smaller number than –60.

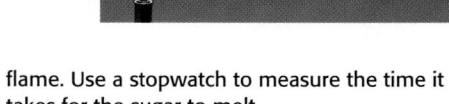 **Inquiry Lab**

Which melts more easily, sugar or salt?

Have test tube racks available so students can place hot test tubes in them until they cool. Remind students that all factors except what is in the test tube should be constant. Be sure students heat the sugar only until it melts. If it burns, the test tube will be difficult to clean.

Analysis

1. Sugar was easier to melt. The salt probably did not melt at all.
2. Sugar is molecular, and the particles have less attraction for each other than the salt particles do. Ions in salt form a network solid with strong attractions between the ions.

RESOURCE LINK
DATASHEETS

Have students use *Datasheet 4.1 Inquiry Lab: Which melts more easily, sugar or salt?* to record their results.

113

Compounds and Molecules

Interpreting Vocabulary

Molecules are affected by both *intermolecular* forces and *intramolecular* forces. Intramolecular forces are those within the molecule. A covalent bond within a molecule is an intramolecular force. Intermolecular forces are those between molecules. The gravitational attraction between molecules and the attraction between the positive part of one polar molecule and the negative part of another are intermolecular forces.

SECTION 4.1 REVIEW

Check Your Understanding

1. a. mixture
   b. compound
   c. compound
   d. compound
2. Silver iodide has a network structure of positive and negative ions. Vanillin consists of molecules. The attraction between particles in silver iodide is much stronger than the attraction between particles of vanillin.
3. Student drawings should show a boron atom surrounded by three equally spaced fluorine atoms in the same plane. A line from each fluorine atom to the boron atom represents a bond. Lines should be of equal length.

Answers continue on p. 141A.

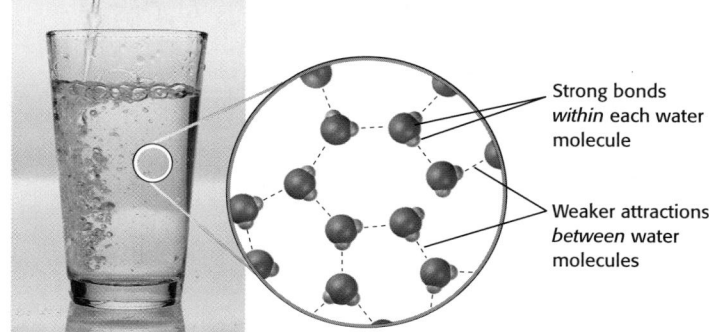

Figure 4-8
Dotted lines indicate the *inter*molecular attractions that occur *between* water molecules, which is often referred to as "hydrogen bonding." Water is a liquid at room temperature because of these attractions.

Strong bonds *within* each water molecule

Weaker attractions *between* water molecules

The higher melting and boiling points of water suggest that water molecules attract each other more than dihydrogen sulfide molecules do. **Figure 4-8** shows how an oxygen atom of one water molecule is attracted to a hydrogen atom of a neighboring water molecule. Water molecules attract each other, but these attractions are not as strong as the bonds holding oxygen and hydrogen atoms together within a molecule.

SECTION 4.1 REVIEW

SUMMARY

▶ Atoms or ions in compounds are joined by chemical bonds.

▶ A compound's chemical formula shows which atoms or ions it is made of.

▶ A model represents a compound's structure visually.

▶ Substances with network structures are usually strong solids with high melting and boiling points.

▶ Substances made of molecules have lower melting and boiling points.

▶ Whether a molecular substance is a solid, a liquid, or a gas depends on the attractions between its molecules at room temperature.

CHECK YOUR UNDERSTANDING

1. **Classify** the following substances as mixtures or compounds:
   a. air   c. SnF_2
   b. CO   d. pure water
2. **Explain** why silver iodide, AgI, a compound used in photography, has a much higher melting point than vanillin, $C_8H_8O_3$, a sweet-smelling compound used in flavorings.
3. **Draw** a ball-and-stick model of a boron trifluoride, BF_3, molecule. In this molecule, a boron atom is attached to three fluorine atoms. Each F—B—F bond angle is 120°, and all B—F bonds are the same length.
4. **Predict** which molecules have a greater attraction for each other, C_3H_8O molecules in liquid rubbing alcohol or CH_4 molecules in methane gas.
5. **Explain** why glass, which is made mainly of SiO_2, is often used to make cookware. (**Hint:** What properties does SiO_2 have because of its structure?)
6. **Predict** whether a compound made of molecules that melts at −77.7°C is a solid, a liquid, or a gas at room temperature.
7. **Creative Thinking** A picometer (pm) is equal to 1×10^{-12} m. O—H bond lengths in water are 95.8 pm, while S—H bond lengths in dihydrogen sulfide are 135 pm. Why are S—H bond lengths longer than O—H bond lengths? (**Hint:** Which is larger, a sulfur atom or an oxygen atom?)

Ionic and Covalent Bonding

OBJECTIVES

▶ Explain why atoms sometimes join to form bonds.
▶ Explain why some atoms transfer their valence electrons to form ionic bonds, while other atoms share valence electrons to form covalent bonds.
▶ Differentiate between ionic, covalent, and metallic bonds.
▶ Compare the properties of substances with different types of bonds.

▶ **KEY TERMS**
ionic bond
metallic bond
covalent bond
polyatomic ion

Scheduling
Refer to pp. 106A–106D for lecture, classwork, and assignment options for Section 4.2.

★ **Lesson Focus**
Use transparency *LT 12* to prepare students for this section.

READING SKILL BUILDER *Reading Hint* Explain the different types of bonding. Then have students form pairs and use the following figures to explain what is happening in terms of bonding. Have them use **Figure 4-11** to explain ionic bonding, **Figures 4-9, 4-14,** and **4-15** to explain nonpolar covalent bonding, **Figure 4-16** for polar covalent bonding, and **Figure 4-13** for metallic bonding.

When two atoms join, a bond forms. You have already seen how bonded atoms form many substances. Because there are so many different substances, it makes sense that atoms can bond in different ways.

What Holds Bonded Atoms Together?

Three different kinds of bonds describe the way atoms bond in most substances. In many of the models you have seen so far, the bonds that hold atoms together are represented by sticks. But what bonds atoms in a real molecule?

The outermost energy level of a bonded atom is full of electrons

Atoms bond when their valence electrons interact. You learned in Chapter 3 that atoms with full outermost energy levels are less reactive than atoms with only partly filled outermost energy levels. Generally, atoms join to form bonds so that each atom has a full outermost energy level. When this happens, each atom has an electronic structure similar to that of a noble gas.

When two hydrogen atoms bond, as shown in **Figure 4-9,** the positive nucleus of one hydrogen atom attracts the negative electron of the other hydrogen atom, and vice versa. This pulls

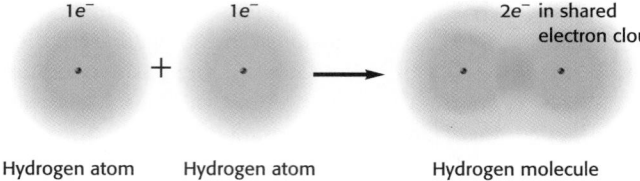

1e⁻   1e⁻   2e⁻ in shared
                                    electron cloud

Hydrogen atom   Hydrogen atom   Hydrogen molecule

Figure 4-9
When two hydrogen atoms are very close together, their electron clouds overlap, and a bond forms. The two electrons of the hydrogen molecule that forms are in the shared electron cloud.

DEMONSTRATION 2 TEACHING

Springy Bonds

Time: Approximately 15 minutes
Materials: pencil; 3 foam balls, one larger than the others; 50 cm pieces of copper wire (2); protractor

Wrap the wire around the pencil to make two springs, each approximately 3 cm long. Leave about 4 cm of wire unwound at each end. Stick one end of a spring into each small ball. Stick the other ends into the large foam ball, forming a bond angle of 105°.

Analysis
1. What element does the large ball represent? *(oxygen)*
2. What element do the small balls represent? *(hydrogen)*
3. Why do springs represent bonds better than sticks do? *(Bonds bend and stretch.)*

Ionic and Covalent Bonding

Did You Know?

Chemists have prepared crystals composed of Na^+ and Na^- ions and others composed of K^+ and K^- ions.

Connection to SOCIAL STUDIES

American scientist Linus Pauling studied how electrons are arranged within atoms. He also studied the ways that atoms share and exchange electrons. In 1954, he won the Nobel Prize in chemistry for his valuable research.

Later, Pauling fought to ban nuclear weapons testing. Pauling was able to convince more than 11 000 scientists from 49 countries to sign a petition to stop nuclear weapons testing. Pauling won the Nobel Peace Prize in 1962 for his efforts. A year later, a treaty outlawing nuclear weapons testing in the atmosphere, in outer space, and underwater went into effect.

Making the Connection
1. *Electronegativity* is an idea first thought of by Pauling. It tells how easily an atom accepts electrons. Which is more electronegative, a fluorine atom or a calcium atom? Why?
2. Nuclear weapons testing is harmful to humans because of the resulting radiation. Write a paragraph explaining how high levels of radiation can affect your body.  **WRITING SKILL**

▶ **ionic bond** a bond formed by the attraction between oppositely charged ions

Figure 4-10
Chemists often use a solid bar to show a bond between two atoms, but real bonds are flexible, like stiff springs.

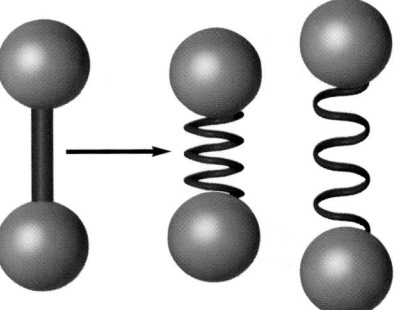

the two atoms closer together. Soon their electron clouds cross each other. The shared electron cloud of the molecule that forms has two electrons (one from each atom). A hydrogen molecule has an electronic structure similar to the noble gas helium. The molecule will not fall apart unless enough energy is added to break the bond.

Bonds can bend and stretch without breaking
Although some bonds are stronger and more rigid than others, all bonds behave more like flexible springs than like sticks, as **Figure 4-10** shows. The atoms move back and forth a little and their nuclei do not always stay the same distance apart. In fact, most reported bond lengths are averages of these distances. Although bonds are not rigid, they still hold atoms together tightly.

Ionic Bonds

Ionic bonds are formed between oppositely charged ions. Atoms of metal elements, such as sodium and calcium, form the positively charged ions. Atoms of nonmetal elements, such as chlorine and oxygen, form the negatively charged ions.

Ionic bonds are formed by the transfer of electrons
Some atoms do not share electrons to fill their outermost energy levels completely. Instead, they transfer electrons. One of the atoms gains the electrons that the other atom loses. Both ions that form usually have filled outermost energy levels. The result is a positive ion and a negative ion, such as the Na^+ ion and the Cl^- ion in sodium chloride.

These oppositely charged ions attract each other and form an ionic bond. Each positive sodium ion attracts several negative chloride ions. These negative chloride ions attract more positive sodium ions, and so on. Soon a network of these bonded ions forms a crystal of table salt.

Graphic Organizer
Ionic and Covalent Bonding

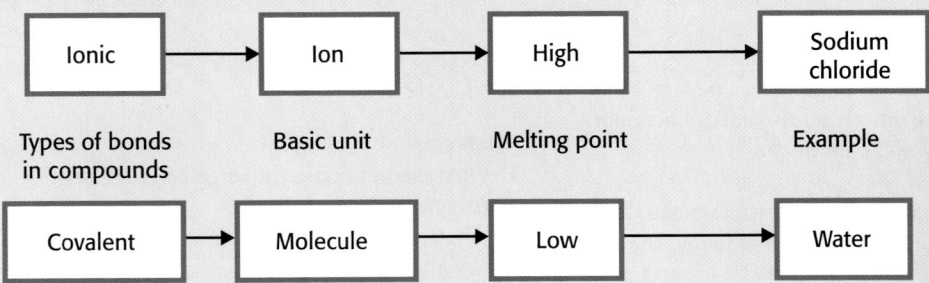

Ionic compounds are in the form of networks, not molecules

Because sodium chloride is a network of ions, it does not make sense to talk about "a molecule of NaCl." In fact, every sodium ion is next to six chloride ions, as shown in **Figure 4-6** on page 112. Instead, chemists talk about the smallest ratio of ions in ionic compounds. Sodium chloride's chemical formula, NaCl, tells us that there is one Na^+ ion for every Cl^- ion, or a 1:1 ratio of ions. This means the compound has a total charge of zero. One Na^+ ion and one Cl^- ion make up a *formula unit* of NaCl.

Not every ionic compound has the same ratio of ions as sodium chloride. An example is calcium fluoride, which is shown in **Figure 4-11.** The ratio of Ca^{2+} ions to F^- ions in calcium fluoride must be 1:2 to make a neutral compound. That is why the chemical formula for calcium fluoride is CaF_2.

When melted or dissolved in water, ionic compounds conduct electricity

Electric current is moving charges. Solid ionic compounds do not conduct electricity because the charged ions are locked into place, causing the melting points of ionic compounds to be very high—often well above 300°C. But if you dissolve an ionic compound in water or melt it, it can conduct electricity. That's because the ions are then free to move, as shown in **Figure 4-12.**

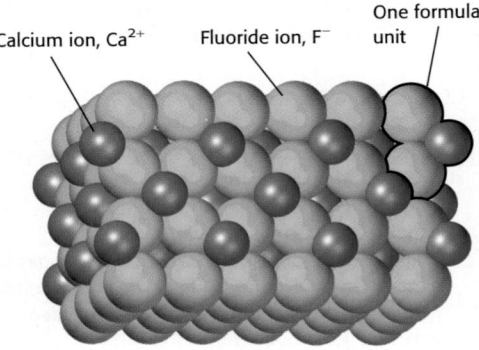

Calcium ion, Ca^{2+} Fluoride ion, F^- One formula unit

Figure 4-11
There are twice as many fluoride ions as calcium ions in a crystal of calcium fluoride, CaF_2. So one Ca^{2+} ion and two F^- ions make up one formula unit of the compound.

Sodium ion, Na^+

Chloride ion, Cl^-

Water molecule, H_2O

Figure 4-12
Like other ionic compounds, sodium chloride conducts electricity when it is dissolved in water.

Ionic and Covalent Bonding

Did You Know ?

The table salt you buy is usually not pure NaCl. It often contains small amounts of finely divided insoluble substances such as silicates or complex salts of aluminum. Particles of these materials stick to the cubic NaCl crystals and keep them from clumping together in high humidity. In addition, much table salt is *iodized* and contains small amounts of KI, which provides dietary iodine for proper thyroid function.

SKILL BUILDER

Graphing The table below shows the melting points of the potassium halides.

Compound	Melting point (°C)
KF	846
KCl	776
KBr	730
KI	686

Have students graph the melting point versus the atomic mass of the halogen. Have them explain the relationship between the melting point and atomic mass as interpreted from the graph. The graph shows that as the atomic mass increases, the melting point decreases.

LINKING CHAPTERS

When studying reaction types in Chapter 5, students will understand the importance of whether a compound is ionic or covalent. Certain types of reactions take place only if the reactants are one type or the other.

Ionic and Covalent Bonding

LINKING CHAPTERS

Tell students they will learn more about electrical current and conductors when they study electricity in Chapter 13.

MISCONCEPTION ALERT

Metallic Bonding

Students are used to thinking that electrons "belong" to one particular atom, ion, or molecule. Emphasize to them that in metallic bonding, metal ions are surrounded by what are known as delocalized electrons. Delocalized electrons are the valence electrons from the metal atoms. They move from one place to another and are not associated with a particular metal atom.

Teaching Tip

Uses of Metals   Show students a periodic table and point out the number of metals on it compared to the number of elements that are not metals. Many more metals exist than nonmetals. Most of their uses are based on properties that result from metallic bonding.

RESOURCE LINK
DATASHEETS

Have students use *Datasheet 4.2 Quick Activity: Building a Close-Packed Structure* to record their results.

Quick ACTIVITY

Building a Close-Packed Structure

Copper and other metals have close-packed structures. This means their atoms are packed very tightly together. In this activity, you will build a close-packed structure using ping pong balls.

1. Place three books flat on a table so that their edges form a triangle.
2. Fill the triangular space between the books with the spherical "atoms." Adjust the books so that the atoms make a one-layer, close-packed pattern, as shown at right.
3. Build additional layers on top of the first layer. How many other atoms does each atom touch? Where have you seen other arrangements that are similar to this one?

---

internet**connect**

SC LINKS
NSTA

TOPIC: Chemical bonding
GO TO: www.scilinks.org
KEYWORD: HK1043

▶ **metallic bond** a bond formed by the attraction between positively charged metal ions and the electrons around them

Figure 4-13
Copper is a flexible metal that melts at 1083°C and boils at 2567°C. Copper conducts electricity because electrons can move freely between atoms.

Metallic Bonds

Metals, like copper, shown in **Figure 4-13,** can conduct electricity when they are solid. Metals are also flexible, so they can bend and stretch without breaking. Copper, for example, can be hammered flat into sheets or stretched into very thin wire. What kind of bonds give copper these properties?

Electrons move freely between metal atoms

The atoms in metals like copper form **metallic bonds.** The attraction between one atom's nucleus and a neighboring atom's electrons packs the atoms closely together. This close packing causes the outermost energy levels of the atoms to overlap, as shown in **Figure 4-13.** Therefore, electrons are free to move from atom to atom. This model explains why metals conduct electricity so well. Metals are flexible because the atoms can slide past each other without their bonds breaking.

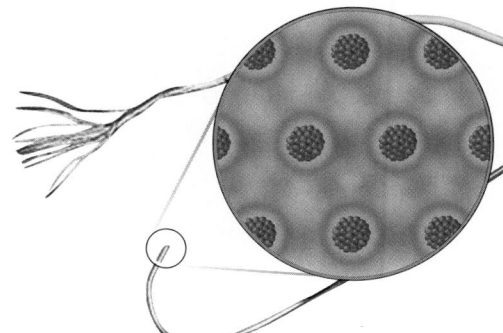

Quick ACTIVITY

Building a Close-Packed Structure   Be sure the spheres are small enough that several of them will fit into the triangle. Students will not see the pattern if too few balls are used. As an alternate activity, use equal numbers of balls of two different sizes, alternating them in the pattern. Students can also use a rectan- gular pattern instead of a triangle. Tell students that sometimes the arrangement of network ionic solids is called *closest packing.* Ask them to explain why this term is accurate. *(The ions in upper layers fill in depressions in the lower levels. This arrangement is the closest the ions can be.)*

Covalent Bonds

Compounds that are made of molecules, like water and sugar, have **covalent bonds.** Compounds existing as networks of bonded atoms, such as silicon dioxide, are also held together by covalent bonds. Covalent bonds are often formed between nonmetal atoms.

Covalent compounds can be solids, liquids, or gases. Except for silicon dioxide and other compounds with network structures, most covalent compounds have a low melting point—usually below 300°C. In compounds that are made of molecules, the molecules are free to move when the compound is dissolved in water or is melted. But these molecules remain intact and do not conduct electricity because they are not charged.

Atoms joined by covalent bonds share electrons

Some atoms, like the hydrogen atoms in **Figure 4-9,** on page 115, bond to form molecules. **Figure 4-14A** shows how two chlorine atoms bond to form a chlorine molecule, Cl_2. Before bonding, each atom has seven electrons in its outermost energy level. The atoms don't transfer electrons to one another because each needs to gain an electron. If each atom shares one electron with the other atom, then both atoms together have a full outermost energy level. That is, both atoms together have eight valence electrons. The way electrons are shared depends on which atoms are sharing the electrons. Two chlorine atoms are exactly alike. When they bond, electrons are equally attracted to the positive nucleus of each atom. Bonds like this one, in which electrons are shared equally, are called *nonpolar covalent bonds*.

The structural formula in **Figure 4-14B** shows how the chlorine atoms are connected in the molecule that forms. A single line drawn between two atoms indicates that the atoms share two electrons and are joined by one covalent bond.

▶ **covalent bond** a bond formed when atoms share one or more pairs of electrons

VOCABULARY *Skills Tip*

Covalent bonds *form when atoms share pairs of* valence electrons.

Section 4.2

Ionic and Covalent Bonding

|SKILL BUILDER

Interpreting Vocabulary
Ask students what the term *polar* means. Definitions will vary but should indicate that it refers to opposites. Point out that Earth's poles are at opposite ends of Earth. The poles of a magnet are opposite in a magnetic field.

The ends of a polar bond are also opposite in charge—one partially negative and one partially positive.

The greater the difference in electronegativity of the joined atoms, the more polar the bond. An ionic bond is the most extreme polar bond, in which one of the atoms is so electronegative that it removes an electron from the other atom. The result is a positive ion and a negative ion.

Figure 4-14

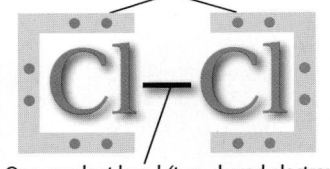

Two electrons are in the shared electron cloud.

Each chlorine atom has six electrons that are not shared.

Chlorine atom   Chlorine atom   Chlorine molecule

One covalent bond (two shared electrons)

A Two chlorine atoms share electrons equally to form a *nonpolar covalent bond.*

B A single line drawn between two chlorine atoms shows that the atoms share two electrons. Dots represent electrons that are not involved in bonding.

THE STRUCTURE OF MATTER **119**

RESOURCE LINK

LABORATORY MANUAL

Have students perform *Lab 4 The Structure of Matter: Determining Which Household Solutions Conduct Electricity* in the lab ancillary.

DATASHEETS

Have students use *Datasheet 4.6* to record their results from the lab.

Ionic and Covalent Bonding

Additional Application

Polar Molecules A process called chromatography can be used to separate mixtures of covalent compounds. One type of chromatography, called paper chromatography, separates molecules based on their polarity. Water or some other liquid solvent carries the components of the mixture through a porous paper. The more polar the compound, the more it is attracted to the paper. Thus, the more polar the component, the less distance the component will travel in the paper.

SKILL BUILDER

Interpreting Vocabulary
The prefix *poly-* means "many." Emphasize to students that polyatomic ions are ions that contain many atoms.

Oxygen
Four electrons are in the shared electron cloud.

$6e^-$ $6e^-$
$2e^-$ $2e^-$

$:\ddot{O}=\ddot{O}:$
Double covalent bond

Nitrogen
Six electrons are in the shared electron cloud.

$5e^-$ $5e^-$
$2e^-$ $2e^-$

$:N\equiv N:$
Triple covalent bond

Figure 4-15
The elements oxygen and nitrogen have covalent bonds. Electrons not involved in bonding are represented by dots.

 **polyatomic ion** an ion made of two or more atoms that are covalently bonded and that act like a single ion

PHYSICAL SCIENCE INTERACTIVE TUTOR
Disc One, Module 4:
Chemical Bonding
Use the Interactive Tutor to learn more about this topic.

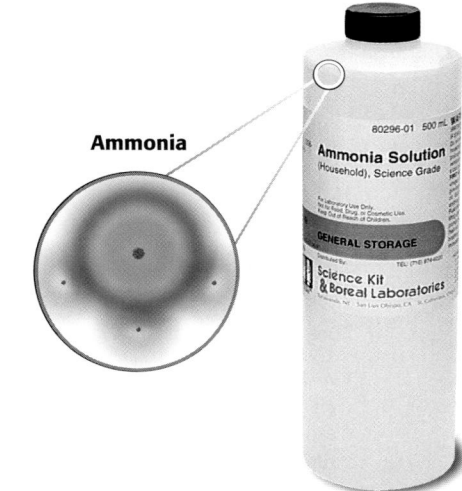
Ammonia

Figure 4-16
The darker shading around the nitrogen atom as compared to the hydrogen atoms shows that electrons are more attracted to nitrogen atoms than to hydrogen atoms. So the bonds in ammonia are *polar covalent bonds.*

Atoms may share more than one pair of electrons

Figure 4-15 shows covalent bonding in oxygen gas, O_2 and nitrogen gas, N_2. Notice that the bond joining two oxygen atoms is represented by two lines. This means that two pairs of electrons (a total of four electrons) are shared to form a double covalent bond.

The bond joining two nitrogen atoms is represented by three lines. Two nitrogen atoms form a triple covalent bond by sharing three pairs of electrons (a total of six electrons). The bond between two nitrogen atoms is stronger than the bond between two oxygen atoms. That's because more energy is needed to break a triple bond than to break a double bond. Triple and double bonds are also shorter than single bonds.

Atoms do not always share electrons equally

When two different atoms share electrons, the electrons are not shared equally. The shared electrons are attracted to the nucleus of one atom more than the other. An unequal sharing of electrons forms a *polar covalent bond*.

Usually, electrons are more attracted to atoms of elements that are located farther to the right and closer to the top of the periodic table. The shading in **Figure 4-16** shows that the shared electrons in the ammonia gas, NH_3, in the headspace of this container, are closer to the nitrogen atom than they are to the hydrogen atoms.

Polyatomic Ions

Until now, we have talked about compounds that have either ionic or covalent bonds. But some compounds have both ionic and covalent bonds. Such compounds are made of **polyatomic ions,** which are groups of covalently bonded atoms that have either lost or gained electrons. A polyatomic ion acts the same as the ions you have already encountered.

ALTERNATIVE ASSESSMENT

Polar Covalent Bond

Have students think of a situation that is analogous to a polar covalent bond. Have them write a paragraph explaining their analogy and telling how the situation is similar to a polar covalent bond. For example, the analogy might be a tug-of-war between ten students who have been lifting weights and ten students who have not. Even though both groups have some pull on the rope, the pull will not be even. The weight lifters will have a greater pull for the shared rope, just as one atom in a polar bond has a greater attraction for the shared electrons.

There are many polyatomic ions

Many compounds you use either contain or are made from polyatomic ions. For example, your toothpaste may contain baking soda. Another name for baking soda is sodium hydrogen carbonate, $NaHCO_3$. Hydrogen carbonate, HCO_3^- is a polyatomic ion. Sodium carbonate, Na_2CO_3, is often used to make soaps and other cleaners and contains the carbonate ion, CO_3^{2-}. Sodium hydroxide, $NaOH$, has hydroxide ions, OH^-, and is also used to make soaps. A few of these polyatomic ions are shown in **Figure 4-17.**

Oppositely charged polyatomic ions, like other ions, can bond to form compounds. Ammonium nitrate, NH_4NO_3, and ammonium sulfate, $(NH_4)_2SO_4$, both contain positively charged ammonium ions, NH_4^+. Nitrate, NO_3^-, and sulfate, SO_4^{2-}, are both negatively charged polyatomic ions.

Parentheses group the atoms of a polyatomic ion

You might be wondering why the chemical formula for ammonium sulfate is written as $(NH_4)_2SO_4$ instead of as $N_2H_8SO_4$. The parentheses around the ammonium ion are there to remind you that it acts like a single ion. Parentheses group the atoms of the ammonium ion together to show that the subscript 2 applies to the whole ion. There are two ammonium ions for every sulfate ion. Parentheses are not needed in compounds like ammonium nitrate, NH_4NO_3, because there is a 1:1 ratio of ions.

Always keep in mind that a polyatomic ion's charge applies not only to the last atom in the formula but to the entire ion. The carbonate ion, CO_3^{2-}, has a 2– charge. This means that CO_3, not just the oxygen atom, has the negative charge.

Some polyatomic anion names relate to their oxygen content

You may have noticed that many polyatomic anions are made of oxygen. Most of their names end with *-ite* or *-ate*. These endings do not tell you exactly how many oxygen atoms are in the ion, but they do follow a pattern. Think about sulfate (SO_4^{2-}) and sulfite (SO_3^{2-}), nitrate (NO_3^-) and nitrite (NO_2^-), and chlorate (ClO_3^-) and chlorite (ClO_2^-). The charge of each ion pair is the same. But notice how the ions have different numbers of oxygen atoms. Their names also have different endings.

An *-ate* ending is used to name the ion with one more oxygen atom. The name of the ion with one less oxygen ends in *-ite*. **Table 4-3,** on the next page, lists several common polyatomic anions. As you look at this table, you'll notice that not all of the anions listed have names that end in *-ite* or *-ate*. That's because some polyatomic anions, like hydroxide (OH^-) and cyanide (CN^-), are not named according to any general rules.

Hydroxide ion, OH^-

Carbonate ion, CO_3^{2-}

Ammonium ion, NH_4^+

Figure 4-17
The hydroxide ion (OH^-), carbonate ion (CO_3^{2-}), and ammonium ion (NH_4^+) are all polyatomic ions.

INTEGRATING

SPACE SCIENCE
Most of the ions and molecules in space are not the same as those that are found on Earth or in Earth's atmosphere. C_3H, C_6H_2, and HCO^+ have all been found in space. So far, no one has been able to figure out how these unusual molecules and ions form in space.

THE STRUCTURE OF MATTER **121**

Ionic and Covalent Bonding

Teaching Tip

Polyatomic Ions Emphasize the difference between monatomic ions and polyatomic ions by writing the names and formulas of a series of compounds containing monatomic ions and a second series containing polyatomic ions. Lists could include the following:

Compounds with monatomic ions

sodium oxide	Na_2O
iron(III) fluoride	FeF_3
barium iodide	BaI_2
copper(II) oxide	CuO

Compounds with polyatomic ions

sodium sulfate	Na_2SO_4
potassium carbonate	K_2CO_3
calcium chlorate	$Ca(ClO_3)_2$
tin(II) acetate	$Sn(CH_3COO)_2$

Stress to students that each polyatomic ion is treated as a single unit. Have students infer the charge of the anions from what they already know about the cations.

INTEGRATING

SPACE SCIENCE The main difference in these ions and molecules in space and similar ions and molecules on Earth is the number of bonds carbon forms in them. Carbon does not form four covalent bonds in many of these space molecules and ions.

Resources Assign students worksheet *4.3 Integrating Space Science—Ion Propulsion in* Deep Space 1 in the **Integration Enrichment Resources** ancillary.

Ionic and Covalent Bonding

Check Your Understanding

1. a. ionic
   b. ionic
   c. covalent
   d. covalent

2. Aluminum foil will conduct because it is a metal and its valence electrons are free to move. KOH dissolved in water will conduct because its ions are free to move.

3. H−C≡C−H
   The carbon atoms share three pairs, or six, electrons.

4. Silver has metallic bonds so it has electrons that are free to move. The coin will conduct electricity.

5. The compound is comprised of Ca^{2+} and OH^- ions held together by ionic bonds. OH^- itself consists of covalently bonded oxygen and hydrogen atoms.

6. Atoms of different elements attract electrons to a different degree. Because all atoms in a molecule of ozone are of the same element, they attract electrons the same amount, and sharing is equal. Carbon and oxygen attract electrons differently, so the sharing is unequal.

7. It has covalent bonds because both elements involved are nonmetals.

Answers continue on p. 141A.

RESOURCE LINK
STUDY GUIDE

Assign students *Review Section 4.2 Ionic and Covalent Bonding.*

Table 4-3 Some Common Polyatomic Anions

Ion name	Ion formula	Ion name	Ion formula
Acetate ion	$CH_3CO_2^-$	Hydroxide ion	OH^-
Carbonate ion	CO_3^{2-}	Hypochlorite ion	ClO^-
Chlorate ion	ClO_3^-	Nitrate ion	NO_3^-
Chlorite ion	ClO_2^-	Nitrite ion	NO_2^-
Cyanide ion	CN^-	Phosphate ion	PO_4^{3-}
Hydrogen carbonate ion	HCO_3^-	Phosphite ion	PO_3^{3-}
Hydrogen sulfate ion	HSO_4^-	Sulfate ion	SO_4^{2-}
Hydrogen sulfite ion	HSO_3^-	Sulfite ion	SO_3^{2-}

SECTION 4.2 REVIEW

SUMMARY

▶ Atoms bond when their valence electrons interact.

▶ Cations and anions attract each other to form ionic bonds.

▶ When ionic compounds are melted or dissolved in water, moving ions can conduct electricity.

▶ Atoms in metals are joined by metallic bonds.

▶ Metals conduct electricity because electrons can move from atom to atom.

▶ Covalent bonds form when atoms share electron pairs. Electrons may be shared equally or unequally.

▶ Polyatomic ions are covalently bonded atoms that have either lost or gained electrons. Their behavior resembles that of simple ions.

CHECK YOUR UNDERSTANDING

1. **Determine** if the following compounds are likely to have ionic or covalent bonds.
   a. magnesium oxide, MgO
   b. strontium chloride, $SrCl_2$
   c. ozone, O_3
   d. methanol, CH_4O

2. **Identify** which two of the following substances will conduct electricity, and explain why.
   a. aluminum foil
   b. sugar, $C_{12}H_{22}O_{11}$, dissolved in water
   c. potassium hydroxide, KOH, dissolved in water

3. **Draw** the structural formula for acetylene. Atoms bond in the order HCCH. Carbon and hydrogen atoms share two electrons, and each carbon atom must have a total of four bonds. How many electrons do the carbon atoms share?

4. **Predict** whether a silver coin can conduct electricity. What kind of bonds does silver have?

5. **Describe** how it is possible for calcium hydroxide, $Ca(OH)_2$, to have both ionic and covalent bonds.

6. **Explain** why electrons are shared equally in ozone, O_3, and unequally in carbon dioxide, CO_2.

7. **Analyze** whether dinitrogen tetroxide, N_2O_4, has covalent or ionic bonds. Describe how you reached this conclusion.

8. **Critical Thinking** *Bond energy* measures the energy per mole of a substance needed to break a bond. Which element has the greater bond energy, oxygen or nitrogen? (**Hint:** Which element has more bonds?)

Compound Names and Formulas

OBJECTIVES

▶ Name simple ionic and covalent compounds.
▶ Predict the charge of a transition metal cation in an ionic compound.
▶ Write chemical formulas for simple ionic compounds.
▶ Distinguish a covalent compound's empirical formula from its molecular formula.

▶ **KEY TERMS**
empirical formula
molecular formula

internetconnect

SCLINKS
NSTA

TOPIC: Naming compounds
GO TO: www.scilinks.org
KEYWORD: HK1044

Just like elements, compounds have names that distinguish them from other compounds. Although the compounds BaF_2 and BF_3 may have similar chemical formulas, they have very different names. BaF_2 is *barium fluoride*, and BF_3 is *boron trifluoride*. When talking about these compounds, there is little chance for confusion. You can see that the names of these compounds reflect the two elements from which they are formed.

Naming Ionic Compounds

Ionic compounds are formed by the strong attractions between cations and anions, as described in Section 4.2. Both ions are important to the compound's structure, so it makes sense that both ions are included in the name.

Names of ionic compounds include the ions of which they are composed

In many cases, the name of the cation is just like the name of the element from which it is made. You have already seen this for many cations. For example, when an atom of the element *sodium* loses an electron, a *sodium ion*, Na^+, forms. Similarly, when a *calcium* atom loses two electrons, a *calcium ion*, Ca^{2+}, forms. And when an *aluminum* atom loses three electrons, an *aluminum ion*, Al^{3+}, forms. These and other common cations are listed in **Table 4-4.** Notice how ions of Group 1 elements have a 1+ charge and ions of Group 2 elements have a 2+ charge.

Table 4-4   Some Common Cations

Ion name and symbol	Ion charge
Cesium ion, Cs^+	1+
Lithium ion, Li^+	
Potassium ion, K^+	
Rubidium ion, Rb^+	
Sodium ion, Na^+	
Barium ion, Ba^{2+}	2+
Beryllium ion, Be^{2+}	
Calcium ion, Ca^{2+}	
Magnesium ion, Mg^{2+}	
Strontium ion, Sr^{2+}	
Aluminum ion, Al^{3+}	3+

THE STRUCTURE OF MATTER **123**

Scheduling

Refer to pp. 106A–106D for lecture, classwork, and assignment options for Section 4.3.

★ **Lesson Focus**
Use transparency *LT 13* to prepare students for this section.

READING SKILL BUILDER *Summarizing*
Have students read about how to name ionic compounds, write formulas for ionic compounds, name covalent compounds, and write formulas for covalent compounds. After reading each topic, ask for volunteers to summarize each process for the rest of the class. Have students ask for clarification of anything they do not understand once each summary is completed.

Teaching Tip

Order in Ionic Formulas
Give examples, such as Einstein Albert, Marie Madame Curie, and Carver Washington George, to illustrate to students the importance of correct order and spelling of a name to accurately denote a person. Extend the discussion to include the naming of ionic compounds. Cations and anions can be thought of as the first and last names, respectively, of ionic compounds. Point out that writing the name in the correct order and with the correct spelling is important for accurately denoting an ionic compound.

DEMONSTRATION 3   TEACHING

Balancing Charge

Time: Approximately 15 minutes
Materials: double-pan balance, pennies, 2 index cards

Let stacks of pennies represent the amount of charge on ions. For example, two pennies represent a charge of two. Place a card with a plus sign on it in front of the left-hand pan of the balance and a card with a minus sign in front of the right-hand pan. Choose several ionic compounds, and use

the stacks to show that a correct formula balances charge. For example, if Fe^{3+} and S^{2-} ions are represented by stacks of three and two pennies, it will take two stacks of three pennies to balance three stacks of two pennies. The final formula is Fe_2S_3.

Analysis

Use the balance and pennies to find the correct formulas for all compounds that would form from the following ions: Au^{3+}, Pb^{2+}, O^{2-}, Cl^-. *(Au_2O_3, $AuCl_3$, $PbCl_2$, PbO)*

Compound Names and Formulas

Teaching Tip

Writing Formulas Students might notice what they consider to be a shortcut in writing ionic formulas. The numerical value of the charge on one ion is usually the subscript of the other ion in the formula for the compound. For example, if Sn^{2+} and PO_4^{3-} form a compound, the charge of 2 for Sn becomes the subscript of the PO_4 part of the formula, and vice versa. The final formula is $Sn_3(PO_4)_2$. If the charges have a common factor, divide by that factor to simplify the formula. For example, Mg^{2+} and O^{2-} form MgO, not Mg_2O_2. Although this procedure is a simple and quick way to write a formula, students should still follow the procedure listed in the Math Skills on the following page. The Math Skills procedure emphasizes the concept of balanced charges and is not just a manipulation of numbers.

Table 4-5 **Some Common Anions**

Element name and symbol	Ion name and symbol	Ion charge
Fluorine, F	Fluoride ion, F^-	1–
Chlorine, Cl	Chloride ion, Cl^-	
Bromine, Br	Bromide ion, Br^-	
Iodine, I	Iodide ion, I^-	
Oxygen, O	Oxide ion, O^{2-}	2–
Sulfur, S	Sulfide ion, S^{2-}	
Nitrogen, N	Nitride ion, N^{3-}	3–

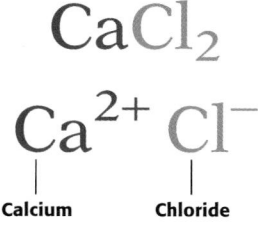

Figure 4-18
Ionic compounds are named for their positive and negative ions.

An anion that is made of one element has a name similar to the element. The only difference is the name's ending. **Table 4-5** lists some common anions and shows how they are named. Just like most cations, anions of elements in the same group of the periodic table have the same charge.

NaF is made of sodium ions, Na^+, and fluoride ions, F^-. Therefore, its name is *sodium fluoride*. **Figure 4-18** shows how calcium chloride, another ionic compound, gets its name.

Some cation names must show their charge

Think about the compounds FeO and Fe_2O_3. According to the rules you have learned so far, both of these compounds would be named *iron oxide*, even though they are not the same compound. Fe_2O_3, the main component of rust, is a reddish brown solid that melts at 1565°C. FeO, on the other hand, is a black powder that melts at 1420°C. These different properties tell us that they are different compounds and should have different names.

Iron is a transition metal. Transition metals may form several cations—each with a different charge. A few of these cations are listed in **Table 4-6.** The charge of the iron cation in Fe_2O_3 is different from the charge of the iron cation in FeO. In cases like this, the cation name must be followed by a Roman numeral in parentheses. The Roman numeral shows the cation's charge. Fe_2O_3 is made of Fe^{3+} ions, so it is named *iron(III) oxide*. FeO is made of Fe^{2+} ions, so it is named *iron(II) oxide*.

Table 4-6 **Some Transition Metal Cations**

Ion name	Ion symbol	Ion name	Ion symbol
Copper(I) ion	Cu^+	Chromium(II) ion	Cr^{2+}
Copper(II) ion	Cu^{2+}	Chromium(III) ion	Cr^{3+}
Iron(II) ion	Fe^{2+}	Cadmium(II) ion	Cd^{2+}
Iron(III) ion	Fe^{3+}	Titanium(II) ion	Ti^{2+}
Nickel(II) ion	Ni^{2+}	Titanium(III) ion	Ti^{3+}
Nickel(III) ion	Ni^{3+}	Titanium(IV) ion	Ti^{4+}

ALTERNATIVE ASSESSMENT

Transition Metals

On the chalkboard, write the following formulas for transition element compounds: CrO, CrCl₃, Cr(SO₄)₃, CoBr₂, Co₂O₃, KMnO₄, MnO₂, MnS, MnO₃, MnN. Have students use the formulas to make a table that gives the ions formed by

chromium, cobalt, and manganese. Review with students how to use the periodic table to find charges of elements in certain families. The ions for chromium are Cr^{2+}, Cr^{3+}, and Cr^{6+}. The ions for cobalt are Co^{2+} and Co^{3+}. Those for manganese are Mn^{2+}, Mn^{3+}, Mn^{4+}, Mn^{6+}, and Mn^{7+}.

Determining the charge of a transition metal cation

How can you tell that the iron ion in Fe_2O_3 has a charge of 3+? Like all compounds, ionic compounds have a total charge of zero. This means that the total positive charges must equal the total negative charges. An oxide ion, O^{2-}, has a charge of 2–. Three of them have a total charge of 6–. That means the total positive charge in the formula must be 6+. For two iron ions to have a total charge of 6+, each ion must have a charge of 3+.

Writing Formulas for Ionic Compounds

You have seen how to determine the charge of each ion in a compound if you are given the compound's formula. Following a similar process, you can determine the chemical formula for a compound if you are given its name.

Math Skills

Writing Ionic Formulas What is the chemical formula for aluminum fluoride?

1 **List the symbols for each ion.**
Symbol for an aluminum ion from **Table 4-4:** Al^{3+}
Symbol for a fluoride ion from **Table 4-5:** F^-

2 **Write the symbols for the ions with the cation first.**
$Al^{3+}F^-$

3 **Find the least common multiple of the ions' charges.**
The least common multiple of 3 and 1 is 3. To make a neutral compound, you need a total of three positive charges and three negative charges.
To get three positive charges: you need only one Al^{3+} ion because $1 \times 3+ = 3+$.
To get three negative charges: you need three F^- ions because $3 \times 1- = 3-$.

4 **Write the chemical formula, indicating with subscripts how many of each ion are needed to make a neutral compound.**
AlF_3

Practice HINT

Once you have determined a chemical formula, always check the formula to see if it makes a neutral compound. For this example, the aluminum ion has a charge of 3+. The fluoride ion has a charge of only 1–, but there are three of them for a total of 3–.

$(3-) + (3+) = 0$, so the charges balance, and the formula is neutral.

Practice

Writing Ionic Formulas
Write formulas for the following ionic compounds.
1. lithium oxide
2. beryllium chloride
3. titanium(III) nitride
4. cobalt(III) hydroxide

THE STRUCTURE OF MATTER **125**

Solution Guide

1. Li_2O
2. $BeCl_2$
3. TiN
4. $Co(OH)_3$

Section 4.3

Compound Names and Formulas

Teaching Tip

Cation-anion Pairs Reinforce the idea of electroneutrality in the following drill. Make a vertical list on the board of the symbols of six cations, and make a parallel list of the symbols of six anions. The ions should have a variety of charges. Point to a cation-anion pair, and ask students how many of each will produce electroneutrality. You may want to ask students to write or state the correct formula, but the main purpose of the exercise is to help students understand how to construct an electroneutral combination.

Math Skills

Resources Assign students worksheet 9: *Writing Ionic Formulas* in the **Math Skills Worksheets** ancillary.

Additional Examples

Writing Ionic Formulas Write formulas for the following ionic compounds.

a. magnesium bromide
Answer: $MgBr_2$

b. rubidium oxide
Answer: Rb_2O

c. lithium nitride
Answer: Li_3N

d. potassium sulfate
Answer: K_2SO_4

125

Teaching Tip

Prefixes Elicit from students examples of words containing prefixes that denote a number. Examples might include *bicycle*, *tricycle*, *octopus*, or *decade*. Other examples might include terms from mathematics, such as *triangle*, *pentagon*, *quadrilateral*, or *hexagon*. Tell students that such prefixes are also used to name molecular compounds.

MISCONCEPTION ALERT

Common Names
Students might think that all compounds have one name only. In addition to a scientific name, a compound might also have a common name. For example, few people would refer to dihydrogen monoxide, H_2O, as anything but water. Ask them to think of other compounds that have common names as well as scientific names. Answers might include vinegar (acetic acid) and rubbing alcohol (isopropanol).

Historical Perspective

Common names are especially frequent among compounds that have been known and used for years, before rules for naming were standard. For example, although many chemical salts exist, sodium chloride, $NaCl$, is what is commonly referred to as salt. Some compounds have common names resulting from old systems of naming or from the compound's effects, not the system currently used. For example, dinitrogen monoxide, N_2O, is commonly referred to as both nitrous oxide and laughing gas. Have students research the common and standard names of some compounds they are familiar with.

Table 4-7
Prefixes Used to Name Covalent Compounds

Number of atoms	Prefix
1	*Mono-*
2	*Di-*
3	*Tri-*
4	*Tetra-*
5	*Penta-*
6	*Hexa-*
7	*Hepta-*
8	*Octa-*
9	*Nona-*
10	*Deca-*

Figure 4-19
One molecule of *di*nitrogen *tetr*oxide has *two* nitrogen atoms and *four* oxygen atoms.

$$N_2O_4$$
Dinitrogen tetroxide

▶ **empirical formula**
the simplest chemical formula of a compound that tells the smallest whole-number ratio of atoms in the compound

Figure 4-20
Emerald gemstones are cut from the mineral beryl. Very tiny amounts of chromium(III) oxide impurity in the gemstones gives them their beautiful green color.

Naming Covalent Compounds

Covalent compounds, like SiO_2 (silicon dioxide) and CO_2 (carbon dioxide), are named using different rules than those used to name ionic compounds.

Numerical prefixes are used to name covalent compounds of two elements

For two-element covalent compounds, numerical prefixes tell how many atoms of each element are in the molecule. **Table 4-7** lists some of these prefixes. If there is only one atom of the first element, it does not get a prefix. Whichever element is farther to the right in the periodic table is named second and ends in *-ide*.

There are one boron atom and three fluorine atoms in *boron trifluoride*, BF_3. *Dinitrogen tetroxide*, N_2O_4, is made of two nitrogen atoms and four oxygen atoms, as shown in **Figure 4-19**. Notice how the *a* in *tetra* is dropped to make the name easier to say.

Chemical Formulas for Covalent Compounds

Emeralds, shown in **Figure 4-20**, are made of a mineral called beryl. The chemical formula for beryl is $Be_3Al_2Si_6O_{18}$. But how did people determine this formula? It took some experiments. Chemical formulas like this one were determined by first measuring the mass of each element in the compound.

A compound's simplest formula is its empirical formula

Once the mass of each element in a sample of the compound is known, scientists can calculate the compound's **empirical formula**, or simplest formula. An empirical formula tells us the smallest whole-number ratio of atoms that are in a compound. Formulas for most ionic compounds are empirical formulas.

Covalent compounds have empirical formulas, too. The empirical formula for water is H_2O. It tells you that the ratio of hydrogen atoms to oxygen atoms is 2:1. Scientists have to analyze unknown compounds to determine their empirical formulas.

ALTERNATIVE ASSESSMENT

Naming Covalent Compounds

Divide students into teams of four. Provide two students on each team with flashcards with the prefixes listed in **Table 4-7** written on them. Supply one of the other students with cards containing names of nonmetals and the other student with *–ide* names based on nonmetals, such as *oxide*. Write the formula for a covalent compound on the chalkboard, and have students use the cards to name it. This assessment can be done as a learning exercise or as a group quiz. Before starting the activity, remind students of the following: *Mono-* is used only with the second part of the name, not the first. For example, CO is carbon monoxide, not monocarbon monoxide. Final *o*'s and *a*'s of prefixes can be dropped if it makes the name easier to pronounce. For example, tetroxide would be used, not tetraoxide.

For example, if a 142 g sample of an unknown compound contains only the elements phosphorus and oxygen and is found to contain 62 g of P and 80 g of O, its empirical formula is easy to calculate. This process is shown in **Figure 4-21.**

Different compounds can have the same empirical formula

It's possible for several compounds to have the same empirical formula because empirical formulas only represent a ratio of atoms. Formaldehyde, acetic acid, and glucose all have the empirical formula CH_2O, as shown in **Table 4-8.** These three compounds are not at all alike, though. Formaldehyde is often used to keep dead organisms from decaying so that they can be studied. Acetic acid gives vinegar its characteristic sour taste and strong smell. And glucose is a sugar that plays a very important role in your body chemistry. Some other formula must be used to distinguish these three very different compounds.

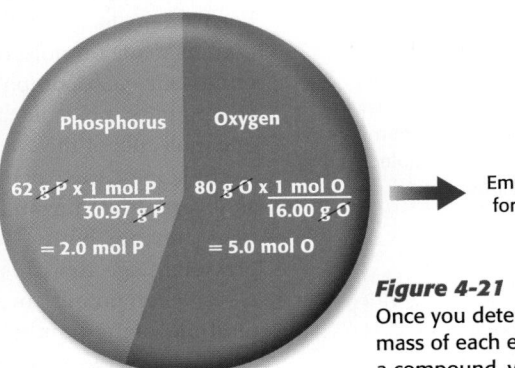

Exactly 142 g of Unknown Compound

Phosphorus

$62 \text{ g P} \times \dfrac{1 \text{ mol P}}{30.97 \text{ g P}}$

$= 2.0 \text{ mol P}$

Oxygen

$80 \text{ g O} \times \dfrac{1 \text{ mol O}}{16.00 \text{ g O}}$

$= 5.0 \text{ mol O}$

$\dfrac{\text{Empirical}}{\text{formula}} = P_2O_5$

Figure 4-21
Once you determine the mass of each element in a compound, you can calculate the amount of each element in moles. The empirical formula for the compound is the ratio of these amounts.

Table 4-8 **Empirical and Molecular Formulas for Some Compounds**

Compound	Empirical formula	Molar mass	Molecular formula	Structure
Formaldehyde	CH_2O	30.03 g/mol	CH_2O	
Acetic acid	CH_2O	60.06 g/mol	$2 \times CH_2O = C_2H_4O_2$	
Glucose	CH_2O	180.18 g/mol	$6 \times CH_2O = C_6H_{12}O_6$	

Compound Names and Formulas

|SKILL BUILDER

Interpreting Vocabulary
Have students look up the meaning of the word *empirical* in the dictionary. Have them use the definition to explain where information is obtained about an empirical formula. Their explanations should reflect that empirical formulas are determined from experimental data.

Teaching Tip

Finding Molecular Formulas
Show students how to find the molecular formula when given the empirical formula and the molar mass of the compound. Use the information in **Table 4-8** as an example. The molar mass of the empirical formula is found by adding the molar mass of each atom, expressed in g/mol. For CH_2O, the molar mass is $(1 \times 12.01) + (2 \times 1.01) + (1 \times 16.00)$, or 30.03. The molecular formula will be a multiple of the empirical formula, so divide the molar mass of the molecule by the molar mass of the empirical formula. For glucose, 180.18 g/mol ÷ 30.03 g/mol = 6. So, the molecule is made up of six units of the empirical formula. The molecular formula is $C_{1\times6}H_{2\times6}O_{1\times6}$, or $C_6H_{12}O_6$. Have students find the molecular formulas for the following molecules:

Molar mass (g/mol)	Empirical formula	Molecular formula
78.12	CH	C_6H_6
32.06	NH_2	N_2H_4
210.33	$C_3H_6N_2$	$C_9H_{18}N_6$

127

Section 4.3

Compound Names and Formulas

Check Your Understanding

1. **a.** nickel(II) phosphate
    b. iron(II) iodide
    c. manganese(III) fluoride
    d. chromium(II) chloride
    e. sodium cyanide
    f. copper(II) sulfide
2. **a.** diarsenic pentoxide
    b. silicon tetriodide
    c. tetraphosphorus trisulfide
    d. tetraphosphorus decoxide
    e. selenium dioxide
    f. phosphorus trichloride
3. Manganese is a transition element, so its ions can vary in charge. Roman numerals are necessary to indicate the charge of manganese in a compound. MnO_2 is manganese(IV) oxide, and Mn_2O_7 is manganese(VII) oxide.
4. The prefix *hexa-* indicates six fluorine atoms.

Math Skills

5. $100.00\% - (49.47\% + 5.20\% + 28.85\%) = 16.48\%$ oxygen
6. The total charge of the compound must be zero. Each of the two cyanide ions has a charge of 1–. The charge of the cadmium ion must be 2+ to add to the $2 \times (1-)$ charge from the cyanide ions to equal zero.
7. **a.** $MgSO_4$ **c.** CrF_2
    b. $RbBr$ **d.** Ni_2CO_3

RESOURCE LINK

STUDY GUIDE

Assign students *Review Section 4.3 Compound Names and Formulas.*

> **molecular formula**
> a chemical formula that reports the actual numbers of atoms in one molecule of a compound

Molecular formulas are determined from empirical formulas

Formaldehyde, acetic acid, and glucose are all covalent compounds made of molecules. They all have the same empirical formula, but each compound has its own **molecular formula**. A compound's molecular formula tells you how many atoms are in one molecule of the compound.

In some cases, a compound's molecular formula is the same as its empirical formula. The empirical and molecular formulas for water are both H_2O. You can see from **Table 4-8** on the previous page that this is also true for formaldehyde. In other cases, a compound's molecular formula is a small whole-number multiple of its empirical formula. The molecular formula for acetic acid is two times its empirical formula, and that of glucose is six times its empirical formula.

SECTION 4.3 REVIEW

SUMMARY

▶ To name an ionic compound, first name the cation and then the anion.

▶ If an element can form cations with different charges, the cation name must include the ion's charge. The charge is written as a Roman numeral in parentheses.

▶ Prefixes are used to name covalent compounds made of two different elements.

▶ An empirical formula tells the relative numbers of atoms of each element in a compound.

▶ A molecular formula tells the actual numbers of atoms in one molecule of a compound.

▶ Covalent compounds have both empirical and molecular formulas.

CHECK YOUR UNDERSTANDING

1. **Name** the following ionic compounds, specifying the charge of any transition metal cations.
    a. $Ni_3(PO_4)_2$ **c.** MnF_3 **e.** NaCN
    b. FeI_2 **d.** $CrCl_2$ **f.** CuS
2. **Name** the following covalent compounds:
    a. As_2O_5 **c.** P_4S_3 **e.** SeO_2
    b. SiI_4 **d.** P_4O_{10} **f.** PCl_3
3. **Explain** why Roman numerals must be included in the names of MnO_2 and Mn_2O_7. Name both of these compounds.
4. **Identify** how many fluorine atoms are in one molecule of sulfur hexafluoride.

Math Skills

5. **Creative Thinking** An unknown compound contains 49.47 percent C, 5.20 percent H, 28.85 percent N, and a certain percentage of oxygen. What percentage of the compound must be oxygen? (**Hint:** The sum of the percentages should equal 100 percent.)
6. What is the charge of the cadmium cation in cadmium cyanide, $Cd(CN)_2$, a compound used in electroplating? Explain your reasoning.
7. Determine the chemical formulas for the following ionic compounds:
    a. magnesium sulfate   **c.** chromium(II) fluoride
    b. rubidium bromide   **d.** nickel(I) carbonate

128 CHAPTER 4

4.4

Organic and Biochemical Compounds

INTEGRATING TECHNOLOGY and Society

Section 4.4

Organic and Biochemical Compounds

OBJECTIVES

▸ Describe how carbon atoms bond covalently to form organic compounds.
▸ Identify the names and structures of groups of simple organic compounds and polymers.
▸ Identify what the polymers essential for life are made of.

▶ **KEY TERMS**
organic compound
polymer
biochemical compound
carbohydrate
protein
amino acid

The word *organic* has many different meanings. Most people associate the word *organic* with living organisms. Perhaps you have heard of or eaten organically grown fruits or vegetables. What this means is that they were grown using fertilizers and pesticides that come from plant and animal matter. In chemistry, the word *organic* is used to describe certain compounds.

Organic Compounds

An **organic compound** is a covalently bonded compound made of molecules. Organic compounds contain carbon and, almost always, hydrogen. Other atoms, such as oxygen, nitrogen, sulfur, and phosphorus, are also found in some organic compounds.

Many ingredients of familiar substances are organic compounds. The effective ingredient in aspirin is a form of the organic compound acetylsalicylic acid, $C_9H_8O_4$. Sugarless chewing gum also has organic compounds as ingredients. Two ingredients are the sweeteners sorbitol, $C_6H_{14}O_6$, and aspartame, $C_{14}H_{18}N_2O_5$, both of which are shown in **Figure 4-22**.

▶ **organic compound** any covalently bonded compound that contains carbon

Figure 4-22
The organic compounds sorbitol and aspartame sweeten some sugarless chewing gums.

Sorbitol   Aspartame

THE STRUCTURE OF MATTER **129**

DEMONSTRATION 4 SCIENCE AND THE CONSUMER

Organic Substances

Time: Approximately 10 minutes
Materials: notebook paper, test tube, test-tube holder, Bunsen burner, sparker to light burner, ice, beaker, tongs

Place a strip of notebook paper into the test tube. Place ice in the beaker. Using the test-tube holder, hold the test tube over the lit burner. At the same time, use tongs to hold the beaker just above the mouth of the test tube.

Analysis

1. What change did you notice in the paper? *(The paper turned black.)*
2. What element could you see after the paper was heated? *(carbon)*
3. What did you notice on the bottom of the beaker? *(condensed water vapor)*
4. What other two elements must be present in the paper? *(the hydrogen and oxygen that make up the water)*

Organic and Biochemical Compounds

SKILL BUILDER

Interpreting Vocabulary
Carbon is one of just a few elements capable of forming chains and rings by bonding to other carbon atoms. *Catenation* is the term that describes this tendency. Carbon exhibits catenation more than any other element does. Silicon also exhibits some catenation. The word *catenation* comes from the Latin word *catena*, which means "chain."

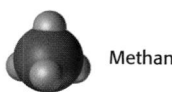

Methane

Figure 4-23
Methane is an alkane that has four C–H bonds.

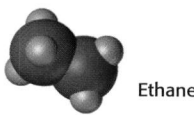

Ethane

Figure 4-24
Ethane, another alkane, has one C–C bond and six C–H bonds.

internet connect

SC*LINKS*
NSTA

TOPIC: Carbon compounds
GO TO: www.scilinks.org
KEYWORD: HK1045

Figure 4-25
This camper is preparing his dinner on a gas grill fueled by propane. Propane is an alkane that has two C–C bonds and eight C–H bonds.

Propane

Carbon atoms form four covalent bonds in organic compounds

When a compound is made of only carbon and hydrogen atoms, it is called a *hydrocarbon*. Methane, CH_4, is the simplest hydrocarbon. Its structure is shown in **Figure 4-23.** Methane gas is formed when living matter, such as plants, decay, so it is often found in swamps and marshes. The natural gas used in Bunsen burners is also mostly methane. Carbon atoms have four valence electrons to use for bonding. In methane, each of these electrons forms a different C–H single bond.

A carbon atom may also share two of its electrons with two from another atom to form a double bond. Or a carbon atom may share three electrons to form a triple bond. However, a carbon atom can never form more than a total of four bonds.

Alkanes have single covalent bonds

Alkanes are hydrocarbons that have only single covalent bonds. **Figure 4-23** shows that methane, the simplest alkane, has only C–H bonds. But alkanes can also have C–C bonds. You can see from **Figure 4-24** that ethane, C_2H_6, has a C–C bond in addition to six C–H bonds. Notice how each carbon atom in both of these compounds bonds to four other atoms.

Many gas grills are fueled by another alkane, propane, C_3H_8. Propane is made of three bonded carbon atoms. Each carbon atom on the end of the molecule forms three bonds with three hydrogen atoms, as shown in **Figure 4-25.** Each of these end carbon atoms forms its fourth bond with the central carbon atom. The central carbon atom shares its two remaining electrons with two hydrogen atoms. You can see only one hydrogen atom bonded to the central carbon atom in **Figure 4-25** because the second hydrogen atom is on the other side.

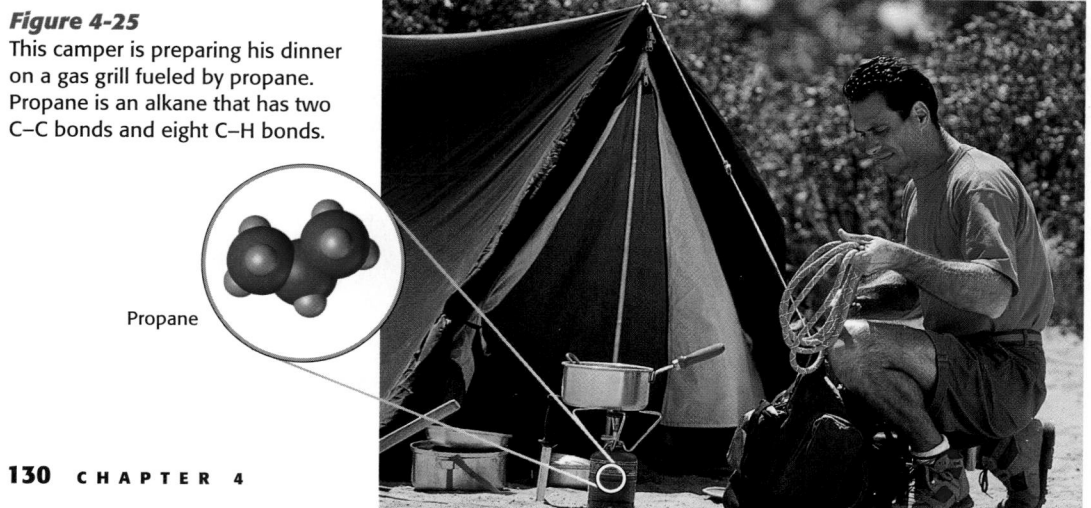

Graphic Organizer
Classifying Alkanes

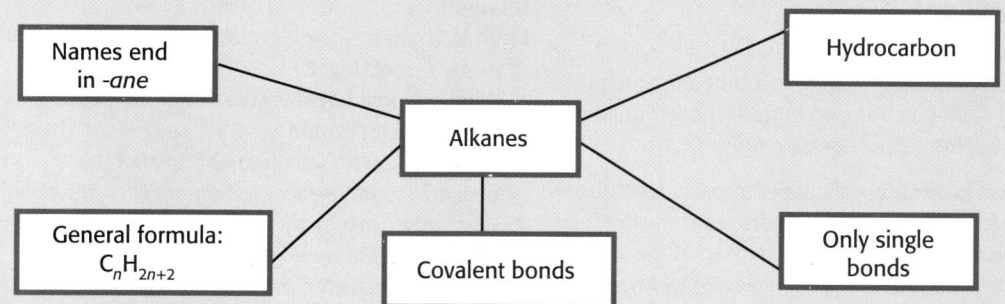

Names end in -*ane*

Hydrocarbon

Alkanes

General formula: C_nH_{2n+2}

Covalent bonds

Only single bonds

Arrangements of carbon atoms in alkanes

The carbon atoms in methane, ethane, and propane all line up in a row because that is their only possible arrangement. When there are more than three bonded carbon atoms, the carbon atoms do not always line up in a row. When they do line up, the alkane is called a *normal alkane,* or *n*-alkane for short. **Table 4-9** shows chemical formulas for the *n*-alkanes that have up to 10 carbon atoms. *Condensed structural formulas* are also included in the table to show how the atoms bond.

The carbon atoms in any alkane with more than three carbon atoms can have more than one possible arrangement. Carbon atom chains may be branched or unbranched, and they can even form rings. **Figure 4-26** shows some of the possible ways six carbon atoms can be arranged when they form hydrocarbons with only single covalent bonds.

Alkane chemical formulas

Except for cyclic alkanes like cyclohexane, the chemical formulas for alkanes follow a special pattern. The number of hydrogen atoms is always two more than twice the number of carbon atoms. This pattern is shown by the chemical formula C_nH_{2n+2}.

Table 4-9   First 10 *n*-Alkanes

n-Alkane	Molecular formula	Condensed structural formula
Methane	CH_4	CH_4
Ethane	C_2H_6	CH_3CH_3
Propane	C_3H_8	$CH_3CH_2CH_3$
Butane	C_4H_{10}	$CH_3(CH_2)_2CH_3$
Pentane	C_5H_{12}	$CH_3(CH_2)_3CH_3$
Hexane	C_6H_{14}	$CH_3(CH_2)_4CH_3$
Heptane	C_7H_{16}	$CH_3(CH_2)_5CH_3$
Octane	C_8H_{18}	$CH_3(CH_2)_6CH_3$
Nonane	C_9H_{20}	$CH_3(CH_2)_7CH_3$
Decane	$C_{10}H_{22}$	$CH_3(CH_2)_8CH_3$

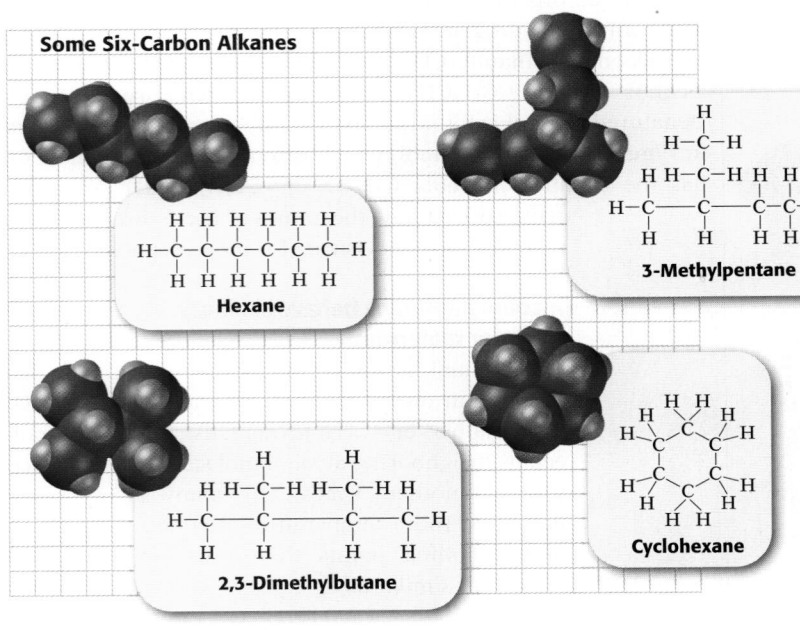

Some Six-Carbon Alkanes

Hexane

3-Methylpentane

2,3-Dimethylbutane

Cyclohexane

Figure 4-26
Hexane, 3-methylpentane, 2,3-dimethylbutane, and cyclohexane are some of the forms six carbon atoms with single covalent bonds may take.

THE STRUCTURE OF MATTER **131**

Teaching Tip

Naming Organic Compounds   Although organic compounds are covalent, they are not named by the conventions used to name other covalent compounds. The prefixes used to name alkanes, as shown in **Table 4-9,** are also used to name alkenes and alkynes. Naming becomes more complex when chains become branched or when other atoms or groups of atoms are substituted for hydrogen atoms on a hydrocarbon. Most high school chemistry books provide complete guidelines for naming organic compounds. In addition to these scientific names, many organic compounds have common names.

|SKILL BUILDER

Interpreting Diagrams   Tell students that the numbers in the names of the organic compounds in **Figure 4-26** are used for locating branches. Carbon atoms in the longest chain in the molecule are numbered, starting with one. A number tells at which carbon atom the chain branches.

Resources   Teaching Transparency 12 shows this visual.

Organic and Biochemical Compounds

Additional Application

General Formulas   Just as the general formula for an alkane is C_nH_{2n+2}, alkenes and alkynes have general formulas. The formula for an alkene is C_nH_{2n}, and that of an alkyne is C_nH_{2n-2}. An alkyne is an organic compound in which two carbon atoms share three pairs of electrons to form a triple bond.

MISCONCEPTION   **ALERT**

Hydroxyl Group
Be sure students understand that the hydroxyl group, —OH, found in alcohols, is not the same as the hydroxide ion, OH⁻. The hydroxyl group is covalently bonded to an organic compound. The hydroxide ion is charged and is ionically bonded to a cation.

Teaching Tip

Substitutions   Compounds known as substituted hydrocarbons form when an atom or group of atoms substitutes for a hydrogen atom in a hydrocarbon. For example, a halogen atom can replace a hydrogen atom. An alcohol is a substituted hydrocarbon, as is an organic acid. Other substituted hydrocarbons include ethers, aldehydes, ketones, and esters.

Propene

Ethene

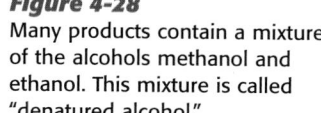

Figure 4-27
The peaches in this plastic container, which is made by joining propene molecules, release ethene gas as they ripen.

Figure 4-28
Many products contain a mixture of the alcohols methanol and ethanol. This mixture is called "denatured alcohol."

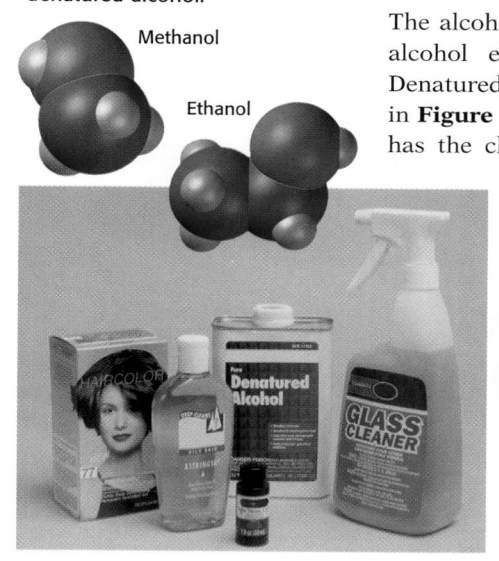

Methanol

Ethanol

Alkenes have double carbon-carbon bonds

Alkenes are also hydrocarbons. Alkenes are different from alkanes because they have at least one double covalent bond between carbon atoms. This is shown by C=C. Alkenes are named like alkanes but with the *-ane* ending replaced by *-ene*.

The simplest alkene is ethene (or ethylene), C_2H_4. Ethene is formed when fruit ripens. Propene (or propylene), C_3H_6, is used to make rubbing alcohol and some plastics. The structures of both compounds are shown in **Figure 4-27.**

Alcohols have —OH groups

Alcohols are organic compounds that are made of oxygen as well as carbon and hydrogen. Alcohols have *hydroxyl*, or –OH, groups. The alcohol methanol, CH_3OH, is sometimes added to another alcohol ethanol, CH_3CH_2OH, to make denatured alcohol. Denatured alcohol is found in many familiar products, as shown in **Figure 4-28.** Isopropanol, which is found in rubbing alcohol, has the chemical formula C_3H_8O, or $(CH_3)_2CHOH$. You may have noticed how the names of these three alcohols all end in *-ol*. This is true for most alcohols.

Alcohol molecules behave similarly to water molecules

A methanol molecule is like a water molecule except that one of the hydrogen atoms is replaced by a methyl, or –CH_3, group. Just like water molecules, neighboring alcohol molecules are attracted to one another. That's why many alcohols are liquids at room temperature. Alcohols have much higher boiling points than other organic compounds of similar size.

Polymers

What do the DNA inside the cells of your body, rubber, wood, and plastic milk jugs have in common? They are all made of large molecules called **polymers.**

Many polymers have repeating subunits

Some small organic molecules bond to form long chains called polymers. Polyethene, which is also known as polythene or polyethylene, is the polymer plastic milk jugs are made of. The name *polyethene* tells its structure. *Poly* means "many." *Ethene* is an alkene whose chemical formula is C_2H_4. Therefore, polyethene is "many ethenes," as shown in **Figure 4-29.** The original molecule, in this case C_2H_4, is called a *monomer.*

Some polymers are natural; others are man-made

Rubber, wood, cotton, wool, starch, protein, and DNA are all natural polymers. Man-made polymers are usually either plastics or fibers. Most plastics are flexible and easily molded, whereas fibers form long, thin strands.

Some polymers can be used as both plastics and fibers. For example, polypropene (polypropylene) is molded to make plastic containers, like the one shown in **Figure 4-27,** as well as some parts for cars and appliances. It is also used to make ropes, carpet, and artificial turf for athletic fields.

The elasticity of a polymer is determined by its structure

As with all substances, the properties of a polymer are determined by its structure. Polymer molecules are like long, thin chains. A small piece of plastic or a single fiber is made of billions of these chains. Polymer molecules can be likened to spaghetti. Like a bowl of spaghetti, the chains are tangled but can slide over each other. Milk jugs are made of polyethene, a plastic made of such noodlelike chains. You can crush or dent a milk jug because the plastic is flexible. Once the jug has been crushed, though, it does not return to its original shape. That's because polyethene is not elastic.

When the chains are connected to each other, or cross-linked, the polymer's properties change. Some become more elastic and can be likened to a volleyball net. Like a volleyball net, an elastic polymer can stretch. When the polymer is released, it returns to its original shape. Rubber bands are elastic polymers. As long as a rubber band is not stretched too far, it can shrink back to its original form.

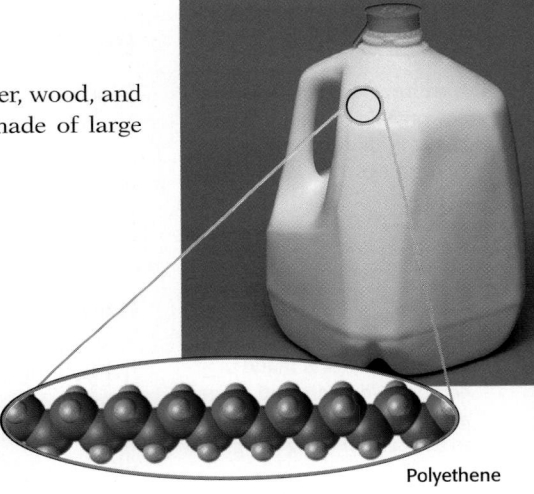

Figure 4-29
Polyethene is a polymer made of many repeating ethene units. As the polymer forms, ethene's double bonds are replaced by single bonds.

Polyethene

▶ **polymer** a large organic molecule made of many smaller bonded units

Quick ACTIVITY

Polymer Memory
Polymers that return to their original shape after stretching can be thought of as having a "memory." In this activity, you will compare the memory of a rubber band with that of the plastic rings that hold a six-pack of cans together.

1. Which polymer stretches better without breaking?
2. Which one has better memory?
3. Warm the stretched six-pack holder over a hot plate, being careful not to melt it. Does it retain its memory?

Organic and Biochemical Compounds

Teaching Tip

Polymers Show students different types of polymers. Examples might include plastic wrap; rubber tubing; polyester thread; nylon pantyhose; foam cups; trash bags; a plastic that is firm but flexible, such as a margarine container; and a rigid, inflexible plastic, such as the material used to make a telephone. Tell students that all of the examples are made up of the same type of compound.

Additional Application

Distinguishing Fibers
Sometimes natural fibers, such as wool and cotton, are difficult to distinguish from synthetic fibers, such as nylon or rayon. One way to tell them apart is to hold them in a flame. The natural fiber will char, and the synthetic fiber will melt.

THE STRUCTURE OF MATTER **133**

Quick ACTIVITY

Polymer Memory Caution students about not touching the hot surface of the hot plate and not melting the plastic. If the plastic accidentally does melt, tell students to notify you immediately. They should not touch the melted plastic and not breathe any of the fumes produced.

1. The rubber band stretches better without breaking.
2. The rubber band has better memory.
3. No. It changes shape and does not return to its original shape.

RESOURCE LINK
IER

Assign students worksheet *4.4 Integrating Environmental Science—Plastics.*

DATASHEETS

Have students use *Datasheet 4.3 Quick Activity: Polymer Memory* to record their results.

Organic and Biochemical Compounds

Did You Know ?

Proteins in the food you eat are necessary to provide amino acids, especially the amino acids that human cells cannot synthesize.

▶ **biochemical compound** any organic compound that has an important role in living things

▶ **carbohydrate** any organic compound that is made of carbon, hydrogen, and oxygen and that provides nutrients to the cells of living things

▶ **protein** a biological polymer made of bonded amino acids

▶ **amino acid** any one of 20 different naturally occurring organic molecules that combine to form proteins

Biochemical Compounds

Biochemical compounds are naturally occurring organic compounds that are very important to living things. Carbohydrates give you energy. Proteins form important parts of your body, like muscles, tendons, fingernails, and hair. The DNA inside your cells gives your body information about what proteins you need. Each of these biochemical compounds is a polymer.

Many carbohydrates are made of glucose

The sugar glucose is a **carbohydrate.** Glucose provides energy to living things. Starch, also a carbohydrate, is made of many bonded glucose molecules. Plants store their energy as chains of starch.

Starch chains pack closely together in a potato or a pasta noodle. When you eat such foods, enzymes in your body break down the starch, making glucose available as a nutrient for your cells. Glucose that is not needed right away is stored as *glycogen.* When you become active, glycogen breaks apart and glucose molecules give you energy. Athletes often prepare themselves for their event by eating starchy foods. They do this so they will have more energy when they exert themselves later on, as shown in **Figure 4-30.**

Proteins are polymers of amino acids

Many polymers are made of only one kind of molecule. Starch, for example, is made of only glucose. **Proteins,** on the other hand, are made of many different molecules that are called **amino acids.** Amino acids are made of carbon, hydrogen, oxygen, and nitrogen. Some amino acids also contain sulfur. There are 20 amino acids found in naturally occurring proteins. The way these amino acids combine determines which protein is made.

Figure 4-30
Athletes often eat lots of foods that are high in carbohydrates the day before a big event. This provides them with a ready supply of stored energy.

DEMONSTRATION 5 TEACHING

Model a Polymer

Time: Approximately 10 minutes
Materials: several spring clothespins

Attach one clothespin onto the leg of another one. Continue the process until a chain of clothespins is formed. Show students that the chain can bend and otherwise move, but it still remains a chain.

Analysis
1. What does each clothespin represent? *(a monomer)*
2. What does the chain represent? *(a polymer)*
3. If the chain represents a protein, what does each clothespin represent? *(an amino acid)*

Inquiry Lab

What properties does a polymer have?

Materials
- ✔ water
- ✔ white glue
- ✔ borax
- ✔ 250 ml beakers (2)
- ✔ plastic spoons
- ✔ plastic sandwich bags

Procedure

SAFETY CAUTION Wear safety goggles, gloves, and a laboratory apron. Be sure to work in an open space and wear clothes that can be cleaned easily.

1. In one beaker, mix 4 g borax with 100 ml water, and stir well.
2. In the second beaker, mix equal parts of glue and water. This solution will determine the amount of new material made. The volume of diluted glue should be between 100 and 200 ml.
3. Pour the borax solution into the beaker containing the glue, and stir well using a plastic spoon.
4. When it becomes too thick to stir, remove the material from the cup and knead it with your fingers. You can store this new material in a plastic sandwich bag.

Analysis

1. What happens to the new material when it is stretched, or rolled into a ball and bounced?
2. Compare the properties of the glue with those of the new material.
3. The properties of the new material resulted from the bonds between the borax and the glue particles. If too little borax were used, in what way would the properties of the new material differ?
4. Does the new material have the properties of a polymer? Explain how you reached this conclusion.

Proteins are long chains made of amino acids. A small protein, insulin, is shown in **Figure 4-31.** Many proteins are made of thousands of bonded amino acid molecules. This means that millions of different proteins can be made with very different properties. When you eat foods that contain proteins, such as cheese, your digestive system breaks down the proteins into individual amino acids. Later, your cells bond the amino acids in a different order to form whatever protein your body needs.

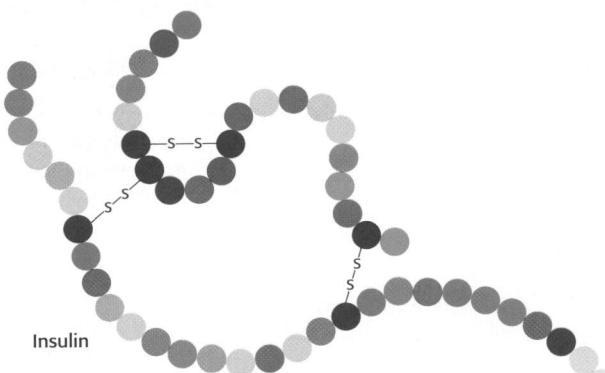

Insulin

Figure 4-31
Insulin controls the use and storage of glucose in your body. Each color in the chain represents a different amino acid.

DNA is a polymer with a complex structure

Your DNA determines your entire genetic makeup. It is made of organic molecules containing carbon, hydrogen, oxygen, nitrogen, and phosphorus.

Figuring out the complex structure of DNA was one of the greatest scientific challenges of the twentieth century. Instead of forming one chain, like many proteins and polymers, DNA is in the form of paired chains, or strands. It has the shape of a twisted ladder known as a *double helix*.

THE STRUCTURE OF MATTER **135**

Organic and Biochemical Compounds

Teaching Tip

Essential Amino Acids Most of the 20 amino acids needed for protein synthesis are made by the human body. However, eight of them—called essential amino acids—are not. Emphasize the importance of eating foods that contain essential amino acids so that the body has the raw materials that it needs to manufacture needed proteins. Eggs, dairy products, and organ meats, such as kidneys and liver, provide all of the essential amino acids, as do the proper combinations of other high-protein foods.

Multicultural Extension

Hemoglobin is the protein contained in red blood cells that carries oxygen throughout the body. Sickle-cell anemia is a genetic disease that results from damaged hemoglobin genes. The red blood cells of affected persons are rigid and have a crescent shape. As a result, the cells are not flexible enough to pass through narrow capillaries and therefore cause blockages. This disorder occurs most frequently among people of African and Mediterranean descent.

RESOURCE LINK
DATASHEETS

Have students use *Datasheet 4.4 Inquiry Lab: What properties does a polymer have?* to record their results.

IER

Assign students worksheet *4.5 Integrating Math—Amino Acid Combinations.*

Inquiry Lab

What properties does a polymer have?
If time allows, have students repeat the activity to find out what happens if less borax is used. Have students compare the result with their prediction in question 3.

Analysis
1. The material stretches and bounces but keeps its shape.
2. Glue is a liquid that flows easily. The new material has properties that are more like a solid than like a liquid.
3. The properties of the material would be closer to the properties of the glue. The material would flow more easily and would not hold its shape as well.
4. The new material has the properties of a polymer because it is elastic and can return to its original shape.

Organic and Biochemical Compounds

Historical Perspective

Scientists Francis Crick and James Watson determined the structure of DNA and were able to correctly predict how DNA replicates, or copies itself. This discovery has led the way for many genetic engineering applications. For their discovery, Crick and Watson won the 1963 Nobel Prize in chemistry.

SECTION 4.4 REVIEW

Check Your Understanding

1. **a.** alkane
   b. alkane
   c. alkene
   d. alcohol
   e. alkene
   f. alcohol
2. Carbon atoms form four bonds, not five. Bromine atoms form one bond, so a carbon-bromine compound would be CBr_4.
3. Each carbon atom must form four bonds. Each end carbon currently has two bonds, so each must further bond to two hydrogen atoms. The two interior carbon atoms each have three bonds, so each can bond to only one hydrogen atom. The total number of bonded hydrogen atoms is six.

Answers continue on p. 141B.

RESOURCE LINK
STUDY GUIDE

Assign students *Review Section 4.4 Organic and Biochemical Compounds.*

Figure 4-32
In DNA, cytosine, C, always pairs with guanine, G. Adenine, A, always pairs with thymine, T.

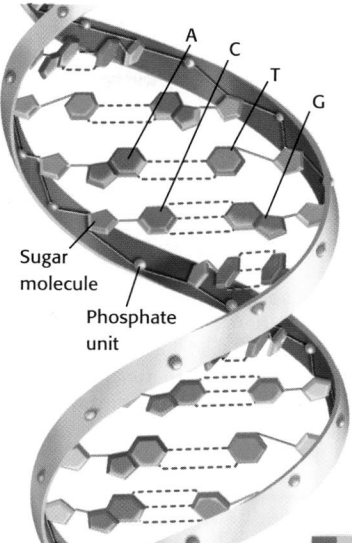

Sugar molecule

Phosphate unit

Your body has many copies of your DNA

Every cell in your body has a copy of your genetic material in the form of chromosomes made of DNA. It is important that DNA has a way of being copied. Copying cannot happen unless the two DNA strands are first separated.

Proteins called helicases unwind DNA by separating the paired strands. Proteins called DNA polymerases then pair up new monomers with those already on the strand. At the end of this process, there are two identical strands of DNA.

DNA's structure resembles a twisted ladder

DNA's structure can be likened to a ladder. Alternating sugar molecules and phosphate units correspond to the ladder's sides, as shown in **Figure 4-32**. Attached to each sugar molecule is one of four possible DNA monomers—adenine, thymine, cytosine, or guanine. These DNA monomers pair up with DNA monomers attached to the opposite strand in a predictable way, as shown in **Figure 4-32.** Together, the DNA monomer pairs make up the rungs of the ladder.

SECTION 4.4 REVIEW

SUMMARY

▶ Alkanes have C–C and C–H bonds.

▶ Alkenes have C=C and C–H bonds.

▶ Alcohols have one or more —OH groups.

▶ Polymers form when small organic molecules bond to form long chains.

▶ Biochemical compounds are polymers important to living things.

▶ Sugars and starches are carbohydrates that provide energy.

▶ Amino acids bond to form polymers called proteins.

▶ DNA is a polymer shaped like a twisted ladder.

CHECK YOUR UNDERSTANDING

1. **Identify** the following compounds as alkanes, alkenes, or alcohols based on their names:
   a. 2-methylpentane   **d.** butanol
   b. 3-methyloctane   **e.** 3-heptene
   c. 1-nonene   **f.** cyclohexanol
2. **Explain** why the compound CBr_5 does not exist. Give an acceptable chemical formula for a compound made of only carbon and bromine.
3. **Determine** how many hydrogen atoms a compound has if it is a hydrocarbon and its carbon atom skeleton is C=C–C=C.
4. **Compare** the structures and properties of carbohydrates with those of proteins.
5. **Identify** which compound is an alkane: CH_2O, C_6H_{14}, or C_3H_4. Explain your reasoning.
6. **Creative Thinking** *Alkynes*, like alkanes and alkenes, are hydrocarbons. Alkynes have carbon-carbon triple covalent bonds, or C≡C bonds. Draw the structure of the alkyne that has the chemical formula C_3H_4. Can you guess the name of this compound? Explain why there aren't any compounds that have C≡C bonds.

Chapter Highlights

Before you begin, review the summaries of the key ideas of each section, found on pages 114, 122, 128, and 136. The key vocabulary terms are listed on pages 108, 115, 123, and 129.

UNDERSTANDING CONCEPTS

1. Which of the following is not true of compounds made of molecules?
   a. They may exist as liquids.
   b. They may exist as solids.
   c. They may exist as gases.
   d. They have very high melting points.
2. Ionic solids _____.
   a. are formed by networks of ions that have the same charge
   b. melt at very low temperatures
   c. have very regular structures
   d. are sometimes found as gases at room temperature
3. A chemical bond can be defined as _____.
   a. a force that joins atoms together
   b. a force blending nuclei together
   c. a force caused by electric repulsion
   d. All of the above
4. Which substance has ionic bonds?
   a. CO   c. KCl
   b. CO_2 d. O_2
5. Covalent bonds _____.
   a. join atoms in some solids, liquids, and gases
   b. usually join one metal atom to another
   c. are always broken when a substance is dissolved in water
   d. join molecules in substances that have molecular structures
6. A compound has an empirical formula CH_2. Its molecular formula could be _____.
   a. CH_2 c. C_4H_8
   b. C_2H_4 d. any of the above

7. The chemical formula for calcium chloride is _____.
   a. CaCl   c. Ca_2Cl
   b. $CaCl_2$ d. Ca_2Cl_2
8. The empirical formula of a molecule _____.
   a. can be used to identify the molecule
   b. is sometimes the same as the molecular formula for the molecule
   c. is used to name the molecule
   d. shows how atoms bond in the molecule
9. All organic compounds _____.
   a. come only from living organisms
   b. contain only carbon and hydrogen
   c. are biochemical compounds
   d. have atoms connected by covalent bonds
10. Which group is not a polymer?
    a. amino acids   c. proteins
    b. carbohydrates   d. plastics

Using Vocabulary

11. Compare the *chemical structure* of oxygen difluoride with that of carbon dioxide. Which compound has the larger *bond angle*? What kind of bonds do both compounds have?

 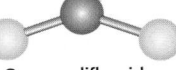

Carbon dioxide   Oxygen difluoride

12. Determine whether the *chemical formula* $C_5H_5N_5$ is the *empirical formula* or *molecular formula* for adenine.
13. Name the following *covalent* compounds:
    a. SF_4 c. PCl_3
    b. N_2O d. P_2O_5
14. Compare the *metallic bonds* of copper with the *ionic bonds* of copper sulfide. Why are metals rather than ionic solids used in electrical wiring?
15. Explain why *proteins* and *carbohydrates* are *polymers*. What is each polymer made of?

THE STRUCTURE OF MATTER **137**

UNDERSTANDING CONCEPTS

1. d	6. d
2. c	7. b
3. a	8. b
4. c	9. d
5. a	10. a

Using Vocabulary

11. Both compounds have two identical atoms covalently bonded to a central atom of a different element. Carbon dioxide has the larger bond angle.
12. molecular formula
13. a. sulfur tetrafluoride
    b. dinitrogen monoxide
    c. phosphorus trichloride
    d. diphosphorus pentoxide
14. Metallic bonds are flexible so that metals can be bent and stretched, while ionic bonds are not flexible. Charges are free to move in a metal when it is solid, but the charges are held in place in an ionic solid. Metals are used in wiring because a solid that carries electrical current is needed.
15. Proteins and most carbohydrates are made from many smaller molecules, or monomers, joined together. The monomers for proteins are amino acids, and glucose is the monomer for carbohydrates that are polymers.

RESOURCE LINK
STUDY GUIDE

Assign students *Mixed Review Chapter 4*.

BUILDING MATH SKILLS

16. Graph C accurately shows the relationship between bond length and bond energy: the shorter the bond length, the greater the bond energy. Graph A incorrectly illustrates that the longer the bond length, the greater the bond energy. Graph B incorrectly illustrates that both short and long bonds have high bond energy, while the relative middle bond length has the lowest bond energy.

17. **a.** The melting point of the compound increases as the atomic mass of the cation increases.
    b. $BeCl_2$ is an ionic compound because it has a relatively high melting point and is a compound of a metal and a nonmetal.
    c. Radium is in the same family as the other cations, and it has a larger atomic mass. Therefore, the melting point will be higher, somewhat over 1000°C.

18. **a.** $Sr(NO_3)_2$
    b. NaCN
    c. $Cr(OH)_3$
    d. AlN
    e. SnF_2
    f. K_2SO_4

THINKING CRITICALLY

19. Because it is a solid at room temperature, is only able to conduct electricity in the liquid state, and has a high melting point, this compound probably has ionic bonds.
20. *See p. 141B.*

BUILDING MATH SKILLS

16. **Graphing** Which of the graphs below shows how bond length and bond energy are related? Describe the flawed relationships shown by each of the other graphs.

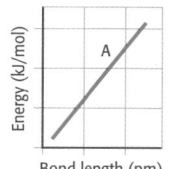 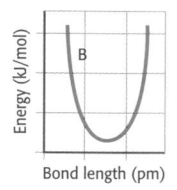 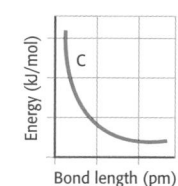

17. **Graphing** The melting points of elements in the same group of the periodic table follow a pattern. A similar pattern is also seen among the melting points of ionic compounds when the cations are made from elements that are in the same group. To see this, plot the melting point of each of the ionic compounds in the table below on the y-axis and the average atomic mass of the element that the cation is made from on the x-axis.
    a. What trend do you notice in the melting points as you move down Group 2?
    b. $BeCl_2$ has a melting point of 405°C. Is this likely to be an ionic compound like the others? Explain. (**Hint:** Locate beryllium in the periodic table.)
    c. Predict the melting point of the ionic compound $RaCl_2$. (**Hint:** Check the periodic table, and compare radium's location with the location of magnesium, calcium, strontium, and barium.)

Compound	Melting point (°C)
$MgCl_2$	712
$CaCl_2$	772
$SrCl_2$	868
$BaCl_2$	963

18. **Writing Ionic Formulas** Determine the chemical formula for each of the following ionic compounds:
    a. strontium nitrate, an ingredient in some fireworks, signal flares, and matches
    b. sodium cyanide, a compound used in electroplating and treating metals
    c. chromium(III) hydroxide, a compound used to tan and dye substances
    d. aluminum nitride, a compound used in the computer-chip-making process
    e. tin(II) fluoride, the source of fluoride for many toothpastes
    f. potassium sulfate, a compound used in the glass-making process

THINKING CRITICALLY

19. **Evaluating Data** A substance is a solid at room temperature. It is unable to conduct electricity as a solid but can conduct electricity as a liquid. This compound melts at 755°C. Would you expect this compound to have ionic, metallic, or covalent bonds?

20. **Creative Thinking** Dodecane is a combustible organic compound used in jet fuel research. It is an n-alkane made of 12 carbon atoms. How many hydrogen atoms does dodecane have? Draw the structural formula for dodecane.

21. **Applying Knowledge** The length of a bond depends upon its type. Predict the relative lengths of the carbon-carbon bonds in the following molecules, and explain your reasoning.

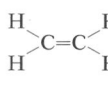

Ethane

Ethene

Ethyne

DEVELOPING LIFE/WORK SKILLS

22. Influencing Others To get crystals to grow from a mixture of dissolved solid and liquid, a small piece of the solid being grown is sometimes added. The added solid is called a seed crystal. As crystals grow, the mixture must not be disturbed. If it is, the crystals that grow are often small and oddly shaped. Pretend you are starting a small business that sells seed crystals to chemists. Design a brochure to promote your product. In your brochure, discuss why chemists should buy your seed crystals instead of a competitor's.

23. Working Cooperatively For one day, write down all of the ionic compounds listed on the labels of the foods you eat. Also write down the approximate mass you eat of each compound. As a class, make a master list in the form of a computer spreadsheet that includes all of the ionic compounds eaten by the whole class. Identify which compounds were eaten by the most people. Together, create a poster describing the dietary guidelines for the ionic compound that was eaten most often.

24. Making Decisions People on low-sodium diets must limit their intake of table salt. Luckily, there are salt substitutes that do not contain sodium. Research different kinds of salt substitutes, and describe how each one affects your body. Determine which salt substitute you would use if you were on a low-sodium diet.

25. Locating Information Numerical recycling codes identify the composition of a plastic so that it can be sorted and recycled. For each of the recycling codes, 1–6, identify the plastic, its physical properties, and at least one product made of this plastic.

INTEGRATING CONCEPTS

26. Concept Mapping Copy the unfinished concept map below onto a sheet of paper. Complete the map by writing the correct word or phrase in the lettered boxes.

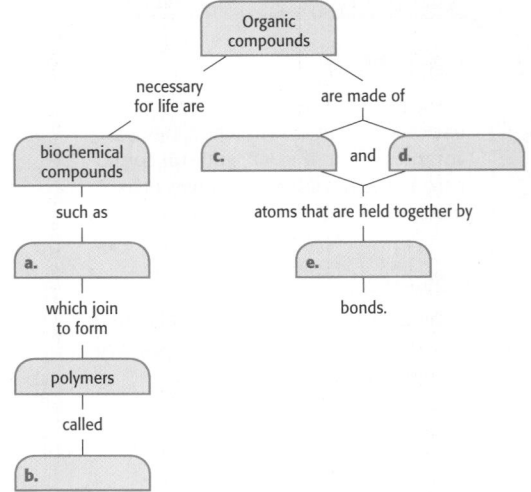

27. Connection to Health The figure below shows how atoms are bonded in a molecule of vitamin C. Which elements is vitamin C made of? What is its molecular formula? Write a paragraph explaining some of the health benefits of taking vitamin C supplements.

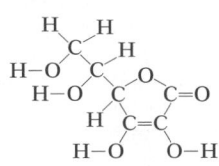

TOPIC: Vitamin C
GO TO: www.scilinks.org
KEYWORD: HK1046

THE STRUCTURE OF MATTER **139**

21. Relatively, bond length increases from ethyne to ethene and from ethene to ethane. In the multiple bonds, more electrons are shared between the two carbon atoms, so the bonds are shorter.

DEVELOPING LIFE/ WORK SKILLS

22. Check brochures for scientific accuracy. Brochures should include that as water evaporates from the solution containing the compound, ions will deposit on the seed crystal, adding to the network structure of ions already there.

23. Answers will vary. Sodium chloride (table salt) probably will be the most common compound. Posters for table salt should include the recommended dietary intake and emphasize that some salt is needed but too much should be avoided.

24. Answers will vary. Many salt substitutes contain KCl. Students who choose to discuss this substance should research the critical Na^+/K^+ balance in the body to learn why excess use of KCl can be dangerous. MSG is not strictly a salt substitute because it, too, contributes sodium ions to the diet.

Answers continue on p. 141B.

Skill Builder Lab

Comparing Polymers

Introduction

Review the material on polymers in Chapter 4. Be certain students understand the differences between a monomer and a polymer. Be sure to relate the properties of polymers, such as strength, flexibility, and elasticity, to the nature of the covalent bonds holding them together.

Objectives

Students will:

▶ **Synthesize** two different polymers, **shape** each into a ball, and **measure** how high each ball bounces.

▶ **Evaluate** which polymer would make a better toy ball.

Planning

Recommended time: 1 lab period
Materials: *(for each lab group)*

▶ liquid latex
▶ 5 percent acetic acid solution (vinegar)
▶ 50 percent ethanol solution
▶ sodium silicate solution
▶ deionized water
▶ 2 L container
▶ 25 mL graduated cylinders
▶ 10 mL graduated cylinder
▶ 2 medium-sized paper cups
▶ 2 wooden craft sticks
▶ paper towels
▶ meterstick

Skill Builder Lab

Introduction

Many polymers are able to "bounce back" after they are stretched, bent, or compressed. In this lab, you will compare the bounce heights of two balls made from different polymers.

Objectives

▶ **Synthesize** two different polymers, **shape** each into a ball, and **measure** how high each ball bounces.

▶ **Evaluate** which polymer would make a better toy ball.

Materials

liquid latex
5 percent acetic acid solution (vinegar)
50 percent ethanol solution
sodium silicate solution
deionized water
2 L container
25 mL graduated cylinders (2)
10 mL graduated cylinder
2 medium-sized paper cups
2 wooden craft sticks
paper towels
meterstick

Safety Needs

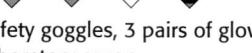

safety goggles, 3 pairs of gloves
laboratory apron

Comparing Polymers

▶ Preparing for Your Experiment

1. Prepare a data table in your lab report similar to the one shown at right.

▶ Making Latex Rubber

SAFETY CAUTION If you get a chemical on your skin or clothing, wash it off with lukewarm water while calling to your teacher. If you get a chemical in your eyes, flush it out immediately at the eyewash station and alert your teacher.

2. Pour 1 L of deionized water into a 2 L container.

3. Use a 25 mL graduated cylinder to pour 10 mL of liquid latex into one of the paper cups.

4. Clean the graduated cylinder thoroughly with soap and water, then rinse it with deionized water and use it to add 10 mL of deionized water to the liquid latex.

5. Use the same graduated cylinder to add 10 mL of acetic acid solution to the liquid latex-water mixture.

6. Stir the mixture with a wooden craft stick. As you stir, a "lump" of the polymer will form around the stick.

7. Transfer the stick and the attached polymer to the 2 L container. While keeping the polymer underwater, gently pull it off the stick with your gloved hands.

8. Squeeze the polymer underwater to remove any unreacted chemicals, shape it into a ball, and remove the ball from the water.

9. Make the ball smooth by rolling it between your gloved hands. Set the ball on a paper towel to dry while you continue with the next part of the lab.

Bounce Heights of Polymers

Polymer	Bounce height (cm)					
	Trial 1	Trial 2	Trial 3	Trial 4	Trial 5	Average
Latex rubber						
Ethanol-silicate						

10. Wash your gloved hands with soap and water, then remove the gloves and dispose of them. Wash your hands again with soap and water.

▶ Making an Ethanol-silicate Polymer

SAFETY CAUTION Put on a fresh pair of gloves. Ethanol is flammable, so make sure there are no flames or other heat sources anywhere in the laboratory.

11. Use a clean 25 mL graduated cylinder to pour 12 mL of sodium silicate solution into the clean paper cup.
12. Use a 10 mL graduated cylinder to add 3 mL of the ethanol solution to the sodium silicate solution.
13. Stir the mixture with the clean wooden craft stick until a solid polymer forms.
14. Remove the polymer with your gloved hands, and gently press it between your palms until you form a ball that does not crumble. This activity may take some time. Occasionally dripping some tap water on the polymer might be helpful.
15. When the ball no longer crumbles, dry it very gently with a paper towel.
16. Repeat step 10, and put on a fresh pair of gloves.
17. Examine both polymers closely. Record in your lab report how the two polymers are alike and how they are different.
18. Use a meterstick to measure the highest bounce height of each ball when each is dropped from a height of 1 m. Drop each ball five times, and record the highest bounce height each time in your data table.

▶ Analyzing Your Results

1. Calculate the average bounce height for each ball by adding the five bounce heights and dividing by 5. Record the averages in your data table.
2. Based on only their bounce heights, which polymer would make a better toy ball?

▶ Defending Your Conclusions

3. Suppose that making a latex rubber ball costs 22 cents and that making an ethanol-silicate ball costs 25 cents. Does this fact affect your conclusion about which polymer would make a better toy ball? Besides cost, what are other important factors that should be considered?

Pre-Lab
Teaching Tips

Ethanol is flammable, so make sure no heat sources are present.

Sodium silicate can irritate if it comes into contact with the skin. Caution students to immediately wash off the affected area with soap and water and to remove contaminated clothing. If inhaled, sodium silicate can irritate the upper respiratory tract. If a student inhales sodium silicate, immediately excuse the student to get fresh air.

Procedure

▶Designing Your Experiment

Students can use either deionized or distilled water when making the polymers.

Show students how to roll the latex and the ethanol-silicate polymer into a ball. Students will have difficulty making a perfect sphere, but they should try to make it as regular as possible. The more irregular the shape is, the more difficulty students will have determining the bounce height because the ball will not bounce straight up.

Remind students to be patient with the ethanol-silicate polymer, which tends to crumble. If it crumbles too much, a few drops of water will rehydrate it so that it can be reshaped into a ball.

Continue on page 141A.

REQUIRED PRECAUTIONS

▶ Read all safety cautions, and discuss them with students. Excuse any student with latex allergies from this experiment.

▶ Wear safety goggles and a lab apron during the lab. Make sure students wear gloves throughout the lab and that they put on fresh gloves when the procedure tells them to.

▶ Be sure to have an MSDS for each of the following chemicals: acetic acid, liquid latex, ethanol, and sodium silicate.

▶ Promptly clean up all spills with paper towels.

▶ Keep the alcohol in a hood, use a container with a lid, and restrict the amount kept in the hood to the minimum needed by students.

▶ Do not allow students to take any ethanol-silicate polymer from the laboratory.

CONTINUATION OF ANSWERS

Skill Builder Lab from page 141
Comparing Polymers

Post-Lab

▶ Disposal

Paper cups, paper towels, disposable gloves, latex, and ethanol-silicate polymer balls and fragments should be thrown in the trash can. Waste liquids from this lab can be poured down the drain.

▶ Analyzing Your Results

1. Student answers will vary.
2. Student answers will vary depending on the measured bounce heights, but the ethanol-silicate polymer tends to bounce higher than the latex rubber.

▶ Defending Your Conclusions

3. Student answers will vary. The lower production cost of toy balls made of latex rubber compared with toy balls made of the ethanol-silicate polymer is a factor in determining which polymer would make a better toy ball. Other important factors that should be considered include texture of the polymer and how well the polymer resists crumbling.

Answers from page 114

SECTION 4.1 REVIEW

4. Molecules in a liquid, such as C_3H_8O, have a greater attraction for each other because they are closer together and are moving more slowly than the molecules in a gas, such as CH_4.
5. SiO_2 has a network structure, resulting in a high melting point. So it does not melt when heated to high cooking temperatures.
6. Because of its low melting point, it is probably a gas at room temperature.
7. Sulfur atoms are larger than oxygen atoms by one electron energy level. Their valence electrons are farther from the nucleus, so the nucleus-to-nucleus distance is greater.

Answers from page 122

SECTION 4.4 REVIEW

8. Nitrogen has greater bond energy. It takes more energy to break the three bonds in a nitrogen molecule than it takes to break the two bonds in an oxygen molecule.

Answers from page 136

4. Carbohydrates contain H, C, and O and may or may not be polymers. Proteins contain H, C, O, N, and S and are polymers of amino acids. In the human body, carbohydrates provide energy, and proteins provide the amino acids needed to create new proteins. Polymers of both are broken down into their monomers before they can be used.

5. An alkane has the general formula C_nH_{2n+2} and contains only H and C. C_6H_{14} is the alkane.

6.
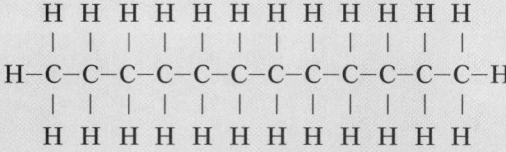

Because the compound has three carbon atoms *(pro-)* and is an alkyne *(-yne)*, the compound is propyne. If one carbon atom could share four bonds with another carbon atom, together they would form a molecular element with no lone pairs of electrons with which to bond to an atom of another element.

Answers from page 138

20. The general formula for *n*-alkanes is C_nH_{2n+2}. With *n*=12, dodecane must have 2(12)+2, or 26 hydrogen atoms.

```
    H H H H H H H H H H H H
    | | | | | | | | | | | |
H−C−C−C−C−C−C−C−C−C−C−C−C−H
    | | | | | | | | | | | |
    H H H H H H H H H H H H
```

Answers from page 139

25. code 1: PETE (polyethylene terephthalate), somewhat flexible and easily molded, soft-drink bottles; code 2: HDPE (high-density polyethylene), rigid but easily molded, milk containers; code 3: V (polyvinyl chloride), flexible but strong, garden hoses; code 4: LDPE (low-density polyethylene), rigid, cottage cheese containers; code 5: PP (polypropylene), somewhat rigid, shampoo bottles; code 6: PS (polystyrene), lightweight because it contains bubbles of air, foam cups and plates

26. **a.** amino acids
    b. proteins
    c. carbon
    d. hydrogen
    e. covalent

27. Vitamin C is made of carbon, hydrogen, and oxygen atoms. Its formula is $C_6H_8O_6$. Linus Pauling advocated large doses of vitamin C to treat the common cold and other conditions and diseases, such as cancer. Little scientific evidence supports his findings.

Analytical Chemist

CareerLink

LINKING CHAPTERS

Analytical chemists use the properties of matter to identify unknown materials. These properties of matter, from density to atomic structure and bonding, were studied in Chapters 2–4.

SKILL BUILDER

Vocabulary The word *analytical* is related to the word *analyze.* The Greek roots of the word are *ana* and *lysis,* meaning "loosen up," as in loosening a knot.

Analytical Chemist

Have you ever looked at something and wondered what chemicals it contained? That's what analytical chemists do for a living. They use a range of tests to determine the chemical makeup of a sample. To find out more about analytical chemistry as a career, read the interview with analytical chemist Roberta Jordan, who works at the Idaho National Engineering and Environmental Laboratory, in Idaho Falls, Idaho.

In addition to working as an analytical chemist, Roberta Jordan mentors students regularly in the local schools.

"Chemistry is in everything we do. Just to take a breath and eat a meal involves chemistry."

 What is your work as an analytical chemist like?

We deal with radioactive waste generated by old nuclear power plants and old submarines, and we try to find a safe way to store the waste. I'm more like a consultant. A group of engineers that are working on a process will come to me. I tell them what things they need to analyze for and why they need to do that. On the flip side, I'll tell them what techniques they need to use.

 What do you like best about your work?

It forces me to stay current with any new techniques, new areas that are going on in analytical chemistry. And I like the team approach because it allows me to work on different projects.

 What do you find most interesting about your work?

Probably the most interesting thing is to observe how different industries and different labs conduct business. It gives you a broad feel for how chemistry is done.

What qualities does a good chemist need?

I think you do need to be good at science and math and to like those subjects. You need to be fairly detail-oriented. You have to be precise. You need to be analytical in general, and you need to be meticulous.

What part of your education do you think was most valuable?

I think it was worthwhile spending a lot of energy on my lab work. With any science, the most important part is the laboratory experience, when you are applying those theories that you learn. I'm really a proponent of being involved in science-fair activities.

What advice do you have for students who are interested in analytical chemistry?

It's worthwhile to go to the career center or library and do a little research. Take the time to find out what kinds of things you could do with your degree. You need to talk to people who have a degree in that field.

Do you think chemistry has a bright future?

I think that there are a lot of things out there that need to be discovered. My advice is to go for it and don't think that everything we need to know has been discovered. Twenty to thirty years down the road, we will have to think of a new energy source, for example.

internetconnect

SCi**LINKS**
NSTA

TOPIC: Analytical chemistry
GO TO: www.scilinks.org
KEYWORD: HK1499

"One of the things necessary to be a good chemist is you have to be creative. You have to be able to think above and beyond the normal way of doing things to come up with new ideas, new experiments."
—ROBERTA JORDAN

Historical Perspective

Originally, analytical chemists worked using tests in which they reacted the unknown substance with other substances. These methods often involved changing the original sample.

In the last 50 years, the field of instrumental analysis (in which instruments are used to analyze substances) has grown. Many of these instruments, such as infrared spectrophotometers and nuclear magnetic resonance spectrometers, are able to analyze a substance without changing it chemically.

Changes in Matter

Did You Know?

Fireworks manufacturers can use a variety of compounds to produce different colors. Strontium compounds produce red light, aluminum compounds produce bright white light, barium compounds produce green light, and sodium compounds produce yellow light. Fireworks manufacturers are constantly striving to produce intense colors; blue is one of the most difficult colors to achieve. Although some copper compounds can produce blue light, they are unstable at the high temperatures found in an exploding firework.

MISCONCEPTION

Chemical Changes ALERT

Many students do not yet understand that the basic parts of matter are not changed during reactions but merely rearranged. Students may believe that when the appearance of matter changes due to a reaction, its atoms have mysteriously changed into other types of atoms.

|SKILL BUILDER

Interpreting Visuals Ask students to explain how the picture relates to the unit's title. Students may associate fireworks with light and energy instead of matter.

Guide students in a discussion to recognize that the light and energy displayed during a fireworks show is caused by the matter that makes up the fireworks. Some students will have seen fireworks before and will remember that they contain chemicals.

145

CHAPTER 5

Chemical Reactions

Annotated Descriptions of the Correlated National Science Standards

The following descriptions summarize the National Science Standards that specially relate to Chapter 5. For the full text of the Standards, see p. 40T.

SECTION 5.1
The Nature of Chemical Reactions
Physical Science
PS 3a, 3b
Life Science
LS 5b
Unifying Concepts and Processes
UCP 1, 2

SECTION 5.2
Reaction Types
Physical Science
PS 3c
Unifying Concepts and Processes
UCP 1, 2

SECTION 5.3
Balancing Chemical Equations
Science as Inquiry
SAI 1

SECTION 5.4
Rates of Change
Physical Science
PS 3d, 3e
Life Science
LS 4a
Unifying Concepts and Processes
UCP 1, 2, 5
Science in Personal and Social Perspectives
SPSP 2

Cross-Discipline Teaching RESOURCES

Cross-Discipline Teaching, ATE p. 146
Physical Education   Mathematics

Integration Enrichment Resources
Real World Applications, **PE** and **ATE** p. 151
  IE 5.1 *Hot Meals on Hand*
Biology, **PE** and **ATE** p. 153
  IE 5.2 *Organisms That Glow*
Earth Science, **PE** and **ATE** p. 156
  IE 5.3 *Limestone Reactions*
Fine Arts, **PE** and **ATE** p. 159
  IE 5.4 *The Chemistry of Art*
Social Studies, **PE** and **ATE** p. 163
  IE 5.5 *Fireworks*
Science and the Consumer, **PE** and **ATE** p. 164
  IE 5.6 *The Right Fire Extinguisher for the Job*
Environmental Science, **PE** and **ATE** p. 175
  IE 5.7 *Fertilizers*

Additional Integration Enrichment Worksheets
  IE 5.8 Social Studies

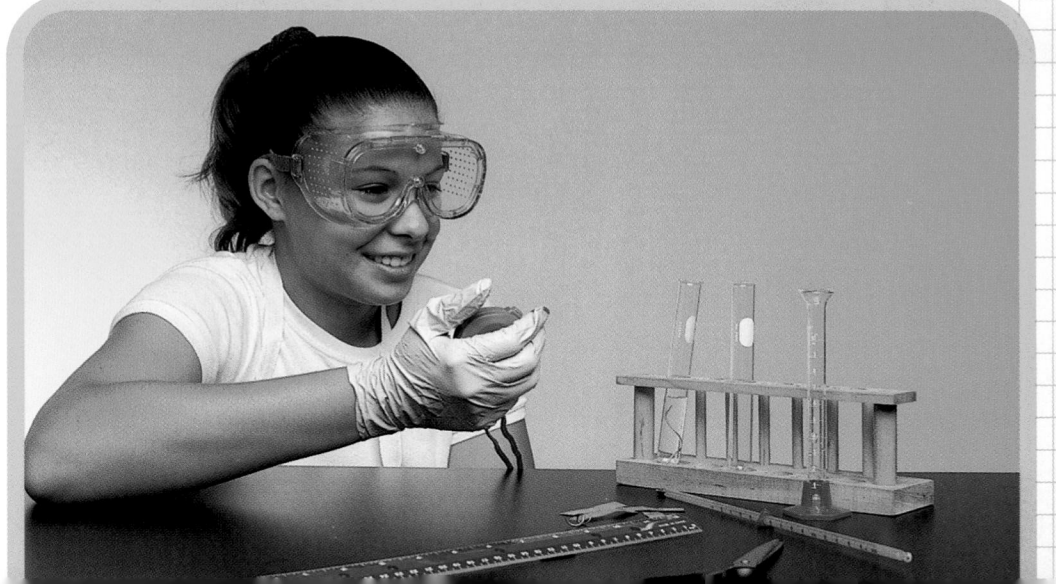

> *Use the Planning Guide on the next page to help you organize your lessons.*

MATH AND COMPUTER RESOURCES

Chapter 5	Math Skills	Assess	Media/Computer Skills
Section 5.1	**ATE** Cross-Discipline Teaching, p. 146		■ Section 5.1
Section 5.2			■ Section 5.2
Section 5.3	**PE** Math Skills Balancing Chemical Equations, p. 165 **ATE** Additional Examples p. 166 **BS** Worksheet 3.3 Balancing Chemical Equations **BS** Worksheet 3.1 Ratios and Proportions	**PE** Practice, p. 166 **MS** Worksheet 10 **PE** Building Math Skills, p. 178, items 16-20 **PE** Problem Bank, p. 695, 46–50	■ Section 5.3 💿 *DISC ONE, MODULE 5* Chemical Equations **PE** Chapter Review, item 22, p. 179
Section 5.4		**PE** Building Math Skills, p. 178, item 15	■ Section 5.4

PE Pupil's Edition   **ATE** Annotated Teacher's Edition   **MS** Math Skills   **BS** Basic Skills
IE Integration Enrichment   ■ Guided Reading Audio   **CRT** Critical Thinking   PHYSICAL SCIENCE INTERACTIVE TUTOR

READING SKILL BUILDER

The following activities found in the Annotated Teacher's Edition provide techniques for developing useful reading strategies to increase your students' reading comprehension skills.

Section 5.1   **Brainstorming,** p. 146
              Prediction Guide, pp. 148, 152

Section 5.2   **Reading Organizer,** p. 154

Section 5.3   **Reading Hint,** p. 161

Section 5.4   **Paired Reading,** p. 169

Smithsonian Institution®

Visit www.si.edu/hrw for additional online resources.

Spanish Resources

The following resources are made available for students who speak Spanish as their first language.

Spanish Resources
Guided Reading Audio CD-ROM
Chapter 5

Spanish Glossary
Chapter 5

Chemical Reactions

CLASSROOM RESOURCES

FOCUS	TEACH	HANDS-ON
Section 5.1: The Nature of Chemical Reactions		
BLOCK 1 45 minutes	**ATE RSB** Brainstorming, p. 146 **ATE RSB** Prediction Guide, p. 148 **ATE** Focus Activities 1, 2, p. 147 **PE** Reactions, pp. 148–149 ★ Focus Transparency LT 15 **ATE Demo 1** Reaction or Not?, p. 148	**ATE Skill Builder** Interpreting Visuals, pp. 147–148	**IE** Worksheet 5.8
BLOCK 2 45 minutes	**ATE RSB** Prediction Guide, p. 152 **PE** Energy, pp. 149–153 **ATE Demo 2** Lemon Cell, p. 150	**ATE Skill Builder** Graphs, p. 152 **TT** 14 Reaction Model **BLM** 16 Exothermic and Endothermic	**PE** Real World Applications *Self-Heating Meals,* p. 151 **IE** Worksheets 5.1, 5.2
Section 5.2: Reaction Types		
BLOCK 3 45 minutes	**ATE RSB** Reading Organizer, p. 154 **ATE Demo 3** Synthesis Reaction, p. 154 **PE** Classifying Reactions, pp. 154–158 ★ Focus Transparency LT 16	**TT** 15 Single-Displacement	**IE** Worksheet 5.3
BLOCK 4 45 minutes	**PE** Electrons and Chemical Reactions, pp. 159–160		**IE** Worksheet 5.4
Section 5.3: Balancing Chemical Equations		
BLOCK 5 45 minutes	**ATE RSB** Reading Hint, p. 161 **ATE Demo 4** A Balancing Act, p. 161 **PE** Describing Reactions, pp. 161–165 ★ Focus Transparency LT 17		**IE** Worksheets 5.5, 5.6 **PE** Science and the Consumer *Fire Extinguishers: Are They All the Same?* p. 164
BLOCK 6 45 minutes	**PE** Determining Mole Ratios, pp. 166–168	**BLM** 17 Balanced Equation	**PE** Quick Activity *Candy Chemistry,* p. 166 **DS** 5.1 **PE** Inquiry Lab *Can you write balanced chemical equations?* p. 167 **DS** 5.2
Section 5.4: Rates of Change		
BLOCK 7 45 minutes	**ATE RSB** Paired Reading, p. 169 **ATE Demo 5** Surface Area, p. 169 **ATE Demo 6** Dissolving, p. 170 **PE** Reaction Rates, pp. 169–172 ★ Focus Transparency LT 18	**ATE Graphic Organizer** Rate of Reaction, p. 171 **ATE Skill Builder** Interpreting Visuals, p. 171	**PE** Inquiry Lab *What affects the rate of chemical reactions?* p. 172 **DS** 5.3 **LE 5** *Investigating the Effect of Temperature on Reaction Rate* **DS** 5.6
BLOCK 8 45 minutes	**PE** Equilibrium Systems, pp. 173–176	**ATE Skill Builder** Vocabulary, p. 174 **TT** 16 Equilibrium **BLM** 18 Changing Equilibrium	**PE** Quick Activity *Catalysts in Action,* p. 173 **DS** 5.4 **IE** Worksheet 5.7 **PE** Design Your Own Lab *Measuring the Rate of a Chemical Reaction,* p. 180 **DS** 5.5

CLASSROOM RESOURCES

HOMEWORK	ASSESS
PE Section Review 1, 2, 4, p. 153 **Chapter 5 Review,** p. 177, item 1	**SG** Chapter 5 Pretest
PE Section Review 3, 5, 6, p. 153 **Chapter 5 Review,** p. 177, items 2, 12	**SG** Section 5.1
PE Section Review 1, 4–8, p. 160 **Chapter 5 Review,** p. 177, items 3, 6, 13	**ATE** *ALTERNATIVE ASSESSMENT,* Carbon Monoxide, p. 156
PE Section Review 2, 3, p. 160 **Chapter 5 Review,** p. 177, items 4, 5	**ATE** *ALTERNATIVE ASSESSMENT,* Oxidation and Reduction, p. 159 **SG** Section 5.2
PE Section Review 1–3, p. 168 **Chapter 5 Review,** p. 177, items 7, 20	**ATE** *ALTERNATIVE ASSESSMENT,* Balanced Chemical Equations, p. 162
PE Section Review 4, 5, p. 168 **Chapter 5 Review,** p. 177, items 16–19	**ATE** *ALTERNATIVE ASSESSMENT,* Coefficients, p. 165 **SG** Section 5.3
PE Section Review 2, 4, 6, p. 176 **Chapter 5 Review,** p. 177, items 9, 15	
PE Section Review 1, 3, 5, 7, 8, p. 176 **Chapter 5 Review,** p. 177, items 8, 10, 11, 14	**ATE** *ALTERNATIVE ASSESSMENT,* Chemical Equilibrium, p. 174 **SG** Section 5.4

REVIEW AND ASSESS

BLOCK 9

Chapter 5 Review
Thinking Critically 21–23, p. 179
Developing Life/Work Skills 24–25, p. 179
Integrating Concepts 26, p. 179
SG Chapter 5 Mixed Review

BLOCK 10

Chapter Tests
Holt Science Spectrum: A Physical Approach
Chapter 5 Test

One-Stop Planner CD-ROM with Test Generator
Holt Science Spectrum Test Generator
FOR MACINTOSH AND WINDOWS
Chapter 5

Teaching Resources
Scoring Rubrics and assignment evaluation checklist.

 internet**connect**

SCI**LINKS**
NSTA

National Science Teachers Association
Online Resources:
www.scilinks.org

The following *sci*LINKS Internet resources can be found in the student text for this chapter.

Page 147 **TOPIC:** Fuels **KEYWORD:** HK1051	**Page 169** **TOPIC:** Factors affecting reaction rate **KEYWORD:** HK1054
Page 151 **TOPIC:** Corrosion **KEYWORD:** HK1052	**Page 171** **TOPIC:** Catalysts **KEYWORD:** HK1055
Page 155 **TOPIC:** Types of reactions **KEYWORD:** HK1053	**Page 179** **TOPIC:** Biodegradable **KEYWORD:** HK1056
Page 164 **TOPIC:** Fire extinguishers **KEYWORD:** HK1057	

CNNfyi.com   www.cnnfyi.com

Visit this site for coverage of current events and related classroom resources.

PE Pupil's Edition   **ATE** Teacher's Edition
RSB Reading Skill Builder   **DS** Datasheets
IE Integrated Enrichment   **SG** Study Guide
LE Laboratory Experiments
TT Teaching Transparencies   **BLM** Blackline Masters
★ Lesson Focus Transparency

Chemical Reactions

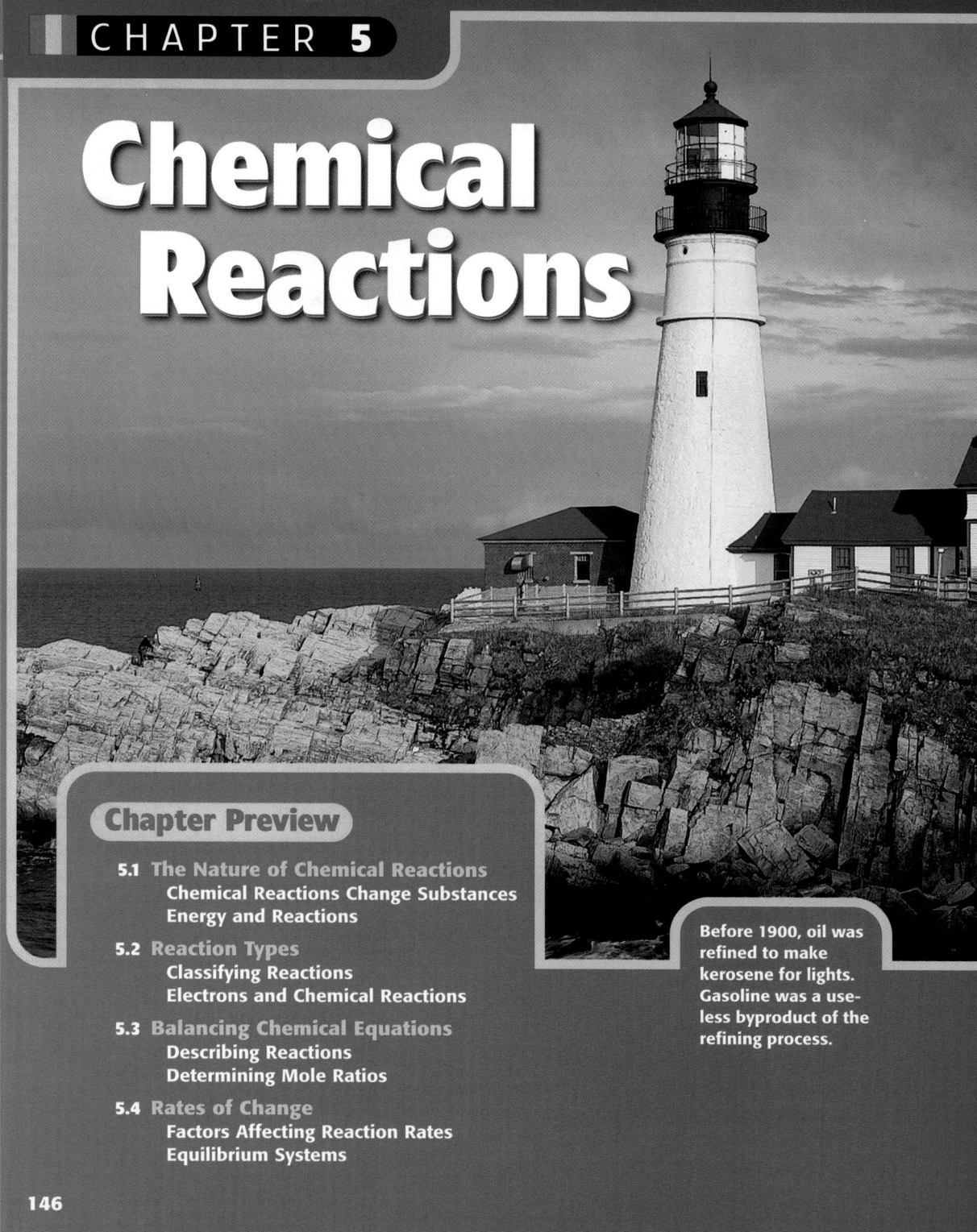

Before 1900, oil was refined to make kerosene for lights. Gasoline was a useless byproduct of the refining process.

146

Tapping Prior Knowledge

Be sure students understand the following concepts:

Chapter 2
Conservation of mass, formulas, chemical changes

Chapter 3
The periodic table, moles, ions, atomic structure, atomic mass

Chapter 4
Chemical structure, bonding, compound names, formulas

READING SKILL BUILDER *Brainstorming*
Have students speculate as to what *reactants* and *products* are. From common usage, they know that *react* indicates action and that a *product* is a result.

RESOURCE LINK
STUDY GUIDE

Assign students *Pretest Chapter 5 Chemical Reactions* before beginning Section 5.1.

CROSS-DISCIPLINE TEACHING

Physical Education   Work with a physical education teacher to emphasize what balance is. Have students walk on a narrow board placed on the floor. Students should notice that they have the greatest balance when their arms are held out the same amount on both sides of their bodies. Ask the physical education teacher to have students do other activities that involve balance.

Mathematics   Review with students how to write and use a ratio, which is a comparison of two numbers. Then have them create a proportion by setting two ratios equal to each other. Show them how to use a proportion to find the value of a variable in the proportion if the other three numbers are known, as in $x/4 = 9/12$; $x = 3$.

Focus ACTIVITY

Background Early in the morning in May 1961, everything was quiet. Then a blindingly bright light flashed. The ground shook. A deafening roar filled the air. A Redstone rocket propelled a Project Mercury capsule toward the sky, and the first United States astronaut, Alan B. Shepard, soared 186 km above Earth's surface.

The Redstone rocket was powered by the chemical reaction that occurs between kerosene and oxygen. Kerosene has been used as a fuel to provide heat and light since the 1860s. The same chemical reaction that provided light from lighthouses and kerosene lamps in the days of the sailing ships was launching the United States manned space program.

These days, the space shuttle, which has a mass of about 2 000 000 kg at liftoff, uses a different chemical reaction. But the chemical reaction that sends the shuttle orbiting is neither exotic nor difficult to understand. It is the reaction between hydrogen and oxygen that yields water.

Activity 1 Kerosene and gasoline are just two of the fuels generally produced from crude oil. Visit a fuel distributor in your community and find out what kinds of fuels are available and what makes them different.

Activity 2 Research the octane rating system for gasolines. Find out what the different octane ratings are and what they mean.

internet**connect**

SC/_LINKS_
NSTA

TOPIC: Fuels
GO TO: www.scilinks.org
KEYWORD: HK1051

147

Focus ACTIVITY

Background Tell students that the same types of changes that release the energy needed to power a rocket also release the energy needed to power the family car. Remind students of the law of conservation of energy that they studied in Chapter 2. Energy is not created to power the rocket or cause the flame in the lamp. The energy released has changed form from another type of energy.

Activity 1 In order of increasing boiling point, fuels include liquified petroleum gas (bottled gas), gasoline, diesel fuel, and fuel oil. All are mixtures of various hydrocarbons. As boiling point increases, so does the size of the hydrocarbon molecules that make up these fuels.

Activity 2 Gasoline is assigned an octane number from 0 to 100 based on how little it explodes suddenly, or "knocks," in an engine. This scale is based on the burning of heptane (0) and isooctane (100). Gasoline with a high octane rating contains more ring and branch structures than does gasoline with a lower octane rating.

|SKILL BUILDER

Interpreting Visuals Have students list things they see in the photos that relate to what they think energy is. Lists might include light from the rocket and the lamp. The rocket is in motion. Although students cannot see it, they might also infer that heat is given off. In this chapter students will learn how energy is released by chemical change.

Scheduling

Refer to pp. 146A–146D for lecture, classwork, and assignment options for Section 5.1.

★ **Lesson Focus**
Use transparency *LT 15* to prepare students for this section.

READING SKILL BUILDER *Prediction Guide* Write the following assertions on the chalkboard:

- In a chemical reaction, atoms change identity.
- A change of color indicates a chemical reaction.
- All chemical reactions give off energy.

Ask students what their opinion of each statement is, then discuss these opinions in small groups. Keep a list of the opinions for discussion at the end of the section.

SKILL BUILDER

Interpreting Visuals Have students study **Figure 5-1.** Ask them to think of examples of when these signs are present but no chemical reaction occurs. For example, dissolved gas can come out of warm water when it cools, and nuclear reactions or other means that do not involve chemical reactions can produce heat and light. Emphasize that the signs are guidelines, not absolutes.

5.1

The Nature of Chemical Reactions

▶ **KEY TERMS**
reactant
product
chemical energy
exothermic reaction
endothermic reaction

OBJECTIVES

▶ Recognize some signs that a chemical reaction is taking place.
▶ Explain chemical changes in terms of the structure and motion of atoms and molecules.
▶ Describe the differences between endothermic and exothermic reactions.
▶ Identify situations involving chemical energy.

I f someone talks about chemical reactions, you might think about scientists doing experiments in laboratories. But words like *grow, ripen, decay,* and *burn* describe chemical reactions you see every day. Even your own health is due to chemical reactions taking place inside your body. The food you eat reacts with the oxygen you inhale in processes such as respiration and cell growth. The carbon dioxide formed in these reactions is carried to your lungs, and you exhale it into the environment.

Figure 5-1
Signs of a Chemical Reaction

A When the calcium carbonate in a piece of chalk reacts with an acid, bubbles of carbon dioxide gas are given off.

B When solutions of sodium sulfide and cadmium nitrate are mixed, a solid—yellow cadmium sulfide—settles out of the solution.

C When ammonium dichromate decomposes, energy is released as light and heat.

Chemical Reactions Change Substances

When sugar, water, and yeast are mixed into flour to make bread dough, a chemical reaction takes place. The yeast acts on the sugar to form new substances, including carbon dioxide and lactic acid. You know that a chemical reaction has happened because lactic acid and carbon dioxide are different from sugar. For example, sugar tastes sweet and lactic acid tastes sour. Sourdough bread gets its characteristic taste from lactic acid.

Chemical reactions occur when substances undergo chemical changes to form new substances. Often you can tell that a chemical reaction is happening because you will be able to see changes, such as those in **Figure 5-1.**

148 CHAPTER 5

DEMONSTRATION 1 TEACHING

Reaction or Not?

Time: Approximately 15 minutes
Materials: 0.1 M silver nitrate solution, 0.1 M copper(II) nitrate solution, 2 test tubes, test-tube rack, piece of copper metal, piece of silver metal

To prepare 0.1 M silver nitrate solution, dissolve 17 g of solid silver nitrate in 100 mL of distilled water.

SAFETY CAUTION: *Silver nitrate stains clothing and skin.*

To prepare 0.1 M copper(II) nitrate solution, dissolve 19 g of solid copper(II) nitrate in 100 mL of distilled water. If the copper(II) nitrate is hydrated [$Cu(NO_3)_2 \cdot 3H_2O$ instead of $Cu(NO_3)_2$], add 24 g instead of 19 g.

Add silver nitrate solution to one test tube and copper(II) nitrate solution to the other test tube until the test tubes are approximately half full.

Production of gas and change of color are signs of chemical reactions

In bread making, the carbon dioxide gas that is produced expands the dough, causing the bread to rise. This release of gas is a sign that a chemical reaction may be happening.

As the dough bakes, old bonds break and new bonds form. Chemical reactions involving starch and protein make food turn brown when heated. A chemical change happens almost every time there is a change in color.

Chemical reactions rearrange atoms

When gasoline is burned in the engine of a car or boat, a lot of different reactions happen with the compounds that are in the mixture we call gasoline. In a typical reaction, isooctane, C_8H_{18}, and oxygen, O_2, are the **reactants.** They react and form two **products,** carbon dioxide, CO_2, and water, H_2O.

The products and reactants contain the same types of atoms: carbon, hydrogen, and oxygen. New product atoms are not created, and old reactant atoms are not destroyed. Atoms are rearranged as bonds are broken and formed. In all chemical reactions, mass is always conserved, as you learned in Chapter 2.

▶ **reactant** a substance that undergoes a chemical change

▶ **product** a substance that is the result of a chemical change

Energy and Reactions

Filling a car's tank with gasoline would be very dangerous if isooctane and oxygen could not be in the same place without reacting. Like most chemical reactions, the isooctane-oxygen reaction needs energy to get started. A small spark provides enough energy to start the reaction. That is why smoking or having any open flame near a gas pump is not allowed.

Energy must be added to break bonds

In each isooctane molecule, like the one shown in **Figure 5-2,** all the bonds to carbon atoms are covalent. In an oxygen molecule, a double covalent bond holds the two oxygen atoms together. For the atoms in isooctane and oxygen to react, all of these bonds have to be broken. This takes energy.

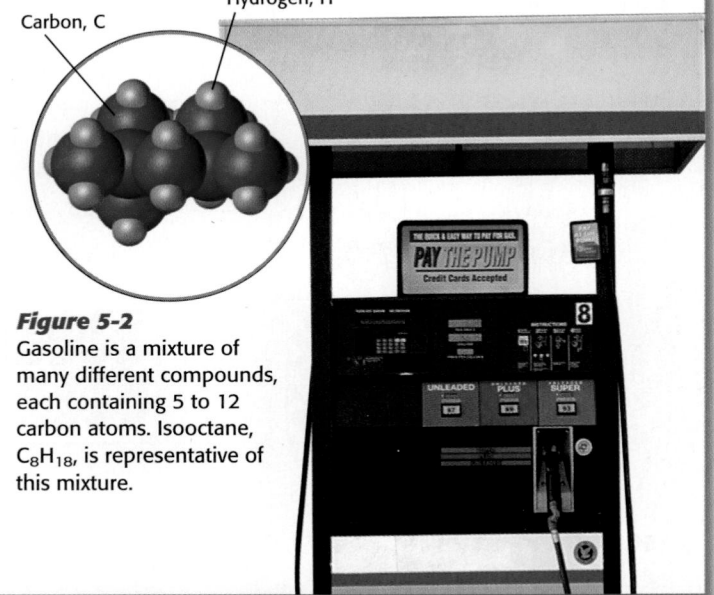

Figure 5-2
Gasoline is a mixture of many different compounds, each containing 5 to 12 carbon atoms. Isooctane, C_8H_{18}, is representative of this mixture.

Teaching Tip

Chemical Reactions Show students several examples of chemical reactions. Include examples of familiar reactions, such as baking soda and vinegar, a cut apple turning brown, or a match burning. For each reaction, have students compare and contrast the appearance of the reactants and the products and note any other signs that a reaction took place, such as the release of bubbles or energy.

Additional Application

Activation Energy Even if a chemical reaction is highly exothermic, energy must be added to start the reaction. This added energy is called activation energy. An example of activation energy is the flame needed to start a newspaper burning. Materials that will burn vary greatly in the amount of activation energy needed to start the reaction. Those materials, such as gasoline, that have low activation energy are considered flammable. Other materials, such as paper, burn but require more energy to start the process. These materials are classified as combustible.

Place the test tubes in the test-tube rack. Add the copper metal to the silver nitrate solution and the silver metal to the copper(II) nitrate solution. Allow the test tubes to remain undisturbed. Observe the results after 15 minutes and then again the next day.

Analysis

1. What did you observe after 15 minutes? *(Crystals of silver appeared on the copper wire in the silver nitrate solution. No change occurred in the other test tube.)*

2. What did you observe the next day? *(More silver appeared. The solution changed from colorless to blue. No change occurred in the other test tube.)*

3. Which combination of substances resulted in a chemical reaction? Which did not? *(Copper and silver nitrate reacted. Silver and copper(II) nitrate did not.)*

4. Do all substances react when they are mixed together? *(no)*

The Nature of Chemical Reactions

Teaching Tip

Voltaic Cells Students are familiar with electricity being produced by a chemical reaction in a device known as a voltaic cell. The two most common types of voltaic cells are the dry cell, such as a flashlight battery, and the wet cell. The reactants in a dry cell vary depending on what type of dry cell it is. The cell contains a shell of some relatively active metal, such as lithium or zinc, and compounds that will react with it. Wet cells are contained in the lead-storage battery that is used in an automobile. It produces electricity by the reaction involving lead, lead(IV) oxide, and sulfuric acid.

MISCONCEPTION

Battery Although **ALERT** a single voltaic cell, such as a dry cell, is commonly called a "battery," a battery is actually formed from several cells operating together as they do in an automobile battery.

LINKING CHAPTERS

Students will learn more about energy transfer when studying heat and temperature in Chapter 10.

Figure 5-3
In photography, light passing through the camera lens causes a chemical reaction on the film. Silver bromide crystals in the gel on the film react to form darker elemental silver, which becomes the negative (A) that is used to make a black and white photograph (B).

A Negative   **B** Photo (positive image)

Many forms of energy can be used to break bonds. Sometimes the energy is transferred as heat, like the spark that starts the isooctane-oxygen reaction. Energy also can be transferred as electricity, sound, or light, as shown in **Figure 5-3.** When molecules collide and enough energy is transferred to separate the atoms, bonds can break.

Forming bonds releases energy

Once enough energy is added to start the isooctane-oxygen reaction, new bonds form to make the products, as shown in **Figure 5-4.** Each carbon dioxide molecule has two oxygen atoms connected to the carbon atom with a double bond. A water molecule is made when two hydrogen atoms each form a single bond with the oxygen atom.

When new bonds form, energy is released. When gasoline burns, energy in the form of heat and light is released as the products of the isooctane-oxygen reaction and other gasoline reactions form. Other chemical reactions can produce electrical energy.

Figure 5-4
The formation of carbon dioxide and water from isooctane and oxygen produces the energy used to power engines.

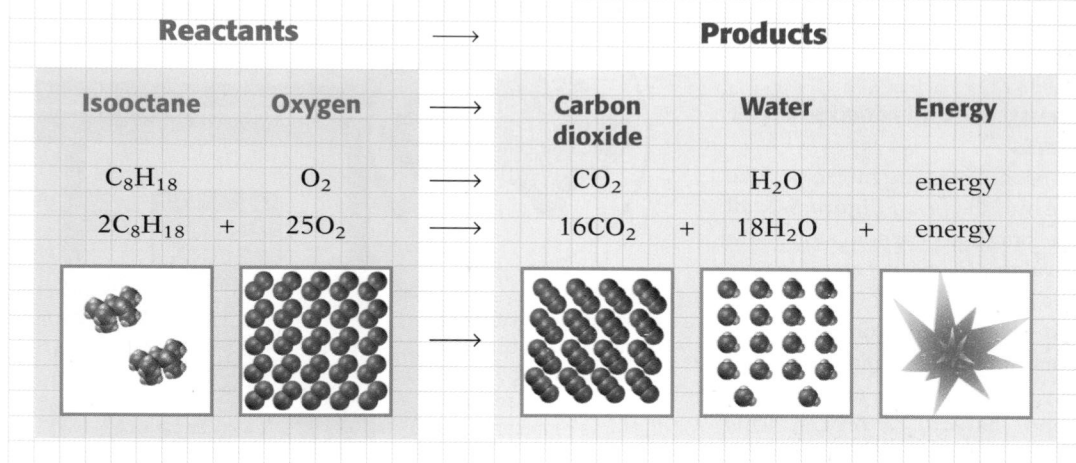

Reactants		→	Products		
Isooctane	Oxygen →		Carbon dioxide	Water	Energy
C_8H_{18}	O_2 →		CO_2	H_2O	energy
$2C_8H_{18}$ +	$25O_2$ →		$16CO_2$ +	$18H_2O$ +	energy

DEMONSTRATION 2 SCIENCE AND THE CONSUMER

Lemon Cell

Time: Approximately 10 minutes
Materials: lemon, iron strip, copper strip, 2 wire leads with alligator clips, voltmeter

Any metallic copper, such as wire or tubing, and iron, such as an iron nail or washer, will work. The metal should be long enough to go into the lemon past the peel.

Because lemons vary in acidity and thickness of the peel, try this demonstration before class to assure that your materials will produce the desired results.

Push the iron strip well into the side of the lemon, near one end, and the copper strip well into the side near the other end. Use the wire leads to attach both metals to the voltmeter. Have students observe the reading on the voltmeter.

If time allows, use four to six such cells to form a battery. Use wire to connect the iron in one

Energy is conserved in chemical reactions

Energy may not appear to be conserved in the isooctane reaction. After all, a tiny spark can set off an explosion. The energy for that explosion comes from the reactants. Often this stored energy is called **chemical energy.** The total energy of isooctane, oxygen, and their surroundings includes this chemical energy. The total energy before the reaction is equal to the total energy of the products and their surroundings.

Reactions that release energy are exothermic

In the isooctane-oxygen reaction, more energy is released as the products form than is absorbed to break the bonds in the reactants. Like all other combustion reactions, this is an **exothermic reaction.** After an exothermic reaction, the temperature of the surroundings rises because energy is released. The released energy comes from the chemical energy of the reactants.

Reactions that absorb energy are endothermic

If you put hydrated barium hydroxide and ammonium nitrate together in a flask, the reaction between them takes so much energy from the surroundings that water in the air will condense and then freeze on the surface of the flask. This is an **endothermic reaction**—more energy is needed to break the bonds in the reactants than is given off by forming bonds in the products.

▶ **chemical energy** the energy stored within atoms and molecules that can be released when a substance reacts

▶ **exothermic reaction** a reaction that transfers energy from the reactants to the surroundings as heat

▶ **endothermic reaction** a reaction in which energy is transferred to the reactants as heat from the surroundings

📷 **internetconnect**

SC**LINKS**
NSTA

TOPIC: Corrosion
GO TO: www.scilinks.org
KEYWORD: HK1052

REAL WORLD APPLICATIONS

Self-Heating Meals

Corrosion, the process by which a metal reacts with the oxygen in air or water, is not often wanted. However, corrosion is encouraged in self-heating meals so that the energy from the exothermic reaction can be used. Self-heating meals, as the name implies, have their own heat source.

Each meal contains a package of precooked food, a bag that holds a porous pad containing a magnesium-iron alloy, and some salt water. When the salt water is poured into the bag, the salt water soaks through the holes in the pad of metal alloy and begins to corrode the metals vigorously. Then the sealed food package is placed in the bag. The exothermic reaction raises the temperature of the food by 38°C in 14 minutes.

Applying Information

1. List some people for whom self-heating meals would be useful.
2. What other uses can you think of for this self-heating technology?

CHEMICAL REACTIONS **151**

lemon to the copper in the next lemon. Connect the end lemons in the series to the voltmeter as was done with the single cell. Such a battery should create enough electricity to power a small radio or light a small light bulb.

Analysis

1. What did you notice when you looked at the voltmeter? *(An electrical current was flowing.)*

2. What must be contained in the lemon for it to conduct a current? *(ions)*

3. Hydrogen ions in a lemon are part of the chemical reaction that produces the electricity. Hydrogen is present in almost all acids. Why do you think a lemon can be used to make a cell and an orange cannot? *(A lemon is more acidic than an orange. As a result, the lemon contains more hydrogen ions to react.)*

The Nature of Chemical Reactions

Self-Heating Meals Be sure students understand that not all "heat packs" result from a chemical reaction. Some materials release heat when they dissolve. For example, calcium chloride, $CaCl_2$, releases heat when it is dissolved in water. The heat produced in this process is called heat of solution.

Applying Information

1. Examples include military personnel and outdoor sports enthusiasts, such as campers and hikers.
2. Answers will vary but might include hand warmers or heat packs used to treat certain injuries.

Resources Assign students worksheet *5.1 RWA—Hot Meals on Hand* in the **Integration Enrichment Resources** ancillary.

Teaching Tip

Hydrates Hydrates are compounds that include molecules of water in their crystal structures. An example of a hydrate is cobalt(II) chloride hexahydrate, $CoCl_2 \cdot 6H_2O$.

MISCONCEPTION ALERT

Bond Energy
Students often do not recognize that bond breaking always requires energy. The overall process of bond breaking (which requires energy) and bond formation (which releases energy) results in either an endothermic or an exothermic reaction.

The Nature of Chemical Reactions

Prediction Guide Review the list of opinions developed in the Active Reading activity from the section opener. Ask students whether their opinions are the same or have changed. Have them cite passages in the text that account for the change or reinforcement of their opinions.

Teaching Tip

Respiration Although the exact chemical reactions are not the reverse, the reactants and products are opposite for the processes of photosynthesis and cellular respiration. Photosynthesis uses carbon dioxide, energy, and water to produce glucose and oxygen. Cellular respiration oxidizes glucose to produce carbon dioxide, energy, and water.

SKILL BUILDER

Interpreting Graphs Have students work in pairs or small groups to use sentences to describe what is happening in the graphs shown in **Figure 5-5.** The graph in **Figure 5-5A** illustrates the general form for exothermic reactions: energy as heat is released as the reactants form the products. The graph in **Figure 5-5B** illustrates the general form for endothermic reactions: energy as heat is absorbed as the reactants form the products.

Resources Blackline Master 16 shows this visual.

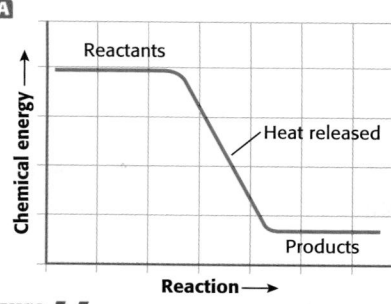
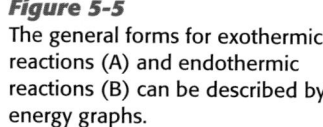
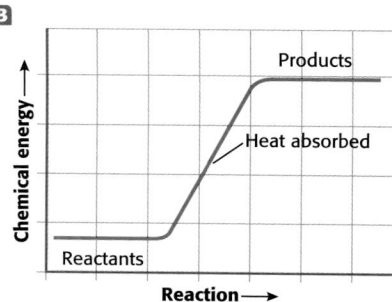

Figure 5-5
The general forms for exothermic reactions (A) and endothermic reactions (B) can be described by energy graphs.

When an endothermic reaction occurs, you may be able to notice a drop in temperature. Some endothermic reactions cannot get enough energy as heat from the surroundings to happen; so energy must be added as heat to cause the reaction to take place. The changes in chemical energy for an exothermic reaction and for an endothermic reaction are shown in **Figure 5-5.**

Photosynthesis, like many reactions in living things, is endothermic. In photosynthesis, plants use energy from light to convert carbon dioxide and water to glucose and oxygen, as shown in **Figure 5-6.**

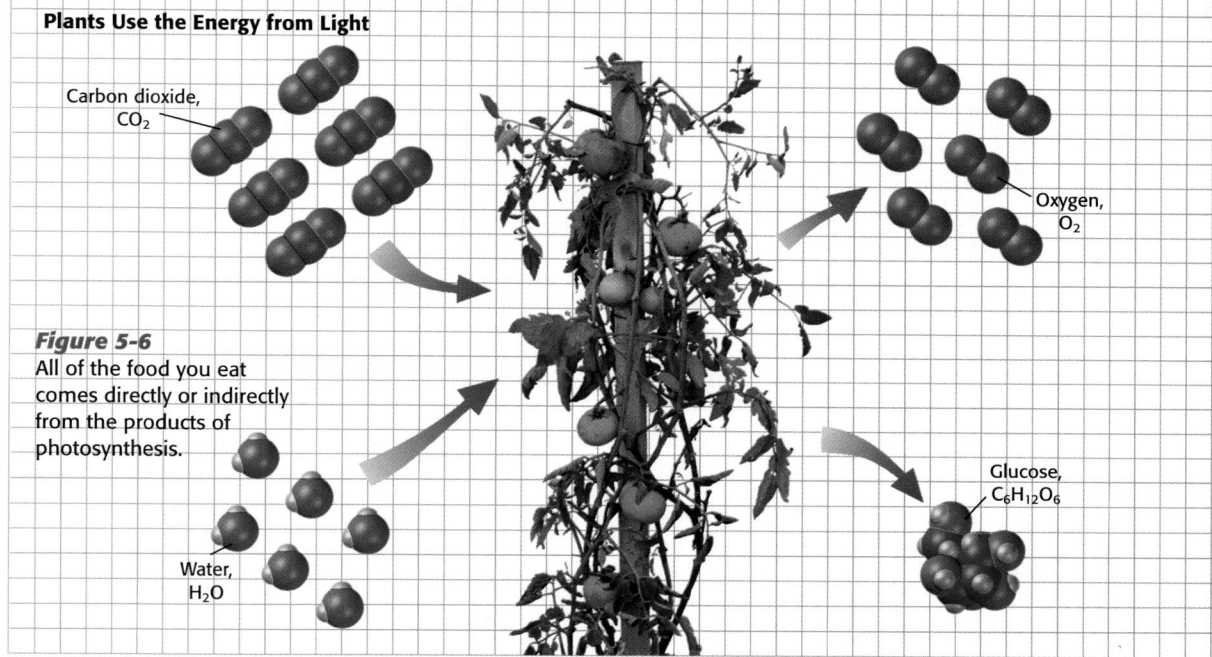

Figure 5-6
All of the food you eat comes directly or indirectly from the products of photosynthesis.

Figure 5-7

A Some living things, such as this firefly, produce light through a chemical process called bioluminescence.

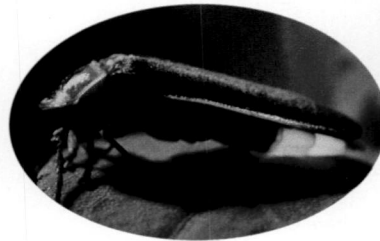

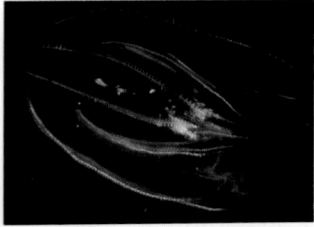

B The comb jelly *(Mnemiopsis leidyi),* shown above, is about 10 cm wide and is native to the Atlantic coast. Comb jellies are not true jellyfish.

Sometimes, reactions are described as exergonic or endergonic. These terms refer to the ease with which the reactions occur. In most cases in this book, exergonic reactions are exothermic and endergonic reactions are endothermic. Bioluminescence, shown in **Figure 5-7,** and respiration are exergonic reactions, and photosynthesis is an endergonic reaction.

SECTION 5.1 REVIEW

SUMMARY

▶ During a chemical reaction, atoms are rearranged.

▶ Signs of a chemical reaction include any of the following: a substance that has different properties than the reactants have; a color change; the formation of a gas or a solid precipitate; or the transfer of energy.

▶ Mass and energy are conserved in chemical reactions.

▶ Chemical energy can be released or absorbed.

▶ Energy must be added to the reactants for bonds between atoms to be broken.

CHECK YOUR UNDERSTANDING

1. **Identify** which of the following is a chemical reaction:
   a. melting ice
   b. burning a candle
   c. rubbing a marker on paper
   d. rusting iron
2. **List** three signs that could make you think a chemical reaction might be taking place.
3. **List** four forms of energy that might be absorbed or released during a chemical reaction.
4. **Classify** the following reactions as exothermic or endothermic:
   a. paper burning with a bright flame
   b. plastics becoming brittle after being left in the sun
   c. a firecracker exploding
5. **Predict** which atoms will be found in the products of the following reactions:
   a. mercury(II) oxide, HgO, is heated and decomposes
   b. limestone, $CaCO_3$, reacts with hydrochloric acid, HCl
   c. table sugar, $C_{12}H_{22}O_{11}$, burns in air to form caramel
6. **Critical Thinking** Calcium oxide, CaO, is used in cement mixes. When water is added, heat is released as CaO forms calcium hydroxide, $Ca(OH)_2$. What signs are there that this is a chemical reaction? Which has more chemical energy, the reactants or the products? Explain your answer.

CHEMICAL REACTIONS **153**

Scheduling

Refer to pp. 146A–146D for lecture, classwork, and assignment options for Section 5.2.

★ **Lesson Focus**
Use transparency *LT 16* to prepare students for this section.

Reading Organizer Have students read the section and then organize what they learn in a concept map. Concept maps should start with *Reaction types*. They should list each type of reaction, describe it, and provide examples.

Teaching Tip

Classifying Chemical Reactions Ask students to describe what the terms *synthesis, decomposition,* and *displacement* mean to them. All are terms that have common usage. Students should associate synthesis with making something, decomposition with things breaking down, and displacement with movement from one place to another. Have students compare their descriptions and discuss any similarities and any differences.

Historical Perspective

In 1869, John Wesley Hyatt (1837–1920), in an attempt to find a substitute for the fragile ivory in billiard balls, discovered the first synthetic polymer. Called celluloid, it is a material that can be molded into different shapes. In 1884, Louis M. H. Berniguad pushed the same substance through tiny holes in a nozzle, making small threads that he called rayon.

154

5.2

Reaction Types

▶ **KEY TERMS**

synthesis reaction

decomposition reaction

electrolysis

combustion reaction

single-displacement reaction

double-displacement reaction

redox reaction

radical

▶ **synthesis reaction** a reaction of at least two substances that forms a new, more complex compound

OBJECTIVES

▶ Distinguish among five general types of chemical reactions.

▶ Predict the products of some reactions based on the reaction type.

▶ Describe reactions that transfer or share electrons between molecules, atoms, or ions.

In the last section, you saw how CO_2 is made from sugar by yeast, how isooctane from gasoline burns, and how photosynthesis happens. These are just a few examples of the many millions of possible reactions.

Classifying Reactions

Even though there are millions of unique substances and many millions of possible reactions, there are only a few general types of reactions. Just as you can follow patterns to name compounds, you also can use patterns to identify the general types of chemical reactions and to predict the products of the chemical reactions.

Synthesis reactions combine substances

Polyethene, a plastic often used to make trash bags and soda bottles, is produced by a synthesis reaction called polymerization. In polymerization reactions, many small molecules join together in chains to make larger structures called polymers. Polyethene, shown in **Figure 5-8,** is a polymer formed of repeating ethene molecules.

Hydrogen gas reacts with oxygen gas to form water. In a synthesis reaction, at least two reactants join to form a product. Synthesis reactions have the following general form.

$$A + B \longrightarrow AB$$

The following is a synthesis reaction in which the metal sodium reacts with chlorine gas to form sodium chloride, or table salt.

$$2Na + Cl_2 \longrightarrow 2NaCl$$

Figure 5-8
A molecule of polyethene is made up of as many as 3500 units of ethene.

Polyethene   Ethene unit

154

DEMONSTRATION 3   TEACHING

Synthesis Reaction

Time: Approximately 10 minutes

Materials: concentrated ammonia solution, concentrated hydrochloric acid solution, 25 mL beaker (2)

SAFETY CAUTION: *Wear safety goggles, protective gloves, and a lab apron. Do not breathe fumes. Students must be 10 ft from demonstration in a well-ventilated area. Neutralize all reactants before disposal.*

Place 5 mL of ammonia solution in one beaker and 5 mL of hydrochloric acid solution in the other beaker. Situate the beakers about 4 in. apart in an area that has no breeze.

Analysis

1. What did you observe? *(A cloud forms.)*

2. What are the reactants? What is the product? *(ammonia and hydrogen chloride; ammonium chloride)*

Synthesis reactions always join substances, so the product is a more complex compound than the reactants.

Photosynthesis is another kind of synthesis reaction—the synthesis reaction that goes on in plants. The photosynthesis reaction is shown in **Figure 5-9.**

Decomposition reactions break substances apart

Digestion is a series of reactions that break down complex foods into simple fuels your body can use. Similarly, in what is known as "cracking" crude oil, large molecules made of carbon and hydrogen are broken down to make gasoline and other fuels. Digestion and "cracking" oil are **decomposition reactions,** reactions in which substances are broken apart. The general form for decomposition reactions is as follows.

$$AB \longrightarrow A + B$$

The following shows the decomposition of water.

$$2H_2O \longrightarrow 2H_2 + O_2$$

The **electrolysis** of water is a simple decomposition reaction—water breaks down into hydrogen gas and oxygen gas when an electric current flows through the water.

Combustion reactions use oxygen as a reactant

In Section 5.1 you learned that isooctane forms carbon dioxide and water during combustion. Oxygen is a reactant in every **combustion reaction,** and at least one product of such reactions always contains oxygen.

If the air supply is limited when a carbon-containing fuel burns, there may not be enough oxygen gas for all the carbon to form carbon dioxide. In that case, some carbon monoxide may form. Carbon monoxide, CO, is a poisonous gas that lowers the ability of the blood to carry oxygen. Carbon monoxide has no color or odor, so you can't tell when it is present. When there is not a good air supply during a combustion reaction, not all fuels are converted completely to carbon dioxide. In some combustion reactions, you can tell if the air supply is limited because carbon is given off as small particles that make a dark, sooty smoke.

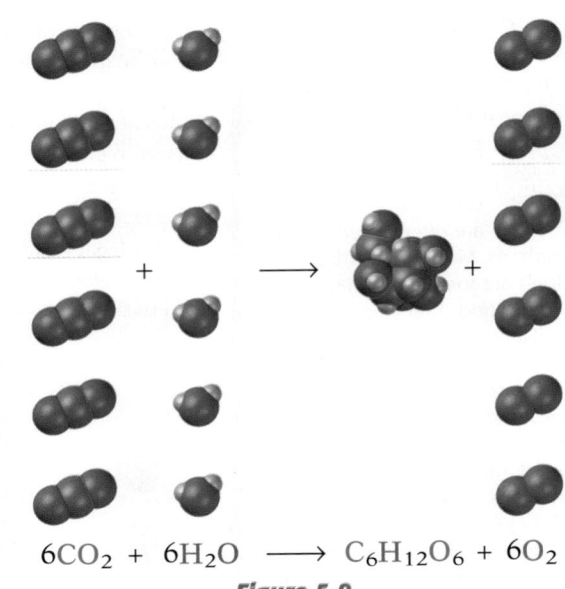

$$6CO_2 + 6H_2O \longrightarrow C_6H_{12}O_6 + 6O_2$$

Figure 5-9
Photosynthesis is the synthesis of glucose and oxygen gas from carbon dioxide and water.

▶ **decomposition reaction** a reaction in which one compound breaks into at least two products

▶ **electrolysis** the decomposition of a compound by an electric current

▶ **combustion reaction** a reaction in which a compound and oxygen burn

internetconnect

SCLINKS
NSTA

TOPIC: Types of reactions
GO TO: www.scilinks.org
KEYWORD: HK1053

MISCONCEPTION **ALERT**
Polymerization
Students might think that all polymers are made by simply combining monomers to form one large molecule. Many polymers, such as polyethylene, are formed that way in what is known as an addition polymerization reaction. When certain other types of polymers form, the reaction forms a small molecule—usually water—as well as the polymer. This type of reaction is condensation polymerization. An example of a condensation polymer is nylon.

Teaching Tip

Carbon Monoxide Remind students that the hemoglobin in red blood cells is the protein that carries oxygen to all parts of the body. The reason that carbon monoxide is so dangerous to humans is that it bonds to hemoglobin more readily than oxygen does. When bonded to carbon monoxide, hemoglobin is incapable of carrying oxygen. Because carbon monoxide is colorless and odorless, it is important for homes to have carbon monoxide detectors.

CHEMICAL REACTIONS **155**

INTEGRATING

EARTH SCIENCE Fossil fuels include not only coal, natural gas, and petroleum but also oil shale, peat, and bitumens. Oil shale is a sedimentary rock that releases hydrocarbons when heated above 500°C. Bitumens are dense, very viscous hydrocarbons similar to asphalt.

Natural gas is the cleanest burning fossil fuel. It is composed primarily of methane. Other fossil fuels do not burn as cleanly as natural gas. Oil and coal compounds pollute by releasing sulfur dioxide, nitrogen oxides, and carbon monoxide into the atmosphere.

Resources Assign students worksheet *5.3: Integrating Earth Science—Limestone Reactions* in the **Integration Enrichment Resources** ancillary.

Did You Know?

If air is used instead of pure oxygen in the combustion process, nitrogen-oxygen compounds—many of which are poisonous—are produced. Some nitrogen-oxygen compounds are also light sensitive and turn brown when exposed to sunlight, causing the brown smog that appears in some cities.

INTEGRATING

EARTH SCIENCE Compounds containing carbon and hydrogen are often called hydrocarbons. Most hydrocarbon fuels are fossil fuels, that is, compounds that were formed millions of years before dinosaurs existed. When prehistoric organisms died, they decomposed, and many were slowly buried under layers of mud, rock, and sand. During the millions of years that passed, the once-living material formed different fuels, such as oil, natural gas, or coal, depending on the kind of material present, the length of time the material was buried, and the conditions of temperature and pressure that existed when the material was decomposing.

Did You Know?

In the United States, natural gas supplies one-fifth of the energy used. The pipelines that carry this natural gas, if laid end-to-end, would stretch to the moon and back twice.

To see how important a good air supply is, look at a series of combustion reactions for methane, CH_4. Because methane has only one carbon atom, it is the simplest carbon-containing fuel. Methane is the primary component in natural gas, the fuel often used in stoves, water heaters, and furnaces.

Methane reacts with oxygen gas to make carbon dioxide and water. Two molecules of oxygen gas are needed for the combustion of each molecule of methane. Therefore, four molecules of oxygen gas are needed for the combustion of two molecules of methane, as shown below.

$$2CH_4 + 4O_2 \longrightarrow 2CO_2 + 4H_2O$$

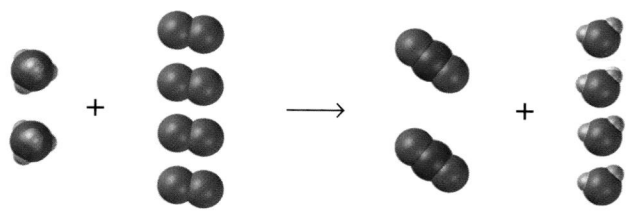

Now look at what happens when less oxygen gas is available. If there are only three molecules of oxygen gas for every two molecules of methane, water and carbon monoxide may form, as shown in the following reaction.

$$2CH_4 + 3O_2 \longrightarrow 2CO + 4H_2O$$

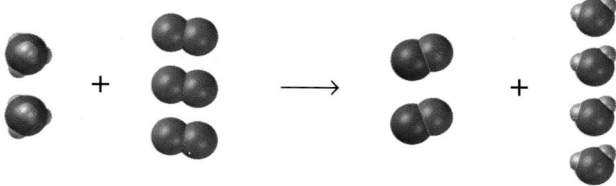

When the air supply is very limited and only two molecules of oxygen gas are available to react with two molecules of methane, water and tiny bits of carbon, or soot, are formed as follows.

$$2CH_4 + 2O_2 \longrightarrow 2C + 4H_2O$$

156 CHAPTER 5

ALTERNATIVE ASSESSMENT

Carbon Monoxide

Have groups of students design and make posters that relate information about carbon monoxide. Information can include how and why carbon monoxide forms, what it does in the human body, and how its dangers can be minimized. Encourage students to find out how carbon monoxide detectors function and to include this information. After the products are evaluated and any incorrect information is corrected, have students acquire permission to place the posters in areas that might be at risk for increased amounts of carbon monoxide. Possible locations include the school auto shop or bus garage and community auto repair shops and transportation sources.

In single-displacement reactions, elements trade places

Copper(II) chloride dissolves in water to make a bright blue solution. If you add a piece of aluminum foil to the solution, the color fades, and clumps of reddish brown material form. The reddish brown clumps are copper metal. Aluminum replaces copper in the copper(II) chloride, forming aluminum chloride. Aluminum chloride does not make a colored solution, so the blue color fades as the amount of blue copper(II) chloride decreases, as shown in **Figure 5-10.**

The copper atoms are in the form of copper(II) ions, as part of copper(II) chloride, and the aluminum atoms are in the aluminum metal. After the reaction, the aluminum atoms become ions, and the copper atoms become neutral in the copper metal. Because the atoms of one element appear to move into a compound, and atoms of the other element appear to move out, this is called a **single-displacement reaction.** Single-displacement reactions have the following general form.

$$XA + B \longrightarrow BA + X$$

The single-displacement reaction between copper(II) chloride and aluminum is shown as follows.

$$3CuCl_2 + 2Al \longrightarrow 2AlCl_3 + 3Cu$$

Generally, in a single-displacement reaction, a more reactive element will take the place of a less reactive one.

▶ **single-displacement reaction** a reaction in which atoms of one element take the place of atoms of another element in a compound

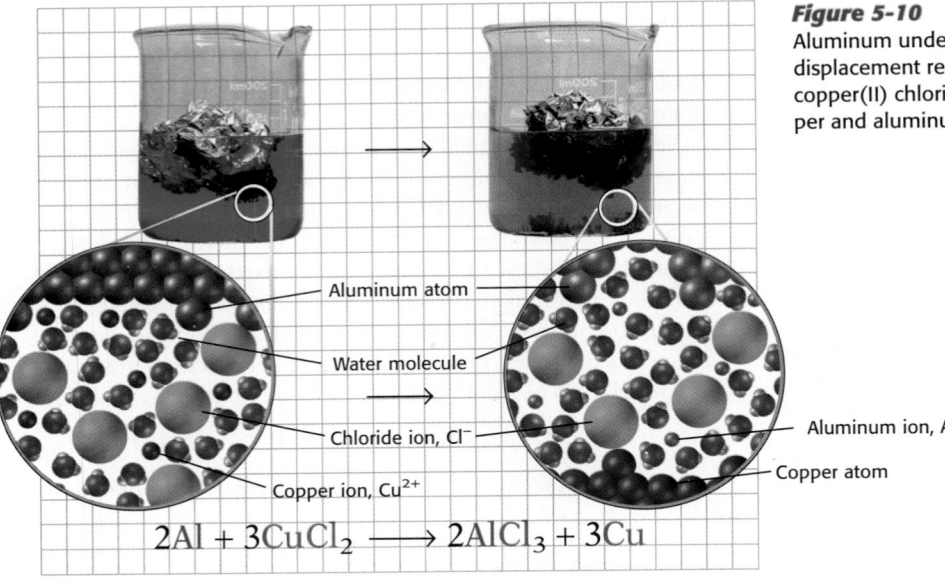

Figure 5-10
Aluminum undergoes a single-displacement reaction with copper(II) chloride to form copper and aluminum chloride.

Aluminum atom
Water molecule
Chloride ion, Cl⁻
Copper ion, Cu²⁺
Aluminum ion, Al³⁺
Copper atom

$$2Al + 3CuCl_2 \longrightarrow 2AlCl_3 + 3Cu$$

Teaching Tip

Single Displacement Activity refers to how readily an element reacts. As shown on the student page, active metals replace less active metals in compounds. In addition, active nonmetals will also replace less active nonmetals. For example, fluorine is more active than chlorine. If fluorine gas, F_2, is bubbled through a sodium chloride, NaCl, solution, the fluorine will replace the chlorine in the compound. The products of the reaction are chlorine, Cl_2, and sodium fluoride, NaF. If chlorine gas is bubbled through a sodium fluoride solution, no reaction occurs because the more active nonmetal is already in the compound. Have students use what they now know about this activity to explain the results of Demonstration 1 in Section 5.1. *(Copper is more active than silver, so copper will replace silver in a compound. No reaction occurs when silver is placed in a copper-containing compound because the more active metal is already in the compound.)*

CHEMICAL REACTIONS **157**

Multicultural Extension

From the time of Hippocrates, an ancient Greek healer, people knew that chewing willow bark would relieve pain. Native Americans and the Chinese also used it. But with the pain relief of willow bark came a problem. In the 1800s, the active ingredient in the bark was isolated. It is salicylic acid, which causes stomach discomfort because of its acidity. Felix Hoffman, a German chemist, used a displacement reaction to make the acid less acidic without destroying its pain-relieving properties. He replaced a hydrogen atom on the acid molecule with an acetyl group, $-OOCCH_3$. The result—acetylsalicylic acid—relieves pain with fewer stomach problems.

Teaching Tip

Double-Displacement Reactions   One common example of a double-displacement reaction is an acid-base reaction. Acid-base reactions fall under the category of neutralization reactions because the two components neutralize each other's properties, producing a salt and water.

LINKING CHAPTERS

Students will learn more about acid/base reactions in Chapter 5.

Figure 5-11
Potassium reacts with water in a single-displacement reaction.

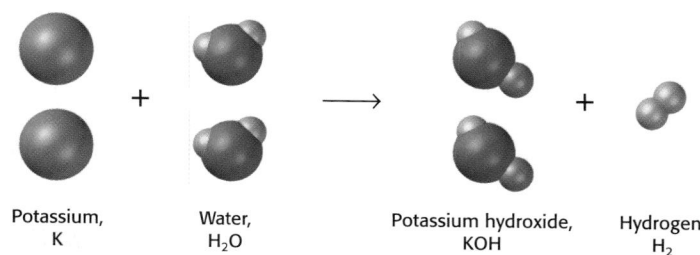

Potassium,
K

Water,
H_2O

Potassium hydroxide,
KOH

Hydrogen,
H_2

Potassium metal is so reactive that it undergoes a single-displacement reaction with water. A potassium ion appears to take the place of one of the hydrogen atoms in the water molecule. Potassium ions, K^+, and hydroxide ions, OH^-, are formed. The hydrogen atoms displaced from the water join to form hydrogen gas, H_2.

The potassium and water reaction, shown in **Figure 5-11,** is so exothermic that the H_2 may explode and burn instantly. All alkali metals and some other metals undergo single-displacement reactions with water to form hydrogen gas, metal ions, and hydroxide ions.

All of these reactions happen rapidly and give off heat but some alkali metals are more reactive than others. Lithium reacts steadily with water to form lithium ions, hydroxide ions, and hydrogen gas. Sodium and water react vigorously to make sodium ions, hydroxide ions, and hydrogen gas. For potassium, the reaction with water is more violent. Rubidium and cesium are so reactive that the hydrogen gas will explode as soon as they are put into water.

In double-displacement reactions, ions appear to be exchanged between compounds

The yellow lines painted on roads are colored with lead chromate, $PbCrO_4$. This compound can be formed by mixing solutions of lead nitrate, $Pb(NO_3)_2$, and potassium chromate, K_2CrO_4. In solution, these compounds form the ions Pb^{2+}, NO_3^-, K^+, and CrO_4^{2-}. When the solutions are mixed, the yellow lead chromate compound that forms doesn't dissolve in water, so it settles to the bottom. A **double-displacement reaction,** such as this one, occurs when two compounds appear to exchange ions. The general form of a double-displacement reaction is as follows.

$$AX + BY \longrightarrow AY + BX$$

The double-displacement reaction that forms lead chromate is as follows.

$$Pb(NO_3)_2 + K_2CrO_4 \longrightarrow PbCrO_4 + 2KNO_3$$

▶ **double-displacement reaction** a reaction in which a gas, a solid precipitate, or a molecular compound is formed from the apparent exchange of ions between two compounds

Electrons and Chemical Reactions

The general classes of reactions described earlier in this section were used by early chemists, who knew nothing about the parts of the atom. With the discovery of the electron and its role in chemical bonding, another way to classify reactions was developed. We can understand many reactions as transfers of electrons.

Electrons are transferred in redox reactions

The following **reduction/oxidation reaction** is an example of electron transfer. When the metal iron reacts with oxygen to form rust, Fe_2O_3, each iron atom loses three electrons to form Fe^{3+} ions, and each oxygen atom gains two electrons to form the O^{2-} ions.

Substances that accept electrons are said to be *reduced;* substances that give up electrons are said to be *oxidized.* One way to remember this is that the gain of electrons will reduce the positive charge on an ion or will make an uncharged atom a negative ion. Reduction and oxidation are linked. In all redox reactions, one or more reactants is reduced and one or more is oxidized.

Some redox reactions do not involve ions. In these reactions, oxidation is a gain of oxygen or a loss of hydrogen, and reduction is the loss of oxygen or the gain of hydrogen. Respiration and combustion are redox reactions because oxygen gas reacts with carbon compounds to form carbon dioxide. Carbon atoms in CO_2 are oxidized, and oxygen atoms in O_2 are reduced.

Radicals have electrons available for bonding

Many synthetic fibers, as well as plastic bags and wraps, are made by polymerization reactions, as you have already learned. Polymerization reactions can occur when **radicals** are formed.

When a covalent bond is broken such that at least one unpaired electron is left on each fragment of the molecule, these fragments are called radicals. Because an uncharged hydrogen atom has one electron available for bonding, it is a radical. Radicals react quickly to form covalent bonds with other substances, making new compounds. Often, when you see chemical radicals mentioned in the newspaper or hear about them on the radio or television, they are called free radicals.

CHEMICAL REACTIONS **159**

Connection to FINE ARTS

Metal sculptures often corrode because of redox reactions. The Statue of Liberty, which is covered with 200 000 pounds of copper, was as bright as a new penny when it was erected. However, after more than 100 years, the statue had turned green. The copper reacted with the damp air of New York harbor. More importantly, oxidation reactions between the damp, salty air and the internal iron supports made the structure dangerously weak. The statue was closed for several years in the 1980s while the supports were cleaned and repaired.

Making the Connection

1. Metal artwork in fountains often rusts very quickly. Suggest a reason for this.
2. Why do you think the most detailed parts of a sculpture are the first to appear worn away?

ALTERNATIVE ASSESSMENT

Oxidation and Reduction

Have students use a number line to explain why gaining electrons (adding a negative charge) during reduction results in a loss of positive charge. Have them also explain why losing electrons (subtracting negative charge) during oxidation results in increased positive charge. Remind students that free elements have zero charge, and provide them with several examples of changes of charge. For each, have them identify the change as oxidation or reduction. Examples of oxidation include Fe to Fe^{2+}, Cr^{2+} to Cr^{3+}, and Cl^- to Cl. Examples of reduction include F to F^-, Pb^{4+} to Pb^{2+}, and Mg^{2+} to Mg. After mastering the concepts of oxidation and reduction, have groups of students create posters that use a number line to explain oxidation and reduction along with examples of each.

Did You Know?

Because they are so reactive, free radicals can be harmful. Ultraviolet radiation from the sun breaks chlorofluorocarbons (CFCs) from certain refrigerants down, forming a chlorine free radical. Each of these free radicals can destroy thousands of ozone molecules.

SECTION 5.2 REVIEW

Check Your Understanding

1. **a.** synthesis
   b. synthesis
   c. decomposition
   d. single-displacement
2. Zinc is oxidized, and copper is reduced.
3. a fragment of a molecule that has at least one electron available for bonding
4. In single-displacement reactions, atoms of one element replace the atoms of another element in a compound. In a double-displacement reaction, positive ions in two compounds trade places, forming two different compounds.
5. Because oxygen might be limited, carbon monoxide might form instead of carbon dioxide. Carbon monoxide is harmful to animals, including humans.
6. In synthesis reactions, two or more substances combine to form a more complex substance. Decomposition is the opposite process.

Answers continue on p. 181A.

RESOURCE LINK
STUDY GUIDE

Assign students *Review Section 5.2 Reaction Types.*

Figure 5-12
Radical reactions are used to make polystyrene. Polystyrene foam is often used to insulate or to protect things that can break.

Radicals are part of many everyday reactions besides the making of polymers, such as those shown in **Figure 5-12.** Radicals can also be formed when coal and oil are processed or burned. The explosive combustion of rocket fuel is another reaction involving the formation of radicals.

SECTION 5.2 REVIEW

SUMMARY

▶ Synthesis reactions make larger molecules.

▶ Decomposition breaks compounds apart.

▶ In combustion, substances react with oxygen.

▶ Elements appear to trade places in single-displacement reactions.

▶ In double-displacement reactions, ions appear to move between compounds, resulting in a solid that settles out of solution, a gas that bubbles out of solution, and/or a molecular substance.

▶ In redox reactions, electrons transfer from one substance to another.

CHECK YOUR UNDERSTANDING

1. **Classify** each of the following reactions by type:
   a. $S_8 + 8O_2 \longrightarrow 8SO_2 + \text{heat}$
   b. $6CO_2 + 6H_2O \longrightarrow C_6H_{12}O_6 + 6O_2$
   c. $2NaHCO_3 \longrightarrow Na_2CO_3 + H_2O + CO_2$
   d. $Zn + 2HCl \longrightarrow ZnCl_2 + H_2$
2. **Identify** which element is oxidized and which element is reduced in the following reaction.
   $$Zn + CuSO_4 \longrightarrow ZnSO_4 + Cu$$
3. **Define** *radical.*
4. **Compare and Contrast** single-displacement and double-displacement reactions based on the number of reactants. Use the terms *compound, atom* or *element,* and *ion.*
5. **Explain** why charcoal grills or charcoal fires should never be used for heating inside a house. (**Hint:** Doors and windows are closed when it is cold, so there is little fresh air.)
6. **Contrast** synthesis and decomposition reactions.
7. **List** three possible results of a double-displacement reaction.
8. **Creative Thinking** Would you expect larger or smaller molecules to be components of a more viscous liquid? Which is likely to be more viscous, crude oil or oil after cracking?

160 CHAPTER 5

5.3

Balancing Chemical Equations

OBJECTIVES

▶ Demonstrate how to balance chemical equations.
▶ Interpret chemical equations to determine the relative number of moles of reactants needed and moles of products formed.
▶ Explain how the law of definite proportions allows for predictions about reaction amounts.
▶ Identify mole ratios in a balanced chemical equation.
▶ Calculate the relative masses of reactants and products from a chemical equation.

▶ **KEY TERMS**
chemical equation
mole ratio

Figure 5-13 shows a combustion reaction you learned about in Section 5.2. You may have seen this reaction in the lab or at home if you have a gas stove. When natural gas burns, methane, the main component, reacts with oxygen gas to form carbon dioxide and water.

Describing Reactions

You can describe this reaction in many ways. You could take a photograph or make a videotape. One way to record the products and reactants of this reaction is to write a word equation.

methane + oxygen $\longrightarrow$ carbon dioxide + water

Chemical equations summarize reactions

In Section 5.1, you learned that all chemical reactions are rearrangements of atoms. This is shown clearly in **Figure 5-13.** A better way to write the methane combustion reaction is as a **chemical equation,** using the formulas for each substance.

▶ **chemical equation** an equation that uses chemical formulas and symbols to show the reactants and products in a chemical reaction

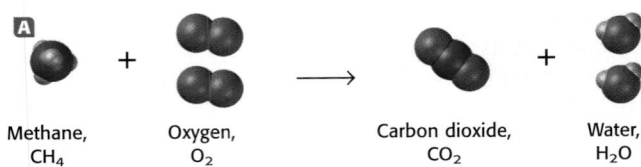

Methane, CH_4 Oxygen, O_2 Carbon dioxide, CO_2 Water, H_2O

Figure 5-13
(A) Methane burns with oxygen gas to make carbon dioxide and water.
(B) A methane flame is used to polish the edges of these glass plates.

CHEMICAL REACTIONS **161**

DEMONSTRATION 4 SCIENCE AND THE CONSUMER

A Balancing Act

Time: Approximately 15 minutes
Materials: 20 index cards, tape or thumbtacks

Divide the index cards into 4 groups of 5 cards. Write the term *center* on the cards of the first group, *guard* on the cards of the second group, *forward* on the cards of the third group, and *basketball team* on the cards of the fourth group. Fasten the cards on the chalkboard or a bulletin

board. Have volunteers create as many basketball teams as they can from the cards.

Analysis
1. Can the leftover cards be used? Explain. *(No; there are not enough of all the positions to form another team.)*
2. Write an equation that shows the formation of a basketball team. *(2 forwards + 1 center + 2 guards = 1 basketball team)*

Scheduling
Refer to pp. 146A–146D for lecture, classwork, and assignment options for Section 5.3.

★ **Lesson Focus**
Use transparency *LT 17* to prepare students for this section.

READING SKILL BUILDER *Reading Hint* As students read through the section, have them use the balanced and unbalanced chemical equations on pp. 162–163 to help them understand the difference between a balanced and an unbalanced equation.

Teaching Tip
An Equation Analogy Write the following items on the board:

1 center + 2 guards + 2 forwards → 1 basketball team

9 girls + 14 boys → 10 lab pairs + 1 group of three

Point out to students that the same number of people are represented on both sides of the arrows. They are just arranged differently. Discuss with students that the same principle applies to atoms represented in a chemical reaction.

Balancing Chemical Equations

Chemical Equations Because students know that the order of elements in a formula is important, they might think that there is a specific order of reactants and products in a chemical equation. Tell them that a chemical equation is just like a mathematical equation in that regard. Items that are added together can be in any order.

Teaching Tip

Equation Information Students might notice chemical equations from other sources that contain more information than is presented in this course. The state of a substance is frequently indicated by a (s), (l), or (g) written after a formula, or (aq) might be used to indicate that the substance is in a water, or aqueous, solution. Information provided above or below the arrow often indicates conditions such as required temperatures or pressure or the presence of a catalyst.

Figure 5-14
This student is giving a talk on reactions that use copper. You can read the chemical equations even if you can't read Japanese.

Unbalanced Chemical Equation

$CH_4 + O_2$	$\longrightarrow$	$CO_2 + H_2O$
reactants	"give" or "yield"	products

In a chemical equation, such as the one above, the reactants, which are on the left-hand side of the arrow, form the products, which are on the right-hand side. When chemical equations are written, $\longrightarrow$ means "gives" or "yields". People all over the world write chemical equations the same way, as shown in **Figure 5-14**.

Balanced chemical equations account for the conservation of mass

The chemical equation shown above can be made more useful. As written, it does not tell you anything about the amount of the products that will be formed from burning a given amount of methane. When the number of atoms of each element on the right-hand side of the equation matches the number of atoms of each element on the left, then the chemical equation is said to be *balanced*. A balanced chemical equation follows the law of conservation of mass.

How to balance chemical equations

In the previous equation, the number of atoms on each side of the arrow did not match for all of the elements in the equation. Carbon is balanced because one carbon atom is on each side of the equation. However, four hydrogen atoms are on the left, and only two are on the right. Also, two oxygen atoms are on the left, and three are on the right. This can't be correct because atoms can't be created or destroyed in a chemical reaction, as you learned in Chapter 2.

Remember that you cannot balance an equation by changing the chemical formulas. You have to leave the subscripts in the formulas alone. Changing the formulas would mean that different substances were in the reaction. An equation can be balanced only by putting numbers, called coefficients, in front of the chemical formulas.

Because there is a total of four hydrogen atoms in the reactants, a total of four hydrogen atoms must be in the products. Instead of a single water molecule, this reaction makes two water molecules to account for all four hydrogen atoms. To show that two water molecules are formed, a coefficient of 2 is placed in front of the formula for water.

$$CH_4 + O_2 \longrightarrow CO_2 + 2H_2O$$

Balanced Chemical Equations

Have students create a concept map that shows the steps necessary to write a balanced chemical equation. The map should definitely include writing the formula for each reactant and product, using plus signs and an arrow where needed, and using coefficients to balance the number of each type of atom on each side of the equation. Maps might also include an initial step of writing a word equation or a final step of double-checking the equation for balance.

Next look at the oxygen. There is a total of four oxygen atoms in the products. Two are in the CO_2, and each water molecule contains one oxygen atom. To get four oxygen atoms on the left side of the equation, two oxygen molecules must react. That would account for all four oxygen atoms.

Balanced Chemical Equation
$CH_4 + 2O_2 \longrightarrow CO_2 + 2H_2O$

Now the numbers of atoms for each element are the same on each side, and the equation is balanced, as shown below.

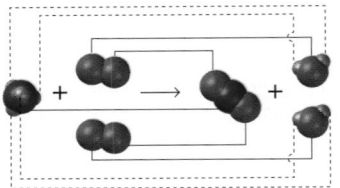

Information from a balanced equation

You can learn a lot from a balanced equation. In our example, you can tell that each molecule of methane requires two oxygen molecules to react. Each methane molecule that burns forms one molecule of carbon dioxide and two molecules of water. Balanced chemical equations are the standard way chemists write about reactions to describe both the substances in the reaction and the amounts involved.

If you know the formulas of the reactants and products in a reaction, like the one shown in **Figure 5-15,** you can always write a balanced equation, as shown on the following pages.

Connection to
SOCIAL STUDIES

No one can be sure when fireworks were first used. When the Mongols attacked China in 1232, the defenders used "arrows of flying fire," which some historians think were rockets fired by gunpowder. The Arabs probably used rockets when they invaded the Spanish peninsula in 1249. For hundreds of years, the main use of rockets was to add terror and confusion to battles. In the late 1700s, rockets were used with some success against the British in India. Because of this, Sir William Congreve began to design rockets for England. Congreve's rockets were designed to explode in the air or be fired along the ground.

Making the Connection

British forces used Congreve's rockets during the War of 1812. Research the battle of Fort McHenry. Find out what happened, who won the battle, and what lyrics the rockets inspired.

PHYSICAL SCIENCE INTERACTIVE TUTOR

Disc One, Module 5:
Chemical Equations
Use the Interactive Tutor to learn more about this topic.

Figure 5-15
Magnesium in these fireworks gives off energy as heat and light when it burns to form magnesium oxide.

CHEMICAL REACTIONS **163**

Connection to
SOCIAL STUDIES

By the fourteenth century, Europe had surpassed China's development of fireworks, or pyrotechnics. During the Renaissance, an Italian school emphasized fireworks for entertainment, and a German school promoted scientific advancement in pyrotechnics. As fireworks became more popular, improper manufacture and use resulted in injuries. As a result, use of fireworks is limited in many countries.

Making the Connection

Fort McHenry, located in Baltimore Harbor, protected the city in the past from invasion by sea. The British were defeated as their leader was killed during an attempt to take the fort by land. The "Star Spangled Banner" was written after this battle.

Resources Assign students worksheet *5.5 Connection to Social Studies—Fireworks* in the **Integration Enrichment Resources** ancillary.

Balancing Chemical Equations

Fire Extinguishers: Are They All The Same?
Have students determine where fire extinguishers are located in their school and at home. Under adult supervision, have them check the codes found on these extinguishers. Are the extinguishers the correct type to put out the type of fire that might occur in their location?

Stress that a fire extinguisher is to be used only on the fire specified on the extinguisher's display code. In the case of chemical fires, it's important to know the properties of the burning chemicals. For example, a carbon dioxide fire extinguisher would not successfully extinguish burning magnesium because magnesium burns at a temperature high enough to decompose carbon dioxide.

Your Choice

1. Water or cold CO_2 reduces a fire's severity by lowering the temperature.
2. The chain reaction is interrupted when the contents of a dry chemical extinguisher react with the intermediates of the chain reaction.

Resources Assign students worksheet *5.6 Science and the Consumer—The Right Fire Extinguisher for the Job* in the **Integration Enrichment Resources** ancillary.

Did You Know ?

If a class D fire is not on a vertical surface, an effective way to extinguish the fire is to cover it with sand.

Fire Extinguishers: Are They All The Same?

A fire is a combustion reaction in progress that is speeded up by high temperatures. Three things are needed for a combustion reaction to occur: a fuel, some oxygen, and an ignition source. If any of these three is absent, combustion cannot occur. So the goal of firefighting is to remove one or more of these parts. Fire extinguishers are effective in firefighting because they separate the fuel from the oxygen supply, which is most commonly air.

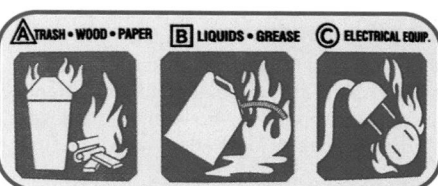

Fire extinguishers display codes indicating which types of fires they can put out.

Classes of Fires

A fire is classified by the type of fuel that combusts to produce it. Class A fires involve solid fuels, such as wood and paper. The fuel in a Class B fire is a flammable liquid, like grease, gasoline, or oil. Class C fires involve "live" electric circuits. And Class D fires are fueled by the combustion of flammable metals.

Types of Fire Extinguishers

Different types of fuels require different firefighting methods. Water extinguishers are used on Class A fires, which involve fuels such as most flammable building materials. The steam that is produced helps to displace the air around the fire, preventing the oxygen supply from reaching the fuel.

A Class B fire, in which the fuel is a liquid, is best put out by cold carbon dioxide gas, CO_2. Because carbon dioxide is more dense than air, it forms a layer underneath the air, cutting off the oxygen supply for the combustion reaction.

Class C fires, which involve a "live" electric circuit, can also be extinguished by CO_2. Liquid water cannot be used, or there will be a danger of electric shock. Some Class C fire extinguishers contain a dry chemical that smothers the fire. The dry chemical smothers the fire by reacting with the intermediates that drive the chain reaction that produces the fire. This stops the chain reaction and extinguishes the fire.

Finally, Class D fires, which involve burning metals, cannot be extinguished with CO_2 or water because these compounds may react with some hot metals. For these fires, nonreactive dry powders are used to cover the metal and keep it separate from oxygen. In many cases, the powders used in Class D extinguishers are specific to the type of metal that is burning.

Most fire extinguishers can be used with more than one type of fire. Check the fire extinguishers in your home and school to find out the kinds of fires they are designed to put out.

Your Choice

1. **Making Decisions** Aside from displacing the air supply, how does water or cold CO_2 gas reduce a fire's severity?
2. **Critical Thinking** How is the chain reaction in a Class C fire interrupted by the contents of a dry chemical extinguisher?

> internet**connect**
>
> SC*LINKS*
> **NSTA**
> **TOPIC:** Fire extinguishers
> **GO TO:** www.scilinks.org
> **KEYWORD:** HK1057

Math Skills

Balancing Chemical Equations Write the equation that describes the burning of magnesium in air to form magnesium oxide.

1 **Identify the reactants and products.**

Magnesium and oxygen gas are the reactants that form the product, magnesium oxide.

2 **Write a word equation for the reaction.**

magnesium + oxygen $\longrightarrow$ magnesium oxide

3 **Write the equation using formulas for the elements and compounds in the word equation.**

Remember that some gaseous elements, like oxygen, are molecules, not atoms. Oxygen in air is O_2, not O.

$$Mg + O_2 \longrightarrow MgO$$

4 **Balance the equation one element at a time.**

The same number of each kind of atom must appear on both sides. So far, there is one atom of magnesium on each side of the equation.

Atom	Reactants	Products	Balanced?
Mg	1	1	✔
O	2	1	✘

But there are two oxygen atoms on the left and only one on the right. To balance the number of oxygen atoms, you need to double the amount of magnesium oxide:

$$Mg + O_2 \longrightarrow 2MgO$$

Atom	Reactants	Products	Balanced?
Mg	1	2	✘
O	2	2	✔

This equation gives you two magnesium atoms on the right and only one on the left. So you need to double the amount of magnesium on the left, as follows.

$$2Mg + O_2 \longrightarrow 2MgO$$

Atom	Reactants	Products	Balanced?
Mg	2	2	✔
O	2	2	✔

Now the equation is balanced. It has an equal number of each type of atom on both sides.

Practice **HINT**

▶ Sometimes changing the coefficients to balance one element may cause another element in the equation to become unbalanced. So always check your work.

Math Skills

Resources Assign students worksheet *10: Balancing Chemical Equations* in the **Math Skills Worksheets** ancillary.

Teaching Tip

Balancing Equations Remind students to watch for elements contained in more than one reactant or more than one product. For example, H is contained in both reactants in the reaction from Demonstration 3 in this chapter: $NH_3 + HCl \rightarrow NH_4Cl$. Both the hydrogen locations must be considered in balancing the equation.

Tell students that polyatomic ions in reactants that remain the same in the products can be balanced as units. For example, in $2Fe + 3H_2SO_4 \rightarrow Fe_2(SO_4)_3 + 3H_2$, the sulfate ion is on both sides. It can be balanced as sulfate ions instead of as oxygen and sulfur. If the ion is changed at all, it cannot be considered a unit.

Additional Application

Real Equations If you or your students write equations to balance, be sure the reactions actually occur. Although an equation for a reaction that does not occur can be balanced, it can be confusing to students. If necessary, refer to a high school or college chemistry text for practice equations to balance.

CHEMICAL REACTIONS **165**

ALTERNATIVE ASSESSMENT

Coefficients

Have students write a paragraph explaining why the sum of the coefficients on one side of a balanced equation doesn't necessarily equal the sum of the coefficients on the other side of the equation. Paragraphs should include the idea that the number of each type of atom must be the same on both sides of the equation. That number is determined by the formulas, including subscripts, not just coefficients.

Balancing Chemical Equations

Quick ACTIVITY

Candy Chemistry Student models should result in the following balanced equations.

1. $C_3H_8 + 5O_2 \rightarrow 3CO_2 + 4H_2O$; combustion
2. $2KI + Br_2 \rightarrow 2KBr + I_2$; single-displacement
3. $H_2 + Cl_2 \rightarrow 2HCl$; synthesis
4. $FeS + 2HCl \rightarrow FeCl_2 + H_2S$; double-displacement

Additional Examples

Balancing Chemical Equations
Write balanced equations for each of the following:

1. Potassium metal reacts violently with water to produce potassium hydroxide and hydrogen gas.

   Answer: $2K + 2H_2O \rightarrow 2KOH + H_2$

2. Calcium oxide, an ingredient in cement, combines with water to produce calcium hydroxide.

   Answer: $CaO + H_2O \rightarrow Ca(OH)_2$

3. Ethanol, C_2H_5OH, produces water and carbon dioxide when it burns.

   Answer: $C_2H_5OH + 3O_2 \rightarrow 2CO_2 + 3H_2O$

Quick ACTIVITY

Candy Chemistry
Look at the partial equations below. Using different-colored gumdrops to show atoms of different elements, make models of the reactions by connecting the "atoms" with toothpicks. Use your models to help you balance the following equations. Classify each reaction.

a. $C_3H_8 + O_2 \longrightarrow CO_2 + H_2O$

b. $KI + Br_2 \longrightarrow KBr + I_2$

c. $H_2 + Cl_2 \longrightarrow HCl$

d. $FeS + HCl \longrightarrow FeCl_2 + H_2S$

Practice

Balancing Chemical Equations

1. Copper(II) sulfate, $CuSO_4$, and aluminum react to form aluminum sulfate, $Al_2(SO_4)_3$, and copper. Write the balanced equation for this single-displacement reaction.
2. In a double-displacement reaction, sodium sulfide, Na_2S, reacts with silver nitrate, $AgNO_3$, to form sodium nitrate, $NaNO_3$, and silver sulfide, Ag_2S. Balance this equation.
3. Hydrogen peroxide, H_2O_2, is sometimes used as a bleach or as a disinfectant. Hydrogen peroxide decomposes to give water and molecular oxygen. Write a balanced equation for the decomposition reaction.
4. Hydrogen sulfide, H_2S, is a gas that smells like rotten eggs. Write and balance an equation for the oxidation by molecular oxygen of hydrogen sulfide to make sulfuric acid, H_2SO_4.
5. Propane gas, C_3H_8, is commonly used as a fuel for camping stoves and gas barbecue grills. Write and balance the equation for the synthesis of propane from methane in which molecular hydrogen, H_2, is also a product.

Determining Mole Ratios

Look at the reaction of magnesium with oxygen to form magnesium oxide.

$$\text{magnesium} + \text{oxygen} \longrightarrow \text{magnesium oxide}$$

$$2Mg + O_2 \longrightarrow 2MgO$$

The single molecule of oxygen in the equation might be shown as $1O_2$. However, a coefficient of 1 is never written.

Balanced equations indicate particles and moles

One way to read the equation is to say that two atoms of magnesium can react with one molecule of oxygen to give two units of magnesium oxide. This is a good way to understand the reaction. But reactions almost always involve more than one or two atoms.

The equation can also be read as describing mole quantities—2 mol of magnesium can react with 1 mol of oxygen to produce 2 mol of magnesium oxide.

Balanced equations show the conservation of mass

Other ways of looking at the amounts in the reaction are shown in **Figure 5-16.** Notice that there are equal numbers of magnesium and oxygen atoms in the product and in the reactants. The total mass of the reactants is always the same as the total mass of the products.

Solution Guide

1. $3CuSO_4 + 2Al \rightarrow Al_2(SO_4)_3 + 3Cu$
2. $Na_2S + 2AgNO_3 \rightarrow 2NaNO_3 + Ag_2S$
3. $2H_2O_2 \rightarrow 2H_2O + O_2$
4. $H_2S + 2O_2 \rightarrow H_2SO_4$
5. $3CH_4 \rightarrow C_3H_8 + 2H_2$

Figure 5-16 Information from the Balanced Equation: $2Mg + O_2 \longrightarrow 2MgO$

Equation:	2Mg	+	O_2	$\longrightarrow$	2MgO
Amount (mol)	2		1	$\longrightarrow$	2
Molecules	$(6.02 \times 10^{23}) \times 2$		$(6.02 \times 10^{23}) \times 1$	$\longrightarrow$	$(6.02 \times 10^{23}) \times 2$
Mass (g)	24.3 g/mol × 2 mol		32.0 g/mol × 1 mol	$\longrightarrow$	40.3 g/mol × 2 mol
Total mass (g)	48.6		32.0	$\longrightarrow$	80.6
Model				$\longrightarrow$	

The law of definite proportions

What if you want 4 mol of magnesium to react completely? If you have twice as much magnesium as the balanced equation calls for, you will need twice as much oxygen. Twice as much magnesium oxide will be formed. No matter what amounts of magnesium and oxygen are combined or how the magnesium oxide is made, the balanced equation does not change. This follows the law of definite proportions, which states:

A compound always contains the same elements in the same proportions, regardless of how the compound is made or how much of the compound is formed.

Inquiry Lab

Can you write balanced chemical equations?

Materials ✔ 7 test tubes ✔ test-tube rack ✔ labels or wax pencil ✔ 10 mL graduated cylinder
✔ bottles of the following solutions: sodium chloride, NaCl; potassium bromide, KBr; potassium iodide, KI; and silver nitrate, $AgNO_3$

Procedure

SAFETY CAUTION Wear safety goggles and an apron. Silver nitrate will stain your skin and clothes.
1. Label three test tubes, one each for NaCl, KBr, and KI.
2. Using the graduated cylinder, measure 5 mL of each solution into the properly labeled test tube. Rinse the graduated cylinder between each use.
3. Add 1 mL of $AgNO_3$ solution to each of the test tubes. Record your observations.

Analysis

1. What did you observe as a sign that a double-displacement reaction was occurring?
2. Identify the reactants and products for each reaction.
3. Write the balanced equation for each reaction.
4. Which ion(s) produced a solid with silver nitrate?
5. Does this test let you identify all the ions? Why or why not?

Inquiry Lab

Can you write balanced chemical equations?

1. the formation of a precipitate
2. reactants: NaCl, $AgNO_3$
   products: AgCl, $NaNO_3$;
   reactants: KBr, $AgNO_3$
   products: AgBr, KNO_3;
   reactants: KI, $AgNO_3$
   products: AgI, KNO_3

3. $NaCl + AgNO_3 \rightarrow AgCl + NaNO_3$
   $KBr + AgNO_3 \rightarrow AgBr + KNO_3$
   $KI + AgNO_3 \rightarrow AgI + KNO_3$
4. Cl^-, Br^-, and I^- all form solids with $AgNO_3$.
5. Solid AgCl is white, AgBr is pale yellow, and AgI is also yellow. Although AgI is a darker yellow than AgBr, it might be difficult to distinguish the two ions by color.

Did You Know?

Review with students what a mole is and how it relates to Avogadro's constant, 6.02×10^{23}.

Teaching Tip

Mole Ratios Explain to students the reason why coefficients in a balanced equation can represent either single units or moles. Write a simple balanced chemical equation on the chalkboard. Multiply all coefficients by a small integer, such as 3. Show that even though the coefficients are not as simple as they could be, the equation is still balanced. Repeat several times, using different integers. Emphasize that a chemical equation is like a mathematical equation in that you can multiply through the entire equation by the same number without changing the relationship among the formulas. For coefficients to represent moles, the number used to multiply the coefficients in a balanced equation is Avogadro's constant.

Balancing Chemical Equations

▌ SECTION 5.3 REVIEW

Check Your Understanding

1. The complete and balanced equation is (c).

2. **a.** $KOH + HCl \rightarrow KCl + H_2O$
   b. $Pb(NO_3)_2 + 2KI \rightarrow 2KNO_3 + PbI_2$
   c. $2NaHCO_3 \rightarrow H_2O + CO_2 + Na_2CO_3$
   d. $2NaCl + H_2SO_4 \rightarrow Na_2SO_4 + 2HCl$

3. Changing subscripts changes the identities of the substances in the reaction. Changing coefficients does not change the identity of a substance, just the number of units of it.

4. You need to know the molar mass of the substance and the mass and molar mass of one other substance in the reaction.

Answers continue on p. 181B.

▶ **mole ratio** the smallest relative number of moles of the substances involved in a reaction

Mole ratios can be derived from balanced equations

Whether the magnesium-oxygen reaction starts with 2 mol or 4 mol of magnesium, the proportions remain the same. One way to understand this is to look at the **mole ratios** from the balanced equation. For 2 mol of magnesium and 1 mol of oxygen, the ratio is 2:1. If 4 mol of magnesium is present, 2 mol of oxygen is needed to react. The ratio is 4:2, which reduces to 2:1.

The mole ratio for any reaction comes from the balanced chemical equation. For example, in the following equation for the synthesis of water, the mole ratio for $H_2:O_2:H_2O$, using the coefficients, is 2:1:2.

$$2H_2 + O_2 \longrightarrow 2H_2O$$

▌ SECTION 5.3 REVIEW

SUMMARY

▶ A chemical equation shows the reactants that combine and the products that result from the reaction.

▶ Balanced chemical equations show the proportions of reactants and products needed for the mass to be conserved.

▶ A compound always contains the same elements in the same proportions, regardless of how the compound is made or how much of the compound is formed.

▶ A mole ratio relates the amounts of any two or more substances involved in a chemical reaction.

CHECK YOUR UNDERSTANDING

1. **Identify** which of the following is a complete and balanced chemical equation:
   a. $H_2O \longrightarrow H_2 + O_2$
   b. $NaCl + H_2O$
   c. $Fe + S \longrightarrow FeS$
   d. $CaCO_3$

2. **Balance** the following equations:
   a. $KOH + HCl \longrightarrow KCl + H_2O$
   b. $Pb(NO_3)_2 + KI \longrightarrow KNO_3 + PbI_2$
   c. $NaHCO_3 \longrightarrow H_2O + CO_2 + Na_2CO_3$
   d. $NaCl + H_2SO_4 \longrightarrow Na_2SO_4 + HCl$

3. **Explain** why the numbers in front of chemical formulas, not the subscripts, must be changed to balance an equation.

4. **Describe** the information needed to calculate the mass of a reactant or product for the following balanced equation:

$$FeS + 2HCl \longrightarrow H_2S + FeCl_2$$

5. **Critical Thinking** Ammonia is manufactured by the Haber process.

$$N_2 + 3H_2 \rightleftharpoons 2NH_3 + \text{heat}$$

This involves the reaction of nitrogen with hydrogen to form ammonia. What mass of nitrogen is needed to make 34 g of ammonia?

5.4

Rates of Change

OBJECTIVES

- Describe the factors affecting reaction rates.
- Explain the effect a catalyst has on a chemical reaction.
- Explain chemical equilibrium in terms of equal forward and reverse reaction rates.
- Apply Le Châtelier's principle to predict the effect of changes in concentration, temperature, and pressure in an equilibrium process.

KEY TERMS

catalyst
enzyme
substrate
equilibrium
Le Châtelier's principle

Chemical reactions can occur at different speeds or rates. Some reactions, such as the explosion of nitroglycerin, shown in **Figure 5-17,** are very fast. Other reactions, such as the burning of carbon in charcoal, are much slower. But what if you wanted to slow down the nitroglycerin reaction to make it safer? What if you wanted to speed up the reaction by which yeast make carbon dioxide, so bread would rise in less time? If you think carefully, you may already know some things about how to change reaction rates.

internetconnect

SCILINKS NSTA

TOPIC: Factors affecting reaction rate
GO TO: www.scilinks.org
KEYWORD: HK1054

Factors Affecting Reaction Rates

Think about the following observations:

- A potato slice takes 5 minutes to fry in oil at 200°C but takes 10 minutes to cook in boiling water at 100°C. Therefore, potatoes cook faster at higher temperatures.
- Potato slices take 10 minutes to cook in boiling water, but whole potatoes take about 30 minutes to boil. Therefore, potatoes cook faster if you cut them up into smaller pieces.

These observations relate to the speed of chemical reactions. For any reaction to occur, the particles of the reactants must collide with one another. In each situation where the potatoes cooked faster, the contact between particles was greater, so the cooking reaction went faster.

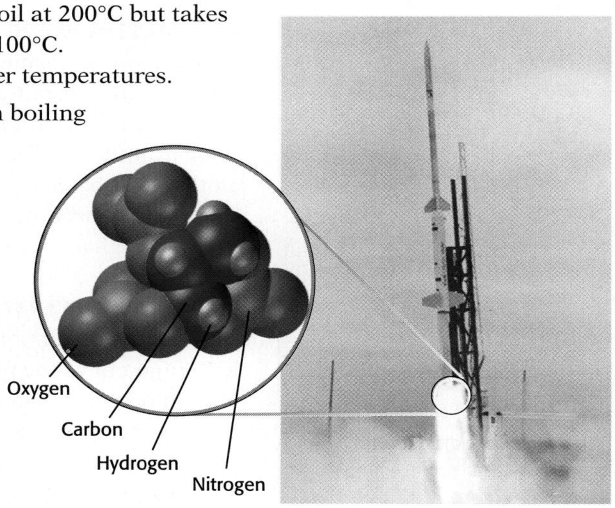
Oxygen
Carbon
Hydrogen
Nitrogen

Figure 5-17
Nitroglycerin can be used as a rocket fuel as well as a medicine for people with heart ailments.

Rates of Change

Scheduling

Refer to pp. 146A–146D for lecture, classwork, and assignment options for Section 5.4.

★ Lesson Focus
Use transparency *LT 18* to prepare students for this section.

READING SKILL BUILDER ***Paired Reading*** Have pairs of students read difficult passages silently and make notes on the sections they do not understand. Be sure students study all figures, captions, and tables to help clarify the relevant passages. Have each pair of students discuss the passages that each student found difficult. If one student is unable to clarify the passage for his or her partner, have the pair pose a question for class discussion or teacher explanation.

Teaching Tip

Reaction Rate Before beginning this section, point out to students that chemical reactions occur when reactant particles collide with each other with sufficient energy to cause a reaction. Ask students to suggest ways that you could increase the frequency of collisions, the energy of the collisions, or both to increase the reaction rate. Lead students to realize that increasing concentration, temperature, or surface area will increase the reaction rate. Ask students to explain how each of these changes would affect the frequency or energy of the collisions.

DEMONSTRATION 5 TEACHING

Effect of Surface Area on Rates of Change

Time: Approximately 15 minutes
Materials: 100 mL graduated cylinder (2), rock salt, table salt, weighing paper, balance, 1 can of carbonated soda

Label one graduated cylinder "rock salt" and the other cylinder "table salt." Pour 75 mL of carbonated soda into each graduated cylinder. Measure the mass of one large crystal of rock salt. Obtain an equivalent mass of table salt. Simultaneously dump each salt sample into the appropriately labeled graduated cylinder.

Analysis
Since the masses of the salt samples are identical, the only variable between the two samples is the amount of surface area. The increased surface area of the table salt provides many more reactive sites for the dissolved CO_2 to form, resulting in a greater amount of foam being formed.

Rates of Change

Teaching Tip

Increasing Concentration
Model the effect of increasing concentration on reaction rate by using a CD case and metal BBs. Remove the plastic insert that holds the CD in the case to get a clear shallow box. Place 25 to 50 BBs in the case, and place the case on an overhead projector. Swirl and jerk the case so that the frequency of collisions between the BBs can be seen. Next double the number of BBs in the box. This doubles the concentration of BBs. Swirl the box again; students should be able to see the increase in the frequency of collisions. If you cover the outer 3/4 in. of the box, students will not be distracted by the BBs hitting the sides.

Figure 5-18

A Mold will grow on bread stored at room temperature.

B Bread stored in the freezer for the same length of time will be free of mold when you take it out.

Figure 5-19
When a solid is divided into pieces, the total surface area becomes larger.

Most reactions go faster at higher temperatures

A potato slice cooks faster in hot oil than in boiling water. Heating food speeds up the chemical reactions that happen in cooking. Cooling food slows down the chemical reactions that result in spoiling, as shown in **Figure 5-18.**

In Chapter 2, you learned that one of the assumptions of the kinetic theory is that particles move faster at higher temperatures. This faster motion increases the energy of the particles and increases the chances that the particles will collide. This means that there are more chances for the particles to react. Because the particles have more chances to react, the reaction will be faster.

A large surface area speeds up reactions

You can save time making mashed potatoes by cutting the potatoes into small pieces before boiling them, because sliced potatoes cook more quickly than whole potatoes. When a whole potato is placed in boiling water, only the outside is in direct contact with the boiling water. As **Figure 5-19** shows, cutting potatoes into pieces allows parts that were inside the potato to be exposed. In other words, the *surface area* of the potato is increased. The surface area of a solid is the amount of the surface that is exposed.

The same holds true for most chemical reactants. If you crush a solid into a powder or dissolve it in a solution, more of the solid surface is exposed. Generally solids that have a large surface area react more rapidly because more particles can come in contact with the other reactants.

Concentrated solutions react faster

Think about a washing machine full of clothes with grass stains on them. If you put a few drops of bleach in the washing machine full of water, little will happen to the dirty clothes. If you pour a bottle of bleach into the washing machine, the stained clothes will be clean. In fact, they may not have any color left. The more concentrated solution has more bleach particles. This means a higher chance for particle collisions with the stains.

Reactions are quicker at higher pressure

Like the concentration of a liquid, the concentration of a gas can be thought of as the number of particles in a given volume. A gas at high pressure is more concentrated than a gas at low pressure because the gas at high pressure has been squeezed into a smaller volume. Gases react faster at higher pressures; the particles have less space, so they have more collisions.

DEMONSTRATION 6   SCIENCE AND THE CONSUMER

Temperature Effects on Dissolving

Time: Approximately 30 minutes
Materials: 400 mL beakers (2), beaker tongs, 2 tea bags, tap water, ice, hot plate

Add 300 mL of water to each 400 mL beaker. Place the first beaker on a hot plate and heat the water until it is almost boiling. Add ice to the second beaker and allow the water to cool to almost 0°C. Remove any remaining ice. Add a tea bag to each beaker. The hot water quickly becomes brown as the tea dissolves into it. The cold water remains colorless because the rate of dissolving is much slower at low temperatures.

Analysis

1. Is it important to keep the volumes of water constant in this demonstration? *(Yes, then temperature will be the only variable.)*
2. How does temperature relate to the rate of molecular motion? *(As temperature increases, so does the rate of molecular motion.)*

Massive, bulky molecules react slower

The size and shape of the reactant molecules affect the rate of reaction. You know from the kinetic theory of matter, which you studied in Chapter 2, that massive molecules move more slowly than less massive molecules at the same temperature. This means that for equal numbers of massive and "light" molecules of about the same size, the molecules with more mass collide less often with other molecules.

Some molecules, such as large biological compounds, must fit together in a particular way to react. They can collide with other reactants many times, but if the collision occurs on the wrong end of the molecule, they will not react. Generally these compounds react very slowly because many unsuccessful collisions may occur before a successful collision begins the reaction.

Catalysts change the rates of chemical reactions

Why add a substance to a reaction if the substance may not react? This is done all the time in industry when **catalysts** are added to make reactions go faster. Catalysts are not reactants or products. They speed up or slow reactions. Catalysts that slow reactions are called *inhibitors*. Catalysts are used to help make ammonia, to process crude oil, and to accelerate making plastics. Catalysts can be expensive and still be profitable because they can be cleaned or renewed and reused.

Catalysts work in different ways. Most solid catalysts, such as those in car exhaust systems, speed up reactions by providing a surface where the reactants can collect and react. Then the reactants can form new bonds to make the products. Most solid catalysts are more effective if they have a large surface area.

Enzymes are biological catalysts

Enzymes are proteins that are catalysts for chemical reactions in living things. Enzymes are very specific. Each enzyme controls one reaction or set of similar reactions. Some common enzymes and the reactions they control are listed in **Table 5-1.** Most enzymes are fragile. If they are kept too cold or too warm, they tend to decompose. Most enzymes stop working above 45°C.

Did You Know?

In our atmosphere at room temperature, a molecule of oxygen, O_2, will have about four billion (4×10^9) collisions in 1 s. In interstellar space due to the differences in both temperature and pressure, hydrogen will have a collision about once every 8 days.

▶ **catalyst** a substance that changes the rate of chemical reactions without being consumed

▶ **enzyme** a protein that speeds up a specific biochemical reaction

internetconnect

SCI**LINKS**
NSTA

TOPIC: Catalysts
GO TO: www.scilinks.org
KEYWORD: HK1055

Table 5-1 **Common Enzymes and Their Uses**

Enzyme	Substrate	What the enzyme does
Amylase	Starch	Breaks down long starch molecules into sugars
Cellulase	Cellulose	Breaks down long cellulose molecules into sugars
DNA polymerase	Nucleic acid	Builds up DNA chains in cell nuclei
Lipase	Fat	Breaks down fat into smaller molecules
Protease	Protein	Breaks down proteins into amino acids.

Graphic Organizer
Rate of Reaction

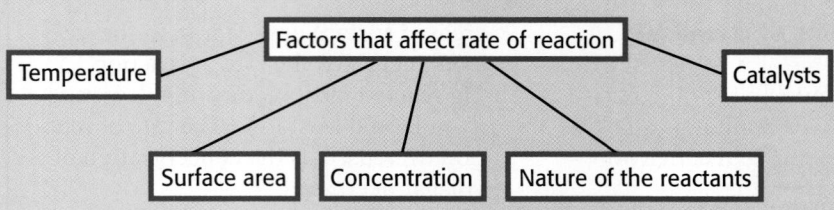

Additional Application

Catalytic Converters Students are probably familiar with catalytic converters. In general, catalytic converters have one section where nitrogen oxides are reduced to N_2 and O_2 using catalysts, such as platinum. The second section uses the same catalysts to completely oxidize unoxidized or only partially oxidized hydrocarbons and carbon monoxide in exhaust gases.

MISCONCEPTION   ALERT

Inhibitors Although inhibitors appear to retard reactions, they actually bind reactants so that they are not available for other reactions. The term *inhibitor* comes from the Latin *in*, which means "in," and *habere*, which means "to have or to hold." Thus, an inhibitor is a substance that holds a reactant, keeping it from reacting with another substance.

|SKILL BUILDER

Interpreting Visuals Few chemical reactions in the human body would occur at a rate fast enough to sustain life without the presence of enzymes. Have students study the enzyme functions listed in **Table 5-1.** Not all enzymes break down large molecules. Some enzymes catalyze the formation of larger molecules, as is shown by the entry for DNA polymerase. Other examples where enzymes catalyze the formation of larger molecules include the formation of proteins from amino acids.

Rates of Change

Teaching Tip

Enzymes Two types of catalysts exist. Heterogeneous catalysts provide a surface where reactants concentrate, increasing reaction rate. This type of catalyst does not actually enter into the reaction. A heterogeneous catalyst is used in the catalytic converters found in vehicles. Homogeneous catalysts, such as enzymes, mix with the reactants and form an intermediate compound with one of them. This intermediate compound reacts more readily with the other reactant than the original reactant does. After this final reaction, the catalyst is released unchanged.

Enzymes Students may think that all enzymes break molecules apart because they have often heard about enzymes "breaking down" food in the digestive system. Enzymes are also responsible for putting together molecules, including large biopolymers such as starch and proteins. These enzymes carry out biosyntheses that are usually endothermic. For this reason they use a large amount of energy stored in the form of ATP, adenosine triphosphate, to carry out their functions. This is one of the reasons why living things require a constant supply of energy.

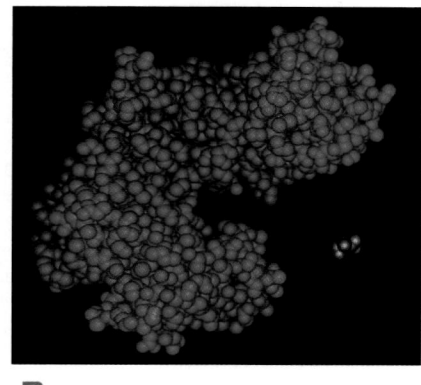
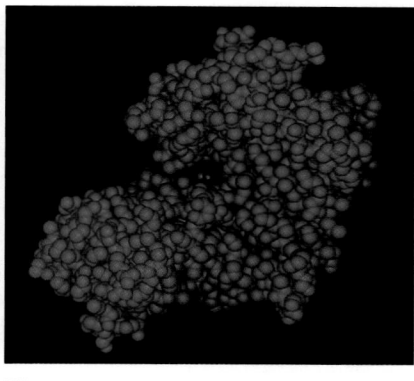

Figure 5-20
The enzyme hexokinase catalyzes the addition of phosphate to glucose. This model shows the enzyme, in blue, before (A) and after (B) it fits with a glucose molecule, shown in red.

A   **B**

► **substrate** the specific substance affected by an enzyme

Catalase, an enzyme produced by humans and most other living organisms, breaks down hydrogen peroxide. Hydrogen peroxide is the **substrate** for catalase.

$$2H_2O_2 \xrightarrow{\text{catalase}} 2H_2O + O_2$$

For an enzyme to catalyze a reaction, the substrate and the enzyme must fit exactly—like a key in a lock. This fit is shown in **Figure 5-20.** Enzymes are very efficient. In 1 minute, one molecule of catalase can catalyze the decomposition of 6 million molecules of hydrogen peroxide.

Inquiry Lab

What affects the rates of chemical reactions?

Materials
- ✔ Bunsen burner
- ✔ paper clip
- ✔ 6 test tubes
- ✔ paper ash
- ✔ sandpaper
- ✔ tongs
- ✔ matches
- ✔ 2 sugar cubes
- ✔ steel wool ball, 2 cm diameter
- ✔ graduated cylinder
- ✔ vinegar
- ✔ magnesium ribbon, copper foil strip, zinc strip; each 3 cm long, uniform width

Procedure

SAFETY CAUTION Wear safety goggles and an apron.
1. Label three test tubes 1, 2, and 3. Place 10 mL of vinegar in each test tube. Sandpaper the metals until they are shiny. Then add the magnesium to test tube 1, the zinc to test tube 2, and the copper to test tube 3. Record your observations.
2. Using tongs, hold a paper clip in the hottest part of the burner flame for 30 s. Repeat with a ball of steel wool. Record your observations.
3. Label three more test tubes A, B, and C. To test tube A, add 10 mL of vinegar; to test tube B, add

5 mL of vinegar and 5 mL of water; and to test tube C, add 2.5 mL of vinegar and 7.5 mL of water. Add a piece of magnesium ribbon to each test tube. Record your observations.
4. Using tongs, hold a sugar cube and try to ignite it with a match. Rub paper ash on another cube and try again. Record your observations.

Analysis

1. Describe and interpret your results.
2. For each step, list the factor(s) that influenced the rate of reaction.

172 CHAPTER 5

Inquiry Lab

What affects the rates of chemical reactions?

1. Mg reacted most quickly, forming bubbles of H_2. Zn reacted but not as quickly, and Cu did not react. The reactivity of the metals differed.
2. The paper clip showed no evidence of reaction. The steel wool had rust, indicating a reaction with oxygen. The increased surface area of iron in the steel wool increased the rate of reaction.
3. Mg reacted most readily in A, less readily in B, and least in C. The rate of reaction decreased as the concentration of vinegar decreased.
4. The sugar cube did not burn. The ash was a catalyst.

Equilibrium Systems

When nitroglycerin explodes, nothing much is left. When an iron nail rusts, given enough time, all the iron is converted to iron(III) oxide and only the rust remains. Even though an explosion occurs rapidly and rusting occurs slowly, both reactions go to completion. Most of the reactants are converted to products, and the amount that is not converted is not noticeable and usually is not important.

Some changes are reversible

You may get the idea that all chemical reactions go to completion if you watch a piece of wood burn or see an explosion. However, reactions don't always go to completion; some reactions are reversible.

For example, carbonated drinks, such as the soda shown in **Figure 5-21,** contain carbon dioxide. These drinks are manufactured by dissolving carbon dioxide in water under pressure. To keep the carbon dioxide dissolved, you need to maintain the pressure by keeping the top on the bottle. Opening the soda allows the pressure to decrease. When this happens, some of the carbon dioxide comes out of solution, and you see a stream of carbon dioxide bubbles. This carbon dioxide change is reversible.

$$CO_2 \text{ (gas above liquid)} \underset{\substack{\text{decrease} \\ \text{pressure}}}{\overset{\substack{\text{increase} \\ \text{pressure}}}{\rightleftharpoons}} CO_2 \text{ (gas dissolved in liquid)}$$

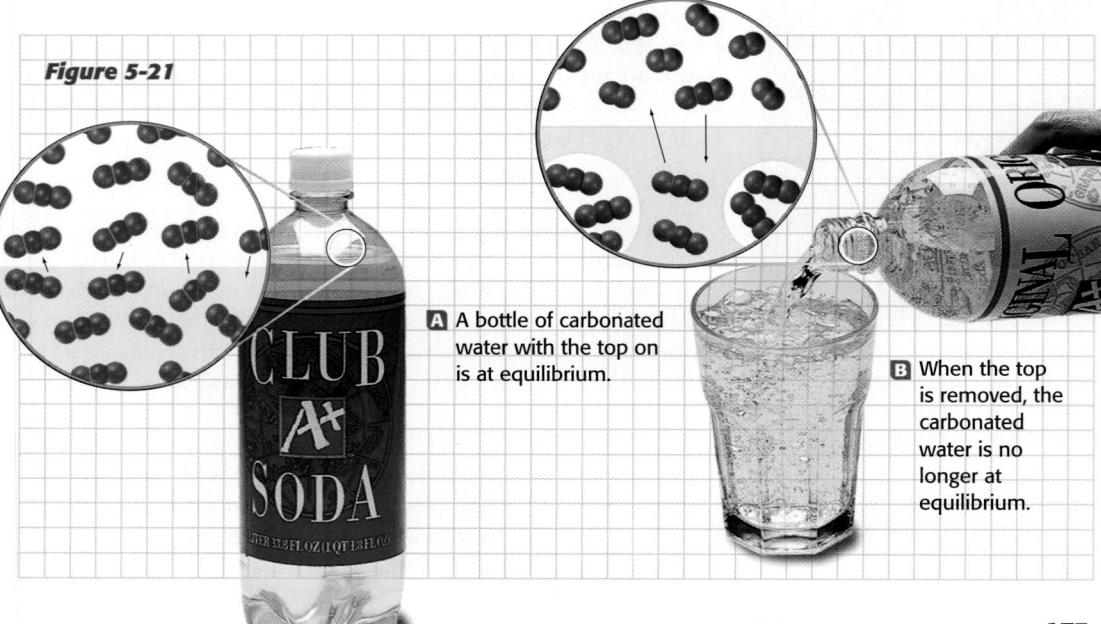

Figure 5-21

A A bottle of carbonated water with the top on is at equilibrium.

B When the top is removed, the carbonated water is no longer at equilibrium.

CHEMICAL REACTIONS **173**

Section 5.4

Rates of Change

Historical Perspective

In the early part of the twentieth century, a rapid increase in use of vehicles that contained internal combustion engines resulted in an equally rapid increase in demand for gasoline. Distillation of petroleum resulted in production of gasoline, but the amount produced was not nearly adequate. Other, heavier petroleum products were available from the distillation, and few uses existed for them. In 1912, gasoline producers started using high temperatures to perform large-scale "cracking" of these larger molecules. The resulting smaller molecules were suitable for gasoline. In 1936, a cracking procedure that used catalysts instead of high temperatures was developed. This procedure was instrumental in providing Allied forces with needed gasoline during World War II.

RESOURCE LINK
DATASHEETS

Have students use *Datasheet 5.4 Quick Activity: Catalysts in Action* to record their results.

The reaction can go in either direction. The $\rightleftarrows$ sign indicates a reversible change. Compare it with the arrow you normally see in chemical reactions, $\longrightarrow$, which indicates a change that goes in one direction—toward completion.

Equilibrium results when rates balance

When a carbonated drink is in a closed bottle, you can't see any changes. The system is in **equilibrium**—a balanced state. This balanced state is dynamic. No changes are apparent, but changes are occurring. If you could see individual molecules in the bottle, you would see continual change. Molecules of CO_2 are coming out of solution constantly. However, CO_2 molecules from the air above the liquid are dissolving at the same time and the same rate.

The result is that the amount of dissolved and undissolved CO_2 doesn't change, even though individual CO_2 molecules are moving in and out of the solution. This is similar to the number of players on the field for a football team. Although different players can be on the field at any time, eleven players are always on the field for each team.

Systems in equilibrium respond to minimize change

When the top is removed from a carbonated drink, the drink is no longer at equilibrium, and CO_2 leaves as bubbles. For equilibrium to be reached, none of the reactants or products can escape.

An example of an equilibrium system is the conversion of limestone, $CaCO_3$, to lime, CaO. Limestone and seashells, which are also made of $CaCO_3$, were used to make lime more than 2000 years ago. By heating limestone in an open pot, lime was produced to make cement. The ancient buildings in Greece and Rome, such as the one shown in **Figure 5-22,** were probably built with cement made by this reaction.

$$CaCO_3 + heat \longrightarrow CaO + CO_2$$

Because the CO_2 gas can escape from an open pot, the reaction proceeds until all of the limestone is converted to lime.

However, if some dry limestone is sealed in a closed container and heated, the result is different. As soon as some CO_2 builds up in the container, the reverse reaction starts. Once the concentrations of the $CaCO_3$, CaO, and CO_2 stabilize, equilibrium is established.

$$CaCO_3 \rightleftarrows CaO + CO_2$$

If there aren't any changes in the pressure or the temperature, the forward and reverse reactions continue to take place at the same rate. The concentration of CO_2 and the amounts of $CaCO_3$ and CaO in the container remain the same.

▶ **equilibrium** the state in which a chemical reaction and its reverse occur at the same time and at the same rate

VOCABULARY *Skills Tip*
Equilibrium comes from the Latin aequilibris *meaning equally balanced. In Latin,* aequil *means equal, and* libra *means a balance scale. You may have seen the constellation called Libra. The stars in the constellation roughly represent a balance.*

Figure 5-22
Cement for ancient buildings, like this one in Limeni, Greece, probably contained lime made from seashells.

ALTERNATIVE ASSESSMENT

Dissolving Gases and Pressure

Have students bring in bottles of carbonated soft drinks. Hold a discussion to establish that there is carbon dioxide in the space above the liquid in the bottle, and that there is carbon dioxide dissolved within the liquid. Explain that the carbon dioxide is in equilibrium. Ask students to identify whether an opened carbonated soft drink is at higher or lower pressure than a sealed one. *(The opened bottle is at lower pressure.)*

Have students write a paragraph predicting how the amount of dissolved gas will be influenced by decreasing the pressure. (**HINT:** See Table 5-2.) When students have made predictions, they can demonstrate the influence of decreasing pressure on the dissolved gas by opening their bottles. In a second paragraph, ask students to discuss how well their observations match their predictions.

Table 5-2 The Effects of Change on Equilibrium

Condition	Effect
Temperature	Increasing temperature favors the reaction that absorbs energy.
Pressure	Increasing pressure favors the reaction that produces less gas.
Concentration	Increasing the concentration of one substance favors the reaction that produces less of that substance.

Le Châtelier's principle predicts changes in equilibrium

Le Châtelier's principle is a general rule that describes the behavior of equilibrium systems.

> **If a change is made to a system in chemical equilibrium, the equilibrium shifts to oppose the change until a new equilibrium is reached.**

The effects of different changes on an equilibrium system are shown in **Table 5-2.**

Ammonia is a chemical building block used to make fertilizers, dyes, plastics, cosmetics, cleaning products, and fire retardants, such as those you see being applied in **Figure 5-23.** The Haber process, which is used to make ammonia industrially, is exothermic; it releases energy.

$$\text{nitrogen} + \text{hydrogen} \rightleftharpoons \text{ammonia} + \text{heat}$$

$$N_2 \text{ (gas)} + 3H_2 \text{ (gas)} \rightleftharpoons 2NH_3 \text{ (gas)} + \text{heat}$$

At an ammonia-manufacturing plant, such as the one shown in **Figure 5-24,** production chemists must choose the conditions that favor the highest yield of NH_3. In other words, the equilibrium should favor the production of NH_3.

Figure 5-24
Ammonia, which is manufactured in plants such as this, is used to make ammonium perchlorate—one of the space shuttle's fuels.

Figure 5-23
Ammonium sulfate and ammonium phosphate are being dropped from the airplane as fire retardants. The red dye used for identification fades away after a few days.

INTEGRATING

ENVIRONMENTAL SCIENCE
All living things need nitrogen, which cycles through the environment. Nitrogen gas, N_2, is changed to ammonia by bacteria in soils. Different bacteria in the soil change the ammonia to nitrites and nitrates. Nitrogen in the form of nitrates is needed by plants to grow. Animals eat the plants and deposit nitrogen compounds back in the soil. When plants or animals die, nitrogen compounds are also returned to the soil. Additional bacteria change the nitrogen compounds back to nitrogen gas, and the cycle can start again.

Rates of Change

Historical Perspective

In 1909, Fritz Haber used what is now known as the Haber process to manufacture ammonia from nitrogen and hydrogen. Carl Bosch, who built an operating ammonia plant in Germany in 1913, further refined the process. Throughout World War I, the factory supplied Germany with ammonia that was needed for explosives. As a result, controversy existed regarding Haber's receiving the Nobel Prize in Chemistry in 1918 and Bosch's receiving the same award in 1931.

INTEGRATING

ENVIRONMENTAL SCIENCE
Soil often lacks sufficient amounts of the organisms that change nitrogen gas to ammonia, so fertilizers containing usable nitrogen compounds are added. To reduce the amount of chemical fertilizers needed, agriculturalists usually rotate crops, alternating a nitrogen-fixing legume crop, such as clover, beans, peas, or peanuts, with other crops.

Nodules in the roots of legumes contain nitrogen-fixing bacteria that convert atmospheric nitrogen to ammonia. Recently, researchers at the University of Sydney, in Australia, have succeeded in adding nitrogen-fixing bacteria to the roots of wheat plants. Similar research is ongoing with other crops, such as corn and rice.

Resources Assign students worksheet *5.7 Integrating Environmental Science—Fertilizers: Friend or Foe?* in the **Integration Enrichment Resource** ancillary.

Check Your Understanding

1. Examples of chemical equilibrium are (a), (c), and (d).

2. surface area, concentration, temperature, presence of a catalyst, pressure, nature of the reactants

3. If a change is made to a system in chemical equilibrium, the equilibrium shifts to oppose the change until a new equilibrium is reached. Carbonic acid, H_2CO_3, decomposes into CO_2 and H_2O. ($H_2CO_3 \rightarrow CO_2 + H_2O$) If the CO_2 is removed as it is produced, the equilibrium will shift to the right to produce more products.

4. A catalyst alters the rate of a reaction, usually by speeding it up. An inhibitor is a type of catalyst that ties up a reactant, the effect being to slow the rate of reaction.

5. If the reaction is in equilibrium, it is proceeding in both directions at equal rates.

6. Most reactions speed up when heated and slow down when cooled.

7. Pressure changes affect gases only. Because there are more moles of gas on the left side of the equation, increasing the pressure forces the reaction to the right.

Answers continue on p. 181B.

If you raise the temperature, Le Châtelier's principle indicates that the equilibrium will shift to the left, the direction that absorbs energy and makes less ammonia. If you raise the pressure, the equilibrium will move to reduce the pressure according to Le Châtelier's principle. One way to reduce the pressure is to have fewer gas molecules. This means the equilibrium moves to the right—more ammonia—because there are fewer gas molecules on the right side. So to get the most ammonia from this reaction, you need to use a high pressure and a low temperature. The Haber process is a good example of balancing equilibrium conditions to make the most product.

SECTION 5.4 REVIEW

SUMMARY

▶ Increasing the temperature, surface area, concentration, or pressure of reactants may speed up chemical reactions.

▶ Catalysts alter the rate of chemical reactions. Most catalysts speed up chemical reactions. Others, called inhibitors, slow reactions down.

▶ In a chemical reaction, chemical equilibrium is achieved when reactants change to products and products change to reactants at the same time and the same rate.

▶ At chemical equilibrium, no changes are apparent even though individual particles are reacting.

▶ Le Châtelier's principle states that for any change made to a system in equilibrium, the equilibrium will shift to minimize the effects of the change.

CHECK YOUR UNDERSTANDING

1. **Identify** which of the following are examples of chemical equilibrium:
   a. $2NO_2 \rightleftharpoons N_2O_4$
   b. $2H_2O \longrightarrow 2H_2 + O_2$
   c. $N_2 + 3H_2 \rightleftharpoons 2NH_3 + heat$
   d. $H_2 + I_2 \rightleftharpoons 2HI$

2. **List** five factors that may affect the rate of a chemical reaction.

3. **Identify and Explain** an example of Le Châtelier's principle.

4. **Compare and Contrast** a catalyst and an inhibitor.

5. **Analyze** the error in reasoning in the following situation: A person claims that because the overall amounts of reactants and products don't change, a reaction must have stopped.

6. **Describe** what can happen to the reaction rate of a system that is heated and then cooled.

7. **Decide** which way an increase in pressure will shift the following equilibrium system involving ethane, C_2H_6, oxygen, O_2, water, H_2O, and carbon dioxide, CO_2.

   $2C_2H_6 \text{ (gas)} + 7O_2 \text{ (gas)} \rightleftharpoons 6H_2O \text{ (liquid)} + 4CO_2 \text{ (gas)}$

8. **Decision Making** Consider the decomposition of solid calcium carbonate to solid calcium oxide and carbon dioxide gas.

   $heat + CaCO_3 \rightleftharpoons CaO + CO_2 \text{ (gas)}$

   What conditions of temperature and pressure would you choose to get the most decomposition of $CaCO_3$? Explain your reasoning.

Chapter Highlights

Before you begin, review the summaries of the key ideas of each section, found on pages 153, 160, 168, and 176. The key vocabulary terms are listed on pages 148, 154, 161, and 169.

UNDERSTANDING CONCEPTS

1. When a chemical reaction occurs, atoms are never _____.
   a. ionized
   c. destroyed
   b. rearranged
   d. vaporized

2. In an exothermic reaction, _____.
   a. energy is conserved
   b. the formation of bonds in the product releases more energy than is required to break the bonds in the reactants
   c. energy is released as bonds form
   d. All of the above

3. A + B $\longrightarrow$ AB is an example of a _____.
   a. synthesis reaction
   b. decomposition reaction
   c. single-displacement reaction
   d. double-displacement reaction
   e. redox reaction

4. Which of the following reactions is not an example of a redox reaction?
   a. combustion
   b. rusting
   c. dissolving in salt water
   d. respiration

5. Radicals _____.
   a. form ionic bonds with other ions
   b. result from broken covalent bonds
   c. usually break apart to form smaller components
   d. bind molecules together

6. In any chemical equation, the arrow means _____.
   a. "equals"
   b. "is greater than"
   c. "yields"

7. Hydrogen peroxide, H_2O_2, decomposes to produce water and oxygen gas. The balanced equation for this reaction is _____.
   a. $H_2O_2 \longrightarrow H_2O + O_2$
   b. $2H_2O_2 \longrightarrow 2H_2O + O_2$
   c. $2H_2O_2 \longrightarrow H_2O + 2O_2$
   d. $2H_2O_2 \longrightarrow 2H_2O + 2O_2$

8. Most reactions speed up when _____.
   a. the temperature is lowered
   b. equilibrium is achieved
   c. the concentration of the products is increased
   d. the reactants are in small pieces

9. Enzymes _____.
   a. can be used to speed up almost any chemical reaction
   b. rely on increased surface area to catalyze reactions
   c. catalyze specific biological reactions
   d. always work faster at higher temperatures

10. A system in chemical equilibrium _____.
    a. has particles that don't move
    b. responds to minimize change
    c. is undergoing visible change
    d. is stable only when all of the reactants have been used

Using Vocabulary

11. Explain what it means when a system in equilibrium shifts to favor the products.

12. When wood is burned, energy is released in the forms of heat and light. Describe the reaction, and explain why this change does not violate the law of conservation of energy. Use the terms *combustion, exothermic,* and *chemical energy*.

WRITING SKILL

13. Translate the following chemical equation into a sentence.
    $$CH_4 + 2O_2 \longrightarrow CO_2 + 2H_2O$$

UNDERSTANDING CONCEPTS

1. c	6. c
2. d	7. b
3. a	8. d
4. c	9. c
5. b	10. b

Using Vocabulary

11. It means that a stress that favors formation of products has been placed on the system. The system will shift to produce more products to relieve that stress.

12. Wood undergoes combustion, which is an exothermic reaction. The total energy released in the reaction plus the chemical energy in the bonds of the products is the same chemical energy contained in the chemical bonds of the reactants. Energy was neither created nor destroyed.

13. Accept any accurate sentence. Sample sentence: One mole of methane reacts with 2 mol of oxygen gas to yield 1 mol of carbon dioxide gas and 2 mol of water.

14. a. forward
    b. forward
    c. forward
    d. forward
    e. reverse

BUILDING MATH SKILLS

15. a. from 10°C to about 42°C
   b. from about 42°C to 50°C
   c. about 42°C
16. $2HgO \rightarrow 2Hg + O_2$
17. a. The mole ratio of $Al_2(SO_4)_3$ and H_2SO_4 is 1:3. If 6 mol of H_2SO_4 are used, 2 mol of $Al_2(SO_4)_3$ are produced.
   b. The mole ratio of Al_2O_3 and H_2O is 1:3. Therefore, 3 mol of Al_2O_3 are needed for 9 mol of H_2O.
   c. 588 mol of $Al_2(SO_4)_3$ and 1764 mol of H_2O
18. 1:12 for $C_{12}H_{22}O_{11}$: O_2 and $C_{12}H_{22}O_{11}$: CO_2; 1:11 for $C_{12}H_{22}O_{11}$:H_2O; 1:1 for O_2:CO_2; 12:11 for O_2:H_2O and CO_2:H_2O
19. a. $64 \text{ g S} \times \dfrac{1 \text{ mol S}}{32.07 \text{ g S}} \times \dfrac{1 \text{ mol } SO_2}{1 \text{ mol S}} \times \dfrac{64.07 \text{ g } SO_2}{1 \text{mol } SO_2} = 130 \text{ g } SO_2$
   b. $256 \text{ g } SO_2 \times \dfrac{1 \text{ mol } SO_2}{64.07 \text{ g } SO_2} \times \dfrac{1 \text{ mol S}}{1 \text{ mol } SO_2} \times \dfrac{32.07 \text{ g S}}{1 \text{ mol S}} = 128 \text{ g S}$
20. $Zn + 2HCl \rightarrow ZnCl_2 + H_2$

---

14. For each of the following changes to the equilibrium system below, predict which reaction will be favored—forward (to the right), reverse (to the left), or neither.

$$H_2 \text{ (gas)} + Cl_2 \text{ (gas)} \rightleftharpoons 2HCl \text{ (gas)} + \text{heat}$$

   a. addition of Cl_2
   b. removal of HCl
   c. increased pressure
   d. decreased temperature
   e. removal of H_2

BUILDING MATH SKILLS

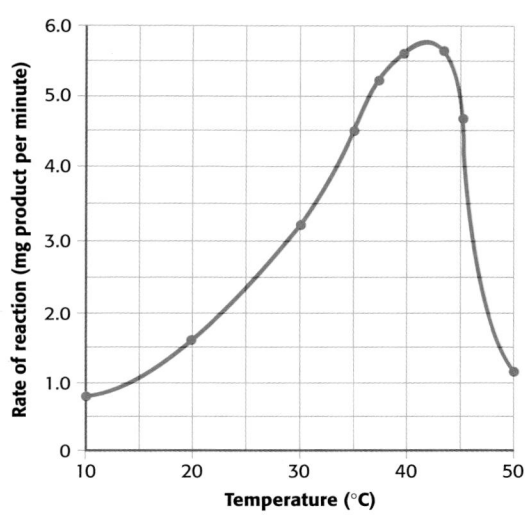

15. Graphing A technician carried out an experiment to study the effect of increasing temperature on a certain reaction. Her results are shown in the graph above.
   a. Between which temperatures does the rate of the reaction rise?
   b. Between which temperatures does the rate of the reaction slow down?
   c. At what temperature is the rate of the reaction fastest?

16. Chemical Equations In 1774, Joseph Priestly discovered oxygen when he heated solid mercury(II) oxide, HgO, and produced the element mercury and oxygen gas. Write and balance this equation.

17. Chemical Equations Aluminum sulfate, $Al_2(SO_4)_3$, is used to fireproof fabrics and to make antiperspirants. It can be formed from a reaction between aluminum oxide, Al_2O_3, and H_2SO_4.

$$Al_2O_3 + 3H_2SO_4 \longrightarrow Al_2(SO_4)_3 + 3H_2O$$

   a. How many moles of $Al_2(SO_4)_3$ would be produced if 6 mol of H_2SO_4 reacted with an unlimited amount of Al_2O_3?
   b. How many moles of Al_2O_3 are required to make 9 mol of H_2O?
   c. If 588 mol of Al_2O_3 reacts with unlimited H_2SO_4, how many moles of each of the products will be produced?

18. Chemical Equations Sucrose, $C_{12}H_{22}O_{11}$, is a sugar used to sweeten many foods. Inside the body, it is broken down to produce H_2O and CO_2.

$$C_{12}H_{22}O_{11} + 12O_2 \longrightarrow 12CO_2 + 11H_2O$$

List all of the mole ratios that can be determined from this equation.

19. Chemical Equations Sulfur burns in air to form sulfur dioxide.

$$S + O_2 \longrightarrow SO_2$$

   a. What mass of SO_2 is formed from 64 g of sulfur?
   b. What mass of sulfur is necessary to form 256 g of SO_2?

20. Chemical Equations Zinc metal will react with hydrochloric acid, HCl, to produce hydrogen gas and zinc chloride, $ZnCl_2$. Write and balance the chemical equation for this reaction.

THINKING CRITICALLY

21. Designing Systems Paper consists mainly of cellulose, a complex compound made up of simple sugars. Suggest a method for turning old newspapers into sugars using an enzyme. What problems would there be? What precautions would need to be taken?

22. Applying Knowledge Molecular models of some chemical reactions are pictured below. Correct the drawings by adding coefficients or drawing molecules with a computer drawing program to reflect balanced equations.

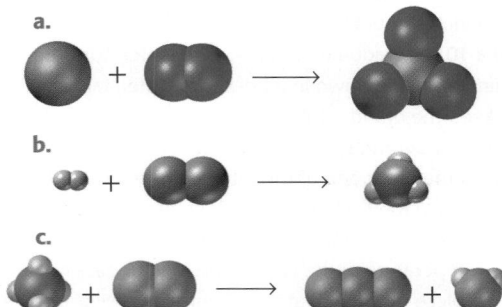

23. Understanding Systems Why is it dangerous to leave a car engine running when the car is in a closed garage?

DEVELOPING LIFE/WORK SKILLS

24. Making Decisions Cigarette smoke contains carbon monoxide. Why do you think carbon monoxide is in the smoke? Why is smoking bad for your health?

25. Interpreting and Communicating Choose several items labeled "biodegradable," and research the decomposition reactions involved. Write balanced chemical equations for the decomposition reactions. Be sure to note any conditions that must occur for the substance to biodegrade. Present your information to the class to inform the students about what products are best for the environment.

INTEGRATING CONCEPTS

26. Concept Mapping Copy the unfinished concept map given below onto a sheet of paper. Complete the map by writing the correct word or phrase in the lettered box.

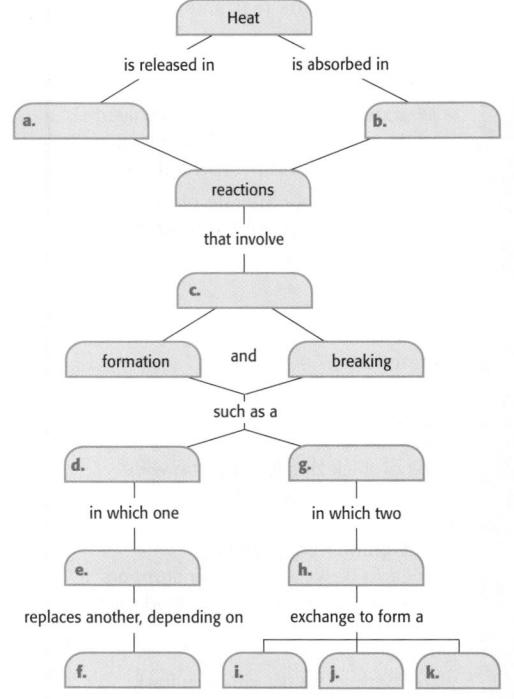

internet**connect**

SC*L*INKS
NSTA

TOPIC: Biodegradable
GO TO: www.scilinks.org
KEYWORD: HK1056

CHEMICAL REACTIONS **179**

21. Answers will vary but might include adding water to shredded newspaper to make a slurry, then adding enzymes that break down cellulose. Problems might include interference from inks or other materials in the paper, using the wrong amount of enzyme, or being unable to separate the sugars from other materials. Precautions might include controlling the temperature so the enzyme stays active.

22. Answers will vary. One general form for the answers follows.
   a. $2A + 3B_2 \rightarrow 2AB_3$
   b. $3A_2 + B_2 \rightarrow 2A_3B$
   c. $AB_4 + 2C_2 \rightarrow C_2A + 2\,CB_2$

23. The combustion reaction uses O_2 and produces CO_2. Therefore, the O_2 concentration will drop and the CO_2 levels will rise. Humans will have difficulty getting enough O_2 to survive. The combustion reaction probably produces some carbon monoxide. If the CO becomes concentrated, it can harm humans.

DEVELOPING LIFE/WORK SKILLS

24. In a cigarette, tobacco combusts with a limited supply of oxygen. In addition to CO, cigarette smoke contains other toxic gases, nicotine, and tars, all of which can damage the lungs and circulatory system.

Answers continue on p. 181B.

Measuring the Rate of a Chemical Reaction

Introduction

Students should review **Figure 1-16** on page 20, which shows gas being collected by volumetric displacement. Ask students to write and balance the equation for the reaction.

$Zn + 2HCl \rightarrow ZnCl_2 + H_2$

The reaction will not go to completion in the approximately 15 minutes allotted for the reaction at room temperature.

Objectives

Students will:

▶ **Measure** the volume of gas evolved to determine the rate of the reaction between zinc and hydrochloric acid.

▶ **Determine** how the rate of this reaction depends on the temperature of the reactants.

Planning

Recommended time: 1 lab period
Materials: (for each lab group)
▶ thermometer
▶ metric ruler
▶ stopwatch
▶ heavy scissors
▶ strips of zinc foil, 10 mm wide
▶ 1.0 M hydrochloric acid
▶ 10 mL graduated cylinder
▶ 25 mL graduated cylinder
▶ 2 sidearm flasks with rubber stoppers
▶ beaker to hold a 10 mL graduated cylinder
▶ rubber tubing
▶ ice
▶ water bath

RESOURCE LINK
DATASHEETS

Have students use *Datasheet 5.5 Design Your Own Lab: Measuring the Rate of a Chemical Reaction* to record their results.

Design Your Own Lab

Introduction

How can you show that the rate of a chemical reaction depends on the temperature of the reactants?

Objectives

▶ **Measure** the volume of gas evolved to determine the rate of the reaction between zinc and hydrochloric acid.

▶ **Determine** how the rate of this reaction depends on the temperature of the reactants.

Materials

thermometer
metric ruler
stopwatch
heavy scissors
strips of thick zinc foil, 10 mm wide
1.0 M hydrochloric acid
10 mL graduated cylinder
25 mL graduated cylinder
2 sidearm flasks with rubber stoppers
beaker to hold a 10 mL graduated cylinder
rubber tubing
ice
water bath to hold a sidearm flask

Safety Needs

lab apron
safety goggles
polyethylene gloves

REQUIRED PRECAUTIONS

▶ Read all safety cautions and discuss them with your students.

▶ Safety goggles and a lab apron must be worn at all times.

▶ Polyethylene gloves must be worn when handling hydrochloric acid.

▶ Hydrogen gas is extremely flammable. Be sure that no open flame or spark source is present in the lab during this experiment.

Measuring the Rate of a Chemical Reaction

▶ Observing the Reaction Between Zinc and Hydrochloric Acid

1. On a blank sheet of paper, prepare a table like the one shown at right.

   SAFETY CAUTION Hydrochloric acid can cause severe burns. Wear a lab apron, gloves, and safety goggles. If you get acid on your skin or clothing, wash it off at the sink while calling to your teacher. If you get acid in your eyes, immediately flush it out at the eyewash station while calling to your teacher. Continue rinsing for at least 15 minutes or until help arrives.

2. Fill a 10 mL graduated cylinder with water. Turn the cylinder upside down in a beaker of water, taking care to keep the cylinder full. Place one end of the rubber tubing under the spout of the graduated cylinder. Attach the other end of the tubing to the arm of the flask. Place the flask in a water bath at room temperature. Record the initial gas volume of the cylinder and the temperature of the water bath in your data table.

3. Cut a piece of zinc about 50–75 mm long. Measure the length, and record this in your data table. Place the zinc in the sidearm flask.

4. Measure 25 mL of hydrochloric acid in a graduated cylinder.

5. Carefully pour the acid from the graduated cylinder into the flask. Start the stopwatch as you begin to pour. Stopper the flask as soon as the acid is transferred.

6. Record any signs of a chemical reaction you observe.

7. After 15 minutes, determine the amount of gas given off by the reaction. Record the volume of gas in your data table.

	Length of zinc strip (mm)	Initial gas volume (mL)	Final gas volume (mL)	Temperature (°C)	Reaction time (s)
Reaction 1					
Reaction 2					

▶ Designing Your Experiment

8. With your lab partners decide how you will answer the question posed at the beginning of the lab. By completing steps 1–7, you have half the data you need to answer the question. How can you collect the rest of the data?

9. In your lab report, list each step you will perform in your experiment. Because temperature is the variable you want to test, the other variables in your experiment should be the same as they were in steps 1–7.

10. Before you carry out your experiment, your teacher must approve your plan.

▶ Performing Your Experiment

11. After your teacher approves your plan, carry out your experiment. Record your results in your data table.

12. How do the two reactions differ?

▶ Analyzing Your Results

1. Express the rate of each reaction as mL of gas evolved in 1 minute.
2. Which reaction was more rapid?
3. Divide the faster rate by the slower rate, and express the reaction rates as a ratio.
4. According to your results, how does decreasing the temperature affect the rate of a chemical reaction?

▶ Defending Your Conclusions

5. How could you test the effect of temperature on this reaction without using an ice bath?
6. How can you express the rate of each of the two reactions you conducted as a function of the surface area of the zinc?
7. How would you design an experiment to test the effect of surface area on this reaction?

Sample Data Table

	Length of zinc strip (mm)	Initial gas volume (mL)	Final gas volume (mL)	Temperature of water bath (°C)	Reaction time (s)
Reaction 1	50	2.6	10.3	21	900
Reaction 2	50	3.2	4.8	0	900

Pre-Lab

Teaching Tips

Sidearm flasks (i.e., filter flasks) are specified rather than test tubes to avoid the risk of students inserting glass tubing through a test-tube stopper. Because of the relatively large head space in a 125 mL sidearm flask, several minutes may pass before enough hydrogen evolves to flow through the rubber tubing to the graduated cylinder. If filter tubes (sidearm test tubes) are available in the laboratory, this experiment can be conducted with 10 mL of 1 M HCl and a piece of zinc approximately 5 mm wide and 25 cm in length. After 15 minutes, about 0.5 mL of H_2 will be evolved at 0°C and about 2 mL of H_2 will be evolved at room temperature.

Procedure

▶ Designing Your Experiment

In the second half of the lab, students need to devise a way to conduct the same chemical reaction at a different temperature. Although student answers may vary, having ice available will point them toward conducting the experiment in an ice bath. An essential part of the student's structuring of the inquiry is the recognition that temperature is the only variable that should change. The amounts of acid and zinc and the duration should be the same as in the first half of the experiment. Because of the risk of igniting the evolved hydrogen, the second half of the experiment should be performed at an elevated temperature only if no spark source or open flame is present.

Continue on p. 181A.

Design Your Own Lab from page 181

Measuring the Rate of a Chemical Reaction

▶ Performing Your Experiment

11. See sample data table.
12. The two reactions differ in that the reaction at an elevated temperature gave off more hydrogen gas than the reaction at the lower temperature.

Post-Lab

▶ Disposal

Neutralize the acid with 0.1 M NaOH, and filter the solution. The filtrate may be poured down the drain. After the $Zn(OH)_2$ precipitate has dried, it may be wrapped in newspaper and discarded in the trash.

▶ Analyzing Your Results

1. Answers will vary. Sample data show 0.51 mL H_2/min at room temperature and 0.11 mL H_2/min at 0°C.
2. The reaction at an elevated temperature is more rapid than the reaction at the lower temperature.
3. The ratio of the sample data is 4.6:1.
4. Decreasing the temperature slows the rate of a chemical reaction.

▶ Defending Your Conclusions

5. The effect of temperature on this reaction could be determined by comparing the results at room temperature with the results at a higher temperature.
6. The rate of the reactions can be given in mL of hydrogen gas/mm^2 of zinc.
7. To test the effect of surface area, the reaction can be conducted with equal amounts of zinc but one sample folded tightly in half so that mass is not a variable.

Answers from page 160

SECTION 5.2 REVIEW

7. formation of a gas; a precipitate; or a covalent molecule, such as water
8. You would expect larger molecules in a more viscous liquid, so crude oil would be more viscous. Cracking breaks large molecules down into smaller ones.

Answers from page 168

5. molar mass of N_2 = 2×14 g/mol = 28 g/mol;
   molar mass of NH_3 = 14 g/mol + (3×1 g/mol) =
   17 g/mol
   $mass_1/(coefficient_1 \times molar\ mass_1) =$
   $mass_2/(coefficient_2 \times molar\ mass_2)$
   $x/(1\ mol \times 28\ g/mol) = 34\ g/(2\ mol \times 17\ g/mol)$;
   $x = 28$ g

Answers from page 176

8. CO_2 is the only substance affected by pressure. Decreasing
   pressure would increase decomposition of $CaCO_3$. Because
   the reaction is endothermic, increasing temperature would
   also increase the rate of decomposition.

Answers from page 179

25. Answers will vary. Biodegradation reactions rely on bacteria
    or other organisms to degrade materials to more basic
    forms, such as the biodegradation of hydrocarbons to CO_2
    and H_2O. The hydrocarbon is converted to a carboxylic
    acid. The acid is broken down by beta oxidation, which
    removes two carbon atoms at a time, as follows.

$$\begin{array}{ccc} H\ H\ H & H & H \\ R-C-C-C-COOH \rightarrow & R-C-COOH\ + & H-C-COOH \\ H\ H\ H & H & H \end{array}$$

    The short-chain acids are used for energy, protoplasm,
    CO_2, and H_2O. In some cases, only 50 percent of a material
    must degrade for a product to be labeled biodegradable,
    and a biodegradable product can endure for years. Some
    newspapers placed in sanitary landfills 40 years ago are
    still readable.

26. a. exothermic
    b. endothermic
    c. bond
    d. single-displacement reaction
    e. element
    f. activity
    g. double-displacement reaction
    h. positive ions in two ionic compounds
    i. precipitate
    j. gas
    k. molecule

How Should Life-Saving Inventions Be Introduced?

view **viewpoints**

How Should Life-Saving Inventions Be Introduced?

> **Your Turn**

1. Critiquing Viewpoints

Students' analyses of a single argument's weak points may vary. Be sure that student responses clearly identify a weakness and respond in some way that provides support. Possible responses are listed below. (Note that students should analyze only *one of the following*.)

Stacey F.: Some companies might conceal their ability to pay to avoid having to do it.

But that would be better than placing an undue burden on airplane manufacturers.

Emily B.: When people make purchases, they don't always consider safety as one of the factors involved.

But airlines could remind people of safety in their advertisements.

Virginia M.: The FAA does not pass laws.

But such a law, if passed by Congress, could help companies make this decision, if they stand to lose even more money without safety.

April R.: For some, the price of a plane ticket will determine whether they travel.

But people should consider safety.

Carlene de C.: Airline passengers already have the right to sue airlines if they've been negligent.

But stronger regulations about safer materials could help make it easier for such suits.

Shannon B.: The airlines may have other ways to keep people safe besides fireproof materials, such as better fire extinguishers and smoke detectors.

Even so, these new materials will do no harm.

2. Critiquing Viewpoints

Students' analyses of strong points in opposing arguments may vary. Be sure that student responses clearly identify the strong points and respond in some way that provides

Researchers are developing better fireproof materials to use inside passenger airplanes. But the new materials are much more expensive than the ones currently used.

Should the Federal Aviation Administration (FAA) require that the new materials be used on all new and old planes, or should it be up to the plane manufacturers and airlines to decide whether to use the new materials?

A similar debate occurs whenever life-saving inventions are introduced, from automobile airbags to better child-safety seats. If the inventions should be used, who should bear the cost? Should it be the federal government, an insurance company, a manufacturer, or the customers?

If the device shouldn't be required at all times, how do you decide when it should be used? When are the risks so small that it doesn't make sense to spend money on another safety device?

What do you think?

> FROM: Stacey F., Rochester, MN.

It should be up to the plane manufacturers because not all companies would be able to afford the cost. The FAA should look into the budgets of all plane companies and companies that can afford it should be required to use the new material.

> FROM: Emily B., Coral Springs, FL

I think it should be up to the plane manufacturers and airlines. The new materials shouldn't be required on planes that are already built or on planes that are being built, because of expenses. However, it would be to an airline's advantage to have the best safety material possible for their customers' sake.

> FROM: Virginia M., Houston, TX

The airlines are responsible for the lives of their passengers, so they should decide. But the FAA should pass a law stating that if the airlines refuse new safety measures, the airlines will accept total responsibility for any accidents that occur.

Leave the Decisions to the Companies Involved

support for the opposite point of view. Possible responses are listed below. (Note that students should analyze only *one of the following*.)

Stacey F. and Emily B.: Providing this safety equipment on all planes could be a substantial financial burden.

A company should not place its profits above the lives of its customers.

Virginia M.: Airline companies should be responsible for safety.

But companies may not realize the risks they are running without regulations to serve as guidelines.

April R.: Lives should be valued more than profits.

But you can't be sure that any safety improvement will solve all problems.

Carlene de C.: Airline companies should minimize their liabilities.

But each company should be able to decide which strategies it wants to use to keep liabilities low.

Shannon B.: Public health should be protected in the event of a malfunction.

Malfunctions that don't cause fires can also cause death, and the addition of these fireproof materials will not solve those problems.

> FROM: April R., Coral Springs, FL

If it can save just one life, it's worth spending money and time on. Eventually the technology will be required on all planes anyway. If an airline chose not to use these materials and there were an accident, there would be liability cases because lives might have been saved. Most people will have no problem spending more for a plane ticket if their safety is ensured.

Require Safety Immediately

> FROM: Carlene de C., Chicago, IL

The FAA should require that all planes—those currently in use and those being built—have fireproof materials. Otherwise, passengers could sue the airline company if they were hurt in a fire and it could have been prevented.

> FROM: Shannon B., Bowling Green, KY

They should put the new fireproof materials on all planes, even the ones that have already been built. The public's health is at risk if a plane malfunctions, and the airlines should want to keep everybody safe. Otherwise they will lose customers.

> Your Turn

1. **Critiquing Viewpoints** Select one of the statements on this page that you *agree* with. Identify and explain at least one weak point in the statement. What would you say to respond to someone who brought up this weak point as a reason you were wrong?

2. **Critiquing Viewpoints** Select one of the statements on this page that you *disagree* with. Identify and explain at least one strong point in the statement. What would you say to respond to someone who brought up this point as a reason they were right?

3. **Life/Work Skills** Imagine that you are preparing to testify in a congressional hearing about this matter. Choose the four most important points you'd make, and draft a statement that explains all of them persuasively.

4. **Working Cooperatively** With your teacher's help, stage a role-playing exercise, with students serving as the panel of congressional representatives preparing to vote on this issue and as witnesses for the airlines, the airplane manufacturers, insurance companies, safety organizations, and a passengers' rights group.

internet connect

go.hrw.com

TOPIC: Lifesaving technology
GO TO: go.hrw.com
KEYWORD: HK1Lifesavers

What do you think should be done? Why? Share your views on this issue and learn about other viewpoints at the HRW Web site.

183

Life/Work Skills continued
4. Working Cooperatively
Students should be given time prior to the role-playing exercise to consider what questions and arguments they will want to state, given their different roles.

Evaluate students' performances using a scale of 1–5 points for each of the following: clarity of presentation, use of logic, attention to role, persuasiveness, and effort. (25 total possible points)

---

3. Life/Work Skills
Evaluate student responses based on whether the four points chosen are pertinent and are persuasively explained in student statements. The following sample statements include some arguments students may use.

Leave the Decisions to the Companies Involved
1. The costs and logistics of adding these materials to existing planes will be burdensome to businesses.
2. The forces of the marketplace should be used rather than regulatory matters. Customers that want safety will reward companies providing it.
3. In the unfortunate event of an accident, customers can still resort to lawsuits if the company has truly been negligent.
4. While these materials resist fires, it is possible that an accident will still result in deaths even with the materials present.

Require Safety Immediately
1. The lives of citizens should be more important than the profits of a private company.
2. Government action can help guide companies to do the right thing.
3. Fireproof materials can help airlines minimize their liability and the damage to their aircraft as well as save lives.
4. Airlines can use the presence of these materials as a demonstration of their commitment to customer safety.

internet connect

The HRW Web site has more opinions from other students and also provides an opportunity for your students to contribute their points of view. Every few months, more opinions will be added from the ones submitted. Student opinions that are posted will be identified only by the student's first name, last initial, and city to protect his or her privacy.

CHAPTER 6

Solutions, Acids, and Bases

Annotated Descriptions of the Correlated National Science Standards

The following descriptions summarize the National Science Standards that specially relate to Chapter 6. For the full text of the Standards, see p. 40T.

SECTION 6.1
Solutions and Other Mixtures
Science as Inquiry
SAI 2

SECTION 6.2
Dissolving and Solubility
Science as Inquiry
SAI 1

SECTION 6.3
Acids, Bases, and pH
Science as Inquiry
SAI 1
Science in Personal and Social Perspectives
SPSP 1

SECTION 6.4
Integrating Technology and Society—Acids and Bases in the Home
Science as Inquiry
SAI 1
History and Nature of Science
HNS 3
Science in Personal and Social Perspectives
SPSP 1, 5

Cross-Discipline Teaching RESOURCES

Cross-Discipline Teaching, ATE p. 184
Social Studies   Chemistry
Fine Arts

Integration Enrichment Resources
Real World Applications, **PE** and **ATE** p. 191
  IE 6.1 *What Is Your Favorite Flavor?*
Biology, **PE** and **ATE** p. 205
  IE 6.4 *A Balance in the Body*
Social Studies, **PE** and **ATE** p. 208
  IE 6.2 *Detergents: Helpful or Harmful?*

Additional Integration Enrichment Worksheets
  IE 6.3 Physics   IE 6.5 Biology

Use the Planning Guide on the next page to help you organize your lessons.

MATH AND COMPUTER RESOURCES

Chapter 6	Math Skills	Assess	Media/Computer Skills
Section 6.1	**BS Worksheet 6.1:** Making and Interpreting Tables		■ Section 6.1 💿 *DISC ONE, MODULE 8* Solutions
Section 6.2		**PE Building Math Skills,** p. 214, item 16	■ Section 6.2 **PE Chapter Review,** p. 214, item 20 **CNN Presents Chemistry Connections Segment 14** Harvesting Salt **CRT** Worksheet 14
Section 6.3			■ Section 6.3 **CNN Presents Chemistry Connections Segment 26** Acids in the Environment **CRT** Worksheet 26
Section 6.4			■ Section 6.4

PE Pupil's Edition **ATE** Annotated Teacher's Edition **MS** Math Skills **BS** Basic Skills

IE Integration Enrichment ■ Guided Reading Audio **CRT** Critical Thinking

PHYSICAL SCIENCE — INTERACTIVE TUTOR

READING SKILL BUILDER

The following activities found in the Annotated Teacher's Edition provide techniques for developing useful reading strategies to increase your students' reading comprehension skills.

Section 6.1   **Brainstorming,** p. 184
              Reading Organizer, p. 186

Section 6.2   **K-W-L,** p. 192

Section 6.3   **Paired Reading,** p. 199

Section 6.4   **Summarizing,** p. 207

Spanish Resources

The following resources are made available for students who speak Spanish as their first language.

**Spanish Resources
Guided Reading Audio CD-ROM**
Chapter 6

Spanish Glossary
Chapter 6

Solutions, Acids, and Bases

Solutions, Acids, and Bases

CLASSROOM RESOURCES

FOCUS	TEACH	HANDS-ON

Section 6.1: Solutions and Other Mixtures

BLOCK 1 — 45 minutes

FOCUS	TEACH	HANDS-ON
ATE **RSB** Brainstorming, p. 184 ATE Focus Activities 1, 2, p. 185 ATE **RSB** Reading Organizer, p. 186 PE Mixtures, pp. 186–188 ★ Focus Transparency LT 19 ATE **Demo 1** Solution or Not?, p. 186	ATE **Skill Builder** Interpreting Visuals, p. 185 Vocabulary, p. 187 TT 17 Suspension	IE Worksheets 6.3, 6.5

BLOCK 2 — 45 minutes

FOCUS	TEACH	HANDS-ON
PE Homogeneous Mixtures, pp. 189–191 ATE **Demo 2** Stirring, p. 190	TT 18 Homogeneous Mixtures	PE Quick Activity *Making Butter*, p. 189 **DS** 6.1 PE Real World Applications *Chromatography*, p. 191 IE Worksheet 6.1

Section 6.2: Dissolving and Solubility

BLOCK 3 — 45 minutes

FOCUS	TEACH	HANDS-ON
ATE **RSB** K-W-L, p. 192 ATE **Demo 3** Solution Rate, p. 192 PE Dissolving Process, pp. 192–195 ★ Focus Transparency LT 20	ATE **Skill Builder** Interpreting Visuals, pp. 193, 195	PE Quick Activity *"Like Dissolves Like,"* p. 195 **DS** 6.2

BLOCK 4 — 45 minutes

FOCUS	TEACH	HANDS-ON
ATE **Demo 4** Solubility, p. 196 PE Concentration, pp. 196–198	ATE **Skill Builder** Vocabulary, p. 197	LE 6 *Determining the Concentration of an Ionic Solution* **DS** 6.7

Section 6.3: Acids, Bases, and pH

BLOCK 5 — 45 minutes

FOCUS	TEACH	HANDS-ON
ATE **RSB** Paired Reading, p. 199 ATE **Demo 5** Indicator, p. 199 PE Acids and Bases, pp. 199–202 ★ Focus Transparency LT 21	ATE **Skill Builder** Interpreting Tables, p. 201	

BLOCK 6 — 45 minutes

FOCUS	TEACH	HANDS-ON
PE pH and Neutralization Reactions, pp. 202–206 ATE **Demo 6** Temperature Affects Solubility, p. 203	ATE **Skill Builder** Interpreting Tables, p. 205 TT 19 pH Scale BLM 19 Common Acids	PE Inquiry Lab *Which household substances are acids, which are bases . . .* p. 204 **DS** 6.3 IE Worksheet 6.4

Section 6.4: Acids and Bases in the Home

BLOCK 7 — 45 minutes

FOCUS	TEACH	HANDS-ON
ATE **RSB** Summarizing, p. 207 ATE **Demo 7** Cabbage, p. 207 ATE **Demo 8** Making Soap, p. 208 PE Cleaning Products, pp. 207–209 ★ Focus Transparency LT 22	TT 20 Soap in Emulsion	IE Worksheet 6.2 PE Quick Activity *Detergents* p. 209 **DS** 6.4 PE Inquiry Lab *What does an antacid do?* p. 210 **DS** 6.5

BLOCK 8 — 45 minutes

FOCUS	TEACH	HANDS-ON
PE Other Household Acids and Bases, pp. 210–212		PE Skill Builder Lab *Temperature and Gas Solubility*, p. 216 **DS** 6.6

CLASSROOM RESOURCES

HOMEWORK	ASSESS
PE Section Review 2, 3, 5, p. 191	**ATE** *ALTERNATIVE ASSESSMENT,* The Advantages of Alloys, p. 188 **SG** Chapter 6 Pretest
PE Section Review 1, 4, 6, 7, p. 191 **Chapter 6 Review,** p. 213, items 1, 2	**SG** Section 6.1
PE Section Review 3, 4, 6, p. 198 **Chapter 6 Review,** p. 213, item 3	
PE Section Review 1, 2, 5, 7, 8, p. 198 **Chapter 6 Review,** p. 213, items 4, 11, 16	**SG** Section 6.2
Chapter 6 Review, p. 213, items 5, 6, 12	**ATE** *ALTERNATIVE ASSESSMENT,* Properties of Acids and Bases, p. 200
PE Section Review 1–7, p. 206 **Chapter 6 Review,** p. 213, items 7, 8, 13, 14	**ATE** *ALTERNATIVE ASSESSMENT,* pH of Blood, p. 202 **SG** Section 6.3
PE Section Review 2–5, 7, p. 212 **Chapter 6 Review,** p. 213, items 10, 15	
PE Section Review 1, 6, 8, p. 212 **Chapter 6 Review,** p. 213, item 9	**SG** Section 6.4

BLOCK 9

Chapter 6 Review
Thinking Critically 17–22, p. 214
Developing Life/Work Skills 23–25, p. 215
Integrating Concepts 26–28, p. 215
SG Chapter 6 Mixed Review

BLOCK 10

Chapter Tests
Chapter 6 Test

One-Stop Planner CD-ROM **with Test Generator**
Chapter 6

Teaching Resources
Scoring Rubrics and assignment checklist.

 **internetconnect**

SCI LINKS **National Science Teachers**
NSTA **Association**
Online Resources:
www.scilinks.org
The following *sci*LINKS Internet resources can be found in the student text for this chapter.

Page 185 **TOPIC:** Vaccines **KEYWORD:** HK1060	HK1063**Page 202** **TOPIC:** pH **KEYWORD:** HK1064 **Page 207** **TOPIC:** Acids and bases at home **KEYWORD:** HK1065
Page 187 **TOPIC:** Colloids **KEYWORD:** HK1061	
Page 190 **TOPIC:** Chromatography **KEYWORD:** HK1062	**Page 210** **TOPIC:** Antacids **KEYWORD:** HK1066
Page 197 **TOPIC:** Solubility **KEYWORD:**	**Page 215** **TOPIC:** Transdermal patch medicines **KEYWORD:** HK1067

CNNfyi.com.   www.cnnfyi.com

Visit this site for coverage of current events and related classroom resources.

PE Pupil's Edition   **ATE** Teacher's Edition
RSB Reading Skill Builder   **DS** Datasheets
IE Integrated Enrichment   **SG** Study Guide
LE Laboratory Experiments
TT Teaching Transparencies   **BLM** Blackline Masters
★ Lesson Focus Transparency

CHAPTER 6

Solutions, Acids, and Bases

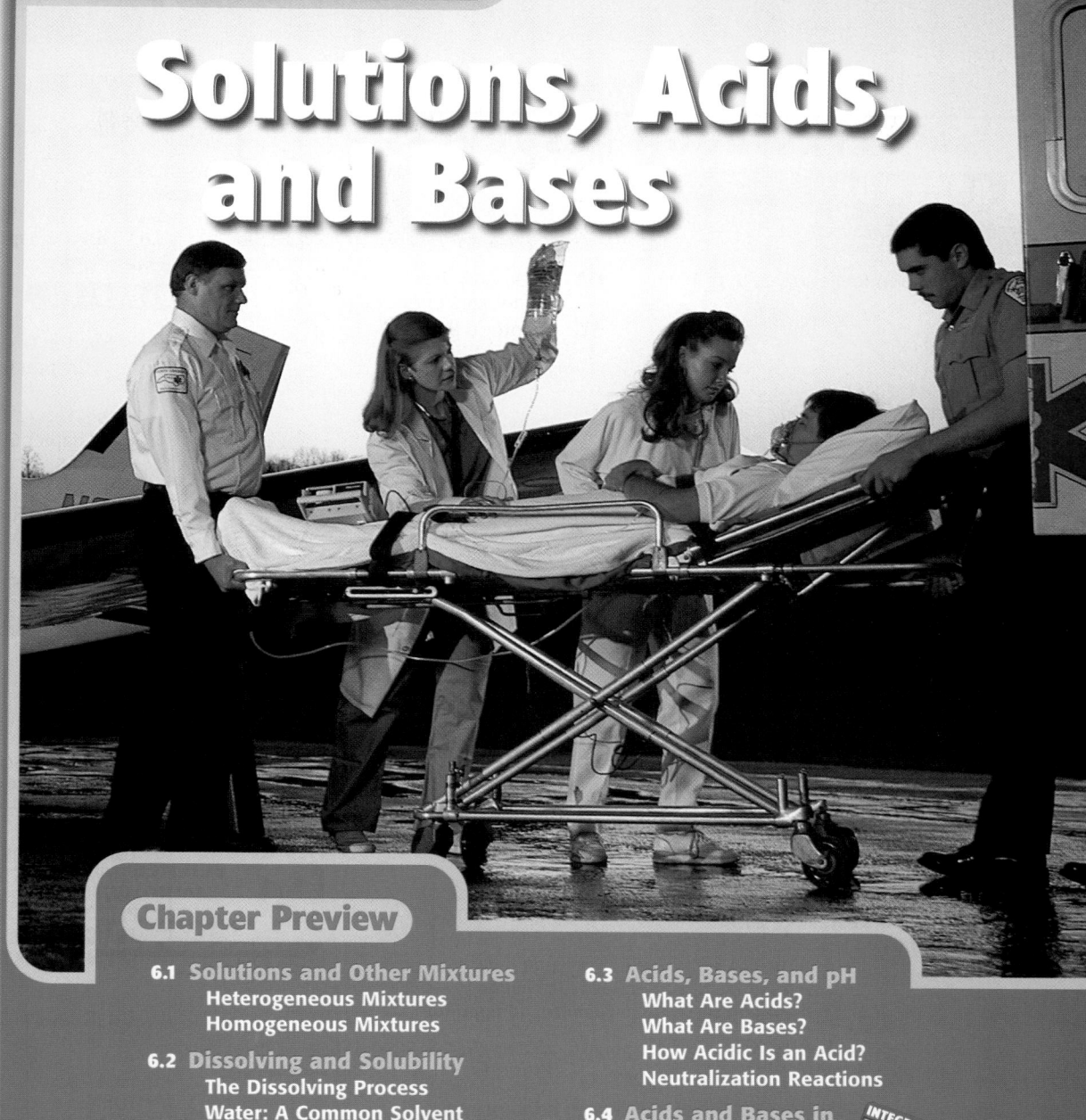

Be sure students understand the following concepts:

Chapter 2
Mixtures

Chapter 3
Moles and ions

Chapter 4
Writing formulas and bonding

Chapter 5
Chemical reactions and chemical equations

READING SKILL BUILDER *Brainstorming*
Have students brainstorm words, phrases, and ideas they associate with *acid*. List students' responses on the board and clarify any ideas that are confusing. Have students make notes of everything they remember from the discussion, then look over the notes to see what they know about acids based on experience and the discussion. Have students refer to their notes at the end of Section 6.4 and use them to evaluate what they have learned.

Chapter Preview

6.1 Solutions and Other Mixtures
Heterogeneous Mixtures
Homogeneous Mixtures

6.2 Dissolving and Solubility
The Dissolving Process
Water: A Common Solvent
Concentration

6.3 Acids, Bases, and pH
What Are Acids?
What Are Bases?
How Acidic Is an Acid?
Neutralization Reactions

6.4 Acids and Bases in the Home *INTEGRATING TECHNOLOGY and Society*
Cleaning Products
Other Household Acids and Bases

184

RESOURCE LINK
STUDY GUIDE

Assign students *Pretest Chapter 6 Solutions, Acids, and Bases* before beginning Chapter 6.

CROSS-DISCIPLINE TEACHING

Social Studies Have students find out what areas of the world are affected by acid rain. Have students relate the geographic location of these areas, the location of nearby areas that are highly industrial, and the direction of prevailing winds.

Fine Arts Have an art teacher speak to the class about solvents used in various art materials. For example, water is used as a solvent for certain

types of paints, but other paints are oil or acrylic based. Water is also used to keep clay moist, to moisten newspaper for papier-mâché, and it is also used in some glues.

Chemistry Show students what happens when water is added to baking powder. The resulting neutralization reaction produces bubbles of carbon dioxide.

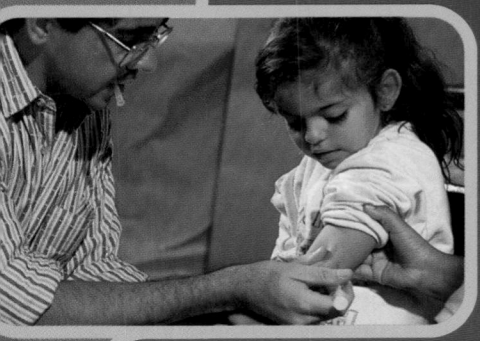

Many solutions can be life-saving. Some solutions replace vital fluids in your body if you are injured, while others protect you from potentially deadly diseases.

Focus ACTIVITY

Background Paramedics rush to the scene of an accident. Someone has been injured, and the person's blood pressure has become dangerously low. Paramedics pump a *saline solution,* a mixture of water and sodium chloride that is similar to blood, into the person's veins. This mixture maintains the blood pressure that is needed to keep the person alive on the way to the hospital.

Throughout your life, you have received many shots, or vaccinations. These shots have helped protect you from many diseases. Surprisingly, vaccines are mixtures that have a tiny amount or some parts of the disease-causing bacterium or virus you are trying to protect yourself from. The shot you get is harmless because the bacterium or virus contained in it is dead, or inactivated. But the shot keeps you from getting the disease. That's because if your body "sees" this harmful bacterium or virus again, your body is able to recognize it and fight it.

Activity 1 Look up the word *saline* in the dictionary. Which group of elements in the periodic table form ionic compounds that can be described by the word *saline*? Explain how this applies to sodium chloride.

Activity 2 Substances must be added to vaccines to make the disease-causing bacterium or virus they contain harmless. Added substances also keep the vaccine from spoiling or becoming less effective over time. Use the Internet to find out which substances are commonly added to vaccines for these reasons.

internet**connect**

SC*i*LINKS
NSTA

TOPIC: Vaccines
GO TO: www.scilinks.org
KEYWORD: HK1060

185

Focus ACTIVITY

Background Have students use LeChâtelier's principle, studied in Chapter 5, to explain what would happen if too much or too little salt were added to the saline solution. Explanations should state that the salt concentrations in the liquid and cellular part of blood are in equilibrium. If a stress is placed on the system, the cells will react in a manner that will equalize salt concentration. If too much salt is added, blood cells lose water and wither. If too little salt is added, the cells swell.

Activity 1 *Saline* refers to salts. The group of elements related to this meaning would be the alkali metals. Sodium chloride contains ions of sodium, an alkali metal.

Activity 2 Information on vaccine composition can be found at the Centers for Disease and Prevention Control at www.cdc.gov/nip/vacsafe/fs/qchem.htm. Antibiotics, aluminum gels and salts, MSG, and sulfites (for stabilization) are commonly added. Egg protein and thimerosal are added as preservatives.

SKILL BUILDER

Interpreting Visuals Ask students what the two photos have in common. In each photo, someone trained in health care is treating another person. Point out that anything added to the human body must be compatible with human body tissue.

Scheduling

Refer to pp. 184A–184D for lecture, classwork, and assignment options for Section 6.1.

★ Lesson Focus

Use transparency *LT 19* to prepare students for this section.

READING SKILL BUILDER *Reading Organizer* Students can work individually or in groups. Have students read Section 6.1 and then organize the ideas presented in a concept map. Maps should start with *Mixtures* and include the two types of mixtures. Students' maps should also describe each type of mixture and provide examples.

Additional Application

Solution or Suspension?

Group students in pairs and distribute paper cups and straws to each group. Also provide each group with a container of warm water and small amounts of vinegar, vegetable oil, ground coffee, instant coffee, and sand. Ask students to determine how many solutions and how many suspensions they can make by mixing any two materials. Have them make a list of solutions and a list of suspensions. *(Possible solutions include: water and sugar, water and instant coffee, water and vinegar; Possible suspensions include: water and oil, water and ground coffee, oil and vinegar, sand and water, sand and oil, sand and vinegar)*

Solutions and Other Mixtures

▶ **KEY TERMS**

suspension
colloid
emulsion
solution
solute
solvent

OBJECTIVES

▶ Distinguish between homogeneous mixtures and heterogeneous mixtures.
▶ Compare and contrast the properties of solutions, colloids, and suspensions.
▶ Identify ways to separate different kinds of mixtures.

Any sample of matter is either a pure substance or a mixture of pure substances. Fruit salad is a mixture because it is a blend of different kinds of fruit. But some mixtures look like they are pure substances. For example, salt water looks the same as pure water. Air is a mixture of several different gases, but you can't tell that just by looking.

Heterogeneous Mixtures

A heterogeneous mixture, such as fruit salad, is not the same throughout. The quantity of each kind of fruit varies with each spoonful, as shown in **Figure 6-1.** Similarly, if you compared two shovelfuls of dirt from a garden, they would not be exactly the same. Each shovelful would have a different mixture of rock, sand, clay, and decayed matter.

Particles in a suspension are large and eventually settle out

Have you ever forgotten to shake the orange juice carton before pouring yourself a glass of juice? The juice probably tasted watery. This is because most brands of orange juice are **suspensions** of orange pulp in orange juice, which is mostly water. If the carton is not shaken, the top layer of liquid in the carton is mostly water because all the pulp has settled to the bottom.

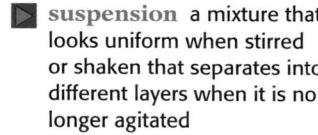

▶ **suspension** a mixture that looks uniform when stirred or shaken that separates into different layers when it is no longer agitated

Figure 6-1
Fruit salad is a heterogeneous mixture. Each spoonful has a different composition of fruit because the fruits are not distributed evenly throughout the salad.

186 CHAPTER 6

DEMONSTRATION 1 CONSUMER FOCUS

Solution or Not?

Time: Approximately 10 minutes
Materials: hot distilled water
gelatin
table sugar
flashlight
2 clear, colorless tumblers or beakers
2 spoons

Add equal amounts of hot water to the two tumblers. To one, add some dry gelatin and stir to dissolve. To the other, add about the same quantity of table sugar and stir to dissolve. Darken the room. Shine the flashlight through both the tumblers from the side. Have students observe. Let the tumblers sit undisturbed until near the end of class. At the end of class, shine the light through them and have students make observations.

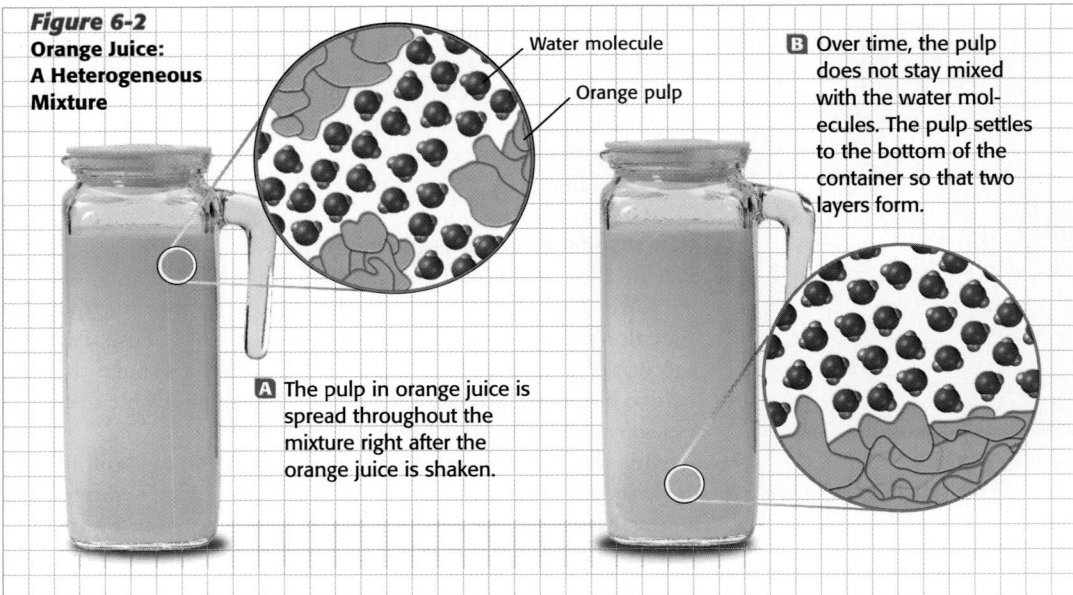

Figure 6-2
Orange Juice: A Heterogeneous Mixture

Water molecule
Orange pulp

B Over time, the pulp does not stay mixed with the water molecules. The pulp settles to the bottom of the container so that two layers form.

A The pulp in orange juice is spread throughout the mixture right after the orange juice is shaken.

Solutions and Other Mixtures

Settled juice is clearly a heterogeneous mixture because the liquid near the top of the container is not the same as the liquid near the bottom. Shaking the container mixes the pulp and water, as shown in **Figure 6-2A.** But the pulp pieces are big enough that they will eventually settle out again, as shown in **Figure 6-2B.** Particles in suspensions are usually larger than the tip of a sharpened pencil, which has a diameter of about 1000 nm.

Not all orange juices available in the grocery store contain pulp. That's because the pulp has been separated from the mixture. Particles in suspensions are usually large enough that they can be filtered out of the mixture. For example, a filter made of porous paper can be used to catch the suspended pulp in orange juice. That is, the pulp stays behind in the filter while tiny water molecules pass through the filter easily.

Particles in a colloid are smaller and do not settle out

Dessert gelatin is another heterogeneous mixture. It is a gel-like substance made of small pieces of solid protein spread throughout water. Gelatin is a **colloid.** There are two important differences between the particles in colloids and those in suspensions. The particles in colloids are much smaller than those in suspensions—ranging from only 1 to 100 nm in diameter. And because the particles in colloids are so small, they do not settle to the bottom of the mixture to form a different layer. Instead, the particles stay dispersed throughout the mixture.

internet connect

SC**LINKS**
NSTA

TOPIC: Colloids
GO TO: www.scilinks.org
KEYWORD: HK1061

▶ **colloid** a mixture of very tiny particles of pure substances that are dispersed in another substance but do not settle out of the substance

SOLUTIONS, ACIDS, AND BASES **187**

Analysis

1. What did you observe? *(The light beam could not be seen in the sugar water but could be seen in the water and gelatin.)*
2. Particles can reflect light. Do you think the particles are larger in the gelatin mixture or in sugar water? Explain. *(Light was reflected from the gelatin and not from the sugar in the other tumbler. The gelatin particles are larger.)*
3. Did anything settle out in either tumbler? *(no)*
4. The water and sugar form a solution, and the gelatin dessert forms a colloid in water. What can you state about the size of the particles in a colloid? *(The particles are small enough to stay suspended but not large enough to settle out. The suspended gelatin particles are larger than the dissolved particles in the sugar-water solution.)*

Solutions and Other Mixtures

Teaching Tip

Stabilizing Emulsions An ingredient that stabilizes an emulsion, such as the egg yolk in mayonnaise, is called an emulsifier. One common emulsifier found in many foods is the group of compounds known as lecithins. Lecithins are found in egg yolks and soybeans. Have students check for lecithin on the ingredient labels of food items such as salad dressings that do not separate, sprays for cooking pans, soft vegetable spreads, and pancake mix.

Did You Know?

Some common colloids, such as milk and mayonnaise, appear white primarily because of the complete scattering of light striking them. On the microscopic level, they generally appear to be made of clear droplets suspended in another clear liquid.

Additional Application

Lipids Lipids are organic compounds that contain hydrogen, carbon, and oxygen, just as carbohydrates do. Lipids include animal fats and vegetable oils. Cholesterol is also a lipid, and it is found in foods that come from animals. The liver also produces cholesterol. In some animals, cholesterol is the base of pheromones, which are chemicals that enable members of the same species to communicate with each other.

Figure 6-3
Because the spout of this special cup is near the bottom, the liquid in the bottom layer (which is denser) is poured out first.

▶ **emulsion** any mixture of immiscible liquids in which the liquids are spread throughout one another

Figure 6-4
Cream looks like a single substance. But when cream is magnified, you can see that it is really an emulsion of droplets of fat, or lipids, dispersed in water.

Many familiar substances are colloids. Egg white, paint, and blood are colloids of solids in liquids. Whipped cream is made by dispersing a gas in a liquid, while marshmallows are made by dispersing a gas in a solid. Fog is made of small droplets of water dispersed in air, and smoke is made of very tiny solid particles dispersed in air.

Heterogeneous liquid-liquid mixtures

When oil is mixed with vinegar to make salad dressing, two layers form. That's because the two liquids are immiscible, meaning they don't mix. Eventually, the oil, which is less dense, floats on top of the vinegar, which is denser. You have to shake the mixture to be sure that the liquids mix so that you get a blend of both vinegar and oil on your salad.

One way to separate two immiscible liquids is to carefully pour the less dense liquid off the top. You can also separate immiscible liquids by using a special cup, like the one shown in **Figure 6-3.** Some health-conscious cooks, for instance, use this kind of cup to separate fat from meat juices. The desired meat juices settle to the bottom of the cup and are poured back onto the meat. The fat, which is less dense, stays behind in the cup.

Some immiscible liquids can mix in emulsions

Mayonnaise is a mixture of tiny droplets of oil suspended in vinegar. Unlike vinegar-and-oil salad dressings, which separate into two layers, the vinegar and oil in mayonnaise stay mixed. That's because mayonnaise has another ingredient that keeps the oil and vinegar together—egg yolk. Egg yolk coats the oil droplets, keeping them from joining to form a separate layer. Mayonnaise is an **emulsion,** a colloid in which liquids that normally do not mix are spread throughout each other.

Like other colloids, emulsions have particles so small that they may appear to be uniform. But a closer look shows that they are not. Cream has only one layer, so it looks like a single substance. Cream is really a mixture of oily fats called *lipids*, proteins, and carbohydrates dispersed in water. The lipid droplets are coated with a protein. The protein is an *emulsifier* that keeps the lipid droplets dispersed in the water so that they can spread throughout the entire mixture, as shown in **Figure 6-4.**

ALTERNATIVE ASSESSMENT

The Advantages of Alloys

Students can work individually or in small groups when performing this activity. Some students are most familiar with liquid solutions. Use this activity to make sure all students become familiar with solid solutions. Have each student choose an alloy, research its makeup and its uses, and report his or her findings to the class. The report can consist of an oral or written report, a poster, or some other method of communicating the infor-

mation. Emphasize that the report should include the advantages the alloy has over the use of the individual components. Possible alloys include brass, bronze, dental amalgam, and many different types of iron (steel) and aluminum alloys. Checking recent sources of information on steel and aluminum should provide many choices of iron and aluminum alloys.

Making Butter

As you have learned, cream is a lipid-in-water emulsion. Churning or shaking cream causes lipid droplets to stick to one another, forming butter. You can make your own butter by doing the following:

1. Pour 250 mL (about 1/2 pt) of heavy cream into an empty 500 mL (about 1 pt) container.
2. Add a clean marble, and seal the container tightly so that it does not leak.
3. Take turns shaking the container. When the cream becomes very thick, you will no longer hear the marble moving.
4. Open the container to look at the substance that formed. Record your observations.
5. If the butter is made of joined lipid droplets, what must make up most of the liquid that is left behind?

Homogeneous Mixtures

Homogeneous mixtures not only look uniform, they *are* uniform. Salt water is an example of a homogeneous mixture. If you add table salt to a glass of water and stir, the mixture soon looks like pure water. The mixture looks uniform even when you examine it under a microscope. That's because the components of the mixture are too small to be seen. The mixture looks like water, but it is really made of sodium ions and chloride ions surrounded by water molecules, as shown in **Figure 6-5A.**

When salt and water are mixed, no chemical reaction occurs. For this reason, it is easy to separate the two substances by evaporating, or boiling away, the water, as shown in **Figure 6-5B.** Once all the water has boiled away, you are left with only salt, as shown in **Figure 6-5C.**

Salt Water: A Homogeneous Mixture

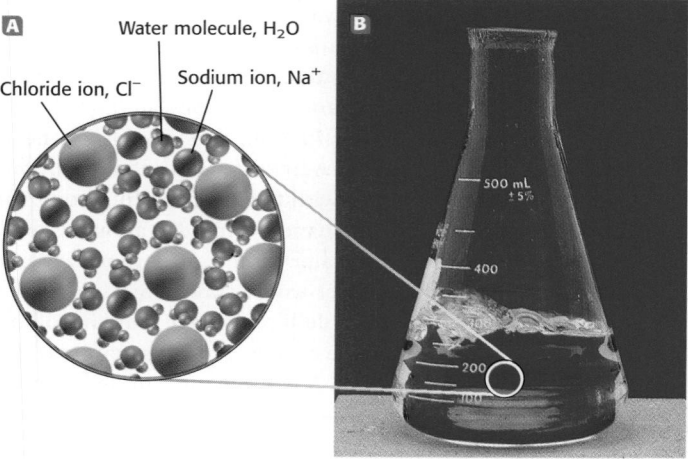

Disc One, Module 8:
Solutions
Use the Interactive Tutor to learn more about this topic.

Figure 6-5
(A) Dissolving table salt in water makes a homogeneous mixture. The salt water has the same chemical makeup throughout. (B) If you heat the mixture to above 100ºC, the water boils and begins to leave a salt residue on the sides of the container. (C) When all of the water has completely evaporated, you are left with only salt.

SOLUTIONS, ACIDS, AND BASES **189**

Making Butter Students will find that the activity produces butter and a liquid that is mostly water and contains a few milk solids. Try to get students to realize that the lipids that formed the emulsion (cream) clumped together to form the butter. If the butter were to be prepared for actual use, the liquid would be drained off and any liquid remaining in the butter would be squeezed out. A small amount of salt might be added to improve the taste.

Solutions and Other Mixtures

Solute or Solvent?
Students might think that water is always the solvent when it is part of a solution. The solvent is the part of the solution that is in the greatest concentration. The solute exists in smaller concentration. For example, if 25 mL of ethanol is mixed with 10 mL of water, ethanol is the solvent, and water is the solute. Nitrogen, which makes up approximately 79 percent of air, is the solvent in air, and the other gases present are solutes.

Teaching Tip

Chromatography Several different types of chromatography are used under different circumstances, but all chromatography is based on differences in polarity. Have interested students investigate the difference between column chromatography, gas chromatography, ion chromatography, and thin layer chromatography and then present their findings to the class.

▶ **solution** a homogeneous mixture of two or more substances uniformly spread throughout a single phase

▶ **solute** the substance that dissolves in a solution

▶ **solvent** the substance that dissolves the solute to make a solution

internet connect

SC*LINKS*
NSTA

TOPIC: Chromatography
GO TO: www.scilinks.org
KEYWORD: HK1062

Figure 6-6
To make a salt-water solution for her tropical fish, this girl is dissolving aquarium salt (a solute) in water (a solvent).

Solutions are homogeneous mixtures

Figure 6-6 shows that when you add aquarium salt to water and stir, the solid seems to disappear. What really happens is the solid dissolves in water to form a **solution.** In this particular solution, aquarium salt is the **solute,** the substance that dissolves. Water is the **solvent,** the substance in which the solute dissolves. When a solute has dissolved completely in a solution, the dissolved particles are so small that you can't see them.

Like the water in the aquarium shown in **Figure 6-6,** many common solutions are solids dissolved in liquids. However, solutes and solvents can be in any state. For instance, vinegar is a solution of acetic acid, a liquid, dissolved in water, another liquid. And a tank of air used by a scuba diver can be thought of as a solution of oxygen and several other gases.

Miscible liquids mix to form solutions

Two or more liquids that form a single layer when mixed are said to be miscible. Sometimes when liquids mix, the resulting solution is useful. Examples are when water mixes with isopropanol to make a solution of rubbing alcohol and when acetic acid mixes with water to make vinegar. Other times, however, you might want to separate miscible liquids. For instance, chemists often have to separate miscible liquids when purifying substances in the laboratory. Because miscible liquids form solutions and do not separate into layers, they are not as easy to separate as immiscible liquids are. One way to separate miscible liquids is by a process called *distillation.*

Separating miscible liquids is a challenging task. A distillation is the easiest way to separate some miscible liquids. A mixture of methanol and water could be separated by a distillation because the boiling points of the two liquids are sufficiently different. (Methanol boils at 64.5°C and water boils at 100.0°C.) To perform the distillation, you would first need to heat the entire mixture until it started boiling. The liquid with the lower boiling point (in this case, methanol) would vaporize first. Some of the water would also vaporize, but most of the water would stay behind.

If two miscible liquids have similar boiling points, it can be even harder to separate them by a distillation. Any time it is hard to separate the components of a mixture, a technique called *chromatography* can be useful.

Effect of Stirring on Dissolving

Time: Approximately 15 minutes
Materials: 500 mL beakers (2), stirring plate, magnetic stirring bar, tap water, powdered drink mix

Fill each beaker with room temperature tap water. Attach white paper to the back of the beakers to increase the effectiveness of the demonstration by making the color changes more dramatic. Add the magnetic stirring bar to one of the beakers. Turn on the stirring plate and adjust the rate of spinning so that a slight vortex is observed at the surface of the water. Carefully drop a small amount of the powdered drink mix into each beaker. The drink mix should quickly dissolve in the stirred beaker. The drink mix will take longer to dissolve in the control (unstirred) beaker.

REAL WORLD APPLICATIONS

Chromatography Chromatography is often used to separate mixtures that can't be separated by simple methods. The figure at right shows how paper chromatography can be used to separate colored dyes in three different samples of black ink.

First ink marks are made on absorbent paper. Then the paper is put in a jar holding a small volume of solvent. The solvent travels upward through the paper, carrying the ink with it. The finished *chromatogram* reveals which dyes make up each of the inks.

Each dye has a different chemical structure. Dyes with structures more like that of the paper than that of the solvent stick to the paper and travel slower. Dyes with structures more like that of the solvent move upward with the solvent and therefore travel farther.

Applying Information
1. Does the blue dye in each ink sample have a structure more like that of the paper or the solvent? Why?
2. How would the result differ if the inks were made from a single dye instead of a mixture of several dyes?

SECTION 6.1 REVIEW

SUMMARY

▶ A heterogeneous mixture is a nonuniform blend of two or more substances.

▶ The particles in a suspension soon settle out of the mixture.

▶ The dispersed particles in a colloid are smaller and do not settle out.

▶ An emulsion is a colloid in which liquids that normally do not mix are spread throughout one another.

▶ A homogeneous mixture, or solution, is a uniform blend of two or more substances.

▶ In a solution, the solute is dissolved in the solvent.

CHECK YOUR UNDERSTANDING

1. **Classify** the following mixtures as homogeneous or heterogeneous:
   a. orange juice without pulp
   b. sweat
   c. cinnamon sugar
   d. dirt
2. **Explain** what would happen if coffee were brewed without a filter. What does the filter do?
3. **Describe** one reason smoke can irritate your eyes, while fog does not. (**Hint:** What is smoke a mixture of?)
4. **Identify** the solute and solvent in a solution containing silver nitrate, an ingredient in some hair dyes, and water.
5. **Arrange** the following mixtures in order of increasing particle size: muddy water (settles after a few hours), sugar water (does not settle), and sand in water (settles quickly).
6. **Explain** why a distillation would not separate a mixture of the miscible liquids formic acid, which boils at 100.7°C, and water, which boils at 100.0°C.
7. **Creative Thinking** Imagine as you are drinking lemonade outside, that some dirt blows into your glass. Write a plan for an experiment to separate the dirt from your lemonade. How could you separate the sugar and other solutes from the water?

WRITING SKILL

REAL WORLD APPLICATIONS

Chromatography Inks can be pure substances or mixtures. Most ballpoint pen inks are complex mixtures containing pigments or dyes that can be separated by paper chromatography.

Applying Information
1. The blue dye has a structure more like that of the solvent because it is near the top of the paper.
2. All parts of the ink would travel at the same rate, and the color on the paper would be the color of the ink.

Resources Assign students worksheet *6.1 Real World Applications—What Is Your Favorite Color?* in the **Integration Enrichment Resources** ancillary.

SECTION 6.1 REVIEW

Check Your Understanding

1. a. homogeneous
   b. homogeneous
   c. heterogeneous
   d. heterogeneous
2. The coffee would contain grounds. The filter separates the brewed coffee from the solid grounds.
3. Fog contains only water droplets. Smoke contains small particles of solids that can irritate eyes.
4. Water is the solvent, and silver nitrate is the solute.

Answers continue on p. 217A.

RESOURCE LINK
STUDY GUIDE

Assign students *Review Section 6.1 Solutions and Other Mixtures.*

Scheduling

Refer to pp. 184A–184D for lecture, classwork, and assignment options for Section 6.2.

★ **Lesson Focus**
Use transparency *LT 20* to prepare students for this section.

 **READING SKILL BUILDER** *K-W-L* Have students list what they think they know about the process of dissolving. Then have them list what they want to know about the topic. After they have studied this section, have students look at their lists and write down what they have learned. Also have them write down any new questions they might have. Have students do further reading in other sources to answer any unanswered questions they have about dissolving.

6.2

Dissolving and Solubility

▶ **KEY TERMS**

concentration
unsaturated solution
saturated solution
solubility
supersaturated solution
molarity

OBJECTIVES

▶ Describe how a substance dissolves in terms of its solubility, molecular motion, and solute-solvent interactions.

▶ Identify several factors that affect the rate at which a substance dissolves.

▶ Relate the structure of water to its ability to dissolve many different substances.

▶ Distinguish between saturated, unsaturated, and supersaturated solutions.

Suppose you and a friend are drinking iced tea. You add one spoonful of loose sugar to your glass of tea and stir. Soon all the sugar dissolves completely. Your friend adds a sugar cube to her tea. Even though your friend has been stirring for some time, a lump of sugar is still at the bottom of your friend's glass. Why does the sugar cube take longer to dissolve?

The Dissolving Process

According to the kinetic theory, the water molecules in each glass of tea are always moving. Some moving water molecules collide with sugar crystals. When this happens, energy is transferred to the sugar molecules at the surface of the crystal.

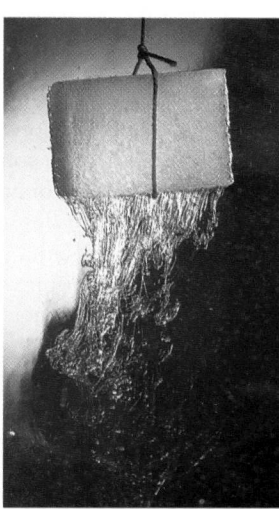

Figure 6-7
Sugar crystals dissolve in water when water molecules bump into sugar molecules at the surface of the crystals. These sugar molecules break away, dissolve, and spread throughout the solution.

Figure 6-7 shows that this energy, as well as the interaction between water and sugar molecules, causes sugar molecules at the surface of the crystal to break away from the rest of the sugar. These sugar molecules dissolve and move about randomly in the water.

Every time a layer of sugar molecules leaves the crystal, another layer of sugar molecules is uncovered. Sugar molecules break away from the crystal layer by layer in this way until the crystal completely dissolves.

DEMONSTRATION 3 SCIENCE AND THE CONSUMER

Temperature and Solution Rate

Time: Approximately 10 minutes
Materials: 2 sugar cubes, hot tap water, cold tap water, 2 Petri dishes, overhead projector

Place the two Petri dishes on the lit overhead projector. Add hot water to one dish and cold water to the other one until they are almost full. At the same time, drop a sugar cube into each one. Be careful not to disturb the dishes.

Analysis

1. Contrast your observations of the two dishes. *(The cube in the hot water dissolved faster.)*

2. What generalization can you make about how quickly a solute dissolves, and how temperature affects the speed of solution? *(In general, an increased temperature results in an increased rate of dissolution.)*

Solutes with a larger surface area dissolve faster

A substance in small pieces dissolves faster than the same substance in big pieces. When a solid is whole, most molecules are buried within it. Breaking the solid uncovers molecules along the break. The broken solid has more surface area, which leads to more solute-solvent collisions. Therefore, the solid dissolves faster.

Loose sugar has much more surface area than a sugar cube. That's why loose sugar dissolves faster. **Figure 6-8** shows how chewing a vitamin C tablet increases its surface area. This causes the vitamin to dissolve faster than it could if the vitamin were contained in a pill that was swallowed whole.

Stirring or shaking a solution helps the solute dissolve faster

If you pour sugar in a glass of water and let it sit without stirring, it will take a long time for the sugar to dissolve completely. That's because sugar is at the bottom of the glass surrounded by dissolved sugar molecules, as shown in **Figure 6-9A.** Dissolved sugar molecules will slowly *diffuse*, or spread out, throughout the entire solution. But until that happens, they keep water molecules from reaching the sugar that has not yet dissolved.

Stirring or shaking the solution moves the dissolved sugar away from the sugar crystals. Now more water molecules can interact with the solid, as shown in **Figure 6-9B,** so the sugar crystals dissolve faster.

Figure 6-8
Chewing a vitamin C tablet exposes molecules inside the tablet. More molecules can then collide with water molecules, so the tablet dissolves faster.

How Stirring Affects the Dissolving Process

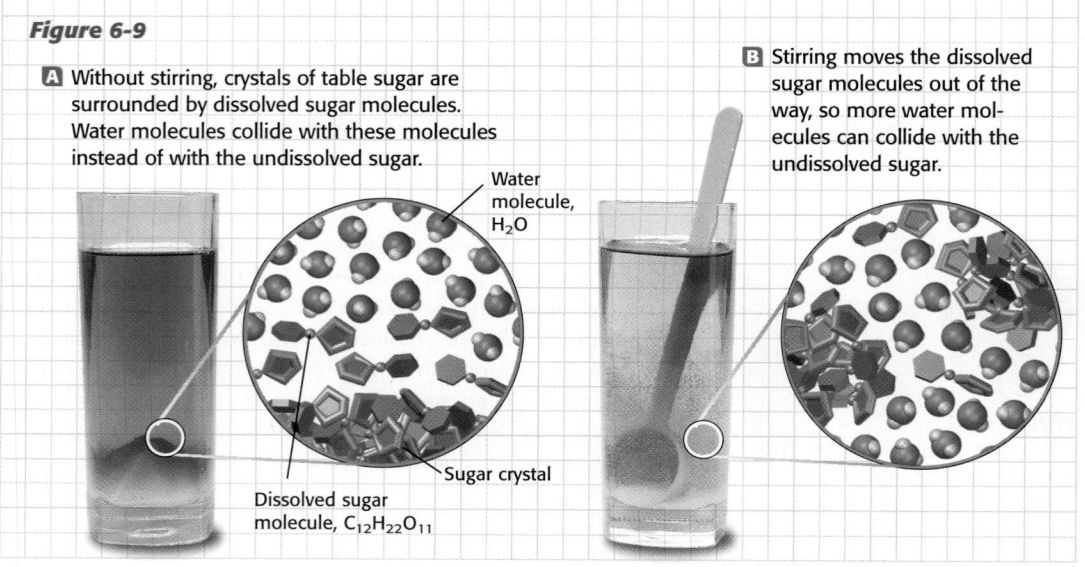

Figure 6-9

A Without stirring, crystals of table sugar are surrounded by dissolved sugar molecules. Water molecules collide with these molecules instead of with the undissolved sugar.

B Stirring moves the dissolved sugar molecules out of the way, so more water molecules can collide with the undissolved sugar.

Water molecule, H_2O

Sugar crystal

Dissolved sugar molecule, $C_{12}H_{22}O_{11}$

SOLUTIONS, ACIDS, AND BASES **193**

Teaching Tip

Rates of Dissolving All the factors that affect the rate of dissolving—surface area, stirring or shaking, and temperature—can be easily demonstrated using water and table sugar or table salt. Demonstration 2 is an example.

Point out the other factors to students, or have students check out the factors themselves. These simple activities are a good opportunity for students and family members to demonstrate scientific concepts at home. Caution students never to eat or drink anything in a laboratory setting and to use only warm, not hot, water when investigating the effect temperature has on the rate of dissolving.

Additional Application

Sugar Versus Artificial Sweetener Pair students in groups and give each group 2 g of granular sugar and 2 g of at least three different kinds of artificial sweetener. Using a stopwatch and a 100 mL beaker, have each group measure the dissolving rate of the sugar and each type of sweetener in distilled water.

SKILL BUILDER

Interpreting Visuals Have students examine **Figure 6-8.** Ask students how many of them have taken chewable vitamin C tablets. Emphasize to students that vitamin C is an acid. It is usually not harmful, but it is important to keep teeth properly brushed after chewing vitamin C so that the acid does not harm tooth enamel.

Dissolving and Solubility

Teaching Tip

Partial Charge The term *partial charge* is used to indicate the amount of charge, not whether the charge is positive or negative. A partial charge indicates that the amount of charge is less than the charge of an electron or a proton.

LINKING CHAPTERS

The role of energy in determining the speed of particles is further discussed in Chapter 10.

Figure 6-10
Olive oil and water form two layers when they are mixed. That's because olive oil is *insoluble* in water.

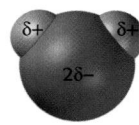

Figure 6-11
The oxygen atom in a water molecule is partially negative, and each hydrogen atom is partially positive. Note that the sum of these partial charges is equal to zero.

Solutes dissolve faster when the solvent is hot

Sugar and other solutes dissolve faster in hot water than in cold water. Remember that as a substance is heated, its particles move faster. As a result, there are more collisions between particles. These collisions also transfer more energy.

Many people like to add salt to the water they boil to cook pasta. In hot water, salt crystals are hit more often by water molecules, and these water molecules have more energy. So it is more likely that these water molecules will strip off sodium ions and chloride ions when they hit salt crystals.

Not every substance dissolves

When you put table salt, or sodium chloride, in water and stir, it seems to disappear. Yet you know it is still there because the water tastes salty. Table salt seems to disappear because it dissolves in water. Table salt and other substances that dissolve in water are described as being *soluble* in water. The olive oil shown in **Figure 6-10** is an example of a substance that is *insoluble* in water, meaning that it does not dissolve. It is also possible to have substances that are only *partly soluble* in water.

Water: A Common Solvent

Two-thirds of Earth's surface is water. The liquids you drink are mostly water, and so is three-fourths of your body weight. There are many substances that can dissolve in water. For this reason, water is sometimes called the universal solvent.

The structure of water helps it dissolve charged particles

To understand what makes water such a good solvent, consider the structure of a single water molecule. Think also about the attractions between water molecules that you learned about in Chapter 4. You have already seen how the oxygen atom on one water molecule is attracted to a hydrogen atom on a neighboring water molecule. These attractions occur because of charges.

Water is not an ionic compound, but it is *polar*. This means the shared electrons of each water molecule are not evenly spread throughout the molecule. The oxygen atom attracts shared electrons more strongly than the hydrogen atoms in a water molecule. As a result, the oxygen atom has a partial negative charge, and each hydrogen atom has a partial positive charge, as shown in **Figure 6-11**. To show that a charge is partial, the lowercase Greek letter delta (δ) is used. You can see from **Figure 6-11** that a partial positive charge is written as $\delta+$, and a partial negative charge is written as $\delta-$.

Figure 6-12

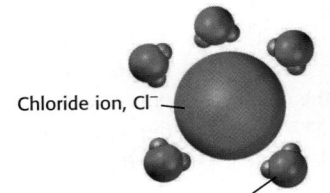

A When sodium chloride dissolves in water, positively charged sodium ions are attracted to the partially negative oxygen atoms of water.

Sodium ion, Na⁺

Water molecule, H₂O

Chloride ion, Cl⁻

Water molecule, H₂O

B Negatively charged chloride ions are attracted to the partially positive hydrogen atoms of water.

Figure 6-12 shows why sodium chloride dissolves easily in water. Sodium ions are attracted to the partially negative oxygen atom, and chloride ions are attracted to the partially positive hydrogen atoms. This interaction between ions and water molecules pulls the ions away from the solid. Substances made of molecules that dissolve in water also have partial charges that interact with water molecules. However, these substances exist as single molecules floating in solution, not as ions, when they dissolve.

"Like dissolves like"

Water can dissolve many substances, but there are many others it can't dissolve. For example, olive oil doesn't dissolve in water, and neither does gasoline. When deciding whether it is likely one substance will dissolve in another substance, chemists often use the rule "like dissolves like."

Methanol is soluble in water because both liquids are polar. They both have partially charged atoms that are attracted to one another. Gasoline is not soluble in water because its components are *nonpolar*, meaning their molecules do not have partial charges on opposite ends, like water molecules have. Substances like gasoline are soluble in oils and in other nonpolar substances.

Quick ACTIVITY

"Like dissolves like"

Tincture of iodine is a solution of iodine in ethanol. It is used to clean cuts and scrapes so that they do not become infected. Iodine, I₂, is a somewhat *nonpolar* element. Ethanol, C₂H₅OH, is a somewhat *polar* compound. In this activity, you will determine whether water or ethanol is more polar.

1. Dip a cotton swab in tincture of iodine, and make two small spots on the palm of your hand. The ethanol will evaporate and make your palm feel cool. The spots that remain are iodine.

2. Dip a second cotton swab in water, and wash one of the iodine spots with it. What happens to the iodine spot?

3. Dip a third cotton swab in ethanol, and wash the other iodine spot with it. What happens to the iodine spot?

4. Did water or ethanol dissolve the iodine spot better? Is water more polar or less polar than ethanol? Write a paragraph explaining your reasoning.

WRITING SKILL

Teaching Tip

Ionization and Dissociation
Ions form in solution by one of two processes. One is dissociation, in which the ions already exist, and they simply dissociate from the solid. Molecular compounds form ions in solution to varying extents by the process of ionization. Sometimes both processes are incorrectly referred to as ionization. Emphasize to students that the terms are not synonymous.

|SKILL BUILDER

Interpreting Visuals Perform the following demonstration to emphasize the polarity of water as shown in **Figure 6-12.** Use a plastic comb to rapidly comb someone's hair. Hold the comb near a small stream of water running from a faucet or poured slowly from a beaker. Show students that the stream bends toward the comb. The comb is charged, and the partial charges of the water molecules are attracted to it.

Quick ACTIVITY

"Like Dissolves Like" Be sure no students in the class have skin reactions to iodine before performing this activity. Warn students that tincture of iodine stains clothing and that iodine is poisonous. Have students wear safety goggles and laboratory aprons. Properly dispose of cotton swabs containing iodine according to your local environmental guidelines.

Students will find that ethanol removes iodine better than water does. Because iodine is nonpolar, it will dissolve better in a solvent that has little or no polarity. Because iodine is more soluble in ethanol than water, ethanol must be less polar than water is.

RESOURCE LINK
DATASHEETS

Have students use *Datasheet 6.2 Quick Activity: "Like Dissolves Like"* to record their results.

Teaching Tip

Saturation Conditions Be sure students understand that "the given conditions" mentioned in the definition of a saturated solution refer to temperature and, if a gas is involved, pressure. Because solubility is so dependent on temperature, solubility values are meaningless unless temperature is stated. Most substances have a unique solubility for each temperature. Pressure has no effect on solubility unless a gas is involved. If a gas is involved, the existing pressure must be stated for the solubility value to have meaning.

MISCONCEPTION

Dilute and Concentrated Be sure students understand that *dilute* and *concentrated* are relative terms based on use. For example, an experiment for a sixth grade class might require dilute hydrochloric acid, HCl. For those students, muriatic acid, which is impure HCl, used by a construction worker to clean brick would be considered concentrated. To the industrial engineer who needs HCl with little water in it for an industrial process, muriatic acid would be too dilute.

concentration the quantity of solute dissolved in a given quantity of solution

unsaturated solution a solution that is able to dissolve more solute

saturated solution a solution that cannot dissolve any more solute at the given conditions

Concentration

You can make a solution by dissolving sodium acetate in water. But how much sodium acetate do you need to add? And to what volume of water? Solutions can have different **concentrations**, depending on how much solute and solvent are present.

If you are not concerned about the exact concentration of a solution, you can express concentration less specifically. If a small quantity of solute is dissolved in a large volume of solvent, the resulting solution is said to be *dilute*. A *concentrated* solution, however, has a large quantity of dissolved solute.

Unsaturated solutions can dissolve more solute

An **unsaturated solution** of sodium acetate has many more water molecules than dissolved sodium ions and acetate ions, as shown in **Figure 6-13A**. A solution is unsaturated as long as it is able to dissolve more solute.

At some point, most solutions become saturated with solute

If you keep adding sodium acetate to the solution, the added sodium acetate dissolves until the solution becomes saturated, as shown in **Figure 6-13B**. A **saturated solution** is in equilibrium. This means that if any more solute dissolves, an equal amount comes out of solution. If you add more solute, it just settles to the bottom of the container. No matter how much you stir, no more sodium acetate will dissolve in a solution that is already saturated with solute.

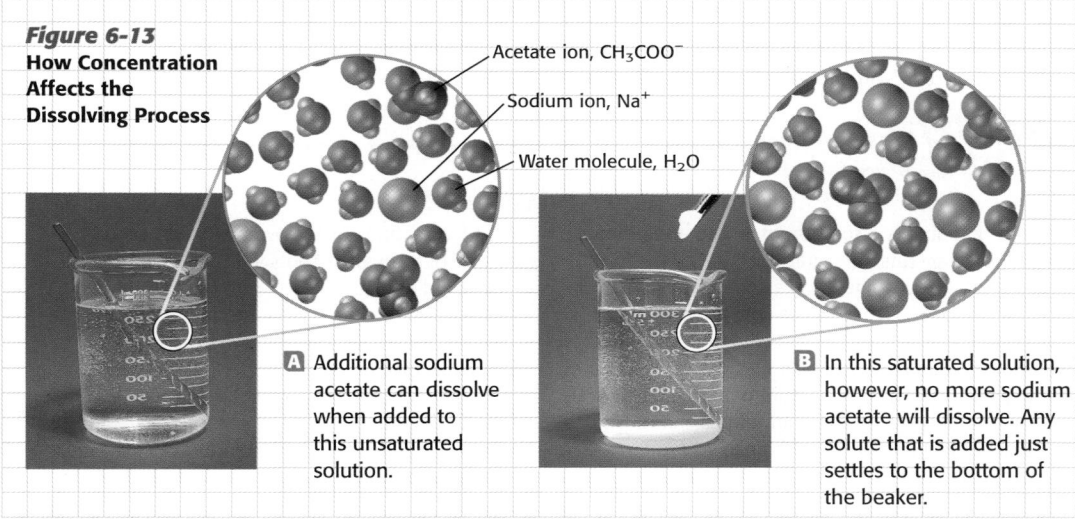

Figure 6-13
How Concentration Affects the Dissolving Process

Acetate ion, CH_3COO^-
Sodium ion, Na^+
Water molecule, H_2O

A Additional sodium acetate can dissolve when added to this unsaturated solution.

B In this saturated solution, however, no more sodium acetate will dissolve. Any solute that is added just settles to the bottom of the beaker.

196 CHAPTER 6

DEMONSTRATION 4 TEACHING

Temperature and Solubility

Time: Approximately 15 minutes

Materials: labels or marking pen, 150 mL beakers (2), 100 mL distilled water, balance, 20 g of calcium acetate, $Ca(CH_3COO)_2$, 20 g of potassium chloride, KCl, 2 stirrers, 100 mL graduated cylinder, 2 hot plates

Step 1 Label one beaker *Calcium acetate* and label the other beaker *Potassium chloride*. Pour 50 mL of distilled water into each beaker.

Step 2 Add 20 g of calcium acetate to one beaker and 20 g of potassium chloride to the other.

Step 3 Stir the contents of each beaker until all of the compound dissolves. Have students observe the results.

A saturated solution contains the greatest quantity of solute that will dissolve in a given quantity of solvent. Exactly how much solute will dissolve to make the solution saturated depends on the solute's **solubility** in the solvent as well as the solvent's temperature. At 20°C, you can dissolve a maximum of 203.9 g of table sugar in 100.0 g of water. At the same temperature, you can dissolve a maximum of 46.4 g of sodium acetate in 100.0 g of water. Although a much greater mass of table sugar will dissolve in water, the molar amounts of table sugar and sodium acetate that will dissolve in 100.0 g of water is nearly equal.

Not all solutions become saturated, though. Some substances can dissolve in each other in any proportion. A methanol-water solution, for example, never becomes saturated. Whether you add a small volume of methanol or a very large volume of methanol to water, it will always dissolve.

Heating a saturated solution usually allows you to dissolve even more solute

The solubility of many solutes, such as sodium acetate, increases as the temperature of the solution increases. If you heat a solution that is already saturated with dissolved sodium acetate, even more sodium acetate can dissolve. If you keep adding sodium acetate, it will keep dissolving until the solution becomes saturated at the higher temperature.

But something interesting happens when the solution cools down again. At the cooler temperature, this **supersaturated solution** holds more solute than it normally can. Supersaturated solutions are unstable systems because the solute's solubility is exceeded for a short time. Adding a small crystal of sodium acetate provides the surface that the excess solute needs to begin crystallizing, as shown in **Figure 6-14.** The solute keeps crystallizing out of the solution until the solution is saturated at the cooler temperature.

▶ **solubility** the greatest quantity of a solute that will dissolve in a given quantity of solvent to produce a saturated solution

📶 internet**connect** ≣

SCI**LINKS**
NSTA

TOPIC: Solubility
GO TO: www.scilinks.org
KEYWORD: HK1063

▶ **supersaturated solution** a solution holding more dissolved solute than is specified by its solubility at a given temperature

Figure 6-14
Adding a single crystal of sodium acetate to this supersaturated solution causes the excess sodium acetate to quickly crystallize out of the solution.

SOLUTIONS, ACIDS, AND BASES **197**

|**SKILL** BUILDER|

Vocabulary The terms *unsaturated, saturated,* and *supersaturated* will have more meaning to students if they are related to common usage of the term *saturated.* Ask students to describe a saturated sponge, saturated air, or becoming saturated with homework. Descriptions should mention that *saturated* refers to the greatest amount of something that normally can be contained. Once an understanding of *saturated* is achieved, students should be able to accurately infer the meanings of *unsaturated* and *supersaturated.*

MISCONCEPTION
Temperature Affects Solubility **ALERT**
Be sure students understand that solubility is so temperature-dependent that a saturated solution usually becomes unsaturated when its temperature is increased. That same saturated solution usually becomes supersaturated when the temperature is decreased.

Step 4 Warm each beaker on a hot plate. Stir and observe the results.

(**Note:** *After discussing the Analysis questions, point out to students that heating usually increases solubility; calcium acetate is an exception.*)

Analysis

1. What did you observe before heating the solutions? *(All the calcium acetate dissolves. Some of the potassium chloride remains undissolved.)*

2. What did you observe after heating the solutions? *(The rest of the potassium chloride dissolves. Some of the calcium acetate comes out of solution.)*

3. What conclusion can you make about the effect of temperature on how much of a substance will dissolve? *In many cases, an increased temperature increases the solubility of a substance. In other cases, an increased temperature decreases the solubility of a substance.*

Dissolving and Solubility

SECTION 6.2 REVIEW

Check Your Understanding

1. The compound hexane is nonpolar, so it will not be soluble in water.

2. Answers will vary but might include adding a crystal of solid to the solution. If it dissolves, the solution was unsaturated. If it remains solid but no solid comes out of solution, the solution was saturated. If solid comes out of the solution, the solution was supersaturated.

3. Chewing the medication increases its surface area so that it can dissolve faster.

4. Answers will vary but might include warming the milk so it will melt the chocolate and stirring the chocolate as it melts.

5. Sweat would evaporate more quickly when there is 37 percent humidity.

6. Water is polar. A partially charged end of a water molecule attracts an oppositely charged ion in an ionic compound or the oppositely charged end of another polar molecule.

7. $\dfrac{x}{200 \text{ g}} \times 100\% = 3\%$;

   $x = 200 \text{ g} \times \dfrac{3}{100} = 6 \text{ g}$

8. If students followed the instructions exactly, the solution would be saturated and would be too sweet. The teacher probably meant that students should add a small amount of sugar and then stir until the sugar they added dissolves.

RESOURCE LINK

STUDY GUIDE

Assign students *Review Section 6.2 Dissolving and Solubility.*

Measuring concentration precisely

Sometimes describing a solution as being unsaturated, saturated, or supersaturated is too general. Often you need to know exactly how much solute is dissolved in a solution. There are many different ways to express concentration. Which one is used depends on what the solution is being used for and how concentrated it is.

You have already seen that the solubility of a substance can be expressed as grams of solute per 100 g of solvent. Concentration can also be expressed as a mass percent, or grams of solute per 100 g of solution. A 5.0 percent solution of sodium chloride is made by dissolving 5.0 g of sodium chloride in 95 g of water. Concentration can also be expressed in units of **molarity**.

▶ **molarity** a concentration unit of a solution that expresses moles of solute dissolved per liter of solution

$$\text{Molarity} = \frac{\text{moles of solute}}{\text{liters of solution}}, \text{ or } M = \frac{\text{mol}}{L}$$

A 1.0 M (pronounced "one *molar*") solution of sodium chloride contains 1.0 mol of dissolved NaCl for every 1.0 L of solution. Molarity is the preferred concentration unit for many chemists because it expresses the molar amount of solute present.

SECTION 6.2 REVIEW

SUMMARY

▶ The larger the surface area a solute has, the faster it will dissolve.

▶ Stirring or shaking the solution dissolves solutes faster.

▶ Heating a solvent also dissolves solutes faster.

▶ So many substances are soluble in water that it is sometimes called the universal solvent.

▶ An unsaturated solution can dissolve more solute.

▶ A saturated solution cannot dissolve any more solute.

▶ A solute's solubility is exceeded in a supersaturated solution.

CHECK YOUR UNDERSTANDING

1. **Decide** if hexane, C_6H_{14}, is likely to be soluble in water.

2. **Propose** a way to determine whether a salt-water solution is unsaturated, saturated, or supersaturated.

3. **Explain** why chewable medication is usually faster-acting in your body than the same medication enclosed in a pill.

4. **Describe** the steps you would take to make hot chocolate as quickly as possible using cold milk and a chocolate candy bar.

5. **Determine** whether your sweat would evaporate more quickly if there were 92 percent humidity or 37 percent humidity. (**Hint:** When there is 100 percent humidity, the air is totally saturated with dissolved water vapor.)

6. **Describe** why water can dissolve some ionic compounds, like NH_4Cl, as well as some nonionic compounds, like methanol.

7. **Determine** what mass of potassium iodide should be dissolved in 200 g of water to make a 3.0 percent solution.

8. **Critical Thinking** A home economics teacher instructs the class to continue adding table sugar to their homemade lemonade until the sugar stops dissolving. Write a paragraph describing how your lemonade would taste if you followed these directions exactly. What did the teacher really mean?

WRITING SKILL

6.3

Acids, Bases, and pH

OBJECTIVES

▶ Compare and contrast acids and bases.
▶ Relate the pH of a solution to the concentration and strength of dissolved acid or base.
▶ Identify the products of neutralization reactions.

▶ **KEY TERMS**
acid
indicator
base
pH
neutralization reaction
salt

Does the thought of eating a lemon make your mouth pucker? You know what to expect: that sour, piercing taste that can sometimes make you shudder. Eating a lime or a dill pickle may cause you to have a similar response.

What Are Acids?

Each of these foods tastes sour because of **acids.** Several fruits, including lemons and limes, contain citric acid. Dill pickles are soaked in vinegar, which contains acetic acid. Acids donate hydrogen ions, H^+, to form hydronium ions, H_3O^+, when they are dissolved in water. **Indicators,** such as litmus, can help you determine if a substance is an acid. Acids turn blue litmus paper red, as shown in **Figure 6-15.**

Acids in lemons and other foods are mixed with lots of water, so they are usually not harmful. But if you have ever gotten lemon juice in your eye accidentally, you know that it is painful. That's because all acids, even very dilute ones, can damage your eyes and other sensitive areas of your body. Concentrated acids, those that aren't mixed with much water, can burn your skin. To be safe, always protect yourself by wearing safety goggles, gloves, and a laboratory apron when working with acids in the laboratory. If possible, work with only very dilute acids.

▶ **acid** a substance that donates hydrogen ions, H^+, to form hydronium ions, H_3O^+, when dissolved in water

▶ **indicator** a compound that can reversibly change color in a solution, depending on the concentration of H_3O^+ ions

VOCABULARY *Skills Tip*

The word acid *originates from the Latin word* acidus, *meaning "sour."*

Figure 6-15
Lemons, limes, and dill pickles taste sour because of acids. Acids turn blue litmus paper red.

Scheduling
Refer to pp. 184A–184D for lecture, classwork, and assignment options for Section 6.3.

★ **Lesson Focus**
Use transparency *LT 21* to prepare students for this section.

Multicultural Extension

The sandbox trees that are found in Central and South America contain sap that is potentially dangerous. The sap contains a strong acid that can burn skin. If someone's eyes are exposed to it, it can cause blindness. However, the sap has an important use for the native populations of the area. When thrown into dammed areas of lakes and streams, the sap has a temporarily paralyzing effect on fish. The fish float to the top of the water and are gathered for food. After all the needed fish are taken, the dams are removed, the added water dilutes the sap, and the remaining fish recover.

READING SKILL BUILDER *Paired Reading* Have students read the section silently and mark on self-adhesive notes those passages that they do not understand. Be sure students study figures and tables to help clarify the relevant passages. Pair students and have them discuss the passages each found difficult. If passages remain unclear, have the pair keep track of their questions for later class discussion or teacher explanation.

DEMONSTRATION 5 SCIENCE AND THE CONSUMER

A Natural Indicator

Time: Approximately 15 minutes
Materials: red cabbage, distilled water, large beaker, hot plate, 8 test tubes, test-tube rack, 8 stirrers
Solutions: vinegar, lemon juice, distilled water, ammonia cleaner, baking soda, drain cleaner, colorless soft drink, liquid soap

Prepare an indicator before class by boiling red cabbage leaves. Cool the purple liquid. Add this indicator to the test tubes in the rack until they are about half full. Add one of the listed liquids to each test tube and stir. Cabbage juice turns red or reddish-purple in an acid.

Analysis

1. Which of the solutions were acids? *(vinegar, lemon juice, soft drink)*

Acids, Bases, and pH

Teaching Tip

Indicators Indicators change color over a range of H_3O^+ concentrations. Some indicators, such as crystal violet, change color in solutions that are quite acidic. Others, such as alizarin yellow, change color in a solution with low H_3O^+ concentration.

MISCONCEPTION

Hydrogen Atoms **ALERT**
Students might think that the more hydrogen atoms an acid has, the stronger it is. Acids that have more than one acidic hydrogen atom per molecule ionize by losing the atoms one at a time. Each atom is more difficult to lose than the one before because it is being lost from a negative ion. Phosphoric acid, H_3PO_4, loses one hydrogen atom relatively easily, leaving an $H_2PO_4^-$ ion. Fewer hydrogen atoms leave the $H_2PO_4^-$ ion because it is negatively charged. Few HPO_4^{2-} ions lose their final hydrogen ion. Phosphoric acid contains three acidic hydrogen atoms, but it does not have a high degree of ionization and is therefore a weak acid.

Figure 6-16

A Strong acids, like nitric acid, ionize completely and are therefore better conductors, as indicated by the brightly lit bulb.

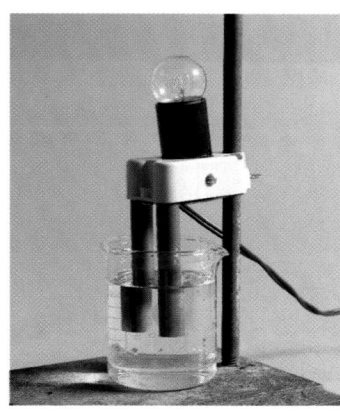

B Weak acids, like acetic acid, only partially ionize. There are not as many ions in solution as there are for a strong acid, so the bulb is only dimly lit.

Some acid solutions form the maximum amount of charged ions

All acids can conduct electricity when dissolved in water because all acids form hydronium ions, H_3O^+, when they are dissolved in water. But some acid solutions conduct electricity better than others. Solutions of some acids, like nitric acid, conduct electricity well. Nitric acid, HNO_3, is a *strong acid*. Strong acids fully ionize when dissolved in water. This means their solutions have as many hydronium ions as the acid can possibly form. The following reaction takes place when nitric acid is added to water.

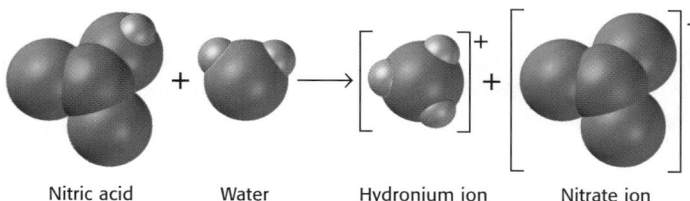

Nitric acid   Water   Hydronium ion   Nitrate ion

The single reaction arrow pointing to the right shows that nitric acid ionizes completely in water to form hydronium ions and nitrate ions. These ions move around in the solution and conduct electricity. Other strong acids behave similarly when dissolved in water. A solution of sulfuric acid in water, for instance, conducts electricity in car batteries.

Other acids do not ionize completely

Solutions of *weak acids*, such as acetic acid, CH_3COOH, do not conduct electricity as well as nitric acid. When acetic acid is added to water, the following equilibrium takes place.

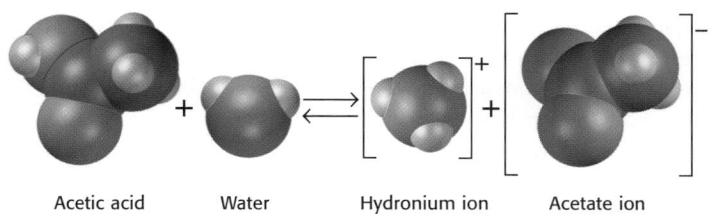

Acetic acid   Water   Hydronium ion   Acetate ion

The reaction arrow pointing to the right shows that some acetic acid molecules combine with water molecules to form ions. The reaction arrow pointing to the left shows that not all of the acetic acid in the solution reacts to form ions. Because there are fewer ions (charges) in the solution, it does not conduct electricity as well as a solution of nitric acid, as shown in **Figure 6-16. Table 6-1** lists several common acids and their uses.

ALTERNATIVE ASSESSMENT

Properties of Acids and Bases

Step 1 Have groups of students brainstorm lists of properties, examples, and uses of acids and bases.

Step 2 After checking the lists for accuracy, have students use the lists to write books for younger students that explain in simple language what acids and bases are and how they are used.

Step 3 Have students create outlines and rough drafts for the books. Check these items for clarity of explanation and scientific accuracy before students finalize their books. Students can use pictures that they draw themselves or acquire from magazines to illustrate their written copy.

Step 4 If possible, have students use the completed books to teach another class about acids and bases.

Table 6-1   Some Common Acids

Acid	Formula	Strength	Uses for dissolved acid
Hydrochloric acid (muriatic acid)	HCl	Strong	Cleaning and food processing; adjusting the pH of swimming pools
Sulfuric acid	H_2SO_4	Strong	Making fertilizers and other chemicals; fluid inside car batteries
Nitric acid	HNO_3	Strong	Making fertilizers and explosives
Acetic acid (ethanoic acid)	CH_3COOH	Weak	Making vinegar; manufacturing chemicals, plastics, and medicines
Formic acid	HCOOH	Weak	Dyeing textiles
Citric acid	$C_6H_8O_7$	Weak	Preparing flavorings, candies, and soft drinks

What Are Bases?

Like acids, all **bases** share common properties. Foods that contain bases taste bitter. Bases are also slippery. Like acidic solutions, basic solutions can conduct electricity and cause indicators to change color. Not all bases are exactly alike, though. Some bases contain hydroxide ions, OH^-, while others do not. But bases that do not will react with water molecules to form hydroxide ions. **Figure 6-17** shows some common household substances that contain bases. Bases turn red litmus paper blue.

Like acids, bases can be very dangerous if they are not diluted with water. To protect yourself when working with bases in the laboratory, always wear safety goggles, gloves, and a laboratory apron. If possible, work with very dilute bases instead of concentrated ones.

▶ **base** a substance that either contains hydroxide ions, OH^-, or reacts with water to form hydroxide ions

Many common bases contain hydroxide ions

Potassium hydroxide, KOH, is a base found in some drain cleaners. Solutions of potassium hydroxide conduct electricity well, so potassium hydroxide must be a *strong base.* In water, potassium hydroxide dissociates completely to form ions, as shown below.

$$KOH \longrightarrow K^+ + OH^-$$

Figure 6-17
These household items all contain bases. Bases turn red litmus paper blue.

SOLUTIONS, ACIDS, AND BASES **201**

SKILL BUILDER

Interpreting Tables Have students examine **Tables 6-1** and **6-2.** Point out that most organic and other nonmetallic acids and bases are weak.

Resources Blackline Master 19 shows **Table 6-1.** Blackline Master 20 shows **Table 6-2.**

Teaching Tip

Slippery Bases Explain to students that bases feel slippery because they actually react with skin. Weak bases, such as soap, do not harm skin, but strong bases will damage human tissue.

Historical Perspective

Inorganic acids such as HCl and H_2SO_4 were first reported in medieval times. The importance of the discovery and use of these acids is considered by some scientific historians to be second only to the manufacture of iron items 3000 years earlier.

MISCONCEPTION

ALERT

Strong Bases
Because students may have a preconceived idea that acids can be harmful, they might assume that bases are not. Emphasize that strong bases are just as reactive as strong acids.

Acids, Bases, and pH

Acids have been used in many cultures for food preservation in a process known as pickling. Pickling inhibits growth of bacteria and other microorganisms. Ancient Greeks ate pickled birds. Pickled fish have been an important food supply in Scandinavia since the Maglemosian culture there used the pickling technique as early as 10 000 B.C.

MISCONCEPTION ALERT

Hydroxide Ions

Explain that strong bases do not always produce a large number of hydroxide ions. For example, calcium hydroxide is a strong base because it completely dissociates when dissolved in water. However, it does not produce a large number of hydroxide ions in solution because its solubility is so low. Although all the calcium hydroxide that dissolves dissociates, not much dissolves.

Other bases react with water to form hydroxide ions

As **Table 6-2** shows, ammonia is a base that does not contain hydroxide ions. When ammonia gas is dissolved in water, water acts like an acid and donates a hydrogen ion. This ion is accepted by ammonia. The result is a mixture of dissolved ammonia, water, ammonium ions, and hydroxide ions.

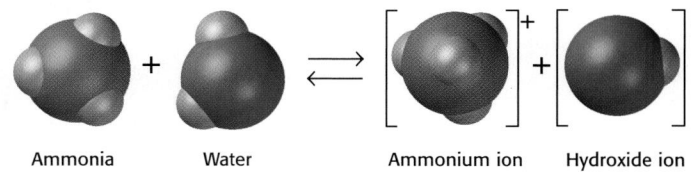

Ammonia   Water   Ammonium ion   Hydroxide ion

A solution of ammonia does not conduct electricity as well as a solution containing an equal concentration of potassium hydroxide. That's because the ammonia solution has fewer dissolved ions.

How Acidic Is an Acid?

You can tell if a solution is acidic, basic, or neutral by using litmus paper. But to determine if one solution is more acidic than another, you must measure the concentration of hydronium ions. The **pH** of a solution indicates its concentration of hydronium ions. The pH of a solution is often critical. For example, enzymes in your body work only in a very narrow pH range. And an abnormal pH of a person's blood can be a sign of health problems.

internetconnect

SCiLINKS
NSTA

TOPIC: pH
GO TO: www.scilinks.org
KEYWORD: HK1064

VOCABULARY *Skills Tip*

The term pH *originates from the French words* pouvoir Hydrogène, *meaning "hydrogen power."*

▶ **pH** a measure of the hydronium ion concentration in a solution

Table 6-2 **Some Common Bases**

Base	Formula	Strength	Uses for dissolved base
Potassium hydroxide (potash)	KOH	Strong	Manufacturing soap and some drain cleaners; bleaching
Sodium hydroxide (lye)	NaOH	Strong	Manufacturing soap, paper, textiles, and some drain cleaners
Calcium hydroxide (lime)	$Ca(OH)_2$	Strong	Making plaster, cement, and mortar
Ammonia	NH_3	Weak	Manufacturing fertilizers and many cleaners
Methylamine	CH_3NH_2	Weak	Manufacturing dyes and medicines
Pyridine	C_5H_5N	Weak	Manufacturing vitamins and medicines

ALTERNATIVE ASSESSMENT

pH of Blood

Have students write a paragraph explaining why hyperventilation, which is breathing too rapidly and deeply, can upset the pH of the blood. Have them include why breathing into a paper bag decreases the effects of hyperventilation. If students need a hint, remind them that the waste produced from cellular respiration is CO_2, and ask them what is formed when this gas reacts with water in the blood. Carbonic acid, H_2CO_3, and

CO_2 and H_2O are in equilibrium in the blood. When hyperventilating, a person breathes out an unusually large amount of CO_2. The equilibrium is upset, and the body decomposes more carbonic acid to replace lost CO_2. The decrease of this acid in the blood raises the pH. Breathing into a paper bag helps reduce the effects of hyperventilation because you are breathing exhaled air, which has a high concentration of CO_2.

pH values correspond to the concentration of hydronium ions

pH is a measure of the hydronium ion concentration in a solution, but it also indicates the solution's hydroxide ion concentration. So a pH value can tell you how acidic or basic a solution is. pH can even tell you if a solution is neutral, or neither an acid nor a base.

Typically, the pH of solutions ranges from 0 to 14, as shown in **Figure 6-18.** Neutral solutions have a pH of 7. In neutral solutions, like pure water, the concentration of hydronium ions equals the concentration of hydroxide ions. Solutions with a pH of less than 7 are acidic. In acidic solutions, like apple juice, the concentration of hydronium ions is greater than the concentration of hydroxide ions. Solutions with a pH of greater than 7 are basic. In basic solutions, such as household ammonia, the concentration of hydroxide ions is greater than the concentration of hydronium ions.

Small differences in pH values mean larger differences in hydronium ion concentration

Figure 6-18 compares the pH values of several common solutions. Notice how the pH value of apple juice differs from that of coffee by two pH units. Each unit of pH represents a factor of 10 in hydronium ion concentration. So apple juice is really 10^2, or 100 times, more acidic than coffee. Likewise, coffee is about 10^3, or 1000 times, more acidic than the antacid shown in **Figure 6-18.**

Did You Know ?

Did you know that the concentration of hydronium ions and the concentration of hydroxide ions are related? In any solution made with water, the more hydronium ions there are (the more acidic the solution), the fewer hydroxide ions there are (the less basic the solution).

Figure 6-18
The pH of a substance is easily measured by comparing the color the substance turns a strip of pH paper with the color scale on the pH paper dispenser.

More acidic — NEUTRAL — More basic

0 1 2 3 4 5 6 7 8 9 10 11 12 13 14

Battery acid | Stomach acid | Apple juice | Black coffee | Pure water | Antacid (when dissolved in water) | Baking soda | Hand soap | Household ammonia | Drain cleaner

SOLUTIONS, ACIDS, AND BASES **203**

DEMONSTRATION 6 TEACHING

Temperature Affects Solubility

Time: Approximately 20 minutes

Materials: 600 mL beaker, Bunsen burner, ring-stand, hot plate, magnetic stirrer, stirring bar, 1 M Na_2CO_3 solution, 5% universal indicator solution, carbonated water (carbon dioxide and water only)

Pour 250 mL of tap water into the beaker. Add 40 mL of the universal indicator to the beaker. Add a few drops of the Na_2CO_3 solution until a blue color

is achieved. Add 50 mL of carbonated water to the beaker. Note the instant color change resulting in a yellow-orange colored solution. This indicates that the solution has become acidic due to the presence of the dissolved CO_2 in the carbonated water. Heat the solution to boiling. As the temperature rises, the solution will become basic. This results from the decreased solubility of the carbon dioxide. When the CO_2 has been removed from the solution, the color will return to the initial blue color.

Section 6.3

Acids, Bases, and pH

Historical Perspective

In 1909, Søren Peter Sørensen, a Danish biochemist, developed the pH scale. He refined the concept of pH and presented his ideas about it in 1923. He also presented his research on dyes that act as indicators. But the pH scale was not widely used until the 1930s.

Teaching Tip

What is pH? The negative base-ten logarithm of the hydronium ion concentration of a solution expressed in molarity is its pH. That is not as scary as it sounds. In solutions, hydronium ion concentrations range from 10^0 (1) M to 10^{-14} M. Suppose an acid has a hydronium ion concentration of 10^{-4} M. The base-ten logarithm of that number is simply its exponent, –4. The negative of that number is 4. The pH of the acid is 4. Similarly, the pH of a basic solution with a hydronium ion concentration of 10^{-11} M is 11. Use the hydronium ion concentration range to help students understand where the 0 to 14 range for pH originates.

Additional Application

Temperature Effects on Solubility Refer students to the results obtained in Demonstration 6. Ask students how the temperature of water can affect fish and other aquatic life. *(Fish breathe dissolved oxygen gas, and the solubility of oxygen is dependent upon the temperature of the water. As the temperature of the water increases, the dissolved oxygen concentration decreases.)*

203

Acids, Bases, and pH

Teaching Tip

pH and Aquariums If possible, set up an aquarium of freshwater fish in the classroom. Discuss with students what factors might cause the pH of the water to change. Factors might include increased acidity from the carbon dioxide in the air bubbled through the tank or increased basicity from ammonia released in fish wastes. Each day, assign a student to check the pH of the water and to decide whether it needs to be adjusted or not. If it does, have the student propose what needs to be added to make the adjustment. Approve student plans before any action is taken. After approval, have the student adjust and recheck the pH.

Additional Application

Spectator Ions Those ions that are "on the sidelines watching the reaction" are called spectator ions. The spectator ions in the reaction shown on the student page are Na^+ and Cl^-. Chemical equations known as *net ionic equations* include only items that change from one side of the equation to the other and do not include spectator ions.

Inquiry Lab

Which household substances are acids, which are bases, and which are neither?

Materials
- ✔ baking powder
- ✔ baking soda
- ✔ bleach
- ✔ mayonnaise
- ✔ milk
- ✔ mineral water
- ✔ soft drinks
- ✔ tap water
- ✔ white vinegar
- ✔ dishwashing liquid
- ✔ laundry detergent
- ✔ pipet bulbs
- ✔ disposable glass pipets
- ✔ several 50 mL beakers
- ✔ blue litmus paper
- ✔ red litmus paper

Procedure

SAFETY CAUTION Wear safety goggles, gloves, and a laboratory apron. Never pipet anything by mouth.

1. Prepare a sample of each substance you will test. If the substance is a liquid, pour about 5 mL of it into a small beaker. If the substance is a solid, place a small amount of it in a beaker, and add about 5 mL of water. Label each beaker clearly with the name of the substance that is in it.
2. Use a pipet to transfer a drop of liquid from one of the samples to red litmus paper. Then transfer another drop of liquid from the same sample to blue litmus paper. Record your observations.
3. Repeat step 2 for each sample. Be sure to use a clean pipet to transfer each sample.

Analysis

1. Which substances are acids? Which are bases? How did you determine this?
2. Which substances are neither acids nor bases? How did you determine this?

▶ **neutralization reaction**
a reaction in which hydronium ions from an acid and hydroxide ions from a base react to produce water molecules

Neutralization Reactions

A **neutralization reaction** is a reaction between hydronium ions and hydroxide ions to form water molecules. The resulting solution is more neutral than either of the reactants.

Strong acids and bases react to form water and a salt

A solution of a strong acid, like hydrochloric acid, will ionize completely, as shown below.

$$HCl + H_2O \longrightarrow H_3O^+ + Cl^-$$

Similarly, a solution of a strong base, like sodium hydroxide, dissociates completely, as shown below.

$$NaOH \longrightarrow Na^+ + OH^-$$

If the two solutions are of equal concentrations and equal volumes are combined, the following reaction takes place.

$$H_3O^+ + Cl^- + Na^+ + OH^- \longrightarrow Na^+ + Cl^- + 2H_2O$$

Notice how Na^+ and Cl^- are on both sides of this balanced equation. That's because they do not react. They are not changed at all in the reaction—it is as if they are on the sidelines, watching the reaction between H_3O^+ and OH^-.

204 CHAPTER 6

RESOURCE LINK
DATASHEETS

Have students use *Datasheet 6.3 Inquiry Lab: Which household substances are acids, which are bases, and which are neither?* to record their results.

Inquiry Lab

Which household substances are acids, which are bases, and which are neither?

If either color of litmus changes color when a liquid is added, it is a clear indication of whether the liquid is an acid or a base. However, students might assume that if a solution does not change red litmus to blue, for example, it is an acid. Be sure students use both red and blue litmus paper to check the liquids. Using only one color might result in erroneous results if the solution is neutral.

Analysis

The acids are soft drinks, milk, white vinegar, and mayonnaise because the liquids turned blue litmus red. The bases are baking soda, bleach, dishwashing liquid, and laundry detergent because they turned red litmus

If you include only the substances that react, the equation can be written as follows.

$$H_3O^+ + OH^- \longrightarrow 2H_2O$$

This equation describes how most acids and bases react. Usually, when an acid reacts with a base, hydronium ions react with hydroxide ions to form water. The other ions—positive ions from the base and negative ions from the acid—form a **salt,** such as sodium chloride. Salts are ionic compounds that are often soluble in water. **Table 6-3** lists some common salts and some of the ways these salts are used.

Some acid-base reactions do not result in neutral solutions

Reactions between acids and bases do not always produce exactly neutral solutions. The pH of the solution depends on the amounts of acid and base that are combined. The pH also depends on whether the combined acid and base are strong or weak.

If a strong acid, like nitric acid, spills and reacts with an equal amount of a weak base, like sodium hydrogen carbonate from an antacid tablet, only some of the acid will be neutralized. The solution will still be acidic. However, if a strong acid reacts with *enough* of a weak base, the solution that results can be neutral or even basic.

A similar situation occurs when a strong base reacts with a weak acid. If the right ratio of amounts react, only some of the base will be neutralized. The solution will still be basic. But if a strong base reacts with *enough* of a weak acid, it's possible that the solution can be neutral or even acidic.

▶ **salt** an ionic compound composed of cations bonded to anions, other than oxide or hydroxide anions

INTEGRATING

BIOLOGY

Adding even small amounts of acids or bases can drastically change the pH of a system. Luckily, reactions take place in the human body to ensure that a proper pH is maintained. In your blood, hydrogen carbonate removes excess hydronium ions by reacting with them to form carbonic acid and water, as shown by the reaction below.

$$HCO_3^- + H_3O^+ \rightarrow$$
$$H_2CO_3 + H_2O$$

Carbonic acid removes basic ions from your blood by reacting with them to form hydrogen carbonate ions and water, as shown by the following reaction.

$$H_2CO_3 + OH^- \rightarrow$$
$$HCO_3^- + H_2O$$

Table 6-3 **Some Common Salts**

Salt	Formula	Uses
Aluminum sulfate	$Al_2(SO_4)_3$	Purifying water
Ammonium sulfate	$(NH_4)_2SO_4$	Fertilizing
Barium sulfate	$BaSO_4$	Medical diagnostic testing
Calcium chloride	$CaCl_2$	De-icing streets
Potassium chloride	KCl	Table-salt substitute
Silver bromide	$AgBr$	Developing photographic film
Sodium carbonate (washing soda)	Na_2CO_3	Manufacturing glass, detergents, and paper
Sodium hydrogen carbonate (baking soda)	$NaHCO_3$	Baking; manufacturing antacids and air fresheners

SOLUTIONS, ACIDS, AND BASES **205**

blue. Depending on the sample tested, baking powder and tap water are probably neutral because they did not cause either litmus paper to change color. As an extension exercise have students test other household products to determine which are acids and which are bases.

INTEGRATING

BIOLOGY
Resources Assign students worksheet *6.4 Integrating Biology—Balance in the Body* in the **Integration Enrichment Resources** ancillary.

Teaching Tip

Hydrolysis The pH of the solution after a neutralization reaction depends on the *hydrolysis* of the salt produced. Hydrolysis is the reaction of a salt with water. Remember that water ionizes to a small extent, forming a few OH^- ions and an equal number of H_3O^+ ions. Suppose the salt produced is sodium chloride, NaCl. Because NaOH is a strong base and HCl is a strong acid, the ions from the salt do not combine with the ions from the water, and the solution is neutral. However, if the salt formed is aluminum nitrate, $Al(NO_3)_3$, the Al^{3+} ion from the salt will combine with the OH^- from the water because $Al(OH)_3$ is a weak base. The H_3O^+ ions stay in solution because HNO_3 is a strong acid. An $Al(NO_3)_3$ solution is therefore acidic. Similarly, a salt formed from a strong base and a weak acid, such as sodium carbonate, Na_2CO_3, will be basic. The result of a neutralization between a weak acid and a weak base depends on the relative strengths of the two reactants.

SKILL BUILDER

Interpreting Tables Have students examine **Table 6-3** and compare the different uses for each listed salt.

Resources Blackline Master 21 shows this table.

Acids, Bases, and pH

Neutral Versus Neutralization
Be sure students do not use the terms *neutral* and *neutralization* synonymously. *Neutral* refers to having a pH of 7. *Neutralization* refers to an acid-base reaction that occurs when an acid is mixed with a base. The resulting solution after a neutralization reaction can be acidic, basic, or neutral.

SECTION 6.3 REVIEW

Check Your Understanding

1. **a.** basic
   b. acidic
   c. acidic
   d. neutral
2. soft drink, gastric juices, vinegar
3. 10^4 (10 000)
4. $Al(OH)_3 + 3HCl \rightarrow AlCl_3 + 3H_2O$
5. $Al_2(SO_4)_3$ is formed from the base aluminum hydroxide, $Al(OH)_3$, and sulfuric acid, H_2SO_4.
6. **a.** $KOH + HNO_3 \rightarrow KNO_3 + H_2O$
   b. $Ca(OH)_2 + H_2SO_4 \rightarrow CaSO_4 + 2H_2O$
   c. $NaOH + HCl \rightarrow NaCl + H_2O$
   d. $CH_3NH_2 + H_2O \rightleftarrows CH_3NH_3^+ + OH^-$
7. A pH of 5.5 is more acidic than a pH of 6.0, so more acid should be added.

Avoiding dangerous reactions at home
Figure 6-19 shows that some household products should never be combined because they react to produce harmful substances. Ammonia and bleach react to produce a poisonous substance called chloramine, NH_2Cl. Combining vinegar and bleach produces chlorine gas, Cl_2, another poisonous substance. To be safe, don't combine household products and always check the warning labels.

Figure 6-19
Ammonia and bleach should never be combined and neither should vinegar and bleach. Both combinations result in reactions that produce poisonous substances.

SECTION 6.3 REVIEW

SUMMARY

▶ Acids are sour, corrosive substances that form hydronium ions when dissolved in water.

▶ Bases are bitter, slippery substances that either contain hydroxide ions or form them when dissolved in water.

▶ Indicators are substances that change color depending on whether a solution is acidic, basic, or neutral.

▶ The pH of a solution is a measure of its concentration of hydronium ions.

▶ Neutral solutions have a pH of 7, acidic solutions have a pH of less than 7, and basic solutions have a pH of greater than 7.

▶ A neutralization reaction occurs when hydronium ions and hydroxide ions react to form water molecules.

CHECK YOUR UNDERSTANDING

1. **Classify** the following substances as acidic, basic, or neutral:
   a. a soapy solution, pH = 9
   b. a sour liquid, pH = 5
   c. a solution with four times as many hydronium ions as hydroxide ions
   d. pure water (a liquid with an equal concentration of hydronium ions and hydroxide ions)
2. **Arrange** the following substances in order of increasing acidity: vinegar (pH = 2.8), gastric juices from inside your stomach (pH = 3.0), and a soft drink (pH = 3.4).
3. **Complete** the following sentence: A solution with a pH of 2 is _____ times more acidic than a solution with a pH of 6.
4. **Write** the balanced equation for the reaction of aluminum hydroxide, $Al(OH)_3$, a common antacid, with hydrochloric acid in your stomach.
5. **Determine** which acid and which base react to form the salt aluminum sulfate, $Al_2(SO_4)_3$.
6. **Complete** the following equations. Make sure that each equation is balanced properly.
   a. $KOH + HNO_3 \longrightarrow$ **c.** $NaOH + HCl \longrightarrow$
   b. $Ca(OH)_2 + H_2SO_4 \longrightarrow$ **d.** CH_3NH_2 (a base) $+ H_2O \rightleftarrows$
7. **Decision Making** Imagine you have made a solution that has a pH of 6.0 by dissolving NaOH and CH_3COOH in water. The solution needs to have a pH of 5.5. Should you add more acid or more base to achieve the desired pH?

206 CHAPTER 6

6.4

Acids and Bases in the Home

OBJECTIVES

▶ Recognize several acidic and basic substances commonly found in homes.

▶ Explain how soap is made and why it can remove dirt and grease.

▶ Describe the acidic or basic characteristics of other household items.

▶ KEY TERMS

soap
detergent
disinfectant
bleach
antacid

A s you have seen, you won't find acids and bases only in a laboratory. Many substances are acids and bases, including many items in your own home. Soaps, detergents, shampoos, antacids, vitamins, and even juices in your kitchen are just a few examples of household acids and bases.

Cleaning Products

If you work in the garden without gloves or if you've been eating potato chips, no amount of water alone will remove the greasy film from your hands. That's because water doesn't mix with grease or oil. Unfortunately, most dirt that ends up on your skin and clothes has some grease or oil. So dirt cannot be removed with water alone. Something else is needed that can work with water to help it clean.

Soaps allow oil and water to mix

Soaps can dissolve in both grease or oil and in water. Soaps are emulsifiers that let oil and water mix and keep them from separating. The fact that soap can make these two very different substances mix makes it a good cleaner. For example, when you wash your face with soap, like the girl in **Figure 6-20,** the oil on your face is suspended in soapy water. The water you rinse with carries away the soap and unwanted oil, leaving your face clean.

internetconnect

SCI LINKS
NSTA

TOPIC: Acids and bases at home
GO TO: www.scilinks.org
KEYWORD: HK1065

▶ **soap** a cleaner that dissolves in both water and oil

Figure 6-20
When you wash with soap, you create an emulsion of oil droplets spread throughout water.

SOLUTIONS, ACIDS, AND BASES **207**

DEMONSTRATION 7 SCIENCE AND THE CONSUMER

A Natural pH Indicator

Time: Approximately 30 minutes
Materials: red cabbage juice, 24-well spot plate, pipets, various household products (ammonia, vinegar, detergent, etc.), blender, strainer, overhead projector

Place 1/2 a head of red cabbage into a blender. Fill the blender with water and chop for a minute. Strain the solid material from the liquid. Place the spot plate on the overhead projector. Add a small amount of each of the household products to the spot plate. Add a squirt of red cabbage juice to each of the wells. Observe the different colors.

pH	Cabbage Juice Color
2-3	Red
3-4	Pink
4-6	Purple
6-8	Blue-Green
8-12	Green

INTEGRATING TECHNOLOGY and Society
Acids and Bases in the Home

Connection to
SOCIAL STUDIES

Soap was also used in Sumer, which is now Iran and Iraq, as early as 2500 B.C. Around 600 B.C., the Phoenicians made soap from wood ashes and goat fat and found it to be valuable for barter or trade. Ancient Mediterranean and British cultures also made soap.

Making the Connection
1. The term is based on the Latin word for soap, *sapo*, which came from the name of the mountain that was the source of soapy water.
2. Ashes provided the base, and the hog fat provided the hydrocarbon chain with a water-soluble end.

Resources Assign students worksheet *6.2: Connection to Social Studies—Detergents: Helpful or Harmful?* in the **Integration Enrichment Resources** ancillary.

Connection to
SOCIAL STUDIES

People have used soap for thousands of years. For instance, ancient Egyptians took baths regularly with soap made from animal fats or vegetable oils and basic solutions of alkali-metal compounds. According to Roman legend, people discovered that the water in the Tiber River near Mount Sapo was good for washing. Mount Sapo was used for elaborate animal-sacrifice rituals, and the combination of animal fat and the basic ash that washed down the mountain made the river soapy. Early-American pioneers made their soap in a similar way.

Making the Connection
1. The process of making soap is sometimes referred to as *saponification*. How does this word relate to the Roman soap legend?
2. American pioneers made lye soap from hog fat and ashes. Which substance provided the base needed to make the soap?

▶ **detergent** a nonsoap water-soluble cleaner that can emulsify dirt and oil

Figure 6-21
A droplet of oil can stay suspended in water because the charged ends of the soap dissolve in water and the uncharged ends dissolve in oil.

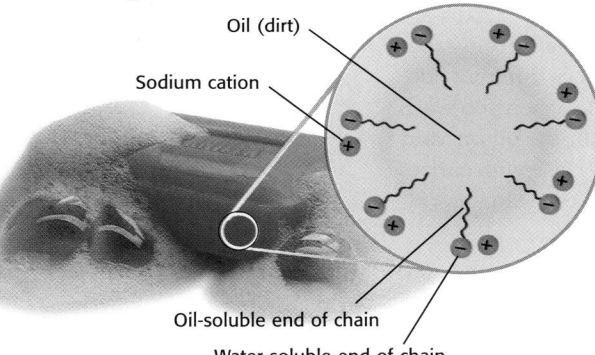

Oil (dirt)

Sodium cation

Oil-soluble end of chain

Water-soluble end of chain

Soaps are made by reacting animal fats or vegetable oils with a solution of sodium hydroxide or potassium hydroxide. The products of the reaction are soap and an alcohol called glycerol. Soap is in the form of long hydrocarbon chains with a negatively charged group of atoms at one end of each chain. For every negatively charged end, there is a corresponding sodium or potassium cation.

Soap is able to remove grease and oil because the cations and the negatively charged ends of the chains ($—COO^-$) dissolve in water while the uncharged ends dissolve in oil, as shown in **Figure 6-21.** Soap acts as an emulsifier and surrounds the oil. This causes the droplets of oil to stay suspended in water. When you are washing your hands with soap, you naturally want to rub them together. Rubbing your hands together actually helps clean them. When you do this, you shift most of the emulsion of grease and water off your hands and into the sink. Rinsing your hands with clean water gets rid of any soap and grease that are left behind.

Detergents are used to wash clothes and dishes

As useful as soap is for cleaning, it does not work well in water that is "hard," that is, water containing dissolved salts of the ions Mg^{2+}, Ca^{2+}, and Fe^{3+}. These ions react with soap to form an insoluble scum that settles out. This is especially a problem when you want to wash clothes and dishes. That's why clothes and dishes are washed with **detergents** instead of soap.

Like soaps, detergents are in the form of long chains that have a negatively charged end and an uncharged end. But the charged end of a detergent is a sulfonate group ($—SO_3^-$) instead of a carboxylate group ($—COO^-$). Detergents are also different from soaps because their chains are derived from petroleum products instead of from compounds that are found in animal fats. Detergents lather well in hard water and do not form a scum, so clothes and dishes washed with detergents are brighter and cleaner than they would be if they were washed with soap.

208 CHAPTER 6

DEMONSTRATION 8 TECH PREP

Making Soap
Time: Approximately 30 minutes
Materials: graduated cylinder, balance, 25 g of solid vegetable shortening, 250 mL beaker, 10 mL of ethanol, 1.2 g of NaOH, 30 mL of distilled water, hot plate, glass stirring rod, 25 mL saturated NaCl solution, cheesecloth

SAFETY CAUTION: *Make sure there are no open flames while ethanol is present.*

Step 1 Mix the shortening, ethanol, NaOH, and 5 mL of water in the beaker.

Step 2 Warm it on the hot plate while stirring for about 15 minutes. Cool the mixture in ice water.

Step 3 Add the rest of the water and the NaCl solution.

Ammonia solutions are common household cleaners

Ammonia solutions, like the ones that are shown in **Figure 6-22**, are also very effective cleaners. Household ammonia is a solution of ammonia gas dissolved in water. Ammonia gas reacts with water to form a basic solution containing dissolved ammonia, water, ammonium ions, and hydroxide ions.

$$NH_3 + H_2O \rightleftharpoons NH_4^+ + OH^-$$

Hydroxide ions interact with greasy dirt, causing the grease to form an emulsion with the water. Scrubbing the area shifts this emulsion from the surface and cleans it.

Disinfectants kill bacteria

A **disinfectant** is a substance that kills harmful bacteria and viruses. **Bleach,** a very good disinfectant, is a solution of sodium chlorite, $NaClO_2$, or sodium hypochlorite, $NaOCl$, in water.

Some hypochlorite ions, OCl^-, react with water to form hypochlorous acid, $HOCl$, and hydroxide ions.

$$OCl^- + H_2O \rightleftharpoons HOCl + OH^-$$

Hypochlorous acid gives bleach its disinfectant properties. Hydroxide ions that are formed in the reaction above make the solution basic. This is why bleach solutions often feel slippery.

You are probably more familiar with bleach because of its ability to remove colors and stains. Bleach does not actually remove the substance causing the stain. Instead, it removes the color of the unwanted stain by oxidizing the compound responsible. Most stains become colorless or white when they are oxidized.

Figure 6-22
The hydroxide ions present in ammonia solutions allow dirt and water to mix and be removed.

▶ **disinfectant** a substance that kills harmful bacteria or viruses

▶ **bleach** a basic solution that can either be used as a disinfectant or to remove colors and stains

Quick ACTIVITY

Detergents

Detergents get their cleaning ability by helping water mix with substances that it normally does not mix with. In this activity, you will demonstrate this idea using a piece of wax paper, a drop of water, a straight pin, and liquid detergent.

1. Lay some wax paper on a flat surface, and put a drop of water on it. Does the water mix at all with the wax paper? How can you tell?

2. Gently touch the drop of water with the tip of the straight pin. What happens to the drop of water?

3. Now dip the tip of the straight pin in liquid detergent.

4. Gently touch the drop of water with the tip of the pin after it has been dipped in detergent. What happens to the drop of water? Why does the detergent have this effect?

Step 4 Filter the soap from the liquid using cheesecloth. Press the soap into a candy or soap mold to shape. Dry for several days.

Analysis

1. Which of the substances actually formed the soap? *(NaOH and the shortening)*

Teaching Tip

Solid Versus Liquid Tell students that in a saponification reaction, sodium hydroxide produces solid soaps and potassium hydroxide produces liquid soaps.

MISCONCEPTION ALERT

Color-Safe Bleaches Explain to students that not all bleaches are disinfectants. Color-safe bleaches contain nonchlorine oxidizing agents and do not disinfect items.

Teaching Tip

Cleaner Sooner Tell students that clothes wash cleaner if they are cleaned soon after they are soiled. Oils from the skin react with oxygen soon after they are deposited on clothes, making the molecules more polar and thus more easily removed by soaps and detergents. However, certain oils change over time, forming large molecules that tend to bond with molecules in fabric. These changes cause yellowing in fabrics, especially cotton, and the yellowing is not easily removed.

Quick ACTIVITY

Detergents Students will notice that when the drop of water is touched with the straight pin, nothing happens to the drop. When detergent is on the pin, the water spreads out. The detergent allowed the water and wax paper to mix.

Resources Have students use *Datasheet 6.4* to record their results.

Acids and Bases in the Home

Antacids

Two types of antacids currently exist. One type is insoluble metallic hydroxides, such as magnesium hydroxide, $Mg(OH)_2$. These undergo a neutralization reaction with stomach acid, forming chloride salts and water. Another type is a carbonate-based antacid, such as calcium carbonate, $CaCO_3$, or sodium hydrogen carbonate, $NaHCO_3$. These react with stomach acid to produce a chloride salt and carbonic acid, which breaks down into carbon dioxide and water.

Teaching Tip

Buffers Tell students that buffers are systems that can dissolve moderate amounts of acids or bases without significantly changing pH. Buffered aspirin minimizes the effects of the acid in aspirin on the stomach. Blood must maintain a narrow pH range, and the HCO_3^- ion acts as a buffer in blood. If blood becomes too acidic, HCO_3^- acts as a base. If blood becomes too basic, HCO_3^- acts as an acid.

Inquiry Lab

What does an antacid do?

Materials
- ✔ plastic stirrer
- ✔ pipet bulbs
- ✔ vinegar
- ✔ 150–200 mL beakers (2)
- ✔ blue litmus paper
- ✔ disposable glass pipets
- ✔ spoon
- ✔ red litmus paper
- ✔ several varieties of antacid tablets
- ✔ wax paper

Procedure

SAFETY CAUTION Wear safety goggles, gloves, and a laboratory apron.

1. Pour 100 mL of water in a beaker. Add vinegar dropwise while stirring with the stirrer. Test the solution with litmus paper after each drop is added. Record the number of drops it takes for the solution to turn blue litmus paper bright red.

2. Use the back of a spoon to crush an antacid tablet on a small piece of wax paper. Pour 100 mL of water in the second beaker, and add the crushed antacid tablet. Stir the solution until the powder dissolves completely.

3. Use litmus paper to find out whether the solution is acidic, basic, or neutral. Record your results.

4. Now add vinegar dropwise to the antacid solution. Record the number of drops it takes the blue litmus paper to turn bright red. Compare this solution with the solution that has only vinegar and water. Compare the brand of antacid you tested with the brands of other groups.

Analysis

1. How does an antacid work to relieve the pain caused by excess stomach acid?

2. Of the brands that were tested, which brand worked the best? Explain your reasoning.

Other Household Acids and Bases

internet connect

SCI*LINKS*
NSTA

TOPIC: Antacids
GO TO: www.scilinks.org
KEYWORD: HK1066

▶ **antacid** a weak base that neutralizes excess stomach acid

You probably have taken many of the acids and bases in your home for granted. For example, many of the clothes in your closet get their color from acidic dyes that are made of sodium salts containing the sulfonic group ($-SO_3H$) or carboxylic acid group ($-COOH$). And if you have ever had an upset stomach because of excess stomach acid, you might have taken an antacid tablet to feel better. The antacid was able to make you feel better because it is basic. Many other useful products throughout your home are also acids or bases.

Many health-care products are acids or bases

Ascorbic acid is another name for vitamin C, which your body needs to grow and repair itself. When you have a headache, you might take some aspirin. The chemical name for aspirin is acetylsalicylic acid. Both sodium hydrogen carbonate and magnesium hydroxide (milk of magnesia) can be used as **antacids**. Antacids are weak bases that you swallow to neutralize excess stomach acid. **Figure 6-23** on the next page shows how adding an antacid tablet to an acidic solution changes the pH of the solution. A similar reaction (without the color change) takes place in your stomach when you take an antacid.

Inquiry Lab

What does an antacid do? Students will find that the antacid dissolved in water produces a basic solution. It takes quite a bit more vinegar to make the antacid solution acidic than it does to make the water acidic.

Emphasize to students that it is normal for stomach contents to be acidic. Acid is necessary for proper digestion in the stomach. The stomach itself is protected from this acid by a layer of mucus. If stomach contents become too acidic, this mucus layer is damaged and the acid starts to attack the stomach wall.

Analysis

1. It neutralizes excess stomach acid.

2. the brand that needs the most acid to neutralize it

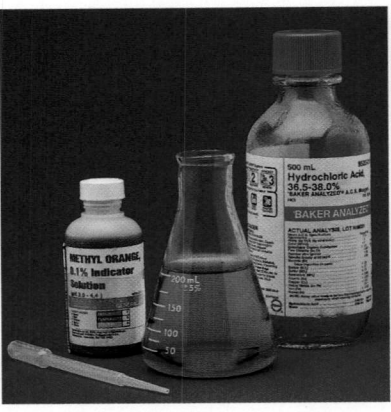
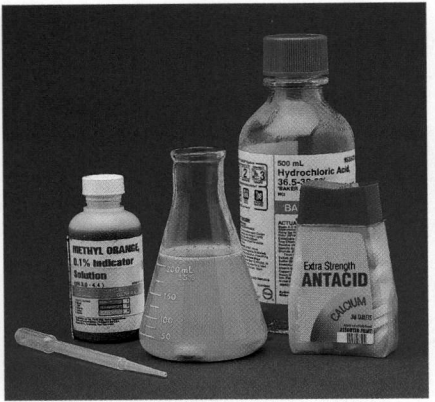

Figure 6-23
Adding antacid tablets to an acidic solution makes the solution less acidic. This is indicated by the color change of the indicator present in the solution.

Shampoos also make use of acid-base properties

Shampoos can be made from soap. But if they are, they can leave a sticky buildup on your hair if you happen to live in an area that has hard water. However, shampoos made from detergents are able to remove dirt as well as most of the oil from your hair without leaving a buildup, even when they are used with hard water. Shampoo is not meant to remove all of the oil from your hair. Some oil is needed to give your hair shine and to keep it from becoming dry and brittle.

The appearance of your hair is greatly affected by the pH of the shampoo you use. Hair—which consists of strands of a protein called keratin—looks best when it is kept at either a slightly acidic pH or very close to neutral. If a shampoo is too basic, it can cause strands of hair to swell, causing them to have a dull, lifeless appearance. Shampoos are usually pH balanced, which means that they are made to be in a specific pH range. The pH of most shampoos is between 5 and 8.

Acids and bases in the kitchen

Some cut fruits slowly turn brown when they are exposed to air, like the right side of the cut apple shown in **Figure 6-24.** This happens because certain molecules in the apple are oxidized. Both sides of the apple were cut at the same time, so why does the left side of the apple in **Figure 6-24** look like it was just cut? The left side was moistened with lemon juice shortly after it was cut. The citric acid in lemon juice keeps the apple from browning.

Did You Know ?

The protein keratin is also found in the outermost layer of cells of your epidermis, or outer layer of your skin. Keratin in these cells makes the skin tough and almost completely waterproof.

The horns, hoofs, claws, feathers, and scales of animals also consist mainly of keratin. Keratin helps keep these structures strong to protect the animal from the environment.

Figure 6-24
Coating the left side of this cut apple with an acidic substance, like lemon juice or pineapple juice, keeps it looking fresh longer.

SOLUTIONS, ACIDS, AND BASES **211**

Historical Perspective

Most of the acids and bases discussed in this chapter fit the definitions of acids and bases that Svante Arrhenius, a Swedish chemist, formulated in 1887. Arrhenius defined an acid as a substance that produces H^+ in water and a base as a substance that produces OH^- in water.

In 1923, the definitions were expanded. The Brønsted-Lowry theory, proposed by a Danish chemist and an English chemist, defines an acid as a proton donor and a base as a proton acceptor. In the same year, Gilbert Lewis expanded the definition even further by defining an acid as an electron-pair acceptor and a base as an electron-pair donor. This last definition includes acids and bases that do not involve hydrogen or its ions.

LINKING CHAPTERS

The effects of acids in the environment will be mentioned in Chapter 17 when chemical weathering is explained and in Chapter 19 when air and water quality are discussed.

Additional Application

Do Detergents Emulsify Lipids? Use this Teaching Tip to extend the Quick Activity on page 209.

Partially fill a Petri dish with whole milk. Drop four different colors of food coloring carefully in the milk near the edge of the dish. Place a drop of liquid detergent in the middle of the dish, and have students observe how the colors mix after the detergent is added.

INTEGRATING TECHNOLOGY and *Society*

Acids and Bases in the Home

SECTION 6.4 REVIEW

Check Your Understanding

1. Answers will vary. Acidic substances might include fruit juices, vinegar, and battery acid. Basic substances might include antacids, baking soda, and soap. Answers can be verified by using litmus paper.

2. Oil is nonpolar; water is polar. Soap has a polar end that will dissolve in water and a nonpolar end that will dissolve in oil. When water containing soap washes away, it carries the oily dirt attached to the soap with it.

3. The scum is iron(III) stearate, $Fe(C_{18}H_{35}O_2)_3$.

4. Agitation moves the soap and dirt away from the clothes.

5. Bleach oxidizes the compound responsible for the stain. Most oxidized compounds are colorless.

6. $CaCO_3$ produces a slightly basic solution.

7. Magnesium stearate forms. It is insoluble in water.

8. Oil and wax are both nonpolar, so wax will dissolve in an oily lubricant. The nonpolar end of the dishwashing liquid will dissolve in the oily lubricant, while the polar end will dissolve in water. The agitation of the washing machine moves the soap, lubricant, and wax away from the clothes.

RESOURCE LINK
STUDY GUIDE

Assign students *Review Section 6.4 Acids and Bases in the Home.*

212

Figure 6-25
If you add vinegar to milk, the acetic acid in vinegar causes the milk to curdle.

Acids have other uses in the kitchen as well. Acidic marinades made of vinegar or wine can be used to tenderize meats. Acids have the ability to do this because they can *denature* proteins in the meat. That is, the proteins unravel and lose their characteristic shapes. As a result, the meat becomes more tender.

Figure 6-25 shows that if you add vinegar to milk, the milk curdles. Although this reaction seems undesirable, a similar reaction occurs in the formation of yogurt. Bacteria convert lactose, a sugar in milk, into lactic acid. This acid changes the texture of milk and makes yogurt.

There are many bases in the kitchen as well. Baking soda, or sodium hydrogen carbonate, $NaHCO_3$, for instance, is used in cooking and also to absorb odors in the refrigerator. Baking powder is used to make light, fluffy batter for cakes and other foods. To unclog a drain in the sink, you might have used a drain cleaner containing potassium hydroxide, KOH, or sodium hydroxide, NaOH, sometimes called lye.

SECTION 6.4 REVIEW

SUMMARY

▶ Soaps are made by reacting fats or oils with a solution of NaOH or KOH.

▶ Soaps consist of long hydrocarbon chains ending with a negatively charged end $(-COO^-)$ that dissolves in water. The uncharged end dissolves in grease or oil.

▶ Detergents are similar to soap, except that their chains have a different negatively charged end, $(-SO_3^-)$.

▶ Disinfectants kill bacteria and viruses.

▶ Antacids neutralize excess stomach acid.

▶ Many foods contain acids or bases that react during food preparation.

CHECK YOUR UNDERSTANDING

1. **List** three acidic household substances and three basic household substances. How can you verify your answers?

2. **Describe** how soap can dissolve in both oil and water. How does soap work with water to remove oily dirt?

3. **Determine** what compound is responsible for the soap scum that develops in bathtubs where the water contains Fe^{3+} ions and the soap is sodium stearate, $NaC_{18}H_{35}O_2$.

4. **Explain** why the agitation of a washing machine helps a detergent clean your clothes. (**Hint:** Compare this agitation to your rubbing your hands together when you wash them.)

5. **Describe** why it is not necessary for bleach to actually remove the substance causing a stain.

6. **Predict** whether $CaCO_3$ is acidic, basic, or neutral. It is the active ingredient in some antacids.

7. **Explain** why soap scum forms in hard water that contains Mg^{2+} ions when a sodium stearate soap is used.

8. **Critical Thinking** Crayon companies recommend treating wax stains on clothes by spraying them with an oily lubricant, applying dishwashing liquid, and then washing them. Explain in a paragraph why this treatment would remove the stain.

WRITING SKILL

212 CHAPTER 6

Chapter Highlights

Before you begin, review the summaries of the key ideas of each section, found on pages 191, 198, 206, and 212. The key vocabulary terms are listed on pages 186, 192, 199, and 207.

UNDERSTANDING CONCEPTS

1. Which of the following is a homogeneous mixture?
   a. tossed salad
   b. soil
   c. a KCl solution
   d. vegetable soup

2. If the label on a bottle of medicine says "Shake well before using," the medicine is probably a _____.
   a. solution
   b. suspension
   c. colloid
   d. gel

3. Which of the following affects the solubility of a solute in a solvent?
   a. the surface area of the solute
   b. stirring the solution
   c. the temperature of the solvent
   d. All of the above

4. Suppose you add a teaspoon of table salt to a cool salt-water solution and stir until all of the salt dissolves. The solution you started with was _____.
   a. unsaturated
   b. supersaturated
   c. saturated
   d. concentrated

5. An acid forms which ions in solution?
   a. oxygen
   b. hydronium
   c. hydroxide
   d. sulfur

6. A base forms which ions in solution?
   a. oxygen
   b. hydronium
   c. hydroxide
   d. sulfur

7. A substance with a pH of 9 has
   a. the same number of H_3O^+ ions as it does OH^- ions.
   b. more H_3O^+ ions than OH^- ions.
   c. no H_3O^+ ions or OH^- ions.
   d. more OH^- ions than H_3O^+ ions.

8. When a solution of nitric acid is added to a solution of calcium hydroxide, the salt formed has the formula _____.
   a. H_2O
   b. CaH
   c. $Ca(NO_3)_2$
   d. None of the above

9. An antacid relieves an acid stomach because antacids are _____.
   a. acidic
   b. neutral
   c. basic
   d. dilute

10. Bleach removes stains by
    a. removing the color of the stain.
    b. covering the stain.
    c. removing the stain-causing substance.
    d. disinfecting the stain.

Using Vocabulary

11. A small amount of *solute* is added to two different solutions. Based on the figures below, which solution was *unsaturated*? Which solution was *saturated*?

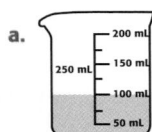 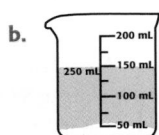

12. Explain how the ionization of a *strong acid* differs from that of a *weak acid* in a solution. Give an example of a strong acid and a weak acid. Show what ions form when each is dissolved in water.

13. What *salt* is produced in the following neutralization reaction?

$$2H_3O^+ + 2Br^- + Ca^{2+} + 2OH^- \longrightarrow Ca^{2+} + 2Br^- + 4H_2O$$

14. Use the terms *pH* and *indicator* to describe a way to determine whether an unknown solution is acidic or basic.

15. How are *detergents* and *soaps* alike? How are they different?

SOLUTIONS, ACIDS, AND BASES **213**

UNDERSTANDING CONCEPTS

1. c
2. b
3. c
4. a
5. b
6. c
7. d
8. c
9. c
10. a

Using Vocabulary

11. a. unsaturated
    b. saturated

12. A strong acid, such as hydrochloric acid, HCl, ionizes completely when dissolved in water. A weak acid, such as formic acid, HCOOH, ionizes little. HCl will form H_3O^+ and Cl^- ions in water. HCOOH will form a few H_3O^+ and $HCOO^-$ ions in water, but most of the HCOOH remains as it is and does not ionize.

13. calcium bromide, $CaBr_2$

14. The color of an indicator in solution depends on the pH of the solution. If an indicator changes color at a pH of approximately 7, that indicator can show whether an unknown solution is acidic or basic by what color it is in the solution.

RESOURCE LINK
STUDY GUIDE

Assign students *Mixed Review Chapter 6.*

15. Both are emulsifiers because the molecules have a charged end and an uncharged end. They differ in that the charged ends contain different groups, the main molecules have different sources, and soap forms a scum when placed in water that contains certain metal ions, while detergent does not.

BUILDING MATH SKILLS

16. a. Solubility increases as temperature increases.
b. Accept values near the following in grams: $AgNO_3$/100 g H_2O: for 35°C, 295; for 55°C, 415; for 75°C, 540
c. approximately 94°C
d. More could dissolve, so it would be unsaturated.

THINKING CRITICALLY

17. methanol, chloroform, ethyl acetate (and ether)
18. basic
19. Sample 1 is a solution, sample 2 is a suspension, and sample 3 is a colloid.
20. Student presentations should show a crystal of KBr with its K^+ and Br^- ions arranged in a cubic pattern, surrounded by water molecules. The partially positive parts of the water molecules attract Br^- in the crystal, and the partially negative parts of the water molecules attract K^+, pulling the ions out of the surface of the crystal. The diagrams should show some K^+ and Br^- ions surrounded by water molecules in the correct orientation.

BUILDING MATH SKILLS

16. Graphing Make a solubility graph for $AgNO_3$ from the data in the table below. Plot the temperature on the x-axis. Plot solubility on the y-axis.

Temperature (°C)	Solubility of $AgNO_3$ (g of $AgNO_3$ /100 g of H_2O)
0	122
20	216
40	311
60	440
80	585
100	733

a. How does the solubility of $AgNO_3$ vary with the temperature of water?
b. Estimate the solubility of $AgNO_3$ at 35°C, at 55°C, and at 75°C.
c. At what temperature would the solubility of $AgNO_3$ be 680 g per 100 g of H_2O?
d. If 100 g of $AgNO_3$ were added to 100 g of H_2O at 10°C, would the solution be saturated or unsaturated?

THINKING CRITICALLY

17. Evaluating Data Based on the chart below, which solvents can be mixed with ether to form a single layer?

X = immiscible	Water	Methanol	Ether	Chloroform	Ethyl acetate
Water			X	X	X
Methanol					
Ether	X				
Chloroform	X				
Ethyl acetate	X				

18. Interpreting Graphics Study the graph shown at right. Is the solution being added acidic or basic? Explain how you determined your answer.

19. Applying Knowledge You have been investigating the nature of suspensions, colloids, and solutions and have made the following observations on three unknown samples. From your data, decide whether each sample is a solution, a suspension, or a colloid.

Sample	Clarity	Settles out?	Diameter of particles
1	Clear	No	Too small to be seen
2	Cloudy	Yes	1.5 mm
3	Clear	No	95 nm

20. Designing Systems Use what you have learned about how substances dissolve to make a diagram or a computer representation that shows how the ionic compound KBr dissolves in water.

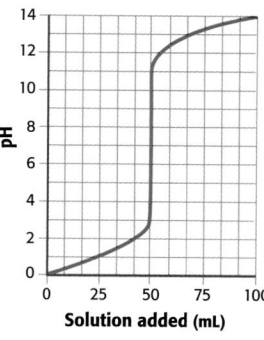
COMPUTER SKILL

21. Creative Thinking If you wish to change the pH of a pH-sensitive solution only very slightly, would it be better to add a strong acid or a weak acid? Explain why.

22. Problem Solving Insect bites hurt because the insect injects a toxin into the victim, often in the form of an acid. When an ant bites you, it injects you with formic acid. Suggest a treatment that might stop an ant bite from itching or hurting.

DEVELOPING LIFE/WORK SKILLS

23. Working Cooperatively The salt you use to flavor foods is usually mined from the ground. **WRITING SKILL** However, when mined, salt is often mixed with soil and minerals. Work with a partner to design a method to purify this crude material to yield pure salt. Write a specific plan that describes your method.

24. Communicating Effectively When there is an oil spill, emergency-response teams use the properties of oil and water along with solubility principles to clean spills and prevent them from spreading. Describe the research behind these techniques, and evaluate the impact this research has had on the environment.

25. Locating Information A reaction between baking soda, $NaHCO_3$, and a baking batter that is made of acidic ingredients produces CO_2 gas. The reaction makes the batter fluffier. Some recipes call for baking powder instead of baking soda. Find out what regular baking powder and double-acting baking powder are made of. Which is more likely to result in a light, fluffy cake? How does each substance differ from baking soda?

INTEGRATING CONCEPTS

26. Connection to History In the eighteenth century, the French chemist Antoine Lavoisier experimented with substances containing oxygen, like CO_2 and SO_2. He observed that these substances formed acidic solutions when dissolved in water. His observations led him to infer that for a solution to be acidic, it must contain oxygen. Provide evidence to disprove Lavoisier's conclusion.

27. Concept Mapping Copy the unfinished concept map below onto a sheet of paper. Complete the map by writing the correct word or phrase in the lettered boxes.

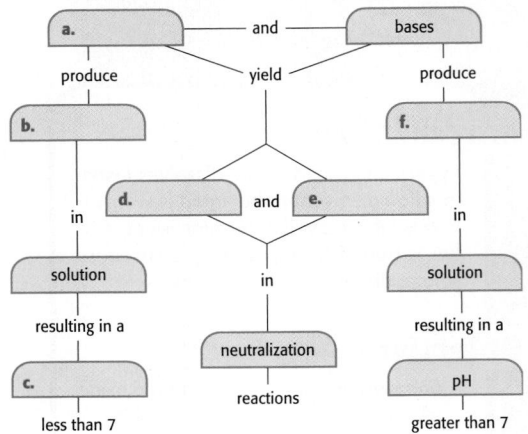

28. Connection to Health One method of taking medicine is known as transdermal infusion. As the name implies, medicine is absorbed into the body through the skin, after being placed in a package fastened to the body like a bandage. Medicines to prevent motion sickness and to treat some coronary conditions are sometimes given in this way. Identify and explore some of the applications of transdermal infusion and the research that made this technique possible. Write a two-page report that evaluates the impact this research has had on society.

internet connect

SCiLINKS
NSTA

TOPIC: Transdermal patch medicines
GO TO: www.scilinks.org
KEYWORD: HK1067

SOLUTIONS, ACIDS, AND BASES **215**

21. A weak acid would be better. It would change the pH more gradually because fewer hydronium ions would be added.

22. A weak base, such as a paste of baking soda, could be applied. A strong base should not be used because it would damage the skin.

DEVELOPING LIFE/ WORK SKILLS

23. Plans might include dissolving the salt in water, filtering out the solid impurities, then evaporating the water to recover the salt.

24. Student answers should focus on the research into chemical clean-up methods for oil spills. Their answer should include both a description of the research and the environmental impact of the clean-up method. Some techniques used in cleaning up oil spills—such as bioremediation—do not primarily involve differences in solubility between oil and water.

25. Regular baking powder contains sodium hydrogen carbonate and an acid. Double-acting baking powder contains two different acids instead of one. The acids react at different stages of baking, increasing the height the batter rises. Baking soda requires an acid, such as lemon juice or buttermilk, to be added.

INTEGRATING CONCEPTS

26. Many common acids, like HF, HCl, HBr, and HI, do not contain oxygen.

Answers continue on p. 217A.

Skill Builder Lab

Investigating How Temperature Affects Gas Solubility

Objectives

Students will:

▶ **Use** appropriate lab safety procedures.

▶ **Compare** the volume of carbon dioxide released from a warm soft drink with that released from a cold soft drink.

▶ **Relate** carbon dioxide's solubility in each soft drink to the temperature of each soft drink.

Planning

Recommended time: 1 lab period
Materials: *(for each lab group)*

▶ 2 carbonated soft drinks in plastic bottles

▶ 2 small plastic bags

▶ 4 twist ties

▶ thermometer

▶ stopwatch

▶ flexible metric tape measure

▶ 1 L beaker

▶ crushed ice

▶ paper towels

Skill Builder Lab

Introduction

In general, a solid solute dissolves faster in a liquid solvent if the liquid is warm. In this lab, you will determine whether this is true of carbon dioxide, a gaseous solute, dissolved in a soft drink.

Objectives

▶ **Compare** the volume of carbon dioxide released from a warm soft drink with that released from a cold soft drink.

▶ **Relate** carbon dioxide's solubility in each soft drink to the temperature of each soft drink.

Materials

2 carbonated soft drinks in plastic bottles
2 small plastic bags
4 twist ties
thermometer
stopwatch
flexible metric tape measure
1 L beaker
crushed ice
paper towels

Safety Needs

safety goggles
gloves
laboratory apron

Investigating How Temperature Affects Gas Solubility

▶ Preparing for Your Experiment

1. Prepare a data table in your lab report similar to the one shown at right.

▶ Testing the Solubility of Carbon Dioxide in a Warm Soft Drink

SAFETY CAUTION Wear safety goggles, gloves, and a laboratory apron.

2. Obtain a bottle of carbonated soft drink that has been stored at room temperature, and carry it to your lab table. Try not to disturb the liquid.

3. Use a thermometer to measure the temperature in the laboratory. Record this temperature in your data table.

4. Remove the bottle's cap, and quickly place the open end of a deflated plastic bag over the bottle's opening. Seal the bag tightly around the bottle's neck with a twist tie. Begin timing with a stopwatch.

5. When the bag is almost fully inflated, stop the stopwatch. Very carefully remove the plastic bag from the bottle, making sure to keep the bag sealed so the carbon dioxide inside does not escape. Seal the bag tightly with another twist tie.

6. Gently mold the bag into the shape of a sphere. Measure the bag's circumference in centimeters by wrapping the tape measure around the largest part of the bag. Record the circumference in your data table.

REQUIRED PRECAUTIONS

▶ Read all safety cautions, and discuss them with your students.

▶ Safety goggles and a lab apron must be worn at all times.

▶ Tie back loose clothing and long hair.

▶ In case of a spill, use a dampened cloth or paper towels to mop up the spill. Then rinse the cloth in running water at the sink, wring it out until it is only damp, and put it in the trash.

Soft Drink Data

	Temperature (°C)	Circumference of bag (cm)	Radius of bag (cm)	Volume of bag (cm³)
Soft drink at room temp.				
Chilled soft drink				

▶ Testing the Solubility of Carbon Dioxide in a Cold Soft Drink

7. Obtain a second bottle of carbonated soft drink that has been chilled. Place the bottle in a 1 L beaker, and pack crushed ice around the bottle. Use paper towels to dry any water on the outside of the beaker, and then carefully move the beaker to your lab table.

8. Repeat step 4. Let the second plastic bag inflate for the same length of time that the first bag was allowed to inflate. Very carefully remove the bag from the bottle as you did before. Seal the plastic bag tightly with a twist tie.

9. Wait for the bag to warm to room temperature. While you are waiting, use the thermometer to measure the temperature of the cold soft drink. Record the temperature in your data table.

10. When the bag has warmed to room temperature, repeat step 6.

▶ Analyzing Your Results

1. Calculate the radius in centimeters of each inflated plastic bag by using the following equation. Record the results in your data table.

$$\text{radius (in cm)} = \frac{\text{circumference (in cm)}}{2\pi}$$

2. Calculate the volume in cubic centimeters of each inflated bag by using the following equation. Record the results in your data table.

$$\text{volume (in cm}^3) = \frac{4}{3}\pi \times [\text{radius (in cm)}]^3$$

3. Compare the volume of carbon dioxide released from the two soft drinks. Use your data to explain how the solubility of carbon dioxide in a soft drink is affected by temperature.

▶ Defending Your Conclusions

4. Suppose someone says that your conclusion is not valid because a soft drink contains many other solutes besides carbon dioxide. How could you verify that your conclusion is correct?

Pre-Lab

Teaching Tips

Show students how to seal the plastic bag with a twist tie without allowing the carbon dioxide gas inside the bag to escape. A better way might be to stopper the soda bottles with a one-hole stopper and collect the gas in a graduated cylinder under a bath of warm water. This method can be used to accelerate the results of the room temperature bottle.

Procedure

▶ Testing the Solubility of Carbon Dioxide in a Soft Drink

Use thin plastic bags like the kind found in the produce section of a supermarket.

Post-lab

▶ Disposal

The soft drinks can be poured down the sink. Discard the plastic bottles, bags, twist ties and paper towels in the trash.

▶ Analyzing Your Results

1. Answers will vary.
2. Answers will vary.
3. The volume of the bag attached to the room-temperature drink should be greater than the volume of the bag attached to the cold drink. This would mean that more carbon dioxide came out of the room-temperature drink, indicating that the solubility of carbon dioxide in the soft drink decreases as temperature increases.

▶ Defending Your Conclusions

4. Students could repeat the experiment using a solution such as seltzer water.

CONTINUATION OF ANSWERS

Answers from page 191

SECTION 6.1 REVIEW

5. sugar water, muddy water, sand in water
6. The boiling points are too similar.
7. Assuming the lemonade contains no pulp, the dirt could be filtered out of the lemonade. Evaporating the water and leaving the solids behind could separate the sugar and other solids dissolved in the lemonade.

Answers from page 215

INTEGRATING CONCEPTS

27. a. acids
   b. hydronium ions
   c. pH
   d. water
   e. a salt
   f. hydroxide ions
28. Transdermal infusion is used to deliver many drugs such as estrogen, nitroglycerin, scopolamine, and nicotine. The students' answers should include information about research into a particular transdermally infused drug. They should also comment on how delivering this drug transdermally has impacted society.

Tailoring the Program to YOUR Classroom

CHAPTER 7

Nuclear Changes

Annotated Descriptions of the Correlated National Science Standards

The following descriptions summarize the National Science Standards that specially relate to Chapter 7. For the full text of the Standards, see p. 40T.

SECTION 7.1
What Is Radioactivity?
Physical Science
PS 1d
Unifying Concepts and Processes
UCP 2

SECTION 7.2
Nuclear Fission and Fusion
Physical Science
PS 1c
Unifying Concepts and Processes
UCP 2

SECTION 7.3
Integrating Technology and Society—Dangers and Benefits of Nuclear Radiation
Science as Inquiry
SAI 1

Cross-Discipline Teaching RESOURCES

Cross-Discipline Teaching, ATE p. 218
Mathematics   Life Science
Social Studies

Integration Enrichment Resources
Earth Science, **PE** and **ATE** p. 227
    IE 7.1 *Radioactivity Within the Earth*
Real World Applications, **PE** and **ATE** p. 238
    IE 7.3 *Radiation and Medicine*
Space Science, **PE** and **ATE** p. 239
    IE 7.4 *Nuclear-Powered Space Probes*
Space Science, **PE** and **ATE** p. 240
    IE 7.2 *The Life Cycle of a Star*

Additional Integration Enrichment Worksheets
    IE 7.5 Social Studies
    IE 7.6 Language Arts
    IE 7.7 Chemistry
    IE 7.8 Environmental Science

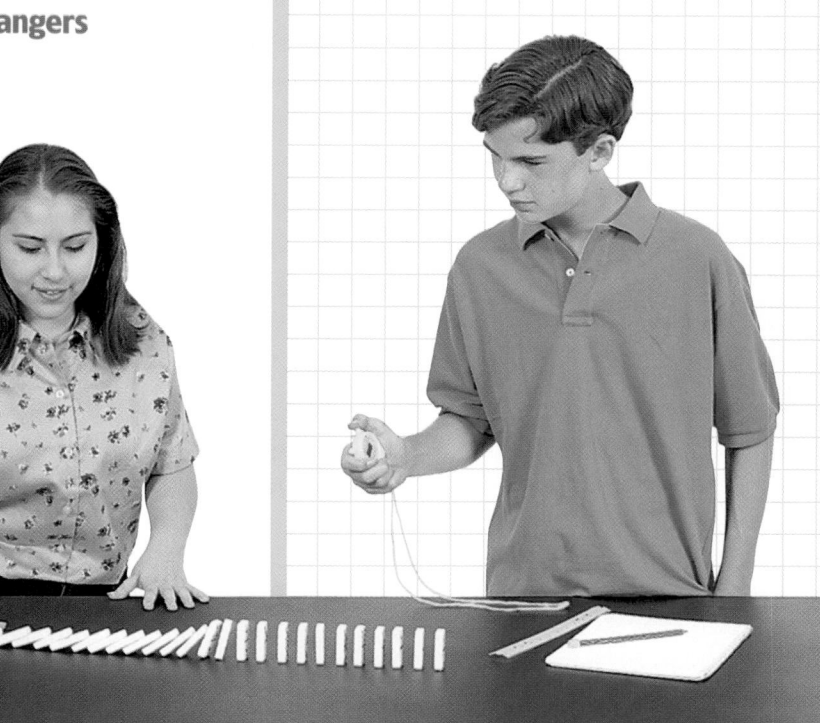

Use the Planning Guide on the next page to help you organize your lessons.

MATH AND COMPUTER RESOURCES

Chapter 7	**Math Skills**	Assess	Media/Computer Skills
Section 7.1	**ATE** **Cross-Discipline Teaching,** p. 218 **PE** **Math Skills** Nuclear Decay, p. 224 **ATE** **Additional Examples** p. 224 **PE** **Math Skills** Half-life, p. 227 **ATE** **Additional Examples** p. 227	**PE** **Practice,** p. 225 **PE** **Practice,** p. 228 **PE** Section Review 4–8, p. 228 **PE** **Building Math Skills,** p. 242, item 17 **MS** Worksheet 11 **MS** Worksheet 12 **PE** **Problem Bank,** p. 696, 51–60	■ Section 7.1
Section 7.2			■ Section 7.2
Section 7.3			■ Section 7.3 **CNN** Presents **Chemistry Connections** **Segment 31** Nuclear Waste **CRT** Worksheet 31 **CNN** Presents **Chemistry Connections** **Segment 32** Radioisotopes in Medicine **CRT** Worksheet 32

PE Pupil's Edition   **ATE** Annotated Teacher's Edition   **MS** Math Skills   **BS** Basic Skills
IE Integration Enrichment   ■ Audio Guided Reading   **CRT** Critical Thinking

The following activities found in the Annotated Teacher's Edition provide techniques for developing useful reading strategies to increase your students' reading comprehension skills.

Section 7.1   **Brainstorming,** p. 218
            Reading Hint, p. 220

Section 7.2   **K-W-L,** p. 229

Section 7.3   **Reader Response Logs,** p. 235

Smithsonian Institution®

Visit www.si.edu/hrw for additional online resources.

Spanish Resources

The following resources are made available for students who speak Spanish as their first language.

Spanish Resources Guided Reading Audio CD-ROM
Chapter 7

Spanish Glossary
Chapter 7

Nuclear Changes

	CLASSROOM RESOURCES		
	FOCUS	**TEACH**	**HANDS-ON**
Section 7.1 What Is Radioactivity?			
BLOCK 1 45 minutes	**ATE RSB** Brainstorming, p. 218 **ATE** Focus Activities 1, 2, p. 219 **ATE RSB** Reading Hint, p. 220 **ATE Demo 1** Radon Detectors, p. 220 **PE** Nuclear Radiation and Decay, pp. 220–225 ★ Focus Transparency LT 23	**ATE Skill Builder** Interpreting Visuals, p. 219 Interpreting Tables, p. 221	**IE** Worksheets 7.5, 7.6, 7.7
BLOCK 2 45 minutes	**PE** Radioactive Decay Rates, pp. 225–228	**ATE Skill Builder** Graphs, p. 226 **BLM** 22 Half-life	**PE** Quick Activity *Modeling Decay and Half-life,* p. 226 **DS** 7.1 **IE** Worksheet 7.1
Section 7.2: Nuclear Fission and Fusion			
BLOCK 3 45 minutes	**ATE RSB** K-W-L, p. 229 **ATE Demo 2** Nuclear Forces, p. 229 **PE** Nuclear Forces, pp. 229–230 ★ Focus Transparency LT 24		
BLOCK 4 45 minutes	**ATE Demo 3** A Chain Reaction, p. 232 **PE** Fission and Fusion, pp. 231–234	**ATE Skill Builder** Interpreting Visuals, p. 232 **TT** 21 Chain Reaction	**PE** Quick Activity *Modeling Chain Reactions,* p. 233 **DS** 7.2
Section 7.3: Dangers and Benefits of Nuclear Radiation			
BLOCK 5 45 minutes	**ATE RSB** Reader Response Logs, p. 235 **ATE Demo 4** Disposal of Nuclear Waste, p. 236 **PE** Dangers of Nuclear Radiation, pp. 235–237 ★ Focus Transparency LT 25	**ATE Skill Builder** Interpreting Visuals, p. 236	**IE** Worksheet 7.8
BLOCK 6 45 minutes	**PE** Beneficial Uses of Nuclear Radiation; Nuclear Power, pp. 237–240 **PE** Real World Applications *Medical Radiation Exposure,* p. 238		**IE** Worksheets 7.2, 7.3, 7.4 **PE** Skill Builder Lab *Simulating Nuclear Decay Reactions,* p. 244 **DS** 7.3 **LE 7** *Determining the Effective Half-life of Iodine-131 in the Human Body* **DS** 7.4

CLASSROOM RESOURCES

HOMEWORK	ASSESS
PE Section Review 1–5, p. 228 **Chapter 7 Review**, p. 241, items 1, 2, 11, 12, 18–20	**SG** Chapter 7 Pretest
PE Section Review 6–8, p. 228 **Chapter 7 Review**, p. 241, items 3–5, 17, 21, 22	**ATE** *ALTERNATIVE ASSESSMENT,* Radiation, p. 226 **SG** Section 7.1
PE Section Review 1, p. 234 **Chapter 7 Review**, p. 241, item 6	**ATE** *ALTERNATIVE ASSESSMENT,* Stable Nuclei, p. 230
PE Section Review 2–4, p. 234 **Chapter 7 Review**, p. 241, items 7, 8, 14, 15	**SG** Section 7.2
PE Section Review 1, p. 240 **Chapter 7 Review**, p. 241, items 9, 16	
PE Section Review 2–5, p. 240 **Chapter 7 Review**, p. 241, items 10, 13	**ATE** *ALTERNATIVE ASSESSMENT,* Radioactive Tracer, p. 238 **SG** Section 7.3

PE Chapter 7 Review
Thinking Critically 23–27, p. 242
Developing Life/Work Skills 28–30, p. 243
Integrating Concepts 31–32, p. 243
SG Chapter 7 Mixed Review

Chapter Tests
Holt Science Spectrum: A Physical Approach
Chapter 7 Test

One-Stop Planner CD–ROM with Test Generator
Holt Science Spectrum Test Generator
FOR MACINTOSH AND WINDOWS
Chapter 7

Teaching Resources
Scoring Rubrics and assignment evaluation
checklist.

internetconnect

National Science Teachers
Association
Online Resources:
www.scilinks.org
The following *sci*LINKS Internet resources can be found
in the student text for this chapter.

Page 219 **TOPIC:** Radioactive isotopes **KEYWORD:** HK1071	**Page 234** **TOPIC:** Fusion **KEYWORD:** HK1074
Page 221 **TOPIC:** Types of radiation **KEYWORD:** HK1072	**Page 237** **TOPIC:** Mutations **KEYWORD:** HK1075
Page 232 **TOPIC:** Fission **KEYWORD:** HK1073	**Page 243** **TOPIC:** Radioactive tracers **KEYWORD:** HK1076

CNNfyi.com   www.cnnfyi.com

Visit this site for coverage of current events and related
classroom resources.

PE Pupil's Edition   **ATE** Annotated Teacher's Edition
RSB Reading Skill Builder   **DS** Datasheets
IE Integrated Enrichment   **SG** Study Guide
LE Laboratory Experiments
TT Teaching Transparencies   **BLM** Blackline Masters
★ Lesson Focus Transparency

Tapping Prior Knowledge

Be sure students understand the following concepts:

Chapter 1
Scientific notation

Chapter 2
Elements, matter and energy

Chapter 3
Atomic structure, isotopes, mass number, atomic number

READING SKILL BUILDER

Brainstorming Write the word *radiation* on the chalkboard. Under the word, list the terms *positive* and *negative* as column heads. Have students brainstorm positive and negative perceptions that they think are true about radiation. Keep a copy of the list and use it as a discussion tool when students complete Section 7.1.

RESOURCE LINK
STUDY GUIDE

Assign students *Pretest Chapter 7 Nuclear Changes* before beginning Section 7.1

Nuclear Changes

Chapter Preview

7.1 What Is Radioactivity?
Nuclear Radiation
Nuclear Decay
Radioactive Decay Rates

7.2 Nuclear Fission and Fusion
Nuclear Forces
Nuclear Fission
Nuclear Fusion

7.3 Dangers and Benefits of Nuclear Radiation
Dangers of Nuclear Radiation
Beneficial Uses of Nuclear Radiation
Nuclear Power

INTEGRATING TECHNOLOGY and Society

CROSS-DISCIPLINE TEACHING

Mathematics Review the use of exponents. Students should have an understanding of exponents before making half-life calculations. When n is the number of half-lives, $\left(\frac{1}{2}\right)^n$ gives the fractional part of the original substance remaining. For example, after three half-lives, $\left(\frac{1}{2}\right)^3$, or $\frac{1}{8}$, of the sample is left.

Life Science Have a radiologist speak to the class on how tracers are used to diagnose certain health problems and why certain radioactive materials are used as tracers and others are not. Also, have the radiologist discuss which health problems are treated with radiation.

Social Studies Have students investigate the effect of nuclear fission on the outcome of World War II.

Focus ACTIVITY

Background The painting "Woman Reading Music" was considered one of a series of great finds discovered by Dutch painter and art dealer Han van Meegeren in the 1930s. The previously unknown paintings were believed to be by the great seventeenth century Dutch artist Jan Vermeer. But after World War II, another painting said to be by Vermeer was found in a Nazi art collection, and its sale was traced to van Meegeren. Arrested for collaborating with the Nazis, van Meegeren confessed that both paintings were forgeries. He claimed that he had used one of the fake Vermeers to lure Nazi Germany into returning many genuine paintings to the Dutch.

Was van Meegeren lying to avoid a long prison sentence, or had he really swindled the Nazis? Although X-ray photographs of the painting suggested that it was a forgery, conclusive evidence did not come about until 20 years later. A fraction of the lead in certain pigments used in the painting proved to be radioactive. By measuring the number of radioactive lead nuclei that decayed each minute, experts were able to determine the age of the painting. The fairly rapid decay rate indicated that the paint—and thus the painting—was less than 40 years old.

Activity 1 Radiation exposes photographic film. To test this observation, obtain a small sheet of unexposed photographic film and a new household smoke detector, which contains a radioactive sample. Remove the casing from the detector. In a dark room, place the film next to the smoke detector in a cardboard box and close the box. Be sure that no light can enter the box. After a day, open the box in a dark room and place the film in a thick envelope. Take the film to be processed. Is there an image on the film? How does the image differ from the rest of the film? How can you tell that the image is related to the radioactive source?

Activity 2 Use library resources to research famous art forgeries. How were the forgeries detected? What techniques use radioactive substances to identify the elements in paintings?

internet connect

SCiLINKS
NSTA

TOPIC: Radioactive isotopes
GO TO: www.scilinks.org
KEYWORD: HK1071

Radioactive substances in the paints and canvases used in painting decay over time. These radioactive substances emit nuclear radiation. The amount of radiation emitted can be used to determine how old the painting is and whether the painting is a forgery or not.

219

Focus ACTIVITY

Background In 1968, an American chemist used uranium-lead dating to prove that van Meegeren was a forger. The parent material for the lead isotope found in paint is uranium-238. The series of reactions that form lead includes steps that form radium-226 and polonium-210. The ratio of these two elements in the paint determines the age of the paint. The higher the ratio, the older the paint.

Activity 1 The film will show a scattering of spots on the otherwise unaffected film. The spots will be more numerous near the radioactive source.

Activity 2 Methods of detection will probably include uranium-lead dating (described above), neutron activation analysis, X ray, and autoradiographs.

In neutron activation analysis, neutrons bombard a sample of paint, making it a temporary gamma emitter. Each element has its own pattern of gamma rays. The pattern detected reveals the paint composition, which can indicate when a painting was painted.

X rays and autoradiographs are used to determine layers of paint.

SKILL BUILDER

Interpreting Visuals Have students examine the photographs shown. Ask students what the difference is between a forgery and a reproduction. (*Both are copies of an original, but the forgery claims to be the original, and the reproduction does not.*)

Scheduling
Refer to pp. 218A–218D for lecture, classwork, and assignment options for Section 7.1.

★ **Lesson Focus**
Use transparency *LT 23* to prepare students for this section.

READING SKILL BUILDER

Reading Hint
Explain the different types of radiation to students. Then group the students in pairs and have them use **Table 7-1** to explain the different types of radiation and the characteristics of each. Encourage students to use the student text as a resource to find additional characteristics of the types of radiation.

7.1

What Is Radioactivity?

▶ **KEY TERMS**
radioactivity
nuclear radiation
alpha particle
beta particle
gamma ray
neutron emission
half-life

OBJECTIVES

▶ Identify four types of nuclear radiation and their properties.
▶ Balance equations for nuclear decay.
▶ Calculate the half-life of a radioactive isotope.

In recent years there has been concern about radon gas in buildings and its impact on health. Detectors are used to check the level of radon in a house or a building. Many elements and compounds are dangerous because of the way they react with substances in our bodies. Radon, however, is a gas that, like helium and neon, does not chemically react with substances in the body. Why, then, is it considered a health hazard?

Nuclear Radiation

▶ **radioactivity** process by which an unstable nucleus emits one or more particles or energy in the form of electromagnetic radiation

Radon is one of many elements that change through **radioactivity**. Radioactive materials, which were mentioned in Chapter 3, have unstable nuclei. These nuclei go through changes by emitting particles or releasing energy, as shown in **Figure 7-1.** After the changes in the nucleus, the element can transform into a different isotope of the same element or change into an entirely different element. This nuclear process is referred to as *nuclear decay.* (Recall from Chapter 3 that isotopes of an element are atoms with the same number of protons but a different number of neutrons in their nuclei.)

▶ **nuclear radiation** charged particles or energy emitted by an unstable nucleus

The released energy and matter is called **nuclear radiation,** and it can cause damage to living tissue. Nuclear radiation from radon that seeps into houses and buildings is the reason for the health concerns. (Note that the term *radiation* also refers to light or to an energy transfer method between objects at different temperatures. *To avoid confusion, the term* nuclear radiation *will be used to describe radiation associated with nuclear changes.*)

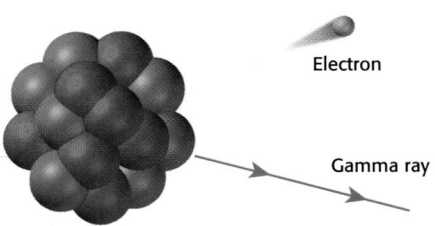
Electron

Gamma ray

Figure 7-1
During radioactivity an unstable nucleus emits one or more particles or high-energy electromagnetic radiation.

220 CHAPTER 7

RESOURCE LINK

IER

Assign students worksheet *7.5: Connection to Social Studies—A Remarkable Discovery* in the **Integration Enrichment Resources** ancillary.

DEMONSTRATION 1 TEACHING

Radon Detectors

Time: Approximately 10 minutes
Materials: radon detection kit

Obtain a short-term radon detection kit from a hardware store. Follow the kit instructions. If more than one class uses a kit, obtain permission from school administrators to place the detectors in different areas of the school where they will not be disturbed. If the school has a basement, be sure one is placed there in a poorly ventilated area.

Analysis

1. Why is it important to place a detector in the lowest area of the building? (*Radon is formed from rocks within the Earth.*)
2. Does the kit tell you how to get rid of radon gas? If so, explain what you should do. (*Answers should include increasing ventilation and sealing cracks.*)

Table 7-1 Types of Nuclear Radiation

Radiation type	Symbol	Mass (kg)	Charge	
Alpha particle	^4_2He	6.646×10^{-27}	+2	
Beta particle	$^0_{-1}e$	9.109×10^{-31}	−1	
Gamma ray	γ	none	0	
Neutron	^1_0n	1.675×10^{-27}	0	

There are different types of nuclear radiation

Essentially, there are four types of nuclear radiation: alpha particles, beta particles, gamma rays, and neutron emission. Some of their properties are listed in **Table 7-1.** When a radioactive atom decays, the nuclear radiation leaves the nucleus. This nuclear radiation then interacts with nearby matter. The interaction with matter depends in part on the properties of nuclear radiation, like charge, mass, and energy, which are discussed below.

Alpha particles consist of protons and neutrons

Uranium is a radioactive element that naturally occurs in three isotope forms. One of its isotopes, uranium-238, undergoes nuclear decay by emitting positively charged particles. Ernest Rutherford, noted for discovering the nucleus, named them *alpha* (α) *rays.* Later, he discovered that alpha rays were actually particles, each made of two protons and two neutrons—the same as helium nuclei. **Alpha particles** are positively charged and more massive than any other type of nuclear radiation.

Alpha particles do not travel far through materials. In fact, they barely pass through a sheet of paper. One factor that limits an alpha particle's ability to pass through matter is the fact that it is massive. Because alpha particles are charged, they remove electrons from—or ionize—matter as they pass through it. This ionization causes the alpha particle to lose energy and slow down further.

Beta particles are electrons produced from neutron decay

Some nuclei emit another type of nuclear radiation consisting of negatively charged particles. Compared to alpha particles, this type of nuclear radiation travels farther through matter. This nuclear radiation is named the **beta particle,** after the second Greek letter, *beta* (β). Beta particles are fast-moving electrons.

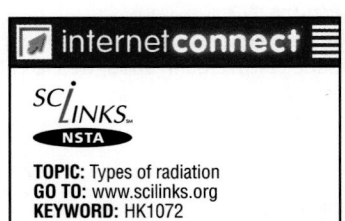
internet**connect**

SCI**LINKS**
NSTA

TOPIC: Types of radiation
GO TO: www.scilinks.org
KEYWORD: HK1072

▶ **alpha particle** a positively charged particle, emitted by some radioactive nuclei, that consists of two protons and two neutrons

▶ **beta particle** an electron emitted during the radioactive decay of a neutron in an unstable nucleus

NUCLEAR CHANGES **221**

|SKILL BUILDER
Interpreting Tables Remind students how to interpret the symbols used in **Table 7-1.**

For practice, provide students with several different elements and a periodic table. Have students write similar symbols for the most common isotope of each element. For example, for phosphorus, the atomic number is 15 and the atomic mass, rounded off, is 31. The symbol for this isotope of phosphorus is $^{31}_{15}\text{P}$.

MISCONCEPTION **ALERT**
Radiation When many students think of radiation, they think of negative aspects. Emphasize to students that many positive aspects of radiation also exist. The radiation that causes sunburn on unprotected skin also keeps Earth at a temperature that can sustain life. The nuclear processes that can cause destruction also provide electricity for many places on Earth. Tell students that they will learn more about the positive and negative aspects of radiation in Section 7.3.

What Is Radioactivity?

Did You Know?

In 1903, Marie Curie, her husband, Pierre, and Henri Becquerel were jointly awarded a Nobel Prize in physics for their studies in the field of radioactivity.

Teaching Tip

Other Radiation Tell students that the main types of radiation are discussed in the student text. However, other types exist. For example, chromium-49 decays forming vanadium-49 and what is known as a *positron*.

A positron is the same as an electron except that it is positively charged. Positrons exist for an extremely short period of time because they are the antiparticles of electrons. When an electron and a positron collide, all the mass in both particles converts to energy in the form of gamma rays.

Figure 7-2
The element radium, which Marie Curie discovered in 1898, was later found to emit gamma rays.

▶ **gamma ray** high-energy electromagnetic radiation emitted by a nucleus during radioactive decay

▶ **neutron emission** the release of a high-energy neutron by some neutron-rich nuclei during radioactive decay

Having negative particles come from a positively-charged nucleus puzzled scientists for years. However, in the 1930s, another discovery helped to clear up the mystery: neutrons, which are not charged, decay to form a proton and an electron. The electron, having very little mass, is then ejected from the nucleus at a high speed as a beta particle.

Beta particles easily go through a piece of paper, but most are stopped by 3 mm of aluminum or 10 mm of wood. This greater penetration occurs because beta particles aren't as massive as alpha particles and therefore move faster. But like alpha particles, beta particles can easily ionize other atoms. As they ionize atoms, beta particles lose energy. This property prevents them from penetrating matter very deeply.

Gamma rays are very high energy light

In 1898, Marie Curie, shown in **Figure 7-2,** and her husband, Pierre, isolated the radioactive element radium. In 1900, studies of radium by Paul Villard revealed that the element emitted a new form of nuclear radiation. This radiation was much more penetrating than even beta particles. Following the pattern established by Rutherford, this new kind of nuclear radiation was named the **gamma ray,** after the third Greek alphabet letter, *gamma* (γ).

Unlike alpha or beta particles, gamma rays are not made of matter and do not have an electric charge. Instead, gamma rays are a form of electromagnetic energy, like visible light or X rays. Gamma rays, however, have more energy than light or X rays.

Because gamma rays have no electrical charge, they do not easily ionize matter. But gamma rays still cause damage because of their high energy. They can go through up to 60 cm of aluminum or 7 cm of lead. Because gamma rays penetrate matter deeply, they are not easily stopped by clothing or most building materials and therefore pose a greater danger to health than either alpha or beta particles.

Neutron radioactivity may occur in a neutron-rich nucleus

Like alpha and beta radiation, **neutron emission** consists of matter that is emitted from an unstable nucleus. In fact, scientists first discovered the neutron by detecting its emission from a nucleus.

Because neutrons have no charge, they do not ionize matter like alpha or beta particles do. Because neutrons do not use their energy ionizing matter, they are able to travel farther through matter than either alpha or beta particles. A block of lead about 15 cm thick is required to stop most fast neutrons emitted during radioactive decay.

Nuclear Decay

When an unstable nucleus emits alpha or beta particles, the number of protons or neutrons changes. For instance, radium-226 (an isotope of radium with the mass number 226) changes to radon-222 by emitting an alpha particle.

A nucleus gives up two protons and two neutrons during alpha decay

Nuclear decay processes can be written as equations similar to those for chemical reactions. The nucleus before decay is like a reactant and is placed on the left side of the equation. The products are placed on the right side. In the case of the alpha decay of radium-226, the decay process is written as follows.

$$\underset{88}{\overset{226}{\text{Ra}}} \longrightarrow \underset{86}{\overset{222}{\text{Rn}}} + \underset{2}{\overset{4}{\text{He}}} \qquad \begin{array}{l} 226 = 222 + 4 \\ 88 = 86 + 2 \end{array}$$

Notice that the mass numbers and the atomic numbers add up. The mass number of the atom before decay is 226 and equals the sum of the mass numbers of the products, 222 and 4. The atomic numbers follow the same principle. The 88 protons in radium before the nuclear decay equals the 86 protons in the radon-222 nucleus and 2 protons in the alpha particle.

A nucleus gains a proton and loses a neutron during beta decay

With beta decay, the form of the equation is the same except the symbol for a beta particle is used. This symbol, with the appropriate mass and atomic numbers, is $\underset{-1}{\overset{0}{e}}$.

Of course, an electron is not an atom and should not have an atomic number, which is the number of positive charges in a nucleus. But for the sake of convenience, since an electron has a single negative charge, an electron is given an atomic number of −1 when you write a nuclear decay equation. Similarly, the beta particle's mass is so much less than that of a proton or neutron that it can be regarded as having a mass number of 0.

A beta decay process occurs when carbon-14 decays to nitrogen-14 by emitting a beta particle.

$$\underset{6}{\overset{14}{\text{C}}} \longrightarrow \underset{7}{\overset{14}{\text{N}}} + \underset{-1}{\overset{0}{e}} \qquad \begin{array}{l} 14 = 14 + 0 \\ 6 = 7 + (-1) \end{array}$$

In all cases of beta decay, the mass number before and after the decay does not change. Note that the atomic number of the product nucleus increases by 1. This occurs because a neutron

Did You Know?

Ernest Rutherford showed that alpha particles are helium nuclei by trapping alpha particles from radon-222 decay in a glass tube. He then passed a high electric voltage across the gas, causing it to glow. The glow was identical to the glow produced by helium atoms, indicating that the two substances are the same.

Teaching Tip

Decay Make sure students are familiar with the word *decay* indicating the breakdown of a substance, such as when food or a tooth decays. Be sure students know that *radioactive decay* is the release of radiation by isotopes that are radioactive. In a sense, the nucleus breaks down as it loses matter or energy in the form of radiation.

Historical Perspective

In 1896, the French scientist Henri Becquerel discovered that uranium gives off penetrating radiation. He tried to prove that uranium's radiation resulted from its absorbing sunlight and releasing this energy in the form of X rays. But after using uranium that had not been exposed to sunlight to expose a photographic plate, he discovered that uranium spontaneously emits radiation.

Pierre and Marie Curie used Becquerel's findings to conclude that a nuclear change takes place within the uranium atoms, resulting in what they first called *radioactivity*.

What Is Radioactivity?

Additional Examples

Nuclear Decay Complete the following radioactive-decay equations by identifying the nuclide X. Indicate whether alpha or beta decay takes place.

$^{14}_{6}C \rightarrow ^{A}_{Z}X + ^{0}_{-1}e$

Answer: $^{14}_{7}N$, beta

$^{238}_{92}U \rightarrow ^{234}_{90}Th + ^{A}_{Z}X$

Answer: $^{4}_{2}He$, alpha

$^{40}_{19}K \rightarrow ^{40}_{20}Ca + ^{A}_{Z}X$

Answer: $^{0}_{-1}e$, beta

$^{219}_{86}Rn \rightarrow ^{A}_{Z}X + ^{4}_{2}He$

Answer: $^{215}_{84}Po$, alpha

Figure 7-3
A nucleus that undergoes beta decay has nearly the same atomic mass afterward, except that it has one more proton and one less neutron.

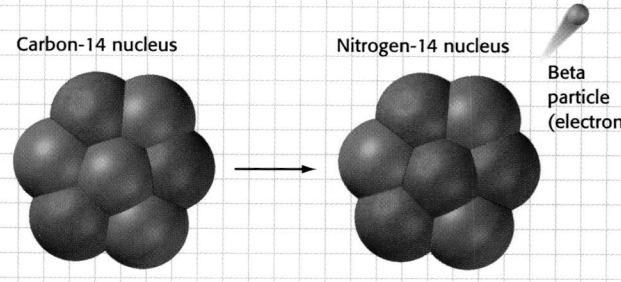

Carbon-14 nucleus   Nitrogen-14 nucleus   Beta particle (electron)

decays into a proton, causing the positive charge of the nucleus to increase by 1, as illustrated in **Figure 7-3.**

When the nucleus undergoes nuclear decay by gamma rays, there is no change in the atomic number of the element. The only change is in the energy content of the nucleus. The results of neutron emission will be discussed in greater detail in the next section.

Math Skills

Nuclear Decay Actinium-217 decays by releasing an alpha particle. Write the equation for this decay process, and determine what element is formed.

1 **Write down the equation with the original element on the left side and the products on the right side.**
  Use the letter X to denote the unknown product. Note that the mass and atomic numbers of the unknown isotope are represented by the letters A and Z.

$$^{217}_{89}Ac \longrightarrow ^{A}_{Z}X + ^{4}_{2}He$$

2 **Write math equations for the atomic and mass numbers.**
  $217 = A + 4 \qquad 89 = Z + 2$

3 **Rearrange the equations.**
  $A = 217 - 4 \qquad Z = 89 - 2$

4 **Solve for the unknown values, and rewrite the equation with all nuclei represented.**
  $A = 213 \qquad Z = 87$
  The unknown decay product has an atomic number of 87, which is francium, according to the periodic table. The element is therefore $^{213}_{87}Fr$.

$$^{217}_{89}Ac \longrightarrow ^{213}_{87}Fr + ^{4}_{2}He$$

Practice

Nuclear Decay

Complete the following radioactive-decay equations by identifying the isotope X. Indicate whether alpha or beta decay takes place.

1. $^{12}_{5}B \longrightarrow \, ^{12}_{6}C + \, ^{A}_{Z}X$

2. $^{225}_{89}Ac \longrightarrow \, ^{221}_{87}Fr + \, ^{A}_{Z}X$

3. $^{63}_{28}Ni \longrightarrow \, ^{A}_{Z}X + \, ^{0}_{-1}e$

4. $^{212}_{83}Bi \longrightarrow \, ^{A}_{Z}X + \, ^{4}_{2}He$

Radioactive Decay Rates

If you were asked to pick up a rock and determine its age, you would probably not be able to do so. After all, old rocks do not look much different from new rocks. How, then, would you go about finding the rock's age? Likewise, how would a scientist find out the age of cloth found at the site of an ancient village?

One way to do it involves radioactive decay. Although it is impossible to predict the moment when any particular nucleus will decay, it is possible to predict the time it takes for half the nuclei in a given radioactive sample to decay. The time in which half a radioactive substance decays is called the substance's **half-life.**

After the first half-life of a radioactive sample has passed, half the sample remains unchanged, as indicated in **Figure 7-4** for carbon-14. After the next half-life, half the remaining half decays, leaving only a quarter of the sample undecayed. Of that quarter, half will decay in the next half-life. Only one-eighth will remain undecayed then. Eventually, the entire sample will decay.

▶ **half-life** the time required for half a sample of radioactive nuclei to decay

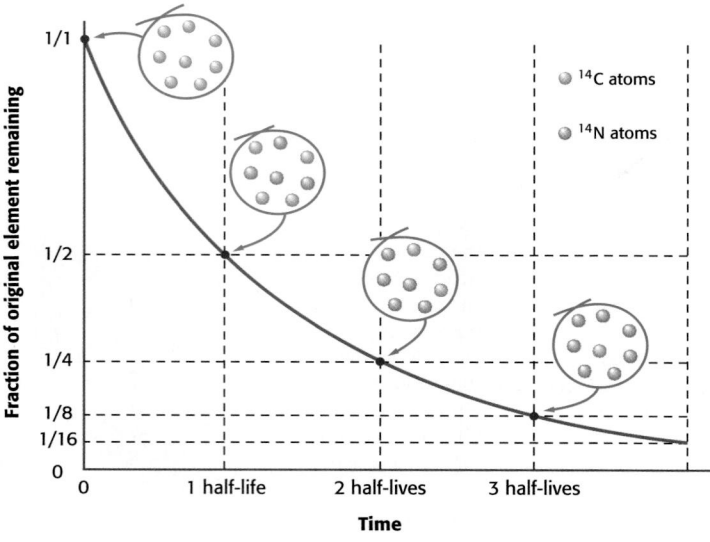

Figure 7-4
With each successive half-life, half the remaining sample decays to form another element.

○ ^{14}C atoms

○ ^{14}N atoms

NUCLEAR CHANGES **225**

What Is Radioactivity?

Table 7-2
Half-lives of Selected Isotopes

Isotope	Half-life	Nuclear radiation emitted
Thorium-219	1.05×10^{-6} s	^4_2He
Hafnium-156	2.5×10^{-2} s	^4_2He
Radon-222	3.82 days	^4_2He, γ
Iodine-131	8.1 days	$^0_{-1}e$, γ
Radium-226	1599 years	^4_2He, γ
Carbon-14	5730 years	$^0_{-1}e$
Plutonium-239	2.412×10^4 years	^4_2He, γ
Uranium-235	7.04×10^8 years	^4_2He, γ
Potassium-40	1.28×10^9 years	$^0_{-1}e$, γ
Uranium-238	4.47×10^9 years	^4_2He, γ

SKILL BUILDER

Graphs Have students graph their results of the Quick Activity. Graphs should show the number of remaining parent pennies on the *y*-axis and the trial number (number of half-lives) on the *x*-axis for each trial. A trial number of zero represents the starting number of pennies.

Make sure student graphs show a curve with a *y*-intercept at 128 that curves downward asymptotic to the *x*-axis.

Quick ACTIVITY

Modeling Decay and Half-life This activity differs from an actual half-life in that eventually all the pennies are removed. Even in a small sample of a radioactive isotope, the number of atoms is so large that theoretically, some parent atoms would always remain. The number would decrease to the point that the parent atoms would not be detectable, but they would be present. Students should find that the ratio of heads-up pennies to the total number of pennies in the trial is approximately 1:2, or $\frac{1}{2}$. Point out that if the actual number of atoms in a sample were considered, the ratio would be even closer to 1:2 because of the large sample size.

RESOURCE LINK
DATASHEETS

Have students use *Datasheet 7.1 Quick Activity: Modeling Decay and Half-life* to record their results.

Half-life is a measure of how quickly a substance decays

Different radioactive isotopes have different half-lives, as indicated in **Table 7-2.** Half-lives can last from nanoseconds to billions of years, depending on the stability of the nucleus.

If you know how much of a particular radioactive isotope was present in an object at the beginning, you can predict how old the object is. Geologists, people who study the Earth, use the half-lives of long-lasting isotopes, such as potassium-40, to calculate the age of rocks. Potassium-40 decays to argon-40, so the ratio of potassium-40 to argon-40 is smaller for older rocks.

Quick ACTIVITY

Modeling Decay and Half-life

For this exercise, you will need a jar with a lid, 128 pennies, pencil and paper, and a flat work surface.
1. Place the pennies in the jar, and place the lid on the jar. Shake the jar, and then pour the pennies onto the work surface.
2. Separate pennies that are heads up from those that are tails up. Count and record the number of heads-up pennies, and set these pennies aside. Place the tails-up pennies back in the jar.
3. Repeat the process until all pennies have been set aside.
4. For each trial, divide the number of heads-up pennies set aside by the total number of pennies used in the trial. Are these ratios nearly equal to each other? What fraction are they closest to?

ALTERNATIVE ASSESSMENT

Radiation

Step 1 Have students review the list of ideas about radiation that they created in the Reading Skill Builder on page 218.

Step 2 Discuss each item, evaluating whether each item is accurate and in the correct category of positive and negative.

Step 3 Have students adjust items based on what they learned about radiation in this section. They should use the text to justify any changes.

Archaeologists use the half-life of radioactive carbon-14 to date more recent materials, such as the remains of an animal or fibers from ancient clothing. All of these materials came from organisms that were once alive. When plants absorb carbon dioxide during photosynthesis, a tiny fraction of the CO_2 molecules contains carbon-14 rather than the more common carbon-12. While the plant is alive, the ratio of the carbon isotopes remains constant. This is also true for animals that eat plants.

When a plant or animal dies, it no longer takes in carbon-14. The amount of carbon-14 decreases through beta decay, while the amount of carbon-12 remains constant. Thus, the ratio of carbon-14 to carbon-12 decreases with time. By measuring this ratio and comparing it with the ratio in a living plant or animal, the age of the once-living organism can be estimated.

Math Skills

Half-life Radium-226 has a half-life of 1599 years. How long would it take seven-eighths of a radium-226 sample to decay?

1 **List the given and unknown values.**
　　Given: half-life = 1599 years
　　　　　　fraction of sample decayed = $\frac{7}{8}$
　　Unknown: fraction of sample remaining = ?
　　　　　　total time of decay = ?

2 **Calculate the fraction of radioactive sample remaining.**
　　To find the fraction of sample remaining, subtract the fraction that has decayed from 1.

　　fraction of sample remaining = 1 − fraction decayed
　　fraction of sample remaining = $1 - \frac{7}{8} = \frac{1}{8}$

3 **Calculate the number of half-lives needed to equal that fraction.**

　　Amount of sample remaining after one half-life = $\frac{1}{2}$
　　Amount of sample remaining after two half-lives
　　= $\frac{1}{2} \times \frac{1}{2} = \frac{1}{4}$

　　Amount of sample remaining after three half-lives
　　= $\frac{1}{2} \times \frac{1}{2} \times \frac{1}{2} = \frac{1}{8}$

　　Three half-lives are needed for one-eighth of the sample to remain undecayed.

4 **Calculate the total time required for the radioactive decay.**
　　Each half-life lasts 1599 years.
　　total time of decay = 3 half-lives × $\dfrac{1599\ y}{\text{half-life}}$ = 4797 years

INTEGRATING

EARTH SCIENCE
The Earth's interior is extremely hot. One reason is because radioactive elements are present in trace amounts beneath the surface of the Earth and their nuclear decay produces energy that raises the temperature of their surroundings.

Many radioactive isotopes, like uranium-238, are very dense, which causes them to sink deep into Earth's interior. This is similar to what happens when dense liquids sink below less dense liquids, like syrup does in water.

The long half-lives of these radioactive isotopes can cause some of the surrounding matter to remain hot for billions of years.

Section 7.1

What Is Radioactivity?

INTEGRATING

EARTH SCIENCE Emphasize to students the great amount of heat released on Earth by radioactive elements. Tell them that 1.0 g of radium during its lifetime releases by natural radiation the same amount of energy released when half a ton of coal is burned.

Resources Assign students worksheet *7.1 Integrating Earth Science—Radioactivity Within the Earth* in the **Integration Enrichment Resources** ancillary.

Teaching Tip

Carbon Dating Have interested students investigate how carbon-14 dating was used to date the Shroud of Turin

Math Skills

Resources Assign students worksheet *12: Half-life* in the **Math Skills Worksheets** ancillary.

Additional Examples

Half-life The half-life of tritium, $^{3}_{1}\text{H}$, is 12.3 years. How long will it take for $\frac{7}{8}$ of a sample to decay?

Answer: $1 - \frac{7}{8} = \frac{1}{8}$ remains

It will take three half-lives.
3 half-lives × 12.3 years/half-life
= 36.9 years

The half-life of cobalt-60 is 5.3 years. How much of a 20.0 g sample will remain after 21.2 years?

Answer: $\dfrac{21.2 \text{ years}}{5.3 \text{ years per half-life}}$
= 4 half-lives.
$20.0 \text{ g} \times \frac{1}{2} \times \frac{1}{2} \times \frac{1}{2} \times \frac{1}{2} = 1.25 \text{ g}$

Section 7.1

What Is Radioactivity?

SECTION 7.1 REVIEW

Check Your Understanding

1. a. beta
   b. neutron
   c. alpha
   d. gamma

2. A neutron in the nucleus of an atom decays, forming a proton, which remains in the nucleus, and an electron, which is released as a beta particle.

3. They ionize the materials they pass through. Each ionization transfers energy from the alpha or beta particle to the ionized particle. Less energy means less penetration.

Math Skills

4. $212 = A + 4$, $A = 208$; $86 = Z + 2$, $Z = 84$; $X = $ Po; The product is $^{208}_{84}$Po.

5. $131 = A + 0$, $A = 131$; $53 = Z + (-1)$, $Z = 54$; $X = $ Xe; The product is $^{131}_{54}$Xe.

6. $1 - \frac{3}{4} = \frac{1}{4}$, or $\frac{1}{2} \times \frac{1}{2}$, remains
Two half-lives is 2×32.2 minutes, or 64.4 minutes.

7. $1 - \frac{7}{8} = \frac{1}{8}$, or $\frac{1}{2} \times \frac{1}{2} \times \frac{1}{2}$, remains
$\frac{6 \times 10^6 \text{ years}}{3 \text{ half-lives}} = 2 \times 10^6$ years / half-life

8. $\frac{1}{16} = \frac{1}{2} \times \frac{1}{2} \times \frac{1}{2} \times \frac{1}{2}$
Four half-lives have passed. The mask is 4 half-lives $\times \frac{5730 \text{ years}}{\text{half-life}}$, or 22 920 years old.

RESOURCE LINK
STUDY GUIDE

Assign students *Review Section 7.1 What Is Radioactivity?* before beginning Section 7.2.

Practice

Half-life

1. The half-life of iodine-131 is 8.1 days. How long will it take for three-fourths of a sample of iodine-131 to decay?

2. Radon-222 is a radioactive gas with a half-life of 3.82 days. How long would it take for fifteen-sixteenths of a sample of radon-222 to decay?

3. Uranium-238 decays very slowly, with a half-life of 4.47 billion years. What percentage of a sample of uranium-238 would remain after 13.4 billion years?

4. A sample of strontium-90 is found to have decayed to one-eighth of its original amount after 87.3 years. What is the half-life of strontium-90?

5. A sample of francium-212 will decay to one-sixteenth its original amount after 80 minutes. What is the half-life of francium-212?

SECTION 7.1 REVIEW

SUMMARY

▶ Nuclear radiation includes alpha particles, beta particles, gamma rays, and neutron emissions.

▶ Alpha particles are helium-4 nuclei.

▶ Beta particles are electrons emitted by neutrons decaying in the nucleus.

▶ Gamma radiation is an electromagnetic wave like visible light but with much greater energy.

▶ In nuclear decay, the sums of the mass numbers and the atomic numbers of the decay products equal the mass number and atomic number of the decaying nucleus.

▶ The time required for half a sample of radioactive material to decay is called its half-life.

228 CHAPTER 7

CHECK YOUR UNDERSTANDING

1. Identify which of the four common types of nuclear radiation correspond to the following descriptions:
   a. an electron
   b. uncharged particle
   c. can be stopped by a piece of paper
   d. high-energy light

2. Describe what happens when beta decay occurs.

3. Explain why charged particles do not penetrate matter deeply.

Math Skills

4. Determine the product denoted by X in the following alpha decay.
$$^{212}_{86}\text{Rn} \longrightarrow {}^{A}_{Z}X + {}^{4}_{2}\text{He}$$

5. Determine the isotope produced in the beta decay of iodine-131, an isotope used to check thyroid-gland function.
$$^{131}_{53}\text{I} \longrightarrow {}^{A}_{Z}X + {}^{0}_{-1}e$$

6. Calculate the time required for three-fourths of a sample of cesium-138 to decay given that its half-life is 32.2 minutes.

7. Calculate the half-life of cesium-135 if seven-eighths of a sample decays in 6×10^6 years.

8. Critical Thinking An archaeologist discovers a wooden mask whose carbon-14 to carbon-12 ratio is one-sixteenth the ratio measured in a newly fallen tree. How old does the wooden mask seem to be, given this evidence?

Solution Guide

1. $1 - \frac{3}{4} = \frac{1}{4}$, or $\frac{1}{2} \times \frac{1}{2}$; 2 half-lives remain
2×8.1 days = 16 days

2. $1 - \frac{15}{16} = \frac{1}{16}$, or $\frac{1}{2} \times \frac{1}{2} \times \frac{1}{2} \times \frac{1}{2}$; 4 half-lives remain
4×3.82 days = 15.3 days

3. $\frac{13.4 \text{ billion years}}{4.47 \text{ billion years / half-life}}$ = 3 half-lives

$\frac{1}{2} \times \frac{1}{2} \times \frac{1}{2} = \frac{1}{8} = 0.125$; $0.125 \times 100 = 12.5\%$

4. $\frac{1}{8} = \frac{1}{2} \times \frac{1}{2} \times \frac{1}{2}$; three half-lives
$\frac{87.3 \text{ years}}{3 \text{ half-lives}} = 29.1$ years / half-life

5. $\frac{1}{16} = \frac{1}{2} \times \frac{1}{2} \times \frac{1}{2} \times \frac{1}{2}$; 4 half-lives
$\frac{80 \text{ min}}{4 \text{ half-lives}} = 20$ min / half-life

Nuclear Fission and Fusion

OBJECTIVES

▶ Describe how the strong nuclear force affects the composition of a nucleus.

▶ Distinguish between fission and fusion, and provide examples of each.

▶ Recognize the equivalence of mass and energy, and why small losses in mass release large amounts of energy.

▶ Explain what a chain reaction is, how one is initiated, and how it can be controlled.

▶ **KEY TERMS**

strong nuclear force
fission
nuclear chain reaction
critical mass
fusion

Scheduling

Refer to pp. 218A–218D for lecture, classwork, and assignment options for Section 7.2.

★ **Lesson Focus**
Use transparency *LT 24* to prepare students for this section.

READING SKILL BUILDER *K-W-L* Students probably have preconceptions about the energy released by a nuclear reaction. Have them list what they know about the topic. Then have them list what they want to know about it. After students read Section 7.2, have them look at their lists and write down what they have learned about the energy released by a nuclear reaction. Students should list questions they still have about the topic and research these questions using other sources.

In 1939, two German scientists, Otto Hahn and Fritz Strassman, conducted experiments in the hope of forming heavy nuclei. Using the apparatus shown in **Figure 7-5,** they bombarded uranium samples with neutrons, expecting a few nuclei to capture one or more neutrons. They were surprised to discover that the result was less-massive nuclei instead of more-massive nuclei.

It wasn't until their colleague Lise Meitner and her nephew Otto Frisch read the results of Hahn and Strassman's work that an explanation was offered. Meitner and Frisch believed that instead of making heavier elements, the uranium nuclei had split into smaller elements.

Nuclear Forces

Protons and neutrons are tightly packed in the tiny nucleus of an atom. As we saw in the previous section, certain nuclei are unstable and undergo decay by emitting nuclear radiation. Also, an element can have both stable and unstable isotopes. For instance, carbon-12 is a stable isotope, while carbon-14 is unstable and radioactive. The stability of a nucleus depends on the nuclear forces that hold the nucleus together. This force acts between the protons and the neutrons.

Figure 7-5
Using this equipment, Otto Hahn and Fritz Strassman first discovered nuclear fission.

DEMONSTRATION 2 TEACHING

Nuclear Forces

Time: Approximately 5 minutes
Materials: 2 bar magnets, rubber band

Show students how like poles of magnets repel each other. Place the magnets so that the like poles are together and the magnets touch. Wrap the rubber band tightly around them so that the magnets are held together.

Analysis

1. What part of a nucleus do the magnets represent? Explain. *(protons; they repel each other)*

2. What does the rubber band represent? *(a force strong enough to hold objects together even though they repel each other)*

Nuclear Fission and Fusion

Multicultural Extension

Hideki Yukawa, a Japanese scientist, first theorized in 1935 that a strong force exists that holds the nucleus together. He described the force as being stronger over short distances than the electrical repulsion that repels protons. He thought that this strong force was the result of the transfer of some unknown particle.

In 1947, the particle Yukawa predicted was found. This particle is the pion, which exists for only about a billionth of a second. After his theory was confirmed by the discovery of this particle, Yukawa received the Nobel Prize in 1949. He was the first Japanese person ever to receive this prestigious award.

MISCONCEPTION ALERT

Nuclear Fission
Students might think that fission in a cell and in a nucleus are identical processes because both involve splitting. The product of cell fission is two cells that are identical to each other and to the parent cell. Nuclear fission produces particles that differ from the parent atom and from each other.

230

▶ **strong nuclear force**
the interaction that binds protons and neutrons together in a nucleus

Nuclei are held together by a special force

You may know that like charges repel. But how is it that so many positively charged protons fit into an atomic nucleus without flying apart?

The answer lies in the existence of the **strong nuclear force.** This force causes protons and neutrons in the nucleus to attract each other. The attraction is much stronger than the electric repulsion between protons. However, this attraction due to the strong nuclear force occurs over a very short distance, less than 3×10^{-15} m, or about the width of three protons.

Neutrons contribute to nuclear stability

Due to the strong nuclear force, neutrons and protons in a nucleus attract other protons and neutrons. Because neutrons have no charge, they do not repel each other or the protons. On the other hand, the protons in a nucleus both repel and attract each other, as shown in **Figure 7-6.** In stable nuclei, the attractive forces are stronger than the repulsive forces.

Too many neutrons or protons can cause a nucleus to become unstable and decay

While more neutrons can help hold a nucleus together, there is a limit to how many neutrons a nucleus can have. Nuclei with too many or too few neutrons are unstable and undergo decay.

Nuclei with more than 83 protons are always unstable, no matter how many neutrons they have. These nuclei will always decay, releasing large amounts of energy and nuclear radiation. Some of this released energy is transferred to the various particles ejected from the nucleus, the least massive of which move very fast as a result. The rest of the energy is emitted in the form of gamma rays.

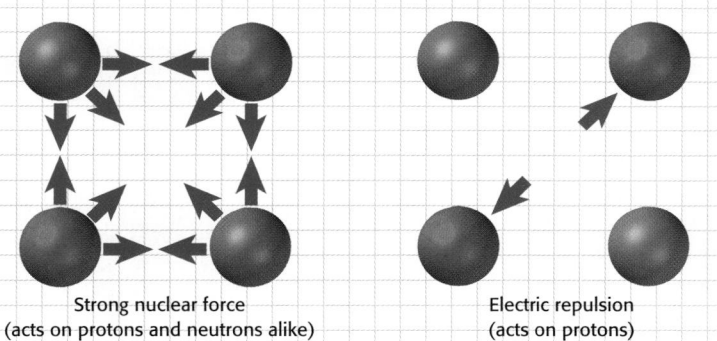

Figure 7-6
The nucleus is held together by the attractions among protons and neutrons. These forces are greater than the electric repulsion among the protons alone.

Strong nuclear force
(acts on protons and neutrons alike)

Electric repulsion
(acts on protons)

ALTERNATIVE ASSESSMENT

Stable Nuclei

Step 1 Have students create a graph with the number of protons on the *x*-axis and the number of neutrons on the *y*-axis.

Step 2 Have them draw a line for $x = y$. Tell them that this line indicates stable atoms that have an equal number of protons and neutrons.

Step 3 Have students make a scatter graph of the number of protons versus the number of neutrons for elements that have atomic numbers 1 through 50. For the number of neutrons, have students use the mass number of the most common isotope of the element, based on its average atomic mass on the periodic table.

Step 4 Students should use these graphs to explain why larger atoms are more likely to be unstable. Point out that not all isotopes of the atoms are represented. Heavier isotopes are more likely to be unstable.

Nuclear Fission

The process of the production of lighter nuclei from heavier nuclei, which Hahn and Strassman observed, is called **fission.** In their experiment, uranium-235 was bombarded by neutrons. The products of this fission reaction included two lighter nuclei barium-137 and krypton-84, together with neutrons and energy.

$$^{235}_{92}U + ^{1}_{0}n \longrightarrow ^{137}_{56}Ba + ^{84}_{36}Kr + 15^{1}_{0}n + energy$$

Notice that the products include 15 neutrons. Uranium-235 can also undergo fission by producing different pairs of lighter nuclei with a different number of neutrons. For example, a different fission of uranium-235 produces strontium-90, xenon-143, and three neutrons. On average, two or three neutrons are released when uranium-235 undergoes fission.

Energy is released during nuclear fission

During fission, as shown in **Figure 7-7,** the nucleus breaks into smaller nuclei. The reaction also releases large amounts of energy. Each dividing nucleus releases about 3.2×10^{-11} J of energy. By comparison, the chemical reaction of one molecule of the explosive trinitrotoluene (TNT) releases only 4.8×10^{-18} J.

In their experiment, Hahn and Strassman determined the masses of all the nuclei and particles before and after the reaction. They found that the overall mass had decreased after the reaction. The missing mass had changed into energy.

The equivalence of mass and energy observed in nature is explained by the special theory of relativity, which Albert Einstein presented in 1905. This equivalence means that matter can be converted into energy and energy into matter. This equivalence is expressed by the following equation.

> **Mass-Energy Equation**
> $$Energy = mass \times (speed\ of\ light)^2$$
> $$E = mc^2$$

Because c, which is constant, has such a large value, 3.0×10^8 m/s, the energy associated with even a small mass is immense. The mass-equivalent energy of 1 kg of matter is 9×10^{16} J. This is more than the chemical energy of 8 million tons of TNT.

Obviously, it would be devastating if objects around us changed into their equivalent energies. Under ordinary conditions of pressure and temperature, matter is very stable. Objects, such as chairs and tables, never spontaneously change into energy.

> ▶ **fission** the process by which a nucleus splits into two or more smaller fragments, releasing neutrons and energy

Figure 7-7
When the uranium-235 nucleus is bombarded by a neutron the nucleus breaks apart. It forms smaller nuclei, such as barium-137 and krypton-84, and releases energy through fast neutrons.

Did You Know?

Enrico Fermi and his associates achieved the first controlled nuclear reaction in December 1942. The reactor was built on squash courts under the unused football stadium at the University of Chicago. The reactor consisted of blocks of uranium-235 for fuel and graphite to slow the neutrons so that they could be captured by the uranium nuclei and cause fission.

Section 7.2

Nuclear Fission and Fusion

Teaching Tip

Relative Energy Students might not understand the immense difference in energies of one nucleus undergoing fission and one molecule of TNT exploding. For clarification, divide the two quantities shown in the student text:
$$\frac{3.2 \times 10^{-11}\ J}{4.8 \times 10^{-18}\ J} = 6.7 \times 10^6,$$
or 6 700 000.
Explain to students that one nucleus undergoing fission releases approximately the same amount of energy as 6.7 million TNT molecules do when they explode.

Did You Know?

Fast-moving neutrons are less likely to cause a fission reaction than slower ones are. The material that slows down neutrons during nuclear fission in a nuclear reactor is called a moderator. A moderator provides particles other than the fuel for the neutrons to collide with. Water and graphite are frequently used as moderators in atomic reactors.

Interpreting Visuals Have students examine **Figure 7-8** and make a concept map that summarizes what happens when a chain reaction occurs.

Maps should start with a neutron hitting a uranium-235 atom, which then splits into barium-140 and krypton-93 atoms. Three other neutrons are released and each neutron hits another uranium-235 atom.

Resources *Teaching Transparency 21* shows this visual.

Teaching Tip

Power from Fission Tell students that the United States receives approximately 20 percent of its electrical power from power plants that use nuclear fission as an energy source. The country that currently receives the greatest percentage of its electrical power from nuclear fission is France.

Additional Application

Controlling Fission Moderators do not absorb neutrons during fission reactions; they just slow them down. Control rods, which are made from materials that readily absorb neutrons, such as boron or cadmium, are used to absorb excess neutrons. The rods are inserted or withdrawn as needed to control the number of neutrons present.

---

internet connect

SC LINKS
NSTA

TOPIC: Fission
GO TO: www.scilinks.org
KEYWORD: HK1073

▶ **nuclear chain reaction** a series of fission processes in which the neutrons emitted by a dividing nucleus cause the division of other nuclei

Figure 7-8
A nuclear chain reaction may be triggered by a single neutron.

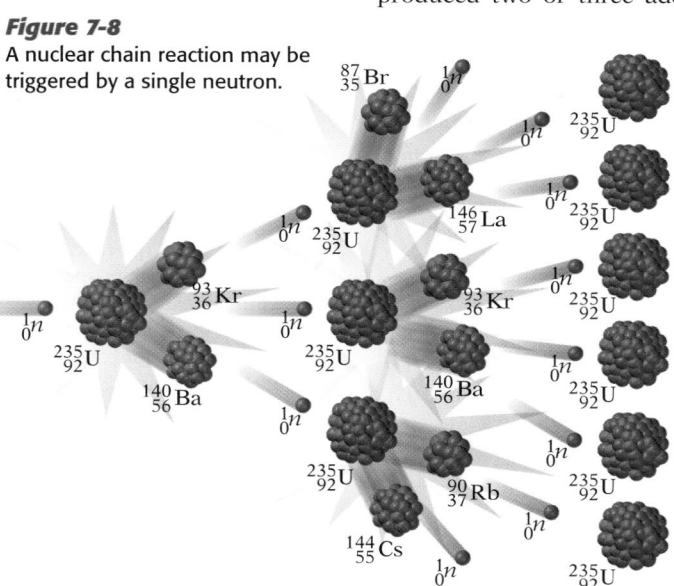

When the total mass of any nucleus is measured, it turns out to be less than the individual masses of the neutrons and protons that make up the nucleus. This missing mass is referred to as the *mass defect*. But what happens to the missing mass? Einstein's equation provides an explanation—it changes into energy. However, the mass defect of a nucleus is very small.

Another way to think about mass defect is to imagine constructing a nucleus by bringing individual protons and neutrons together. During this process a small amount of mass changes into energy, as described by $E = mc^2$.

Neutrons released by fission can start a chain reaction

Have you ever played marbles with lots of marbles in the ring? When one marble is shot into the ring, the resulting collisions cause some of the marbles to scatter. Some nuclear reactions are like this, where one reaction triggers another.

A nucleus that splits when it is struck by a neutron forms smaller product nuclei. These smaller nuclei need fewer neutrons to be held together. Therefore, excess neutrons are emitted. One of these neutrons can collide with another large nucleus, triggering another nuclear reaction. This reaction releases more neutrons, and so it is possible to start a chain reaction.

When Hahn and Strassman continued experimenting, they discovered that each dividing uranium nucleus, on average, produced two or three additional neutrons. Therefore, two or three new fission reactions could be started from the neutrons ejected from one reaction.

If each of these three new reactions produce three additonal neutrons, a total of nine neutrons become available to trigger nine additional fission reactions. From these nine reactions, a total of 27 neutrons are produced, setting off 27 new reactions, and so on. You can probably see from **Figure 7-8** how the reaction of uranium-235 nuclei would quickly result in an uncontrolled **nuclear chain reaction**. Therefore, the ability to create a chain reaction partly depends on the number of neutrons released.

DEMONSTRATION 3 TEACHING

A Chain Reaction

Time: Approximately 10 minutes
Materials: 8 books of matches, ring stand, tape

SAFETY CAUTION: *Work in a well-ventilated area. Have water available to extinguish the matches.*
Open the books of matches. Starting at the top of the ring stand, use tape to attach the matches so that the heads of the matches form a vertical row on the stand. Light the bottom match.

Analysis
1. Have students explain their observations. *(Each match supplied enough energy to the next match to light it.)*
2. How is this demonstration a model of a nuclear chain reaction? *(Just like each match supplies energy to the next match, each neutron emitted in one fission reaction causes another fission reaction.)*

The chain-reaction principle is used in the nuclear bomb. Two or more masses of uranium-235 are contained in the bomb. These masses are surrounded by a powerful chemical explosive. When the explosive is detonated, all of the uranium is pushed together to create a **critical mass.** The critical mass refers to the minimum amount of a substance that can not only undergo a fission reaction but also sustain a chain reaction. If the amount of fissionable substance is less than the critical mass, a chain reaction will not continue.

In a nuclear bomb, a chain reaction is started and proceeds very quickly. The result is the release of a large amount of energy in a very short time, causing devastation to the environment and to the life-forms within it for many miles.

The ease with which uranium-235 can make an uncontrolled chain reaction makes it extremely dangerous. Fortunately, the concentration of uranium-235 in nature is too low to start a chain reaction. Almost all of the escaping neutrons are absorbed by the more common and more stable isotope uranium-238.

Chain reactions can be controlled

Not all neutrons released in a fission reaction succeed in triggering a fission reaction. For this reason, the more neutrons that are produced per reaction, the better the chances are of a chain reaction sustaining itself. It is also possible to use materials that will slow a fission chain reaction by absorbing some of the neutrons. In this way, the reaction is controlled, unlike in a nuclear bomb. The energy produced in a controlled reaction can be used to generate electricity.

▶ **critical mass** the minimum mass of a fissionable isotope in which a nuclear chain reaction can occur

Section 7.2

Nuclear Fission and Fusion

Additional Application

Chain Reactions Have students list examples of non-nuclear chain reactions that they come in contact with daily. For example, one person tells another a secret, that person tells two other people, each of them tells two others, and the information chain continues.

Quick ACTIVITY

Modeling Chain Reactions

1. To model a fission chain reaction, you will need a small wooden building block and a set of dominoes.
2. Place the building block on a table or counter. Stand one domino upright in front of the block and parallel to one of its sides, as shown at right.
3. Stand two more dominoes vertically, parallel, and symmetrical to the first domino. Continue this process until you have used all the dominoes and a triangular shape is created, as shown at right.
4. Gently push the first domino away from the block so that it falls and hits the second group. Note how more dominoes fall with each step.

Quick ACTIVITY

Modeling Chain Reactions
Encourage students to try other domino arrangements to model chain reactions. For example, they could arrange dominoes in a chain that continually branches, so that one domino falling in the first step causes 16 dominoes to fall in the fifth step. If possible, use a video camera to tape the chain reaction. If a VCR that has a slow-motion feature is available, play the tape back at slow speed. If students arranged their dominoes in branches, have them use the video to examine which domino caused each branch to fall.

NUCLEAR CHANGES **233**

RESOURCE LINK
DATASHEETS

Have students use *Datasheet 7.2 Quick Activity: Modeling Chain Reactions* to record their results.

Teaching Tip

Containing Fusion One of the most difficult problems with nuclear fusion is containing the reaction. For the reaction to readily occur, it must happen at temperatures of approximately 10^8 °C, where the fuel is in the plasma state. No known material could contain such a reaction without melting. Because plasma consists of charged particles, some success has been achieved by containing the reaction in a magnetic field. However, the moving, charged particles produce magnetic fields that interfere with the magnetic field.

SECTION 7.2 REVIEW

Check Your Understanding

1. The strong force acts over such a small distance that large nuclei are difficult to hold together. These unstable nuclei undergo nuclear reactions that make them more stable.

2. **a.** fusion
   b. fission
   c. fusion
   d. fusion

3. The total mass of this nucleus—56 amu—will be greater than 55.847 amu. The mass is not equal to 55.847 amu because that value is an average of the masses of several different isotopes.

4. A continued chain reaction will not occur. Each step of fission reactions requires more neutrons than the previous fission releases.

fusion the process in which light nuclei combine at extremely high temperatures, forming heavier nuclei and releasing energy

internetconnect

SCiLINKS
NSTA

TOPIC: Fusion
GO TO: www.scilinks.org
KEYWORD: HK1074

Nuclear Fusion

Just as energy is obtained when heavy nuclei break apart, energy can also be obtained when very light nuclei are combined to form heavier nuclei. This type of nuclear process is called **fusion**.

In stars, including the sun, energy is primarily produced when hydrogen nuclei combine, or fuse together, and release tremendous amounts of energy. However, a large amount of energy is needed to start a fusion reaction. This is because all nuclei are positively charged, and they repel each other with an electrical force. Energy is required to bring the hydrogen nuclei close together until the electrical forces are overcome by the attractive nuclear forces between two protons. In stars, the extreme temperatures provide the energy needed to bring hydrogen nuclei together.

Four hydrogen atoms fuse together in the sun to produce a helium atom and enormous energy in the form of gamma rays. This occurs in a multistep process that involves two isotopes of hydrogen: ordinary hydrogen ($_1^1H$), and deuterium ($_1^2H$).

$$_1^1H + _1^1H \longrightarrow _1^2H + \text{two particles}$$
$$_1^2H + _1^1H \longrightarrow _2^3He + _0^0\gamma$$
$$_2^3He + _2^3He \longrightarrow _2^4He + _1^1H + _1^1H$$

SECTION 7.2 REVIEW

SUMMARY

▶ Neutrons and protons in the nucleus are held together by the strong nuclear force.

▶ Nuclear fission takes place when a large nucleus divides into smaller nuclei.

▶ Nuclear fusion occurs when two light nuclei combine.

▶ Mass is converted into energy during both fusion and fission reactions.

CHECK YOUR UNDERSTANDING

1. **Explain** why most isotopes of elements with a high atomic number are radioactive.

2. **Indicate** if the following are fission or fusion reactions.
   a. $_1^1H + _1^2H \longrightarrow _2^3He + \gamma$
   b. $_0^1n + _{92}^{235}U \longrightarrow _{57}^{146}La + _{35}^{87}Br + 3_0^1n$
   c. $_{10}^{21}Ne + _2^4He \longrightarrow _{12}^{24}Mg + _0^1n$
   d. $_{82}^{208}Pb + _{26}^{58}Fe \longrightarrow _{108}^{265}Hs + _0^1n$

3. **Predict** whether the total mass of the 26 protons and 30 neutrons that make up the iron nucleus will be more, less, or equal to 55.847 amu, the mass of an iron atom, $_{26}^{56}Fe$. If it is not equal, explain why.

4. **Critical Thinking** Suppose a nucleus captures two neutrons and decays to produce one neutron, is this process likely to produce a chain reaction? Explain your reasoning.

7.3

Dangers and Benefits of Nuclear Radiation

INTEGRATING TECHNOLOGY and Society

OBJECTIVES

▶ Describe the dangers and possible health effects of exposure to nuclear radiation.
▶ Identify several beneficial uses of nuclear radiation.
▶ Explain the benefits and drawbacks of nuclear power.

▶ **KEY TERMS**
background radiation
radioactive tracer

When you think about nuclear radiation, do you have a negative reaction? Do you immediately think about danger? The plots of many science-fiction movies and television shows have revolved around the dangers of nuclear radiation, showing it causing mutations or death and destruction.

Dangers of Nuclear Radiation

In many cases, especially when it is used carelessly, nuclear radiation can be extremely dangerous. However, it may surprise you to know that we are exposed to nuclear radiation of some sort every day. This kind of radiation is called **background radiation.** Most of it comes from natural sources, such as the sun, soil, water, and plants, as shown in **Figure 7-9.** The living tissues of most organisms are adapted to survive these low levels of natural nuclear radiation. Only when these background levels are exceeded do problems arise.

▶ **background radiation**
nuclear radiation that arises naturally from cosmic rays and from radioactive isotopes in the soil and air

Figure 7-9
Sources of background radiation are all around us.

NUCLEAR CHANGES **235**

Scheduling

Refer to pp. 218A–218D for lecture, classwork, and assignment options for Section 7.3.

★ **Lesson Focus**
Use transparency *LT 25* to prepare students for this section.

READING SKILL BUILDER *Reader Response Logs* Have students draw a vertical line down the middle of a piece of paper. On the left, have them write down passages from Section 7.3 about which they have reactions, thoughts, feelings, questions, or associations. On the right, have them write those reactions, thoughts, feelings, questions, or associations. Encourage quality over quantity. It is acceptable to have only one, well-developed passage with reactions to it. Have student volunteers share their entries.

RESOURCE LINK
IER

Assign students worksheet *7.8 Integrating Environmental Science—Environmental Radiation* in the **Integration Enrichment Resources** ancillary.

Danger and Benefits of Nuclear Radiation

SKILL BUILDER

Interpreting Visuals As they examine **Figure 7-10,** tell students that radon tests are either short term or long term, depending on whether the testing period is more or less than 90 days. If a short-term test shows high levels of radon, it should be followed by another test. The advantage of long-term testing is that it allows for seasonal variations in radon levels.

LINKING CHAPTERS

Energy uses, including energy produced by nuclear reactions, are discussed in Chapter 10.

Figure 7-10
Radon-222 levels in the air of basements and cellars can become dangerously high. Radon detectors are used to monitor radon-222 levels.

Nuclear radiation can ionize atoms in living tissue

When hemoglobin—the molecule in blood that carries oxygen throughout the body—is exposed to excessive amounts of nuclear radiation, its structure is changed. This changed hemoglobin can no longer draw oxygen into the blood, so the body cannot get oxygen as easily.

Most of your body's tissues are made of large molecules. Among these are proteins, carbohydrates, and fats. The chemical properties of these molecules change when the molecules lose or gain electrons through ionization caused by nuclear radiation. If enough molecules in a cell are ionized, the cell no longer functions properly. This can affect the overall health of the body.

Fortunately, the outer skin keeps most radiation outside the body. But if a source of alpha and beta particles is introduced into the body through air, water, or food, the nuclear radiation can severely damage the delicate linings of the body's organs.

Energetic gamma rays and fast neutrons can damage tissues regardless of whether the source of these types of nuclear radiation is inside or outside the body. Nuclear radiation can cause burns in the skin, and it also destroys bone marrow cells, which form red and white blood cells.

High concentrations of radon gas can be dangerous

The potential for internal damage by alpha particles explains the public concern over radon gas. Radon-222 is produced through a series of nuclear reactions of uranium-238 in the Earth's crust. The gas drifts up through the rock and enters the air we breathe.

Outdoors, the radon concentration is low and the gas is less harmful. However, radon can accumulate in the basements of buildings, as shown in **Figure 7-10,** until it reaches dangerous concentrations. The alpha particles emitted by inhaled radon-222 can destroy lung tissue. Prolonged exposure to radon-222 can lead to lung cancer, especially among smokers.

Radiation sickness results from exposure to high levels of nuclear radiation

Not all nuclear radiation causes intense damage to the body's cells. A person exposed for long periods or to high intensities of nuclear radiation will have more damage in his or her cells than a person who is exposed for short periods or to low intensities.

Observable effects from nuclear radiation exposure often do not appear for days or even years. Some common symptoms after serious exposure include a decrease in the number of white blood cells (leucopenia), hair loss, sterility, destruction and death of bones (bone necrosis), and cancer.

DEMONSTRATION 4 TEACHING

Disposal of Nuclear Waste

Time: Approximately 15 minutes
Materials: phenolphthalein indicator
4 NaOH pellets
plastic wrap and twist tie
modeling clay
aluminum foil
400 mL beakers (4)
water

SAFETY CAUTION: *Do not touch the NaOH pellets or solution.*

Step 1 Add water and four drops of phenolphthalein, which turns pink in a base, to each beaker.

Step 2 Add one pellet to a beaker.

Nuclear radiation can cause genetic mutations

Long-term effects of nuclear radiation appear when DNA molecules in the body are damaged. As described in Chapter 4, DNA directs the synthesis of proteins by the body, so it contains all the information cells need to function. DNA also carries all the genetic information of an organism. If DNA molecules are extensively damaged by nuclear radiation, the cell may repair them incorrectly, as shown in **Figure 7-11.** When the DNA in reproductive cells is damaged, there is a strong chance of birth defects.

Biologists have observed birth defects in animals that have been exposed to large amounts of nuclear radiation in water or soil. An example of this occurred near the Shiprock Uranium Mine, which operated from 1954 to 1968 in northwestern New Mexico. Radioactive waste from the mine contaminated water that the nearby Navajo used for their sheep and cattle. Although the animals that drank the water remained healthy, the nuclear radiation from the water damaged the DNA in their reproductive cells. This caused their offspring to be born with birth defects.

Beneficial Uses of Nuclear Radiation

In spite of their dangers, radioactive substances are highly useful. They have a wide range of applications from medicine to archeological dating.

Small radioactive sources are present in smoke alarms, as shown in **Figure 7-12.** They release alpha particles, which are charged and produce an electric current. If smoke is present in the air, the smoke particles reduce the flow of this current. The drop in current sets off the alarm before dangerous levels of smoke build up.

Nuclear radiation therapy is used to treat cancer

Controlled doses of nuclear radiation are used for treating diseases such as cancer. For example, certain brain tumors can be targeted with small beams of gamma rays. These beams are focused to kill only the tumor cells. The surrounding healthy tissue is harmed only minimally. Different kinds of tumors throughout the body can be treated in a similar way.

A **B**

Radiation damage

Figure 7-11
After extensive radiation damage, a normal DNA molecule (A) is likely to be rebuilt with its nitrogen bases out of sequence (B).

---

internetconnect

SCiLINKS
NSTA

TOPIC: Mutations
GO TO: www.scilinks.org
KEYWORD: HK1075

Figure 7-12
In a smoke alarm, a small alpha-emitting isotope detects smoke particles in the air.

NUCLEAR CHANGES **237**

Historical Perspective

Point out to students that many aspects of nuclear radiation are either positive or negative, depending on how safely they are used.

On April 26, 1986, the operators of a nuclear reactor at Chernobyl, in Ukraine, improperly managed the water coolant levels. Overheating and an explosion resulted in radioactive materials being blown high into the air. Had the explosion occurred in a containment vessel, such as that required for any nuclear power plant in the United States, no nuclear materials would have escaped into the environment.

MISCONCEPTION ALERT

Irradiation Some foods are irradiated by gamma rays from cobalt-60 or cesium-137 to retard spoilage. Irradiation is FDA approved and most commonly used on fruits, vegetables, and spices. Irradiation kills bacteria, so irradiated food requires fewer chemicals to keep it fresh. Students might think that such foods become radioactive. Irradiated food is not radioactive and is safe to eat.

Step 3 Wrap one pellet in clay, one in a plastic wrap with a twist tie, and one in foil.

Step 4 Drop each covered pellet into a separate beaker.

Step 5 Have students make observations at the end of class and for the next 3 days.

Analysis
1. What does NaOH represent? *(nuclear waste)*
2. Based on the results, how would you store nuclear waste? *(The clay did not leak at all. Waste should be sealed in insoluble, waterproof materials.)*

Danger and Benefits of Nuclear Radiation

Medical Radiation Exposure

Iodine-131 is also used in diagnosing thyroid problems. Because iodine accumulates in the thyroid gland, the amount of radiation detected from iodine-131 indicates how well the thyroid is functioning.

Applying Information

1. Answers might include that the risk increases by approximately 3 percent.
2. Answers will vary but might include the benefits received from radiation, such as an increased recovery rate.

Resources Assign students worksheet *7.3: Real World Applications—Radiation and Medicine* in the **Integration Enrichment Resources** ancillary.

Teaching Tip

Medical Tracers Tell students that examples of medical tracers include technetium-99, which emits gamma rays and has a half-life of 6 hours. It accumulates in areas of rapid cell growth and can be used to detect tumors. Gadolinium-153 is absorbed by bone and is used to diagnose osteoporosis.

238

▶ **radioactive tracer** a radioactive material added to a substance so that the substance's location can be detected later

Radioactive tracers are used in agriculture, medicine, and scientific research

Radioactive tracers are short-lived isotopes, like magnesium-28, that can be observed with sensitive detectors. On research farms, tracers in flowing water can show how fast water moves through the soil or through the stems and leaves of crops. Geologists use tracers to follow underground water flow.

Tracers are widely used in medicine as well. Tracers that tend to concentrate in affected cells are used to locate tumors. Other tracers can follow the path of drugs in the body to help doctors be sure they are delivered to the desired area.

Nuclear Power

Today, nuclear reactors are used in dozens of countries to generate electricity. Energy produced from fission is used to light the homes of millions of families. There are numerous benefits to this source of energy. Nuclear fission does not produce gaseous pollutants, and there is much more energy in the known uranium reserves than in the known reserves of coal and oil.

Medical Radiation Exposure

Graves's disease is an illness in which the thyroid gland produces excess hormones. This excess causes an increase in metabolism, weight loss (despite a healthy appetite), and an irregular heartbeat.

Graves's disease and similar illnesses can be treated in several ways. Parts of the thyroid gland can be surgically removed, or patients can be treated with radioactive

iodine-131. The thyroid cells need iodine to make hormones. When they take in the radioactive iodine-131, the overactive cells are destroyed, and hormone levels drop.

There is some concern that low-level nuclear radiation might cause cancers, such as leukemia. Examine the table below, which shows radiation exposures for different situations and the resulting increased risks in leukemia rates. Note that a *rem* is a unit for measuring doses of nuclear radiation.

Applying Information

1. Given that the typical exposure for radioisotope therapy is about 10 rems, mostly delivered at once, do you think leukemia rates are likely to go up for this group? If so, estimate what risk you would expect.
2. Low-level nuclear radiations and its link to cancers such as leukemia is still in question. Describe what other information would help you evaluate the risks. **WRITING SKILL**

Person tested	Radiation exposure	Measured increased leukemia risk
Hiroshima atomic bomb survivor	27 rem at once	6%
U.S. WW II radiology technician	50 rem over 2 years	0%
Austrian citizen after the nuclear accident at Chernobyl	0.025 rem	0%

ALTERNATIVE ASSESSMENT

Radioactive Tracer

Ask students to write a short paragraph explaining why the half-life of a medical radioactive tracer is so important. The half-life of a medical radioactive tracer must be long enough to reach its destination and be detected but short enough to minimize the length of time healthy cells are exposed to radiation. Paragraphs might include the effects on the human body if either of these requirements is not met.

Nuclear fission has disadvantages

In nuclear fission reactors, energy is produced by triggering a controlled fission reaction in uranium-235. However, the products of fission reactions are often radioactive isotopes. Therefore, serious safety concerns must be addressed. Radioactive products of fission must be handled carefully so they do not escape in the environment releasing nuclear radiation.

Another safety issue involves the safe operation of the nuclear reactors in which the controlled fission reaction is carried out. A nuclear reactor must be equipped with many safety features in case of a reactor failure. The reactor requires considerable shielding and must meet stricter safety requirements than those required for fossil-fuel-burning power plants. Thus, nuclear power plants are expensive to build.

According to regulations, nuclear power plants can be operated for only about 40 years. After that time, they must be shut down. To avoid accidental contamination, this process is very slow and expensive. Equipment used to take the reactor apart can become contaminated and must also be disposed of as radioactive waste. Because of political opposition, few nuclear power plants have operated for 40 years. This is one of the many factors that limit how effective nuclear power can be.

Nuclear waste must be safely stored

Besides the expenses that occur during the life of a nuclear power plant, there is the expense of storing radioactive materials, such as the fuel rods used in the reactors. After their use they must be placed in safe facilities that are well shielded, as shown in **Figure 7-13.** These precautions are necessary to keep nuclear radiation from leaking out which harms living things and taints ground water.

Ideal places for such facilities are sparsely populated areas with little water on the surface or underground. These areas must be free from earthquakes. Even with these considerations, one cannot be sure about long-term safety. Little nuclear waste is stored this way because of debates about where to put facilities.

INTEGRATING

SPACE SCIENCE
Unmanned space probes have greatly increased our knowledge of the solar system. Nuclear-powered probes can venture far from the sun without losing power, as solar-powered probes do. *Cassini,* which has been sent to explore Saturn, has been powered by the heat generated by the radioactive decay of plutonium.

Figure 7-13
Storage facilities for nuclear waste must be designed to contain radioactive materials safely for thousands of years.

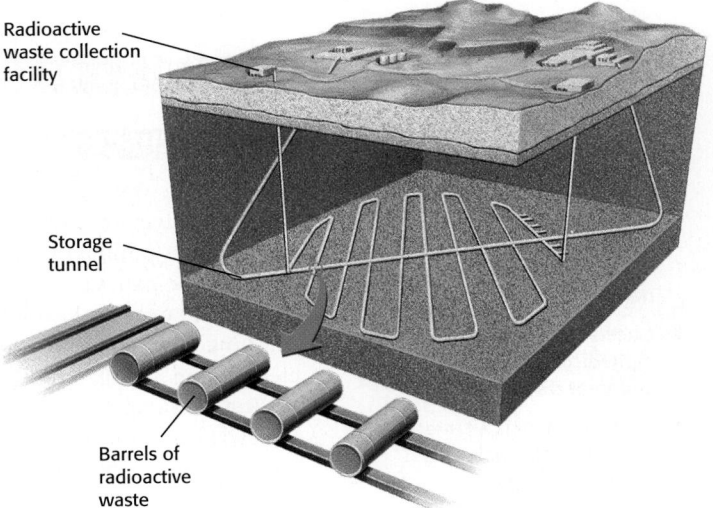

Radioactive waste collection facility

Storage tunnel

Barrels of radioactive waste

INTEGRATING

SPACE SCIENCE Nuclear-powered probes eventually lose power. The older the plutonium in the probe, the less energy the plutonium releases. As time passes, it will no longer be able to release enough energy to operate all the instruments and some of the instruments will be turned off. Eventually, the plutonium will not release enough energy for the probe's vital functions.

Resources Assign students worksheet *7.4: Integrating Space Science—Nuclear-Powered Space Probes* in the **Integration Enrichment Resources** ancillary.

Teaching Tip

Decommissioning Nuclear Reactors Tell students that nuclear power plants are initially commissioned for 40 years, but the license might be renewed for 20 more years. After the license expires or the operation of the plant ceases, the plant must be removed and the area returned to a condition that is not dangerous to the environment. The decommissioning process is long and expensive. It must be completed within 60 years after the license expires.

NUCLEAR CHANGES **239**

Danger and Benefits of Nuclear Radiation

INTEGRATING

SPACE SCIENCE In regular fusion reactions in stars, elements lighter than and including iron are formed. Elements heavier than iron are not formed because they consume instead of release energy when they form. When fuel in the star is spent, the star collapses, ending in a tremendous explosion called a supernova. Supernovas release enough energy to produce elements heavier than iron.

Resources Assign students worksheet *7.2: Integrating Space Science—The Life Cycle of a Star* in the **Integration Enrichment Resources** ancillary.

SECTION 7.3 REVIEW

Check Your Understanding

1. Radiation ionizes and tears apart molecules in the human body. These damaged molecules do not function properly. If enough molecules in a cell are damaged, the cell will not function correctly.
2. Several small beams are focused so that they target the cancerous tissue but are not concentrated in the tissue around it.
3. They can be used to trace water underground, through soil, and through crops. In the human body, tracers locate tumors and trace the path of drugs.

Answers continue on p. 245A.

RESOURCE LINK
STUDY GUIDE

Assign students *Review Section 7.3 Danger and Benefits of Nuclear Radiation.*

The main problem with some radioactive wastes is that they have long half-lives, from hundreds of thousands to millions of years. The oldest human-made structures that are still standing, such as the pyramids of Egypt, are only about 5000 years old. It is hard to imagine whether people could ever build structures that could last 20 to 200 times as long.

Nuclear-fusion reactors are being tested

Another option that holds some promise as an energy source is nuclear fusion. Recall from the last section that fusion takes place when light nuclei, such as hydrogen, are forced together to produce heavier nuclei, such as helium, and energy. Because fusion requires that the electrical repulsion between protons be overcome, these reactions are difficult to produce in the laboratory and have never been produced in a power plant.

The most attractive feature of fusion is that the fuel for it is abundant. Hydrogen is the most common element in the universe and is plentiful in many compounds on Earth, such as water. Earth's oceans could provide enough hydrogen to meet current world energy demands for millions of years.

Unfortunately, practical fusion-based power is far from being a reality. Fusion reactions have some drawbacks. They can produce fast neutrons, a highly energetic and dangerous form of nuclear radiation. Shielding material in the reactor would have to be replaced periodically, increasing the expense of operating a fusion power plant. Lithium can be used to slow down these neutrons, but it is chemically reactive and rare, making its use impractical.

INTEGRATING

SPACE SCIENCE
All heavy elements, from cobalt to uranium, are made when massive stars explode. The pressure produced in the explosion causes nearby nuclei to fuse together, in some cases more than once.

The explosion carries the newly created elements into space. These elements later become parts of new stars and planets. The elements of Earth are believed to have formed in the outer layers of an exploding star.

SECTION 7.3 REVIEW

SUMMARY

▶ Nuclear radiation can damage living cells, causing radiation sickness and birth defects, even death.

▶ Nuclear radiation is used in medicine to diagnose and treat diseases.

▶ Nuclear fission is an alternative to fossil fuels as a source of energy.

CHECK YOUR UNDERSTANDING

1. **Describe** the ways in which nuclear radiation can cause damage to living tissues.
2. **Explain** how gamma rays are used in cancer therapy without harming the patient.
3. **List** several uses for low-level radioactive tracers.
4. **Describe** how sea water could be a source of hydrogen for nuclear fusion.
5. **Critical Thinking** Suppose uranium-238 could undergo fission as easily as uranium-235. Predict how that would change the advantages and drawbacks of fission reactors.

Chapter Highlights

Before you begin, review the summaries of the key ideas of each section, found on pages 228, 234, and 240. The key vocabulary terms are listed on pages 220, 229, and 235.

UNDERSTANDING CONCEPTS

1. When a heavy nucleus decays, it may emit _____.
   a. alpha particles   **c.** gamma rays
   b. neutrons   **d.** All of the above

2. A neutron decays to form a proton and a(n) _____.
   a. alpha particle   **c.** gamma ray
   b. beta particle   **d.** emitted neutron

3. After three half-lives, _____ of a radioactive sample remains.
   a. all   **c.** one-third
   b. one-half   **d.** one-eighth

4. Carbon dating can be used to measure the age of each of the following except _____.
   a. a 7000-year-old human body
   b. a 1200-year-old wooden statue
   c. a 2600-year-old iron sword
   d. a 3500-year-old piece of fabric

5. Of the following elements, only the isotopes of _____ are all radioactive.
   a. nitrogen   **c.** sulfur
   b. gold   **d.** uranium

6. The strong nuclear force _____.
   a. attracts protons to electrons
   b. holds molecules together
   c. holds the atomic nucleus together
   d. attracts electrons to neutrons

7. The process in which a heavy nucleus splits into two lighter nuclei is called _____.
   a. fission   **c.** alpha decay
   b. fusion   **d.** a chain reaction

8. Which condition is not necessary for a chain reaction to occur?
   a. The radioactive sample must have a short half-life.
   b. The neutrons from one split nucleus must cause other nuclei to divide.
   c. The radioactive sample must be at critical mass.
   d. Not too many neutrons must be allowed to leave the radioactive sample.

9. Alpha emitters can be dangerous when they are _____.
   a. inhaled into the lungs
   b. consumed in drinking water
   c. eaten in food
   d. All of the above

10. Which of the following is *not* a use for radioactive isotopes?
   a. as tracers for diagnosing disease
   b. as an additive to paints to increase their durability
   c. as a way of treating forms of cancer
   d. as a way to check the thickness of newly made metal sheets

Using Vocabulary

11. How can *radioactivity* affect the atomic number and mass number of a nucleus that changes after undergoing decay?

12. Describe the main differences between the four main types of nuclear *radiation: alpha particles, beta particles, gamma rays,* and *neutron emission.*

13. Would a substance with an extremely short *half-life* be effective as a *radioactive tracer*?

14. For the nuclear *fission* process, how is *critical mass* important in a *chain reaction*?

15. How does nuclear *fusion* account for the energy produced in stars?

16. What is *background radiation,* and what are its sources?

UNDERSTANDING CONCEPTS

1. d   **6.** c
2. b   **7.** a
3. d   **8.** a
4. c   **9.** d
5. d   **10.** b

Using Vocabulary

11. Radioactivity can increase atomic number (β), decrease it (α), or leave it unaffected (γ). It can either decrease mass number (α) or not affect it (β and γ). When mass number is decreased, the atom is more stable because the strong nuclear force is greater in a smaller nucleus.

12. An alpha particle is a helium nucleus with a charge of +2 and is only slightly penetrating. A beta particle is an electron emitted when a neutron in a nucleus changes into a proton and an electron; its charge is –1 and it is moderately penetrating. A gamma ray is high-energy, penetrating, electromagnetic radiation. Neutron emission occurs as an uncharged particle is emitted when an unstable nucleus undergoes fission.

13. The half-life of the tracer must be long enough to reach its destination and be detected.

14. Enough of the radioactive substance must be present for fission to release enough radiation to cause other nuclei to undergo fission in a continuing process.

15. Nuclear fusion occurs when two small nuclei combine or fuse to form a larger more stable nucleus. This process occurs at extremely high temperatures with the release of energy. The energy in stars is produced when hydrogen nuclei fuse together and release tremendous amounts of energy.

16. Background radiation is radiation that arises naturally from cosmic rays and from radioactive isotopes in the soil and in the air.

BUILDING MATH SKILLS

17. Graphs may vary. One possibility is to graph number of half-lives on the x-axis and percentage of sample remaining on the y-axis.

a. $\dfrac{4 \text{ days}}{8.1 \text{ days/half-life}} =$ 0.494 half-lives; 29%

b. 64.5%

c. 82%

d. 8.8%

18. a. 212 − 4 = 208
$^{212}_{83}\text{Bi} \rightarrow {}^{208}_{81}\text{Tl} + {}^{4}_{2}\text{He}$
83 − 2 = 81
$^{208}_{81}\text{Tl} \rightarrow {}^{208}_{82}\text{Pb} + {}^{0}_{-1}e$

b. 212 − 0 = 212
$^{212}_{83}\text{Bi} \rightarrow {}^{212}_{84}\text{Po} + {}^{0}_{-1}e$
83 − (−1) = 84
$^{212}_{84}\text{Po} \rightarrow {}^{208}_{82}\text{Pb} + {}^{4}_{2}\text{He}$

19. $^{130}_{52}\text{Te} \rightarrow {}^{130}_{53}\text{I} + {}^{0}_{-1}e$

20. $^{149}_{62}\text{Sm} \rightarrow {}^{145}_{60}\text{Nd} + {}^{4}_{2}\text{He}$

BUILDING MATH SKILLS

17. Graphing Using a graphing calculator or computer graphing program, create a graph for the decay of iodine-131, which has a half life of 8.1 days. Use the graph to answer the following questions:

a. Approximately what percentage of the iodine-131 has decayed after 4 days?

b. Approximately what percentage of the iodine-131 has decayed after 12.1 days?

c. What fraction of iodine-131 has decayed after 2.5 half-lives have elapsed?

d. What percentage of the original iodine-131 remains after 3.5 half-lives?

18. Nuclear Decay Bismuth-212 undergoes a combination of alpha and beta decays to form lead-208. Depending on which decay process occurs first, different isotopes are temporarily formed during the process. Identify these isotopes by completing the equations given below:

a. $^{212}_{83}\text{Bi} \longrightarrow {}^{\square}_{\square}\text{X} + {}^{4}_{2}\text{He}$

$^{\square}_{\square}\text{X} \longrightarrow {}^{208}_{82}\text{Pb} + {}^{0}_{-1}e$

b. $^{212}_{83}\text{Bi} \longrightarrow {}^{\blacksquare}_{\square}\text{Y} + {}^{0}_{-1}e$

$^{\square}_{\square}\text{Y} \longrightarrow {}^{208}_{82}\text{Pb} + {}^{4}_{2}\text{He}$

19. Nuclear Decay The longest-lived radioactive isotope yet discovered is the beta-emitter tellurium-130. It has been determined that it would take 2.5×10^{21} years for 99.9% of this isotope to decay. Write the equation for this reaction, and identify the isotope into which tellurium-130 decays.

20. Nuclear Decay It takes about 10^{16} years for just half the samarium-149 in nature to decay by alpha-particle emission. Write the decay equation, and find the isotope that is produced by the reaction.

21. Half-life The ratio of carbon-14 to carbon-12 in a prehistoric wooden artifact is measured to be one-eighth of the ratio measured in a fresh sample of wood from the same region. The half-life of carbon-14 is 5730 years. Determine its age.

22. Half-life Health officials are concerned about radon levels in homes. The half-life of radon-222 is 3.82 days. If a sample of gas taken from a basement contains 4.38 μg of radon-222, how much will remain in the sample after 15.2 days?

THINKING CRITICALLY

23. Applying Knowledge Explain how the equivalence of mass and energy accounts for the small difference between the mass of a uranium-235 nucleus and the masses of the nuclei of its fission fragments.

24. Applying Knowledge Describe the similarities and differences between atomic electrons and beta particles.

25. Creative Thinking Why do people working around radioactive waste in a radioactive storage facility wear badges containing strips of photographic film?

26. Creative Thinking Many radioactive isotopes have half-lives of several billion years. Other radioactive isotopes have half-lives of billionths of a second. Suggest a way in which the half-lives of such isotopes are measured.

27. Problem Solving A radioactive tracer can be used to measure water movement through soil. In order to avoid contamination of ground water, 99.9% of the tracer must decay between the time it is introduced into the soil and the time it reaches the ground-water supply. Estimate this time and calculate the half-life of an ideal tracer that could be used in this application.

DEVELOPING LIFE/WORK SKILLS

28. Allocating Resources An archeologist has collected seven samples from a site: two scraps of fabric, two strips of leather, and three bone fragments. The age of each item must be determined, but the budget for carbon-14 dating is only $4500. Carbon-14 mass spectrometry is an accurate way to find a sample's age, but it costs $820 per sample. Carbon-14 dating by liquid scintillation costs only $400 a sample, but is less reliable. How would you apply either or both of these techniques to the samples to obtain the most reliable information and still stay within your budget?

29. Making Decisions Suppose you are an energy consultant who has been asked to evaluate a proposal to build a power plant in a remote area of the desert. Investigate the requirements for and possible hazards of nuclear-fission power plants, coal-burning power plants, and solar-energy farms. Study research about their environmental impacts. Using this information and what you have learned from this chapter, write a paragraph supporting your decision about which of these power plants would be best for its surroundings.

WRITING SKILL

30. Working Cooperatively Read the following, and discuss with a group of classmates a possible solution to the problem that makes use of radioactivity.

A person believed to be suffering from cancer has been admitted to a hospital. What are some possible methods of diagnosing the patient's conditions? Assuming that cancer is found, how might the disease be treated? Suppose you suspect that another patient is suffering from radiation poisoning. How would you be able to tell?

INTEGRATING CONCEPTS

31. Concept Mapping Copy the unfinished concept map below onto a sheet of paper. Complete the map by writing the correct word or phrase in the lettered boxes.

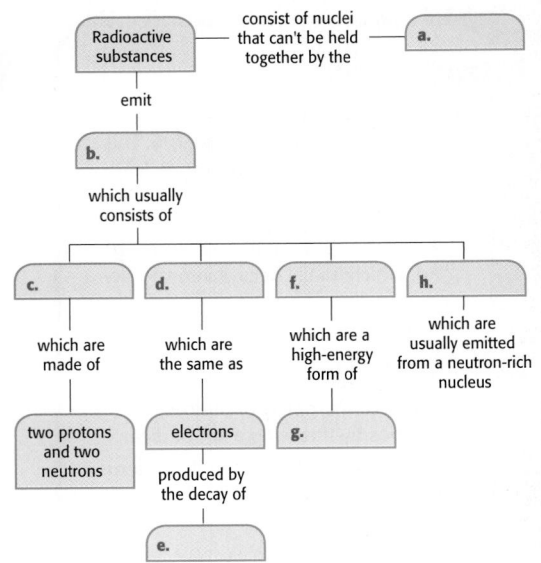

32. Connection to Social Studies Research the philosophical debate surrounding the discovery of radioactive decay. Examine the arguments against the transmutation of elements as presented by scientists such as Lord Kelvin. What ideas were these arguments based on? What experiments convinced most scientists that radioactive elements changed into other elements?

internetconnect

SC*i*LINKS₋ NSTA

TOPIC: Radioactive tracers
GO TO: www.scilinks.org
KEYWORD: HK1076

NUCLEAR CHANGES **243**

21.
$$\frac{1}{8} = \frac{1}{2} \times \frac{1}{2} \times \frac{1}{2}; \text{ three half-lives}$$
$3 \times 5730 \text{ years} = 1.72 \times 10^4$ years

22. $15.2 \text{ days} \times \dfrac{1 \text{ half-life}}{3.82 \text{ days}} =$ about 4 half-lives
$$\frac{1}{2} \times \frac{1}{2} \times \frac{1}{2} \times \frac{1}{2} = \frac{1}{16}$$
$$\frac{1}{16} \times 4.38 \text{ μg} = 0.274 \text{ μg}$$

THINKING CRITICALLY

23. The mass of the nucleus is slightly more than the mass of the fission fragments. During the fission, a small amount of mass is transformed to energy. The total amount of mass and energy is the same in the nucleus and in the products of the fission reaction.

24. They are alike in mass and charge. Beta particles are higher in energy and are not part of a particular atom.

25. Where radioactivity strikes the plate, it will expose it. The amount and pattern of exposure indicates the amount of radiation exposure.

26. Answers might include that it is calculated mathematically using an equation based on current and original amounts of radioactivity and lapsed time.

27. The time lapsed is approximately 10 half-lives.

Answers continue on p. 245B.

Simulating Nuclear Decay Reactions

Introduction

This lab will reinforce students' understanding of radioactive decay and half-life by allowing students to simulate a radioactive decay reaction that converts one isotope into another in a decay series. Students should be able to write the nuclear equations for the different decays represented once they have completed this lab.

Objectives

Students will

► **Use** appropriate lab safety procedures.

► **Simulate** the decay of radioactive isotopes by throwing a set of dice.

► **Graph** the results to identify patterns in the amounts of each isotope present.

Planning

Recommended time: 1 lab period
Materials: *(for each lab group)*

► 10 dice

► large paper cup with plastic lid

► roll of masking tape

► scissors

Introduction

In this lab we will simulate the decay of lead-210 into its isotope lead-206. This decay of lead-210 into its isotope lead-206 occurs in a multistep process. Lead-210, $^{210}_{82}Pb$, first decays into bismuth-210, $^{210}_{83}Bi$, which decays into polonium-210, $^{210}_{84}Po$, which finally decays into the isotope lead-206, $^{206}_{82}Pb$.

Objectives

► **Simulate** the decay of radioactive isotopes by throwing a set of dice.

► **Graph** the results to identify patterns in the amounts of each isotope present.

Materials

10 dice
large paper cup with plastic lid
roll of masking tape
scissors

Simulating Nuclear Decay Reactions

► Preparing for Your Experiment

1. On a sheet of paper, prepare a table as shown below. Leave room to add extra rows at the bottom, if necessary.

Throw #	# of dice representing each Isotope			
	$^{210}_{82}Pb$	$^{210}_{83}Bi$	$^{210}_{84}Po$	$^{206}_{82}Pb$
0 (start)	10	0	0	0
1				
2				
3				
4				

2. Place all 10 dice in the cup. Each die represents an atom of $^{210}_{82}Pb$, a radioactive isotope.

3. Put the lid on the cup, and shake it a few times. Then remove the lid, and spill the dice. In this simulation, each throw represents a *half-life*.

4. All the dice that land with *1, 2,* or *3* up represent atoms of $^{210}_{82}Pb$ that have decayed into $^{210}_{83}Bi$. The remaining dice still represent $^{210}_{82}Pb$ atoms. Separate the two sets of dice. Count the dice, and record the results in your data table.

5. To keep track of the dice representing the decayed atoms, you will make a small mark on them. On a die, the faces with *1, 2,* and *3* share a corner. With a pencil, draw a small circle around this shared corner, and this die represents the $^{210}_{83}Bi$ atoms.

6. Put all the dice back in the cup, shake them and roll them again. In a decay process, there are two possibilities: some atoms decay and some do not. See the diagram below to track your results.

$$^{210}_{82}Pb$$

no decay | decay

$^{210}_{82}Pb$ $^{210}_{83}Bi$ *After Throw 1*

no decay | decay   no decay | decay

$^{210}_{82}Pb$ $^{210}_{83}Bi$ $^{210}_{83}Bi$ $^{210}_{84}Po$ *After Throw 2*

Original radioactive sample

REQUIRED PRECAUTIONS

► Read all safety precautions and discuss them with your students.

► Safety goggles and a lab apron must be worn at all times.

► Long hair and loose clothing must be tied back.

Isotope type	Decays into	Signs of decay	Identifying the atoms in column 2
$^{210}_{82}Pb$	$^{210}_{83}Bi$	Unmarked dice lands on *1*, *2*, or *3*	Mark $^{210}_{83}Bi$ by drawing a circle around the corner where faces *1*, *2*, and *3* meet.
$^{210}_{83}Bi$	$^{210}_{84}Po$	Dice with one loop lands on *1*, *2*, or *3*	Draw a circle around the corner where faces *4*, *5*, and *6* meet.
$^{210}_{84}Po$	$^{206}_{82}Pb$	Dice with two loops lands on *1*, *2*, or *3*	Put a small piece of masking tape over the two circles.
$^{206}_{82}Pb$	Decay ends		

7. After the second throw, we have three types of atoms. Sort the dice into three sets.
   a. The first set consists of dice with a circle drawn on them that landed with *1*, *2*, or *3* facing up. These represent $^{210}_{83}Bi$ atoms that have decayed into $^{210}_{84}Po$.
   b. The second set consists of two types of dice: the dice with one circle that did not land on *1*, *2*, or *3* (undecayed $^{210}_{83}Bi$) and the unmarked dice that landed with *1*, *2*, or *3* facing up (representing the decay of original $^{210}_{82}Pb$ into $^{210}_{83}Bi$).
   c. The third set includes unmarked dice that did not land with *1*, *2*, or *3* facing up. These represent the original undecayed $^{210}_{82}Pb$ atoms.
8. After each throw, do the following: separate the different types of atoms in groups, count the atoms in each group, record your data in your table, and mark the dice to identify each isotope. Use the table above as a guide.
9. For your third throw, put all the dice back into the cup. After the third throw, some of the $^{210}_{84}Po$ will decay into the stable isotope $^{206}_{82}Pb$. Use the table above and step 8 to figure out what else happens after the third throw.
10. Continue throwing the dice until all the dice have decayed into $^{206}_{82}Pb$, which is a stable isotope. Hence, these dice will remain unchanged in all future throws.

▶ Analyzing Your Results

1. Write nuclear decay equations for the nuclear reactions modeled in this lab.
2. In your lab report, prepare a graph like the one shown at right. Using a different color or symbol for each atom, plot the data for all four atoms on the same graph.
3. What do your results suggest about how the amounts of $^{210}_{82}Pb$ and $^{206}_{82}Pb$ on Earth are changing over time?

▶ Defending Your Conclusions

4. $^{210}_{82}Pb$ is continually produced through a series of nuclear decays that begin with $^{238}_{92}U$. Does this information cause you to modify your answer to item 3? Explain why.

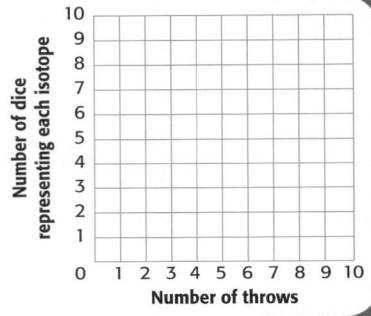

Pre-Lab
Teaching Tips

Some students may have difficulty understanding the concept of probability. Begin the lab with the following activity to illustrate the concept of probability.

- Have each student write his or her name on a strip of paper. Collect all the strips and place them in a container. Ask students how likely it is that his or her name will be picked if someone were to draw a name from the container.

Post-Lab

▶Disposal

▶Analyzing Your Results

1. $^{210}_{82}Pb \rightarrow {}^{210}_{83}Bi + {}^{0}_{-1}e$
   $^{210}_{83}Bi \rightarrow {}^{210}_{84}Po + {}^{0}_{-1}e$
   $^{210}_{84}Po \rightarrow {}^{206}_{82}Pb + {}^{4}_{2}He$
2. Students' graphs will vary. The graphs will depend on the results of throwing 10 dice (governed by probability) as described in the lab. A graph of the sample data in Data Table 1 is shown on p. 245A.
3. Lead-210 decays into lead-206. The amount of lead-210 gradually decreases, while lead-206 increases. Eventually, all the lead-210 will be used up.

Continue on p. 245A.

RESOURCE LINK
DATASHEETS

Have students use *Datasheet 7.3: Skill Builder Lab—Simulating Nuclear Decay Reactions* to record their results.

Skill Builder Lab from page 245

Simulating Nuclear Decay Reactions

Post-Lab

▶ Defending Your Conclusions

4. If lead-210 is continually produced through the decay of uranium-238, then the amount of lead-210 will not necessarily decrease. This depends on how much new lead-210 is produced in a given time and how much lead-210 decays into lead-206.

Data Table 1				
Throw	$^{210}_{82}Pb$	$^{210}_{83}Bi$	$^{210}_{84}Po$	$^{206}_{82}Pb$
0	10	0	0	0
1	6	4	0	0
2	3	5	2	0
3	2	3	4	1
4	0	4	3	3
5	0	2	4	4
6	0	0	3	7
7	0	0	2	8
8	0	0	0	10

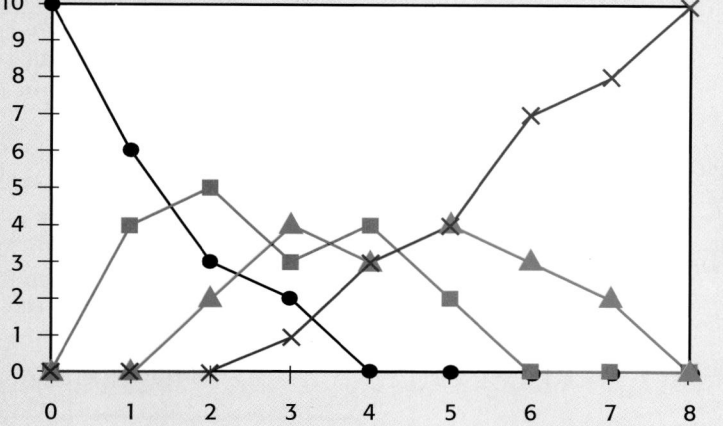
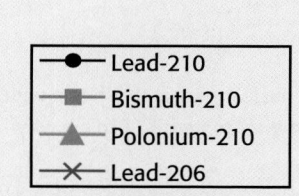

Answers from page 240

SECTION 7.3 REVIEW

4. Hydrogen is a fuel for nuclear fusion. Each molecule of water in the ocean contains two hydrogen atoms, and the electrolysis of this water will supply the hydrogen needed.

5. Advantages might include that fuel would be more abundant, thus lowering expense. The relative radioactivity and usefulness of waste products would need to be evaluated.

Answers from page 243

28. Answers might include assuming that all samples of each type are of approximately the same age. Date one fabric sample, one leather sample, and two bone samples by mass spectrometry for a cost of 4 × $820, or $3280. Confirm these ages by dating the other samples by liquid scintillation for a cost of 3 × $400, or $1200. The total cost is $3280 + $1200, or $4480, which is within the budget.

29. Answers might include the following: Nuclear fission power plants require large amounts of water, which are not present in the desert. Water would have to be piped in or shipped by truck or rail. The local landscape would have to be altered to support the pipeline, roads, or railway. An accidental release of radiation could be harmful to local organisms. Coal would have to be shipped in. If the coal were shipped in by truck, pollution from vehicle exhaust could cause a problem. In addition, burning the coal would produce large amounts of pollution. A solar-energy farm would require the fewest alterations to the landscape and would not release pollutants as part of normal operations or in an accident. However, solar-energy technology needs more development to be practical and cost-efficient.

30. A tracer that concentrates in fast-growing cells, such as tumors, could be used to detect any cancer. Depending on the type of cancer, it could be treated by focused gamma radiation. Symptoms of radiation poisoning include lower white cell count in the blood, hair loss, sterility, unhealthy bones, and cancer.

31. a. strong force
  b. radiation
  c. alpha particles
  d. beta particles
  e. neutrons
  f. gamma rays
  g. electromagnetic radiation
  h. neutrons

32. In 1862, Lord Kelvin estimated that the Earth could not be older than 100 million years, assuming that the Earth was once molten and has been gradually giving off energy as heat. His estimate was, in addition, based on the assumption that the Earth does not produce any new energy as heat on its own.

  However, around that time, Henri Becquerel discovered radioactivity.

  Scientists also discovered that radioactive isotopes, like uranium, in Earth's crust undergo radioactive decay and generate energy as heat. This discovery showed the flaw in Lord Kelvin's estimate of Earth's age based on his assumption that the Earth does not produce any new energy as heat.

  Using dating techniques based on radioactivity, the American chemist Bertram Boltwood estimated in 1905 that Earth's age is between 410 million to 2 billion years old.

  For almost three decades, geologists did not question Lord Kelvin's estimate about Earth's age. In his time, he was very well respected (and he still is for his scientific contributions). Also, his estimates were mathematically obtained and many geologists were too intimidated by the mathematics to question his calculations.

CareerLink

Science Reporter

LINKING CHAPTERS

Corinna Wu reports on matters involving chemistry and materials science, including the topics covered in Chapters 5–7.

Science reporters are usually among the first people to hear about scientific discoveries. News organizations hire science reporters to explain these discoveries to the general public in a clear, understandable, and entertaining way. To learn more about science reporting as a career, read the interview with science reporter Corinna Wu, who writes for Science News *magazine, in Washington, D.C.*

Corinna Wu describes scientific research and discovery in the articles she writes.

"I think writing is something you can learn —it's a craft. Lots of people talk about talents, but I think it's something you can do if you work at it."

 What does a science reporter do?

I write and report news and feature articles for a weekly science news magazine. That entails finding news stories—generally about research. I have to call the researchers and ask them questions about how they did their work and the significance of the work. Then I write a short article explaining the research to ordinary people.

 What is your favorite part of your work?

I like learning about a new subject every week. I get to ask all the stupid questions I was afraid to ask in school.

 How did you become interested in science reporting as a career?

After college, I had a summer internship at NASA, at the Johnson Space Center in Houston, Texas, doing materials research there. I had lots of time to read space news magazines. It was at that time that I realized, "Hey, people write this stuff."

 What kinds of skills are important for a science reporter?

One thing that is really important is to really love writing. If you don't like to write already, it's pretty hard to make yourself do it every day. It helps to have a creative bent, too. It also helps to enjoy explaining things. Science writing by nature is explanatory, more so than other kinds of journalism.

 You have a science background. How does that help you do your job?

I majored in chemistry as an undergraduate and got a master's degree in materials science. I find that I draw on that academic background a lot, in terms of understanding the research.

Do you think a science reporter needs a science background?

Ideally, you should be studying science while writing on the side. But if you have to do one or the other, I'd do science first. It's harder to pick up the science later. Science builds on itself. It takes years to really get a grasp of it.

 Why do you think science reporting is important?

Science and technology are becoming part of our everyday lives. It's important for people to keep up on research in these areas. There is an element of education in everything you write.

 What advice do you have for students who are interested in science reporting?

Read as much as you can—newspapers, magazines, books. Nothing beats getting real experience writing. If you have a newspaper or magazine at school, get involved in that. You draw on academic experiences—you don't know when they will become useful.

 internet**connect**

 SCLINKS NSTA

TOPIC: Science writer
GO TO: www.scilinks.org
KEYWORD: HK1799

Musical Metal

Science catches up with the shimmering sound of steel drums

By CORINNA WU

"Science is a strong tool, a strong way of looking at the world. I feel that trying to introduce people to that way of looking at the world is very important."
—CORINNA WU

247

Historical Perspective

Science Service, the organization which publishes *Science News* magazine, has been in existence since 1921. It was originally founded to provide reliable science news for newspapers in the United States. The first editors of the service were concerned that most other science reporting was overly sensationalized.

The weekly *Science News* magazine, originally entitled *Science News Letter*, was first published on March 13, 1922. The publication was an outgrowth of Science Service's wire reports for newspapers. It was intended to explain scientific news to nonscientists. While the wire service was discontinued when many newspapers began to assign reporters to cover science in the 1960s, the magazine has been published ever since.

In 1941, Science Service began the Science Talent Search, an annual competition that showcases original research work by high school students.

UNIT
3

READING SKILL BUILDER

Brainstorming Write the titles of the chapters on the chalkboard. In a class discussion, ask students to discuss these terms and create definitions for each one. Record the definitions so they can be referenced later when the specific scientific meaning of words, like *force, work,* and *heat,* are taught in the chapters that follow.

MISCONCEPTION ALERT

Forces Many students' views of the causes of motion do not take into account the laws of Newton, which will be studied in Chapter 8. A common misconception is that most motion can be explained by the phrase "What goes up must come down."

Motion and Energy

249

Tailoring the Program to YOUR Classroom

CHAPTER 8

Motion and Forces

Annotated Descriptions of the Correlated National Science Standards

The following descriptions summarize the National Science Standards that specially relate to Chapter 8. For the full text of the Standards, see p. 40T.

SECTION 8.1
Motion
Science as Inquiry
SAI 1

SECTION 8.2
Acceleration and Force
Physical Science
PS 4b
Unifying Concepts and Processes
UCP 2

SECTION 8.3
Newton's Laws of Motion
Physical Science
PS 4a
Unifying Concepts and Processes
UCP 2

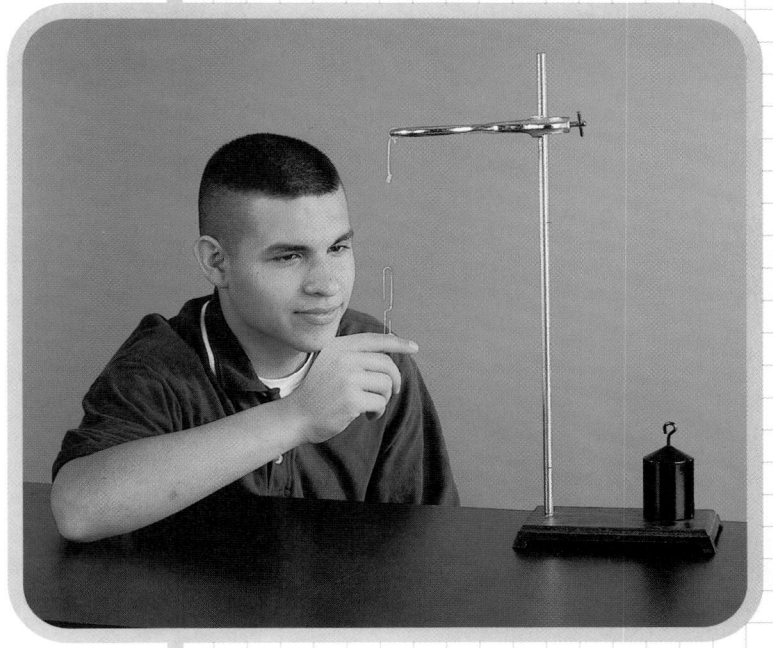

Use the Planning Guide on the next page to help you organize your lessons.

MATH AND COMPUTER RESOURCES

Chapter 8	Math Skills	Assess	Media/Computer Skills
Section 8.1	**ATE** **Cross-Discipline Teaching,** p. 250 **BS** **Worksheet 3.6:** Rates of Change **BS** **Worksheet 6.5:** Slope of a Line **PE** **Math Skills** Velocity, p. 255 **ATE** **Additional Examples** p. 255 **PE** **Math Skills** Momentum, p. 257 **ATE** **Additional Examples** p. 257	**MS** Worksheet 13 **MS** Worksheet 14 **PE** **Practice,** p. 255 **PE** **Practice,** p. 257 **PE** Section Review 7–9, p. 258 **PE** **Building Math Skills,** pp. 275–276, items 15–19 **PE** **Problem Bank,** p. 696, 61–70	■ Section 8.1 💿 *DISC TWO, MODULE 11* Conservation of Momentum **PE** Real World Applications, p. 256 **CNN** Presents **Physical Science Segment 2** Land Speed Record **CRT** Worksheet 2
Section 8.2	**BS** **Worksheet 5.5:** Rearranging Algebraic Equations **PE** **Math Skills** Acceleration, p. 260 **ATE** **Additional Examples** p. 260	**MS** Worksheet 15 **PE** **Practice,** p. 260 **PE** Section Review 7, 8, p. 267 **PE** **Building Math Skills,** pp. 275–276, items 14, 20, 21 **PE** **Problem Bank,** p. 697, 71–75	■ Section 8.2 💿 *DISC TWO, MODULE 9* Speed and Acceleration **CNN** Presents **Physical Science Segment 4** Crash-Test Dummies **CRT** Worksheet 4
Section 8.3	**PE** **Math Skills** Newton's Second Law, p. 270 **ATE** **Additional Examples** p. 270	**MS** Worksheet 16 **PE** **Practice,** p. 270 **PE** Section Review 5, 6, p. 274 **PE** **Problem Bank,** p. 697, 76–80	■ Section 8.3 **CNN** Presents **Physical Science Segment 6** Egg Drop Contest **CRT** Worksheet 6 **CNN** Presents **Physical Science Segment 7** Zero-Gravity Plane **CRT** Worksheet 7

PE Pupil's Edition **ATE** Annotated Teacher's Edition **MS** Math Skills **BS** Basic Skills
IE Integration Enrichment ■ Guided Reading Audio **CRT** Critical Thinking

PHYSICAL SCIENCE INTERACTIVE TUTOR

READING SKILL BUILDER
The following activities found in the Annotated Teacher's Edition provide techniques for developing useful reading strategies to increase your students' reading comprehension skills.

Section 8.1 **Brainstorming,** p. 250
          Paired Reading, p. 256
Section 8.2 **Discussion,** p. 260
Section 8.3 **Paired Reading,** p. 269

Smithsonian Institution®
Visit www.si.edu/hrw for additional online resources.

Spanish Resources
The following resources are made available for students who speak Spanish as their first language.

Spanish Resources Guided Reading Audio CD-ROM
Chapter 8

Spanish Glossary
Chapter 8

Motion and Forces

CLASSROOM RESOURCES		
FOCUS	**TEACH**	**HANDS-ON**

Section 8.1 Motion

BLOCK 1
45 minutes

ATE **RSB** Brainstorming, p. 250 **ATE** Focus Activities 1, 2, p. 251 **PE** Speed and Velocity, pp. 252–256 ★ Focus Transparency LT 26	**ATE** **Skill Builder** Interpreting Visuals, p. 251 Interpreting Diagrams, p. 253 Graphs, p. 254 **BLM** 23 Distance–Time Graph	**IE** Worksheet 8.1 **IE** Worksheet 8.2 **PE** Real World Applications *Hiking,* p. 256

BLOCK 2
45 minutes

ATE **RSB** Paired Reading, p. 256 **PE** Momentum, pp. 256–258		**IE** Worksheet 8.9

Section 8.2: Acceleration and Force

BLOCK 3
45 minutes

ATE **RSB** Discussion, p. 260 **ATE** **Demo 1** Acceleration, p. 259 **PE** Acceleration, pp. 259–262 ★ Focus Transparency LT 27	**ATE** **Skill Builder** Graphing, p. 261 **BLM** 24 Constant Velocity Graph **BLM** 25 Acceleration Graphs	**IE** Worksheet 8.3 **LE 8** *Determining Your* *Acceleration on a Bicycle* **DS** 8.4

BLOCK 4
45 minutes

ATE **Demo 2** Gravity Is a Weak Force, p. 266 **PE** Force, pp. 262–267	**TT** 22 Balanced Forces	**PE** Science and the Consumer, p. 264 **IE** Worksheet 8.4

Section 8.3: Newton's Laws of Motion

BLOCK 5
45 minutes

ATE **RSB** Paired Reading, p. 269 **PE** Newton's First and Second Laws, pp. 268–270 ★ Focus Transparency LT 28	**ATE** **Skill Builder** Interpreting Visuals, p. 268	**PE** Quick Activity *Newton's First Law,* p. 269 **DS** 8.1 **IE** Worksheet 8.7

BLOCK 6
45 minutes

PE Free Fall and Weight; Newton's Third Law, pp. 271–274	**TT** 23 Terminal Velocity	**IE** Worksheets 8.5, 8.6, 8.8 **PE** Inquiry Lab *How are action and* *reaction forces related?* p. 273 **DS** 8.2 **PE** Design Your Own Lab *Testing the* *Strength of a Human Hair,* p. 278 **DS** 8.3

CLASSROOM RESOURCES

HOMEWORK	ASSESS
PE Section Review 2–8, p. 258 **Chapter 8 Review,** p. 275, items 1, 2, 9, 15–17	**SG** Chapter 8 Pretest
PE Section Review 1, 9, p. 258 **Chapter 8 Review,** p. 275, items 18, 19	**SG** Section 8.1
PE Section Review 1, 7, 8, p. 267 **Chapter 8 Review,** p. 275, items 3, 14, 20, 21	
PE Section Review 2–6, p. 267 **Chapter 8 Review,** p. 275, items 5, 10, 13	**SG** Section 8.2
PE Section Review 1, 3–5, p. 274 **Chapter 8 Review,** p. 275, items 4, 6–8, 22–24	
PE Section Review 2, 6, p. 274 **Chapter 8 Review,** p. 275, items 11, 12, 25	**SG** Section 8.3

BLOCK 7

PE Chapter 8 Review
  Thinking Critically 26–32, p. 277
  Developing Life/Work Skills 33–35, p. 277
  Integrating Concepts 36–38, p. 277
SG Chapter 8 Mixed Review

BLOCK 8

Chapter Tests
  Holt Science Spectrum: A Physical Approach
  Chapter 8 Test

One-Stop Planner CD–ROM with Test Generator
  Holt Science Spectrum Test Generator
  FOR MACINTOSH AND WINDOWS
  Chapter 8

Teaching Resources
  Scoring Rubrics and assignment evaluation
  checklist.

---

internet connect

SCiLINKS
NSTA

National Science Teachers
Association
Online Resources:
www.scilinks.org

The following *sci*LINKS Internet resources can be found
in the student text for this chapter.

Page 251 **TOPIC:** Forces **KEYWORD:** HK1081	Page 277 **TOPIC:** Graphing speed, velocity, acceleration **KEYWORD:** HK1085
Page 264 **TOPIC:** Friction **KEYWORD:** HK1083	

CNNfyi.com   www.cnnfyi.com

Visit this site for coverage of current events and related
classroom resources.

PE Pupil's Edition   **ATE** Annotated Teacher's Edition
RSB Reading Skill Builder   **DS** Datasheets
IE Integrated Enrichment   **SG** Study Guide
LE Laboratory Experiments
TT Teaching Transparencies   **BLM** Blackline Masters
★ Lesson Focus Transparency

CHAPTER 8

Motion and Forces

Tapping Prior Knowledge

Be sure students understand the following concepts:

Chapter 1 Units of measurement

Chapter 2 Mass

READING SKILL BUILDER

Brainstorming Write on the chalkboard the words *movement* and *force*. Ask students to come up with words or phrases that relate to the concepts of movement and force. This exercise should help identify your students' preconceptions about motion and forces. Encourage each student to write their ideas down.

Based on their ideas, ask them to predict if a force (acting on an object) is removed, would the object *necessarily* come to a stop. Ask them the same question when the chapter is finished.

Based on everyday experiences that are dominated by frictional forces, many of us develop inaccurate preconceptions about forces and motion.

Chapter Preview

250

RESOURCE LINK
STUDY GUIDE

Assign students *Pretest Chapter 8 Motion and Forces* before beginning Section 8.1.

CROSS-DISCIPLINE TEACHING

Fine Arts The technology for creating motion films was developed by inventing a way to photograph a live action many times per second and then rapidly playing the photo frames. In regular films, 24 frames per second are projected to produce the perception of continuous motion.

Life Science Ask a biology teacher to visit your classroom and explain the effects of space flight on the human body.

Social Studies During your discussion of gravity, rent and play the video of Neil Armstrong's first step on the moon during the Apollo 11 mission.

Mathematics Present the mathematical form of Newton's universal law of gravitation:

$$F_g = \frac{Gm_1m_2}{r^2}$$

Use the equation to explain how gravitational force, F_g, varies depending on the masses, m, of the objects and the distance, r, between their centers.

Focus ACTIVITY

Background A car cruises down a track at 48 km/h (30 mi/h). Suddenly, the car smashes into an immovable block of steel and concrete, stopping in only fifteen-hundredths of a second. The occupant is not wearing a seat belt and is thrown against the steering wheel. The occupant's torso experiences the same force of impact it would have received if the occupant had fallen off the roof of a one-story house! The occupant escapes without any injuries because the occupant is a crash-test dummy.

Crash-test dummies come in various sizes and shapes. Each dummy is outfitted with sensors that record how the dummy moves and how hard it presses against different parts of the car during a crash when the dummy is strapped in by a seat belt. Automobile manufacturers use this information to develop and improve seat belts and other safety devices, such as air bags and padded dashboards.

Activity 1 Sit in the driver's seat of a parked car. Without your seat belt fastened, move forward to see what parts of your body would strike the car if you were in a head-on crash. Repeat this test with your seat belt fastened, and then perform the same two tests while sitting in the front passenger seat. Based on your results, where do you think sensors should be placed on a crash-test dummy to provide the most useful information when the dummy is wearing a seat belt? Where should sensors be placed on the dummy when the dummy is not wearing a seat belt?

Activity 2 You can investigate the Earth's pull on objects by using a stopwatch, a board, and two balls of different sizes. Set one end of the board on a chair and the other end on the ground. Time each ball as it rolls down the board. Do this several times with the board at different angles. Does the heavier ball move faster, slower, or take the same amount of time as the lighter one? What factors do you think might have affected the motion of the two balls?

internetconnect

SC*LINKS*.
NSTA

TOPIC: Forces
GO TO: www.scilinks.org
KEYWORD: HK1081

Scientists use crash-test dummies to learn what happens to passengers involved in an automobile accident. During a crash, sensors inside each dummy gather information and feed it to a computer outside the car.

Focus ACTIVITY

Background The number of accidental deaths in the United States related to inflating air bags has steadily increased among small children and women. Automobile manufacturers are now required by the federal government to test air bag safety on infant and female crash-test dummies. In the past, only male crash-test dummies were used.

Activity 1 The sensors should be located in the waist and torso of a crash test dummy when the dummy is wearing the seat belt. The sensors should be located in the torso and head of a crash test dummy when the dummy is not wearing the seat belt.

Activity 2 Do not allow students to use hollow balls for this activity. The weight of the balls is not important. The greater the angle, the faster the ball accelerates.

SKILL BUILDER

Interpreting Visuals The effect of head-on collisions can be easily carried out by running the car containing the crash-test dummy into a barrier. How would the car manufacturer test the effectiveness of the seatbelt in a rear-end collision without using two cars?

Scheduling

Refer to pp. 250A–250D for lecture, classwork, and assignment options for Section 8.1.

★ **Lesson Focus**

Use transparency *LT 26* to prepare students for this section.

Historical Perspective

After the failed effort of ancient Greeks like Aristotle and Zeno in describing motion, almost 1900 years passed before Galileo found himself conducting "scientific experiments" to understand motion.

During students' first exposure to ideas like speed, velocity, and acceleration, research shows that very few students grasp the subtleties of describing motion. The definitions of average speed, average velocity, and average acceleration are deceivingly simple. But the idea of speed at a particular moment (instantaneous speed) involves sophisticated mathematical ideas.

To help students grasp the concept of speed, first introduce constant motion. The definition of constant motion—an object covering equal distances in equal amounts of time—naturally motivates the concept of speed.

Describing nonconstant motion—an object that does not cover equal distances in equal intervals of time—provides the motivation to develop the concept of average speed.

252

8.1

Motion

▶ **KEY TERMS**

speed
velocity
momentum

OBJECTIVES

▶ Relate speed to distance and time.
▶ Distinguish between speed and velocity.
▶ Recognize that all moving objects have momentum.
▶ Solve problems involving time, distance, velocity, and momentum.

We are surrounded by moving things. From a car moving in a straight line to a satellite traveling in a circle around the Earth, objects move in a variety of ways. In everyday life motion is so common, it seems to appear very simple. But, in fact, understanding motion requires some new and advanced ideas. How do we know when an object is moving?

Speed and Velocity

An object is moving if its position changes against some background that stays the same. In **Figure 8-1,** a horse is seen galloping against the background of stationary trees. This stationary background is called a *reference frame.* The change in position in a reference frame is measured in terms of the distance traveled by an object from a fixed point.

Our everyday experience shows that some objects move faster than others. **Speed** describes how fast an object moves. **Figure 8-1** shows speeds for some familiar things. A flying eagle moves faster than a galloping horse. But how do we determine speed?

▶ **speed** distance traveled divided by the time interval during which the motion occurred

Figure 8-1
We encounter a wide range of speeds in our everyday life.

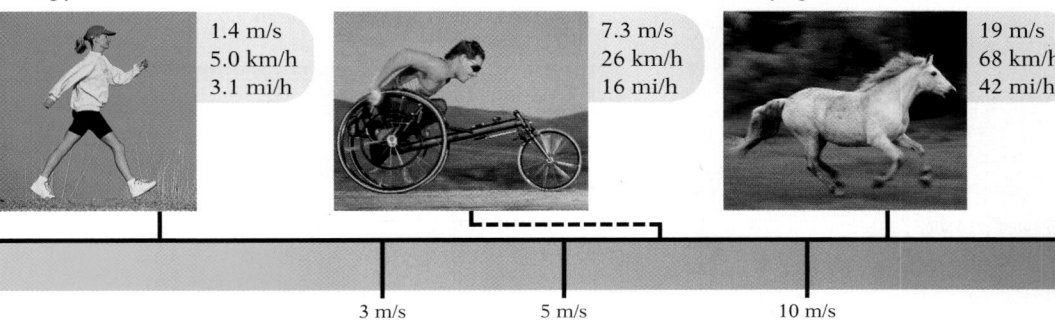

Walking person
1.4 m/s
5.0 km/h
3.1 mi/h

Wheelchair racer
7.3 m/s
26 km/h
16 mi/h

Galloping horse
19 m/s
68 km/h
42 mi/h

3 m/s   5 m/s   10 m/s

Speed measurements involve distance and time

To find speed, you must measure two quantities: distance traveled by an object and the time it takes to travel that distance. Notice that all the speeds shown in **Figure 8-1** are expressed as a distance unit divided by a time unit. The SI unit for speed is meters per second (m/s). Speed is sometimes expressed in other units, such as kilometers per hour (km/h) or miles per hour (mi/h).

Constant speed is the simplest type of motion

When an object covers equal distances in equal amounts of time, it is moving at a **constant speed**. So what does it mean if a race car has a constant speed of 96 m/s? It means that the race car travels a distance of 96 m every second, as shown in **Table 8-1**.

Speed can be determined from a distance-time graph

We can investigate the relationship between speed, distance, and time by plotting a distance-time graph. The distance covered by an object is noted at regular intervals of time. The time and distance values are plotted along the horizontal and vertical axes respectively. For a race car moving with constant speed, the distance-time graph is a straight line as shown in **Figure 8-2**. The speed of the race car can be found by calculating the slope of the line.

Suppose all objects in **Figure 8-1** are moving at a constant speed. The distance-time graph of each object is drawn in **Figure 8-2**. Notice that the distance-time graph of a faster moving object is steeper than a slower moving object. An object at rest, such as a parked car, has a speed of 0 m/s. Its position does not change as time goes by. So, the distance-time graph of a resting object is a flat line with a slope of zero.

Table 8-1 Distance-Time Values for a Racing Car

Time (s)	Distance (m)
0	0
1	96
2	192
3	288
4	384

Figure 8-2
When the motion of an object is graphed by plotting the distance it travels versus time, the slope of the resulting line is the object's speed.

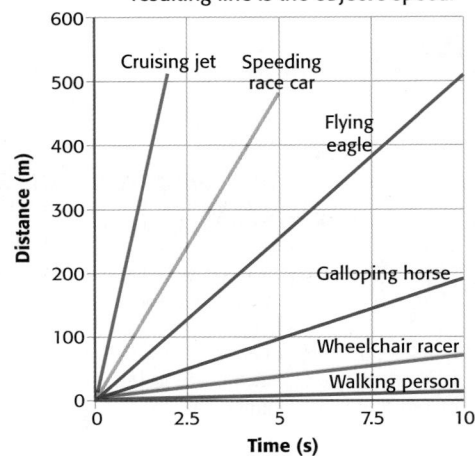

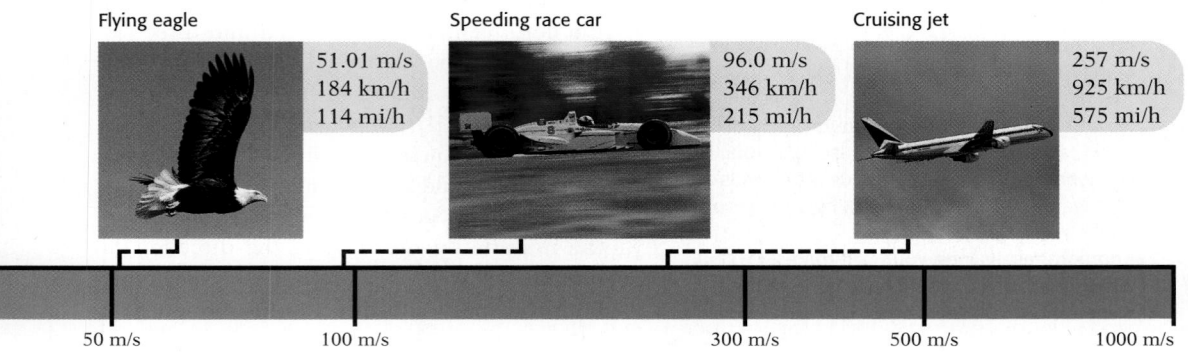

MOTION AND FORCES **253**

Teaching Tip

Average Speed Calculating speed as distance divided by time always yields average speed. Because the time you divide by is some finite amount (even if very small), the speed is always the average speed for that time interval.

SKILL BUILDER

Interpreting Diagrams Explain to students that the scale in **Figure 8-1** is adjusted so that objects with vastly different speeds can be shown on a page spread. If the figure were drawn using a linear scale in which 3 m/s was at the same position on the page, the position for the jet's speed (257 m/s) would be 5.65 m, or about 18 ft, to the right of the starting point. Therefore, a logarithmic scale is used to arrange the different objects of varying speeds shown in **Figure 8-1**.

RESOURCE LINK
BASIC SKILLS

Assign students worksheet *6.5: Slope of a Line* in the **Basic Skills Worksheets** ancillary as a review of the concept of slopes, which provides a geometrical approach of speed, velocity, and acceleration.

Motion

Graphs Plot on the chalk-board a graph of the following data for a runner.

Time (s)	Position (m)
0	0
10	20
20	30
30	30

Ask students during which time interval the runner is moving faster, *(0 s to 10 s)*, moving slower, *(10 s to 20 s)*, and standing still, *(20 s to 30 s)*. Point out that the steeper the slope of the line, the faster the runner moves.

Connection to SOCIAL STUDIES

City planners are struggling with balancing urban sprawl and its impact on the air quality of the city due to greater car emissions.

Making the Connection
Check student answers for items 1, 2, and 3.

Resources Assign students worksheet *8.1: Connection to Social Studies—An Expanding City* in the **Integration Enrichment Resources** ancillary.

Figure 8-3
A wheelchair racer's speed can be determined by timing the racer on a set course.

▶ **velocity** quantity describing both speed and direction

Connection to SOCIAL STUDIES

Many inventions have increased the speed at which people can travel. Cars have greatly changed the relationship between where people live and where they work. This has led to the growth of suburbs surrounding cities.

Making the Connection

1. Use a map to find the shortest straight-line path between your home and school. Calculate how long it would take you to walk to school along this path at a speed of 5.0 km/h.
   (**Hint:** 1 mi = 1.6 km)
2. Now determine the shortest route a school bus could take to go from your house to school. If you were to ride in a school bus that travels an average of 70 km/h (40 mi/h), how long would it take you to get to school?
3. Compare results with your classmates. Explain whether all of you would have gone to the same school 100 years ago.

Speed is calculated as distance divided by time

Most objects do not move with constant speed. The speed of an object can change from one instant to another. A useful quantity called *average* speed can be defined. Average speed is simply the distance covered by an object divided by the time it takes to travel that distance. From this definition, we can write a simple mathematical formula to calculate average speed.

Speed Equation

$$speed = \frac{distance}{time} \qquad v = \frac{d}{t}$$

Suppose a wheelchair racer finishes a 132 m race in 18 s. By inserting the time and distance measurements in the formula, you can calculate the racer's average speed.

$$v = \frac{d}{t} = \frac{132 \text{ m}}{18 \text{ s}} = 7.3 \text{ m/s}$$

The racer's average speed over the entire distance is 7.3 m/s. But the racer probably did not travel at this speed for the whole race. The racer's pace might have been faster at the start of the race and slower near the end as the racer got tired. Suppose we are interested in the average speed during just the first half of the race. To calculate the average speed during the first half, we need to find the time it takes to travel the first 66 m.

Velocity describes both speed and direction

Sometimes, describing the speed of an object is not enough; you may also need to know the direction in which the object is moving. In 1997, a 200 kg (450 lb) lion escaped from a zoo in Florida. The lion was located by searchers in a helicopter. The helicopter crew was able to guide searchers on the ground by reporting the lion's **velocity,** or its speed and direction of motion. The escaped lion's velocity may have been reported as 4.5 m/s *to the north* or 2.0 km/h *toward the highway*.

Without knowing the direction of the lion's motion, it would have been impossible to predict the lion's position. This example shows the importance of knowing the direction of motion, as well as its speed. By specifying both the speed and direction of motion, you get an object's velocity.

The direction of motion can be described in various ways. For instance, you can indicate the direction as east, west, south, or north of some fixed point, or you can specify the angle from a fixed line. Also, the direction can be described as positive or negative along the line of motion. So, if a body is moving in one direction, then it has positive velocity, and if it is moving in the opposite direction, then it has negative velocity. *In this book, velocity will always be considered to be positive in the direction of motion.*

MISCONCEPTION **ALERT**

Are Speed and Velocity the Same? Help students distinguish between speed and velocity by describing a car moving at constant speed as it turns a corner. The speed remains constant, but its velocity has changed because the direction in which the car is moving has changed.

Math Skills

Velocity Metal stakes are sometimes placed in glaciers to help measure a glacier's movement. For several days in 1936, Alaska's Black Rapids glacier surged as swiftly as 89 m per day down the valley. Find the glacier's velocity in meters per second. Remember, velocity includes the direction of motion.

1 **List the given and unknown values.**
Given: *time*, $t = 1$ day
distance, $d = 89$ m
Unknown: *velocity*, $v = ?$ (m/s and direction)

2 **Perform any necessary conversions.**
To find the velocity in meters per second, the value for time must be in seconds.

$$t = 1 \text{ day} = 24 \text{ h} \times \frac{60 \text{ min}}{1 \text{ h}} \times \frac{60 \text{ s}}{1 \text{ min}}$$

$$t = 86\,400 \text{ s} = 8.64 \times 10^4 \text{ s}$$

3 **Write the equation for speed.**

$$speed = \frac{distance}{time} \qquad v = \frac{d}{t}$$

4 **Insert the known values into the equation, and solve.**

$$v = \frac{d}{t} = \frac{89 \text{ m}}{8.64 \times 10^4 \text{ s}} \quad \text{(For velocity, include direction.)}$$

$$v = 1.0 \times 10^{-3} \text{ m/s down the valley}$$

Practice

Practice HINT

▶ When a problem requires you to calculate velocity, you can use the speed equation on the previous page.
▶ The speed equation can also be rearranged to isolate distance on the left side of the equation in the following way.

$$v = \frac{d}{t}$$

Multiply both sides by *t*.

$$v \times t = \frac{d}{t} \times t$$

$$d = vt$$

You will need to use this form of the equation in Practice Problem 3.
▶ In Practice Problem 4, you will need to rearrange the equation to isolate time on the left side of the equation.

Velocity
1. Find the velocity in meters per second of a swimmer who swims exactly 110 m toward the shore in 72 s.
2. Find the velocity in meters per second of a baseball thrown 38 m from third base to first base in 1.7 s.
3. Calculate the distance in meters a cyclist would travel in 5.00 hours at an average velocity of 12.0 km/h to the southwest.
4. Calculate the time in seconds an Olympic skier would take to finish a 2.6 km race at an average velocity of 28 m/s downhill.

Math Skills

Resources Assign students worksheet *13: Velocity* in the **Math Skills Worksheets** ancillary.

Additional Examples

Velocity Suppose the lion in the previous discussion moves due east at different speeds so that it travels 25 km in 4.0 hours. What is the lion's average velocity? What is its speed?

Answer: velocity: 6.2 km/h east = 1.7 m/s east; speed: 6.2 km/h = 1.7 m/s

What would the lion's velocity be if it traveled 15 km due north in 2 hours and 15 minutes?

Answer: 6.7 km/h north = 1.9 m/s north

Solution Guide

1. $v = \dfrac{d}{t} = \dfrac{110 \text{ m}}{72 \text{ s}} = 1.5$ m/s toward shore

2. $\dfrac{38 \text{ m}}{1.7 \text{ s}} = 22$ m/s toward first base

3. $d = vt = (12.0 \text{ km/h})(5.00 \text{ h}) = 60.0 \text{ km}(1000 \text{ m/km}) = 6.00 \times 10^4$ m

4. $t = \dfrac{d}{v} = \dfrac{(2.6 \text{ km})(1000 \text{ m/km})}{(28 \text{ m/s})} = 93$ s

Hiking
Applying Information

1. about 4 km
2. 754 ft
3. (4 km)(1 h/5 km) + (754 ft)(1 h/2000 ft) = 0.8 h + 0.4 h = 1.2 h
4. Check students' programs for accuracy.

Resources Assign students worksheet *8.2: Real World Applications—Hiking in Yellowstone* in the **Integration Enrichment Resources** ancillary.

Paired Reading
Pair each student with a partner. Have each student read silently about momentum. As students read, have them place a check mark on a self-adhesive note next to passages they understand and a question mark on a self-adhesive note next to passages they find confusing or have questions about.

After students finish reading, ask one student to summarize what he or she understood, referring to the text when needed. The second student should add anything omitted. The second student should then continue the discussion by pointing out the passages that he or she did not understand.

The first reader should help the second with ideas that were unclear and discuss passages that he or she did not understand. Both readers should work together to come to an understanding of all the passages. Have each paired group create a list of questions to pose to the class about ideas or passages that are still unclear after their discussion.

Hiking Experienced hikers use Naismith's rule to help them calculate the length of a trip. Naismith's rule is as follows:

Allow 1 hour for every 5 km (3 mi) you measure on the map, then add 1 hour for every 600 m (2000 ft) you have to climb.

This rule works for a fit walker who is not carrying a lot of equipment.

Applying Information
1. A group of hikers need to travel from Ambition Lake, at 3293 m (10 805 ft), to Blackcap Mountain, at 3523 m (11 559 ft).

They plan to travel by the route shown on the map at right. Use the map's distance scale to determine how far the hikers have to travel.
2. How many feet must the hikers climb?
3. Use Naismith's rule to calculate how long it will take the hikers to reach their destination.
4. Create a spreadsheet or graphing calculator program that applies Naismith's rule. **COMPUTER SKILL**

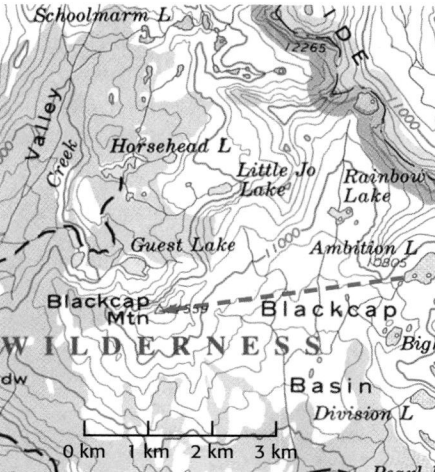

   The velocity of an object changes if its speed or direction changes or both change. If you watch a car's speedometer, you will notice that the speed changes from time to time. This shows a change in the velocity of the car. Even when a car has a constant speed, its velocity can change if the car turns. Why? Because the car's direction has changed.

Momentum

Velocity is not the only important quantity when objects are in motion. For example, a train is more difficult to stop than a car moving along the same path at the same speed. The train is more difficult to stop because it has a greater mass than the car. What if the car is moving very fast and the train is moving very slowly? In that case, is it possible that the car would be more difficult to stop? How do we know which object would be more difficult to stop?

Moving objects have momentum

The object with more **momentum** would be more difficult to stop. The momentum of an object depends on both its velocity and its mass. For an object moving in a straight line, momentum is calculated by simply multiplying an object's mass by its velocity.

▶ **momentum** a quantity defined as the product of an object's mass and its velocity

Like velocity, momentum also has direction. An object's momentum is in the same direction as its velocity. The momentum of the bowling ball shown in **Figure 8-4** is directed toward the pins and is calculated by multiplying its mass and its velocity. The SI unit for momentum is kilograms times meters per second (kg•m/s).

> **Momentum Equation (for straight-line motion)**
> $$momentum = mass \times velocity$$
> $$p = mv$$

The momentum equation shows that for a given velocity, the more mass an object has, the greater its momentum is. A massive semi truck on the highway, for example, has much more momentum than a sports car traveling at the same velocity. The momentum equation also shows that the faster an object is moving, the greater its momentum is. For instance, a fast-moving train has much more momentum than a slow-moving train with the same mass. If an object is not moving, its momentum is zero.

Figure 8-4
Because of the large mass and high speed of this bowling ball, it has a lot of momentum and is able to knock over the pins easily.

Math Skills

Momentum Calculate the momentum of a 6.00 kg bowling ball moving at 10.0 m/s down the alley.

1 **List the given and unknown values.**
  Given: *mass*, $m = 6.00$ kg
  velocity, $v = 10.0$ m/s down the alley
  Unknown: *momentum*, $p = ?$ kg•m/s (and direction)

2 **Write the equation for momentum.**
  $momentum = mass \times velocity$
  $p = mv$

3 **Insert the known values into the equation, and solve.**
  $p = mv = 6.00$ kg $\times 10.0$ m/s
  $p = 60.0$ kg•m/s down the alley

Practice

Momentum

1. Calculate the momentum of the following objects:
  a. a 75 kg speed skater moving forward at 16 m/s
  b. a 135 kg ostrich running north at 16.2 m/s
  c. a 5.0 kg baby on a train moving eastward at 72 m/s
  d. a 0.8 kg kitten running to the left at 6.5 m/s
  e. a 48.5 kg passenger on a train stopped on the tracks

MOTION AND FORCES **257**

Section 8.1

Motion

Math Skills

Resources Assign students worksheet *14: Momentum* in the **Math Skills Worksheets** ancillary.

Additional Examples

Momentum An athlete with a mass of 73.0 kg runs with a constant forward velocity of 1.50 m/s. What is the athlete's momentum?

Answer: 110. kg • m/s forward

If a car with a mass of 925 kg has the same momentum as the athlete, what is the car's speed?

Answer: 0.119 m/s

Solution Guide

1. $p = mv$
  a. (75 kg)(16 m/s) = 1200 kg • m/s forward
  b. (135 kg)(16.2 m/s) = 2190 kg • m/s north
  c. (5.0 kg)(72 m/s) = 360 kg • m/s eastward
  d. (0.8 kg)(6.5 m/s) = 5 kg • m/s to the left
  e. (48.5 kg)(0 m/s) = 0 kg • m/s

Motion

SECTION 8.1 REVIEW

Check Your Understanding

1. **a.** speed
   b. velocity
   c. momentum
   d. velocity

2. To find the average speed of a moving train, the distance the train traveled and the time it took to travel that distance must be measured.

3. cm/minute

4. Velocity is more important to a traveler than speed because velocity indicates how fast and in what direction the traveler is going. Speed only indicates how fast the traveler is going.

5. As the ferris wheel turns, you are moving in a different direction at each instant of time. Since the direction changes, the velocity changes.

6. Answers may vary but students should suggest that if a ball moves in a straight line at a constant speed, the velocity is constant. If the ball changes direction or speed, the velocity changes.

Math Skills

7. 43 km/h
8. 8.87 m/s away from shore
9. 5.06 kg • m/s away from home plate

RESOURCE LINK
STUDY GUIDE

Assign students *Review Section 8.1 Motion.*

258

PHYSICAL SCIENCE

Disc Two, Module 11:
Conservation of Momentum
Use the Interactive Tutor to learn more about this topic.

The law of conservation of momentum

Imagine that two cars of different masses and traveling with different velocities collide head on. Can you predict what will happen after the collision? Momentum can be used to predict the motion of the cars after the collision. This is because in the absence of outside influences, the momentum is conserved.

The total amount of momentum in a system is conserved.

In other words, the total momentum of the two cars before a collision is the same as the total momentum after the collision. This is true if the cars bounce off each other or get tangled together. Cars can bounce off each other to move in opposite directions. If the cars stick together after a head-on collision, the cars will continue in the direction of the car that originally had the greater momentum.

SECTION 8.1 REVIEW

SUMMARY

▶ The average speed of an object is defined as the distance the object travels divided by the time of travel.

▶ The distance-time graph of an object moving at constant speed is a straight line. The slope of the line is the object's speed.

▶ The SI unit for speed is meters per second (m/s).

▶ The velocity of an object consists of both its speed and direction of motion.

▶ The momentum of an object moving in a straight line is calculated by multiplying the object's mass and velocity. An object's momentum is in the same direction as its velocity.

▶ The SI unit for momentum is kilograms times meters per second (kg•m/s).

CHECK YOUR UNDERSTANDING

1. **Identify** the following measurements as speed, velocity, or momentum:
   a. 88 km/h   **c.** 18 kg•m/s down
   b. 10 m/s straight up   **d.** 19 m/s to the west

2. **Describe** the measurements necessary to find the average speed of a moving train.

3. **Determine** the units of a caterpillar's speed if you measure the distance the caterpillar travels in centimeters and the time it takes to travel this distance in minutes.

4. **Explain** why knowing the velocity of an airplane is more important to a traveler than knowing only the airplane's speed.

5. **Describe** why your velocity changes when you ride a Ferris wheel even if the wheel turns at a constant speed.

6. **Creative Thinking** Describe the motion of a ball in a typical sport. Identify times when the ball moves with a constant velocity and times when its velocity changes.

Math Skills

7. What is the speed in kilometers per hour of a train that travels 3701 km in 87 hours?

8. What is the velocity in meters per second of a sailboat that travels 149 m away from the shore in 16.8 s?

9. What is the momentum of a 1.35 kg baseball moving at 3.75 m/s away from home plate after a hit?

Acceleration and Force

OBJECTIVES

▶ Calculate the acceleration of an object.
▶ Describe how force affects the motion of an object.
▶ Distinguish between balanced and unbalanced forces.
▶ Explain how friction affects the motion of an object.

▶ **KEY TERMS**
acceleration
force
balanced forces
unbalanced forces
friction
gravity

When you pedal hard to gain speed on your bicycle, your velocity changes. It changes again when you slow down to stop. Your velocity also changes as you round a curve in the road because your direction of motion changes. Any change in velocity is called an **acceleration**. The cyclist in **Figure 8-5** is accelerating as he turns the corner.

▶ **acceleration** change in velocity divided by the time interval in which the change occurred

Acceleration

To find the acceleration of an object moving in a straight line, we need to measure the object's velocity at different times. For an object moving in a straight line, acceleration can be calculated by dividing the change in the object's velocity by the time in which the change occurs. The change in an object's velocity is symbolized by Δv. The SI unit for acceleration is meters per second per second, or meters per second squared (m/s^2).

Acceleration Equation (for straight-line motion)

$$acceleration = \frac{final\ velocity - initial\ velocity}{time} \qquad a = \frac{\Delta v}{t}$$

What does an acceleration value tell you? If the acceleration is small, that means the speed is increasing very gradually. If the acceleration has a greater value, the object is speeding up more rapidly. For example, a human runner's acceleration is about $2\ m/s^2$. On the other hand, a sports car that goes from 0 to 96 km/h (60 mi/h) in 3.7 s has an acceleration of $7.2\ m/s^2$.

Because we use only positive velocity in this book, positive acceleration means the object's velocity will increase—it will speed up. Negative acceleration means the object's velocity will decrease—it will slow down.

Figure 8-5
This cyclist accelerates when he turns a corner even if his speed doesn't change.

MOTION AND FORCES **259**

Acceleration and Force

READING SKILL BUILDER *Discussion* Have students read aloud or silently the passage on acceleration. Start a class discussion about scenarios that involve acceleration. Be sure to emphasize that any change in velocity (including change of direction) is acceleration.

Math Skills

Resources Assign students worksheet *15: Acceleration* in the **Math Skills Worksheets** ancillary.

Additional Examples

Acceleration A car accelerates from 0 m/s to 45 m/s northward in 15 s. What is the acceleration of the car?

Answer: 3.0 m/s² northward

After reaching 45 m/s, the car slows down to 0 m/s in 10.0 s. What is the acceleration of the car?

Answer: 4.5 m/s² southward (or –4.5 m/s² northward)

PHYSICAL SCIENCE INTERACTIVE TUTOR

Disc Two, Module 9:
Speed and Acceleration
Use the Interactive Tutor to learn more about these topics.

Practice HINT

▶ When a problem asks you to calculate acceleration, you can use the acceleration equation on page 259.
▶ The acceleration equation can also be rearranged to isolate time on the left in the following way.

$$a = \frac{\Delta v}{t}$$

Multiply both sides by t.

$$a \times t = \frac{\Delta v}{\cancel{t}} \times \cancel{t}$$

$$\Delta v = at$$

Divide both sides by a.

$$\frac{\Delta v}{a} = \frac{\cancel{a}t}{\cancel{a}}$$

$$t = \frac{\Delta v}{a}$$

You will need to use this form of the equation in Practice Problem 4.
▶ In Practice Problem 5, you will need to rearrange the equation to isolate final velocity on the left:

$$final\ v = initial\ v + at$$

Math Skills

Acceleration A flowerpot falls off a second-story windowsill. The flowerpot starts from rest and hits the sidewalk 1.5 s later with a velocity of 14.7 m/s. Find the average acceleration of the flowerpot.

1 **List the given and unknown values.**
   Given: *time*, $t = 1.5$ s
   initial velocity, initial v = 0 m/s down
   final velocity, final v = 14.7 m/s down
   Unknown: *acceleration*, a = ? m/s² (and direction)

2 **Write the equation for acceleration.**

$$acceleration = \frac{final\ v - initial\ v}{time} \qquad a = \frac{\Delta v}{t}$$

3 **Insert the known values into the equation, and solve.**

$$a = \frac{\Delta v}{t} = \frac{final\ v - initial\ v}{t} = \frac{14.7\ \text{m/s} - 0\ \text{m/s}}{1.5\ \text{s}}$$

$$a = \frac{14.7\ \text{m/s}}{1.5\ \text{s}} = 9.8\ \text{m/s}^2\ \text{down}$$

Practice

Acceleration

1. Natalie accelerates her skateboard along a straight path from 0 m/s to 4.0 m/s in 2.5 s. Find her average acceleration.
2. A turtle swimming in a straight line toward shore has a speed of 0.50 m/s. After 4.0 s, its speed is 0.80 m/s. What is the turtle's average acceleration?
3. Find the average acceleration of a northbound subway train that slows down from 12 m/s to 9.6 m/s in 0.8 s.
4. Marisa's car accelerates at an average rate of 2.6 m/s². Calculate how long it takes her car to accelerate from 24.6 m/s to 26.8 m/s.
5. A cyclist travels at a constant velocity of 4.5 m/s westward, then speeds up with a steady acceleration of 2.3 m/s². Calculate the cyclist's speed after accelerating for 5.0 s.

When you press on the gas pedal in a car, you speed up and your acceleration is in the direction of the car's motion. When you press on the brake pedal, your acceleration is opposite to the direction of motion and you slow down. And when you turn the steering wheel, your velocity changes whether or not you speed up or slow down as you make the turn. This is because as you turn a corner the direction of your velocity changes. So acceleration is a common part of many types of motion.

RESOURCE LINK
LABORATORY MANUAL

Have students perform *Lab 8 Forces: Determining Your Acceleration on a Bicycle* in the lab ancillary.

DATASHEETS

Have students use *Datasheet 8.4* to record their results from the lab.

Solution Guide

1. $\frac{(4.0\ \text{m/s} - 0\ \text{m/s})}{2.5\ \text{s}} = 1.6\ \text{m/s}^2$ along her path

2. $\frac{(0.80\ \text{m/s} - 0.50\ \text{m/s})}{4.0\ \text{s}} = 0.075\ \text{m/s}^2$ toward the shore

3. $\frac{(9.6\ \text{m/s} - 12\ \text{m/s})}{(0.8\ \text{s})} = -3\ \text{m/s}^2\ \text{north} = 3\ \text{m/s}^2\ \text{south}$

4. $t = \frac{v}{a} = \frac{(26.8\ \text{m/s} - 24.6\ \text{m/s})}{2.6\ \text{m/s}^2} = 0.85\ \text{s}$

5. $v_f = v_i + at = 4.5\ \text{m/s} + (2.3\ \text{m/s}^2)(5.0\ \text{s}) = 16\ \text{m/s}$

Acceleration can be determined from a velocity-time graph

In the last section you learned that an object's speed can be determined from a distance-time graph of its motion. You can make a velocity-time graph by plotting velocity on the vertical axis and time on the horizontal axis.

A straight line on a velocity-time graph means that the velocity changes by the same amount each time. This is called constant acceleration. The slope of a line on a velocity-time graph gives you the value of the acceleration. A line with a positive slope represents an object that is speeding up. A line with a negative slope represents a slowing object.

The acceleration of an object is zero if its velocity is constant. If you ride your bike in a straight line at a constant speed, you are not accelerating. The bicyclist in **Figure 8-6A** is riding in a straight line with a constant speed of 13.00 m/s, as shown by the data in **Table 8-2**. If you move with a constant speed in a straight line, you are moving with a constant velocity. **Figure 8-6B** and **Figure 8-6C** show two different graphs that tell us about the motion of a cyclist traveling at a constant velocity.

Did You Know?

The faster a car goes, the longer it takes a given braking force to bring the car to a stop. Braking distance describes how far a car travels between the moment the brakes are applied and the moment the car stops. As a car's speed increases, so does its *braking distance*. For example, when a car's speed is doubled, its braking distance is four times as long.

Section 8.2

Acceleration and Force

|SKILL BUILDER

Graphing Have students create a distance-time graph from the data in **Table 8-2.** To do this, have them first create a new data table. Students should create a new data table that contains the information in **Table 8-2** in the first two columns. Have students add two more columns—the distance traveled in the time interval and the total distance traveled.

To calculate the distance traveled in a time interval, students should use $d = vt$. To calculate the total distance traveled, students should add the distance traveled in the time interval (column 3) to the previous total distance.

For an extension exercise, give students a data table with an increasing velocity (3 m/s, 6 m/s, 9 m/s, 12 m/s corresponding to the times 1 s, 2 s, 3 s, 4 s). Have them create both a velocity–time graph and a distance–time graph. Discuss the differences between the two graphs.

Figure 8-6

A When you ride your bike straight ahead at a constant speed, you are not accelerating because your velocity does not change.

Table 8-2   Data for a Bicycle with Unchanging Velocity

Time (s)	Velocity (m/s)
0	13.00
1	13.00
2	13.00
3	13.00
4	13.00

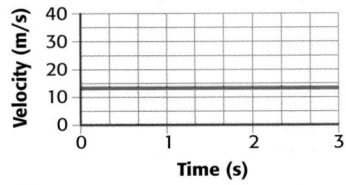

B If you plot the distance traveled against the time it takes, the resulting graph is a straight line with a slope of 13.00 m/s.

C Plotting the velocity against time results in a horizontal line because the velocity does not change. The acceleration is 0 m/s².

MOTION AND FORCES   **261**

Teaching Tip

Forces Because the direction of a force is important, the description of a force includes both a size and direction, just like velocity and acceleration. To emphasize the importance of direction, pose the following question to students:

- What is the net (or total) force acting on a piano if two students are each putting a force of 100 N on it?

After a brief discussion, draw two scenarios on the board. The first scenario should show two forces (drawn as arrows) acting on an object in the same direction. The net force in this case would be 200 N in the direction of the forces. The second scenario should show the forces acting in opposite directions. The net force in this case would be zero.

Figure 8-7

A When you slow down, your velocity changes. Your acceleration is negative because you are decreasing your velocity.

Table 8-3
Data for a Slowing Bicycle

Time (s)	Velocity (m/s)
0	13.00
1	9.75
2	6.50
3	3.25
4	0

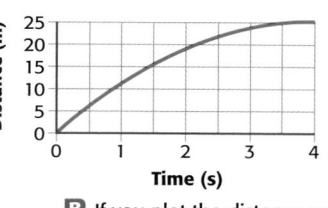

B If you plot the distance you travel against the time it takes you, the distance you travel each second becomes shorter and shorter until you finally stop.

C Plotting the velocity against time results in a line with a negative slope, which means the acceleration is negative.

▶ **force** the cause of acceleration, or change in an object's velocity

The rider in **Figure 8-7A** is slowing down from 13.00 m/s to 3.25 m/s over a period of 3.00 s, as shown by the data in **Table 8-3.** You can find out the rate at which velocity changes by calculating the acceleration.

$$a = \frac{3.25 \text{ m/s} - 13.00 \text{ m/s}}{3.00 \text{ s}} = \frac{-9.75 \text{ m/s}}{3.00 \text{ s}} = -3.25 \text{ m/s}^2$$

The rider's velocity decreases by 3.25 m/s each second. The acceleration value has a negative sign because the rider is slowing down. **Figure 8-7B** and **Figure 8-7C** show two different graphs describing the motion of an object that is slowing down.

Force

When you throw or catch a ball, you exert a **force** to change the ball's velocity. What causes an object to change its velocity, or accelerate? Usually, many forces act on an object at any given time. The **net force,** the combination of all of the forces acting on an object, determines whether the velocity of the object will change. An object accelerates in the direction of the net force. It won't accelerate if the net force is zero.

Balanced forces do not change motion

In **Figure 8-8A,** the two teams are engaged in a tug-of-war. Both the teams pull the rope by using their weight and by pushing on the ground. You can imagine that the combined effect of the forces exerted by each team is acting at the center of the rope. If each team exerts an equal force, the rope will not move. **Balanced forces,** such as these, completely cancel each other. The combined force equals zero.

Unbalanced forces do not cancel completely

If opposing forces acting on an object do not have the same strength, they do not cancel each other completely. Such **unbalanced forces** are present in the tug-of-war shown in **Figure 8-8B.** Team 2 moves the rope in its direction because the combined effect from its team members results in a greater force. Although part of the force exerted by Team 2 is canceled by the force exerted by Team 1, the additional, or net, force provided by Team 2 causes the rope to move toward Team 2. Team 1 accelerates to the right because the leftward force is smaller than the rightward force.

What if the forces act in different directions but are not exactly opposite? In this situation, the combination of forces acts like a single force on the object. Like all unbalanced forces, the net force will cause the object to accelerate.

▶ **balanced forces** forces acting on an object that combine to produce a net force equal to zero

▶ **unbalanced forces** forces acting on an object that combine to produce a net nonzero force

VOCABULARY *Skills Tip*

The word force *comes from the Latin word* fortis, *meaning "strength." The word* fortress *comes from the same root.*

Figure 8-8

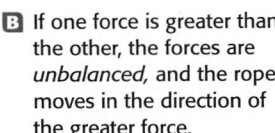

A In a tug-of-war, each side exerts a force on the rope. If the opposing forces are equal, they are *balanced,* and the rope does not move.

B If one force is greater than the other, the forces are *unbalanced,* and the rope moves in the direction of the greater force.

Balanced forces: no acceleration

Team 1   Team 2

Unbalanced forces: acceleration

Team 1   Team 2

MOTION AND FORCES **263**

MISCONCEPTION
Balanced Forces **ALERT**
Be sure to emphasize that balanced forces do not *change* the motion of an object. That does not imply that the object is not moving. For example, a car moving at a constant speed in a straight line has balanced forces acting on it. The force exerted by the engine is balanced by the frictional forces within the car's components, by the road, and by the air. Because the car is not accelerating, we can tell that the forces are balanced. If the car speeds up, slows down, or turns, then the forces are no longer balanced.

Historical Perspective

Aristotle believed that a moving object must have a force acting on it or it would stop moving. His belief was suggested by everyday experiences. If you slide an object and then remove your hand, it will stop sliding. What Aristotle did not realize was that when you remove your hand, you remove a force that is balancing another opposing force—friction. So the object stops moving because friction is still acting on it.

Should a Car's Air Bags Be Disconnected?

Should a Car's Air Bags Be Disconnected?
The key to an air bag's success during a crash is the speed at which it inflates. Inside the bag is a gas generator that contains the compounds sodium azide, potassium nitrate, and silicon dioxide. At the moment of a crash, an electronic sensor in the vehicle detects the sudden decrease in speed. The sensor sends a small electric current to the gas generator, providing the energy needed to start the chemical reaction.

The force that triggers the inflation of an air bag is approximately the same as that of hitting a solid barrier head-on at 20 km/h. The chemicals sodium azide and potassium nitrate react to form nontoxic, nonflammable nitrogen gas, which is what actually inflates the bag. (Several toxic chemicals are also formed, but they quickly react with other substances to make them less hazardous.)

The rate at which the reaction occurs is very fast. In 0.04 s—less than the blink of an eye—the gas formed in the reaction inflates the bag. By filling the space between the person and the car's dashboard, the air bag protects the person from injury.

Your Choice

1. No, because your body would move toward the seat back and not toward the dashboard, where the air bag deploys.

2. Student's reports will vary.

Resources Assign students worksheet *8.4: Science and the Consumer—Car Seat Safety* in the Integration Enrichment Resources ancillary.

Air bags are standard equipment in every new automobile sold in the United States. These safety devices are credited with saving almost 1700 lives between 1986 and 1996. However, air bags have also been blamed for the deaths of 36 children and 20 adults during the same period. In response to public concern about the safety of air bags, the National Highway Traffic Safety Administration has proposed that drivers be allowed to disconnect the air bags on their vehicles.

In a collision, air bags explode from a compartment to cushion the passenger's upper body and head.

How Do Air Bags Work?

When a car equipped with air bags crashes into another object, the car comes to an abrupt stop. Sensors in the car detect the sudden change in speed (negative acceleration) and trigger a chemical reaction inside the air bags. This reaction very quickly produces nitrogen gas, causing the bags to inflate and explode out of their storage compartment in a fraction of a second. The inflated air bags cushion the head and upper body of the driver and passengers in the front seat, who keep moving forward at the time of impact because of their inertia. Also, the inflated air bag increases the amount of time over which the stopping force acts. So as the rider moves forward, the air bag absorbs the impact.

What Are the Risks?

Because an air bag inflates suddenly and with great force, it can cause serious head and neck injuries in some circumstances. Seat belts reduce this risk by holding passengers against the seat back, allowing the air bag to inflate before the passenger's head comes into contact with it. In fact, most of the people killed by air bags either were not using seat belts or had not adjusted the seat belts properly.

However, two groups of people are at risk of being injured by air bags even with seat belts on: drivers shorter than about 157 cm (5 ft 2 in.) and infants who ride next to the driver in a rear-facing safety seat.

Alternatives to Disconnecting Air Bags

Always wearing a seat belt and placing child safety seats in the back seat of the car are two easy ways to reduce the risk of injury from air bags. Shorter drivers can buy pedal extenders that allow them to sit farther back and still safely reach the pedals. If the vehicle has a back seat, parents can put their child's safety seat there. Some vehicles without a back seat have a switch that can deactivate the passenger-side air bag. Automobile manufacturers are also working on air bags that inflate less forcefully.

Your Choice

1. **Critical Thinking** Are air bags useful if your car is struck from behind by another vehicle?

2. **Locating Information** Use library resources or the Internet to prepare a report about "smart" air-bag systems.

internetconnect

SCI**LINKS**
NSTA

TOPIC: Friction
GO TO: www.scilinks.org
KEYWORD: HK1083

264 CHAPTER 8

Friction and Air Resistance

Imagine a car that is rolling along a flat, evenly paved street. If no force is acting on the car, the car should keep moving at a constant speed. Experience tells you, however, that the car will keep slowing down until it eventually stops. This steady change in the car's speed gives you a clue that a force must be acting on the car. This unbalanced force that acts against the car's direction of motion is **friction.**

Because of friction, a constant force must be applied to a car on a flat road just to keep it moving. In order for the car to reach a certain speed from rest, the forces on the car must be unbalanced. The force pushing the car forward must be greater than the force of friction opposing the car's motion, as shown in **Figure 8-9A.** Once the car reaches its desired speed, the car will maintain this speed if the forces acting on the car are balanced, as shown in **Figure 8-9B.**

Friction also affects objects that aren't moving. For example, when a truck is parked on a hill with its brakes set, as shown in **Figure 8-9C,** friction provides the force needed to balance the force of gravity and prevent the truck from moving downhill.

Frictional force varies depending on the surfaces in contact

New jogging shoes often have rough rubber soles. Friction between the new shoes and a carpeted floor will be large enough to prevent you from slipping. Frictional forces are relatively great when both surfaces are rough.

> ▶ **friction** the force between two objects in contact that opposes the motion of either object

Did You Know ?

Another way to think about the effect of force on an object's motion is to use the concept of momentum. The change in momentum for an object is greater when the force is larger or when the force acts over a longer time.

Figure 8-9
Frictional Force and Acceleration

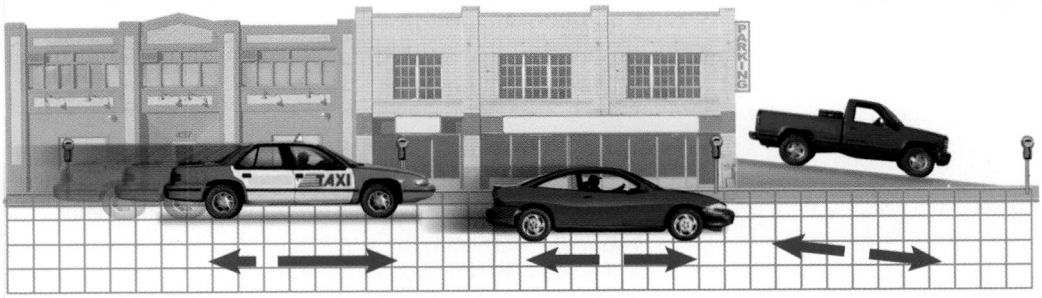

Unbalanced forces: acceleration

A When a car is accelerating, the forces are unbalanced. The force moving the car forward is greater than the opposing force of friction.

Balanced forces: constant speed

B When a car is cruising at constant speed, the force moving the car forward is balanced by the force of friction.

Balanced forces: no motion

C This truck does not roll because the force of friction between the brakes and the wheels balances the force of gravity.

MOTION AND FORCES **265**

MISCONCEPTION ALERT

Static Friction
The force of static friction is only a reaction force. Static frictional forces do not exist if there is no other force trying to change the motion of an object. For example, when trying to slide a crate to the left, there is an opposing frictional force to the right. However, if you stop pushing the crate, the frictional force stops. Otherwise the crate would start to move backward and to the right.

Also, consider a sliding crate. If you stop pushing, the crate will slow down due to friction. As the relative motion between the crate and the floor decreases, so does the frictional force. So when the crate stops, the frictional force is zero. If the frictional force was not a reaction force, the crate would slow down, stop, and start moving backward due to friction.

Teaching Tip

Friction Vehicle tires are designed to use friction to increase grip. Have students find information about as many different kinds of tires, tire compounds, and tread designs as they can. Have them make a poster or other project showing some of the types of tires and treads they have learned about.

Acceleration and Force

Teaching Tip

Gravity Emphasize the concept that every object exerts a gravitational attraction toward every other object. The apple exerts a gravitational force on Earth that is the same magnitude as the force that Earth exerts on the apple. The reason we do not notice Earth moving toward the apple is because of Earth's extremely large mass. The apple accelerates toward Earth's center because of its smaller mass.

Figure 8-10
With the need for better fuel efficiency and increased speed, car designs have been changed to reduce air resistance. Modern cars are much more aerodynamic.

▷ **gravity** the attraction between two particles of matter due to their mass

However, if the soles of your shoes are smooth or if the floor you are walking on has been waxed, you may find it difficult to walk steadily. That's because there is less frictional force if one surface is rough and the other is smooth. Smooth soles and a smooth floor can make it even more difficult to walk because of even less frictional force.

Air resistance is a form of friction

Although friction between a car's tires and the road allows a car to move forward, another type of friction, air resistance, opposes the car's motion. Air resistance is caused by the interaction between the surface of a moving object and the air molecules.

The amount of air resistance on an object depends on its size and shape as well as on the speed with which it moves. Objects with larger surfaces can experience greater air resistance. Air resistance also increases as the object's speed increases. As shown in **Figure 8-10,** car design has changed dramatically over the years. One factor taken into account in designing cars is reducing air resistance. To make cars, trains, and planes move faster without using more fuel, designers have changed the shapes of these vehicles to reduce the resistance between the vehicle and the surrounding air.

Gravity

Gravity is given as the reason why an apple falls down from a tree. But you may not realize that every object exerts a gravitational force on every other object. When an apple breaks from its stem, the apple falls down because the gravitational force between Earth and the apple is much greater than the gravitational force between the apple and the tree. The force of gravity is different from forces such as friction; the force of gravity acts even when the objects do not touch.

Mass and distance affect gravitational force

The force of gravity between two objects depends on their masses and on the distance between the two objects. The gravitational force between two objects is proportional to the product of their masses. The greater the mass of an object is, the larger the gravitational force it exerts on other objects. For instance, the gravitational force that the person sitting next to you in the classroom exerts on you is so small that you don't even notice it. You can't help but notice Earth's gravitational force because Earth is extremely massive. The gravitational force between most objects around you is very small.

266 CHAPTER 8

DEMONSTRATION 2 TEACHING

Gravity Is a Weak Force

Time: Approximately 10 minutes
Materials: magnet
      paper clip
      thread
      tape

Step 1 Tie a 30 cm piece of thread to a paper clip and tape the other end of the thread to a desk. Explain to students that the entire mass of Earth is pulling down on the paper clip.

Step 2 Lift the paper clip up with your hand until the thread is taut.

Step 3 Hold the magnet approximately 1 cm above the paper clip (close enough to hold the paper clip suspended but without touching it). Show students the suspended paper clip and explain that the magnetic force between the paper clip and the magnet is stronger than the gravitational force between the paper clip and Earth.

Gravitational force also depends on the distance between two objects, as shown in **Figure 8-11.** The force of gravity changes as the distance between the balls changes. If the distance between the two balls is doubled, the gravitational force between them decreases to one-fourth its original value. If the original distance is tripled, the gravitational force decreases to one-ninth its original value. Gravitational force is weaker than other types of forces, even though it holds the planets, stars, and galaxies together.

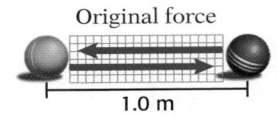

Original force
1.0 m

$\dfrac{\text{Original force}}{9}$
3.0 m

Figure 8-11
Gravitational force rapidly grows weaker as the distance between two objects increases.

SECTION 8.2 REVIEW

Check Your Understanding

1. speeding up, slowing down, turning
2. When an object moves at constant velocity including when the object is at rest, the resulting force is zero. The motion of the object does not change.
3. When an object speeds up, slows down, or turns, the resulting force is in the direction of the change in velocity. If an object is speeding up, the force is in the direction of motion. If an object is turning, the force is in a sideways direction to the direction of motion.
4. **a.** yes
   b. no
   c. yes
   d. yes
5. c, a, b
6. Venus is much closer to the sun than Earth is.

Math Skills

7. 1.5 m/s² along the road
8. the cyclist

SECTION 8.2 REVIEW

SUMMARY

▶ Acceleration is a change in the velocity of an object. An object accelerates when it speeds up, slows down, or changes direction. Acceleration is caused by a force.

▶ For straight-line motion, average acceleration is defined as the change in an object's velocity per unit of time.

▶ The SI unit for acceleration is meters per second squared (m/s²).

▶ The forces that act on an object combine to act effectively as one force.

▶ Friction is the force between two objects in contact; it opposes the motion of either object.

▶ Gravity is the attraction between two particles due to their mass. The force of gravity is proportional to their mass and inversely proportional to the square of the distance between them.

CHECK YOUR UNDERSTANDING

1. **Describe** three ways in which a car's velocity will change.
2. **Identify** a situation involving balanced forces. Describe the net force, and explain how this force affects the motion of an object.
3. **Identify** a situation involving unbalanced forces. Describe the net force, and explain how it affects the motion of an object.
4. **Evaluate** the following situations, and decide if an unbalanced force is present:
   a. A car turns right without slowing down.
   b. A spacecraft moves in one direction at a constant speed.
   c. A cyclist coasts downhill, going faster and faster.
   d. A tennis racket hits a tennis ball.
5. **Arrange** the following pairs of surfaces in order of most friction to least friction:
   a. a shoe sole and a waxed basketball court
   b. a shoe sole and the frozen surface of a lake
   c. a shoe sole and the sidewalk
6. **Creative Thinking** Explain why Venus, which is slightly less massive than Earth, experiences a stronger gravitational pull from the sun than Earth does.

Math Skills

7. What is the average acceleration of a car that starts from rest and moves straight ahead at 18 m/s in 12 s?
8. Which will be moving faster after 3.0 s, a cyclist maintaining a constant velocity of 15 m/s straight ahead or a race car accelerating forward from a stoplight at 4.0 m/s²?

MOTION AND FORCES **267**

Using this setup, you can also discuss the effect of distance. If you pull the magnet farther away, the paper clip will fall to the desk. This is because the magnetic force depends on distance just like the gravitational force does.

RESOURCE LINK
STUDY GUIDE

Assign students *Review Section 8.2 Acceleration and Force.*

Newton's Laws of Motion

▶ **KEY TERMS**

inertia
free fall
terminal velocity

OBJECTIVES

▶ State Newton's three laws of motion, and apply them to physical situations.

▶ Calculate force, mass, and acceleration with Newton's second law.

▶ Recognize that the free-fall acceleration near Earth's surface is independent of the mass of the falling object.

▶ Explain the difference between mass and weight.

▶ Identify paired forces on interacting objects.

Every motion you observe or experience is related to a force. Sir Isaac Newton described the relationship between motion and force in three laws that we now call Newton's laws of motion. Newton's laws apply to a wide range of motion—a caterpillar crawling on a leaf, a person riding a bicycle, or a rocket blasting off into space.

Newton's First Law

If you slide your book across a rough surface, such as carpet, the book will soon come to rest. On a smooth surface, such as ice, the book will slide much farther before stopping. Because there is less frictional force between the ice and the book, the force must act over a longer time before the book comes to a stop. Without friction, the book would keep sliding forever. This is an example of Newton's first law, which is stated as follows.

An object at rest remains at rest and an object in motion maintains its velocity unless it experiences an unbalanced force.

You experience the effect described by Newton's first law when you ride in a car. As the car comes to a stop, you can feel your body continue to move forward. Your seat belt and the friction between your pants and the seat stop your forward motion. They provide the unbalanced rearward force needed to bring you to a stop as the car stops.

Because infants are more fragile than adults, they are placed in special backward-facing car seats, as shown in **Figure 8-12.** The force that is needed to bring the baby to a stop is safely spread out over the baby's entire body.

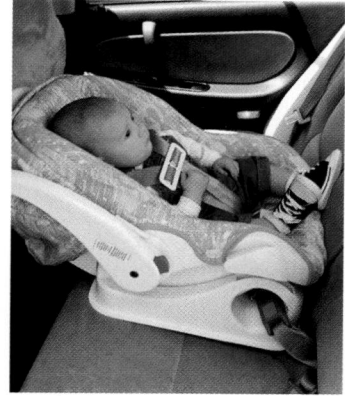

Figure 8-12
During an abrupt stop, this baby would continue to move forward. The backward-facing car seat distributes the force that holds the baby in the car.

Newton's First Law

1. Place an index card over a glass, and set a coin on top of the index card.
2. With your thumb and forefinger, quickly flick the card sideways off the glass. Observe what happens to the coin. Does the coin move with the index card?
3. Try again, but this time slowly pull the card sideways and observe what happens to the coin.
4. Use Newton's first law to explain your results.

Inertia is the tendency of an object at rest to remain at rest or, if moving, to continue moving with a constant velocity. All objects have inertia because they resist changes in motion. An object with very little mass, such as a baseball, can be accelerated with a small force. But it takes a much larger force to accelerate a car, which has a large mass.

▶ **inertia** the tendency of an object to remain at rest or in motion with a constant velocity

Newton's Second Law

Newton's first law describes what happens when the net force acting on an object is zero: the object either remains at rest or continues moving at a constant velocity. What happens when the net force acting on an object is not zero? Newton's second law describes the effect of this unbalanced force on the motion of an object.

Force equals mass times acceleration

Newton's second law, which describes the relationship between mass, force, and acceleration, can be stated as follows.

The unbalanced force acting on an object equals the object's mass times its acceleration.

Mathematically, Newton's second law can be written as follows.

Newton's Second Law
$$force = mass \times acceleration$$
$$F = ma$$

Consider the difference between pushing an empty shopping cart and pushing the same cart filled with groceries, as shown in **Figure 8-13.** If you push the cart with the same amount of force in each situation, the empty cart will have a greater acceleration because it has a smaller mass than the full cart. The same amount of force in each case produces different accelerations because the masses are different.

Figure 8-13
Because the full cart has a larger mass than the empty cart, the same force gives the empty cart a greater acceleration.

MOTION AND FORCES **269**

Section 8.3

Newton's Laws of Motion

READING SKILL BUILDER *Paired Reading* Have students read silently the section on Newton's laws of motion. Instruct them to mark on self-adhesive notes those portions of the text that they do not understand. Be sure that students study all illustrations and legends that accompany the passage. Group students together in pairs, and have one student in each pair discuss with the other student the parts of the passage that he or she found difficult. The listener should either clarify the difficult passages or should help frame a common question for later explanation.

RESOURCE LINK
DATASHEETS

Have students use *Datasheet 8.1 Quick Activity: Newton's First Law* to record their results.

Newton's First Law In step 2, students should observe the coin fall into the glass. The coin may move slightly sideways with the card. If students are having difficulty, emphasize that they must flick the card very quickly.

Make sure that students understand that in step 3, the coin should not fall into the glass; it should remain resting on the card. The force of friction caused the coin to move sideways with the card.

269

Additional Examples

Newton's Second Law A 1200 kg car has a force of 1500 N from the engine pushing it forward. The car also has a combined frictional force of 1100 N pushing it backward. What is the acceleration of the car? (**Hint:** You will need to calculate the net force first.)

Answer: 0.33 m/s² forward

If the driver eases up on the gas pedal, the frictional force remains the same, and the engine is only exerting a force of 950 N, what is the new acceleration?

Answer: –0.13 m/s² forward = 0.13 m/s² backward (The car is slowing down.)

What would happen if you and a friend each pushed an empty cart but you used more force? The cart you pushed would have a greater acceleration. When two masses are the same, a greater force provides a greater acceleration.

Although the force in these cases is a push, Newton's second law applies regardless of the type of force involved. The acceleration is always in the direction of the net force.

Force is measured in newtons

Newton's second law can be used to derive the SI unit of force, the newton (N). One newton is the force that can give a mass of 1 kg an acceleration of 1 m/s², expressed as follows.

$$1 \text{ N} = 1 \text{ kg} \times 1 \text{ m/s}^2$$

The pound (lb) is sometimes used as a unit of force. One newton is equivalent to 0.225 lb. Conversely, 1 lb is equal to 4.448 N.

Practice HINT

▶ When a problem requires you to calculate the unbalanced force on an object, you can use Newton's second law on the previous page.

▶ The equation for Newton's second law can be rearranged to isolate mass on the left side of he equation in the following way.

$$F = ma$$

Divide both sides by a.

$$\frac{F}{a} = \frac{m\cancel{a}}{\cancel{a}}$$

$$m = \frac{F}{a}$$

You will need to use this form of the equation in Practice Problem 2.

▶ In Practice Problem 3 you will need to rearrange the equation to isolate acceleration on the left side.

Math Skills

Newton's Second Law Zookeepers lift a stretcher that holds a sedated lion. The total mass of the lion and stretcher is 175 kg, and the lion's upward acceleration is 0.657 m/s². What is the unbalanced force necessary to produce this acceleration of the lion and the stretcher?

1 List the given and unknown values.
  Given: *mass*, $m = 175$ kg
  acceleration, $a = 0.657$ m/s²
  Unknown: *force*, $F = ?$ N

2 Write the equation for Newton's second law.
  force = mass × acceleration
  $F = ma$

3 Insert the known values into the equation, and solve.
  $F = 175 \text{ kg} \times 0.657 \text{ m/s}^2$
  $F = 115 \text{ kg} \cdot \text{m/s}^2 = 115$ N

Practice

Newton's Second Law

1. What is the net force necessary for a 1.6×10^3 kg automobile to accelerate forward at 2.0 m/s²?

2. A baseball accelerates downward at 9.8 m/s². If the gravitational force acting on the baseball is 1.4 N, what is the baseball's mass? (**Hint:** Assume gravity is the only force acting on the ball.)

3. A sailboat and its crew have a combined mass of 655 kg. If the sailboat experiences an unbalanced force of 895 N pushing it forward, what is the sailboat's acceleration?

Solution Guide

1. $F = ma = (1.6 \times 10^3 \text{ kg})(2.0 \text{ m/s}^2) = 3.2 \times 10^3$ N

2. $m = \dfrac{F}{a} = \dfrac{1.4 \text{ N}}{9.8 \text{ m/s}^2} = 0.14$ kg

3. $a = \dfrac{F}{m} = \dfrac{895 \text{ N}}{655 \text{ kg}} = 1.37$ m/s² in the direction of the force

Free Fall and Weight

When the force of gravity is the only force acting on an object, the object is said to be in **free fall.** The free-fall acceleration of an object is directed toward the center of the Earth. Because free-fall acceleration results from gravity, it is often abbreviated as the letter g. Near Earth's surface, g is approximately 9.8 m/s^2.

Free-fall acceleration near Earth's surface is constant

In the absence of air resistance, all objects near Earth's surface accelerate at the same rate, regardless of their mass. This means that if you dropped a 1.5 kg book and a 15 kg rock from the same height, they would hit the ground at about the same moment. For simplicity, we will disregard air resistance for all calculations in this book. We will assume that all objects on Earth accelerate at exactly 9.8 m/s^2.

Why do all objects have the same free-fall acceleration? Newton's second law shows that acceleration depends on both the force on an object and its mass. A heavier object experiences a greater gravitational force than a lighter object. But a heavier object is also harder to accelerate because it has more mass. The extra mass of the heavy object exactly compensates for the additional gravitational force.

Weight equals mass times free-fall acceleration

The force on an object due to gravity is called its weight. On Earth, your weight is simply the amount of gravitational force exerted on you by Earth. If you know the free-fall acceleration, g, acting on a body, you can use $F = ma$ (Newton's second law) to calculate the body's weight. Weight equals mass times free-fall acceleration. Mathematically, this is expressed as follows.

$$weight = mass \times free\text{-}fall\ acceleration$$
$$w = mg$$

Note that because weight is a force, the SI unit of weight is the newton. For example, a small apple weighs about 1 N. A 1.0 kg book has a weight of 1.0 kg $\times$ 9.8 m/s^2 = 9.8 N.

You may have seen pictures of astronauts floating in the air, as shown in **Figure 8-14.** Does this mean that they don't experience gravity? In orbit, astronauts, the space shuttle, and all objects on board experience free fall due to the Earth's gravity. In fact, the astronauts and their surroundings all accelerate at the same rate. Therefore, the floor of the shuttle does not push up against the astronauts and the astronauts appear to be floating. This situation is referred to as *apparent weightlessness.*

▶ **free fall** the motion of a body when only the force of gravity is acting on it

Figure 8-14
In the environment of the orbiting space shuttle, astronauts experience apparent weightlessness.

Newton's Laws of Motion

Teaching Tip
Apparent Weightlessness
Many students will have experienced a temporary sensation of weightlessness in an elevator, on a roller coaster, or on a free-fall type of ride as it begins to descend. This is similar to what astronauts experience. Because the seat and the car around you begin descending at the acceleration of gravity, there is no gravitational force holding you into your seat. This causes the sensation of weightlessness. In reality, you do have weight, as evidenced by your rapid fall toward the Earth!

Did You Know ?

In the reduced gravity of space, astronauts lose bone and muscle mass, even after a very short time. Sleep patterns may be affected and so may cardiovascular strength and the immune response. These same effects happen more gradually as people age on Earth. Scientists are interested in studying the effects of microgravity so they can find ways to counteract them in space and here on Earth.

Newton's Laws of Motion

INTEGRATING

SPACE SCIENCE
Earth: 570 N
Mars: 210 N
Venus: 510 N
Neptune: 680 N

Resources Assign students worksheet *8.5: Integrating Space Science—Gravity and the Planets* in the **Integration Enrichment Resources** ancillary.

Teaching Tip

Weight Influences Shape

The dramatic necessity of having a shape correct for your size can be shown by comparing an ant's legs to the legs of an elephant. An ant has very thin legs relative to the size of its body, while an elephant has thick legs. Students may have seen science fiction movies with giant ants, but in reality these giant ants could never exist. If an ant were somehow enlarged to the size of an elephant, it wouldn't even be able to walk. This is because strength is proportional to the cross-sectional area—how big the muscle is. In order to support its new, larger body, the ant would have to grow thick, strong legs like an elephant!

RESOURCE LINK

IER

Assign students worksheet *8.6: Integrating Biology—How Fish Maintain Neutral Buoyancy* in the **Integration Enrichment Resources** ancillary.

INTEGRATING

SPACE SCIENCE
Because the planets in our solar system have different masses and sizes, the value of *g* is different on each planet. Find the weight of a 58 kg person on the following planets:

Earth, where $g = 9.8$ m/s^2

Mars, where $g = 3.7$ m/s^2

Venus, where $g = 8.8$ m/s^2

Neptune, where $g = 11.8$ m/s^2

▶ **terminal velocity** the maximum velocity reached by a falling object that occurs when the resistance of the medium is equal to the force due to gravity

Figure 8-15
When a sky diver reaches terminal velocity, the force of gravity is balanced by air resistance.

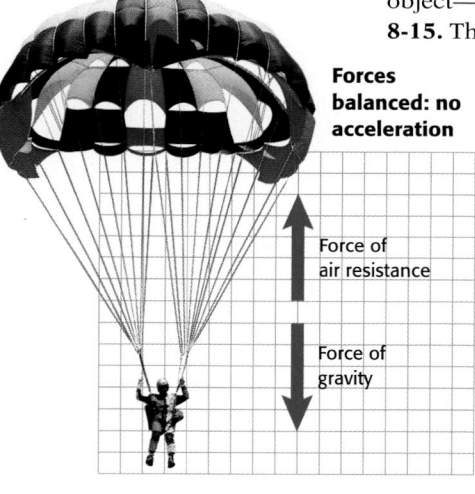

Forces balanced: no acceleration

Force of air resistance

Force of gravity

Weight is different from mass

Mass and weight are easy to confuse. Although mass and weight are proportional to one another, they are not the same. Mass is a measure of the amount of matter in an object. Weight is the gravitational force an object experiences due to its mass.

The weight of an object depends on gravity, so a change in an object's location will change the object's weight. For example, consider a 66 kg astronaut. On Earth, this astronaut weighs 66 kg $\times$ 9.8 m/s^2 = 650 N (about 150 lb), but on the moon's surface, where *g* is only 1.6 m/s^2, the astronaut would weigh 66 kg $\times$ 1.6 m/s^2 = 110 N (about 24 lb). The astronaut's mass remains the same on Earth, the moon, or an orbiting space shuttle, but the gravitational force acting on the astronaut changes in each place.

Weight influences shape

Gravitational force influences the shapes of living things. On land, large animals must have strong skeletons to support their mass against the force of gravity. The woody trunks of trees serve the same function. For organisms that live in water, however, the downward force of gravity is balanced by the upward forces of the water. For many of these creatures, strong skeletons or other supporting structures are unnecessary. Because a jellyfish has no skeleton, it can drift gracefully through the water but collapses if it washes up on the beach.

Velocity is constant when air resistance balances weight

Both air resistance and gravity act on objects moving through Earth's atmosphere. For a falling object, when the force of air resistance becomes equal to the gravitational force on the object—the weight—it stops accelerating, as shown in **Figure 8-15.** This happens because the air resistance acts in the opposite direction to the weight. When these two forces are equal, the object stops accelerating and reaches its maximum velocity, the **terminal velocity.**

When sky divers start a jump, their parachutes are closed, and they are accelerated toward Earth by the force of gravity. As their velocity increases, the force they experience due to air resistance increases. When air resistance and the force of gravity are equal, sky divers reach a terminal velocity of about 320 km/h (200 mi/h). But when they open the parachute, air resistance increases greatly. For a while, this slows them down. Eventually, they reach a new terminal velocity of several kilometers per hour, allowing them to land safely.

272 CHAPTER 8

Inquiry Lab

How are action and reaction forces related? If students have difficulty with item 1, encourage them to list the forces acting on each object separately. For example, the forces acting on the middle spring scale are: its weight, the downward pull of the 2 kg mass, and the upward pull of the top spring scale.

The reaction forces that correspond with each force are: the upward force on the Earth from the mass of the spring scale, the upward force on the 2 kg mass, and the downward pull on the top spring scale.

The pairs are much easier to identify if students list all forces acting on each object

Newton's Third Law

When you kick a soccer ball with your foot, as shown in **Figure 8-16,** you notice the effect of the force exerted by your foot on the ball. The ball experiences a change in motion. But is this the only force present? Do you feel a force on your foot when kicking the ball? In fact, the soccer ball exerts an equal and opposite force on your foot. The force exerted on the ball by your foot is the action force, and the force exerted on your foot by the ball is the reaction force.

Note that the action and reaction forces are applied to different objects. These forces are equal and opposite, but this is not a case of balanced forces because two different objects are involved. The action force acts on the ball, and the reaction force acts on the foot. This is an example of Newton's third law, also called the law of action and reaction.

For every action force, there is an equal and opposite reaction force.

Newton's third law implies that forces always occur in pairs. But the action and reaction force of a force pair act on different objects. Also, action and reaction forces occur at the same time.

Newton's third law is used in rocketry. Rockets were invented many centuries ago. They have many different sizes and designs, but the basic principle remains the same.

Figure 8-16
According to Newton's third law, the soccer ball and the foot shown in this photo exert equal and opposite forces on one another.

Section 8.3

Newton's Laws of Motion

MISCONCEPTION ALERT

Newton's Third Law Emphasize that the equal but opposite forces in Newton's third law act on different objects. Action/reaction forces never cancel out—they cannot because they act on different objects. The only time forces could cancel out (add up to zero) would be if they acted on the same object.

RESOURCE LINK

IER

Assign students worksheet *8.8: Integrating Technology—Hydraulic Lift Force* in the **Integration Enrichment Resources** ancillary.

DATASHEETS

Have students use *Datasheet 8.2 Inquiry Lab: How are action and reaction forces related?* to record their results.

Inquiry Lab

How are action and reaction forces related?

Materials ✔ *2 spring scales*   ✔ *2 kg mass*

Procedure

1. Hang the 2 kg mass from one of the spring scales.
2. Observe the reading on the spring scale.
3. While keeping the mass connected to the first spring scale, link the two scales together. The first spring scale and the mass should hang from the second spring scale, as shown in the figure at right.
4. Observe the readings on each spring scale.

Analysis

1. What are the action and reaction forces involved in the spring scale–mass system you have constructed?
2. How did the readings on the two spring scales in step 4 compare? Explain how this is an example of Newton's third law of motion.

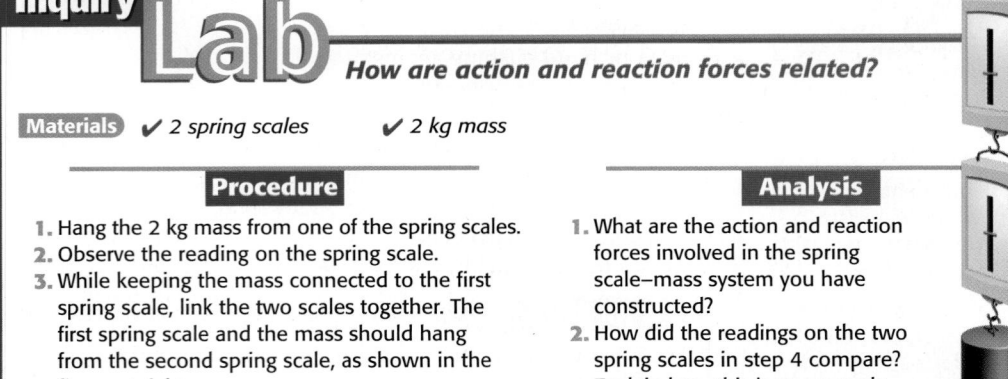

separately. Scan the lists for pairs like: A pulls down on B, and B lifts up on A.

Students should be able to determine in question 2 that the reading on the top spring scale should be the weight of the 2 kg mass plus the weight of the other spring scale. The reading on the bottom spring scale should be the weight of the 2 kg mass. Since the bottom spring scale is pulling down on the top spring scale with a force equal to its weight plus the weight of the 2 kg mass, the top scale must exert an upward force on the bottom scale that is equal to the weight of the bottom spring scale and the 2 kg mass.

Check Your Understanding

1. Accept all reasonable responses.

2. Mass is the amount of matter in an object. Weight is the force of gravity on the mass. The weight of an object depends on where the object is. For example, in space an astronaut weighs much less than she does on Earth.

3. **a.** hand pushing wall, wall pushing hand
   b. hammer pounding nail, nail pushes hammer
   c. stone hits well, well pushes stone
   d. book pushes ground, ground pushes book

4. **a.** The car may be unable to turn. Newton's first law states that the object (car) will continue to travel in a straight line unless an unbalanced force acts on the object. Since the road is icy, the friction between the tires and the ice may not be large enough to turn the car.
   b. The car will slide for the same reasons in (a). Also, the car will decelerate much less than it would on a dry road. Newton's second law states that acceleration is proportional to force. Since the friction force is much smaller on an icy road, the acceleration (deceleration) is much smaller.

Answers continue on p. 279B.

Figure 8-17
All forces occur in action-reaction pairs. In this case, the upward push on the rocket equals the downward push on the exhaust gases.

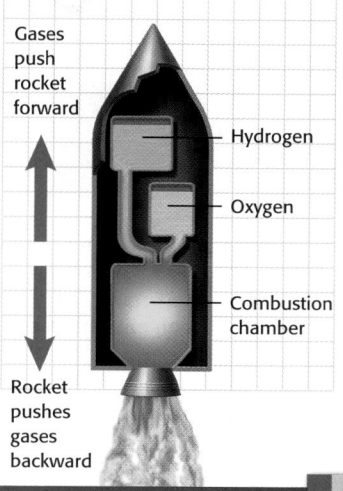

Gases push rocket forward

Hydrogen

Oxygen

Combustion chamber

Rocket pushes gases backward

The push of the hot gases through the nozzle is matched by an equal push in the opposite direction on the combustion (burning) chamber, which accelerates the rocket forward.

Figure 8-17 is a representation of a liquid-fuel rocket. Liquid oxygen and liquid hydrogen are held in separate compartments, as shown. The oxygen and hydrogen react in a combustion chamber to produce a gas with a great deal of energy. This energy causes the gas to press out equally in all directions inside the rocket. The pressure of the gas against one side of the rocket balances the pressure of the gas against the opposite side. However, because the bottom of the combustion chamber is open, gas escapes through the nozzle. Thus, the force of the gas against the front of the rocket is not balanced at the back of the rocket. This unbalanced force pushes the rocket forward.

Rockets burn up most of their fuel during the early stages of flight, mainly because the rocket has more mass to accelerate because of the unused fuel it carries. As the fuel is used, the rocket's mass decreases and the force needed to produce a given acceleration decreases. Because air is more dense in Earth's lower atmosphere, the rocket also experiences greater air resistance initially.

SECTION 8.3 REVIEW

SUMMARY

▶ An object at rest remains at rest and an object in motion maintains a constant velocity unless it experiences an unbalanced force (Newton's first law).

▶ The unbalanced force acting on an object equals the object's mass times its acceleration, or $F = ma$ (Newton's second law).

▶ The SI unit for force is the newton (N). Weight equals mass times free fall acceleration, or $W = mg$.

▶ For every action force, there is an equal and opposite reaction force (Newton's third law).

CHECK YOUR UNDERSTANDING

1. **State** each of Newton's three laws of motion in your own words, and give an example that demonstrates each law.

2. **Explain** the difference between mass and weight. Does the weight of an object ever change? If so, when?

3. **Identify** the action and reaction forces in each of the following cases:
   a. your hand pushing against a wall
   b. a hammer pounding a nail
   c. a stone striking the bottom of a well
   d. a book sliding to a stop on the ground

4. **Critical Thinking** Using Newton's laws, predict what will happen when a car traveling on an icy road
   a. comes to a sharp bend.
   b. has to stop quickly.

Math Skills

5. What is the acceleration of a boy on a skateboard if the unbalanced forward force on the boy is 15 N? The total mass of the boy and skateboard is 58 kg.

6. How much does a 5.0 kg puppy weigh on Earth?

Chapter Highlights

Before you begin, review the summaries of the key ideas of each section, found on pages 258, 267, and 274. The key vocabulary terms are listed on pages 252, 259, and 268.

UNDERSTANDING CONCEPTS

1. If you jog for 1 hour and travel 10 km, 10 km/h describes your _____.
   a. momentum
   b. average speed
   c. displacement
   d. acceleration

2. _____ is speed in a certain direction.
   a. Acceleration
   b. Friction
   c. Momentum
   d. Velocity

3. Which of the following objects is not accelerating?
   a. a ball being juggled
   b. a woman walking at 2.5 m/s along a straight road
   c. a satellite circling Earth
   d. a braking cyclist

4. The newton is a measure of _____.
   a. mass
   b. length
   c. force
   d. acceleration

5. _____ is a force that opposes the motion between two objects in contact with each other.
   a. Motion
   b. Friction
   c. Acceleration
   d. Velocity

6. Automobile seat belts are necessary for safety because of a passenger's _____.
   a. inertia
   b. weight
   c. speed
   d. gravity

7. The winner of the shot-put event in the Olympics is the person who best uses _____.
   a. Newton's first law
   b. Newton's second law
   c. air resistance
   d. the law of gravity

8. An example involving action-reaction forces is _____.
   a. air escaping from a toy balloon
   b. a rocket traveling through the air
   c. a ball bouncing off a wall
   d. All of the above

Using Vocabulary

9. State whether 30 m/s to the west represents a *speed*, a *velocity*, or both.

10. Describe the motion of a cyclist at the start of a race. In your answer, use the terms *velocity, acceleration, force,* and *friction.*

11. A wrestler weighs in for the first match on the moon. Will he weigh more or less on the moon? Explain your answer using the terms *weight, mass, force,* and *gravity.*

12. "There is no *gravity* in outer space." Write a paragraph explaining whether this statement is true or false. **WRITING SKILL**

13. Describe a sky diver's jump from the airplane to the ground. In your answer, use the terms *air resistance, gravity,* and *terminal velocity.*

BUILDING MATH SKILLS

14. **Graphing** The following graphs describe the motion of four different balls—*a, b, c,* and *d.* Using the graphs below, state whether each ball is accelerating, sitting still, or moving at a constant velocity.

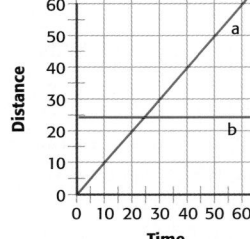
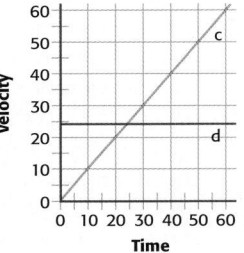

UNDERSTANDING CONCEPTS

1. b	5. b
2. d	6. a
3. b	7. b
4. c	8. d

Using Vocabulary

9. Velocity includes the speed of an object and its direction of motion; therefore, 30 m/s to the west is a velocity.

10. At the start of a race, a cyclist has a speed of 0 m/s. As the race begins, the cyclist exerts a force and begins to accelerate. The cyclist's velocity increases in the direction of the acceleration. The friction between the tires and the road allows the bike to move forward.

11. The wrestler will weigh less on the moon than he does on Earth, because the force exerted on him will be different at these locations. Since he has the same mass in both places, his weight will depend on the acceleration due to gravity at each location. The moon causes a much smaller acceleration due to gravity, so the wrestler will weigh less there.

12. The statement is false. Since every mass interacts with every other mass via gravity, the force of gravity is everywhere. In outer space, the force of gravity is very small if you are far from other masses.

RESOURCE LINK
STUDY GUIDE

Assign students *Mixed Review Chapter 8.*

13. As a skydiver jumps from a plane, gravity pulls her downward. Air resistance pushes upward against the downward motion. The skydiver accelerates downward until the force of air resistance equals the downward force of gravity. Then the skydiver stops accelerating and falls downward at a constant speed. This is called terminal velocity.

BUILDING MATH SKILLS

14. Objects a and d are moving with constant velocity; object b is at rest; object c is moving with constant acceleration.

15. $v = \dfrac{d}{t} = \dfrac{1260 \text{ km}}{3.5 \text{ h}} =$ 360 km/h northeast

16. $v = \dfrac{d}{t} = \dfrac{72 \text{ m}}{45 \text{ s}} = 1.6$ m/s eastward

17. $t = \dfrac{d}{v} = \dfrac{560 \text{ km}}{85 \text{ km/h}} = 6.6$ h

18. $p = mv = (85 \text{ kg})(2.65 \text{ m/s})$ $= 230$ kg • m/s north

19. $p = mv = (9.1 \text{ kg})(89 \text{ km/h})$ (1000 m/km) $\left(\dfrac{1 \text{ h}}{60 \text{ min}}\right)\left(\dfrac{1 \text{ min}}{60 \text{ s}}\right) =$ 220 kg • m/s east

20. $a = \dfrac{\Delta v}{t} = \dfrac{5.5 \text{ m/s} - 14.0 \text{ m/s}}{6.0 \text{ s}}$ $= -1.4$ m/s² east $= 1.4$ m/s² west

21. $t = \dfrac{\Delta v}{a} = \dfrac{0 \text{ m/s} - 13.5 \text{ m/s}}{-0.50 \text{ m/s}^2} =$ 27 s

22. $F = ma = (5.5 \text{ kg})(4.2 \text{ m/s}^2)$ $= 23$ N

23. $m = \dfrac{F}{a} = \dfrac{13.5 \text{ N}}{6.5 \text{ m/s}^2} =$ 2.1 kg

24. $a = \dfrac{F}{m} = \dfrac{37 \text{ N}}{925 \text{ kg}} =$ 4.0×10^{-2} m/s² away from the stop sign

25. $W = \dfrac{1}{6} mg =$ $\dfrac{(2.26 \text{ kg})(9.8 \text{ m/s}^2)}{6} =$ 3.7 N

15. Velocity An airplane traveling from San Francisco northeast to Chicago travels 1260 km in 3.5 hours. What is the airplane's velocity?

16. Velocity Heather and Matthew take 45 s to walk eastward along a straight road to a store 72 m away. What is their average velocity?

17. Velocity Simpson drives his car with an average velocity of 85 km/h toward the east. How long will it take him to drive 560 km on a perfectly straight highway?

18. Momentum Calculate the momentum of an 85 kg man jogging north along the highway at 2.65 m/s.

19. Momentum Calculate the momentum of a 9.1 kg toddler who is riding in a car moving east at 89 km/h.

20. Acceleration A driver is traveling east on a dirt road when she spots a pothole ahead. She slows her car from 14.0 m/s to 5.5 m/s in 6.0 s. What is the car's acceleration?

21. Acceleration How long will it take a cyclist with a forward acceleration of –0.50 m/s² to bring a bicycle with an initial forward velocity of 13.5 m/s to a complete stop?

22. Force A 5.5 kg watermelon is pushed across a table. If the acceleration of the watermelon is 4.2 m/s² to the right, what is the net force exerted on the watermelon?

23. Force A block pushed with a force of 13.5 N accelerates at 6.5 m/s² to the left. What is the mass of the block?

24. Force The net force on a 925 kg car is 37 N as it pulls away from a stop sign. Find the car's acceleration.

25. Weight A bag of sugar has a mass of 2.26 kg. What is its weight in newtons on the moon, where the acceleration due to gravity is one-sixth that on Earth? (**Hint:** On Earth, $g = 9.8$ m/s².)

THINKING CRITICALLY

26. Interpreting Graphics Two cars are traveling east on a highway, as shown in the figure below. After 5.0 s, they are side by side at the *next* telephone pole. The distance between the poles is 70.0 m. Determine the following quantities:
  a. the distance car A has traveled during the 5.0 s interval
  b. the distance car B has traveled during the 5.0 s interval
  c. the average velocity of car A during this 5.0 s time interval
  d. the average velocity of car B during this 5.0 s time interval

27. Applying Knowledge If the average velocity of a sea gull in a given time interval is 0 m/s, what can you say about the position of the sea gull at the end of the time interval?

28. Applying Knowledge Which object has more momentum in each of the following?
  a. a car and train with the same velocity
  b. a moving ball and a still bat
  c. two identical balls moving with the same speed in the same direction
  d. two identical balls moving at the same speed in opposite directions

29. Problem Solving Why will a boat use more fuel to travel 32 km/h against the wind in a rainstorm than it would to travel at the same velocity for the same time on a sunny day with no wind?

30. Creative Thinking According to Newton's second law, twice the net force results in twice the acceleration. Explain why a stone weighing 20 N doesn't fall twice as fast as a stone weighing 10 N.

31. Applying Knowledge If you doubled the net force acting on a moving object, how would the object's acceleration be affected?

32. Problem Solving How will acceleration change if the mass being accelerated is tripled but the net force is halved?

DEVELOPING LIFE/WORK SKILLS

33. Allocating Resources A pizza-delivery car can travel 11 km for every liter (L) of gasoline it uses (26 mi/gal). If the driver's average speed is 28 km/h (18 mi/h), how many hours can the driver travel before emptying a full 35 L gas tank?

34. Making Decisions If you were an engineer designing an air-bag system, would you want the air bag to release vertically or horizontally from its storage compartment? Explain your reasoning. (**Hint:** Consider the direction of the force of the air bag.)

35. Working Cooperatively Read the following arguments about rocket propulsion. With a small group, determine which is correct. Use a diagram to explain your answer.

  a. Rockets cannot travel in outer space because there is nothing for the gas exiting the rocket to push against.

  b. Rockets can travel in outer space because gas exerts an unbalanced force on the front of the rocket. This net force causes the acceleration.

  c. Argument b can't be true. The action and reaction forces will be equal and opposite. Therefore, the forces will balance, and no movement would be possible.

INTEGRATING CONCEPTS

36. Concept Mapping Copy the unfinished concept map below onto a sheet of paper. Complete the map by writing the correct word or phrase in the lettered boxes.

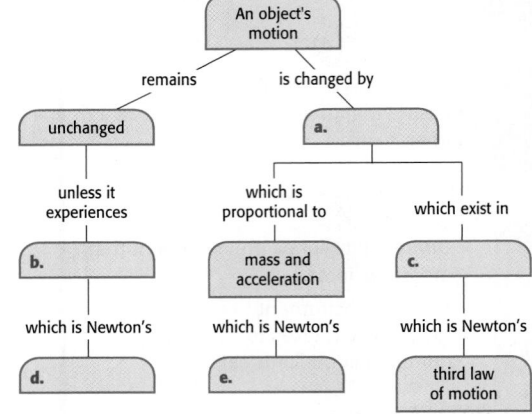

37. Connection to Social Studies Research Galileo's work on falling bodies. What did he want to demonstrate? What theories did he try to refute? What arguments did he use to persuade others that he was right? Did he depend on experiments and observations, logic, or other approaches?

38. Integrating Health When you exercise, you move all or parts of your body to oppose various forces. Identify the forces that oppose your body during the following exercises: push-ups, running, and swimming.

internet connect

SCi LINKS
NSTA

TOPIC: Graphing speed, velocity, acceleration
GO TO: www.scilinks.org
KEYWORD: HK1085

26. a. 140.0 m
  b. 70.0 m
  c. $v = \dfrac{d}{t} = \dfrac{140.0 \text{ m}}{5.0 \text{ s}} = 28 \text{ m/s}$
  d. $\dfrac{70.0 \text{ m}}{5.0 \text{ s}} = 14 \text{ m/s}$

27. The position at the end must be the same as the starting position.

28. a. train
  b. ball
  c. equal
  d. equal but opposite

29. The boat engine must exert more force in order to overcome air resistance.

30. The force on the 20 N stone is twice as great, but the mass is also twice as great, so the acceleration is the same.

31. The object's acceleration would be doubled.

32. The acceleration will be 1/6 what it was.

DEVELOPING LIFE/ WORK SKILLS

33. 14 hours

34. An air bag that is released vertically is less likely to injure a person.

35. a. cannot be correct because rockets *do* travel in outer space
  b. true; the gas in the tank is pushing in all directions. Some pushes forward on the rocket, and some exits through the back of the rocket. This is an imbalance that pushes the rocket forward.
  c. cannot be true because action/reaction pairs never cancel

Answers continue on p. 279B.

Measuring Forces

Introduction

In 1660, Robert Hooke (1635–1703) stated that for small deformations, the stretching of a solid body is directly proportional to the applied force. Under these conditions, the object will return to the original configuration after the load is removed. Hooke's law is given as $F = kx$, where F is the applied force; k is a constant, which depends on the material, its dimensions, and shape; and x is the change in length.

Hooke was employed by Robert Boyle to build Boyle's air pump, was the first to use the word *cell* to name microscopic units in a piece of cork, was a proponent of the theory of evolution based on his studies of fossils, and was the first to make the general observation that matter expands when heated and that air is a mixture of particles separated by relatively large distances.

Objectives

Students will:

► **Build** and calibrate an instrument that measures force.

► **Measure** how much force it takes to stretch a human hair until it breaks.

Planning

Recommended Time: 1 lab period
Materials: (for each lab group)

► large rubber bands of various sizes

► large and small paper clips

► pen or pencil

► metric ruler

► standard hooked masses ranging from 10–200 g

► comb or hairbrush

Design Your Own Lab

Introduction

How can you use a rubber band to measure the force necessary to break a human hair?

Objectives

► **Build** and calibrate an instrument that measures force.

► **Use** your instrument to measure how much force it takes to stretch a human hair until it breaks.

Materials

rubber bands of various sizes
large and small metal paper clips
pen or pencil
metric ruler
standard hooked masses ranging from 10–200 g
comb or hairbrush

Safety Needs

safety goggles

Measuring Forces

► Testing the Strength of a Human Hair

1. Obtain a rubber band and a paper clip.
2. Carefully straighten the paper clip so that it forms a double hook. Cut the rubber band and tie one end to the ring stand and the other end to one of the paper clip hooks. Let the paper clip dangle.
3. In your lab report, prepare a table as shown below.
4. Measure the length of the rubber band. Record this length in **Table 1**.
5. Hang a hooked mass from the lower paper clip hook. Supporting the mass with your hand, allow the rubber band to stretch downward slowly. Then remove your hand carefully so the rubber band does not move.
6. Measure the stretched rubber band's length. Record the mass that is attached and the rubber band's length in **Table 1**. Calculate the change in length by subtracting your initial reading of the rubber band's length from the new length.
7. Repeat steps 5 and 6 three more times using different masses each time.
8. Convert each mass (in grams) to kilograms using the following equation.
$$\text{mass (in kg)} = \text{mass (in g)} \div 1000$$
Record your answers in **Table 1**.
9. Calculate the force (weight) of each mass in newtons using the following equation.
$$\text{Force (in N)} = \text{mass (in kg)} \times 9.81 \text{ m/s}^2$$
Record your answers in **Table 1**.

Table 1 **Calibration**

Rubber-band length (cm)	Change in length (cm)	Mass on hook (g)	Mass on hook (kg)	Force (N)
	0	0	0	0

REQUIRED PRECAUTIONS

► Safety goggles must be worn at all times.

► Read all safety precautions and discuss them with your students.

► Remind students that horseplay will not be allowed in the lab.

► Long hair and loose clothing must be tied back.

▶ Designing Your Experiment

10. With your lab partner(s), devise a plan to measure the force required to break a human hair using the instrument you just calibrated. How will you attach the hair to your instrument? How will you apply force to the hair?
11. In your lab report, list each step you will perform in your experiment.
12. Have your teacher approve your plan before you carry out your experiment.

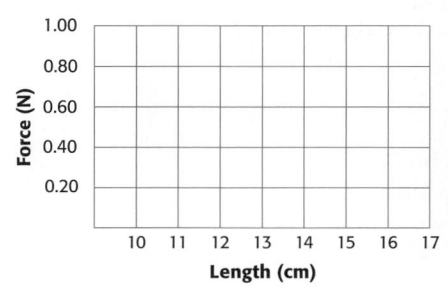

▶ Performing Your Experiment

13. After your teacher approves your plan, gently run a comb or brush through a group member's hair several times until you find a loose hair at least 10 cm long that you can test.
14. In your lab report, prepare a data table similar to the one shown at right to record your experimental data.
15. Perform your experiment on three different hairs from the same person. Record the maximum rubber-band length before the hair snaps for each trial in **Table 2**.

Table 2 **Experimentation**

Trial	Rubber-band length (cm)	Force (N)
Hair 1		
Hair 2		
Hair 3		

▶ Analyzing Your Results

1. Plot your calibration data in your lab report in the form of a graph like the one shown at right. On your graph draw the line or smooth curve that fits the points best.
2. Use the graph and the length of the rubber band for each trial of your experiment to determine the force that was necessary to break each of the three hairs. Record your answers in **Table 2**.

[Graph: Force (N) on vertical axis with values 0.20, 0.40, 0.60, 0.80, 1.00; Length (cm) on horizontal axis with values 10, 11, 12, 13, 14, 15, 16, 17]

▶ Defending Your Conclusions

3. Suppose someone tells you that your results are flawed because you measured length and not force. How can you show that your results are valid?

Pre-Lab

Teaching Tips

The rubber bands used in this experiment can be compared to spring balances or car shock absorbers.

Procedure

▶ Designing Your Experiment

The calibration mass depends on the size of the rubber band. Some students may find it easier to hang a mass of 10 g or 50 g on the rubber band to straighten the rubber band, and call that mass a zero mass. Alternatively, the rubber band can be cut and loops tied at the end to hang the masses. This method eliminates the need to use a token mass to keep the rubber band straight. Tying a hair into a knot is often difficult. Longer hair is generally easier to tie than short hair. Measurements made to 0.1 cm may be easier for most students to estimate.

▶ Performing Your Experiment

15. Answers will vary. Sample data is given in the calibration table.

Post Lab

▶ Disposal

None. The equipment can be kept for future use.

Continue on p. 279A.

Design Your Own Lab from page 279

Measuring Forces

Sample Data Table Calibration

Rubber-band length (cm)	Mass on hook (g)	Mass on hook (kg)	Force (N)
0	0	0	0
2.1	200	0.200	1.96
7.1	500	0.500	4.90
11.2	1000	1.000	9.81

Sample Data Table Experimentation

Trial	Rubber-band length (cm)	Force (N)
Hair 1	1.1	1
Hair 2	1.1	1
Hair 3	1.2	1

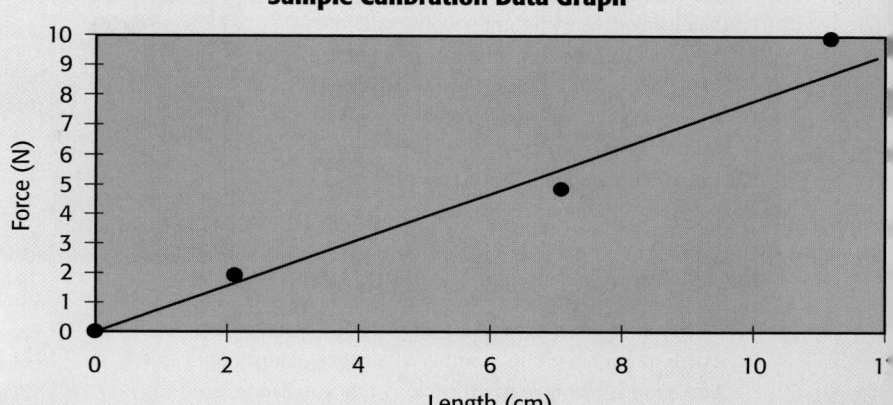

Sample Calibration Data Graph

▶ Analyzing Your Results

1. Answers will vary. Sample data is given in the graph.
2. Answers will vary. Sample data is given in the data table. In the sample data table, length is given as the change in length. The absolute length can be used also. The force is extrapolated from the sample data graph.

▶ Defending Your Conclusions

3. Although length was measured and not force, the applied force is proportional to the change in length. Therefore, length and force are directly related and to measure one is to have a way to know the other.

Answers from page 274

Math Skills

5. 0.26 m/s^2 forward
6. 49 N

Answers from page 277

INTEGRATING CONCEPTS

36. a. force
  b. unbalanced force
  c. action/reaction pairs
  d. first law
  e. second law
37. He wanted to demonstrate that the gravitational acceleration is the same for all objects. He was trying to disprove the theory that heavier bodies fall faster. He conducted experiments with rolling and dropping balls. He used logic, observations, and experiments.
38. push-ups—gravity; running—gravity and air resistance; swimming—water resistance (friction)

viewpoints

Should Bicycle Helmets Be Required by Law?

> Your Turn

1. Critiquing Viewpoints
Students' analyses of a single argument's weak points may vary. Be sure that student responses clearly identify a weakness and respond in some way that provides support. Possible responses for each of the viewpoints in the feature are listed below. (Note that students should analyze only *one of the following.*)
Chad A.: Some objections to helmet use are more serious than appearance, such as decreases in peripheral vision and ability to hear.

But bicycle helmets can still protect you from serious head injuries.
Laurel R.: Ticketing children is not likely to change matters.

But children are at greater risk because they are more likely to be riding bicycles and have less experience.
Jocelyn B.: The unfortunate accident described happened to one person. That does not necessarily mean everyone's at risk.

But this single incident does show that accidents that could be less tragic with bicycle helmets do occur, even when people don't expect them.
Megan J. and Heather R.: The argument that individual rights exceed the public health benefits do not take into account the fact that preventable injuries are a waste of money for insurance companies, hospitals, the government, and taxpayers.

But laws limiting individual freedom can have unintended consequences.
Melissa F.: If people can't afford to bicycle safely and with helmets, perhaps they shouldn't bicycle at all.

But is it right to deny someone access to such a simple vehicle because of their financial situation?

2. Critiquing Viewpoints
Students' analyses of strong points

in some communities, bicyclists are required by law to wear a helmet and can be ticketed if they do not. Few people dispute the fact that bicycle helmets can save lives when used properly.

But others say that it is a matter of private rights and that the government should not interfere. Should it be up to bicyclists to decide whether or not to wear a helmet and to suffer any consequences?

But are the consequences limited to the rider? Who will pay when the rider gets hurt? Should the rider bear the cost of an injury that could have been prevented?

Is this an issue of public health or private rights? What do you think?

> FROM: Chad A., Rochester, MN

More and more people are getting head injuries every year because they do not wear a helmet. Nowadays helmets look so cool— I wouldn't be ashamed to wear one.

> FROM: Laurel R., Coral Springs, FL

I believe that this is a public issue only for people under the age of 12. Children 12 and under still need guidance and direction about safety and they are usually the ones riding their bicycles out in the road or in traffic. Often they don't pay attention to cars or other motor vehicles around them.

> FROM: Jocelyn B., Chicago, IL

They should treat helmets the same way they treat seatbelts. I was in a tragic bike accident when I was 7. I was jerked off my bike, and I slid on the glass-laden concrete. To make a long story short, I think there should be a helmet law because people just don't know the danger.

Require Bicycle Helmets

in opposing arguments may vary. Be sure that student responses clearly identify the strong points and respond in some way that provides support for the opposite point of view. Possible responses for each of the viewpoints in the feature are listed below. (Note that students should analyze *only one of the following.*)
Chad A. and Jocelyn B.: More and more injuries that are preventable are occurring.

But the government should not get involved in every risk someone takes.

Laurel R.: Children need to be protected the most from such accidents.

But because they are children, they can't force their parents to get them helmets anyway.
Megan J.: Individual rights are important.

But when an individual decides to risk his life, others do have the right to try to stop him.
Melissa F.: Bicycle helmets are not cheap.

But far more money can be saved by preventing a costly accident.
Heather R.: This is not likely to be a high-priority for police enforcement.

> FROM: Megan J., Bowling Green, KY.

Although wearing a bicycle helmet can be considered a matter of public health, the rider is the one at risk. It is a personal choice, no matter what the public says.

> FROM: Melissa F., Houston, TX

Bicycle helmets shouldn't be required by law. Helmets are usually a little over $20, and if you have five kids, the helmets alone cost $100. You'd still have to buy the bikes.

Don't Require Bicycle Helmets

> FROM: Heather R., Rochester, MN

It has to do with private rights. The police have more serious issues to deal with, like violent crimes. Bicycle riders should choose whether or not they want to risk their life by riding without a helmet.

> Your Turn

1. **Critiquing Viewpoints** Select one of the statements on this page that you *agree* with. Identify and explain at least one weak point in the statement. What would you say to respond to someone who brought up this weak point as a reason you were wrong?

2. **Critiquing Viewpoints** Select one of the statements on this page that you *disagree* with. Identify and explain at least one strong point in the statement. What would you say to respond to someone who brought up this point as a reason they were right?

3. **Creative Thinking** Suppose you live in a community that does not have a bicycle helmet law. Design a campaign to persuade people to wear helmets, even though it isn't required by law. Your campaign could include brochures, posters, and newspaper ads.

4. **Acquiring and Evaluating Data** When a rider falls off a bicycle, the rider continues moving at the speed of the bicycle until the rider strikes the pavement and slows down rapidly. For bicycle speeds ranging from 5.0 m/s to 25.0 m/s, calculate what acceleration would be required to stop the rider in just 0.50 s. How large is the force that must be applied to a 50.0 kg rider to cause this acceleration? Organize your data and results in a series of charts or graphs.

 internet**connect**

 go. hrw .com

TOPIC: Bicycle helmets
GO TO: go.hrw.com
KEYWORD: HK1Helmet

Should helmets be required by law? Why or why not? Share your views on this issue and learn about other viewpoints at the HRW Web site.

281

Many other laws are rarely enforced, but have been instituted so society can go on record in favor of or opposing something.

3. Creative Thinking
Student answers will vary. Evaluate students' plans for campaigns using a scale of 1–5 points for each of the following: thought behind the planning of the advertising strategy, clarity in the advertising message, persuasiveness, creativity, and effort. (25 total possible points)

4. Acquiring and Evaluating Data
Student answers should indicate that an acceleration of 10 m/s^2 (nearly the same as gravity) and a force of 500 N would be required to stop the slowest bicyclist, and an acceleration of 50 m/s^2 and 2500 N would be required to stop the fastest one.

Students should probably choose a bar graph to display their results if they evaluated specific speeds. Some may choose to show all values in between the maximum and minimum by plotting a line graph.

Evaluate students' charts or graphs using a scale of 1–5 points for each of the following: accuracy of calculation, accuracy of graphing, neatness of graph, explanation of significance of data, and effort. (25 total possible points)

internet**connect**

The HRW Web site has more opinions from other students and also provides an opportunity for your students to contribute their points of view. Every few months, more opinions will be added from the ones submitted. Student opinions that are posted will be identified only by the student's first name, last initial, and city to protect his or her privacy.

Tailoring the Program to YOUR Classroom

CHAPTER 9

Work and Energy

Annotated Descriptions of the Correlated National Science Standards

The following descriptions summarize the National Science Standards that specially relate to Chapter 9. For the full text of the Standards, see p. 40T.

SECTION 9.1
Work, Power, and Machines
Physical Science
PS 4a
Unifying Concepts and Processes
UCP 1–3
Science as Inquiry
SAI 1

SECTION 9.2
Simple Machines
Physical Science
PS 4a
Unifying Concepts and Processes
UCP 1–3, 5
Science and Technology
ST 2

SECTION 9.3
What Is Energy?
Physical Science
PS 1a, 1c, 2a–2e, 3b, 4b, 5a–5d, 6a, 6b
Life Science
LS 1b, 1f, 4a, 5a–5c, 5f
Earth and Space Science
ES 1a
Unifying Concepts and Processes
UCP 1–3
Science in Personal and Social Perspectives
SPSP 2

SECTION 9.4
Conservation of Energy
Physical Science
PS 5a, 5d
Life Science
LS 5f
Unifying Concepts and Processes
UCP 1–3

Cross-Discipline Teaching RESOURCES

Cross-Discipline Teaching, ATE p. 282
Social Studies   Mathematics
Life Science

Integration Enrichment Resources
Biology, **PE** and **ATE** p. 285
    IE 9.1 *Muscles and Work*
Social Studies, **PE** and **ATE** p. 295
    IE 9.2 *The Pyramids*
Real World Applications, **PE** and **ATE** p. 303
    IE 9.3 *Calories and Nutrition*
Computers and Technology, **PE** and **ATE** p. 310
    IE 9.4 *Batteries and Emerging Technology*

Additional Worksheets
    IE 9.5 Language Arts   **IE 9.6** Chemistry
    IE 9.7 Environmental Science

Use the Planning Guide on the next page to help you organize your lessons.

MATH AND COMPUTER RESOURCES

Chapter 9	Math Skills	Assess	Media/Computer Skills
Section 9.1	**ATE Cross-Discipline Teaching,** p. 282 **BS Worksheet 5.7** Equations with Three Parts **PE Math Skills** Work, p. 285 **PE Math Skills** Power, p. 286 **ATE Additional Examples** p. 286 **PE Math Skills** Mechanical Advantage, p. 289 **ATE Additional Examples** p. 289	**PE Practice,** p. 285 **PE Practice,** p. 287 **PE Practice,** p. 290 **PE Section Review** 5–8, p. 290 **MS** Worksheets 17–19 **PE Problem Bank,** p. 697, 81–95	■ Section 9.1 ◉ *DISC TWO, MODULE 10* Work
Section 9.2			■ Section 9.2 **CNN** Presents **Physical Science Segment 3** Trebuchet Design **CRT** Worksheet 3
Section 9.3	**PE Math Skills** Gravitational Potential Energy, p. 299 **ATE Additional Examples** p. 299 **PE Math Skills** Kinetic Energy, p. 301 **ATE Additional Examples** p. 301 **BS Worksheet 3.4** Squares and Square Roots	**PE Practice,** p. 299 **PE Practice,** p. 301 **MS** Worksheets 20, 21 **PE Section Review** 7–9, p. 305 **PE Problem Bank,** pp. 698–699, 96–105	■ Section 9.3
Section 9.4	**PE Math Skills** Efficiency, p. 313 **ATE Additional Examples** p. 313 **BS Worksheet 3.2** Percentages	**PE Practice,** p. 313 **MS** Worksheet 22 **PE Section Review** 7–9, p. 314 **PE Problem Bank,** p. 699, 106–110	■ Section 9.4

PE Pupil's Edition **ATE** Annotated Teacher's Edition **MS** Math Skills **BS** Basic Skills **IE** Integration Enrichment ■ Guided Reading Audio **CRT** Critical Thinking

PHYSICAL SCIENCE INTERACTIVE TUTOR

READING SKILL BUILDER

The following activities found in the Annotated Teacher's Edition provide techniques for developing useful reading strategies to increase your students' reading comprehension skills.

Section 9.1 **Brainstorming,** p. 282
          L.I.N.K., p. 284

Section 9.2 **Anticipation (Prediction),** p. 291

Section 9.3 **K-W-L,** p. 297

Section 9.4 **Brainstorming,** p. 306

Smithsonian Institution®

Visit www.si.edu/hrw for additional online resources.

Spanish Resources

The following resources are made available for students who speak Spanish as their first language.

Spanish Resources Guided Reading Audio CD-ROM
Chapter 9

Spanish Glossary
Chapter 9

282B

Work and Energy

CLASSROOM RESOURCES

FOCUS	TEACH	HANDS-ON
Section 9.1: Work, Power, and Machines		
BLOCK 1 45 minutes	**ATE RSB** Brainstorming, p. 282 **ATE** Focus Activities 1, 2, p. 283 **ATE RSB** L.I.N.K., p. 284 **PE** Work and Power, pp. 284–287 ★ Focus Transparency LT 29 **ATE Demo 1** Work, p. 284	**ATE Skill Builder** Interpreting Visuals, p. 283	**IE** Worksheet 9.1 **PE** Inquiry Lab *What is your power output when you climb the stairs?* p. 287 **DS** 9.1
BLOCK 2 45 minutes	**PE** Machines and Mechanical Advantage, pp. 288–290	**ATE Skill Builder** Interpreting Visuals, p. 288	
Section 9.2: Simple Machines		
BLOCK 3 45 minutes	**ATE RSB** Anticipation, p. 291 **ATE Demo 2** Pulley Power, p. 291 **PE** The Lever Family, pp. 291–294 ★ Focus Transparency LT 30	**ATE Skill Builder** Interpreting Visuals, p. 293 **TT** 24 Levers **TT** 25 Pulleys	**PE** Quick Activity *A Simple Lever*, p. 292 **DS** 9.2
BLOCK 4 45 minutes	**PE** Inclined Planes and Compound Machines, pp. 294–296	**ATE Skill Builder** Interpreting Visuals, p. 294	**PE** Quick Activity *A Simple Inclined Plane*, p. 294 **DS** 9.3 **IE** Worksheet 9.2
Section 9.3: What Is Energy?		
BLOCK 5 45 minutes	**ATE RSB** K-W-L, p. 297 **PE** Energy and Work; Potential Energy, pp. 297–299 ★ Focus Transparency LT 31	**ATE Skill Builder** Vocabulary, p. 298 Interpreting Visuals, p. 298	**IE** Worksheet 9.5
BLOCK 6 45 minutes	**PE** Kinetic Energy, pp. 300–301 **PE** Other Forms of Energy, pp. 302–305	**BLM** 26 Kinetic Energy Graph	**PE** Real World Applications *The Energy in Food*, p. 303 **IE** Worksheets 9.3, 9.6
Section 9.4: Conservation of Energy		
BLOCK 7 45 minutes	**ATE RSB** Brainstorming, p. 306 **ATE Demo 3** Bouncing Ball, p. 308 **PE** Energy Transformations, pp. 306–309 ★ Focus Transparency LT 32	**ATE Skill Builder** Interpreting Visuals, p. 306 **TT** 26 Kinetic and Potential Energy **BLM** 27 Energy Graphs	**PE** Quick Activity *Energy Transfer*, p. 309 **DS** 9.4
BLOCK 8 45 minutes	**PE** Conservation of Energy; Efficiency of Machines, pp. 310–314		**PE** Inquiry Lab *Is energy conserved in a pendulum?* p. 311 **DS** 9.5 **PE** Skill Builder Lab *Determining Energy for a Rolling Ball*, p. 318 **DS** 9.6 **LE** 9 *Determining Which Ramp Is More Efficient* **DS** 9.7 **IE** Worksheets 9.4, 9.7

CLASSROOM RESOURCES

HOMEWORK	ASSESS
PE Section Review 1, 2, 5, 7, 8, p. 290 **Chapter 9 Review,** p. 315, items 1, 4, 10, 14	**SG** Chapter 9 Pretest
PE Section Review 3, 4, 6, p. 290 **Chapter 9 Review,** p. 315, items 2, 16	**SG** Section 9.1
PE Section Review 1–4, 7, p. 296	
PE Section Review 5, 6, 8, p. 296 **Chapter 9 Review,** p. 315, items 3, 12	**SG** Section 9.2
PE Section Review 2, 5–7, p. 305 **Chapter 9 Review,** p. 315, item 15	
PE Section Review 1, 3, 4, 8, 9, p. 305 **Chapter 9 Review,** p. 315, items 5, 7, 8, 11, 13	**SG** Section 9.3
PE Section Review 2, 3, p. 314 **Chapter 9 Review,** p. 315, item 6	
PE Section Review 1, 4–9, p. 314 **Chapter 9 Review,** p. 315, items 9, 17, 18	**SG** Section 9.4

BLOCK 9

Chapter 9 Review
Thinking Critically 19–22, pp. 316–317
Developing Life/Work Skills 23–24, p. 317
Integrating Concepts 25–28, p. 317
SG Chapter 9 Mixed Review

BLOCK 10

Chapter Tests
Chapter 9 Test

One-Stop Planner CD-ROM **with Test Generator**
Chapter 9

Teaching Resources
Scoring Rubrics and assignment checklist.

internet connect

SCI LINKS
NSTA

National Science Teachers Association
Online Resources:
www.scilinks.org

The following *sci*LINKS Internet resources can be found in the student text for this chapter.

Page 283 **TOPIC:** Machines **KEYWORD:** HK1091	**Page 301** **TOPIC:** Kinetic energy **KEYWORD:** HK1095
Page 289 **TOPIC:** Mechanical advantage **KEYWORD:** HK1092	**Page 308** **TOPIC:** Energy transformations **KEYWORD:** HK1096
Page 298 **TOPIC:** Potential energy **KEYWORD:** HK1094	**Page 317** **TOPIC:** Energy and sports **KEYWORD:** HK1097

CNN fyi.com   www.cnnfyi.com

Visit this site for coverage of current events and related classroom resources.

PE Pupil's Edition   **ATE** Teacher's Edition
RSB Reading Skill Builder   **DS** Datasheets
IE Integrated Enrichment   **SG** Study Guide
LE Laboratory Experiments
TT Teaching Transparencies   **BLM** Blackline Masters
★ Lesson Focus Transparency

Work and Energy

Tapping Prior Knowledge

Be sure students understand the following concepts:

Chapter 8
Speed, velocity, forces, gravity, and the difference between mass and weight

READING SKILL BUILDER *Brainstorming*
Write the words *work* and *energy* on the chalkboard. Ask students to come up with words or phrases that relate to the concepts of work and energy. Have two student volunteers write down students' contributions in a list under each word. Have students use the section headings and objectives in the chapter to devise a hypothesis about how the terms are related.

Chapter Preview

282

RESOURCE LINK
STUDY GUIDE

Assign students *Pretest Chapter 9 Work and Energy* before beginning Section 9.1.

CROSS-DISCIPLINE TEACHING

Social Studies Invite a history teacher to be a guest lecturer during your discussion of power or energy transformation. Have the History teacher explain the impact of new sources of power during the Industrial Revolution.

Life Science Plants use energy from the sun to carry out photosynthesis. Invite a biology teacher to be a guest lecturer during your discussion of

energy. Have the biology teacher explain the energy transformations that take place during the process of photosynthesis.

Mathematics Discuss the possibility of joint assignments with an algebra teacher. Possible overlaps include ratios, square roots, and basic concepts of algebra.

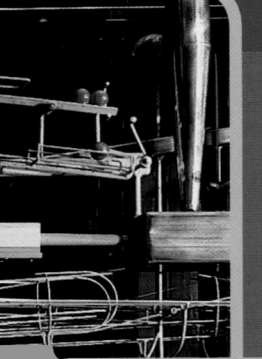

Kinetic sculptures are sculptures that have moving parts. The changes in the motion of different parts of a kinetic sculpture can be explained in terms of forces or in terms of energy transformations.

Focus ACTIVITY

Background The collection of tubes, tracks, balls, and blocks of wood shown at left is an audio-kinetic sculpture. A conveyor belt lifts the balls to a point high on the track, and the balls wind their way down as they are pulled by the force of gravity and pushed by various other forces. They twist through spirals, drop straight down tubes, and sometimes go up and around loops as if on a roller coaster. Along the way, the balls trip levers and bounce off elastic membranes. The sculpture uses the energy of the falling balls to produce sounds in wood blocks and metal tubes.

This kinetic sculpture can be considered a machine or a collection of many small machines. It uses the motion of the balls to produce a desired musical effect. Other kinetic sculptures may incorporate simple machines such as levers, wheels, and screws. The American artist Alexander Calder, shown at left, is well known for his hanging mobiles that move in response to air currents.

This chapter introduces the basic principles of energy that explain the motions and interactions of machines and of parts within machines—including kinetic sculptures.

Activity 1 Look around your kitchen or garage. What kinds of tools or utensils do you see? How do these tools help with different kinds of projects? For each tool, consider where force is applied to the tool and how the tool may apply force to another object. Is the force transferred to another part of the tool? Is the force that the tool can exert on an object larger or smaller than the force exerted on the tool?

Activity 2 Any piece of artwork that moves is a kinetic sculpture. Design and construct a kinetic sculpture of your own. Some ideas for materials include hangers, rubber bands, string, wood and metal scraps, and old toys.

internet connect

SCI**LINKS**
NSTA

TOPIC: Machines
GO TO: www.scilinks.org
KEYWORD: HK1091

Focus ACTIVITY

Background The artist Alexander Calder was born in Philadelphia, Pennsylvania, in 1898. He is best known for inventing the mobile. He died at the age of 78, after creating 16 000 works of art.

Activity 1 Answers may vary. Students should have lists of tools around the home and should have given some thought to the function of each tool, where forces act on the tools, and how the tools apply forces to other objects.

Activity 2 Encourage students to model simple machines from Section 9.2. Students may also construct a kinetic sculpture by combining simple machines into a compound machine.

SKILL BUILDER

Interpreting Visuals Have students examine the illustrations at left and identify as many simple machines in the kinetic sculptures as they can. Students may refer to **Figure 9-4** on page 291 for examples of the six simple machines.

Work, Power, and Machines

Scheduling

Refer to pp. 282A–282D for lecture, classwork, and assignment options for Section 9.1.

★ **Lesson Focus**
Use transparency *LT 29* to prepare students for this section.

READING SKILL BUILDER *L.I.N.K.* Write the word *work* on the board. Have students brainstorm all the words, phrases, and ideas that they associate with work. Have a volunteer write students' contributions on the board. Lead students in a discussion about the listed terms.

Allow students to ask you and other students for clarification of the listed ideas. At the end of the discussion have students make notes of everything they remember from the discussion. Have the students look over their notes to see what they know about work based on experience and the discussion.

Which of their examples involve work in the scientific sense? Which examples use a different definition of *work*?

MISCONCEPTION ALERT

Work Students may confuse the scientific meaning of *work* with the common, everyday meaning. In order to clarify the proper scientific meaning, point out that when used in the scientific sense, *work* is always done *by* a force, *on* an object, changing the motion of the object. Have students come up with sentences using *work* in both the common sense and the scientific sense.

9.1

Work, Power, and Machines

▶ **KEY TERMS**
work
power
mechanical advantage

OBJECTIVES

▶ Define *work* and *power*.
▶ Calculate the work done on an object and the rate at which work is done.
▶ Use the concept of mechanical advantage to explain how machines make doing work easier.
▶ Calculate the mechanical advantage of various machines.

Disc Two, Module 10: Work
Use the Interactive Tutor to learn more about this topic.

▶ **work** quantity of energy transferred by a force when it is applied to a body and causes that body to move in the direction of the force

Figure 9-1
As this weightlifter holds the barbell over her head, is she doing any work on the barbell?

If you needed to change a flat tire, you would probably use a car jack to lift the car. Machines—from complex ones such as a car to relatively simple ones such as a car jack, a hammer, or a ramp—help people get things done every day.

What Is Work?

Imagine trying to lift the front of a car without using a jack. You could exert a lot of force without moving the car at all. Exerting all that force might seem like hard work. In science, however, the word **work** has a very specific meaning.

Work is done only when force causes a change in the motion of an object in the direction of the applied force. Work is calculated by multiplying the force by the distance over which the force is applied. We will always assume that the force used to calculate work is acting along the same line as the direction of motion.

Work Equation

$$work = force \times distance$$
$$W = F \times d$$

In the case of trying to lift the car, you might apply a large force, but if the distance that the car moves is equal to zero, the work done on the car is also equal to zero.

However, once the car moves even a small amount, you have done some work on it. You could calculate how much by multiplying the force you have applied by the distance the car moves.

The weightlifter in **Figure 9-1** is applying a force to the barbell as she holds it overhead, but the barbell is not moving. Is she doing any work on the barbell?

284 CHAPTER 9

DEMONSTRATION 1 TEACHING

Work

Time: Approximately 15 minutes
Materials: textbook
spring scale
string

Step 1 Hang the textbook from the spring scale with string. Hold the top of the scale stationary and have students note the reading on the scale. Is there a force acting on the book? *(Yes, the force of gravity is pulling down on the book and the*

spring is exerting an equal and opposite upward force.) Is work being done on the book? *(No, the work on the book is zero because the displacement of the book is zero.)*

Step 2 Now lift the book (using the scale) through a distance of about 1 m. Try to move the book at a constant velocity. Does the reading on the scale change? *(The reading changes only at the beginning and the end of the motion, while the book is accelerating or decelerating.)* Is work

Work is measured in joules

Because work is calculated as force times distance, it is measured in units of newtons times meters, N•m. These units are also called *joules* (J). In terms of SI base units, a joule is equivalent to 1 kg•m²/s².

$$1 \text{ N•m} = 1 \text{ J} = 1 \text{ kg•m}^2/\text{s}^2$$

Because these units are all equal, you can choose whichever unit is easiest for solving a particular problem. Substituting equivalent units will often help you cancel out other units in a problem.

You do about 1 J of work when you slowly lift an apple, which weighs about 1 N, from your waist to the top of your head, a distance of about 1 m. Three push-ups require about 1000 J of work.

Math Skills

Work Imagine a father playing with his daughter by lifting her repeatedly in the air. How much work does he do with each lift, assuming he lifts her 2.0 m and exerts an average force of 190 N?

1 List the given and unknown values.
> **Given:** *force*, F = 190 N
> *distance*, d = 2.0 m
> **Unknown:** *work*, W = ? J

2 Write the equation for work.
> *work = force × distance* $W = F \times d$

3 Insert the known values into the equation, and solve.
> $W = 190 \text{ N} \times 2.0 \text{ m} = 380 \text{ N•m} = 380 \text{ J}$

Practice

Work

1. A crane uses an average force of 5200 N to lift a girder 25 m. How much work does the crane do on the girder?

2. An apple weighing 1 N falls through a distance of 1 m. How much work is done on the apple by the force of gravity?

3. The brakes on a bicycle apply 125 N of frictional force to the wheels as the bicycle travels 14.0 m. How much work have the brakes done on the bicycle?

4. While rowing in a race, John uses his arms to exert a force of 165 N per stroke while pulling the oar 0.800 m. How much work does he do in 30 strokes?

5. A mechanic uses a hydraulic lift to raise a 1200 kg car 0.5 m off the ground. How much work does the lift do on the car?

Practice HINT

▶ In order to use the work equation, you must use units of newtons for force and units of meters for distance. Practice Problem 5 gives a mass in kilograms instead of a weight in newtons. To convert from mass to force (weight), use the definition of weight from Section 8.3:

$$w = mg$$

where *m* is the mass in kilograms and g = 9.8 m/s². Then plug the value for weight into the work equation as the force.

Section 9.1

Work, Power, and Machines

INTEGRATING

LIFE SCIENCE *Resources* Assign students worksheet *9.1: Integrating Biology—Muscles and Work* in the **Integration Enrichment Resources** ancillary.

Historical Perspective

The unit of work and energy was named in honor of the English physicist James Prescott Joule (1818–1889). Joule was the first to recognize that mechanical work and non-mechanical energy could be interchangeable, which was the foundation of the law of conservation of energy.

Math Skills

Resources Assign students worksheet *17: Work* in the **Math Skills Worksheets** ancillary.

Solution Guide

1. $W = F \times d = (5200 \text{ N})(25 \text{ m}) = 1.3 \times 10^5 \text{ J}$
2. $W = (1 \text{ N})(1 \text{ m}) = 1 \text{ J}$
3. $W = (125 \text{ N})(14.0 \text{ m}) = 1750 \text{ J}$
4. $W = (30)(165 \text{ N})(0.800 \text{ m}) = 3960 \text{ J}$
5. $F = mg = (1200 \text{ kg})(9.8 \text{ m/s}) = 1.2 \times 10^4 \text{ N}$
   $W = (1.2 \times 10^4 \text{ N})(0.5 \text{ m}) = 6000 \text{ J}$

being done on the book? *(Yes, because the book is moving through a distance, while a force is acting on it in the same direction as its motion.)*

Step 3 Now hold the book at shoulder height and carry it across the room (again using the scale). Try to move at a constant velocity. Does the reading on the scale change? *(No, the reading should not change significantly.)* Is work being done on the book? *(No, because the motion is perpendicular to the direction of force.)*

Historical Perspective

The unit of power was named for James Watt (1736–1819), a Scottish inventor who played an important role in the development of the steam engine.

Math Skills

Resources Assign students worksheet *18: Power* in the **Math Skills Worksheets** ancillary.

Additional Examples

Power A student lifts a 12 N textbook 1.5 m in 1.5 s and carries the book 5 m across the room in 7 s.

a. How much work does the student do on the textbook?

Answer: (12 N)(1.5 m) = 18 J

b. What is the power output of the student?

Answer: (18 J)/(1.5 s) = 12 W

Compare the work and power used in the following cases:
a. A 43 N force is exerted through a distance of 2.0 m over a time of 3.0 s.

Answer: $W = 86$ J, $P = 29$ W

b. A 43 N force is exerted through a distance of 3.0 m over a time of 2.0 s.

Answer: $W = 130$ J, $P = 65$ W

▷ **power** a quantity that measures the rate at which work is done

Did You Know ❓

Another common unit of power is horsepower (hp). This originally referred to the average power output of a draft horse. One horsepower equals 746 W. With that much power, a horse could raise a load of 746 apples, weighing 1 N each, by 1 m every second.

Power

Running up a flight of stairs doesn't require any more work than walking up slowly, but it is definitely more exhausting. The amount of time it takes to get work done is another important factor when considering work and machines. The quantity that measures this is **power**. Power is defined as the rate at which work is done, that is, how much work is done in a certain amount of time.

Power Equation

$$power = \frac{work}{time} \qquad P = \frac{W}{t}$$

Running up the stairs takes less time than walking. How does reducing the time in this equation affect the power if the amount of work stays the same?

Power is measured in watts

Power is measured in SI units called *watts* (W). A watt is the amount of power required to do 1 J of work in 1 s, about as much power as you need to lift an apple over your head in 1 s. You must be careful not to confuse the abbreviation for watts, W, with the symbol for work, *W*. You can tell which one is meant by the context in which it appears and by whether it is in italics.

Math Skills

Power It takes 100 kJ of work to lift an elevator 18 m. If this is done in 20 s, what is the average power of the elevator during the process?

1 List the given and unknown values.
   Given: *work*, $W = 100$ kJ $= 1 \times 10^5$ J
   time, $t = 20$ s
   The distance of 18 m will not be needed to calculate power.
   Unknown: *power*, $P = ?$ W

2 Write the equation for power.
   $$power = \frac{work}{time} \qquad P = \frac{W}{t}$$

3 Insert the known values into the equation, and solve.
   $$P = \frac{1 \times 10^5 \text{ J}}{20 \text{ s}} = 5 \times 10^3 \text{ J/s} = 5 \times 10^3 \text{ W}$$
   $$P = 5 \text{ kW}$$

286 CHAPTER 9

Practice

Power

1. While rowing in a race, John does 3960 J of work on the oars in 60.0 s. What is his power output in watts?
2. Every second, a coal-fired power plant produces enough electricity to do 9×10^8 J (900 MJ) of work. What is the plant's power output in watts (or in megawatts)?
3. Using a jack, a mechanic does 5350 J of work to lift a car 0.500 m in 50.0 s. What is the mechanic's power output?
4. Suppose you are moving a 300 N box of books. Calculate your power output in the following situations:
   a. You exert a force of 60.0 N to push the box 12.0 m in 20.0 s.
   b. You lift the box 1 m onto a truck in 3 s.
5. Anna walks up the stairs on her way to class. She weighs 565 N and the stairs go up 3.25 m vertically.
   a. Calculate her power output if she climbs the stairs in 12.6 s.
   b. What is her power output if she climbs the stairs in 10.5 s?

▶ In order to calculate power in Practice Problems 4 and 5, you must first use the work equation to calculate the work done in each case.

Inquiry Lab

What is your power output when you climb the stairs?

Materials ✔ flight of stairs   ✔ stopwatch   ✔ meterstick

Procedure

1. Determine your weight in newtons. If your school has a scale that weighs in kilograms, multiply your mass in kilograms by 9.8 m/s² to determine your weight in newtons. If your school has a scale that weighs in pounds, you can use the conversion factor of 4.45 N/lb.
2. Divide into pairs. Have your partner use the stopwatch to time how long it takes you to walk quickly up the stairs. Record the time. Then switch roles and repeat.
3. Measure the height of one step in meters. Multiply the number of steps by the height of one step to get the total height of the stairway.
4. Multiply your weight in newtons by the height of the stairs in meters to get the work you did in joules. Recall the work equation: *work = force × distance*, or $W = F \times d$.
5. To get your power in watts, divide the work done in joules by the time in seconds that it took you to climb the stairs.

Analysis

1. How would your power output change if you walked up the stairs faster?
2. What would your power output be if you climbed the same stairs in the same amount of time while carrying a stack of books weighing 20 N?
3. Why did you use your weight as the force in the work equation?

Inquiry Lab

What is your power output when you climb the stairs?

SAFETY CAUTION *Instruct students not to run on the stairs. Also caution students not to overexert themselves. Emphasize to students that this is not a contest.*

Analysis

1. Your power output would be greater if you walked up the stairs faster.
2. Answers will vary depending on data. Answer should be a power output in watts, slightly larger than the power output calculated in item 5 of the procedure.
3. The students' weight is the force used to calculate power because the students are lifting themselves up the stairs against the force of gravity. The gravitational force is equivalent to their weight.

Solution Guide

1. $P = \dfrac{W}{t} = \dfrac{3960 \text{ J}}{60.0 \text{ s}} = 66.0 \text{ W}$

2. $P = \dfrac{900 \text{ MJ}}{1 \text{ s}} = 900 \text{ MW}$

3. $P = \dfrac{5350 \text{ J}}{50.0 \text{ s}} = 107 \text{ W}$

4. a. $W = (60.0 \text{ N})(12.0 \text{ m}) = 720 \text{ J}$

$P = \dfrac{W}{t} = \dfrac{720 \text{ J}}{20.0 \text{ s}} = 36 \text{ W}$

b. $W = (300 \text{ N})(1 \text{ m}) = 300 \text{ J}$

$P = \dfrac{W}{t} = \dfrac{300 \text{ J}}{3 \text{ s}} = 100 \text{ W}$

5. a. $P = \dfrac{W}{t} = \dfrac{(565 \text{ N})(3.25 \text{ m})}{12.6 \text{ s}} = 146 \text{ W}$

b. $P = \dfrac{(565 \text{ N})(3.25 \text{ m})}{10.5 \text{ s}} = 175 \text{ W}$

RESOURCE LINK
DATASHEETS

Have students use *Datasheet 9.1 Inquiry Lab: What is your power output when you climb the stairs?* to record their results.

Teaching Tip

Machines Be sure to emphasize that machines do not increase the quantity of work that one can do. The machine simply spreads the work out over a longer distance, so that the required input force is reduced. Use the equation W = F × d to show that a longer distance implies a smaller force (for the same amount of work). You may want to use concrete examples with numbers. For example, to lift a 225 N box into the back of a truck that is 1.00 m off the ground requires 225 J of work. If you lift the box straight up into the truck, the force needed is 225 N, but if you use a 3.00 m ramp, the force needed is only 75 N (ignoring friction).

SKILL BUILDER

Interpreting Visuals Use **Figure 9-3** with the concrete example above to help students learn the concept of mechanical advantage. Be sure to point out that whether or not you use the ramp, the box ends up in the same place—a sure sign that the work done on the box is the same in either case.

Additional Application

Work Input and Output

The statement that different forces can do the same amount of work is really an expression of the law of conservation of energy. The law is implicit throughout Chapter 9, but it is not stated explicitly until Section 9.4. Have students look back to this discussion of work and mechanical advantage after finishing Section 9.4.

Figure 9-2
A jack makes it easier to lift a car by multiplying the input force and spreading the work out over a large distance.

Figure 9-3
(A) When lifting a box straight up, a mover applies a large force over a short distance.
(B) Using a ramp to lift the box, the mover applies a smaller force over a longer distance.

Machines and Mechanical Advantage

Which is easier, lifting a car yourself or using a jack as shown in **Figure 9-2**? Which requires more work? Using a jack is obviously easier. But you may be surprised to learn that using a jack doesn't require less work. You do the same amount of work either way, but the jack makes the work easier by allowing you to apply less force at any given moment.

Machines multiply and redirect forces

Machines help us do work by redistributing the work that we put into them. Machines can change the direction of an input force, or they can increase an output force by changing the distance over which the force is applied. This process is often called multiplying the force.

Different forces can do the same amount of work

Compare the amount of work required to lift a box straight onto the bed of a truck, as shown in **Figure 9-3A**, with the amount of work required to push the same box up a ramp, as shown in **Figure 9-3B.** When the mover lifts straight up, he must apply 225 N of force for a short distance. Using the ramp, he can apply a smaller force over a longer distance. But the work done is about the same in both cases.

Both a car jack and a loading ramp make doing work easier by increasing the distance over which the force is applied. As a result, the force required at any point is reduced. The same amount of work can be done either with greater forces and shorter distances, or lesser forces and longer distances.

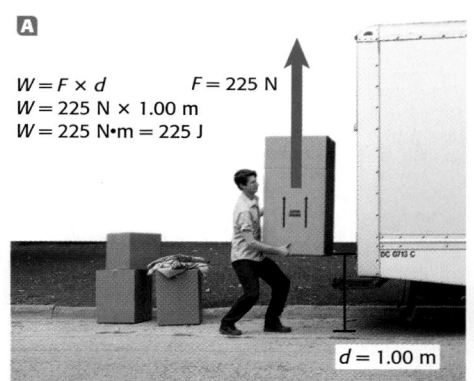

A

$W = F \times d$ $F = 225$ N
$W = 225$ N $\times$ 1.00 m
$W = 225$ N•m $= 225$ J

$d = 1.00$ m

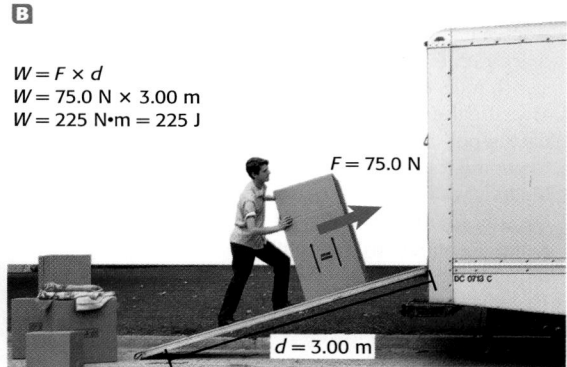

B

$W = F \times d$
$W = 75.0$ N $\times$ 3.00 m
$W = 225$ N•m $= 225$ J

$F = 75.0$ N

$d = 3.00$ m

Mechanical advantage tells how much a machine multiplies force or increases distance

A ramp makes doing work easier by increasing the distance over which force is applied. But how long should the ramp be? An extremely long ramp would allow the mover to use very little force, but he would have to push the box a long distance. A very short ramp, on the other hand, would be too steep and would not help him very much.

To solve problems like this, scientists and engineers use a number that describes how much the force or distance is multiplied by a machine. This number is called the **mechanical advantage,** and it is defined as the ratio between the output force and the input force. It is also equal to the ratio between the input distance and the output distance.

Mechanical Advantage Equation

$$\text{mechanical advantage} = \frac{\text{output force}}{\text{input force}} = \frac{\text{input distance}}{\text{output distance}}$$

A machine with a mechanical advantage of greater than 1 multiplies the input force. Such a machine can help you move or lift heavy objects, such as a car or a box of books. A machine with a mechanical advantage of less than 1 does not multiply force, but increases distance and speed. When you swing a baseball bat, your arms and the bat together form a machine that increases speed without multiplying force.

▶ **mechanical advantage**
a quantity that measures how much a machine multiplies force or distance

🌱 internet**connect**

SC**LINKS**
NSTA

TOPIC: Mechanical advantage
GO TO: www.scilinks.org
KEYWORD: HK1092

Math Skills

Mechanical Advantage Calculate the mechanical advantage of a ramp that is 5.0 m long and 1.5 m high.

1 List the given and unknown values.
> **Given:** *input distance* = 5.0 m
> *output distance* = 1.5 m
> **Unknown:** *mechanical advantage* = ?

2 Write the equation for mechanical advantage.
> Because the information we are given involves only distance, we only need part of the full equation:
>
> $$\text{mechanical advantage} = \frac{\text{input distance}}{\text{output distance}}$$

3 Insert the known values into the equation, and solve.
> $$\text{mechanical advantage} = \frac{5.0 \text{ m}}{1.5 \text{ m}} = 3.3$$

Teaching Tip
Mechanical Advantage
Point out to students that the mechanical advantage equation does not take friction into account. If a ramp has a mechanical advantage of 3 (it is three times longer than it is high), the true input force will be greater than one-third of the output force because of friction.

Math Skills

Ask students: What are the units of mechanical advantage? *(There are none; all units cancel out in the equation.)*

Resources Assign students worksheet *19: Mechanical Advantage* in the **Math Skills Worksheets** ancillary.

Additional Examples

Mechanical Advantage A mover uses a pulley system with a mechanical advantage of 10.0 to lift a 1500 N piano 3.5 m.
a. What force must the mover use?

Answer: 150 N

b. How far must the mover pull the rope?

Answer: 35 m

A person pushes a 950 N box up an incline. If the person exerts a force of 350 N along the incline, what is the mechanical advantage of the incline?

Answer: 2.7

Check Your Understanding

1. If the object does not move, then no work is done because work is equal to force times distance.

2. a. yes
   b. no
   c. yes (by gravity)

3. A ramp can make lifting a box easier without changing the work done because it allows the use of a smaller input force exerted over a longer distance.

4. The long ramp has a greater mechanical advantage than the short ramp.

Math Skills

See p. 319A for worked-out solutions.

5. $W = 75$ J
6. $MA = 2.40$
7. a. $W = 1000$ J
   b. $P = 300$ W
8. $P = 2.0 \times 10^4$ W (27 hp)

RESOURCE LINK

STUDY GUIDE

Assign students *Review Section 9.1 Work, Power, and Machines.*

Practice HINT

▶ The mechanical advantage equation can be rearranged to isolate any of the variables on the left.

▶ For practice problem 4, you will need to rearrange the equation to isolate output force on the left.

▶ For practice problem 5, you will need to rearrange to isolate ouput distance. When rearranging, use only the part of the full equation that you need.

SUMMARY

▶ Work is done when a force causes an object to move. This meaning is different from the everyday meaning of *work.*

▶ Work is equal to force times distance. The most commonly used SI unit for work is joules.

▶ Power is the rate at which work is done. The SI unit for power is watts.

▶ Machines help people by redistributing the work put into them. They can change either the size or the direction of the input force.

▶ The mechanical advantage of a machine describes how much the machine multiplies force or increases distance.

Practice

Mechanical Advantage

1. Calculate the mechanical advantage of a ramp that is 6.0 m long and 1.5 m high.
2. Determine the mechanical advantage of an automobile jack that lifts a 9900 N car with an input force of 150 N.
3. A sailor uses a rope and pulley to raise a sail weighing 140 N. The sailor pulls down with a force of 140 N on the rope. What is the mechanical advantage of the pulley?
4. Alex pulls on the handle of a claw hammer with a force of 15 N. If the hammer has a mechanical advantage of 5.2, how much force is exerted on a nail in the claw?
5. While rowing in a race, John pulls the handle of an oar 0.80 m on each stroke. If the oar has a mechanical advantage of 1.5, how far does the blade of the oar move through the water on each stroke?

SECTION 9.1 REVIEW

CHECK YOUR UNDERSTANDING

1. **Explain** how you can exert a large force on an object without doing any work.
2. **Determine** if work is being done on the objects in the following three situations:
   a. lifting a spoonful of soup to your mouth
   b. holding a stack of books motionless over your head
   c. letting a pencil fall to the ground
3. **Describe** how a ramp can make lifting a box easier without changing the amount of work being done.
4. **Critical Thinking** A short ramp and a long ramp both reach a height of 1 m. Which ramp has a greater mechanical advantage?

Math Skills

5. How much work in joules is done by a person who uses a force of 25 N to move a desk 3.0 m?
6. A bus driver applies a force of 55.0 N to the steering wheel, which in turn applies 132 N of force on the steering column. What is the mechanical advantage of the steering wheel?
7. A student who weighs 400 N climbs a 3 m ladder in 4 s.
   a. How much work does the student do?
   b. What is the student's power output?
8. An outboard engine on a boat can do 1.0×10^6 J of work in 50.0 s. Calculate its power in watts. Convert your answer to horsepower (1 hp = 746 W).

Solution Guide

1. $MA = \dfrac{input\ distance}{output\ distance} = \dfrac{6.0\ m}{1.5\ m} = 4.0$

2. $MA = \dfrac{output\ force}{input\ force} = \dfrac{9900\ N}{150\ N} = 66$

3. $MA = \dfrac{140\ N}{140\ N} = 1.0$

4. $output\ force = (MA)(input\ force) = (5.2)(15\ N) = 78\ N$

5. $output\ distance = \dfrac{input\ distance}{MA} = \dfrac{0.80\ m}{1.5} = 0.53\ m$

9.2

Simple Machines

OBJECTIVES

▶ Name and describe the six types of simple machines.
▶ Discuss the mechanical advantage of different types of simple machines.
▶ Recognize simple machines within compound machines.

▶ **KEY TERMS**
simple machines
compound machines

The most basic machines of all are called **simple machines**. Other machines are either modifications of simple machines or combinations of several simple machines. **Figure 9-4** shows examples of the six types of simple machines. Simple machines are divided into two families, the lever family and the inclined plane family.

▶ **simple machine** one of the six basic types of machines of which all other machines are composed

The Lever Family

To understand how levers do work, imagine using a claw hammer to pull out a nail. As you pull on the handle of the hammer, the head turns around the point where it meets the wood. The force you apply to the handle is transferred to the claw on the other end of the hammer. The claw then does work on the nail.

Figure 9-4 **The Six Simple Machines**

The lever family

Simple lever

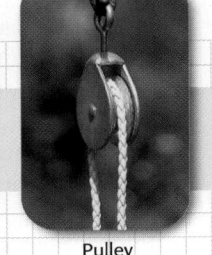
Pulley

Wheel and axle

The inclined plane family

Simple inclined plane

Wedge

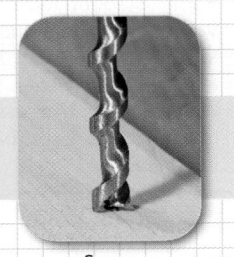
Screw

WORK AND ENERGY **291**

Scheduling

Refer to pp. 282A–282D for lecture, classwork, and assignment options for Section 9.2.

★ **Lesson Focus**
Use transparency *LT 30* to prepare students for this section.

READING SKILL BUILDER *Anticipation (Prediction)* Write the following statement on the board. "All machines are simple machines." Have students read Section 9.2 with this statement in mind. Group the students into pairs or small groups and have the groups debate the statement. Each group should decide whether they agree or disagree with the statement and should provide some evidence to support their opinion. Have a class discussion to compare opinions and justifications.

Students who disagree with the statement will usually point out that compound machines are more complicated because they are combinations of simple machines, as defined at the end of the section. On the other hand, students who agree with the statement may point out that a compound machine is really nothing more than a collection of simple machines.

DEMONSTRATION 2 TEACHING

Pulley Power

Time: Approximately 10 minutes
Materials: ring stand
2 fixed pulleys
1 free pulley
string
75 g and 100 g masses

Step 1 Attach the fixed pulleys to the horizontal arm of the ring stand. Tie the string to the hook on the free pulley, as in **Figure 9-6C** on p. 293.

Thread the string over one fixed pulley, under the free pulley, then over the other fixed pulley.

Step 2 Attach the 100 g mass to the bottom of the free pulley and the 75 g mass to the free end of the string. Hold the masses in place, and ask students what they think will happen when you let go.

Step 3 Let go of the masses. The 75 g mass should fall and the 100 g mass should rise, showing that a lighter mass can lift a heavier mass with the help of simple machines.

291

Interpreting Visuals *Figure 9-5* shows the three classes of levers. Have the students examine **Figure 9-5.** For each of the three examples, where is force input and where is force output? Do the levers multiply force or increase distance on the output side? *(Second-class levers always multiply force, third-class levers always increase distance, and first-class levers may either multiply force or increase distance.)*

Resources Teaching Transparency 24 shows this visual.

Teaching Tip

Three Classes of Levers
Point out that levers that students may see every day, like scissors (first-class), nutcrackers (second-class), and tweezers (third-class), are actually compound machines combining two levers together.

The Three Classes of Levers

Figure 9-5

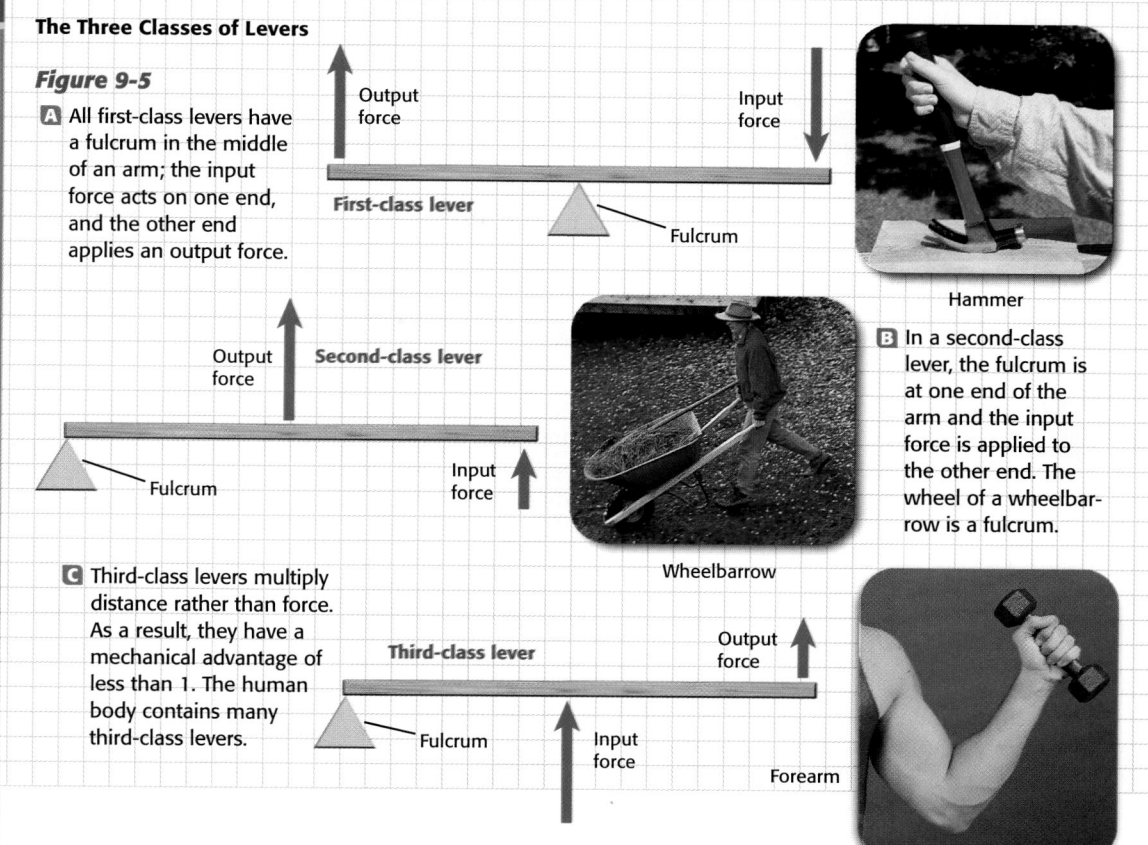

A All first-class levers have a fulcrum in the middle of an arm; the input force acts on one end, and the other end applies an output force.

Output force

Input force

First-class lever

Fulcrum

Hammer

Output force

Second-class lever

Fulcrum

Input force

B In a second-class lever, the fulcrum is at one end of the arm and the input force is applied to the other end. The wheel of a wheelbarrow is a fulcrum.

Wheelbarrow

C Third-class levers multiply distance rather than force. As a result, they have a mechanical advantage of less than 1. The human body contains many third-class levers.

Third-class lever

Output force

Fulcrum

Input force

Forearm

Quick ACTIVITY

A Simple Lever
1. Make a first-class lever by placing a rigid ruler across a pencil or by crossing two pencils at right angles. Use this lever to lift a small stack of books.
2. Vary the location of the fulcrum and see how that affects the lifting strength. Why are the books easier to lift in some cases than in others?

Levers are divided into three classes

All levers have a rigid *arm* that turns around a point called the *fulcrum.* Force is transferred from one part of the arm to another. In that way, the original input force can be multiplied or redirected into an output force. Levers are divided into three classes depending on the location of the fulcrum and of the input and output forces.

Figure 9-5A shows a claw hammer as an example of a first-class lever. First-class levers are the most common type. A pair of pliers is made of two first-class levers joined together.

Figure 9-5B shows a wheelbarrow as an example of a second-class lever. Other examples of second-class levers include nutcrackers and hinged doors.

Figure 9-5C shows the human forearm as an example of a third-class lever. The biceps muscle, which is attached to the bone near the elbow, contracts a short distance to move the hand a large distance.

292 CHAPTER 9

Quick ACTIVITY

A Simple Lever It is important to use very stiff rulers for this activity—plastic rulers will not work well. A rubber eraser makes a good fulcrum. Caution students not to push too hard or too fast on the lever arm; the lever may break or fly away.

Students should find that when the fulcrum is placed near the books, the input force is much less than when the fulcrum is placed farther away from the books. This is due to the mechanical advantage of the lever. When the fulcrum is near the books, the input distance is large and the output distance is small, yielding a large mechanical advantage. The reverse is true when the fulcrum is far away from the books.

Pulleys are modified levers

You may have used pulleys to lift things, as when raising a flag to the top of a flagpole or hoisting a sail on a boat. A pulley is another type of simple machine in the lever family.

Figure 9-6A shows how a pulley is like a lever. The point in the middle of a pulley is like the fulcrum of a lever. The rest of the pulley behaves like the rigid arm of a first-class lever. Because the distance from the fulcrum is the same on both sides of a pulley, a single, fixed pulley has a mechanical advantage of 1.

Using moving pulleys or more than one pulley at a time can increase the mechanical advantage, as shown in **Figure 9-6B** and **Figure 9-6C.** Multiple pulleys are sometimes put together in a single unit called a *block and tackle*.

Figure 9-6   **The Mechanical Advantage of Pulleys**

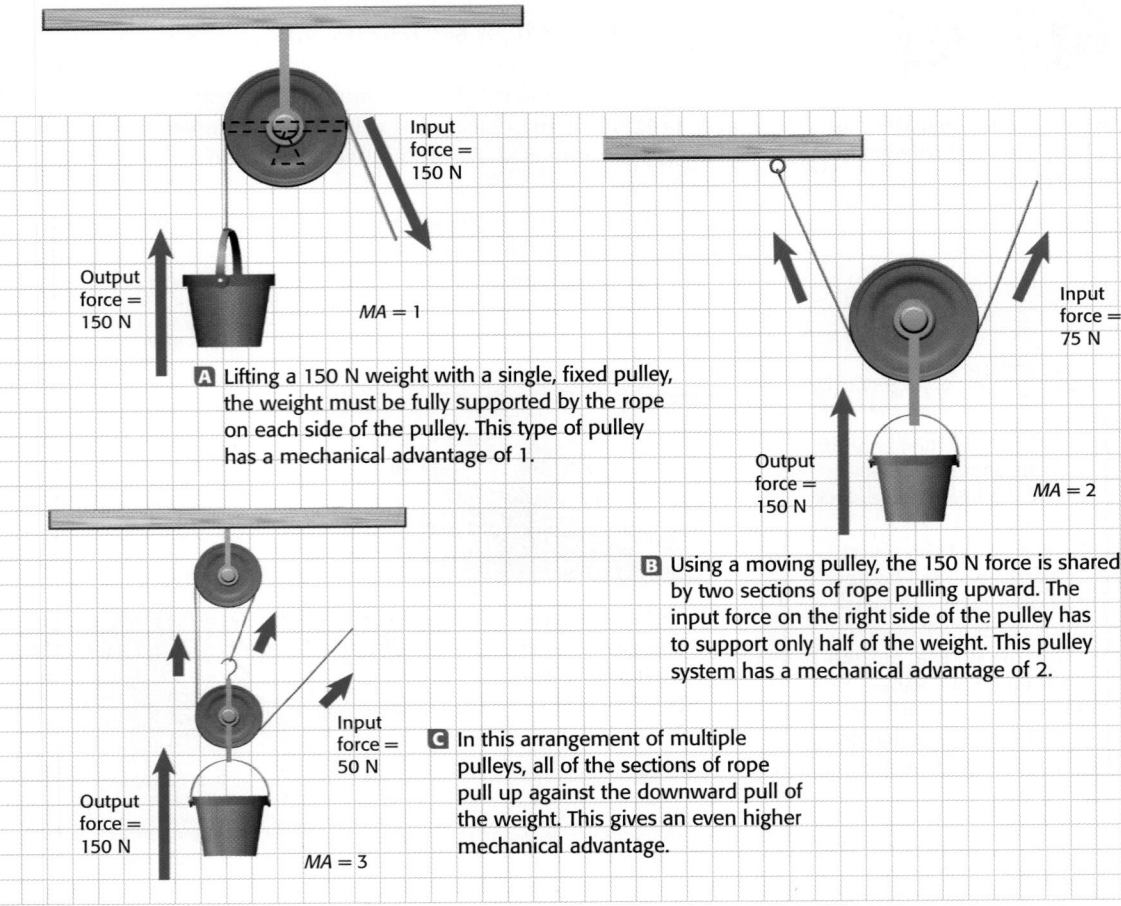

Input force = 150 N

Output force = 150 N

MA = 1

A Lifting a 150 N weight with a single, fixed pulley, the weight must be fully supported by the rope on each side of the pulley. This type of pulley has a mechanical advantage of 1.

Input force = 75 N

Output force = 150 N

MA = 2

B Using a moving pulley, the 150 N force is shared by two sections of rope pulling upward. The input force on the right side of the pulley has to support only half of the weight. This pulley system has a mechanical advantage of 2.

Input force = 50 N

Output force = 150 N

MA = 3

C In this arrangement of multiple pulleys, all of the sections of rope pull up against the downward pull of the weight. This gives an even higher mechanical advantage.

WORK AND ENERGY   **293**

Teaching Tip

Weight of the Pulley   Some students may ask about the weight of the pulleys and the rope in **Figure 9-6.** First, point out that students are correct to consider this.

In part A, the ceiling holds the weight of the pulley, and the weight of the rope is evenly distributed (half on each side), so the "real world" force would be the same as the diagram. In part B, the input force would have to be greater than 75 N by a small amount—the weight of the pulley and the rope. In part C, the input force would have to be greater than 50 N by an amount equal to the weight of the moveable pulley and the section of rope from the pulley to the person. (The rest of the rope is evenly distributed on either side of the stationary pulley.)

You should also point out that these small deviations are omitted in order to simplify calculations. This is usually justified because the weight of the rope and pulleys is often much smaller than the weight of the load. Friction is also ignored in these examples.

SKILL BUILDER

Interpreting Visuals   Have students read the explanation of how **Figure 9-6A** is like a first-class lever with the fulcrum in the middle. Tell students that **Figure 9-6B** is like a second class lever. Have students discuss this.

Resources   Teaching Transparency 25 shows this visual.

Simple Machines

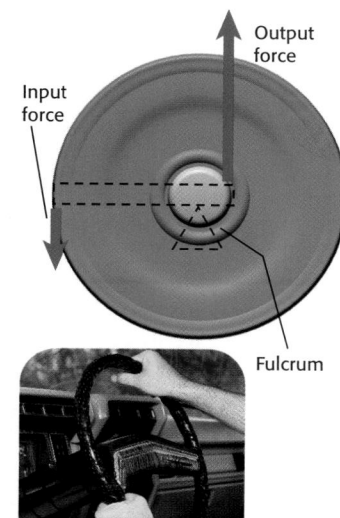

Figure 9-7
How is a wheel and axle like a lever? How is it different from a pulley?

A wheel and axle is a lever or pulley connected to a shaft

The steering wheel of a car is another kind of simple machine: a wheel and axle. A wheel and axle is made of a lever or a pulley (the wheel) connected to a shaft (the axle), as shown in **Figure 9-7.** When the wheel is turned, the axle also turns. When a small input force is applied to the steering wheel, the force is multiplied to become a large output force applied to the steering column, which turns the front wheels of the car. Screwdrivers and cranks are other common wheel-and-axle machines.

The Inclined Plane Family

Earlier we showed how pushing an object up a ramp requires less force than lifting the same object straight up. A loading ramp is another type of simple machine, an inclined plane.

Inclined planes multiply and redirect force

When you push an object up a ramp, you apply a force to the object in a direction parallel to the ramp. The ramp then redirects this force to lift the object upward. For that reason, the output force of the ramp is shown in **Figure 9-8A** as an arrow pointing straight up.

An inclined plane turns a small input force into a large output force by spreading the work out over a large distance. Pushing something up a long ramp that climbs gradually is easier than pushing something up a short, steep ramp.

Quick ACTIVITY

A Simple Inclined Plane
1. Make an inclined plane out of a board and a stack of books.
2. Tie a string to an object that is heavy but has low friction, such as a metal toy car or a roll of wire. Use the string to pull the object up the plane.
3. Still using the string, try to lift the object straight up through the same distance.
4. Which action required more force? In which case did you do more work?

Figure 9-8 **The Inclined Plane Family**

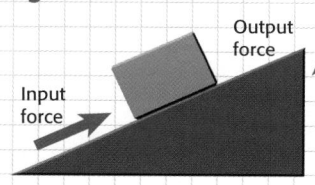

A An inclined plane changes both the magnitude and the direction of force.

Quick ACTIVITY

A Simple Inclined Plane The object used in this activity can be any heavy rolling object or simply a heavy object with low friction, such as a stapler turned upside down. A wheeled dynamics cart makes a great object to pull up the ramp, since the rolling friction is small. A roll of wire works well, too. Tie the string through the hollow shaft through the middle of the roll so that the roll may move freely when dragged up the ramp.

Students should find that pulling the object up the ramp requires less force than lifting the object straight up. If students do not find this to be so, prompt them to consider the additional friction on the ramp. Students should also consider that the work done is the same in either case (if friction is ignored).

A wedge is a modified inclined plane

When an ax blade or a splitting wedge hits a piece of wood, it pushes through the wood and breaks it apart, as shown in **Figure 9-8B**. An ax blade is an example of a wedge, another kind of simple machine in the inclined plane family. A wedge functions like two inclined planes back to back. Using a wedge is like pushing a ramp instead of pushing an object up the ramp. A wedge turns a single downward force into two forces directed out to the sides. Some types of wedges, such as nails, are used as fasteners.

A screw is an inclined plane wrapped around a cylinder

A type of simple machine that you probably use often is a screw. The threads on a screw look like a spiral inclined plane. In fact, a screw is an inclined plane wrapped around a cylinder, as shown in **Figure 9-8C.** Like pushing an object up a ramp, tightening a screw with gently sloping threads requires a small force acting over a large distance. Tightening a screw with steeper threads requires more force. Jar lids are screws that people use every day. Spiral staircases are also common screws.

The ancient Egyptians built dozens of large stone pyramids as tombs for the bodies of kings and queens. The largest of these is the pyramid of Khufu at Giza, also called the Great Pyramid. It is made of more than 2 million blocks of stone. These blocks have an average weight of 2.5 tons, and the largest blocks weigh 15 tons. How did the Egyptians get these huge stones onto the pyramid?

Making the Connection

1. The Great Pyramid is about 140 m tall. How much work would be required to raise an average-sized pyramid block to this height? (2.5 tons = 2.2×10^4 N)
2. If the Egyptians used ramps with a mechanical advantage of 3, then an average block could be moved with a force of 7.3×10^3 N. If one person can pull with a force of 525 N, how many people would it take to pull an average block up such a ramp?

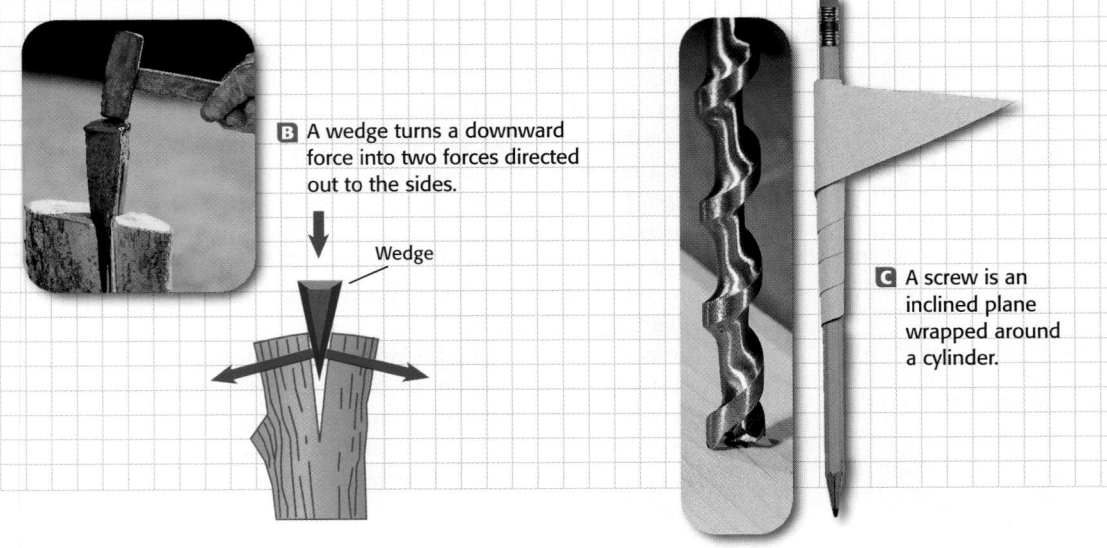

B A wedge turns a downward force into two forces directed out to the sides.

Wedge

C A screw is an inclined plane wrapped around a cylinder.

Connection to SOCIAL STUDIES

The builders of the Great Pyramid lifted approximately 300 blocks per day, at an average weight of 2.5 tons per block. It took the Egyptians around 30 years to complete this enormous project.

There is some uncertainty about how the blocks were lifted, although simple machines must have been involved. One theory posits that the Egyptians primarily used ramps coated with mud to reduce friction. The exercise here is based on that method. Another theory holds that they used levers, mounted on either side of each block, to lift the blocks to successively higher levels.

For an extension project have your students research how the Egyptians might have used simple machines to build the Great Pyramid.

Making the Connection

1. $(2.2 \times 10^4 \text{ N})(140 \text{ m}) = 3.1 \times 10^6$ J or 3.1 MJ
2. $\dfrac{7.3 \times 10^3 \text{ N}}{525 \text{ N/person}} = 14$ people

Resources Assign students worksheet *9.2: Connection to Social Studies—The Pyramids* in the **Integration Enrichment Resources** ancillary.

Figure 9-9
A bicycle is made of many simple machines.

▶ **compound machine**
a machine made of more than one simple machine

Compound Machines

Many devices that you use every day are made of more than one simple machine. A machine that combines two or more simple machines is called a **compound machine**. A pair of scissors, for example, uses two first class levers joined at a common fulcrum; each lever arm has a wedge that cuts into the paper. Most car jacks use a lever in combination with a large screw.

Of course, many machines are much more complex than these. How many simple machines can you identify in the bicycle shown in **Figure 9-9**? How many can you identify in a car?

■■■ **SECTION 9.2 REVIEW**

SUMMARY

▶ The most basic machines are called simple machines. There are six types of simple machines in two families.

▶ Levers have a rigid arm and a fulcrum. There are three classes of levers.

▶ Pulleys and wheel-and-axle machines are also in the lever family.

▶ The inclined plane family includes inclined planes, wedges, and screws.

▶ Compound machines are made of two or more simple machines.

CHECK YOUR UNDERSTANDING

1. **List** the six types of simple machines.
2. **Identify** the kind of simple machine represented by each of these examples:
   a. a drill bit   **b.** a skateboard ramp   **c.** a boat oar
3. **Describe** how a lever can increase the force without changing the amount of work being done.
4. **Explain** why pulleys are in the lever family.
5. **Compare** the mechanical advantage of a long, thin wedge with that of a short, wide wedge. Which is greater?
6. **Critical Thinking** Can an inclined plane have a mechanical advantage of less than 1?
7. **Critical Thinking** Using the principle of a lever, explain why it is easier to open a door by pushing near the knob than by pushing near the hinges. What class of lever is a door?
8. **Creative Thinking** Choose a compound machine that you use every day, and identify the simple machines that it contains.

296 CHAPTER 9

What Is Energy?

 **KEY TERMS**
potential energy
kinetic energy
mechanical energy

OBJECTIVES

▶ Explain the relationship between energy and work.
▶ Define *potential energy* and *kinetic energy*.
▶ Calculate kinetic energy and gravitational potential energy.
▶ Distinguish between mechanical and nonmechanical energy.
▶ Identify nonmechanical forms of energy.

The world around you is full of energy. When you see a flash of lightning and hear a thunderclap, you are observing light and sound energy. When you ride a bicycle, you have energy just because you are moving. Even things that are sitting still have energy waiting to be released. We use other forms of energy, like nuclear energy and electrical energy, to power things in our world, from submarines to flashlights. Without energy, living organisms could not survive. Our bodies use a great deal of energy every day just to stay alive.

Energy and Work

When you stretch a slingshot, as shown in **Figure 9-10,** you are doing work, and you transfer energy to the elastic band. When the elastic band snaps back, it may in turn transfer that energy again by doing work on a stone in the slingshot. Whenever work is done, energy is transformed or transferred to another system. In fact, one way to define energy is as the ability to do work.

Energy is measured in joules

While work is done only when an object experiences a change in its motion, energy can be present in an object or a system when nothing is happening at all. But energy can be observed only when it is transferred from one object or system to another, as when a slingshot transfers the energy from its elastic band to a stone in the sling.

The amount of energy transferred from the slingshot can be measured by how much work is done on the stone. Because energy is a measure of the ability to do work, energy and work are expressed in the same units—joules.

Figure 9-10
A stretched slingshot has the ability to do work.

WORK AND ENERGY **297**

Section 9.3

What Is Energy?

Scheduling
Refer to pp. 282A–282D for lecture, class work, and assignment options for Section 9.3.

★ **Lesson Focus**
Use transparency *LT 31* to prepare students for this section.

READING SKILL BUILDER *K-W-L* Write the word *energy* on the board. Have students list what they know or think they know about energy. Then have them list what they want to know. After they have read the section, have them look at their lists and write down what they have learned about energy.

Teaching Tip
Work and Energy When defining energy as the ability to do work, point out that an acceptable definition for work is the transfer of energy from one object (or system) to another. When a force is applied through a distance, work is done by one object on another object. The energy to do the work comes from one object, and is transferred to the second object. Section 9.4 will discuss energy transfer and conservation of energy in more detail, but the idea may be introduced here.

RESOURCE LINK
IER
Assign students worksheet *9.5: Connection to Language Arts—The Concept of Energy* as an extension exercise.

SKILL BUILDER

Vocabulary Potential energy is a term that encompasses many types of energy. Gravitational potential energy will be studied in detail in this section. Other forms of potential energy include elastic, chemical, electrical, and magnetic. These may seem like very different concepts to students, but all forms of potential energy deal with position.

Gravitational potential energy depends on distances between masses; elastic potential energy depends on the shape of elastic materials. Chemical potential energy depends on bonds (position) between atoms within molecules. Electrical potential energy depends on distances between charged particles, and magnetic potential depends on position within a magnetic field.

Teaching Tip

Gravitational Potential Energy Equation Gravitational potential energy is different from weight because gravitation takes potential energy height into account. The equation for gravitational potential energy is really weight, *mg*, times height, *h*. This is also a measurement of the work that the gravitational field would do on an object if it were to fall through a certain distance (the height).

Figure 9-11
This apple has gravitational potential energy. The energy results from the gravitational attraction between the apple and Earth.

▶ **potential energy** the stored energy resulting from the relative positions of objects in a system

internetconnect

SCI LINKS
NSTA

TOPIC: Potential energy
GO TO: www.scilinks.org
KEYWORD: HK1094

Potential Energy

Stretching a rubber band requires work. If you then release the stretched rubber band, it will fly away from your hand. The energy used to stretch the rubber band is stored so that it can do work at a later time. But where is the energy between the time you do work on the rubber band and the time you release it?

Potential energy is stored energy

A stretched slingshot or a rubber band stores energy in a form called **potential energy**. Potential energy is sometimes called energy of position because it results from the relative positions of objects in a system. The rubber band has potential energy because the two ends of the band are far away from each other. The energy stored in any type of stretched or compressed elastic material, such as a clock spring or a bungee cord, is called *elastic potential energy*.

The apple in **Figure 9-11** will fall if the stem breaks off the branch. The energy that could potentially do work on the apple results from its position above the ground. This type of stored energy is called *gravitational potential energy*. Any system of two or more objects separated by a distance contains gravitational potential energy resulting from the gravitational attraction between the objects.

Gravitational potential energy depends on both mass and height

An apple at the top of the tree has more gravitational potential energy with respect to the Earth than a similar apple on a lower branch. But if two apples of different mass are at the same height, the heavier apple has more gravitational potential energy than the lighter one.

Because it results from the force of gravity, gravitational potential energy depends both on the mass of the objects in a system and on the distance between them.

> **Gravitational Potential Energy Equation**
>
> *grav. PE = mass × free-fall acceleration × height*
> $$PE = mgh$$

In this equation, notice that *mg* is the weight of the object in newtons, which is the same as the force on the object due to gravity. So this equation is really just a calculation of force times distance, like the work equation.

The height used in the equation for gravitational potential energy is usually measured from the ground. However, in some cases, a relative height might be more important. For example, if an apple were in a position to fall into a bird's nest on a lower branch, the apple's height above the nest could be used to calculate the apple's potential energy relative to the nest.

Math Skills

Gravitational Potential Energy A 65 kg rock climber ascends a cliff. What is the climber's gravitational potential energy at a point 35 m above the base of the cliff?

1 **List the given and unknown values.**
  Given: *mass, m* = 65 kg
  height, h = 35 m
  free-fall acceleration, g = 9.8 m/s^2
  Unknown: *gravitational potential energy, PE* = ? J

2 **Write the equation for gravitational potential energy.**
  $PE = mgh$

3 **Insert the known values into the equation, and solve.**
  $PE = (65 \text{ kg})(9.8 \text{ m/s}^2)(35 \text{ m})$
  $PE = 2.2 \times 10^4 \text{ kg} \cdot \text{m}^2/\text{s}^2 = 2.2 \times 10^4 \text{ J}$

Practice

Gravitational Potential Energy

1. Calculate the gravitational potential energy in the following systems:
  a. a car with a mass of 1200 kg at the top of a 42 m high hill
  b. a 65 kg climber on top of Mount Everest (8800 m high)
  c. a 0.52 kg bird flying at an altitude of 550 m

2. Lake Mead, the reservoir above Hoover Dam, has a surface area of approximately 640 km^2. The top 1 m of water in the lake weighs about 6.3×10^{12} N. The dam holds that top layer of water 220 m above the river below. Calculate the gravitational potential energy of the top 1 m of water in Lake Mead.

3. A science student holds a 55 g egg out a window. Just before the student releases the egg, the egg has 8.0 J of gravitational potential energy with respect to the ground. How far is the student's arm from the ground in meters? (**Hint:** Convert the mass to kilograms before solving.)

4. A diver has 3400 J of gravitational potential energy after stepping up onto a diving platform that is 6.0 m above the water. What is the diver's mass in kilograms?

Practice HINT

▶ The gravitational potential energy equation can be rearranged to isolate height on the left.
  $mgh = PE$
Divide both sides by *mg*, and cancel.
  $$\frac{\cancel{mg}h}{\cancel{mg}} = \frac{PE}{mg}$$
  $$h = \frac{PE}{mg}$$

You will need this version of the equation for practice problem 3.

▶ For practice problem 4, you will need to rearrange the equation to isolate mass on the left. When solving these problems, use *g* = 9.8 m/s^2.

Math Skills

Resources Assign students worksheet *20: Gravitational Potential Energy* in the **Math Skills Worksheets** ancillary.

Additional Examples

Gravitational Potential Energy
A spider has 0.080 J of gravitational potential energy as it reaches the halfway point climbing up a 2.8 m wall. What is the potential energy of the spider at the top of the wall? (**HINT:** You do not need to find the mass first.)

Answer: 0.16 J

A 0.50 g leaf falls from a branch 4.0 m off the ground to a bird's nest 2.5 m off the ground. How much gravitational potential energy did the leaf lose?

Answer: 7.4×10^{-3} J

Solution Guide

1. a. $PE = mgh = (1200 \text{ kg})(9.8 \text{ m/s}^2)(42 \text{ m})$
  $= 4.9 \times 10^5 \text{ J}$
  b. $PE = (65 \text{ kg})(9.8 \text{ m/s}^2)(8800 \text{ m}) =$
  $5.6 \times 10^6 \text{ J}$
  c. $PE = (0.52 \text{ kg})(9.8 \text{ m/s}^2)(550 \text{ m}) =$
  2800 J

2. $PE = (6.3 \times 10^{12} \text{ N})(220 \text{ m}) = 1.4 \times 10^{15} \text{ J}$

3. $h = \dfrac{PE}{mg} = \dfrac{8.0 \text{ J}}{(0.055 \text{ kg})(9.8 \text{ m/s}^2)} = 15 \text{ m}$

4. $m = \dfrac{PE}{gh} = \dfrac{3400 \text{ J}}{(9.8 \text{ m/s}^2)(6.0 \text{ m})} = 58 \text{ kg}$

Teaching Tip

Kinetic Energy Kinetic energy, like all other kinds of energy, is an ability to do work. Kinetic energy is probably the most obvious form of energy. If students have had problems grasping energy, now is a good time to drive it home. When you think of an "energetic" person, you may think of someone who moves around a lot. Something moving has, by nature of its motion, an ability to do work.

SKILL BUILDER

Interpreting Graphs Have students examine the graph in **Figure 9-12B.** The graph shows kinetic energy versus speed for a falling apple that weighs 1 N. Point out that as the speed increases, the kinetic energy increases rapidly. That is because kinetic energy depends on the square of the speed. The curve on this graph is half of a parabola.

Resources Blackline Master 26 shows this visual.

MISCONCEPTION ALERT

Kinetic Energy and Momentum
Some students may be confused about the distinction between kinetic energy and momentum. For those students, write the equations for momentum and for kinetic energy side-by-side. Have students consider how they are similar and how they are different. *(Both quantities depend on mass and velocity, but kinetic energy has a more sensitive dependence on velocity because of the square.)*

▶ **kinetic energy** the energy of a moving object due to its motion

VOCABULARY *Skills Tip*

Kinetic comes from the Greek word kinetikos, *which means "motion."*

Kinetic Energy

Once an apple starts to fall from the branch of a tree, as in **Figure 9-12A,** it has the ability to do work. Because the apple is moving, it can do work when it hits the ground or lands on the head of someone under the tree. The energy that an object has because it is in motion is called **kinetic energy.**

Kinetic energy depends on mass and speed

A falling apple can do more work than a cherry falling at the same speed. That is because the kinetic energy of an object depends on the object's mass.

As an apple falls, it accelerates. The kinetic energy of the apple—its ability to do work—increases as it speeds up. In fact, the kinetic energy of a moving object depends on the square of the object's speed.

Kinetic Energy Equation

$$kinetic\ energy = \frac{1}{2} \times mass \times speed\ squared$$

$$KE = \frac{1}{2}mv^2$$

Figure 9-12B shows a graph of kinetic energy versus speed for a falling apple that weighs 1.0 N. Notice that kinetic energy is expressed in joules. Because kinetic energy is calculated using both mass and speed squared, the base units are kg•m²/s², which are equivalent to joules.

A

Figure 9-12
(A) A falling apple can do work on the ground underneath—or on someone's head.
(B) A small increase in the speed of an apple results in a large increase in kinetic energy.

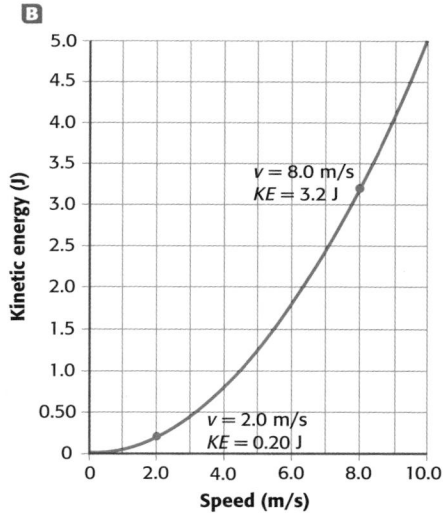

B

v = 8.0 m/s
KE = 3.2 J

v = 2.0 m/s
KE = 0.20 J

Kinetic energy (J)

Speed (m/s)

Kinetic energy depends on speed more than mass

The line on the graph of kinetic energy versus speed curves sharply upward as speed increases. At one point, the speed is 2.0 m/s and the kinetic energy is 0.20 J. At another point, the speed has increased four times to 8.0 m/s. But the kinetic energy has increased 16 times, to 3.2 J. In the kinetic energy equation, speed is squared, so a small increase in speed produces a large increase in kinetic energy.

You may have heard that car crashes are much more dangerous at speeds above the speed limit. The kinetic energy equation provides a scientific reason for that fact. Because a car has much more kinetic energy at higher speeds, it can do much more work—which means much more damage—in a collision.

internetconnect

SCI**LINKS**
NSTA

TOPIC: Kinetic energy
GO TO: www.scilinks.org
KEYWORD: HK1095

Math Skills

Rearranging the kinetic energy equation involves working with squares and square roots. The Practice Hint shows students how to solve the equation for velocity and also gives them the equation rearranged to isolate mass.

Resources Assign students worksheet *21: Kinetic Energy* in the **Math Skills Worksheets** ancillary.

Math Skills

Kinetic Energy What is the kinetic energy of a 44 kg cheetah running at 31 m/s?

1 List the given and unknown values.
   Given: *mass, m* = 45 kg
   speed, v = 31 m/s
   Unknown: *kinetic energy, KE* = ? J

2 Write the equation for kinetic energy.
   kinetic energy $= \frac{1}{2} \times mass \times speed\ squared$

   $KE = \frac{1}{2}mv^2$

3 Insert the known values into the equation, and solve.
   $KE = \frac{1}{2}(44\ \text{kg})(31\ \text{m/s})^2$

   $KE = 2.1 \times 10^4\ \text{kg} \cdot \text{m}^2/\text{s}^2 = 2.1 \times 10^4\ \text{J}$

Practice HINT

▶ The kinetic energy equation can be rearranged to isolate speed on the left.

   $\frac{1}{2}mv^2 = KE$

   Multiply both sides by $\frac{2}{m}$.

   $\left(\frac{2}{m}\right) \times \frac{1}{2}mv^2 = \left(\frac{2}{m}\right) \times KE$

   $v^2 = \frac{2KE}{m}$

   Take the square root of each side.

   $\sqrt{v^2} = \sqrt{\frac{2KE}{m}}$

   $v = \sqrt{\frac{2KE}{m}}$

   You will need this version of the equation for Practice Problem 2.

▶ For Practice Problem 3, you will need to use the equation rearranged with mass isolated on the left:

   $m = \frac{2KE}{v^2}$

Practice

Kinetic Energy

1. Calculate the kinetic energy in joules of a 1500 kg car moving at the following speeds:
   a. 29 m/s
   b. 18 m/s
   c. 42 km/h (**Hint:** Convert the speed to meters per second before substituting into the equation.)

2. A 35 kg child has 190 J of kinetic energy after sledding down a hill. What is the child's speed in meters per second at the bottom of the hill?

3. A bowling ball traveling 2.0 m/s has 16 J of kinetic energy. What is the mass of the bowling ball in kilograms?

Additional Examples

Kinetic Energy A 2.0 kg ball and a 4.0 kg ball are traveling at the same speed. If the kinetic energy of the 2.0 kg ball is 5.0 J, what is the kinetic energy of the 4.0 kg ball? (**HINT:** You do not have to solve for the speed.)

Answer: 10. J

A 2.0 kg ball has 4.0 J of energy when traveling at a certain speed. What is the kinetic energy of the ball when traveling at twice the original speed? (**HINT:** You do not have to solve for the original speed.)

Answer: 16 J

WORK AND ENERGY **301**

Solution Guide

1. a. $KE = \frac{1}{2}mv^2 = \left(\frac{1}{2}\right)(1500\ \text{kg})(29\ \text{m/s})^2 = 6.3 \times 10^5\ \text{J}$

   b. $KE = \left(\frac{1}{2}\right)(1500\ \text{kg})(18\ \text{m/s})^2 = 2.4 \times 10^5\ \text{J}$

   c. $v = 42\ \text{km/h}(1000\ \text{m/km})(1\ \text{h}/3600\ \text{s}) = 12\ \text{m/s}$
   $KE = \left(\frac{1}{2}\right)(1500\ \text{kg})(12\ \text{m/s})^2 = 1.1 \times 10^5\ \text{J}$

2. $v = \sqrt{\frac{2KE}{m}} = \sqrt{\frac{(2)(190\ \text{J})}{35\ \text{g}}} = 3.3\ \text{m/s}$

3. $m = \left(\frac{2KE}{v^2}\right) = \frac{(2)(16\ \text{J})}{(2.0\ \text{m/s})^2} = 8.0\ \text{kg}$

RESOURCE LINK
BASIC SKILLS

Assign students worksheet *3.4: Squares and Square Roots* to help them with the kinetic energy equation.

What Is Energy?

Teaching Tip

Nonmechanical Energy The distinction between mechanical energy and nonmechanical energy is vague by nature. Nonmechanical energy is often called "internal energy," also a vague concept. In most cases, nonmechanical energy can be reduced to some kind of mechanical energy. For each type of energy introduced in the next few pages, discuss how it can also be considered as either kinetic or potential energy.

Additional Application

Nonmechanical Energy Explain to students that the practice of considering only major effects and ignoring small effects is a very common practice in science. As students read this page they may ask how scientists can consider some energy to be nonmechanical at some times and not at others. Explain that scientists are quite often investigating one certain aspect of things.

For example, a physicist trying to explain the flight of a horseshoe could include the motion of the molecules (with the help of a computer), but the physicist would probably ignore the motion of the molecules because that motion is so small compared to the horseshoe flying through the air.

LINKING CHAPTERS

Chapter 10 will further explain how the kinetic energy of atoms and molecules is related to heat and temperature. These concepts are also related to the kinetic theory of matter, covered in Chapter 2.

▶ **mechanical energy**
the sum of the kinetic and potential energy of large-scale objects in a system

Other Forms of Energy

Apples have potential energy when they are hanging on a branch above the ground, and they have kinetic and potential energy when they are falling. The sum of the potential energy and the kinetic energy in a system is called **mechanical energy**.

Apples can also give you energy when you eat them. What kind of energy is that? In almost every system, there are hidden forms of energy that are related to the motion and arrangement of atoms that make up the objects in the system.

Energy that lies at the level of atoms and that does not affect motion on a large scale is sometimes called *nonmechanical energy*. However, a close look at the different forms of energy in a system usually reveals that they are in most cases just special forms of kinetic or potential energy.

Atoms and molecules have kinetic energy

You learned in Chapter 2 that atoms and molecules are constantly in motion. Therefore, these tiny particles have kinetic energy. Like a bowling ball hitting pins, kinetic energy is transferred between particles through collisions. The average kinetic energy of particles in an object increases as the object gets hotter and decreases as it cools down. In Chapter 10, you will learn more about how the kinetic energy of particles relates to heat and temperature.

Figure 9-13 shows the motion of atoms in two parts of a horseshoe at different temperatures. In both parts, the iron atoms inside the horseshoe are vibrating. The atoms in the hotter part of the horseshoe are vibrating more rapidly than the atoms in the cooler part, so they have greater kinetic energy.

Figure 9-13
The atoms in a hot object, such as this horseshoe, have kinetic energy. The kinetic energy is related to the object's temperature.

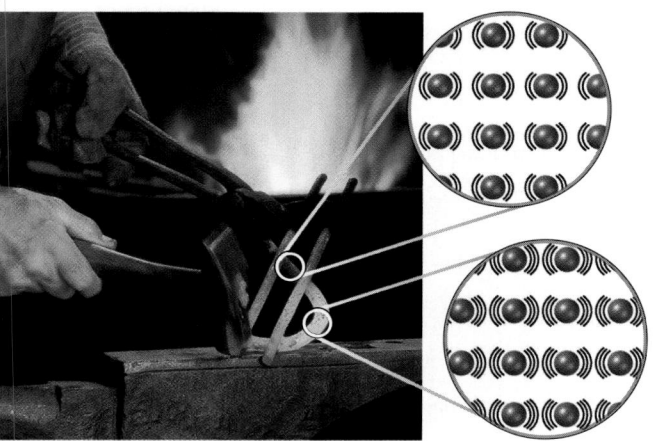

If a scientist wanted to analyze the motion of a horseshoe in a game of "horseshoes," the motion of particles inside the shoes would not be important. For the sake of that study, the energy due to the motion of the atoms would be considered nonmechanical energy.

However, if the same scientist wanted to study the change in the properties of iron when heated in a blacksmith's shop, the motion of the atoms would become significant to the study, and the kinetic energy of the particles within the horseshoe would then be viewed as mechanical energy.

Chemical reactions involve potential energy

In a chemical reaction, bonds between atoms break apart. When the atoms bond together again in a new pattern, a different substance is formed. Both the formation of bonds and the breaking of bonds involve changes in energy. The amount of *chemical energy* associated with a substance depends in part on the relative positions of the atoms it contains.

Because chemical energy depends on position, it is a kind of potential energy. Reactions that release energy involve a decrease in the potential energy within substances. For example, when a match burns, as shown in **Figure 9-14,** the release of stored energy from the match head produces light and an explosion of hot gas. For more on chemical energy, review Chapter 5.

Figure 9-14
When a match burns, the chemical energy stored inside the head of the match is released, producing light and an explosion of hot gas.

Living things get energy from the sun

Where do you get the energy you need to live? It comes in the form of chemical energy stored in the food you eat. But where did that energy come from? When you eat a meal, you are eating either plants or animals, or both. Animals also eat plants or other animals, or both. At the bottom of the food chain are plants and algae that derive their energy directly from sunlight.

Plants use *photosynthesis* to turn the energy in sunlight into chemical energy. This energy is stored in sugars and other organic molecules that make up cells in living tissue. When your body digests food, these molecules from plants or animals are transferred to your own cells. When your body needs energy, some of the organic molecules are broken down through *respiration.* Respiration releases the energy your body needs to live.

REAL WORLD APPLICATIONS

The Energy in Food

We get energy from the food we eat. This energy is often measured by another unit, the Calorie. One Calorie is equivalent to 4186 J.

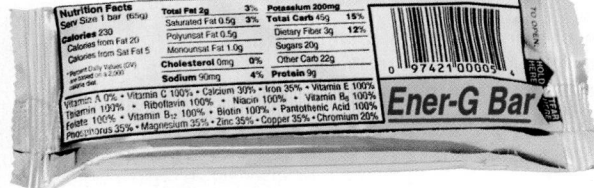

Ener-G Bar

Applying Information

1. Look at the nutrition label on this "energy bar." How many Calories of energy does the bar contain?

2. Calculate how many joules of energy the bar contains by multiplying the number of Calories by the conversion factor of 4186 J/Cal.

3. An average person needs to take in about 10 million joules of energy every day. How many energy bars would you have to eat to get this much energy?

WORK AND ENERGY **303**

What Is Energy?

LINKING **CHAPTERS**

Students will learn more about nuclear energy in Chapter 7. The energy processes in stars will be described in more detail in Chapter 16. Students will learn more about electricity in Chapter 13.

Teaching Tip

Nuclear Fission Tell students to imagine a large water balloon filled almost to the breaking point. You have to carry a balloon like that very carefully because the slightest bump will cause it to break. Now have students imagine two smaller water balloons that are not as full. There is still a large amount of flexibility in the "wrapper" (or balloon). Large nuclei are like an overfilled water balloon. The wrapper (strong nuclear forces that hold the nucleus together) is stretched to the breaking point. When a nucleus undergoes fission, it splits into smaller nuclei, where the nuclear forces are not stretched as much. The energy that is released is the difference in the energy required to contain the nuclei. It takes less energy to contain two small nuclei than it does to contain one very large one.

Additional Application

Tons of TNT Nuclear energy, especially as contained in nuclear weapons, is sometimes expressed in units of tons of TNT. One ton of TNT is equal to the amount of energy released from the explosion of 1 ton of TNT explosive. 1 ton of TNT = 4.2×10^9 J.

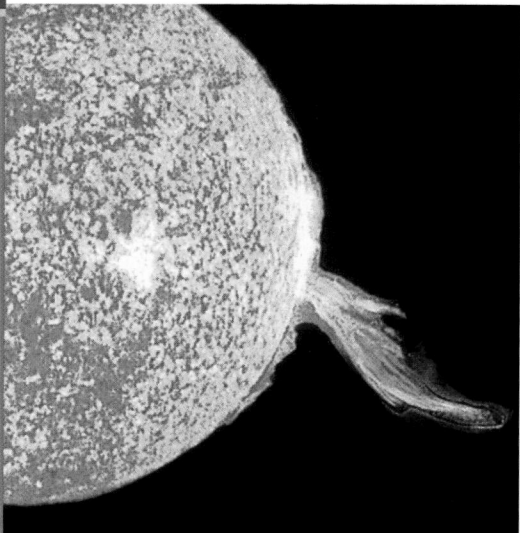

Figure 9-15
The nuclei of atoms contain enormous amounts of energy. The sun is fueled by nuclear fusion reactions in its core.

Figure 9-16
Electrical energy is derived from the flow of charged particles, as in a bolt of lightning or in a wire. We can harness electricity to power appliances in our homes.

304 CHAPTER 9

The sun gets energy from nuclear reactions

The sun, shown in **Figure 9-15,** not only gives energy to living things but also keeps our whole planet warm and bright. And the energy that reaches Earth from the sun is only a small portion of the sun's total energy output. How does the sun produce so much energy?

The sun's energy comes from nuclear fusion, a type of reaction in which light atomic nuclei combine to form a heavier nucleus. Nuclear power plants use a different process, called nuclear fission, to release nuclear energy. In fission, a single heavy nucleus is split into two or more lighter nuclei. In both fusion and fission, small quantities of mass are converted into large quantities of energy.

In Section 7.2, you learned that mass is converted to energy during nuclear reactions. This nuclear energy is a kind of potential energy stored by the forces holding subatomic particles together in the nuclei of atoms.

Electricity is a form of energy

The lights and appliances in your home are powered by another form of energy, electricity. Electricity results from the flow of charged particles through wires or other conducting materials. Moving electrons can increase the temperature of a wire and cause it to glow, as in a light bulb. Moving electrons also create magnetic fields, which can do work to power a motor or other devices. The lightning shown in **Figure 9-16** is caused by electrons traveling through the air between the ground and a thundercloud. You will learn more about electricity in Chapter 13.

Light can carry energy across empty space

An asphalt surface on a bright summer day is hotter where light is shining directly on it than it is in the shade. Light energy travels from the sun to Earth across empty space in the form of *electromagnetic waves*.

A beam of white light can be separated into a color spectrum, as shown in **Figure 9-17.** Light toward the blue end of the spectrum carries more energy than light toward the red end. You will learn more about electromagnetic waves and the electromagnetic spectrum in Chapter 11 and Chapter 12.

Figure 9-17
Light is composed of electromagnetic waves, which can carry energy across empty space.

SECTION 9.3 REVIEW

SUMMARY

▶ Energy is the ability to do work.

▶ Like work, energy is measured in joules.

▶ Potential energy is stored energy.

▶ Elastic potential energy is stored in any stretched or compressed elastic material.

▶ The gravitational potential energy of an object is determined by its mass, its height, and *g*, the free-fall acceleration due to gravity. *PE* = *mgh*.

▶ An object's kinetic energy, or energy of motion, is determined by its mass and speed. $KE = \frac{1}{2}mv^2$.

▶ Potential energy and kinetic energy are forms of mechanical energy.

▶ In addition to mechanical energy, most systems contain nonmechanical energy.

▶ Nonmechanical energy does not usually affect systems on a large scale.

CHECK YOUR UNDERSTANDING

1. **List** three different forms of energy.
2. **Explain** how energy is different from work.
3. **Explain** the difference between potential energy and kinetic energy.
4. **Determine** what form or forms of energy apply to each of the following situations, and specify whether each form is mechanical or nonmechanical:
   a. a Frisbee flying though the air
   b. a hot cup of soup
   c. a wound clock spring
   d. sunlight
   e. a boulder sitting at the top of a cliff
5. **Critical Thinking** Water storage tanks are usually built on towers or placed on hilltops. Why?
6. **Creative Thinking** Name one situation in which gravitational potential energy might be useful, and name one situation where it might be dangerous.

Math Skills

7. Calculate the gravitational potential energy of a 93.0 kg sky diver who is 550 m above the ground.
8. What is the kinetic energy in joules of a 0.02 kg bullet traveling 300 m/s?
9. Calculate the kinetic or potential energy in joules for each of the following situations:
   a. a 2.5 kg book held 2.0 m above the ground
   b. a 15 g snowball moving through the air at 3.5 m/s
   c. a 35 kg child sitting at the top of a slide that is 3.5 m above the ground
   d. an 8500 kg airplane flying at 220 km/h

WORK AND ENERGY **305**

What Is Energy?

SECTION 9.3 REVIEW

Check Your Understanding

1. Answers may include: kinetic energy, potential energy (gravitational or elastic), mechanical energy, nonmechanical energy, chemical energy, electrical energy, nuclear energy, light energy
2. Energy is the ability to do work. Or when work is done, energy is transferred from one object to another.
3. Potential energy is energy due to position. Kinetic energy is the energy of motion.
4. a. gravitational PE and KE, both mechanical
   b. kinetic energy of the molecules (nonmechanical), chemical energy of the molecules (nonmechanical)
   c. elastic potential energy (mechanical) and some kinetic energy as the spring slowly unwinds (mechanical)
   d. light energy (nonmechanical)
   e. gravitational PE (mechanical)
5. Storing the water up high gives the water gravitational potential energy, so the water will naturally flow out of the tower if needed.

Answers continued on p. 319A.

RESOURCE LINK
STUDY GUIDE

Assign students *Review Section 9.3 What Is Energy?*

Scheduling

Refer to pp. 282A–282D for lecture, classwork, and assignment options for Section 9.4.

★ **Lesson Focus**
Use transparency *LT 32* to prepare students for this section.

READING SKILL BUILDER *Brainstorming* Write the words *conservation* and *law* on the chalkboard. Have students come up with words or phrases that relate to the words. Have students devise a hypothesis about the subject of the section based on the objectives and headings. Have students create a concept map or graphic organizer to show the structure of the section.

|SKILL BUILDER

Interpreting Visuals Have students discuss how the roller car in **Figure 9-18** behaves going up and down the hills. Ask them to describe the types and magnitudes of energy the roller car has at the highest and lowest points. The students should be able to express that the roller car has its maximum potential energy at the highest point, and it has its maximum kinetic energy at the lowest point.

Conservation of Energy

▶ **KEY TERMS**

efficiency

╭─ **OBJECTIVES**
▶ Identify and describe transformations of energy.
▶ Explain the law of conservation of energy.
▶ Discuss where energy goes when it seems to disappear.
▶ Analyze the efficiency of machines.

Figure 9-18
The tallest roller coaster in the world is the Fujiyama, in Fujikyu Highland Park, Japan. It spans 70 m from its highest to lowest points.

Imagine you are sitting in the front car of a roller coaster, such as the one shown in **Figure 9-18.** The car is pulled slowly up the first hill by a conveyor belt. When you reach the crest of the hill, you are barely moving. Then you go over the edge and start to race downward, speeding faster and faster until you reach the bottom of the hill. The wheels are roaring along the track. You continue to travel up and down through a series of smaller humps, twists, and turns. Finally, you climb another hill almost as big as the first, drop down again, and then coast to the end of the ride.

Energy Transformations

In the course of a roller coaster ride, energy changes form many times. You may not have noticed the conveyor belt at the beginning, but in terms of energy it is the most important part of the ride. All of the energy required for the entire ride comes from work done by the conveyor belt as it lifts the cars and the passengers.

The energy from that initial work is stored as gravitational potential energy at the top of the first hill. After that, the energy goes through a series of transformations, or changes, turning into kinetic energy and turning back into potential energy. A small quantity of this energy is transferred as heat to the wheels and as vibrations that produce a roaring sound in the air. But whatever form the energy takes during the ride, it is all there from the very beginning.

Potential energy can become kinetic energy

Almost all of the energy of a car on a roller coaster is potential energy at the top of a tall hill. The potential energy gradually changes to kinetic energy as the car accelerates downward. At the bottom of the lowest hill, the car has a maximum of kinetic energy and a minimum of potential energy.

Figure 9-19A shows the potential energy and kinetic energy of a car at the top and the bottom of the biggest hill on the Fujiyama roller coaster. Notice that the system has the same amount of energy, 354 kJ, whether the car is at the top or the bottom of the hill. That is because all of the gravitational potential energy at the top changes to kinetic energy as the car goes down the hill. When the car reaches the lowest point, the system has no potential energy because the car cannot go any lower.

Kinetic energy can become potential energy

When the car is at the lowest point on the roller coaster, it has no more potential energy, but it has a lot of kinetic energy. This kinetic energy can do the work to carry the car up another hill. As the car climbs the hill, the car slows down, decreasing its kinetic energy. Where does that energy go? Most of it turns back into potential energy as the height of the car increases.

At the top of a smaller hill, the car will still have some kinetic energy, along with some potential energy, as shown in **Figure 9-19B.** The kinetic energy will carry the car forward over the crest of the hill. Of course, the car could not climb a hill taller than the first one without an extra boost. The car does not have enough energy.

Figure 9-19

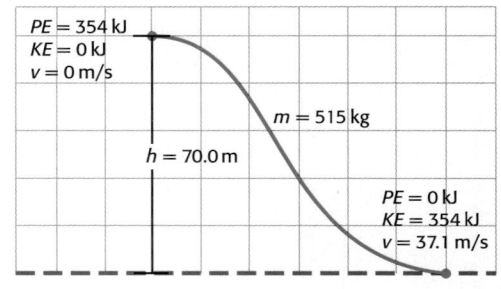

A As a car goes down a hill on a roller coaster, potential energy changes to kinetic energy.

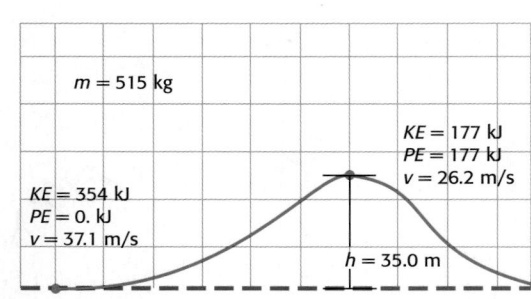

B At the top of this small hill, half the kinetic energy has become potential energy. The rest of the kinetic energy carries the car over the crest of the hill at high speed.

WORK AND ENERGY   **307**

SKILL BUILDER

Interpreting Diagrams
Figure 9-19 shows diagrams of two different hills on a roller coaster. Walk students through the equations, which are the same equations learned in Section 9.3. What assumption is made in each diagram about the energy of the roller car? *(The energy of the car at a later time is equal to the energy of the car at any earlier time. This is based on the law of conservation of energy.)*

Resources   Blackline Master 27 shows this visual.

Teaching Tip

Friction   Point out to students that in a world with no friction, the exchange of energy—from potential to kinetic and back again—could go on forever. In the real world, some energy is lost as the car rolls along the track experiencing friction and air resistance, so the roller coaster could not continue forever without some energy input (the motor that pulls the cars up the first hill).

Conservation of Energy

Interpreting Visuals

Figure 9-20 shows a tennis player tossing a ball for a serve. The height of the ball toss is important in tennis because the tennis player wants to hit the ball near the top of the arc, when it is not moving or is barely moving. If the ball is thrown too high, it would be harder to time the serve and hit the ball at the right point. If the ball is too low, the tennis player would not be able to extend his or her arm and would not have as much power.

Resources Teaching Transparency 26 shows this visual.

MISCONCEPTION

Flight of a Ball

ALERT

On the board, draw the flight of a ball thrown from one person to another. This should be drawn as an inverted parabola. Ask students to identify where the ball has the maximum kinetic energy (at the bottom on either side) and where the ball has the maximum potential energy (at the top). Point out to students that the ball you have just drawn on the board does not have 0 J KE at the top, unlike the tennis ball shown in **Figure 9-20.** Because the ball drawn on the board is traveling sideways as well as up and down, the ball still has some KE at the top. If it did not, it would fall straight down, because there would be no energy at the top to carry the ball sideways.

internet connect

SCLINKS
NSTA

TOPIC: Energy transformations
GO TO: www.scilinks.org
KEYWORD: HK1096

Energy transformations explain the flight of a ball

The relationship between potential energy and kinetic energy can explain motion in many different situations. Let's look at some other examples.

A tennis player tosses a 0.05 kg tennis ball into the air to set up for a serve, as shown in **Figure 9-20.** He gives the ball 0.5 J of kinetic energy, and it travels straight up. As the ball rises higher, the kinetic energy is converted to potential energy. The ball will keep rising until all the kinetic energy is gone. At its highest point, the ball has 0.5 J of potential energy. As the ball falls down again, the potential energy changes back to kinetic energy.

Imagine that a tennis trainer wants to know how high the ball will go when it is given 0.5 J of initial kinetic energy by a tennis player. The trainer could make a series of calculations using force and acceleration, but in this case using the concept of energy transformations is easier. The trainer knows that the ball's initial kinetic energy is 0.5 J and that its mass is 0.05 kg. To find out how high the ball will go, the trainer has to find the point where the potential energy equals its initial kinetic energy, 0.5 J. Using the equation for gravitational potential energy, the height turns out to be 1 m above the point that the tennis player releases the ball.

Figure 9-20
The kinetic energy of the ball at the bottom of its path equals the potential energy at the top of the path.

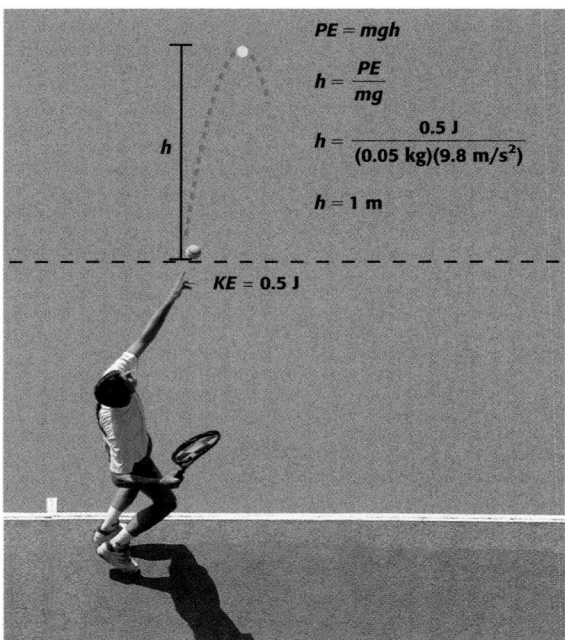

$$PE = mgh$$

$$h = \frac{PE}{mg}$$

$$h = \frac{0.5 \text{ J}}{(0.05 \text{ kg})(9.8 \text{ m/s}^2)}$$

$$h = 1 \text{ m}$$

$$KE = 0.5 \text{ J}$$

DEMONSTRATION 3 TEACHING

Bouncing Balls

Time: Approximately 10 minutes

Materials: several different types of balls (super ball, tennis ball, racquet ball, squash ball, ball made of clay, steel ball bearing, etc.)

If possible, perform the Quick Activity before this demonstration.

Rotating through all the types of balls, hold two at a time approximately 1 m above the floor or a desk. Drop the balls simultaneously. Lead a discussion about the different reactions (heights) of the balls' bounces. Discuss the energy conversions mentioned in the text. Ask students to hypothesize about the "disappearance" of the energy. Explain to students that each ball has a different ability to store elastic energy—the super ball is

Energy transformations explain a bouncing ball

Before a serve, a tennis player usually bounces the ball a few times while building concentration. The motion of a bouncing ball can also be explained using energy principles. As the tennis player throws the ball down, she adds kinetic energy to the potential energy the ball has at the height of her hand. The kinetic energy of the ball then increases steadily as the ball falls because the potential energy is changing to kinetic energy.

When the ball hits the ground, there is a sudden energy transformation as the kinetic energy of the ball changes to elastic potential energy stored in the compressed tennis ball. The elastic potential energy then quickly changes back to kinetic energy as the ball bounces upward.

If all of the kinetic energy in the ball changed to elastic potential energy, and that elastic potential energy all changed back to kinetic energy during the bounce, the ball would bounce up to the tennis player's hand. Its speed on return would be exactly the same as the speed at which it was thrown down. If the ball were dropped instead of thrown down, it would bounce up to the same height from which it was dropped.

Mechanical energy can change to other forms of energy

If changes from kinetic energy to potential energy and back again were always complete, then balls would always bounce back to the same height they were dropped from and cars on roller coasters would keep gliding forever. But that is not the way things really happen.

When a ball bounces on the ground, not all of the kinetic energy changes to elastic potential energy. Some of the kinetic energy compresses the air around the ball, making a sound, and some of the kinetic energy makes the ball, the air, and the ground hotter. Because these other forms of energy are not directly due to the motion or position of the ball, they can be considered nonmechanical energy. With each bounce, the ball loses some mechanical energy, as shown in **Figure 9-21.**

Likewise, a car on a roller coaster cannot keep moving up and down the track forever. The total mechanical energy of a car on a roller coaster constantly decreases due to friction and air resistance. This energy does not just disappear though. Some of it increases the temperature of the track, the car's wheels, and the air. Some of the energy compresses the air, making a roaring sound. Often, when energy seems to disappear, it has really just changed to a nonmechanical form.

Figure 9-21
With each bounce of a tennis ball, some of the mechanical energy changes to nonmechanical energy.

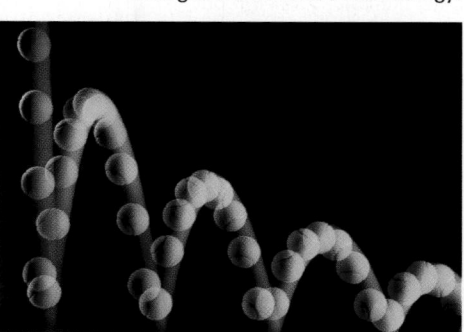

Conservation of Energy

Quick ACTIVITY
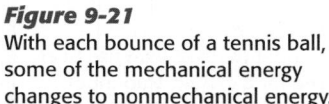

Energy Transfer   Caution students to avoid flexing the wire too many times, as it may break or heat up enough to cause burns.

Students should discover that the wire heats up as a result of the work done on the wire. The mechanical energy involved in moving the wire is transformed into nonmechanical energy, namely, the kinetic energy of the atoms in the wire. Performing this activity before Demonstration 3 will increase the student's ability to identify the "disappearing" energy.

Teaching Tip

Transformations to Nonmechanical Energy   Many examples in the chapter so far have assumed "ideal" circumstances, disregarding friction and air resistance. Once the idea that mechanical energy can change to nonmechanical energy is introduced, deviations from the ideal in "real world" situations can be explained. After reading this page, students may want to look back at earlier examples in the chapter to consider if energy would be lost from the system in realistic circumstances. (When pushing a box up a ramp, energy is lost to friction. On a roller coaster, energy is lost to both friction and air resistance).

Quick ACTIVITY

Energy Transfer
1. Flex a piece of thick wire or part of a coat hanger back and forth about 10 times with your hands. Are you doing work?
2. After flexing the wire, cautiously touch the part of the wire where you bent it. Does the wire feel hot? What happened to the energy you put into it?

RESOURCE LINK
DATASHEETS

Have students use *Datasheet 9.4 Quick Activity: Energy Transfer* to record their results.

very elastic, while the ball of clay is definitely not. The students should be able to conclude that some energy is lost in the collision with the floor or table. Lead the students to the realization that some energy is released as sound, and some is stored internally as the temperature of the ball rises. If you throw the ball of clay down hard several times in succession, you may be able to feel an increase in the temperature of the clay.

INTEGRATING ——

COMPUTERS AND TECHNOLOGY
Resources Assign students worksheet *9.4: Integrating Technology—Batteries and Emerging Technology* in the **Integration Enrichment Resources** ancillary.

MISCONCEPTION **ALERT**

Conservation of Energy Students may confuse the conservation of energy with the kind of energy conservation that is important to ecologists and environmentalists. They are related but not the same. Conservationists want to preserve energy in a useable form. Most energy technologies are inefficient, and after the energy has been used once or a few times, it is no longer useful. (For example, once gasoline is burned, the energy has been used to move the car, heat the tires and road, and so on.)

RESOURCE LINK

IER

Assign students worksheet *9.7: Integrating Environmental Science—The Conservation of Energy* as an extension exercise.

310

INTEGRATING

COMPUTERS AND TECHNOLOGY
In order for a flashlight to work, there must be a supply of energy.

A flashlight battery contains different chemicals that can react with each other to release energy. When the flashlight is turned on, chemical potential energy changes to electrical energy, and electrons begin to flow through a wire attached to the battery. Inside the bulb, the wire filament begins to glow, and the energy is transformed into light energy.

After the flashlight has been used for a certain amount of time, the battery will run out of energy. It will have to be replaced or recharged. You will learn more about batteries in Chapter 13.

The Law of Conservation of Energy

In our study of machines in Section 9.1, we saw that the work done on a machine is equal to the work that it can do. Similarly, in our study of the roller coaster, we found that the energy present at the beginning of the ride is present throughout the ride and at the end of the ride, although the energy continually changes form. The energy in each system does not appear out of nowhere and never just disappears.

This simple observation is based on one of the most important principles in all of science—the law of conservation of energy. Here is the law in its simplest form.

Energy cannot be created or destroyed.

In a mechanical system such as a roller coaster or a swinging pendulum, the energy in the system at any time can be calculated by adding the kinetic and potential energy to get the total mechanical energy. The law of conservation of energy requires that at any given time, the total energy should be the same.

Energy doesn't appear out of nowhere

Energy cannot be created from nothing. Imagine a girl jumping on a trampoline. After the first bounce, she rises to a height of 0.5 m. After the second bounce, she rises to a height of 1 m. Because she has greater gravitational potential energy after the second bounce, we must conclude that she added energy to her bounce by pushing with her legs. Whenever the total energy in a system increases, it must be due to energy that enters the system from an external source.

Energy doesn't disappear

Because mechanical energy can change to nonmechanical energy due to friction, air resistance, and other factors, tracing the flow of energy in a system can be difficult. Some of the energy may leak out of the system into the surrounding environment, as when the roller coaster produces sound as it compresses the air. But none of the energy disappears; it just changes form.

Systems may be open or closed

Energy has many different forms and can be found almost everywhere. Accounting for all of the energy in a given situation can be complicated. To make studying a situation easier, scientists often limit their view to a small area or a small number of objects. These boundaries define a system.

A system might include a gas burner and a pot of water. A scientist could study the flow of energy from the burner into the pot and ignore the small amount of energy going into the pot from the lights in the room, from a hand touching the pot, and so on.

When the flow of energy into and out of a system is small enough that it can be ignored, the system is called a *closed system*. Most systems are *open systems*, which exchange energy with the outside. Earth is an open system, as shown in **Figure 9-22.** Is your body an open or closed system?

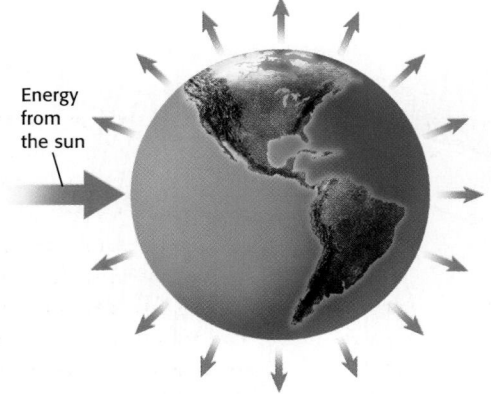

Energy from the sun

Figure 9-22
Earth is an open system because it receives energy from the sun and radiates some of its own energy out into space.

Conservation of Energy

READING SKILL BUILDER ***Brainstorm*** Have students think of different systems (just about anything can be considered a system). For each idea, ask what boundaries define the system. Is the system open or closed? *(Almost all systems are open to some degree.)* If open, where does energy come into and leak out of the system?

RESOURCE LINK
DATASHEETS

Have students use *Datasheet 9.5 Inquiry Lab: Is energy conserved in a pendulum?* to record their results.

Inquiry Lab

Is energy conserved in a pendulum?

Materials
- ✔ 1–1.5 m length of string
- ✔ pencil with an eraser
- ✔ meterstick
- ✔ nail or hook in the wall above a chalkboard
- ✔ pendulum bob
- ✔ level

Procedure

1. Hang the pendulum bob from the string in front of a chalkboard. On the board, draw the diagram as shown in the photograph at right. Use the meterstick and the level to make sure the horizontal line is parallel to the ground.
2. Pull the pendulum ball back to the "X." Make sure everyone is out of the way; then release the pendulum and observe its motion. How high does the pendulum swing on the other side?
3. Let the pendulum swing back and forth several times. How many swings does the pendulum make before the ball noticeably fails to reach its original height?
4. Stop the pendulum and hold it again at the "X" marked on the board. Have another student place the eraser end of a pencil on the intersection of the horizontal and vertical lines. Make sure everyone is out of the way again, especially the student holding the pencil.
5. Release the pendulum again. This time its motion will be altered halfway through the swing as the string hits the pencil. How high does the pendulum swing now? Why?
6. Try placing the pencil at different heights along the vertical line. How does this affect the motion of the pendulum? If you put the pencil down close enough to the arc of the pendulum, the pendulum will do a loop around it. Why does that happen?

Analysis

1. Use the law of conservation of energy to explain your observations in steps 2–6.
2. If you let the pendulum swing long enough, it will start to slow down, and it won't rise to the line any more. That suggests that the system has lost energy. Has it? Where did the energy go?

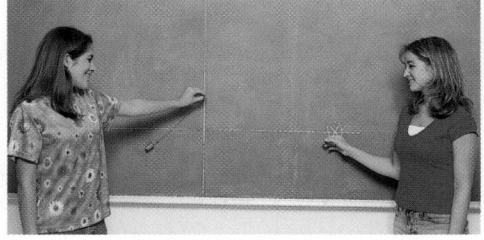

Inquiry Lab

Is energy conserved in a pendulum? Attach the string and hooks or nails before students arrive. Try to make sure that the string is far enough from the wall that the plumb bob and string do not rub against anything as they swing.

Analysis

1. The PE of the bob at the beginning is converted into KE at the bottom of the swing. The KE at the bottom is converted back into PE as the bob rises. When the pencil is low enough, the bob cannot rise enough to convert all of the KE into PE, so the bob continues to travel, looping over the pencil.
2. The energy of the pendulum is lost to air friction and internal friction in the string and hook. This causes the air to move and the string to heat up.

Figure 9-23
Like all machines, the pulleys on a sailboat are less than 100 percent efficient.

efficiency a quantity, usually expressed as a percentage, that measures the ratio of useful work output to work input

Efficiency of Machines

If you use a pulley to raise a sail on a sailboat like the one in **Figure 9-23,** you have to do work against the forces of friction in the pulley. You also have to lift the added weight of the rope and the hook attached to the sail. As a result, only some of the energy that you transfer to the pulley is available to raise the sail.

Not all of the work done by a machine is useful work

Because of friction and other factors, only some of the work done by a machine is applied to the task at hand; the machine also does some incidental work that does not serve any intended purpose. In other words, there is a difference between the total work done by a machine and the *useful* work done by the machine, that is, work that the machine is designed or intended to do.

Although all of the work done on a machine has some effect on the output work that the machine does, the output work might not be in the form that you expect. In lifting a sail, for example, some of the work available to lift the sail, which would be useful work, is transferred away as heat that warms the pulley, which is not a desired effect. The amount of useful work might decrease slightly more if the pulley squeaks, because some energy is "lost" as it dissipates into forces that vibrate the pulley and the air to produce the squeaking sound.

Efficiency is the ratio of useful work out to work in

The efficiency of a machine is a measure of how much useful work it can do. Efficiency is defined as the ratio of useful work output to total work input.

Efficiency Equation

$$efficiency = \frac{useful\ work\ output}{work\ input}$$

Efficiency is usually expressed as a percentage. To change an answer found using the efficiency equation into a percentage, just multiply by 100 and add the percent sign, "%."

A machine with 100 percent efficiency would produce exactly as much useful work as the work done on the machine. Because every machine has some friction, no machine has 100 percent efficiency. The useful work output of a machine never equals—and certainly cannot exceed—the work input.

Math Skills

Efficiency A sailor uses a rope and an old, squeaky pulley to raise a sail that weighs 140 N. He finds that he must do 180 J of work on the rope in order to raise the sail by 1 m (doing 140 J of work on the sail). What is the efficiency of the pulley? Express your answer as a percentage.

1 List the given and unknown values.

Given: *work input* = 180 J
useful work output = 140 J
Unknown: *efficiency* = ? %

2 Write the equation for efficiency.

$$efficiency = \frac{useful\ work\ output}{work\ input}$$

3 Insert the known values into the equation, and solve.

$$efficiency = \frac{140\ J}{180\ J} = 0.78$$

To express this as a percentage, multiply by 100 and add the percent sign, "%."
$$efficiency = 0.78 \times 100 = 78\%$$

Practice

Efficiency

1. Alice and Jim calculate that they must do 1800 J of work to push a piano up a ramp. However, because they must also overcome friction, they actually must do 2400 J of work. What is the efficiency of the ramp?
2. It takes 1200 J of work to lift the car high enough to change a tire. How much work must be done by the person operating the jack if the jack is 25 percent efficient?
3. A windmill has an efficiency of 37.5 percent. If a gust of wind does 125 J of work on the blades of the windmill, how much output work can the windmill do as a result of the gust?

Perpetual motion machines are impossible

Figure 9-24 shows a machine designed to keep on going forever without any input of energy. These theoretical machines are called *perpetual motion machines*. Many clever inventors have devoted a lot of time and effort to designing such machines. If such a perpetual motion machine could exist, it would require a complete absence of friction.

Practice HINT

▶ The efficiency equation can be rearranged to isolate any of the variables on the left
▶ For practice problem 2, you will need to rearrange the equation to isolate *work input* on the left side.
▶ For practice problem 3, you will need to rearrange to isolate *useful work output*.
▶ When using these rearranged forms to solve the problems, you will have to plug in values for *efficiency*. When doing so, do not use a percentage, but rather convert the percentage to a decimal by dropping the percent sign and dividing by 100.

Figure 9-24
Theoretically, a perpetual motion machine could keep going forever without any energy loss or energy input.

WORK AND ENERGY **313**

Section 9.4

Conservation of Energy

Math Skills

Resources Assign students worksheet *22: Efficiency* in the **Math Skills Worksheets** ancillary.

Additional Examples

Efficiency How much work must you do using a pulley that has an efficiency of 65 percent to raise a 120 N box up to a 3.0 m shelf? (**Hint:** First solve for the work done on the box.)

Answer: 550 N

If you improve the efficiency of the pulley to 85 percent by oiling it, how much work would you have to do?

Answer: 420 N

Solution Guide

1. *efficiency* = (1800 J)/(2400 J) = 0.75 or 75%
2. *work input* = $\frac{useful\ work\ output}{efficiency} = \frac{1200\ J}{0.25} = 4800\ J$
3. *useful work output* = (*efficiency*)(*work input*) = (0.375)(125 J) = 46.9 J

RESOURCE LINK
LABORATORY MANUAL

Have students perform *Lab 9 Work: Determining Which Ramp Is More Efficient* in the lab ancillary.

DATASHEETS

Have students use *Datasheet 9.7* to record their results from the lab.

▌ **SECTION 9.4 REVIEW**

Check Your Understanding

1. Energy can neither be created nor destroyed.
2. a falling ball, anything rolling downhill, a pendulum on the downswing; a rising ball, anything rolling uphill, a pendulum on the upswing
3. The player throws the ball, giving it KE. The ball begins to rise and slow down, transforming KE into PE. At its peak, the ball has maximum PE, then begins to fall, transforming PE into KE.
4. Friction prevents machines from being 100 percent efficient.
5. A child on a swing undergoes energy transformations from PE at the top (both sides) to maximum KE at the bottom and back to PE at the top of the opposite side. The child needs a push every now and then to make up for the energy lost to air resistance and friction in the rope.
6. The driver must keep transferring energy from the gas to the KE of the car to make up for the losses due to air resistance and friction between the tires and the road.

Answers continue on p. 319B.

Answers continue on p. 319B.

314

Because energy always leaks out of a system, no machine has 100 percent efficiency. In other words, every machine needs at least a small amount of energy input to keep going. Unfortunately, that means that perpetual motion machines are impossible. But new technologies, from magnetic trains to high speed microprocessors, reduce the amount of energy leaking from systems so that energy can be used as efficiently as possible.

▌ **SECTION 9.4 REVIEW**

SUMMARY

▶ Energy readily changes from one form to another.

▶ In a mechanical system, potential energy can become kinetic energy, and kinetic energy can become potential energy.

▶ Mechanical energy can change to nonmechanical energy as a result of friction, air resistance, or other means.

▶ Energy cannot be created or destroyed, although it may change form. This is called the law of conservation of energy.

▶ A machine cannot do more work than the work required to operate the machine. Because of friction, the work output of a machine is always somewhat less than the work input.

▶ The efficiency of a machine is the ratio of the useful work performed by the machine to the work required to operate the machine.

CHECK YOUR UNDERSTANDING

1. **State** the law of conservation of energy in your own words.
2. **List** three situations in which potential energy becomes kinetic energy and three situations in which kinetic energy becomes potential energy.
3. **Describe** the rise and fall of a basketball using the concepts of kinetic energy and potential energy.
4. **Explain** why machines are not 100 percent efficient.
5. **Applying Knowledge** Use the concepts of kinetic energy and potential energy to describe the motion of a child on a swing. Why does the child need a push from time to time?
6. **Creative Thinking** Using what you have learned about energy transformations, explain why the driver of a car has to continuously apply pressure to the gas pedal in order to keep the car cruising at a steady speed, even on a flat road. Does this situation violate the law of conservation of energy? Why or why not?

Math Skills

7. **Efficiency** When you do 100 J of work on the handle of a bicycle pump, it does 40 J of work pushing the air into the tire. What is the efficiency of the pump?
8. **Efficiency and Power** A river does 6500 J of work on a water wheel every second. The wheel's efficiency is 12 percent.
   a. How much work in joules can the axle of the wheel do in a second?
   b. What is the power output of the wheel?
9. **Efficiency and Work** John is using a pulley to lift the sail on his sailboat. The sail weighs 150 N and he must lift it 4.0 m.
   a. How much work must be done on the sail?
   b. If the pulley is 50 percent efficient, how much work must John do on the rope in order to lift the sail?

Chapter Highlights

Before you begin, review the summaries of the key ideas of each section, found on pages 290, 296, 305, and 314. The key vocabulary terms are listed on pages 284, 291, 297, and 306.

UNDERSTANDING CONCEPTS

1. _____ is defined as force acting over a distance.
   a. Power
   b. Energy
   c. Work
   d. Potential energy

2. The quantity that measures how much a machine multiplies force is called _____.
   a. mechanical advantage
   b. leverage
   c. efficiency
   d. power

3. Scissors are an example of _____.
   a. a lever
   b. a wedge
   c. a wheel and axle
   d. a compound machine

4. The unit that measures 1 J of work done each second is the _____.
   a. power
   b. newton
   c. watt
   d. mechanical advantage

5. Joules could be used to measure _____.
   a. the work done in lifting a bowling ball
   b. the potential energy of a bowling ball held in the air
   c. the kinetic energy of a rolling bowling ball
   d. All of the above

6. Which of the following situations does *not* involve potential energy being changed into kinetic energy?
   a. an apple falling from a tree
   b. shooting a dart from a spring-loaded gun
   c. pulling back on the string of a bow
   d. a creek flowing downstream

7. _____ is determined by both mass and velocity.
   a. Work
   b. Power
   c. Potential energy
   d. Kinetic energy

8. Energy that does not involve the large-scale motion or position of objects in a system is called _____.
   a. potential energy
   b. mechanical energy
   c. nonmechanical energy
   d. conserved energy

9. The law of conservation of energy states that _____.
   a. the energy of a system is always decreasing
   b. no machine is 100 percent efficient
   c. energy is neither lost nor created
   d. Earth has limited energy resources

Using Vocabulary

10. Write one sentence using *work* in the scientific sense, and write another sentence using it in a different, nonscientific sense. Explain the difference in the meaning of *work* in the two sentences.

    WRITING SKILL

11. The first page of this chapter shows an example of *kinetic sculpture.* You have now also learned the definition of *kinetic energy.* Given your knowledge of these two terms, what do you think the word *kinetic* means?

12. A can opener is a *compound machine.* Name three *simple machines* that it contains.

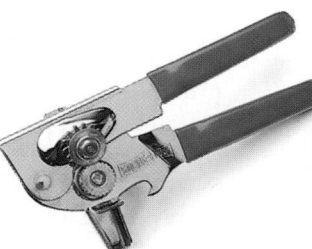

1. c
2. a
3. d
4. c
5. d
6. c
7. d
8. c
9. c

Using Vocabulary

10. Answers will vary. *Work* used in the scientific sense should imply a force acting on an object and changing the object's motion, while *work* in other contexts may have other meanings.

11. Answers should contain some statement that the word *kinetic* relates to motion.

12. wheel and axle, wedge, lever

13. a. PE b. KE c. PE d. KE

14. Because work is force times distance, the elephant does much more work than the mouse; the distance is the same, but the elephant weighs much more. Power is work divided by time, and because the mouse beat the elephant by a small amount of time, the fact that the elephant did much more work means that the power of the elephant is much greater than the power of the mouse.

RESOURCE LINK
STUDY GUIDE

Assign students *Mixed Review Chapter 9.*

CHAPTER 9 REVIEW

15. Energy is the ability to do work. Doing work is transferring or transforming energy. Energy is changed by doing work, which is exerting a force through a distance. An object that has energy has the ability to exert a force through a distance. The rate of changing energy per unit time is power.

BUILDING MATH SKILLS

See p. 319B for worked-out solutions.

16. a. 850 J
    b. 170 W
    c. 4.0

17. a. 55 000 J (or 55 kJ)
    b. 50%
    c. 55 kJ

18. a. 240 J
    b. 240 J
    c. 15 m/s
    d. It is transferred into the kinetic energy of the sand, sound energy (KE of air), and increased temperature (KE of the molecules of the rock and sand).

THINKING CRITICALLY

19. a. A, E, B, D, C
    b. C, D, B, E, A
    c. The lists are identical, except in reverse order.

20. Because energy cannot be created, the machine can only put out an amount of work equal to or less than the energy within the machine, which is less than or equal to the work input.

13. For each of the following, state whether the system contains primarily *kinetic energy* or *potential energy:*
    a. a stone in a stretched slingshot
    b. a speeding race car
    c. water above a hydroelectric dam
    d. the water molecules in a pot of boiling water

14. An elephant and a mouse race up the stairs. The mouse beats the elephant by a full second, but the elephant claims, "I am more powerful than you are, and this race has proved it." Use the definitions of *work* and *power* to support the elephant's claim.

15. How is *energy* related to *work, force,* and *power*?

BUILDING MATH SKILLS

16. You and two friends apply a force of 425 N to push a piano up a 2.0 m long ramp.
    a. **Work** How much work in joules has been done when you reach the top of the ramp?
    b. **Power** If you make it to the top in 5.0 s, what is your power output in watts?
    c. **Mechanical Advantage** If lifting the piano straight up would require 1700 N of force, what is the mechanical advantage of the ramp?

17. A crane uses a block and tackle to lift a 2200 N flagstone to a height of 25 m.
    a. **Work** How much work is done on the flagstone?
    b. **Efficiency** In the process, the crane's hydraulic motor does 110 kJ of work on the cable in the block and tackle. What is the efficiency of the block and tackle?
    c. **Potential Energy** What is the potential energy of the flagstone when it is 25 m above the ground?

18. A 2.0 kg rock sits on the edge of a cliff 12 m above the beach.
    a. **Potential Energy** Calculate the potential energy in the system.
    b. **Energy Transformations** The rock falls off the cliff. How much kinetic energy will it have just before it hits the beach? (Ignore air resistance.)
    c. **Kinetic Energy** Calculate the speed of the rock just before it hits the beach. (For help, see Practice Hint on page 301.)
    d. **Conservation of Energy** What happens to the energy after the rock hits the beach?

THINKING CRITICALLY

19. **Interpreting Graphics** The diagram below shows five different points on a roller coaster.

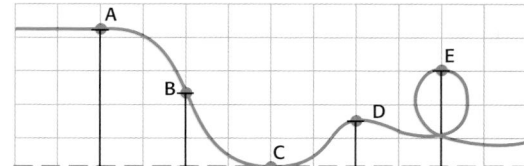

   a. List the points in order from the point where the car would have the greatest potential energy to the point where it would have the least potential energy.
   b. Now list the points in order from the point where the car would have the greatest kinetic energy to the point where it would have the least kinetic energy.
   c. How are your two lists related to each other?

20. **Critical Thinking** Use the law of conservation of energy to explain why the work output of a machine can never exceed the work input.

21. Applying Knowledge If a bumper car triples its speed, how much more work can it do on a bumper car at rest? (**Hint:** Use the equation for kinetic energy.)

22. Understanding Systems When a hammer hits a nail, there is a transfer of energy as the hammer does work on the nail. However, the kinetic energy and potential energy of the nail do not change very much. What happens to the work done by the hammer? Does this violate the law of conservation of energy?

23. Applying Knowledge You are trying to pry the lid off a paint can with a screwdriver, but the lid will not budge. Should you try using a shorter screwdriver or a longer screwdriver? Explain.

24. Designing Systems Imagine you are trying to move a piano into a second-floor apartment. It will not fit through the stairwell, but it will fit through a large window 3.0 m off the ground. The piano weighs 1800 N and you can exert only 290 N of force. Design a compound machine or system of machines you could use to lift the piano to the height of the window.

25. Connection to Sports A baseball pitcher applies a force to the ball as his arm moves a distance of 1.0 m. Using a radar gun, the coach finds that the ball has a speed of 18 m/s after it is released. A baseball has a mass of 0.15 kg. Calculate the average force that the pitcher applied to the ball. (**Hint:** You will need to use both the kinetic energy equation and the work equation.)

26. Concept Mapping Copy the unfinished concept map below onto a sheet of paper. Complete the map by writing the correct word or phrase in the lettered boxes.

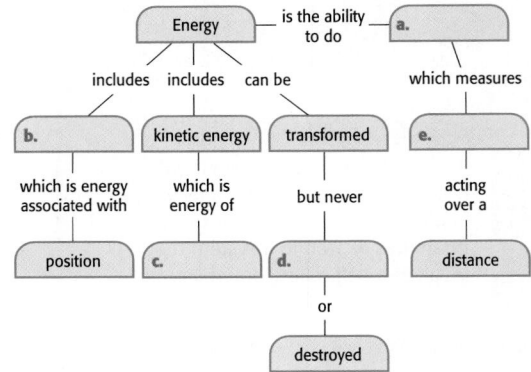

27. Connection to Earth Science Many fuels come from fossilized plant and animal matter. How is the energy stored in these fuels? How do you think that energy got into the fuels in the first place?

28. Connection to Biology When lifting an object using the biceps muscle, the forearm acts as a lever with the fulcrum at the elbow. The input work is provided by the biceps muscle pulling up on the bone. Assume that the muscle is attached 1.0 cm from the elbow and that the total length of the forearm from elbow to palm is 32 cm. How much force must the biceps exert to lift an object weighing 12 N? What class of lever is the forearm in this example?

internet connect

SC**LINKS**
NSTA

TOPIC: Energy and sports
GO TO: www.scilinks.org
KEYWORD: HK1097

WORK AND ENERGY **317**

21. nine times
22. The work done by the hammer is converted into kinetic energy of the nail and then into useful work on the wood, splitting it open so the nail can enter. Much of the energy goes into heating the hammer, nail, and wood. Some of the energy goes into the air as sound. This does not violate the law of conservation of energy.

23. You should use a longer screwdriver. The output length remains the same (the distance from the fulcrum to the output force), but the input length increases with a longer screwdriver, creating a larger mechanical advantage.
24. Answers may vary. One option is to use a ramp that is 19 m long, but that is not practical. Another option is a block and tackle with a mechanical advantage of 6.2 (three moving pulleys).

25. 24 N; *See p. 319B for a worked-out solution.*
26. a. work; b. potential energy; c. motion; d. created; e. force
27. Chemical energy; light (solar) energy was converted into chemical energy through photosynthesis
28. 380 N; The forearm is acting as a third-class lever. *See p. 319B for a worked-out solution.*

Determining Energy for a Rolling Ball

Introduction

Raised objects have gravitational potential energy. Moving objects have kinetic energy. How are these two quantities related in a system that involves a ball rolling down a ramp? Before the lab, review the law of conservation of energy with the students.

Objectives

Students will:

▶ **Use** appropriate lab safety procedures.

▶ **Measure** the heights, distances traveled, and time intervals for several balls rolling down ramps.

▶ **Calculate** the ball's potential energy at the top of the ramp and its speed and kinetic energy at the bottom of the ramp.

▶ **Analyze** the relationship between potential energy and kinetic energy.

Planning

Recommended Time: 1 lab period
Materials: *(for each lab group)*

▶ golf ball, racquet ball, or handball

▶ board, at least 90 cm in length

▶ stack of books, at least 60 cm in height

▶ box

▶ meterstick

▶ masking tape

▶ stopwatch

▶ balance

RESOURCE LINK
DATASHEETS

Have students use *Datasheet 9.6 Skill Builder Lab: Determining Energy for a Rolling Ball* to record their results.

Introduction

Raised objects have gravitational potential energy. Moving objects have kinetic energy. How are these two quantities related in a system that involves a ball rolling down a ramp?

Objectives

▶ **Measure** the height, distance traveled, and time interval for a ball rolling down a ramp.

▶ **Calculate** the ball's potential energy at the top of the ramp and its kinetic energy at the bottom of the ramp.

▶ **Analyze** the relationship between potential energy and kinetic energy.

Materials

golf ball, racquet ball, or handball
board, at least 90 cm (3 ft) long
stack of books, at least 60 cm (2 ft) high
box
meterstick
masking tape
stopwatch
balance

Safety Needs

safety goggles

REQUIRED PRECAUTIONS

▶ Read all safety precautions and discuss them with your students.

▶ Safety goggles must be worn at all times.

▶ Remind students that no horseplay will be allowed in the lab.

▶ The balls used for the experiment could cause trip and fall hazards. Be sure that students use a catch box at the end of the ramp.

Determining Energy for a Rolling Ball

▶ Preparing for Your Experiment

1. On a blank sheet of paper, prepare a table like the one shown below.

Table I **Potential Energy and Kinetic Energy**

	Height 1	Height 2	Height 3
Mass of ball (kg)			
Length of ramp (m)			
Height of ramp (m)			
Time ball traveled, first trial (s)			
Time ball traveled, second trial (s)			
Time ball traveled, third trial (s)			
Average time ball traveled (s)			
Final speed of ball (m/s)			
Final kinetic energy of ball (J)			
Initial potential energy of ball (J)			

2. Measure the mass of the ball, and record it in your table.

3. Place a strip of masking tape across the board close to one end, and measure the distance from the tape to the opposite end of the board. Record this distance in the row labeled "Length of ramp."

4. Make a catch box by cutting out one side of a box.

5. Make a stack of books approximately 30 cm high. Build a ramp by setting the taped end of the board on top of the books, as shown in the photograph on the next page. Place the other end in the catch box. Measure the vertical height of the ramp at the tape, and record this value in your table as "Height of ramp."

▶ Making Time Measurements

6. Place the ball on the ramp at the tape. Release the ball, and measure how long it takes the ball to travel to the bottom of the ramp. Record the time in your table.

7. Repeat step 6 two more times and record the results in your table. After three trials, calculate the average travel time and record it in your table.

8. Repeat steps 5–7 with a stack of books approximately 45 cm high, and repeat the steps again with a stack approximately 60 cm high.

▶ Analyzing Your Results

1. Calculate the average speed of the ball using the following equation:

$$average\ speed = \frac{length\ of\ ramp}{average\ time\ ball\ traveled}$$

2. Multiply average speed by 2 to obtain the final speed of the ball, and record the final speed.

3. Calculate and record the final kinetic energy of the ball by using the following equation:

$$KE = \frac{1}{2} \times mass\ of\ ball \times (final\ speed)^2$$

$$KE = \frac{1}{2}mv^2$$

4. Calculate and record the initial potential energy of the ball by using the following equation:

$$grav.\ PE = mass\ of\ ball \times (9.8\ m/s^2) \times height\ of\ ramp$$

$$PE = mgh$$

▶ Defending Your Conclusions

5. For each of the three heights, compare the ball's potential energy at the top of the ramp with its kinetic energy at the bottom of the ramp.

6. How did the ball's potential and kinetic energy change as the height of the ramp was increased?

7. Suppose you perform this experiment and find that your kinetic energy values are always just a little less than your potential energy values. Does that mean you did the experiment wrong? Why or why not?

WORK AND ENERGY **319**

Pre-Lab
Teaching Tips

Expand on the concepts of kinetic and potential energy and energy conservation. Give students an example of each such as a speeding car or a skydiver for kinetic energy and a coconut in a tree or a book on the edge of a desk as examples of potential energy.

Procedure

▶ **Designing Your Experiment**

Explain to students that they may have some difficulty obtaining precise measurements of the time it takes the ball to roll down the ramp. Have the students try the experiment a few times to decide on their best method for timing.

Post Lab

▶ **Disposal**

None. The equipment can be kept for future use.

▶ **Analyzing Your Results**

1. Answers will vary. All answers should be greater than the average speed of a falling body, between 0.25 s and 0.35 s for the ramp heights used in the experiment.

2. Answers will vary.

3. Answers will vary. Answers should all be less than 1.0 J.

4. Answers will vary. Answers should all be less than 1.0 J.

Continue on p. 319A.

CONTINUATION OF ANSWERS

Skill Builder Lab from page 319

Determining Energy for a Rolling Ball

Sample Data Table Potential Energy and Kinetic Energy	Height 1	Height 2	Height 3
Mass of ball (kg)	0.045	0.045	0.045
Length of ramp (m)	1.513	1.513	1.513
Height of ramp (m)	0.28	0.445	0.583
Time ball traveled, first trial (s)	1.59	1.31	1.09
Time ball traveled, second trial (s)	1.62	1.28	1.06
Time ball traveled, third trial (s)	1.56	1.25	1.04
Average time ball traveled (s)	1.59	1.28	1.06
Final speed of ball (m/s)	1.90	2.36	2.86
Final kinetic energy of ball (J)	0.081	0.125	0.184
Initial potential energy of ball (J)	0.123	0.196	0.257

▶ **Defending Your Conclusions**

5. The gravitational potential energy at the top and the kinetic energy at the bottom should be the same.

6. The higher the ramp, the greater the energy.

7. No. Not all of the gravitational potential energy is converted to kinetic energy because some energy changes into heat and sound due to friction.

Answers from page 290

SECTION 9.1 REVIEW

5. $W = F \times d = (25 \text{ N})(3.0 \text{ m}) = 75 \text{ J}$

6. $mechanical \; advantage = \dfrac{output \; force}{input \; force} = \dfrac{132 \text{ N}}{55.0 \text{ N}} = 2.40$

7. a. $W = F \times d = (400 \text{ N})(3 \text{ m}) = 1000 \text{ J}$

b. $P = \dfrac{W}{t} = \dfrac{1000 \text{ J}}{4 \text{ s}} = 300 \text{ W}$

8. $P = \dfrac{W}{t} = \dfrac{1.0 \times 10^6 \text{ J}}{50.0 \text{ s}} = 2.0 \times 10^4 \text{ W}$

$P = 2.0 \times 10^4 \text{ W} \times \dfrac{1 \text{ hp}}{746 \text{ W}} = 27 \text{ hp}$

Answers from page 296

SECTION 9.2 REVIEW

7. A door is normally a second-class lever, with mechanical advantage greater than 1. Pushing near the knob, rather than near the hinges, is easier because the input distance is longer. If you push near the hinges, the input arm is less than the output arm, so the door becomes a third-class lever, which has a mechanical advantage less than 1.

8. Answers will vary. A pencil sharpener, for example, is a compound machine that consists of a couple of screws (the blades to sharpen the pencil), wedges (the edges of those blades), and a wheel and axle (the crank).

Answers from page 305

SECTION 9.3 REVIEW

6. The water tower in item 5 is a case where gravitational PE is useful. Gravitational PE is dangerous to people hanging from the side of a cliff or building.

Math Skills

7. $PE = mgh = (93.0 \text{ kg})(9.8 \text{ m/s}^2)(550 \text{ m}) = 5.0 \times 10^5 \text{ J}$

8. $KE = \dfrac{1}{2}mv^2 = \dfrac{1}{2}(0.02 \text{ kg})(300 \text{ m/s})^2 = 900 \text{ J}$

9. a. $PE = mgh = (2.5 \text{ kg})(9.8 \text{ m/s}^2)(2.0 \text{ m}) = 49 \text{ J}$

b. $KE = \dfrac{1}{2}mv^2 = \dfrac{1}{2}(0.015 \text{ kg})(3.5 \text{ m/s})^2 = 9.2 \times 10^{-2} \text{ J}$

c. $PE = mgh = (35 \text{ kg})(9.8 \text{ m/s}^2)(3.5 \text{ m}) = 1.2 \times 10^3 \text{ J}$

d. $v = 220 \text{ km / h} \times \dfrac{1 \text{ h}}{60 \text{ min}} \times \dfrac{1 \text{ min}}{60 \text{ s}} \times \dfrac{1000 \text{ m}}{1 \text{ km}} = 61 \text{ m/s}$

$KE = \dfrac{1}{2}mv^2 = \dfrac{1}{2}(8500 \text{ kg})(61 \text{ m/s})^2 = 1.6 \times 10^7 \text{ J}$

Answers from page 314

Math Skills

7. $efficiency = \dfrac{useful\ work\ output}{work\ input} = \dfrac{40\ J}{100\ J} = 0.4\ or\ 40\%$

8. a. $useful\ work\ output = work\ input \times efficiency =$
$(6500\ J)(0.12) = 780\ J$

    b. $P = \dfrac{W}{t} = \dfrac{780\ J}{1\ s} = 780\ W$

9. a. $W = F \times d = (150\ N)(4.0\ m) = 600\ J$

    b. $work\ input = \dfrac{useful\ work\ output}{efficiency} = \dfrac{600\ J}{0.50} = 1200\ J$

Answers from page 316

**BUILDING
MATH SKILLS**

16. a. $W = F \times d = (425\ N)(2.0\ m) = 850\ J$

    b. $P = \dfrac{W}{t} = \dfrac{850\ J}{5.0\ s} = 170\ W$

    c. $mechanical\ advantage = \dfrac{output\ force}{input\ force} = \dfrac{1700\ N}{425\ N} = 4.0$

17. a. $W = F \times d = (2200\ N)(25\ m) = 5.5 \times 10^4\ J$

    b. $efficiency = \dfrac{useful\ work\ output}{work\ input} = \dfrac{5.5 \times 10^4\ J}{1.1 \times 10^5\ J} =$
    $0.50,\ or\ 50\%$

    c. $PE = mgh = (2200\ N)(25\ m) = 5.5 \times 10^4\ J$

18. a. $PE = mgh = (2.0\ kg)(9.8\ m/s^2)(12\ m) = 240\ J$

    b. $KE\ at\ end = PE\ at\ beginning = 240\ J$

    c. $v = \sqrt{\dfrac{2KE}{m}} = \sqrt{\dfrac{2(240\ J)}{2.0\ kg}} = 15\ m/s$

Answers from page 317

**INTEGRATING
CONCEPTS**

25. $W = KE;\ F \times d = \dfrac{1}{2}mv^2$

$F = \dfrac{mv^2}{2d} = \dfrac{(0.15\ kg)(18\ m/s)^2}{2(1.0\ m)} = 24\ N$

28. $work\ input = work\ output;\ F_i \times d_i = F_o \times d_o$

$F_i = F_o\dfrac{d_o}{d_i} = 12\ N\left(\dfrac{32\ cm}{1.0\ cm}\right) = 380\ N$

CareerLink

CareerLink

Civil Engineer [S]

Civil engineers rely on many of the principles of physics to plan their projects and be certain they are appropriate. In Grace Pierce's work with Traffic Systems, Inc., she uses the concepts of speed, acceleration, and force from Chapter 8.

Did You Know?

According to the Southern California Association of Governments, by the year 2020, traffic in Los Angeles will move twice as slow as it does now.

Civil Engineer

In a sense, civil engineering has been around since people started to build structures. Civil engineers plan and design public projects, such as roads, bridges, and dams, and private projects, such as office buildings. To learn more about civil engineering as a career, read the profile of civil engineer Grace Pierce, who works at Traffic Systems, Inc., in Orlando, Florida.

 What do you do as a civil engineer?

I'm a transportation engineer with a bachelor's degree in civil engineering. I do a lot of transportation studies, transportation planning, and engineering—anything to do with moving cars. Right now, my clients are about a 50-50 mix of private and public.

 What part of your job do you like best?

Transportation planning. On the planning side, you get to be involved in developments that are going to impact the community . . . being able to tap into my creative sense to help my clients get what they want.

 What do you find most rewarding about your job?

Civil engineering in civil projects. They are very rewarding because I get to see my input on a very fast time scale.

As a civil engineer, Grace Pierce designs roads and intersections.

"I get to help in projects that provide a better quality of life for people. It's a good feeling."

 What kinds of skills do you think a good civil engineer needs?

You need a good solid academic background. You need communication skills and writing ability. Communication is key. You should get involved in things like Toastmasters, which can help you with your presentation skills. You should get involved with your community.

What part of your education do you think was most important?

Two years before graduation, I was given the opportunity to meet with the owner of a company who gave me a good preview of what he did. It's really important to get out there and get the professional experience as well as the academic experience before you graduate.

What advice do you have for anyone interested in civil engineering?

Have a vision. Have a goal, whatever that might be, and envision yourself in that arena. Work as hard as you can to realize that vision. Find out what you want to do, and find someone who can mentor you. Use every resource available to you in high school and college, including professors and people in the community. And in the process, have fun. It doesn't have to be dreary.

 You didn't enter college immediately after high school. Did you have to do anything differently from a younger student?

I went to school as an older student. I didn't go back to college until age 27. I knew that because I was competing with younger folks, I really had to hustle.

internetconnect

SCI*LINKS*
NSTA

TOPIC: Engineer
GO TO: www.scilinks.org
KEYWORD: HK1999

INTEGRATING

COMPUTERS AND TECHNOLOGY One fast-growing area of traffic research is in building new models that can predict traffic flow patterns. Many of these models are computer simulations of traffic situations, either generated with a few key equations or with simulations of independent vehicles whose movement is governed by a few basic rules.

Another promising field of inquiry compares the creation and dilution of traffic jams by individual drivers' behaviors to the behavior of the particles in a liquid as the liquid undergoes a phase change to become a solid.

" *I think my industry is going toward the 'smart' movement of vehicles and people. The future is intelligent transportation systems using automated systems.*"
—GRACE PIERCE

321

CHAPTER 10

Heat and Temperature

Annotated Descriptions of the Correlated National Science Standards

The following descriptions summarize the National Science Standards that specially relate to Chapter 10. For a full text of the Standards, see p. 40T.

SECTION 10.1
Temperature
Science as Inquiry
SAI 1

SECTION 10.2
Energy Transfer
Physical Science
PS 5d

SECTION 10.3
Integrating Technology and Society —Using Heat
Physical Science
PS 5d

Cross-Discipline Teaching RESOURCES

Cross-Discipline Teaching, ATE p. 322
Language Arts   Mathematics

Integration Enrichment Resources
Space Science, **PE** and **ATE** p. 328
   IE 10.1 *Starlight, Star Heat*
Health, **PE** and **ATE** p. 330
   IE 10.2 *Skin Temperature*
Earth Science, **PE** and **ATE** p. 337
   IE 10.3 *Sea Breezes*
Social Studies, **PE** and **ATE** p. 340
   IE 10.4 *Early Central Heating*
Biology, **PE** and **ATE** p. 344
   IE 10.5 *Hibernation and Torpor*
Real World Applications, **PE** and **ATE** p. 346
   IE 10.6 *Appliance Energy Use and Cost*

Additional Integration Enrichment Worksheets
   IE 10.7 Social Studies
   IE 10.8 Environmental Science

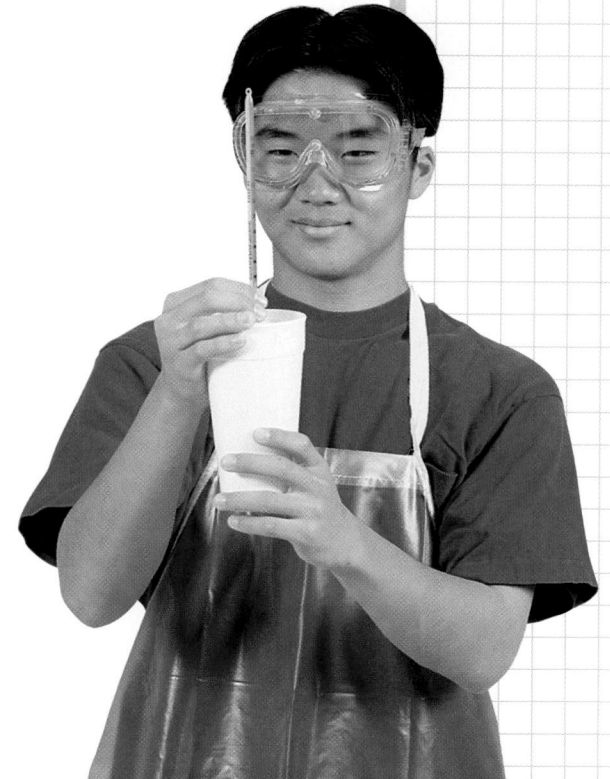

Use the Planning Guide on the next page to help you organize your lessons.

MATH AND COMPUTER RESOURCES

Chapter 10	Math Skills	Assess	Media/Computer Skills
Section 10.1	**ATE** **Cross-Discipline Teaching,** p. 322 **PE** **Math Skills** Temperature Scale Conversions, p. 328	**PE** **Practice**, p. 328 **PE** Section Review 6, 7, p. 330 **MS** Worksheet 23 **PE** **Building Math Skills,** p. 348, items 19, 20 **PE** **Problem Bank,** p. 699, 111–115	■ Section 10.1 🔆 *DISC ONE, MODULE 7* Heat
Section 10.2	**PE** **Math Skills** Specific Heat, p. 337 **ATE** **Additional Examples** p. 338	**PE** **Practice,** p. 338 **PE** Section Review 6, 7, p. 338 **MS** Worksheet 24 **PE** **Building Math Skills,** p. 348, items 21, 22 **PE** **Problem Bank,** p. 699, 116–120	■ Section 10.2 **CNN** Presents **Physical Science** Segment 12 Urban Heat Islands **CRT** Worksheet 12
Section 10.3			■ Section 10.3 **PE** Section Review 6, p. 346

PE Pupil's Edition   **ATE** Annotated Teacher's Edition   **MS** Math Skills   **BS** Basic Skills
IE Integration Enrichment   ■ Guided Reading Audio   **CRT** Critical Thinking

PHYSICAL SCIENCE INTERACTIVE TUTOR

READING SKILL BUILDER

The following activities found in the Annotated Teacher's Edition provide techniques for developing useful reading strategies to increase your students' reading comprehension skills.

Section 10.1 **Brainstorming,** p. 322

Section 10.2 **Anticipation (Prediction) Guide,** p. 331

Section 10.3 **K-W-L,** p. 339
Discussion, p. 344

Spanish Resources

The following resources are made available for students who speak Spanish as their first language.

Spanish Resources
Guided Reading Audio CD-ROM
Chapter 10

Spanish Glossary
Chapter 10

Heat and Temperature

CLASSROOM RESOURCES		
FOCUS	**TEACH**	**HANDS-ON**

Section 10.1 Temperature

BLOCK 1 — 45 minutes

FOCUS	TEACH	HANDS-ON
ATE RSB Brainstorming, p. 322 **ATE** Focus Activities 1, 2, p. 323 **ATE** **Demo 1** How Hot Is It?, p. 324 **ATE** **Demo 2** Building a Thermometer, p. 326 **PE** Temperature and Energy, pp. 324–328 ★ Focus Transparency LT 33	**ATE** **Skill Builder** Interpreting Visuals, pp. 323, 327 Graphs, p. 324 Graphing, p. 326 **TT** 27 Temperature Scales	**PE** Quick Activity *Sensing Hot and Cold,* p. 325 **DS** 10.1 **IE** Worksheet 10.1

BLOCK 2 — 45 minutes

FOCUS	TEACH	HANDS-ON
ATE **Demo 3** Energy Transfer, p. 330 **PE** Relating Temperature to Energy Transfer as Heat, pp. 329–330		**PE** Inquiry Lab *How do temperature and energy relate?* p. 329 **DS** 10.2 **IE** Worksheet 10.2

Section 10.2: Energy Transfer

BLOCK 3 — 45 minutes

FOCUS	TEACH	HANDS-ON
ATE RSB Anticipation (Prediction) Guide, p. 331 **ATE** **Demo 4** Energy Transfer in Boiling Water, p. 332 **PE** Methods of Energy Transfer, pp. 331–333 ★ Focus Transparency LT 34	**ATE** **Skill Builder** Interpreting Visuals, p. 332	**PE** Quick Activity *Convection,* p. 333 **DS** 10.3

BLOCK 4 — 45 minutes

FOCUS	TEACH	HANDS-ON
ATE **Demo 5** Heat Versus Temperature, p. 336 **PE** Conductors and Insulators; Specific Heat, pp. 334–338	**ATE** **Skill Builder** Interpreting Tables, p. 336 Graphing, p. 336 **BLM** 28 Specific Heats	**PE** Inquiry Lab *What color absorbs more radiation?* p. 334 **DS** 10.4 **PE** Quick Activity *Conductors and Insulators,* p. 335 **DS** 10.5 **IE** Worksheet 10.3 **LE 10** *Determining the Better Insulator for Your Feet* **DS** 10.7

Section 10.3: Using Heat

BLOCK 5 — 45 minutes

FOCUS	TEACH	HANDS-ON
ATE RSB K-W-L, p. 339 **ATE** **Demo 6** Conduction, p. 339 **PE** Heating Systems, pp. 339–343 ★ Focus Transparency LT 35	**ATE** **Skill Builder** Interpreting Visuals, pp. 339, 341, 343 **TT** 28 Air Conditioner **BLM** 29 Insulation *R*-Values	**IE** Worksheet 10.4 **IE** Worksheet 10.7

BLOCK 6 — 45 minutes

FOCUS	TEACH	HANDS-ON
ATE RSB Discussion, p. 344 **ATE** **Demo 7** Heat Pumps, p. 344 **PE** Cooling Systems, pp. 343–346		**IE** Worksheet 10.5 **PE** Real World Applications *Buying Appliances,* p. 346 **IE** Worksheets 10.6, 10.8 **PE** Design Your Own Lab *Investigating the Conduction of Heat,* p. 350 **DS** 10.6

CLASSROOM RESOURCES

HOMEWORK	ASSESS
PE Section Review 1–3, 5–7, p. 330 **Chapter 10 Review,** p. 347, items 1–4, 13, 19, 20	**SG** Chapter 10 Pretest
PE Section Review 4, p. 330 **Chapter 10 Review,** p. 347, items 11, 12	**SG** Section 10.1
PE Section Review 1, 3–5, p. 338 **Chapter 10 Review,** p. 347, items 5, 6, 14, 15, 17	
PE Section Review 2, 6, 7, p. 338 **Chapter 10 Review,** p. 347, items 7, 16, 21, 22	**SG** Section 10.2
PE Section Review 2–6, p. 346 **Chapter 10 Review,** p. 347, item 10	
PE Section Review 1, p. 346 **Chapter 10 Review,** p. 347, items 8, 9, 18	**SG** Section 10.3

REVIEW AND ASSESS

BLOCK 7

PE Chapter 10 Review
Thinking Critically 23–32, p. 348
Developing Life/Work Skills 33–34, p. 349
Integrating Concepts 35–36, p. 349
SG Chapter 10 Mixed Review

BLOCK 8

Chapter Tests
Chapter 10 Test

One-Stop Planner CD–ROM **with Test Generator**
Chapter 10

Teaching Resources
Scoring Rubrics and assignment checklist.

 internet**connect**

SCiLINKS
NSTA

National Science Teachers
Association
Online Resources:
www.scilinks.org
The following *sci*LINKS Internet resources can be found
in the student text for this chapter.

Page 323 **TOPIC:** Electromagnetic spectrum **KEYWORD:** HK1101	**Page 340** **TOPIC:** Heating and cooling systems **KEYWORD:** HK1104
Page 326 **TOPIC:** Temperature scales **KEYWORD:** HK1102	**Page 349** **TOPIC:** Insulators **KEYWORD:** HK1105
Page 331 **TOPIC:** Energy transfer **KEYWORD:** HK1103	

CNNfyi.com   www.cnnfyi.com

Visit this site for coverage of current events and related
classroom resources.

PE Pupil's Edition   **ATE** Annotated Teacher's Edition
RSB Reading Skill Builder   **DS** Datasheets
IE Integrated Enrichment   **SG** Study Guide
LE Laboratory Experiments
TT Teaching Transparencies   **BLM** Blackline Masters
★ Lesson Focus Transparency

Tapping Prior Knowledge

Be sure students understand the following concepts:

Chapter 1
Units of measurement

Chapter 9
Energy and conservation of energy

READING SKILL BUILDER

Brainstorming
Have the students create a table of the planets in our solar system. Have the students compare the temperature of each planet with the classroom's temperature. Record the table on the board or on an overhead transparency.

Develop some general principles that can guide the students to classify which planets are "hotter" or "colder." General principles that should be suggested to students are the distance of a planet from the sun and the type of atmosphere of the planet.

LINKING CHAPTERS

Table 16-1, p. 543 lists the average surface temperature of each planet and each planet's type of atmosphere.

Heat and Temperature

Chapter Preview

10.1 Temperature
Temperature and Energy
Relating Temperature to
Energy Transfer as Heat

10.2 Energy Transfer
Methods of Energy Transfer
Conductors and Insulators
Specific Heat

10.3 Using Heat
Heating Systems
Cooling Systems

INTEGRATING TECHNOLOGY and Society

322

RESOURCE LINK
STUDY GUIDE

Assign students *Pretest Chapter 10 Heat and Temperature* before beginning Section 10.1

CROSS-DISCIPLINE TEACHING

Language Arts Since ancient times, fire has stirred the imagination of people all over the world. Many myths and legends about fire have originated in various civilizations. Have your students write their own legend describing the origin of fire and how it came to be used on Earth.

Mathematics Obtain a price for 1 kWh of electricity from the local power company or from your electric bill. Have students calculate the cost of using the following combinations of power levels and times: a 100 W light bulb for 2 hours and a 60 W stereo for 3 hours.

Focus ACTIVITY

Background The fire started at night. By the time firefighters arrived the next morning, the forest was filled with thick smoke. The firefighters knew the fire was still raging in the forest, but they had to see through the smoke to find the fire's exact location.

Fortunately, firefighters have instruments that detect infrared radiation. Infrared radiation is a form of light that is invisible to the eye and is given off by hot objects, such as burning wood. Infrared radiation passes through the smoke and is picked up by infrared detectors. The images formed by these instruments are then converted into pictures that we can see. From these pictures, the fire's exact location can be determined, and the firefighters can keep the fire from spreading.

Activity 1 Use a prism to separate a beam of sunlight into its component colors, and project these onto a sheet of paper. Use a thermometer to record the temperature of the air in the room, and then place the thermometer bulb in each colored band for 3 minutes. Record the final temperature of each colored band. Place the thermometer on the dark side of the red band, where infrared radiation is found, for 3 minutes. How do the final temperature readings differ? Do your results suggest why infrared radiation is associated with hot objects?

Activity 2 Obtain several cups that are about the same size but are made of different materials (glass, metal, ceramic, plastic foam). Fill one cup with hot tap water, and measure the time it takes for the outside of the cup to feel hot (at a temperature of about 35°C). Repeat this for each cup. List the materials, with the one that warms fastest listed first. Note any differences such as cup thickness, cup volume, or changes in the temperature of your hand.

internet connect

SCI LINKS.
NSTA

TOPIC: Electromagnetic spectrum
GO TO: www.scilinks.org
KEYWORD: HK1101

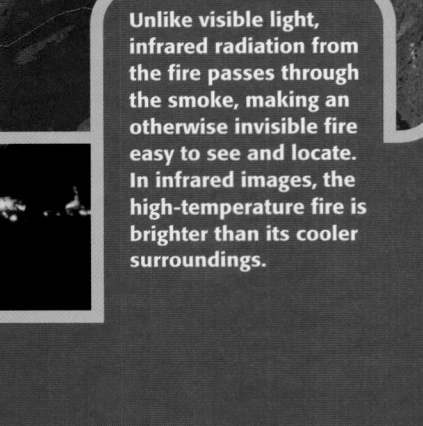

Unlike visible light, infrared radiation from the fire passes through the smoke, making an otherwise invisible fire easy to see and locate. In infrared images, the high-temperature fire is brighter than its cooler surroundings.

323

Focus ACTIVITY

Background Infrared detectors are also useful to firefighters trying to find people trapped in smoke-filled buildings. Since the temperature of a living human body is higher than the temperature of most objects in a room, a firefighter can use the detector to find the people.

Activity 1 This activity will work best with a sheet of white paper.

Students should find that the temperature of the bands increases as they move from violet to red, and the infrared region (the dark side of the red band) should be the highest temperature.

Activity 2 Answers will vary depending on which materials are used as well as the thickness of each. Students should find that metal heats up faster, followed by glass, ceramic, and plastic foam.

|SKILL BUILDER

Interpreting Visuals Have students look at the photo and identify "hot spots." Lead a discussion about how a firefighter might use this image to guide his or her actions.

Discuss how different colors of a flame have different temperatures. Blue, for instance, is hotter than the yellow part of the flame.

Scheduling

Refer to pp. 322A–322D for lecture, class work, and assignment options for Section 10.1.

★ **Lesson Focus**
Use transparency *LT 33* to prepare students for this section.

INTEGRATING

MATHEMATICS Using a simple model of a gas consisting of 10 atoms, discuss the difference between each atom's average kinetic energy and total kinetic energy. Assign each atom a value for kinetic energy.

▌SKILL BUILDER

Graphs Plot a graph of the total energy versus number of atoms in the gas model. Also, plot a graph of average energy versus the number of atoms. Use the gas model for your data. Ask the students what they have learned from the graph. You can pose the following questions:

- Can a glass of water and a lake have the same average kinetic energy?
- Can a glass of water and a lake have the same total energy?

10.1

Temperature

▶ **KEY TERMS**
temperature
thermometer
absolute zero
heat

OBJECTIVES

▶ Define *temperature* in terms of the average kinetic energy of atoms or molecules.

▶ Convert temperature readings between the Fahrenheit, Celsius, and Kelvin scales.

▶ Recognize heat as a form of energy transfer.

▶ **temperature** a measure of the average kinetic energy of all the particles within an object

People use **temperature** readings, such as those shown in **Figure 10-1**, to make a wide variety of decisions every day. You check the temperature of the outdoor air to decide what to wear. The temperature of a roasting turkey is monitored to see if it is properly cooked. A nurse monitors the condition of a patient by checking the patient's body temperature. But what exactly is it that you, the cook, and the nurse are measuring? What does the temperature indicate?

Temperature and Energy

When you touch the hood of an automobile, you sense how hot or cold it is. In everyday life, we associate this sensation of hot or cold with the temperature of an object. However, this sensation serves only as a rough indicator of temperature. The Quick Activity on the next page illustrates this point.

Figure 10-1
Many decisions are made based on temperature.

 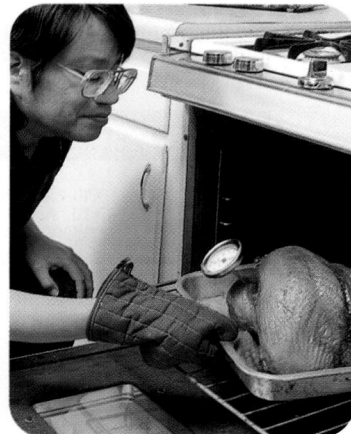 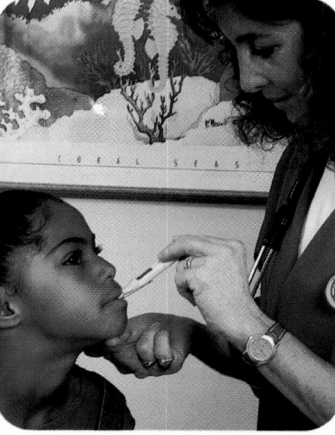

DEMONSTRATION 1 TEACHING

How Hot Is It?

Time: Approximately 10 minutes
Materials: dry ice (available at most supermarkets), beaker, water, hot plate, thermometer

Before class begins, place the beaker on the hot plate. Be sure the hot plate is turned off and that students cannot see the plug or power light. Fill the beaker halfway with water and add some dry ice. Place the thermometer in the water. When

students enter the class, the water in the beaker should be bubbling as if it were boiling.

Analysis

1. Ask the students to observe the beaker for 1 minute and write their observations.
2. Have the students write down their best guess of the temperature of the water.
3. Have a student read the thermometer.
4. Discuss the importance of using scientific instruments to make observations.

Quick ACTIVITY

Sensing Hot and Cold

For this exercise you will need three bowls.
1. Put an equal amount of water in all three bowls. In the first bowl, put some cold tap water. Put some hot tap water in the second bowl. Then, mix equal amounts of hot and cold tap water in the third bowl.
2. Place one hand in the hot water and the other hand in the cold water. Leave them there for 15 s.
3. Place both hands in the third bowl, which contains the mixture of hot and cold water. How does the water temperature feel to each hand? Explain.

In Chapter 2, you learned that all particles in a substance are constantly moving. Like all moving objects, each particle has kinetic energy. If we average the kinetic energy of all the particles in an object, it turns out that this average kinetic energy is related to the temperature of the object. In fact, the temperature is proportional to the average kinetic energy.

In other words, as the average kinetic energy of an object increases, its temperature will increase. Compared to a cool car hood, the particles in a hot hood move faster because they have more kinetic energy. But how do we measure the temperature of an object? It is impossible to find the kinetic energy of every particle in an object and calculate its average. Actually, nature provides a very simple way to measure temperature directly.

Common thermometers rely on expansion

Icicles forming on trees, flowers wilting in the sun, and the red glow of a stove-top burner are all indicators of certain temperature ranges. You feel these temperatures as hot or cold. How you sense hot and cold depends not only on an object's temperature but also on other factors, such as the temperature of your skin.

To measure temperature accurately, we rely on a simple physical property of substances: most objects expand when their temperature increases. Ordinary **thermometers** are based on this principle and use liquid substances like mercury or colored alcohol that expand as their temperature increases and contract as their temperature falls. The expansion and contraction is the result of energy exchange between the thermometer and its surroundings.

For example, the thermometer shown in **Figure 10-2** can measure the temperature of air on a sunny day. As the temperature rises, the particles in the liquid inside the thermometer gain kinetic energy and move faster. With this increased motion, the particles in the liquid move farther apart causing it to expand and rise up the narrow tube.

▶ **thermometer** a device that measures temperature

Figure 10-2
A liquid thermometer uses the expansion of liquid alcohol or mercury to indicate changes in temperature.

Historical Perspective

It is generally believed that Galileo built the first thermometer around 1592. Galileo's thermometer consisted of a glass vessel that was inverted and placed in a trough of water, partially submerging the open-mouthed end of the glass vessel in the water. As the temperature of the air inside the glass vessel changed, the air expanded or contracted, changing the water level in the glass vessel. The change in the water level indicated change in temperature, which was measured against a temperature scale.

INTEGRATING

LIFE SCIENCE The human body maintains a fairly constant body temperature of 98.6°F. This is in contrast to reptiles, like snakes and lizards, whose temperature adjusts according to the temperature of their surroundings.

REAL WORLD APPLICATIONS

Building and Roads Because most substances expand when their temperature increases, bridges and roads are built to account for this expansion when the weather gets hotter. Expansion joints are built between sections of the road to prevent it from breaking when the road expands.

Quick ACTIVITY

Sensing Hot and Cold

SAFETY CAUTION *Monitor "hot" tap water carefully to ensure students do not burn themselves.*

If tap water is not cold, have students add one or two ice cubes to the "cold" bowl.

Be sure students grasp the idea that terms like *hot* and *cold* are qualitative measures of temperature. Professionals in all disciplines prefer measurements that are quantitative, so a scientist uses a thermometer to measure temperature. The main conclusion from the Quick Activity is that the hot and cold sensations are not accurate and can be misleading.

RESOURCE LINK
DATASHEETS

Have students use *Datasheet 10.1 Quick Activity: Sensing Hot and Cold* to record their results.

Temperature

Teaching Tip

Temperature Scale Draw two horizontal number lines on the chalkboard, one above the other. At the left end of the lines, draw a vertical line and write "Water Freezes." At the right end, draw another vertical line and write "Water Boils." Label the top line °F and the bottom line °C. Label the left end of the top line "32" and the bottom line "0." Label the right ends "212" and "100."

Show the students that the temperatures mean the same thing, but they have different units, like 75 cm or 0.75 m. Also point out that there are 180 spaces in between water freezing and boiling on the top line, but there are only 100 spaces on the bottom line. That means that a °C must be almost twice as big as a °F.

INTEGRATING

MATHEMATICS Show students the origin of the factor $\frac{9}{5}$ in the Fahrenheit-to-Celsius conversions.

100 °C divisions = 180 °F divisions; therefore,

1°C division = $\frac{180}{100}$°F divisions

1°C division = $\frac{9}{5}$°F divisions

SKILL BUILDER

Graphing Use a spreadsheet program to draw a graph of °F versus °C. Copy the graph onto an overhead transparency. Show the students the linear relationship between the two scales. Point out the slope $\left(\frac{9}{5}\right)$ and the *y*-intercept (32°) in the equation.

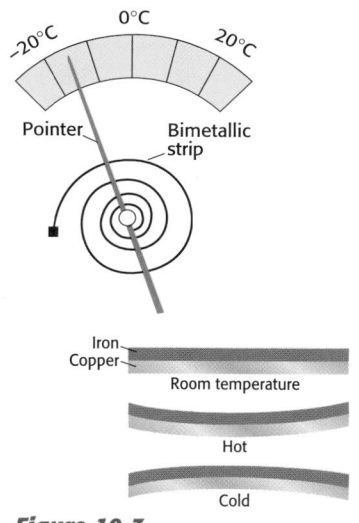

Figure 10-3
A refrigerator thermometer uses the bending of a strip made from two metals to indicate the correct temperature.

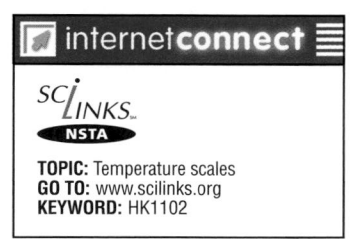

Figure 10-4
A digital thermometer uses changes in electricity to measure temperature.

internet connect

SC**LINKS**
NSTA

TOPIC: Temperature scales
GO TO: www.scilinks.org
KEYWORD: HK1102

Liquid thermometers can measure only temperatures within a certain range. This is because below a certain temperature, the liquid used in the thermometer freezes. Also, above a certain temperature the liquid boils. Therefore, different types of thermometers are designed to measure extreme temperatures.

The thermometer used in a refrigerator is based on the expansion of metal, as shown in **Figure 10-3.** The thermometer contains a coil made from two different metal strips pressed together. Both strips expand and contract at different rates as the temperature changes. As the temperature falls, the coil unwinds moving the pointer to the correct temperature. A digital thermometer, shown in **Figure 10-4,** is designed to measure temperature by noting the change in current. Changes in temperature also cause electric current to change in a circuit.

Fahrenheit and Celsius are common scales used for measuring temperatures

The temperature scale that is probably most familiar to you from weather reports and cookbooks is the Fahrenheit scale. The units on the Fahrenheit scale are called degrees Fahrenheit, or °F. On the Fahrenheit scale, water freezes at 32°F and boils at 212°F.

Most countries other than the United States use the Celsius (or centigrade) scale. This scale is widely used in science. The Celsius scale gives a value of zero to the freezing point of water and a value of 100 to the boiling point of water at standard atmospheric pressure. The difference between these two points is divided into 100 equal parts, called degrees Celsius, or °C.

A degree Celsius is nearly twice as large as a degree Fahrenheit. Also, the temperature at which water freezes differs for the two scales by 32 degrees. To convert from one scale to the other, use one of the following formulas.

Celsius-Fahrenheit Conversion Equation

$$Fahrenheit\ temperature = \left(\frac{9}{5} \times Celsius\ temperature\right) + 32.0$$

$$T_F = \frac{9}{5}t + 32.0$$

Fahrenheit-Celsius Conversion Equation

$$Celsius\ temperature = \frac{5}{9}(Fahrenheit\ temperature - 32.0)$$

$$t = \frac{5}{9}(T_F - 32.0)$$

DEMONSTRATION 2 TEACHING

Building a Thermometer

Time: Approximately 30 minutes
Materials: ring stand
         Bunsen burner
         500 mL flask
         roughly 8 in. long glass tube
         stopper with one hole (stopper
           should fit the flask)
         water trough

Step 1 Cover the open end of the flask with the stopper containing the glass tube. Invert the flask through the ring on the ring stand.

Step 2 The length of the glass tube inside the flask should be very small. Place the other end of the glass tube in a trough of water.

Step 3 Build a temperature scale as long as the length of the glass tube, using an arbitrary unit.

The Kelvin scale is based on absolute zero

You have probably heard of negative temperatures, such as those reported on extremely cold winter days in the northern United States and Canada. Remember that temperature is a measure of the average kinetic energy of the particles in an object. Even far below 0°C these particles are moving and therefore have some kinetic energy. But how low can the temperature fall? Physically, the lowest possible temperature is –273.13°C. This temperature is referred to as absolute zero. At absolute zero the energy of an object is minimal, that is, the energy of the object cannot be any lower.

Absolute zero is the basis for another temperature scale called the Kelvin scale. On this scale, 0 kelvin, or 0 K, is absolute zero. Since the lowest possible temperature is assigned a zero value, there are no negative temperature values on the Kelvin scale. The Kelvin scale is used in many fields of science, especially those involving low temperatures. The three temperature scales are compared in **Figure 10-5.**

In magnitude, a unit of kelvin is equal to a degree on the Celsius scale. Therefore, the temperature of any object in kelvins can be found by simply adding 273 to the object's temperature in degrees Celsius. The equation for this conversion is given below.

Temperature Values on Different Scales

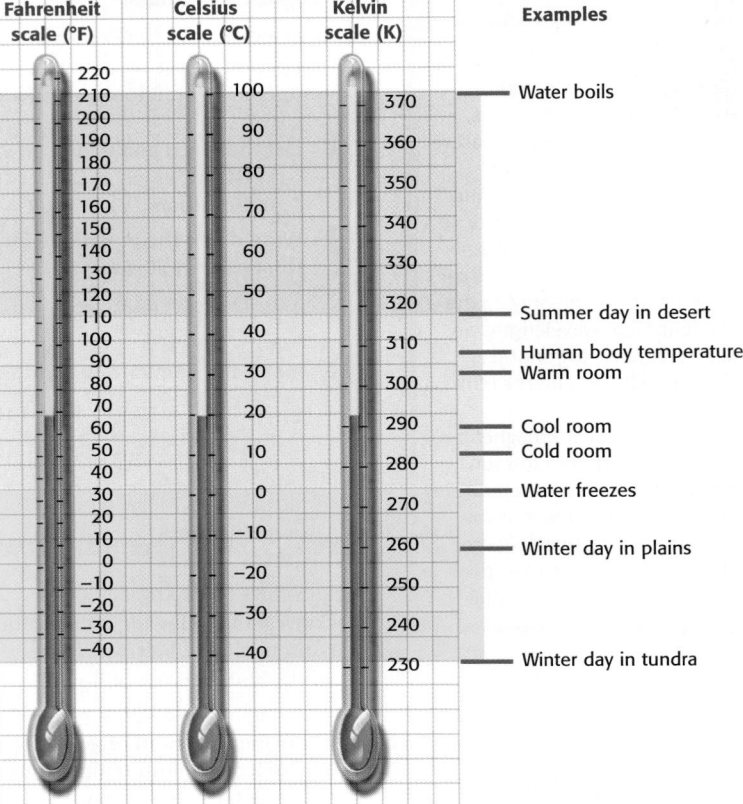

Figure 10-5
Temperatures on the Celsius scale can be converted to both Fahrenheit and Kelvin scales. Note that all Kelvin temperatures are positive.

▶ **absolute zero** the temperature at which an object's energy is minimal

---

Celsius-Kelvin Conversion Equation

$$Kelvin\ temperature = Celsius\ temperature + 273$$

$$T = t + 273$$

Step 4 Using the Bunsen burner, gently heat the glass vessel until a few bubbles escape from the trough. Stop heating at this point. As the air inside the flask cools down, the water level in the glass tube will increase.

Step 5 The temperature scale allows you to quantify the temperature.

Temperature

|SKILL BUILDER|

Interpreting Visuals Write three or four Fahrenheit temperatures on the board. Have students use **Figure 10-5** to determine the Celsius and Kelvin equivalents. Possible choices are 98.6°F (body temperature), 70°F (room temperature), 32°F (water freezes), and –40°F (the same on the Celsius scale).

Resources *Teaching Transparency 27* shows this visual.

Historical Perspective

The Kelvin scale is named after the British physicist Lord Kelvin (1824–1907). The Fahrenheit scale is named after the German physicist Gabriel Fahrenheit (1686–1736). The Celsius scale is named for the Swedish astronomer Anders Celsius (1701–1744). The Celsius scale was originally called the centigrade scale because there are 100 degrees between the freezing and boiling points of water. In Latin, *centi* means "100" and *gradus* means "degree."

Teaching Tip

Superconductors Copper and aluminum, like most metals, are good conductors of electric current, which is the flow of electrons in a substance. At very low temperatures, certain substances lose all their resistance to electric current and become excellent conductors of electric current. These substances are called superconductors. The temperature at which a substance becomes a superconductor is close to absolute zero. For example, aluminum becomes a superconductor at 1.2 K.

Temperature

INTEGRATING

SPACE SCIENCE
From cold deep space to hot stars, astronomers measure a wide range of temperatures of objects in the universe. All objects produce different types of electromagnetic waves depending on their temperature. By identifying the distribution of wavelengths an object radiates, astronomers can estimate the object's temperature.

Light (an electromagnetic wave) received from the sun indicates that the temperature of its surface is 6000 K. If you think that is hot, try the center of the sun, where the temperature increases to 15 000 000 K!

PHYSICAL SCIENCE INTERACTIVE TUTOR

***Disc One, Module 7:* Heat**
Use the Interactive Tutor to learn more about this topic.

Math Skills

Temperature Scale Conversion The highest atmospheric temperature ever recorded on Earth was 57.8°C. Express this temperature both in degrees Fahrenheit and in kelvins.

1 List the given and unknown values.
  Given: $t = 57.8°C$
  Unknown: $T_F = ?°F, T = ?K$

2 Write down the equations for temperature conversions from pages 326 and 327.
$$T_F = \frac{9}{5}t + 32.0$$
$$T = t + 273$$

3 Insert the known values into the equations, and solve.
$$T_F = \left(\frac{9}{5} \times 57.8\right) + 32.0 = 104 + 32.0 = 136°F$$
$$T = 57.8 + 273 = 331 \text{ K}$$

Practice

Temperature Scale Conversion
1. Convert the following temperatures to both degrees Fahrenheit and kelvins.
  a. the boiling point of liquid hydrogen (–252.87°C)
  b. the temperature of a winter day at the North Pole (–40.0°C)
  c. the melting point of gold (1064°C)
2. For each of the four temperatures given in the table below, make the necessary conversions to complete the table.

Example	Temp. (°C)	Temp. (°F)	Temp. (K)
Air in a typical living room	21	?	?
Metal in a running car engine	?	?	388
Liquid nitrogen	–200.	?	?
Air on a summer day in the desert	?	110.	?

3. Use **Figure 10-5** to determine which of the following is a likely temperature for ice cubes in a freezer.
  a. –20°C   **c.** 253 K
  b. –4°F   **d.** all of the above
4. Use **Figure 10-5** to determine which of the following is the nearest value for normal human body temperature.
  a. 50°C   **c.** 310 K
  b. 75°F   **d.** all of the above

Solution Guide

1. a. $\frac{9}{5}(-252.87) + 32.0 = -423.2$ °F
$-252.87 + 273 = 20.$ K

b. $\frac{9}{5}(-40.0) + 32.0 = -40.0°F$
$-40.0 + 273 = 233$ K

c. $\frac{9}{5}(1064) + 32.0 = 1947°F$
$1064 + 273 = 1337$ K

2. $\frac{9}{5}(21) + 32.0 = 70.°F$
$21 + 273 = 294$ K

$388 - 273 = 115°C$
$\frac{9}{5}(115) + 32.0 = 239°F$

$\frac{9}{5}(-200.) + 32.0 = -328°F$
$-200. + 273 = 73$ K

$\frac{5}{9}(110. - 32.0) = 43°C$
$43 + 273 = 316$ K

3. d
4. c

Relating Temperature to Energy Transfer as Heat

When you grab a piece of ice, it feels very cold. When you step into a hot bath, the water feels very hot. Clasping your hands together usually produces neither sensation. These three cases can be explained by comparing the temperatures of the two objects making contact with each other.

The feeling associated with temperature difference results from energy transfer

Imagine that you are holding a piece of ice. The temperature of ice is lower than your hand; therefore, the molecules in the ice move very slowly compared with the molecules in your hand. As the molecules on the surface of your hand collide with those on the surface of the ice, energy is transferred to the ice. As a result, the molecules in the ice speed up and their kinetic energy increases. This causes the ice to melt.

Inquiry Lab

How do temperature and energy relate?

Materials
- ✔ glass beaker
- ✔ tongs
- ✔ 2 pieces of string, 20 cm each
- ✔ thermometer
- ✔ clock
- ✔ electric hot plate
- ✔ graduated cylinder
- ✔ 40 identical small metal washers
- ✔ 2 plastic-foam cups

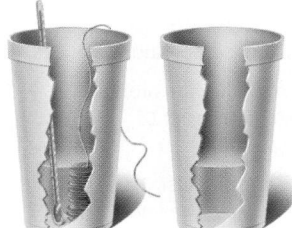

Procedure

1. Tie 10 washers on one piece of string and 30 washers on another piece of string.
2. Fill the beaker two-thirds full with water, lower the washers in, and set the beaker on the hot plate.
3. Heat the water to boiling.
4. While the water heats, put exactly 50 mL of cool water in each plastic-foam cup.
5. Use a thermometer to measure and record the initial temperature of water in each cup.
6. When the water in the beaker has boiled for about 3 minutes, use tongs to remove the group of 30 washers. Gently shake any water off the washers back into the beaker, and quickly place the washers into one of the plastic-foam cups.
7. Observe the change in temperature of the cup's water. Record the highest temperature reached.

8. Repeat steps 6 and 7 by placing the 10 washers in the other plastic-foam cup.

Analysis

1. Which cup had the higher final temperature?
2. Both cups had the same starting temperature. Both sets of washers started at 100°C. Why did one cup reach a higher final temperature?

HEAT AND TEMPERATURE **329**

Inquiry Lab

How do temperature and energy relate?

Suppose we have three objects—A, B, and C. A and B have the same initial temperature, T_1, but A is more massive than B. The temperature of C, T_2, is lower than T_1. If A and B are separately brought in contact with C, which has an even lower temperature, then the temperature of C will rise. Because A has more mass than B, one would expect that A is capable of transferring more energy as heat into C than B is.

Analysis

If students have trouble answering item 2, guide them with further questions like the following:
- Why did the water temperature rise?
- Which set of washers had more energy available to transfer?

MISCONCEPTION ALERT

Heat The concept of heat refers to energy transfer when two objects at different temperatures interact with each other. The term *heat* should be used with care, so as not to imply that heat is contained in an object. Common phrases like "heat is given off" or "heat is absorbed" can be clarified by using the phrase "energy is transferred as heat" instead.

INTEGRATING

LIFE SCIENCE Some animals, like lizards and frogs, do not have an internal mechanism to regulate their body temperature. Lizards and frogs bask in the sun to increase their body temperature by absorbing energy as heat. When it is very cold outside, these animals become inactive because they do not have a lot of extra energy to spend.

Teaching Tip

Burns The painful sensation of a burn is caused by a rapid transfer of energy as heat. This is usually caused by touching a very hot object, but it can also be caused by touching a very cold object. When you touch a hot object, energy flows from the object into your skin cells very rapidly, causing damage. When you touch a very cold object, energy transfers as heat from your skin into the object, also resulting in tissue damage.

RESOURCE LINK
DATASHEETS

Have students use *Datasheet 10.2 Inquiry Lab: How do temperature and energy relate?* to record their results.

INTEGRATING

HEALTH Active people use more energy when they exercise than less active people, so they need to take in more than 2000 Calories per day.

Resources Assign students worksheet *10.2 Integrating Health—Skin Temperature* from the **Integration Enrichment Resources** ancillary.

SECTION 10.1 REVIEW

Check Your Understanding

1. Absolute zero is the temperature at which particles no longer have any energy that can be transferred.
2. Water molecules in a cup of hot soup will move faster on average than water molecules in a glass of iced lemonade because the temperature of the soup is higher.
3. A chamber at 100 K is very cold (–173°C), so you would wear clothes designed for arctic conditions. A chamber at 100°C is very hot (the temperature of boiling water), so you would wear clothes designed for firefighting.
4. More energy would be transferred as heat between water at 10°C and a freezer at –15°C because the temperature difference is greater.

Answers continue on p. 351A.

▶ **heat** the transfer of energy from the particles of one object to those of another object due to a temperature difference between the two objects

INTEGRATING

HEALTH
Food supplies the human body with the energy it needs. A person on a typical diet takes in and expends about 2400 Calories (about 10^7 J) per day, or about 100 J/s. Much of this energy is eventually transferred away by heat, which is why a full classroom feels hotter toward the end of class.

In a similar manner, a hot-water bottle transfers energy from the hot water to your skin. However, when both your hands are at the same temperature, neither hand feels warm or cold because there is no energy transfer.

The transfer of energy between the particles of two objects due to a temperature difference between the two objects is called **heat.** This transfer of energy always takes place from a substance at a higher temperature to a substance at a lower temperature.

Because temperature is an indicator of the particles' average kinetic energy, you can use it to predict which way energy will be transferred. The warmer object, such as the hot-water bottle, will transfer energy to the cooler object, such as your skin. When energy is transferred as heat from the hot water to your skin, the temperature of the water falls while the temperature of your skin rises.

When both your skin and the hot-water bottle approach the same temperature, less energy is transferred from the bottle to your skin. To continue the transfer of energy, the temperature of the hot water must be kept at a higher temperature than your skin. The greater the difference in the temperatures of the two objects, the more energy that will transfer as heat.

SECTION 10.1 REVIEW

SUMMARY

▶ Temperature is a measure of the average kinetic energy of an object's particles.

▶ A thermometer is a device that measures temperature.

▶ On the Celsius temperature scale, water freezes at 0° and boils at 100°.

▶ A kelvin is the same size as a degree Celsius. The lowest temperature possible—absolute zero—is 0 K.

▶ At absolute zero the particles of an object have no kinetic energy to transfer.

▶ Heat is the transfer of energy between objects with different temperatures.

CHECK YOUR UNDERSTANDING

1. **Define** *absolute zero* in terms of particles and their kinetic energy.
2. **Predict** which molecules will move faster on average: water molecules in a cup of hot soup or water molecules in a glass of iced lemonade.
3. **Explain** how your precautions would differ if you were preparing to enter a chamber at 100 K as opposed to one at 100°C.
4. **Predict** whether a greater amount of energy will be transferred as heat between 1 kg of water at 10°C and a freezer at –15°C or between 1 kg of water at 60°C and an oven at 65°C.
5. **Critical Thinking** Determine which of the following has a higher temperature and which contains a larger amount of total kinetic energy: a cup of boiling water or Lake Michigan.

Math Skills

6. Convert the temperature of the air in an air-conditioned room, 20.0°C, to equivalent values on the Fahrenheit and Kelvin temperature scales.
7. Convert the coldest outdoor temperature ever recorded, –128.6°F, to equivalent Celsius and Kelvin temperatures.

330 CHAPTER 10

DEMONSTRATION 3 TEACHING

Energy Transfer

Time: Approximately 15 minutes
Materials: 1 tablespoon of baking soda, 2 L soda bottle, 500 mL graduated cylinders (2), 200 mL of distilled water, 200 mL of vinegar, cork, coffee filter, twist tie (optional)

SAFETY CAUTION: *Be sure not to lean over the bottle or have it pointing towards your students once the baking soda is placed inside.*

Put a tablespoon of baking soda into the center of a coffee filter. Twist the ends of the filter tightly shut. (You can use a twist tie if necessary.) Use a graduated cylinder to pour 200 mL of water into an empty 2 L soda bottle. Use another graduated cylinder to pour 200 mL of vinegar into the same soda bottle. Place the bottle upright on several pieces of newspaper on a table or on the floor. Drop the coffee filter into the soda bottle, and

Energy Transfer

OBJECTIVES

▶ Investigate and demonstrate how energy is transferred by conduction, convection, and radiation.
▶ Identify and distinguish between conductors and insulators.
▶ Solve problems involving specific heat.

▶ **KEY TERMS**
conduction
convection
convection current
radiation
conductor
insulator
specific heat

While water is being heated for your morning shower, your breakfast food is cooking. In the freezer, water in ice trays becomes solid after the freezer cools the water to 0°C. Outside, the morning dew evaporates soon after light from the rising sun strikes it. These are all examples of energy transfers from one object to another.

internet**connect**

SCI**LINKS**
NSTA

TOPIC: Energy transfer
GO TO: www.scilinks.org
KEYWORD: HK1103

Methods of Energy Transfer

The energy transfer as heat from a hot object can occur in three ways. Roasting marshmallows around a campfire, as shown in **Figure 10-6,** provides an opportunity to experience each of these three ways.

Ways of Transferring Energy

Figure 10-6

🅰 Conduction transfers energy as heat along the wire and into the hand.

🅱 Embers swirl upward in the convection currents that are created as warmed air above the fire rises.

🅲 Electromagnetic waves emitted by the hot campfire transfer energy by radiation.

HEAT AND TEMPERATURE **331**

Section 10.2

Energy Transfer

Scheduling

Refer to pp. 322A–322D for lecture, classwork, and assignment options for Section 10.2.

★ **Lesson Focus**
Use transparency *LT 34* to prepare students for this section.

READING SKILL BUILDER *Anticipation (Prediction) Guide* Ask the students how energy from the sun is transferred as heat to Earth and its atmosphere. At this stage, students are not expected to know terms like *conduction* and *convection*.

Teaching Tip

Popping Popcorn Cooking popcorn is a familiar example of energy transfer by heat, as well as a dramatic example of what happens when water rapidly undergoes a phase change to become steam. The hard kernels absorb energy until, at a high temperature, superheated water inside the kernel suddenly turns to steam and rushes outward, and the kernels burst open to form popcorn.

---

quickly place a cork in the mouth of the bottle. Take several steps back from the bottle. Instruct your students to observe what happens inside the bottle and what happens to the cork.

Analysis
1. Does the water, vinegar, or baking soda have energy? *(Answers will vary, but students should infer that the water, vinegar, and baking soda*

have energy because they produced a reaction that popped the cork.)
2. How does what happened to the cork show that the cork has energy? *(Answers will vary, but students should mention that the movement of the cork indicates that it has energy.)*

Interpreting Visuals Have students examine **Figure 10-8.** Have them brainstorm explanations for why you can put your hand close to the side of a candle flame and not get burned but putting your hand above the flame will burn your hand. Much of the candle's energy is transferred as heat by convection as hot air rises. Therefore, the air next to the flame is not as hot as the air above the flame.

Teaching Tip

Convection Essentially, a convection current is generated when a layer of fluid becomes hot and rises as it becomes less dense. Suppose a glass tube containing water is heated by putting a flame next to the top portion of the water layer. Ask the students if energy transfer as heat will occur by convection, causing the bottom layer of water to get hot.

Did You Know?

Both heat and work are ways in which energy can be transferred from one substance to another.

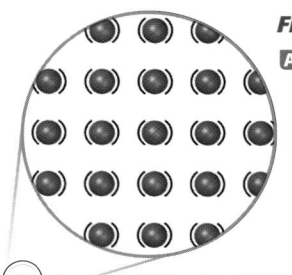

Figure 10-7

A Before conduction takes place, the average kinetic energy of the particles in the metal wire is the same throughout.

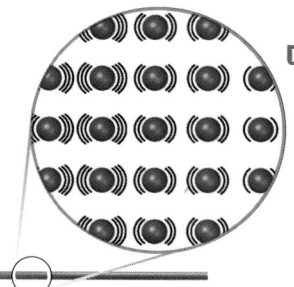

B During conduction, the rapidly moving particles in the wire transfer some of their energy to slowly moving particles nearby.

▶ **conduction** the transfer of energy as heat between particles as they collide within a substance or between two objects in contact

▶ **convection** the transfer of energy by the movement of fluids with different temperatures

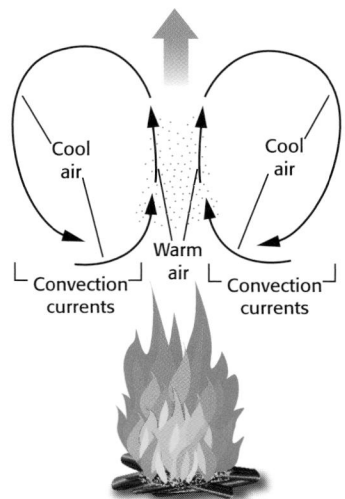

Cool air — Cool air

Warm air

Convection currents — Convection currents

Figure 10-8
During convection, energy is carried away by a heated gas or liquid that expands and rises above cooler, denser gas or liquid.

Conduction involves objects in direct contact

Imagine you place a marshmallow on one end of a wire made from a metal coat hanger. Then you hold the other end of the wire while letting the marshmallow cook in the campfire flame. Soon you will notice that the end of the wire you are holding is getting warmer. This is an example of energy transfer by **conduction.**

Conduction is one of the methods of energy transfer. Conduction takes place when two objects that are in contact are at unequal temperatures. It also takes place between particles within an object. In the case of the wire in the campfire, the rapidly moving air molecules close to the flame collide with the atoms at the end of the wire. The energy transferred to the atoms in the wire causes them to vibrate rapidly. As shown in **Figure 10-7,** these rapidly vibrating atoms collide with slowly vibrating atoms, transferring energy as heat all along the wire. The energy is then transferred to you as the wire's atoms collide with the molecules in your skin, creating a hot sensation in your hand.

Convection results from the movement of warm fluids

While roasting your marshmallow, you may notice that tiny glowing embers from the fire rise and begin to swirl, as shown in **Figure 10-6.** They are following the movement of air away from the fire. The air close to the fire becomes hot and expands so that there is more space between the air particles. As a result, the air becomes less dense and moves upward, carrying its extra energy with it, as shown in **Figure 10-8.** The rising warm air is replaced by cooler, denser air. The cooler air then becomes hot by the fire until it also expands and rises. Eventually, the rising hot air cools, contracts, becomes denser, and sinks. This is an example of energy transfer by **convection.**

Convection involves the movement of the heated substance itself. This is possible only if the substance is a fluid—either a liquid or a gas—because particles within solids are not as free to move.

DEMONSTRATION 4 TEACHING

Energy Transfer in Boiling Water

Time: Approximately 10 minutes
Materials: hot plate
    beaker
    water
    metal spoon
    wooden spoon

Step 1 Fill the beaker with water, and place it on the hot plate.

Step 2 Place the two spoons in the water, and bring the water to a boil. Have students observe the setup, and write down all the energy transfers that are occurring.

Analysis

1. Which spoon is safe to touch? *(wooden spoon)*
2. Why is one spoon cool and one hot? *(Metal is a conductor, so it will be hot. Wood is an insulator, so it will not be hot.)*

The cycle of a heated fluid that rises and then cools and falls is called a **convection current.** The glowing embers rising from the campfire are caught up in the convection currents created in the air surrounding the fire. The proper heating and cooling of a building requires the use of convection currents. Warm air expands and rises from vents near the floor. It cools and contracts near the ceiling and then sinks back to the floor. Eventually, the temperature of all the air in the room is increased by convection currents.

Radiation does not require physical contact between objects

As you stand close to a campfire, you can feel its warmth. This warmth can be felt even when you are not in the path of a convection current. The energy transfer as heat from the fire in this case is in the form of *electromagnetic waves*, which include infrared radiation, visible light, and ultraviolet rays. The transfer of energy by electromagnetic waves is called **radiation.** You will learn more about electromagnetic radiation in Chapters 11 and 12.

When you stand near a fire, your skin absorbs the energy radiated by the fire. As the molecules in your skin absorb this energy, the average kinetic energy of these molecules—and thus the temperature of your skin—increases. A hot object radiates more energy than a cool object or cool surroundings, as shown in **Figure 10-9.**

Radiation differs from conduction and convection in that it does not involve the movement of matter. Radiation is therefore the only method of energy transfer that can take place in a vacuum, such as outer space. Much of the energy we receive from the sun is transferred by radiation.

▶ **convection current** the flow of a fluid due to heated expansion followed by cooling and contraction

Quick ACTIVITY

Convection
Light a candle. Carefully observe the motion of the tiny soot particles in smoke. They move because of convection currents.

▶ **radiation** the transfer of energy by electromagnetic waves

Changes in Radiated Energy

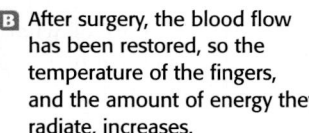

Figure 10-9

A Before surgery, as seen in the infrared photo, the fingers are cooler than the rest of the hand. This results from poor blood flow in this patient's fingers.

B After surgery, the blood flow has been restored, so the temperature of the fingers, and the amount of energy they radiate, increases.

HEAT AND TEMPERATURE **333**

Energy Transfer

MISCONCEPTION
Electromagnetic Waves The electromagnetic waves from the sun provide energy as heat, causing the temperature of our planet to increase. It is often assumed that the temperature of the atmosphere rises due to the direct energy transfer as heat between the electromagnetic waves and the air molecules. In fact, very little energy is absorbed by the air molecules as the electromagnetic waves pass through the atmosphere.

First the electromagnetic waves transfer energy as heat to the ground, raising its temperature. The hot ground then transfers energy as heat to the layer of air next to the ground by conduction. This is followed by the generation of convection currents, which rise up and transfer energy as heat to subsequent layers of the atmosphere. The hot ground also produces infrared radiation, which travels upward in the air. The infrared radiation is mostly absorbed by water vapor and CO_2 in the air.

Quick ACTIVITY

Convection
The motion of the soot particles should resemble that shown in **Figure 10–8.**

RESOURCE LINK
STUDY GUIDE

Have students use *Datasheet 10.3 Quick Activity: Convection* to describe the motion of the soot particles.

3. Where are all the energy transfers occurring? Name the type of each transfer. *(The hot pad heats the beaker, the beaker is heating the water, and the water is heating both spoons, all by conduction. The steam escaping is convection. The air around the setup is being heated by conduction, convection, and radiation.)*

Energy Transfer

Dark Objects Absorb and Emit Radiation The radiator in a hot-water heating system should effectively transfer energy as heat by conduction and radiation.

The radiator should have a dark surface.

As we have seen, a dark surface becomes hotter by absorbing radiation more effectively than surfaces with light colors.

It turns out that dark objects are not only good absorbers but they are also very effective emitters of radiation. In fact, all good absorbers of radiation are also good emitters of radiation. Therefore, most radiators consist of a dark surface, particularly, a dull black surface.

Inquiry Lab

What color absorbs more radiation?

Materials
- ✔ empty soup can, painted black inside and out, label removed
- ✔ empty soup can, label removed
- ✔ 2 thermometers
- ✔ clock
- ✔ graduated cylinder
- ✔ bright lamp or sunlight

Procedure

1. Prepare a data table with three columns and at least seven rows. Label the first column "Time," the second column "Temperature of painted can (°C)," and the third column "Temperature of un- painted can (°C)."
2. Pour 50 mL of cool water into each can.
3. Place a thermometer in each can, and record the temperature of the water in each can at the start. Leave the thermometers in the cans. Aim the lamp at the cans, or place them in sunlight.
4. Record the temperature of the water in each can every 3 minutes for at least 15 minutes.

Analysis

1. Prepare a graph. Label the *x*-axis "Time" and the *y*-axis "Temperature". Plot your data for each can of water.
2. Which color absorbed more radiation?
3. Which variables in the lab were controlled (unchanged throughout the experiment)? For each of the following variables, explain your answer.
   a. starting temperature of water in cans
   b. volume of water in cans
   c. distance of cans from light
   d. size of cans
4. Use your results to explain why panels used for solar heating are often painted black.
5. Based on your results, what color would you want your car to be in the winter? in the summer? Justify your answer.

Conductors and Insulators

When you are cooking, the energy transfer as heat from the stove to the food must occur effectively. However, it is important that the handle does not get uncomfortably hot.

Energy is transferred as heat quickly in conductors

To increase the temperature of a substance using conduction, we must use materials through which energy can be quickly transferred as heat. Cooking pans are made of metal because energy is passed easily and quickly between the particles in most metals. Any material through which energy can be easily transferred as heat is called a **conductor**.

Part of what determines how well a substance conducts is whether it is a gas, liquid, or solid. Gases are extremely poor conductors because their particles are far apart, and the particle collisions necessary to transfer energy rarely occur. The particles

▶ **conductor** a material through which energy can be easily transferred as heat

Inquiry Lab

What color absorbs more radiation? Have students bring cans from home, but be sure each group gets two cans that are matched in size. If you decide to use sunlight, try to take students outside, since the glass in the class- room windows will reflect or absorb the in- frared and ultraviolet light. If you go outside, you will need stopwatches. If you use lamps, try to use 100 W bulbs.

Analysis

1. Both sets of data should show an in- crease in the temperature of the water.
2. The black can should absorb more energy.

in liquids are more closely packed. However, while liquids conduct better than gases, they are not very effective conductors.

Some solids, like rubber and wood, conduct energy about as well as liquids. However, metals such as copper and silver conduct energy transfer as heat very well. Some solids are better conductors than other solids. Metals, in general, are better conductors than non-metals.

Figure 10-10
The skillet conducts energy from the stove element to the food. The wooden spoon and handle insulate the hands from the energy of the skillet.

Insulators slow the transfer of energy as heat

Because energy costs money, we try to avoid wasting it. This waste is most often due to unwanted energy transfer. To reduce or stop unwanted energy transfer, we use materials that are poor conductors. A material of this type is called an **insulator**.

Examples of conductors and insulators are shown in **Figure 10-10.** The skillet is made of iron, a good conductor, so that energy is transferred effectively as heat to the food. Wood is an insulator, so the energy from the hot skillet won't reach your hand through the wooden spoon or the wooden handle.

▶ **insulator** a material that is a poor energy conductor

Teaching Tip

Liquids: Are They Conductors? Liquids, in general, are poor conductors of energy transfer as heat. An exception is molten or liquid metals, which are very good conductors.

Quick ACTIVITY

Conductors and Insulators
Students should readily identify factors, such as thickness, shape, and color, that may affect the results.

After completing the activity, you may want to have students brainstorm ways to improve the accuracy of the activity, such as using thermometers or using materials of uniform thickness and shape.

Resources Have students use *Datasheet 10.5 Quick Activity: Conductors and Insulators* to record their results.

Quick ACTIVITY

Conductors and Insulators

For this activity you will need several flatware utensils. Each one should be made of a different material, such as stainless steel, aluminum, and plastic. You will also need a bowl and ice cubes.

1. Place the ice cubes in the bowl. Position the utensils in the bowl so that an equal length of each utensil lies under the ice.
2. Check the utensils' temperature by briefly touching each utensil at the same distance

from the ice every 20 s. Which utensil becomes colder first? What variables might affect your results?

3. **a.** The starting temperature of the water in each can should be the same.
   b. The volume of the water was controlled (50 mL in each can).
   c. The distance should be the same for each can, although some groups might not have been careful about this.
   d. The size of each can should be the same.
4. Black absorbs more energy, which is why solar panels are often black.
5. In winter, a black car would absorb wanted energy, and in summer, a white or silver car would reflect unwanted energy.

Energy Transfer

Teaching Tip

Specific Heat Tell students the specific heat is the "price" to raise the temperature of 1 kg of a substance. Water changes its "price" as the temperature changes. At 20°C, water's specific heat is 4181 J/kg•K, while its specific heat changes to 4196 J/kg•K at 80°C.

SKILL BUILDER

Interpreting Tables Have students examine **Table 10-1.** Point out that the numbers in the chart represent how much energy is required to raise the temperature of the substance by 1 K (or 1°C). Have students make a list ranking the substances from the ones that absorb energy as heat the easiest (gold and lead) to the one that absorbs the least energy as heat (water).

Resources Blackline Master 28 shows this visual.

SKILL BUILDER

Graphing Have students prepare a graph of the following data (for a 1.0 kg sample) with energy on the *y*-axis and the temperature change on the *x*-axis. Students should note the constant nature of the relationship. You may wish to have advanced students calculate the slope (140 J/kg•K) and use **Table 10-1** to determine the substance (mercury).

Energy (J)	Temperature change (K)
700	5
1400	10
2100	15
2800	20
3500	25

Figure 10-11
The spoon's temperature increases rapidly because of the spoon's low specific heat.

▶ **specific heat** the amount of energy transferred as heat that will raise the temperature of 1 kg of a substance by 1 K.

Specific Heat

You have probably noticed that a metal spoon, like the one shown in **Figure 10-11,** becomes hot when it is placed in a cup of hot liquid. You have also probably noticed that a spoon made of a different material, such as plastic, does not become hot as quickly. The difference between the final temperatures of the two spoons depends on whether they are good conductors or good insulators. But what makes a substance a good or poor conductor depends in part on how much energy a substance requires to change its temperature by a certain degree.

Specific heat describes how much energy is required to raise an object's temperature

Not all substances behave the same when they absorb energy by heat. For example, a metal spoon left in a metal pot becomes hot seconds after the pot is placed on a hot stovetop burner. This is because a few joules of energy are enough to raise the spoon's temperature substantially. However, if an amount of water with the same mass as the spoon is placed in the same pot, that same amount of energy will produce a much smaller temperature change in the water.

For all substances, the amount of energy that must be transferred to the substance in order to raise the temperature of 1 kg of the substance by 1 K is a characteristic physical property. This property is known as **specific heat** and is denoted by c.

Some values for specific heat are given in **Table 10-1.** These values are in units of J/kg•K, meaning each is the amount of energy in J needed to raise the temperature of 1 kg of the substance by exactly 1 K.

Table 10-1 **Specific Heats at 25°C**

Substance	c (J/kg•K)	Substance	c (J/kg•K)
Water (liquid)	4186	Copper	385
Steam	1870	Gold	129
Ammonia (gas)	2060	Iron	449
Ethanol (liquid)	2440	Mercury	140
Aluminum	897	Lead	129
Carbon (graphite)	709	Silver	234

DEMONSTRATION 5 TEACHING

Heat Versus Temperature

Time: Approximately 15 minutes
Materials: 400 mL beaker, 250 mL beakers (2), ice cubes, water, hot plate, beaker tongs, thermometer

SAFETY CAUTION: *Monitor "hot" tap water carefully, so that you do not burn yourself.*

Step 1 Use a hot plate to heat 200 mL of water to boiling in a 400 mL beaker. Measure the tempera-

ture of the boiling water.

Step 2 Fill the two 250 mL beakers with equal amounts of ice.

Step 3 Use the beaker tongs to pour a small portion (about 40 mL) of the boiling water to one beaker containing the ice.

Step 4 Then dump the remaining boiling water directly into the other beaker with ice.

On a hot summer day, the temperature of the water in a swimming pool remains much lower than the air temperature and the temperature of the concrete around the pool. This is due to water's relatively high specific heat as well as the large mass of water in the pool. Similarly, at night, the concrete and the air cool off quickly, while the water changes temperature only slightly.

Specific heat can be used in calculations

Because specific heat is a ratio, it can be used to predict the effects of larger temperature changes for masses other than 1 kg. For example, if it takes 4186 J to raise the temperature of 1 kg of water by 1 K, twice as much energy, 8372 J, will be required to raise the temperature of 2 kg of water by 1 K. Three times that amount, 25 120 J, will be required to raise the temperature of the 2 kg of water by 3 K. This relationship is summed up in the equation below.

Specific Heat Equation

energy = (specific heat) × (mass) × (temperature change)

$$energy = cm\Delta t$$

Specific heat can change slightly with changing pressure and volume. *However, problems and questions in this chapter will assume that specific heat does not change.*

Math Skills

Specific Heat How much energy must be transferred as heat to the 420 kg of water in a bathtub in order to raise the water's temperature from 25°C to 37°C?

1 List the given and unknown values.

> **Given:** $\Delta t = 37°C - 25°C = 12°C = 12$ K
> $m = 420$ kg
> $c = 4186$ J/kg•K
>
> **Unknown:** *energy* = ? J

2 Write down the specific heat equation from this page.

> $energy = cm\Delta t$

3 Substitute the specific heat, mass, and temperature change values, and solve.

> $$energy = \left(\frac{4186 \text{ J}}{\text{kg}\bullet\text{K}}\right) \times (420 \text{ kg}) \times (12\text{ K})$$
>
> $energy = 21\ 000\ 000$ J $= 2.1 \times 10^4$ kJ

INTEGRATING

EARTH SCIENCE Sea breezes result from both convection currents in the coastal air and differences in the specific heats of water and sand or soil. During the day, the temperature of the land increases more than the temperature of the ocean water, which has a larger specific heat. As a result, the temperature of the air over land increases more than the temperature of air over the ocean. This causes the warm air over the land to rise and the cool ocean air to move inland to replace the rising warm air. At night, the temperature of the dry land drops below that of the ocean, and the direction of the breezes is reversed.

INTEGRATING

EARTH SCIENCE This is true on a local level. There are many other factors affecting the direction of the wind: convection currents on a global scale, weather disturbances such as thunderstorms or hurricanes, the size of the landmass and water mass, etc.

Resources Assign students worksheet *10.3 Integrating Earth Science—Land and Sea Breezes* in the **Integration Enrichment Resources** ancillary.

Math Skills

Resources Assign students worksheet *24: Specific Heat* in the **Math Skills Worksheets** ancillary.

RESOURCE LINK

LABORATORY MANUAL

Have students perform *Lab 10 Heat and Temperature: Determining the Better Insulator for Your Feet* in the lab ancillary.

DATASHEETS

Have students use *Datasheet 10.7* to record their results.

HEAT AND TEMPERATURE **337**

Analysis

1. What was the temperature of the boiling water? *(Answers will vary.)*

2. Which of the beakers received more heat energy when the boiling water was added? *(The beaker that received the larger volume of boiling water received more heat energy. All of the ice cubes melted whereas not all of the ice cubes in the other beaker melted.)*

Energy Transfer

Additional Examples

Specific Heat Identify an unknown substance with a mass of 0.455 kg that absorbs 6.33×10^3 J, in which a temperature change of 15.5°C is observed.

Answer: aluminum

What temperature change would copper experience under the same conditions as those above (same mass and energy)?

Answer: 36.1°C or 36.1 K

SECTION 10.2 REVIEW

Check Your Understanding

1. Energy transfer by conduction involves direct contact. The molecules of higher energy bump into molecules with lower energy and transfer some of the energy. Energy transfer by convection involves the movement of the higher energy molecules from one place to another. Energy transfer by radiation involves the emission and absorption of electromagnetic waves.

2. gold, iron, water, air

3. The hottest part of the room should be near the ceiling because hot air from the vent will rise to the ceiling.

Answers continue on p. 351A.

RESOURCE LINK
STUDY GUIDE

Assign students *Review Section 10.2 Energy Transfer.*

Practice HINT

▶ To rearrange the equation to isolate temperature change, divide both sides of the equation by *mc*.

$$\frac{energy}{mc} = \left(\frac{mc}{mc}\right)\Delta t$$

$$\Delta t = \frac{energy}{mc}$$

▶ Use this version of the equation for Practice Problem 4.
▶ For Practice Problems 5 and 6, you will need to isolate *m* and *c*.

Practice

Specific Heat

1. How much energy is needed to increase the temperature of 755 g of iron from 283 K to 403 K?
2. How much energy must a refrigerator absorb from 225 g of water so that the temperature of the water will drop from 35°C to 5°C?
3. A 144 kg park bench made of iron sits in the sun, and its temperature increases from 25°C to 35°C. How many kilojoules of energy does the bench absorb?
4. An aluminum baking sheet with a mass of 225 g absorbs 2.4×10^4 J from an oven. If its temperature was initially 25°C, what will its new temperature be?
5. What mass of water is required to absorb 4.7×10^5 J of energy from a car engine while the temperature increases from 298 K to 355 K?
6. A vanadium bolt gives up 1124 J of energy as its temperature drops 25 K. If the bolt's mass is 93 g, what is its specific heat?

SECTION 10.2 REVIEW

SUMMARY

▶ Conduction is the transfer of energy as heat between particles as they collide within a substance or between objects in contact.

▶ Convection currents are the movement of gases and liquids as they become heated, expand, and rise, then cool, contract, and fall.

▶ Radiation is the transfer of energy by electromagnetic waves.

▶ Conductors are materials through which energy is easily transferred as heat.

▶ Insulators are materials that conduct energy poorly.

▶ Specific heat is the energy required to heat 1 kg of a substance by 1 K.

CHECK YOUR UNDERSTANDING

1. **Describe** how energy is transferred by conduction, convection, and radiation.
2. **Rank** the following in order from the best conductor to the best insulator:
   a. iron   c. water
   b. air   d. gold
3. **Predict** whether the hottest part of a room will be near the ceiling, in the center, or near the floor, given that there is a hot-air vent near the floor. Explain your reasoning.
4. **Explain** why there are temperature differences on the moon's surface, even though there is no atmosphere present.
5. **Critical Thinking** Explain why cookies baked near the turned-up edges of a cookie sheet receive more energy than those baked near the center.

Math Skills

6. When a shiny chunk of metal with a mass of 1.32 kg absorbs 3250 J of energy, the temperature of the metal increases from 273 K to 292 K. Is this metal likely to be silver, lead, or aluminum?
7. A 0.400 kg sample of glass requires 3190 J for its temperature to increase from 273 K to 308 K. What is the specific heat for this type of glass?

Solution Guide

1. *energy* = (449 J/kg•K)(0.755 kg)(403 K – 283 K) = 40 700 J
2. *energy* = (4180 J/kg•K)(0.225 kg)(35°C – 5°C) = 28 000 J
3. *energy* = (449 J/kg•K)(144 kg)(35°C – 25°C)(1 kJ/1000 J) = 650 kJ
4. ΔT = (2.4 × 10⁴ J)/[(897 J/kg•K)(0.225 kg)]
   ΔT = 120 K = 120°C
   T_f – 25°C = 120°C
   T_f = 145°C
5. *m* = *energy*/(*c* × ΔT) = (4.7 × 10⁵ J)/[(4180 J/kg•K)(355 K – 298 K)] = 2.0 kg
6. $c = \dfrac{1124 \text{ J}}{93 \text{ g} (1 \text{ kg}/1000 \text{ g}) 25 \text{ K}}$ = 480 J/kg•K

10.3

Using Heat

INTEGRATING TECHNOLOGY and Society

OBJECTIVES

▶ Describe the mechanisms of different heating and cooling systems, and discuss their advantages and drawbacks.

▶ Compare different heating and cooling systems in terms of how they decrease the amount of usable energy.

▶ **KEY TERMS**
heating system
cooling system
refrigerant

Heating a house in the winter, cooling an office building in the summer, or preserving food throughout the year is possible because of machines that transfer energy as heat from one place to another. An example of one of these machines, an air conditioner, is shown in **Figure 10-12.** An air conditioner does work to remove energy as heat from the warm air inside a room and then transfers the energy to the warmer air outside the room. An air conditioner can do this because of two principles about energy that you have already studied.

The first principle, from Chapter 9, is that the total energy used in any process—whether that energy is transferred as a result of work, heat, or both—is conserved. This principle of conservation of energy is called the first law of thermodynamics.

The second principle, from this chapter, is that the energy transferred as heat always moves from an object at a high temperature to an object at a low temperature.

Gaseous refrigerant   Liquid refrigerant

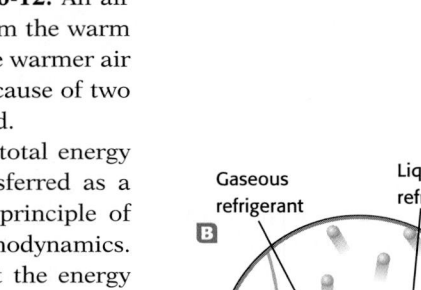

Figure 10-12

A A substance that easily evaporates and condenses is used in air conditioners to transfer energy from a room to the air outside.

B When the liquid evaporates, it absorbs energy from the surrounding air, thereby cooling it.

C Outside, the air conditioner causes the gas to condense, releasing energy.

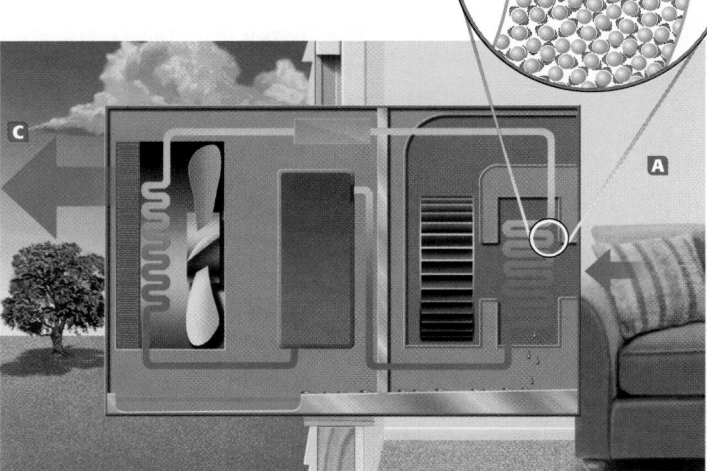

Scheduling

Refer to pp. 322A–322D for lecture, classwork, and assignment options for Section 10.3.

★ **Lesson Focus**
Use transparency *LT 35* to prepare students for this section.

READING SKILL BUILDER *K-W-L* Have students list what they know or think they know about heating and cooling systems, then have them list what they want to know. After the students read this section, have them write down what they have learned about heating and cooling systems.

SKILL BUILDER

Interpreting Visuals Discuss the energy transfers in **Figure 10-12** with students. Have them work in pairs to describe how a heat pump would work to heat a room. Discuss proposed solutions with the class.

Resources Teaching Transparency 28 shows this visual.

DEMONSTRATION 6 TEACHING

Conduction

Time: Approximately 10 minutes
Materials: 4 spoons (silver, wooden, plastic, metal)
4 cups of hot water
thermometer

SAFETY CAUTION: *Monitor "hot" tap water carefully, so that you do not burn yourself.*

Fill each of the cups with the same amount of hot water. Verify that the water in each of the cups is the same temperature. Place a different spoon in each cup. After several minutes, have students feel the handle of each spoon and rank the materials as heat conductors from best to poorest.

Analysis

1. Which spoon is the best heat conductor? (*Silver spoons will rank at the top.*)

Using Heat

Connection to
SOCIAL STUDIES

In honor of James Watt's contribution, the metric unit of power was named the watt (W). One watt is one joule per second.

Making the Connection
1. Answers will vary but may include: WWII boats and submarines in movies, nuclear reactors, trains, and vegetable steamers.
2. radiators

Resources Assign students worksheet *10.4 Connection to Social Studies—Early Central Heating* in the **Integration Enrichment Resources** ancillary.

LINKING CHAPTERS

The importance of work is emphasized in Chapter 9.

Teaching Tip

Detecting Energy Electromagnetic radiation emitted by the human body cannot be seen by humans because the radiation's wavelengths are primarily in the infrared portion of the electromagnetic spectrum. However, this radiation can be seen by some snakes. By detecting infrared radiation, these snakes seek out their prey in what appears to humans to be complete darkness. A similar approach is used in some types of night-vision goggles.

Connection to
SOCIAL STUDIES

In 1769, a Scottish engineer named James Watt patented a new design that made steam engines more efficient. During the next 50 years, the improved steam engines were used to power trains and ships. Previously, transportation had depended on the work done by horses or the wind.

Watt's new steam engines were used in machines and factories of the industrial revolution. In 1784, Watt used steam coils to heat his office. This was the first practical use of steam for heating.

Making the Connection
1. Old steam-powered riverboats are popular tourist attractions in many cities. Make a list of at least three other instances in which the energy in steam is used for practical purposes.
2. What devices in older buildings function like the steam coils Watt used for heating his office?

▶ **heating system** any device or process that transfers energy to a substance to raise the temperature of the substance

internet connect

SC**LINKS**
NSTA

TOPIC: Heating and cooling systems
GO TO: www.scilinks.org
KEYWORD: HK1104

Heating Systems

People generally feel and work their best when the temperature of the air around them is in the range of 21°C–25°C (70°F–77°F). To raise the indoor temperature on colder days, energy must be transferred into a room's air by a **heating system.** Most heating systems use a source of energy to raise the temperature of a substance such as air or water.

Work can be done to increase temperature

When you rub your hands together, they become warmer. The energy you transfer to your hands by work is transferred to the molecules of your hands, and their temperature increases. Processes that involve energy transfer by work are called mechanical processes.

Another example of a mechanical heating process is a device used in the past by certain American Indian tribes to start fires. The device consists of a bow with a loop in the bowstring that holds a pointed stick. The sharp end of the stick is placed in a small indentation in a stone. A small pile of wood shavings is then put around the place where the stick and stone make contact. A person then does work to move the bow back and forth. This energy is transferred to the stick, which turns rapidly. The friction between the stick and stone causes the temperature to rise until the shavings are set on fire.

The energy from food is transferred as heat to blood moving throughout the human body

You may not think of yourself as a heating system. But unless you are sick, your body maintains a temperature of about 37°C (98.6°F), whether you are in a place that is cool or hot. Maintaining this temperature in cool air requires your body to function like a heating system.

If you are surrounded by cold air, energy will be transferred as heat from your skin to the air, and the temperature of your skin will drop. To compensate, stored nutrients are broken down by your body to provide energy, and this energy is transferred as heat to your blood. The warm blood circulates through your body, transferring energy as heat to your skin and increasing your skin's temperature. In this way your body can maintain a constant temperature.

Heated water or air transfers energy as heat in central heating systems

Most modern homes and large buildings have a central heating system. As is the case with your body, when the building is surrounded by cold air, energy is transferred as heat from the building to the outside air. The temperature of the building begins to drop.

A central heating system has a furnace that burns coal, fuel oil, or natural gas. The energy released in the furnace is transferred as heat to water, steam, or air, as shown in **Figure 10-13.** The steam, hot water, or hot air is then moved to each room through pipes or ducts. Because the temperature of the pipe is higher than that of the air, energy is transferred as heat to the air in the room.

Solar heating systems also use warmed air or water

Cold-blooded animals, such as lizards and turtles, increase their body temperature by using external sources, such as the sun. You may have seen these animals sitting motionless on rocks on sunny days, as shown in **Figure 10-14.** During such behavior, called basking, energy is absorbed by the reptile's skin through conduction from the warmer air and rocks, and by radiation from sunlight. This absorbed energy is then transferred as heat to the reptile's blood. As the blood circulates, it transfers this energy to all parts of the reptile's body.

Solar heating systems, such as the one illustrated in **Figure 10-15,** use an approach similar to that of a basking reptile. A solar collector uses panels to gather energy radiated from the sun. This energy is used to heat water. The hot water is then moved throughout the house by the same methods other hot-water systems use.

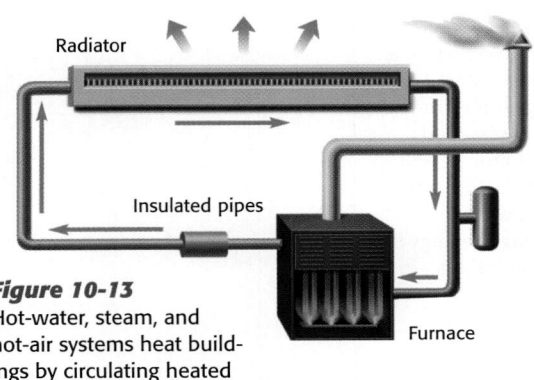

Figure 10-13
Hot-water, steam, and hot-air systems heat buildings by circulating heated fluids to each room.

Figure 10-14
Reptiles bask in the sun to raise their body temperature.

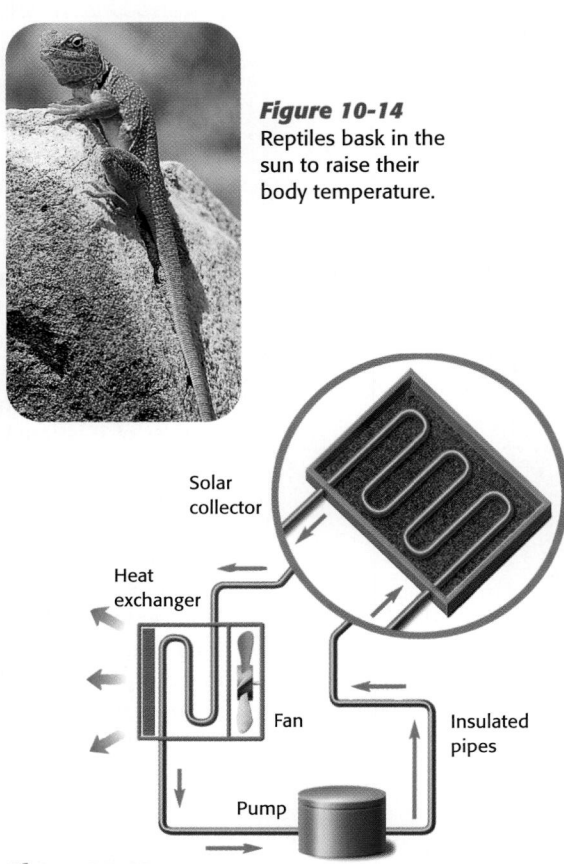

Figure 10-15
An active solar heating system moves water heated by sunlight through pipes and a heat exchanger.

HEAT AND TEMPERATURE **341**

Using Heat

|SKILL BUILDER

Interpreting Visuals Have students examine **Figure 10-15.** Discuss the various energy transfers that are occurring. Have students work in pairs to describe what would happen on a cold, cloudy day when the temperature inside the house is higher than the temperature outside the house. Have them brainstorm ways to prevent energy loss.

Science and the Consumer

Heating From the Ground Up As the earliest cave dwellers knew, a good way to stay warm in the winter is to go underground. Now scientists and engineers are using the same premise to heat aboveground homes for a fraction of the cost of conventional air-conditioning and heating systems.

Although the average specific heat capacity of Earth has a smaller value than the specific heat capacity of air, Earth has a greater density. That means there are more kilograms of earth than there are of air near a house and that 1°C change in temperature involves transferring more energy to or from the ground than to or from the air. Thus in wintertime, the ground will probably have a higher temperature than the air above it, while in the summer the ground will likely have a lower temperature than the air.

An earth-coupled heat pump enables homeowners to tap Earth's belowground temperature to heat their homes in the winter or cool them in the summer.

Using Heat

Teaching Tip

Loss of Useful Energy

Point out to students that transferring energy is like pouring water from one cup into another, and then another, etc. Each time you pour into a new cup, some leftover water remains in the "empty" cup. Even if you hold the cup upside down and wait, some of the water still remains in the "empty" cup. Each time you pour water into a cup, you will end up with less water than you started with.

Historical Perspective

Benjamin Thompson Rumford (1753–1814) was a physicist who made an early connection between work and heat. He also made many practical innovations such as central heating and thermal underwear.

Figure 10-16
(A) In a passive solar heating system, energy from sunlight is absorbed in a rooftop panel. (B) Pipes carry the hot fluid that exchanges energy as heat with the air in each room.

The warm water can also be pumped through a device called a heat exchanger, which transfers energy from the water to a mass of air by conduction and radiation. The warmed air is then blown through ducts as with other warm-air heating systems.

Both of these types of solar heating systems are called active solar heating systems. They require extra energy from another source, such as electricity, in order to move the heated water or air around.

Passive solar heating systems, as shown in **Figure 10-16,** require no extra energy to move the hot fluids through the pipe. In this type of system, energy transfer is accomplished by radiation and convection currents created in heated water or air. In warm, sunny climates, passive solar heating systems are easy to construct and maintain and are clean and inexpensive to operate.

Usable energy decreases in all energy transfers

When energy can be easily transformed and transferred to accomplish a task, such as heating a room, we say that the energy is in a usable form. After this transfer, the same amount of energy is present, according to the law of conservation of energy. Yet less of it is in a form that can be used.

The energy used to increase the temperature of the water in a hot-water tank should ideally stay in the hot water. However, it is impossible to keep some energy from being transferred as heat to parts of the hot-water tank and its surroundings. The amount of usable energy decreases even in the most efficient heating systems.

Due to conduction and radiation, some energy is lost to the tank's surroundings, such as the air and nearby walls. Cold water in the pipes that feed into the water heater also draw energy from some of the hot water in the tank. When energy from electricity is used to heat water in the hot-water heater, some of the energy is used to increase the temperature of the electrical wire, the metal cover of the water heater, and the air around the water heater. All of these portions of the total energy put into the hot-water heater can no longer be used to heat the water, and therefore are no longer in a usable form. In general, the amount of usable energy always decreases whenever energy is transferred or transformed.

Figure 10-17
Insulating materials, such as fiberglass and cellulose, are used in most buildings to reduce the transfer of energy as heat.

Table 10-2
R-Values for Some Common Building Materials

Substance	R-value
Drywall, 1.3 cm (0.50 in.)	0.45
Wood shingles, (overlapping)	0.87
Flat glass, 0.318 cm (0.125 in.)	0.89
Hardwood siding, 2.54 cm (1.00 in.)	0.91
Vertical air space, 8.9 cm (3.5 in.)	1.01
Insulating glass, 0.64 cm (0.25 in.)	1.54
Cellulose fiber, 2.54 cm (1.00 in.)	3.70
Brick, 10.2 cm (4.00 in.)	4.00
Fiberglass batting, 8.9 cm (3.5 in.)	10.90

Insulation minimizes undesirable energy transfers

During winter, some of the energy from the warm air inside a building is lost to the cold outside air. Similarly, during the summer, energy from warm air outside seeps into an air-conditioned building, raising the temperature of the cool inside air. Good insulation can reduce, but not entirely eliminate, the unwanted transfer of energy to and from the building's surroundings. As shown in **Figure 10-17,** insulation material is placed in the walls and attics of homes and other buildings to reduce the unwanted transfer of energy as heat.

A standard rating system has been developed to measure the effectiveness of insulation materials. This rating, called the *R-value*, is determined by the type of material used and the material's thickness. *R*-values for several common building and insulating materials of a given thickness are listed in **Table 10-2.** The greater the *R*-value, the greater the material's ability to decrease unwanted energy transfers.

Cooling Systems

If you quickly let the air out of a compressed-air tank like the one used by scuba divers, the air from the tank and the tank's nozzle feel slightly cooler than they did before the air was released. This is because the molecules in the air lose some of their kinetic energy as the air's pressure and volume change and the temperature of the air decreases. This process is a simple example of a **cooling system.** In all cooling systems, energy is transferred as heat from one substance to another, leaving the first substance with less energy and thus a lower temperature.

▶ **cooling system** a device that transfers energy as heat out of an object to lower its temperature

HEAT AND TEMPERATURE **343**

Using Heat

Did You Know ?

Many people believe that glass is a good insulator because fiberglass (thin glass fibers that resemble cotton candy) is used for insulating homes. However, glass is actually a poor insulator (Have you ever touched a window when the air outside is cold?), which is why many people install double-paned windows for energy efficiency. The reason fiberglass is used for insulation is because there is so much trapped air in the material, and air is a good insulator—as long as it cannot flow and transfer energy by convection.

SKILL BUILDER

Interpreting Visuals Have students look at **Figure 10-17.** Explain to them that the insulation being spread relies on the trapped air. If the insulating material (cellulose or fiberglass) were compressed so that more would fit in the same space, the *R*-factor would actually decrease because there would be less trapped air. However, if the homeowner relied just on the air in the attic, the insulating effect would be less because air would be free to circulate, setting up convection currents.

RESOURCE LINK
IER

Assign students worksheet *10.7: Connection to Social Studies—The Little Ice Age* in the **Integration Enrichment Resources** ancillary.

BIOLOGY Elephants flap their ears to increase the air circulation and thus increase the energy transfer from the blood vessels in their ears to the air.

Resources Assign students worksheet *10.5 Integrating Biology—Hibernation and Torpor* in the **Integration Enrichment Resources** ancillary.

READING SKILL BUILDER *Discussion* Have students read the section on refrigerators. Ask students to brainstorm reasons why leaving the refrigerator door open will not cool down the house. Be sure to guide the discussion to the correct explanation.

The refrigerator removes energy from the air inside the refrigerator and then releases that energy to the air outside the refrigerator (in the house). If the refrigerator did nothing else, the house would still not cool because the energy removed from the air in the refrigerator is released into the air in the house. The refrigerator transfers extra energy from the motor to the air in the house. The result of leaving the refrigerator door open would be to heat up the house!

▶ **refrigerant** a substance used in cooling systems that transfers large amounts of energy as it changes state

INTEGRATING

BIOLOGY
In hot regions, the ears of many mammals serve as cooling systems. Larger ears provide more area for energy to be transferred from blood to the surrounding air, helping the animals to maintain their body temperature. Rabbits and foxes that live in the desert have much longer ears than rabbits and foxes that live in temperate or arctic climates.

Cooling systems often use evaporation to transfer energy from their surroundings

In the case of a refrigerator, the temperature of the air and food inside is lowered. But because the first law of thermodynamics requires energy to be conserved, the energy inside the refrigerator must be transferred to the air outside the refrigerator. If you place your hand near the rear or base of a refrigerator, you will feel warm air being discharged. Much of the energy in this air was removed from inside the refrigerator.

Hidden in the back wall of a refrigerator is a set of coiled pipes through which a substance called a **refrigerant** flows, as shown in **Figure 10-18.** During each operating cycle of the refrigerator, the refrigerant evaporates into a gas and then condenses back into a liquid.

Recall from Chapter 2 and the beginning of this section that evaporation produces a cooling effect. Changes of state always involve the transfer of relatively large amounts of energy. In liquids that are good refrigerants, such as Freon®, evaporation occurs at a much lower temperature than that of the air inside the refrigerator. When the liquid refrigerant is in a set of pipes near the inside of the refrigerator, energy is transferred by heat from the air to the refrigerant. This exchange causes the air and food to cool.

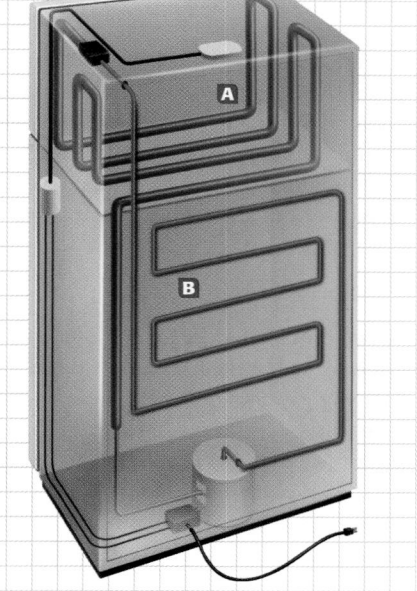

Figure 10-18

A Liquid refrigerant flowing through the pipes inside a refrigerator cools the compartment by evaporation.

B Energy is removed by the outside coils as the warmed refrigerant vapor cools and condenses back into a liquid.

Heat Pumps

Time: Approximately 5 minutes
Materials: none

A simple experiment can demonstrate the cooling effect of a heat pump, which relies on the expansion of a gas. Have students breathe on their palms with their mouth wide open. They should note warm air. (Body temperature is much warmer than the air in the room.) Now have stu-

dents purse their lips and blow on their hand through the small hole in their lips. Students should feel a cooling effect. Even though the air inside their lungs is the same each time, the cooling effect of the second try is due to the expansion of the air. In this scenario, their body (or more accurately, the diaphragm) is the pump in the heat pump.

Condensation transfers energy to the surroundings

The refrigerant has become a gas by absorbing energy. This gas moves to the section of coils outside the refrigerator, where electrical energy is used to power a compressor. Pressure is used to condense the refrigerant back into a liquid. Because condensation involves transferring energy from the vapor as heat, the temperature of the air outside the refrigerator increases. This explains why the outside coils stay warm.

Air-conditioning systems in homes and buildings use the same process refrigerators use. As air near the evaporation coils is cooled, a fan blows this air through ducts into the rooms and hallways. Convection currents in the room then allow the cool air to circulate as displaced warmer air flows into return ducts.

Heat pumps can transfer energy to or from rooms

Heat pumps use the evaporation and condensation of a refrigerant to provide heating in the winter and cooling in the summer. A heat pump is a refrigeration unit in which the cooling cycle can be reversed.

As shown in **Figure 10-19A,** the liquid refrigerant travels through the outdoor coils during the winter and absorbs enough energy from the outside air to evaporate. Work is done on the gas by a compressor, increasing the refrigerant's energy. Then the refrigerant moves through the coils inside the house, as shown in **Figure 10-19B.** The hot gas transfers energy as heat to the air inside the house. This process warms the air while cooling the refrigerant gas enough for it to condense back into a liquid.

In the summer, the refrigerant is pumped in the opposite direction, so that the heat pump functions like a refrigerator or an air conditioner. The liquid refrigerant absorbs energy from the air inside the house as it evaporates. The hot refrigerant gas is then moved to the coils which are outside the house. The refrigerant then condenses, transferring energy as heat to the outside air.

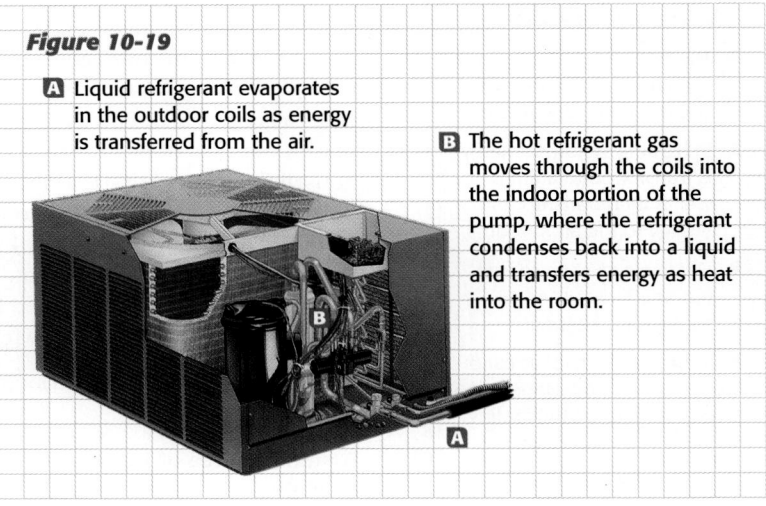

Figure 10-19

A Liquid refrigerant evaporates in the outdoor coils as energy is transferred from the air.

B The hot refrigerant gas moves through the coils into the indoor portion of the pump, where the refrigerant condenses back into a liquid and transfers energy as heat into the room.

HEAT AND TEMPERATURE **345**

Using Heat

REAL WORLD APPLICATIONS

Buying Appliances Most major appliances, including those that involve the transfer of energy as heat, are required by law to have an *Energyguide* label attached to them.

The label indicates the average amount of energy used by the appliance in a year. It also gives the average cost of using the appliance based on a national average of cost per energy unit.

The *Energyguide* label provides consumers a way to compare various brands and models of appliances.

Applying Information

1. Use the *Energyguide* label shown to find how much energy the appliance uses each hour.
2. What is the daily operating cost of the appliance?

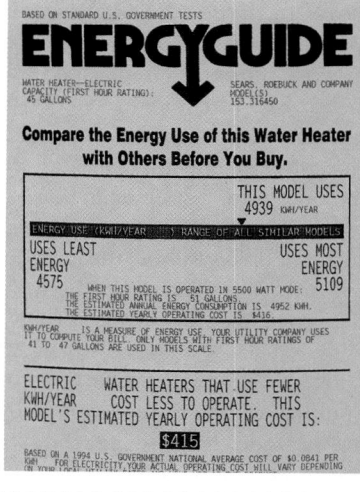

SECTION 10.3 REVIEW

SUMMARY

▶ Heating and cooling systems regulate temperature by transferring energy.

▶ Usable energy decreases during any process in which energy is transferred.

▶ The total amount of energy, both usable and unusable, is constant in any process.

▶ In heating systems, energy is transferred to a fluid, which then transfers its energy to the air in rooms.

▶ Heating systems use fuel-burning furnaces or sunlight for heating.

▶ Refrigerators and air conditioners use the evaporation of a refrigerant for cooling.

CHECK YOUR UNDERSTANDING

1. **Explain** how evaporation is a cooling process.
2. **List** one type of home heating system, and describe how it transfers energy to warm the air inside the rooms.
3. **Describe** how energy changes from a usable form to a less usable form in a building's heating system.
4. **Compare** the advantages and disadvantages of using a solar heating system in your geographical area.
5. **Critical Thinking** Water has a high specific heat, meaning it takes a good deal of energy to raise its temperature. For this reason, the cost of heating water is a large part of a monthly household energy bill. Describe two ways the people in your household could change their routines, without sacrificing results, in order to save money by using less hot water.
6. **Create** a spreadsheet to calculate the rate of energy transfer for each of the substances listed in **Table 10-2**. This rate can be determined using the following equation.

$$rate\ of\ energy\ transfer = \frac{(area) \times (temp.\ diff.)}{(R\text{-}value)}$$

Assume an area of 1.0 m² and a temperature difference of 20.0°C.

Chapter Highlights

Before you begin, review the summaries of the key ideas of each section, found on pages 330, 338, and 346. The key vocabulary terms are listed on pages 324, 331, and 339.

UNDERSTANDING CONCEPTS

1. Temperature is proportional to the average kinetic energy of particles in an object. Thus an increase in temperature results in a(n) _____.
   a. increase in mass
   b. decrease in average kinetic energy
   c. increase in average kinetic energy
   d. decrease in mass

2. As measured on the Celsius scale, the temperature at which ice melts is _____.
   a. –273°C   c. 32°C
   b. 0°C   d. 100°C

3. As measured on the Fahrenheit scale, the temperature at which water boils is _____.
   a. 32°F   c. 100°F
   b. 212°F   d. 451°F

4. The temperature at which the particles of a substance have no more kinetic energy to transfer is _____.
   a. –273 K   c. 0°C
   b. 0 K   d. 273 K

5. Which kind of energy transfer can occur in empty space?
   a. convection   c. conduction
   b. contraction   d. radiation

6. Campfires transfer energy as heat to their surroundings by methods of _____.
   a. convection and conduction
   b. convection and radiation
   c. conduction and radiation
   d. convection, conduction, and radiation

7. The amount of energy required to raise the temperature of 1 kg of a substance by 1 K is determined by its _____.
   a. *R*-value
   b. usable energy
   c. specific heat
   d. convection current

8. The amount of usable energy decreases when _____.
   a. systems are used only for heating
   b. systems are used only for cooling
   c. systems are used for heating or cooling
   d. the heating or cooling system is poorly designed

9. A refrigerant in a cooling system cools the surrounding air _____.
   a. as it evaporates
   b. as it condenses
   c. both as it evaporates and as it condenses
   d. when it neither evaporates nor condenses

10. Solar heating systems are classified as _____.
    a. positive and negative
    b. active and passive
    c. AC and DC
    d. active and indirect

Using Vocabulary

11. Why is it incorrect to say that an object contains *heat*?

12. Use the concepts of average particle kinetic energy, *temperature,* and *absolute zero* to predict whether an object at 0°C or an object at 0 K will transfer more energy as heat to its surroundings.

13. How would a *thermometer* that measures temperatures using the Kelvin scale differ from one that measures temperatures using the Celsius scale?

14. Explain how water can transfer energy by *conduction* and by *convection.*

HEAT AND TEMPERATURE **347**

UNDERSTANDING CONCEPTS

1. c	**6.** d
2. b	**7.** c
3. b	**8.** d
4. b	**9.** a
5. d	**10.** b

Using Vocabulary

11. Heat is the transfer of energy.

12. An object at 0 K cannot transfer energy to its surroundings because 0 K is absolute zero, which is the temperature at which the molecules of an object have no transferrable energy. An object at 0°C (273 K) has particles with a much higher average kinetic energy and can transfer that energy to its surroundings.

13. The difference would be how the thermometer is numbered because $T = t + 273$.

14. Water can transfer energy by conduction when an object is placed in the water. For example, a raw egg placed in 100°C water will absorb energy by conduction and become a boiled egg. Water can transfer energy by convection as it flows around an object. For example, a warm soda in a river transfers energy to the cold water, making it warm, but then the warm water moves away and more cold water surrounds the soda.

RESOURCE LINK
STUDY GUIDE

Assign students *Mixed Review Chapter 10.*

347

15. During the day, the hot desert sand raises the temperature of the surrounding air, which rises up along the mountain wall. As the air rises up, it loses energy through conduction. After reaching the top, this cool air becomes dense and sinks down along the opposite wall of the mountain, creating a downdraft.

16. Metal is a conductor with a low specific heat, so pouring a hot beverage in a metal cup would make the cup hot also. This cup would be unpleasant to hold. A china cup is a better insulator with a higher specific heat, so it will not become hot as rapidly.

17. The dark clothing absorbs energy transferred from the sun by radiation.

18. The ammonia would evaporate very easily in a room, absorbing energy from the room. Even a cold room is warmer than –33.4°C, so the ammonia would still evaporate, taking energy from the room rather than adding energy to the room.

BUILDING MATH SKILLS

19. –100. + 273 = 173 K

$\frac{9}{5}$(–100.) + 32.0 = –148°F

20. 3 – 273 = –270°C

$\frac{9}{5}$(–270) + 32.0 = –454°F

21. (234 J/kg•K)(0.0225 kg) (12 K) = 63 J

22. (385 J/kg•K)(0.55 kg) (21 K) = 4400 J

15. Explain how *convection currents* form updrafts near tall mountain ranges along deserts, as shown in the figure below.

16. Use the differences between a *conductor* and an *insulator* and the concept of *specific heat* to explain whether you would rather drink a hot beverage from a metal cup or from a china cup.

17. If you wear dark clothing on a sunny day, the clothing will become hot after a while. Use the concept of *radiation* to explain this.

18. Explain why ammonia, which has a boiling point of –33.4°C, is sometimes used as a *refrigerant* in a *cooling system*. Why would ammonia be less effective in a *heating system*?

BUILDING MATH SKILLS

19. Temperature Scale Conversion A piece of dry ice, solid CO_2, has a temperature of –100.°C. What is its temperature in kelvins and in degrees Fahrenheit?

20. Temperature Scale Conversion The temperature in deep space is thought to be around 3 K. What is 3 K in degrees Celsius? in degrees Fahrenheit?

21. Specific Heat How much energy is needed to raise the temperature of a silver necklace chain with a mass of 22.5 g from room temperature, 25°C, to body temperature, 37°C? (**Hint:** Refer to **Table 10-1** on p. 336)

22. Specific Heat How much energy would be absorbed by 550 g of copper when it is heated from 24°C to 45°C? (**Hint:** Refer to **Table 10-1** on p. 336.)

THINKING CRITICALLY

23. Interpreting Graphics Graph the Celsius-Fahrenheit conversion equation, plotting Celsius temperature along the *x*-axis and Fahrenheit temperature on the *y*-axis. Use an *x*-axis range from –100°C to 100°C, then use the graph to find the following values:
a. the Fahrenheit temperature equal to 77°C
b. the Fahrenheit temperature equal to –40°C
c. the Celsius temperature equal to 23°F
d. the Celsius temperature equal to –17°F

24. Applying Knowledge If two objects that have the same temperature come into contact with each other, what can you say about the amount of energy that will be transferred between them as heat?

25. Applying Knowledge If two objects that have different temperatures come into contact with each other, what can you say about their temperatures after several minutes of contact?

26. Creative Thinking Why does a metal doorknob feel cooler to your hand than a carpet feels to your bare feet?

27. Creative Thinking Why do the metal shades of desk lamps have small holes at the top?

28. Creative Thinking Why does the temperature of hot chocolate decrease faster if you place a metal spoon in the liquid?

29. Creative Thinking If you bite into a piece of hot apple pie, the pie filling might burn your mouth while the crust, at the same temperature, will not. Explain why.

348 CHAPTER 10

30. Applying Technology Glass can conduct some energy. Double-pane windows consist of two plates of glass separated by a small layer of insulating air. Explain why a double-pane window prevents more energy from escaping your house than a single-pane window.

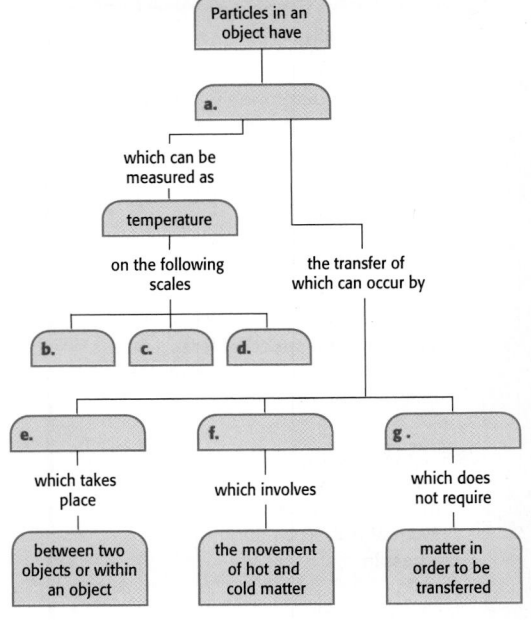

31. Understanding Systems Explain why window unit air conditioners always have the back part of the air conditioner hanging outside. Why is it that the entire air-conditioner cannot be in the room?

32. Making Decisions If the only factor considered were specific heat, which would make a better coolant for automobile engines: water or ethanol? Explain your answer.

DEVELOPING LIFE/WORK SKILLS

33. Allocating Resources In one southern state the projected yearly costs for heating a home were $463 using a heat pump, $508 using a natural-gas furnace, and $1220 using electric radiators. Contact your local utility company to determine the projected costs for the three different systems in your area. Make a table comparing the costs of the three systems.

34. Working Cooperatively Read the following statements, and discuss with a group of classmates which statement is correct. Explain your answer.
  a. Energy is lost when water is boiled.
  b. The energy used to boil water is still present, but it is no longer in a usable form unless you use work or heat to make it usable.

INTEGRATING CONCEPTS

35. Concept Mapping Copy the unfinished concept map below onto a sheet of paper. Complete the map by writing the correct word or phrase in the lettered boxes.

Particles in an object have

a.

which can be measured as

temperature

on the following scales

the transfer of which can occur by

b. **c.** **d.**

e. **f.** **g.**

which takes place

which involves

which does not require

between two objects or within an object

the movement of hot and cold matter

matter in order to be transferred

36. Connection to Social Studies
Research the work of Benjamin Thompson, also known as Count Rumford. What was the prevailing theory of heat during Thompson's time? What observations led to Thompson's theory?

WRITING SKILL

internetconnect

SCiLINKS **NSTA**
TOPIC: Insulators
GO TO: www.scilinks.org
KEYWORD: HK1105

HEAT AND TEMPERATURE **349**

THINKING CRITICALLY

23. a. 170°F
  b. −40°F
  c. −5°C
  d. −27°C

24. No net transfer of energy; the amount leaving an object will equal the amount entering the object.

25. Their temperatures will be closer together than they were at the start.

26. The metal is a better conductor than the carpet, so energy flows more easily away from you.

27. to let hot air escape

28. The metal spoon is a good conductor, so energy flows into the spoon. The spoon transfers energy to the surrounding air.

29. The crust is an insulator, whereas the filling is a conductor, so energy flows easily out of the filling.

30. The thicker glass is a better insulator than thin glass and the layer of air (or other gas) is an even better insulator.

31. The air conditioner must exhaust some energy. If the air conditioner were contained entirely within the room, the exhaust energy would also be in the room, heating the room up.

32. Water would be better because it has a higher specific heat. For a certain amount of water or ethanol, the water would absorb more energy from the engine per degree of temperature change.

Answers continue on p. 351B.

Investigating Conduction of Heat

Introduction

Energy is transferred as heat by conduction, convection, and radiation. This lab examines conduction, the transfer of energy as heat through a wire as atoms collide. A brief review of the kinetic theory from Chapter 2 may help the students visualize conduction.

Objectives

Students will:

▶ **Use** appropriate lab safety procedures.

▶ **Develop** a plan to measure how quickly energy is transferred as heat through a metal wire.

▶ **Compare** the speed of heat conduction in metal wires of different thicknesses.

Planning

Recommended Time: 1 lab period
Materials: (for each lab group)

▶ 3 metal wires of different thicknesses, each about 30 cm long
▶ clothespin
▶ candle
▶ lighter or matches
▶ candle holder
▶ metric ruler
▶ stopwatch

Design Your Own Lab

Introduction

How can you determine whether the thickness of a metal wire affects its ability to conduct energy as heat?

Objectives

▶ **Develop** a plan to measure how quickly energy is transferred as heat through a metal wire.

▶ **Compare** the speed of heat conduction in metal wires of different thicknesses.

Materials

3 metal wires of different thicknesses, each about 30 cm long
clothespin
candle
lighter or matches
candle holder
metric ruler
stopwatch

Safety Needs

goggles
apron

Investigating Conduction of Heat

▶ Demonstrating Conduction in Wires

1. Obtain three wires of different thicknesses. Clip a clothespin on one end of one of the wires. Lay the wire and attached clothespin on the lab table.
2. Light the candle and place it in the holder.
   SAFETY CAUTION Tie back long hair and confine loose clothing. Never reach across an open flame. Always use the clothespin to hold the wire as you heat it and move it to avoid burning yourself. Remember that the wires will be hot for some time after they are removed from the flame.
3. Hold the lighted candle in its holder above the middle of the wire, and tilt the candle slightly so that some of the melted wax drips onto the middle of the wire.
4. Wait a couple of minutes for the wire and dripped wax to cool completely. The dripped wax will harden and form a small ball. Using the clothespin to hold the wire, place the other end of the wire in the candle's flame. When the ball of wax melts, remove the wire from the flame, and place it on the lab table. Think about what caused the wax on the wire to melt.

▶ Designing Your Experiment

5. With your lab partner(s), decide how you will use the materials available in the lab to compare the speed of conduction in three wires of different thicknesses. Form a hypothesis about whether a thick wire will conduct energy more quickly or more slowly than a thin wire.
6. In your lab report, list each step you will perform in your experiment.
7. Have your teacher approve your plan before you carry out your experiment.

SOLUTION/MATERIAL PREPARATION

The wires should be bare, solid rather than braided, and made of the same metal. Copper wires of various diameters are available in electronics stores, electrical supply stores, and hardware stores.

Select candle holders that are designed to catch wax drips.

▶ Performing Your Experiment

8. After your teacher approves your plan, you can carry out your experiment.
9. Prepare a data table in your lab report that is similar to the one shown below.
10. Record in your table how many seconds it takes for the ball of wax on each wire to melt. Perform three trials for each wire, allowing the wires to cool to room temperature between trials.

Conductivity Data

	Wire diameter (mm)	Time to melt wax (s)			
		Trial 1	Trial 2	Trial 3	Average time
Wire 1					
Wire 2					
Wire 3					

▶ Analyzing Your Results

1. Find the diameter of each wire you tested. If the diameter is listed in inches, convert it to millimeters by multiplying by 25.4. If the diameter is listed in mils, convert it to millimeters by multiplying by 0.0254. In your data table, record the diameter of each wire in millimeters.
2. Calculate the average time required to melt the ball of wax for each wire. Record your answers in your data table.
3. Plot your data in your lab report in the form of a graph like the one shown. On your graph, draw the line or smooth curve that fits the points best.
4. **Reaching Conclusions** Based on your graph, does a thick wire or a thin wire conduct energy more quickly?
5. When roasting a large cut of meat, some cooks insert a metal skewer into the meat to make the inside cook more quickly. If you were roasting meat, would you insert a thick skewer or a thin skewer? Why?

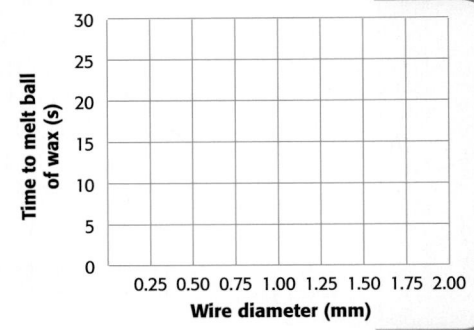

▶ Defending Your Conclusions

6. Suppose someone tells you that your conclusion is valid only for the particular metal you tested. How could you show that your conclusion is valid for other metals as well?

REQUIRED PRECAUTIONS

- ▶ Read all safety precautions and discuss them with your students.
- ▶ Caution students to tie back long hair and confine loose clothing.
- ▶ Never allow students to reach across an open flame.
- ▶ Clothespins can be a fire hazard with students. As an alternative, wires can be strung between two test-tube clamps on ring stands or lab supports.
- ▶ Be sure students always use a clamp or clothespin to hold the wire as it heats.
- ▶ Remind students that the wires will be hot for some time after they are removed from the flame.

Pre-Lab

Teaching Tips

The success of this experiment depends on the experimental design. Results may vary because of flickering of the candle flames and some difficulty in determining when melting begins to occur. The data may overlap if the diameters of the wires are close. Ask the students how they will decide when melting has started. One way to determine the beginning of melting is to tilt the wire slightly at an angle of 15 to 20 degrees, such that a drop will slide down the wire as the wax begins to melt.

Procedure

▶ Designing Your Experiment

Students should control all variables except for wire diameter. A distance from the end of the wire should be specified that is consistent among the three wires and across the three trials. The end of each wire should be held in the same part of the flame, so the temperature at the end will be the same for all wires. The wax balls on the wires should be close to the same size. If the thinnest wires are too flexible, students can hold both ends of the wire (with two clamps or clothespins) and heat the wire somewhere between the clamps. However, the wax balls should always be the same distance from the flame.

Continue on p. 351A.

RESOURCE LINK
DATASHEETS

Have students use *Datasheet 10.6: Design Your Own Lab—Investigating Conduction of Heat* to record their results.

Design Your Own Lab from page 351

Investigating Conduction of Heat

▶Analyzing Your Results

1. Answers will vary. See sample data.
2. Answers will vary. See sample data.
3. See sample graph. Results will vary, but times should be greater for smaller-diameter wires. The line that best fits the data points should decrease as diameter increases.
4. Students should find that thicker wires conduct energy as heat more quickly than thin wires.
5. A thicker skewer will conduct energy as heat more quickly than a thin skewer.

▶Defending Your Conclusions

6. Students could test wires made from different kinds of metals.

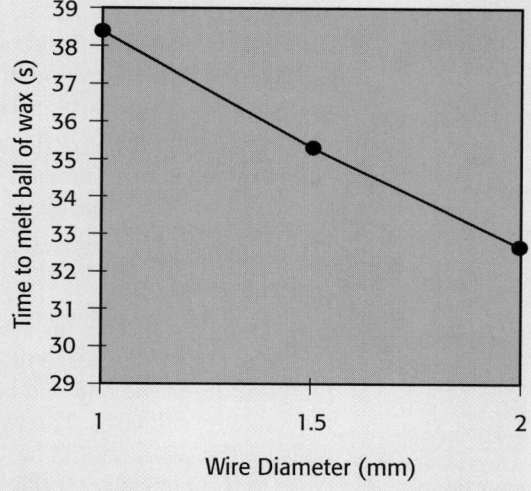

Wire Diameter (mm)

Sample Data Table Heat Conductivity for Copper Wire				
	Wire	Time to melt wax (s)		
	diameter (mm)	Trial 1	Trial 2	Trial 3	Average time
Wire 1	1.0	39.1	37.8	38.4	38.4
Wire 2	1.5	35.0	36.1	34.8	35.3
Wire 3	2.0	34.0	33.3	30.9	32.7

Answers from page 330

SECTION 10.1 REVIEW

5. A cup of boiling water has a higher temperature than Lake Michigan, but Lake Michigan has more total kinetic energy since it has more particles.

Math Skills

6. $\frac{9}{5}(20.0) + 32.0 = 68.0°F$

$20 + 273 = 293$ K

7. $\frac{5}{9}(-128.6 - 32.0) = -89.2°C$

$-89.2 + 273 = 184$ K

Answers from page 338

SECTION 10.2 REVIEW

4. The temperature differences on the moon's surface are due to two things. One is the composition of the moon's surface, which varies from place to place. The other factor is whether or not the spot in question is on the sunny side of the moon (hot) or the shadow side (cold).
5. The cookies near the turned-up edge receive conduction energy from the cookie sheet, just like the cookies in the middle. However, those near the edge also receive more energy from air convection currents and radiation from the turned up edge.

Math Skills

6. $c = \dfrac{3250 \text{ J}}{(1.32 \text{ kg})(292 \text{ K} - 273 \text{ K})} = 130$ J/kg•K; lead

7. 228 J/kg•K

Answers from page 346

4. Answers will depend on your area, but some possibilities are:
   advantages—free energy from sun, less pollution; disadvantages—not much sun available, expensive to set up, difficult to install
5. Accept all reasonable responses.
6. Students' spreadsheets should calculate the following values for rate of energy transfer:

drywall: $\dfrac{1.0 \text{ m}^2 \times 20°C}{0.45} = 44$

wood shingles: $\dfrac{1.0 \text{ m}^2 \times 20.0°C}{0.87} = 23$

flat glass: $\dfrac{1.0 \text{ m}^2 \times 20.0°C}{0.89} = 22$

hardwood siding: $\dfrac{1.0 \text{ m}^2 \times 20.0°C}{0.91} = 22$

vertical air space: $\dfrac{1.0 \text{ m}^2 \times 20.0°C}{1.01} = 20.$

insulating glass: $\dfrac{1.0 \text{ m}^2 \times 20.0°C}{1.54} = 13$

cellulose fiber: $\dfrac{1.0 \text{ m}^2 \times 20.0°C}{3.70} = 5.4$

brick: $\dfrac{1.0 \text{ m}^2 \times 20.0°C}{4.00} = 5.0$

fiberglass batting: $\dfrac{1.0 \text{ m}^2 \times 20.0°C}{10.90} = 1.8$

Answers from page 349

33. Answers will vary.
34. Statement (b) is correct. Energy can never be lost; it is always conserved.

35. a. kinetic energy
    b. Celsius
    c. Kelvin
    d. Fahrenheit
    e. conduction
    f. convection
    g. radiation
36. http://www.treasure-troves.com/bios/Rumford.html

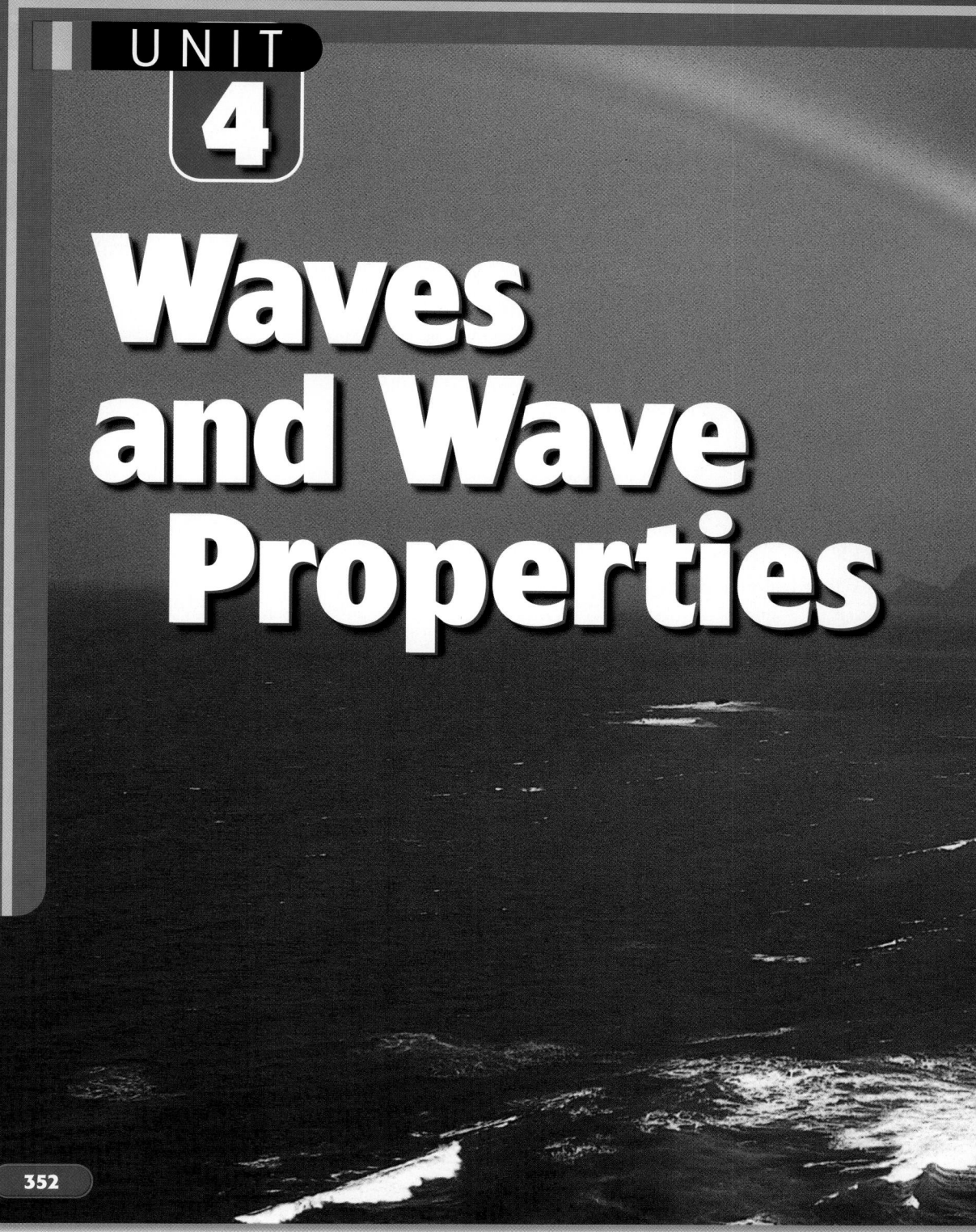

Waves and Wave Properties

Historical Perspective

Before Isaac Newton, people generally believed that the colors of the rainbow were caused by changes from "white light" to "colored light."

Newton showed that white light actually contains light of all the colors of the rainbow. In one of his most convincing demonstrations, Newton showed that the spectrum of light from a prism could be recombined to form white light.

Another part of Newton's evidence was that while a prism could easily create green light from white light, it could not make green light from red light. Today we understand the reason is because the frequency of the waves in light do not change.

MISCONCEPTION ALERT

Waves Many students are accustomed to thinking that motion applies only to objects. They may be unfamiliar with the concept that a wave is a means by which matter can move energy from one place to another without the matter changing location.

You may want to prepare students for this idea, which is explored further in Chapter 11, by asking them to consider a wave in water. Point out that when a pebble is dropped in the center of a bowl of water, the ripples spread outward. But most of the water that was in the center of the bowl remains there.

352

|SKILL BUILDER

Interpreting Visuals Ask students to identify what waves can be seen in this photograph. While many will notice the waves in the water shown near the bottom of the page, some may not realize that the colors of the rainbow shown closer to the top of the page are due to differences in the wavelengths of the light waves detected by the camera taking this picture.

This may also be an opportunity to point out that there are many other common kinds of waves, from sound waves to seismic waves.

Tailoring the Program to YOUR Classroom

CHAPTER 11

Waves

Annotated Descriptions of the Correlated National Science Standards

The following descriptions summarize the National Science Standards that specially relate to Chapter 11. For the full text of the Standards, see p. 40T.

SECTION 11.1
Types of Waves
Physical Science
PS 4a, 5a, 5b, 5d
Unifying Concepts and Processes
UCP 1, 2, 4, 5
Science as Inquiry
SAI 1
Science and Technology
ST 1, 2
Science in Personal and Social Perspectives
SPSP 5

SECTION 11.2
Characteristics of Waves
Physical Science
PS 2e, 4a, 4e, 5a, 5d
Earth and Space Science
ES 3c
Unifying Concepts and Processes
UCP 1, 2, 3
Science and Technology
ST 2
History and Nature of Science
HNS 1
Science in Personal and Social Perspectives
SPSP 5

SECTION 11.3
Wave Interactions
Physical Science
PS 4a
Unifying Concepts and Processes
UCP 1, 2, 4
Science as Inquiry
SAI 1
Science and Technology
ST 1, 2
Science in Personal and Social Perspectives
SPSP 5

Cross-Discipline Teaching RESOURCES

Cross-Discipline Teaching, ATE p. 354
Fine Arts   Social Studies

Integration Enrichment Resources
Engineering, **PE** and **ATE** p. 357
   IE 11.1 *Wave Energy*
Science and the Consumer, **PE** and **ATE** p. 360
   IE 11.2 *Bicycle Design and Shock Absorption*
Earth Science, **PE** and **ATE** p. 369
   IE 11.3 *Earthquake Waves*
Architecture, **PE** and **ATE** p. 379
   IE 11.4 *Architectural Acoustics*

Additional Integration Enrichment Worksheets
   IE 11.5 Technology
   IE 11.6 Language Arts
   IE 11.7 Mathematics

Use the Planning Guide on the next page to help you organize your lessons.

MATH AND COMPUTER RESOURCES

Chapter 11	Math Skills	Assess	Media/Computer Skills
Section 11.1			■ Section 11.1
Section 11.2	**PE** **Math Skills** Wave Speed, p. 370 **ATE** **Additional Examples** p. 370	**PE** **Practice,** p. 370 **MS** Worksheet 25 **PE** Section Review 7–9, p. 373 **PE** **Problem Bank,** p. 700, 121–125	■ Section 11.2 💿 *DISC TWO, MODULE 12* Frequency and Wavelength 　**PE** **Developing Life/Work Skills,** 　p. 383, item 30
Section 11.3			■ Section 11.3 💿 *DISC TWO, MODULE 13* Reflection 💿 *DISC TWO, MODULE 14* Refraction

PE Pupil's Edition　**ATE** Annotated Teacher's Edition　**MS** Math Skills　**BS** Basic Skills
IE Integration Enrichment　■ Guided Reading Audio　**CRT** Critical Thinking

The following activities found in the Annotated Teacher's Edition provide techniques for developing useful reading strategies to increase your students' reading comprehension skills.

Section 11.1 **Brainstorming,** p. 354
　　　　　　Reading Organizer, p. 356

Section 11.2 **Reading Organizer,** p. 365

Section 11.3 **Summarizing,** p. 374

Smithsonian Institution®
Visit
www.si.edu/hrw
for additional
online resources.

Spanish Resources

The following resources are made available for students who speak Spanish as their first language.

Spanish Resources
Guided Reading Audio CD-ROM
Chapter 11

Spanish Glossary
Chapter 11

Waves

	CLASSROOM RESOURCES		
	FOCUS	**TEACH**	**HANDS-ON**
Section 11.1: Types of Waves			
BLOCK 1 45 minutes	ATE **RSB** Brainstorming, p. 354 ATE Focus Activities 1, 2, p. 355 ATE **RSB** Reading Organizer, p. 356 ATE **Demo 1** Wave Motion, p. 357 ATE **Demo 2** Harmonic Motion, p. 358 PE What Is a Wave? pp. 356–358 ★ Focus Transparency LT 36	ATE **Skill Builder** Interpreting Visuals, p. 355	IE Worksheet 11.1
BLOCK 2 45 minutes	ATE **Demo 3** Longitudinal Waves in Air, p. 363 PE Vibrations and Waves; Transverse and Longitudinal Waves, pp. 359–364	ATE **Skill Builder** Interpreting Visuals, pp. 359, 361, 362 TT 29 Wave Model TT 30 Water Wave Motion	PE Science and the Consumer *Shock Absorbers: Why Are They Important?* p. 360 IE Worksheet 11.2 PE Inquiry Lab *How do particles move in a medium?* p. 362 **DS** 11.1 PE Quick Activity *Polarization,* p. 363 **DS** 11.2
Section 11.2: Characteristics of Waves			
BLOCK 3 45 minutes	ATE **RSB** Reading Organizer, p. 365 ATE **Demo 4** Graphically Representing Longitudinal Waves, p. 366 PE Wave Properties, pp. 365–368 ★ Focus Transparency LT 37	ATE **Skill Builder** Vocabulary, p. 365 Interpreting Diagrams, p. 365 Interpreting Visuals, pp. 366–368 Interpreting Data, p. 368 ATE **Graphic Organizer** Properties of Waves, p. 365 BLM 30 Transverse Wave BLM 31 Longitudinal Wave TT 31 Frequency TT 32 Visible Light BLM 32 The Electromagnetic Spectrum	IE Worksheet 11.6 IE Worksheet 11.5
BLOCK 4 45 minutes	ATE **Demo 5** Doppler Effect, p. 372 PE Wave Speed; The Doppler Effect, pp. 369–373	TT 33 Doppler Effect	IE Worksheet 11.3 PE Quick Activity *Wave Speed,* p. 371 **DS** 11.3
Section 11.3: Wave Interactions			
BLOCK 5 45 minutes	ATE **RSB** Summarizing, p. 374 ATE **Demo 6** Observing Reflection and Refraction, p. 376 PE Reflection, Diffraction, and Refraction, pp. 374–376 ★ Focus Transparency LT 38		IE Worksheet 11.7
BLOCK 6 45 minutes	PE Interference; Standing Waves, pp. 376–380	ATE **Skill Builder** Interpreting Graphs, pp. 377, 378 BLM 33 Interference BLM 34 Beats	IE Worksheet 11.4 PE Design Your Own Lab *Modeling Transverse Waves,* p. 384 **DS** 11.4 LE 11 *Tuning a Musical Instrument* **DS** 11.5

CLASSROOM RESOURCES

HOMEWORK	ASSESS
PE Section Review 1, 2, p. 364 **Chapter 11 Review,** p. 381, items 1, 11	**SG** Chapter 11 Pretest
PE Section Review 3–6, p. 364 **Chapter 11 Review,** p. 381, items 2–5, 12	**ATE** *ALTERNATIVE ASSESSMENT,* Transverse and Longitudinal Waves, p. 364 **SG** Section 11.1
PE Section Review 1, 2, p. 373 **Chapter 11 Review,** p. 381, items 6, 7, 13, 17	
PE Section Review 3–9, p. 373 **Chapter 11 Review,** p. 381, items 8, 14, 18	**ATE** *ALTERNATIVE ASSESSMENT,* Sound Wave, p. 373 **SG** Section 11.2
PE Section Review 1, 2, 4, p. 380 **Chapter 11 Review,** p. 381, item 10	
PE Section Review 3, 5–8, p. 380 **Chapter 11 Review,** p. 381, items 9, 15, 16	**ATE** *ALTERNATIVE ASSESSMENT,* Standing Waves on a Rope, p. 378 **ATE** *ALTERNATIVE ASSESSMENT,* Wave Phenomena, p. 380 **SG** Section 11.3

BLOCK 7

PE Chapter 11 Review
Thinking Critically p. 382, 23–28
Developing Life/Work Skills p. 383, 29–33
Integrating Concepts p. 383, 34–36
SG Chapter 11 Mixed Review

BLOCK 8

Chapter Tests
Holt Science Spectrum: A Physical Approach
Chapter 11 Test

One-Stop Planner CD–ROM **with Test Generator**
Holt Science Spectrum Test Generator
FOR MACINTOSH AND WINDOWS
Chapter 11

Teaching Resources
Scoring Rubrics and assignment evaluation
checklist.

---

internetconnect

SC/LINKS
NSTA

**National Science Teachers
Association
Online Resources:
www.scilinks.org**
The following *sci*LINKS Internet resources can be found
in the student text for this chapter.

Page 355 **TOPIC:** Waves **KEYWORD:** HK1111	**Page 375** **TOPIC:** Reflection, refraction, diffraction **KEYWORD:** HK1115
Page 359 **TOPIC:** Vibrations and waves **KEYWORD:** HK1112	**Page 383** **TOPIC:** Seismic waves **KEYWORD:** HK1116
Page 373 **TOPIC:** Doppler effect **KEYWORD:** HK1114	

CNNfyi.com   **www.cnnfyi.com**

Visit this site for coverage of current events and related
classroom resources.

PE Pupil's Edition   **ATE** Annotated Teacher's Edition
RSB Reading Skill Builder   **DS** Datasheets
IE Integrated Enrichment   **SG** Study Guide
LE Laboratory Experiments
TT Teaching Transparencies   **BLM** Blackline Masters
★ Lesson Focus Transparency

CHAPTER 11

Waves

Be sure students understand the following concepts:

Chapter 2
Interactions of matter and energy

Chapter 8
Motion and forces

Chapter 9
Work, forms of energy, energy transformations

READING SKILL BUILDER

Brainstorming Write the word *wave* on the chalkboard. Ask students to brainstorm a list of words that can precede wave to describe different kinds of *waves*. Words can include *water, ocean, tidal, heat, cold, sound, radio, light,* and so on. Invite students to speculate on what all these waves have in common. Help them to realize that these phrases usually represent some sort of back-and-forth or up-and-down motion or change, or a coming and going of some condition or event. Wave motion is a periodic recurrence.

Chapter Preview

354

CROSS-DISCIPLINE TEACHING

Social Studies Waves have been used in artworks to convey serenity, drama, danger, and the helplessness of humans in the face of nature. Ask an art teacher or art historian to show visual examples of art depicting waves, including paintings by American artists Winslow Homer, Thomas Moran, and John F. Kensett. Their work can be contrasted with artworks by Japanese artists that also depict waves.

Fine Arts Find out if your school has an electronic device or computer for tuning instruments to a common pitch. Either borrow the device or take the class to its location, and ask students who play instruments to demonstrate beats and the techniques of tuning.

Focus ACTIVITY

Background The energy in an ocean wave can lift a surfboard up into the air and carry the surfer into shore. Ocean waves get most of their energy from the wind. A wave may start as a small ripple in a calm sea, then build up as the wind pushes it along. Waves that start on the coast of northern Canada may be very large by the time they reach a beach in the Hawaiian Islands.

The winds that create ocean waves are caused by convection currents in the atmosphere, which are driven by energy from the sun. Energy travels across empty space from the sun to Earth—in the form of waves.

Waves are all around us. As you read this book, you are depending on light waves. Light bounces off the pages and into your eyes. When you talk with a friend you are depending on sound waves traveling through the air. Sometimes the waves can be gentle, such as those that rock a canoe in a pond. Other times waves can be very destructive, such as those created by earthquakes.

Activity 1 Fill a long, rectangular pan with water. Experiment with making waves in different ways. Try making waves by sticking the end of a pencil into the water, by moving a wide stick or board back and forth, and by striking the side of the pan. Place wooden blocks or other obstacles into the pan, and watch how the waves change when they encounter the obstacles.

Activity 2 Make a list of things that you do every day that depend on waves. Next to each item, write down what kind of waves you think are involved. Write a short paragraph describing some properties that you think these different kinds of waves may have in common.

internet connect

SC*LINKS*
NSTA

TOPIC: Waves
GO TO: www.scilinks.org
KEYWORD: HK1111

A surfer takes advantage of the energy in ocean waves. Energy travels from the sun to Earth in the form of waves.

355

Focus ACTIVITY

Background Ask students to describe what they think sound waves and light waves would look like if they could be observed directly. Many students will have trouble getting away from the up-and-down undulations they associate with water waves.

Activity 1 See Demonstration 1 on page 357 for additional information about observing waves in a pan.

Activity 2 Help students realize that waves transfer energy. The evidence is that they can do mechanical work (or destruction) or cause things to become warmer (transferring energy as heat).

SKILL BUILDER

Interpreting Visuals Ask students where you would go to find surf. Ask students to speculate on why these waves occur reliably near shore and how they are able to lift a surfer high in the air and propel the surfer toward shore.

RESOURCE LINK
STUDY GUIDE

Assign students *Pretest Chapter 11 Waves* before beginning Section 11.1.

Scheduling

Refer to pp. 354A–354D for lecture, classwork, and assignment options for Section 11.1.

★ **Lesson Focus**
Use transparency *LT 36* to prepare students for this section.

 **READING SKILL BUILDER** *Reading Organizer* Have students read Section 11.1. Then have students prepare a blank table with the title *Properties of Waves,* like the one shown below. Students should use the text as a resource to gather information on wave properties. Have students fill in the table once they have finished reading Section 11.1. Answers shown in italics may vary slightly.

Types of Waves

▶ **KEY TERMS**
wave
medium
mechanical wave
electromagnetic wave
transverse wave
longitudinal wave

OBJECTIVES

▶ Recognize that waves transfer energy.
▶ Distinguish between mechanical waves and electromagnetic waves.
▶ Explain the relationship between particle vibration and wave motion.
▶ Distinguish between transverse waves and longitudinal waves.

When a stone is thrown into a pond, it creates ripples on the surface of the water, as shown in **Figure 11-1.** If there is a leaf floating on the water, the leaf will bob up and down and back and forth as each ripple, or wave, disturbs it. But after the waves pass, the leaf will return to its original position on the water.

What Is a Wave?

Like the leaf, individual drops of water do not travel outward with a wave. They move only slightly from their resting place as each ripple passes by. If drops of water do not move very far as a wave passes, and neither does a leaf on the surface of the water, then what moves along with the wave? Energy does. A wave is not made of matter. A wave is a disturbance that carries energy through matter or space.

▶ **wave** a disturbance that transmits energy through matter or space

Figure 11-1
A stone thrown into a pond creates waves.

356 CHAPTER 11

356

Properties of Waves

Type of wave	Mechanical		Electromagnetic
Form	*Longitudinal*	*Transverse*	*Modeled as transverse*
Medium	*Solids, liquids, gases*	*Solids and liquids*	*None required*
Travel as	*Compression and rarefactions in matter*	*Back-and-forth (or up-and-down) movement of matter*	*Oscillating electric and magnetic fields*
Examples	*Sound waves, some earthquake waves*	*Water waves, rope waves, some earthquake waves*	*Visible light waves, radio waves, X rays*

Most waves travel through a medium

The waves in a pond are disturbances traveling through water. Sound also travels as a wave. The sound from a stereo is a pattern of changes in the air between the stereo speakers and your ear. Earthquakes create waves, called *seismic waves*, that travel through Earth.

In each of these examples, the waves involve the movement of some kind of matter. The matter through which a wave travels is called the medium. In the example of the pond, the water is the medium. For sound from a stereo, air is the medium. And in earthquakes, Earth itself is the medium.

Waves that require a medium are called mechanical waves. Almost all waves are mechanical waves, with one important exception: electromagnetic waves.

Light does not require a medium

Light can travel from the sun to Earth across the empty space between them. This is possible because light waves do not need a medium through which to travel. Instead, light waves consist of changing electric and magnetic fields in space. For that reason, light waves are also called electromagnetic waves.

Visible light waves are just one example of a wide range of electromagnetic waves. Radio waves, such as those that carry signals to your radio or television, are also electromagnetic waves. Other kinds of electromagnetic waves will be introduced in Section 11-2. *In this book, the terms light and light wave may refer to any electromagnetic wave, not just visible light.*

Waves transfer energy

In Chapter 9, you learned that energy can be defined as the ability to do work. We know that waves carry energy because they can do work. For example, water waves can do work on a leaf, on a boat, or on a beach. Sound waves can do work on your eardrum. Light waves can do work on your eye or on photographic film.

A wave caused by dropping a stone in a pond might carry enough energy to move a leaf up and down several centimeters. The bigger the wave is, the more energy it carries. A cruise ship moving through water in the ocean could create waves big enough to move a fishing boat up and down a few meters.

Connection to ENGINEERING

If you have ever been hit by an ocean wave at the beach, you know these waves carry a lot of energy. Could this energy be put to good use? Research is currently underway to find ways to harness the energy of ocean waves. Some small floating navigation buoys, which shine lights to help ships find their way in the dark, obtain energy solely from the waves. A few larger systems are in place that harness wave energy to provide electricity for small coastal communities.

Making the Connection

1. In a library or on the Internet, research different types of devices that harness wave energy. How much power do some of these devices provide? Is that a lot of power?
2. Design a device of your own to capture the energy from ocean waves. The device should take the motion of waves and convert it into a motion that could be used to drive a machine, such as a pump or a wheel.

▶ **medium** the matter through which a wave travels

▶ **mechanical wave** a wave that requires a medium through which to travel

▶ **electromagnetic wave** a wave caused by a disturbance in electric and magnetic fields and that does not require a medium; also called a light wave

Types of Waves

Connection to ENGINEERING

Making the Connection

1. Remind students that ordinary ocean waves (except for tsunamis) are produced by wind, so wave power is just another form of wind power. In addition, winds are caused by differential heating of Earth by the sun. Thus, you can also say that wave power is another form of solar power.
2. Students should recall from Chapter 9 that "capturing the energy" means using it to do useful work and that work is done whenever a force is used to move an object.

Resources Assign students worksheet *11.1: Connection to Engineering—Wave Energy* in the **Integration Enrichment Resources** ancillary.

Teaching Tip

Mechanical Waves Remind students of the definition of mechanical energy. Mechanical energy is the kinetic and potential energy of large-scale objects in a system. Mechanical waves involve mechanical energy passing through the medium.

MISCONCEPTION ALERT

Wave Motion
Stress at this point that wave motion transfers only energy, not matter. Even though mechanical waves are transferred by the motion of matter, no matter itself is transferred.

WAVES **357**

DEMONSTRATION 1 TEACHING

Observing Wave Motion

Time: Approximately 10 minutes
Materials: ripple tank or shallow, clear baking dish, wooden dowel (cut to the width of the dish), overhead projector, wood scraps, corks

Step 1 If you do not have access to a ripple tank, you can assemble a makeshift tank with a clear baking dish. Put about 3 cm of water in the dish and place it on the overhead projector.

Step 2 Make waves in the dish by holding the dowel along the surface of the water and moving it up and down at a constant frequency. You can also make circular waves with the end of the dowel.

Step 3 Have students observe how the waves reflect off the walls of the pan or off pieces of wood placed in the water. Also demonstrate the motion of corks floating on the surface.

Multicultural Extension

People who live on Pacific islands or in Pacific Coast countries, including Chile and Australia, have great respect for the power of tsunamis. These tidal waves occur more frequently around the Pacific than in other oceans because of earthquakes and underwater volcanic activity associated with the movement of the continental plates in that region. It may surprise students to know that if they were on a ship in the deep part of the ocean when a tidal wave passed, it would cause only a smooth rise and fall of a few inches. In other words, no one would notice. However, a lot of energy is required to lift a great depth of water a few inches. When that energy becomes concentrated in shallow water, it will produce a fast and fearsome tsunami.

Teaching Tip

Spreading of Waves Mechanical waves spread out through the medium evenly and spherically from the source if the source is open to the medium in all directions. If the source, such as a speaker, is pointed in a particular direction, the sound waves will spread spherically but will be stronger in the direction the speaker points. Note that the spherical wave fronts are represented as circles in **Figure 11-3.**

Figure 11-2
This portrait of a tsunami was created by the Japanese artist Hokusai in 1830.

Figure 11-3
Sound waves from a stereo speaker spread out in spherical wave fronts.

358 CHAPTER 11

Figure 11-2 shows a woodblock print of a *tsunami*, a huge ocean wave caused by earthquakes. A tsunami may be as high as 30 m when it reaches shore, taller than a 10-story building. Such waves carry enough energy to cause a lot of damage to coastal towns and shorelines. Normal-sized ocean waves do work on the shore, too, breaking up rocks into tiny pieces to form sandy beaches.

Energy may spread out as a wave travels

If you stand next to the speakers at a rock concert, the sound waves may damage your ears. Likewise, if you look at a bright light bulb from too close, the light may damage your eyes. But if you are 100 m away, the sound of the rock band or the light from the bulb is harmless. Why?

Think about waves created when a stone falls into a pond. The waves spread out in circles that get bigger as the waves move farther from the center. Each of these circles, called a *wave front*, has the same amount of total energy. But as the circles get larger, the energy spreads out over a larger area.

When sound waves travel in air, the waves spread out in spheres, as shown in **Figure 11-3.** These spheres are similar to the circular ripples on a pond. As they travel outward, the spherical wave fronts get bigger, so the energy in the waves spreads out over a larger area. This is why large amplifiers and speakers are needed to fill a concert hall with sound, even though the same music can sound just as loud if it is played on a portable radio and listened to with a small pair of headphones.

DEMONSTRATION 2 TEACHING

Harmonic Motion

Time: Approximately 5 minutes
Materials: spring
        support for spring
        chalkboard
        chalk
        mass

Step 1 Set up a demonstration of the system illustrated in **Figure 11-4.** The mass must be heavy enough to stretch the spring significantly without permanently deforming it. The spring should not completely collapse at the top of the vibration.

Step 2 Demonstrate the up and down vibration (oscillation) of the mass when it is pulled down or pushed up from its resting position.

Vibrations and Waves

When a singer sings a note, vocal cords in the singer's throat move back and forth. That motion makes the air in the throat vibrate, creating sound waves that eventually reach your ears. The vibration of the air in your ears causes your eardrums to vibrate. The motion of the eardrum triggers a series of electrical pulses to your brain, and your brain interprets them as sounds.

Waves are related to vibrations. Most waves are caused by a vibrating object. Electromagnetic waves may be caused by vibrating charged particles. In a mechanical wave, the particles in the medium also vibrate as the wave passes through the medium.

Vibrations involve transformations of energy

Figure 11-4 shows a mass hanging on a spring. If the mass is pulled down slightly and released, it will begin to move up and down around its original resting position. This vibration involves transformations of energy, much like those in a swinging pendulum.

When the mass is pulled away from its resting place, the mass-spring system gains elastic potential energy. The spring exerts a force that pulls the mass back to its original position.

As the spring moves back toward the original position, the potential energy in the system changes to kinetic energy. The mass moves beyond its original resting position to the other side.

At the top of its motion, the mass has lost all its kinetic energy. But the system now has both elastic potential energy and gravitational potential energy. The mass moves downward again, past the resting position, and back to the beginning of the cycle.

internet connect

SC*LINKS*.
NSTA

TOPIC: Vibrations and waves
GO TO: www.scilinks.org
KEYWORD: HK1112

Figure 11-4
When a mass hanging on a spring is disturbed from rest, it starts to vibrate up and down around its original position.

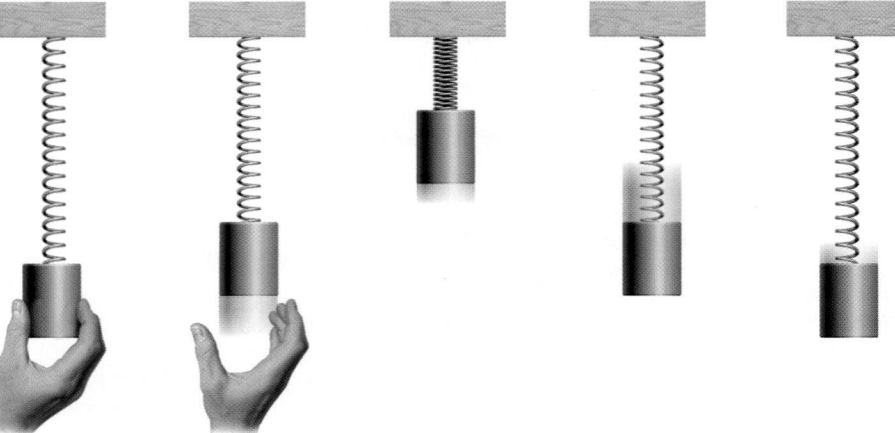

WAVES **359**

Teaching Tip

The Nature of Mechanical Waves Mechanical waves of a given frequency travel as regular, repeating disturbances or displacements of matter. These displacements are caused by a vibrating object. When mechanical waves pass a certain point in the medium, particles in the medium also vibrate. These vibrations will have the same frequency as the source of the vibrations unless the source is moving relative to the medium.

▌ SKILL BUILDER

Interpreting Visuals Have students examine **Figure 11-4.** Ask students to determine when the mass has the highest potential energy and the lowest kinetic energy *(when the mass is at the top and bottom points of its oscillation, with a velocity of zero).* When does the mass have the highest kinetic energy and the lowest potential energy *(just as it crosses its resting position).*

You may want to show that the mass has potential energy for two reasons, depending on whether it is at the top or bottom of its oscillation. At the top, the mass has gravitational potential energy. As the mass falls, this energy is transformed into elastic potential energy due to the stretching of the spring.

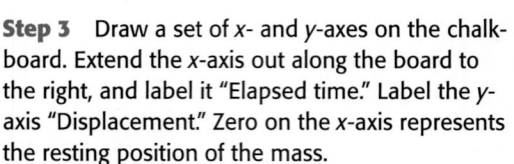

Step 3 Draw a set of *x*- and *y*-axes on the chalkboard. Extend the *x*-axis out along the board to the right, and label it "Elapsed time." Label the *y*-axis "Displacement." Zero on the *x*-axis represents the resting position of the mass.

Step 4 Set the mass in motion and walk along the board to the right at a steady pace while reproducing the up-and-down motion of the mass

with chalk. The resulting curve should be a reasonable approximation of a sine curve that describes the harmonic motion of the weight. Point out that any vibration can be graphed in this way.

Science and the Consumer

Shock Absorbers: Why Are They Important? This feature puts the distinction between simple harmonic motion and damped harmonic motion into a real-world context. Ask students if they have ever ridden in a car with poor suspension. What did it feel like? Did the car continue bouncing up and down after going over a bump? Did the shock from hitting a bump transfer more directly to the passengers in the car?

Students may also be familiar with shock absorbers on a bicycle. Ask students if they have or know someone who has a bike with shock absorbers. Have them find out if the shock absorbers contain springs or a fluid such as oil or pressurized air.

Your Choice

1. Students' answers should indicate that they would look for a vehicle with leaf springs, because these types of springs can bear heavier loads than coil springs can.

2. Shock absorbers stop an automobile from continually bouncing by dampening the vibrations of the springs.

Resources Assign students worksheet *11.2: Science and the Consumer—Bicycle Design and Shock Absorption* in the **Integration Enrichment Resources** ancillary.

Science and the Consumer

Shock Absorbers: Why Are They Important?

Bumps in the road are certainly a nuisance, but without strategic use of dampening devices, they could also be very dangerous. To control a car going 100 km/h (60 mi/h), a driver needs all the wheels of the vehicle on the ground. Bumps in the road lift the wheels off the ground and may rob the driver of control of the car.

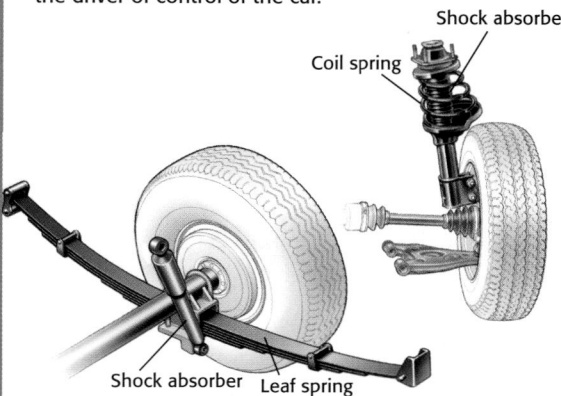

Coil spring

Shock absorber

Shock absorber   Leaf spring

Springs Absorb Energy

To solve this problem, cars are fitted with springs at each wheel. When the wheel of a car goes over a bump, the spring absorbs kinetic energy so that the energy is not transferred to the rest of the car. The energy becomes elastic potential energy in the spring, which then allows the spring to push the wheel back down onto the road.

Springs Alone Prolong Vibrations

Once a spring is set in motion, it tends to continue vibrating up and down in simple harmonic motion. This can create an uncomfortable ride, and it may also affect the driver's control of the car. One way to cut down on unwanted vibrations is to use stiff springs that compress only a few centimeters with thousands of newtons of force. However, the stiffer the spring is, the rougher the ride is and the more likely the wheels are to come off the road.

Shock Absorbers Dampen Vibrations

Modern automobiles are fitted with devices known as shock absorbers that absorb energy without prolonging vibrations. Shock absorbers are fluid-filled tubes that turn the simple harmonic motion of the springs into a damped harmonic motion. In a damped harmonic motion, each cycle of stretch and compression of the spring is much smaller than the previous cycle. Modern auto suspensions are set up so that all a spring's energy is absorbed by the shock absorbers in just one up-and-down cycle.

Shock Absorbers and Springs Come in Different Arrangements

Different types of springs and shock absorbers are combined to give a wide variety of responses. For example, many passenger cars have coil springs with shock absorbers parallel to the springs, or even inside the springs, as shown at near left. Some larger vehicles have heavy-duty leaf springs made of stacks of steel strips. Leaf springs are stiffer than coil springs, but they can bear heavier loads. In this type of suspension system, the shock absorber is perpendicular to the spring, as shown at far left.

The stiffness of the spring can affect steering response time, traction, and the general feel of the car. Because of the variety of combinations, your driving experiences can range from the luxurious "floating-on-air" ride of a limousine to the bone-rattling feel of a true sports car.

Your Choice

1. **Making Decisions** If you were going to haul heavy loads, would you look for a vehicle with coil springs or leaf springs? Why?
2. **Critical Thinking** How do shock absorbers stop an automobile from continually bouncing?

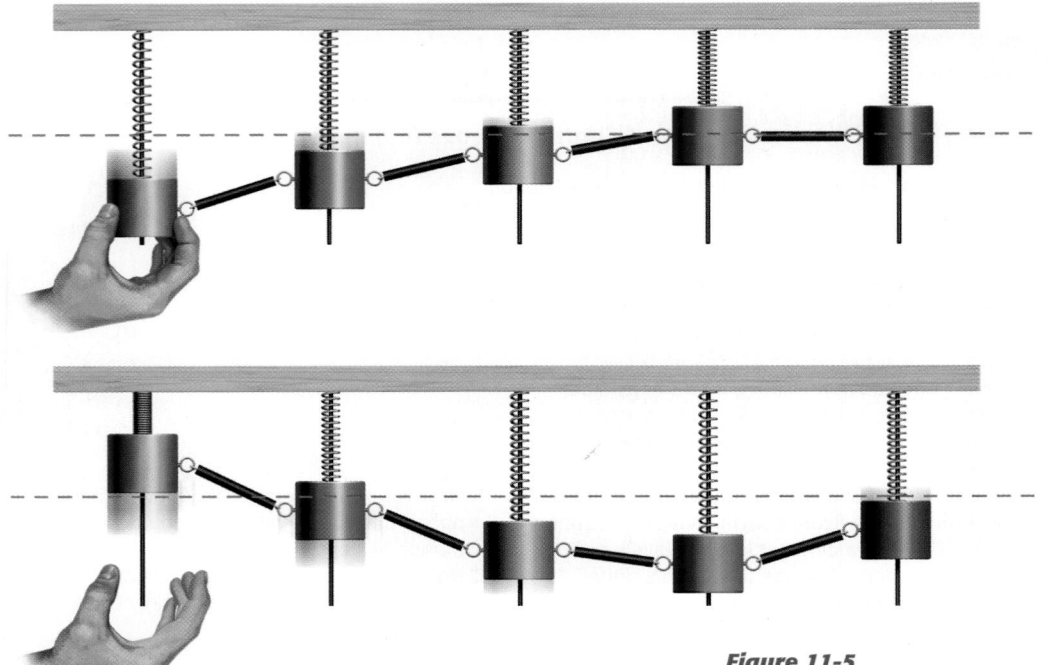

Figure 11-5
A wave can pass through a series of masses on springs. The masses act like the particles in a medium.

At every point in the motion of the mass, the spring is exerting a force that pushes it back to the original resting position. As a result, the mass could keep bouncing up and down forever. This type of vibration is called *simple harmonic motion.*

A wave can pass through a series of vibrating objects

Imagine a series of masses and springs tied together in a row, as shown in **Figure 11-5.** If you push down on a mass at the end of the row, that mass will begin to vibrate up and down. As the mass on the end moves, it pulls on the mass next to it, causing that mass to vibrate. The energy in the vibration of the first mass, which is a combination of kinetic energy and elastic potential energy, is transferred to the mass-spring system next to it. In this way, the disturbance that started with the first mass travels down the row. This disturbance is a wave that carries energy from one end of the row to the other.

If the first mass were not connected to the other masses, it would keep vibrating up and down on its own. However, because it transfers its energy to the second mass, it slows down and then returns to its resting position. A vibration that fades out as energy is transferred from one object to another is called *damped harmonic motion.*

WAVES **361**

Teaching Tip

Soundproofing Have students find out how rooms and buildings are soundproofed and what sorts of material are used. There are contractors who specialize in this work. Recording studios typically have soundproofed booths and rooms. An effective soundproofing or acoustic deadening material must be able to absorb the energy of sound waves of all frequencies. This energy is usually absorbed by mats of fibers, which move slightly and rub against each other, changing the energy of the sound wave to heat. The amount of absorbed energy is small in relation to the amount of fiber, so the mats do not get hot.

|SKILL BUILDER

Interpreting Visuals **Figure 11-5** shows a simple model of wave motion in a medium. Have students look at the top part of the figure and predict what will happen. Then look at the bottom part and see if their predictions were correct. What will happen when the wave reaches the end of the series? *(The wave will be reflected.)*

Resources Teaching Transparency 29 shows this visual.

Teaching Tip

Transverse Waves Transfer of energy by transverse mechanical waves depends on the attraction or bonds of the molecules of matter to each other, so that the motion of one particle is easily transferred to the next. This explains why transverse waves in nature occur commonly in the condensed states of matter—solid and liquid—but seldom in gases.

SKILL BUILDER

Interpreting Visuals Have students examine **Figure 11-6.** Ask students if the ribbon's position will change after the wave passes. Ask students to relate the ribbon to other examples they may have seen, such as a leaf on the surface of a pond or corks floating in the ripple tank in Demonstration 1.

RESOURCE LINK
DATASHEETS

Have students use *Datasheet 11.1 Inquiry Lab: How do particles move in a medium?* to record their results.

Inquiry Lab

How do particles move in a medium?

Materials ✔ long, flexible spring ✔ colored ribbon

Procedure

1. Have two people each grab an end of the spring and stretch it out along a smooth floor. Have another person tie a small piece of colored ribbon to a coil near the middle of the spring.
2. Swing one end of the spring from side to side. This will start a wave traveling along the spring. Observe the motion of the ribbon as the wave passes by.
3. Take a section of the spring and bunch it together as shown in the figure at right. Release the spring. This will create a different kind of wave traveling along the spring. Observe the motion of the ribbon as this wave passes by.

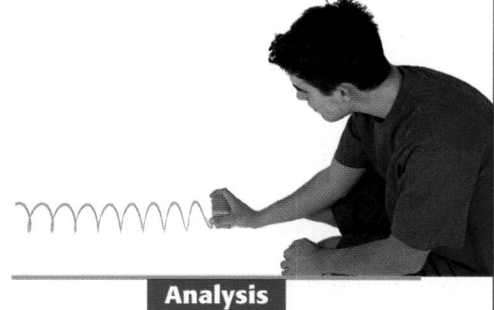

Analysis

1. How would you describe the motion of the ribbon in step 2? How would you describe its motion in step 3?
2. How can you tell that energy is passing along the spring? Where does that energy come from?

The motion of particles in a medium is like the motion of masses on springs

If you tie one end of a rope to a doorknob, pull it straight, and then rapidly move your hand up and down once, you will generate a single wave along the rope, as shown in **Figure 11-6.** A small ribbon tied to the middle of the rope can help you visualize the motion of a single particle of matter in the rope.

As the wave approaches, the ribbon moves up in the air, away from its resting position. As the wave passes farther along the rope, the ribbon drops below its resting position. Finally, after the wave passes by, the ribbon returns to its original starting point. Like the ribbon, each part of the rope moves up and down as the wave passes by.

The motion of each part of the rope is like the vibrating motion of a mass hanging on a spring. As one part of the rope moves up and down, it pulls on the part next to it, transferring energy. In this way, a wave passes along the length of the rope.

Figure 11-6
As this wave passes along a rope, the ribbon moves up and down while the wave moves to the right.

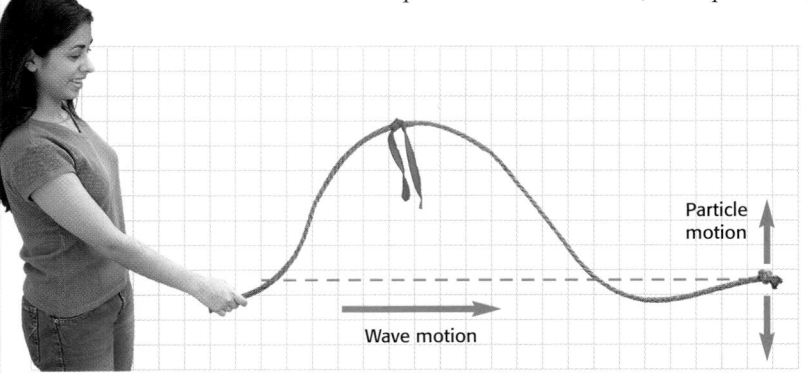

Particle motion

Wave motion

Inquiry Lab

How do particles move in a medium? Be sure students do not stretch the spring enough to permanently deform it. A metal spring toy is preferable to a plastic one.

Students should first send single wave pulses along the spring and observe the ribbon as this wave passes. In step 3, students can also make longitudinal waves by rapidly pushing and pulling on the end of the spring.

Analysis

1. Students should observe the ribbon move from the resting position to one side, to the other side, and then back to the resting position.
2. The energy was able to set matter in motion along the length of the spring. The energy came from the motion (vibration) of the hand holding the spring.

Transverse and Longitudinal Waves

Particles in a medium can vibrate either up and down or back and forth. Waves are often classified by the direction that the particles in the medium move as a wave passes by.

Transverse waves have perpendicular motion

When a crowd does "the wave" at a sporting event, people in the crowd stand up and raise their hands into the air as the wave reaches their part of the stadium. The wave travels around the stadium in a circle, but the people move straight up and down. This is similar to the wave in the rope. Each particle in the rope moves straight up and down as the wave passes by from left to right.

In these cases, the motion of the particles in the medium (in the stadium, the people in the crowd) is perpendicular to the motion of the wave as a whole. Waves in which the motion of the particles is perpendicular to the motion of the wave as a whole are called **transverse waves.**

Light waves are another example of transverse waves. The fluctuations in electric and magnetic fields that make up a light wave are perpendicular to the direction the light travels. For an illustration, see Section 14.3.

Longitudinal waves have parallel motion

Suppose you stretch out a long, flexible spring on a table or a smooth floor, grab one end, and move your hand back and forth, directly toward and directly away from the other end of the spring. You would see a wave travel along the spring as it bunches up in some spots and stretches in others, as shown in **Figure 11-7.**

As a wave passes along the spring, a ribbon tied to one of the coils of the spring will move back and forth, parallel to the direction that the wave travels. Waves that cause the particles in a medium to vibrate parallel to the direction of wave motion are called **longitudinal waves.**

Sound waves are an example of longitudinal waves that we encounter every day. Sound waves traveling in air compress and expand the air in bands. As sound waves pass by molecules in the air move backward and forward parallel to the direction that the sound travels.

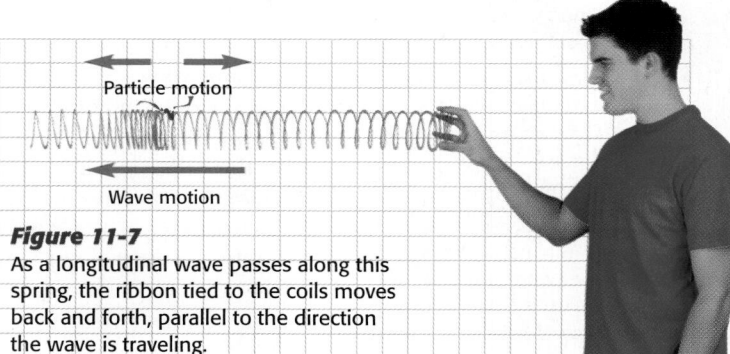

Figure 11-7
As a longitudinal wave passes along this spring, the ribbon tied to the coils moves back and forth, parallel to the direction the wave is traveling.

WAVES **363**

Teaching Tip

Longitudinal Waves Point out that longitudinal waves are often called *compression waves.* Ask students to explain why that term fits this type of wave. Repeat Demonstration 2, on page 358, and have students look again at **Figure 11-4.** Point out that the vibration of a mass on a spring is also a model of how longitudinal waves are created. As the weight moves down, the bottom surface compresses the air in front of it. As it moves up, the bottom surface "stretches" the air behind it. We don't hear this wave as sound because its frequency is much too low for human hearing.

Quick ACTIVITY

Polarization The planes of vibration of electromagnetic waves in a beam of light are oriented randomly around an axis passing along the direction of the motion of the light. A polarizing filter has tiny transparent slits that allow only electromagnetic waves of a single orientation to pass through. As a result, the light is dimmed as it passes through the filter. If two filters are placed together with the slits aligned, the second filter will not dim the light much further. If the filters are rotated so that the slits are perpendicular, almost all the light may be blocked.

DEMONSTRATION 3 TEACHING

Longitudinal Waves in Air

Time: Approximately 10 minutes
Materials: source of amplified music, such as a boom box, raw speaker about 5 inches in diameter (or a mounted speaker with an exposed cone), connecting cables

Step 1 Connect a speaker (with its cone exposed) to an amplifier. A raw, unmounted speaker is the most interesting.

Step 2 Play music and speech through the speaker and invite students to gently touch the vibrating cone. Ask students to describe what the cone is doing and how they think the speaker produces sound waves in air. Ask students what happens to the air when the speaker cone moves forward *(the cone pushes air molecules closer together, causing a compression)* and when the speaker cone moves backward *(the cone pulls air molecules farther apart, causing a rarefaction).*

Types of Waves

SECTION 11.1 REVIEW

Check Your Understanding

1. a. water
   b. air
   c. Earth's crust and interior
2. electromagnetic (light) waves
3. The mass vibrates up and down from a low point to a high point. Particles in a medium vibrate like masses on springs when a wave passes.
4. In a transverse wave, particles in the medium move back and forth at right angles to the direction the wave is moving. A wave along a rope is a transverse wave. In a longitudinal wave, particles in the medium move back and forth in the same direction the wave is moving. A sound wave is a longitudinal wave.
5. The wave causes the molecule to move up and down as well as forward and backward at the same time. This combination causes the molecule to move in a circular path.
6. Answers will vary. Students should cite any instance in which waves move objects from their positions. Examples include tsunamis, beach erosion during storms, and waves destroying waterfront buildings in a hurricane.

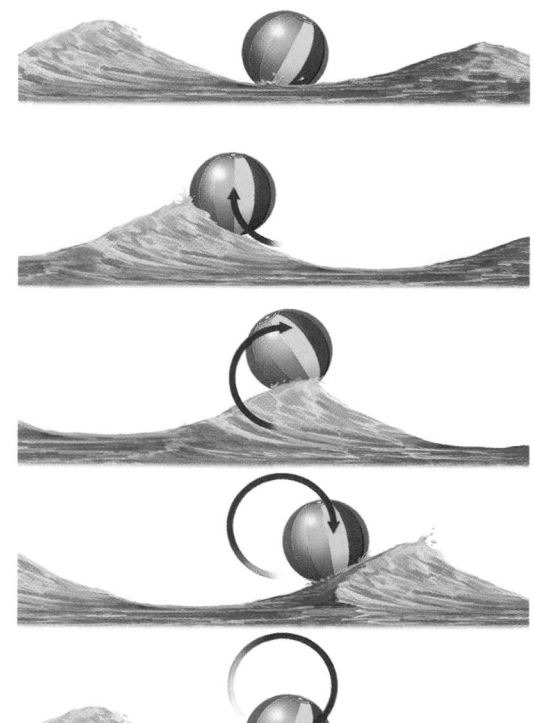

In a surface wave, particles move in circles

Waves on the ocean or in a swimming pool are not simply transverse waves or longitudinal waves. Water waves are an example of *surface waves*. Surface waves occur at the boundary between two different mediums, such as between water and air. The particles in a surface wave move both perpendicularly and parallel to the direction that the wave travels.

Follow the motion of the beach ball in **Figure 11-8** as a wave passes by traveling from left to right. At first, the ball is in a trough. As the crest approaches, the ball moves to the left and upward. When the ball is very near the crest, it starts to move to the right. Once the crest has passed, the ball starts to fall back downward, then to the left. The up and down motions combine with the side to side motions to produce a circular motion overall.

The beach ball helps to make the motion of the wave more visible. Particles near the surface of the water also move in a similar circular pattern.

Figure 11-8
Ocean waves are surface waves at the boundary between air and water.

SECTION 11.1 REVIEW

SUMMARY

▶ A wave is a disturbance that carries energy through a medium or through space.

▶ Mechanical waves require a medium through which to travel. Light waves, also called electromagnetic waves, do not require a medium.

▶ Particles in a medium may vibrate perpendicularly to or parallel to the direction a wave is traveling.

CHECK YOUR UNDERSTANDING

1. **Identify** the medium for the following waves:
   a. ripples on a pond
   b. the sound waves from a stereo speaker
   c. seismic waves
2. **Name** the one kind of wave that does not require a medium.
3. **Describe** the motion of a mass vibrating on a spring. How does this relate to wave motion?
4. **Explain** the difference between transverse waves and longitudinal waves. Give an example of each type.
5. **Describe** the motion of a water molecule on the surface of the ocean as a wave passes by.
6. **Critical Thinking** Describe a situation that demonstrates that water waves carry energy.

ALTERNATIVE ASSESSMENT

Transverse and Longitudinal Waves

Step 1 Ask students to draw diagrams that model transverse and longitudinal waves.

Step 2 Have students draw lines between the two kinds of waves connecting corresponding parts (crest = compression, trough = rarefaction).

Step 3 Students should then describe the motion of the medium as each type of wave passes through it.

11.2

Characteristics of Waves

OBJECTIVES

▶ Identify the crest, trough, amplitude, and wavelength of a wave.
▶ Define the terms *frequency* and *period*.
▶ Solve problems involving wave speed, frequency, and wavelength.
▶ Describe the Doppler effect.

KEY TERMS

crest
trough
amplitude
wavelength
period
frequency
wave speed
Doppler effect

I f you have spent any time at the beach or on a boat, you have probably observed many properties of waves. Sometimes the waves are very large; other times they are smaller. Sometimes they are close together, and sometimes they are farther apart. How can these differences be described and measured in more detail?

Wave Properties

All transverse waves have somewhat similar shapes, no matter how big they are or what medium they travel through. An ideal transverse wave has the shape of a *sine curve*, such as the curve on the graph in **Figure 11-9A.** A sine curve looks like an S lying on its side. Sine curves can be used to represent waves and to describe their properties.

Waves that have the shape of a sine curve, such as those on the rope in **Figure 11-9B,** are called *sine waves*. Although many waves, such as water waves, are not ideal sine waves, they can still be modeled with the graph of a sine curve.

Figure 11-9

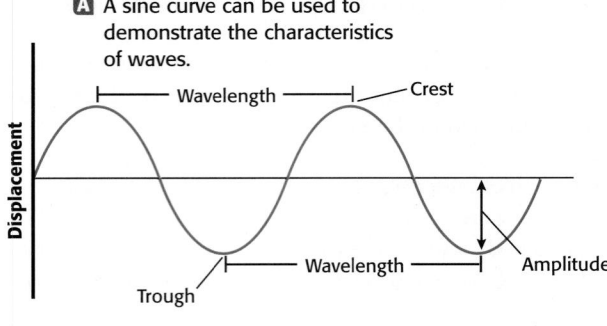

A A sine curve can be used to demonstrate the characteristics of waves.

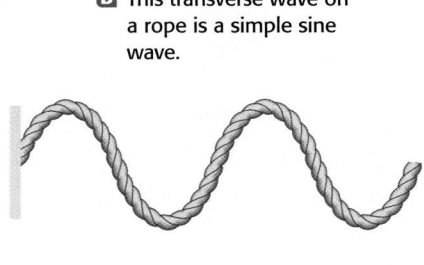

B This transverse wave on a rope is a simple sine wave.

WAVES **365**

Section 11.2

Characteristics of Waves

Scheduling
Refer to pp. 354A–354D for lecture, classwork, and assignment options for Section 11.2.

★ **Lesson Focus**
Use transparency *LT 37* to prepare students for this section.

READING SKILL BUILDER *Reading Organizer* Have students read Section 11.2 and add to their table, *Properties of Waves,* from page 356. Information in the table may vary slightly for each student.

|SKILL BUILDER
Vocabulary Ask students to define the word *sinuous* and give examples of things that are described as sinuous, such as climbing vines and snakes. Both sinuous and sine are derived from the Latin *sinus,* which means "curve." It can also mean "hollow," as in the nasal sinus cavities.

|SKILL BUILDER
Interpreting Diagrams
Have students identify the crests and the troughs in **Figure 11-9A,** and have them indicate where wavelength and amplitude can be measured.

Resources Blackline Master 30 shows this visual.

Properties of Waves

Type of wave	Mechanical		Electromagnetic
Form	*Longitudinal*	*Transverse*	*Modeled as transverse*
Description	*Compressions and rarefactions of matter*	*Sine-wave-shaped movement of matter*	*Oscillating electric and magnetic fields*
Measure of wavelength	*Distance between two successive compressions or rarefactions*	*Distance between two successive crests or troughs*	*Distance between two successive crests or troughs*
Measure of amplitude	*Difference in pressure between maximum compression and the resting state of matter*	*Difference in height between a crest and the resting state of matter*	*Modeled as the difference between maximum field strength and zero*

365

Characteristics of Waves

MISCONCEPTION ALERT

Representing Sound Waves
Students often see sound waves and electrical signals represented as transverse waves. In fact, neither is a transverse wave, but sine curves can represent sound waves in a useful way. Ask students to suppose they needed to represent several different sound waves on paper. Would it be better to depict longitudinal waves, as in **Figure 11-10A,** or sine waves, as in **Figure 11-10B?**

Teaching Tip

Period and Wavelength
Demonstrate differences in period and wavelength with the ripple tank from Demonstration 1. Varying the frequency of vibration of the dowel will produce waves of varying wavelength and period.

366

▶ **crest** the highest point of a transverse wave

▶ **trough** the lowest point of a transverse wave

▶ **amplitude** the greatest distance that particles in a medium move from their normal position when a wave passes

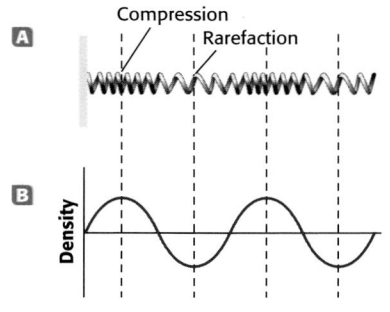

Figure 11-10
(A) A longitudinal wave has compressions and rarefactions. (B) The high and low points of this sine curve correspond to compressions and rarefactions in the spring.

▶ **wavelength** the distance between any two successive identical parts of a wave

PHYSICAL SCIENCE INTERACTIVE TUTOR

Disc Two, Module 12:
Frequency and Wavelength
Use the Interactive Tutor to learn more about these topics.

Amplitude measures the amount of particle vibration

The highest points of a transverse wave are called **crests.** The lowest parts of a transverse wave are called **troughs.** The greatest distance that particles are displaced from their normal resting positions because of a wave is called the **amplitude.** The amplitude is also half the vertical distance between a crest and a trough. Larger waves have bigger amplitudes and carry more energy.

But what about longitudinal waves? These waves do not have crests and troughs because they cause particles to move back and forth instead of up and down. If you make a longitudinal wave in a spring, you will see a moving pattern of areas where the coils are bunched up alternating with areas where the coils are stretched out. The crowded areas are called *compressions.* The stretched-out areas are called *rarefactions.* **Figure 11-10A** illustrates these properties of a longitudinal wave.

Figure 11-10B shows a graph of a longitudinal wave. Density or pressure of the medium is plotted on the vertical axis; the horizontal axis represents the distance along the spring. The resulting curve is a sine curve. The amplitude of a longitudinal wave is the maximum deviation from the normal density or pressure of the medium, which is shown by the high and low points on the graph.

Wavelength measures the distance between two equivalent parts of a wave

Waves crashing on the shore at a beach may be several meters apart, while ripples in a pond may be only a few centimeters apart. Crests of a light wave may be separated by only billionths of a meter.

The distance from one crest of a wave to the next crest, or from one trough to the next trough, is called the **wavelength.** In a longitudinal wave, the wavelength is the distance between two compressions or between two rarefactions. The wavelength is the measure of the distance between any two successive identical parts of a wave.

When used in equations, wavelength is represented by the Greek letter lambda, λ. Because wavelength is a distance measurement, it is expressed in the SI unit meters.

The period measures how long it takes for waves to pass by

If you swim out into the ocean until your feet can no longer touch the bottom, your body will be free to move up and down as waves come into shore. As your body rises and falls, you can count off the number of seconds between two successive waves.

The time required for one full wavelength of a wave to pass a certain point is called the **period** of the wave. The period is also the time required for one complete vibration of a particle in a medium—or of a swimmer in the ocean. In equations, the period is represented by the symbol T. Because the period is a time measurement, it is expressed in the SI unit seconds.

Frequency measures the rate of vibrations

While swimming in the ocean or floating in an inner tube, as shown in **Figure 11-11**, you could also count the number of crests that pass by in a certain time, say in 1 minute. The **frequency** of a wave is the number of full wavelengths that pass a point in a given time interval. The frequency of a wave also measures how rapidly vibrations occur in the medium, at the source of the wave, or both.

The symbol for frequency is f. The SI unit for measuring frequency is hertz (Hz), named after Heinrich Hertz, who in 1888 became the first person to experimentally demonstrate electromagnetic waves. Hertz units measure the number of vibrations per second. One vibration per second is 1 Hz, two vibrations per second is 2 Hz, and so on. You can hear sounds with frequencies as low as 20 Hz and as high as 20 000 Hz. When you hear a sound at 20 000 Hz, there are 20 000 compressions hitting your ear every second.

The frequency and period of a wave are related. If more vibrations are made in a second, each one takes a shorter amount of time. In other words, the frequency is the inverse of the period.

Frequency-Period Equation

$$frequency = \frac{1}{period} \qquad f = \frac{1}{T}$$

In the inner tube example, a wave crest passes the inner tube every 2 s, so the period is 2 s. The frequency can be found by dividing the number of crests in a 4 s time interval by 4 s. Because 2 waves pass every 4 s, the frequency is 0.5 Hz, or half a wave per second. Note that 0.5 (1/2) is the inverse of 2.

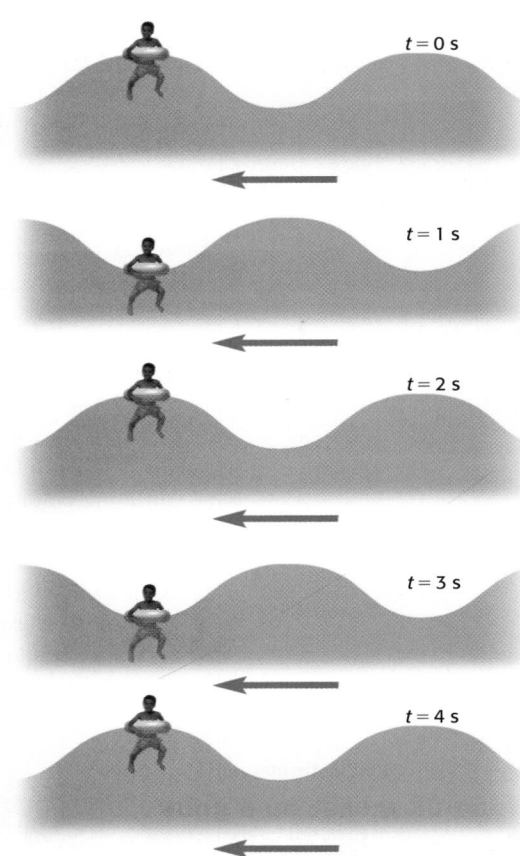

$t = 0$ s

$t = 1$ s

$t = 2$ s

$t = 3$ s

$t = 4$ s

Figure 11-11
A person floating in an inner tube can determine the period and frequency of the waves by counting off the number of seconds between wave crests.

▶ **period** the time required for one full wavelength to pass a certain point

▶ **frequency** the number of vibrations that occur in a 1 s time interval

WAVES **367**

Characteristics of Waves

Teaching Tip

Frequency One wave every 5 s or more is the equivalent of 0.2 waves per second. Point out that there is no such thing as 0.2 waves, but wave frequencies are always expressed as waves per second, or Hz.

Additional Application

Period and Frequency To help students understand the inverse relationship between wave period and wave frequency, try this analogy. Suppose you are at a railroad crossing waiting for a freight train to pass. All of the boxcars are the same length, and you find that 120 cars pass in 5.0 minutes. Calculate the period and frequency at which the cars pass. ($T = 2.5$ s/car; $f = 0.4$ Hz)

|SKILL| BUILDER

Interpreting Visuals **Figure 11-11** shows a boy floating in an innertube as waves pass by. Each successive image is one second later than the previous image. Have students determine the frequency and period of these waves. ($T = 2$ s; $f = 0.5$ Hz)

Resources Teaching Transparency 31 shows this visual.

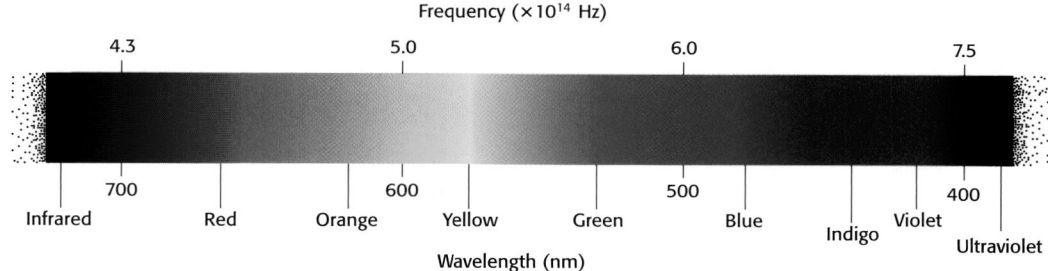

Figure 11-12
The part of the electromagnetic spectrum that we can see is called visible light.

MISCONCEPTION ALERT
Visible Light
Help students understand that visible light has no special properties when compared to other electromagnetic waves. In addition, visible light makes up only a tiny fraction of the entire electromagnetic spectrum.

SKILL BUILDER
Interpreting Visuals Have students examine **Figure 11-12.** Ask students to formulate a general statement comparing the wavelengths and frequencies at the red and violet extremes of the visible spectrum. They should observe that the radiation at the violet end of the spectrum has the shortest wavelengths and the highest frequencies. Radiation at the red end has the longest wavelengths and the lowest frequencies.

Resources Teaching Transparency 32 shows this visual.

SKILL BUILDER
Interpreting Data **Table 11-1** shows the ranges of the different parts of the electromagnetic spectrum. Point out that the range for visible light is very small compared to some of the other ranges. Also point out that as frequency increases, wavelength decreases.

Resources Blackline Master 32 shows this table.

RESOURCE LINK
IER
Assign students worksheet *11.5: Integrating Computers and Technology—Radio Waves* as an extension exercise.

Light comes in a wide range of frequencies and wavelengths
Our eyes can detect light with frequencies ranging from 4.3×10^{14} Hz to 7.5×10^{14} Hz. Light in this range is called *visible light.* The differences in frequency in visible light account for the different colors we see, as shown in **Figure 11-12.**

Electromagnetic waves also exist at other frequencies that we cannot see directly. The full range of light at different frequencies and wavelengths is called the *electromagnetic spectrum.* **Table 11-1** lists several different parts of the electromagnetic spectrum, along with some real-world applications of the different kinds of waves.

Table 11-1 **The Electromagnetic Spectrum**

Type of waves	Range of frequency and wavelength	Applications
Radio waves	$f < 1 \times 10^9$ Hz $\lambda > 30$ cm	AM and FM radio; television broadcasting; radar; aircraft navigation
Microwaves	1×10^9 Hz $< f < 3 \times 10^{11}$ Hz 30 cm $> \lambda > 1$ mm	Atomic and molecular research; microwave ovens
Infrared (IR) waves	3×10^{11} Hz $< f < 4.3 \times 10^{14}$ Hz 1 mm $> \lambda > 700$ nm	Infrared photography; physical therapy; heat radiation
Visible light	4.3×10^{14} Hz $< f < 7.5 \times 10^{14}$ Hz 700 nm (red) $> \lambda > 400$ nm (violet)	Visible-light photography; optical microscopes; optical telescopes
Ultraviolet (UV) light	7.5×10^{14} Hz $< f < 5 \times 10^{15}$ Hz 400 nm $> \lambda > 60$ nm	Sterilizing medical instruments; identifying fluorescent minerals
X rays	5×10^{15} Hz $< f < 3 \times 10^{21}$ Hz 60 nm $> \lambda > 1 \times 10^{-4}$ nm	Medical examination of bones, teeth, and organs; cancer treatments
Gamma rays	3×10^{18} Hz $< f < 3 \times 10^{22}$ Hz 0.1 nm $> \lambda > 1 \times 10^{-5}$ nm	Food irradiation; studies of structural flaws in thick materials

368 CHAPTER 11

Wave Speed

Imagine watching as water waves move past a post at a dock such as the one in **Figure 11-13.** If you count the number of crests passing the post for 10 s, you can determine the frequency of the waves by dividing the number of crests you count by 10 s. If you measure the distance between crests, you can find the wavelength of the wave. But how fast are the water waves moving?

Wave speed equals frequency times wavelength

In Chapter 8, you learned that the speed of a moving object is found by dividing the distance an object travels by the time interval during which it travels that distance. Recall the speed equation from Section 8.1.

$$speed = \frac{distance}{time}$$

$$v = \frac{d}{t}$$

The **wave speed** is simply how fast a wave moves. Finding the speed of a wave is just like finding the speed of a moving object. You need to measure how far a wave travels in a certain amount of time.

For a wave, it is most convenient to use the wavelength as the distance traveled. The amount of time it takes the wave to travel a distance of one wavelength is the period. Substituting these into the speed equation gives an equation that can be used to calculate the speed of a wave.

$$speed = \frac{wavelength}{period}$$

$$v = \frac{\lambda}{T}$$

Because the period is the inverse of the frequency, dividing by the period is equivalent to multiplying by the frequency. Therefore, the speed of a wave can also be calculated by multiplying the wavelength by the frequency.

Wave Speed Equation

$$wave\ speed = frequency \times wavelength$$

$$v = f \times \lambda$$

Suppose that waves passing by a post at a dock have a wavelength of 5 m, and two waves pass by in 10 s. In other words, 10 m of wave pass by in 10 s. Each second 1 m of the wave passes by the post. The waves in this case travel with a wave speed of 1 m/s.

Figure 11-13
By observing the frequency and wavelength of waves passing a dock, you can calculate the speed of the waves.

▶ **wave speed** the speed at which a wave passes through a medium

INTEGRATING

EARTH SCIENCE
Earthquakes create waves, called *seismic waves,* that travel through Earth. There are two main types of seismic waves, *P waves* (primary waves) and *S waves* (secondary waves).

P waves travel faster than S waves, so the P waves arrive at a given location first. P waves are longitudinal waves that tend to shake the ground from side to side.

S waves move more slowly than P waves but also carry more energy. S waves are transverse waves that shake the ground up and down, often damaging buildings and roads.

INTEGRATING

EARTH SCIENCE   P waves and S waves travel through Earth from the focus of an earthquake. In addition, earthquakes produce L waves and R waves. L waves are up-and-down transverse waves that travel along Earth's surface. R waves are side-to-side transverse waves that also travel along Earth's surface.

Resources   Assign students worksheet *11.3: Integrating Earth Science—Earthquake Waves* from the **Integration Enrichment Resources** ancillary.

Teaching Tip

Wave Speed   Use the ripple tank from Demonstration 1 to show differences in wave speed. Adjust the water depth for the best effect.

The speed of water waves changes in shallow water. Place a block with a large horizontal surface in the tank so that it is submerged less than 1 cm. Students will observe that the ripples change speed as they pass over the block.

WAVES   **369**

Characteristics of Waves

Math Skills

Resources Assign students worksheet *25: Wave Speed* in the **Math Skills Worksheets** ancillary.

Additional Examples

Wave Speed The speed of sound in dry, desert air at 40°C is 355 m/s. The speed at 0°C is 331 m/s. Will a sound of a given frequency have a longer or shorter wavelength at 40°C than at 0°C? Explain.

Answer: longer; the waves will be farther apart because the speed is greater.

Calculate the frequency of microwaves that have a wavelength of 0.0085 m and a speed of 3.00×10^8 m/s.

Answer: 3.5×10^{10} Hz

The speed of sound in sea water is 1530 m/s at 25°C. A sonar device emits a pulse of sound of 922 Hz. What is the wavelength of sound at this frequency in sea water? If an echo from the sonar device returns 4.76 s after the pulse is sent, how deep is the object that reflected the sonar?

Answer: 1.66 m; 3640 m in depth (using one-half the total travel time for *t*)

Practice HINT

▶ When a problem requires you to calculate wave speed, you can use the wave speed equation on the previous page.

▶ The wave speed equation can also be rearranged to isolate frequency on the left in the following way:

$$v = f \times \lambda$$

Divide both sides by λ.

$$\frac{v}{\lambda} = \frac{f \times \cancel{\lambda}}{\cancel{\lambda}}$$

$$f = \frac{v}{\lambda}$$

You will need to use this form of the equation in Practice Problem 3.

▶ In Practice Problem 4, you will need to rearrange the equation to isolate wavelength on the left.

Math Skills

Wave Speed The string of a piano that produces the note middle C vibrates with a frequency of 264 Hz. If the sound waves produced by this string have a wavelength in air of 1.30 m, what is the speed of sound in air?

1 List the given and unknown values.
　　Given: *frequency, f* = 264 Hz
　　　　　wavelength, λ = 1.30 m
　　Unknown: *wave speed, v* = ? m/s

2 Write the equation for wave speed.
　　$v = f \times \lambda$

3 Insert the known values into the equation, and solve.
　　$v = 264 \text{ Hz} \times 1.30 \text{ m} = 264 \text{ s}^{-1} \times 1.30 \text{ m}$
　　$v = 343$ m/s

Practice

Wave Speed

1. The average wavelength in a series of ocean waves is 15.0 m. A wave arrives on average every 10.0 s, so the frequency is 0.100 Hz. What is the average speed of the waves?

2. An FM radio station broadcasts electromagnetic waves at a frequency of 94.5 MHz (9.45×10^7 Hz). These radio waves have a wavelength of 3.17 m. What is the speed of the waves?

3. Green light has a wavelength of 5.20×10^{-7} m. The speed of light is 3.00×10^8 m/s. Calculate the frequency of green light waves with this wavelength.

4. The speed of sound in air is about 340 m/s. What is the wavelength of a sound wave with a frequency of 220 Hz (on a piano, the A below middle C)?

The speed of a wave depends on the medium

Sound waves travel through air. If they didn't, you wouldn't be able to have a conversation with a friend or hear music from a radio across the room. Because sound travels very fast, you don't notice a time delay in most normal situations. The speed of sound in air is about 340 m/s.

If you swim with your head underwater, you may hear certain sounds very clearly. Sound waves travel better—and three to four times faster—in water than in air. Dolphins, such as those in **Figure 11-14,** use sound waves to communicate with one another over long distances underwater. Sound waves travel even faster in solids than in air or in water. Sound waves have speeds 15 to 20 times faster in rock or metal than in air.

370 CHAPTER 11

Solution Guide

1. $v = f \times \lambda$
　$v = 0.100 \text{ Hz} \times 15.0 \text{ m} = 1.50$ m/s

2. $v = f \times \lambda$
　$v = (9.45 \times 10^7 \text{ Hz})(3.17 \text{ m}) = 3.00 \times 10^8$ m/s

3. $f = \dfrac{v}{\lambda}$
　$f = \dfrac{3.00 \times 10^8 \text{ m/s}}{5.20 \times 10^{-7} \text{ m}} = 5.77 \times 10^{14}$ Hz

4. $\lambda = \dfrac{v}{f}$
　$\lambda = \dfrac{340 \text{ m/s}}{220 \text{ Hz}} = 1.5$ m

If someone strikes a long steel rail with a hammer at one end and you listen for the sound at the other end, you might hear two bangs. The first sound comes through the steel rail itself and reaches you shortly before the second sound, which travels through the air.

The speed of a wave depends on the medium. In a given medium, though, the speed of waves is constant. No matter how fast you shake your hand up and down to create waves on a rope, the waves will travel the same speed. Shaking your hand faster just increases the frequency and decreases the wavelength.

Kinetic theory explains differences in wave speed

The arrangement of particles in a medium determines how well waves travel through it. As you learned in Chapter 2, the different states of matter are due to different degrees of organization at the particle level.

In gases, the molecules are far apart and move around randomly. A molecule must travel through a lot of empty space before it bumps into another molecule. Waves don't travel as fast in gases.

In liquids, such as water, the molecules are much closer together. But they are also free to slide past one another. As a result, vibrations are transferred more quickly from one molecule to the next than they are in a gas. This situation can be compared to vibrating masses on springs that are so close together that the masses rub against each other.

In a solid, molecules are not only closer together but also tightly bound to each other. The effect is like having vibrating masses that are glued together. When one mass starts to vibrate, all the others start to vibrate almost immediately. As a result, waves travel very quickly through solids.

Light has a finite speed

When you flip a light switch, light seems to fill the room instantly. However, light does take time to travel from place to place. All electromagnetic waves in empty space travel at the same speed, the speed of light, which is 3×10^8 m/s (186 000 mi/s). The speed of light constant is often represented by the symbol c. Light travels slower when it has to pass through a medium such as air or water.

Figure 11-14
Dolphins use sound waves to communicate with one another. Sound travels three to four times faster in water than in air.

Quick ACTIVITY

Wave Speed
1. Place a rectangular pan on a level surface, and fill the pan with water to a depth of about 2 cm.
2. Cut a wooden dowel (3 cm in diameter or thicker) to a length slightly less than the width of the pan, and place the dowel in one end of the pan.
3. Move the dowel slowly back and forth, and observe the length of the wave generated.
4. Now roll the dowel back and forth faster (increased frequency). How does that affect the wavelength?
5. Do the waves always travel the same speed in the pan?

WAVES **371**

Characteristics of Waves

Teaching Tip

Elasticity and Sound Transmission The speed of sound in a material depends on the elasticity of the material. Elasticity is the tendency of a material to restore itself or "bounce back" after being deformed by an external force. A sound wave is a compression wave, so it is reasonable that a material that quickly bounces back from a compression can transmit sound at a high velocity.

Very elastic materials include steel, glass, and aluminum. Lead, on the other hand, is very inelastic by comparison because it deforms semi-permanently rather than bouncing back. The speed of sound in lead is about one-third of the speed of sound in steel. Materials thought of as elastic, such as rubber, actually have relatively poor elasticity. Materials such as dough and modeling clay are very inelastic.

MISCONCEPTION ALERT

Speed of Light Reinforce the idea that light requires no medium for transmission. It does, however, interact with matter that it passes through by slowing down somewhat, depending on the material. For example, light slows down from 3.00×10^8 m/s to around 2.25×10^8 m/s when it enters water. The speed of light in diamond is only about 40 percent the speed of light in air.

Quick ACTIVITY

Wave Speed You may also use the setup for Demonstration 1. Students should observe that the velocity of the waves stays the same because it is determined by the medium. Waves of higher frequency will have shorter wavelengths, and waves of lower frequency will have longer wavelengths.

RESOURCE LINK
DATASHEETS

Have students use *Datasheet 11.3 Quick Activity: Wave Speed* to record their results.

The Doppler Effect Ask students to relate experiences in which they heard the Doppler effect, such as along highways, at airports, or near railroad tracks. Ask students to explain the characteristic sound that allows you to identify an auto race on TV, even if you can't see the picture. Consider having students use an audio recorder or a video camera to record examples of the Doppler effect. Reinforce the idea that the pitch of sound you hear depends entirely on the frequency at which compressions strike the eardrum, even if the source of vibration is at a higher or lower frequency. Emphasize that the frequency of vibration of the sound source remains constant. However, the waves are pushed closer together ahead of the moving vehicle and stretched farther apart behind it. Stress the point that the speed of the waves does not change; it is determined by the nature of the medium.

MISCONCEPTION ALERT

Ambulance Siren
Point out that the siren sound does not become noticeably higher as the ambulance approaches. It will be high when it is first heard. The only observable change in pitch occurs as the sound source passes.

The Doppler Effect

Imagine that you are standing on a corner as an ambulance rushes by. As the ambulance passes, the sound of the siren changes from a high pitch to a lower pitch. Why? Do the sound waves produced by the siren change as the ambulance goes by? How does the motion of the ambulance affect the sound?

Pitch is determined by the frequency of sound waves

The *pitch* of a sound, how high or low it is, is determined by the frequency at which sound waves strike the eardrum in your ear. A higher-pitched sound is caused by sound waves of higher frequency. As you know from the wave speed equation, frequency and wavelength are also related to the speed of a wave.

Suppose you could see the sound waves from the ambulance siren when the ambulance is at rest. You would see the sound waves traveling out from the siren in circular wave fronts, as shown in **Figure 11-15A.** The distance between two successive wave fronts shows the wavelength of the sound waves. When the sound waves reach your ears, they have a frequency equal to the number of wave fronts that strike your eardrum each second. That frequency determines the pitch of the sound that you hear.

Figure 11-15

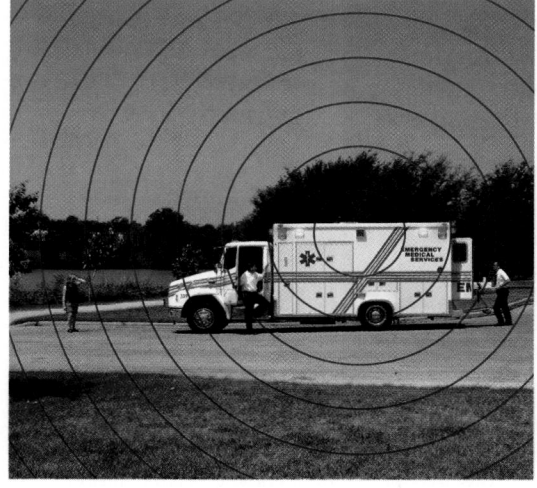

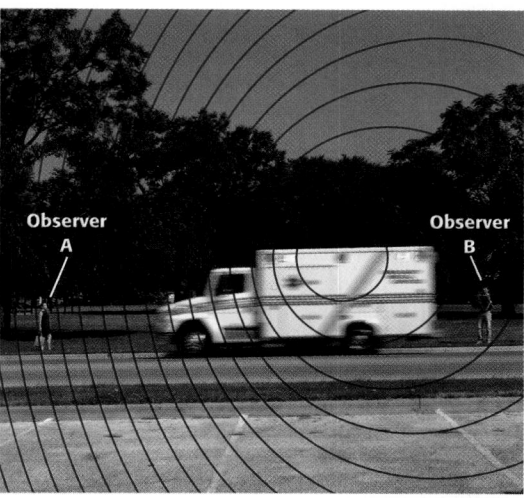

A When an ambulance is not moving, the sound waves produced by the siren spread out in circles. The frequency of the waves is the same at any location.

B When an ambulance is moving, the sound waves produced by the siren are closer together in front and farther apart behind. Observer A hears a higher-pitched sound than Observer B hears.

DEMONSTRATION 5 TEACHING

Doppler Effect

Time: Approximately 5 minutes
Materials: strong mesh bag
battery-powered alarm
clock
1 m of heavy cord

Step 1 Adjust the clock to start the alarm. Place the clock in a mesh bag tied securely to a sturdy cord about 1 m long.

Step 2 Swing the bag containing the clock in a circle over your head. To hear the changes in pitch, students should stand just below the plane of the circle. Do not allow students to stand in the plane in case the bag or cord should break. If necessary, add mass to the bag to slow the circular motion.

Frequency changes when the source of waves is moving

If the ambulance is moving toward you, the sound waves from the siren are compressed in the direction of motion, as shown in **Figure 11-15B.** Between the time that one sound wave and the next sound wave are emitted by the siren, the ambulance moves a short distance. This shortens the distance between successive wave fronts. As a result, the sound waves reach your ear at a faster rate, that is, at a higher frequency.

Because the waves now have a higher frequency, you hear a higher-pitched sound than you would if the ambulance were at rest. Similarly, if the ambulance were moving away from you, the frequency at which the waves reached your ear would be less than if the ambulance were at rest, and you would hear the sound of the siren at a lower pitch. This change in the observed frequency of a wave resulting from the motion of the source or observer is called the **Doppler effect.** The Doppler effect occurs for light and other types of waves as well.

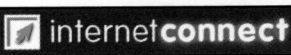

internetconnect

SCI**LINKS.**
NSTA

TOPIC: Doppler effect
GO TO: www.scilinks.org
KEYWORD: HK1114

▶ **Doppler effect** an observed change in the frequency of a wave when the source or observer is moving

---

SECTION 11.2 REVIEW

SUMMARY

▶ The highest points of a transverse wave are called crests; the lowest parts are called troughs.

▶ The amplitude of a transverse wave is half the vertical distance between a crest and a trough.

▶ The wavelength is the distance between two successive identical parts of a wave.

▶ The period of a wave is the time it takes a wavelength to pass a certain point.

▶ The frequency of a wave is the number of vibrations that occur in 1 s. (1 Hz = 1 vibration/s)

▶ The speed of a wave equals the frequency times the wavelength. ($v = f \times \lambda$)

CHECK YOUR UNDERSTANDING

1. **Draw** a sine curve, and label a crest, a trough, and the amplitude.
2. **State** the SI units used for wavelength, period, frequency, and wave speed.
3. **Describe** how the frequency and period of a wave are related.
4. **Explain** why sound waves travel faster in liquids or solids than in air.
5. **Critical Thinking** What happens to the wavelength of a wave when the frequency of the wave is doubled but the wave speed stays the same?
6. **Critical Thinking** Imagine you are waiting for a train to pass at a railroad crossing. Will the train whistle have a higher pitch as the train approaches you or after it has passed you by?

Math Skills

7. A wave along a guitar string has a frequency of 440 Hz and a wavelength of 1.5 m. What is the speed of the wave?
8. The speed of sound in air is about 340 m/s. What is the wavelength of sound waves produced by a guitar string vibrating at 440 Hz?
9. The speed of light is 3×10^8 m/s. What is the frequency of microwaves with a wavelength of 1 cm?

WAVES **373**

Section 11.2

Characteristics of Waves

SECTION 11.2 REVIEW

Check Your Understanding

1. Students drawings should resemble **Figure 11-9A.**
2. wavelength, m
   period, s
   frequency, Hz
   speed, m/s
3. Frequency and period are the inverse of each other.
4. Sound travels faster in liquids and solids because the particles of the medium are closer together than particles in air.
5. The wavelength is halved.
6. The pitch will sound higher as the train approaches and will become lower as the whistle passes.

Math Skills

7. $v = f \times \lambda$
   $v = (440 \text{ Hz})\,(1.5 \text{ m}) = 660 \text{ m/s}$

8. $\lambda = \dfrac{v}{f}$
   $\lambda = \dfrac{340 \text{ m/s}}{440 \text{ Hz}} = 0.77 \text{ m}$

9. $f = \dfrac{v}{\lambda}$
   $f = \dfrac{3 \times 10^8 \text{ m/s}}{0.01 \text{ m}}$
   $f = 3 \times 10^{10} \text{ Hz}$

ALTERNATIVE ASSESSMENT

Sound Wave

Have students draw examples of two transverse waves, making the second wave have a higher frequency and lower amplitude than the first. Ask students to label wavelength and amplitude on the two waves. Ask students to explain the nature of a sound wave and how it travels through matter (*as compressions and rarefactions*). Ask them what measure constitutes wavelength in a sound wave (*distance between compressions or rarefactions*).

RESOURCE LINK
STUDY GUIDE

Assign students *Review Section 11.2 Characteristics of Waves.*

11.3

Scheduling

Refer to pp. 354A–354D for lecture, classwork, and assignment options for Section 11.3.

★ **Lesson Focus**
Use transparency *LT 38* to prepare students for this section.

READING SKILL BUILDER *Summarizing* Have students read the material on reflection, diffraction, and refraction, one topic at a time. After each topic, ask for volunteers to summarize each phenomenon, giving particular attention to what happens to the waves and the conditions that are necessary to make this happen.

MISCONCEPTION ALERT
Electromagnetic Waves Mechanical waves will always spread out from a source into the available medium. However, spreading out is not an inherent property of electromagnetic waves. If light waves are given out from a point source in space, they will travel in all directions. But light waves can also be focused into a beam that does not spread out. For example, a laser beam consists of light waves traveling parallel to each other and not spreading out.

Wave Interactions

▶ **KEY TERMS**
reflection
diffraction
refraction
interference
constructive interference
destructive interference
standing wave

Disc Two, Module 13: **Reflection**
Use the Interactive Tutor to learn more about this topic.

▶ **reflection** the bouncing back of a wave as it meets a surface or boundary

OBJECTIVES

▶ Describe how waves behave when they meet an obstacle, pass into another medium, or pass through another wave.
▶ Explain what happens when two waves interfere.
▶ Distinguish between constructive interference and destructive interference.
▶ Explain how standing waves are formed.

When waves are simply moving through a medium or through space, they may move in straight lines like waves on the ocean, spread out in circles like ripples on a pond, or spread out in spheres like sound waves in air. But what happens when a wave meets an object or another wave in the medium? And what happens when a wave passes into another medium?

Reflection, Diffraction, and Refraction

You probably already know what happens when light waves strike a shiny surface: they reflect off the surface. Other waves reflect, too. **Figure 11-16** shows two ways that a wave on a rope may be reflected. **Reflection** is simply the bouncing back of a wave when it meets a surface or boundary.

Figure 11-16
(A) If the end of a rope is free to slide up and down a post, a wave on the rope will reflect from the end. (B) If the end of the rope is fixed, the reflected wave is turned upside down.

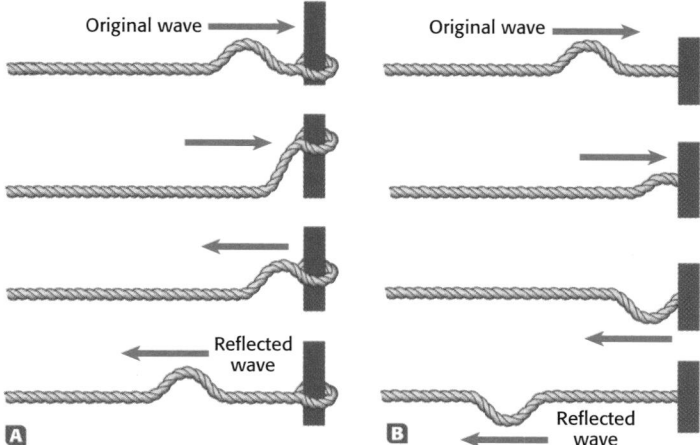

Waves reflect at a free boundary

Figure 11-16A shows the reflection of a single wave traveling on a rope. The end of the rope is free to move up and down on a post. When the wave reaches the post, the loop on the end moves up and then back down. This is just what would happen if someone were shaking that end of the rope to create a new wave. The reflected wave in this case is exactly like the original wave.

At a fixed boundary, waves reflect and turn upside down

Figure 11-16B shows a slightly different situation. In this case, the end of the rope is not free to move because it is attached to a wall. When the wave reaches the wall, the rope exerts an upward force on the wall. The wall is too heavy to move, but it exerts an equal and opposite downward force on the rope, following Newton's third law. The force exerted by the wall causes another wave to start traveling down the rope. This reflected wave is like the original wave, but it is turned upside down and travels in the opposite direction.

Diffraction is the bending of waves around an edge

If you stand outside the doorway of a classroom, you may be able to hear the sound of voices inside the room. But if the sound waves cannot travel in a straight line to your ear, how are you able to hear the voices?

When waves pass the edge of an object or pass through an opening, such as a door, they spread out as if a new wave were created there. In effect, the waves bend around an object or opening. This bending of waves as they pass an edge is called **diffraction**.

Figure 11-17A shows waves passing around a block in a tank of water. Before they reach the block, the waves travel in a straight line. After they pass the block, the waves near the edge bend and spread out into the space behind the block.

The tank in **Figure 11-17B** contains two blocks placed end to end with a small gap in between. In this case, waves bend around two edges and spread out as they pass through the opening. Sound waves passing through a door behave the same way. Because sound waves spread out into the space beyond the door, a person near the door on the outside can hear sounds from inside the room.

> **diffraction** the bending of a wave as it passes an edge or an opening

Figure 11-17
(A) Waves bend when they pass the edge of an obstacle.
(B) When they pass through an opening, waves bend around both edges.

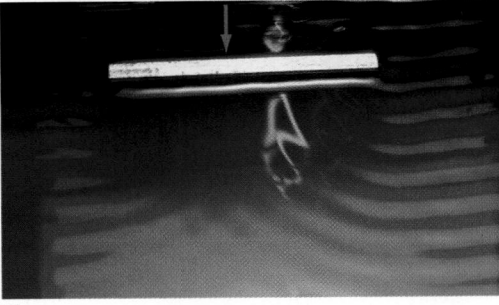

A

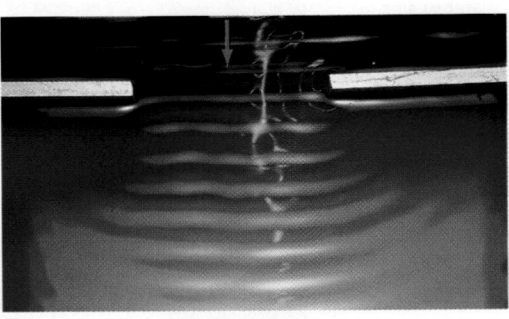

B

WAVES **375**

LINKING CHAPTERS

Students will take up reflection, diffraction, and refraction of light in more detail in Chapter 12.

MISCONCEPTION ALERT

Bending Waves
Caution students that the word *bend*, when applied to light waves, seldom means that they bend in a curving path like a highway. In diffraction and refraction, light waves change direction abruptly.

Teaching Tip

Change in Direction Waves change direction when they pass at an angle from one medium into another (unless both mediums have exactly the same refractive qualities). However, if the waves meet the boundary between mediums at a right angle, the waves will cross the boundary without changing direction.

Figure 11-18
Because light waves bend when they pass from one medium to another, this spoon looks like it is in two pieces.

▶ **refraction** the bending of waves as they pass from one medium to another

▶ **interference** the combination of two or more waves that exist in the same place at the same time

Figure 11-19
Water waves passing through each other produce interference patterns.

Waves can also bend by refraction

Figure 11-18 shows a spoon in a glass of water. Why does the spoon look like it is broken into two pieces? This strange sight results from light waves bending, but not because of diffraction. This time, the waves are bending because of **refraction**. Refraction is the bending of waves when they pass from one medium into another. All waves are refracted when they pass from one medium to another at an angle.

Light waves from the top of the spoon handle pass straight through the air from the spoon to your eyes. But the light waves from the rest of the spoon start out in the water, then pass into the glass, then into the air. Each time the waves enter a new medium, they bend slightly. By the time those waves reach your eyes, they are coming from a different angle than the waves from the top of the spoon handle. But your eyes don't know that; they just see that one set of light waves are coming from one direction, and another set of waves are coming from a different direction. As a result, the spoon appears to be broken.

Interference

What would happen if you and another person tried to walk through the exact same place at the same time? You would run into each other. Material objects, such as a human body, cannot share space with other material objects. More than one wave, however, can exist in the same place at the same time.

Waves in the same place combine to produce a single wave

When several waves are in the same location, the waves combine to produce a single, new wave that is different from the original waves. This is called **interference**. **Figure 11-19** shows interference occurring as water waves pass through each other. Once the waves have passed through each other and moved on, they return to their original shape.

You can show the interference of two waves by drawing one wave on top of another on a graph, as in **Figure 11-20.** The resulting wave can be found by adding the height of the waves at each point. Crests are considered positive, and troughs are considered negative.

376 CHAPTER 11

RESOURCE LINK
IER

Assign students worksheet *11.7: Integrating Math—Bending Light Waves to Magnify* as an extension exercise.

DEMONSTRATION 6 TEACHING

Observing Reflection and Refraction

Time: Approximately 5 minutes

Materials: aquarium tank (5 or 10 gal) or other large transparent container, milk, small mirror, laser pointer or focusing flashlight

Step 1 Fill the aquarium with water. Leave enough space above the water so that you can reach to the bottom of the tank without it spilling over. Add three drops of milk to the water, and stir.

Shine the laser into the water to see if the beam is visible. Add more milk as needed.

Step 2 Demonstrate refraction by directing the laser beam straight down into the water and then moving it in an arc to change the angle at which the beam enters the water. Students will be able to see the beam bend toward the normal (vertical) as it enters the water.

Step 3 Demonstrate reflection by placing the small mirror on the bottom of the tank.

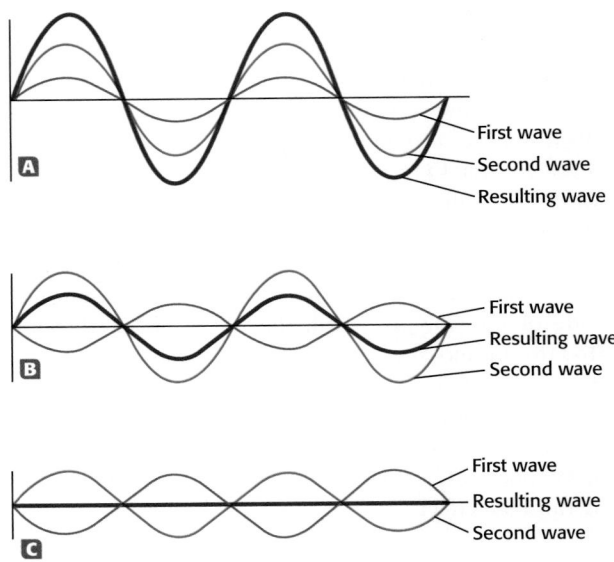
A — First wave / Second wave / Resulting wave

B — First wave / Resulting wave / Second wave

C — First wave / Resulting wave / Second wave

Figure 11-20
Constructive and Destructive Interference
(A) When two waves line up so their crests overlap, they add together to make a larger wave.
(B) When the crest of a large wave overlaps with the trough of a smaller wave, subtraction occurs.
(C) Two waves of the same size may completely cancel each other out.

Disc Two, Module 14: Refraction
Use the Interactive Tutor to learn more about this topic.

In constructive interference, amplitudes are added

When the crest of one wave overlaps the crest of another wave, the waves reinforce each other, as shown in **Figure 11-20A.** Think about what happens at the particle level. Suppose the crest of one wave would move a particle up 4 cm from its original position, and another wave crest would move the particle up 3 cm.

When both waves hit at the same time, the particle moves up 4 cm due to one wave and 3 cm due to the other for a total of 7 cm. The result is a wave whose amplitude is the sum of the amplitudes of the two individual waves. This is called **constructive interference.**

In destructive interference, amplitudes are subtracted

When the crest of one wave meets the trough of another wave, the resulting wave has a smaller amplitude than the larger of the two waves, as shown in **Figure 11-20B.** This is called **destructive interference.**

To understand how this works, imagine again a single particle. Suppose the crest of one wave would move the particle up 4 cm, and the trough of another wave would move it down 3 cm. If the waves hit the particle at the same time, the particle would move in response to both waves, and the new wave would have an amplitude of just 1 cm. When destructive interference occurs between two waves that have the same amplitude, the waves may completely cancel each other out, as shown in **Figure 11-20C.**

▶ **constructive interference** any interference in which waves combine so that the resulting wave is bigger than the original waves

▶ **destructive interference** any interference in which waves combine so that the resulting wave is smaller than the largest of the original waves

Wave Interactions

SKILL BUILDER

Interpreting Graphs **Figure 11-20** shows one example of constructive interference, one example of partial destructive interference, and one example of total destructive interference. You may make this more quantitative by treating the diagrams as graphs. Points above the horizontal axis are positive, and points below the axis are negative. Ask students to add together the crests of the first wave and the second wave on each diagram to show how the resulting wave is generated.

Resources Blackline Master 33 shows this visual.

WAVES **377**

Wave Interactions

Teaching Tip

Color by Interference Other examples of color in nature may be attributed to light interference rather than colored pigments. Ask students to give examples of where they have seen colors similar to those in soap bubbles. The colors are typically jewel-like colors that we associate with the term *iridescent*. Students may think of thin oil slicks they see after a rain or the colors of liquid-crystal thermometers that you press to the forehead. The colors on the wings of butterflies and moths and the colors of many beetles' shells are produced by interference. Interference also produces colors in bird feathers, as in the tail of a peacock.

SKILL BUILDER

Interpreting Graphs **Figure 11-22** shows two waves interfering constructively and destructively to produce beats. Have students add the amplitudes of the top two waves to see how the resulting "beat wave" is produced.

Resources Blackline Master 34 shows this visual.

Figure 11-21
The colorful swirls on a bubble result from the constructive interference of some colors and the destructive interference of other colors.

Figure 11-22
(A) When two waves of slightly different frequencies interfere with each other, they produce beats.
(B) A piano tuner can listen for beats to tell if a string is out of tune.

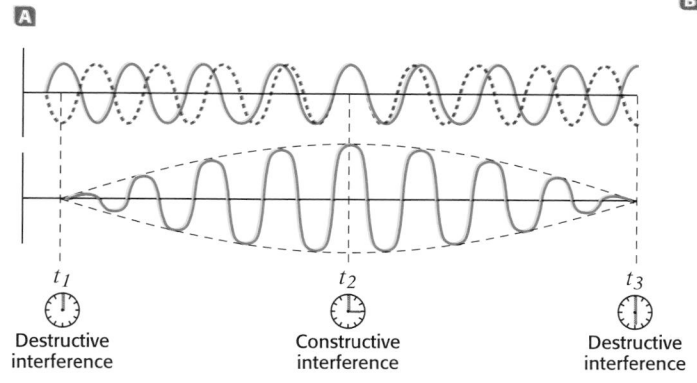

A

t_1
Destructive interference

t_2
Constructive interference

t_3
Destructive interference

378 CHAPTER 11

Interference of light waves creates colorful displays

The interference of light waves often produces colorful displays. You can see a rainbow of colors when oil is spilled onto a watery surface. Soap bubbles, like the ones shown in **Figure 11-21,** have reds, blues, and yellows on their surfaces. The colors in these examples are not due to pigments or dyes. Instead, they are due to the interference of light.

When you look at a soap bubble, some light waves bounce off the outside of the bubble and travel directly to your eye. Other light waves travel into the thin shell of the bubble, bounce off the inner side of the bubble's shell, then travel back through the shell, into the air and to your eye. Those waves travel farther than the waves reflected directly off the outside of the bubble. At times the two sets of waves are out of step with each other. The two sets of waves interfere contructively at some frequencies (colors) and destructively at other frequencies (colors). The result is a swirling rainbow effect.

Interference of sound waves produces beats

The sound waves from two tuning forks of slightly different frequencies will interfere with each other as shown in **Figure 11-22A.** Because the frequencies of the tuning forks are different, the compressions arrive at your ear at different rates.

When the compressions from the two tuning forks arrive at your ear at the same time, constructive interference occurs, and the sound is louder. A short time later, the compression from one and the rarefaction from the other arrive together. When this happens, destructive interference occurs, and a softer sound is heard. After a short time, the compressions again arrive at the same time, and again a loud sound is heard. Overall, you hear a series of loud and soft sounds called *beats*.

B

LABORATORY MANUAL

Have students perform *Lab 11 Waves: Tuning a Musical Instrument* in the lab ancillary.

DATASHEETS

Have students use *Datasheet 11.5* to record their results from the lab.

ALTERNATIVE ASSESSMENT

Standing Waves on a Rope

Students can experience standing waves by using a rope. They can also observe the basics of harmonics and resonance.

Step 1 Have two students stand about 5 m apart holding a rope or piece of rubber tubing between them. The rope should be several meters long. Adjust the rope so that there is only a little slack between the students.

Step 2 Ask one student to make the entire rope vibrate in a single standing wave by moving the end up and down continuously. The rope should vibrate in a single standing wave only at a certain frequency.

Step 3 After students get the rhythm of this vibration, tell them to make the rope vibrate in two segments, with a node in the middle. They will discover that this will happen only at twice the frequency of the previous wave.

Figure 11-22B shows a piano tuner tuning a string. Piano tuners listen for beats between a tuning fork of known frequency and a string on a piano. By adjusting the tension in the string, the tuner can change the pitch (frequency) of the string's vibration. When no beats are heard, the string is vibrating with the same frequency as the tuning fork. In that case, the string is said to be in tune.

Standing Waves

Waves can also interfere in another way. Suppose you send a wave through a rope tied to a wall at the other end. The wave is reflected from the wall and travels back along the rope. If you continue to send waves down the rope, the waves that you make will interfere with those waves that reflect off the wall and travel back toward you.

Interference can cause standing waves

If the reflected waves have the same amplitude, frequency, and speed as the original waves, then **standing waves** are formed. Standing waves look very different from normal traveling waves. Standing waves do not move through the medium. Instead, the waves cause the medium to vibrate in a loop or in a series of loops.

Standing waves have nodes and antinodes

Each loop of a standing wave is separated from the next loop by points that have no vibration, called *nodes*. Nodes lie at the points where the crests of the original waves meet the troughs of the reflected waves, causing complete destructive interference.

One of the nodes on a fixed rope string lies at the point of reflection, where the rope cannot vibrate. Another node is near your hand. If you shake the rope up and down fast enough, you can create standing waves with several nodes along the length of the string.

Midway between the nodes lie points of maximum vibration, called *antinodes*. Antinodes form where the crests of the original waves line up with the crests of the reflected waves so that complete constructive interference occurs.

▶ **standing wave** a wave form caused by interference that appears not to move along the medium and that shows some regions of no vibration (nodes) and other regions of maximum vibration (antinodes)

Connection to ARCHITECTURE

Making the Connection

1. Lower-pitched sounds will be more effective than higher-pitched sounds because the lower sounds will have wavelengths closer to the dimensions of the room.
2. Students should discuss sound reflection and wave interference.
3. Proposals should include the placement of objects with reflective surfaces at varying distances and in varying directions. Breaking up flat walls by adding multiple surfaces (baffles) or sound-absorbing materials is another technique.

Resources Assign students worksheet *11.4: Connection to Architecture* from the **Integration Enrichment Resources** ancillary.

Caution students to hold the rope tightly as considerable energy can build up in the standing waves.

Step 4 Ask students to make the rope vibrate at a frequency somewhere between the two observed frequencies. They will find this impossible to do. Ask students to find the next higher natural frequency of the rope. This will occur at three times the original frequency, and the rope will exhibit a standing wave of three parts with two nodes.

Step 5 Have students suggest ways to make the rope vibrate at different frequencies. Almost any change in length or tension will result in standing waves of different frequencies. Point out that the rope is a model for a string on a violin, guitar, piano, or other stringed instrument.

Check Your Understanding

1. The waves will reflect off of the rock.
2. Sound waves diffract when they pass the edge of a barrier, spreading into the medium beyond the barrier.
3. The waves must be in the same place and the crest of one wave must overlap the crest of the other.
4. When light strikes a bubble, some light reflects off the outer surface of the bubble, while other light passes through the thickness of the bubble membrane and reflects off the inner surface. The two sets of reflected waves interfere. Some wavelengths are reinforced while others are canceled, producing colors.
5. See answer to question 16 in the Chapter 11 Review.
6. The waves must match in amplitude and frequency, and the crests of one wave must exactly overlap the troughs of the other.
7. Decide which guitar will be used as the standard pitch. Pluck the strings of both guitars and listen for beats as the tones fade. Adjust the tension of the string on the second guitar until no beats are heard.
8. The longest possible wavelength is twice the length of the string, 4 m.

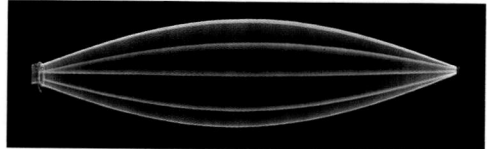
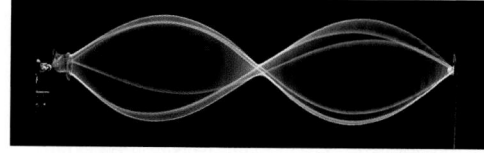
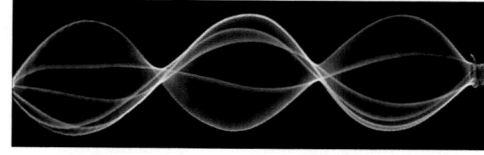
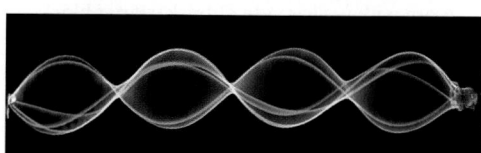

Standing waves can have only certain wavelengths

Figure 11-23 shows several different possible standing waves on a string fixed at both ends. Only a few waves with specific wavelengths can form standing waves in any given string.

The simplest standing waves occur when the wavelength of the waves is twice the length of the string. In that case, it just looks like the entire string is shaking up and down. The only nodes are on the two ends of the string.

If the string vibrates with a higher frequency, the wavelength becomes shorter. At a certain frequency, the wavelength is exactly equal to the length of the string. In the middle of the string, complete destructive interference occurs, producing a node.

In general, standing waves can exist whenever a multiple of half-wavelengths will fit exactly in the length of the string.

Figure 11-23
These photos of standing waves were captured using a strobe light that flashes different colors at different times.

■ SECTION 11.3 REVIEW

SUMMARY

▶ Waves bouncing off a surface is called reflection.

▶ Diffraction is the bending of waves as they pass an edge or corner.

▶ Refraction is the bending of waves as they pass from one medium to another.

▶ Interference results when two waves exist in the same place and combine to make a single wave.

▶ Interference may cause standing waves.

CHECK YOUR UNDERSTANDING

1. **Describe** what may happen when ripples on a pond encounter a large rock in the water.
2. **Explain** why you can hear two people talking even after they walk around a corner.
3. **Name** the conditions required for two waves to interfere constructively.
4. **Explain** why colors appear on the surface of a soap bubble.
5. **Draw** a standing wave, and label the nodes and antinodes.
6. **Critical Thinking** What conditions are required for two waves on a rope to interfere completely destructively?
7. **Critical Thinking** Imagine that you and a friend are trying to tune the lowest strings on two different guitars to the same pitch. Explain how you could use beats to determine if the strings are properly tuned.
8. **Critical Thinking** Determine the longest possible wavelength of a standing wave on a string that is 2 m long.

ALTERNATIVE ASSESSMENT

Wave Phenomena

Step 1 Ask students to draw diagrams showing reflection, refraction, and diffraction of waves. Students do not need to draw waves but simply sketch the geometry of each phenomenon.

Step 2 Tell them to label each of the diagrams clearly as to which phenomenon it represents. Students should also label the objects and boundaries involved and use arrows to show the direction of wave travel both before and after the encounter between the waves and the objects.

Chapter Highlights

Before you begin, review the summaries of the key ideas of each section, found on pages 364, 373, and 380. The key vocabulary terms are listed on pages 356, 365, and 374.

UNDERSTANDING CONCEPTS

1. Waves that need a medium in which to travel are called _____.
   a. longitudinal waves
   b. transverse waves
   c. mechanical waves
   d. All of the above

2. Most waves are caused by _____.
   a. velocity
   b. amplitude
   c. a vibration
   d. earthquakes

3. For which type of waves do particles in the medium vibrate perpendicularly to the direction in which the waves are traveling?
   a. transverse waves
   b. longitudinal waves
   c. P waves
   d. none of the above

4. A sound wave is an example of _____.
   a. an electromagnetic wave
   b. a transverse wave
   c. a longitudinal wave
   d. a surface wave

5. In an ocean wave, the molecules of water _____.
   a. move perpendicularly to the direction of wave travel
   b. move parallel to the direction of wave travel
   c. move in circles
   d. don't move at all

6. Half the vertical distance between the crest and trough of a wave is called the _____.
   a. frequency
   b. crest
   c. wavelength
   d. amplitude

7. The number of waves passing a given point each second is called the _____.
   a. frequency
   b. wave speed
   c. wavelength
   d. amplitude

8. The Doppler effect of a passing siren results from an apparent change in _____.
   a. loudness
   b. wave speed
   c. frequency
   d. interference

9. The combining of waves as they meet is known as _____.
   a. a crest
   b. noise
   c. interference
   d. the Doppler effect

10. Waves bend when they pass through an opening. This is called _____.
    a. interference
    b. diffraction
    c. refraction
    d. the Doppler effect

Using Vocabulary

11. How is an *electromagnetic wave* different from a *mechanical wave*?

12. You have a long metal rod and a hammer. How would you hit the metal rod to create a *longitudinal wave*? How would you hit it to create a *transverse wave*?

13. Identify each of the following as a distance measurement, a time measurement, or neither.
    a. *amplitude*
    b. *wavelength*
    c. *period*
    d. *frequency*
    e. *wave speed*

14. Imagine a train approaching a crossing where you are standing safely behind the gate. Explain the changes in sound of the horn that you may hear as the train passes. Use the following terms in your answer: *frequency, wavelength, wave speed, Doppler effect.*

15. Explain the difference between *constructive interference* and *destructive interference*.

16. Draw a picture of a *standing wave,* and label a *node* and an *antinode.*

WAVES **381**

UNDERSTANDING CONCEPTS

1. c
2. c
3. a
4. c
5. c
6. d
7. a
8. c
9. c
10. b

Using Vocabulary

11. Mechanical waves involve the movement of matter. Electromagnetic waves do not require a material medium.

12. To cause a longitudinal wave in a rod, you would strike the end of the rod, along the axis of the rod. To cause a transverse wave, you would strike the rod at right angles to its axis.

13. a. distance in a transverse mechanical wave; neither in other waves
    b. distance
    c. time
    d. neither (inverse time)
    e. neither (distance and time)

RESOURCE LINK
STUDY GUIDE

Assign students *Review Chapter 11.*

14. As the train approaches, you hear a sound with a frequency slightly higher than the actual pitch of the train's horn. The waves emitted by the train's horn travel at a fixed speed through air. The motion of the train squeezes the waves closer together in the forward direction, shortening their wavelength. The waves strike your ear with a frequency greater than that emitted by the horn. As the train moves past you, the wavelength of the waves increases, and as it moves away, the waves are stretched farther apart and strike your ear at a lower frequency. This is called the Doppler effect.

15. In constructive interference, the crests of one wave align with the crests of another wave. Their energies combine to give a wave with energy greater than either wave alone. In destructive interference, the crests of one wave align with the troughs of the other. Their energies combine to give a wave with less energy than either of the waves alone.

16.

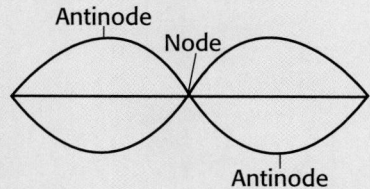

Antinode

Node

Antinode

BUILDING MATH SKILLS

17. Graphing Draw a sine curve, and label a crest, a trough, and the amplitude.

18. Interpreting Graphics The wave shown in the figure below has a frequency of 25.0 Hz. Find the following values for this wave:

  a. amplitude   **c.** speed

  b. wavelength   **d.** period

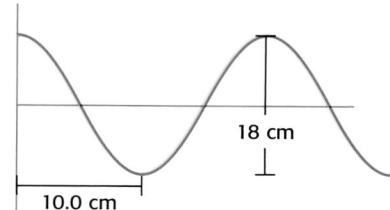

18 cm

10.0 cm

19. Wave Speed Suppose you tie one end of a rope to a doorknob and shake the other end with a frequency of 2 Hz. The waves you create have a wavelength of 3 m. What is the speed of the waves along the rope?

20. Wave Speed Ocean waves are hitting a beach at a rate of 2.0 Hz. The distance between wave crests is 12 m. Calculate the speed of the waves.

21. Wavelength All electromagnetic waves have the same speed in empty space, 3.0×10^8 m/s. Using that speed, find the wavelengths of the electromagnetic waves at the following frequencies:

  a. radio waves at 530 kHz

  b. visible light at 6.0×10^{14} Hz

  c. X rays at 3.0×10^{18} Hz

22. Frequency Microwaves range in wavelength from 1 mm to 30 cm. Calculate their range in frequency. Use 3×10^8 m/s as the speed of electromagnetic waves.

THINKING CRITICALLY

23. Understanding Systems A friend standing 2 m away strikes two tuning forks at the same time, one at a frequency of 256 Hz and the other at 240 Hz. Which sound will reach your ear first? Explain.

24. Applying Knowledge When you are watching a baseball game, you may hear the crack of the bat a short time after you see the batter hit the ball. Why does this happen? (**Hint:** Consider the relationship between the speed of sound and the speed of light.)

25. Understanding Systems You are standing on a street corner, and you hear a fire truck approaching. Does the pitch of the siren stay constant, increase, or decrease as it approaches you? Explain.

26. Applying Knowledge If you yell or clap your hands while standing at the edge of a large rock canyon, you may hear an echo a few seconds later. Explain why this happens.

27. Interpreting Graphics Draw the wave that results from interference between the two waves shown below.

  a.    **b.**

28. Understanding Systems An orchestra is playing in a huge outdoor amphitheater, and thousands of listeners sit on a hillside far from the stage. To help those listeners hear the concert, the amphitheater has speakers halfway up the hill. How could you improve this system? A computer delays the signal to the speakers by a fraction of a second. Why is this computer used? What might happen if the signal were not delayed at all?

DEVELOPING LIFE/WORK SKILLS

29. Applying Knowledge Describe how you interact with waves during a typical school day. Document the types of waves you encounter and how often you interact with each. Decide if one type of wave is more important in your life than the others.

30. Applying Technology With your teacher's help, use a microphone and an oscilloscope or a CBL interface to obtain an image of a sound. Determine the frequency and wavelength of the sound. COMPUTER SKILL

31. Making Decisions A new car is advertised as having antinoise technology. The manufacturer claims that inside the car any sounds are negated. Evaluate the possibility of such a claim. What would have to be created to cause destructive interference with any sound in the car? Would it be possible to have destructive interference everywhere inside the car? Do you believe that the manufacturer is correct in its statement?

32. Working Cooperatively Work with two other classmates to research the types of architectural acoustics that would affect a restaurant. Investigate some of the acoustics problems in places where many people gather. How do odd-shaped ceilings, decorative panels, and glass windows affect echoes and noise. Prepare a model of your school cafeteria showing what changes you would make to reduce the level of noise.

33. Applying Knowledge A piano tuner listens to a tuning fork vibrating at 440 Hz to tune the string of a piano. He hears beats between the tuning fork and the piano string. Is the string in tune? Explain your answer.

INTEGRATING CONCEPTS

34. Concept Mapping Copy the unfinished concept map below onto a sheet of paper. Complete the map by writing the correct word or phrase in the lettered boxes.

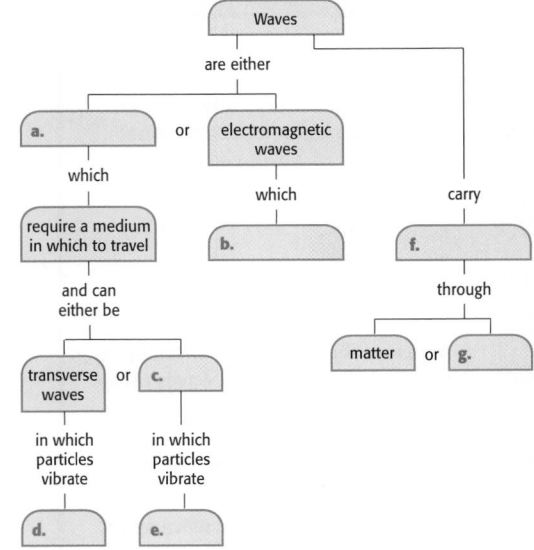

35. Connection to Earth Science What is the medium for seismic waves?

36. Connection to Architecture Explore and describe research on earthquake-proof buildings and materials. Evaluate the impact of this research on society in terms of building codes and architectural styles in earthquake-prone areas such as Los Angeles, San Francisco, and Tokyo.

internet**connect**

SC**LINKS**
NSTA

TOPIC: Seismic waves
GO TO: www.scilinks.org
KEYWORD: HK1116

WAVES **383**

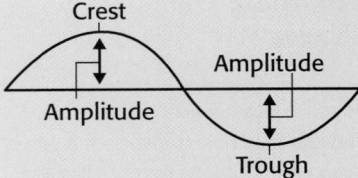

Design Your Own Lab

Modeling Transverse Waves

Introduction

Review the characteristics of a wave with your students before allowing them to perform this experiment.

Objectives

Students will:

► **Use** appropriate lab safety procedures.
► **Create** the curves by pulling paper under a sand pendulum.
► **Measure** the amplitude, wavelength, and period of transverse waves using sine curves as models.
► **Predict** how changes to the experiment may change the amplitude and wavelength.
► **Calculate** frequency and wave speed using measurements.

Planning

Recommended Time: 1 lab period
Materials *(for each lab group)*

► paper or plastic-form cup
► nail
► string
► scissors
► masking tape
► colored sand
► ring stand or other support
► rolls of white paper, about 30 cm wide
► meterstick
► stopwatch

RESOURCE LINK
DATASHEETS

Have students use *Datasheet 11.4: Design Your Own Lab— Modeling Transverse Waves* to record their results.

Design Your Own Lab

Introduction

A model of a transverse wave may be created with a sand pendulum. What characteristics of waves can you measure using such a model?

Objectives

► **Create** sine curves by pulling paper under a sand pendulum.
► **Measure** the amplitude, wavelength, and period of transverse waves using sine curves as models.
► **Predict** how changes to the experiment may change the amplitude and wavelength.
► **Calculate** frequency and wave speed using your measurements.

Materials

paper or plastic-foam cup
nail
string and scissors
masking tape
colored sand
ring stand or other support
rolls of white paper, about 30 cm wide
meterstick
stopwatch

Safety Needs

safety glasses, gloves

REQUIRED PRECAUTIONS

► Read all safety precautions, and discuss them with your students.
► Safety goggles and a lab apron must be worn at all times.
► Long hair and loose clothing must be tied back.
► Wear gloves while handling nails and use caution when punching holes.

Modeling Transverse Waves

► Making Sine Curves with a Sand Pendulum

1. Review the discussion in Section 11.2 on the use of sine curves to represent transverse waves.
2. On a blank sheet of paper, prepare a table like the one shown at right.
3. Use a nail to puncture a small hole in the bottom of a paper cup. Also punch two holes on opposite sides of the cup near the rim. Tie strings of equal length through the upper holes. Make a pendulum by tying the strings from the cup to a ring stand or other support. Clamp the stand down at the end of a table, as shown in the photograph at right. Cover the bottom hole with a piece of tape, then fill the cup with sand. **SAFETY CAUTION** Wear gloves while handling the nails and punching holes.
4. Unroll some of the paper, and mark off a length of 1 m using two dotted lines. Then roll the paper back up, and position the paper under the pendulum, as shown in the photograph at right.
5. Remove the tape over the hole. Start the pendulum swinging as your lab partner pulls the paper in a direction perpendicular to the cup's swing. Another lab partner should loosely hold the paper roll. Try to pull the paper in a straight line with a constant speed. The sand should trace a sine curve on the paper, as in the photograph at right.
6. As your partner pulls the paper under the pendulum, start the stopwatch when the sand trace reaches the first dotted line marking the length of 1 m. When the sand trace reaches the second dotted line, stop the watch. Record the time in your table.
7. When you are finished making a curve, stop the pendulum and cover the hole in the bottom of the cup. Be careful not to jostle the paper; if you do, your trace may be erased. You may want to tape the paper down.

Length along paper = 1m	Time (s)	Average wavelength (m)	Average amplitude (m)
Curve 1			
Curve 2			
Curve 3			

8. For the part of the curve between the dotted lines, measure the distance from the first crest to the last crest, then divide that distance by the total number of crests. Record your answer in the table under "Average wavelength."

9. For the same part of the curve, measure the vertical distance between the first crest and the first trough, between the second crest and the second trough, and so on. Add the distances together, then divide by the number of distances you measured. Record your answer in the table under "Average amplitude."

▶ Designing Your Experiment

10. With your lab partners, decide how you will work together to make two additional sine curve traces, one with a different average wavelength than the first trace and one with a different average amplitude.

11. In your lab report, write down your plan for changing these two factors. Before you carry out your experiment, your teacher must approve your plan.

▶ Performing Your Experiment

12. After your teacher approves your plan, carry out your experiment. For each curve, measure and record the time, the average wavelength, and the average amplitude.

13. After each trace, return the sand to the cup and roll the paper back up.

▶ Analyzing Your Results

1. For each of your three curves, calculate the average speed at which the paper was pulled by dividing the length of 1 m by the time measurement. This is equivalent to the speed of the wave that the curve models or represents.

2. For each curve, use the wave speed equation to calculate average frequency.

$$\text{average frequency} = \frac{\text{average wave speed}}{\text{average wavelength}} \qquad f = \frac{v}{\lambda}$$

▶ Defending Your Conclusions

3. What factor did you change to alter the average wavelength of the curve? Did your plan work? If so, did the wavelength increase or decrease?

4. What factor did you change to alter the average amplitude? Did your plan work?

Pre-Lab

Teaching Tips

Review Section 11.2 *Characteristics of Waves* with students before beginning this lab.

Procedure

▶ Making Sine Curves with a Sand Pendulum

If students find it difficult punching holes in a plastic or paper cup without ruining the entire cup, they can melt holes in a cup with a nail that has been slightly heated in the flame of a laboratory burner. As always, use tongs and gloves when working with the Bunsen burner. You may want to prepare the cups before your students perform the lab.

To make sure the hole in the bottom of the cup is the right size: cover the bottom hole with a piece of tape, then fill the cup with sand. Uncover the hole and swing the cup in a small arc over a sheet of test paper. If the sand does not leak fast enough to make a continuous track on the sheet, increase the diameter of the hole until it does. Once the flow seems right, cover the hole again and pour the sand back into the cup. Students may use a whisk broom and dustpan when returning the sand to the cup or make a crimp at one end of the paper and pour the sand into the cup.

Have students perform a trial run before doing the actual experiment. Students should identify the following on the wave trace: crests, troughs, amplitude, wavelength.

The students will not pull the paper at exactly the same rate for the entire time; as a result all the values are calculated as averages. (The pendulum will slow down slightly over time.)

Continue on p. 385A.

CONTINUATION OF ANSWERS

Design Your Own Lab from page 385

Modeling Transverse Waves

▶ **Designing Your Experiment**

To make a curve with a different average amplitude, students simply have to change the initial displacement of the pendulum (so it swings through a smaller or larger arc).
To make a curve with a different average wavelength, students will have to pull the paper at a different average speed.

▶ **Performing Your Experiment**

If students want to change the length of the pendulum, make sure the strings are still tied securely to the ringstand.

Post-Lab

▶ **Disposal**

The sand can be collected and reused.

▶ **Analyzing Your Results**

1. Calculate the average speed of the paper by dividing the length measurement by the time measurement.
2. Students should use the wave speed equation to calculate the average frequency. Another way to calculate frequency is to count the number of times the cup swings back and forth during a 10 s interval. Divide the number of swings by 10 to calculate the average period of the pendulum. Then use the frequency-period equation to calculate the frequency of the wave.

   The frequency will be close to the same in every case, unless the length of the pendulum was changed. (A pendulum of given length has a more or less fixed period. Increasing the length increases the period.)

▶ **Defending Your Conclusions**

3. To make a curve with a different average wavelength, students should have pulled the paper at a different average speed, and/or have changed the frequency of the pendulum (by altering the length of the pendulum).
4. To make a curve with a different average amplitude, students should have changed the initial displacement of the pendulum (so it swings through a smaller or larger arc).

   Additional question to pose to students: How could the same apparatus be used to model longitudinal waves? *(The sand pendulum could be used to model a longitudinal wave if the paper were moved parallel to the motion of the pendulum. Compressions would appear as areas with more sand and rarefactions as areas with less sand.)*

Answers from page 383

22. $f = \dfrac{v}{\lambda} = \dfrac{3 \times 10^8 \text{ m / s}}{1 \text{ mm}} \times \dfrac{1000 \text{ mm}}{1 \text{ m}} = 3 \times 10^{11} \text{ Hz}$

   $f = \dfrac{v}{\lambda} = \dfrac{3 \times 10^8 \text{ m / s}}{30 \text{ cm}} \times \dfrac{100 \text{ cm}}{1 \text{ m}} = 1 \times 10^9 \text{ Hz}$

   f range $= 1 \times 10^9$ Hz to 3×10^{11} Hz.

25. As a fire truck approaches, the pitch of the siren is higher than it would be if the fire truck were at rest. However, the pitch of the truck does not change noticeably until the fire truck is passing right in front of you, when the pitch rapidly drops. In fact, as the truck approaches, the pitch from the siren is always dropping to some degree.
26. You hear an echo because the sound waves you produced by clapping or shouting have reflected off the walls of the canyon and returned to your ears.
27. **a.** Drawings should have three crests (high points), two troughs (low points) and be twice as large (tall) as the waves shown.
    b. Drawings should show a straight line (the waves completely cancel each other.)
28. To avoid cancellation, the amplifier delays the sound so that the sound waves will be in phase with those directly from the orchestra.

29. Students will probably think of sound waves, visible light waves, and maybe water waves. Encourage them to look at the entire electromagnetic spectrum, including infrared light, microwaves, and radio waves.

30. The oscilloscope image will be a transverse wave. Ask students to explain how that image can represent a longitudinal wave.

31. Ask students to consider how they would listen to music if the antinoise device canceled all interior noise. They should consider the effect of such cancellation on safety. Students may be interested in exploring the current status of these devices and which cars have them. The technology is called Active Noise Reduction or ANR.

32. Have students also learn about materials used for acoustic control including the use of carpet and upholstered furniture.

33. If beats are heard, the string is not in tune. The string and the tuning fork vibrate at slightly different frequencies. As a result, the two sounds interfere constructively and destructively in succession. These successive reinforcements and cancellations are heard as beats. When the frequencies are exactly equal, no beats are heard.

34. **a.** mechanical waves
    b. can travel through empty space or require no medium
    c. longitudinal waves
    d. at right angles to the path of the wave
    e. parallel to the path of the wave
    f. energy
    g. space

35. Earth, or the ground

36. Building codes are often updated when engineers study the damage to buildings after an earthquake. Computer models allow scientists and engineers to evaluate how new building designs may be affected by earthquakes. Students may be surprised to learn that many modern buildings in earthquake-prone regions are built to be able to sway, slide, or move horizontally. Some even have giant rollers, springs, or rubber shock absorbers that let the ground move beneath the building.

CareerLink

Ultrasonographer

As described in Chapter 11 and in the feature on these pages, ultrasonographers use the properties of sound waves in order to generate images of structures within the body.

When the ultrasound waves pass from one material to a different material, such as from muscle tissues to the lungs, some of the waves are reflected back toward the source. In addition, the speed of sound is slightly different in these different materials, so the time it takes for a reflection to arrive back at the detector depends on the material the reflection passes through.

A computer is able to build an image based on the patterns of reflections detected.

SKILL BUILDER

Vocabulary The word *sonograph* comes from two different root words. The Latin word *sonos* means "sound," and the Greek word *graphein* means "to write."

Ultrasonographer

Most people have seen a sonogram showing an unborn baby inside its mother's womb. Ultrasound technologists make these images with an ultrasound machine, which sends harmless, high-frequency sound waves into the body. Ultrasonographers work in hospitals, clinics, and doctors' offices. Besides checking on the health of unborn babies, ultrasonographers use their tools to help diagnose cancer, heart disease, and other health problems. To find out more about this career, read the interview with Estela Zavala, a registered diagnostic medical sonographer who works at Austin Radiological Association in Austin, Texas.

"Ultrasound is a helpful diagnostic tool that allows you to see inside the body without the use of X rays."

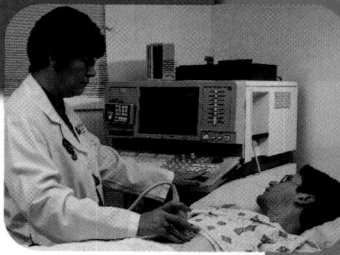

Estela Zavala uses an ultrasound machine to check this man's kidneys.

 What does an ultrasonographer do?

We scan various organs of the body with an ultrasound machine to see if there are any abnormalities. For example, we can check a gallbladder to see if there are any stones in it. We already know what healthy organs look like, so anything unusual shows up in these pictures. This can help a doctor make a diagnosis.

 How does the ultrasound machine make pictures?

The machine creates high-frequency sound waves. When the sound waves reflect off of the organs in the body, the waves strike a piezoelectric crystal in the detector. Piezoelectric crystals can convert the pressure energy from the ultrasound wave into an electrical signal. The ultrasound system processes the signal to create an image.

 What part of your job do you find most satisfying?

I like helping people find out what is wrong with them in a noninvasive way. Before ultrasound, invasive surgery was often the only option.

 What is challenging about your job?

The technology is constantly changing. We are using ultrasound in more ways than ever before. For example, we can create images of veins and arteries with vascular technology.

 What skills does an ultrasonographer need?

First you need excellent hand-eye coordination, so you can move the equipment over the parts of the body you need to image. You also have to know a lot about all of the organs in the body. It is very important to be able to work quickly, because sometimes patients are uncomfortable because they are sick.

How much training and education did you receive before becoming an ultrasonographer?

After graduating from high school, I went to an X-ray school to be licensed as an X-ray technologist. A medical background like this is necessary for entering ultrasound training. First I went to an intensive 1-month training program, which involved 2 weeks of hands-on work and 2 weeks of classwork. After that, I worked for a licensed radiologist for about a year. Finally, I attended an accredited year-long ultrasound program at a local community college before becoming fully licensed.

 What part of your education do you think was the most valuable?

The best part was the on-the-job training that was involved. You need to do a lot of ultrasounds before you can become proficient.

 Would you recommend ultrasound technology as a career to students?

Yes, I would recommend it. Just remember that you must have some medical experience first, such as being a nurse or an X-ray technician, if you want to continue into other areas of radiology, like ultrasound.

 internet**connect**

 SC**LINKS** NSTA

TOPIC: Ultrasound
GO TO: www.scilinks.org
KEYWORD: HK1127

Additional Application

Ultrasound Cauterization

Scientists at the University of Washington in Seattle have developed a technique that focuses ultrasound waves in one spot to cause clots in some blood vessels in a certain organ. This technique can be used before surgery on organs such as the spleen, liver, and brain. Usually, surgery on these organs is very difficult because their tissue is so fragile, and doctors have trouble stopping the bleeding after an operation.

A related technology could allow doctors to use ultrasound to detect internal bleeding, which otherwise could lead to death in minutes.

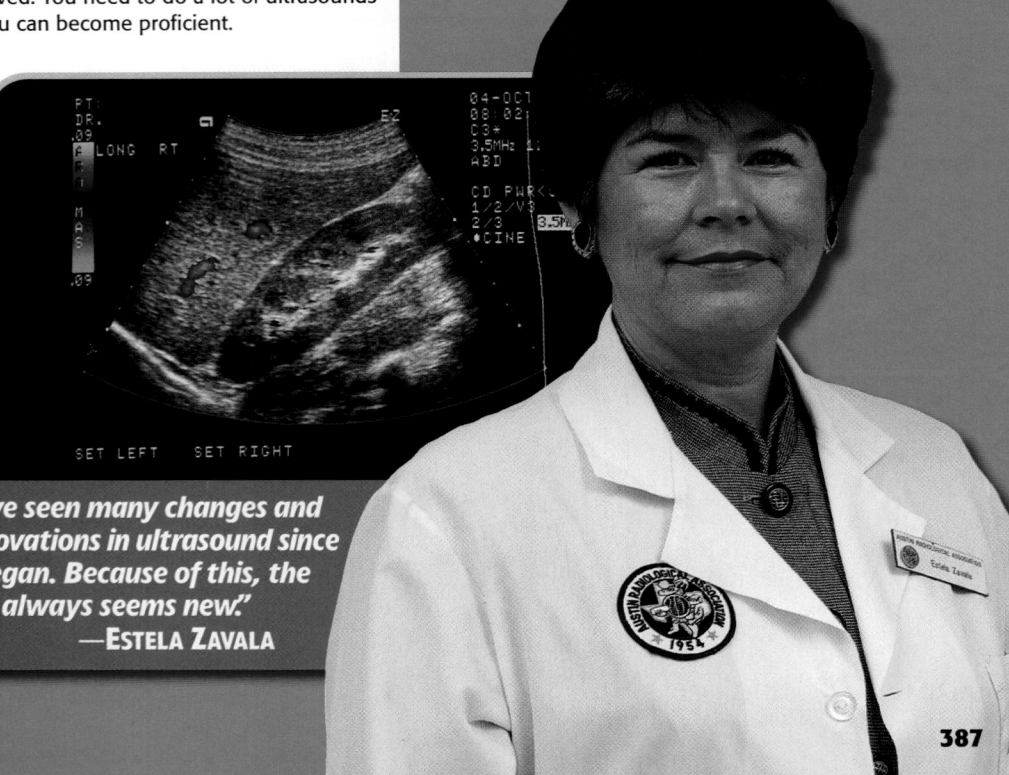

"I've seen many changes and innovations in ultrasound since I began. Because of this, the job always seems new."
—ESTELA ZAVALA

CHAPTER 12

Sound and Light

Annotated Descriptions of the Correlated National Science Standards

The following descriptions summarize the National Science Standards that specially relate to Chapter 12. For the full text of the Standards, see p. 40T.

SECTION 12.1
Sound

Physical Science
PS 2e, 5a, 5c, 5d

Life Science
LS 6a

Unifying Concepts and Processes
UCP 2, 3, 5

Science and Technology
ST 2

Science in Personal and Social Perspectives
SPSP 2, 4, 5

SECTION 12.2
The Nature of Light

Physical Science
PS 5d

Unifying Concepts and Processes
UCP 1, 2

Science and Technology
ST 2

History and Nature of Science
HSN 1–3

Science in Personal and Social Perspectives
SPSP 2–5

SECTION 12.3
Reflection and Color

Unifying Concepts and Processes
UCP 2, 5

SECTION 12.4
Refraction, Lenses, and Prisms

Life Science
LS 6a

Unifying Concepts and Processes
UCP 2

Science and Technology
ST 2

History and Nature of Science
HNS 1

Cross-Discipline Teaching RESOURCES

Cross-Discipline Teaching, ATE p. 388
Earth Science   Fine Arts
Life Science

Integration Enrichment Resources
Real World Applications, **PE** and **ATE** p. 403
  IE 12.1 *How Does Sunscreen Work?*
Space Science, **PE** and **ATE** p. 407
  IE 12.2 *Telescopes*

Use the Planning Guide on the next page to help you organize your lessons.

MATH AND COMPUTER RESOURCES

Chapter 12	Math Skills	Assess	Media/Computer Skills
Section 12.1		**Building Math Skills,** p. 420, items 19–21 **CRT** Worksheet 14	■ Section 12.1 **CNN. Presents Physical Science** **Segment 14** Virtual Practice Room
Section 12.2		**Building Math Skills,** p. 420, items 22, 23	■ Section 12.2
Section 12.3		**CRT** Worksheet 16	■ Section 12.3 **CNN. Presents Physical Science** **Segment 16** Color-Deficiency Lenses
Section 12.4			■ Section 12.4

PE Pupil's Edition   **ATE** Annotated Teacher's Edition   **MS** Math Skills   **BS** Basic Skills
IE Integration Enrichment   ■ Guided Reading Audio   **CRT** Critical Thinking

READING SKILL BUILDER

The following activities found in the Annotated Teacher's Edition provide techniques for developing useful reading strategies to increase your students' reading comprehension skills.

Section 12.1 **Brainstorming,** p. 388, 390

Section 12.2 **Summarizing,** p. 399

Section 12.3 **Discussion,** p. 406

Section 12.4 **Paired Reading,** p. 412

Smithsonian Institution®

Visit www.si.edu/hrw for additional online resources.

Spanish Resources

The following resources are made available for students who speak Spanish as their first language.

Spanish Resource Package
Guided Reading Audio CD-ROM
Chapter 12

Spanish Glossary
Chapter 12

Sound and Light

CLASSROOM RESOURCES

	FOCUS	TEACH	HANDS-ON

Section 12.1: Sound

BLOCK 1
45 minutes

FOCUS	TEACH	HANDS-ON
ATE RSB Brainstorming, pp. 388, 390 **ATE** Focus Activities 1, 2, p. 389 **ATE** **Demo 1** Pitch and Loudness, p. 390 **ATE** **Demo 2** Resonance, p. 396 **PE** Properties of Sound; Musical Instruments, pp. 390–396 ★ Focus Transparency LT 39	**ATE** **Skill Builder** Interpreting Visuals, pp. 389, 390, 392, 393 Vibrating Strings, p. 394 Vocabulary, p. 395 **TT** 34 Sound Intensity	**PE** Quick Activity *Sound in Different Mediums*, p. 391 **DS** 12.1 **PE** Quick Activity *Frequency and Pitch*, p. 392 **DS** 12.2 **PE** Inquiry Lab *How can you amplify the sound of a tuning fork?* p. 395 **DS** 12.3

BLOCK 2
45 minutes

FOCUS	TEACH	HANDS-ON
PE Hearing and the Ear; Ultrasound and Sonar, pp. 396–398	**ATE** **Skill Builder** Interpreting Visuals, p. 396 **TT** 35 The Ear	

Section 12.2: The Nature of Light

BLOCK 3
45 minutes

FOCUS	TEACH	HANDS-ON
ATE RSB Summarizing, p. 399 **PE** Waves and Particles, pp. 399–402 ★ Focus Transparency LT 40	**ATE** **Skill Builder** Interpreting Visuals, pp. 400, 401 Interpreting Tables, p. 401	**LE 12** Choosing a Pair of Sunglasses **DS** 12.5

BLOCK 4
45 minutes

FOCUS	TEACH	HANDS-ON
PE The Electromagnetic Spectrum, pp. 402–405	**BLM** 35 Spectrum Diagram	**PE** Real World Applications *Sun Protection*, p. 403 **IE** Worksheet 12.1

Section 12.3: Reflection and Color

BLOCK 5
45 minutes

FOCUS	TEACH	HANDS-ON
ATE RSB Discussion, p. 406 **ATE** **Demo 3** Observing Reflection and Refraction, p. 406 **ATE** **Demo 4** Reflection from Curved Mirrors, p. 408 **PE** Reflection of Light; Mirrors, pp. 406–409 ★ Focus Transparency LT 41	**ATE** **Skill Builder** Interpreting Diagrams, pp. 407, 408 **BLM** 36 Reflection **BLM** 37 Law of Reflection **BLM** 38 Flat Mirror	**IE** Worksheet 12.2

BLOCK 6
45 minutes

FOCUS	TEACH	HANDS-ON
PE Seeing Colors, pp. 410–411		

Section 12.4: Refraction, Lenses, and Prisms

BLOCK 7
45 minutes

FOCUS	TEACH	HANDS-ON
ATE RSB Paired Reading, p. 412 **ATE** **Demo 5** Total Internal Reflection, p. 414 **PE** Refraction of Light, pp. 412–414 ★ Focus Transparency LT 42	**ATE** **Skill Builder** Interpreting Diagrams, p. 413 **TT** 36 Refraction	

BLOCK 8
45 minutes

FOCUS	TEACH	HANDS-ON
ATE **Demo 6** Dispersion, p. 416 **PE** Lenses; Dispersion and Prisms, pp. 415–418	**ATE** **Skill Builder** Vocabulary, p. 415 Interpreting Visuals, p. 416 **TT** 37 The Eye	**PE** Skill Builder Lab *Forming Images with Lenses*, p. 422 **DS** 12.4

CLASSROOM RESOURCES

HOMEWORK	ASSESS
PE Section Review 1, 2, 4–7, 10, p. 398 **Chapter 12 Review,** p. 419, items 1, 2, 11–14	**SG** Chapter 12 Pretest
PE Section Review 3, 8, 9, p. 398 **Chapter 12 Review,** p. 419, items 3, 4, 19–21	**SG** Section 12.1
PE Section Review 1, p. 405 **Chapter 12 Review,** p. 419, item 5	**ATE** *ALTERNATIVE ASSESSMENT,* Comparing Frequency and Intensity, p. 399
PE Section Review 2–5, p. 405 **Chapter 12 Review,** p. 419, items 6–8, 22, 23	**SG** Section 12.2
PE Section Review 1–4, 7, 8, p. 411 **Chapter 12 Review,** p. 419, items 9, 15	
PE Section Review 5, 6, p. 411 **Chapter 12 Review,** p. 419, items 10, 16	**ATE** *ALTERNATIVE ASSESSMENT,* Law of Reflection, p. 410 **SG** Section 12.3
PE Section Review 1–3, 7, 8, p. 418	
PE Section Review 4–6, p. 418 **Chapter 12 Review,** p. 419, items 17, 18	**ATE** *ALTERNATIVE ASSESSMENT,* Light Rays, p. 418

BLOCK 9

PE Chapter 12 Review
Thinking Critically 24–28, p. 420
Developing Life/Work Skills 29, 30, p. 421
Integrating Concepts 31–36, p. 421
SG Chapter 12 Mixed Review

BLOCK 10

Chapter Tests
Chapter 12 Test

One-Stop Planner CD–ROM with Test Generator
Chapter 12

Teaching Resources
Scoring Rubrics and assignment checklist.

internetconnect

SCILINKS
NSTA

National Science Teachers Association
Online Resources:
www.scilinks.org

The following *sci*LINKS Internet resources can be found in the student text for this chapter.

Page 389 **TOPIC:** Transfer of sound and light energy **KEYWORD:** HK1120	**Page 402** **TOPIC:** The electromagnetic spectrum **KEYWORD:** HK1124
Page 391 **TOPIC:** Properties of sound **KEYWORD:** HK1121	**Page 407** **TOPIC:** Reflection **KEYWORD:** HK1125
Page 396 **TOPIC:** The ear **KEYWORD:** HK1122	**Page 417** **TOPIC:** Refraction **KEYWORD:** HK1126
Page 399 **TOPIC:** Properties of light **KEYWORD:** HK1123	**Page 421** **TOPIC:** Ultrasound **KEYWORD:** HK1127

CNNfyi.com   www.cnnfyi.com

Visit this site for coverage of current events and related classroom resources.

PE Pupil's Edition   **ATE** Annotated Teacher's Edition
RSB Reading Skill Builder   **DS** Datasheets
IE Integrated Enrichment   **SG** Study Guide
LE Laboratory Experiments
TT Teaching Transparencies   **BLM** Blackline Masters
★ Lesson Focus Transparency

 **READING SKILL BUILDER** *Brainstorming* Write the words *sound* and *light* on the chalkboard. Have students brainstorm words and phrases commonly used to describe sound and light. Allow a student volunteer to write the student contributions on the board under the appropriate term.

Students should provide words such as *waves, strong, bright, dim, colored, loud, soft, musical, high-pitched,* and *low-pitched.* Next have students pair a word used for sound with a word used for light when the words have the same meaning in terms of wave motion. For example, *loud* would pair with *bright* because both are related to the energy of the wave. *Color* would pair with *pitch* because both depend on frequency.

CHAPTER 12

Sound and Light

Chapter Preview

12.1 Sound
Properties of Sound
Musical Instruments
Hearing and the Ear
Ultrasound and Sonar

12.2 The Nature of Light
Waves and Particles
The Electromagnetic Spectrum

12.3 Reflection and Color
Reflection of Light
Mirrors
Seeing Colors

12.4 Refraction, Lenses, and Prisms
Refraction of Light
Lenses
Dispersion and Prisms

CROSS-DISCIPLINE TEACHING

Earth Science Invite an Earth science teacher to be a guest lecturer in your class, and ask the teacher to display maps of the sea floor. If a relief globe is available, have the teacher show the sea floors and continental shelves. Discuss how these maps were obtained using both sonar and satellite radar.

Life Science If a biology teacher has done dissections of a sheep's or a cow's eye, ask that teacher to display some dissected eyes and conduct a lesson on their structure and function.

Fine Arts Ask the school's instrumental music director to conduct a lesson on pitch and quality of sound by demonstrating or having players demonstrate instruments having similar or contrasting sounds.

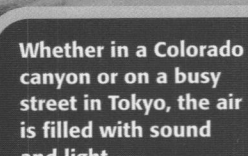

Whether in a Colorado canyon or on a busy street in Tokyo, the air is filled with sound and light.

Focus ACTIVITY

Background Imagine that you are walking through a canyon at sunset. As the red light of the setting sun fades, you see the first stars of the night sky. Your footsteps make a faint echo that bounces around the rocky canyon walls. As you approach your destination, you hear the sounds of people talking around a campfire.

Now imagine that you are walking down a street in a big city. You see the flash of neon signs and the colors of street lights. You hear the sound of cars, and you hear music from a car radio. Through the open door of a restaurant, you hear dishes clanking and people laughing.

Sound and light carry information about the world around us. In Chapter 11, you learned that sound waves are longitudinal waves, which require a medium, while light waves are transverse waves that can pass through empty space. You also learned some of the ways that waves behave in different situations.

This chapter will focus on the behavior of sound waves and light waves. You will learn how sound is produced, how mirrors and lenses work, how we see and hear, and how sound and light are used in different applications, ranging from music to medicine.

Activity 1 Stand outside in front of a large wall, and clap your hands. Do you hear an echo? How much time passes between the time you clap your hands and the time you hear the echo? Use this estimated time to estimate the distance to the wall. You will need two other pieces of information: the speed of sound in air, about 340 m/s, and the speed equation, $v = d/t$.

Activity 2 Find a crosswalk with a crossing signal. Watch as the signal changes from "Walk" to "Don't Walk" and back again. Does the crossing signal ever produce a sound? If so, why? If not, why would it be a good idea for the signal to produce a sound?

internetconnect

SC**LINKS**
NSTA

TOPIC: Transfer of sound and light energy
GO TO: www.scilinks.org
KEYWORD: HK1120

389

Focus ACTIVITY

Background Students will study electric charge and electric current in Chapter 13. Then in Chapter 15, the concepts of this chapter are combined with the concepts of electricity to show how sound and images can be transmitted as electrical signals and electromagnetic waves, including light signals in fiber optics.

Activity 1 Encourage students to find a location where echoes return in a second or more. This would require a distance of 170 m from the wall. In many cases this will be possible only outdoors with a large, isolated building or in some type of geological feature.

Activity 2 Some crosswalks use bells, buzzers, or other audible signals. These devices help the visually impaired. In some cases, the light-changing device produces sounds as a result of electrical relays opening and closing switches.

SKILL BUILDER

Interpreting Visuals Ask students to describe information they might receive from their sense of sound. Students should imagine themselves hiking alone in an area similar to the one in the photo at left. What are the sources of the sound? How are those sounds produced? How are all sounds produced? What are we responding to when we hear sounds? Repeat this exercise for the information we receive by sight.

Scheduling

Refer to pp. 388A–388D for lecture, classwork, and assignment options for Section 12.1.

★ Lesson Focus

Use transparency *LT 39* to prepare students for this section.

READING SKILL BUILDER *Brainstorming* Write the words *sound* and *music* on the chalkboard. Ask students to list words and phrases that apply to both terms and that are exclusive to one term or the other. Students should generally conclude that musical sounds have organized or regular properties, such as pitch and quality, that other sounds do not have.

SKILL BUILDER

Interpreting Visuals Have students examine **Figure 12-1.** Call attention to the fact that the motion of the drumhead in one direction compresses air while the motion in the other direction "stretches" the air causing a rarefaction. Similarly, the sound waves both push and pull on the eardrum when they strike it.

Sound

▶ **KEY TERMS**
pitch
ultrasound
infrasound
resonance
sonar

OBJECTIVES

▶ Recognize what factors affect the speed of sound.
▶ Relate loudness and pitch to properties of sound waves.
▶ Explain how harmonics and resonance affect the sound from musical instruments.
▶ Describe the function of the ear.
▶ Explain how sonar and ultrasound imaging work.

When you listen to your favorite musical group, you hear a variety of sounds. You may hear the steady beat of a drum, the twang of guitar strings, the wail of a saxophone, chords from a keyboard, or human voices.

Although these sounds all come from different sources, they are all longitudinal waves produced by vibrating objects. How does a musical instrument or a stereo speaker make sound waves in the air? What happens when those waves reach your ears? Why does a guitar sound different from a violin?

Properties of Sound

Figure 12-1

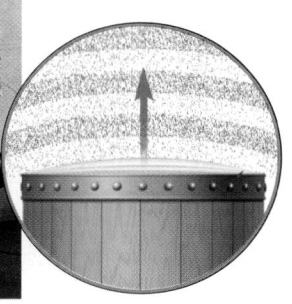

A The head of a drum vibrates up and down when it is struck by the drummer's hand.

B The vibrations of the drumhead create sound waves in the air.

When a drummer hits a drum, the head of the drum vibrates up and down, as shown in **Figure 12-1A.** Each time the drumhead moves upward, it compresses the air above it. As the head moves back down again, it leaves a small region of air that has a lower pressure. As this happens over and over, the drumhead creates a series of compressions and rarefactions in the air, as shown in **Figure 12-1B.**

The sound waves from a drum are longitudinal waves, like the waves along a stretched spring that were discussed in Chapter 11. Sound waves are caused by vibrations, and carry energy through a medium. Unlike waves along a spring, however, sound waves in air spread out in all directions away from the source. When sound waves from the drum reach your ears, the waves cause your eardrums to vibrate.

DEMONSTRATION 1 TEACHING

Pitch and Loudness

Time: Approximately 10 minutes
Materials: piano, guitar, other musical instruments as available

Step 1 Use musical instruments to demonstrate the concepts of sound in this section. Try to borrow a practice piano that you can take to your classroom on rollers. If no piano is available, have an acoustic guitar on hand and any other musical instruments students might volunteer to bring in.

Step 2 Use the piano or other instruments to demonstrate differences in loudness using notes of the same pitch. Use a sound level meter to reinforce the judgment of students.

Step 3 Demonstrate difference in pitch. Students may be able to see that the lowest string of a guitar vibrates with noticeably lower frequency than the highest string. Having students touch the strings lightly as they vibrate will also help convey this idea.

Table 12-1   Speed of Sound in Various Mediums

Medium	Speed of sound (m/s)	Medium	Speed of sound (m/s)
Gases		**Liquids at 25°C**	
air (0°C)	331	water	1490
air (25°C)	346	sea water	1530
air (100°C)	386	**Solids**	
helium (0°C)	972	copper	3813
hydrogen (0°C)	1290	iron	5000
oxygen (0°C)	317	rubber	54

The speed of sound depends on the medium

If you stand a few feet away from a drummer, it may seem that you hear the sound from the drum at the same time that the drummer's hand strikes the drum head. Sound waves travel very fast, but not infinitely fast. The speed of sound in air at room temperature is about 346 m/s (760 mi/h).

Table 12-1 shows the speed of sound in various materials and at various temperatures. The speed of sound in a particular medium depends on how well the particles can transmit the compressions and rarefactions of sound waves. In a gas, such as air, the speed of sound depends on how often the molecules of the gas collide with one another. At higher temperatures, the molecules move around faster and collide more frequently. An increase in temperature of 10°C increases the speed of sound in a gas by about 6 m/s.

Sound waves travel faster through liquids and solids than through gases. In a liquid or solid the particles are much closer together than in a gas, so the vibrations are transferred more rapidly from one particle to the next. However, some solids, such as rubber, dampen vibrations so that sound travels very slowly. Materials like rubber can be used for soundproofing.

Loudness is determined by intensity

How do the sound waves change when you increase the volume on your stereo or television? The loudness of a sound depends partly on the energy contained in the sound waves. The energy of a mechanical wave is determined by its amplitude. So the greater the amplitude of the sound waves, the louder the sound. For more on the energy of waves, review Section 11.1.

Loudness also depends on your distance from the source of the sound waves. The *intensity* of a sound describes its loudness at a particular distance from the source of the sound.

internetconnect

SC*LINKS*
NSTA

TOPIC: Properties of sound
GO TO: www.scilinks.org
KEYWORD: HK1121

Quick ACTIVITY

Sound in Different Mediums

1. Tie a spoon or other utensil to the middle of a 1–2 m length of string.
2. Wrap the loose ends of the string around your index fingers and place your fingers against your ears.
3. Swing the spoon so that it strikes a tabletop, and compare the volume and quality of the sound received with those received when you listen to the sound directly through the air.
4. Does sound travel better through the string or through the air?

SOUND AND LIGHT   **391**

Sound

Teaching Tip

Speed of Sound in Gases
Students may wonder why the speed of sound in hydrogen and helium is much greater than it is in air. The speed of sound in a gas depends on the velocity of the molecules. Temperature is a measure of the average kinetic energy of molecules, so the average kinetic energy of the molecules of any matter at the same temperature is the same. Therefore, at 0°C, molecules in air have the same average kinetic energy as molecules of hydrogen or helium. However, the molecules in air have an average mass of about 29 amu, whereas hydrogen molecules have a mass of 2 amu, and helium, 4 amu. The kinetic energy of any object depends on the object's mass and velocity. Therefore, in order to have the same kinetic energy, molecules of hydrogen and helium must be moving much faster than the molecules of air.

MISCONCEPTION ALERT

Sound Waves
Make clear that sound waves are not transverse waves even though they are usually represented in a transverse wave form. Amplitude in a sound wave is determined by the degree of compression (and the degree of rarefaction) compared to the normal pressure of the medium.

RESOURCE LINK
DATASHEETS

Have students use *Datasheet 12.1 Quick Activity: Sound in Different Mediums* to record their results.

Quick ACTIVITY

Sound in Different Mediums   The utensil should be a one-piece object, not one with parts that can rattle against one another. It is better to use hard kite string instead of yarn. Students should wrap the string near their fingertips and try to arrange the string so that the last loop before the downward part passes over the ends of their fingers. This will ensure that the string is pushed against their ears.

Heavier objects, such as one-piece wrenches, make the loudest sounds. A welded oven rack is truly impressive. Try striking the object with a soft object such as a rubber stopper.

Students should find that the object produces a ringing, bell-like sound that is louder when transmitted by the string than when transmitted through air.

Sound Level If you have or can borrow a sound level meter, let students measure the intensity of various sounds around school. Have them take note of the decibel, dB, scale on the meter. These meters are inexpensive and available at local electronic stores.

MISCONCEPTION ALERT

Pitch Versus Sound Students unfamiliar with the language of music may confuse the idea of high and low pitch with loud and soft sounds. All students should understand these words before proceeding. Also, students should understand that the words *fast* and *slow*—when applied to vibration—refer to the frequency, or "oftenness," of the back and forth movement.

SKILL BUILDER

Interpreting Visuals Figure 12-2 shows the decibel levels of several common sounds. Have students examine the figure. What is the decibel level of normal conversation? *(50 dB)* What is the level of a vacuum cleaner? *(70 dB)* How many times louder would a vacuum cleaner sound than a normal conversation? *(Four times as loud; an increase of 10 dB makes a sound seem twice as loud.)*

Resources Teaching Transparency 34 shows this visual.

RESOURCE LINK
DATASHEETS

Have students use *Datasheet 12.2 Quick Activity: Frequency and Pitch* to record their results.

Relative Intensities of Common Sounds

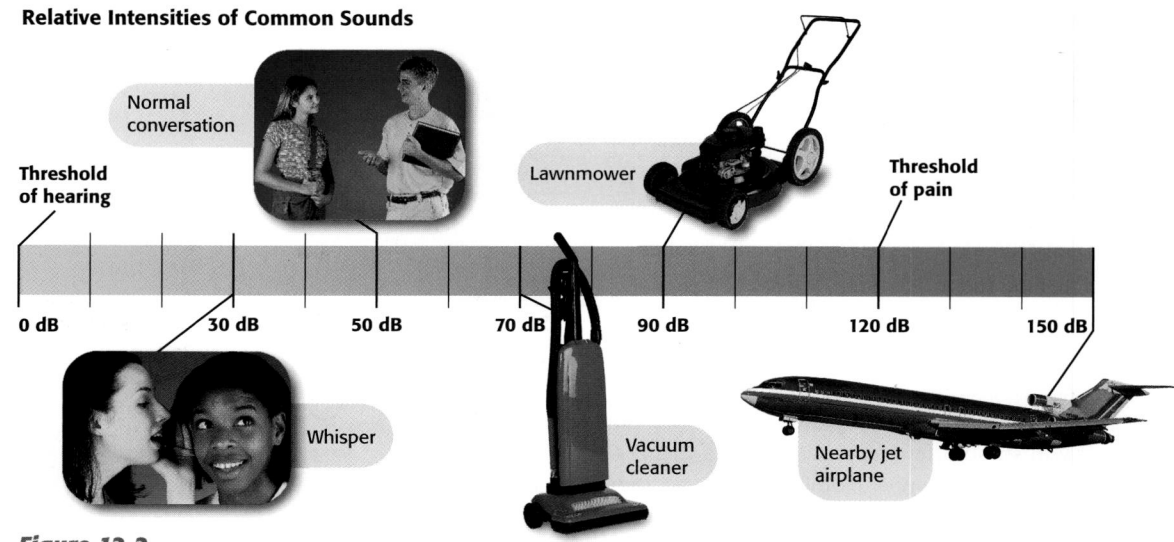

Figure 12-2
Sound intensity is measured on a logarithmic scale of decibels.

▶ **pitch** the perceived highness or lowness of a sound, depending on the frequency of sound waves

Quick ACTIVITY

Frequency and Pitch
1. Hold one end of a flexible metal or plastic ruler on a desk with about half of the ruler hanging off the edge. Bend the free end of the ruler and then release it. Can you hear a sound?
2. Try changing the position of the ruler so that less hangs over the edge. How does that change the sound produced?

However, a sound with twice the intensity of another sound does not seem twice as loud. Humans perceive loudness on a logarithmic scale. This means that a sound seems twice as loud when its intensity is 10 times the intensity of another sound.

The *relative intensity* of sounds is found by comparing the intensity of a sound with the intensity of the quietest sound a person can hear, the threshold of hearing. Relative intensity is measured in units called *decibels,* dB. A difference in intensity of 10 dB means a sound seems about twice as loud. **Figure 12-2** shows some common sounds and their decibel levels.

The quietest sound a human can hear is 0 dB. A sound of 120 dB is at the threshold of pain. Sounds louder than this can hurt your ears and give you headaches. Extensive exposure to sounds above 120 dB can cause permanent deafness.

Pitch is determined by frequency

Musicians use the word **pitch** to describe how high or low a note sounds. The pitch of a sound is related to the frequency of sound waves. Small instruments generally produce higher-pitched sounds than large instruments. A high-pitched note is made by something vibrating very rapidly, like a violin string or the air in a flute. A low-pitched sound is made by something vibrating more slowly, like a cello string or the air in a tuba.

In other words, a high-pitched sound corresponds to a high frequency, and a low-pitched sound corresponds to a low frequency. Trained musicians are capable of detecting subtle differences in frequency, even as slight as a change of 2 Hz.

392 CHAPTER 12

Quick ACTIVITY

Frequency and Pitch Have students relate their observations to the idea of pitch. A possible conclusion is that, given a longer and a shorter object of the same form and material, the shorter object will vibrate at a higher frequency (pitch).

Ranges of Hearing for Various Mammals

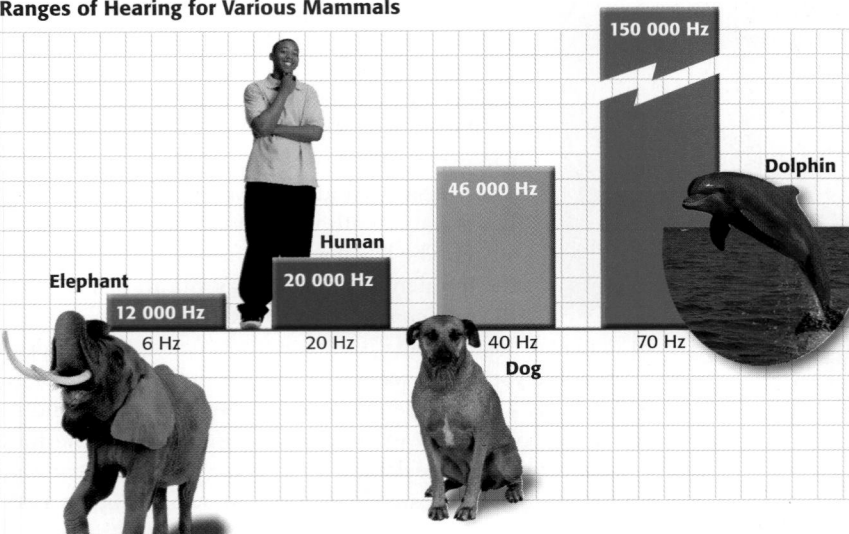

Figure 12-3
Humans can hear sounds ranging from 20 Hz to about 20 000 Hz, but many other animals can hear sounds well into the infrasound and ultrasound ranges.

Humans hear sound waves in a limited frequency range

The human ear can hear sounds from sources that vibrate as slowly as 20 vibrations per second (20 Hz) and as rapidly as 20 000 Hz. Any sound with a frequency below the range of human hearing is known as **infrasound**; any sound with a frequency above human hearing range is known as **ultrasound**. Many animals can hear frequencies of sound outside the range of human hearing, as shown in **Figure 12-3.**

Musical Instruments

Musical instruments, from deep bassoons to twangy banjos, come in a wide variety of shapes and sizes and produce a wide variety of sounds. But musical instruments can be grouped into a small number of categories based on how they make sound. Most instruments produce sound through the vibration of strings, air columns, or membranes.

Musical instruments rely on standing waves

When you pluck the string of a guitar, particles in the string start to vibrate. Waves travel out to the ends of the string, and then reflect back toward the middle. These vibrations cause a standing wave on the string, as shown in **Figure 12-4.** The two ends of the strings are nodes, and the middle of the string is an antinode.

▶ **infrasound** any sound consisting of waves with frequencies lower than 20 Hz

▶ **ultrasound** any sound consisting of waves with frequencies higher than 20 000 Hz

Figure 12-4
Vibrations on a guitar string produce standing waves on the string. These standing waves in turn produce sound waves in the air.

SOUND AND LIGHT **393**

|SKILL BUILDER

Interpreting Visuals Have students examine **Figure 12-3.** Tell students that several years ago, scientist Katherine Payne of Cornell University discovered that elephants can make and hear sounds having pitches well below the range of human hearing, which ends at about 20 Hz. She found that elephants in the wild communicate over long distances with these sounds, which were in the range of 6 to 18 Hz. Few objects or materials can absorb the energy of sound waves of these frequencies, so the sounds can be heard by other elephants long distances away.

Teaching Tip

Standing Waves Repeat *Alternate Assessment, Standing Waves on a Rope* from Chapter 11, page 378. Stress to students that only certain frequencies of standing waves are possible because these are the "natural" frequencies of that particular rope at a certain state of tension and length.

Teaching Tip

Fundamental Frequency To explain how standing waves relate to fundamental frequency, point out that any object, when disturbed, will vibrate at certain natural frequencies that are characteristic of that object. Certain objects vibrate better than others and produce sounds of recognizable pitch. Ask students to name objects that fit into this category. Responses may include bells, stretched strings, xylophone bars (metal), marimba bars (wood), and cymbals.

SKILL BUILDER

Vibrating Strings Have students examine **Figure 12-6.** Point out that string instruments do not usually vibrate in only one segment. The string will also vibrate in two, three, or more segments at the same time. These multiple vibrations produce the sound characteristic of string instruments. A guitar player can increase harmonics by plucking a string nearer to one end than in the middle.

Figure 12-5
Colored dust lies along the nodes of the two-dimensional standing waves on the head of this drum.

Figure 12-6
The note A-natural on a clarinet sounds different from the same note on a tuning fork due to the relative intensity of harmonics.

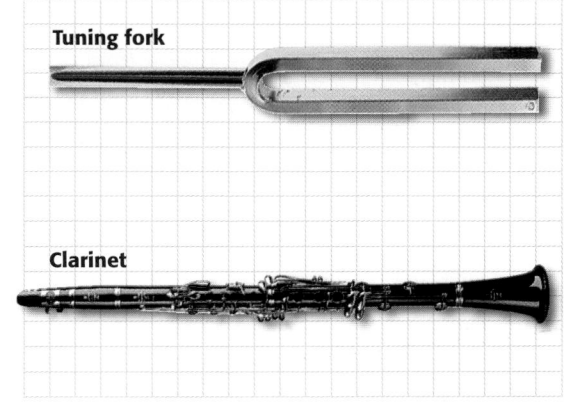
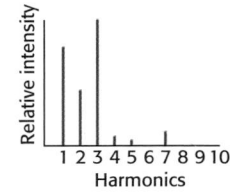
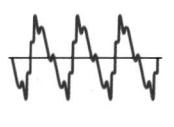

By placing your finger on the string somewhere along the neck of the guitar, you can change the pitch of the sound. This happens because a shorter length of string vibrates more rapidly, or in other words, at a higher frequency.

Recall from Section 11.3 that standing waves can exist only at certain frequencies on a string. The primary standing wave on a vibrating string has a wavelength that is twice the length of the string. The frequency of this wave, which is also the frequency of the string's vibrations, is called the *fundamental frequency.*

All musical instruments use standing waves to produce sound. In a flute, standing waves are formed in the column of air inside the flute. The wavelength and frequency of the standing waves can be changed by opening or closing holes in the flute body, which changes the length of the air column. Standing waves also form on the head of a drum, as shown in **Figure 12-5.**

Harmonics give every instrument a unique sound

If you play notes of the same pitch on a tuning fork and a clarinet, the two notes will sound different from each other. If you listen carefully, you may be able to hear that the clarinet is actually producing sounds at several different pitches, while the tuning fork produces a pure tone of only one pitch.

A tuning fork vibrates only at its fundamental frequency. The air column in a clarinet, however, vibrates at its fundamental frequency and at certain whole-number multiples of that frequency, called *harmonics.* **Figure 12-6** shows the harmonics present in a tuning fork and a clarinet when each sounds the note A-natural.

Inquiry Lab

How can you amplify the sound of a tuning fork? You should provide each group performing the lab at least one pair of forks of the same frequency. If you have a hollow resonance box, you may include it with the other items provided for the students, along with blocks of wood, metal bars, and so on.

Caution students not to strike the tuning forks against anything hard, such as a table-top or any of the solid objects provided. Dents and dings will eventually make a tuning fork useless. Tuning forks may be activated with a rubber stopper if rubber blocks are not available.

In step 3, students should touch the bases, not the tines, of the two forks.

In step 4, have students try bringing the tines of the active fork very near, but not

In the clarinet, several harmonics combine to make a complex wave. Note, however, that this wave still has a primary frequency that is the same as the frequency of the wave produced by the tuning fork. This is the fundamental frequency, which makes the note sound a certain pitch. The unique sound quality of a clarinet results from the relative intensity of different harmonics in each note that it plays. Every musical instrument has a characteristic sound quality resulting from the mixture of harmonics.

Instruments use resonance to amplify sound

When you pluck a guitar string, you can feel that the bridge and the body of the guitar also vibrate. These vibrations, which are a response to the vibrating string, are called *forced vibrations*. The body of the guitar is more likely to vibrate at certain specific frequencies called *natural frequencies*.

The sound produced by the guitar will be loudest when the forced vibrations cause the body of the guitar to vibrate at a natural frequency. This effect is called **resonance**. When resonance occurs, the sound is amplified because both the string and the guitar itself are vibrating at the same frequency.

▶ **resonance** an effect in which the vibration of one object causes the vibration of another object at a natural frequency

Inquiry Lab

How can you amplify the sound of a tuning fork?

Materials
✔ tuning forks of various frequencies
✔ rubber block for activating forks
✔ various objects made of metal and wood

Procedure

1. Activate a tuning fork by striking the tongs of the fork against a rubber block.
2. Touch the base of the tuning fork to different wood or metal objects, as shown in the figure at right. Listen for any changes in the sound of the tuning fork.
3. Activate the fork again, but now try touching the end of the tuning fork to the ends of other tuning forks (make sure that the tongs of the forks are free to vibrate, not touching anything). Can you make another tuning fork start vibrating in this way?
4. If you find two tuning forks that resonate with each other, try activating one and holding it near the tongs of the other one. Can you make the second fork vibrate without touching it?

Analysis

1. What are some characteristics of the objects that helped to amplify the sound of the tuning fork in step 2?
2. What is the relationship between the frequencies of tuning forks that resonate with each other in steps 3 and 4?

SOUND AND LIGHT **395**

touching, the tines of another fork of the same frequency. Students can also get the second fork to vibrate by touching the bases of both forks simultaneously to a resonant surface.

Analysis

1. Answers will vary. Generally, objects will be made of hard, thin materials with a relatively large surface area, such as desktops, boxes, tabletops, and sheets of poster board.
2. The forks will have the same pitch. If one fork has a pitch double (one octave above) that of another, the forks may also resonate.

internet**connect**

SC*LINKS*
NSTA

TOPIC: The ear
GO TO: www.scilinks.org
KEYWORD: HK1122

The natural frequency of an object depends on its shape, size, and mass, as well as the material it is made of. Complex objects such as a guitar have many natural frequencies, so they resonate well at many different pitches. However, some musical instruments, such as an electric guitar, do not resonate well and must be amplified electronically.

Hearing and the Ear

The head of a drum or the strings and body of a guitar vibrate to create sound waves in air. But how do you hear these waves and interpret them as different sounds?

The human ear is a very sensitive organ that senses vibrations in the air, amplifies them, and then transmits signals to the brain. In some ways, the process of hearing is the reverse of the process by which a drum head makes a sound. In the ear, sound waves cause membranes to vibrate.

Vibrations pass through three regions in the ear

Your ear is divided into three regions—outer, middle, and inner—as shown in **Figure 12-7.** Sound waves are funneled through the fleshy part of your outer ear and down the ear canal. The ear canal ends at the eardrum, a thin, flat piece of tissue.

When sound waves strike the eardrum, they cause the eardrum to vibrate. These vibrations pass from the eardrum through the three small bones of the middle ear—known as the hammer, the anvil, and the stirrup. When the vibrations reach the stirrup, the stirrup strikes a membrane at the opening of the inner ear, sending waves through the spiral-shaped cochlea.

Figure 12-7
Sound waves are transmitted as vibrations through the ear. Vibrations in the cochlea stimulate nerves that send impulses to the brain.

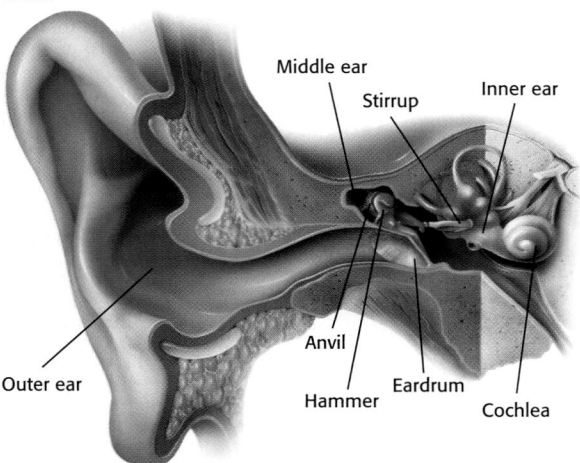

Middle ear
Stirrup
Inner ear
Outer ear
Anvil
Hammer
Eardrum
Cochlea

Resonance occurs in the inner ear

The cochlea contains a long, flexible membrane called the *basilar membrane.* Different parts of the basilar membrane vibrate at different natural frequencies. As waves pass through the cochlea, they resonate with specific parts of the basilar membrane.

A wave of a particular frequency causes only a small portion of the basilar membrane to vibrate. Hair cells near that part of the membrane then stimulate nerve fibers that send an impulse to the brain. The brain interprets this impulse as a sound with a specific frequency.

DEMONSTRATION 2 TEACHING

Resonance

Time: Approximately 10 minutes
Materials: piano, guitar, or other string instruments

Step 1 When one object vibrates at the natural frequency of another object, vibrations can be induced in the second object. This is an example of sympathetic vibration caused by resonance. A piano works best for this demonstration, but other acoustic, string instruments may work also.

Step 2 Press down the loud pedal of the piano to lift the felt dampers from all the strings. Sing or have a student sing a single note very loudly for 2 s and then stop. When the singing stops, you will hear the same note coming from the piano. This is caused by the induced vibration of the string of the same pitch (along with its harmonics). Try several other pitches. With a guitar, match the pitch of the sung note to the pitch of one of the strings.

Ultrasound and Sonar

If you shout over the edge of a rock canyon, you may hear the sound reflected back to you in an echo. Like all waves, sound waves can be reflected. The reflection of sound waves can be used to determine distances and to create maps and images.

Sonar is used for underwater location

How can a person on a ship measure the distance to the ocean floor, which may be thousands of meters from the surface of the water? One way is to use **sonar.**

A sonar system determines distance by measuring the time it takes for sound waves to be reflected back from a surface. A sonar device on a ship sends a pulse of sound downward, and measures the time, t, that it takes for the sound to be reflected back from the ocean floor. Using the average speed of the sound waves in water, v, the distance, d, can be calculated using a form of the speed equation from Section 8.1.

$$d = vt$$

If a school of fish or a submarine passes under the ship, the sound pulse will be reflected back much sooner.

Ultrasound waves—sound waves with frequencies above 20 000 Hz—work particularly well in sonar systems because they can be focused into narrow beams and can be directed more easily than other sound waves. Bats, like the one in **Figure 12-8,** use reflected ultrasound waves to navigate in flight and to locate insects for food.

Ultrasound imaging is used in medicine

The echoes of very high frequency ultrasound waves, between 1 million and 15 million Hz, are used to produce computerized images called *sonograms.* Using sonograms, doctors can safely view organs inside the body without having to perform surgery. Sonograms can be used to diagnose problems, to guide surgical procedures, or even to view unborn fetuses, as shown in **Figure 12-9.**

Figure 12-8
Bats use ultrasound echoes to navigate in flight.

▶ **sonar** a system that uses reflected sound waves to determine the distance to, and location of, objects

VOCABULARY *Skills Tip*

Sonar stands for **so**und **n**avigation **a**nd **r**anging.

Figure 12-9
An image of an unborn fetus can be generated from reflected ultrasound waves.

Sound

Teaching Tip

Using Sonar In the case of sonar, the speed equation becomes $D = \frac{1}{2}vt$, where D is the depth to the object causing the reflection; the wave travels a total distance of twice the depth.

Additional Application

Ultrasound Students may be interested in investigating the many other medical and non-medical uses for ultrasound, in addition to sonograms and sonar. For example, kidney stones can be disintegrated with frequencies between 20 000 Hz and 30 000 Hz. Tumors have be treated by ultrasound beams from outside the body. The beams come to a focus at the site of the tumor and kill the tissue by heating it. Students may also look into some of the dangers of the mis-use of ultrasound. In addition to heating, some frequencies can cause cells to disintegrate.

In nonmedical applications, ultrasound can be used to locate hairline fractures in metal support beams and machinery. High-intensity ultrasonic waves passing through a liquid-filled tank are used to clean jewelry, dentures, or small machinery placed in the tank.

Step 3 Students will also hear evidence that the human voice has several strong harmonics, or overtones, because several other strings will also sound along with the fundamental. In addition, all strings will vibrate a little due to forced vibrations.

Sound

SECTION 12.1 REVIEW

Check Your Understanding

1. Students may list state of matter, nature of the medium, or temperature.

2. In air, molecules are very far apart and collide less often than in water, where molecules are packed closely together.

3. Audible sound can be heard by the human ear. Its frequency range is about 20 Hz to 20 000 Hz. Sounds with frequencies lower than 20 Hz make up infrasound. Ultrasound has frequencies higher than 20 000 Hz.

4. Frequency increases and wavelength decreases.

5. Amplitude and intensity both increase.

6. Although the two notes have the same fundamental pitch, they sound different because they emphasize different harmonics.

7. The acoustic guitar is constructed so that the hollow body vibrates in resonance with the string. Electric guitars usually have a solid body that vibrates very little.

Answers continue on p. 423A.

RESOURCE LINK

STUDY GUIDE

Assign students *Review Section 12.1 Sound.*

At high frequencies, ultrasound waves can travel through most materials. But some sound waves are reflected when they pass from one type of material into another. How much sound is reflected depends on the density of the materials at each boundary. The reflected sound waves from different boundary surfaces are compiled into a sonogram by a computer.

The advantage of using sound to see inside the human body is that it doesn't harm living cells as X rays may do. However, to see details, the wavelengths of the ultrasound must be slightly smaller than the smallest parts of the object being viewed. That is another reason that such high frequencies are used. According to the wave speed equation from Section 11.2, the higher the frequency of waves in a given medium, the shorter the wavelength will be. Sound waves with a frequency of 15 million Hz have a wavelength of less than 1 mm when they pass through soft tissue.

SECTION 12.1 REVIEW

SUMMARY

▶ The speed of sound waves depends on temperature, density, and other properties of the medium.

▶ Pitch is determined by the frequency of sound waves.

▶ Infrasound and ultrasound lie beyond the range of human hearing.

▶ The loudness of a sound depends on intensity. Relative intensity is measured in decibels (dB).

▶ Musical instruments use standing waves and resonance to produce sound.

▶ The ear converts vibrations in the air into nerve impulses to the brain.

▶ Reflection of sound or ultrasound waves can be used to determine distances or to create sonograms.

CHECK YOUR UNDERSTANDING

1. **Identify** two factors that affect the speed of sound.
2. **Explain** why sound travels faster in water than in air.
3. **Distinguish** between infrasound, audible sound, and ultrasound waves.
4. **Determine** which of the following must change when pitch gets higher.
   a. amplitude   d. intensity
   b. frequency   e. speed of the sound waves
   c. wavelength
5. **Determine** which of the following must change when a sound gets louder.
   a. amplitude   d. intensity
   b. frequency   e. speed of the sound waves
   c. wavelength
6. **Explain** why the note middle C played on a piano sounds different from the same note played on a violin.
7. **Explain** why an acoustic guitar generally sounds louder than an electric guitar without an electronic amplifier.
8. **Describe** the process through which sound waves in the air are translated into nerve impulses to the brain.
9. **Critical Thinking** Why are sonograms made with ultrasound waves instead of audible sound waves?
10. **Creative Thinking** Why do most pianos contain a large *sounding board* underneath the strings? (**Hint:** The piano would be harder to hear without it.)

12.2

The Nature of Light

OBJECTIVES

▶ Recognize that light has both wave and particle characteristics.
▶ Relate the energy of light to the frequency of electromagnetic waves.
▶ Describe different parts of the electromagnetic spectrum.
▶ Explain how electromagnetic waves are used in communication, medicine, and other areas.

KEY TERMS
photon
intensity
radar

Scheduling

Refer to pp. 388A–388D for lecture, classwork, and assignment options for Section 12.2.

★ **Lesson Focus**
Use transparency *LT 40* to prepare students for this section.

Most of us see and feel light almost every moment of our lives, from the first rays of dawn to the warm glow of a campfire. Even people who cannot see can feel the warmth of the sun on their skin, which is an effect of infrared light. We are very familiar with light, but how much do we understand about what light really is?

internet connect

SC*LINKS*
NSTA

TOPIC: Properties of light
GO TO: www.scilinks.org
KEYWORD: HK1123

READING SKILL BUILDER *Summarizing*
The speed of light and the wave-particle duality of light are fundamental ideas of science. To help students grasp these concepts, proceed in a stepwise fashion by having students read the subsections on pp. 399–402 one at a time. At the end of each subsection, stop and ask for volunteers to summarize that part. After the student finishes, ask students whether they agree on the summary given. If not, ask for other volunteers to offer their insights.

Waves and Particles

It is difficult to describe all of the properties of light with a single scientific model. The two most commonly used models describe light either as a wave or as a stream of particles.

Light produces interference patterns like water waves

In 1801, the English scientist Thomas Young devised an experiment to test the nature of light. He passed a beam of light through two narrow openings and then onto a screen on the other side. He found that the light produced a striped pattern on the screen, like the pattern in **Figure 12-10A**. This pattern is similar to the pattern caused by water waves interfering in a ripple tank, as shown in **Figure 12-10B**.

LINKING CHAPTERS

Have students review wave interference in Chapter 11.

Figure 12-10

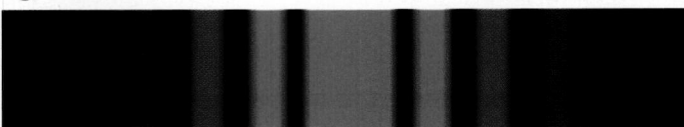

A Light passed through two small openings produces light and dark bands on a screen.

B Two water waves in a ripple tank also produce an interference pattern with light and dark bands.

ALTERNATIVE ASSESSMENT

Comparing Frequency and Intensity

Have students use common objects or musical instruments to demonstrate the following:
• two sounds of different intensities but the same frequency; two sounds of different frequencies but about the same intensity
• two sounds of different pitches but about the same amplitude; two sounds of different amplitudes but the same pitch
• two sounds of different wavelengths but the same amplitude

RESOURCE LINK
LABORATORY MANUAL

Have students perform *Lab 12 Light: Choosing a Pair of Sunglasses* in the lab ancillary.

DATASHEETS

Have students use *Datasheet 12.5* to record their results.

The Nature of Light

Historical Perspective

In 1905, Albert Einstein introduced photons to explain the photoelectric effect, which is the ejection of electrons from a metal plate by light. Einstein's theory was based on the earlier (1900) quantum theory of Max Planck, who said that atoms absorb and release energy in certain discrete amounts or quanta. The photoelectric effect was once widely used in devices called "electric eyes," which detected when a light beam was broken and caused an action such as setting off an alarm or opening a door.

SKILL BUILDER

Interpreting Visuals To help students understand the photon concept pictured in **Figure 12-11,** have them visualize a brick wall being struck by streams of thousands of ping-pong balls. No single ball has enough kinetic energy to chip the bricks. Then imagine the same wall being struck at the same speed by only a few steel bolts. Even though just a few strike the wall, each has enough energy to break chips out of the bricks. The many ping-pong balls represent bright red light and the few bolts represent dim blue light. Thus, the brightness of light corresponds to the number of photons striking a surface per unit time, and the color of light corresponds to the energy per photon.

Figure 12-11

A Bright red light cannot knock electrons off this metal plate.

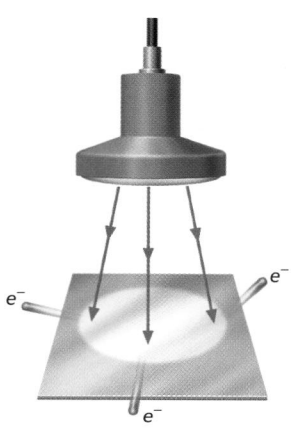

B Dim blue light can knock electrons off the plate. The wave model of light cannot explain this effect, but the particle model can.

▶ **photon** a particle of light

Light can be modeled as a wave

Because the light in Young's experiment produced interference patterns, Young concluded that light must consist of waves. The model of light as a wave is still used today to explain many of the basic properties of light and its behavior.

Chapter 11 describes light waves as transverse waves that do not require a medium in which to travel. Light waves are also called electromagnetic waves because they consist of changing electric and magnetic fields, which will be discussed further in Chapter 13 and Chapter 14. The properties of transverse waves that you have already learned are all that you need to know to understand the wave model of light as it is used in this chapter.

The wave model of light explains much of the observed behavior of light. For example, light waves may reflect when they meet a mirror, refract when they pass through a lens, or diffract when they pass through a narrow opening.

The wave model of light cannot explain some observations

In the early part of the twentieth century, physicists began to realize that some observations could not be explained with the wave model of light. For example, when light strikes a piece of metal, electrons may fly off the metal's surface. Experiments show that in some cases, dim blue light may knock some electrons off a metal plate, while very bright red light cannot knock off any electrons, as shown in **Figure 12-11.**

According to the wave model, very bright red light should have more energy than dim blue light because the waves in bright light should have greater amplitude. But this does not explain how the blue light can knock electrons off the plate while the red light cannot.

Light can be modeled as a stream of particles

One way to explain the effects of light striking a metal plate is to assume that the energy of the light is contained in small packets. A packet of blue light carries more energy than a packet of red light, enough to knock an electron off the plate. Bright red light contains many packets, but no single one has enough energy to knock an electron off the plate.

In the particle model of light, these packets are called **photons,** and a beam of light is considered to be a stream of photons. Photons are considered particles, but they are not like ordinary particles of matter. Photons do not have mass; they are more like little bundles of energy. But unlike the energy in a wave, the energy in a photon is located in a particular place.

400 CHAPTER 12

The model of light used depends on the situation

Light can be modeled as either waves or particles; so which explanation is correct? The success of any scientific theory depends on how well it can explain different observations. Some effects, such as the interference of light, are more easily explained with the wave model. Other cases, like light knocking electrons off a metal plate, are explained better by the particle model. The particle model also easily explains how light can travel across empty space without a medium.

Most scientists currently accept both the wave model and the particle model of light, and use one or the other depending on the situation that they are studying. Some believe that light has a "dual nature," so that it actually has different characteristics depending on the situation. In many cases, using either the wave model or the particle model of light gives good results.

The energy of light is proportional to frequency

Whether modeled as a particle or as a wave, light is also a form of energy. Each photon of light can be thought of as carrying a small amount of energy. The amount of this energy is proportional to the frequency of the corresponding electromagnetic wave, as shown in **Figure 12-12.**

A photon of red light, for example, carries an amount of energy that corresponds to the frequency of waves in red light, 4.5×10^{14} Hz. A photon with twice as much energy corresponds to a wave with twice the frequency, which lies in the ultraviolet range of the electromagnetic spectrum. Likewise, a photon with half as much energy, which would be a photon of infrared light, corresponds to a wave with half the frequency.

The speed of light depends on the medium

In a vacuum, all light travels at the same speed, called c. The speed of light is very large, 3×10^8 m/s (about 186 000 mi/s). Light is the fastest signal in the universe. Nothing can travel faster than the speed of light.

Light also travels through transparent mediums, such as air, water, and glass. When light passes through a medium, it travels slower than it does in a vacuum. **Table 12-2** shows the speed of light in several different mediums.

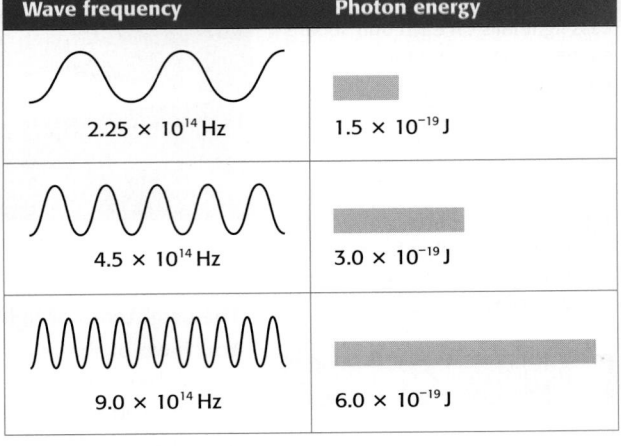

Wave frequency	Photon energy
2.25×10^{14} Hz	1.5×10^{-19} J
4.5×10^{14} Hz	3.0×10^{-19} J
9.0×10^{14} Hz	6.0×10^{-19} J

Figure 12-12
The energy of photons of light is related to the frequency of electromagnetic waves.

Table 12-2 Speed of Light in Various Mediums

Medium	Speed of light ($\times 10^8$ m/s)
Vacuum	2.997925
Air	2.997047
Ice	2.29
Water	2.25
Quartz (SiO_2)	2.05
Glass	1.97
Diamond	1.24

SOUND AND LIGHT **401**

|SKILL BUILDER

Interpreting Visuals Use **Figure 12-12** to remind students that light color relates to the energy per photon. In the wave model, color relates to frequency, as pointed out in the next subsection. Therefore, frequency and energy per photon correspond to each other.

|SKILL BUILDER

Interpreting Tables The speed of light in air is slower than the speed of light in a vacuum, but the difference is very small, as students can see in **Table 12-2.**

The speed of light in a diamond is less than half the speed of light in a vacuum but still on the same order of magnitude ($\times 10^8$ m/s).

Teaching Tip

Speed of Light Unlike sound, which travels better in liquids and solids than in air, light travels more slowly as the density of the medium increases. When light passes through a medium, it encounters the many atoms that make up the medium. If light hits an atom, the light is absorbed and emitted again, which takes a (very) small amount of time. As light passes through the empty space between atoms in the medium, the light moves at its full speed of 3.0×10^8 m/s. The speed of light in the medium is really an average speed that takes into account the stopping and starting of the light as it encounters atoms.

The Nature of Light

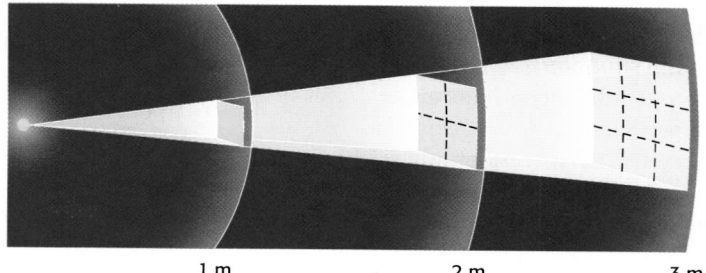

Figure 12-13
Less light falls on each unit square as the distance from the source increases.

> ▶ **intensity** the rate at which light or any other form of energy flows through a given area of space

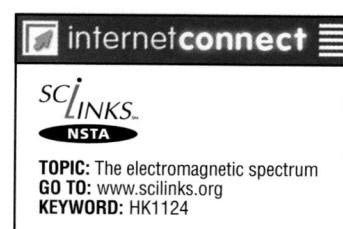

internet connect

SC*LINKS*
NSTA

TOPIC: The electromagnetic spectrum
GO TO: www.scilinks.org
KEYWORD: HK1124

Figure 12-14
The electromagnetic spectrum includes all possible kinds of light.

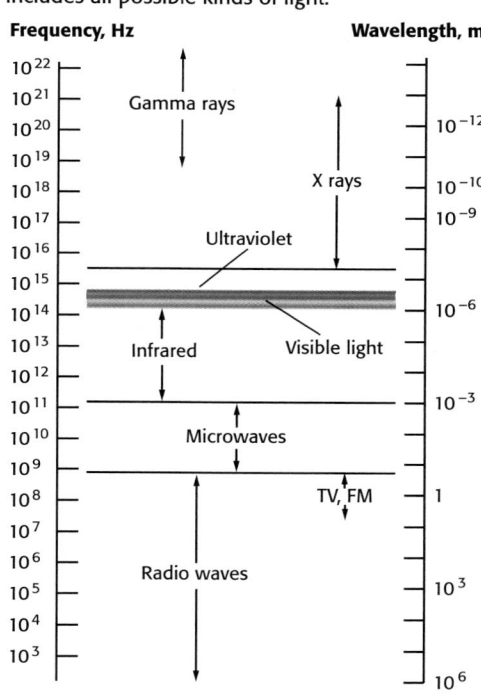

The brightness of light depends on intensity

You have probably noticed that it is easier to read near a lamp with a 100 W bulb than near a lamp with a 60 W bulb. That is because a 100 W bulb is brighter than a 60 W bulb. The quantity that measures the amount of light illuminating a surface is called **intensity**, and it depends on the amount of light—the number of photons or waves—that passes through a certain area of space.

Like the intensity of sound, the intensity of light from a light source decreases as the light spreads out in spherical wave fronts. Imagine a series of spheres centered around a source of light, as shown in **Figure 12-13.** As light spreads out from the source, the number of photons or waves passing through a given area on a sphere, say 1 cm^2, decreases. An observer farther from the light source will therefore see the light as dimmer than will an observer closer to the light source.

The Electromagnetic Spectrum

Light fills the air and space around us. Our eyes can detect light waves ranging from 400 nm (violet light) to 700 nm (red light). But the visible spectrum is only one small part of the entire electromagnetic spectrum, shown in **Figure 12-14.** We live in a sea of electromagnetic waves, ranging from the sun's ultraviolet light to radio waves transmitted by television and radio stations.

The electromagnetic spectrum consists of light at all possible energies, frequencies, and wavelengths. Although all electromagnetic waves are similar in certain ways, each part of the electromagnetic spectrum also has unique properties. Many modern technologies, from radar guns to cancer treatments, take advantage of the different properties of electromagnetic waves.

Sunlight contains ultraviolet light

The invisible light that lies just beyond violet light falls into the *ultraviolet* (UV) portion of the spectrum. Ultraviolet light has higher energy and shorter wavelengths than visible light does. Nine percent of the energy emitted by the sun is UV light. Because of its high energy, some UV light can pass through thin layers of clouds, causing you to sunburn even on overcast days.

X rays and gamma rays are used in medicine

Beyond the ultraviolet part of the spectrum lie waves known as *X rays,* which have even higher energy and shorter wavelengths than ultraviolet waves. X rays have wavelengths less than 10^{-8} m. The highest energy electromagnetic waves are gamma rays, which have wavelengths as short as 10^{-14} m.

An X-ray image at the doctor's office is made by passing X rays through the body. Most of them pass right through, but a few are absorbed by bones and other tissues. The X rays that pass through the body to a photographic plate produce an image such as the one in **Figure 12-15.**

X rays are useful tools for doctors, but they can also be dangerous. Both X rays and gamma rays have very high energies, so they may kill living cells or turn them into cancer cells. However, gamma rays can also be used to treat cancer by killing the diseased cells.

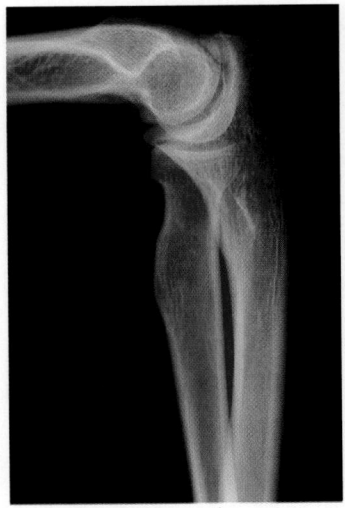

Figure 12-15
X-ray images are negatives. Dark areas show where the rays passed through, while bright areas show denser structures in the body.

REAL WORLD APPLICATIONS

Sun Protection Short-term exposure to UV light can cause sunburn; prolonged or repeated exposure may lead to skin cancer. To protect your skin, you should shield it from UV light whenever you are outdoors by covering your body with clothing, wearing a hat, and using a sunscreen.

Sunscreen products contain a chemical that blocks some or all UV light, preventing it from penetrating your skin. The Skin Protection Factor (SPF) of sunscreens varies as shown in the table at right.

Applying Knowledge
1. A friend is taking an antibiotic, and his doctor tells him to avoid UV light while on the medication. What SPF factor should he use, and why?

2. You and another friend decide to go hiking on a cloudy day. Your friend claims that she does not need any sunscreen because the sun is not out. What is wrong with her reasoning?

SPF factor	Effect on skin
None	Offers no protection from damage by UV
4 to 6	Offers some protection if you tan easily
7 to 8	Offers extra protection but still permits tanning
9 to 10	Offers excellent protection if you burn easily but would still like to get a bit of a tan
15	Offers total protection from burning
22	Totally blocks UV

SOUND AND LIGHT **403**

Teaching Tip

Energy and Penetrating Power Reiterate the connection between color and energy by pointing out that ultraviolet light can damage cells because of the high energy of its photons, which also give it penetrating ability. Call students' attention to the fact that X rays lie just beyond the ultraviolet part of the spectrum and have enough penetrating power to pass completely through the body. Also point out that X rays are even more damaging to cells than UV of the same intensity.

REAL WORLD APPLICATIONS

Sun Protection Have students poll others in the student body as to whether they use sunscreen or sunblock on a regular basis. Allow students to brainstorm facts about sun protection that might persuade their classmates to use sunscreen or sunblock.

Applying Knowledge
1. He or she should use SPF 22. Certain tetracycline antibiotics cause skin sensitivity to UV light. To totally block UV, the friend should use sunscreen with SPF 22 or higher.
2. Although visible light is dimmer and diffused, ultraviolet light has greater energy that can pass through clouds unaffected.

Resources Assign students worksheet *12.1 RWA—How Does Sunscreen Work?* in the **Integration Enrichment Resources** ancillary.

The Nature of Light

Teaching Tip

Incandescence Infrared radiation is sometimes called radiant heat because it increases the velocity of molecules when it is absorbed by matter. The warm matter also radiates energy as infrared waves. As a sample of matter becomes hotter, the average frequency of radiated energy becomes higher. At some temperature, the matter begins to radiate visible light (become incandescent) and appears to be dull red. As matter is heated further, it becomes orange and then yellow. When it is hot enough that significant amounts of blue light are emitted, the object appears white and we say it is "white-hot." In fact, all matter above 0 K emits radiation.

Additional Application

Microwave Radiation Although microwaves are reflected by metals, powdered metals absorb a significant amount of microwaves and become very hot. This technology is used in packaging microwavable foods. A paper or plastic sheet containing metal powder becomes hot and browns or fries the food.

In the 1960s, scientists detected microwave radiation of 7.3 cm wavelength (or 4.1 GHz) coming from all directions. It is theorized that this is the residual radiation from the big bang, the birth of the universe.

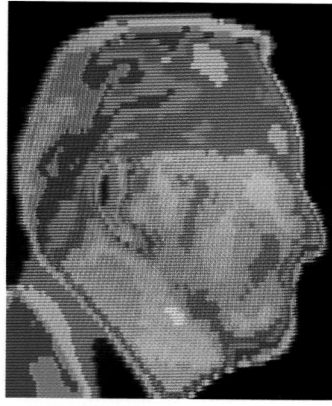

Figure 12-16
An infrared camera reveals the temperatures of different parts of an object.

Did You Know ?

Because microwaves reflect off the inside walls of a microwave oven, they may form standing waves. Food lying at the antinodes, where the vibrations are at a maximum, gets cooked more than food lying at the nodes, where there are no vibrations. For that reason, most microwave ovens rotate food items to ensure even heating.

▶ **radar** a system that uses reflected radio waves to determine the distance to, and location of, objects

VOCABULARY Skills Tip

*Radar stands for **ra**dio **d**etection **a**nd **r**anging.*

Infrared light can be felt as warmth

Electromagnetic waves with wavelengths slightly longer than red light fall into the *infrared* (IR) portion of the spectrum. Infrared light from the sun, or from a heat lamp, warms you. Infrared light is used to keep food warm. You might have noticed reddish lamps above food in a cafeteria. The energy provided by the infrared light is just enough to keep the food hot without continuing to cook it.

Devices and photographic film that are sensitive to infrared light can reveal images of objects like the one in **Figure 12-16.** An infrared sensor can be used to measure the heat that objects radiate and then create images that show temperature variations. By detecting infrared radiation, areas of different temperature can be mapped. Remote sensors on weather satellites that record infrared light can track the movement of clouds and record temperature changes in the atmosphere.

Microwaves are used in cooking and communication

Electromagnetic waves with wavelengths in the range of centimeters, longer than infrared waves, are known as *microwaves.* The most familiar application of microwaves today is in cooking.

Microwave ovens in the United States use microwaves with a frequency of 2450 MHz (12.2 cm wavelength). Microwaves are reflected by metals and are easily transmitted through air, glass, paper, and plastic. However, water, fat, and sugar all absorb microwaves. Microwaves can travel about 3–5 cm into most foods.

As microwaves penetrate deeper into food, they are absorbed along with their energy. The rapidly changing electric field of the microwaves causes water and other molecules to vibrate. The energy of these vibrations is delivered to other parts of the food as energy is transferred by heat.

Microwaves are also used to carry telecommunication signals. Communication technologies using microwaves will be discussed in Chapter 15.

Radio waves are used in communications and radar

Electromagnetic waves longer than microwaves are classified as *radio waves.* Radio waves have wavelengths that range from tenths of a meter to millions of meters. This portion of the electromagnetic spectrum includes TV signals, AM and FM radio signals, and other radio waves. The ways that these waves are used to transmit signals will be described in Chapter 15.

Air-traffic control towers at airports use **radar** to determine the locations of aircraft. Antennas at the control tower emit radio waves, or sometimes microwaves, out in all directions.

When the signal reaches an airplane, a transmitter on the plane sends another radio signal back to the control tower. This signal gives the plane's location and elevation above the ground.

At shorter range, the original signal sent by the antenna may reflect off the plane and back to a receiver at the control tower. A computer then calculates the distance to the plane using the time delay between the original signal and the reflected signal. The locations of various aircraft around the airport are displayed on a screen like the one shown in **Figure 12-17.**

Radar is also used by police to monitor the speed of vehicles. A radar gun fires a radar signal of known frequency at a moving vehicle and then measures the frequency of the reflected waves. Because the vehicle is moving, the reflected waves will have a different frequency, according to the Doppler effect as described in Section 11.2. A computer chip converts the difference in frequency into a speed and shows the result on a digital display.

Figure 12-17
The radar system in an air traffic control tower uses reflected radio waves to monitor the location and speed of airplanes.

MISCONCEPTION
Division Point **ALERT**
The division point between microwaves and radio waves is arbitrarily set as are other division points on the electromagnetic spectrum. The exception is visible light, which is limited by the eye's sensitivity. There is no significant difference between the waves on either side of a division point.

SECTION 12.2 REVIEW

SUMMARY

▶ Light can be modeled as electromagnetic waves or as a stream of particles called photons.

▶ The energy of a photon is proportional to the frequency of the corresponding light wave.

▶ The speed of light in a vacuum, c, is 3.0×10^8 m/s. Light travels more slowly in a medium.

▶ The electromagnetic spectrum includes light at all possible values of energy, frequency, and wavelength.

CHECK YOUR UNDERSTANDING

1. **State** one piece of evidence supporting the wave model of light and one piece of evidence supporting the particle model of light.
2. **Name** the regions of the electromagnetic spectrum from the shortest wavelengths to the longest wavelengths.
3. **Determine** which photons have greater energy, those associated with microwaves or those associated with visible light.
4. **Determine** which band of the electromagnetic spectrum has the following:
   a. the lowest frequency   **c.** the greatest energy
   b. the shortest wavelength   **d.** the least energy
5. **Critical Thinking** You and a friend are looking at the stars, and you notice two stars close together, one bright and one fairly dim. Your friend comments that the bright star must emit much more light than the dimmer star. Is he necessarily right? Explain your answer.

SOUND AND LIGHT **405**

Check Your Understanding

1. Interference, reflection, and refraction support the wave model. The fact that blue light can knock electrons off a metal plate while red light cannot (the photoelectric effect) supports the particle model.
2. gamma rays, X rays, ultraviolet light, visible light (from violet to red), infrared light, microwaves, radio waves
3. Photons of visible light have higher energy than photons associated with microwaves because their frequency is greater.
4. **a.** radio waves
   b. gamma rays
   c. gamma rays
   d. radio waves
5. He may be wrong because there is no way to judge. The star that appears brighter may actually be dimmer but much closer than the less-bright star.

RESOURCE LINK
STUDY GUIDE

Assign students *Review Section 12.2 The Nature of Light.*

Scheduling

Refer to pp. 388A–388D for lecture, classwork, and assignment options for Section 12.3.

★ **Lesson Focus**
Use transparency *LT 41* to prepare students for this section.

READING SKILL BUILDER *Discussion* Write the following questions on the chalkboard and conduct a short discussion on possible responses.
• How do you know things reflect light?
• What kinds of things reflect light best?
• Why can you see your image in some reflectors and not in others?
• Is there any way to predict what direction a light ray will travel after it hits a reflecting surface?
After students have read pages 406–409, discuss the questions again.

MISCONCEPTION

 **ALERT**

Vision In ancient times, people believed that vision was a result of mysterious rays sent out from the eyes. The idea still survives in language, when we cast a glance at something, or in "She threw him a disgusted look." Even recent studies show that many people still believe this idea, probably because they have never been asked to analyze it. Questioning may reveal some students who interpret vision in this way. In the eleventh century, the Arabian scholar Alhazen proved that light was not created by the eyes. He pointed out that light must come from the sun because people who look directly at the sun become blinded.

Reflection and Color

▶ **KEY TERMS**
light ray
virtual image
real image

OBJECTIVES
▶ Describe how light reflects off smooth and rough surfaces.
▶ Explain the law of reflection.
▶ Show how mirrors form real and virtual images.
▶ Explain why objects appear to be different colors.
▶ Describe how colors may be added or subtracted.

You may be used to thinking about light bulbs, candles, and the sun as objects that send light to your eyes. But everything else that you see, including this textbook, also sends light to your eyes. Otherwise, you would not be able to see them.

Of course, there is a difference between the light from the sun and the light from a book. The sun emits its own light. The light that comes from a book is created by the sun or a lamp, then bounces off the pages of the book to your eyes.

▶ **light ray** a model of light that represents light traveling through space in an imaginary straight line

Figure 12-18
This solar collector in the French Pyrenees uses mirrors to reflect and focus light into a huge furnace, which can reach temperatures of 3000°C.

Reflection of Light

Every object reflects some light and absorbs some light. Mirrors, such as those on the solar collector in **Figure 12-18,** reflect almost all incoming light. Because mirrors reflect light, it is possible for you to see an image of yourself in a mirror.

Light can be modeled as a ray
To describe reflection, refraction, and many other effects of light at the scale of everyday experience, it is useful to use another model for light, the **light ray.** A light ray is an imaginary line running in the direction that the light travels. It is the same as the direction of wave travel in the wave model of light or the path of photons in the particle model of light.

Although they do not represent a full picture of the complex nature of light, light rays are a good approximation of light in many situations. The study of light in circumstances where it behaves like a ray makes up the science of *geometrical optics.* Using light rays, the path of light can be traced in geometrical drawings called ray diagrams.

406 CHAPTER 12

DEMONSTRATION 3 TEACHING

Observing Reflection and Refraction

Time: Approximately 5 minutes
Materials: aquarium tank (5 or 10 gal) or other large transparent container, milk, small mirror, laser pointer or focusable flashlight, transparent plastic protractor

Step 1 Repeat Demonstration 6 from Chapter 11 with emphasis on reflection. Simulate **Figure 12-19A** with the shiny side of crumpled aluminum foil and **Figure 12-19B** with a flat mirror lying at the bottom of the tank.

Step 2 Demonstrate the angles of incidence and reflection with the flat mirror on the bottom of the tank. Move the light source to achieve various angles to show the validity of the law of reflection. Tape a transparent protractor to the outside of the tank to measure angles.

Figure 12-19

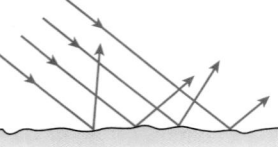

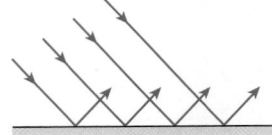

A Light rays reflected from a rough surface are reflected in many directions.

B Light rays reflected from a smooth surface are reflected in the same direction.

Rough surfaces reflect light rays in many directions

Many of the surfaces that we see every day, such as paper, wood, cloth, and skin, reflect light but do not appear shiny. When a beam of light is reflected, the path of each light ray in the beam changes from its initial direction to another direction. If a surface is rough, light striking the surface will be reflected at all angles, as shown in **Figure 12-19A.** Such reflection of light into random directions is called *diffuse reflection.*

Smooth surfaces reflect light rays in one direction

When light hits a smooth surface, such as a polished mirror, it does not reflect diffusely. Instead, all the light hitting a mirror from one direction is reflected together into a single new direction, as shown in **Figure 12-19B.**

The new direction of the light rays is related to the old direction in a definite way. The angle of the light rays reflecting off the surface, called the *angle of reflection,* is the same as the angle of the light rays striking the surface, called the *angle of incidence.* This is called the *law of reflection.*

The angle of incidence equals the angle of reflection.

Both of these angles are measured from a line perpendicular to the surface at the point where the light hits the mirror. This line is called the *normal.* **Figure 12-20** is a ray diagram that illustrates the law of reflection.

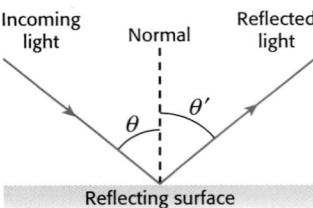

Figure 12-20
When light hits a smooth surface, the angle of incidence (θ) equals the angle of reflection (θ').

INTEGRATING

SPACE SCIENCE

There are two primary types of telescopes, refracting and reflecting. Refracting telescopes use glass lenses to focus light into an image at the eyepiece; reflecting telescopes use curved mirrors to focus light.

The lens of a refracting telescope cannot be very large, because the weight of the glass would cause the lens to bend out of shape. Curved mirrors are thinner and lighter than lenses, so they are stable at larger diameters.

The largest refracting telescope, at the Yerkes Observatory in Wisconson, has a lens that is 1 m in diameter. The Mauna Kea Observatory in Hawaii houses four of the largest reflecting telescopes. Two of them have single mirrors that are over 8 m in diameter, and two use multiple mirrors for a total diameter of 10 m.

TOPIC: Reflection
GO TO: www.scilinks.org
KEYWORD: HK1125

SKILL BUILDER

Interpreting Diagrams **Figure 12-19** shows reflection of light from a smooth and a rough surface. This may be the first time students have seen a ray diagram. Explain that the small arrows on the rays indicate direction of travel.

Point out to the students that in both cases, the incoming light rays are parallel. After reflecting from the rough surface, the rays are no longer parallel, but the rays reflected from the smooth surface remain parallel.

Resources Blackline Master 36 shows this visual.

INTEGRATING

SPACE SCIENCE

Resources Assign students worksheet *12.2 Integrating Space Science—Telescopes* in the **Integration Enrichment Resources** ancillary.

SKILL BUILDER

Interpreting Diagrams **Figure 12-20** illustrates the law of reflection. The normal is shown as a line perpendicular to the surface at the point where the light ray strikes. The angle θ is the angle of incidence, and the angle θ' is the angle of reflection.

Point out that the angle of incidence and angle of reflection are measured from the normal, not from the surface of the mirror.

Stress that the normal is perpendicular to the surface at the point a light ray strikes and that the incident and reflected angles are measured against the normal, not the mirror's surface.

Resources Blackline Master 37 shows this visual.

Interpreting Diagrams The ray diagram in **Figure 12-21B** does not, of course, show every light ray involved in producing the image. One ray from the feet and one ray from the eye itself are shown as they reflect off the surface and to the eye of the observer. The diagram also shows dotted lines, which represent the straight-line paths that your brain thinks the rays have taken.

Ask students to trace out other paths on the diagram. Where would the light rays travel to produce an image of a knee or a shirt button? From what point would the rays appear to come?

Resources Blackline Master 38 shows this visual.

Teaching Tip

Virtual or Real? The words *seem* and *appear* are useful when talking about virtual images. A virtual image is not real; it only seems to be located at the position you see it. The opposite of a virtual image is a real image. A real image can be projected on a screen. The images you see projected from film and slides are real images, as is the image that is focused on the film in a camera. The ultimate test is to use a screen. If you put a screen where an image is or appears to be, only a real image can be seen on the screen. At the place a virtual image appears to be, you would see no image. All mirrors produce virtual images, but only concave mirrors can also produce real images.

Figure 12-21

A A virtual image appears behind a flat mirror.

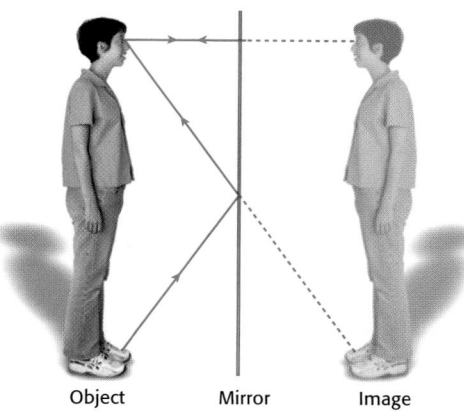

Object   Mirror   Image

B A ray diagram shows where the light actually travels as well as where you perceive that it has come from.

Mirrors

When you look into a mirror, you see an image of yourself behind the mirror, as in **Figure 12-21A.** It is like seeing a twin or copy of yourself standing on the other side of the glass, although flipped from left to right. You also see a whole room, a whole world of space beyond the mirror, even if the mirror is placed against a wall. How is this possible?

Flat mirrors form virtual images by reflection

The ray diagram in **Figure 12-21B** shows the path of light rays striking a flat mirror. When a light ray is reflected by a flat mirror, the angle it is reflected is equal to the angle of incidence, as described by the law of reflection. Some of the light rays reflect off the mirror into your eyes.

However, your eyes do not know where the light rays have been. They simply sense light coming from certain directions, and your brain interprets the light as if it traveled in straight lines from an object to your eyes. As a result, you perceive an image of yourself behind the mirror.

Of course, there is not really a copy of yourself behind the mirror. If someone else looked behind the mirror, they would not see you, an image, or any source of light. The image that you see results from the apparent path of the light rays, not an actual path. An image of this type is called a **virtual image.** The virtual image appears to be as far behind the mirror as you are in front of the mirror.

▶ **virtual image** an image that forms at a point from which light rays appear to come but do not actually come

---

DEMONSTRATION 4 TEACHING

Reflection from Curved Mirrors

Time: Approximately 10 minutes
Materials: aquarium tank and equipment from Demonstration 3, concave mirror, convex mirror

Step 1 Place the convex ("wide-angle") mirror at the bottom of the tank. Shine the laser pointer vertically downward onto the mirror, and move it from side to side over the mirror. Rays will reflect increasingly outward as you move the beam in any direction away from the center of the mirror. Reverse the rays by shining the beam onto the mirror from many different angles. Prompt students to conclude why this type of mirror is called a wide-angle mirror.

Curved mirrors can distort images

If you have ever been to the "fun house" at a carnival, you may have seen a curved mirror like the one in **Figure 12-22.** Your image in a curved mirror does not look exactly like you. Parts of the image may be spread out, making you look wide or tall. Other parts may be compressed, making you look thin or short. How does such a mirror work?

Curved mirrors still create images by reflecting light according to the law of reflection. But because the surface is not flat, the line perpendicular to the mirror (the normal) points in different directions for different parts of the mirror.

Where the mirror bulges out, two light rays that start out parallel are reflected into different directions, making an image that is stretched out. Mirrors that bulge out are called *convex mirrors*.

Similarly, parts of the mirror that are indented reflect two parallel rays in toward one another, making an image that is compressed. Indented mirrors are called *concave mirrors*.

Concave mirrors create real images

Concave mirrors are used to focus reflected light. A concave mirror can form one of two kinds of images. It may form a virtual image behind the mirror or a **real image** in front of the mirror. A real image results when light rays from an object are focused onto a single point or small area.

If a piece of paper is placed at the point where the light rays come together, the real image appears on the paper. If you tried this with a virtual image, say by placing a piece of paper behind a mirror, you would not see the image on the paper. That is the primary difference between a real and a virtual image. With a real image, light rays really exist at the point where the image appears; a virtual image appears to exist in a certain place, but there are no light rays there.

Telescopes use curved surfaces to focus light

Many reflecting telescopes use curved mirrors to reflect and focus light from distant stars and planets. Radio telescopes, such as the one in **Figure 12-23,** gather radio waves from extremely distant objects, such as galaxies and quasars.

Because radio waves reflect off almost any solid surface, these telescopes do not need to use mirrors. Instead, parallel radio waves bounce off a curved dish, which focuses the waves onto another, smaller curved surface poised above the dish. The waves are then directed into a receiver at the center of the dish.

Figure 12-22
A curved mirror produces a distorted image.

▶ **real image** an image of an object formed by many light rays coming together in a specific location

Figure 12-23
A radio telescope dish reflects and focuses radio waves into the receiver at the center of the dish.

Reflection and Color

Teaching Tip

Mirrors The advantage of a larger mirror in a telescope is that more light from a star strikes it, forming a brighter image. Point out that mirrors used in telescopes and in other optical applications are first-surface mirrors. They have a reflective coating, usually aluminum, on the top surface of the mirror rather than the back surface, like most household mirrors. Point out that the reflective coating in modern mirrors is nearly always aluminum. Silver is used only to achieve an antique decorative look.

Step 2 Place a concave mirror at the bottom of the tank. Again shine the beam straight down at the mirror, and move it back and forth while keeping it vertical. Students will observe that all of the rays reflect inward through a common point. Use two beams if you can to show that they cross at a common point no matter where the beams strike the mirror.

Step 3 Place both mirrors in the tank and adjust a flashlight to produce a straight beam. Shine the beam into the mirrors. Students will see the light spread from the convex mirror and focus to a point from the concave mirror.

Reflection and Color

Teaching Tip

Color Perception When the brain receives signals from certain combinations of photoreceptor cells in the retina, it interprets them as the color green. These receptors are three kinds of cone cells, one each for red, green, and blue.

Be sure students understand that there is nothing inherently green about electromagnetic waves in one part of the visible spectrum. "Green" is just the way our brains interpret certain signals. Some students may be interested in conducting a more in-depth project on vision and how cells in the retina respond to light.

Additional Application

Lighting and Color Ask students if they know of any instances in which light color is used to make something look different from how it would look in white light. Examples include the lights over produce displays to make the produce look lush green and deep red, the lighting at makeup counters and some clothing sales areas, and stage lighting to achieve a wide variety of effects.

Teaching Tip

Additive Color TV If some students have never used a magnifying glass to look at the glowing phosphors of a color TV or monitor, this would be an ideal time because it will help reinforce the idea of additive colors.

Seeing Colors

As you learned in Chapter 11, the different wavelengths of visible light correspond to the colors that you perceive. When you see light with a wavelength of about 550 nm, your brain interprets it as *green*. If the light comes from the direction of a leaf, then you may think, "That leaf is green."

A leaf does not emit light on its own; in the darkness of night, you may not be able to see the leaf at all. So where does the green light come from?

Objects have color because they reflect certain wavelengths of light

If you pass the light from the sun through a prism, the prism separates the light into a rainbow of colors. White light from the sun actually contains light from all the visible wavelengths of the electromagnetic spectrum.

When white light strikes a leaf, as shown in **Figure 12-24A,** the leaf reflects light with a wavelength of about 550 nm, corresponding to the color green. The leaf absorbs light at other wavelengths. When the light reflected from the leaf enters your eyes, your brain interprets it as *green*.

Likewise, the petals of a rose reflect red light and absorb other colors, so the petals appear to be red. If you view a rose and its leaves under red light, as shown in **Figure 12-24B,** the petals will still appear red but the leaves will appear black. Why?

Figure 12-24
A Rose in White and Red Light

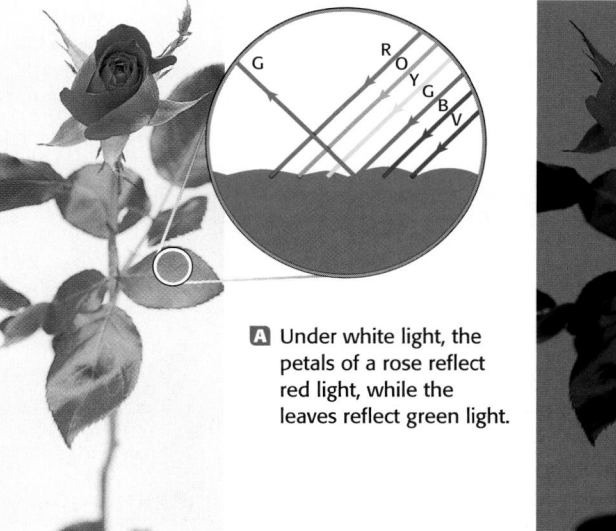

A Under white light, the petals of a rose reflect red light, while the leaves reflect green light.

B Under red light, the petals still look red, but the leaves look black because there is no green light for them to reflect.

410 CHAPTER 12

ALTERNATIVE ASSESSMENT

Law of Reflection

Give students a diagram of a plane mirror with three rays of light approaching it at different angles. Have them draw the resulting reflected rays. Evaluate to see if students understand the law of reflection. Repeat with a concave mirror, but have the rays parallel to each other and the middle ray striking the exact center of the mirror. The reflected rays should meet at a common point. The ray in the center is reflected straight back along the same path.

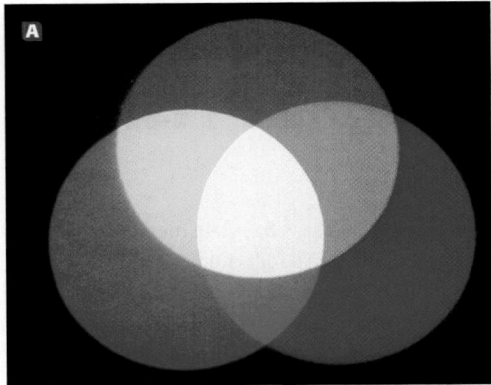

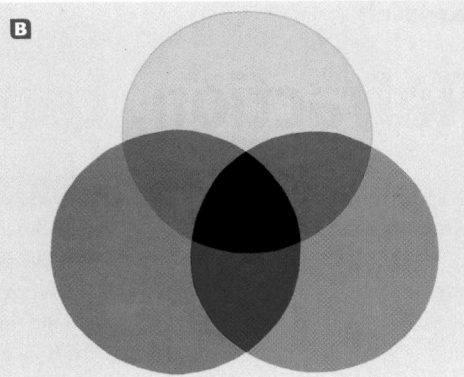

Colors may add or subtract to produce other colors

Televisions and computer monitors display many different colors by combining light of the *additive primary colors*, red, green, and blue. Adding light of two of these colors together can produce the secondary colors yellow, cyan, and magenta, as shown in **Figure 12-25A.** Mixing all three additive primary colors makes white.

In the reverse process, pigments, paints, or filters of the *subtractive primary colors*, yellow, cyan, and magenta, can be combined to create red, green, and blue as shown in **Figure 12-25B.** If filters or pigments of all three colors are combined in equal proportions, all the light is absorbed, leaving black. Black is not really a color at all; it is the absence of color.

Figure 12-25
(A) Red, green, and blue lights can combine to produce yellow, magenta, cyan, or white.
(B) Yellow, magenta, and cyan filters can be combined to produce red, green, blue, or black.

Did You Know ?

Another way to think of subtractive colors is as minus colors. Each subtractive color is the full spectrum minus a color. Magenta is minus green, cyan is minus red, and yellow is minus blue. When all three are mixed, all colors are taken away, and the result is black.

SECTION 12.3 REVIEW

Check Your Understanding

1. Examples may include bicycle reflectors, clothing, and paper. Almost anything that is visible, except a direct source of light, reflects light. Only polished surfaces, such as mirrors, reflect light non-diffusely.
2. Answers should restate the law that states that the angle of incidence of a light ray equals the angle of reflection.
3. Diagrams should resemble **Figure 12-20.**
4. Light that reaches your eyes from the mirror comes from in front of the mirror. But because the rays come from the mirror, you see an image that appears to be behind the mirror.
5. Students should express the idea that the blue object reflects blue light while absorbing colors in the rest of the visible spectrum. A yellow object reflects yellow light while absorbing other colors.

Answers continue on p. 423A.

SECTION 12.3 REVIEW

SUMMARY

▶ Light is reflected when it strikes a boundary between two different mediums.

▶ When light reflects off a surface, the angle of reflection equals the angle of incidence.

▶ Mirrors form images according to the law of reflection.

▶ The color of an object depends on the wavelengths of light that the object reflects.

CHECK YOUR UNDERSTANDING

1. **List** three examples of the diffuse reflection of light.
2. **Describe** the law of reflection in your own words.
3. **Draw** a diagram to illustrate the law of reflection.
4. **Discuss** how a plane mirror forms a virtual image.
5. **Discuss** the difference, in terms of reflection, between objects that appear blue and objects that appear yellow.
6. **Explain** why a plant may look green in sunlight but black under red light.
7. **Critical Thinking** A friend says that only mirrors and other shiny surfaces reflect light. Explain what is wrong with this reasoning.
8. **Creative Thinking** A convex mirror can be used to see around a corner at the intersection of hallways. Draw a simple ray diagram illustrating how this works.

SOUND AND LIGHT **411**

RESOURCE LINK
STUDY GUIDE

Assign students *Review Section 12.3 Reflection and Color.*

Scheduling

Refer to pp. 388A–388D for lecture, classwork, and assignment options for Section 12.4.

★ **Lesson Focus**
Use transparency *LT 42* to prepare students for this section.

READING SKILL BUILDER *Paired Reading*
Have students read the basics of light refraction in the first three pages of this section and write notes about concepts they do not understand. After reading, students should organize in pairs and discuss the passages that each person found difficult. Each member of the pair should help the other to understand the material.

MISCONCEPTION **ALERT**
Does Light Bend?
Remind students that when we say light bends when it passes into a different medium, we mean that it changes direction abruptly.

Refraction, Lenses, and Prisms

▶ **KEY TERMS**
total internal reflection
lens
magnification
prism
dispersion

OBJECTIVES
▶ Describe how light is refracted as it passes between mediums.
▶ Explain how fiber optics use total internal reflection.
▶ Explain how converging and diverging lenses work.
▶ Describe the function of the eye.
▶ Describe how prisms disperse light and how rainbows form.

Light travels in a straight line through empty space. But in our everyday experience, we encounter light passing through various mediums, such as the air, windows, a glass of water, or a pair of eyeglasses. Under these circumstances, the direction of a light wave may be changed by refraction.

Refraction of Light

In Chapter 11, you learned that waves bend when they pass from one medium to another. If light travels from one transparent medium to another at any angle other than straight on, the light changes direction when it meets the boundary, as shown in **Figure 12-26.** Light bends when it changes mediums because the speed of light is different in each medium.

Imagine pushing a lawn mower at an angle from a sidewalk onto grass, as in **Figure 12-27.** The wheel that enters the grass first will slow down due to friction. If you keep pushing on the lawn mower, the wheel on the grass will act like a moving pivot, and the lawn mower will turn to a different angle.

Figure 12-26
Light refracts when it passes from one medium into another.

Figure 12-27
This lawn mower changes direction as it passes from the sidewalk onto the grass.

412 CHAPTER 12

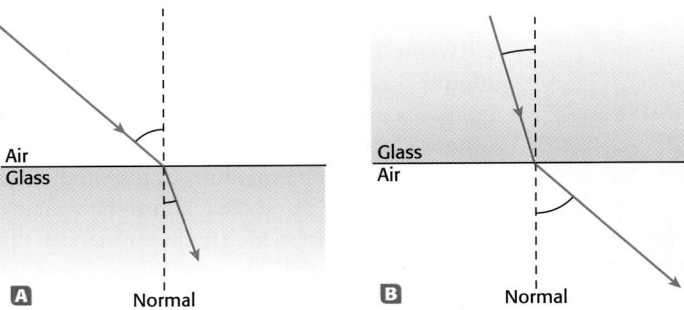

A   Normal   **B**   Normal

Figure 12-28
(A) When the light ray moves from air into glass, its path is bent toward the normal.
(B) When the light ray passes from glass into air, its path is bent away from the normal.

When light moves from a material in which its speed is higher to a material in which its speed is lower, such as from air to glass, the ray is bent toward the normal, as shown in **Figure 12-28A.** This is like the lawnmower moving from the sidewalk onto the grass. If light moves from a material in which its speed is lower to one in which its speed is higher, the ray is bent away from the normal, as shown in **Figure 12-28B.**

Refraction makes objects appear to be in different positions

When a cat looks at a fish underwater, the cat perceives the fish as closer than it actually is, as shown in the ray diagram in **Figure 12-29A.** On the other hand, when the fish looks at the cat above the surface, the fish perceives the cat as farther than it really is, as shown in **Figure 12-29B.**

The misplaced images that the cat and the fish see are virtual images like the images that form behind a mirror. The light rays that pass from the fish to the cat bend away from the normal when they pass from water to air. But the cat's brain doesn't know that. It interprets the light as if it traveled in a straight line, and sees a virtual image. Similarly, the light from the cat to the fish bends toward the normal, again causing the fish to see a virtual image.

Refraction in the atmosphere creates mirages

Have you ever been on a straight road on a hot, dry summer day and seen what looks like water on the road? If so, then you may have seen a *mirage.* A mirage is a virtual image caused by refraction of light in the atmosphere.

Light travels at slightly different speeds in air of different temperatures. Therefore, when light from the sky passes into the layer of hot air just above the asphalt on a road, it refracts, bending upward away from the road. Because you see an image of the sky coming from the direction of the road, your mind may assume that there is water on the road causing a reflection.

Figure 12-29

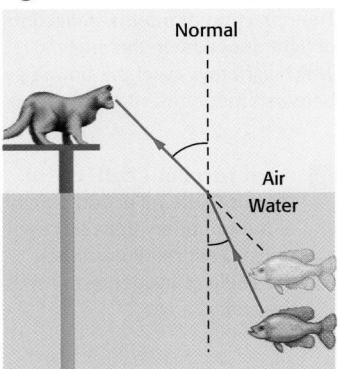

A To the cat on the pier, the fish appears to be closer than it really is.

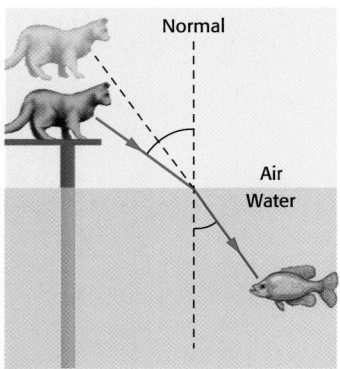

B To the fish, the cat seems to be farther from the surface than it actually is.

SOUND AND LIGHT   **413**

Refraction, Lenses, and Prisms

Teaching Tip

Light Refraction Steering bulldozers and tanks is analogous to light refraction. Ask students if any of them have ever steered a track-driven vehicle such as a bulldozer or have played with radio-controlled miniature bulldozers or tanks. Ask them how the vehicle is steered. It has no wheels that can be turned to point in a different direction. A track vehicle changes direction by the driver either applying a brake to slow down the track on one side or by speeding up the track on the other side (or both actions for sharp turns). Another analogy is making a turn while rowing a boat.

▐ SKILL BUILDER

Interpreting Diagrams **Figure 12-29,** like **Figure 12-20** in the previous section, shows both light rays and dotted lines. The dotted lines show the perceived, or apparent, path of the light rays.

Ask students whether the images in the figure are virtual images or real images. *(They are virtual images.)*

Resources Teaching Transparency 36 shows this visual.

Teaching Tip

Underwater Reflection Ask the class if anyone has ever looked up at the air/water interface while swimming underwater. Ask those who have done this to describe what they saw. Those who are observant will recall that they can see things above the water, but as they look farther off to the side, the surface begins to look like a mirror. This happens when the angle of view is greater than the critical angle. Beyond this point, the swimmer can no longer see anything above water.

Additional Application

Fiber optics There are two primary types of fiber-optic cables. In those used for imaging purposes, the fibers at each end have the same arrangement so that the images will not be jumbled. In those used for transmitting signals, the arrangement of the fibers is less important.

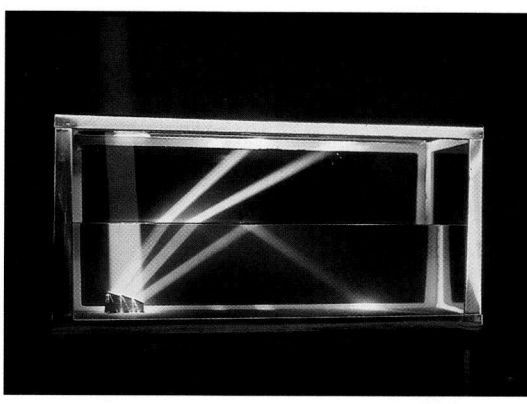

Figure 12-30
The refraction or internal reflection of light depends on the angle at which light rays meet the boundary between mediums.

▶ **total internal reflection**
the complete reflection of light at the boundary between two transparent mediums when the angle of incidence exceeds the critical angle

Light can be reflected at the boundary between two transparent mediums

Figure 12-30 shows four different beams of light approaching a boundary between air and water. Three of the beams are refracted as they pass from one medium to the other. The fourth beam is reflected back into the water.

If the angle at which light rays meet the boundary between two mediums becomes large enough, the rays will be reflected as if the boundary were a mirror. This angle is called the *critical angle,* and this type of reflection is called **total internal reflection.**

Fiber optics use total internal reflection

Fiber-optic cables are made by fusing bundles of transparent fibers together, as shown in **Figure 12-31A.** Light inside a fiber in a fiber-optic cable bounces off of the walls of the fiber due to total internal reflection, as shown in **Figure 12-31B.**

If the fibers are arranged in the same pattern at both ends of the cable, the light that enters one end can produce a clear image at the other end. Fiber-optic cables of that sort are used to produce images of internal organs during surgical procedures.

Because fiber-optic cables can carry many different frequencies at once, they transmit computer data or signals for telephone calls more efficiently than standard metal wires. Fiber-optic communications will be discussed further in Chapter 15.

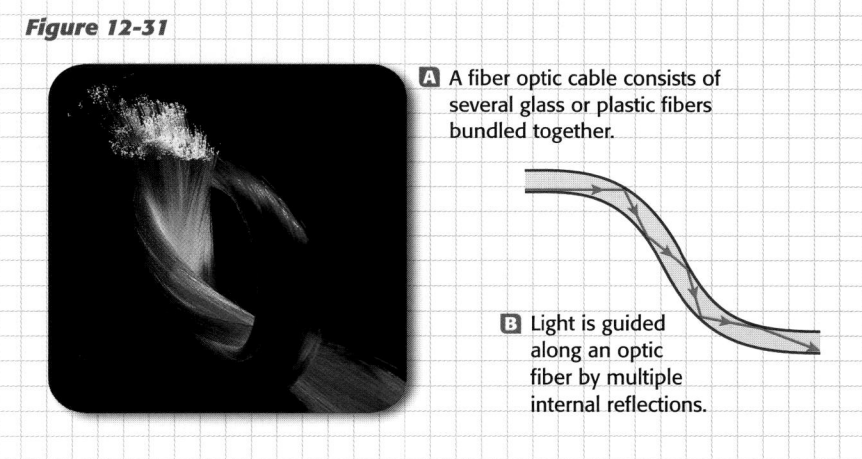

Figure 12-31

Ⓐ A fiber optic cable consists of several glass or plastic fibers bundled together.

Ⓑ Light is guided along an optic fiber by multiple internal reflections.

414 CHAPTER 12

DEMONSTRATION 5 TEACHING

Total Internal Reflection

Time: Approximately 10 minutes
Materials: equipment from Demonstration 3

Step 1 Demonstrate total internal reflection as in **Figure 12-30** by shining the laser pointer upward through the side of the tank toward the water surface. Slowly increase the angle at which the beam strikes the interface. Just as the critical angle is

reached, the beam will be refracted enough that it shines across the interface, which seems to light up. Beyond that angle, the beam reflects back into the water.

Step 2 Repeat step 1 using a wider beam from a flashlight.

Figure 12-32

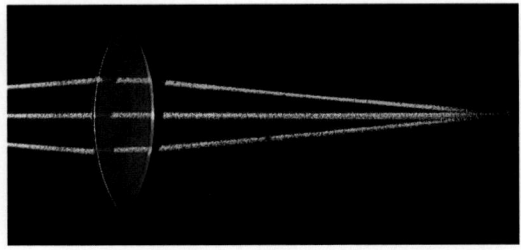

A When rays of light pass through a converging lens (thicker at the middle), they are bent inward.

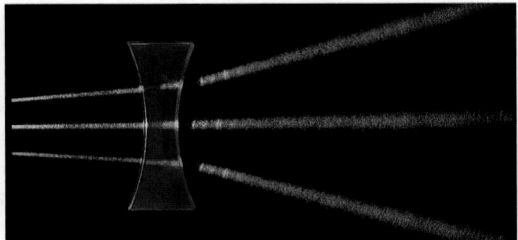

B When they pass through a diverging lens (thicker at the ends), they are bent outward.

Lenses

You are probably already very familiar with one common application of the refraction of light: lenses. From cameras to microscopes, eyeglasses to the human eye, lenses change the way we see the world.

Lenses rely on refraction

Light traveling at an angle through a flat piece of glass is refracted twice—once when it enters the glass and again when it reenters the air. The light ray that exits the glass is still parallel to the original light ray, but it has shifted to one side.

On the other hand, when light passes through a curved piece of glass, a **lens**, there is a change in the direction of the light rays. This is because each light ray strikes the surface of a curved object at a slightly different angle.

A *converging lens*, as shown in **Figure 12-32A,** bends light inward. A lens that bends light outward is a *diverging lens*, as shown in **Figure 12-32B.**

A converging lens can create either a virtual image or a real image, depending on the distance from the lens to the object. A diverging lens, however, can only create a virtual image.

Lenses can magnify images

A magnifying glass is a familiar example of a converging lens. A magnifying glass reveals details that you would not normally be able to see, such as the pistils of the flower in **Figure 12-33.** The large image of the flower that you see through the lens is a virtual image. **Magnification** is any change in the size of an image compared with the size of the object. Magnification usually produces an image larger than the object, but not always.

▶ **lens** a transparent object that refracts light rays, causing them to converge or diverge to create an image

▶ **magnification** a change in the size of an image compared with the size of an object

Figure 12-33
A magnifying glass makes a large virtual image of a small object.

S O U N D   A N D   L I G H T   **415**

SKILL BUILDER

Vocabulary The words *converge* and *diverge* derive from the Latin verb *vergere,* "to slant, slope, or incline." The prefix *con-* means "together," and the prefix *di-* means "apart." Thus, a converging lens slants light rays together, and a diverging lens slants light rays apart.

Teaching Tip

Eyeglass Lenses Students can determine the correction in eyeglasses with the following tests. Hold the lens horizontally above a page of type, and move the lens back and forth. If the lens is convex (used to correct farsightedness), the type will seem to move opposite the direction that the lens moves. With a concave lens (for nearsightedness), the type seems to move in the same direction as the lens moves. If a lens has correction for astigmatism, rotating the lens over the type will cause the type to distort as the lens turns.

Refraction, Lenses, and Prisms

SKILL BUILDER

Interpreting Visuals Figure 12-34 shows that light from a point on the specimen is focused to a point somewhere inside the body tube. If a screen were placed at this point, a small image of the specimen would appear on it. However, a real image can be viewed without a screen. A magnifying lens—the eyepiece—at the top of the tube, lets you view a magnified image of the already-magnified real image inside the tube. A telescope works in the same way as a microscope, except that the objective lens is large to capture a lot of light, and it brings light to a focus much farther from the lens.

MISCONCEPTION **ALERT**

The Eye Lens
Some students were probably taught in the past that the lens of the eye is solely responsible for forming an image on the retina. Help them overcome this error by calling their attention to the fact that the curved cornea is a lens too. The cornea does 70 percent of the focusing of light rays to form an image. The lens is still important, though, because muscles change its curvature to adjust the focus for nearby and distant objects. Some students may be interested in exploring the use of surgery to reshape the cornea to correct vision defects that could otherwise be corrected by contact lenses or eyeglasses.

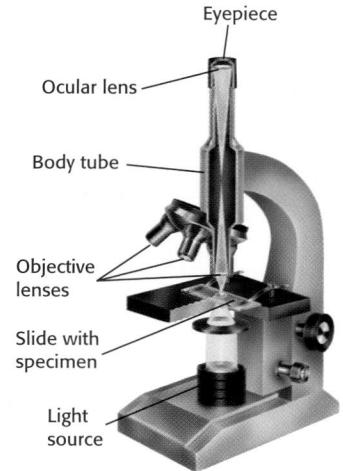

Figure 12-34
A compound microscope uses several lens to produce a highly magnified image.

Figure 12-35
The cornea and lens refract light onto the retina at the back of the eye.

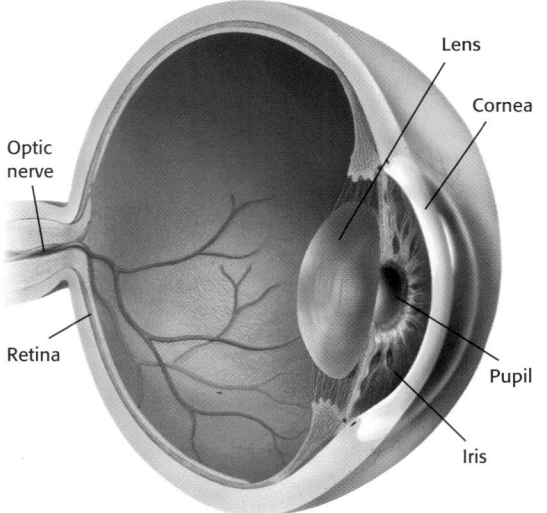

If you hold a magnifying glass over a piece of paper in bright sunlight, you can see a real image of the sun on the paper. By adjusting the height of the lens above the paper, you can focus the light rays together into a small area or a point, called the *focal point*. At the focal point, the image of the sun may contain enough energy to set the paper on fire.

Microscopes and refracting telescopes use multiple lenses

A compound microscope uses multiple lenses to provide greater magnification than a magnifying glass. **Figure 12-34** illustrates a basic compound microscope. The objective lens first forms a large real image of the object. The eyepiece then acts like a magnifying glass and creates an even larger virtual image that you see when you peer through the microscope.

Section 12.3 explained how reflecting telescopes use curved mirrors to create images of distant objects such as planets and galaxies. Refracting telescopes work more like a microscope, focusing light through several lenses. Light first passes through a large lens at the top of the telescope, then through another lens at the eyepiece. The eyepiece focuses an image onto your eye.

The eye depends on refraction and lenses

The refraction of light by lenses is not just used in microscopes and telescopes. Without refraction, you could not see at all.

The operation of the human eye, shown in **Figure 12-35,** is in many ways similar to that of a simple camera. Light enters a camera through a large lens, which focuses the light into an image on the film at the back of the camera.

Light first enters the eye through a transparent tissue called the cornea. The cornea is responsible for 70 percent of the refraction of light in the eye. After the cornea, light passes through the pupil, a hole in the colorful iris.

From there, light travels through the lens, which is composed of glassy fibers situated behind the iris. The curvature of the lens determines how much further the lens refracts light. Muscles can adjust the curvature of the lens until an image is focused on the back layer of the eye, the retina.

The retina is composed of tiny structures, called rods and cones, that are sensitive to light. When light strikes the rods and cones, signals are sent to the brain where they are interpreted as images.

DEMONSTRATION 6 TEACHING

Dispersion

Time: Approximately 10 minutes
Materials: aquarium tank, prism, slide projector, focusable halogen flashlight

Step 1 Darken the room for this demonstration. Focus the flashlight to produce a beam that does not diverge. Shine the beam through a prism, as shown in **Figure 12-36**. Arrange the prism and beam so that a light spectrum appears on a light-colored wall or on white paper.

Step 2 Fill the aquarium with clear water. Shine the projector beam through the side of the tank so that it reflects and refracts, as shown in the diagram on page 417. Arrange the aquarium so that a bright spectrum falls on a light-colored wall. You will need to adjust the lens of the projector to produce the narrowest possible beam. If you do not get a good spectrum, place a sheet of aluminum foil with a $\frac{1}{8}$ in. wide vertical slit over the

Cones are concentrated in the center of the retina, while rods are mostly located on the outer edges. The cones are responsible for color vision, but they only respond to bright light. That is why you cannot see color in very dim light. The rods are more sensitive to dim light, but cannot resolve details very well. That is why you can glimpse faint movements or see very dim stars out of the corners of your eyes.

Dispersion and Prisms

A **prism,** like the one in **Figure 12-36,** can separate white light into its component colors. Water droplets in the air can also do this, producing a rainbow. But why does the light separate into different colors?

Different colors of light are refracted differently

In Chapter 11, you learned that all waves travel the same speed in a given medium. That is true for mechanical waves, but not for electromagnetic waves. Light waves at different wavelengths travel at different speeds in a given medium. In the visible spectrum, violet light travels the slowest and red light travels the fastest.

Because violet light travels slower than red light, violet light refracts more than red light when it passes from one medium to another. When white light passes from air to the glass in the prism, violet bends the most, red the least, and the rest of the visible spectrum appears in between. This effect, in which light separates into different colors because of differences in wave speed, is called **dispersion.**

► **internet**connect ≡

*SC**L**INKS***
NSTA

TOPIC: Refraction
GO TO: www.scilinks.org
KEYWORD: HK1126

► **prism** a transparent block with a triangular cross section

► **dispersion** an effect in which white light separates into its component colors

Figure 12-36
A prism separates white light into its component colors. Notice that violet light is bent more than red light.

Teaching Tip

Dispersion of Light Be sure students understand that the speed of all colors of light in a vacuum (in space) is the same, 3.00×10^8 m/s. It is only when light enters a material medium that the speeds of different colors become different.

Students may wonder why violet light slows down more than red light. This happens because, as you move toward the violet end of the spectrum, the light's frequency (energy) becomes closer to the natural frequency of electron transitions between energy levels of the atom. Thus, photons of violet light are more likely to be absorbed temporarily by atoms than are photons of lower frequency (less energy). As a result, the higher the frequency of light, the more likely it will be delayed.

projector lens. This should produce a narrow beam. You may have to adjust the placement of the projector for the best results.

Step 3 Place colored plastic sheets in front of the projector lens to see which colors they absorb and transmit. You can also place colored objects in the light of the projected spectrum to see how the color of the objects appears under various colors of light.

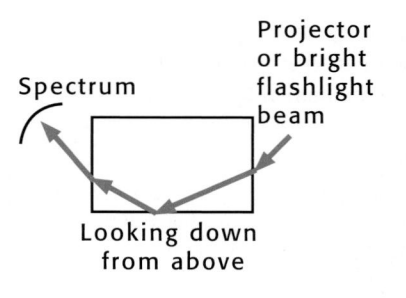

Spectrum

Projector or bright flashlight beam

Looking down from above

Refraction, Lenses, and Prisms

SECTION 12.4 REVIEW

Check Your Understanding

1. The wheels turn slower in the grass. When one wheel is in the grass, the wheel on the sidewalk turns faster, pushing the lawn-mower into a turn.

2. Diagrams should resemble **Figure 12-28A**.

3. When an optical fiber bends, light rays will encounter a wall of the fiber. The rays bounce off the walls of the fiber by total internal reflection.

4. A magnifying lens refracts light rays from an object near the lens so that the light from points on the object appear to be coming from points that are farther apart. This produces an enlarged virtual image.

5. A light ray is first refracted as it passes into the cornea of the eye. From there it passes through the pupil and then on to the lens. The lens refracts the light further so that light is focused on the retina, forming a real image.

6. violet light

7. It is a virtual image because the displaced part of the spoon only seems to be where it is seen.

Answers continue on p. 423A.

Answers continue on p. 423A.

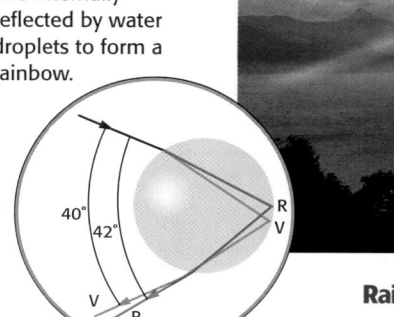

Figure 12-37
Sunlight is dispersed and internally reflected by water droplets to form a rainbow.

Rainbows are caused by dispersion and internal reflection

Rainbows, like the one in **Figure 12-37,** may form any time there is water in the air. When sunlight strikes a droplet of water, the light is dispersed into different colors as it passes from the air into the water. Some of the light then reflects off the back surface of the droplet by total internal reflection. The light disperses further when it passes out of the water back into the air.

When light finally leaves the droplet, violet light emerges at an angle of 40 degrees, red light at 42 degrees, with the other colors in between. We see light from many droplets as arcs of color, forming a rainbow. Red light comes from droplets higher in the air and violet light comes from lower droplets.

SECTION 12.4 REVIEW

SUMMARY

▶ Light may refract when it passes from one medium to another.

▶ Light rays may also be reflected at a boundary between mediums.

▶ Lenses form real or virtual images by refraction.

▶ Converging lenses cause light rays to converge to a point. Diverging lenses cause light rays to spread apart, or diverge.

▶ A prism disperses white light into a color spectrum.

CHECK YOUR UNDERSTANDING

1. **Explain** why a lawn mower turns when pushed at an angle from a sidewalk onto the grass.

2. **Draw** a ray diagram showing the path of light when it travels from air into glass.

3. **Explain** how light can bend around corners inside an optical fiber.

4. **Explain** how a simple magnifying glass works.

5. **Describe** the path of light from the time it enters the eye to the time it reaches the retina.

6. **Critical Thinking** Which color of visible light travels the slowest through a glass prism?

7. **Critical Thinking** A spoon partially immersed in a glass of water may appear to be in two pieces. Is the image of the spoon in the water a real image or a virtual image?

8. **Creative Thinking** If light traveled at the same speed in raindrops as it does in air, could rainbows exist? Explain.

RESOURCE LINK
STUDY GUIDE

Assign students *Review Section 12.4 Refraction, Lenses, and Prisms.*

ALTERNATIVE ASSESSMENT

Light Rays

Give students a sketch showing a light ray passing from air into water at an angle. Have students predict and draw the path of the light ray in the water. Do the same thing with sketches of a convex lens, a concave lens, and a prism. With the prism, have students show the dispersion of white light as well as the path of the ray. Allow leeway in judging student responses. The criterion in each case should be whether the ray bends in the correct direction.

Chapter Highlights

Before you begin, review the summaries of the key ideas of each section, found on pages 398, 405, 411, and 418. The key vocabulary terms are listed on pages 390, 399, 406, and 412.

UNDERSTANDING CONCEPTS

1. All sound waves are _____.
   a. longitudinal waves
   b. transverse waves
   c. electromagnetic waves
   d. standing waves

2. The speed of sound depends on _____.
   a. the temperature of the medium
   b. the density of the medium
   c. how well the particles of the medium transfer energy
   d. All of the above

3. A sonar device can use the echoes of ultra-sound underwater to find the _____.
   a. speed of sound
   b. depth of the water
   c. temperature of the water
   d. height of waves on the surface

4. During a thunderstorm, you see lightning before you hear thunder because _____.
   a. the thunder occurs after the lightning
   b. the thunder is farther away than the lightning
   c. sound travels faster than light
   d. light travels faster than sound

5. The speed of light _____.
   a. depends on the medium
   b. is fastest in a vacuum
   c. is the fastest speed in the universe
   d. All of the above

6. Which of the following forms of light has the most energy?
   a. X rays
   b. microwaves
   c. infrared light
   d. ultraviolet light

7. Light can be modeled as _____.
   a. electromagnetic waves
   b. a stream of particles called photons
   c. rays that travel in straight lines
   d. All of the above

8. The energy of light is proportional to ____.
   a. amplitude
   b. wavelength
   c. frequency
   d. the speed of light

9. A flat mirror forms an image that is _____.
   a. smaller than the object
   b. larger than the object
   c. virtual
   d. real

10. Which of the following wavelengths of visible light bends the most when passing through a prism?
    a. red
    b. yellow
    c. green
    d. blue

Using Vocabulary

11. How is the loudness of a sound related to *amplitude* and *intensity*?

12. How is *pitch* related to *frequency*?

13. Explain how a guitar produces sound. Use the following terms in your answer: *standing waves, resonance.*

14. Why does a clarinet sound different from a tuning fork, even when played at the same pitch? Use these terms in your answer: *fundamental frequency, harmonics.*

15. Explain the difference between a *virtual image* and a *real image*. Give an example of each type of image.

16. Explain why a leaf may appear green in white light but black in red light. Use the following terms in your answer: *wavelength, reflection.*

17. What is the difference between a *converging lens* and a *diverging lens*?

18. Sketch the path of a white *light ray* into a water droplet that is forming a rainbow and indicate where the light is (a) *refracted,* (b) *internally reflected,* and (c) *dispersed.*

UNDERSTANDING CONCEPTS

1. a
2. d
3. b
4. d
5. d
6. a
7. d
8. c
9. c
10. d

Using Vocabulary

11. Both amplitude and intensity are directly related to the energy of sound waves. The more energy the waves contain, the louder the sound is.

12. Pitch is the way the brain interprets the frequency of a sound wave. Higher frequency corresponds to higher pitch, and lower frequency corresponds to lower pitch.

13. When a guitar string is plucked, it vibrates in standing waves, producing a fundamental pitch plus harmonics. The body of the guitar is resonant at all the frequencies produced by the strings and vibrates at these same frequencies, moving more air and thus amplifying the sound.

14. Both are producing sounds of the same fundamental frequency, but the clarinet's sound includes several strong harmonics, whole-number multiples of the fundamental frequency. The tuning fork produces almost no harmonics.

15. When you view a virtual image, you are seeing light rays that only appear to be coming from the location of the image. Examples include a reflection in a flat mirror and the image seen through a magnifying glass. When you view a real image, you are seeing light rays actually coming from the location of the image. A real image can be projected on a screen. Examples are projected movies and the images formed in the tubes of microscopes and telescopes.

16. The leaf appears green because it reflects green light and absorbs other wavelengths. Red light contains no green wavelengths, so the leaf can reflect no light and appears black.

17. A converging lens bends light inward, while a diverging lens bends light outward.

18. Sketches should resemble the diagram in **Figure 12-37**. The ray is refracted when it enters the drop and when it leaves the drop. The ray is internally reflected at the back of the drop. The light is dispersed in the first refraction and dispersed further in the second.

BUILDING MATH SKILLS

You may use the following for items 19–23:
- ▶ the wave speed equation from Section 11.2, $v = f \times \lambda$
- ▶ a rearranged form of the speed equation from Section 8.1, $d = vt$
- ▶ the average speed of sound in water or soft tissue, 1500 m/s
- ▶ the speed of light, 3.0×10^8 m/s

19. **Sound Waves** Calculate the wavelength of ultrasound used in medical imaging if the frequency is 15 MHz.

20. **Sonar** Calculate the distance to the bottom of a lake when a ship using sonar receives the reflection of a pulse in 0.055 s.

21. **Graphing** As a ship travels across a lake, a sonar device on the ship sends out pulses of ultrasound and detects the reflected pulses. The table below gives the ship's distance from the shore and the time for each pulse to return to the ship. Construct a graph of the depth of the lake as a function of distance from the shore.

Distance from shore (m)	Time to receive pulse ($\times 10^{-2}$ s)
100	1.7
120	2.0
140	2.6
150	3.1
170	3.2
200	4.1
220	3.7
250	4.4
270	5.0
300	4.6

22. **Electromagnetic Waves** Calculate the wavelength of radio waves from an AM radio station broadcasting at 1200 kHz.

23. **Electromagnetic Waves** Waves composing green light have a wavelength of about 550 nm. What is their frequency?

THINKING CRITICALLY

24. **Interpreting Graphics** Review the chart on page 393 that illustrates ranges of frequencies of sounds that different animals can hear. Which animal on the chart can hear sounds with the highest pitch?

25. **Aquiring and Evaluating Data** A guitar has six strings, each tuned to a different pitch. Research what pitches the strings are normally tuned to and what frequencies correspond to each pitch. Then calculate the wavelength of the sound waves that each string produces. Assume the speed of sound in air is 340 m/s.

26. **Creative Thinking** Imagine laying this page flat on a table, then standing a mirror upright at the top of the page. Using the law of reflection, draw the image of each of the following letters of the alphabet in the mirror.

A B C F W T

27. **Understanding Systems** The glass in greenhouses is transparent to certain wavelengths and opaque to others. Research this type of glass, and write a paragraph explaining why it is an ideal material for greenhouses.

WRITING SKILL

28. **Applying Knowledge** Why is white light not dispersed into a spectrum when it passes through a flat pane of glass like a window?

DEVELOPING LIFE/WORK SKILLS

29. Teaching Others Your aunt is scheduled for an ultrasound examination of her gall bladder and she is worried that it will be painful. All she knows is that the examination has something to do with sound. How would you explain the procedure to her?

30. Applying Technology Meteorologists use Doppler radar to measure the speed of approaching storms and the velocity of the swirling air in tornadoes. Research this application of radar, and write a short paragraph describing how it works.

WRITING SKILL

INTEGRATING CONCEPTS

31. Connection to Earth Science Landsat satellites are remote sensing satellites that can detect electromagnetic waves at a variety of wavelengths to reveal hidden features on Earth. Research the use of Landsat satellites to view Earth's surface. What kind of electromagnetic waves are detected? What features do Landsat images reveal that cannot be seen with visible light?

32. Connection to Health Research the effect of UV light on skin. Are all wavelengths of UV light harmful to your skin? What problems can too much exposure to UV light cause? Is UV light also harmful to your eyes? If so, how can you protect your eyes?

33. Connection to Biology While most people can see all the colors of the spectrum, people with *colorblindness* are unable to see at least one of the primary colors. What part of the eye do you think is malfunctioning in colorblind people?

34. Concept Mapping Copy the unfinished concept map below onto a sheet of paper. Complete the map by writing the correct word or phrase in the lettered boxes.

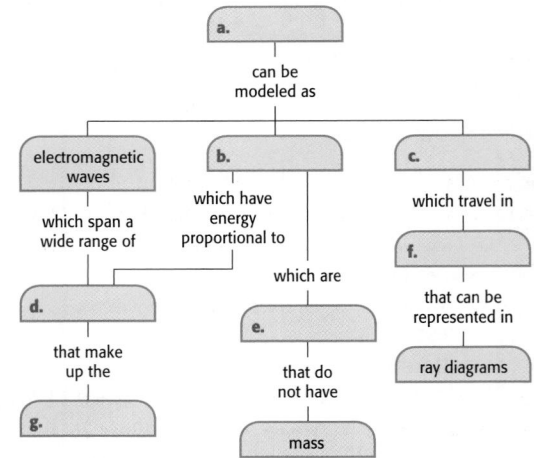

35. Connection to Fine Arts Describe how you can make red, green, blue, and black paint with a paint set containing only yellow, magenta, and cyan paint.

36. Connection to Space Science Telescopes can produce images in several different regions of the electromagnetic spectrum. Research photos of areas of the galaxy taken with infrared light, microwaves, and radio waves. What features are revealed by infrared light that are hidden in visible light? What kinds of objects are often studied with radio telescopes?

internet**connect**

SCILINKS
NSTA

TOPIC: Ultrasound
GO TO: www.scilinks.org
KEYWORD: HK1127

Skill Builder Lab

Forming Images with Lenses

Introduction

Have the students list or discuss items that rely on the focusing ability of lenses to be useful. Students are probably familiar with the concept of focus in relation to cameras, eyeglasses, binoculars, and perhaps even light microscopes and telescopes. However, digital technologies may change most of these items. For example, digital cameras, electron microscopes, and radio telescopes extend our capabilities.

Objectives

Students will:

- ► **Use** appropriate lab safety precautions.
- ► **Observe** images formed by a convex lens.
- ► **Measure** the distance of objects from the lens.
- ► **Measure** the distance of images from the lens.
- ► **Analyze** the data to determine the focal length of the lens.

Planning

Recommended time: 1 lab period
Materials: *(for each lab group)*

- ► cardboard screen, 10 cm x 20 cm
- ► screen holder
- ► meterstick
- ► supports for meterstick
- ► lens holder
- ► convex lens of 10 cm to 15 cm focal length
- ► light box with illuminated design or light bulb

422

Skill Builder Lab

Introduction

How can you find the focal length of a lens and verify the value?

Objectives

- ► **Observe** images formed by a convex lens.
- ► **Measure** the distance of objects and images from the lens.
- ► **Analyze** the data to determine the focal length of the lens.

Materials

cardboard screen 10 × 20 cm
screen holder
meterstick
supports for meterstick
lens holder
convex lens, 10 cm to 15 cm
   focal length
light box with light bulb

Safety Needs

safety goggles

Forming Images with Lenses

► Preparing for Your Experiment

1. The shape of a lens determines the size, position, and types of images that it may form. When parallel rays of light from a distant object pass through a converging lens, they come together to form an image at a point called the focal point. The distance from this point to the lens is called the focal length. In this experiment, you will find the focal length of a lens, and then verify this value by forming images, measuring distances, and using the lens formula shown below.

$$\frac{1}{d_o} + \frac{1}{d_i} = \frac{1}{f}$$

where d_o = object distance,
     d_i = image distance, and
     f = focal length.

2. On a clean sheet of paper, make a table like the one shown at right.
3. Set up the equipment as illustrated in the figure below. Make sure the lens and screen are securely fastened to the meterstick.

► Determining Focal Length

4. Stand about 1 m from a window, and point the meterstick at a tree, parked car, or similar object. Slide the screen holder along the meterstick until a clear image of the distant object forms on the screen. Measure the distance between the lens and the screen in centimeters. This distance is very close to the focal length of the lens you are using. Record this value at the top of your data table.

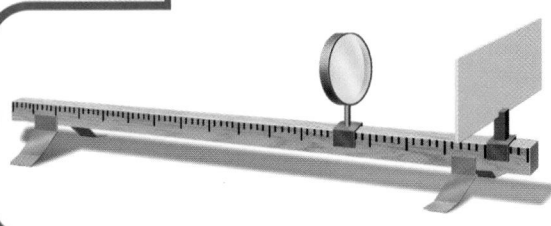

Focal length of lens, f: _____ cm	Object distance, d_o (cm)	Image distance, d_i (cm)	$\frac{1}{d_o}$	$\frac{1}{d_i}$	$\frac{1}{d_o} + \frac{1}{d_i}$	$\frac{1}{f}$	Size of object (mm)	Size of image (mm)
Trial 1								
Trial 2								
Trial 3								

▶ Forming Images

5. Set up the equipment as illustrated in the figure at right. Again, make sure that all components are securely fastened.

6. Place the lens more than twice the focal length from the light box. For example, if the lens has a focal length of 10 cm, place the lens 25 or 30 cm from the light.

7. Move the screen along the meterstick until you get a good image. Record the distance from the light to the lens, d_o, and the distance from the lens to the screen, d_i, in centimeters as Trial 1 in your data table. Also record the height of the object and of the image in millimeters. The object in this case may be either the filament of the light bulb or a cut-out shape in the light box.

8. For Trial 2, place the lens exactly twice the focal length from the object. Slide the screen along the stick until a good image is formed, as in step 7. Record the distances from the screen and the sizes of the object and image as you did in step 7.

9. For Trial 3, place the lens at a distance from the object that is greater than the focal length but less than twice the focal length. Adjust the screen, and record the measurements as you did in step 7.

▶ Analyzing Your Results

1. Perform the calculations needed to complete your data table.

2. How does $\frac{1}{d_o} + \frac{1}{d_i}$ compare with $\frac{1}{f}$ in each of the three trials?

▶ Defending Your Conclusions

3. If the object distance is greater than the image distance, how will the size of the image compare with the size of the object?

SOUND AND LIGHT **423**

Pre-Lab

Teaching Tips

Be sure that students understand that light is refracted and results in an image; the image is called a *refracted image*.

In step 4, a partially darkened room produces a closer approximation of f. The actual point of focus is a judgment call. As a result, the students may have some difficulty measuring the actual size of the image in step 7. Stress that the value of f obtained in step 4 is an approximation. Therefore, if students expect an image at exactly $2f$ in step 8, they will see some discrepancy. Another step can be added to show the effects of the object when it is inside f. Emphasize the relationship between f measured in step 1 and $\frac{1}{f}$ calculated in the analysis of results.

Continue on p. 423A.

RESOURCE LINK
DATASHEETS

Have students use *Datasheet 12.4: Skill Builder Lab—Forming Images with Lenses* to record their results.

Sample Data

Focal length of lens: 10.2 cm	Object distance d_o (cm)	Image distance d_i (cm)	$\frac{1}{d_o}$	$\frac{1}{d_i}$	$\frac{1}{d_o} + \frac{1}{d_i}$	$\frac{1}{f}$	Size of object (mm)	Size of image (mm)
Trial 1	22.0	18.2	0.045	0.055	0.100	0.100	19	16
Trial 2	20.4	21.6	0.049	0.046	0.095	0.095	19	18
Trial 3	16.5	28.0	0.061	0.036	0.097	0.097	19	32

CONTINUATION OF ANSWERS

Skill Builder Lab from page 423

Forming Images with Lenses

Procedure

▶ **Determining Focal Length**

You may find that a partially darkened room creates a clearer image on the card and therefore, a better approximation of f.

In step 5, a 15 W light bulb works best with the lettering on the bulb acting as the object. The bulb can be arranged such that the lettering is upright. This creates an inverted image on the card.

Post-Lab

▶ **Disposal**

None required.

▶ **Analyzing Your Results**

1. Results will vary. Sample data are given in the sample data table.

2. The value of $\frac{1}{d_o} + \frac{1}{d_i}$ is generally very close to the value of $\frac{1}{f}$.

▶ **Defending Your Conclusions**

3. If the object distance is greater than the image distance, the image will be smaller than the object.

Answers from page 398

SECTION 12.1 REVIEW

8. Compressions and rarefactions in sound waves strike the eardrum, causing it to move back and forth. This vibration is transmitted through three small bones of the middle ear, then to the basilar membrane in the cochlea, a fluid-filled, snail-shaped organ. As the vibrations pass through the cochlea, they stimulate hair cells, which, in turn, stimulate nerves leading to the brain.

9. Ultrasound vibrations travel easily through tissue, but audible waves do not.

10. As the strings vibrate, the sound board vibrates at the same frequency (through resonance), causing stronger compressions and rarefactions in the air than the vibrating string alone could cause. This produces a louder sound.

Answers from page 411

SECTION 12.3 REVIEW

6. The appearance of an object partly depends on the color of light striking it. A green leaf reflects green light only if green light is in the light shining on it. Light from the sun contains all colors, so the leaf looks green. Red light contains no green, so the leaf reflects no light and appears black.

7. You see (opaque) objects by light reflected from them. Therefore, anything you can see, except for direct sources of light, reflects light.

8. Diagrams should show how reflected light is directed outward.

Answers from page 418

SECTION 12.4 REVIEW

8. No, rainbows are seen as a result of the dispersion of the colors of the spectrum, resulting from refraction. Refraction results from the change in the speed of light as it passes from one medium to another. If light traveled the same speed in water as in air, no refraction would occur.

BUILDING MATH SKILLS

19. $\lambda = \dfrac{v}{f} = \dfrac{1500 \text{ m/s}}{1.5 \times 10^7 \text{ Hz}} = 1.0 \times 10^{-4} \text{ m}$

20. $d = vt = (1500 \text{ m/s})\left(\dfrac{0.055 \text{ s}}{2}\right) = 41 \text{ m}$

22. $\lambda = \dfrac{v}{f} = \dfrac{3.0 \times 10^8 \text{ m/s}}{1.2 \times 10^6 \text{ Hz}} = 250 \text{ m}$

23. $f = \dfrac{v}{\lambda} = \dfrac{3.0 \times 10^8 \text{ m/s}}{5.5 \times 10^{-7} \text{ m}} = 5.5 \times 10^{14} \text{ Hz}$

THINKING CRITICALLY

27. Students should find that it allows most wavelengths of visible light to pass through. When the light is absorbed by objects inside the greenhouse, it warms those objects. The objects reradiate the energy they have absorbed as long-wave infrared light, which cannot pass through the glass. The energy stays in the greenhouse, keeping it warm.

28. It is dispersed slightly as it refracts when entering the glass. However, when it emerges, it is refracted in exactly the opposite way and is recombined into white light.

DEVELOPING LIFE/WORK SKILLS

29. Answers will vary. They should reflect the idea that the procedure is non-invasive, the sound is above the range of human hearing, and that the sound will reflect from the gallstones to produce an image showing their size and location.

30. Answers will vary. Students will find that meteorologists can measure the speed of approach in the same way as police radar determines the speed of cars. In addition, Doppler radar can show the velocities on either side of a storm cell. If one side is moving forward and the other side is moving away, the storm must be rotating.

INTEGRATING CONCEPTS

31. Landsat uses visible light and infrared wavelengths. The Landsat program monitors agricultural activities, forests, population change, urbanization, water resources, desert growth, disasters, geology of Earth's surface, and wildlife habitat.

32. The shortest wavelengths of UV radiation are absorbed or reflected before reaching Earth's surface. Medium wavelengths that are not absorbed by the ozone layer reach Earth's surface. Their high energy gives them penetrating power, and they can damage DNA and the eyes, but they also help the body produce vitamin D. UV rays in this range cause the most severe sunburns. The longest wavelengths contribute to smog formation and cause fading of paints and dyes. Otherwise, they are not that harmful to humans.

33. Colors are perceived primarily by the cones of the eye. On the retina, there is one set of cones for red light, one set for green light, and one set for blue light. Different types of colorblindness are caused by malfunctions of one or more of these sets of cones.

34. **a.** light
b. photons
c. light rays
d. frequencies
e. particles
f. straight lines
g. electromagnetic spectrum

35. Paints are subtractive pigments. Red paint can be made by combining yellow and magenta. Green paint can be made by combining yellow and cyan. Blue paint can be made by combining magenta and cyan. Black paint can be made by combining yellow, magenta, and cyan. If students have trouble, refer them to **Figure 12-25** on page 411.

36. Infrared light can penetrate interstellar matter, so telescopes that can detect infrared light are used to study the interiors of interstellar clouds and to view the center of the galaxy (which is surrounded by interstellar matter). Radio telescopes are often used to study extremely distant objects, such as galaxies and quasars. Light from these objects may be red shifted entirely into radio frequencies.

viewpoints

Should the Electromagnetic Spectrum Be Auctioned?

> ## Your Turn

1. Critiquing Viewpoints

Students' analyses of a single argument's weak points may vary. Be sure that student responses clearly identify a weakness and respond in some way that provides support. Possible responses for each of the viewpoints in the feature are listed below. (Note that students should analyze only *one of the following*.)

Derek K.: The government doesn't always know what it is doing.

Even so, it is true that wireless communications systems can benefit the public.

Phillip V.: The payments for the spectrum are one-time sums. While this income can be used to fund new programs, what happens to these programs when the money runs out?

Increasing government revenues is still a good goal, even if it will only have a temporary effect.

Komal V.: How can you know how much to save in case of an emergency?

You could auction some of the spectrum with the provision that, in the event of an emergency, ownership of a specific part of the spectrum would revert back to the government.

Chris C.: Companies may not feel that a lease is worth their investment in time, technology, and money.

But leasing it would allow for more flexibility due to changing conditions.

Stacy G.: Better wireless communications can benefit the public.

It is possible that some companies could make a lot of money for a limited fee they pay to the government.

Maria D.: If the government "saves the spectrum for everyone," will citizens really be able to use it?

Even so, the spectrum is so important that the fact the govern-

In the late 1990s, the Federal Communications Commission (FCC) auctioned off several portions of the electromagnetic spectrum that were not being used for broadcasting or other communications. Many private companies, especially those involved in wireless communications, bought the rights to use parts of the spectrum.

Is this a good way for the government to raise money without increasing taxes? Or should the spectrum be reserved for other uses that will benefit everyone, not just a communications company and its subscribers?

If the spectrum had not been auctioned, would that have left inventors with no way to market new technologies? What will happen if new technologies are invented that require use of the spectrum, but there's not enough of it available?

> **FROM: Derek K., Coral Springs, FL**

Private companies, like those involved in wireless communications, do benefit the public even though the companies make a profit. I think we should give the government a little credit. They must know what they are doing.

Auction the Spectrum

> **FROM: Phillip V., Chicago, IL**

By selling unused parts of the spectrum to private companies, the government can earn more money that can be used to fund different programs, without increasing the tax rate. Since no one is currently using the spectrum, why not sell it to someone who will?

> **FROM: Komal V., Chicago, IL**

I think that some of the spectrum should be reserved. All of it should not be auctioned off. Some of the spectrum might be needed in an emergency.

> **FROM: Chris C., Lockport, IL**

Many companies who bought parts of the spectrum are on the cutting edge of technology. While they advance, they will use their part of the spectrum for newer technologies. However, the spectrum never should have been sold. It should have been leased, because there might be better uses for it in the future.

Don't Auction ALL of the Spectrum

424

ment can make some money should not be the only factor considered.

2. Critiquing Viewpoints

Students' analyses of strong points in opposing arguments may vary. Be sure that student responses clearly identify the strong points and respond in some way that provides support for the opposite point of view. Possible responses for each of the viewpoints in the feature are listed below. (Note that students should analyze only *one of the following*.)

Derek K.: Better wireless communications systems can benefit the public even if private companies prosper as a result.

But giving up some of the spectrum without knowing what the future brings can be dangerous.

Phillip V.: Increasing government revenues without raising taxes will be very popular.

But now may not be the best time to sell the spectrum.

Komal V.: It's good to make spectrum use flexible enough to allow for an emergency.

> FROM: Stacy G., Rochester, MN

I think the spectrum shouldn't be sold. It should be used in ways that will help out many people instead of helping a company become richer.

Don't Auction ANY of the Spectrum

> FROM: Maria D., Chicago, IL

The spectrum should be saved for everyone. Why does it have to be a benefit for the government? If the government collected the $3 trillion that haven't been paid in taxes, along with all the money given to foreign countries, the government could focus on things that would be more beneficial.

But you might reserve some of the spectrum and never need it. That would represent a lost opportunity for revenue.

Chris C.: Leasing the spectrum provides more flexibility for the future.

But companies may not want to make long-term investments in improving technology if their lease on the spectrum will expire in a few years.

Stacy G.: Companies may get very rich using parts of the spectrum bought at an auction.

Making a profit is not against the law.

Maria D.: The federal government is not always efficient and effective.

But that's all the more reason why getting the spectrum out of the government's hands will help spur creativity and service.

> Your Turn

1. Critiquing Viewpoints Select one of the statements on this page that you *agree* with. Identify and explain at least one weak point in the statement. What would you say to respond to someone who brought up this weak point as a reason you were wrong?

2. Critiquing Viewpoints Select one of the statements on this page that you *disagree* with. Identify and explain at least one strong point in the statement. What would you say to respond to someone who brought up this point as a reason they were right?

3. Creative Thinking If the spectrum were leased instead of sold, what should the terms be? For how long and for how much money? Develop a plan and an argument in favor of it, either as a written report, or as a poster or other form of presentation.

4. Allocating Resources Suppose you could decide what should be done with eight available frequencies in the electromagnetic spectrum. How would you distribute them among the following categories: emergency use, military use, National Weather Service, radio, television, wireless communication, and remote-control devices? How many frequencies would you leave open for future inventions? Write a paragraph to justify your decisions.

 internet connect

go.hrw.com

TOPIC: Spectrum auction
GO TO: go.hrw.com
KEYWORD: HK1Spectrum

Should the spectrum be auctioned? Why or why not? Share your views on this issue and find out what others think about it at the HRW Web site.

425

3. Creative Thinking
Student answers will vary. Evaluate students' plans for selling the spectrum and their arguments in support of it using a scale of 1–5 points for each of the following: organization of plan, clarity in explanation, persuasiveness, creativity, and effort. (25 total possible points)

4. Allocating Resources
Student answers will vary. Evaluate students' paragraphs describing their opinions about how to ration the spectrum using a scale of 1–5 points for each of the following: organization of plan, clarity in explanation, persuasiveness, creativity, and effort. (25 total possible points)

internet connect

The HRW Web site has more opinions from other students and also provides an opportunity for your students to contribute their points of view. Every few months, more opinions will be added from the ones submitted. Student opinions that are posted will be identified only by the student's first name, last initial, and city to protect his or her privacy.

UNIT 5

MISCONCEPTION ALERT

Electricity and Magnetism

Many students do not recognize that electricity and magnetism are simply two manifestations of a single electromagnetic force.

To prepare students for this idea, which is covered more extensively in Chapter 14, remind them about the discussion of light as an electromagnetic wave, which was briefly described in Chapter 11.

 **READING SKILL BUILDER** **Reading Organizer** Write the words *electric charge* and *magnetic pole* on the chalkboard. Ask students to give descriptions of each of these terms. Once they have come up with positive and negative charges and S and N poles, ask them to describe how these interact. The fact that both obey the simple rule "likes repel/opposites attract" can be used to help students recognize that electricity and magnetism are simply two manifestations of the electromagnetic force.

426

UNIT 5

Electricity and Magnetism

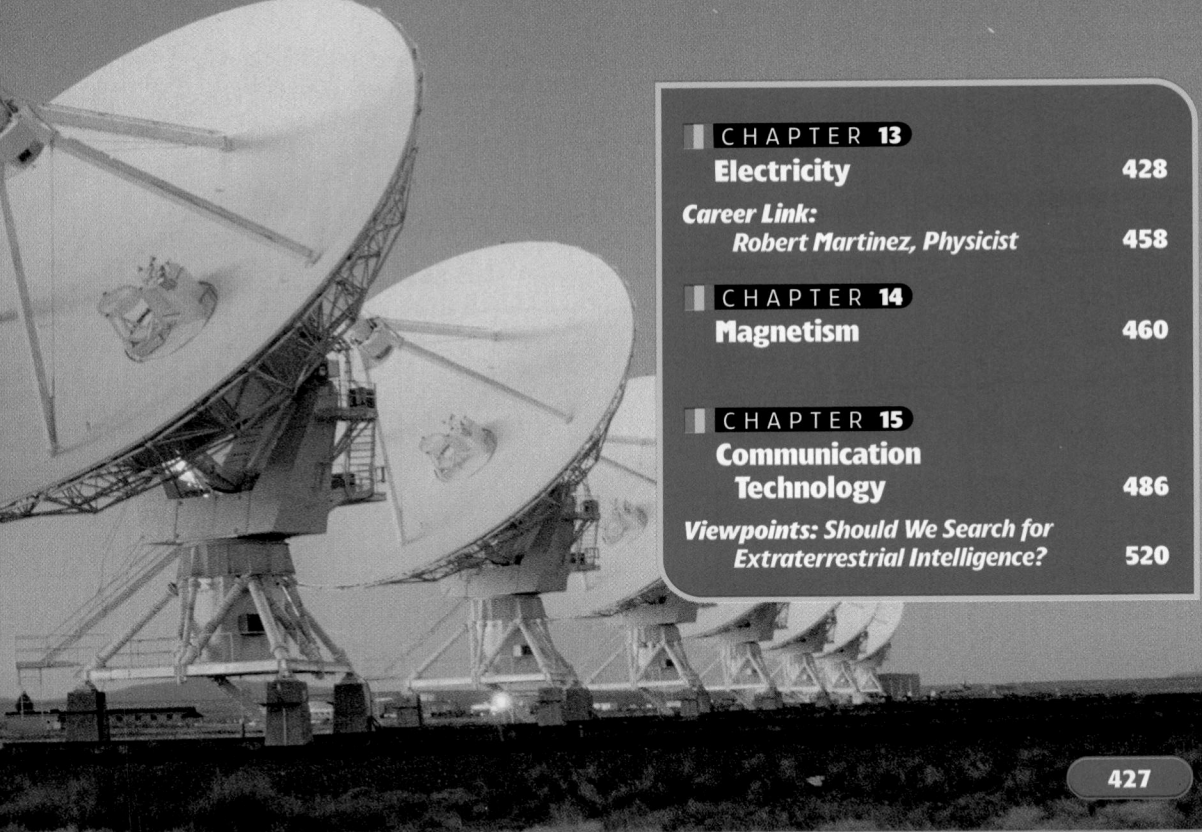

427

SKILL BUILDER

Interpreting Visuals Ask students to explain how the titles of the chapters in this unit relate to the photograph of the radiotelescope antennas.

They should know from their study of waves that radio waves are a form of electromagnetic radiation.

Students may not realize the way these antennas detect a signal: As an electromagnetic wave passes into the detector, its changing electric and magnetic fields cause charges in the detector to oscillate. This signal is amplified and interpreted.

This system works for antennas in car radios, televisions, cellular telephones, and also for satellite dishes.

CHAPTER 13

Electricity

Annotated Descriptions of the Correlated National Science Standards

The following descriptions summarize the National Science Standards that specially relate to Chapter 13. For the full text of the Standards, see p. 40T.

SECTION 13.1
Electric Charge and Force
Physical Science
PS 1a, 4b, 4d, 4c, 5b, 6c
Unifying Concepts and Processes
UCP 1, 2, 3
Science as Inquiry
SAI 1, 2
Science and Technology
ST 1, 2
Science in Personal and Social Perspectives
SPSP 5

SECTION 13.2
Current
Physical Science
PS 5b, 6c
Unifying Concepts and Processes
UCP 1, 2, 3
Science as Inquiry
SAI 1, 2
Science and Technology
ST 1, 2
Science in Personal and Social Perspectives
SPSP 4, 5

SECTION 13.3
Circuits
Physical Science
PS 5b
Unifying Concepts and Processes
UCP 1, 2, 3
Science as Inquiry
SAI 1, 2
Science and Technology
ST 1, 2
Science in Personal and Social Perspectives
SPSP 5

Cross-Discipline Teaching RESOURCES

Cross-Discipline Teaching, ATE p. 428
Technology   Biology
Mathematics

Integration Enrichment Resources
Social Studies, **PE** and **ATE** p. 431
 IE 13.1 *Incandescent Light Bulbs*
Biology, **PE** and **ATE** p. 432
 IE 13.2 *Electric Eels*
Science and the Consumer, **PE** and **ATE** p. 440
 IE 13.3 *Battery Issues*
Real World Applications, **PE** and **ATE** p. 442
 IE 13.4 *Electric Shock: Caution!*

Additional Integration Enrichment Worksheets
 IE 13.5 Chemistry   IE 13.6 Health

Use the Planning Guide on the next page to help you organize your lessons.

MATH AND COMPUTER RESOURCES

Chapter 13	Math Skills	Assess	Media/Computer Skills
Section 13.1	**ATE Cross-Discipline Teaching,** p. 428	**PE Building Math Skills,** p. 454, item 13	■ Section 13.1 💿 *DISC TWO, MODULE 15* Force Between Charges
Section 13.2	**PE Math Skills** Resistance, p. 443 **ATE Additional Examples** p. 443	**PE Practice,** p. 443 **MS** Worksheet 26 **PE** Section Review 7, 8, p. 445 **PE Building Math Skills,** p. 454, items 14–16 **PE Problem Bank,** p. 700, 126–130	■ Section 13.2 💿 *DISC ONE, MODULE 8* Batteries and Cells  Presents **Chemistry Connections** Segment 4 Student Superconductors **CRT** Worksheet 4
Section 13.3	**PE Math Skills** Electric Power, p. 450 **ATE Additional Examples** p. 451	**PE Practice,** p. 451 **MS** Worksheet 27 **PE** Section Review 7, 8, p. 452 **PE Building Math Skills,** p. 454, items 17–19 **PE Problem Bank,** p. 700, 131–135	■ Section 13.3 💿 *DISC TWO, MODULE 16* Electrical Circuits **PE Developing Life/Work Skills,** p. 454, item 26 Presents **Physical Science** Segment 20 Eagle Electrocution **CRT** Worksheet 20

PE Pupil's Edition   **ATE** Annotated Teacher's Edition   **MS** Math Skills   **BS** Basic Skills
IE Integration Enrichment   ■ Guided Reading Audio   **CRT** Critical Thinking

PHYSICAL SCIENCE INTERACTIVE TUTOR

READING SKILL BUILDER

The following activities found in the Annotated Teacher's Edition provide techniques for developing useful reading strategies to increase your students' reading comprehension skills.

Section 13.1 **Brainstorming,** p. 428

Section 13.2 **Reading Organizer,** p. 437

Section 13.3 **Summarizing,** p. 446
Paired Summarizing, p. 449

Smithsonian Institution®

Visit www.si.edu/hrw for additional online resources.

Spanish Resources

The following resources are made available for students who speak Spanish as their first language.

Spanish Resources Guided Reading Audio CD-ROM Chapter 13

Spanish Glossary Chapter 13

Electricity

CLASSROOM RESOURCES

	FOCUS	TEACH	HANDS-ON
Section 13.1: Electric Charge and Force			
BLOCK 1 45 minutes	**ATE RSB** Brainstorming, p. 428 **ATE** Focus Activities 1, 2, p. 429 **ATE Demo 1** Pith Ball Electroscope, p. 430 **ATE Demo 2** Charging by Friction and Induction, p. 432 **PE** Electric Charge, pp. 430–434 ★ Focus Transparency LT 43	**ATE Skill Builder** Interpreting Visuals, pp. 430, 433, 434 **TT** 38 Charging by Contact **TT** 39 Induced Charges	**IE** Worksheet 13.1 **IE** Worksheet 13.2 **PE** Quick Activity *Charging Objects*, p. 434 **DS** 13.1
BLOCK 2 45 minutes	**PE** Electric Force, pp. 434–436	**ATE Skill Builder** Graphing, p. 434 Interpreting Diagrams, pp. 435, 436 **BLM** 39 Point Charges **BLM** 40 Electric Fields	
Section 13.2: Current			
BLOCK 3 45 minutes	**ATE RSB** Reading Organizer, p. 437 **ATE Demo 3** Van de Graaff Generator, p. 438 **ATE Demo 4** Comparing Batteries, p. 440 **PE** Voltage and Current, pp. 437–440 ★ Focus Transparency LT 44	**ATE Skill Builder** Interpreting Visuals, p. 438 **BLM** 41 Electric Potential Energy	**PE** Science and the Consumer *Which Is the Best Type of Battery?* p. 440 **IE** Worksheet 13.3 **IE** Worksheet 13.5
BLOCK 4 45 minutes	**PE** Electrical Resistance, pp. 441–445		**PE** Quick Activity *Using a Lemon as a Cell*, p. 441 **DS** 13.2 **PE** Real World Applications *The Danger of Electric Shock*, p. 442 **IE** Worksheet 13.4 **PE** Inquiry Lab *How can materials be classified by resistance?* p. 444 **DS** 13.3 **LE** 13 *Investigating How Length Affects Resistance* **DS** 13.6
Section 13.3: Circuits			
BLOCK 5 45 minutes	**ATE RSB** Summarizing, p. 446 **ATE RSB** Paired Summarizing, p. 449 **PE** What Are Circuits? pp. 446–449 ★ Focus Transparency LT 45	**ATE Skill Builder** Interpreting Visuals, p. 447 Diagrams, p. 448 **TT** 40 Series and Parallel **BLM** 42 Circuit Diagram	**PE** Quick Activity *Series and Parallel Circuits*, p. 449 **DS** 13.4
BLOCK 6 45 minutes	**PE** Electric Power and Electrical Energy, pp. 450–452		**PE** Skill Builder Lab *Constructing Electric Circuits*, p. 456 **DS** 13.5 **IE** Worksheet 13.6

CLASSROOM RESOURCES

HOMEWORK	ASSESS
PE Section Review 1–4, p. 436 **Chapter 13 Review,** p. 453, items 1, 2	**SG** Chapter 13 Pretest
PE Section Review 5, 6, p. 436 **Chapter 13 Review,** p. 453, items 3, 4, 10, 13	**SG** Section 13.1
PE Section Review 1, 2, 5, p. 445 **Chapter 13 Review,** p. 453, items 5, 6	
PE Section Review 3, 4, 6–8, p. 445 **Chapter 13 Review,** p. 453, items 11, 14–16	**SG** Section 13.2
PE Section Review 1–4, p. 452 **Chapter 13 Review,** p. 453, items 7, 8, 12	**ATE** *ALTERNATIVE ASSESSMENT,* Wiring Circuits, p. 448
PE Section Review 5–8, p. 452 **Chapter 13 Review,** p. 453, items 9, 17–19	**ATE** *ALTERNATIVE ASSESSMENT,* Energy Use in Home Appliances, p. 450 **SG** Section 13.3

BLOCK 7

PE Chapter 13 Review
  Thinking Critically 20–25, p. 454
  Developing Life/Work Skills 26–28, p. 454
  Integrating Concepts 29–33, p. 455
SG Chapter 13 Mixed Review

BLOCK 8

Chapter Tests
  Chapter 13 Test

One-Stop Planner CD–ROM **with Test Generator**
  Chapter 13

Teaching Resources
Scoring Rubrics and assignment checklist.

---

internetconnect

**National Science Teachers
Association
Online Resources:
www.scilinks.org**
The following *sci*LINKS Internet resources can be found
in the student text for this chapter.

Page 429 **TOPIC:** Applications of the electric spark **KEYWORD:** HK1131	**Page 447** **TOPIC:** Electric circuits **KEYWORD:** HK1135
Page 431 **TOPIC:** Static electricity **KEYWORD:** HK1132	**Page 455** **TOPIC:** Electrostatic precipitators **KEYWORD:** HK1136
Page 440 **TOPIC:** Batteries **KEYWORD:** HK1134	

CNNfyi.com   www.cnnfyi.com

Visit this site for coverage of current events and related
classroom resources.

PE Pupil's Edition   **ATE** Annotated Teacher's Edition
RSB Reading Skill Builder   **DS** Datasheets
IE Integrated Enrichment   **SG** Study Guide
LE Laboratory Experiments
TT Teaching Transparencies   **BLM** Blackline Masters
★ Lesson Focus Transparency

CHAPTER 13

Tapping Prior Knowledge

Be sure students understand the following concepts:

Chapter 1
Scientific notation

Chapter 3
Atomic structure

Chapter 8
Force, acceleration

Chapter 9
Potential energy

READING SKILL BUILDER *Brainstorming* Have students brainstorm words that they believe are related to electricity. Write these relevant words on the chalkboard. Have students suggest potential applications of electricity in industry and in daily life. Students should write down these terms so that they can define them at the end of the unit, using what they have learned about electricity and electric fields. Some suggested terms: electrical current, DC (direct current), AC (alternating current), electrical power, electrical generators, light bulbs, electric motors, voltage, circuits, fuses.

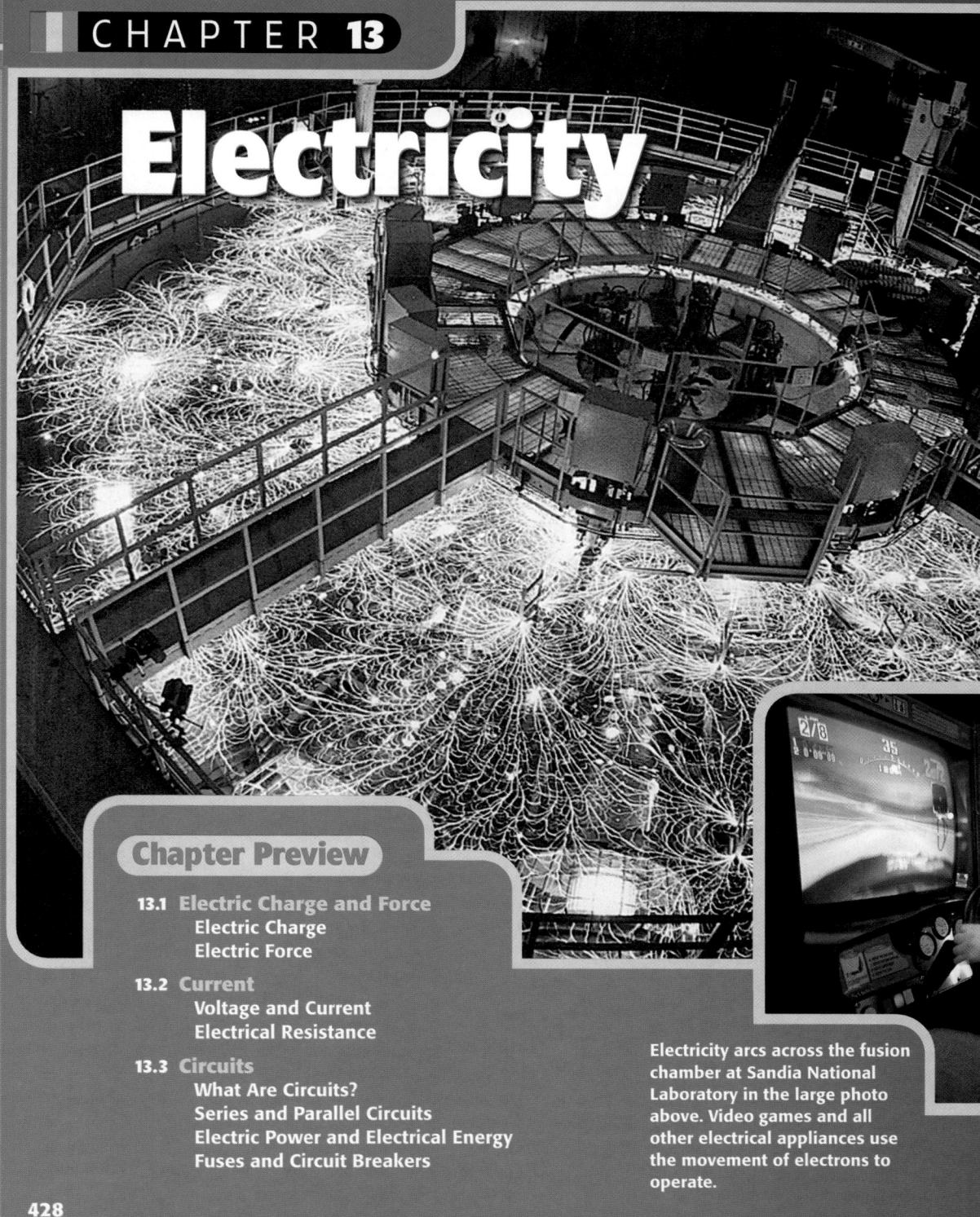

CHAPTER 13
Electricity

Chapter Preview

13.1 Electric Charge and Force
Electric Charge
Electric Force

13.2 Current
Voltage and Current
Electrical Resistance

13.3 Circuits
What Are Circuits?
Series and Parallel Circuits
Electric Power and Electrical Energy
Fuses and Circuit Breakers

428

Electricity arcs across the fusion chamber at Sandia National Laboratory in the large photo above. Video games and all other electrical appliances use the movement of electrons to operate.

RESOURCE LINK
STUDY GUIDE

Assign students *Pretest Chapter 13 Electricity* before beginning Section 13.1.

CROSS-DISCIPLINE TEACHING

Technology Have the technology teacher come into class and lecture on the use of electrical circuits in technology. The technology teacher can discuss the different uses of basic analog circuits and digital circuits as well as the historical development of electrical circuits.

Mathematics Have a math teacher visit your class and discuss the inverse square law, or $1/r^2$ dependence. Discuss the asymptotic behavior of this law and its implications as to how far you

must be away from an electrical source for the effects of that source to be zero. Have the math teacher discuss how changing the distance between charged objects changes the electric force between them.

Biology Sharks have specialized organs (ampullae of Lorenzini) that can sense the minute electrical fields generated by all marine animals and that assist in the detection of prey. Scientists have developed a device called the Shark POD (Protective

Focus ACTIVITY

Background A race car rounds a curve and speeds to the finish line in first place. Afterward, the screen darkens and the driver's score is displayed. Video games let you pretend to drive race cars, fly airplanes, and fight warriors. They are complex pieces of electrical equipment with a detailed video display and computer chips that use electric power supplied by a power plant miles away. And in turn, that energy comes from burning fossil fuels, falling water, the wind, or nuclear fission.

At the Sandia National Laboratory, in New Mexico, powerful electrical arcs are generated in a split second when scientists fire a fusion device. Each electrical arc is similar to a bolt of lightning. A huge number of electrons move across the chamber with each arc. Although they cannot be seen, electrons move inside all electrical devices, including video games. Without electricity, we couldn't make telephone calls, use computers, watch television, or ride in high-speed trains. But electricity is not just important in technology; it is also a vital part of the natural world and every living organism.

Activity 1 Remove the bulb and battery from a flashlight. Can you use the bulb, battery, and a small piece of wire or some aluminum foil to make the light bulb light up? Try connecting the light bulb to the battery in several different ways. What makes the light bulb light up?

Activity 2 Find your electric meter at home. Observe how the horizontal gear moves and the numbers on the dials change. If you have an electric clothes dryer or air conditioner, observe the dials on the meter when one of these appliances is operating. Compare this with the rate of movement of the dials when all the electrical appliances and lights are turned off. Based on your results, what do you think the electric meter measures?

internetconnect

SC*LINKS*
NSTA

TOPIC: Applications of the electric spark
GO TO: www.scilinks.org
KEYWORD: HK1131

429

Focus ACTIVITY

Background Sandia National Laboratory uses X rays to implode a tiny capsule containing deuterium and tritium in order to produce nuclear fusion. In the implosion, the capsule is compressed to a density of about 200 g/cm^3 and reaches a temperature of 5.5×10^7 K.

Three electron beams strike the screen in a carefully controlled manner to produce the picture in a video game. Video games contain many other electrical components, such as switches, computer chips, and speakers.

Activity 1 To light the bulb, students should connect the bottom of the bulb to one terminal of the battery and the side of the bulb's base to the other terminal. The bulb can be lit with one wire or piece of foil by holding the base of the bulb to one of the battery's terminals and using the wire to connect the side of the bulb's base to the other terminal.

Activity 2 Refrigerators and electric heaters use the most electricity of home appliances. Ask students to bring in their electric bills for the month. Have students compare their family's electrical usage over a given billing period with that of other students' families and with the class average.

Oceanic Device) for scuba divers to use against sharks. The Shark POD produces an electric field so strong that sharks cannot come near the divers. This would be analogous to humans being unable to look into extremely bright lights. It is believed that the Shark POD causes mild pain in the sharks' ampullae, repelling the sharks from distances of 1–7 m.

Scheduling

Refer to pp. 428A–428D for lecture, classwork, and assignment options for Section 13.1.

★ **Lesson Focus**
Use transparency *LT 43* to prepare students for this section.

Teaching Tip

Electrostatics Use the triboelectric series shown below to determine the charge on two objects that are rubbed together for Demonstration 1. A material that is closer to the positive end of the series charges positively and a material that is closer to the negative end charges negatively when they are rubbed together.

Positive
glass
nylon
wool
silk
aluminum
paper
cotton
steel
hard rubber
nickel and copper
brass and silver
synthetic rubber
Orlon™
saran
polyethylene
Teflon™
silicone rubber
Negative

SKILL BUILDER

Interpreting Visuals Have students consider all the forces that may be acting on the balloons in **Figure 13-1**. Ask students how it can be assumed that some force is acting on the balloons in **Figure 13-1B**. *(The balloons' strings are at an angle so there must be a horizontal force pushing them apart.)*

Electric Charge and Force

▶ **KEY TERMS**
electric charge
conductor
insulator
electric force
electric field

▶ Indicate which pairs of charges will repel and which will attract.
▶ Explain what factors affect the strength of the electric force.
▶ Describe the characteristics of the electric field due to a charge.

Disc Two, Module 15:
Force Between Charges
Use the Interactive Tutor to learn more about this topic.

▶ **electric charge** an electrical property of matter that creates a force between objects

Figure 13-1

A If you rub a balloon across your hair on a dry day, the balloon and your hair become charged and are attracted to each other.

B The two charged balloons, on the other hand, repel one another.

When you speak into a telephone, the microphone in the handset changes your sound waves into electric signals. Light shines in your room when you flip a switch. And if you step on a pin with bare feet, your nerves send messages back and forth between your brain and your muscles so that you react quickly. These messages are carried by electric pulses moving through your nerve cells.

Electric Charge

You have probably been shocked from touching a doorknob after walking across a rug on a dry day. This happens because your body picks up **electric charge** as your shoes move across the carpet. Although you may not notice these charges when they are spread throughout your body, you notice them as they pass from your finger to the metal doorknob. You experience this movement of charges as a shock.

Like charges repel, and opposite charges attract

One way to observe charge is to rub a balloon back and forth across your hair. You may find that the balloon is attracted to your hair, as shown in **Figure 13-1A.** If you rub two balloons across your hair and then gently bring them near each other, as shown in **Figure 13-1B,** the balloons will push away from, or repel, each other.

Pith Ball Electroscope

Time: Approximately 20 minutes
Materials: 2 pith balls, string, PVC pipe 6 in. long, wool, aluminum pipe, plastic cling wrap

Step 1 Attach each pith ball to a piece of string with a plastic hook or other fastening device. Then hang the pith balls together from a hook so they touch.

Step 2 Students will rub the PVC pipe with the wool. The PVC pipe will become charged. Have

students touch the PVC pipe to the pith balls to charge them. The pith balls will repel each other.

Step 3 Remove both of the pith balls, with the strings still attached, and discharge them by touching them to a faucet. Hang them back on the hook.

Step 4 Have students rub the aluminum with the plastic, giving the aluminum a positive charge. Then have them touch the aluminum to the pith balls. The balls will again repel each other.

After this experiment, the balloons and your hair have some kind of charge on them. Your hair is attracted to both balloons, yet the two balloons are repelled by each other. This means there must be two types of charges—the type on the balloons and the type on your hair.

The two balloons must have the same kind of charge because each became charged in the same way. Because the two charged balloons repel each other, we see that like charges repel. However, a rubbed balloon and your hair, which did not become charged in the same way, are attracted to one another. This is because unlike charges attract.

The two types of charges are called *positive* and *negative*. When you rub a balloon on your hair, the charge on your hair is positive and the charge on the balloon is negative. When there is an equal amount of positive and negative charges on an object, it has no net charge.

An object's electric charge depends on the imbalance of its protons and electrons

Recall from Section 3.1 that all matter, including you, is made up of atoms. Atoms in turn are made up of even smaller building blocks—electrons, protons, and neutrons. Electrons are negatively charged, protons are positively charged, and neutrons are neutral (no charge).

Objects are made up of an enormous number of neutrons, protons, and electrons. Whenever there is an imbalance in the number of protons and electrons in an atom, molecule, or other object, it has a net electric charge. The difference in the numbers of protons and electrons determines an object's electric charge. Negatively charged objects have more electrons than protons. Positively charged objects have fewer electrons than protons.

The SI unit of electric charge is the *coulomb*, C. The electron and proton have exactly the same amount of charge, 1.6×10^{-19} C. Because they are oppositely charged, a proton has a charge of $+1.6 \times 10^{-19}$ C, and an electron has a charge of -1.6×10^{-19} C. An object with a total charge of -1.0 C has 6.25×10^{18} excess electrons. Because the amount of electric charge on an object depends on the numbers of protons and electrons, the net electric charge of a charged object is always a multiple of 1.6×10^{-19} C.

internet**connect**

SC*LINKS*
NSTA

TOPIC: Static electricity
GO TO: www.scilinks.org
KEYWORD: HK1132

Connection to
SOCIAL STUDIES

Making the Connection
1. As Philadelphia's Postmaster, he made many improvements, including speeding up domestic and foreign delivery by hiring more couriers. In 1731, he founded the Philadelphia Library, America's first circulating library. In 1736, he organized the Union Fire Company of Philadelphia, the world's first volunteer fire department.
2. The Franklin stove has metal baffles, which increase its heating efficiency.

Resources Assign students worksheet *13.1: Connection to Social Studies—Incandescent Light Bulbs* in the **Integration Enrichment Resources** ancillary.

Students can try rubbing different materials together to see if the materials can be charged. To test if the materials are charged, touch each material to the pith ball electroscope and see if the pith balls repel.

Remember to discharge the pith balls between each trial.

You can also charge each pith ball separately and then test whether the charges on different materials are alike or unalike.

Electric Charge and Force

INTEGRATING

BIOLOGY

Resources Assign students worksheet *13.2: Integrating Biology—Electric Eels* in the **Integration Enrichment Resources** ancillary.

Additional Application

Materials Science Optical engineers make optical components to be used for laser experiments. The mirrors being used with the lasers must be extremely good reflectors. Scientists have found that materials that are good conductors are also good reflectors of light. The best conductor of electricity is gold. As a result, gold mirrors tend to be very good reflectors.

Gold mirrors are made by cooling a flat piece of glass then holding it over molten gold that is starting to boil. The evaporating gold condenses onto the flat glass, just like steam condensing on a bathroom mirror, coating it with a smooth layer of gold.

Historical Perspective

Sir Joseph John Thomson is credited for being the scientist that discovered the electron. He was the first to recognize that negatively charged beams, known as cathode rays, were actually made up of electrons. He received the Nobel Prize for his discovery in 1906.

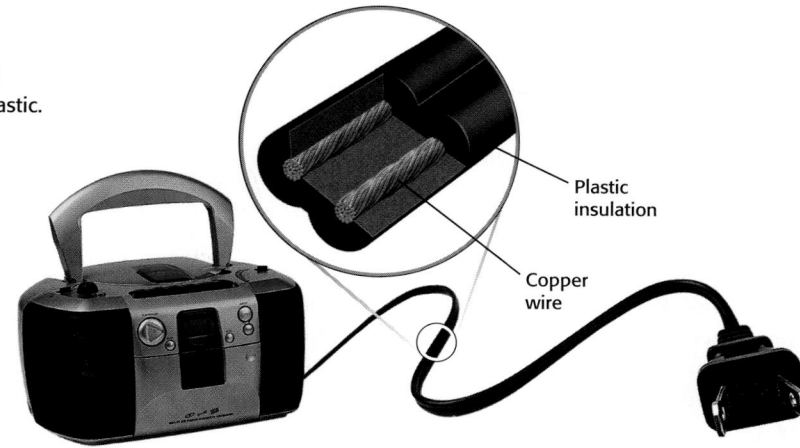

Figure 13-2
Appliance cords are made of metal wire surrounded by plastic. Electric charges move easily through the wire, but the plastic insulation prevents them from leaking into the surroundings.

Plastic insulation

Copper wire

▶ **conductor** a material that transfers charge easily

▶ **insulator** a material that does not transfer charge easily

INTEGRATING

BIOLOGY

All living cells contain ions. Most cells also need to be bathed in solutions of ions to stay alive. As a result, most living things are fairly good conductors.

Dry skin can be a good insulator. But if your skin gets wet it becomes a conductor, and charge can move through your body more easily. So there is a greatly increased risk of electrocution when your skin is wet.

Conductors allow charges to flow; insulators do not

Have you ever noticed that the electric cords attached to appliances, such as the stereo shown in **Figure 13-2,** are plastic? These cords are not plastic all the way through, however. The center of an electric cord is made of thin copper wires twisted together. Cords are layered like this because of the electric properties of each material.

Materials like the metal in cords are called **conductors.** Conductors allow electric charges to move relatively freely. The plastic in the cord, however, does not allow electric charges to move freely. Materials that do not transfer charge easily are called **insulators.** Cardboard, glass, silk, and plastic are insulators.

Charges in the electric cord attached to an appliance can move through the conducting center but cannot escape through the surrounding insulator. This design makes the appliances more efficient and helps protect people from dangerous electric shock.

Objects can be charged by the transfer of electrons

Protons and neutrons are relatively fixed in the nucleus of the atom, but the outermost electrons can be easily transferred from one atom to another. When different materials are rubbed together, electrons can be transferred from one material to the other. The direction in which the electrons are transferred depends on the materials.

For example, when you slide across a fabric car seat, some electrons are transferred between your clothes and the car seat. Depending on the types of materials involved, the electrons can be transferred from your clothes to the seat or from the seat to your clothes. One material gains electrons and becomes negatively charged, and the other loses electrons and becomes positively charged. This is an example of *charging by friction.*

DEMONSTRATION 2 TEACHING

Charging by Friction and Induction

Time: Approximately 10 minutes
Materials: PVC pipe 6 in. long, wool, aluminum pipe, plastic cling wrap, electroscope

Using the wool, rub the PVC pipe. The pipe will become negatively charged by friction. Now bring the end of the PVC pipe near the top of the electroscope. The negative charges on the PVC pipe will repel the negative charges in the electroscope, causing them to move downward towards the leaves. The leaves will now repel each other and separate. Try again with the aluminum. Rub the aluminum with the plastic. Bring the aluminum pipe near the top of the electroscope. This time the electroscope leaves are positively charged, so they repel each other. Try this demonstration with other materials from the list on page 430.

A

B

Figure 13-3
(A) When a negative rod touches a neutral doorknob, electrons move from the rod to the doorknob.
(B) The transfer of electrons to the metal doorknob gives the doorknob a net negative charge.

Objects can also be charged without friction. One way to charge a neutral object without friction is by touching it with a charged object. As shown in **Figure 13-3A,** when the negatively charged rubber rod touches a neutral object, like the doorknob, some electrons move from the rod to the doorknob. The doorknob then has a net negative charge, as shown in **Figure 13-3B.** The rubber rod still has a negative charge, but the charge is smaller. If a positively charged rod touches a neutral doorknob, electrons move into the rod from the neutral doorknob, giving the doorknob a positive charge. Objects charged in this manner are said to be charged by *contact*.

Charges move within uncharged objects

The charges in a neutral conductor can be redistributed without contacting a charged object. If you just bring a negatively charged rubber rod close to the doorknob, the movable electrons in the doorknob will be repelled. Because the doorknob is a conductor, the electrons will move away from the rod. As a result, the portion of the doorknob closest to the negatively charged rod will have an excess of positive charge. The portion farthest from the rod will have a negative charge. But the doorknob will be neutral. Although the total charge on the doorknob will be zero, the opposite sides will have an *induced* charge, as shown in **Figure 13-4.**

Figure 13-4
A negatively charged rod brought near a metal doorknob induces a positive charge on the side of the doorknob closest to the rod and a negative charge on the side farthest from the rod.

Figure 13-5
The negatively charged comb induces a positive charge on the surface of the tissue paper closest to the comb, so the comb and the paper are attracted to each other.

Quick ACTIVITY

Charging Objects
1. Rub two air-filled balloons vigorously on a piece of wool.
2. Hold your balloons near each other.
3. Now try to attach one balloon to the wall.
4. Turn on a faucet, and hold a balloon near the stream of tap water.
5. Explain what happens to the charges in the balloons, wool, water, and wall.

▶ **electric force** the force of attraction or repulsion between objects due to charge

How can the negatively charged comb in **Figure 13-5** pick up pieces of neutral tissue paper? The electrons in tissue paper cannot move about freely because the paper is an insulator. But when a charged object is brought near an insulator, the positions of the electrons within the individual molecules of the insulator change slightly. One side of a molecule will be slightly more positive or negative than the other side. This *polarization* of the atoms or molecules of an insulator produces an induced charge on the surface of the insulator. The surface of the tissue paper nearest the comb has an induced positive charge. The surface farthest from the comb has an induced negative charge.

Electric Force

The attraction of tissue paper to a negatively charged comb and the repulsion of the two balloons are examples of **electric force.** It is also the reason clothes sometimes cling to each other when you take them out of the dryer. Such pushes and pulls between charges are all around you. For example, a table feels solid, even though its atoms contain mostly empty space. The electric force between the electrons in the table's atoms and your hand is strong enough to prevent your hand from going through the table. In fact, the electric force at the atomic and molecular level is responsible for most of the common forces we can observe, such as the force of a spring and the force of friction.

The electric force is also responsible for effects that we can't see; it is part of what holds an atom together. The bonding of atoms to form molecules is also due to the electric force. The electric force plays a part in the interactions among molecules, such as the proteins and other building blocks of our bodies. Without the electric force, life itself would be impossible.

Quick ACTIVITY

Charging Objects When the balloons are rubbed on wool, the balloons become negatively charged and the wool becomes positively charged. The two negatively charged balloons repel each other. A negatively charged balloon will be attracted to the wall because it will polarize molecules in the wall, creating a positively charged area on the wall. The charged balloon will deflect a stream of water. Be sure that the faucet is turned on low, so that you cannot see any air bubbles in the water stream. If the water stream is too turbulent, the electric force will not be strong enough to deflect it. The side of the water stream nearest the balloon will be positively charged and the side farthest will be negatively charged. This is due to the polar nature of water molecules—which will rotate so the positive hydrogen end faces the balloon—and the presence of ions in the water.

Electric force depends on charge and distance

The electric force between two charged objects varies depending on the amount of charge on each object and the distance between them. The electric force between two balloons is proportional to the product of the charges on the balloons.

The electric force is inversely proportional to the square of the distance between two objects. For example, if the distance between two charged balloons is doubled, the electric force between them decreases to one-fourth its original value. If the distance between two charged balloons is quadrupled, the electric force between them decreases to one-sixteenth its original value. Chapter 8 showed that the gravitational force depends on distance in the same way.

Electric force acts through a field

As described earlier, electric force does not require that objects touch. How do charges interact over a distance? One way to model this property of charges is with the concept of an **electric field**. A charged particle produces an electric field in the space around it. Another charged particle in that field will experience an electric force. This force is due to the electric field associated with the first charged particle.

One way to show an electric field is by drawing *electric field lines*. Electric field lines point in the direction of the electric force on a positive charge. Because two positive charges repel one another, the electric field lines around a positive charge point outward, as shown in **Figure 13-6A.** In contrast, the electric field lines around a negative charge point inward, as shown in **Figure 13-6B.** Regardless of the charge, electric field lines never cross one another.

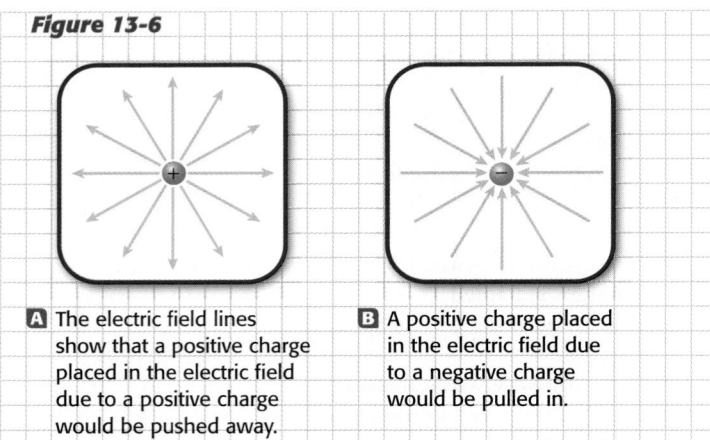

Figure 13-6

A The electric field lines show that a positive charge placed in the electric field due to a positive charge would be pushed away.

B A positive charge placed in the electric field due to a negative charge would be pulled in.

Electric force and gravitational force both depend on a physical property of objects—charge and mass, respectively—and the distance between the objects. They have the same mathematical form. But gravitational force is attractive, while electric force is both attractive and repulsive. Also, the electric force between two charged particles separated by a given distance is much greater than the gravitational force between the particles.

▶ **electric field** the region around a charged object in which other charged objects experience an electric force

MISCONCEPTION
Electric Field Lines

ALERT

Some students may think that electric field lines are a physical phenomenon. Students should be told explicitly that electric field lines do not actually exist. The lines are a visual representation of the field that would be experienced by a test charge.

|SKILL BUILDER

Interpreting Diagrams Figure 13-6 shows the electric fields for a positive source charge and a negative source charge. Be sure students understand the similarities and differences between the two cases shown in this figure. Ask students what can be concluded about the charges in **Figure 13-6A** and **B** by comparing the electric field lines for each case. *(Because the number of field lines in **A** is equal to the number of field lines approaching the charge in **B**, the charges must be equal in magnitude. The field lines also show that the charge in **A** is positive because they are pointing away from the charge. Because the field lines point toward the charge in **B**, they show that the charge is negative.)*

Resources Blackline Master 39 shows this visual.

Electric Charge and Force

SKILL BUILDER

Interpreting Diagrams

Have students look at **Figure 13-7** while you discuss how each diagram demonstrates the rules for drawing electric field lines.

Resources Blackline Master 40 shows this visual.

Teaching Tip

Drawing Electric Field Lines

Students may have difficulty remembering that the electric field points in the direction of the electric force on a positive charge. When teaching this idea, draw a positive test charge at the location where the electric field will be drawn. Ask students if this positive charge will be attracted to or repelled from the source charge. The electric field will point in the direction that this positive charge would move. Negatively charged particles will move in the opposite direction of the electric field.

SECTION 13.1 REVIEW

Check Your Understanding

1. proton—positive; neutron—neutral, no charge; electron—negative
2. Like charges repel each other.

Answers continue on p. 457A.

RESOURCE LINK

STUDY GUIDE

Assign students *Review Section 13.1 Electric Charge and Force.*

Figure 13-7
(A) The electric field lines for two positive charges show the repulsion between the charges. (B) Half the field lines starting on the positive charge end on the negative charge because the positive charge is twice as great as the negative charge.

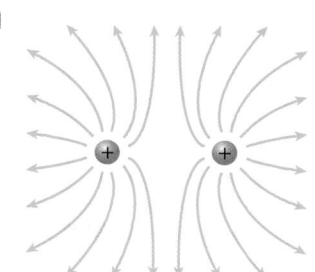 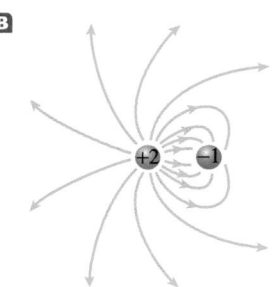

You can see from **Figure 13-7** that the electric field between two charges can be represented using these rules. The field lines in **Figure 13-7A** point away from the positive charges, showing that the positive charges repel each other. Field lines show not only the direction of an electric field but also the relative strength due to a given charge. As shown in **Figure 13-7B**, there are twice as many field lines pointing outward from the +2 charge as there are ending on the −1 charge. More lines are drawn for greater charges to indicate greater force.

SECTION 13.1 REVIEW

SUMMARY

▶ There are two types of electric charge, positive and negative.

▶ Like charges repel; unlike charges attract.

▶ The electric force between two charged objects is proportional to the product of the charges and inversely proportional to the distance between them squared.

▶ Electric force acts through electric fields.

▶ Electric fields surround charged objects. Any charged object that enters a region with an electric field experiences an electric force.

CHECK YOUR UNDERSTANDING

1. **Identify** the electric charge of each of the following atomic particles: a proton, a neutron, and an electron.
2. **Describe** the interaction between two like charges.
3. **Diagram** what will happen if a positively charged rod is brought near the following objects:
   a. a metal washer **b.** a plastic disk
4. **Categorize** the following as conductors or insulators:
   a. copper wire
   b. rubber tubing
   c. your body when your skin is wet
   d. a plastic comb
5. **Explain** how the electric force between two positive charges changes if
   a. the distance between the charges is tripled.
   b. the amount of one charge is doubled.
6. **Critical Thinking** What missing electric charge would produce the electric field shown at right?

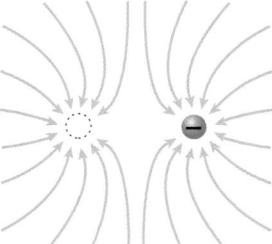

Current

OBJECTIVES

▶ Describe how batteries are sources of voltage.
▶ Explain how a potential difference produces a current in a conductor.
▶ Define *resistance.*
▶ Calculate the resistance, current, or voltage, given the other two quantities.
▶ Distinguish between conductors, superconductors, semiconductors, and insulators.

▶ **KEY TERMS**
electrical potential
  energy
potential difference
cell
current
resistance

PHYSICAL SCIENCE
Disc One, Module 8:
Batteries and Cells
Use the Interactive Tutor to learn more about these topics.

W hen you wake up in the morning, you reach up and turn on the light switch. The light bulb is powered by moving charges. How do charges move through a light bulb? And what causes the charges to move?

Voltage and Current

Gravitational potential energy depends on the relative position of the ball, as shown in **Figure 13-8A.** A ball rolling downhill moves from a position of higher gravitational potential energy to one of lower gravitational potential energy. An electric charge also has potential energy—**electrical potential energy**—that depends on its position in an electric field.

Just as a ball will roll downhill, a negative charge will move away from another negative charge. This is because of the first negative charge's electric field. The electrical potential energy of the moving charge decreases, as shown in **Figure 13-8B,** because the electric field does work on the charge.

▶ **electrical potential energy** potential energy of a charged object due to its position in an electric field

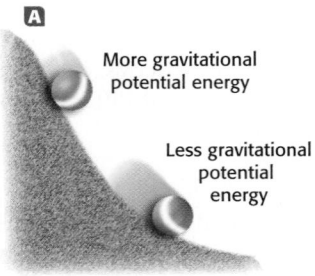
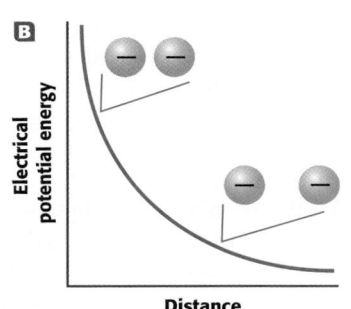

More gravitational potential energy

Less gravitational potential energy

Electrical potential energy

Distance

Figure 13-8
(A) The gravitational potential energy of a ball decreases as it rolls downhill. (B) The electrical potential energy between two negative charges decreases as the distance between them increases.

Scheduling
Refer to pp. 428A–428D for lecture, classwork, and assignment options for Section 13.2.

★ **Lesson Focus**
Use transparency *LT 44* to prepare students for this section.

READING SKILL BUILDER *Reading Organizer* Have students read pp. 437–439 and then organize the ideas presented in an outline. The outline should be organized in terms of the details presented for each heading.

Teaching Tip

Electrical Potential Energy
The electrical potential energy of a charged object depends on the object's position relative to another charged object. If two charged objects repel each other, the electrical potential energy will be greatest when the objects are near each other, as shown in **Figure 13-8**. If two charged objects attract each other, the electrical potential energy will be greatest when they are far apart. In either case, the electrical potential energy can be converted to kinetic energy if either charge is free to move.

ELECTRICITY **437**

Teaching Tip

Car Batteries The battery in a car contains two different metals as well as a strong acid. The acid allows electrons from one metal to be attracted to the other metal. This flow of electrons is used by the car in the form of electricity.

As the battery uses its energy, the voltage stays the same but the internal resistance rises until the battery cannot supply any more current. Attached to the motor is a generator that recharges the battery as the car is driven. The motor converts the chemical potential energy of gasoline into kinetic energy. The generator then converts this kinetic energy into electrical energy.

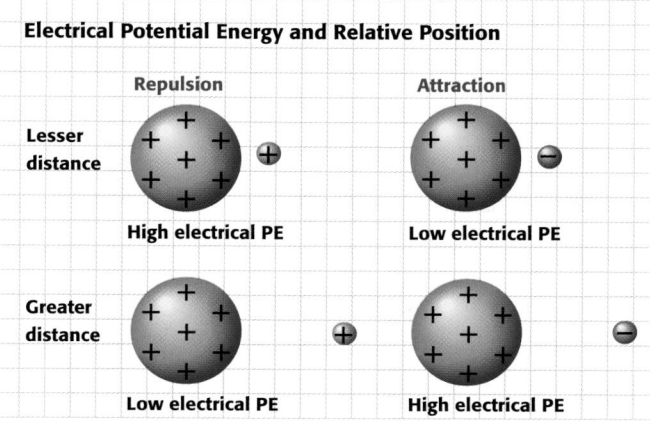

Electrical Potential Energy and Relative Position

Repulsion	Attraction
Lesser distance — High electrical PE	Lesser distance — Low electrical PE
Greater distance — Low electrical PE	Greater distance — High electrical PE

Figure 13-9
The electrical potential energy of a charge depends on its position in an electric field.

▶ **potential difference** the change in the electrical potential energy per unit charge

▶ **cell** a device that is a source of electric current because of a potential difference, or voltage, between the terminals

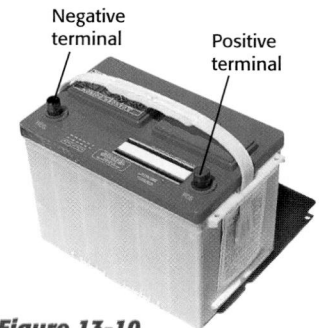

Negative terminal

Positive terminal

Figure 13-10
For a typical car battery, there is a voltage of 12 V across the negative (black) terminal and the positive (red) terminal.

You can do work on a ball to move it uphill. This will increase the ball's gravitational potential energy. In the same way, a force can push a charge in the opposite direction of the electric force. This increases the electrical potential energy associated with the charge's relative position. **Figure 13-9** shows how the electrical potential energy depends on the distance between two charged objects for both an attractive and a repulsive electric force.

Potential difference is measured in volts

When studying electricity, it is more practical to consider the **potential difference** than the electrical potential energy. Potential difference is the change in the electrical potential energy of a charged particle divided by its charge. This change occurs as a charge moves from one place to another in an electric field.

The SI unit for potential difference is the *volt,* V, which is equivalent to one joule per coulomb (1 J/C). For this reason, potential difference is often called *voltage.*

There is a voltage across the terminals of a battery

The voltage across the two *terminals* of a battery can range from about 1.5 V for a small battery to about 12 V for a car battery, as shown in **Figure 13-10.** Most common batteries are an electric **cell**—or a combination of connected electric cells—that convert chemical energy into electrical energy. One terminal is positive, and the other is negative. A summary of various types of electric cells is given in **Table 13-1.**

Electrochemical cells contain an *electrolyte,* a solution that conducts electricity, and two *electrodes,* each a different conducting material. These cells can be dry cells or wet cells. Dry cells, such as those used in flashlights, contain a paste-like electrolyte. Wet cells, such as those used in almost all car batteries, contain a liquid electrolyte. An average cell has a potential difference of 1.5 V between the positive and negative terminals.

A voltage sets charges in motion

When a flashlight is switched on, the terminals of the battery are connected through the light bulb. Electrons move through the light bulb from the negative terminal to the positive terminal.

DEMONSTRATION 3 TEACHING

Van de Graaf Generator

Time: Approximately 10 minutes
Materials: Van de Graaf generator, small fluorescent light bulb (tube-shaped)

SAFETY CAUTION: *Use a plastic fluorescent tube cover to protect students from possible shattering glass. Be careful to discharge the generator before touching it.*

Borrow a Van de Graaf generator from the physics teacher. Turn on the generator and allow it to build up a charge. The fluorescent tube can be taped to the end of a meterstick for better visibility. Hold the tube near the generator so that it points out radially, but do not touch the ball of the generator. Turn the lights off in the room. There will be a potential difference across the tube, and it will light up slightly.

Table 13-1 Types of Electric Cells

Electrical cell	Basic principle	Uses
Electrochemical	Electrons are transferred between different metals immersed in an electrolyte.	Common batteries, automobile batteries
Photoelectric and photovoltaic	Electrons are released from a metal when struck by light of sufficient energy.	Artificial satellites, calculators, streetlights
Thermoelectric	Two different metals are joined together, and the junctions are held at different temperatures, causing electrons to flow.	Thermostats for furnaces and ovens
Piezoelectric	Opposite surfaces of certain crystals become electrically charged when under pressure.	Crystal microphones and headsets, computer keypads, record stylus

When charges are accelerated by an electric field to move to a position of lower potential energy, an electric **current** is produced. Current is the rate that these charges move through a conductor. The SI unit of current is the *ampere*, A. One ampere, or *amp*, equals 1 C of charge moving past a point in 1 second.

A battery is a *direct current* source because the charges always move from one terminal to the other in the same direction. Current can be made up of positive, negative, or a combination of both positive and negative charges. In metals, moving electrons make up the current. In gases and many chemical solutions, current is the result of both positive and negative charges in motion.

In our bodies, current is mostly positive charge movement. Nerve signals are in the form of a changing voltage across the nerve cell membrane. **Figure 13-11A** shows that a resting cell has more negative charges on the inside than on the outside. **Figure 13-11B** shows how a nerve impulse moves along the cell membrane. As one end of the cell is stimulated, channels nearby in the cell membrane open, allowing Na^+ ions to enter. Later, potassium channels open, and K^+ ions exit the cell, restoring the original voltage across the cell membrane.

Conventional current is defined as movement of positive charge

A negative charge moving in one direction has the same effect as a positive charge moving in the opposite direction. *Conventional current* is defined as the current made of positive charge that would have the same effect as the actual motion of charge in the material. *In this book, the direction of current will always be given as the direction of positive charge movement that is equivalent to the actual motion of charges in the material.* So the direction of current in a wire is opposite the direction that electrons move in that wire.

▶ **current** the rate that electric charges move through a conductor

Figure 13-11

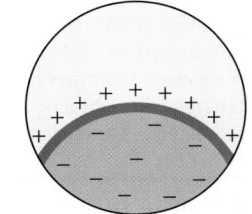

A A resting nerve cell is more negatively charged than its surroundings.

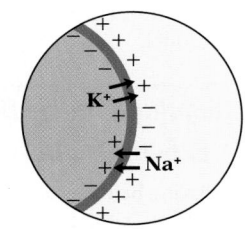

B As a nerve impulse moves along the cell membrane, the voltage across it changes.

ELECTRICITY **439**

Lightning is the flow of charge from a cloud to the Earth, from the Earth to the cloud, or between clouds. In the first situation, negative charges build up in the cloud. As the charge increases, an electric field forms between the Earth and the cloud. When the potential difference between the cloud and the ground is great enough, the air acts as a conductor. At that point, the lightning strikes the closest point on the ground, delivering up to 1 million joules of electrical energy. Students will learn more about atmospheric conditions that may cause lightning in Chapter 18.

Teaching Tip

Current Currents that consist of both positive and negative charge carriers in motion include those that exist in batteries, in the human body, in the ocean, and in the ground. Electric currents in the brain and nerves of the human body consist of moving sodium ions and potassium ions. Remind students that current refers to the movement of matter, not energy.

Additional Application

Lightning Protection If a house is hit by lightning, the electrical charges flow through any metal material throughout the house until the charges reach the Earth. Lightning can explode brick walls and concrete and start fires. A lightning protection system provides a designated path for the current. The system neither attracts nor repels a lightning strike, but simply intercepts the current and guides it harmlessly to the ground.

Science and the Consumer

Which Is the Best Type of Battery?
The first battery was developed and constructed by Alessandro Volta in about 1800. He was a professor of natural philosophy at the University of Pavia, in Italy. His device was made of a series of silver and zinc disks in pairs, each separated with a sheet of pasteboard saturated with salt water. This type of battery is called a voltaic pile. A current is generated when the first silver disk is connected with a wire to the last zinc disk.

Your Choice

1. rechargeable alkaline; they hold a charge like a regular alkaline so they can be left in the stereo and are cheapest in the long run.
2. NiCads lose about 1 percent of their stored energy every day. A smoke detector needs to have a battery that will hold its charge for a longer period of time.
3. Answers may vary. Lead acid storage batteries are used in gasoline-powered cars. They use lead-antimony electrodes with lead or lead dioxide, and sulfuric acid as the electrolyte. Electric vehicles can use several types of rechargeable batteries, such as Ni-Cd, nickel-metal hydride, lead acid, or sodium-sulfur. Sodium-sulfur batteries, for example, use liquid sodium and sulfur, with a solid aluminum oxide electrolyte.

Resources Assign students worksheet *13.3: Science and the Consumer—Battery Issues* in the **Integration Enrichment Resources** ancillary.

Science and the Consumer

Which Is the Best Type of Battery?

"Heavy-duty," "long-lasting alkaline," and "environmentally friendly rechargeable" are some of the labels that manufacturers put on batteries. But how do you know which type to use?

The answer depends on how you will use the battery. Some batteries are used continuously, but others are turned off and on frequently, such as those used in a stereo. Still other batteries must be able to hold a charge without being used, such as those used in smoke detectors and flashlights.

Heavy-duty Batteries Are Inexpensive

In terms of price, a heavy-duty battery typically costs the least but lasts only about 30 percent as long as an alkaline battery. This makes heavy-duty batteries impractical for most uses and an unnecessary source of landfill clutter.

Regular Alkaline Batteries Are Expensive but Long-lasting

Regular alkaline batteries are more expensive but have longer lives, lasting up to 6 hours with continuous use and up to 18 hours with intermittent use. They hold a full charge for years, making them good for use in flashlights and similar devices. They are less

of an environmental problem than they previously were because manufacturers have stopped using mercury in them. However, because they are single-use batteries, they also end up in landfills very quickly.

Rechargeable Batteries Don't Clutter Landfills

Rechargeable batteries are the most expensive to purchase initially. If recycled, however, they are the most economical in the long run and are the most environmentally sound choice. The most common rechargeable cells are either NiCads—containing nickel, Ni, and cadmium, Cd, metals—or alkaline. Either type of rechargeable battery can be recharged hundreds of times. Although rechargeable batteries last only about half as long on one charge as regular alkaline batteries, the energy to recharge them costs pennies. NiCads lose about 1 percent of their stored energy each day they are not used and should therefore never be used in smoke detectors or flashlights. However, rechargeable alkaline batteries retain a charge like regular batteries and can be used in such devices.

Your Choice

1. **Making Decisions** Which type of battery would you use in a portable stereo? Explain your reasoning.
2. **Critical Thinking** Why is it important not to use NiCads in smoke detectors?
3. **Locating Information** Use library resources or the Internet to learn more about batteries used in gasoline-powered and electric cars. Prepare a summary of the types of rechargeable car batteries available.

internet connect

SCiLINKS
NSTA

TOPIC: Batteries
GO TO: www.scilinks.org
KEYWORD: HK1134

DEMONSTRATION 4 SCIENCE AND THE CONSUMER

Comparing Batteries

Time: Approximately 1 hour
Materials: AA or AAA batteries, battery holders, holiday lights, wire connectors with alligator clips, wire strippers

Buy a strand of holiday lights. Cut the lights apart and strip the insulation off the ends of each light.

Use the wire connectors to make a complete circuit using the battery, battery holder, and holiday lights. Give each student lab group a different brand of battery, but each battery must be the same size and same voltage. Start all the circuits at the same time. By the end of class, some of the light bulbs will be dimmer than the others. You should be able to easily see which batteries last the longest.

Quick ACTIVITY

Using a Lemon as a Cell

Because lemons are very acidic, their juice can act as an electrolyte. If various metals are inserted into a lemon to act as electrodes, the lemon can be used as an electrochemical cell.

SAFETY CAUTION Handle the wires only where they are insulated.

1. Using a knife, make two parallel cuts 6 cm apart along the middle of a juicy lemon. Insert a copper strip into one of the cuts and a zinc strip the same size into the other.
2. Cut two equal lengths of insulated copper wire. Use wire cutters to remove the insulation from both ends of each wire. Connect one end of each wire to one of the terminals of a galvanometer.
3. Touch the free end of one wire to the copper strip in the lemon. Touch the free end of the other wire to the zinc strip, as shown in the figure at right. Record the galvanometer reading for the zinc-copper cell.

4. Replace the strips of copper and zinc with equally sized strips of different metals. Record the galvanometer readings for each pair of electrodes. Which pair of electrodes resulted in the largest current?
5. Construct a table of your results.

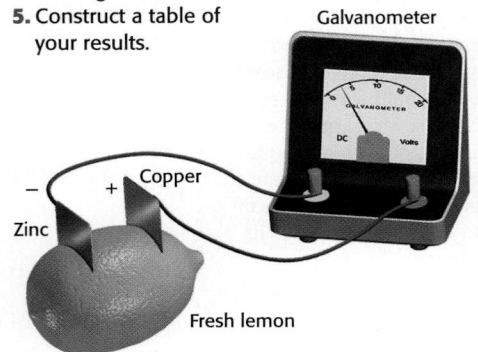

Galvanometer

Copper

Zinc

Fresh lemon

Electrical Resistance

Most electrical appliances you plug into an outlet are designed for the same voltage: 120 V. But light bulbs come in many varieties, from dim 40 W bulbs to bright 100 W bulbs. These bulbs shine differently because they have different amounts of current in them. The difference in current between these bulbs is due to their **resistance.** Resistance is caused by internal friction, which slows the movement of charges through a conducting material. Because it is difficult to measure the internal friction directly, resistance is defined by a relationship between the voltage across a conductor and the current through it.

The resistance of the *filament* of a light bulb, as shown in **Figure 13-12,** determines how bright the bulb is. The filament of a dim 40 W light bulb has a higher resistance than the filament of a bright 100 W light bulb.

▶ **resistance** the ratio of the voltage across a conductor to the current it carries

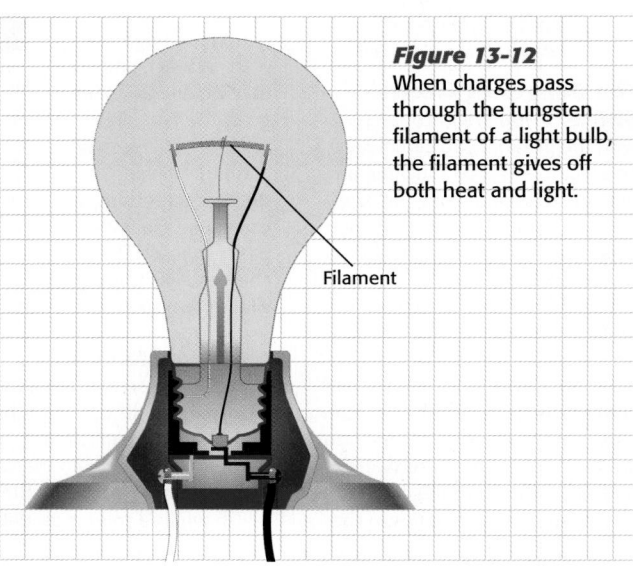

Figure 13-12
When charges pass through the tungsten filament of a light bulb, the filament gives off both heat and light.

Filament

ELECTRICITY **441**

Historical Perspective

The first commercially viable incandescent light bulb was made by Thomas Edison on October 21, 1879. Between October 21 and December 31, Edison and his crew worked day and night to construct the huge number of components necessary for a complete electric lighting system—including wires, insulators, bulb sockets, and connectors. This electrical system was then used for the first public demonstration of electrical lighting on New Year's Eve in 1879.

RESOURCE LINK
DATASHEETS

Have students use *Datasheet 13.2 Quick Activity: Using a Lemon as a Cell* to record their results.

IER

Assign students worksheet *13.5: Integrating Chemistry—Rechargeable Ni-Cd Batteries.*

Quick ACTIVITY

Using a Lemon as a Cell The electrodes need to be of a uniform size. It is important that the electrodes are inserted as deeply as possible into the lemon so that there is maximum contact between the metal and the lemon juice. If zinc is not available, use magnesium. Be sure to review any safety concerns regarding the magnesium.

Any fruit with an acidic juice, such as an orange or grapefruit, will work. Potatoes will also work.

Answers will vary depending on the metals used as electrodes. Larger electrodes will produce greater current. Consult an electrochemical series to determine which pair of electrodes should produce the greatest current.

Did You Know ?

Use the following two analogies to help students understand why resistance in wires decreases with increasing cross-sectional area and increases with increasing length.

The fire department uses very thick hoses so that the resistance to the flow of water is less, just like with electrical wires. In addition, they use hoses that can be connected together to make a longer hose. In this way the length of the hose can be controlled and kept as short as possible, thus minimizing the resistance in the hose to the flow of water.

Speaker wire is used to connect speakers to a stereo. If the stereo is to be played at high volume, then you want a low resistance in the speaker wires. The thicker the wire, the louder and the better quality the sound will be. Longer speaker wires will cause the speakers to play a little softer.

The Danger of Electric Shock

Applying Information

1. $I = \dfrac{V}{R} = \dfrac{24 \text{ V}}{10^5 \ \Omega} = 2.4 \times 10^{-4} \text{ A}$

   This much current could not even be felt.

2. $I = \dfrac{V}{R} = \dfrac{24 \text{ V}}{10^3 \ \Omega} = 2.4 \times 10^{-2} \text{ A}$

   This amount of current is enough to cause you to lose muscle control and probably enough to cause a bad burn.

Resources   Assign students worksheet *13.4: RWA—Electric Shock: Caution!* in the **Integration Enrichment Resources** ancillary.

Did You Know ?

Resistance depends on the material used as well as the material's length, cross-sectional area, and temperature. Longer pieces of a material have greater resistance. Increasing the cross-sectional area of a material decreases its resistance. Lowering the temperature of a material also decreases its resistance.

REAL WORLD APPLICATIONS

The Danger of Electric Shock   If you are in contact with the ground, you can receive an electric shock by touching an uninsulated conducting, or "live," wire. An electric shock from such a wire can result in serious burns or even death.

The degree of damage to your body by an electric shock depends on several factors. Large currents are more dangerous than smaller currents. A current of 0.1 A is often fatal. But the amount of time you are exposed to the current also matters. If the current is larger than about 0.01 A, the muscles in the

hand touching the wire contract, and you may be unable to let go of the wire. In this case, the charges will continue moving through your body and can cause great damage, especially if the charges pass through a vital organ, such as the heart.

Applying Information

1. You can use the definition of *resistance* to calculate the amount of current that would be in a body, given the voltage and resistance. Using the table above as a reference, determine

Resistance can be calculated from current and voltage

You have probably noticed that electrical devices such as televisions or stereos become warm after they have been on for a while. As moving electrons collide with the atoms of the material, some of their kinetic energy is transferred to the atoms. This energy transfer causes the atoms to vibrate, and the material warms up. In most materials, some of the kinetic energy of electrons is lost as heat.

A conductor's resistance indicates how much the motion of charges within it is resisted because of collisions. Resistance is found by dividing the voltage across the conductor by the current.

Resistance Equation

$$resistance = \frac{voltage}{current} \qquad R = \frac{V}{I}$$

The SI unit of resistance is the *ohm*, Ω, which is equal to volts per ampere. If a voltage across a conductor of 1 V produces a current of 1 A, then the resistance of the conductor is 1 Ω.

A *resistor* is a special type of conductor used to control current. Every resistor is designed to have a specific resistance. For example, for any applied voltage, the current in a 10 Ω resistor is half the current in a 5 Ω resistor.

Current (A)	Effect
0.001	Slight tingle
0.005	Pain
0.010	Muscle spasms
0.015	Loss of muscle control
0.070	Probably fatal (if contact is more than 1 second)

the effect of touching the terminals of a 24 V battery. Assume that your body is dry and has a resistance of 100 000 Ω.

2. If your skin is moist, your body's resistance is only about 1000 Ω. How would touching the terminals of a 24 V battery affect your body if your skin is moist?

Math Skills

Resistance The headlights of a typical car are powered by a 12 V battery. What is the resistance of the headlights if they draw 3.0 A of current when turned on?

1 **List the given and unknown values.**

Given: *current, I* = 3.0 A
voltage, V = 12 V

Unknown: *resistance, R* = ? Ω

2 **Write the equation for resistance.**

$$resistance = \frac{voltage}{current} \quad R = \frac{V}{I}$$

3 **Insert the known values into the equation, and solve.**

$$R = \frac{V}{I} = \frac{12\ V}{3.0\ A}$$

$$R = 4.0\ \Omega$$

Practice

Resistance

1. Find the resistance of a portable lantern that uses a 24 V power supply and draws a current of 0.80 A.

2. The current in a resistor is 0.50 A when connected across a voltage of 120 V. What is its resistance?

3. The current in a handheld video game is 0.50 A. If the resistance of the game's circuitry is 12 Ω, what is the voltage produced by the battery?

4. A 1.5 V battery is connected to a small light bulb with a resistance of 3.5 Ω. What is the current in the bulb?

Practice HINT

▶ When a problem requires you to calculate the resistance of an object, you can use the resistance equation as shown on the previous page.

▶ The resistance equation can also be rearranged to isolate voltage on the left in the following way:

$$R = \frac{V}{I}$$

Multiply both sides by *I*.

$$IR = \frac{V\cancel{I}}{\cancel{I}}$$

$$V = IR$$

You will need this version of the equation for Practice Problem 3.

▶ For Practice Problem 4, you will need to rearrange the equation to isolate current on the left.

Conductors have low resistances

Whether or not charges will move in a material depends partly on how tightly electrons are held in the atoms of the material. A good conductor is any material in which electrons can flow easily under the influence of an electric field. Metals, like the copper found in wires, are some of the best conductors because electrons can move freely throughout them. Certain metals, conducting alloys, or carbon are used in resistors.

When you flip the switch on a flashlight, the light seems to come on immediately. But the electrons don't travel that rapidly. The electric field is directed through the conductor at almost the speed of light when a voltage source is connected to the conductor. Electrons everywhere throughout the conductor simultaneously experience a force due to the electric field and move in the opposite direction of the field lines. This is why the light comes on so quickly in a flashlight.

Math Skills

Resources Assign students worksheet *26: Resistance* in the **Math Skills Worksheets** ancillary.

Additional Examples

Resistance A battery-operated CD player uses 12 V from the wall socket and draws a current of 2.5 A. Calculate the resistance of the CD player.

Answer: $R = \frac{V}{I} = \frac{12\ V}{2.5\ A} = 4.8\ \Omega$

A light bulb has a resistance of 12 Ω. It is attached to a battery that has a voltage of 24 V. Calculate the current in the light bulb.

Answer: $I = \frac{V}{R} = \frac{24\ V}{12\ \Omega} = 2.0\ A$

Teaching Tip

Electron Movement in a Conductor Free electrons in a conductor move about randomly until there is a potential difference across the conductor. Then the electrons move through the conductor in the opposite direction of the electric field. The electrons do not move in straight lines, but collide repeatedly with the vibrating metal atoms of the conductor. Despite these collisions, electrons move slowly along the conductor toward the positive terminal of the battery.

ELECTRICITY **443**

Solution Guide

1. $R = \frac{V}{I} = \frac{24\ V}{0.80\ A} = 3.0 \times 10^1\ \Omega$

2. $R = \frac{V}{I} = \frac{120\ V}{0.50\ A} = 240\ \Omega$

3. $V = IR = (0.50\ A)(12\ \Omega) = 6.0\ V$

4. $I = \frac{V}{R} = \frac{1.5\ V}{3.5\ \Omega} = 0.43\ A$

RESOURCE LINK
LABORATORY MANUAL

Have students perform *Lab 13 Electricity: Investigating How the Length of a Conductor Affects Resistance* in the lab ancillary.

DATASHEETS

Have students use *Datasheet 13.6* to record their results from the lab.

Current

Variable Resistors The resistance of electrical circuits is not always fixed. This can be demonstrated by changing the volume control on a portable stereo. The volume control is an example of a variable resistor. Ask students to speculate how a variable resistor works based on their knowledge of resistance. Have students think of other devices, such as indoor light-dimmer switches or electric oven controls, that also have variable resistors.

Multicultural Extension

Have students research the Japanese or German Maglev trains. These Maglev trains levitate on a magnetic field provided by superconducting electromagnets. Have students discuss whether Maglev trains would be practical in the United States.

Historical Perspective

Superconductivity was first observed in 1911 when H. K. Onnes cooled mercury to below 3 K, or –270°C, and found that the resistance went almost to zero ($3 \times 10^{-6}\ \Omega$, which is one ten-millionth its resistance at 0°C). Onnes was able to cool the mercury using liquid helium because he had developed the method to liquify helium 3 years earlier.

Some materials become superconductors below a certain temperature

Certain metals and compounds have zero resistance when their temperature falls below a certain temperature called the *critical temperature*. These types of materials are called *superconductors*. The critical temperature varies among materials, from less than −272°C (−458°F) to as high as −123°C (−189°F).

Metals such as niobium, tin, and mercury and some metallic compounds containing barium, copper, and oxygen become superconductors below their respective critical temperatures. Superconductors have been used in electrical devices such as filters, powerful magnets, and Maglev high-speed express trains.

Insulators have high resistance

Insulators have high resistance to charge movement. So insulating materials are used to prevent electric current from leaking. For example, plastic coating around the copper wire of an electric cord keeps the current from escaping into the floor or your body.

Sometimes it is important to provide a pathway for current to leave a charged object. So a conducting wire is run between the charged object and the ground, thereby *grounding* the object. Grounding is an important part of electrical safety.

How can materials be classified by resistance?

Materials
- ✔ 6 V battery
- ✔ flashlight bulb in base holder
- ✔ 2 wire leads with alligator clips
- ✔ 2 metal hooks
- ✔ block of wood
- ✔ glass stirring rod
- ✔ iron nail
- ✔ wooden dowel
- ✔ copper wire
- ✔ piece of chalk
- ✔ strip of cardboard
- ✔ plastic utensil
- ✔ aluminum nail
- ✔ brass key
- ✔ strip of cork

Procedure

1. Construct a conductivity tester, as shown in the diagram.
2. Test the conductivity of various materials by laying the objects one at a time across the hooks of the conductivity tester.

Analysis

1. What happens to the conductivity tester if a material is a good conductor?
2. Which materials were good conductors?
3. Which materials were poor conductors?
4. Explain the results in terms of resistance.

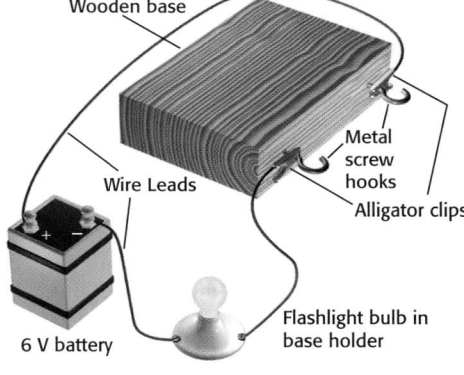

Wooden base
Metal screw hooks
Alligator clips
Wire Leads
6 V battery
Flashlight bulb in base holder

Inquiry Lab

How can materials be classified by resistance?

SAFETY CAUTION: *Students should be careful not to touch both terminals of the battery.*

Analysis

1. The conductivity tester lights up.
2. The iron nail, copper wire, aluminum nail, and brass key were good conductors.
3. The glass stirring rod, wooden dowel, chalk, cardboard, plastic utensil, and cork were poor conductors.
4. Good conductors have low resistance and allow charges to pass through, while insulators have high resistance.

Many electrical sockets are wired with three connections: two current-carrying wires and the ground wire. If there is any charge buildup, or if the live wire contacts an appliance, the ground wire conducts the charge to the Earth. The excess charge can spread over the planet safely.

Semiconductors are intermediate to conductors and insulators

Semiconductors belong to a third class of materials with electrical properties between those of insulators and conductors. In their pure state, semiconductors are insulators. The controlled addition of specific atoms of other materials as impurities dramatically increases a semiconductor's ability to conduct electric charge. Silicon and germanium are two common semiconductors. Complex electrical devices, like the computer board shown in **Figure 13-13,** are made of conductors, insulators, and semiconductors.

Figure 13-13
Most electrical devices contain conductors, insulators, and semiconductors.

SECTION 13.2 REVIEW

SUMMARY

▶ A charged object has electrical potential energy due to its position in an electric field.

▶ Potential difference, or voltage, is the difference in electrical potential energy per unit charge.

▶ A voltage causes charges to move, producing a current.

▶ Current is the rate of charge movement.

▶ Electrical resistance can be calculated by dividing voltage by current.

▶ Conductors are materials in which electrons flow easily.

▶ Superconductors have no resistance below their critical temperature.

▶ Insulators are materials with high resistance.

CHECK YOUR UNDERSTANDING

1. **Identify** which of the following could produce current:
   a. a wire connected across a battery's terminals
   b. two electrodes in a solution of positive and negative ions
   c. a salt crystal, whose ions cannot move
   d. a sugar-water mixture
2. **Predict** which way charges are likely to move between two positions of different electrical potential energy, one high and one low.
   a. from low to high
   b. from high to low
   c. back and forth between high and low
3. **State** the quantities needed to calculate an object's resistance.
4. **Explain** the function of insulation around a wire.
5. **Describe** the motion of charges through a flashlight, from one terminal of a battery to the other.
6. **Classify** the following materials as conductors or insulators: wood, paper clip, glass, air, paper, plastic, steel nail, water, aluminum can.

Math Skills

7. If the current in a certain resistor is 6.2 A and the voltage across the resistor is 110 V, what is its resistance?
8. If the voltage across a flashlight bulb is 3 V and the bulb's resistance is 6 Ω, what is the current through the bulb?

ELECTRICITY **445**

SECTION 13.2 REVIEW

Check Your Understanding

1. a. yes
   b. yes; The ions can move, causing a current.
   c. no; If the ions cannot move, then no current can be generated.
   d. no
2. b
3. You need the voltage across the object and the current.
4. Insulation electrically isolates the wire from the surrounding environment.
5. Electrons move away from the negative terminal of the battery and travel through the filament in the light bulb where they heat the filament causing it to give off light. The electrons then travel toward the positive terminal of the battery.
6. wood – insulator
   paper clip – conductor
   glass – insulator
   air – insulator
   paper – insulator
   plastic – insulator
   steel nail – conductor
   pure water – insulator
   aluminum can – conductor

Math Skills

7. $R = \dfrac{V}{I} = \dfrac{110\,\text{V}}{6.2\,\text{A}} = 18\ \Omega$

8. $I = \dfrac{V}{R} = \dfrac{3\,\text{V}}{6\,\Omega} = 0.5\ \text{A}$

RESOURCE LINK
STUDY GUIDE

Assign students *Review Section 13.2 Current.*

Circuits

Scheduling

Refer to pp. 428A–428D for lecture, classwork, and assignment options for Section 13.3.

★ **Lesson Focus**
Use transparency *LT 45* to prepare students for this section.

Summarizing
Have students read pp. 446–448 and write out a summary of the ideas on these pages. Ask for a volunteer to read his or her summary. The class, as listeners, should ask for clarification of parts of the passage once the "reteller" has finished. All students may consult the text during the clarification process.

Teaching Tip

Materials Science Light bulbs are slightly damaged each time they are turned on and then turned off. When the filament becomes hot, it expands slightly. When the light bulb is turned off, it cools and contracts slightly. The process of expansion and contraction stresses the surface of the filament, causing it to crack slightly over time. Repeated expansion and contraction causes the filament to crack even more. Eventually, the filament cracks too much and breaks, causing the light bulb to burn out. If the light bulb were kept on all the time, it would last much longer.

▶ **KEY TERMS**
electric circuit
schematic diagram
series
parallel
electrical energy
fuse
circuit breaker

Disc Two, Module 16:
Electrical Circuits
Use the Interactive Tutor to learn more about this topic.

▶ **electric circuit** an electrical device connected so that it provides one or more complete paths for the movement of charges

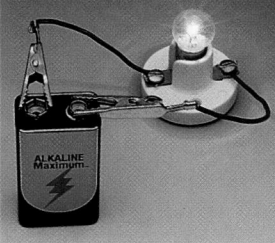

Figure 13-14
When this battery is connected to a light bulb, the voltage across the battery generates a current that lights the bulb.

OBJECTIVES

▶ Use schematic diagrams to represent circuits.
▶ Distinguish between series and parallel circuits.
▶ Calculate electric power using voltage and current.
▶ Explain how fuses and circuit breakers are used to prevent circuit overload.

Think about how you would get the bulb shown in **Figure 13-14** to light up. Would the bulb light if the bulb were not fully screwed into the socket? How about if one of the clips were removed from the battery?

What Are Circuits?

When a wire connects the terminals of the battery to the light bulb, as shown in **Figure 13-14,** charges that built up on one terminal of the battery have a path to follow to reach the opposite charges on the other terminal. Because there are charges moving uniformly, a current exists. This current causes the filament inside the light bulb to give off heat and light.

An electric circuit is a path through which charges can be conducted

Together, the bulb, battery, and wires form an **electric circuit.** In the circuit shown in **Figure 13-14,** the path from one battery terminal to the other is complete. Because of the voltage of the battery, electrons move through the wires and bulb from the negative terminal to the positive terminal. Then the battery adds energy to the charges as they move within the battery from the positive terminal back to the negative one.

In other words, there is a closed-loop path for electrons to follow. The conducting path produced when the light bulb is connected across the battery's terminals is called a *closed circuit.* Without a complete path, there is no charge flow and therefore no current. This is called an *open circuit.*

The inside of the battery is part of the closed path of current through the circuit. The voltage source, whether a battery or an outlet, is always part of the conducting path of a closed circuit.

If a device called a *switch* is added to the circuit, as shown in **Figure 13-15,** you can use the switch to open and close the circuit. You have used a switch many times. The switches on your wall at home are used to turn lights on and off. Although they look different from the switch in **Figure 13-15,** their function is the same. When you flip a switch at home, you either close or open the circuit to turn a light on or off.

The switch shown in **Figure 13-15** is called a knife switch. The metal bar is a conductor. When the bar is touching both sides of the switch, as shown in **Figure 13-15,** the circuit is closed. Electrons can move through the bar to reach the other side of the switch and light the bulb. If the metal bar on the switch is lifted, the circuit is open. Then there is no current, and the bulb does not glow.

Schematic diagrams are used to represent circuits

Suppose you wanted to describe to someone the contents and connections in the photo of the light bulb and battery in **Figure 13-15.** How might you draw each element? Could you use the same representations of the elements to draw a bigger circuit, such as a string of lights?

A diagram that depicts the construction of an electrical circuit or apparatus is called a **schematic diagram. Figure 13-16** shows how the battery and light bulb can be drawn as a schematic diagram. The symbols that are used in this figure can be used to describe any other circuit with a battery and one or more bulbs. All electrical devices, from toasters to computers, can be described using schematic diagrams. Because schematic diagrams use standard symbols, they can be read by people all over the world.

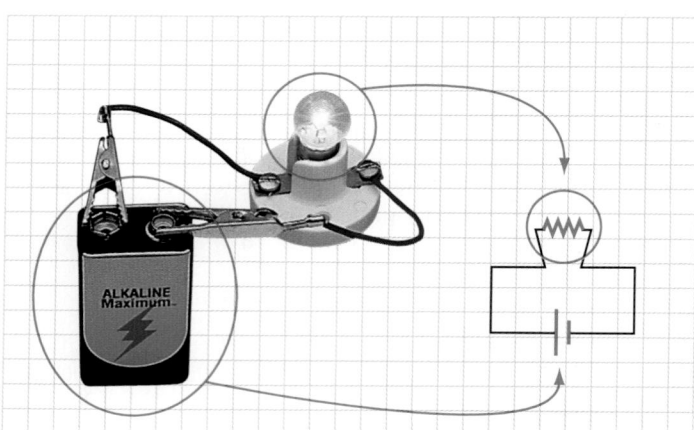

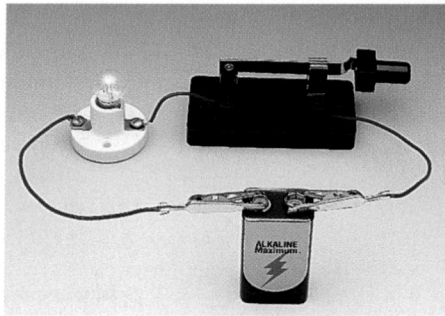

Figure 13-15
When added to the circuit, a switch can be used to open and close the circuit.

internet**connect**

SCI**LINKS**
NSTA

TOPIC: Electric circuits
GO TO: www.scilinks.org
KEYWORD: HK1135

▶ **schematic diagram**
a graphic representation of an electric circuit or apparatus, with standard symbols for the electrical devices

Figure 13-16
The connections between the light bulb and battery can be represented by symbols. This type of illustration is called a schematic diagram.

SKILL BUILDER

Interpreting Visuals Students should recognize that the straight-line symbols connecting the battery symbol with the bulb symbol in **Figure 13-16** represent not only the wires but also all parts of the conducting connection between the bulb and battery. Ask the students to list the parts of the photo symbolized by the black straight lines in **Figure 13-16.** *(The black lines symbolize the conducting path provided by the wires, clips, and socket.)* Then have students compare the circuits in **Figures 13-15** and **13-16.** Ask them to consider the length of the conducting path in each. Ask them which circuit probably has more resistance. *(The circuit in Figure 13-15 has more resistance because the wire connectors are longer, and the knife switch also has resistance.)* Based on this observation, what is one way to decrease the resistance in a given circuit? *(decrease the lengths of the wires connecting electrical components)*

Resources Blackline Master 42 shows this visual.

Historical Perspective

The first computer chips, called integrated circuits, were invented by Jack Kilby and Robert Noyce in the late 1950s. Since 1962, the number of electrical components on a chip has nearly doubled every year. Both the size of the components and the distance between them has become much smaller. Discuss with your class whether this trend is likely to continue.

Circuits

Diagrams If you were to draw out the entire schematic diagram for a computer chip using components the same size as in **Table 13-2,** the circuit schematic would probably cover the entire wall of your classroom.

INTEGRATING

TECHNOLOGY Mercury is the only metal that is a liquid at room temperature. Some switches make use of mercury in what is called a rocker switch. When the switch is rocked in one direction, the liquid mercury flows downhill and will cover two electrodes. Because mercury is a conductor, it makes an electrical connection with these two electrodes and closes the circuit. When the switch is rocked in the opposite direction, the liquid flows in the opposite direction and moves off the electrodes. This breaks the connection between the electrodes and opens the circuit, stopping charges from flowing.

As shown in **Table 13-2,** each element used in a piece of electrical equipment is represented by a symbol that reflects the element's construction or function. For example, the schematic-diagram symbol that represents an open switch resembles the open-knife switch shown in the corresponding photograph. Any circuit can be drawn using a combination of these and other, more-complex schematic diagram symbols.

Table 13-2 Schematic Diagram Symbols

Component	Symbol used in this book	Explanation
Wire or conductor		Wires that connect elements are conductors.
Resistor		Resistors are shown as wires with multiple bends, indicating resistance to a straight path.
Bulb or lamp		The winding of the filament indirectly indicates that the light bulb is a resistor, something that impedes the movement of electrons or the flow of charge.
Battery or other direct current source		The difference in line height indicates a voltage between positive and negative terminals of the battery. The taller line represents the positive terminal of the battery.
Switch	Open / Closed	The small circles indicate the two places where the switch makes contact with the wires. Most switches work by breaking only one of the contacts, not both.

ALTERNATIVE ASSESSMENT

Wiring Circuits
Draw different basic circuit diagrams having 4, 5, or 6 light bulbs on the board. Have groups of students wire these diagrams using a 6 V battery, wire connectors with alligator clips on the ends, and lights cut off of a set of holiday lights.

Have students work in pairs and take turns drawing simple schematic diagrams and wiring the circuits.

Series and Parallel Circuits

Section 13.2 showed that the current in a circuit depends on voltage and the resistance of the device in the circuit. What happens when there are two or more devices connected to a battery?

Series circuits have a single path for current

When appliances or other devices are connected in a **series** circuit, as shown in **Figure 13-17A,** they form a single pathway for charges to flow. Charges cannot build up or disappear at a point in a circuit. For this reason, the amount of charge that enters one device in a given time interval equals the amount of charge that exits that device in the same amount of time. Because there is only one path for a charge to follow when devices are connected in series, the current in each device is the same. Even though the current in each device is the same, the resistances may be different. Therefore, the voltage across each device in a series circuit can be different.

If one element along the path in a series circuit is removed, the circuit will not work. For example, if either of the light bulbs in **Figure 13-17A** were removed, the other one would not glow. The series circuit would be open. Several kinds of breaks may interrupt a series circuit. The opening of a switch, the burning out of a light bulb, a cut wire, or any other interruption can cause the whole circuit to fail.

Parallel circuits have multiple paths for current

When devices are connected in **parallel,** rather than in series, the voltage across each device is the same. The current in each device does not have to be the same. Instead, the sum of the currents in all of the devices equals the total current. A simple parallel circuit is shown in **Figure 13-17B.** The two lights are connected to the same points. The electrons leaving one end of the battery can pass through either bulb before returning to the other terminal. If one bulb has less resistance, more charge moves through that bulb because the bulb offers less opposition to the movement of charges.

Even if one of the bulbs in the circuit shown in **Figure 13-17B** were removed, charges would still move through the other loop. Thus, a break in any one path in a parallel circuit does not interrupt the flow of electric charge in the other paths.

ELECTRICITY **449**

Quick ACTIVITY

Series and Parallel Circuits

1. Connect two flashlight bulbs, a battery, wires, and a switch so that both bulbs light up.
2. Make a diagram of your circuit. Is it a series or a parallel circuit?
3. Now make the other type of circuit. Compare the brightness of the bulbs in the two types of circuits.

▶ **series** describes a circuit or portion of a circuit that provides a single conducting path

▶ **parallel** describes components in a circuit that are connected across common points, providing two or more separate conducting paths

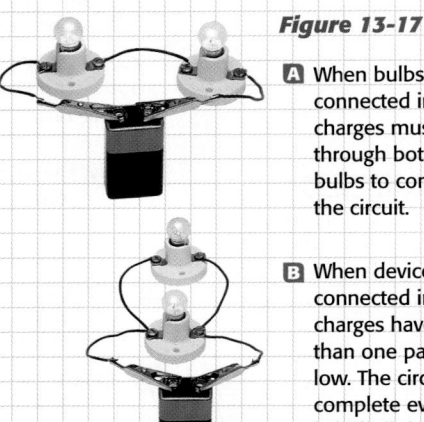

Figure 13-17

A When bulbs are connected in series, charges must pass through both light bulbs to complete the circuit.

B When devices are connected in parallel, charges have more than one path to follow. The circuit can be complete even if one light bulb burns out.

Section 13.3

Circuits

READING SKILL BUILDER *Paired Summarizing* Pair students together and have them silently read the section on series circuits. Choose one of the pair to be the "reteller" and the other the "listener." The reteller then summarizes the selection for the listener, who does not interrupt until the reteller has finished, or if there is a portion of the summary that requires clarification. The reteller may consult the text during his or her summary. The listener should then state any inaccuracies or omissions, and the students should work together to refine the summary. The students then change roles and read the section on parallel circuits.

Teaching Tip

Fluid Model of Electric Current Many teachers use a fluid model of electric current. In this model, charges moving due to potential difference are analogous to water moving to a level of lower gravitational potential energy. Wires are analogous to horizontal pipes, and resistors are analogous to water wheels, which transform the energy to another form. Batteries and generators act like pumps in that they lift water upward, increasing its potential energy.

Quick ACTIVITY

Series and Parallel Circuits When students have finished building both types of circuits, choose two of them to use as examples. Have students draw schematic diagrams for both circuits. Then ask them to trace the path for the movement of charges in both types of circuits on their diagrams and to describe the energy transformations involved. Ask students to explain how the difference in brightness of the lights between the series and parallel circuits relates to the current in each circuit. *(Lights in the parallel circuit must have more current in them because they are brighter.)*

RESOURCE LINK
DATASHEETS

Have students use *Datasheet 13.4 Quick Activity: Series and Parallel Circuits* to record their results.

Teaching Tip

Light Bulbs The rate of energy a lamp uses depends on the type of bulb in it. You may want to discuss the advantages and disadvantages of incandescent, fluorescent, and lower-wattage bulbs with students.

Math Skills

Resources Assign students worksheet *27: Electric Power* in the **Math Skills Worksheets** ancillary.

▶ **electrical energy** the energy associated with electrical charges, whether moving or at rest

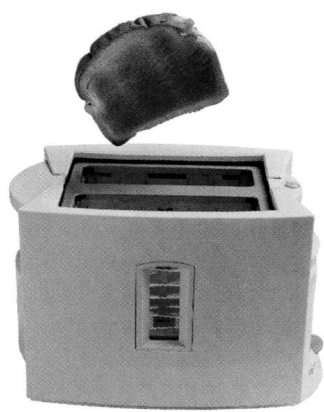

Figure 13-18
Household appliances use electrical energy to do useful work. Some of that energy is lost as heat.

VOCABULARY *Skills Tip*
The SI unit of power, the watt, *was named after the Scottish inventor James Watt in honor of his important work on steam engines.*

Electric Power and Electrical Energy

Many of the devices you use on a daily basis, such as the toaster shown in **Figure 13-18,** require electrical energy to run. The energy for these devices may come from a battery or from a power plant miles away.

Electric power is the rate at which electrical energy is used in a circuit

When a charge moves in a circuit, it loses energy. This energy is transformed into useful work, such as the turning of a motor, and is lost as heat in a circuit. The rate at which electrical work is done is called *electric power.* Electric power is the product of total current (I) in and voltage (V) across a circuit.

> **Electric Power Equation**
> $$power = current \times voltage$$
> $$P = IV$$

The SI unit for power is the watt (W), as shown in Chapter 9. A watt is equivalent to 1 A × 1 V. Light bulbs are rated in terms of watts. For example, a typical desk lamp uses a 60 W bulb.

If you combine the electric power equation above with the equation $V = IR$, the power lost, or *dissipated*, by a resistor can be calculated.

$$P = I^2R = \frac{V^2}{R}$$

Math Skills

Electric Power When a hair dryer is plugged into a 120 V outlet, it has a 9.1 A current in it. What is the hair dryer's power rating?

1 List the given and unknown values.
 Given: *voltage,* $V = 120$ V
   current, $I = 9.1$ A
 Unknown: *electric power,* $P = ?$ W

2 Write the equation for electric power.
 $power = current \times voltage$
 $P = IV$

3 Insert the known values into the equation, and solve.
 $P = (9.1 \text{ A})(120 \text{ V})$
 $P = 1.1 \times 10^3$ W

ALTERNATIVE ASSESSMENT

Energy Use in Home Appliances

SAFETY CAUTION: *Unplug appliances and use caution when handling electrical equipment.*
 Determine the power ratings for a few large appliances, such as a refrigerator, an air conditioner, or an electric heater. Bring a household electric-company bill (optional) and a few small appliances to class, such as a toaster, a clock/radio, and a hand-held vacuum cleaner.

 Look for a label on the back or bottom of each appliance. Record the power rating, which is given in units of watts (W). Use the billing statement to find the cost of energy per kilowatt-hour. Ask the students to calculate the cost of running each appliance for 1 hour. Then have them estimate how many hours a day each appliance is used, and calculate the monthly cost of using each appliance based on their estimate.

Practice

Electric Power

1. An electric space heater requires 29 A of 120 V current to adequately warm a room. What is the power rating of the heater?
2. A graphing calculator uses a 6.0 V battery and draws 2.6×10^{-3} A of current. What is the power rating of the calculator?
3. A color television has a power rating of 320 W. How much current is in the television when it is connected across 120 V?
4. The operating voltage for a light bulb is 120 V. The power rating of the bulb is 75 W. Find the current in the bulb.
5. The current in the heating element of an electric iron is 5.0 A. If the iron dissipates 590 W of power, what is the voltage across it?

Electric companies measure energy consumed in kilowatt-hours

Power companies charge for energy used in the home, not power. The unit of energy that electric companies use to track consumption of energy is the kilowatt-hour (kW•h). One kilowatt-hour is the energy delivered in 1 hour at the rate of 1 kW. In SI units, $1 \text{ kW•h} = 3.6 \times 10^{6}$ J.

Depending on where you live, the cost of energy ranges from 5 to 20 cents per kilowatt-hour. All homes and businesses have an electric meter, like the one shown in **Figure 13-19.** Electric meters are used by an electric company to determine how much electrical energy is consumed over a certain time interval.

Fuses and Circuit Breakers

When too many appliances, lights, CD players, televisions, and other devices are connected across a 120 V outlet, the overall resistance of the circuit is lowered. That means the electrical wires carry more than a safe level of current. When this happens, the circuit is said to be *overloaded.* The high currents in overloaded circuits can cause fires.

Worn insulation on wires can also be a fire hazard. If a wire's insulation wears down, two wires may touch, creating an alternative pathway for current. This is called a *short circuit.* The decreased resistance greatly increases the current in the circuit. Short circuits can be very dangerous. Grounding appliances reduces the risk of electric shock from a short circuit.

Practice HINT

▶ When a problem requires you to calculate power, you can use the power equation as shown on the previous page.
▶ The electric power equation can also be rearranged to isolate current on the left in the following way:

$$P = IV$$

Divide both sides by V.

$$\frac{P}{V} = \frac{IV}{V}$$

$$I = \frac{P}{V}$$

You will need this version of the equation for Practice Problems 3 and 4.

▶ For Practice Problem 5, you will need to rearrange the equation to isolate voltage on the left.

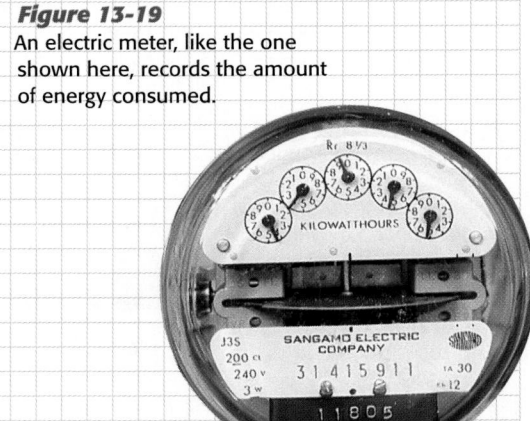

Figure 13-19
An electric meter, like the one shown here, records the amount of energy consumed.

ELECTRICITY **451**

Additional Examples

Electric Power A certain electrical motor needs a 9.0 V battery to operate and has a power output of 1.6 W. Calculate the current in the motor.

Answer: $I = \dfrac{P}{V} = \dfrac{1.6 \text{ W}}{9.0 \text{ V}} = 0.18 \text{ A}$

A single solar panel for home use puts out 550 W of electrical power. If the electrical current produced by this panel is 4.2 A, calculate the voltage generated by the panel.

Answer: $V = \dfrac{P}{I} = \dfrac{550 \text{ W}}{4.2 \text{ A}} = 130 \text{ V}$

Solution Guide

1. $P = IV = (29 \text{ A})(120 \text{ V}) = 3.5 \times 10^{3} \text{ W}$
2. $P = IV = (2.6 \times 10^{-3} \text{ A})(6.0 \text{ V}) = 1.6 \times 10^{-2} \text{ W}$
3. $I = \dfrac{P}{V} = \dfrac{320 \text{ W}}{120 \text{ V}} = 2.7 \text{ A}$
4. $I = \dfrac{P}{V} = \dfrac{75 \text{ W}}{120 \text{ V}} = 0.62 \text{ A}$
5. $V = \dfrac{P}{I} = \dfrac{590 \text{ W}}{5.0 \text{ A}} = 120 \text{ V}$

Circuits

Teaching Tip

GFIs Ground Fault Circuit Interrupters and Ground Fault Interrupters are mounted in electrical outlets and in certain appliances to prevent electrocution. GFCIs and GFIs are usually installed in the kitchen, bathroom, and outdoor outlets. They function by comparing the current in both wires of a socket. If there is a difference in current, the device opens the circuit within a few milliseconds. If you were to touch a bare wire, the device would detect the change in current and open the circuit; you would get only a small shock. Some circuit breakers are equipped with a GFI.

SECTION 13.3 REVIEW

Check Your Understanding

1. battery = 1, switch = 1, resistor = 2, light bulb = 3

2. In a parallel arrangement, if one light burns out, the rest will still keep working. In a series arrangement, if one burns out, all of the lights will stop working.

3.
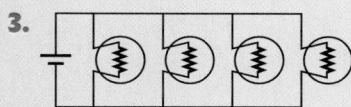

4.
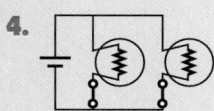

Answers continue on p. 457A.

RESOURCE LINK
STUDY GUIDE

Assign students *Review Section 13.3 Circuits.*

▷ **fuse** an electrical device containing a metal strip that melts when current in the circuit becomes too great

▷ **circuit breaker** a device that protects a circuit from current overloads

---

Fuses melt to prevent circuit overloads

To prevent overloading in circuits, **fuses** are connected in series along the supply path. A fuse is a ribbon of wire with a low melting point. If the current in the line becomes too large, the fuse melts and the circuit is opened.

Fuses "blow out" when the current in the circuit reaches a certain level. For example, a 20 A fuse will melt if the current in the circuit exceeds 20 A. A blown fuse is a sign that a short circuit or a circuit overload may exist somewhere in your home. It is best to find out what made a fuse blow out before replacing it.

Circuit breakers open circuits with high current

Many homes are equipped with **circuit breakers** instead of fuses. A circuit breaker uses a magnet or *bimetallic strip*, a strip with two different metals welded together, that responds to current overload by opening the circuit. The circuit breaker acts as a switch. As with blown fuses, it is wise to determine why the circuit breaker opened the circuit. Unlike fuses, circuit breakers can be reset by turning the switch back on.

SECTION 13.3 REVIEW

SUMMARY

▷ An electric circuit is a path along which charges can move.

▷ In a series circuit, devices are connected along a single pathway. A break anywhere along the path will stop the movement of charges.

▷ In a parallel circuit, two or more paths are connected to the voltage source. A break along one path will not stop the movement of charges in the other paths.

▷ Electric power supplied to a circuit or dissipated in a circuit is calculated as the product of the current and voltage.

CHECK YOUR UNDERSTANDING

1. Identify the types of elements in the schematic diagram at right and the number of each type.

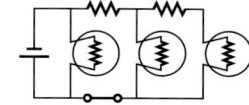

2. Describe the advantage of using a parallel arrangement of decorative lights rather than a series arrangement.

3. Draw a schematic diagram with four lights in parallel.

4. Draw a schematic diagram of a circuit with two light bulbs in which you could turn off either light and still have a complete circuit. (**Hint:** You will need to use two switches.)

5. Contrast how a fuse and a circuit breaker work to prevent overloading in circuits.

6. Predict whether a fuse will work successfully if it is connected in parallel with the device it is supposed to protect.

═ Math Skills ═

7. When a VCR is connected across a 120 V outlet, the VCR has a 9.5 A current in it. What is the power rating of the VCR?

8. A 40 W light bulb and a 75 W light bulb are in parallel across a 120 V outlet. Which bulb has the greater current?

Chapter Highlights

Before you begin, review the summaries of the key ideas of each section, found on pages 436, 445, and 452. The key vocabulary terms are listed on pages 430, 437, and 446.

UNDERSTANDING CONCEPTS

1. Which of the following particles is electrically neutral?
   a. a proton
   b. an electron
   c. a hydrogen atom
   d. a hydrogen ion

2. Which of the following is not an example of charging by friction?
   a. sliding over a plastic-covered car seat
   b. scraping food from a metal bowl with a metal spoon
   c. walking across a woolen carpet
   d. brushing dry hair with a plastic comb

3. The electric force between two objects depends on all of the following except _____.
   a. the distance between the objects
   b. the electric charge of the first object
   c. how the two objects became electrically charged
   d. the electric charge of the second object

4. A positive charge placed in the electric field of a second positive charge will _____.
   a. experience a repulsive force
   b. accelerate away from the second positive charge
   c. have greater electrical potential energy when near the second charge than when farther away
   d. All of the above

5. The _____ is the change in the electrical potential energy of a charged particle per unit charge.
   a. circuit
   b. voltage
   c. induction
   d. power

6. The type of electrical cell in a common battery is _____.
   a. piezoelectric
   b. thermoelectric
   c. electrochemical
   d. photoelectric

7. An electric current does not exist in _____.
   a. a closed circuit
   b. a series circuit
   c. a parallel circuit
   d. an open circuit

8. Which of the following schematic diagrams represent circuits that cannot have current in them as drawn.

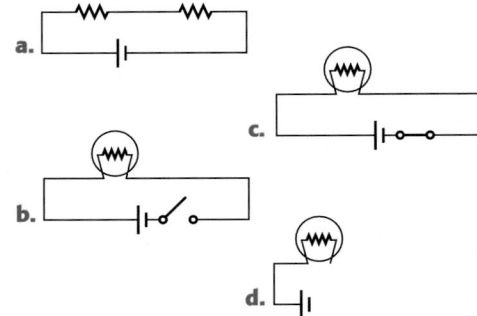

9. Which of the following can help prevent a circuit from overloading?
   a. a fuse
   b. a switch
   c. a circuit breaker
   d. both (a) and (c)

Using Vocabulary

10. Explain the energy changes involved when a positive charge moves because of a nearby, negatively charged object. Use the terms *electrical potential energy, work,* and *kinetic energy* in your answer.

11. How do charges move through an insulated wire connected across a battery? Use the terms *potential difference, current, conductor,* and *insulator* in your answer.

12. Contrast the movement of charges in a *series circuit* and in a *parallel circuit*. Use a diagram to aid in your explanation.

ELECTRICITY **453**

BUILDING MATH SKILLS

13. b

14. $R = \dfrac{V}{I} = \dfrac{12\,\text{V}}{0.30\,\text{A}} = 4.0 \times 10^1\ \Omega$

15. $V = IR = (1.6\,\text{A})(75\ \Omega) = 120\,\text{V}$

16. $I = \dfrac{V}{R} = \dfrac{3.0\,\text{V}}{25\,\Omega} = 0.12\,\text{A}$

17. $P = IV = (0.33\,\text{A})(3.0\,\text{V}) = 0.99\,\text{W}$

18. $I = \dfrac{P}{V} = \dfrac{2.4\,\text{W}}{1.5\,\text{V}} = 1.6\,\text{A}$

19. $V = \dfrac{P}{I} = \dfrac{7.0 \times 10^8\,\text{W}}{1.0 \times 10^3\,\text{A}} = 7.0 \times 10^5\,\text{V}$

THINKING CRITICALLY

20. Protons are trapped in the nucleus and cannot escape. As a result, electrons are the only subatomic particles that can be transferred. Metals transfer electrons most easily. In gases and certain chemical solutions, current can be the result of positive charge movement.

21. Your skin's resistance decreases when it gets wet because the ions on your skin dissolve in the water, making your skin a good conductor.

22. Decreases—shocks from static electricity would be worse in dry air. Dryer air is more insulating, allowing more charge to build up on an object.

23. Masses are always positive, while charges can be either positive or negative.

24. four (ignoring the position of the battery and as long as the light bulbs are identical): all in series, all in parallel, two in parallel in series with the third, two in series in parallel with the third

BUILDING MATH SKILLS

13. Electric Force The electric force is proportional to the product of the charges and inversely proportional to the square of the distance between them. If q_1 and q_2 are the charges on two objects, and d is the distance between them, which of the following represents the electric force, F, between them?

a. $F \propto \dfrac{q_1 q_2}{d}$

c. $F \propto \dfrac{d^2}{q_1 q_2}$

b. $F \propto \dfrac{q_1 q_2}{d^2}$

d. $F \propto \dfrac{(q_1 q_2)^2}{d}$

14. Resistance A potential difference of 12 V produces a current of 0.30 A in a piece of copper wire. What is the resistance of the copper wire?

15. Resistance What is the voltage across a 75 Ω resistor with 1.6 A of current?

16. Resistance A nickel wire with a resistance of 25 Ω is connected across the terminals of a 3.0 V flashlight battery. How much current is in the wire?

17. Power A portable cassette player uses 3.0 V (two 1.5 V batteries in series) and has 0.33 A of current. What is its power rating?

18. Power Find the current in a 2.4 W flashlight bulb powered by a 1.5 V battery.

19. Power A high-voltage transmission line carries 1.0×10^3 A of current. The power transmitted is 7.0×10^8 W. Find the voltage of the transmission line.

THINKING CRITICALLY

20. Understanding Systems Why is charge usually transferred by electrons? Which materials transfer electrons most easily? In what situations can positive charge move?

21. Applying Knowledge Why does the electrical resistance of your body decrease if your skin gets wet?

22. Problem Solving Humid air is a better electrical conductor because it has a higher water content than dry air. Do you expect shocks from static electricity to be worse as the humidity increases or as it decreases? Explain your answer.

23. Understanding Systems The gravitational force is always attractive, while the electric force is both attractive and repulsive. What accounts for this difference?

24. Designing Systems How many ways can you connect three light bulbs in a circuit with a battery? Draw a schematic diagram of each circuit.

25. Applying Knowledge At a given voltage, which light bulb has the greater resistance, a 200 W light bulb or a 75 W light bulb?

DEVELOPING LIFE/WORK SKILLS

26. Interpreting and Communicating A metal can is placed on a wooden table. If a positively charged ball suspended by a thread is brought close to the can, the ball will swing toward the can, make contact, then move away. Explain why this happens, and predict what will happen to the ball next. Use presentation software or a drawing program to make diagrams showing the charges on the ball and on the can at each phase.

COMPUTER SKILL

27. Working Cooperatively With a small group of classmates, make a chart about electrical safety in the home and outdoors. Use what you have learned in this chapter and information from your local fire department. Include how to prevent electric shock.

28. Allocating Resources Use the electric bill shown below to calculate the average amount of electrical energy used per day and the average cost of fuel to produce the electricity per day.

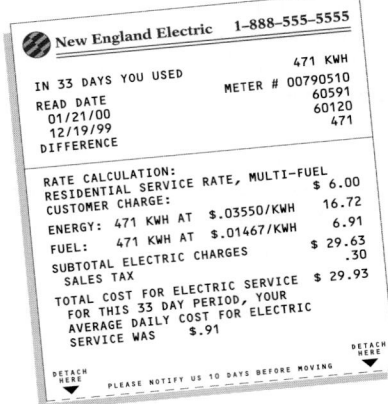

INTEGRATING CONCEPTS

29. Concept Mapping Copy the unfinished concept map below onto a sheet of paper. Complete the map by writing the correct word or phrase in the lettered boxes.

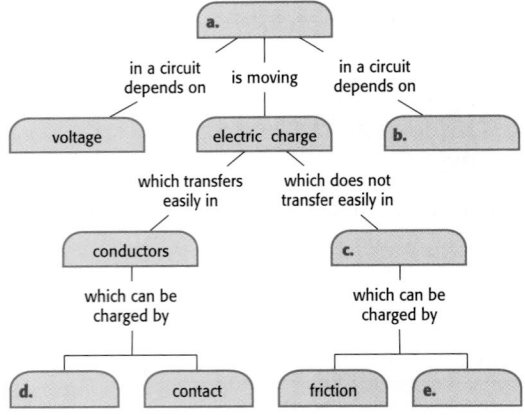

30. Connection to Social Studies The units of measurement you learned about in this chapter were named after three famous scientists—Alessandro Volta, André-Marie Ampère, and Georg Simon Ohm. Create a presentation about one of these scientists. Research the life, work, discoveries, and contributions of the scientist. The presentation can be in the form of a report, poster, short video, or computer presentation.

31. Connection to Engineering Research one of the four types of electrical cells. Write a report describing how it works. **WRITING SKILL**

32. Connection to Environmental Science Research how an *electrostatic precipitator* removes smoke and dust particles from the polluting emissions of fuel-burning industries. Find out what industries in your community use a precipitator. What are the advantages and costs of using this device? What alternatives are available? Summarize your findings in a brochure, poster, or chart.

33. Connection to Chemistry Atoms are held together partly because of the electric force between electrons and protons. Chemical bonding is also explained by the attraction between positive and negative particles. Prepare a poster that explains the types of bonding within substances using information from this book and the library. Give examples of common substances that contain these bonds. Describe the relative strengths of the bonds and the types of atoms these bonds form between.

TOPIC: Electrostatic precipitators
GO TO: www.scilinks.org
KEYWORD: HK1136

ELECTRICITY **455**

25. $R = \dfrac{V^2}{P} = \dfrac{V^2}{200\ W}$

$R = \dfrac{V^2}{P} = \dfrac{V^2}{75\ W}$

The 75 W bulb has a greater resistance. Alternatively, students may argue that a dimmer bulb (75 W) has a greater resistance than a brighter bulb (200 W) does.

DEVELOPING LIFE/WORK SKILLS

26. The positively charged ball induces a negative charge on the surface of the can closest to it. The ball is then attracted to the can and swings toward it. Upon contact, some of the electrons from the can are transferred to the ball, leaving the can positively charged. The ball is still positively charged, but the amount of charge is less. The ball is unlikely to touch the can after this.

27. Your local fire department will have electrical safety brochures. You can also find information in the public library as well as on the Internet.

28. $\dfrac{average\ electrical\ energy}{day} =$
$\dfrac{471\ kWh}{33\ days} = \dfrac{14\ kWh}{day}$
$\dfrac{cost\ of\ fuel}{day} = \dfrac{\$6.91}{33\ days} = \dfrac{\$0.21}{day}$

Answers continue on p. 457B.

Skill Builder Lab

Constructing Electric Circuits

Objectives

Students will:

▶ **Use** appropriate lab safety procedures.

▶ **Construct** parallel and series circuits.

▶ **Predict** voltage and current using the resistance law.

▶ **Measure** voltage, current, and resistance.

Planning

Recommended time: 1 lab period
Materials: *(for each lab group)*

▶ 1.5 V dry-cell battery

▶ battery holder

▶ 100 Ω resistor

▶ 200 Ω resistor

▶ 3 connecting wires

▶ masking tape

▶ multimeter

Note: Most new batteries will have 1.55–1.6 V. Battery holders that have tabs or wires attached to the positive and negative terminals will make it easier for students to connect the batteries in a circuit. To connect components, students may use miniature test leads with spring clips at each end, or wires approximately 10 cm long with small alligator clips soldered to each end. The test leads attached to the multimeter should also have alligator clips at their ends.

Skill Builder Lab

Introduction

How can you show how the current that flows through an electric circuit depends on voltage and resistance?

Objectives

▶ **Construct** parallel and series circuits.

▶ **Predict** voltage and current using the resistance law.

▶ **Measure** voltage, current, and resistance.

Materials

dry-cell battery
battery holder
2 resistors
3 connecting wires
masking tape
multimeter

Safety Needs

safety goggles
heat-resistant gloves

Constructing Electric Circuits

▶ Preparing for Your Experiment

1. In this laboratory exercise, you will use an instrument called a multimeter to measure voltage, current, and resistance. Your teacher will demonstrate how to use the multimeter to make each type of measurement.

2. As you read the steps listed below, refer to the diagrams for help making the measurements. Write down your predictions and measurements in your lab notebook. **SAFETY CAUTION** Handle the wires only where they are insulated.

▶ Circuits with a Single Resistor

3. Measure the resistance in ohms of one of the resistors. Write the resistance on a small piece of masking tape, and tape it to the resistor. Repeat for the other resistor.

4. Use the resistance equation to predict the current in amps that will be in a circuit consisting of one of the resistors and one battery. (**Hint:** You must rearrange the equation to solve for current.)

5. Test your prediction by building the circuit. Do the same for the other resistor.

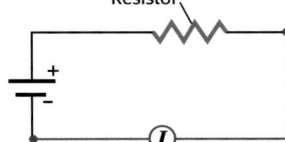

▶ Circuits with Two Resistors in Series

6. Measure the total resistance across both resistors when they are connected in series.

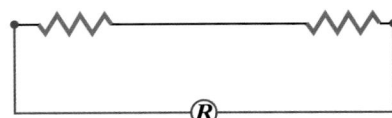

7. Using the total resistance you measured, predict the current that will be in a circuit consisting of one battery and both resistors in series. Test your prediction.

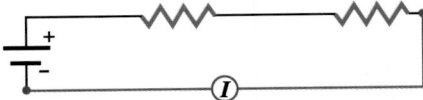

8. Using the current you measured, predict the voltage across each resistor in the circuit you just built. Test your prediction.

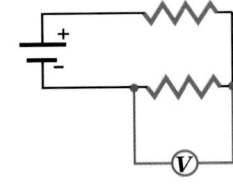

▶ Circuits with Two Resistors in Parallel

9. Measure the total resistance across both resistors when they are connected in parallel.

10. Using the total resistance you measured, predict the total current that will be in an entire circuit consisting of one battery and both resistors in parallel. Test your prediction.

11. Predict the current that will be in each resistor individually in the circuit you just built. Test your prediction.

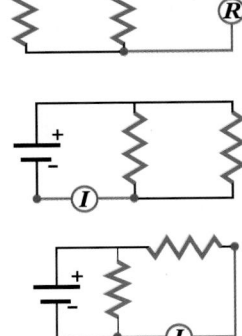

▶ Analyzing Your Results

1. If you have a circuit consisting of one battery and one resistor, what happens to the current if you double the resistance?

2. What happens to the current if you add a second, identical battery in series with the first battery?

3. What happens to the current if you add a second resistor in parallel with the first resistor?

4. Reaching Conclusions Suppose you have a circuit consisting of one battery plus a 10 Ω resistor and a 5 Ω resistor in series. Which resistor will have the greater voltage across it?

5. Reaching Conclusions Suppose you have a circuit consisting of one battery plus a 10 Ω resistor and a 5 Ω resistor in parallel. Which resistor will have more current in it?

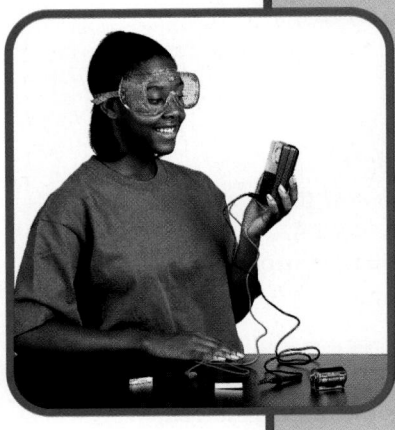

▶ Defending Your Conclusions

6. Suppose someone tells you that you can make the battery in a circuit last longer by adding more resistors in parallel. Is that correct? Explain your reasoning.

Continue on p.457A

CONTINUATION OF ANSWERS

Skill Builder Lab from page 457
Constructing Electric Circuits

Post-Lab

▶ **Disposal**

The batteries should be tested. Discharged batteries should be taken to hazardous waste disposal.

▶ **Circuits with a Single Resistor**

3. The resistances should be about 100 Ω and 200 Ω.

4. $I = \dfrac{V}{R} = \dfrac{1.5\,\text{V}}{100\,\Omega} = 0.015$ A in the 100 Ω circuit

$I = \dfrac{V}{R} = \dfrac{1.5\,\text{V}}{200\,\Omega} = 0.0075$ A in the 200 Ω circuit

5. About 0.015 A should be in the 100 Ω circuit and 0.0075 A should be in the 200 Ω circuit.

▶ **Circuits with Two Resistors in Series**

6. The total resistance should be about 300 Ω.
7. The total current should be about 0.005 A.
8. The voltage should be about 0.5 V across the 100 Ω resistor and 1.0 V across the 200 Ω resistor.

▶ **Circuits with Two Resistors in Parallel**

9. The total resistance should be about 67 Ω.
10. The total current should be about 0.022 A.
11. About 0.015 A should be in the 100 Ω resistor and 0.0075 A should be in the 200 Ω resistor.

▶ **Analyzing Your Results**

1. The current will be half as much as the original current.
2. The total current will be double the original current.
3. The total current will increase.
4. The 10 Ω resistor will have the greater voltage across it.
5. The 5 Ω resistor will have more current in it.

▶ **Defending Your Conclusions**

6. No, adding more resistors will increase the amount of current in the circuit, which will drain the battery more quickly.

Answers from page 436
SECTION 13.1 REVIEW

3. a. The drawing should show negative charges on the side of the metal washer nearest the rod and positive charges on the side of the washer farthest from the rod.
b. The drawing should show "polarized molecules" (refer to **Fig. 13-5**) with the side of each "molecule" nearest the rod negative and the side farthest from the rod positive.
4. a. conductor
b. insulator
c. conductor
d. insulator
5. a. The force will become one-ninth as large as the original force.
b. The force will double.
6. a negative charge of equal amount

Answers from page 452
SECTION 13.3 REVIEW

5. Fuses melt when the current exceeds their current rating, while circuit breakers break the connection when the current exceeds their current rating. Circuit breakers can also be reset and reused.
6. If a fuse is attached in parallel, it will not protect the intended device because even if the fuse blows out, there will still be current in the device.

Math Skills

7. $P = IV = (9.5\,\text{A})(120\,\text{V}) = 1.1 \times 10^3$ W
8. $I = \dfrac{P}{V} = \dfrac{40\,\text{W}}{120\,\text{V}} = 0.3$ A

$I = \dfrac{P}{V} = \dfrac{75\,\text{W}}{120\,\text{V}} = 0.62$ A

The 75 W bulb has more current in it.

INTEGRATING CONCEPTS

29. a. current
b. resistance
c. insulators
d. friction
e. contact

30. Alessandro Volta (1745–1827) was an Italian physicist who served as chair of physics at the University of Pavia. He invented the battery and was the first to discover and isolate methane gas.

André-Marie Ampère (1775–1836) was a French physicist and mathematics professor at the Ecole Polytechnique, in Paris. He founded and named electrodynamics. He developed techniques for measuring electricity that were later refined to produce the galvanometer (see Chapter 14). He is responsible for recognizing several of the fundamental principles of electromagnetism. Ampère's law describes the magnetic field induced by electric currents.

George Simon Ohm (1789–1854) was a German physicist and professor of mathematics at the Polytechnic School of Nürnberg. He discovered that the current in a conductor is proportional to the potential difference across the conductor and inversely proportional to its resistance.

31. Refer to **Table 13-1** for the basic principle for each type of electrical cell.

32. Students' answers will vary. Electrostatic precipitators can remove either solid particles or liquid drops that are suspended in a gas. They can handle large volumes of gas, even at high temperatures, and can remove particles in the micrometer range. However, they must be designed and tested for each application, making them more expensive than other methods. Alternatives include scrubbers (gas passes through streams of water), air filters (gas passes through coated fiber filters or dry filters), packed-bed particle separation devices (gas passes through layers of materials such as sand, glass, or steel wool), gravity settling chambers (velocity of gas is decreased so particles settle out), cloth collectors (gas passes through layers of fabric), and inertial separators (direction of gas motion is changed suddenly and particles settle out due to their greater inertia).

33. The three types of bonds are covalent bonds, ionic bonds, and metallic bonds. Many substances have covalent bonds, such as water, sand, and many organic compounds. Covalent bonds form between nonmetal atoms and are usually very strong. Table salt, NaCl, is an example of a compound with ionic bonds. Ionic bonds form between metal and nonmetal atoms and are also very strong. Other examples of compounds with ionic bonds are CaF_2 and KI. All metals have metallic bonds. Examples include copper, aluminum, silver, and gold. Metallic bonds form between metal atoms. They are fairly strong but flexible so that metals can be bent and stretched.

CareerLink

LINKING CHAPTERS

Dr. Martinez's research work involves exploring the electrical and magnetic properties of individual molecules and how these molecules interact with the electromagnetic fields associated with light. The concepts associated with electricity in Chapter 13 and magnetism in Chapter 14 are key to his work.

SKILL BUILDER

Vocabulary The word *spectroscopy* comes from two different root words. The Latin word *spectrum* means "appearance" or "apparition," and the Greek word *skopein* means "to see."

Physicist

Physicists are scientists who are trying to understand the fundamental rules of the universe. Physicists pursue these questions at universities, private corporations, and government agencies. To learn more about physics as a career, read the interview with physicist Robert Martinez, who works at the University of Texas in Austin, Texas.

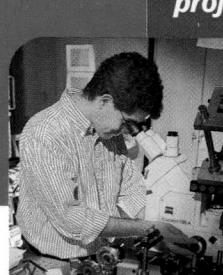

Robert Martinez uses a microscope that he has developed to identify single molecules.

 What kinds of problems are you studying?

We're working on a technique that will allow us to study single molecules. We could look at, say, molecules on the surface of a cell. What we're doing is building a kind of microscope for optical spectroscopy, which is a way to find out the colors of molecules. Studying the colors of molecules can tell us what those molecules are made of.

 How does this allow you to identify molecules?

Atoms act as little beams, and the bonds act as little springs. By exciting them with light, we can get them to vibrate and give off different colors of light. It's a little bit like listening to a musical instrument and telling from the overtones that a piano is different from a trumpet or a clarinet.

"I think of our current project a little bit like the nineteenth century explorers did. They didn't know what they would find on the other side of the ridge or the other side of the ocean, but they had to go look."

 What facets of your work do you find most interesting?

The thing that I like about what we're doing is that it's very practical, very hands-on. Also, the opportunity exists to explore whole new areas of physics and chemistry that no one has explored before. What we are doing has the promise of giving us new tools—new "eyes"—to look at important problems.

 What qualities do you think a physicist needs?

You've got to be innately curious about how the world works, and you've got to think it's understandable and you are capable of understanding it. You've got to be courageous. You've got to be good at math.

Can you remember any experiences that were particularly valuable for you?

When I was growing up, my dad was a pipe fitter for the city of Los Angeles, and I got to be his apprentice. I got a lot of practical experience that way. I think it's important to take the lawn mower engine apart, take the toaster apart—unplug it first—and see how it works.

 Which part of your education was most important?

I liked graduate school a great deal. When I started in research, I had an adviser who was very hands off. What I got was the freedom to go as high as I could or to fall on my face. It was a place where I could stretch out and use things I had under my belt but didn't get to use in the classroom. Outside of school, my dad was my best teacher. He was very bright and had a lot of practical experience.

 What advice would you give someone interested in physics?

If it interests you at all, stick with it. If you have doubts, try to talk to people who know what physicists do and know about physics training. The number of people with physics training far exceed the number of people who work as physicists. A good fraction of engineering is physics, for instance.

 internet**connect**

 SC*L*INKS
NSTA

TOPIC: Physicist
GO TO: www.scilinks.org
KEYWORD: HK1139

"I think that children are born scientists. It's just a matter of keeping your eyes open—keeping your curiosity alive."
—ROBERT MARTINEZ

459

CareerLink

Physicist

Historical Perspective

Spectroscopy While Dr. Martinez's work with molecular spectroscopy is cutting-edge research, other types of spectroscopy have been used for many years.

Isaac Newton first studied the spectra of sunlight in 1672.

In 1802, W. H. Wollaston, and in 1814, Joseph Fraunhofer independently demonstrated that by passing sunlight through a slit first, a spectrum could be made that contained a series of dark lines.

In 1859, G. R. Kirchoff explained that the dark lines Fraunhofer had found in the solar spectrum years before were due to elements in the sun's atmosphere absorbing wavelengths of light.

In the 1860s, working with R. Bunsen, Kirchoff demonstrated that spectral analysis of light from sparks or flames could be used to identify specific elements. In 1861, Bunsen and Kirchoff co-discovered the elements cesium and rubidium as the sources for previously undescribed lines in some spectra of alkali metals.

CHAPTER 14

Magnetism

Annotated Descriptions of the Correlated National Science Standards

The following descriptions summarize the National Science Standards that specially relate to Chapter 14. For a full text of the Standards, see p. 40T.

SECTION 14.1
Magnets and Magnetic Fields
Physical Science
PS 5b
Unifying Concepts and Processes
UCP 1–3, 5
Science as Inquiry
SAI 1, 2
Science and Technology
ST 1, 2
History and Nature of Science
HNS 1–3
Science in Personal and Social Perspectives
SPSP 5

SECTION 14.2
Magnetism from Electric Currents
Physical Science
PS 4e, 5b
Unifying Concepts and Processes
UCP 1–3, 5
Science as Inquiry
SAI 1, 2
Science and Technology
ST 1, 2
History and Nature of Science
HNS 1–3
Science in Personal and Social Perspectives
SPSP 5

SECTION 14.3
Electric Currents from Magnetism
Physical Science
PS 4e, 5b, 6b
Unifying Concepts and Processes
UCP 1–3, 5
Science as Inquiry
SAI 1, 2
Science and Technology
ST 1, 2
History and Nature of Science
HNS 1–3
Science in Personal and Social Perspectives
SPSP 5

Cross-Discipline Teaching RESOURCES

Cross-Discipline Teaching, ATE p. 460
Biology

Integration Enrichment Resources
Social Studies, **PE** and **ATE** p. 465
IE 14.1 *The Natural Forces and Laws of Compasses*

Additional Integration Enrichment Worksheets
IE 14.2 Chemistry   IE 14.3 Technology

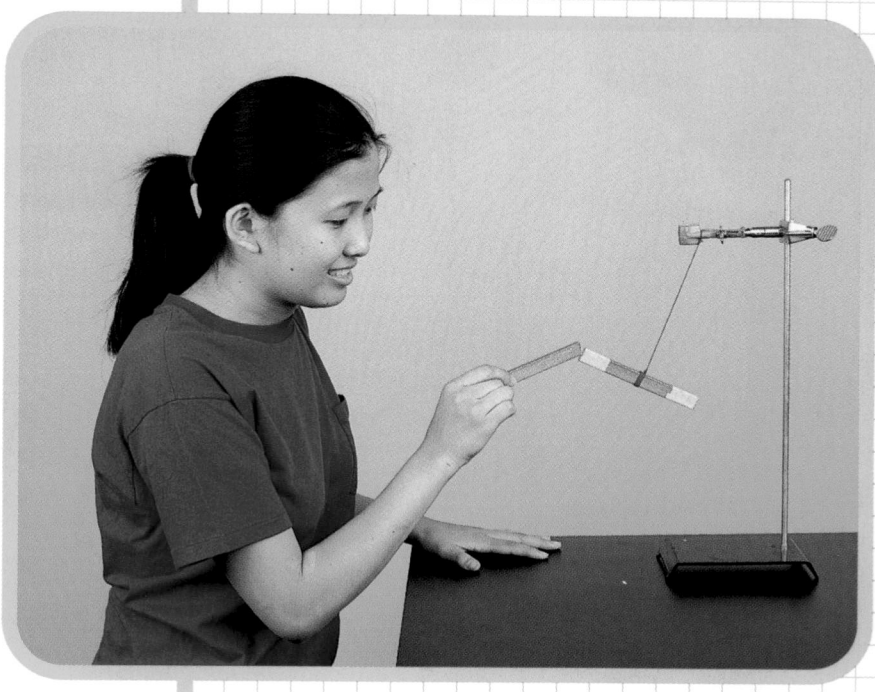

Use the Planning Guide on the next page to help you organize your lessons.

MATH AND COMPUTER RESOURCES

Chapter 14	Math Skills	Assess	Media/Computer Skills
Section 14.1			■ Section 14.1 **CNN Presents Physical Science** **Segment 21** Magnetic Attractions **CRT** Worksheet 21
Section 14.2			■ Section 14.2 **DISC TWO, MODULE 17** Magnetic Field of a Wire **PE Developing Life/Work Skills,** p. 483, item 24
Section 14.3		**PE Building Math Skills,** p. 482, items 16, 17	■ Section 14.3

PE Pupil's Edition   **ATE** Annotated Teacher's Edition   **MS** Math Skills   **BS** Basic Skills
IE Integration Enrichment   ■ Guided Reading Audio   **CRT** Critical Thinking

PHYSICAL SCIENCE INTERACTIVE TUTOR

READING SKILL BUILDER

The following activities found in the Annotated Teacher's Edition provide techniques for developing useful reading strategies to increase your students' reading comprehension skills.

Section 14.1 **Brainstorming,** p. 460
Paired Reading, p. 462

Section 14.2 **Reading Organizer,** p. 468

Smithsonian Institution®

Visit
www.si.edu/hrw
for additional
online resources.

Spanish Resources

The following resources are made available for students who speak Spanish as their first language.

Spanish Resources
Guided Reading Audio CD-ROM
Chapter 14

Spanish Glossary
Chapter 14

Magnetism

CLASSROOM RESOURCES

FOCUS	TEACH	HANDS-ON
Section 14.1 Magnets and Magnetic Fields		
BLOCK 1 45 minutes	ATE RSB Brainstorming, p. 460 ATE Focus Activities 1, 2, p. 461 ATE RSB Paired Reading, p. 462 ATE **Demo 1** Magnetizing a Nail, p. 462 PE Magnets, pp. 462–464 ★ Focus Transparency LT 46	ATE **Skill Builder** Interpreting Visuals, pp. 461, 463	PE Quick Activity *Test Your Knowledge of Magnetic Poles,* p. 464 **DS** 14.1
BLOCK 2 45 minutes	ATE **Demo 2** Shapes of Magnetic Fields, p. 465 PE Magnetic Fields, pp. 464–467	ATE **Skill Builder** Interpreting Visuals, p. 466 BLM 43 Magnetic Field BLM 44 Earth's Magnetic Field	IE Worksheet 14.1 PE Quick Activity *Magnetic Field of a File Cabinet,* p. 466 **DS** 14.2
Section 14.2: Magnetism from Electric Currents		
BLOCK 3 45 minutes	ATE RSB Reading Organizer, p. 468 ATE **Demo 3** Magnetic Field of a Current Loop, p. 469 PE Producing Magnetism from Electric Currents, pp. 468–471 ★ Focus Transparency LT 47	ATE **Skill Builder** Interpreting Visuals, p. 469 BLM 45 Right Hand Rule BLM 46 Solenoid	PE Inquiry Lab *How can you make an electromagnet?* p. 470 **DS** 14.3
BLOCK 4 45 minutes	ATE **Demo 4** Magnetic Force on a Current Loop, p. 472 PE Electromagnetic Devices, pp. 471–473	ATE **Skill Builder** Interpreting Visuals, pp. 471–473 TT 41 Electric Motor BLM 47 Galvanometer	LE 14 *Testing Magnets for an Electric Motor* **DS** 14.6 IE Worksheet 14.2
Section 14.3: Electric Currents from Magnetism		
BLOCK 5 45 minutes	ATE **Demo 5** Measuring Energy, p. 476 PE Electromagnetic Induction and Faraday's Law, pp. 474–478 ★ Focus Transparency LT 48	ATE **Skill Builder** Interpreting Visuals, pp. 474, 476, 477 TT 42 Induced Current TT 44 AC Generator	PE Inquiry Lab *Can you demonstrate electromagnetic induction?* p. 475 **DS** 14.4 IE Worksheet 14.3
BLOCK 6 45 minutes	ATE **Demo 6** DC Transformer, p. 479 PE Transformers, pp. 479–480	ATE **Skill Builder** Interpreting Visuals, pp. 479, 480 TT 43 Transformers	PE Design Your Own Lab *Making a Better Electromagnet,* p. 485 **DS** 14.5

CLASSROOM RESOURCES

HOMEWORK	ASSESS
PE Section Review 1, 2, p. 467 **Chapter 14 Review,** p. 481, items 1–3	**SG** Chapter 14 Pretest
PE Section Review 3-5, p. 467 **Chapter 14 Review,** p. 481, items 4, 11	**SG** Section 14.1
PE Section Review 1–5, p. 473 **Chapter 14 Review,** p. 481, items 5, 6	
PE Section Review 6, p. 473 **Chapter 14 Review,** p. 481, items 7, 12	**SG** Section 14.2
PE Section Review 1, 2, 4, 5, p. 480 **Chapter 14 Review,** p. 481, items 8–10, 13, 14, 16, 17	**ATE** *ALTERNATIVE ASSESSMENT,* Generators, p. 478
PE Section Review 3, p. 480 **Chapter 14 Review,** p. 481, item 15	**SG** Section 14.3

BLOCK 7

PE Chapter 14 Review
Thinking Critically 18–22, p. 482
Developing Life/Work Skills 23–25, pp. 482–483
Integrating Concepts 26–30, p. 483
SG Chapter 14 Mixed Review

BLOCK 8

Chapter Tests
Holt Science Spectrum: A Physical Approach
Chapter 14 Test

One-Stop Planner CD–ROM with Test Generator
Holt Science Spectrum Test Generator
FOR MACINTOSH AND WINDOWS
Chapter 14

Teaching Resources
Scoring Rubrics and assignment evaluation checklist.

 **internetconnect**

SC/LINKS
NSTA

National Science Teachers
Association
Online Resources:
www.scilinks.org

The following *sci*LINKS Internet resources can be found in the student text for this chapter.

Page 461
TOPIC: Maglev trains
KEYWORD: HK1141

Page 463
TOPIC: Properties of
magnets
KEYWORD: HK1142

Page 466
TOPIC: Earth's magnetic
field
KEYWORD: HK1143

Page 470
TOPIC: Electromagnetism
KEYWORD: HK1144

Page 476
TOPIC: Generators
KEYWORD: HK1145

Page 483
TOPIC: Magnetic fields
of power lines
KEYWORD: HK1146

CNNfyi.com   www.cnnfyi.com

Visit this site for coverage of current events and related classroom resources.

PE Pupil's Edition   **ATE** Annotated Teacher's Edition
RSB Reading Skill Builder   **DS** Datasheets
IE Integrated Enrichment   **SG** Study Guide
LE Laboratory Experiments
TT Teaching Transparencies   **BLM** Blackline Masters
★ Lesson Focus Transparency

CHAPTER 14

Magnetism

Chapter Preview

14.1 Magnets and Magnetic Fields
 Magnets
 Magnetic Fields

14.2 Magnetism from Electric Currents
 Producing Magnetism from Electric Currents
 Electromagnetic Devices

14.3 Electric Currents from Magnetism
 Electromagnetic Induction and Faraday's Law
 Transformers

The iron filings in the photo above are moved into a pattern by the magnetic force of the magnet. Maglev trains, like the one shown above, levitate above their tracks using magnetic force.

460

Focus ACTIVITY

Background Just as a magnet exerts a force on the iron filings in the small photo at left, a modern type of train called a *Maglev* train is levitated and accelerated by magnets. A Maglev train uses magnetic forces to lift the train off the track, reducing the friction and allowing the train to move faster. These trains, in fact, have reached speeds of more than 500 km/h (310 mi/h).

In addition to enabling the train to reach high speeds, the lack of contact with the track provides a smoother, quieter ride. With improvements in the technologies that produce the magnetic forces used in levitation, these trains may become more common in high-speed transportation.

Activity 1 You can see levitation in action with two ring-shaped magnets and a pencil.

Hold the pencil near the eraser with the tip pointing upward. Drop one of the ring magnets over the tip of the pencil so that it rests on your hand. Now drop the other magnet over the tip of the pencil. If the magnets are oriented correctly, the second ring will levitate above the other. If the magnets attract, remove the second ring, flip it over, and again drop it over the tip of the pencil.

The magnetic force exerted on the levitating magnet is equal to the magnet's weight. Use a scale to find the magnet's mass; then use the weight equation from Section 8.3 to calculate the magnetic force necessary to levitate this magnet.

Activity 2 The small photo at left shows how one magnet aligns iron filings. How does the pattern differ for two magnets?

Place two bar magnets flat on a table with the N poles about 2 cm apart. Cover the magnets with a sheet of plain paper. Sprinkle iron filings on the paper. Tap the paper gently until the filings line up. Make a sketch showing the orientation of the filings. Where does the magnetic force seem to be the strongest?

internet connect

SC*LINKS*
NSTA

TOPIC: Maglev trains
GO TO: www.scilinks.org
KEYWORD: HK1141

461

Focus ACTIVITY

Background Modern Maglev trains are levitated above guideways by on-board superconducting electromagnets and coils on the guideway. The electromagnets move at a high speed very close to the coils, inducing an electric current within the coils, which then act as electromagnets temporarily. The interaction between the coils and the on-board magnets levitates the train, keeps it centered on the guideway, and propels it forward.

Activity 1 The top magnet will levitate if the magnets' north poles are next to each other or if the south poles are next to each other. If the north and south poles are next to each other, the magnets will be attracted, and the top magnet will not levitate.

Activity 2 When you try this experiment, it is advisable to put the magnet into a plastic sandwich bag. Have students try many different arrangements of magnets to see the resulting magnetic fields.

SKILL BUILDER

Interpreting Visuals The magnetic force between the train and the track increases as the poles of the electromagnets on the train and those on the track are pushed together. This automatically compensates for variations in weight along the train. Students can observe the increase in repulsion as the distance between like poles decreases by pushing the like poles of two different magnets together.

Magnets and Magnetic Fields

Scheduling

Refer to pp. 460A–460D for lecture, classwork, and assignment options for Section 14.1.

★ Lesson Focus

Use transparency *LT 46* to prepare students for this section.

READING SKILL BUILDER *Paired Reading* Have students read Section 14.1 and note the concepts that are difficult to understand. Be sure students study legends, captions, diagrams, and illustrations to help clarify the material. Divide students into pairs after the reading. Each student within a pair will either clarify the other student's difficult passage or help determine a question concerning the passage for later class discussion or teacher explanation.

Teaching Tip

Levitating Magnets As shown in Activity 1 on page 461, ring magnets can be placed on a pencil so that they will levitate if their magnetic fields are oriented correctly. Try putting many ring magnets on the same pencil so that they all repel each other. You will notice that the spacing between magnets gradually decreases as you go from top to bottom. This is because the bottom magnet must support the weight of all the levitated magnets, while the middle magnet must support only half the weight. Now turn the pencil 90° so that it is parallel to the ground. The gaps between magnets are equal because each magnet exerts the same amount of force when the pencil is horizontal.

14.1

Magnets and Magnetic Fields

▶ **KEY TERMS**

magnetic pole
magnetic field

OBJECTIVES

▶ Recognize that like magnetic poles repel and unlike poles attract.
▶ Describe the magnetic field around a permanent magnet.
▶ Explain how compasses work.
▶ Describe the orientation of Earth's magnetic field.

You may think of magnets as devices used to attach papers or photos to a refrigerator door. But magnets are involved in many different devices, such as alarm systems like the one in **Figure 14-1.** This type of alarm system uses the simple magnetic attraction between a piece of iron and a magnet to alert homeowners that a window or door has been opened.

As shown in **Figure 14-1A,** when the window is closed, the iron switch is attracted to the magnet. Thus, the switch completes the circuit, and a current is in the system when it is turned on. When the window slides open, as shown in **Figure 14-1B,** the magnet is no longer close enough to the iron to attract it strongly. The spring pulls the switch open, and the circuit is broken. When this happens, the alarm sounds.

Figure 14-1

A When the window is closed, the magnet holds the switch closed so that current is in the circuit.

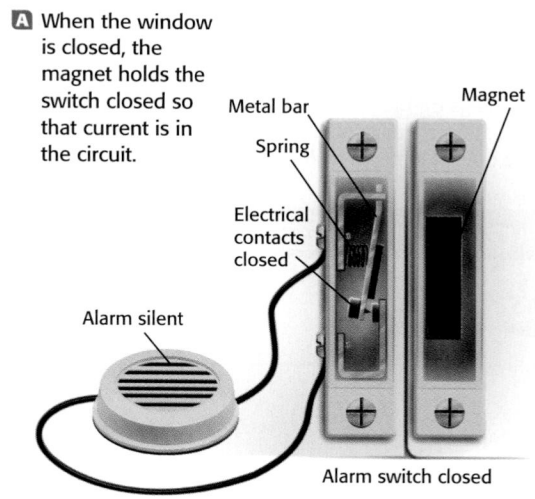

Metal bar
Magnet
Spring
Electrical contacts closed
Alarm silent
Alarm switch closed

B If the window is opened, the switch will open, and the alarm will sound.

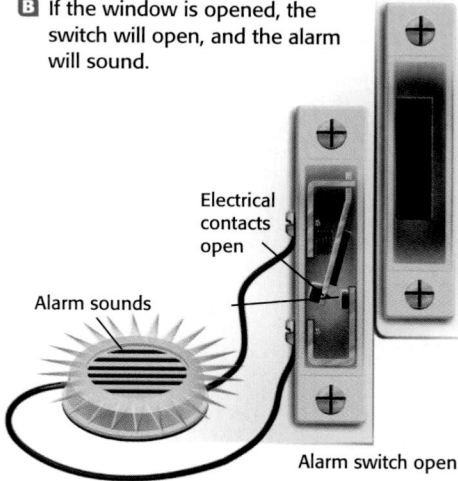

Electrical contacts open
Alarm sounds
Alarm switch open

DEMONSTRATION 1 TEACHING

Magnetizing a Nail

Time: Approximately 10 minutes
Materials: bar magnet
           iron nail
           paper clips

Step 1 Magnetize the nail with the bar magnet by rubbing the magnet on the end of the nail. Rub the nail in only one direction, and do not change direction. If you rub back and forth in two directions, the nail will not become magnetized. Have

a student rub the magnet on the nail 10 times and then determine how many paper clips the nail will lift.

Step 2 Rub the nail 10 more times and see how many paper clips the nail will lift. If you continue to rub the nail, the magnetic force will increase. At some point, additional rubbing with the bar magnet will not increase the strength of the magnetized nail because the nail becomes saturated.

Magnets

Magnets got their name from the region of Magnesia, which is now part of modern-day Greece. The first naturally occurring magnetic rocks, called *lodestones*, were found in this region almost 3000 years ago. A lodestone, shown in **Figure 14-2**, is composed of an iron-based material called *magnetite*.

Some materials can be made into permanent magnets

Some substances, such as lodestones, are magnetic all the time. These types of magnets are called *permanent magnets*. You can change any piece of iron, such as a nail, into a permanent magnet by stroking it several times with a permanent magnet. A slower method is to place the piece of iron near a strong magnet. Eventually the iron will become magnetic and will remain magnetic even when the original magnet is removed.

Although a magnetized piece of iron is called a "permanent" magnet, its magnetism can be weakened or even removed. Possible ways to do this are to heat or hammer the piece of iron. Even when this is done, some materials retain their magnetism longer than others.

Scientists classify materials as either magnetically *hard* or magnetically *soft*. Iron is a soft magnetic material. Although a piece of iron is easily magnetized, it also tends to lose its magnetic properties easily. In contrast, hard magnetic materials, such as cobalt and nickel, are more difficult to magnetize. Once magnetized, however, they don't lose their magnetism easily.

Magnets exert magnetic forces on each other

As shown in **Figure 14-3,** a magnet lowered into a bucket of nails will often pick up several nails. As soon as a nail touches the magnet, the nail acts as a magnet and attracts other nails. More than one nail is lifted because each nail in the chain becomes temporarily magnetized and exerts a *magnetic force* on the nail below it. This ability disappears when the chain of nails is no longer touching the magnet.

There is a limit to how long the chain of nails can be. The length of the chain depends on the ability of the nails to become magnetized and the strength of the magnet. The farther from the magnet each nail is, the smaller its magnetic force. Eventually, the magnetic force between the two lowest nails is not strong enough to overcome the force of gravity, and the bottom nail falls.

Figure 14-2
A naturally occurring magnetic rock, called a lodestone, will attract a variety of iron objects.

internetconnect

SC*LINKS*
NSTA

TOPIC: Properties of magnets
GO TO: www.scilinks.org
KEYWORD: HK1142

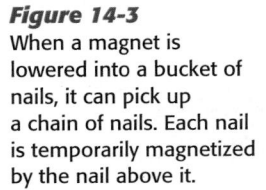

Figure 14-3
When a magnet is lowered into a bucket of nails, it can pick up a chain of nails. Each nail is temporarily magnetized by the nail above it.

Magnets and Magnetic Fields

┃SKILL BUILDER

Interpreting Visuals Magnetite, Fe_3O_4, is a lustrous black magnetic mineral that occurs in crystals with cubic structure. It is one of the important ores of iron and is a common constituent of igneous and metamorphic rocks. It is found in Norway, Sweden, the Urals, and various parts of the United States. A variety of magnetite—lodestone, shown in **Figure 14-2**—has been noted for its natural magnetism since antiquity.

Teaching Tip

Bar Magnets Bar magnets do not start out magnetic. They must be magnetized during the manufacturing process. They are made by melting steel and pouring the molten steel into a mold. As the molten steel is cooling, it is exposed to a strong magnetic field. This magnetic field makes all the magnetic fields of the iron atoms inside the molten steel reorient themselves to point in the same direction.

As a result, the magnetic field from each iron atom combines with the magnetic fields of all the other iron atoms to generate an overall magnetic field. Once the molten iron has hardened, the external magnetic field is turned off.

One way to demagnetize a bar magnet is to hit it hard with a hammer many times. Striking with a hammer can change the orientation of the individual atoms' magnetic fields. This has the effect of reducing the strength of the bar magnet.

Magnets and Magnetic Fields

MISCONCEPTION

Magnetic Poles **ALERT**

Students often think the poles of a magnet are named for the North and South Poles. This leads to confusion about which pole of a magnet points toward geographic north.

Did You Know ?

Some permanent magnets are made out of ceramic materials, such as barium or strontium ferrite. These magnets can be extremely strong, are resistant to demagnetization, and are inexpensive, but they are also extremely brittle.

Ceramic magnets must be machined when they are unmagnetized. Then they can be magnetized in the desired direction. These magnets are used for a wide range of applications from motors and loudspeakers to toys.

Quick ACTIVITY

Test Your Knowledge of Magnetic Poles

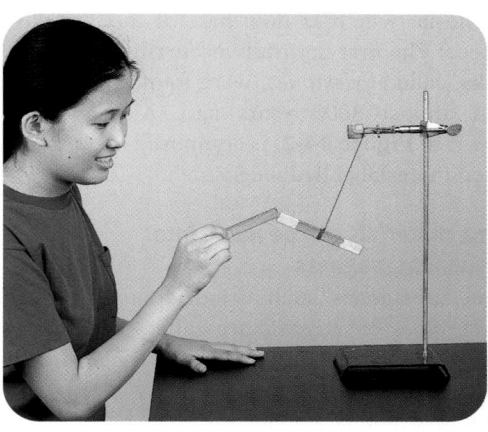

1. Tape the ends of a bar magnet so that its pole markings are covered.
2. Tie a piece of string to the center of the magnet and suspend it from a support stand, as shown in the figure at right.
3. Use another bar magnet to determine which pole of the hanging magnet is the north pole and which is the south pole. What happens when you bring one pole of your magnet near each end of the hanging magnet?
4. Now try to identify the poles of the hanging magnet using the other pole of your magnet.
5. After you have decided the identity of each pole, remove the tape to check. Can you determine which are north poles and which are south poles if you cover the poles on both magnets?

▶ **magnetic pole** an area of a magnet where the magnetic force appears to be the strongest

VOCABULARY *Skills Tip*

The word pole *is used in physics for two related opposites that are separated by some distance along an axis. The word* polar, *used in chemistry, has the same origin.*

Like poles repel, and opposite poles attract

As explained in Section 13.1, the closer two like electrical charges are brought together, the more they repel each other. The closer two opposite charges are brought together, the more they attract each other. A similar situation exists for **magnetic poles.**

Magnets have a pair of poles, a north pole and a south pole. The poles of magnets exert a force on one another. Two like poles, such as two south poles, repel each other. Two unlike poles, however, attract each other. Thus, the north pole of one magnet will attract the south pole of another magnet. Also, the north pole of one magnet repels the north pole of another magnet.

It is impossible to isolate a south magnetic pole from a north magnetic pole. If a magnet is cut, each piece will still have two poles. No matter how small the pieces of a magnet are, each piece still has both a north and a south pole.

Magnetic Fields

Try moving the south pole of one magnet toward the south pole of another that is free to move. As you do this, the magnet you are not touching will move away. A force is being exerted on the second magnet even though it never touches the magnet in your hand. The force is acting at a distance. This may seem unusual, but you are already familiar with other forces that act at a distance. Gravitational forces and the force between electric charges also act at a distance.

Quick ACTIVITY

Test Your Knowledge of Magnetic Poles
The string should be tied in such a way that the magnet will be balanced and hang parallel to the ground. A small piece of tape will keep the string from moving while the magnet is suspended. Be sure you perform this experiment away from metal objects like metal cabinets and faucets. Metal objects may attract the magnet and change the outcome of the experiment.

Like poles repel each other, and opposite poles attract each other. If left alone, the hanging magnet will align itself with Earth's magnetic field, with its N pole pointing north. Using this fact, you can determine the unknown poles of both magnets.

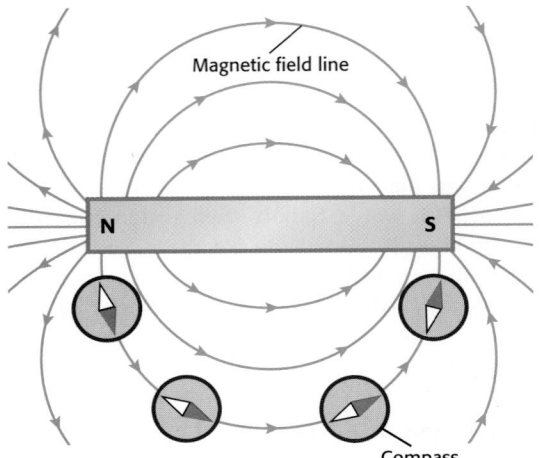

Magnetic field line

Compass

Figure 14-4
The magnetic field of a bar magnet can be traced with a compass. Note that the north pole of each compass points in the direction of the field lines from the magnet's north pole to its south pole.

Magnets are sources of magnetic fields

Magnetic force is a field force. When magnets repel or attract each other, it is due to the interaction of their **magnetic fields.**

All magnets produce a magnetic field. Some magnetic fields are stronger than others. The strength of the magnetic field depends on the material from which the magnet is made and the degree to which it has been magnetized.

Recall from Chapter 13 that electric field lines are used to represent an electric field. Similarly, magnetic field lines are used to represent the magnetic field of a bar magnet, as shown in **Figure 14-4.** These field lines all form closed loops. **Figure 14-4** shows only the field near the magnet. The field also exists within the magnet and farther away from the magnet. The magnetic field, however, gets weaker with distance from the magnet. Magnetic field lines that are close together indicate a strong magnetic field. Field lines that are farther apart indicate a weaker field. Knowing this, you can tell from **Figure 14-4** that a magnet's field is strongest near its poles.

Compasses can track magnetic fields

One way to analyze a magnetic field's direction is to use a compass, as shown in **Figure 14-4.** A compass is a magnet suspended on top of a pivot so that the magnet can rotate freely. You can make a simple compass by hanging a bar magnet from a support with a string tied to the magnet's midpoint.

▶ **magnetic field** a region where a magnetic force can be detected

With the invention of iron and steel ships in the late 1800s, it became necessary to develop a new type of compass. The *gyrocompass*, a device containing a spinning loop, was the solution. Because of inertia, the gyrocompass always points toward Earth's geographic North Pole, regardless of which way the ship turns.

Making the Connection

1. Why does the metal hull of a ship affect the function of magnetic compasses?
2. A gyrocompass contains a device called a gyroscope. Research gyroscopes, and briefly explain how they work.

MAGNETISM **465**

Field Lines Many people believe that the magnetic field lines associated with a magnet show the direction in which the magnet will push another magnet. This is not correct. The magnetic field lines indicate how a second magnet will align itself if placed in the magnetic field of the first magnet.

The steel hulls of ships become magnetized due to exposure to Earth's magnetic field. A gyrocompass, consisting of a compass and a motorized gyroscope, provides a stable reference because it maintains a north-south orientation of its spin axis due to conservation of momentum.

Making the Connection

1. The magnetic field produced by the hull of the ship interferes with the compass.
2. A gyroscope is a device with a wheel or disk mounted in a set of mutually perpendicular rings so that its axis of rotation is free to turn in any direction. When turning, a gyroscope always points in the same direction, regardless of any movement of its base.

Resources Assign students worksheet *14.1: Connection to Social Studies—The Natural Force and Laws of Compasses* in the **Integration Enrichment Resources** ancillary.

DEMONSTRATION 2 TEACHING

Shapes of Magnetic Fields

Time: Approximately 10 minutes
Materials: two bar magnets, one horseshoe magnet, one blank transparency, iron filings, overhead projector

Step 1 Set two bar magnets about 4 cm apart, aligned with opposite poles facing each other on

the overhead projector, and lay the blank transparency over the magnets. Sprinkle the iron filings onto the transparency, and have students observe the behavior of the filings.

Step 2 Repeat the demonstration using the horseshoe magnet.

Magnets and Magnetic Fields

Interpreting Visuals The orientation of Earth's magnetic field, shown in **Figure 14-5,** can be confusing for many students. Emphasize that the N and S poles of a magnet are named for the geographical poles they point to.

Resources Blackline Master 44 shows this visual.

INTEGRATING

SPACE SCIENCE The sun also has a magnetic field. The sun periodically ejects charged particles into space. This stream of particles is called the *solar wind.* Earth's magnetic field acts like a shield and deflects most of these particles. The only place where the charged particles can enter Earth's atmosphere is at the magnetic poles. These charged particles collide with atoms in the atmosphere, resulting in the emission of visible light. This light causes the sky at the North and South Poles to glow with different colors. These colors are called the Northern and Southern Lights, or the aurora borealis and aurora australis.

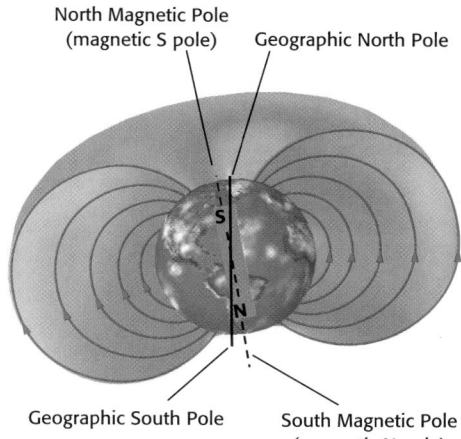

North Magnetic Pole (magnetic S pole)   Geographic North Pole

Geographic South Pole   South Magnetic Pole (magnetic N pole)

Figure 14-5
Earth's magnetic field is similar to that of a bar magnet.

internetconnect

SC*LINKS*
NSTA

TOPIC: Earth's magnetic field
GO TO: www.scilinks.org
KEYWORD: HK1143

A compass aligns with Earth's magnetic field just as iron filings align with the field of a bar magnet. The compass points in a direction that lies along, or is tangent to, the magnetic field at that point.

The first compasses were made using lodestones. A lodestone was placed on a small plank of wood and floated in calm water. Sailors then watched as the wood turned and pointed toward the north star. In this way, sailors could gauge their direction even during the day, when stars were not visible. Later, sailors found that a steel or iron needle rubbed with lodestone acted in the same manner.

Earth's magnetic field is like that of a bar magnet

A compass can be used to determine direction because Earth acts like a giant bar magnet. As shown in **Figure 14-5,** Earth's magnetic field has both direction and strength. If you were to move northward along Earth's surface with a compass whose needle could point up and down, the needle of the compass would slowly tilt forward. At a point in northeastern Canada, the needle would point straight down. This point is one of Earth's magnetic poles. There is an opposite magnetic pole in Antarctica.

The source of Earth's magnetism is a topic of scientific debate. Although Earth's core is made mostly of iron, the iron in the core is too hot to retain any magnetic properties. Instead, many researchers believe that the circulation of ions or electrons in the liquid layer of Earth's core may be the source of the magnetism. Others believe it is due to a combination of several factors.

Earth's magnetic field has changed direction throughout geologic time. Evidence of more than 20 reversals in the last 5 million years is preserved in the magnetization of sea-floor rocks.

Quick ACTIVITY

Magnetic Field of a File Cabinet

1. Stand in front of a metal file cabinet, and hold a compass face up and parallel to the ground.
2. Move the compass from the top of the file cabinet to the bottom, and check to see if the direction of the compass needle changes. If the compass needle changes direction, the file cabinet is magnetized.
3. Can you explain what might have caused the file cabinet to become magnetized? Remember that Earth's magnetic field not only points horizontal to Earth but also points up and down.

Have students use *Datasheet 14.2 Quick Activity: Magnetic Field of a File Cabinet* to record their results.

Quick ACTIVITY

Magnetic Field of a File Cabinet The file cabinet can become magnetized because of prolonged exposure to the Earth's magnetic field. However, the amount of magnetization that occurs is dependent upon the kind of metal from which the cabinet is made. If the cabinet is aluminum, for example, it will not be magnetic at all. If the cabinet is steel, it is probably slightly magnetic and will cause the compass needle to be deflected. If you are performing this lab in class, test the file cabinet before the lab. Possible substitutes include iron flagpoles and iron fence posts, such as those around tennis courts. Remind the students that Earth's magnetic field has both a vertical and horizontal component. The file cabinet is magnetized by the vertical component. Have them try to find an object that has been magnetized by the horizontal component of Earth's magnetic field.

Earth's magnetic poles are not the same as its geographic poles

One of the interesting things about Earth's magnetic poles is that they are not in the same place as the geographic poles, as shown in **Figure 14-5.** Another important distinction that should be made about Earth's magnetic poles is the orientation of the magnetic field. Earth's magnetic field points from the geographic South Pole to the geographic North Pole. This orientation is similar to an upside-down bar magnet, like the one shown in **Figure 14-5.** The magnetic pole in Antarctica is actually a magnetic N pole, and the magnetic pole in northern Canada is actually a magnetic S pole.

For historical reasons, the poles of magnets are named for the geographic pole they point toward. Thus, the end of the magnet labeled *N* is a "north-seeking" pole, and the end of the magnet labeled *S* is a "south-seeking" pole.

SECTION 14.1 REVIEW

SUMMARY

▶ All magnets have two poles that cannot be isolated.

▶ Like poles repel each other, and unlike poles attract each other.

▶ The magnetic force is the force due to interacting magnetic fields.

▶ The magnetic field of a magnet is strongest near its poles and gets weaker with distance.

▶ The direction of a magnetic field can be traced using a compass.

▶ Earth's magnetic field has both north and south poles.

▶ Earth's magnetic poles are not at the same location as the geographic poles. The magnetic N pole is in Antarctica, and the magnetic S pole is in northern Canada.

CHECK YOUR UNDERSTANDING

1. **Determine** whether the magnets will attract or repel each other in each of the following cases.

   a. [S   N] [N   S]

   b. [S   N] [S   N]

   c.

2. **State** how many poles each piece of a magnet will have when you break it in half.

3. **Identify** which of the compass-needle orientations in the figure below correctly describe the direction of the bar magnet's magnetic field.

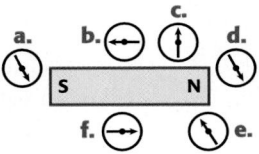

4. **Describe** the direction a compass needle would point if you were in Australia.

5. **Critical Thinking** The north pole of a magnet is attracted to the geographic North Pole, yet like poles repel. Explain why.

MAGNETISM **467**

LINKING CHAPTERS

Evidence for reversals of Earth's magnetic field is provided by basalt (an iron-containing rock) on the ocean floor. Volcanic activity along mid-ocean ridges produces new ocean floor. As the lava cools and solidifies, it retains a picture of Earth's magnetic field direction at that time. Radioactive dating of these rocks provides evidence for periodic reversals of Earth's magnetic field. In Chapter 17, students will learn more about how Earth's magnetism is used to understand Earth's history.

SECTION 14.1 REVIEW

Check Your Understanding

1. a. repel
   b. attract
   c. attract
2. Each piece of the magnet will have two poles. It is impossible for a magnet to have only one pole.
3. a, b
4. The compass needle would point toward the geographic North Pole.
5. The north pole of a magnet is attracted to Earth's magnetic south pole, which is near the geographic North Pole.

Scheduling

Refer to pp. 460A–460D for lecture, classwork, and assignment options for Section 14.2.

★ **Lesson Focus**
Use transparency *LT 47* to prepare students for this section.

READING SKILL BUILDER *Reading Organizer* Have students read Section 14.2 and then organize the ideas presented in the section in the form of a concept map or other reading organizer. The organization can be in terms of the order presented in the chapter or in terms of detailed characteristics listed for each idea. Students' concept maps or reading organizers should have areas left blank so that students can add to them while learning about the section.

Did You Know?

Wire taps are possible because the electrical current that is carrying the telephone conversation produces a magnetic field. Because magnetic fields travel through most materials, it is not necessary to cut the wire; coils are placed around the wire to measure the magnetic field. The pattern of changes in the magnetic field is converted to current (a current is induced by the changing magnetic field—covered in Section 14.3), which is converted to sound by a speaker, reproducing the conversation. Fiber-optic cables cannot be tapped in this way because they do not produce an external magnetic field.

14.2
Magnetism from Electric Currents

▶ **KEY TERMS**
solenoid
electromagnet
domain
galvanometer
electric motor

OBJECTIVES
▶ Describe how magnetism is produced by electric currents.
▶ Interpret the magnetic field of a solenoid and of an electromagnet.
▶ Explain the magnetic properties of a material in terms of magnetic domains.
▶ Explain how galvanometers and electric motors work.

Figure 14-6
The iron filings show that the magnetic field of a current-carrying wire forms concentric circles around the wire.

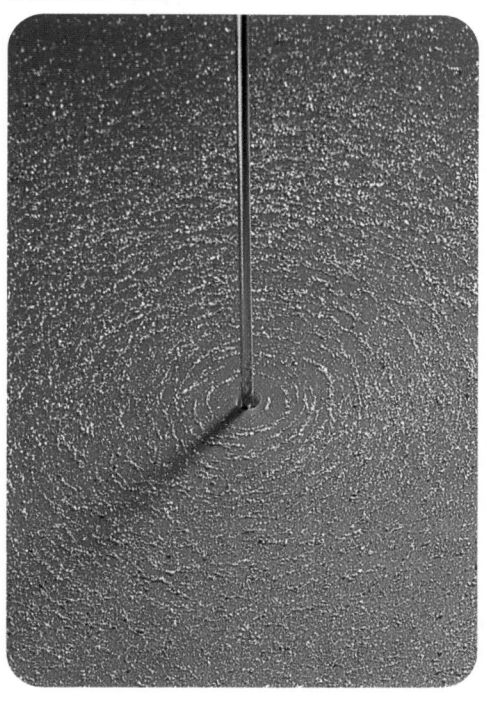

468 CHAPTER 14

During the eighteenth century, people noticed that a bolt of lightning could change the direction of a compass needle. They also noticed that iron pans sometimes became magnetized during lightning storms. Although these observations suggested a relationship between electricity and magnetism, it wasn't until 1820 that the relationship was understood.

Producing Magnetism from Electric Currents

In 1820, a Danish science teacher named Hans Christian Oersted first experimented with the effects of an electric current on the needle of a compass. He found that magnetism is produced by moving electric charges.

Electric currents produce magnetic fields

The experiment shown in **Figure 14-6** uses iron filings to demonstrate that a current-carrying wire creates a magnetic field. Because of this field, the iron filings make a distinct pattern around the wire.

As you learned in Section 14.1, pieces of iron will align with a magnetic field. The pattern of the filings in **Figure 14-6** suggests that the magnetic field around a current-carrying wire forms concentric circles around the wire. If you were to bring a compass close to a current-carrying wire, as Oersted did, you would find that the needle points in a direction tangent to the circles of iron filings.

DEMONSTRATION 3 **TEACHING**

Magnetic Field of a Current Loop

Time: Approximately 15 minutes
Materials: 6 V battery, spool of insulated wire, compass, 2 ring stands

Step 1 Make a large coil of wire, perhaps 1 ft in diameter. Use many loops around the coil so that the magnetic field is strong. An easy way to make the coil is to wrap the wire around a soccer ball or basketball. Use a ring stand to hold the loop off

the table. The loop must be oriented perpendicular to the ground in order to use the compass.

Step 2 Attach the wire to the battery so that a current is going through the loop, creating a magnetic field at its center.

Step 3 Place the compass at the center of the loop and turn the circuit on and off. The compass

Use the right-hand rule to find the direction of the magnetic field produced by a current

Is the direction of the wire's magnetic field clockwise or counterclockwise? Repeated measurements have shown an easy way to predict the direction: the *right-hand rule*. The right-hand rule is explained below.

> **If you imagine holding the wire in your right hand with your thumb pointing in the direction of the positive current, the direction your fingers would curl is in the direction of the magnetic field.**

Figure 14-7 illustrates the right-hand rule. Pretend the wire is grasped with the right hand with the thumb pointing upward, in the direction of the current. When the hand holds the wire, the fingers encircle the wire with the fingertips pointing in the direction of the magnetic field, counterclockwise in this case. If the current were toward the bottom of the page, the thumb would point downward, and the magnetic field would point clockwise. *Remember—never grasp or touch an uninsulated wire. You could be electrocuted.*

The magnetic field of a coil of wire resembles that of a bar magnet

As Oersted demonstrated, the magnetic field of a current-carrying wire exerts a force on a compass needle. This force causes the needle to turn in the direction of the wire's magnetic field. However, this force is very weak. One way to increase the force is to increase the current in the wire, but large currents can be fire hazards. A safer way to create a strong magnetic field that will provide a greater force is to wrap the wire into a coil, as shown in **Figure 14-8.** This device is called a **solenoid.**

In a solenoid, the magnetic field of each loop of wire adds to the strength of the magnetic field of the loop next to it. The result is a strong magnetic field similar to the magnetic field produced by a bar magnet. A solenoid even has a north and south pole, just like a magnet.

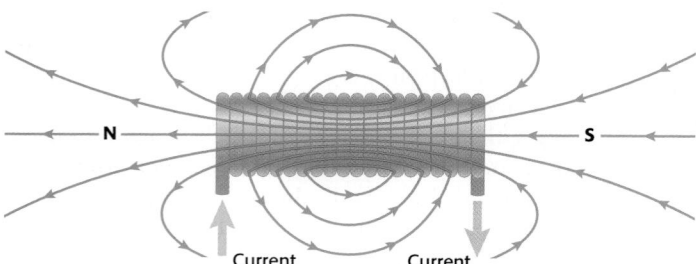

Figure 14-7
Use the right-hand rule to find the direction of the magnetic field around a current-carrying wire.

PHYSICAL SCIENCE INTERACTIVE TUTOR

Disc Two, Module 17:
Magnetic Field of a Wire
Use the Interactive Tutor to learn more about this topic.

▶ **solenoid** a long, wound coil of insulated wire

Figure 14-8
The magnetic field of a coil of wire resembles the magnetic field of a bar magnet.

needle should move when the circuit is activated. The compass does not need to be at the exact center; however, that is where the magnetic field is the strongest. Trace the magnetic field around the loop with the compass.

Magnetism from Electric Currents

▌SKILL BUILDER

Interpreting Visuals Have students practice using the right-hand rule by confirming that the direction of the magnetic field shown in **Figure 14-8** is correctly drawn for the solenoid. Ask them which end of the solenoid would be the N pole if the current were reversed. *(the right side)*

Resources Blackline Master 46 shows this visual.

Did You Know?

CERN, the Center for European Nuclear Research, studies subatomic particles. This is done by accelerating charged particles to speeds near the speed of light and then smashing them into other particles. Large wire coils are used to generate strong magnetic fields to help accelerate and steer the particles.

Additional Application

MRI Prior to 1973, the most common way that doctors looked inside the human body was with X rays. In 1973, Mansfield and Grannell invented Magnetic Resonance Imaging. When an MRI is done, the patient is placed inside a large coil of wire. A current is sent through the coil, exposing the patient to a strong magnetic field. This magnetic field, used in conjunction with low-frequency radio waves, can cause hydrogen atoms to emit low-frequency electromagnetic waves. These waves are used to do the imaging. Molecules of water contain hydrogen, and water is prevalent in soft tissue.

Magnetism from Electric Currents

Teaching Tip

Electromagnets Electromagnets are used in many different industries. Perhaps their best-known use is for lifting junk cars at a junkyard. These electromagnets are suspended at the end of a crane. Large currents are used to power the electromagnet so that its magnetic field is strong enough to lift a car off the ground.

These heavy-duty electromagnets are also used to lift machine parts that are being cast in foundries. After parts have been cast, they must cool in their molds. Once they solidify but are not completely cool, they must be removed from the mold for additional processing. Electromagnets are used to lift the cooling parts and continue the manufacturing process because the parts are still too hot to touch.

Additional Application

Electromagnetic Card Keys Many hotels use electromagnetic card keys instead of traditional keys. Within the door lock mechanism are small solenoids with many loops. These solenoids read the magnetic signature on a key to determine whether the lock should unlock. The same kind of readers are also used in ATMs and credit card reading machines.

 **Inquiry Lab**

How can you make an electromagnet?

Materials
✔ D-cell
✔ compass
✔ 1 m length of insulated wire
✔ large iron or steel nail

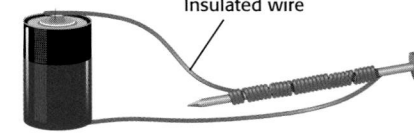

Insulated wire

Procedure

1. Wind the wire around the nail, as shown at right. Remove the insulation from the ends. Hold the insulated wire with the ends against the terminals.
2. Determine whether the nail is magnetized. If it is magnetized, the compass needle will spin to align with the nail's magnetic field.
3. Switch connections to the cell so the current is reversed. Again bring the compass toward the same part of the nail.

Analysis

1. What type of device have you produced? Explain your answer.
2. What happens to the direction of the compass needle after you reverse the direction of the current? Why does this happen?
3. After detaching the coil from the cell, what can you do to make the nail nonmagnetic?

The strength of the magnetic field of a solenoid depends on the number of loops of wire and the amount of current in the wire. In particular, more loops or more current can create a stronger magnetic field.

The strength of a solenoid's magnetic field can be increased by inserting a rod made of iron (or some other potentially magnetic metal) through the center of the coils. The resulting device is called an **electromagnet.** The magnetic field of the solenoid causes the rod to become a magnet as well. The magnetic field of the rod then adds to the coil's field, creating a stronger magnet than the solenoid alone.

▶ **electromagnet** a strong magnet created when an iron core is inserted into the center of a current-carrying solenoid

Magnetism is caused by moving charges

The movement of charges causes all magnetism. The magnetic properties of bar magnets, for instance, can be attributed to the movement of charged particles.

But what charges are moving in a bar magnet? Recall from Section 3.1 that electrons are negatively charged particles that move around the nuclei of atoms. All electrons have a property called *electron spin.* Electron spin produces a tiny magnetic field around every electron.

In some cases, the magnetic fields of the electrons in an atom cancel each other and the material is not magnetic. However, in materials such as iron, nickel, and cobalt, not all of the magnetic fields of the electrons cancel. Thus, each atom in those metals has its own magnetic field.

 **internetconnect**

SC/LINKS
NSTA

TOPIC: Electromagnetism
GO TO: www.scilinks.org
KEYWORD: HK1144

Inquiry Lab

How can you make an electromagnet?
The electromagnet will work better if the wire is wound very tightly together.
SAFETY CAUTION: *The wires will get warm. Students should use heat-resistant gloves to handle the electromagnet. Be sure students disconnect the battery after making their observations.*

Analysis

1. an electromagnet—the coil of wire is the solenoid, and the nail is the magnetic core
2. The direction of the compass needle should reverse because the current is in the opposite direction when the battery is flipped.
3. Hit the nail on its side sharply with a hammer.

Figure 14-9

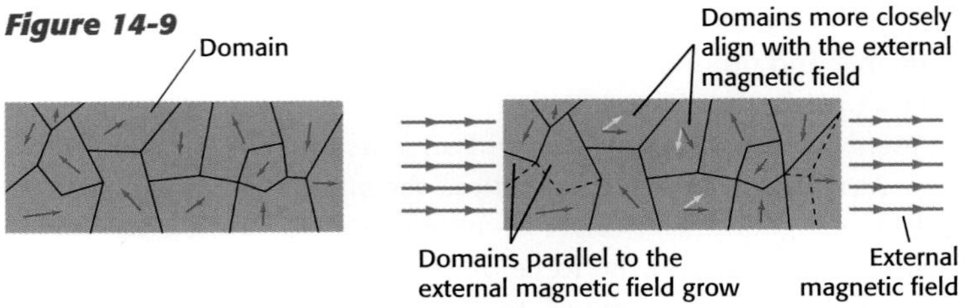

Domain

Domains more closely
align with the external
magnetic field

Domains parallel to the
external magnetic field grow

External
magnetic field

A When a potentially
magnetic substance is
unmagnetized, its domains
are randomly oriented.

B When in an external magnetic field,
the direction of the domains becomes
more uniform, and the material
becomes magnetized.

Just as a compass needle rotates to align with a magnetic
field, magnetic atoms rotate to align with the magnetic fields of
nearby atoms. The result is small regions within the material
called **domains.** The magnetic fields of atoms in a domain point
in the same direction.

As shown in **Figure 14-9A,** the magnetic fields of the domains inside an unmagnetized piece of iron are not aligned.
When a strong magnet is brought nearby, the domains line up
more closely with the magnetic field. **Figure 14-9B** shows the
two ways this can happen. The result of the reorientation of the
domains is an overall magnetization of the iron.

▶ **domain** a microscopic
magnetic region composed
of a group of atoms whose
magnetic fields are aligned in
a common direction

▶ **galvanometer** an instrument that measures the
amount of current in a circuit

Electromagnetic Devices

Many modern devices make use of the magnetic field produced
by coils of current-carrying wire. Devices as different as hair
dryers and stereo speakers function because of
the magnetic field produced by these current-
carrying conductors.

Galvanometers detect current

Galvanometers are devices used to measure
current in *ammeters* and voltage in *voltmeters.*
The basic construction of a galvanometer is
shown in **Figure 14-10.** In all cases, a galvanometer detects current, or the movement of
charges in a circuit.

As shown in **Figure 14-10,** a galvanometer
consists of a coil of insulated wire wrapped
around an iron core that can spin between the
poles of a permanent magnet. When the galvanometer is attached to a circuit, a current will

Figure 14-10

When there is current in the coil
of a galvanometer, magnetic
repulsion between the coil and
the magnet causes the coil to twist.

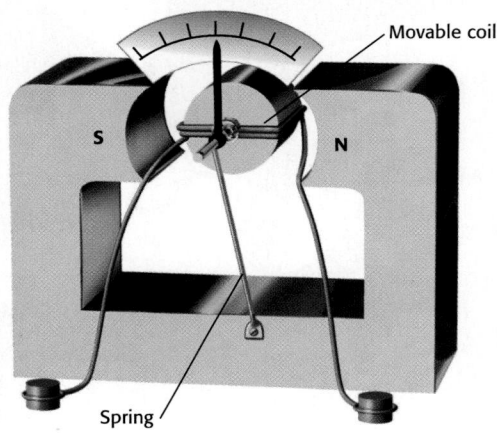

Movable coil

S

N

Spring

MAGNETISM **471**

SKILL BUILDER

Interpreting Visuals Have
students use the right-hand
rule to show how the gal-
vanometer reading in **Figure
14-10** depends on the direction
of current through the circuit.
If charges move through the
coil from the left terminal to
the right terminal, which direction will the needle rotate?
(clockwise)

Resources Blackline Master
47 shows this visual.

Teaching Tip

Galvanometers Remove the
case of a galvanometer. The
meter portion is typically
screwed into a plastic case with
four small screws. Many times
the back portion of the meter
is clear, and the internal parts
can be seen. Remove the meter
from the case and show it to
students. You can hook the
meter to a small 1.5 V battery
and show students the coils of
wire being deflected. Alternatively, your physics department
may have a demonstration galvanometer with clear sides.

RESOURCE LINK

IER

Assign students worksheet
*14.2: Integrating Chemistry—
Molecular Magnetism* in the
**Integration Enrichment Re-
sources** ancillary.

Magnetism from Electric Currents

Interpreting Diagrams
Have students trace the path of electric charge through the motor in **Figure 14-11.** In which direction does the magnetic field of the loop point? *(toward the upper right of the page)*

Resources Teaching Transparency 41 shows this visual.

Teaching Tip

Electric Motors Obtain some small electric motors. It doesn't matter if these motors work or not. Remove the outer casing with a pair of pliers. Once this casing is removed, the inner components of the motor will be visible to students. Let them investigate the inner components. Students will see the wire coils, which have hundreds of turns each, as well as the permanent magnets in the casing. They will also be able to see the brushes and commutator. Describe what happens during one rotation of the coil.

▶ **electric motor** a device that converts electrical energy to mechanical energy

Figure 14-11
In an electric motor, the current in the coil produces a magnetic field that interacts with the magnetic field of the surrounding magnet, causing the coil to turn.

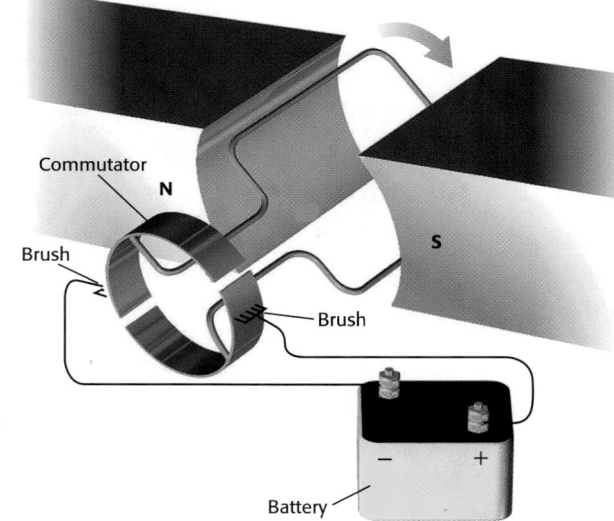

Commutator

Brush

Brush

Battery

472 CHAPTER 14

be in the coil of wire. The coil and iron core will act as an electromagnet and produce a magnetic field. This magnetic field will interact with the magnetic field of the surrounding permanent magnet. The resulting forces will turn the core.

As stated earlier in this section, the greater the current in the electromagnet, the stronger its magnetic field. If the core's magnetic field is strong, the force on the core will be great, and the core will rotate through a large angle. A needle extends upward from the core to a scale. As the core rotates, the needle moves across the scale. The greater the movement across the scale, the larger the current.

Electric motors convert electrical energy to mechanical energy

Electric motors are another type of device that uses magnetic force to cause motion. **Figure 14-11** is an illustration of a simple direct current, or DC, motor.

As shown by the arrow in **Figure 14-11,** the coil of wire in a motor turns when a current is in the wire. But unlike the coil and core in a galvanometer, the coil in an electric motor keeps spinning. If the coil is attached to a shaft, it can do work. The end of the shaft is connected to some other device, such as a propeller or wheel. This design is often used in mechanical toys.

A device called a *commutator* is used to make the current change direction every time the flat coil makes a half revolution. This commutator is two half rings of metal. Devices called *brushes* connect the wires to the commutator. Because of the slits in the commutator, charges must move through the coil of wire to reach the opposite half of the ring. As the coil and commutator spin, the current in the coil changes direction every time the brushes come in contact with a different side of the ring.

So the magnetic field of the coil changes direction as the coil spins. In this way, the coil is repelled by both the north and south poles of the magnet surrounding it. Because the current keeps reversing, the loop rotates in one direction. If the current did not keep changing direction, the loop would just bounce back and forth in the magnetic field until the force of friction caused it to come to rest.

DEMONSTRATION 4 TEACHING

Magnetic Force on a Current Loop

Time: Approximately 20 minutes
Materials: strong horseshoe magnet, wire, 2 ring stands and supports, variable DC power supply

Step 1 Lay the horseshoe magnet on its side so that one pole is above the other. Connect the wire to the power supply, and support the wire so that it passes through the center of the poles of the horseshoe magnet.

Step 2 Turn on the power supply, and gradually increase the current in the wire until the wire is forced to one side or the other. Ask students what will happen if the direction of the current is reversed. *(The wire will move in the opposite direction.)*

Step 3 Turn off the power supply, detach the wires, and attach them to the opposite terminals. Test the students' hypotheses. Have students sketch the magnetic fields of the magnet and the wire for both cases.

Stereo speakers use magnetic force to produce sound

Motion caused by magnetic force can even be used to produce sound waves. This is how most stereo speakers work. The speaker shown in **Figure 14-12** consists of a permanent magnet and a coil of wire attached to a flexible paper cone. When a current is in the coil, a magnetic field is produced. This field interacts with the field of the permanent magnet, causing the coil and cone to move in one direction. When the current reverses direction, the magnetic force on the coil also reverses direction. As a result, the cone accelerates in the opposite direction.

This alternating force on the speaker cone makes it vibrate. Varying the magnitude of the current changes how much the cone vibrates. These vibrations produce sound waves. In this way, an electric signal is converted to a sound wave.

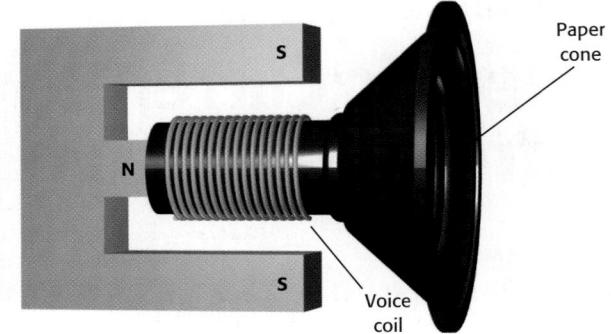

Figure 14-12
In a speaker, when the direction of the current in the coil of wire changes, the paper cone attached to the coil moves, producing sound waves.

SKILL BUILDER

Interpreting Visuals In **Figure 14-12,** the voice coil makes the speaker move forward and backward in a line. When a speaker is turned up too loud, it tries to move in another direction, side to side. The speaker generates distortion in the sound, and the paper cone begins to tear, causing the speaker to buzz.

SECTION 14.2 REVIEW

Check Your Understanding

1. The magnetic field generated by a straight current-carrying wire is in the shape of concentric rings, with the wire at the center.
2. Using the right-hand rule, point your thumb west. Your fingers curl in the direction of the magnetic field. Above the wire, your fingers would point north.
3. b
4. A very strong magnet is able to change the orientation of the domains in a weak magnet. As a result, the strong magnet is able to attract both poles of a weak magnet.

Answers continue on p. 485A.

SECTION 14.2 REVIEW

SUMMARY

▶ A magnetic field is produced around a current-carrying wire.

▶ A current-carrying solenoid has a magnetic field similar to that of a bar magnet.

▶ An electromagnet consists of a current-carrying solenoid with an iron core.

▶ A domain is a group of atoms whose magnetic fields are aligned.

▶ Galvanometers measure the current in a circuit using the magnetic field produced by a current in a coil.

▶ Electric motors convert electrical energy to mechanical energy.

CHECK YOUR UNDERSTANDING

1. **Describe** the shape of the magnetic field produced by a straight current-carrying wire.
2. **Determine** the direction in which a compass needle will point when held above a wire with positive charges moving west. (**Hint:** Use the right-hand rule.)
3. **Identify** which of the following would have the strongest magnetic field. Assume the current in each is the same.
   a. a straight wire
   b. an electromagnet with 30 coils
   c. a solenoid with 20 coils
   d. a solenoid with 30 coils
4. **Explain** why a very strong magnet attracts both poles of a weak magnet. Use the concept of magnetic domains in your explanation.
5. **Predict** whether a solenoid suspended by a string could be used as a compass.
6. **Critical Thinking** A friend claims to have built a motor by attaching a shaft to the core of a galvanometer and removing the spring. Can this motor rotate through a full rotation? Explain your answer.

MAGNETISM **473**

RESOURCE LINK
STUDY GUIDE

Assign students *Review Section 14.2 Magnetism from Electric Currents.*

Electric Currents from Magnetism

Scheduling

Refer to pp. 460A–460D for lecture, classwork, and assignment options for Section 14.3.

★ **Lesson Focus**
Use transparency *LT 48* to prepare students for this section.

SKILL BUILDER

Interpreting Visuals Have students look at **Figure 14-13.** Ask them to state the condition required for current to exist in the loop in the figure. *(There must be relative motion between the loop and the magnetic field.)* Some students may have trouble distinguishing between the external magnetic field and the magnetic field that is created by the induced current. Point out that only when the loop is moved will there be a magnetic field created by the induced current in the loop. Use the right hand rule to show that it will point in the same direction as the magnetic field between the pole pieces.

Did You Know?

The operation of detectors at traffic signals is based on Faraday's law. A wire is placed in a groove cut into the road so that the wire makes a loop where the first car will sit. The ends of the wire go back to the computer controller. Earth's magnetic field goes through this loop. When a car sits on top of the loop, the amount of magnetic field going through the loop decreases. This change in magnetic field induces a current in the loop and tells the computer that a car is waiting.

Electric Currents from Magnetism

▶ **KEY TERMS**
electromagnetic induction
generator
alternating current
transformer

OBJECTIVES

▶ Describe the conditions required for electromagnetic induction.

▶ Apply the concept of electromagnetic induction to generators.

▶ Explain how transformers increase or decrease voltage across power lines.

▶ **electromagnetic induction** the production of a current in a conducting circuit by a change in the strength, position, or orientation of an external magnetic field

Can you have current in a wire without a battery or some other source of voltage? In 1831, Michael Faraday discovered that a current can be produced by pushing a magnet through a coil of wire. In other words, moving a magnet in and out of a coil of wire causes charges in the wire to move. This process is called **electromagnetic induction**.

Electromagnetic Induction and Faraday's Law

Electromagnetic induction is so fundamental that it has become one of the laws of physics—*Faraday's law.* Faraday's law states the following:

An electric current can be produced in a circuit by a changing magnetic field.

Figure 14-13
When the loop moves in or out of the magnetic field, a current is induced in the wire.

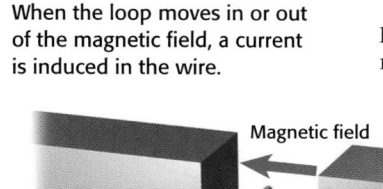
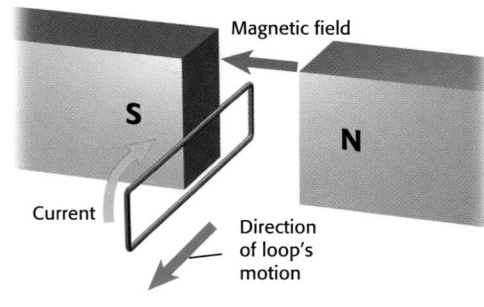

Magnetic field

S

N

Current

Direction of loop's motion

Consider the loop of wire moving between the two magnetic poles in **Figure 14-13.** As the loop moves in and out of the magnetic field of the magnet, a current is *induced* in the circuit. As long as the wire continues to move in or out of the field in a direction that is not parallel to the field, an induced current will exist in the circuit.

Rotating the circuit or changing the strength of the magnetic field will also induce a current in the circuit. In each case, there is a changing magnetic field passing through the loop. You can predict whether a current will be induced using the concept of magnetic field lines. A current will be induced if the number of field lines that pass through the loop changes.

It would seem that electromagnetic induction creates energy from nothing, but this is not true. Electromagnetic induction does not violate the law of conservation of energy. Pushing a loop through a magnetic field requires work. The greater the magnetic field, the stronger the force required to push the loop through the field. The energy required for this work comes from an outside source, such as your muscles pushing the loop through the magnetic field. So while electrical energy is produced by electromagnetic induction, energy is required to move the loop.

Moving electric charges experience a magnetic force when in a magnetic field

When studying electromagnetic induction, it is helpful to imagine the individual charges in a wire. A charged particle moving in a magnetic field will experience a force due to the magnetic field. Experiments have shown that this magnetic force is zero when the charge moves along or opposite the direction of the magnetic field lines. The force is at its maximum value when the charge moves perpendicular to the field. As the angle between the charge's direction and the direction of the magnetic field decreases, the force on the charge decreases.

INTEGRATING

BIOLOGY
Many types of bacteria contain magnetic particles of iron oxide and iron sulfide. These particles are encased in a membrane within the cell, forming a magnetosome. The magnetosomes in a bacterium spread out in a line and align with Earth's magnetic field. In this way, as the cell uses its flagella to swim, it travels along a north-south axis. Recently, magnetite crystals have been found in human brain cells, but the role these particles play remains uncertain.

Did You Know?

Physicists first studied protons, neutrons, and electrons by firing them through magnetic fields. They found that when a charged particle goes through a constant magnetic field, the particle moves in a circular path. The radius of the path is directly related to the mass of the particle and inversely related to the particle's charge. Electrons and protons fired through a constant magnetic field curve in different directions, indicating that they are oppositely charged. Neutrons travel straight, indicating no charge.

Additional Application

Tethered Satellites These satellites are connected to a spacecraft through a long cable (10 km), called a tether. As the tether moves through Earth's magnetic field, the charges in the tether experience a force due to the magnetic field and try to move to one end of the tether. This motion ends up producing a voltage across the tether. The tether can then be used as an energy source. A tethered satellite should be able to generate more than 1 A of current.

Inquiry Lab

Can you demonstrate electromagnetic induction?

Materials
✔ galvanometer ✔ 2 insulated wire leads
✔ solenoid   ✔ 2 bar magnets

Procedure

1. Set up the apparatus as shown in the photo at right. With this arrangement, current induced in the solenoid will pass through the galvanometer.
2. Holding one of the bar magnets, insert its north pole into the solenoid while observing the galvanometer needle. What happens?
3. Pull the magnet out of the solenoid, and record the movement of the galvanometer needle.
4. Turn the magnet around, and move the south pole in and out of the solenoid. What happens?
5. Vary the speed of the magnet. What happens if you do not move the magnet at all?
6. Try again using two magnets alongside each other with north poles and south poles together. How does the amount of current induced depend on the strength of the magnetic field?

Analysis

1. What evidence did you find that current is induced by a changing magnetic field?
2. Compare the current induced by a south pole with that induced by a north pole.
3. What two observations did you make that show that more current is induced if the magnetic field changes rapidly?

Inquiry Lab

Can you demonstrate electromagnetic induction?   If the magnetic field is changing, then an electrical current will be induced in the wire loop. The greater the rate of change, the greater the induced current. As a result, if you move the magnet more quickly, it should induce a stronger current than if it is moved slowly.

Analysis

1. As the magnet is being brought toward the coil, the strength of the magnetic field in the coil increases, current is induced in the coil, and the galvanometer needle deflects.
2. in opposite directions
3. The induced current increases with speed and with the number of magnets.

Electric Currents from Magnetism

|SKILL BUILDER

Interpreting Visuals Have students use **Figure 14-14** to explain why a current is not induced in a loop that is moving parallel to a magnetic field. *(There is no force on charges in the wire when the loop moves parallel to a magnetic field. The magnetic field through the loop is constant, so no current is induced.)*

Resources Teaching Transparency 44 shows this visual.

Teaching Tip

Mechanical Energy to Electrical Energy Obtain a hand crank generator from the physics department. Use this generator to light up a light bulb. This demonstrates that different types of energy can be converted into electrical energy. The energy flow for this device is the following: chemical energy in your muscles is converted into kinetic energy to make your hand crank the motor. This kinetic energy is converted into electrical energy when a magnet or coil rotates inside the generator. The magnetic field through the wire loop generates an electrical current, lighting the bulb.

Figure 14-14
(A) When the wire in a circuit moves perpendicular to a magnetic field, the current induced in the wire is at a maximum. (B) When the wire moves parallel to a magnetic field, there is zero current induced in the wire.

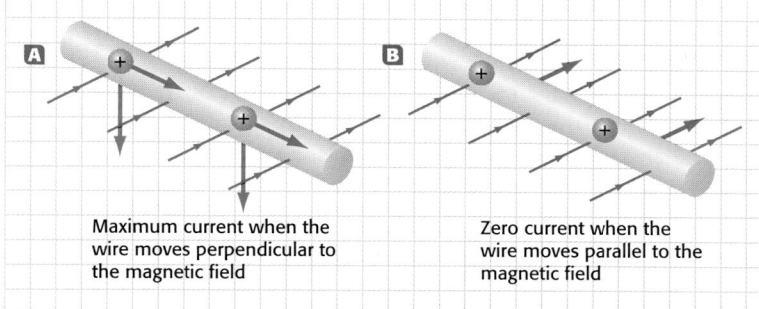

Maximum current when the wire moves perpendicular to the magnetic field

Zero current when the wire moves parallel to the magnetic field

internet connect

SCiLINKS.
NSTA

TOPIC: Generators
GO TO: www.scilinks.org
KEYWORD: HK1145

▶ **generator** a device that uses electromagnetic induction to convert mechanical energy to electrical energy

▶ **alternating current** an electric current that changes direction at regular intervals; also called AC

Figure 14-15
In an alternating current generator, the mechanical energy of the loop's rotation is converted to electrical energy when a current is induced in the wire. The current lights the light bulb.

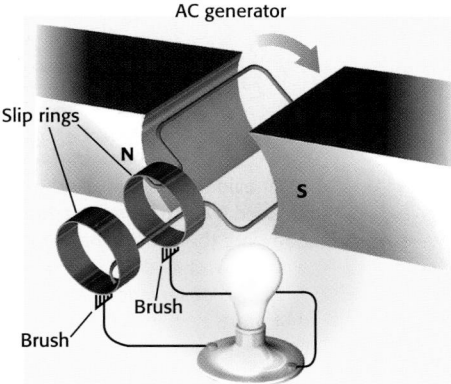

AC generator

Slip rings

N

S

Brush

Brush

Now apply this concept to current. Imagine the wire in a circuit as a tube full of charges, as shown in **Figure 14-14.** When the wire is moving perpendicular to a magnetic field, the force on the charges is at a maximum. In this case, there will be a current in the wire and circuit, as shown in **Figure 14-14A.** When a wire is moving parallel to the field, as in **Figure 14-14B,** no current is induced in the wire. Because the charges are moving parallel to the field, they experience no magnetic force.

Generators convert mechanical energy to electrical energy

Generators are similar to motors except that they convert mechanical energy to electrical energy. If you exert energy to do work on a simple generator, like the one in **Figure 14-15,** the loop of wire inside turns within a magnetic field and current is produced. For each half rotation of the loop, the current produced by the generator reverses direction. This type of generator is therefore called an **alternating current,** or *AC,* generator. The generators that produce the electrical energy that you use at home are alternating current generators. The current supplied by the outlets in your home and in most of the world is alternating current.

As can be seen by the glowing light bulb in **Figure 14-15,** the coil turning in the magnetic field of the magnet creates a current. The magnitude and direction of the current that results from the coil's rotation vary depending on the orientation of the loop in the field.

DEMONSTRATION 5 TEACHING

Measuring Energy

Time: Approximately 30 minutes
Materials: small electrical motor, galvanometer, string, various weights, ring stand, test-tube clamp

Attach the motor to the ring stand with the test-tube clamp. Raise it to the highest position. Put something heavy on top of the ring stand base to keep it from falling over. The shaft of the motor should hang over the edge of the table. Tape or glue the end of the string to the shaft of the motor and wind it around the shaft. Tie a small mass to the string. The mass should be heavy enough so that, when released, the weight of the mass will cause the motor to turn. Attach the galvanometer. Release the weight and record the reading of the galvanometer when the mass reaches the floor or some fixed position. Repeat the experiment with different weights. Discuss the energy transformations involved.

Table 14-1   **Induced Current in a Generator**

Position of loop	Amount of current	Graph of current versus angle of rotation
Magnetic field	Zero current	Current vs. Rotation angle (0° 90° 180° 270° 360°)
Magnetic field	Maximum current	Current vs. Rotation angle (0° 90° 180° 270° 360°)
Magnetic field	Zero current	Current vs. Rotation angle (0° 90° 180° 270° 360°)
Magnetic field	Maximum current (opposite direction)	Current vs. Rotation angle (0° 90° 180° 270° 360°)
Magnetic field	Zero current	Current vs. Rotation angle (0° 90° 180° 270° 360°)

Table 14-1 shows how the magnitude of the current produced by an alternating current generator varies with time. When the loop is perpendicular to the field, the current is zero. Recall that a charge moving parallel to a magnetic field experiences no magnetic force. This is the case here. The charges in the wire experience no magnetic force, so no current is induced in the wire.

As the loop continues to turn, the current increases until it reaches a maximum. When the loop is parallel to the field, charges on either side of the wire move perpendicular to the magnetic field. Thus, the charges experience the maximum magnetic force, and the current is large. Current decreases as the loop rotates, reaching zero when it is again perpendicular to the magnetic field. As the loop continues to rotate, the direction of the current reverses.

MAGNETISM   **477**

Electric Currents from Magnetism

|SKILL BUILDER

Interpreting Diagrams
Have students work in pairs and use **Table 14-1** to describe the changing magnetic field through the wire loop and the force on charged particles as the loop rotates in the magnetic field.

Resources   Teaching Transparency 42 shows this visual.

Teaching Tip

AC   By using an overhead projector and a piece of colored cellophane mounted in a frame (like a 35 mm slide), you can illustrate the effects of the changing cross-sectional area of a loop on induced current and show how generators create AC. Tell students that the light from the overhead projector represents a uniform magnetic field and the frame represents a wire loop. The amount of colored light that reaches the screen represents the magnetic field that passes through the wire loop, the change in which is related to the induced current. Slowly rotate the filter over the overhead projector, starting with the frame parallel to the ground, and allow changing amounts of colored light to reach the screen. Have students observe the changing intensity. Draw a graph of the changes in intensity over time on the board. (The graph is a sine curve.) Point out the analogy between the changing intensity and a changing current. Note that the intensity is at a maximum (with the frame perpendicular to the light source) when the induced current would be at a minimum (when the loop is perpendicular to the magnetic field).

Electric Currents from Magnetism

Did You Know?

Many dams and hydro-electric power plants stop or inhibit the migration of salmon and other fish on the waterway. This prevents the fish from migrating upstream to spawn. As a result of legislation, power companies in many states are required to build a "fish ladder" to enable the fish to swim past the dam in order to reproduce.

Additional Application

Electric Guitars When an electric guitar is played, a small electrical current goes through the strings. Beneath each string is a series of solenoids with iron cores, called pickups. As the string moves across the pickups, the magnetic field generated by the strings goes through the solenoids. The moving string also causes the strength of the magnetic field going through the solenoids to change, inducing a current. This induced current is then sent to the amplifier to be increased in magnitude and then to the speakers to convert the signal into sound. Some guitars have removable pickups, and the solenoids can be seen. Guitar players can change the sound of their guitars by changing how the solenoids are wound.

Did You Know?

Although the light from an incandescent light bulb appears to be constant, the current in the bulb actually varies, changing direction 60 times each second. The light appears to be steady because the changes are too rapid for our eyes to perceive.

Figure 14-16
An electromagnetic wave consists of electric and magnetic field waves at right angles to each other.

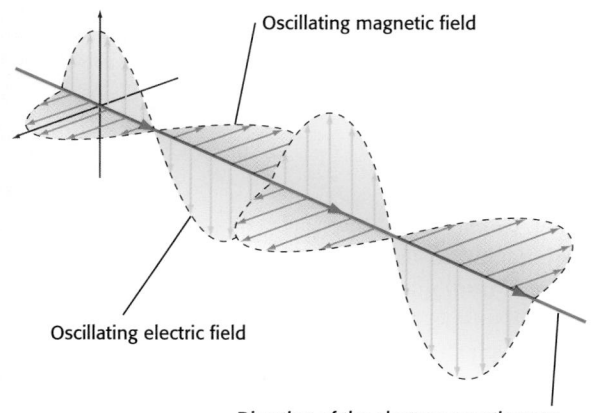

Oscillating magnetic field

Oscillating electric field

Direction of the electromagnetic wave

Generators produce the electrical energy you use in your home

Large power plants use generators to convert mechanical energy to electrical energy. The mechanical energy used in a commercial power plant comes from a variety of sources. One of the most common sources is running water. Dams are built to harness the kinetic energy of falling water. Water is forced through small channels at the top of the dam. As the water falls to the base of the dam, it turns the blades of large turbine fans. The fans are attached to a core wrapped with many loops of wire that rotate within a strong magnetic field. The end result is electrical energy.

Coal power plants use the heat from burning coal to make steam that eventually turns the blades of the turbines. Other sources of energy are nuclear fission, wind, hot water from geysers (geothermal), and solar power.

Unfortunately, much of the electrical energy produced by generators is lost to external sources. Many power plants are not very efficient. More-efficient and safer methods of producing energy are continually being sought.

Electricity and magnetism are two aspects of a single electromagnetic force

So far you've read that a moving charge produces a magnetic field and that a changing magnetic field causes an electric charge to move. The energy that results from these two forces is called electromagnetic energy.

You learned in Section 12.2 that light is a form of electromagnetic energy. Visible light travels as electromagnetic waves, or *EM* waves, as do other forms of radiation, such as radio signals and X rays. These waves are also called *EMF* (electromagnetic frequency) waves. As shown in **Figure 14-16,** EM waves are made up of oscillating electric and magnetic fields that are perpendicular to each other. This is true of any type of EM wave, regardless of the frequency.

Both the electric and magnetic fields in an EM wave are perpendicular to the direction the wave travels. So EM waves are transverse waves. As the wave moves along, the changing electric field generates the magnetic field. The changing magnetic field generates the electric field. Each field regenerates the other, allowing EM waves to travel through empty space.

ALTERNATIVE ASSESSMENT

Generators

There are many different types of electrical power generation techniques. Assign groups of students different generation techniques, and have them research how they work. They can prepare a poster or oral presentation on how the power generation technique works, show a diagram or schematic of the system, show what it uses for fuel, give a typical power output, research whether the electricity generated is expensive or inexpensive to make, and show what effect this method has on the environment. Students should also research "green energy" and decide if the technique is a green energy method. Some generation methods are: nuclear, coal burning, oil/gasoline burning, natural gas burning, solar, wind, hydroelectric, geothermal, co-generation, biomass, and tidal power plants.

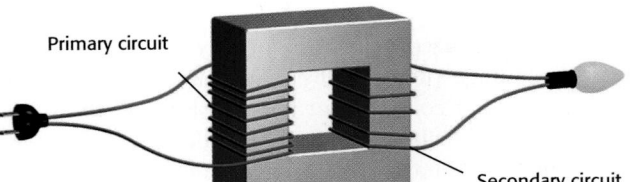

Figure 14-17
A transformer uses the alternating current in the primary circuit to induce an alternating current in the secondary circuit.

Primary circuit

Secondary circuit

Transformers

You may have seen metal cylinders on power line poles in your neighborhood. These cylinders hold electromagnetic devices called **transformers. Figure 14-17** is a simple representation of a transformer. Two wires are coiled around opposite sides of a closed iron loop. In this transformer, one wire is attached to a source of alternating current, such as a power outlet in your home. The other wire is attached to an appliance, such as a lamp.

When there is current in the primary wire, this current creates a changing magnetic field that magnetizes the iron core. The changing magnetic field of the iron core then induces a current in the secondary coil. The direction of the current in the secondary coil changes every time the direction of the current in the primary coil changes.

Transformers can increase or decrease voltage

The voltage induced in the secondary coil of a transformer depends on the number of loops, or *turns*, in the coil. As shown in **Figure 14-18A,** both the primary and secondary wires are coiled only once around the iron core. If the incoming current has a voltage of 5 V, then the voltage measured in the other circuit will be close to 5 V. When the number of turns in the two coils is equal, the voltage induced in the secondary coil is about the same as the voltage in the primary coil.

In **Figure 14-18B,** two secondary coils with just one turn each are placed on the iron core. In this case, a voltage of slightly less than 5 V is induced in each coil. If these turns are joined together to form one coil with two turns, as shown in **Figure 14-18C,** the voltmeter

▶ **transformer** a device that can change one alternating-current voltage to a different alternating-current voltage

Figure 14-18

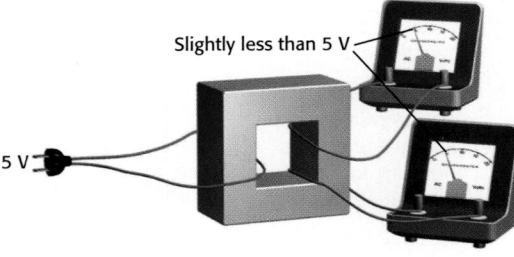

Slightly less than 5 V

5 V

A When the primary and secondary circuits in a transformer each have one turn, the voltage across each is about equal.

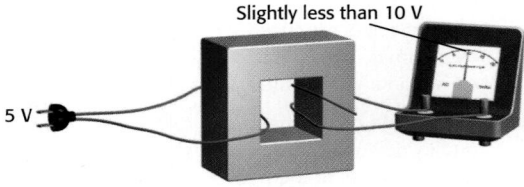

Slightly less than 5 V

5 V

B When an additional secondary circuit is added, the voltage across each is again about equal.

Slightly less than 10 V

5 V

C When the two secondary circuits are combined, the secondary circuit has about twice the voltage of the primary circuit. Actual transformers have thousands of turns.

MAGNETISM **479**

DEMONSTRATION 6 TEACHING

DC Transformer

Time: Approximately 15 minutes
Materials: iron bar, 9 V battery, knife switch, flashlight bulb in holder, two wires (each about 1 m long)

Set up the primary side of the transformer before class by connecting the battery and the switch in series with one of the wires coiled around the iron bar. The primary coil should have 50 turns. Set up the secondary coil with 25 turns, and con-

nect the flashlight bulb to the secondary coil. In class, demonstrate this step-down transformer by momentarily closing the switch and then opening it again. Have students discuss the transfer of energy that occurs in this situation. Close the switch and keep it closed. Have students note the behavior of the bulb. Discuss the brief illumination and fading of the bulb with students. Lead students to consider the concept of changing current. Again, open the switch and note the illumination.

Electric Currents from Magnetism

| SKILL | BUILDER |

Interpreting Visuals Voltages are transformed down near homes and businesses with step-down transformers on utility poles, like the one shown in **Figure 14-19,** and at substations. Have students locate their neighborhood transformers or substations. In areas with underground wiring, the transformers may be installed on the ground.

SECTION 14.3 REVIEW

Check Your Understanding

1. c
2. The moving water rotates a turbine. The turbine is attached to a core wrapped with many loops of wire that rotates within a magnetic field. Alternating current is induced in the wire loop as it turns.
3. step-down transformer
4. a. The needle will be deflected to the left.
   b. The needle will fall back to the zero reading because the magnetic field is no longer changing.
   c. The needle will be deflected to the left. The south end of the magnet going into the loop is the same as the north end of the magnet going out of the loop.

Answers continue on p. 485A.

RESOURCE LINK
STUDY GUIDE

Assign students *Review Section 14.3 Electric Currents from Magnetism.*

Figure 14-19
Step-down transformers like this one are used to reduce the voltage across power lines so that the electrical energy supplied to homes and businesses is safer to use.

will measure an induced voltage of slightly less than twice as much as the voltage produced by one coil. Thus, the voltage across the secondary coil is about twice as large as the voltage across the primary coil. This device is called a *step-up transformer* because the voltage across the secondary coil is greater than the voltage across the primary coil.

If the secondary coil has fewer loops than the primary coil, then the voltage is lowered by the transformer. This type of transformer is called a *step-down transformer.*

Step-up and step-down transformers are used in the transmission of electrical energy from power plants to homes and businesses. A step-up transformer is used at or near the power plant to increase the voltage of the current to about 120 000 V. At this high voltage, less energy is lost due to the resistance of the transmission wires. A step-down transformer, like the one shown in **Figure 14-19,** is then used near your home to reduce the voltage of the current to about 120 V. This lower voltage is much safer. Many appliances in the United States operate at 120 V.

SECTION 14.3 REVIEW

SUMMARY

▶ A current is produced in a circuit by a changing magnetic field.

▶ In a generator, mechanical energy is converted to electrical energy by a conducting loop turning in a magnetic field.

▶ Electromagnetic waves consist of magnetic and electric fields oscillating at right angles to each other.

▶ In a transformer, the magnetic field produced by a primary coil induces a current in a secondary coil.

▶ The voltage across the secondary coil of a transformer is proportional to the number of loops, or turns, it has relative to the number of turns in the primary coil.

CHECK YOUR UNDERSTANDING

1. **Identify** which of the following will *not* increase the current induced in a wire loop moving through a magnetic field.
   a. increasing the strength of the magnetic field
   b. increasing the speed of the wire
   c. rotating the loop until it is perpendicular to the field
2. **Explain** how hydroelectrical power plants use moving water to produce electricity.
3. **Determine** whether the following statement describes a step-up transformer or a step-down transformer: The primary coil has 7000 turns, and the secondary coil has 500 turns.
4. **Predict** the movement of the needle of a galvanometer attached to a coil of wire for each of the following actions. Assume that the north pole of a bar magnet has been inserted into the coil, causing the needle to deflect to the right.
   a. pulling the magnet out of the coil
   b. letting the magnet rest in the coil
   c. thrusting the south pole of the magnet into the coil
5. **Critical Thinking** A spacecraft orbiting Earth has a coil of wire in it. An astronaut measures a small current in the coil, even though there is no battery connected to it and there are no magnets on the spacecraft. What is causing the current?

Chapter Highlights

Before you begin, review the summaries of the key ideas of each section, found on pages 467, 473, and 480. The key vocabulary terms are listed on pages 462, 468, and 474.

UNDERSTANDING CONCEPTS

1. If the poles of two magnets repel each other, _____.
   a. both poles must be south poles
   b. both poles must be north poles
   c. one pole is a south pole and the other is a north pole
   d. the poles are the same type

2. The part of a magnet where the magnetic field and forces are strongest is called a magnetic _____.
   a. field   c. attraction
   b. pole   d. repulsion

3. A _____ magnetic material is easy to magnetize but loses its magnetism easily.
   a. hard
   b. magnetically unstable
   c. soft
   d. No such material exists.

4. An object's ability to generate a magnetic field depends on its _____.
   a. size   c. composition
   b. location   d. direction

5. A straight current-carrying wire produces _____.
   a. an electric field
   b. a magnetic field
   c. beams of white light
   d. All of the above

6. A compass held directly below a current-carrying wire with a positive current moving north will point _____.
   a. east   c. south
   b. north   d. west

7. An electric motor uses an electromagnet to change _____.
   a. mechanical energy to electrical energy
   b. magnetic fields in the motor
   c. magnetic poles in the motor
   d. electrical energy to mechanical energy

8. An electric generator is a device that converts _____.
   a. nuclear energy to electrical energy
   b. wind energy to electrical energy
   c. energy from burning coal to electrical energy
   d. All of the above

9. The process of producing an electrical current by moving a magnet in and out of a coil of wire is called _____.
   a. magnetic deduction
   b. electromagnetic induction
   c. magnetic reduction
   d. magnetic production

10. In a generator, the current produced is _____ when the loop is parallel to the surrounding magnetic field.
    a. at a maximum
    b. very small
    c. zero
    d. none of the above

Using Vocabulary

11. Use the terms *magnetic pole* and *magnetic field* to explain why the N pole of a compass points toward northern Canada.

12. What is made by inserting an iron core into a *solenoid*?

13. Use the terms *generator* and *electromagnetic induction* to explain how *electrical energy* can be produced using the *kinetic energy* of falling water.

14. What does the abbreviation *EM* stand for?

15. What is used to increase or decrease the voltage across a power line?

MAGNETISM **481**

UNDERSTANDING CONCEPTS

1. d	6. d
2. b	7. d
3. c	8. d
4. c	9. b
5. b	10. a

Using Vocabulary

11. Earth's magnetic S pole is located in northern Canada. The magnetic field of the Earth points from the magnetic N pole in Antarctica (South Magnetic Pole) to the magnetic S pole in northern Canada (North Magnetic-Pole). The N pole of a compass needle is attracted to the magnetic S pole and ends up pointing to the north.

12. An electromagnet is made by inserting an iron core into a solenoid.

13. Falling water can be used to generate electricity by converting the kinetic energy of the water into electrical energy. This is done by having the water turn a coil of wire that is inside a magnetic field, inducing a current in the wire. This is called electromagnetic induction, which is the basis of all power generators.

14. EM stands for electromagnetic.

15. A step-up transformer increases the voltage and a step-down transformer decreases the voltage across a power line.

BUILDING MATH SKILLS

16. a. *A, C, E*
b. more
c. more
d. Current at *D* is moving in the opposite direction to current at *B*.

17. parallel

THINKING CRITICALLY

18. If a steel nail is magnetized, then the compass needle will point to the S end of the nail. As you move the compass from one end of the nail to the other, the compass should rotate to align with the nail's magnetic field. If it does not rotate, the nail is not magnetized. Refer to **Figure 14-4** for the orientation of the compass needle as it is moved around a magnetized object.

19. The faint crackling sound is the sound of the domains in the iron nail aligning with the magnetic field of the strong magnet.

20. Hold your arm still with the bracelet parallel to the magnetic field.

21. Usually, a transformer would not work if DC current were used; however, it would work if the current were turned off and on repeatedly.

22. b

BUILDING MATH SKILLS

16. Graphing The figure below is a graph of current versus rotation angle for the output of an alternating-current generator.
 a. At what point(s) does the generator produce no current?
 b. Is less or more current being produced at point *B* than at points *C* and *E*?
 c. Is less or more current being produced at point *D* than at points *C* and *E*?
 d. What does the negative value for the current at *D* signify?

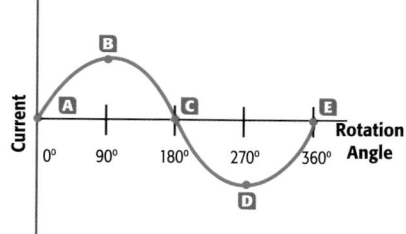

17. Interpreting Graphics If the coil of the generator referred to in item 16 were like the one shown in **Table 14-1,** what would the coil orientation be relative to the magnetic field in order to produce the maximum current at *B*?

THINKING CRITICALLY

18. Problem Solving How could you use a compass with a magnetized needle to determine if a steel nail were magnetized?

19. Applying Knowledge If you place a stethoscope on an unmagnetized iron nail and then slowly move a strong magnet toward the nail, you can hear a faint crackling sound. Use the concept of domains to explain this sound.

20. Problem Solving You walk briskly into a strong magnetic field while wearing a copper bracelet. How should you hold your wrist relative to the magnetic field lines to avoid inducing a current in the bracelet?

21. Understanding Systems Transformers are usually used to raise or lower the voltage across an alternating-current circuit. Could a transformer be used in a direct-current circuit? How about if the direct current were pulsating (turning on and off)?

22. Understanding Systems Which of the following might be the purpose of the device shown below?
 a. to measure the amount of voltage across the wire
 b. to determine the direction of the current in the wire
 c. to find the resistance of the wire

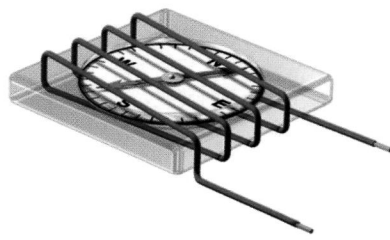

DEVELOPING LIFE/WORK SKILLS

23. Working Cooperatively During a field trip, you find a round chunk of metal that attracts iron objects. In groups of three, design a procedure to determine whether the object is magnetic and, if so, to locate its poles. What materials would you need? How would you draw your conclusions? List all the possible results and the conclusions you could draw from each result.

24. Applying Technology Use your imagination and your knowledge of electromagnetism to invent a useful electromagnetic device. Use a computer-drawing program to make sketches of your invention, and write a description of how it works.

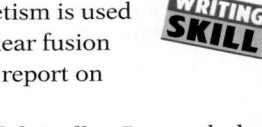

25. Interpreting and Communicating Research one of the following electromagnetic devices. Write a half-page description of how electromagnetism is used in the device, using diagrams where appropriate.
 a. hair dryer   c. doorbell
 b. electric guitar   d. tape recorder

INTEGRATING CONCEPTS

26. Concept Mapping Copy the unfinished concept map below onto a sheet of paper. Complete the map by writing the correct word or phrase in the lettered boxes.

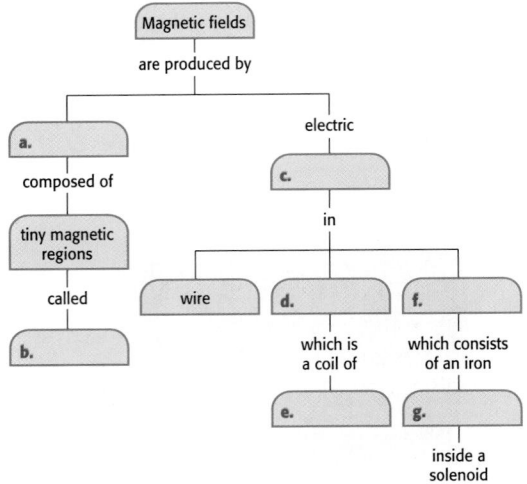

27. Connection to Social Studies Why was the discovery of lodestones in Greece important to navigators hundreds of years later?

28. Connection to Health Some studies indicate that magnetic fields produced by power lines may contribute to leukemia among children who grow up near high-voltage power lines. Research the history of scientific studies of the connection between leukemia and power lines. What experiments show that growing up near power lines increases risk of leukemia? What evidence is there that there is no relation between leukemia and the magnetic fields produced by power lines?

29. Connection to Physics Find out how electromagnetism is used in containing nuclear fusion reactions. Write a report on your findings.

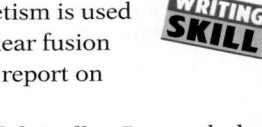

30. Connection to Social Studies Research the debate between proponents of alternating current and proponents of direct current in the 1880s and 1890s. How were Thomas Edison and George Westinghouse involved in the debate? What advantages and disadvantages did each side claim? What kind of current was finally generated in the Niagara Falls hydroelectric plant? If you had been in a position to fund the projects at that time, which projects would you have funded? Prepare your arguments so that you can reenact a meeting of businesspeople in Buffalo in 1887.

TOPIC: Magnetic fields of power lines
GO TO: www.scilinks.org
KEYWORD: HK1146

MAGNETISM **483**

DEVELOPING LIFE/WORK SKILLS

23. Students' plans should be logical, based on principles from the text or previous experiences. A compass could be used to determine if a material is magnetic. The needle would point toward the magnetic south pole of the metal.
24. Check students' drawings. They may include a combination of the following: a source of a magnetic field, wire loops, solenoids, electromagnets, and a voltage source.
25. a. A hair dryer uses an electric motor to blow air. The air is warmed by resistance coils.
 b. Refer to TE page 478.
 c. A doorbell uses an electromagnet to pull a striker that hits a bell.
 d. A tape consists of a thin coating of magnetic particles on a plastic tape. The record head magnetizes the tape in the pattern of the changing magnetic field that corresponds to the intensity of sound being recorded. The playback head reads the pattern and produces an output voltage, which is used to control the speakers.

INTEGRATING CONCEPTS

26. a. magnets
 b. domains
 c. current
 d. solenoid
 e. insulated wire
 f. electromagnet
 g. core

Answers continue on p. 485B.

483

Design Your Own

Lab

Making a Better Electromagnet

Introduction

Electromagnets are used in many devices, from televisions and camcorders to computers and MRI scanners. Electromagnets in a television steer the beams of electrons to hit the right parts of the screen at the right time, while tiny electromagnets in computers are used as read/write heads. The basic structure of these electromagnets is the same, but their designs are optimized for different situations. Encourage students to think about how each factor in the design of an electromagnet influences how it will operate.

Objectives

Students will:

▸ **Use** appropriate lab safety procedures.

▸ **Build** several electromagnets.

▸ **Identify** the features of a strong electromagnet.

▸ **Determine** how many paper clips each electromagnet can lift.

Planning

Recommended Time: 1 lab period
Materials: *(for each lab group)*

▸ 2 D-cell batteries

▸ 2 battery holders

▸ 1 m of 22-gauge insulated single-strand Cu wire

▸ 1 m of 30-gauge insulated single-strand Cu wire

▸ extra insulated wire

▸ 4 metal rods with the same dimensions (iron, tin, aluminum, and nickel)
(for entire class)

▸ wire stripper

▸ electrical tape

▸ box of small paper clips

Design Your Own

Lab

Introduction

How can you build the strongest electromagnet from a selection of batteries, wires, and metal rods?

Objectives

▸ **Build** several electromagnets.

▸ **Identify** the features of a strong electromagnet.

▸ **Determine** how many paper clips each electromagnet can lift.

Materials

2 D-cell batteries
2 battery holders
1 m thick insulated wire
1 m thin insulated wire
extra insulated wire
4 metal rods
    (iron, tin, aluminum, and nickel)
wire stripper
electrical tape
box of small paper clips

Safety Needs

safety goggles
heat-resistant gloves

Making a Better Electromagnet

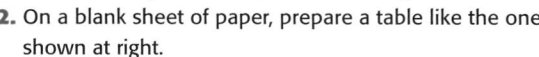

▸ Building an Electromagnet

1. Review the Inquiry Lab in Section 14.2 on the basic steps in making an electromagnet.

2. On a blank sheet of paper, prepare a table like the one shown at right.

3. Wind the thin wire around the thickest metal core. Carefully pull the core out of the center of the thin wire coil. Repeat the above steps with the thick wire. You now have two wire coils that can be used to make electromagnets.
   SAFETY CAUTION Handle the wires only where they are insulated.

▸ Designing Your Experiment

4. With your lab partners, decide how you will determine what features combine to make a strong electromagnet. Think about the following before you predict the features that the strongest electromagnet would have.
   a. Which metal rod would make the best core?
   b. Which of the two wires would make a stronger electromagnet?
   c. How many coils should the electromagnet have?
   d. Should the batteries be connected in series or in parallel?

Electromagnet number	Wire (thick or thin)	# of coils	Core (iron, tin, alum., or nickel)	Batteries (series or parallel)	# of paper clips lifted
1					
2					
3					
4					
5					
6					

5. In your lab report, list each step you will perform in your experiment.
6. Before you carry out your experiment, your teacher must approve your plan.

▶ Performing Your Experiment

7. After your teacher approves your plan, carry out your experiment. You should test all four metal rods, both thicknesses of wire, and both series and parallel battery connections. Count the number of coils of wire in each electromagnet you build.
8. Record your results in your data table.

▶ Analyzing Your Results

1. Did the thick wire or the thin wire make a stronger electromagnet? How can you explain this result?
2. Which metal cores made the strongest electromagnets? Why?
3. Could your electromagnet pick up more paper clips when the batteries were connected in series or in parallel? Explain why.
4. What combination of wire, metal core, and battery connection made the strongest electromagnet?

▶ Defending Your Conclusions

5. Suppose someone tells you that your conclusion is invalid because each time you tested a magnet on the paper clips, the paper clips themselves became more and more magnetized. How could you show that your conclusion is valid?

Pre-Lab

Teaching Tips

Review the construction of an electromagnet with the students before beginning the activity. Discuss the parts of an electromagnet, the solenoid and metal core, and their functions in an electromagnet. Remind the students that the strength of the magnetic field produced by a solenoid increases with increasing current in the solenoid and with the number of coils.

Review the relationship between current, voltage, and resistance. Remind students that a thin wire will have a greater resistance than a thick wire. Encourage them to discuss how the diameter of a wire will affect how many times it can be wound around a core. Also review series and parallel circuits. Ask students to draw schematic diagrams for two batteries and a resistor in series and in parallel. Have them trace the path of a charge through each circuit and discuss the energy changes involved.

Procedure

▶ Designing Your Experiment

Students should propose a systematic testing procedure, changing only one variable (wire thickness, type of metal core, or battery connection) from one test to the next.

Continue on p. 485A.

> ### RESOURCE LINK
> #### DATASHEETS
> Have students use *Datasheet 14.5 Design Your Own Lab: Making a Better Electromagnet* to record their results.

Design Your Own Lab from page 485
Making a Better Electromagnet

Post-Lab

▶ Disposal

The metal cores can be kept for future use. The wire can be unwound and stored. The batteries should be tested. Discharged batteries should be taken to hazardous waste disposal.

▶ Analyzing Your Results

1. Answers will depend on the diameter of the copper conductor in each wire, the thickness of each wire's insulation, and the number of coils made with each wire. A larger-diameter conductor can carry more current, but a thinner wire (conductor plus insulator) allows more coils to be made. Both effects increase the strength of an electromagnet.
2. The iron and nickel cores should make the strongest electromagnets. Both metals contain domains that are aligned in the same direction.
3. The electromagnet should pick up more paper clips with the batteries connected in series. With a series connection, the voltages of the two batteries add together. A larger voltage produces a greater current in the wire, making the magnetic field stronger.
4. The strongest electromagnet should have resulted from using the iron or nickel core, the series arrangement of batteries, and the thicker wire (as long as the difference in number of coils for the thin and thick wires is small).

▶ Defending Your Conclusions

5. Answers may vary. To account for the magnetism of the paper clips, students could determine how many paper clips stick to each electromagnet when the batteries are disconnected. They could also use a different set of paper clips for each electromagnet design that they test.

Answers from page 473

SECTION 14.2 REVIEW

5. A solenoid suspended by a string could be used as a compass. The magnetic field of the solenoid would align itself with the magnetic field of the Earth just as a bar magnet would. The N pole of the solenoid would point to Earth's magnetic south pole in northern Canada.
6. This motor will not be able to make a complete rotation because of the lack of a commutator. This motor will only oscillate back and forth.

Answers from page 480

SECTION 14.3 REVIEW

5. As the spacecraft orbits, the coil encounters a change in both the strength and orientation of Earth's magnetic field, inducing a current in the coil.

Answers from page 483

INTEGRATING
CONCEPTS

27. Lodestone was the first magnetic material discovered. It was used to make the first crude compasses. These compasses enabled travelers to determine directions even when the stars were not visible. Compasses have been used in navigation for hundreds of years.

28. There is a statistical association observed between leukemia and chronic exposure to electromagnetic fields in populations with childhood leukemia. (Chronic lymphocytic leukemia has been detected in adults who are exposed to EM fields in their jobs, such as electrical utility work or welding). Based on these epidemiological studies, there is a fairly consistent pattern of a small increased risk of leukemia with increasing exposure to EM fields. However, lab studies with animals, humans, and specific cells do not support a cause-and-effect relationship between EM fields and leukemia. These lab studies have not been able to find a mechanism for EM fields to cause leukemia. The National Institute of Environmental Health Sciences has determined that the evidence for a risk of cancer from the EM fields around power lines is weak but that EM fields should be regarded as possible carcinogens because this possibility has not been ruled out.

29. The plasmas used in nuclear fusion reactions have extremely high temperatures, usually more than 100 000 000°C, so they cannot be contained in a vessel. Because plasmas are made up of charged particles (atomic nuclei and electrons), they can be contained by electromagnetic fields.

30. Thomas Edison and General Electric wanted DC, while George Westinghouse and Nikola Tesla wanted AC. Edison claimed that DC was safer. Westinghouse claimed that AC would have less loss in transmission and that AC was more appropriate for use in large motors, such as in washing machines and refrigerators. The Niagara Falls power plant produced alternating current. Students should be able to defend their arguments based on their research.

485B

CHAPTER 15

Communication Technology

Annotated Descriptions of the Correlated National Science Standards

The following descriptions summarize the National Science Standards that specially relate to Chapter 15. For the full text of the Standards, see p. 40T.

SECTION 15.1
Signals and Telecommunications
Physical Science
PS 5d, 6b
Science and Technology
ST 2

SECTION 15.2
Telephone, Radio, and Television
Physical Science
PS 5d, 6b
Science in Personal and Social Perspectives
SPSP 5
Science and Technology
ST 2

SECTION 15.3
Integrating Technology and Society—Computers and the Internet
Physical Science
PS 5d, 6b
Science in Personal and Social Perspectives
SPSP 5
Science and Technology
ST 2

Cross-Discipline Teaching RESOURCES

Cross-Discipline Teaching, ATE p. 486
Technology   Mathematics

Integration Enrichment Resources
Social Studies, **PE** and **ATE** p. 489
  IE 15.1 *Morse Code and Computers*
Biology, **PE** and **ATE** p. 498
  IE 15.2 *The Brain's Signals*
Science and the Consumer, **PE** and **ATE** p. 504
  IE 15.3 *HDTV: Why Make the Switch?*
Physics, **PE** and **ATE** p. 508
  IE 15.4 *Building a Computer*
Architecture, **PE** and **ATE** p. 511
  IE 15.5 *Computers and Design Fields*
Real World Applications, **PE** and **ATE** p. 513
  IE 15.6 *World Wide Web Robots*

Additional Integration Enrichment Worksheets
  IE 15.7 *Fine Arts*   IE 15.8 *Mathematics*

Use the Planning Guide on the next page to help you organize your lessons.

MATH AND COMPUTER RESOURCES

Chapter 15	Math Skills	Assess	Media/Computer Skills
Section 15.1	**ATE** Cross-Discipline Teaching, p. 486		■ Section 15.1
Section 15.2			■ Section 15.2
Section 15.3	**BS** Worksheet 1.2: Basic Exercises in Logic	**PE** Building Math Skills, p. 516, item 17	■ Section 15.3

PE Pupil's Edition **ATE** Annotated Teacher's Edition **MS** Math Skills **BS** Basic Skills
IE Integration Enrichment ■ Guided Reading Audio **CRT** Critical Thinking

READING SKILL BUILDER

The following activities found in the Annotated Teacher's Edition provide techniques for developing useful reading strategies to increase your students' reading comprehension skills.

Section 15.1 **Brainstorming,** p. 486
K-W-L, p. 488

Smithsonian Institution®

**Visit
www.si.edu/hrw
for additional
online resources.**

Spanish Resources

The following resources are made available for students who speak Spanish as their first language.

**Spanish Resources
Guided Reading Audio CD-ROM**
Chapter 15

Spanish Glossary
Chapter 15

Communication Technology

CLASSROOM RESOURCES

FOCUS	TEACH	HANDS-ON

Section 15.1: Signals and Telecommunications

BLOCK 1
45 minutes

FOCUS	TEACH	HANDS-ON
ATE **RSB** Brainstorming, p. 486 **ATE** Focus Activities 1, 2, p. 487 **ATE** **RSB** K-W-L, p. 488 **ATE** **Demo 1** Building a Communication System, p. 490 **PE** Signals and Codes; Telecommunication, pp. 488–493 ★ Focus Transparency LT 49	**ATE** **Skill Builder** Interpreting Visuals, pp. 487, 492 **TT** 45 Transducers **BLM** 48 Binary Code	**IE** Worksheet 15.1 **PE** Quick Activity *Examining Optical Fibers*, p. 493 **DS** 15.1 **LE 15** *Sending and Receiving a Message Using a Binary Code* **DS** 15.5 **IE** Worksheet 15.8

BLOCK 2
45 minutes

FOCUS	TEACH	HANDS-ON
ATE **Demo 2** Model of Radio Wave Transmission, p. 494 **PE** Telecommunication Today, pp. 493–496	**ATE** **Skill Builder** Interpreting Visuals, p. 494	

Section 15.2: Telephone, Radio, and Television

BLOCK 3
45 minutes

FOCUS	TEACH	HANDS-ON
ATE **Demo 3** Fiber Optics Cable, p. 498 **PE** Telephones, pp. 497–499 ★ Focus Transparency LT 50	**ATE** **Skill Builder** Graphing, p. 499 **TT** 46 Telephone	**IE** Worksheet 15.2

BLOCK 4
45 minutes

FOCUS	TEACH	HANDS-ON
ATE **Demo 4** Internal Reflection, p. 500 **PE** Radio and Television, pp. 500–505	**ATE** **Skill Builder** Interpreting Diagrams, p. 503 **TT** 47 Television	**PE** Science and the Consumer *TV by the Numbers: High-Definition Digital TV*, p. 504 **IE** Worksheet 15.3 **PE** Inquiry Lab *How do red, blue, and green phosphors produce other colors?* p. 505 **DS** 15.2

Section 15.3: Computers and the Internet

BLOCK 5
45 minutes

FOCUS	TEACH	HANDS-ON
PE Computers, pp. 506–512 ★ Focus Transparency LT 51	**ATE** **Skill Builder** Interpreting Visuals, p. 512 **BLM** 49 Logic Gates	**PE** Quick Activity *How Fast Are Digital Computers?* p. 508 **DS** 15.3 **IE** Worksheet 15.4 **IE** Worksheet 15.5

BLOCK 6
45 minutes

FOCUS	TEACH	HANDS-ON
PE Computer Networks and the Internet, pp. 512–514		**PE** Real World Applications *Using a Search Engine*, p. 513 **IE** Worksheet 15.6 **IE** Worksheet 15.7 **PE** Skill Builder Lab *Determining the Speed of Sound*, p. 518 **DS** 15.4

CLASSROOM RESOURCES

HOMEWORK	ASSESS
PE Section Review 1–4, p. 496 **Chapter 15 Review,** p. 515, items 1, 2, 10, 11	**SG** Chapter 15 Pretest **ATE** *ALTERNATIVE ASSESSMENT,* Deciphering Codes, p. 489
PE Section Review 5–8, p. 496 **Chapter 15 Review,** p. 515, item 3	**SG** Section 15.1
PE Section Review 1, 2, p. 505 **Chapter 15 Review,** p. 515, items 12, 14	
PE Section Review 3–7, p. 505 **Chapter 15 Review,** p. 515, items 4–6, 13	**ATE** *ALTERNATIVE ASSESSMENT,* Deflecting Electron Beams, p. 502 **SG** Section 15.2
PE Section Review 1–8, 10, p. 514 **Chapter 15 Review,** p. 515, items 7–9, 15–17	**ATE** *ALTERNATIVE ASSESSMENT,* Researching Computer Technology, p. 506
PE Section Review 9, p. 514	**SG** Section 15.3

PE Chapter 15 Review
Thinking Critically 18–23, p. 516
Developing Life/Work Skills 24–27, p. 517
Integrating Concepts 28–29, p. 517
SG Chapter 15 Mixed Review

Chapter Tests
Chapter 15 Test

One-Stop Planner CD–ROM **with Test Generator**
Chapter 15

Teaching Resources
Scoring Rubrics and assignment checklist.

🖉 internet connect

National Science Teachers Association
Online Resources:
www.scilinks.org
The following *sci*LINKS Internet resources can be found in the student text for this chapter.

Page 487
TOPIC: Space messages
KEYWORD: HK1501

Page 502
TOPIC: Television
KEYWORD: HK1505

Page 490
TOPIC: Morse code
KEYWORD: HK1502

Page 513
TOPIC: Internet
KEYWORD: HK1506

Page 491
TOPIC: Analog/digital signals
KEYWORD: HK1503

Page 517
TOPIC: Communication technology
KEYWORD: HK1507

Page 495
TOPIC: Communications satellites
KEYWORD: HK1504

CNNfyi.com www.cnnfyi.com

Visit this site for coverage of current events and related classroom resources.

PE Pupil's Edition **ATE** Annotated Teacher's Edition
RSB Reading Skill Builder **DS** Datasheets
IE Integrated Enrichment **SG** Study Guide
LE Laboratory Experiments
TT Teaching Transparencies **BLM** Blackline Masters
★ Lesson Focus Transparency

CHAPTER 15

Communication Technology

Tapping Prior Knowledge

Be sure students understand the following concepts:

Chapter 12
Electromagnetic waves

Chapter 13
Electric current, circuits

Tapping Prior Knowledge

Be sure students understand the following concepts:

Chapter 12
Electromagnetic waves

Chapter 13
Electric current, circuits

READING SKILL BUILDER *Brainstorming* Have students brainstorm words that they believe are related to communications and communications technology. Write these relevant words on the chalkboard. Have students suggest how some of these words affect their daily life. They encounter many of these words on a daily basis, whether they know it or not. The students should write down the brainstormed terms so that they can define them at the end of the unit, using what they have learned about communications and communications technology.

Chapter Preview

15.1 Signals and Telecommunication
Signals and Codes
Telecommunication
Telecommunication Today

15.2 Telephone, Radio, and Television
Telephones
Radio and Television

15.3 Computers and the Internet *INTEGRATING TECHNOLOGY and Society*
Computers
Computer Networks and the Internet

486

RESOURCE LINK
STUDY GUIDE

Assign students *Pretest Chapter 15 Communication Technology* before beginning Section 15.1.

CROSS-DISCIPLINE TEACHING

Technology Ask the technology teacher to come into class and discuss digital communications and the Internet. Discuss how the use of the Internet has changed over the past few years, including how some companies do "e-business" entirely over the Internet. In addition, discuss the use of digital signals in communications.

Mathematics Ask a math teacher to come into class and discuss the base-2 numbering system. Have this math teacher show how to do basic addition in base 2 and how to count to 32.

Focus ACTIVITY

Background When you write a letter, you assume that the recipient can read and understand what you have written. But how would you send a message to intelligent life on another planet?

NASA had to consider this question in the early 1970s when it began sending spacecraft to the outer regions of the solar system. Like bottles drifting on an ocean, these probes would eventually drift out of the solar system into deep space. With messages attached to these spacecraft, any extraterrestrial beings that discover a craft could learn where the craft came from and who made it if they could understand the message.

When the *Voyager 1* and *2* spacecraft were launched, large gold-plated copper disks were sent with them. Each disk was a large phonograph record consisting of sounds of nature, music from various nations, and greetings in all modern languages.

Activity 1 Suppose you are chosen to develop a visual message to be sent with a probe into deep space. Make a list of information you think would be most important to convey to intelligent extraterrestrial beings. What assumptions have you made about the receivers of this information?

Activity 2 On a piece of plain paper, draw the design for the space message you developed in Activity 1. Share your design with your classmates. See if they understand what you tried to communicate. Are there parts of your design that your classmates have trouble understanding? What might you do to remedy this?

internetconnect

SC*i*LINKS
NSTA

TOPIC: Space messages
GO TO: www.scilinks.org
KEYWORD: HK1501

Improvements in communications satellites (left) make it possible for more telephone, radio, and television signals to travel from one place to another. These advancements, in both satellites and other communication equipment, are largely the result of improvements in the speed and storage capacity of modern computers (above).

487

Focus ACTIVITY

Background Students can research the *Voyager 2* satellite launched by NASA. On board this satellite is a gold record. This record has a visual message for any alien culture that may eventually find this space craft. It also has an audio message.

Activity 1 You can suggest images of humans, images of different plants and animals, and images of our solar system, for example. Students can also put sample languages on their messages, and perhaps images of sample mathematical theorems. Extraterrestrial beings could receive this information assuming they have sight and hearing, or some other way to understand the messages.

Activity 2 Have students find out what image is etched into the gold record that is attached to the *Voyager 2* satellite and compare it to their own designs. See if the students can understand the message of *Voyager 2*.

SKILL BUILDER

Interpreting Visuals Telephone calls, which include voice, fax, and computer data, are routed through large telecommunication networks. A network is made of *nodes* and *links*. A node is a switching station where incoming and outgoing calls are properly routed using computers. The photo on the left shows a switching station. A link is a path consisting of cable wires, fiber-optic cables, satellite links, or microwave links across which the calls are routed.

Scheduling

Refer to pp. 486A–486D for lecture, classwork, and assignment options for Section 15.1.

★ **Lesson Focus**
Use transparency *LT 49* to prepare students for this section.

READING SKILL BUILDER *K-W-L*
Have students list what they know about signals and telecommunications, then have them list what they want to know about signals and telecommunications. After they have studied the chapter, have them look at their lists and write down what they have learned about the subject. Also have them write down any new questions that they have after reading the section.

Did You Know ?

Typically, infants are not able to speak until they reach the age of 12–14 months. This is partly because they have not learned communication codes, or language. However, they are able to communicate with their parents. Infants use nonverbal communication skills, and they interpret the nonverbal reactions that their parents present back to them.

15.1

Signals and Telecommunication

▶ **KEY TERMS**

signal
code
telecommunication
analog signals
digital signals
optical fiber

OBJECTIVES

▶ Distinguish between signals and codes.
▶ Define and give an example of telecommunication.
▶ Compare analog signals with digital signals.
▶ Describe two advantages of optical fibers over metal wires for transmitting signals.
▶ Describe how microwave relays transmit signals using Earth-based stations and communications satellites.

Y ou communicate with people every day. Each time you talk to a friend, wave goodbye or hello, or give someone a "thumbs up," you are sending and receiving information. Even actions such as shaking someone's hand and frowning are forms of communication.

Signals and Codes

▶ **signal** a sign that represents information, such as a command, a direction, or a warning

All of the different forms of communication just mentioned use **signals.** A signal is any sign or event that conveys information. People often use nonverbal signals along with words to communicate. Some signals, such as those shown in **Figure 15-1,** are so common that almost everyone in the United States recognizes their meaning. Signals can be sent in the form of gestures, flags, lights, shapes, colors, or even electric current.

Figure 15-1
(A) A handshake indicates friendship or good will.
(B) A green light means "go."
(C) A football referee's raised hands tell the crowd and the scorekeeper that the kick was good.

Codes are used to send signals

In a baseball game, the catcher often sends signals to the pitcher. These signals can tell the pitcher what type of pitch to throw. In order for the catcher's signals to be understood by the pitcher, the two players must work out the meaning of the signals, or **code,** before the game starts.

You hear and use codes every day, perhaps without even being aware of it. The language you speak is a code. Not everybody in the world understands it. An idea or message can be represented in different languages using very different symbols. The phrase "thank you" in English, for instance, is expressed as *gracias* in Spanish, شكران in Arabic, and 謝謝 in Chinese.

Some codes are routinely used by particular groups. For example, chemists around the world recognize Au, Pb, and O as symbols for the elements gold, lead, and oxygen, respectively. Also, all mathematicians recognize $=$, $-$, and $+$ as symbols that mean *equal to, minus,* and *plus.*

In addition to signals and codes, communication requires a sender and a receiver. A sender transmits, or sends, a message to a receiver.

Signals are sent in many different forms

Signals like waving or calling out to someone can be received only if the person at the other end can see or hear the signal. As a result, these signals cannot be sent very far. To send a message over long distances, the signal needs to be converted into a form that can travel long distances easily. Both electricity and electromagnetic waves offer excellent ways to send such signals.

To send sound using electricity, the first step is to convert the sound into an electric current. This electrical signal is produced by using a microphone. The microphone matches the changes in sound waves with comparable changes in electric current. You can imagine the microphone making a copy of the sound in the form of electricity. Next, this electrical signal travels along a wire over longer distances. At the other end, the electrical signal is amplified and converted back into sound using a speaker.

COMMUNICATION TECHNOLOGY **489**

Connection to SOCIAL STUDIES

In 1837, an American named Samuel Morse received a patent on a device called the electric telegraph. The telegraph uses a code made of a series of pulses of electric current to send messages. A machine at the other end marks a paper tape—a dot in response to a short pulse and a dash in response to a long pulse. Morse code, as shown below, represents letters and numbers as a series of dashes and dots.

A ·—	N —·	1 ·————
B —···	O ———	2 ··———
C —·—·	P ·——·	3 ···——
D —··	Q ——·—	4 ····—
E ·	R ·—·	5 ·····
F ··—·	S ···	6 —····
G ——·	T —	7 ——···
H ····	U ··—	8 ———··
I ··	V ···—	9 ————·
J ·———	W ·——	0 —————
K —·—	X —··—	
L ·—··	Y —·——	
M ——	Z ——··	

Making the Connection
1. Write a simple sentence, such as, "I am here."
2. Translate it into Morse code, and send it to a partner using sounds, tapping, or a flashlight.
3. Have your partner write down the code and try to translate the message using Morse code.

▶ **code** a set of rules used to interpret signals that convey information

---

Connection to SOCIAL STUDIES

The invention of the telegraph provided a reliable framework for the communication of news and information over long distances. The Associated Press (AP) is a wire service that traces its beginnings to 1848, when six newspapers in New York City collaborated to finance a telegraph system to relay foreign news.

Making the Connection
1–3. Sentences will vary, but should be written correctly using the key provided. Be sure students differentiate between the dashes and dots when relaying messages to their partners.

Resources Assign students worksheet *15.1: Connection to Social Studies—Morse Code and Computers* in the **Integration Enrichment Resources** ancillary.

Multicultural Extension

For more than 3000 years, the Egyptians used hieroglyphics, a unique method of written communication. Hieroglyphics are a series of pictures, and each picture represents a sound or letter. In 1799, an officer under Napoleon's command found the Rosetta Stone. The top section of the Rosetta Stone had hieroglyphics written on it, the middle had something known as demotic script, and the bottom language was Greek. The Rosetta Stone became the key to deciphering hieroglyphics.

ALTERNATIVE ASSESSMENT

Deciphering Codes

Have students break the following code:

tdjfodf jt gvo   *science is fun*

The letters are transposed by one place. Have students design their own code for sending short messages. Have them make a code key by listing the standard alphabet and then show the coded version next to it. Then ask them to write a short message with their code so that another student can decipher it with the code key.

Signals and Telecommunication

Historical Perspective

The Romans had a sophisticated communication system for their time. They could send messages over long distances by the use of fire.

They would build towers approximately 20 mi apart and place large piles of dry wood and kindling near the towers. Generals in the field would decide what message the fire indicated.

When it was time to pass along the message, the general would order the pile of wood to be lit. The lookout in the next tower, 20 mi away, would see the fire, and then set his wooden pile on fire for the next tower to see.

Because the wooden piles were large, the fires could be seen over great distances, carrying a message faster than a horse and rider could. The drawback of this system was that only one message could be sent at a time.

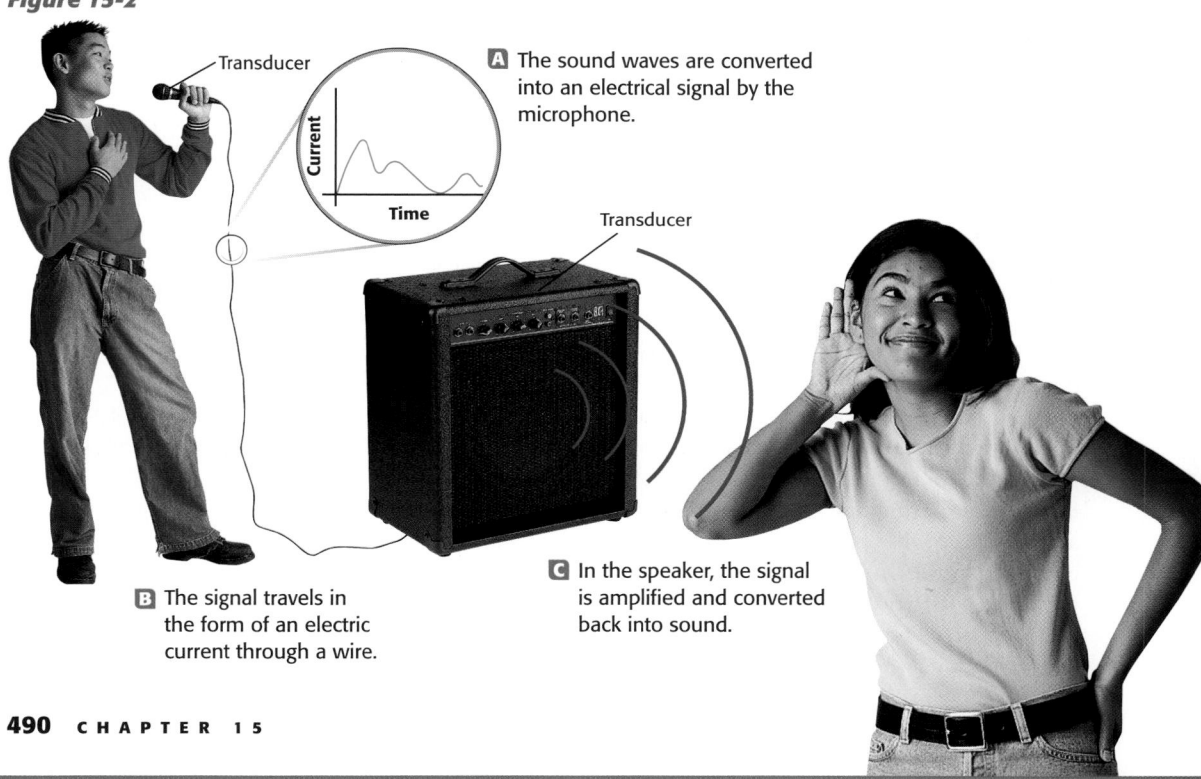

internet connect

SCI LINKS
NSTA

TOPIC: Morse code
GO TO: www.scilinks.org
KEYWORD: HK1502

▶ **telecommunication** a communication method that uses electromagnetic means

Figure 15-2

A speaker is a type of transducer, which is a device that converts a signal from one form to another. A speaker converts an incoming signal in the form of electricity into sound. After the conversion, the original sound is re-created. Two types of transducers, a speaker and a microphone, are shown in **Figure 15-2.** The microphone is a transducer that converts a sound signal into an electrical signal.

Telecommunication

Not long after the discovery of electric current, people tried to find ways of using electricity to send messages over long distances. In 1844, the first telegraph line provided a faster way to send messages between Baltimore and Washington, D.C. With this success, more telegraph lines were installed. By 1861, messages could be sent rapidly between the West Coast and the East Coast.

About 30 years after the first electric telegraph service was provided, the telephone was developed. In another 25 years, the wireless telegraph was invented. With wireless technology, a telegraph message could be sent by radio waves without the use of wires and cables. Sending and receiving signals by using electromagnetic means is referred to as **telecommunication.**

Transducer

Current
Time

A The sound waves are converted into an electrical signal by the microphone.

Transducer

B The signal travels in the form of an electric current through a wire.

C In the speaker, the signal is amplified and converted back into sound.

490 CHAPTER 15

DEMONSTRATION 1 TEACHING

Building a Communication System

Time: Approximately 30 minutes
Materials: string, paper clips, plastic cups with small holes in the bottom

Step 1 Putting holes in the bottom of the cups can be difficult with scissors. The easiest way is to use a large paper clip, a pair of pliers, and a Bunsen burner. Heat the paper clip and melt a small hole in the bottom of each cup.

Step 2 Divide the class into groups of 2–3 students per group. Give each group a long piece of string (10 ft) and a cup and a paper clip for each student.

Step 3 Have students make a communication system with these materials. To attach the string to the cup, students should thread the string through the hole in the bottom of the cup. The

Figure 15-3
This weight scale is an analog device. The spring inside the scale stretches continuously in proportion to the weight.

An analog signal varies continuously within a range

What do a thermometer, a speedometer, and a spring scale have in common? They are analog devices, which means that their readings change continuously as the quantity they are measuring—temperature, wheel rotation, or weight—changes. Readings given by each of these measuring devices are analog signals.

An example of an analog device is shown in **Figure 15-3.** As the weight on the scale increases, the needle moves in one direction. As the weight decreases, the needle moves in the opposite direction. The position of the needle on this scale can have any possible value between 0 lb and 20.0 lb (0 N and 89 N).

The audio signal from the microphone in **Figure 15-2** is an analog signal in the form of a changing electric current. Analog signals consisting of radio waves can be used to transmit picture, sound, and telephone messages.

Digital signals consist of separate bits of information

Unlike an analog signal, which can change continuously, a digital signal consists of only discrete, or fixed, values. The binary number system consists of two discrete values, 0 and 1. The combination for a lock, shown in **Figure 15-4,** is in a digital form. It is composed of discrete values, or digits, each of which can have one of six values—1, 2, 3, 4, 5, or 6.

A simple type of digital signal uses a flashing light. Sailors sometimes use a flashing *signal lamp* to send Morse code for ship-to-ship and ship-to-shore communication. Morse code, which was developed by Samuel Morse for transmitting information by telegraph, uses three "digits": a short interval between clicks, a long interval between clicks, and no click at all.

---

internet connect

SCI**LINKS**
NSTA

TOPIC: Analog/digital signals
GO TO: www.scilinks.org
KEYWORD: HK1503

▶ **analog signal** a signal corresponding to a quantity whose values can change continuously

▶ **digital signal** a signal that can be represented as a sequence of discrete values

Figure 15-4
The code to open this lock is in a digital form, consisting of a series of whole numbers.

COMMUNICATION TECHNOLOGY **491**

Teaching Tip

Digital Coding Morse code was among the first digital coding systems. This system of dots and dashes is similar to the 1's and 0's used in computers. Additional uses of digital signals are in video tape recording, computer information storage, and CD-ROMs. Bar codes in retail stores are also an example of digital systems. The black strips do not reflect light, while the white section between the bars does reflect light. When laser light hits the bar code, the light detectors see a pattern of light, no light, light, no light. The thickness of the bars and the number of the bars changes the pattern, identifying the merchandise to the computer.

Did You Know ?

A scanner used with a computer can digitize an image. It looks at every part of the picture, subdivides the picture into small squares, and assigns a number to each square. This number, or digit, represents the color and brightness of the image in the square.

---

string will stay connected to the cup better if the string is tied to the paper clip inside the cup; the paper clip will keep the knot in the string from pulling through the hole. Students can experiment with having only two cups on the string, or they can attach many cups by connecting multiple strings together at the center so that the strings form a star pattern.

Step 4 You can also have students experiment with different kinds of string, such as fishing line, twine, or guitar strings. Some strings will transmit vibrations better than others.

Signals and Telecommunication

|SKILL BUILDER

Interpreting Visuals **Figure 15-6** shows a CD and the pattern of pits on the CD. The pits etched on the CD surface are microscopically small, just one-thousandth of a millimeter wide. Each CD is marked by roughly 3 billion pits in a spiral track. The area between two pits is called a flat. The digital copy of the sound or any other type of data is etched on the CD in a pattern of pits and flats. **Figure 15-6** shows the playback mechanism of a CD player. The data are read by a laser beam. When the light hits the pit, light is dispersed and no light is reflected back to the detector. But when the light hits a flat, the light is reflected back to the detector. As the laser reads the pattern of pits and flats, the digital copy is converted back into analog signal, which is used to recreate the sound by the speakers.

RESOURCE LINK

IER

Assign students worksheet *15.8: Integrating Math—Converting Binary Numbers.*

LABORATORY MANUAL

Have students perform *Lab 15 Communication Technology: Transmitting and Receiving a Message Using a Binary Code* in the lab ancillary.

DATASHEETS

Have students use *Datasheet 15.5* to record their results from the lab.

Figure 15-5
The English alphabet can be represented by combinations of the binary digits 1 and 0.

Alphabetic Characters and Their Binary Codes							
A	01000001	H	01001000	O	01001111	V	01010110
B	01000010	I	01001001	P	01010000	W	01010111
C	01000011	J	01001010	Q	01010001	X	01011000
D	01000100	K	01001011	R	01010010	Y	01011001
E	01000101	L	01001100	S	01010011	Z	01011010
F	01000110	M	01001101	T	01010100		
G	01000111	N	01001110	U	01010101		

On (1) Off (0)　On (1) Off (0)　On (1) Off (0)

0 1 0 0 0 0 1 1　0 1 0 0 0 0 0 1　0 1 0 1 0 1 0 0

C　　**A**　　**T**

A binary digital signal consists of a series of zeros and ones

Most digital signals use *binary digital code*, which consists of two values, usually represented as 0 and 1. Each binary digit is called a *bit*. In electrical form, 0 and 1 are represented by the two states of an electric current: *off* (no current present) and *on* (current present). Information such as numbers, words, music, and pictures can be represented in binary code. **Figure 15-5** shows a binary digital code that is used to represent the English alphabet.

Most modern telecommunication systems transmit and store data in binary digital code. A compact disc (CD) player, shown in **Figure 15-6,** uses a laser beam to read the music that is digitally stored on the disc.

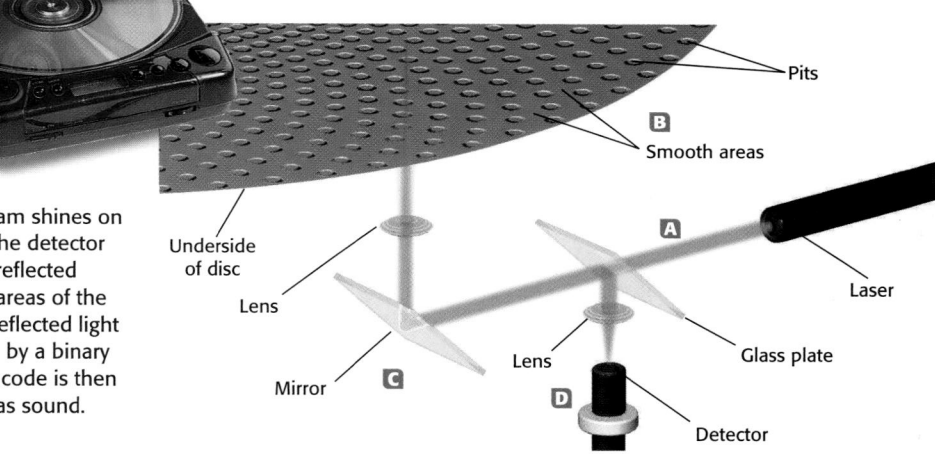

Figure 15-6
(A) A laser beam shines on the disc. (B) The detector receives light reflected from smooth areas of the disc. (C) The reflected light is represented by a binary code. (D) The code is then reinterpreted as sound.

Pits

Smooth areas

Underside of disc

Lens

Mirror

Lens

Laser

Glass plate

Detector

But how can sound be stored digitally? Sound is a wave of compressions (high air pressure) and rarefactions (low air pressure). Therefore, a sound can be described by noting the air pressure changes. The air pressure is measured in numbers and represented in binary digits.

How is the air pressure measured in numbers? This process is indirect. First, a microphone is used to convert the sound into an analog signal as a changing electric current. Then, an electronic device measures this changing current in numbers or digits at regular intervals. In fact, for CD sound recordings, the current is measured 44 100 times every second! The air pressure measurement is converted into binary digits in terms of 16 bits. For instance, 0000000010000010 is the digital representation of air pressure at a particular moment.

This conversion process is basically the same for creating digital signals from analog signals. Another device where this conversion occurs is in a digital telephone.

Digital signals can be sent quickly and accurately

Digital signals have many advantages over analog signals. Some digital "switches," consisting of electronic components, can be turned on and off up to a billion times per second. This allows a digital signal to send a lot of data in a small amount of time.

Noise and static have less effect on digital transmissions. Most digital signals include codes that constantly check the pattern of the received signal and correct any errors that may occur in the signal. By contrast, analog signals must be received, amplified, and retransmitted several times by components along the transmission route. Each time, the signal can get a little more distorted.

Telecommunication Today

Many telecommunication devices, such as telephones, transmit signals along metal wires. However, other ways are more efficient. Metal wires are being replaced with glass fibers that carry signals using pulses of light. Radio waves are also used to send signals. A call to another part of the world is likely to involve sending a signal by way of a communication satellite.

Optical fibers are more efficient than metal wires

A thin glass or plastic fiber, called an optical fiber, can be used to carry a beam of light. The light is reflected by the inside walls of the fiber, so it does not escape. Instead of carrying signals that are coded into electric currents, these fibers carry signals that are represented by pulses of light emitted by a laser.

▶ **optical fiber** a hair-thin, transparent strand of glass or plastic that transmits signals using pulses of light

Quick ACTIVITY

Examining Optical Fibers
SAFETY CAUTION
Wear goggles for this activity.
1. Carefully take apart a piece of fiber-optic cable.
2. Draw and label a diagram of what you find.
3. Point one end of a fiber toward a light source, and curve the fiber to the side.
4. Look at the other end. Does this show that light can move in a curved path? Explain.

Did You Know ?

Gasoline companies are beginning to distribute to their customers key chains with a small radio transmitter attached. This radio transmitter is as thick as a pencil and approximately 1 in. long. When placed near the gasoline pump, the computer in the pump receives the code being transmitted by the device and searches its files for the proper account. In this way, a credit card is not needed to purchase gasoline.

The same kind of technology is being used in states that require drivers to pay tolls on the highways. Drivers that frequently use toll highways can purchase a device that broadcasts a radio signal to the toll booths. When the car drives through a toll booth, the computer in the booth receives the signal, identifies the account number, and charges the account the proper amount. In this way, the driver does not need to stop and does not need to have money in the car at all times.

COMMUNICATION TECHNOLOGY **493**

Quick ACTIVITY

Examining Optical Fibers Optical fibers can be obtained by either purchasing them or asking for donations. You can write a local telecommunications company and ask for 10 to 20 ft of fiber, or you can ask a local university. The engineering department probably experiments with different types of optical fiber, and might donate some to your school.

You can try to look at the fiber through a microscope to view the sides clearly. It would be interesting to look at the end of the fiber with a microscope, but it is extremely difficult to see.

Signals and Telecommunication

Interpreting Visuals One advantage of using optical-fiber cable, shown in **Figure 15-7B,** in the telecommunication industry is that a light signal traveling through the cable loses very little energy. With standard electrical cable, shown in **Figure 15-7A,** an electrical signal loses energy as the signal travels. If the signal is being sent over a large distance, then signal repeaters are needed. Because light can travel farther without losing energy in an optical fiber, fewer repeaters are needed to boost the original signal.

Historical Perspective

Originally, telephone cables were strung from city to city, and from state to state. Eventually, people wanted to be able to call people who were in different countries. As a result, a telephone cable that would span the Atlantic Ocean was needed. The transatlantic cable, completed in July 1866, marked the beginning of rapid communication across the seas. The establishment of this cable is credited to Massachusetts merchant and financier Cyrus W. Field. He first proposed running the 2000 mi long copper cable from Newfoundland to Ireland in 1854. The first three attempts ended in broken cables, but eventually Field succeeded. Messages that would have taken weeks took hours to reach Europe. Cyrus Field was showered with honors and recognition for his accomplishment.

Figure 15-7
A single standard metal-wire cable (A) is much thicker than an optical-fiber cable (B), yet it carries much less information than an optical fiber does.

Many telephone lines now in use in the United States consist of optical fibers. The optical-fiber system is lighter and smaller than the wire-cable system, as shown in **Figure 15-7,** making it much easier to put in place. A standard metal-wire cable, which is about 7.6 cm in diameter, can carry up to 1000 coded conversations at one time. A single optical fiber can carry 11 000 conversations at once using the present coding system.

As the use of the Internet and telephones dramatically increases, telephone companies are busy expanding fiber-optic networks. The materials used to make the optical fibers are so pure that a half-mile-thick slab made from them would transmit as much light as a clean windowpane.

Figure 15-8
A microwave relay tower picks up a signal, amplifies it, and relays it to the next tower.

Relay systems make it possible to send messages across the world

If you've traveled around the United States, you may have noticed tall steel towers with triangular or cone-shaped boxes and perhaps some dish-shaped antennas. These are microwave relay towers. They use microwave frequencies to transmit and relay signals over land.

As shown in **Figure 15-8,** a tower picks up a signal transmitted by another tower, amplifies the signal, and retransmits it toward the next tower. The next tower repeats the process, passing the signal along until it reaches its destination. Microwave transmission is often used to connect distant places with telephone signals.

494 CHAPTER 15

Model of Radio Wave Transmission

Time: Approximately 15 minutes
Materials: large beach ball
      string
      plastic straws
      tape

Step 1 Cut a plastic straw in half and tape it to the beach ball so that it stands straight up.

Step 2 Tie or tape the end of a long piece of string to the end of the straw that is pointed away from the center of the beach ball. The beach ball represents the Earth, and the straw represents a transmission tower. The string represents the radio wave that is being transmitted by the tower.

Step 3 Pull the string so that it is straight. Notice that the straight string can reach only so far from

Microwaves are a form of electromagnetic waves. For the microwave signals to be sent from one tower to the next, each tower must be almost visible from the top of the other. A tower built high in the Rocky Mountains would be able to relay signals for 80 to 160 km. However, a tower built in the plains can relay only a little farther than the horizon, or about 40 km.

Communications satellites receive and transmit electromagnetic waves

Microwave transmission allows you to make telephone calls across deserts or other areas without wires or fiber-optic networks. But how could you call a friend who lives across the ocean in Australia?

In the past, your call would have been carried by one of the cables that run along the ocean floor between continents. Because there are so many telephones, online computers, and fax machines today, the demand is too much for these cables. Communication satellites that orbit Earth help send these messages.

These satellites use solar power to generate electricity. This allows them to operate receivers, transmitters, and antennas. These satellites receive and send microwaves just like the towers described earlier. Because they are so high above the ground, these satellites can relay signals between telephone exchanges thousands of kilometers apart.

A satellite receives a microwave signal, called an *uplink*, from a ground station on Earth. The satellite then processes and transmits a *downlink* signal to another ground station. To keep the signals separate, the uplink signal consists of electromagnetic waves with a frequency of around 6 GHz (gigahertz, or 10^9 Hz), while the downlink signal typically has a lower frequency of about 4 GHz.

For maximum efficiency, the transmitting antenna of a communications satellite must be aimed so that it covers the largest area of land without the signal becoming too weak. This area is called a *satellite footprint*. The satellite footprint increases as the distance between the satellite and Earth's surface increases. With several satellites with large footprints, a signal from one location can be transmitted and received anywhere in the world.

Many communications satellites have geostationary orbits

If you live in an area where people receive television signals from satellites by using dish-shaped antennas, you may have noticed that the dish always points in one direction. If a satellite orbits Earth, its position would change. Why does the dish not have to be moved in order to stay pointed at the orbiting satellite?

Teaching Tip

Satellites A satellite cannot stay in orbit around the Earth forever. The orbit of the satellite gradually degrades. This is because the Earth is not a perfectly smooth ball. The planet is inhomogeneous, which means that the gravitational force generated by the Earth can fluctuate slightly. As a result, satellites must have the ability to correct their orbit over time. They accomplish this by two methods: the satellites may have thrusters that can correct the orbit, or the satellite may require a visit from the space shuttle in order to correct its orbit. If it is cheaper, however, to construct and launch a new satellite, then the old satellite will be left alone. The old satellite's orbit will eventually degrade and the satellite will finally spiral into the Earth's atmosphere, burning up on re-entry.

the tower before the curvature of the Earth (beach ball) blocks the string. A radio tower can basically transmit only as far as the horizon. Similarly, if someone were on the opposite side of the Earth, he or she could not receive this radio signal.

Step 4 Add another transmission tower by taping another straw to the beach ball so that it stands straight out from the ball.

Step 5 Tie another string to that tower. As long as the towers can "see" each other, they can transmit a signal to one another. The signal is transmitted from the first tower to the second tower. The second tower then transmits the original signal, giving the original signal a greater transmission range. With multiple towers, it should be possible to transmit a signal completely around the Earth.

Signals and Telecommunication

SECTION 15.1 REVIEW

Check Your Understanding

1. telephone communication, television transmission, radio communication, satellite communication, fiber-optic communication
2. Telecommunication is when you communicate with someone over a large distance and by electronic means. While talking face to face does not fit this definition, talking on the telephone does.
3. Sound can be converted into an analog signal through the use of a microphone. Sound waves cause a diaphragm to vibrate, which also vibrates the voice coil. The vibrating voice coil generates an electrical current that vibrates in the same way that the sound wave does, converting it to an electrical analog signal.
4. **a.** digital
   b. analog
   c. digital
   d. analog
   e. digital
5. Optical-fiber cable can carry more telephone calls, can transmit signals over a greater distance, and lose less energy. Standard metal wires can do none of these.

Answers continue on p. 519A.

RESOURCE LINK
STUDY GUIDE

Assign students *Review Section 15.1 Signals and Telecommunication.*

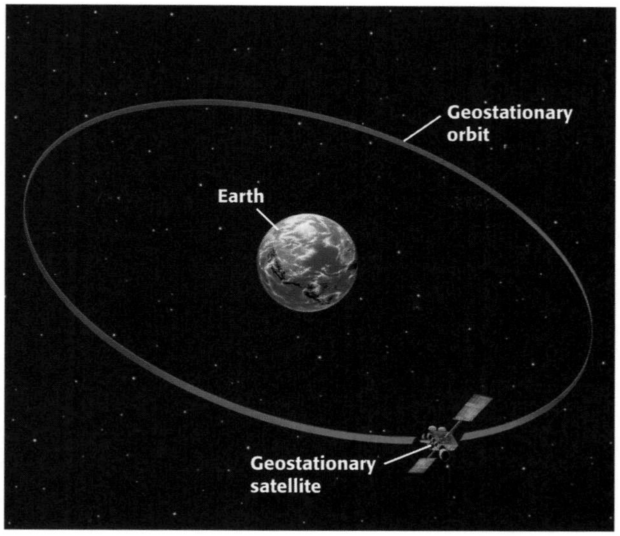

The answer is that these satellites orbit Earth every 24 hours, the same amount of time it takes for Earth to rotate once. Therefore the position of the satellite relative to the ground doesn't change. The orbit of this type of satellite is called a *geostationary orbit,* or a *geosynchronous orbit.* To be in a geostationary orbit, a satellite must be 35 880 km directly over Earth's equator and have a speed of 11 050 km/h, as shown in **Figure 15-9.**

Figure 15-9
A geostationary satellite appears to stay in a fixed position above the same spot on Earth. Once a dish is aimed at one of these satellites, it does not have to be moved again.

SECTION 15.1 REVIEW

SUMMARY

- A signal is a sign or event that conveys a message that can be sent using gestures, shapes, colors, electricity, or light.
- An analog signal varies continuously.
- A digital signal represents information in the form of discrete digits.
- A two-number code, called a binary digital code, represents the signal conditions of "on" or "off" by either a 1 or a 0.
- Telecommunication sends a signal long distances by means of electricity or light.
- Satellites are used to relay microwave signals around the world.

CHECK YOUR UNDERSTANDING

1. **List** five examples of telecommunication.
2. **Explain** why talking to your friend on the telephone is an example of telecommunication but talking to her face to face is not.
3. **Describe** how a sound is translated into an analog signal.
4. **Indicate** which of the following are analog signals and which are digital:
   a. music recorded on a compact disc
   b. speed displayed by the needle on a speedometer dial
   c. time displayed on a clock with three or four numerals
   d. time displayed on a clock with hands and a circular dial
   e. a motion picture on film
5. **Discuss** the advantages of optical fibers over metal wires as media for carrying signals.
6. **Explain** how communications satellites transmit messages around the world.
7. **Explain** what a geostationary orbit is and why many communications satellites are put in geostationary orbits.
8. **Critical Thinking** Explain why a taller microwave relay tower on Earth's surface has a longer transmission range than a shorter relay tower.

15.2

Telephone, Radio, and Television

OBJECTIVES

▶ Describe how a telephone converts sound waves to electric current during a phone call.
▶ Distinguish between physical transmission and atmospheric transmission for telephone, radio, and television signals.
▶ Explain how radio and television signals are broadcast using electromagnetic waves.
▶ Explain how radio and television signals are received and changed into sound and pictures.

▶ **KEY TERMS**

physical transmission
atmospheric transmission
modulate
carrier
cathode-ray tube
pixel

What sort of information do communication satellites relay around the world? Some information is vital business information, and some is secret government and military communication. Much of the information, however, consists of radio and television programming and telephone conversations.

Telephones

When you talk on the telephone, the sound waves of your voice are converted to an electrical signal by a transducer, a microphone in the mouthpiece of the telephone. As you hear the voice from the earpiece, a speaker, another transducer, is changing an electrical signal back into sound waves.

The electret microphone vibrates with sound waves, creating an analog signal

Most newer telephones use an *electret microphone*. In this type of microphone, an electrically charged membrane is mounted over an electret, which is a material that has a constant electric charge. The membrane vibrates up and down with the sound waves of your voice, as shown in **Figure 15-10.**

This motion causes a changing electric field so that an analog electrical signal that corresponds to your voice is produced. This signal is then transmitted as variations in an electric current between your telephone and that of the person you are talking to.

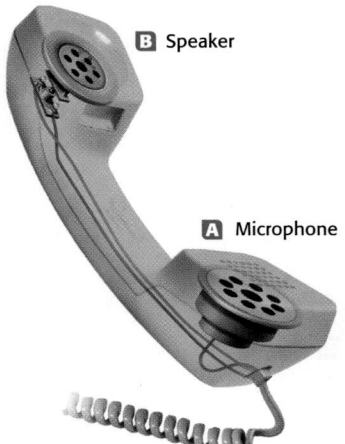

B Speaker

A Microphone

Figure 15-10
The sound waves from your voice are transformed by the microphone (A) into an analog electrical signal. A speaker (B) converts the analog electrical signal back to sound waves.

COMMUNICATION TECHNOLOGY **497**

Section 15.2

Telephone, Radio, and Television

Scheduling
Refer to pp. 486A–486D for lecture, classwork, and assignment options for Section 15.2.

★ **Lesson Focus**
Use transparency *LT 50* to prepare students for this section.

Teaching Tip

Electret Membranes Electret microphones use a membrane that is 1 μm (0.000 001 m) thick. These membranes can also be used as particle detectors, primarily for detecting radioactive alpha particles and radioactive radon gas.
   When these small particles hit the membrane, they alter the total charge. Detectors near the membrane can measure this change in charge and identify the captured particles.
   In addition, these membranes are excellent for filtering very small particles out of the air.

Did You Know ?

   Modems were developed to allow computers to communicate with each other. Originally, the first modems converted the digital signals in the computer into analog sound waves, to be transmitted through the phone lines. Later it was found that digital signals worked better than analog signals. As a result, modems today convert the digital electrical signals in the computer into digital sound waves.

Telephone, Radio, and Television

INTEGRATING

BIOLOGY The nervous system extends throughout the body. Sometimes a person can become injured and lose feeling in a part of his or her body. This loss of feeling may be the result of nerve cells being damaged or torn. Damaged nerve cells break the pathway for the nerve impulses. This is similar to breaking a wire in an electrical circuit, which interrupts the electrical current.

Resources Assign students worksheet *15.2: Integrating Biology—The Brain's Signals* in the **Integration Enrichment Resources** ancillary.

Historical Perspective

Before the development of automatic switches, operators had to connect a call to the next circuit manually so that the call would be routed to its final destination. This would increase the time it took to have a call connected and increase the number of wrong phone connections.

INTEGRATING

BIOLOGY
Biologists have discovered that information is transmitted through the human body by the nervous system. The nervous system contains billions of nerve cells that form bundles of cordlike fibers. Nerve signals, known as *impulses,* can travel along nerve fibers at speeds ranging from about 1 m/s to 90 m/s. Nerve signals are relayed through the body by a combination of electrical and chemical processes.

▶ **physical transmission** a transmission of a signal using wires, cables, or optical fibers

▶ **atmospheric transmission** a transmission of a signal using electromagnetic waves

The movement of the speaker cone converts the analog signal back into sound waves

When you get a telephone call, the electrical signal enters your telephone. As you listen, the incoming electrical signal travels through a coil of wire that is fastened to a thin membrane called a *speaker cone.*

The wire coil is placed in a constant magnetic field and can move back and forth. The varying electric current of the incoming signal creates a varying magnetic field that interacts with the constant magnetic field. This causes the coil to move back and forth, which in turn causes the speaker cone to move in the same way. The movement of the speaker cone creates sound waves in the air that match the sound of your caller's voice. Speakers in radios, televisions, and stereo systems work the same way.

Telephone messages are sent through a medium in physical transmission

Telephone messages can be voice calls, faxes, or computer data. But how do the messages arrive at the right place? When you make a call, the signal is sent along wires to a local station. Telephone wires arrive at and leave the station in bundles called cables that are strung along poles or run underground. The station's switching equipment detects the number called.

If you are calling someone who lives nearby, such as a neighbor, the switching equipment sends the signal down wires that connect your phone through the station to your neighbor's phone. When the signal reaches your neighbor's phone, the phone rings. When your neighbor picks up the phone, the circuit is completed.

Sometimes telephone conversations travel a short distance by wire and then are carried by light through fiber optic cables. In this case, the varying current is fed to a laser diode, causing its laser light to brighten and dim. In this way, the electrical signal is converted into a light or optical signal. This light passes through an optical fiber to its destination, where a sensor changes light back to an electrical signal. Transmission of signals by wires or optical fibers is called **physical transmission.**

Messages traveling longer distances are sent by atmospheric transmission

Long-distance calls may be transmitted over wire or fiber-optic cables, or they may be sent through the atmosphere using microwave radiation. The transfer of information by means of electromagnetic waves through the atmosphere or space is called **atmospheric transmission.** The use of microwaves for telephone signals is one example of atmospheric transmission.

DEMONSTRATION 3 SCIENCE AND THE CONSUMER

Fiber Optics Cable

Time: Approximately 15 minutes
Materials: laser
demonstration optical-fiber cable
blank white paper

Step 1 Borrow a helium neon laser and a thick demonstration optical-fiber cable (in the shape of a spiral) from the physics department. Show the optical fiber to students, and explain that this one

is thick so that it can be easily seen by students in a classroom. The actual size of a piece of optical cable is approximately the same thickness as a human hair.

Step 2 Shine the laser beam into one end of the cable and let students gather around so that they can see the beam bouncing inside the cable. Project the light that is coming out of the end of the

Most broadcast carrier waves are modulated either by *amplitude modulation* (AM) or *frequency modulation* (FM). In amplitude modulation, the audio signal increases and decreases the amplitude of the carrier wave in a pattern that matches the audio signal. In frequency modulation, the audio signal affects

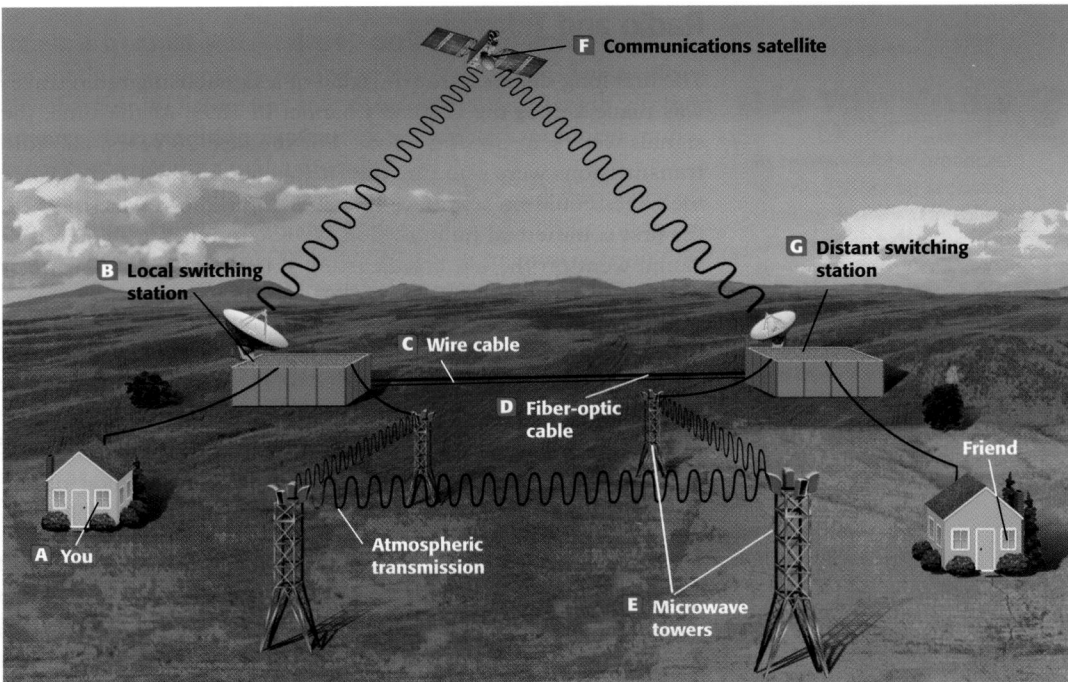

When you make a call, computers are used to find the most direct form of routing. Either physical or atmospheric transmission or a combination of the two may be used for long-distance calls, as shown in **Figure 15-11.** If the telephone system is very busy, computers may route your call indirectly through a combination of cables and microwave links. Your call to someone 100 mi away could actually travel for thousands of miles.

Cellular phones transmit messages in the form of electromagnetic waves

A cellular phone is just a small radio transmitter/receiver, or *transceiver*. Cellular phones communicate with one of an array of antennas mounted on towers or tall buildings. The area covered by each antenna is called a *cell*.

As the user moves from one cell to another, the phone switches to communicate with the next antenna. The user may not even notice the switching. As long as the telephone is not too far from a cellular antenna, the user can make and receive calls.

A cordless phone is also a radiowave transceiver. The phone sends signals to and receives signals from its base station, which is also a transceiver. The base station is connected to a standard phone line.

Figure 15-11
Your telephone call (A) arrives at a local switching station (B). Depending on its destination, the call is routed through a wire cable (C), fiber-optic cable (D), microwave towers (E), or communication satellites (F). The telephone signal then arrives at another switching station (G) where it travels to your friend's house, and the phone rings.

COMMUNICATION TECHNOLOGY **499**

Section 15.2

Telephone, Radio, and Television

|SKILL BUILDER

Graphing Below is a table of data that shows the total number of people using cellular phones in each year. Have students graph the data. What conclusions can you draw from the graph?

Year	# of cell phone users
1985	340 213
1986	681 825
1987	1 230 855
1988	2 069 441
1989	3 508 944
1990	5 283 055
1991	7 557 148
1992	11 032 753
1993	16 009 461
1994	24 134 421
1995	33 785 661
1996	44 042 992
1997	55 312 293
1998	69 209 321

Additional Application

Cellular Technology Have students research the development and history of the cellular telephone. Have the students create a timeline that describes the chronological history of cellular technology.

cable onto a piece of white paper, so that they can see that the light is being transmitted.

Most optical-fiber cables have three parts: the core, the cladding, and the outer coating. The core is where the light travels through the optical-fiber cable. It is located at the very center of the cable. Outside of the core is the cladding. The cladding keeps the light rays reflecting inside the core. Be-

cause of the optical properties of the cladding, when the light hits the boundary between the core and the cladding, the beam of light is reflected back into the core and keeps traveling through the fiber. Outside of the cladding is the outer coating. This is a plastic coating that increases the strength of, and protects, the cladding and the core.

Telephone, Radio, and Television

Did You Know ?

Satellite dishes are becoming more common in our society. However, their operation is not well understood by most people. The large curved dish is called the reflector dish, and the part that sticks out of the center of the dish is the antenna. Electromagnetic (EM) waves are emitted from a satellite that is in orbit. When these waves hit the dish, they are reflected to the antenna. The EM waves generate an electrical signal. The electrical signal then goes into your house via a cable and is amplified by an amplifier. This amplified signal is then sent to your television.

Teaching Tip

Television Sets A television works by the firing of a beam of electrons at the screen. The screen glows where the beam of electrons hits. The electrons are guided by strong electric and magnetic fields so that the beam of electrons spreads across the screen, recreating the image that is contained in the video signal.

The television signal that is broadcast to your TV tells the set how to change the electric and magnetic fields. A magnet placed near a TV screen will cause the electron beam to be deflected and will change the color on the screen. Do not leave magnets near the television set because they can damage it with permanent distortion.

Figure 15-13
After the detector removes the audio signal from the carrier, the signal is amplified and sent to a speaker. (Note that the amplifiers and detector shown as boxes correspond to different circuits that are part of the radio.)

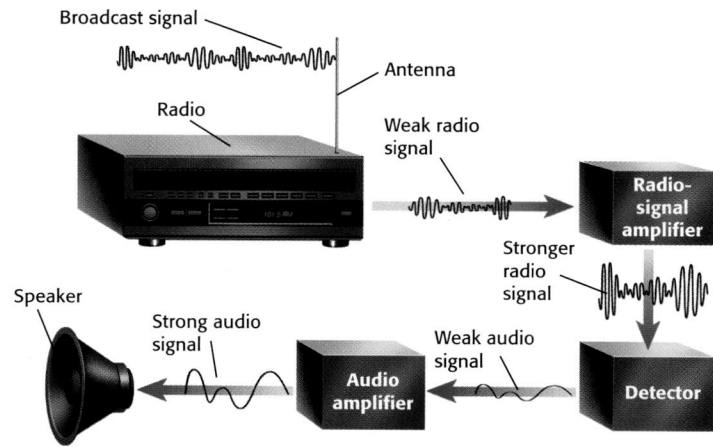

Next the modulated signal from the antenna is sent to a detector, as shown in **Figure 15-13.** The carrier wave has a very high frequency compared with the original electrical signal, so the two can be separated easily. The electrical signal then goes to an amplifier, which increases the signal's power. Finally, the amplified signal is sent to a speaker, where the sound that was originally broadcast is recreated.

Television sets convert electromagnetic waves back into images and sound

Television signals are also received by an antenna. By selecting a channel, you tune the television to the carrier frequency of the station of your choice. The carrier is passed to a detector that separates the audio and video electrical signals from the carrier. The audio electrical signals are sent to an audio amplifier and speaker, just as in a radio. The video electrical signal, which contains the color and brightness information, is used to create an image on the face of a picture tube.

The picture tube of a black-and-white television is a large **cathode-ray tube**, or CRT. A CRT makes a beam (ray) of electrons from a negatively charged cathode. The beam is directed toward the face of the tube that is covered with *phosphors*, which are made of a material that glows when an electron beam strikes them. Electromagnets arranged around the neck of the tube deflect the beam, causing it to move across the phosphor-coated face. The moving beam lights up the phosphors in a pattern that recreates the shot taken by the television camera. Each pass of the beam is called a *scan line*. In the United States, each complete image is made up of 525 scan lines.

internet connect

SC*LINKS*

NSTA

TOPIC: Television
GO TO: www.scilinks.org
KEYWORD: HK1505

▶ **cathode-ray tube** a tube that uses an electron beam to create a display on a phosphorescent screen

ALTERNATIVE ASSESSMENT

Deflecting Electron Beams

Borrow an oscilloscope or CRT from the physics department. Turn on the oscilloscope or CRT and position the screen so that students can easily see it.

These devices work just like televisions. A beam of electrons is fired at the screen from inside the device. Magnetic and electric fields deflect the beam to form the different images on the screen.

Place a magnet near the screen. This should have the effect of distorting the image seen on the screen. It may also be possible to distort the image with a strong electric field. Charge a piece of PVC pipe by rubbing it with a piece of wool. Depending on the strength of the electron beam, this may also deflect the beam and distort the image.

ring stand
test-tube clamp

Step 1 Fill the flask with water and put a little salt into the water. The salt makes it possible to see the laser beam when it is inside the water.

beam should emerge from the other side of the flask without too much distortion.

When you have the correct salt concentration, attach the flask to a tall ring stand with a test-tube clamp.

Color picture tubes in some televisions, like the one shown in **Figure 15-14,** produce three electron beams, one for each of the primary colors of light: red, blue, and green. The phosphors on the face of the tube glow either red, blue, or green. The phosphors are arranged in groups of three dots, one of each color. Each group of three dots is a **pixel,** the smallest piece of an electronically produced picture.

To make sure the beam for red strikes only red phosphors, two different approaches can be used. In one, a screen with holes, called a *shadow mask*, lies just behind the face of the tube. The beam for each color passes through a hole in the shadow mask at an angle so that the beam strikes only the phosphor dot that glows the correct color. Another approach in some televisions use a single electron beam deflected toward the phosphor of the correct color by a charged wire grid.

▶ **pixel** the smallest element of a display image

VOCABULARY *Skills Tip*

The term pixel *is derived from the phrase* **pix**ture **el**ement

Telephone, Radio, and Television

|SKILL BUILDER

Interpreting Diagrams
Figure 15-14 illustrates the path of a video signal from an electromagnetic wave to an image on a television screen.

Resources Teaching Transparency 47 shows this visual.

Teaching Tip

Computer Scanners A computer scanner operates in a manner similar to a television set. It scans the entire image and breaks it up into individual pixels. It then identifies the color and brightness of each pixel and digitally records the location of the pixel and the color and brightness of the pixel. When it re-forms the image on the screen, the series of small colored dots that are generated on the screen form a continuous image to our eyes.

Figure 15-14

A The video signals modulating the television carrier are detected and are then used to control the electron beams in the cathode-ray tube. The sound signal is amplified and sent to a speaker, while video signals vary the intensity of the three electron beams.

B Electromagnets sweep the beams across the face of the screen. The intensity of each beam determines how bright the phosphor dots light up.

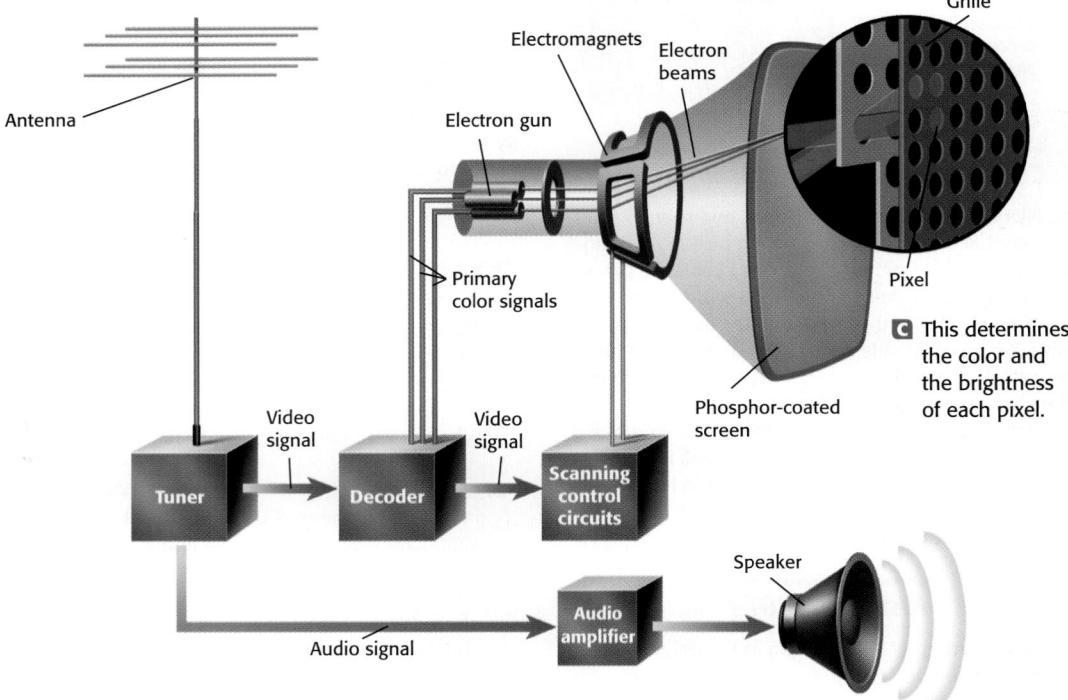

Antenna
Electromagnets
Electron beams
Electron gun
Grille
Primary color signals
Pixel
Video signal
Video signal
Phosphor-coated screen
Tuner
Decoder
Scanning control circuits
C This determines the color and the brightness of each pixel.
Speaker
Audio signal
Audio amplifier

COMMUNICATION TECHNOLOGY **503**

Telephone, Radio, and Television

Science and the Consumer

TV by the Numbers: High-Definition Digital TV
High Definition Television (HDTV) represents a radical change in the television industry. This new format will require broadcasters to transmit their television signals in a different way. This is because the number of scan lines and the number of pixels are increased to create sharper images. In addition to increased video picture quality, the HDTV systems will also incorporate six audio channels for surround sound systems. This further changes the requirements for broadcasting companies to implement this technology in their businesses.

Consumers are not yet willing to purchase HDTVs because HDTVs are currently extremely expensive, and there are not enough shows in the HDTV format to make them a worthwhile purchase.

Your Choice
1. Accept all reasonable answers.
2. Have students search the Internet or call an electronics store in the area to determine the current cost of an HDTV. The cost of VCRs dropped by 76% in the 5 years after their introduction. To project the cost of an HDTV in 5 years, calculate 76% of the current cost of an HDTV, and subtract that value from the current cost of an HDTV.

Resources Assign students worksheet *15.3: Science and the Consumer—HDTV: Why Make the Switch?* in the **Integration Enrichment Resources** ancillary.

504

TV by the Numbers: High-Definition Digital TV

When you turn on a television in the year 2006, it may look a lot different than the one you watch now. That's because the Federal Communications Commission (FCC) has decided that all television stations in the United States must broadcast only digital, high-definition television, called HDTV for short, by 2006.

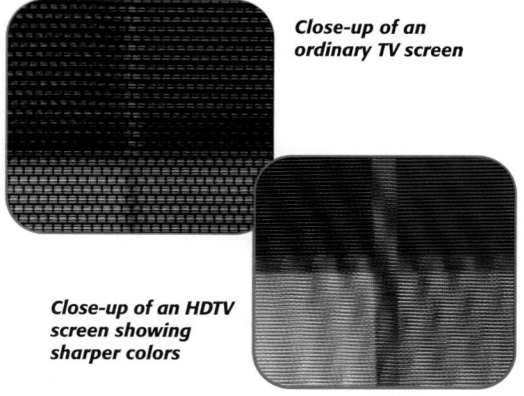

Close-up of an ordinary TV screen

Close-up of an HDTV screen showing sharper colors

Comparing HDTV with Ordinary TV

The HDTV picture looks very detailed and sharp compared with an ordinary television picture. You can even see the faces of fans at a sports event. The picture has a width-to-height ratio of 16:9, similar to many movies that you see in a theater. By 2006, you may have a TV with a large flat screen that hangs on the wall like a painting or mirror. HDTV sound is clear, digital sound, like that recorded on a CD.

However, you won't have to throw out your old television set in 2006. A converter box will let your old TV show pictures that are broadcast in HDTV. However, the picture won't look any better than if it is a regular broadcast.

History of HDTV

The development of HDTV began in the early 1980s when engineers realized that newer microprocessors

would be able to both send and decode data fast enough to transmit a detailed television picture digitally. In 1988, 23 different HDTV systems were proposed to the FCC. In 1993, several companies joined the Massachusetts Institute of Technology in what was called the Grand Alliance. Its purpose was to create HDTV standards for broadcasters. In 1996, the FCC approved an entirely digital system, and by late 1998, the first commercial HDTV receivers were on sale at prices between $10 000 and $20 000.

HDTV Technology

HDTV achieves its sharp picture by using almost 1200 scan lines, compared with 525 on analog TV. The digital signal can also be continuously checked for accuracy, so the picture remains clear.

The movie industry is very interested in HDTV. It will be able to release new HDTV tapes and discs of movies already released on other video formats. Another possibility is that some movies can be released to pay-per-view HDTV at the same time they are released in theaters. The HDTV picture and sound quality should be so good that some people may prefer to stay at home to watch a new movie.

Your Choice

1. **Making Decisions** What effect do you think HDTV will have on movie theaters, especially if studios make movies available on HDTV for the same price as a theater ticket? Explain whether you think people will still want to go to theaters.
2. **Critical Thinking** When home VCRs were introduced in the mid-1970s, they cost about $2500. By 1980, the price was about $600. By 1985, the price was about $450. By the mid-1990s, you could buy a good-quality VCR for about $250. Check the current price of an HDTV, and use the VCR example to project what one will cost in 5 years.

Inquiry Lab

How do red, blue, and green TV phosphors produce other colors?

Materials
- ✔ three adjustable flashlights with bright halogen bulbs
- ✔ several pieces of red, blue, and green cellophane
- ✔ white paper

Procedure

1. Adjust the focus of each flashlight so that it produces a circle of light about 15 cm in diameter on a white sheet of paper. Turn off the flashlights.
2. Place a piece of red cellophane over the lens of one flashlight, green cellophane over the lens of another, and blue over the lens of the third.
3. Turn on the flashlights, and shine the three beams on white paper so the circles of light overlap slightly.
4. Adjust the distance between the flashlights and the paper until the area where all three circles overlap appears white. Add more cellophane if necessary.

Analysis

1. Describe the three colors formed where two of the beams overlap.
2. What combinations of light produced the colors yellow and cyan?

SECTION 15.2 REVIEW

SUMMARY

▶ Telephones change sound to electrical signals and electrical signals to sound.

▶ Signals can be sent by physical transmission or by atmospheric transmission.

▶ Signals modulate carrier waves by amplitude modulation (AM) and frequency modulation (FM).

CHECK YOUR UNDERSTANDING

1. **Describe** how telephones convert sound to electrical signals and electrical signals to sound.
2. **List** three ways that telephone signals can travel.
3. **Identify** which have a higher frequency—AM or FM signals.
4. **Describe** the function of phosphors in a cathode-ray tube.
5. **Explain** the function of the magnetic coils at the rear of a television picture tube.
6. **Describe** how a radio receiver converts a broadcast signal into sound waves.
7. **Critical Thinking** Why do you think there is increasing interest in using fiber-optic cables to provide homes with cable television service?

COMMUNICATION TECHNOLOGY **505**

Inquiry Lab

How do red, blue, and green TV phosphors produce other colors? Color filters can be purchased inexpensively at theatrical supply stores. You want to choose primary red, primary green, and primary blue. These will give the best color mixing.

In addition, you can also purchase colored flood lights from a hardware store. You can then project these three lights onto the over- head projector screen and the screen will appear white. If you separate the lights by approximately 1 m and then shine the light onto the projector screen, you will get interesting shadowing effects. Have a student stand in front of these lights, and you will see six different-colored shadows. Each shadow is the mixture of two different colors.

Section 15.2

Telephone, Radio, and Television

SECTION 15.2 REVIEW

Check Your Understanding

1. Sound waves cause a thin membrane in the microphone in the mouthpiece of a telephone to vibrate. This membrane is attached to an electronic component that generates an electrical current. The electrical signal is then transmitted through the telephone lines to its destination. The process works in the reverse in the speaker to change the electrical signal back into sound.
2. Telephone signals can travel through conventional cable wires, through optical-fiber cable, and through orbiting satellites.
3. FM radio waves have higher frequencies than AM radio waves.
4. The purpose of phosphors in a cathode-ray tube is to glow when struck by the electron beam.
5. Magnetic coils in the back of televisions are used to steer the electron beam towards the TV screen.

Answers continue on p. 519A.

RESOURCE LINK
DATASHEETS

Have students use *Datasheet 15.2 Inquiry Lab: How do red, blue, and green TV phosphors produce other colors?* to record their results.

STUDY GUIDE

Assign students *Review Section 15.2 Telephone, Radio, and Television.*

505

15.3

Computers and the Internet

INTEGRATING TECHNOLOGY and Society

▶ **KEY TERMS**
computer
random-access memory
read-only memory
hardware
software
operating system
Internet

▶ computer an electronic device that can accept data and instructions, follow the instructions, and output the results

OBJECTIVES

▶ Describe a computer, and list its four basic functions.
▶ Describe the binary nature of computer data and the use of logic gates.
▶ Distinguish between hardware and software, and give examples of each.
▶ Explain how the Internet works.

Did you heat a pastry in the microwave for breakfast? Have you ever inserted a card in a slot to pay your fare on a bus or subway? Maybe you rode to school in a car. Did you stop for a traffic light? Was the temperature in your classroom comfortable? Did a clerk scan a bar code on an item you bought at the store?

All of these situations involve computers or the use of computers to function. The computer that controls traffic lights may be large and complex, while the one in the microwave oven is likely to be small and simple.

Figure 15-15
ENIAC, the world's first practical digital computer, used 18 000 vacuum tubes, like the one shown here. The modern microprocessor has thousands of times ENIAC's computing power.

Computers

A **computer** is a machine that can receive data, perform high-speed calculations or logical operations, and output the results. Although computers operate automatically, they do only what they are programmed to do. Computers respond to commands that humans give them, even though they sometimes may appear to "think" on their own.

Computers have been changing greatly since the 1940s

The first electronic computer was the Electronic Numerical Integrator And Computer (ENIAC), shown in **Figure 15-15.** It was developed during World War II. ENIAC was as big as a house and weighed 30 tons. Its 18 000 vacuum tubes consumed 180 000 W of electric power. During the late 1940s, computers began to be used in business and industry. As they became smaller, faster, and cheaper, their use in offices and homes dramatically increased.

506 CHAPTER 15

Today computers are so common that we hardly notice them. Try to imagine what computer developers in the 1940s would think if they could see a modern personal computer, or PC, which fits on a desk and computes thousands of times faster than the earlier cumbersome computers like ENIAC.

Computers carry out four functions

Digital computers perform four basic functions: input, storage, processing, and output. The input function can be carried out using any number of devices, as shown in **Figure 15-16.** When you use a personal computer, you can use a keyboard to input data and instructions for the computer. A mouse is another input device. You may use a mouse to draw or select text in a document.

Other input devices include a scanner, which can enter drawings or photographs, and a joystick, which sends data about the movement of the stick. A modem connected to a telephone line can be both an output and an input device.

Microphones, musical instruments, and cameras can be used as input devices. Once the data are processed, the result, or output, may be displayed on a monitor. You can also send output to a printer. Sound output goes to speakers or to a recording device.

Figure 15-16
A computer can receive data from many devices, store information on a hard drive, process data as needed, and store results or send them to an output device.

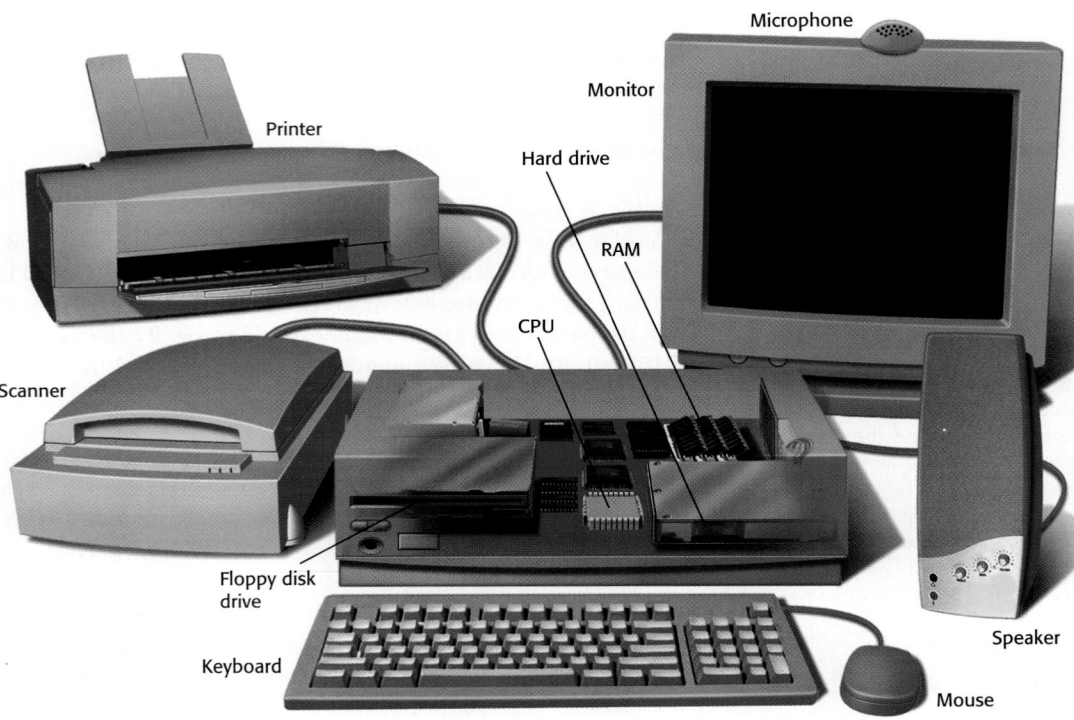

Did You Know?

Computer engineers have developed computer interface cards that allow musicians to play music into the computer. These cards allow a musical keyboard to communicate directly with the computer. A musician can play music on the keyboard, and the computer will not only record the music and play it back, but will also write out the notes with musical symbols in standard five-staff notation. This music can then be printed out for other musicians to use. In addition, the computer can be used to mix different sounds together and to add special effects. This makes it possible to have a basic recording studio in the home.

Additional Application

Digital Images Computers have not only integrated musical sounds but also color images. The recent advances in image capturing and image enhancing have made it affordable for people to design and print graphics on their computers. Scanners scan the image, and photo enhancement programs make it possible to touch up the image. This software makes it possible to alter images in many different ways. Digital cameras make it possible to capture images and copy them directly into the computer for printing or enhancement. Video capture cards make it possible to capture video images and store them on a computer or CD-ROM.

COMMUNICATION TECHNOLOGY **507**

Computers and the Internet

INTEGRATING

PHYSICS Electricity is used in the current generation of analog and digital computers to activate circuits and resistors. The next generation is expected to be optical computers. The optical computer will use light instead of electricity as an energy source.

Resources Assign students worksheet *15.4: Integrating Physics—Building a Computer* in the **Integration Enrichment Resources** ancillary.

Historical Perspective

Initially, inputting data on a computer was a difficult task. A popular method in the 1970s was batch-card processing. This method used computer cards with holes punched in them for the computer to read. Programmers would type a command into a batch console. The console would punch holes into the cards, and each card represented only one command. Large programs might have 10 000 cards. When the card entered the computer, it would pass between a light source and a light detector. The computer "read" the holes by measuring the light that passed through the holes to the detector.

RESOURCE LINK
DATASHEETS

Have students use *Datasheet 15.3 Quick Activity: How Fast Are Digital Computers?* to record their results.

508

Quick ACTIVITY

How Fast Are Digital Computers?

1. With a partner, time how long it takes for each of you to solve problems involving adding, subtracting, multiplying, and dividing large numbers. Do each problem first by hand and then with the help of a hand-held calculator, which is a form of digital computer. Solve at least five problems using each method.

2. Find the average amount of time spent doing the problems by hand and with a calculator. Compare the two averages, and discuss your results.

VOCABULARY Skills Tip

Most disks used for computer work today are not actually floppy. The name floppy disk *originally referred to a larger-sized disk that was encased in softer plastic sleeves.*

INTEGRATING

PHYSICS
All PCs are digital computers, but analog computers also exist. An example of an analog computer in a car is the gasoline gauge, whose needle moves in response to a voltage sent from a sensor in the gas tank.

Computer input is in the form of binary code

All input devices provide data to the computer in the form of binary code. For example, a keyboard contains a small processor that detects which key is pressed and sends the computer a binary code that represents the character you typed. Devices such as temperature sensors, pressure sensors, and light sensors provide information in the form of varying voltage. This information is analog; that is, it changes continuously over the range of the quantity being measured. Such information must be passed through an analog-to-digital converter (A to D converter) before the data can be used by a computer.

Computers process binary data, including numbers, letters, and other symbols, in groups of eight *bits*. Each bit can have only one of two values, usually represented as 1 and 0. A group of eight bits is called a *byte*.

As shown in **Figure 15-5,** when you type the capital letter *W* on the keyboard, the computer receives the data byte 01010111. Similarly, the lowercase letter *e* is received as 01100101. Thus, if you type the word *We*, the computer would recognize the word as 0101011101100101, a combination of the *W* byte and the *e* byte in sequence.

Computers must have a means of storing data

Both input and output data can be stored on long-term storage devices. The most common of these devices is the *hard-disk drive*, which is sometimes simply called the hard drive. Some hard drives can store as much or more than 20 billion bytes, or 20 gigabytes (20 Gigs) of information. Hard drives are so-called to distinguish them from disk drives that use removable "floppy" disks. Floppy disks can be removed from one computer and used in another.

Quick ACTIVITY

How Fast Are Digital Computers? Some calculators show the entire calculation on their screens, rather than just the answer. As a result, you may find a difference in the calculation speed depending upon the type of calculator being used. Compare these calculator speed variances to an average computer, which can do millions of calculations per second.

Figure 15-17
The head of the hard drive moves over the surface of the disk, reading and recording data in narrow tracks.

Disk coated with magnetizable substance

Read-write head

Both hard drives and floppy drives use disks coated with a magnetizable substance. Disks of this type are generally referred to as *magnetic media*. A small read-write head, similar to the record-play head in a cassette tape recorder, transfers data to and from the disk, as shown in **Figure 15-17.** Each data bit consists of a very small area that is magnetized in one direction for 0 and in the opposite direction for 1. These magnetized areas are arranged in tracks around the disk.

When data are being read, the disk spins and the head detects the magnetic direction of each area that passes. When data are being recorded, or "written" on the disk, a current passes through a small coil of wire in the head. The direction of the current at any time creates a magnetic field in one direction or the other. This allows the head to record information on the disks in bits of 0's and 1's.

On a disk, the time required to access (read or write) data depends on where the information is stored on the disk and the position of the read-write head. Therefore, access time for two different pieces of data on a disk will be different.

Random-access memory is used for short-term storage of data and instructions

For working memory, the computer needs to be able to access data quickly. This type of memory is contained on microchips as shown in **Figure 15-18** and is called **random-access memory,** or RAM.

Each RAM microchip is covered with millions of tiny transistors. Like a light switch, each transistor can be placed in one of two electrical states: *on* or *off*. Each transistor represents either a 0 or a 1 and can therefore store one data bit. This memory is called random-access because any of the data stored in RAM can be accessed in the same time. Unlike the data stored on the disk, accessing information in RAM doesn't depend on location.

▶ **random-access memory**
a storage device that allows stored data to be read in the same access time

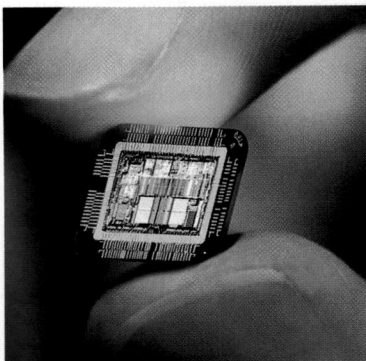

Figure 15-18
This chip is covered with tiny transistors that function as two-position switches. This feature allows the computer to operate as a binary machine.

COMMUNICATION TECHNOLOGY **509**

Additional Application

Data Security Many businesses store their vital business information on computers. This information could be payroll and bookkeeping information, product information, or customer lists. It is important that this information is kept safe for a business. There are a variety of ways to ensure data security. The most common is the magnetic tape cassette. A magnetic tape drive can be installed into a computer, and a copy of all the information can be saved onto a magnetic cassette tape. In the event that the hard disk fails, the data will be backed up onto the magnetic tape. For large amounts of information that is mission critical, hard disk RAID array systems are used. RAID stands for Redundant Array of Independent Disks. Multiple identical hard drives are installed into a computer. As information is written onto a hard disk, a copy is made and stored on the other redundant disks. In this way, if one hard disk fails, the other disks have copies of the information. Some RAID systems use what are called hot swappable drives. "Hot swappable" means that the hard disk can be removed, and a new hard disk can be installed without ever turning off the computer.

Computers and the Internet

Teaching Tip

Artificial Intelligence Some computer programs have the ability to "learn" from past experience in order to make better decisions. These types of systems are called Artificial Intelligence systems, or AI for short. Recently, the first AI computer beat the best human chess player in a game of chess. The computer was always defeated in the past, but because the AI system was able to "learn," it was able to defeat the human player.

▶ **read-only memory** a memory device containing data that cannot be changed

▶ **hardware** the equipment that makes up a computer system

▶ **software** the instructions, data, and programming that make a computer system work

▶ **operating system** the software that controls a computer's activities

Figure 15-19
The motherboard is the nervous system of a computer and contains the CPU, memory chips, and logic circuits.

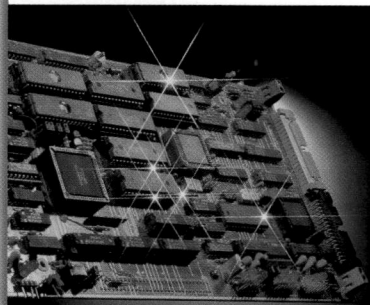

Read-only memory is for long-term storage of operating instructions

Another type of memory is called **read-only memory,** or ROM. The information in ROM is permanently stored when the chip is manufactured. As a result, it can be read but not changed. When you first turn on a computer, instructions that are stored in ROM set up the computer so that it is ready to receive input data from the keyboard or the hard drive.

Optical storage devices can be more permanent than magnetic disks

Information can also be stored on *compact discs* (CDs) and *digital versatile discs* (DVDs). These discs are called optical media because the information in it is read by a laser light. When they are used to store computer data, they are referred to as CD-ROMs and DVD-ROMs because the data they hold are permanently recorded on them.

Computers are guided by programs

All of the physical components of a computer are called **hardware.** The hardware of the computer can compute and store data only if we provide it with the necessary instructions. These instructions are called computer programs, or **software.**

When a computer is turned on, one of the first programs executed by the computer is the **operating system,** or OS. The OS controls the computer hardware—memory, keyboard, disks, printer, mouse, and monitor—so they work together. It also handles the transfer of computer files to and from disks and organizes the files.

The operating system provides the environment in which other computer programs run. These other programs are called applications. Applications include word processors, drawing programs, spreadsheet programs, and programs to organize and manipulate large amounts of information, such as a store's inventory or polling data. Applications also include computer games and programs that allow you to browse the Internet.

The processing function is the primary operation of a computer

The processing function is where computing actually takes place. Computing or data processing is carried out by the *central processing unit*, or CPU. The CPU of a personal computer usually consists of one microchip, which is not much larger than a postage stamp. The CPU is one of the many chips located on the motherboard, as shown in **Figure 15-19.**

This chip, or microprocessor, consists of millions of tiny electronic parts, including resistors, capacitors, diodes, and transistors, most of which act as switches. These components form huge numbers of circuits on the surface of the chip.

Logic circuits in the CPU make decisions

The heart of the CPU is an *arithmetic/logic unit,* or ALU, which performs calculations and logic decisions. The CPU also contains temporary data storage units, called *registers,* which hold results from previous calculations and other data waiting to be processed. A control section coordinates all of the processor activities. Finally, there are conductors that connect the various parts of the CPU to one another and to the rest of the computer.

When you start a program, the program first loads into random-access memory. Next the CPU performs a "fetch" operation, which brings in the first program instruction. Then it carries out that instruction and fetches the next instruction. The CPU proceeds in this fashion, fetching new instructions and obtaining data from the keyboard, mouse, disk, or other input device. Then it processes the data and creates output that is sent to the monitor or printer.

The CPU's logic gates can be built up to evaluate data and make decisions

As with memory chips, transistors in the CPU act as switches. Here, though, the switches can operate as devices called *logic gates.* Just as a real gate can be open or shut, a logic gate can open or close a circuit depending on the condition of two inputs. One kind of logic gate, called an AND gate, closes the circuit and allows current to pass only when both inputs are in the "on" position.

You could use a device like this to alert you when it is both cold and raining so that you will know what kind of clothing to wear. You could connect moisture and temperature sensors to an AND gate and arrange to have it close a circuit and ring a bell.

The bell will ring only when the temperature falls below 40°F and it is raining. If it is raining but is not cold, the bell will not ring. Similarly, the bell will not ring if it is cold but dry outside.

Architects, industrial designers, and engineers often use computer-aided design (CAD) to model new products. With CAD, you can construct a visual model of an object. Then you can rotate it to see how it looks from different positions, and you can make parts of the model transparent so that you can see how it fits together. You can test the model by subjecting it to computer-simulated wind, rain, heat, cold, and other real-world conditions.

Making the Connection

1. Suppose you are designing a bridge that will replace an old bridge across a river in a large city. What real-world conditions would you need to simulate to test your model?
2. What factors would you consider when trying to design a house that will absorb and use solar energy?

Computers and the Internet

CAD systems are used to design just about everything these days, from bridges to toasters to windows and doors. You can find some good 3-D CAD images to show to students on the Internet by searching for CAD Images. There are also systems called CAD-CAM, which stands for Computer Assisted Design – Computer Assisted Machining. With CAD-CAM systems, a diagram is drawn using the computer. When the diagram is finished, the engineer hits "make" instead of "print," and the machines in the machine shop make a three-dimensional version of the drawing made with the CAD system.

Making the Connection

1. weather conditions, such as wind, average rainfall, and temperature.
2. the climate of the proposed location of the house, particularly the average amount of sunlight available throughout the year

Resources Assign students worksheet *15.5: Connection to Architecture—Computers and Design Fields* in the **Integration Enrichment Resources** ancillary.

Computers and the Internet

Teaching Tip

Computer Networks Computer networks can be connected in many different ways. When a series of computers are connected together in an office or a library, this is called a Local Area Network, or LAN. This terminology is used when the computers are in the same building. Multiple LANs in different buildings can be connected together, perhaps at a college or a university. This type of network is called a Wide Area Network, or WAN. The Internet is a WAN because it connects computers in different locations over great distances.

SKILL BUILDER

Interpreting Visuals A logic system, like the one shown in **Figure 15-20**, controls circuits based on the kinds of logic gates used and the condition of the inputs received.

Resources Blackline Master 49 shows this visual.

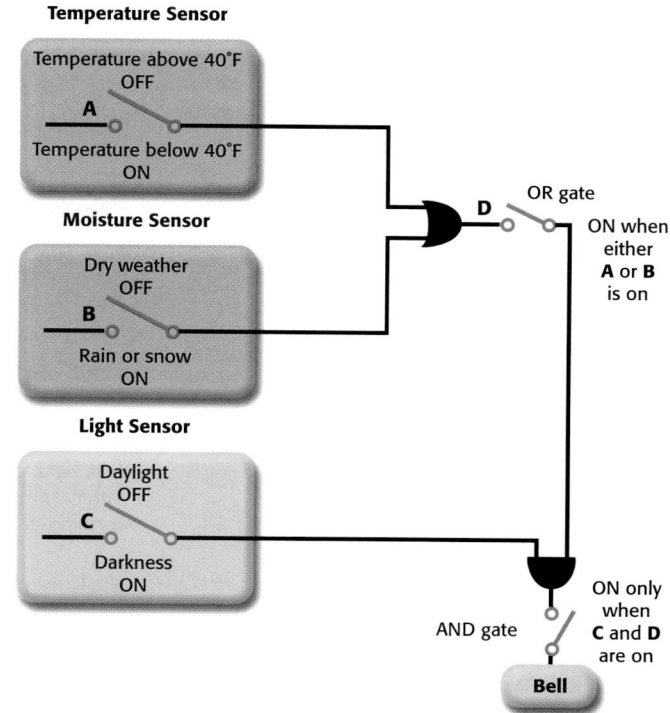

Figure 15-20
This logic system evaluates three variables—temperature, moisture, and light—in order to make a decision.

If you use a type of logic gate called an OR gate, the bell will ring when it is cold or when it is raining. If you want the bell to ring when it is cold or when it is raining, but only if it is dark outside, you could use an OR gate followed by an AND gate, as shown in **Figure 15-20**.

Computer Networks and the Internet

As the use of desktop personal computers became common in the 1980s, people looked for ways to link all of the computers within a single business, university, or government agency. The development of local area networks, or LANs, was the solution. In a LAN, all PCs are connected by cables to a central computer called a *server*. A server consists of a computer with lots of memory and several hard-disk drives for storing huge amounts of information.

This system allows workers to share data files that are stored on the server. One can also send a document to another person on the network. Soon after LANs were established, people were exchanging memos and documents over the network. This type of communication is called electronic mail, or E-mail.

The Internet is a worldwide network of computers

As the number of powerful computers increased, especially in government and universities, the U.S. Department of Defense wanted to connect them in a nationwide network. However, the department's computer experts worried about setting up a network that depended on only a few computers acting as distribution centers for information. If anything went wrong, the entire network would stop working.

Instead, a network in which every computer could communicate with every other computer was created. If part of the network were destroyed, the remainder would still be able to transmit information. This was the beginning of the **Internet.**

Because many companies had set up internal networks that used the same communication methods as the Defense Department's network, it was easy for them to connect to the network by telephone lines. Many other governments and corporations around the world joined to form a worldwide network that we now call the Internet, which is really a network of other networks.

If you have used the Internet, you are probably most familiar with the part known as the *World Wide Web,* or WWW, or just the Web. The Web was created in Europe in 1989 as a way for scientists to use the Internet to share data and other information.

The Web was mostly a resource for scientific information. It has since exploded into a vast number of sites created by individuals, government agencies, companies, and any other group with an interest in communicating or selling on the Internet.

▶ **Internet** a large computer network that connects many local and smaller networks

internet connect

SC*LINKS*
NSTA

TOPIC: Internet
GO TO: www.scilinks.org
KEYWORD: HK1506

Using a Search Engine

Search engines provide a way to find specific information in the vast amount of information that is available on the Internet. Finding information successfully depends on several things, one of which is picking appropriate keywords for your search.

Applying Information

1. Pick a science topic that interests you. Write down a few keywords that you think will occur in information about the topic.

2. Use an Internet search engine to find three Web sites that have information on the topic. Experiment with keywords until you find the kinds of sites you want.

3. Try the same keywords on other search engines. Do they all find the same sites?

4. How did the results differ? Can you detect whether an engine specializes in certain types of information?

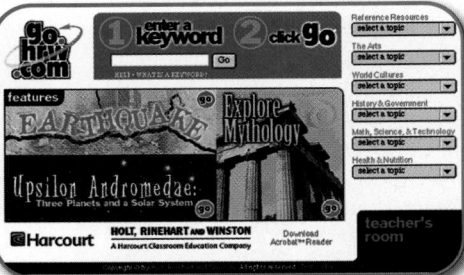

Computers and the Internet

Using a Search Engine The most common way to connect to the Internet is to use a modem. Modems come in various speeds, measured in BAUD rates. The higher the BAUD rate, the faster the rate of communication. If a cable modem is used instead of a telephone modem, then the communication speed is much faster. Cable modems run at 10 MB or 10 000 000 bits per second, which is much faster than the 56 000 bits per second of standard modems.

Resources Assign students worksheet *15.6: RWA—World Wide Web Robots* in the **Integration Enrichment Resources** ancillary.

RESOURCE LINK
IER

Assign students worksheet *15.7: Connection to Fine Arts—Arts and the Internet.*

Computers and the Internet

SECTION 15.3 REVIEW

Check Your Understanding

1. input devices: mouse, keyboard, modem; output devices: monitor screen, printer

2. Computers perform input, storage, process, and output.

3. Optical media use lasers to read the information while magnetic media use magnetic fields and solenoids to detect the information stored on diskettes.

4. Data is stored on magnetic media through the use of a current-carrying coil. Current is sent through the coil, generating a magnetic field. This magnetic field causes the magnetic domains within the diskette to change, storing the information in those magnetic domains.

5. a. hardware
   b. software
   c. software
   d. hardware

6. The operating system controls the computer hardware, memory, keyboard, disks, printer, mouse, and monitor.

Answers continue on p. 519B.

RESOURCE LINK
STUDY GUIDE

Assign students *Review Section 15.3 Computers and the Internet.*

You need three things to use the Internet

To use the Internet, you need a computer with a modem to connect the computer to a telephone line. The word *modem* is short for modulator/demodulator, a device that codes the output data of your computer and uses it to modulate a carrier wave that is transmitted over telephone lines. The modem also extracts data from an incoming carrier wave and sends that data to your computer.

Next you need a software program called an Internet, or Web, browser. This program interprets signals received from the Internet and shows the results on your monitor. It also changes your input into signals that can be sent out.

Finally, you need a telephone connection to an Internet service provider, or ISP. An ISP is usually a company that connects the modem signal of your computer to the Internet for a monthly fee.

Communication across the Internet uses transmission pathways—physical and atmospheric—just like those used to relay television, radio, and telephone signals. The Internet system has advanced to the point that you can begin to communicate with a Web site anywhere on Earth in a matter of seconds.

SECTION 15.3 REVIEW

SUMMARY

▶ Computers are machines that carry out operations as instructed by programs.

▶ Computers perform four functions: input, storage, processing, and output.

▶ The physical components of computers are called hardware.

▶ Programs and instructions are called software.

▶ Computing activity takes place in a central processing unit, which also carries out logic functions.

▶ The Internet is a worldwide network of computers that can store and transmit vast amounts of data.

CHECK YOUR UNDERSTANDING

1. **List** three computer input devices and three output devices.
2. **Describe** each of the four main functions performed by a digital computer.
3. **Distinguish** between the way optical media and magnetic media function.
4. **Explain** how data are stored on and read from a magnetic hard-disk drive.
5. **Identify** which of the following components are part of a computer's hardware and which are part of its software.
   a. a CPU microchip
   b. a program to calculate when a car needs an oil change
   c. the instructions for the computer clock to be displayed
   d. RAM memory
6. **Explain** the purpose of an operating system.
7. **Indicate** how ROM and RAM differ and why RAM is necessary.
8. **Compare** an AND gate's functions with those of an OR gate.
9. **Restate** the three things, in addition to a computer, that you need to use the Internet.
10. **Creative Thinking** What is the connection between the binary operation of computers and the function of transistors?

Chapter Highlights

Before you begin, review the summaries of the key ideas of each section, found on pages 496, 505, and 514. The key vocabulary terms are listed on pages 488, 497, and 506.

UNDERSTANDING CONCEPTS

1. A _____ is necessary in order to interpret a signal.
   a. CPU
   c. operating system
   b. modulation
   d. code
2. The microphone in the mouthpiece of a telephone produces a(n) _____ signal.
   a. microwave
   c. light
   b. analog
   d. digital
3. A communications signal from a ground station to a satellite is an example of _____ transmission.
   a. atmospheric
   c. physical
   b. cellular
   d. ground-wave
4. The up-and-down movement of electrons in the wire of a transmitting antenna produces _____ waves.
   a. electromagnetic
   c. sound
   b. visible light
   d. television
5. By adjusting the _____, a radio can receive a certain station.
   a. amplifier voltage
   c. tuner circuit
   b. speaker circuit
   d. carrier frequency
6. Materials that glow when struck by an electron beam are called _____.
   a. phosphors
   c. cathode rays
   b. pixels
   d. transistors
7. A computer program that coordinates all of the computer hardware is a(n) _____.
   a. read-only memory
   b. application
   c. operating system
   d. browser

8. A modem connects a computer to a _____.
   a. printer
   b. transmitting antenna
   c. hard-disk drive
   d. telephone line
9. The most common data-storage device on a modern personal computer is the _____.
   a. ROM
   c. hard-disk drive
   b. keyboard
   d. CPU

Using Vocabulary

10. How does *telecommunication* differ from ordinary communication?
11. Describe the differences between *analog signals* and *digital signals*.
12. How does *physical transmission* differ from *atmospheric transmission*?
13. Describe two ways that a broadcasting station can *modulate* a carrier wave.
14. Which of the following diagrams correctly represents the path of a light beam through an *optical fiber*? Explain your choice. How is a binary digital signal sent through an optical fiber?

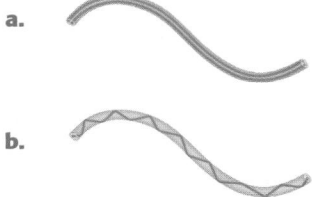

a.

b.

15. List two examples of computer *hardware* that are input devices and two that are output devices.
16. RAM stands for *random-access memory*. Why is this kind of computer memory called "random access"?

UNDERSTANDING CONCEPTS

1. d	**6.** a
2. b	**7.** c
3. a	**8.** d
4. a	**9.** c
5. c	

Using Vocabulary

10. Telecommunication occurs over large distances using electromagnetic means, while other forms of communication occur without electro magnets.
11. Analog signals can vary continuously within a range, whereas digital signals consist of separate bits of information. Digital signals cannot vary continuously; rather, they are discrete values.
12. Physical transmission involves sending signals through a medium like a telephone wire or a cable. Atmospheric transmission involves transmitting signals through the air over larger distances. Microwave communications are an example of atmospheric transmission.
13. A carrier wave can be modulated by changing either the frequency or the amplitude of the carrier wave. Frequency modulation is used in FM radio signals and amplitude modulation is used in AM radio signals.

RESOURCE LINK
STUDY GUIDE

Assign students *Mixed Review Chapter 15.*

CHAPTER 15 REVIEW

14. b; Light travels through an optical fiber by total internal reflection. A binary signal is sent through a piece of optical fiber by pulsing the light—that is, turning it on and off. "On" represents a 1 and "off" represents a 0.

15. Answers will vary. Two input devices might be a mouse and a keyboard, and two output devices might be a printer and a monitor.

16. It is called "random" because the time to access—read or write—information does not depend on the location of the information on a memory chip.

BUILDING MATH SKILLS

17. The number of transistors on an integrated circuit chip for the year 2010 seems rather unrealistic. What will probably happen is that a change in technology will occur so that the number of transistors is not as great.

THINKING CRITICALLY

18. The signals are the hand gestures being sent from the coach to the players. The code is the meaning of these signals—pass, stall, etc.

19. **a.** B
    b. A
    c. C

20. As the height of a transmitter tower is increased, the FM signal can be broadcast over a greater distance. This is because the tower is higher and the Earth's horizon appears to be farther away than it does from a shorter tower. The same is true for higher TV antennas.

BUILDING MATH SKILLS

17. **Graphing** In 1965, an engineer named Moore stated that the number of transistors on integrated-circuit chips would double every 18 to 24 months. This idea became known as Moore's law. The data in the table below show the actual numbers of transistors on the CPU chips that have been introduced since 1972. Make a graph with "Years" on the x-axis and "Number of transistors" on the y-axis. Describe the shape of the graph. Does your graph support Moore's law? Does the projected value for the year 2010 seem realistic?

Year	Microprocessor	Number of transistors
1972	4004	2300
1973	8008	3500
1974	8080	6000
1978	8086	29 000
1982	80286	134 000
1986	80386	275 000
1989	80486	1.2 million
1993	Pentium	3.1 million
1996	Pentium Pro	5.5 million
1997	Pentium II	7.5 million
1999	Pentium III	9.5 million
2010	?	800 million (estimated)

THINKING CRITICALLY

18. **Applying Knowledge** Your basketball team and coach have a meeting in which you decide that certain hand gestures and finger positions will convey certain messages such as pass, stall, or play zone defense, etc. Use this example to explain the difference between a signal and a code.

19. **Interpreting Graphics** Identify the diagram that represents each of the following:
    a. a carrier wave
    b. an audio signal
    c. an amplitude-modulated carrier

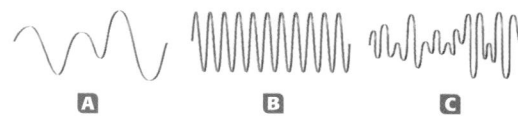

20. **Applying Knowledge** Use words or draw a diagram to explain why an FM radio signal can be received farther away as the height of the transmitting tower is increased. Also explain why you can receive more-distant television stations by using a higher television antenna.

21. **Applying Knowledge** Visible light from a laser can be used as a signal carrier. Describe what you would see if laser light is amplitude modulated and frequency modulated, assuming the modulation is slow enough for you to see the result. Which type of modulation do you think is more practical for visible light? Explain.

22. **Problem Solving** Suppose you want a light to come on automatically when someone comes to your door but only if it is dark outside. You have a proximity sensor, which is a device that closes an electric circuit when a person comes close to the door. What other sensor and what kind of logic gate do you need?

23. **Applying Knowledge** Suppose you are attempting to connect your computer to the World Wide Web, but it is not working. List two possible reasons why your computer is not able to connect, and explain how you could check for each one.

DEVELOPING LIFE/WORK SKILLS

24. Applying Technology AM radio antennas are usually as tall as one-fourth the wavelength of the carrier. How tall is the antenna of a radio station transmitting at 650 kHz? Use the equation relating wavelength, velocity, and frequency from Chapter 11.

25. Applying Technology FM stations usually broadcast with antennas that are 1/2 the wavelength of the carrier. What is the length of an antenna for a station broadcasting at 105.5 MHz? Compare your answer with the answer in item 23, and explain why FM stations broadcast from towers much taller than the actual antenna length.

26. Applying Technology What computer-input device would work best in each of the following situations? Justify your choices.
a. You want to use a picture from a magazine in a report for history class.
b. You want to play a computer game in which you fly a plane.
c. You want to compose an E-mail message and send it to a friend.
d. You want to copy parts of several different documents on the Internet and put them all into one document.

27. Working Cooperatively Working with a group of classmates, research the achievements of the following people in the fields of communication and computer technology. Construct a classroom display that includes a picture of each person and a summary of his or her contributions.
a. Edwin Armstrong
b. Grace Murray Hopper
c. An Wang
d. Lewis Latimer
e. Vladimir Zwyorkin
f. John W. Mauchly

INTEGRATING CONCEPTS

28. Concept Mapping Copy the unfinished concept map below onto a sheet of paper. Complete the map by writing the correct word or phrase in the lettered boxes.

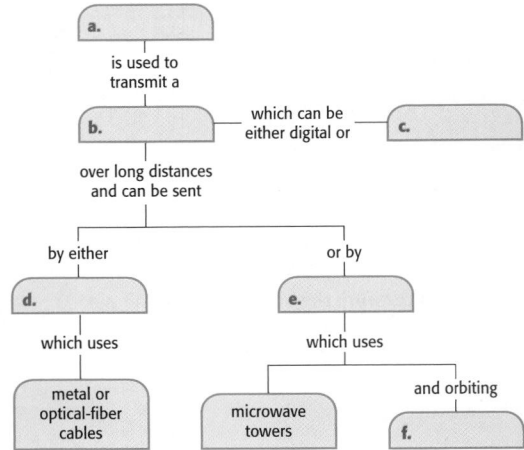

29. Connection to Social Studies Internet access has led to problems involving free speech and privacy. Should there be controls to prevent the spread of potentially dangerous or offensive information? Should others have free access to information about you? Research specific examples of these problems and find out what laws have been passed to address them. What arguments are made for and against free speech? An important fact to consider is that the Internet is not limited to one country.

TOPIC: Communication technology
GO TO: www.scilinks.org
KEYWORD: HK1507

21. If a laser beam were amplitude modulated, you would see the beam get brighter and dimmer as it transmits the signal. If the laser beam were frequency modulated, you would see the beam change color as the frequency changes. Frequency modulation is probably more efficient because of energy losses that occur over the distance traveled. If the beam is to be sent over a large distance, then losses in beam intensity would alter an amplitude-modulated signal but would not affect a frequency-modulated signal.

22. You would need a light sensor outside that can tell the system that it is dark or light outside. In addition, you would need an AND gate that reads the information from the proximity sensor and the light sensor. These two would form the inputs for the AND gate. If both are true, it is dark <u>and</u> someone is nearby, then the system activates.

23. Student answers will vary but might include that the computer does not have a modem or an Internet browser software program. Accept all reasonable answers.

DEVELOPING LIFE/ WORK SKILLS

24. $\lambda = \dfrac{v}{f} = \dfrac{3.0 \times 10^8 \text{ m/s}}{6.5 \times 10^5 \text{ Hz}} =$
460 m

length of antenna $= \dfrac{1}{4} \lambda =$

$\dfrac{1}{4} \times 460 \text{ m} = 120 \text{ m}$

Answers continue on p. 519B.

Skill Builder Lab

Determining the Speed of Sound

Introduction

We communicate through data transmissions, images, and sound. In this experiment, students will determine the speed of sound.

Objectives

Students will:

▶ **Observe** the reinforcement of sound in a column of air.

▶ **Determine** the speed of sound in air by calculating the wavelength of sound at a known frequency.

Planning

Recommended time: 1 lab period
Materials: *(for each lab group)*

▶ two tuning forks of known frequency

▶ glass tube about 4 cm in diameter and 50 cm in length

▶ tall glass cylinder

▶ thermometer

▶ meterstick

▶ large rubber stopper

▶ wood dowel or wire handle for stopper

Skill Builder Lab

Introduction

Can you determine the speed of sound in air?

Objectives

▶ **Observe** the reinforcement of sound in a column of air.

▶ **Determine** the speed of sound in air by calculating the wavelength of sound at a known frequency.

Materials

two tuning forks of known frequency
glass tube about 4 cm in diameter and 50 cm in length
tall glass cylinder
thermometer
meterstick
large rubber stopper
wood dowel or wire handle for stopper

Safety Needs

safety goggles

Determining the Speed of Sound

▶ Preparing for Your Lab

1. The speed of sound is equal to the product of frequency and wavelength. The frequency is known in this experiment, and the wavelength will be determined.

2. If you hold a vibrating tuning fork above a column of air, the note or sound produced by the fork is strongly reinforced when the air column in the glass tube is just the right length. This reinforcement is called resonance and the length is called the resonant length. The resonant length of a closed tube is about one-fourth the wavelength of the note produced by the fork.

3. On a paper, copy **Table 15-1** at right.

▶ Determining the Speed of Sound

SAFETY CAUTION Make sure the tuning fork does not touch the glass tube or cylinder, as the glass may shatter from the vibrations.

4. Set up the equipment as shown in the figure at right.

5. Record the frequency of the tuning fork as the number of vibrations per second (vps) in your **Table 15-1**.

6. Make the tuning fork vibrate by striking it with a large rubber stopper mounted on a dowel or heavy wire.

7. Hold the tube in a cylinder nearly full of water, as illustrated in the figure.

8. Hold the vibrating fork over the open end of the tube. Adjust the air column by moving the tube up and down until you find the point where the resonance causes the loudest sound. Then hold the tube in place while your partner measures the distance from the top of the glass tube to the surface of the water (which is the part of the tube sticking out of water). Record this length to the nearest millimeter as Trial 1 in **Table 15-1**.

9. Repeat steps 6–8 two more times using the same tuning fork, and record your data in **Table 15-1**.

10. Using a different tuning fork, repeat steps 4 through 8.

Table 15-1   Data Needed to Determine the Speed of Sound in Air

	Tuning fork 1	Tuning fork 2
Vibration rate of fork (vps)		
Length of tube above water (mm), Trial 1		
Length of tube above water (mm), Trial 2		
Length of tube above water (mm), Trial 3		

▶ Analyzing Your Results

1. On a clean sheet of paper, make a table like the one shown below.
2. Measure the inside diameter of your tube and record this measurement in your **Table 15-2**. The reflection of sound at the open end of a tube occurs at a point about 0.4 of its diameter above the end of the tube. Calculate this value and record it in **Table 15-2**. This distance is added to the length to get the resonant length. Record the resonant length in **Table 15-2**.
3. Complete the calculations shown in **Table 15-2**.
4. Measure the air temperature, and calculate the speed of sound using the information shown below. Record your answer in **Table 15-2**.

   Speed of sound = 332 m/s at 0 °C + 0.6 m/s for every degree above 0°C

Table 15-2   Calculating the Speed of Sound

	Tuning fork 1	Tuning fork 2
Average measured length of air column (mm)		
Inside diameter (mm)		
Inside diameter × 0.4 (mm)		
Resonant length		
Wavelength of sound (mm), 4 × resonant length		
Wavelength of sound (m), wavelength of sound (mm) × $\frac{1}{1000}$		
Speed of sound (m/s), wavelength × vibration rate of fork		
Speed of sound (m/s), calculated from step 4		

(Illustration labels: Tuning fork; Open-ended glass tube)

▶ Defending Your Conclusions

5. Should the speed of sound determined with the two tuning forks be the same?
6. How does the value for the speed of sound you calculated compare with the speed of sound you determined by measuring the air column?
7. How could you determine the frequency of a tuning fork that had an unknown value?

COMMUNICATION TECHNOLOGY   **519**

Sample Data Table 1

Calculating the Speed of Sound		
	Tuning fork 1	**Tuning fork 2**
Average measured length of air column (mm)	179.6	213.0
Inside diameter (mm)	35	35
Inside diameter × 0.4 (mm)	14	14
Resonant length (mm)	193.6	227.0
Wavelength of sound (mm), 4 × resonant length	774.4	908.0
Speed of sound (m/s), wavelength × vibration rate of fork	340.7	348.7
Speed of sound (m/s), calculated from step 4	344.6	344.6

Pre-Lab

Teaching Tips

To obtain the greatest sound volume, the tuning fork tines should be aligned for the maximum amplitude to enter the tube. Have students start with the tube totally withdrawn from the water.

In this experiment, the frequency of the tuning forks is described as vibrations per second (vps). The SI unit for frequency is the hertz (Hz). Students may be familiar with megahertz (MHz) in reference to the clock speed of personal computers. The SI unit for frequency was named for Heinrich R. Hertz, who experimentally demonstrated electromagnetic waves.

Procedure

▶ Designing Your Experiment

Each setup can accommodate 2–3 students. Students may try to match harmonics of the tuning fork to what they hear in the resonance tube rather than the fundamental frequency.

Frequencies of 250 to 700 vps work best to stay within convenient measurements. Not all tuning forks are equal in amplitude (volume). Each tuning fork should be tested prior to the lab.

If a strobe light is available, students can observe the vibrations of the tines on the tuning fork and estimate their amplitudes. As an extension, ask students why temperature affects the speed of sound. (*Temperature affects the movement of the molecules of the medium.*)

Post-Lab

▶ Disposal

None required.

Continue on p. 519A.

CONTINUATION OF ANSWERS

Skill Builder Lab from page 519
Determining the Speed of Sound

▶ **Analyzing Your Results**

1.–4. Sample answers are given in **Sample Data Table 1.**

▶ **Defending Your Conclusions**

5. The speed of sound should be the same regardless of tuning fork frequency.
6. The speed of sound calculated from step 4 is similar to the lab calculations.
7. The frequency of the tuning fork can be determined by first determining the wavelength of the sound produced by the tuning fork and then applying the appropriate equation, using the value for the speed of sound at room temperature.

Answers from page 496
SECTION 15.1 REVIEW

6. Communication satellites can transmit signals around the world by passing the signal from satellite to satellite. The signal reaches the satellite through the uplink, then passes from satellite to satellite until it reaches its destination, then is transmitted to the ground through a downlink.
7. A geostationary satellite is one that stays fixed in its position over the Earth. This is important in satellite communication because the satellite does not appear to move in the sky. As a result, a satellite dish does not need to be re-aimed over time.
8. Taller microwave relay towers have a longer transmission range because the taller the tower is, the farther away the horizon appears to be. As a result, the taller tower can transmit farther than the shorter transmission tower.

Answers from page 505
SECTION 15.2 REVIEW

6. The broadcast signal is an electromagnetic wave that causes the electrons in a radio antenna to vibrate at the same frequency as the radio wave. The vibrating electrons carry the signal into a radio to be amplified and filtered. The final signal then goes to the speakers, where it recreates the broadcast sound.
7. Optical-fiber cable offers cleaner signals in transmission, fewer signal losses, and fewer power losses.

Answers from page 514

7. ROM is read only memory, while RAM is random access memory. Programs are stored on CD-ROMs, where the computer can read the program but not rewrite it. RAM stores the program when the computer is running it. Without RAM, the computer program would not run.

8. An AND gate gives a TRUE response (1) if both inputs are on. An OR gate gives a TRUE response (1) if only one of the inputs is on.

9. a modem, an Internet browser, and an Internet service provider (ISP)

10. Binary code allows transistors to read the input and output signals. A 1 in binary means "on" or high voltage, a 0 in binary means "off" or low voltage.

Answers from page 517

DEVELOPING LIFE/ WORK SKILLS

25. $\lambda = \dfrac{v}{f} = \dfrac{3.0 \times 10^8 \text{ m/s}}{1.055 \times 10^8 \text{ Hz}} = 2.8 \text{ m}$

length of antenna $= \dfrac{1}{2}\lambda = \dfrac{1}{2} \times 2.8 \text{ m} = 1.4 \text{ m}$

FM antenna towers are taller than AM towers because the FM station can broadcast farther with a taller tower.

26. a. scanner
b. joy stick
c. keyboard
d. mouse

27. Have students make use of the references section of a public library and the Internet to find information on these people.

INTEGRATING CONCEPTS

28. a. telephone
b. signal
c. analog
d. physical transmission
e. atmospheric transmission
f. satellites

29. Student answers will vary. Students can research specific cases involving free speech and privacy issues on the Internet or at the library.

Should We Search for Extraterrestrial Life?

LINKING CHAPTERS

The search for extraterrestrial intelligence represents a challenge for communication technology. All of the different aspects of communications described in Chapter 15 are required here. Radio frequencies are scanned by computers that search for unexpected regularities that could be signs of a signal.

Your Turn

1. Critiquing Viewpoints

Students' analyses of a single argument's weak points may vary. Be sure that student responses clearly identify a weakness and respond in some way that provides support. Possible responses for each of the viewpoints in the feature are listed below. (Note that students should analyze only *one of the following.*)

Lauren L.: It is also possible that if we find extraterrestrial life, we may find out that it is not friendly.

Either way, it is better to find out and be prepared to meet other forms of life than to act as if they aren't there.

Ghautam P. and Thuy N.: Although the search is not too expensive, it isn't free either. Those resources could be doing something better.

Advances in technology will make it cheaper and cheaper to continue pursuing evidence of extraterrestrial life.

Samuel S.: Perhaps the reason there's no evidence yet is because we haven't looked hard enough.

But how will we ever know when we've looked hard enough. Better to abandon the search now.

Zack J.: While requiring extraterrestrial life to have advanced technology makes it less likely to find, that doesn't mean it will never be found.

But why spend resources on something this unlikely?

viewpoints
Should We Search for Extraterrestrial Life?

Since the world's first Search for Extraterrestrial Intelligence, or SETI, in 1960, scientists have been developing more advanced technology for listening to possible radio signals from outer space. Today SETI programs monitor billions of radio frequencies—a huge advance over the 100 listened to in 1960.

No definite extraterrestrial signals have ever been detected, but some promising signals have been recorded. Perhaps the most famous signal—called "Wow"—was picked up in 1977. The transmission lasted only one minute and was never picked up again, so scientists are not sure of the signal's source.

Opponents point out that there is no evidence that life exists on other planets and little evidence that it could. Some scientists say we won't know unless we keep searching. Others say that SETI projects are a waste of time and resources. What do you think?

> FROM: Lauren L., Austin, TX

I believe that the search for ET life should continue. There are thousands of planets in this universe that could have intelligent life on them. The possibility of other life existing besides Earthkind is very high. If we can reach intelligent beings, we may gain knowledge from them.

Continue the Search

> FROM: Ghautam P., Portland, OR

Advances in technology are made each day to help in the search for ET life. It's not that expensive so it doesn't hurt to keep looking, even if the chances of picking up a signal are small. It would be awesome if we actually found life somewhere else in the universe!

> FROM: Thuy N., Huxley, NC

Just because we haven't heard from an ET doesn't mean that ET life doesn't exist. It just means they haven't tried to contact us or we weren't listening. Besides, we have recorded signals that might have been ET life. We just won't know unless we continue to search.

Samantha J.: The amount being spent on this search is small enough that it wouldn't have much of an impact on problems here on Earth.

Every little bit of money that can be used to address real problems will help make them less difficult.

2. Critiquing Viewpoints

Students' analyses of strong points in opposing arguments may vary. Be sure that student responses clearly identify the strong points and respond in some way that provides support for the opposite point of view. Possible responses for each of the viewpoints in the feature are listed below. (Note that students should analyze only *one of the following.*)

Lauren L.: Thousands of planets in the universe could have intelligent life.

Just because intelligent life is possible does not mean that it is definitely out there.

Ghautam P.: It would be a great discovery if life was found elsewhere in the universe.

But life may not be found. Then, all of the work and expense would be in vain.

Thuy N.: We just won't know if extraterrestrial life has tried to contact us if we don't continue the search.

Abandon the Search

> FROM: Samuel S., Ouray, CO

The decision to keep looking should be based on fact, not fantasy or science fiction. The fact is there is no evidence. If ET life exists we would have found it by now. We have instruments that are capable of detecting life in outer space. But they haven't found any real evidence.

> FROM: Zack J., Cincinnati, OH

Even if ET life does exist what are the chances of communicating with it? You have to assume that ET life not only exists, but that it has advanced technology. Communication doesn't seem likely to me.

> FROM: Samantha J., Seattle, WA

Although communications technology is improving quickly, it's not cheap. The millions of dollars spent looking for ET life could be spent on real problems here on Earth rather than chasing dreams in the sky.

But if we continue the search and find nothing, we won't know if that means there really is no life out there or that we just didn't find it. Samuel S. and Zack J.: There has been no evidence yet, and the odds are so small that we will find anything.

Perhaps that's because we haven't been looking long enough or hard enough. Samantha J.: There are many other things the money could be spent on.

There are always many more things to spend money on than there is money. The amount being spent on the search is fairly small.

3. Life/Work Skills
Student answers will vary. Evaluate students' presentations or brochures proposing further projects in searching for extraterrestrial life using a scale of 1–5 points for each of the following: organization, clarity in explanation, persuasiveness, creativity, and effort. (25 total possible points)

internet**connect**

The HRW Web site has more opinions from other students and also provides an opportunity for your students to contribute their points of view. Every few months, more opinions will be added from the ones submitted. Student opinions that are posted will be identified only by the student's first name, last initial, and city to protect his or her privacy.

> Your Turn

1. **Critiquing Viewpoints** Select one of the statements on this page that you *agree* with. Identify and explain at least one weak point in the statement. What would you say to respond to someone who brought up this weak point as a reason you were wrong?

2. **Critiquing Viewpoints** Select one of the statements on this page that you *disagree* with. Identify and explain at least one strong point in the statement. What would you say to respond to someone who brought up this point as a reason they were right?

3. **Life/Work Skills** Assume that you are a member of a SETI committee that is trying to obtain funding for a project. Develop a presentation or a brochure that you could use to convince others to invest in the project.

4. **Creative Thinking** Assume that life does exist on another planet in the universe. How might we communicate without a common language? What other codes and signals might we share?

internet**connect**

TOPIC: Search for extraterrestrial life
GO TO: go.hrw.com
KEYWORD: HK1SETI

Should the search continue? Why or why not? Share your views on this issue, and find out what others think about it at the HRW web site.

521

4. Creative Thinking
Student answers about how to communicate with living beings from other planets will vary. Answers should involve using items that we are likely to share with other living things. For example, a code could be worked out using samples of different elements because the same elements should be found throughout the universe. Another way could be to use waves of varying frequencies because presumably the same electromagnetic spectrum occurs throughout the universe.

Evaluate students' suggestions using a scale of 1–5 points for each of the following: practicality, clarity in explanation, probable ease of use, creativity, and effort. (25 total possible points)

UNIT
6

Exploring Earth and Space

READING SKILL BUILDER

Reading Organizer Ask a student to list on the chalkboard the street address of the school. Continue by asking other students to add to the address as follows: which city it is in, which state it is in, which nation it is in, which continent it is in, which hemisphere it is in, which planet it is on, which solar system it is in, and which galaxy it is in.

This quick exercise will help students get a sense of the scale and scope of the matters discussed in Chapter 16.

LINKING CHAPTERS

This unit is the capstone of the entire course. In this unit, concepts from most of the preceding chapters are used to explain a variety of scientific concepts.

For example, the study of nuclear changes (Chapter 7) and light (Chapter 12) are essential to understanding the discussion of stars in Chapter 16. The study of chemical and physical changes (Chapter 2) are needed for the discussion of the rock cycle in Chapter 17. Concepts from chemistry, such as the kinetic theory of matter (Chapter 2), and from physics, such as heat and temperature (Chapter 10), are used to explain atmospheric phenomena in Chapter 18.

523

CHAPTER 16

The Universe

Annotated Descriptions of the Correlated National Science Standards

The following descriptions summarize the National Science Standards that specially relate to Chapter 16. For the full text of the Standards, see p. 40T.

SECTION 16.1
The Universe and Galaxies
Physical Science
PS 4b, 5a, 5c, 6c
Earth and Space Science
ES 4a, 4b
Unifying Concepts and Processes
UCP 1, 2, 3, 4, 5
Science as Inquiry
SAI 1, 2
Science and Technology
ST 2
History and Nature of Science
HNS 1, 2, 3

SECTION 16.2
Stars and the Sun
Physical Science
PS 1c, 4c, 5c, 6b, 6c
Earth and Space Science
ES 3a, 4c
Unifying Concepts and Processes
UCP 1, 2, 3, 4, 5
Science as Inquiry
SAI 1, 2
Science and Technology
ST 2
History and Nature of Science
HNS 1, 3

SECTION 16.3
The Solar System
Earth and Space Science
ES 3a
Unifying Concepts and Processes
UCP 1, 2, 3, 4, 5
Science as Inquiry
SAI 2
Science and Technology
ST 2
History and Nature of Science
HNS 1, 2, 3
Science in Personal and Social Perspectives
SPSP 5

Cross-Discipline Teaching RESOURCES

Cross-Discipline Teaching, **ATE** p. 524
Space Science   Language Arts
Social Studies

Additional Integration Enrichment Worksheets
IE 16.1 Language Arts
IE 16.2 Physics
IE 16.3 Mathematics
IE 16.4 Health

Use the Planning Guide on the next page to help you organize your lessons.

MATH AND COMPUTER RESOURCES

Chapter 16	Math Skills	Assess	Media/Computer Skills
Section 16.1	**BS** **Worksheet 3.1:** Ratios and Proportions		■ Section 16.1 **CNN** **Presents** **Physical Science** **Segment 24** Wisp of Creation **CRT** Worksheet 24
Section 16.2			■ Section 16.2
Section 16.3			■ Section 16.3 **PE** Chapter 16 Review, p. 552, items 21, 22

PE Pupil's Edition **ATE** Annotated Teacher's Edition **MS** Math Skills **BS** Basic Skills
IE Integration Enrichment ■ Guided Reading Audio **CRT** Critical Thinking

READING SKILL BUILDER

The following activities found in the Annotated Teacher's Edition provide techniques for developing useful reading strategies to increase your students' reading comprehension skills.

Section 16.1 **L.I.N.K.,** p. 524
Discussion, p. 526
K-W-L, p. 532

Section 16.2 **Reading Organizer,** p. 539

Section 16.3 **K-W-L,** p. 542
Reading Hint, p. 543
Reading Organizer, p. 544, 546
Paired Summarizing, p. 548

Smithsonian Institution®
Visit
www.si.edu/hrw
for additional online resources.

Spanish Resources

The following resources are made available for students who speak Spanish as their first language.

Spanish Resources
Guided Reading Audio CD-ROM
Chapter 16

Spanish Glossary
Chapter 16

The Universe

CLASSROOM RESOURCES

FOCUS	TEACH	HANDS-ON
Section 16.1: The Universe and Galaxies		
BLOCK 1 45 minutes ATE RSB L.I.N.K., p. 524 ATE Focus Activities 1, 2, p. 525 ATE RSB Discussion, p. 526 PE What Is the Universe?; Galaxies, pp. 526–530 ★ Focus Transparency LT 52 ATE **Demo 1** See the Universe in the Past, p. 527	ATE **Skill Builder** Interpreting Visuals, pp. 525, 528, 529, 530 Visual Strategy, p. 526	IE Worksheet 16.3
BLOCK 2 45 minutes ATE RSB K-W-L, p. 532 PE The Origin of the Universe, pp. 531–534	ATE **Skill Builder** Interpreting Visuals, p. 533 TT 48 Red-Shift Spectrum BLM 50 Timeline of Universe BLM 51 Fates of Universe	PE Quick Activity *Modeling the Universe,* p. 532 **DS** 16.1 IE Worksheet 16.2
Section 16.2: Stars and the Sun		
BLOCK 3 45 minutes ATE **Demo 2** Understanding Stellar Brightness, p. 536 PE What Are Stars? pp. 535–538 ★ Focus Transparency LT 53	ATE **Skill Builder** Interpreting Visuals, pp. 535, 537, 538 TT 49 Starlight Intensity Graph TT 50 Absorption Spectra TT 51 Structure of the Sun	PE Quick Activity *Using a Star Chart,* p. 538 **DS** 16.2 IE Worksheet 16.4
BLOCK 4 45 minutes ATE RSB Reading Organizer, p. 539 PE The Life and Death of Stars, pp. 539–541	ATE **Skill Builder** Interpreting Visuals, pp. 539, 540	
Section 16.3: The Solar System		
BLOCK 5 45 minutes ATE RSB K-W-L, p. 542 ATE RSB Reading Hint, p. 543 ATE RSB Reading Organizer, pp. 544, 546 ATE **Demo 3** The Reflection of Light from Venus, p. 544 PE The Planets, pp. 542–548 ★ Focus Transparency LT 54	ATE **Skill Builder** Interpreting Visuals, pp. 542, 544, 545 BLM 52 Solar System BLM 53 Properties of the Planets	IE Worksheet 16.1
BLOCK 6 45 minutes ATE RSB Paired Summarizing, p. 548 ATE **Demo 4** Phases of the Moon, p. 549 PE Formation of the Solar System, pp. 548–550	ATE **Skill Builder** Interpreting Visuals, p. 549 TT 52 Phases of the Moon TT 53 Eclipses	PE Skill Builder Lab *Estimating the Size and Power Output of the Sun,* p. 554 **DS** 16.3 LE 16 *Determining the Speed of an Orbiting Moon* **DS** 16.4

CLASSROOM RESOURCES

HOMEWORK	ASSESS
PE Section Review 1–6, p. 534 **Chapter 16 Review,** p. 551, items 1, 11, 12	**ATE** *ALTERNATIVE ASSESSMENT,* Spiral and Elliptical Galaxies, p. 529 **SG** Chapter 16 Pretest
PE Section Review 7–9, p. 534 **Chapter 16 Review,** p. 551, items 2, 13, 14	**SG** Section 16.1
PE Section Review 1–3, p. 541 **Chapter 16 Review,** p. 551, items 3, 4, 20	**ATE** *ALTERNATIVE ASSESSMENT,* p. 535
PE Section Review 4–7, p. 541 **Chapter 16 Review,** p. 551, items 5, 16	**SG** Section 16.2
PE Section Review 1–4, 9, p. 550 **Chapter 16 Review,** p. 551, items 6, 7, 17, 21, 22	
PE Section Review 5–8, p. 550 **Chapter 16 Review,** p. 551, items 8–10, 15, 18, 19	**SG** Section 16.3

BLOCK 7

PE Chapter 16 Review
Thinking Critically 23–29, p. 552
Developing Life/Work Skills 30–31, p. 553
Integrating Concepts 32–35, p. 553
SG Chapter 16 Mixed Review

BLOCK 8

Chapter Tests
Holt Science Spectrum: A Physical Approach
Chapter 16 Test

One-Stop Planner CD–ROM with Test Generator
Holt Science Spectrum Test Generator
FOR MACINTOSH AND WINDOWS
Chapter 16

Teaching Resources
Scoring Rubrics and assignment evaluation checklist.

---

internet connect

National Science Teachers Association
Online Resources:
www.scilinks.org

The following *sci*LINKS Internet resources can be found in the student text for this chapter.

Page 525 **TOPIC:** Meteors **KEYWORD:** HK1161	**Page 539** **TOPIC:** Stars **KEYWORD:** HK1164
Page 529 **TOPIC:** Milky Way galaxy **KEYWORD:** HK1162	**Page 546** **TOPIC:** Planets **KEYWORD:** HK1165
Page 531 **TOPIC:** Origin of the universe **KEYWORD:** HK1163	**Page 553** **TOPIC:** Formation of the elements **KEYWORD:** HK1166

CNNfyi.com   www.cnnfyi.com

Visit this site for coverage of current events and related classroom resources.

PE Pupil's Edition **ATE** Annotated Teacher's Edition
RSB Reading Skill Builder **DS** Datasheets
IE Integrated Enrichment **SG** Study Guide
LE Laboratory Experiments
TT Teaching Transparencies **BLM** Blackline Masters
★ Lesson Focus Transparency

The Universe

Tapping Prior Knowledge

Be sure students understand the following concepts:

Chapter 2
Matter

Chapter 7
Radioactivity

Chapter 8
Motion and forces

Chapter 10
Heat and temperature

Chapter 12
Sound and light

READING SKILL BUILDER *L.I.N.K.* Write the following terms on the chalkboard: *universe, galaxy,* and *light-year.* Have students list all the words, phrases, and ideas that they associate with those terms. Write the relevant terms on the board and begin a discussion in which students seek clarification of the listed ideas. At the end of the discussion have students make notes of everything they remember from the discussion. Students should be allowed to review these notes at the end of the chapter and clarify any misconceptions.

Chapter Preview

524

RESOURCE LINK
STUDY GUIDE

Assign students *Pretest Chapter 16 The Universe* before beginning Section 16.1.

CROSS-DISCIPLINE TEACHING

Space Science Have students go to their local library and research the life and work of Edwin Powell Hubble and the Hubble Space Telescope. If some students need guidance to start their research, have them answer the following questions: What significant contributions did Edwin Powell Hubble make in the field of astronomy? When was HST first launched into space? What problems did it encounter? What role does the Hubble Telescope play in space exploration?

Language Arts Have students write a short story that describes a meteor shower. The students should write the story as if they are a scientist or an astronaut collecting data about the size, color, shape, and composition of the falling meteors.

Social Studies The telescope was one of many instruments that came out of the Scientific Revolution of the seventeenth century. Have students research some of the other instruments produced during this era.

Focus ACTIVITY

Background Have you ever seen a shooting star? You may already know that a shooting star is not a star at all; shooting stars are meteors, tiny pieces of rock or ice that burn brightly as they enter the Earth's atmosphere. But you may not realize that more than 10 000 meteors enter the Earth's atmosphere every night.

When Earth's orbit carries the planet through a cloud of debris, observers on the ground can see a spectacular show of lights in the sky: a meteor shower.

Most meteors burn away completely in the atmosphere, forming tiny particles of dust and ash that float down to the ground. According to estimates, this matter from meteors adds an average of almost half a million kilograms of mass to Earth every day.

A few meteors survive their trip through the atmosphere and reach Earth's surface intact, producing an impact crater like Meteor Crater, in Arizona. A meteor that hits Earth is called a meteorite. Scientists study meteorites to learn more about our solar system.

Early in the history of the solar system, the moon, Earth, and all the planets were constantly bombarded with meteors. Geological activity has erased most of the impact craters on Earth. But the moon, which has less geologic activity than Earth does, is still pocked with thousands of craters.

Activity 1 Go outside on a clear evening at dusk, sit down, and look up at the sky. Spend 20 minutes counting stars as they become visible. What do you think about the first stars you see? Are they the biggest? the brightest? the closest? How many did you count in the 20 minutes? Do you see any lights in the sky that might not be stars? If so, what might they be?

Activity 2 Research the conditions on at least three other planets in the solar system. Try to find data, including surface temperature, thickness and composition of atmosphere, and the amount of water on the planet. For two of the planets, give at least two reasons why they probably could not support life as we know it.

A shooting star is really a meteor burning up in Earth's atmosphere. If a meteor survives its trip through the atmosphere, it may produce a crater when it strikes the ground.

internet connect

SCLINKS.
NSTA

TOPIC: Meteors
GO TO: www.scilinks.org
KEYWORD: HK1161

525

Focus ACTIVITY

Background Meteoroids are small, rocky objects floating in the space between planets in the solar system. Meteoroids are similar to asteroids, only smaller.

Once a meteoroid enters Earth's atmosphere, it is called a meteor. Friction in the atmosphere slows the speed of a meteor, and also heats the meteor, causing partial or complete vaporization. When scientists use the term *meteor*, they may be referring either to the object itself or to the streak of light seen as a meteor travels through the Earth's atmosphere, as shown in the large photo at left.

Any leftover portion of a meteor that reaches Earth's surface is known as a meteorite. The small photo shown at left is Meteor Crater, in Arizona. Meteor Crater is an impact crater created when a large meteor crashed to Earth.

Activity 1 Answers will vary.

Activity 2 Tell students that research sources may include their textbook, encyclopedias, and Internet Web sites.

SKILL BUILDER

Interpreting Visuals Have students examine the shooting star shown in the photo. Ask students to describe differences between the shooting star and the other stars in the photo.

16.1

The Universe and Galaxies

▶ **KEY TERMS**

universe
star
galaxy
light-year
interstellar matter
cluster
red shift
big bang theory

OBJECTIVES

▶ Describe the basic structure of the universe.
▶ Introduce the light-year as a unit of distance.
▶ Describe the structure of the Milky Way galaxy, and include the location of our solar system.
▶ List the three main types of galaxies.
▶ State the main features of the big bang theory and evidence supporting the expansion of the universe.

J ust imagine the following: colliding galaxies that rip stars from each other; a dead star so dense that 1 teaspoon of its matter would contain as much material as all the cars and trucks in the United States; a volcano on Mars that is nearly three times taller than Mount Everest and that has a base larger than Louisiana. All of these are part of the universe.

What Is the Universe?

By the term **universe**, scientists mean everything physical that exists in space and time. The universe consists of all matter and energy that exists, now, in the past, and in the future. There is only one universe.

▶ **universe** the sum of all matter and energy that exists, that ever has existed, and that ever will exist

Figure 16-1
The sizes of astronomical objects are so great that new measuring units, such as the light-year, are needed to describe them.

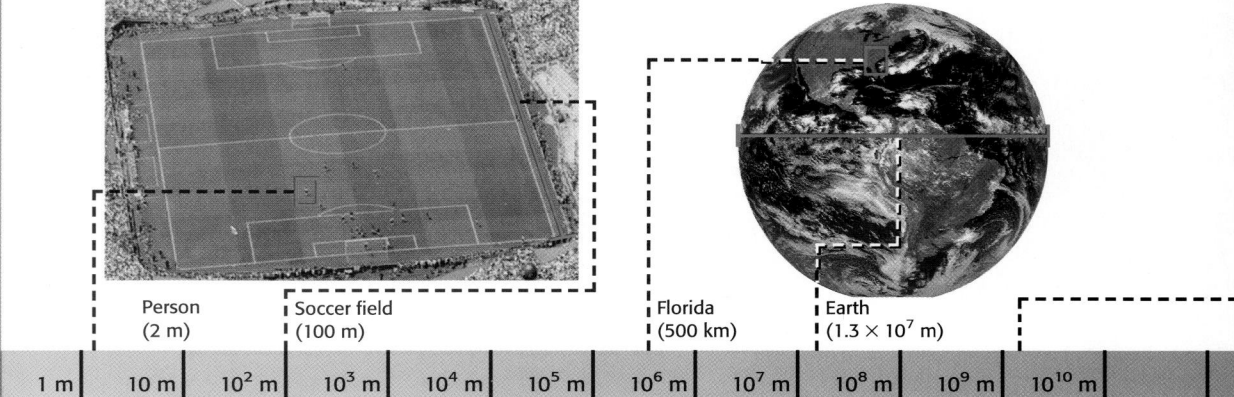

| Person (2 m) | Soccer field (100 m) | | | | | Florida (500 km) | Earth (1.3×10^7 m) | |
| 1 m | 10 m | 10^2 m | 10^3 m | 10^4 m | 10^5 m | 10^6 m | 10^7 m | 10^8 m | 10^9 m | 10^{10} m |

526 CHAPTER 16

You are part of the universe, as is Earth and everything on it. Most of the objects beyond Earth that we can see with the unaided eye are **stars,** huge balls of hot gas that emit light. Stars are grouped together in **galaxies,** collections of millions, billions, or even trillions of stars bound together by gravity.

Astronomical distances are measured in light-years

To measure distances in the universe beyond Earth, scientists use a unit of distance called a **light-year** (ly). A light-year is the distance light travels in one year. Because light travels at a speed of 3.0×10^8 m/s in empty space, a light-year is a very large distance: 9.5×10^{15} m. This distance is so large that driving it in a car moving at highway speed would take over 10 million years.

Figure 16-1 shows objects and systems found in the universe, spanning a wide range of sizes. Beyond the solar system, the light-year is a more convenient unit of length or distance than the meter. Remember, while a *year* is a unit of time, a *light-year* is a unit of distance; it measures how far light travels in a year.

We see the universe now as it was in the past

When you go outside on a sunny day, the light that hits your skin left the sun more than 8 minutes earlier. It takes time for light to travel in space. The farther away an object is, the older the light is that we get from that object.

The three stars nearest to Earth besides the sun are 4.3 light-years away, in the star system Alpha Centauri. When you see their light from Earth, you see light that left the stars 4.3 years ago. A typical cluster of galaxies may be 10 million light-years across. How long would it take for light to travel from one side of such a cluster to the other side?

▶ **star** a huge ball of hot gas that emits light

▶ **galaxy** a collection of millions or billions of stars bound together by gravity

▶ **light-year** a unit of distance equal to the distance light travels in one year; 1 ly = 9.5×10^{15} m

Did You Know ?

Distances within the solar system are sometimes measured in *astronomical units* (AU). This is the average distance between Earth and the sun. 1 AU = 1.5×10^{11} m

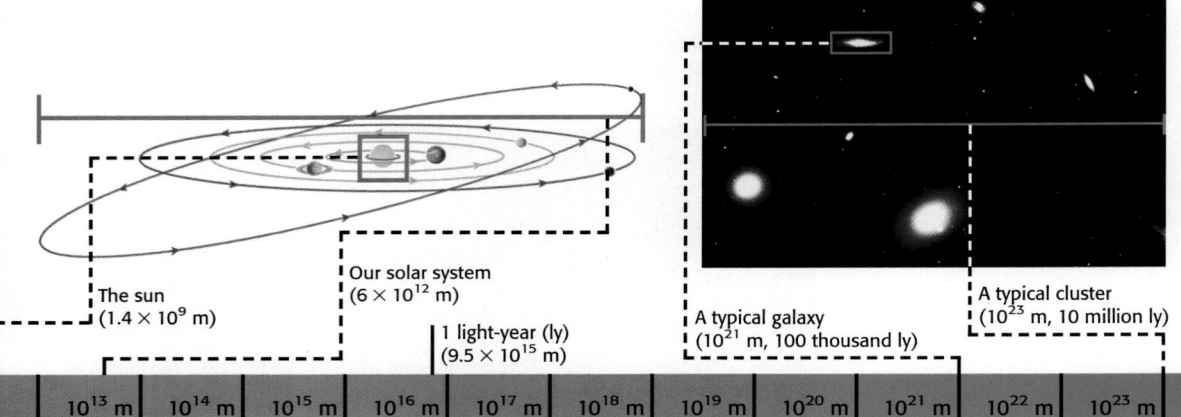

The sun (1.4×10^9 m)

Our solar system (6×10^{12} m)

1 light-year (ly) (9.5×10^{15} m)

A typical galaxy (10^{21} m, 100 thousand ly)

A typical cluster (10^{23} m, 10 million ly)

10^{13} m | 10^{14} m | 10^{15} m | 10^{16} m | 10^{17} m | 10^{18} m | 10^{19} m | 10^{20} m | 10^{21} m | 10^{22} m | 10^{23} m

THE UNIVERSE **527**

Connection to
LANGUAGE ARTS

Have students write a short fictional story describing an alternate universe different in some way from the one we live in. Students should include the relative sizes, shapes, and composition of objects in the universe. Students should also include various life-forms in their story.

Teaching Tip

The Speed of Light Turn out the lights in the room, and tell students that you are going to project a flashlight beam on a spot on the wall. For the first part of the demonstration, gather the students around you, and focus the flashlight's beam on the spot from a few centimeters away. Ask students the following questions: What does the beam look like? How does the light look on the wall?

After generating ideas, move as far as possible away from the spot on the wall, and ask students: What is different about the light on the wall this time? Shine the light on the wall, and although the speed of light will not be noticeable, have this demonstration lead into a discussion of the speed of light and the concept of light-years.

DEMONSTRATION 1 TEACHING

See the Universe in the Past

Time: Approximately 10 minutes

Materials: 3 photographs (1 showing a baby, another showing a 30-year-old, and 1 showing a 70-year-old)

Post the three pictures up on the chalkboard in order of youngest to oldest. Label the picture of the baby "Farthest star, 70 light-years away." Label the picture of the 30-year-old, "Nearer star," and label the picture of the 70-year-old, "Earth." Tell students that each individual was born the same day of the same year. Ask students how many light-years away the 30-year-old is. *(40 light-years).* Ask students why the ages of the individuals appear so different if they were born at the same time. *(The ages appear so different because the images that students are looking at would be 70-light-years in the past for the baby and 40-light-years in the past for the 30-year-old.)*

Figure 16-2
The Andromeda galaxy is 2.2 million light-years from Earth. It is one of the closest galaxies to the Milky Way galaxy, and it can be seen with the unaided eye.

▶ **interstellar matter** the gas and dust located between the stars in a galaxy

Figure 16-3
When we see the band of light called the Milky Way, we are looking along the plane of the Milky Way galaxy.

528 CHAPTER 16

Galaxies

While the nearest stars are 4.3 light-years away, the nearest full-sized galaxy to our own galaxy is more than 2 million light-years away. **Figure 16-2** shows this galaxy, the Andromeda galaxy. Many galaxies contain billions or even trillions of stars, but because they are so far away, galaxies usually look like small smudges in the sky, even through a telescope.

The deeper scientists look into the universe, the more galaxies they find. Astronomers now estimate that the universe contains 100 billion galaxies. To get a sense of how big this number is, consider this: If you counted 1000 new galaxies every night, it would take 275 000 years to count all of them.

We live in the Milky Way galaxy

If you live away from bright outdoor lights, you may be able to see a faint, narrow band of light and dark patches across the sky. **Figure 16-3** shows this band, called the Milky Way. The Milky Way consists of stars, gases, and dust in our own galaxy, the Milky Way galaxy. The Milky Way galaxy contains clouds of gas and dust between the stars, called **interstellar matter**. These clouds provide materials for new stars to form.

Almost every star you can see in the night sky is also part of the Milky Way galaxy. That is because our solar system is inside the Milky Way galaxy. Because we are inside the galaxy, we cannot see all of it at once. But scientists can use astronomical data to piece together a picture of the Milky Way galaxy like the one in **Figure 16-4** on the next page.

Types of Galaxies

Property	Spirals	Giant ellipticals	Dwarf ellipticals	Irregulars
diameter (light-years)	100 000	150 000	30 000	20 000
mass (number of suns)	100 billion	1 trillion	10 billion	100 million
Color of most stars	bluish	reddish	reddish	bluish
Gas as fraction of mass	5%	less than 1%	less than 1%	greater than 15%

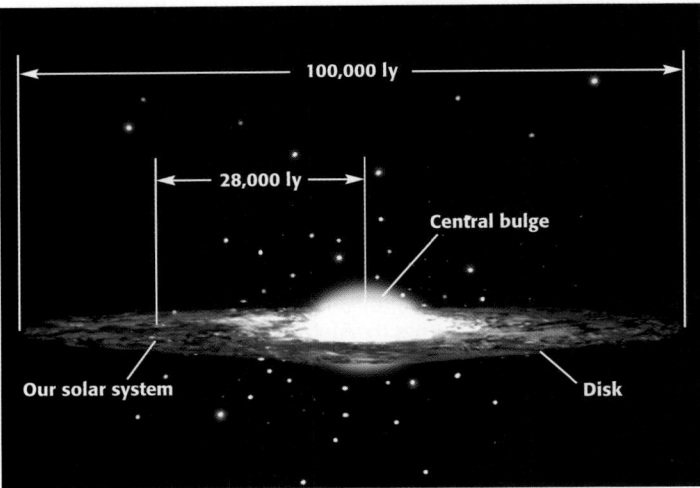

Figure 16-4
A picture of what the Milky Way galaxy might look like from the outside can be pieced together from astronomical data.

Our galaxy is a huge spiraling disk of stars and interstellar matter. The Milky Way galaxy has a huge bulge in its center. Earth, the sun, and the rest of the solar system are about midway between the galaxy's edge and its center.

There are three types of galaxies

Galaxies are classified into three types, based on their shape. The basic types are spiral, elliptical, and irregular.

Spiral galaxies, like the one shown in **Figure 16-5,** usually have spiral arms that contain gas and dust that provide materials for new stars to form. Young stars tend to be bluer in color than old stars, so spiral galaxies often have a bluish tint, especially in the spiral arms.

While spiral galaxies are disk-shaped, elliptical galaxies are spherical or egg-shaped. Elliptical galaxies are generally older than spiral galaxies. They contain mostly older stars, have no spiral arms, and contain relatively little gas and dust. Older stars are generally redder in color than young stars, so elliptical galaxies often have a reddish color.

Elliptical galaxies are found in a wide range of sizes and masses. Giant elliptical galaxies contain trillions of stars and can be as large as 200 000 light-years in diameter. Dwarf elliptical galaxies contain only a few million stars and are much smaller than spiral galaxies or giant ellipticals.

Irregular galaxies, as the name suggests, do not have a well-defined shape or structure. Some irregular galaxies contain relatively little gas and dust, while others are like clouds of intergalactic matter that have never given birth to stars.

internetconnect

SC*LINKS*

NSTA

TOPIC: Milky Way galaxy
GO TO: www.scilinks.org
KEYWORD: HK1162

Figure 16-5
Seen from above, the Milky Way galaxy might look similar to this spiral galaxy.

THE UNIVERSE **529**

The Universe and Galaxies

■SKILL BUILDER

Interpreting Visuals Have students examine **Figure 16-4** and imagine themselves standing within the Milky Way but outside the central bulge. In what direction would they need to look to see a band of light? *(The students could look left, right, or straight ahead along the plane of the galaxy to see the band of light. If students look up or down and out of the plane, they would see stars but no continuous band of light.)*

Connection to
LANGUAGE ARTS

Have students write a short paragraph describing how our galaxy would look to an alien observer in another galaxy.

■SKILL BUILDER

Interpreting Visuals **Figure 16-5** shows the spiral galaxy NGC 2997. Have students examine **Figure 16-5.** Which parts of the galaxy appear to have the most gas and dust? *(the spiral arms)* What color are the spiral arms primarily? *(blue)* Where are the stars that appear in the photograph located? *(The individual stars that can be seen are in the Milky Way galaxy, much closer to Earth than NGC 2997. The stars in that galaxy are too far away to be resolved as separate lights.)*

ALTERNATIVE ASSESSMENT

Spiral and Elliptical Galaxies

Before allowing students to perform this activity, you will need to prepare the hangers by unravelling or cutting the hangers with a pair of wire cutters. (If you use wire cutters, cut the hanger at the top, just below the neck.) Shape the wire into a connected circle and bend the hook toward the top so that it can hang.

Divide students into pairs. Give each group a bag of pipe cleaners, several loose sheets of newspaper, string, and a circular wire clothes hanger. Have the students use the pipe cleaners and newspaper to create their own spiral, giant elliptical, and dwarf elliptical galaxies. *(To create elliptical galaxies, students should crumple the loose sheets of newspaper into a ball and wrap pipe cleaners around the ball.)*

Have each group create a mobile by hanging its galaxies on the clothes hanger.

The Universe and Galaxies

SKILL BUILDER

Interpreting Visuals Have students examine **Figure 16-6** and identify which objects are galaxies and which are stars. Have students identify which galaxies are spiral and which are elliptical.

Did You Know ?

Because they are attracted to each other, galaxies that are close together sometimes orbit around each other and occasionally even collide. These collisions can last millions of years and span over a trillion cubic light-years of space.

The distance from star to star is so great that a galactic collision produces very few actual star collisions; only one pair of stars out of trillions is likely to collide. But the motion of the stars in each galaxy is affected by the gravitational pull of the stars in the other galaxy, so the galaxies are almost completely transformed by the encounter.

Figure 16-6
A cluster like the one shown here may contain thousands of galaxies held together by gravity.

▶ **cluster** a group of galaxies bound by gravity

Gravity holds galaxies together in clusters

Without gravity, the universe might just be a thin veil of gas spread out through space. With gravity, clouds of gas and dust draw together to form stars. Because of gravity, stars, gas, and dust collect into larger units, the galaxies.

Galaxies are not spread out evenly through the universe. They are grouped together in **clusters**, like the one shown in **Figure 16-6.** The members of a cluster of galaxies are bound together by gravity.

The Milky Way galaxy and the Andromeda galaxy are two of the largest members of a cluster of more than 30 galaxies called the Local Group. New members of the Local Group are being discovered as larger telescopes and better instruments are available to astronomers.

Clusters of galaxies can form even larger groups called *superclusters*. A typical supercluster contains thousands of galaxies containing trillions of stars in individual clusters. Superclusters can be as large as 100 million light-years across. They are the largest structures in the universe.

Figure 16-7

 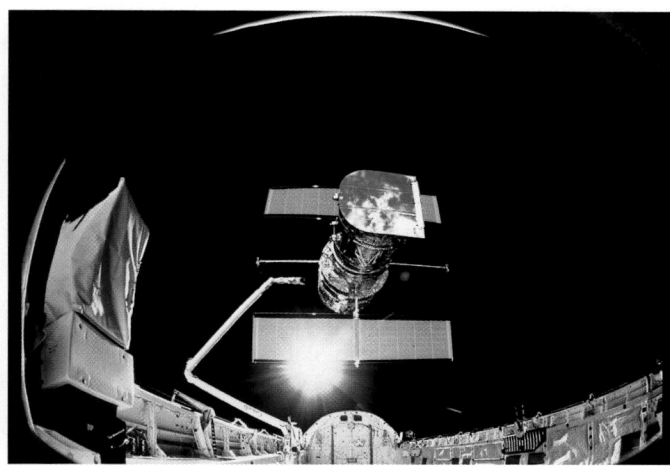

Ⓐ Edwin Hubble used the telescopes at Mount Wilson Observatory, in California, to explore galaxies beyond the Milky Way galaxy.

Ⓑ The Hubble Space Telescope, named in Hubble's honor, now probes the depths of the universe from its orbit high above the Earth's atmosphere.

530 CHAPTER 16

The Origin of the Universe

How did the universe come to be? This is an age-old question. Scientists today study stars and galaxies for clues to the origin of the universe.

The universe is expanding

The astronomer Edwin Hubble, shown in **Figure 16-7,** spent many years studying light from distant galaxies. In 1929, he announced his conclusion that the universe is expanding.

The atoms contained in stars emit light in a characteristic pattern of spectral lines. When Hubble examined the light from stars in other galaxies, he found this pattern of lines was shifted toward the red end of the spectrum. This is called a **red shift,** and it can be interpreted using the Doppler effect.

When an object is moving away from us, any waves coming from that object get stretched out. The faster a light source moves away, the more that light is stretched to longer wavelengths, or shifted toward the red end of the spectrum. **Figure 16-8** illustrates a red shift in spectral lines from a galaxy. For more on spectral lines, see Section 16.2.

The red shift in light from galaxies shows that every galaxy is moving away from Earth. Hubble also found another surprising result: galaxies farther away have greater red shifts. Since the time that those older galaxies emitted the light we see now, space has stretched out, increasing the wavelength of the light. In effect, all the galaxies are moving away from each other. Or in other words, the universe is expanding.

Expansion now implies that the universe was once smaller

Imagine time running backward, like a rewinding movie. If every galaxy normally moves away from every other galaxy, then as time goes backward, the galaxies appear to move closer together. This suggests that long ago the whole universe was contained in an extremely small volume.

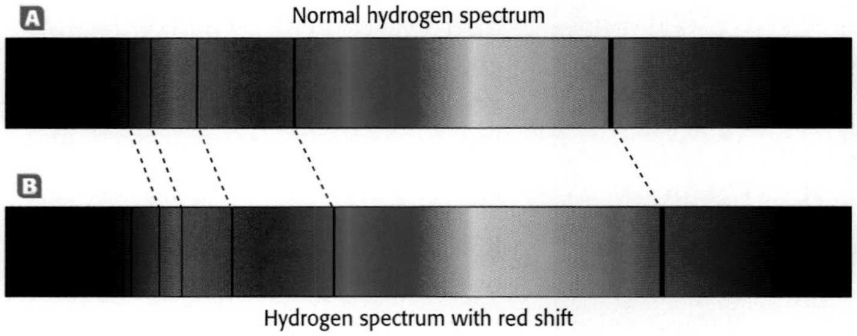

Figure 16-8
(A) The spectral lines of hydrogen gas can be seen and measured in a laboratory. (B) When this pattern appears in starlight, we know the star contains hydrogen. In this case, the lines are shifted toward the red because the star is in a galaxy that is moving away from us.

internetconnect

SciLINKS NSTA

TOPIC: Origin of the universe
GO TO: www.scilinks.org
KEYWORD: HK1163

red shift a shift toward the red end of the spectrum in the observed spectral lines of stars or galaxies

The Universe and Galaxies

LINKING CHAPTERS

Chapter 11 explains that the frequency of sound waves increases when the source of the sound is moving toward you and decreases when the source is moving away from you. The same is true of the frequency of light waves. Have students examine **Figure 11-12** on page 368. Would a decrease in the frequency of light from a galaxy make the galaxy appear more red or more blue? *(more red)*

Did You Know?

Not every galaxy exhibits a red shift. Some nearby galaxies, including the Andromeda galaxy, show a *blue shift,* meaning that spectral lines in light from the galaxy are shifted toward the blue end of the spectrum. That is because galaxies in our local cluster of galaxies, the Local Group, are gravitationally attracted to each other. While the universe is expanding on a very large scale, galaxies within a single cluster may move toward each other and even collide.

RESOURCE LINK
IER

Assign students worksheet *16.2 Integrating Physics—Red Shift, Blue Shift* in the **Integration Enrichment Resources** ancillary.

The Universe and Galaxies

K-W-L Have students list what they know or think they know about the big bang theory. After students read the section on the big bang theory and discuss it, have students look at their lists and write down what they have learned about the subject.

Teaching Tip

Theories on the Origin of the Universe Inform students that although the big bang theory is the theory most widely accepted by the scientific community, there are other scientific theories that explain the origin of the universe. The inflationary theory states that during earlier stages of development, the universe expanded at a faster rate than it is expanding today. This theory is somewhat of an extension of the big bang theory. The steady-state theory states that the universe has always existed in relatively the same state it is in now and that it will remain the same forever. This theory does not propose a beginning of time.

▶ **big bang theory** a scientific theory that states that the universe began 10 billion to 20 billion years ago in an enormous explosion

Quick ACTIVITY

Modeling the Universe
1. Inflate a round balloon to about half full, then pinch it closed to keep the air inside.
2. Use a marker to draw several dots close together on the balloon. Mark one of the dots with an *M* to represent the Milky Way galaxy.
3. Now continue inflating the balloon. How do the dots move relative to each other?
4. How is this a good model of the universe?
5. In what ways might this not be a good model of the universe?

Figure 16-9
The colors in this skywide map of cosmic background radiation represent slight differences in temperature above and below 2.7 K.

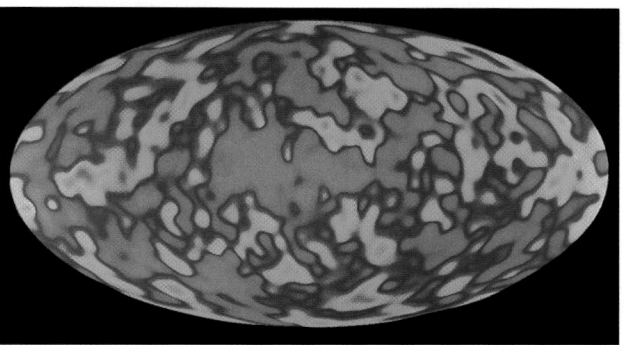

If time starts forward again from that point, all of the matter in the universe appears to expand rapidly outward. This would look like the result of a gigantic explosion. Scientists call this hypothetical explosion the "big bang."

Did the universe start with a big bang?
Although scientists have proposed several different theories to explain the expansion of the universe, the most complete and most widely accepted is the **big bang theory**. The big bang theory proposes that the universe began with a gigantic explosion 10 billion to 20 billion years ago. *In this book, we will assume that the universe is 15 billion years old.*

According to this theory, nothing existed before the big bang. There was no time and no space. But out of this nothingness came the vast system of space, time, matter, and energy that we now see as the universe. The explosion released all of the matter and energy that still exists in the universe today.

Cosmic background radiation supports the big bang theory
In 1965, Arno Penzias and Robert Wilson, of Bell Laboratories in New Jersey, discovered new evidence in support of the big bang theory. While making adjustments to a new radio antenna they had built, they detected a steady but very dim signal from the sky in the form of radiation at microwave wavelengths. This radiation, called the *cosmic background radiation*, had already been predicted by the big bang theory.

Imagine the changes in color as the burner on an electric stove cools off. At first the hot burner glows yellow or white. As it cools, it becomes dimmer and glows orange, then red. At all times, the burner produces light across a wide range of the electromagnetic spectrum. The color you see corresponds to the wavelength at which it radiates the most. If a burner were in outer space, it could keep cooling until the primary radiation reached very long, invisible wavelengths, such as microwaves.

Many scientists believe that the microwaves Penzias and Wilson discovered are dim remains of the energetic radiation produced during the big bang. Using computerized maps of cosmic background radiation, such as the one in **Figure 16-9,** scientists have found that the universe has an overall temperature of about 2.7 kelvins (K).

Quick ACTIVITY

Modeling the Universe The balloon represents the universe, and the dots represent galaxies. Students should observe that each dot moves away from the other dots as the balloon expands. This is a good model for demonstrating that as the universe expands (represented by the balloon), the matter in the universe (represented by the dots) expands as well. The model is limited because the dots are all on the surface of the balloon, which is a two-dimensional surface.

Another common model for the expanding universe is a loaf of raisin bread. As the bread rises, every raisin moves away from every other raisin. This is a three-dimensional model, but it is hard to observe directly because you cannot actually see into the bread. The raisin bread is more useful as a conceptual model.

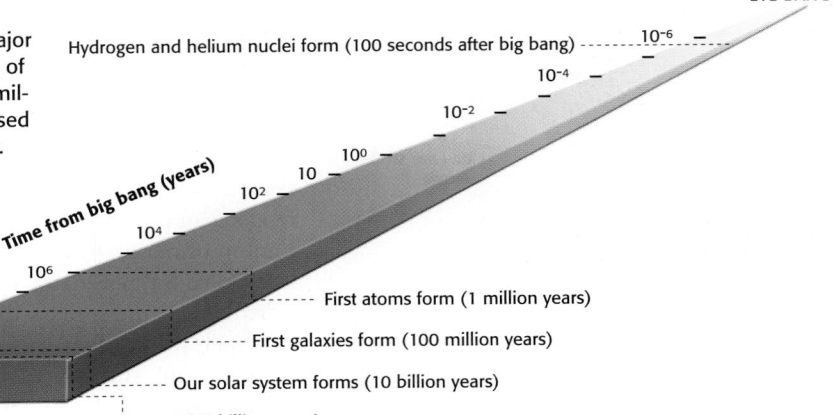

Figure 16-10
This timeline shows major events in the evolution of the universe. The first million (10^6) years are based on the big bang theory.

Hydrogen and helium nuclei form (100 seconds after big bang) ------ 10^{-6}

BIG BANG

10^{-4}

10^{-2}

10^0

Time from big bang (years)

10

10^2

10^4

10^6 ------- First atoms form (1 million years)

10^8 ------ First galaxies form (100 million years)

10^{10} ----- Our solar system forms (10 billion years)

Present (15 billion years)

From the big bang to atoms and beyond

According to the big bang theory, expansion cooled the universe enough for matter such as protons, neutrons, and electrons to form just a few seconds after the big bang. But the temperature was still too high for entire atoms to form and remain stable.

After about a million years, the universe expanded and cooled enough for regular hydrogen atoms to form. Since that time hydrogen has been the most abundant element in the universe. It serves as a fuel for stars and as a building block for stars to make other elements. Once the universe reached this point, the stage was set for the formation of stars, galaxies, and planets.

Figure 16-10 shows several key points in the evolution of the universe, following the model of the big bang theory. Note that the timeline uses a logarithmic scale, so that the last 5 billion years are squeezed into a small area at the end of the line.

The future of the universe is uncertain

The universe is still expanding, but it may not do so forever. The combined gravity of all the mass in the universe is also pulling the universe inward, in the direction opposite the expansion. The competition between these two forces leaves three possible outcomes for the universe:

1. The universe will keep expanding forever.

2. The expansion of the universe will gradually slow down, and the universe will approach a limit in size.

3. The universe will stop expanding and start to fall back in on itself.

Did You Know ?

Scientists estimate that some quasars, the most distant objects we can detect, may be as far as 15 billion light-years away. If this is true, the universe must be at least 15 billion years old in order for light from those quasars to have reached Earth.

THE UNIVERSE **533**

The Universe and Galaxies

|SKILL BUILDER

Interpreting Visuals **Figure 16-10** is a timeline of the evolution of the universe. Have the students examine **Figure 16-10**. How long after the big bang did the first nuclei form? *(100 s)* How long after the big bang did the first atoms form? *(1 million years)* the first galaxies form? *(100 million years)* According to the timeline, how long ago did the big bang occur? *(15 billion years ago)*

Resources Blackline Master 50 shows this visual.

Teaching Tip

Big Bang Theory Students may wonder how we can know what happened in the first seconds of the universe. The study of the origin and evolution of the universe is called *cosmology*. Cosmologists start with a hypothesis, such as "All of the matter in the universe was once contained in an extremely small region," and then use scientific laws to extrapolate what would happen from there. If a theoretical model of the early universe makes a prediction that matches, to some degree, what we observe in today's universe, then the cosmologists know they may be on the right track.

The Universe and Galaxies

Check Your Understanding

1. planets, stars, galaxies, clusters, superclusters
2. 4.1×10^{16} m
3. A typical cluster is about 100 times the size of the Milky Way galaxy.
4. spiral, elliptical, and irregular
5. Sketches from a side view should be similar to **Figure 16-4** on page 529. Sketches from the top should appear similar to **Figure 16-5** on page 529. Only the top view should show spiral arms. In both views, the solar system should be marked at a point that is neither in the central bulge nor on the very edge of the galaxy.
6. Answers should indicate that the Milky Way is a narrow band because (a) we are inside the galaxy and (b) the galaxy has a flat (planar) shape.
7. Evidence that the universe is expanding is provided by the fact that light from other galaxies is shifted toward the red end of the spectrum. That means all galaxies are moving away from each other.

Answers continue on p. 555A.

Answers continue on p. 555A.

RESOURCE LINK

STUDY GUIDE

Assign students *Review Section 16.1 The Universe and Galaxies.*

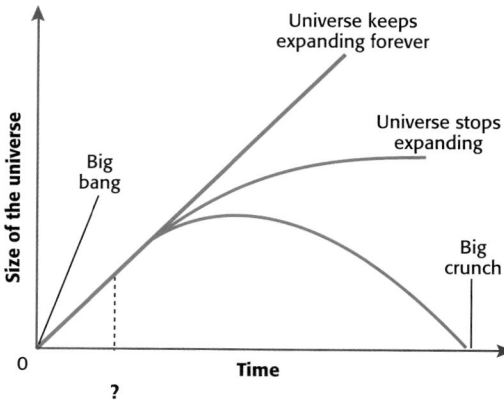

Figure 16-11
This graph shows three possible fates of the universe.

The fate of the universe depends on mass

Figure 16-11 shows three possible fates of the universe. Which one will be the outcome depends in large part on the amount of matter in the universe. If there is not enough mass in the universe, the gravitational force will be too weak to stop the expansion, so the universe will keep expanding forever. If there is just the right amount of mass, the expansion will continually slow down but never stop completely.

If there is more mass than this, gravity will eventually win out over the expansion, and the universe will start to contract. Eventually, a contracting universe might collapse back to a point in a "big crunch." This could be the end of the universe, or it could produce another big bang, starting the cycle all over again.

SUMMARY

▶ The universe consists of all matter and energy that exists, that ever has existed, and that ever will exist.

▶ A light-year is the distance that light travels in one year, 9.5×10^{15} m.

▶ Galaxies consist of billions of stars held together by their own gravity. Galaxies are grouped together in clusters and superclusters.

▶ Earth and the sun are located in a spiral arm of the Milky Way galaxy. Our galaxy is about 100 000 light-years in diameter.

▶ The big bang theory describes the origin of the universe as an enormous explosion that occurred 10 to 20 billion years ago.

CHECK YOUR UNDERSTANDING

1. **Arrange** the following astronomical structures from the smallest to the largest: galaxies, planets, superclusters, stars, clusters.
2. **Determine** the distance in meters to the Alpha Centauri star system, which is 4.3 light-years from Earth. The speed of light is 3.0×10^8 m/s.
3. **Compare** the size of the Milky Way galaxy with the size of a cluster of galaxies. How many times bigger is a typical cluster?
4. **List** the three main types of galaxies.
5. **Draw** sketches of the Milky Way galaxy viewed from the side and from overhead. Label the following on each: central bulge, disk, solar system.
6. **Explain** why the Milky Way appears as a narrow band of light in the night sky.
7. **Describe** the evidence that the universe is expanding.
8. **Critical Thinking** If we observe that all the galaxies are expanding away from the Milky Way galaxy, does that mean that we are at the center of the universe? Explain. (**Hint:** Imagine an inflating balloon with dots on the surface, and picture our galaxy as one of the dots.)
9. **Creative Thinking** How would other galaxies appear to move relative to Earth if the universe were shrinking?

16.2

Stars and the Sun

OBJECTIVES

▸ Describe the basic structure and properties of stars.
▸ Explain how the composition and surface temperatures of stars are measured.
▸ Recognize that all normal stars are powered by fusion reactions that form elements.
▸ Discuss the evolution of stars.

▶ **KEY TERMS**
constellation
red giant
white dwarf
supergiant
supernova
neutron star
black hole

O n any clear night you can gaze upward and see the stars. About 6000 stars are bright enough to be seen from Earth with the unaided eye. The same stars have been observed by people on Earth for many centuries.

What Are Stars?

The ancient Greeks thought that all the stars were at an equal distance from Earth, like lights attached to a giant spherical roof. They grouped the stars together in patterns called **constellations.** The patterns often outlined characters from Greek mythology. For example, the constellation Orion, shown in **Figure 16-12,** depicts Orion the Hunter. The red star Betelgeuse represents Orion's left shoulder; the blue star Rigel represents his right foot.

We still divide the sky into constellations, but we now know that the stars in a constellation are not necessarily grouped together in space. The patterns seen from Earth are merely products of the locations of stars along our line of sight. Although the stars appear close together in the sky, they are actually quite far apart. In Orion, Rigel is almost three times farther away from Earth than is Betelgeuse.

▶ **constellation** a group of stars appearing in a pattern as seen from Earth

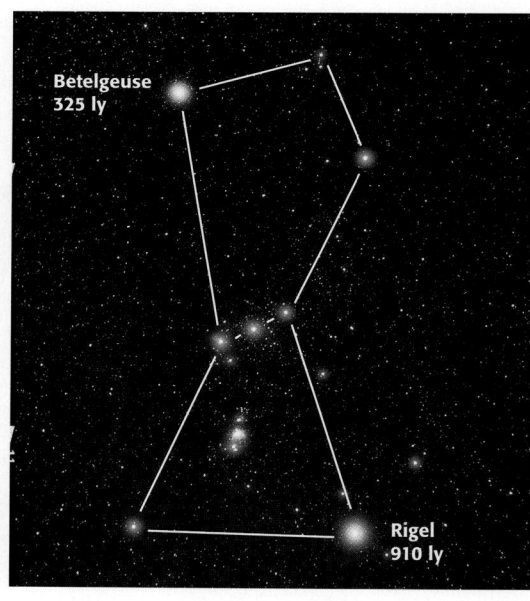

Figure 16-12
Although the stars in Orion appear close together in the sky, they are actually quite far away from each other.

THE UNIVERSE **535**

Section 16.2

Stars and the Sun

Scheduling
Refer to pp. 524A–524D for lecture, classwork, and assignment options for Section 16.2.

★ **Lesson Focus**
Use transparency *LT 53* to prepare students for this section.

▌SKILL BUILDER

Interpreting Visuals
Figure 16-12 shows the constellation Orion. Have the students examine **Figure 16-12.** Do they recognize Orion? Have they seen it in the sky before? What key features make it easy to locate in the sky?

Orion represents a human figure, a hunter. The red star Betelgeuse is Orion's shoulder, and the blue star Rigel represents Orion's foot. What might the three stars across the middle represent? *(traditionally, a belt. The cloudy smudge below the belt, called the Orion nebula, represents a sword.)*

ALTERNATIVE ASSESSMENT

Social Studies The constellations are often modeled after characters from Greek and Roman mythology. Have students pick a constellation from the star chart in Appendix B (or another constellation that they know) and research the origin of its name.

Language Arts Have students draw and name their own star pattern. Then have them write a myth about their constellation.

535

Stars and the Sun

Many people do not realize that the sun is a star. In fact, the sun is a very ordinary star. It appears bright only because it is much closer to Earth than other stars are.

One simple piece of evidence that the sun is close to Earth is the fact that it has an observable diameter. Most stars are so far away that they appear as mere points of light, even through powerful telescopes. Some stars appear larger than mere points in the sky due to the dispersion of starlight in the atmosphere.

Did You Know ?

The part of the sun that we see from Earth is actually a layer of the sun's atmosphere called the photosphere. This layer is composed of gas clouds hundreds of miles thick and of cells called granules. These cells are the size of Earth.

REAL WORLD APPLICATIONS ················

Protection Against Ultraviolet Rays While sunlight is beneficial to life on Earth, ultraviolet rays from the sun are harmful to people. Have your students research the role that ultraviolet rays from the sun play in the lives of humans. What are some of the ways that people protect themselves from the sun's UV rays? *(sunscreen, clothing)* How does Earth's atmosphere protect us from UV rays? *(The ozone layer blocks the most energetic UV light.)*

················

Figure 16-13
People on Earth are very familiar with one star in particular—the sun.

Figure 16-14
Many telescopes detect light that is beyond the visible spectrum. Data from such telescopes must be processed and displayed by a computer.

The sun is a typical star

Of all the stars, astronomers know the most about one in particular: our own sun. The sun, shown in **Figure 16-13,** is an average star, not particularly hot or cool and of average size.

Although the sun is not very big for a star, it is much bigger than Earth. The sun's diameter is about 1.4 million kilometers, or about 110 times Earth's diameter. If Earth were the size of a dime, the sun would be about 2 m in diameter and 200 m away from the dime-sized Earth.

The mass of the sun is about 2×10^{30} kg, or more than 300 000 times the mass of Earth. Although the core of the sun is extremely dense, its overall density—its total mass divided by its total volume—is about 1.4 g/cm^3, only slightly denser than water.

Why do some stars appear brighter than others?

The brightness of a star depends on the star's temperature, size, and distance from Earth. Rigel is the brightest star in the constellation Orion. Although Rigel is much farther away than Betelgeuse, it appears brighter because it is about four times hotter than Betelgeuse. Betelgeuse is not very hot for a star, but it appears brighter than the other stars in Orion because it is very large, with a diameter hundreds of times larger than the sun's.

The brightest star in the night sky is Sirius, in the constellation Canis Major. The main reason that it appears so bright is that it is relatively close to Earth, only about 9 light-years away. The sun is just an average star, but it is so close to Earth that its light dominates the entire sky during the day.

We learn about stars by studying light

Starlight is our only source for information about the nature of stars. But there is much more to starlight than meets the eye. When we look with our unaided eyes or through a telescope, we can detect only light in the visible part of the spectrum.

Stars also produce electromagnetic radiation at other wavelengths, ranging from high-energy X rays to low-energy radio waves. Astronomers today use telescopes with instruments that can detect radiation from all these different wavelengths. The data collected with such telescopes can be processed and displayed on computer screens, as shown in **Figure 16-14.**

536 CHAPTER 16

DEMONSTRATION 2 TEACHING

Understanding Stellar Brightness

Time: Approximately 10 minutes
Materials: 1 large, bright flashlight
3 small, dim flashlights

Step 1 Have the students line up at one end of the classroom, and turn out the lights. Give one student the large flashlight and give another student one of the small flashlights.

Step 2 Send those two students to the other end of the classroom. Ask which light appears to be brightest.

Step 3 Now have the student with the dimmer light walk across the room until the lights appear equally bright. Ask students how this situation relates to the stars Sirius and Rigel. Which flashlight corresponds to which star? *(The large flashlight corresponds to Rigel, the small to Sirius).*

The color of a star is related to its temperature

When light from a glowing hot object passes through a prism, it displays a continuous spectrum of light's many different colors. This spectrum changes with temperature in a definite way: hotter objects glow with light that is more intense at shorter wavelengths (toward the blue end of the spectrum), while cooler objects have greater intensity at longer wavelengths (toward the red end).

Although the light from a glowing object contains many colors, the color that we see when we look directly at any hot object, including a star, is determined by the wavelength at which the object emits the most light.

Figure 16-15 is a graph that shows the intensity, or brightness, of light at different wavelengths for three different stars. The sun appears yellow because the peak wavelength of the sun corresponds to the color yellow. This color also corresponds to a temperature of 6000 K.

Spectral lines reveal the composition of stars

How do we know what stars are made of? The spectra of most stars have dark lines where light is missing at certain wavelengths. The light at these wavelengths has been absorbed by gases in the outer layers of the stars.

Because each element produces a unique pattern of spectral lines, astronomers can match the dark lines in starlight to lines absorbed by gases of elements found on Earth and tested in the lab. **Figure 16-16** shows how the spectral lines of hydrogen and helium match lines found in the spectrum of sunlight.

Figure 16-15
This graph shows the intensity of light at different wavelengths for the sun and two other stars.

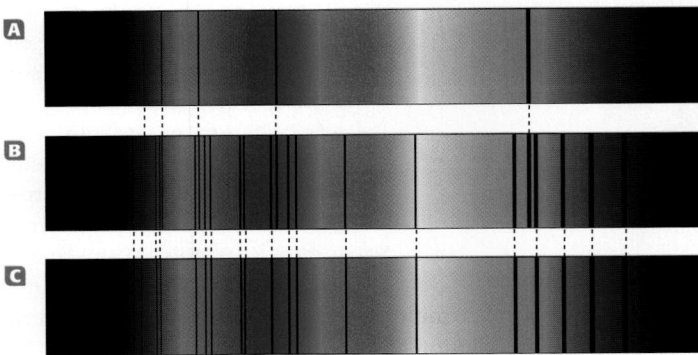

Figure 16-16
When light is passed through hydrogen gas (A) or helium gas (C), then through a prism, dark lines appear in the spectrum. Those lines match lines observed in the sun's spectrum (B).

THE UNIVERSE **537**

SKILL BUILDER

Interpreting Visuals Have students examine **Figure 16-15.** Explain that the three curves represent light from three different stars. Each star emits light across a wide range of the electromagnetic spectrum.

The color that the star appears is the color corresponding to the peak of the curve. For the curve representing the sun, what color of the spectrum is the highest point of the graph? *(yellow)*

The color of a star also corresponds to the surface temperature of the star. Which of the stars has the highest temperature? *(the blue star)* Which has the lowest temperature? *(the red star)*

The total area under each curve corresponds to the total energy output of the star. Which star produces the most energy? *(the blue star)*

Resources *Teaching Transparency 49 shows this visual.*

RESOURCE LINK
IER

Assign students worksheet *16.4 Integrating Health—Exercise in Space* in the **Integration Enrichment Resources** ancillary.

Step 4 Repeat the procedure, but this time have one student hold all three dim flashlights bundled together. In this case, the large flashlight still corresponds to Rigel, and the bundle of dim flashlights corresponds to Betelgeuse.

Stars and the Sun

Quick ACTIVITY

Using a Star Chart
Locate the following stars on the star chart in Appendix B: Betelgeuse, Rigel, Sirius, Capella, and Aldebaran. What constellation is each star in? Which of these stars appears closest in the sky to Polaris, the North Star?

Astronomers have analyzed more than 20 000 lines in the sun's spectrum to find the composition and chemical abundance of the sun's atmosphere. Of all the atoms in the sun, 90 percent are hydrogen, 9.9 percent are helium, and 0.1 percent are other elements. Most other stars have similar compositions.

Stars are driven by nuclear fusion reactions

Stars such as the sun are basically huge, hot balls of hydrogen and helium gas that emit light. They are held together by the enormous gravitational forces caused by their own mass. Inside the core of a star, these forces create a harsh environment. The pressure is more than a billion times the atmospheric pressure on Earth. The temperature is hotter than 15 million kelvins, and the density is over 150 times greater than that of water.

In these extreme conditions, nuclear fusion reactions combine the nuclei of hydrogen atoms into helium with a release of energy. This energy flows outward, balancing the inward pull of gravity. However, the energy released in fusion reactions inside a star does not directly produce the light we see.

Energy moves slowly through the layers of a star

Figure 16-17 shows the major parts of the sun. Other stars have similar structures, although the temperatures may be different. The energy from fusion moves through the layers of a star by a combination of radiation and convection, two of the primary ways that energy is transferred.

These processes are not very fast. In fact, it may take millions of years for the energy generated by a nuclear reaction to work its way through a star. When the energy finally reaches the surface, it is released into space as radiation, or starlight.

Once light leaves the surface of a star, it radiates across space at the speed of light in a vacuum, 3×10^8 m/s. At this speed, it takes light from the sun about 8 minutes to reach Earth. For more on radiation and convection, review Section 10.2.

Figure 16-17
Energy slowly works its way through the layers of the sun by radiation and convection.

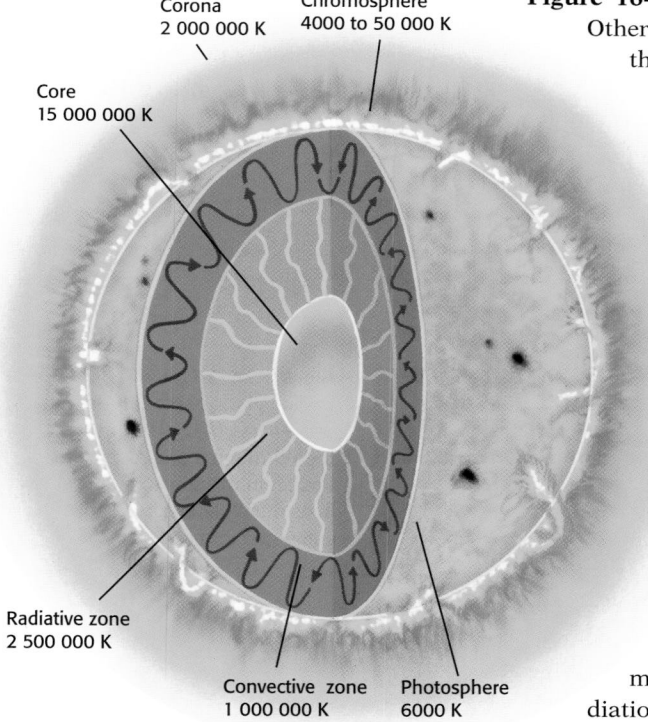

Corona
2 000 000 K

Chromosphere
4000 to 50 000 K

Core
15 000 000 K

Radiative zone
2 500 000 K

Convective zone
1 000 000 K

Photosphere
6000 K

Quick ACTIVITY

Using a Star Chart The star chart in Appendix B shows the sky as it appears in northern latitudes at 8 P.M. on March 1 or midnight on January 1. To use the chart when observing the sky, hold the page overhead and face north (for the upper half of the chart) or south (for the lower half).

Betelgeuse and Rigel are in the constellation Orion; Sirius is in Canis Major; Capella is in Auriga; and Aldebaran is in Taurus. All of these are primarily in the southern sky, except Auriga. Capella is the closest to Polaris, the North Star. Polaris is in the constellation Ursa Minor, and it marks the end of the "handle" of the Little Dipper.

The Life and Death of Stars

Figure 16-18 shows stars being formed in a cloud of gas and dust called a *nebula*. Like living creatures, stars are born, go through different stages of development, and eventually die. Stars appear different from one another in part because they are at different stages in their life cycles. Nearly 90 percent of all stars, including the sun, are in midlife, converting hydrogen into helium in their interiors.

Some stars, such as Rigel, are younger than the sun, while others, such as Betelgeuse, are farther along in their life cycles. Some objects in the universe are remnants of very old stars long since dead. But how do stars get started? And how do they keep on shining for billions of years?

The sun formed from a cloud of gas and dust

About 5 billion years ago, in an arm of the Milky Way galaxy, a thin, invisible cloud of gas and dust collapsed inward, pulled by the force of its own gravity. As the cloud fell together, it began to spin, and the smaller the cloud got, the faster it spun.

About 30 million years after the cloud started to collapse, the center of the cloud reached a temperature of 15 million kelvins. Under these extreme conditions, electrons were stripped from hydrogen atoms, leaving positively charged protons.

Ordinarily, positively charged protons repel each other. But at very high temperatures, protons move very rapidly and may get as close to each other as 10^{-15} m. At such a small distance, the strong nuclear force can overpower the electrical repulsion. Through the process of nuclear fusion, the protons may combine to form helium with a release of energy.

Once nuclear fusion started in the core of the cloud, the star we call the sun was born. For more on nuclear fusion, see Chapter 7. The formation of the rest of the solar system will be covered in more detail in Section 16.3.

The sun now has a balance of inward and outward forces

The fusion reactions in the core of the sun produce an outward force that balances the inward force due to gravity. With those two forces evenly balanced, the sun has maintained an equilibrium for 5 billion years.

The sun is now in the prime of its life, fusing hydrogen into helium. Scientists estimate that the sun has enough fuel to continue nuclear fusion in its core for another 5 billion years.

Figure 16-18
New stars are constantly being born in clouds of gas and dust such as these columns in the Eagle nebula. This image was taken by the Hubble Space Telescope.

internetconnect

SCI LINKS
NSTA

TOPIC: Stars
GO TO: www.scilinks.org
KEYWORD: HK1164

THE UNIVERSE **539**

READING SKILL BUILDER *Reading Organizer* Have students read the section on the life and death of stars. Then have them organize the ideas presented in the section in a sequence of events.

SKILL BUILDER

Interpreting Visuals Figure 16-18 shows star birth in the Eagle nebula. Although some stars are visible in the picture, the stars that are being born are hidden deep within the pillars of gas. The pillars form as lighter gases are blown away by radiation from nearby stars. The stars form as the denser material is drawn together due to gravity.

The image has an unusual outline because of the manner in which the data were compiled by NASA.

REAL WORLD APPLICATIONS ....

Nuclear Power Plants   The sun fuses hydrogen into helium. Have students research nuclear power plants and answer the following questions: How do these facilities produce energy? Compare nuclear power plants with the sun. How similar or different are the two methods of producing energy? (*Nuclear power plants rely on nuclear fission reactions, while the sun derives energy from nuclear fusion.*)

....

Stars and the Sun

SKILL BUILDER

Interpreting Visuals **Figure 16-19** shows the size of the sun after it expands to become a red giant. Theoretical calculations show that it will expand to somewhere between the orbits of Earth and Mars. When that happens, life will no longer be able to exist on Earth. Thankfully, this will happen only in about 5 billion years.

You may pose a math problem to the students. The sun presently has a diameter of 1.4×10^9 m, and the radius of Earth's orbit is 1.5×10^{11} m. How many times larger will the sun be as a red giant than it is now, in terms of diameter? How much larger will it be in terms of volume?

$(V = \frac{4}{3}\pi r^3)$

Connection to SOCIAL STUDIES

In the year 1054, Chinese observers witnessed what seemed to be the birth of a "new star" in the sky. They actually witnessed a supernova. The original star was too far away to be seen from Earth, but when it exploded, it became the brightest light in the night sky for a short time. The remnants of that very same supernova can now be seen in the Crab nebula, shown on page 541.

The most famous supernova sighting in recent times was Supernova 1987A, observed in 1987. Supernova 1987A occurred in the Large Magellanic Cloud, an irregular galaxy very near the Milky Way galaxy. Have students research Supernova 1987A. Prompt them to answer the following questions: Where did the supernova occur? Who first identified it as a supernova? What did scientists learn from studying Supernova 1987A?

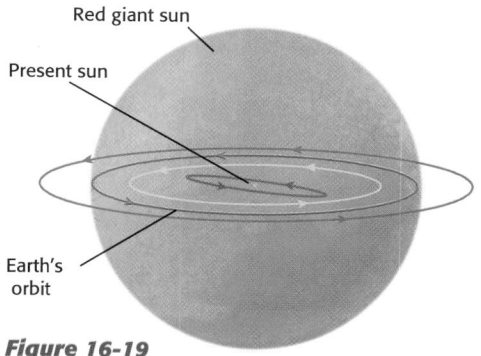

Red giant sun
Present sun
Earth's orbit

Figure 16-19
When the sun becomes a red giant, it will expand out past Earth's orbit.

▶ **red giant** a large, reddish star late in its life cycle that fuses helium into carbon or oxygen

▶ **white dwarf** a small, very dense star that remains after fusion in a red giant stops

▶ **supergiant** an extremely large star that creates elements as heavy as iron

▶ **supernova** a powerful explosion that occurs when a massive star dies

The sun will become a red giant before it dies

When fusion of hydrogen slows, the core of the sun will start to contract, and the temperature in the core will rise. The outer layers of the sun will expand out past Earth's orbit, and the sun will become a **red giant**, as shown in **Figure 16-19.** While the outer layers of the red giant sun will remain relatively cool, the core will reach temperatures high enough to spark the fusion of helium into carbon and oxygen.

After about 100 million years, the core of the red giant sun will become entirely carbon and oxygen, the core will contract further, and the outer layers will expand again. At this point, though, the temperature will not rise high enough to start the fusion of carbon or oxygen into heavier elements.

The outer layers of the sun will continue to expand out from the core, forming a *planetary nebula,* a glowing cloud or ring of gas. The remaining core of the sun will become a **white dwarf,** a dim ember about the size of Earth but extremely dense. The dwarf sun will slowly cool, producing no more energy.

Any star that ends up, after its initial stage of helium fusion, with a mass less than or equal to 1.4 times the mass of the sun will have a life cycle like the sun's and will die as a white dwarf. Most of the stars in the Milky Way Galaxy will end their lives as white dwarfs. But larger stars burn hotter and brighter, and have more dramatic deaths.

Supergiant stars explode in supernovas

Stars more than 1.4 times the mass of the sun do not become red giants. They become **supergiants.** Because of their greater mass, supergiant stars do not stop with carbon fusion. These stars produce successively heavier elements until their cores become iron.

The formation of an iron core signals the beginning of a supergiant star's violent death. This is because fusing iron atoms together to make heavier elements requires energy rather than producing energy. So when the entire core finally becomes iron, fusion stops.

When the fusion stops, there is no longer any outward pressure to balance the gravitational force. The star's core collapses and then rebounds with a shock wave that violently blows the star's outer layers away from the core. The huge, bright explosion that results is called a **supernova.** A supernova is the only natural event in the universe energetic enough to spark fusion that can create elements heavier than iron. The remains of one such explosion can still be seen in the Crab nebula, shown in **Figure 16-20.**

After a supernova, either a neutron star or a black hole forms

If the core that remains after a supernova has a mass of 1.4 to about 3 times that of the Sun, it can become a **neutron star**. Neutron stars are only a few kilometers in diameter—about the size of a small city—but they are very massive. The density of a neutron star is equal to that of matter in the nuclei of atoms, about 10^{17} kg/m³. A thimbleful of the matter in a neutron star would weigh more than 100 million tons on Earth. Neutron stars can sometimes be detected as *pulsars*, rapidly rotating sources of radio waves.

If the core remaining after a supernova has a mass greater than three times that of the sun, it will collapse to form an even stranger object—a **black hole.** A black hole consists of matter so massive and compressed that nothing, not even light, can escape from its gravity.

Because no light comes out of a black hole, a black hole cannot be seen directly. However, black holes have a powerful gravitational influence on objects around them, so they may be detected indirectly.

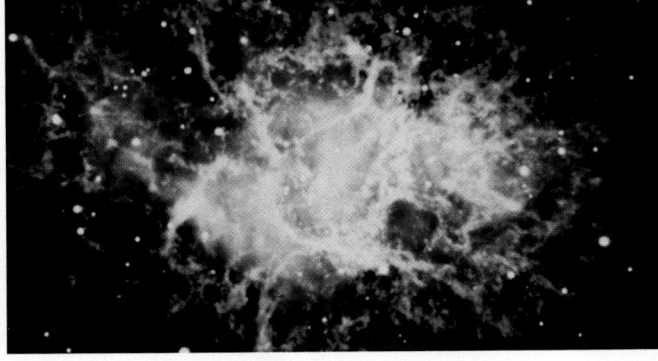

Figure 16-20
The Crab nebula is the remains of a supernova seen by Chinese observers in the year 1054.

▶ **neutron star** a dead star with the density of atomic nuclei

▶ **black hole** an object so massive and dense that not even light can escape its gravity

---

SECTION 16.2 REVIEW

SUMMARY

▶ Stars are huge balls of gas that generate light through fusion in their cores.

▶ Starlight reveals the temperature and composition of stars.

▶ The sun is a typical star. It formed in a cloud of gas and dust; it will become a red giant and then die as a white dwarf.

▶ Supergiant stars die in supernovas; the cores left behind become neutron stars or black holes.

CHECK YOUR UNDERSTANDING

1. **Name** three different kinds of stars.
2. **Describe** how a star generates light.
3. **Explain** why cooler stars are red and hotter stars are blue.
4. **Describe** the formation of the sun.
5. **Describe** the final stages in the lives of the following stars:
   a. the sun
   b. a star 20 times the mass of the sun
6. **Critical Thinking** Which of the following elements are likely to be formed in the sun at some time in its life?
   a. helium   c. iron
   b. carbon   d. uranium
7. **Critical Thinking** You and a friend are looking at the stars. Your friend says, "Stars must always be shrinking because gravity is constantly pulling their particles together." Explain what is wrong with your friend's reasoning.

THE UNIVERSE **541**

SECTION 16.2 REVIEW

Check Your Understanding

1. red giant, white dwarf, supergiant (neutron star, black hole)
2. Stars generate light through the fusion that occurs in their cores.
3. Cooler stars are red because they glow with light that is more intense at longer wavelengths (toward the red end of the light spectrum), and hotter stars are blue because they glow with light that is more intense at shorter wavelengths (toward the blue end of the light spectrum).
4. The sun formed as a cloud of gas and dust collapsed inward, pulled by the force of its own gravity. Nuclear fusion started at the core of the spinning cloud, where protons began to combine, forming helium with a release of energy.
5. a. After the sun has become a red giant, its core will eventually become entirely composed of carbon and oxygen, and the core will contract. The temperature will not rise high enough to start fusion, and the sun will become a white dwarf, which will slowly cool off, no longer producing energy.

Answers continue on p. 555A.

RESOURCE LINK
STUDY GUIDE

Assign students *Review Section 16.2 Stars and the Sun.*

Scheduling

Refer to pp. 524A–524D for lecture, classwork, and assignment options for Section 16.3.

★ Lesson Focus
Use transparency *LT 54* to prepare students for this section.

READING SKILL BUILDER  **K-W-L** Have students list what they know or think they know about the solar system, then have them list what they want to learn about the solar system. After students read Section 16.3, tell them to look at their lists and write down what they have learned about the subject. Students should write down any new questions that they have after reading the section. Encourage students to do further reading in other sources on the aspects of the solar system if they still have unanswered questions.

SKILL BUILDER

Interpreting Visuals **Figure 16-21** shows an ancient map of the heavens alongside a modern representation of the solar system.

Have students identify Earth, the sun, the moon, and the planets in **Figure 16-21A.** *(Earth is in the center, the sun, the moon, and the planets orbit Earth. The names of the planets are in Latin.)* Are all the planets represented? *(The farthest known planet at that time was Saturn.)*

Now have students identify Earth, the sun, and the planets in **Figure 16-21B.** Which object do all the others orbit? *(the sun)* Are the planets in the same order in each of the two models? *(They are the same in terms of distance from Earth.)*

Resources *Blackline Master 52 shows a visual of* **Figure 16-21B.**

16.3

The Solar System

▶ **KEY TERMS**
planet
solar system
asteroid
nebular model
phases
eclipse

OBJECTIVES

▶ Identify the planets of the solar system and their features.
▶ Describe the formation of the solar system.
▶ Explain eclipses and the phases of the moon.

Because the Earth spins on its axis, the stars overhead appear to move in regular, circular paths across the night sky. However, a few lights in the sky deviate from these paths. The ancient Greeks named these strange lights "planets," which in their language meant "wanderers."

▶ **planet** any of the nine primary bodies orbiting the sun; a similar body orbiting another star

The View from Earth

For centuries, people have known about five of the **planets:** Mercury, Venus, Mars, Jupiter, and Saturn. Each of these can be seen from Earth with the unaided eye. **Figure 16-21A** shows an ancient model of the solar system with Earth at the center.

In 1543, the astronomer Nicolaus Copernicus argued that all of the planets—including Earth—orbit the sun. Shortly after that, the astronomer Kepler showed that the orbits of the planets are ellipses, not perfect circles. **Figure 16-21B** shows a modern representation of the solar system.

Figure 16-21

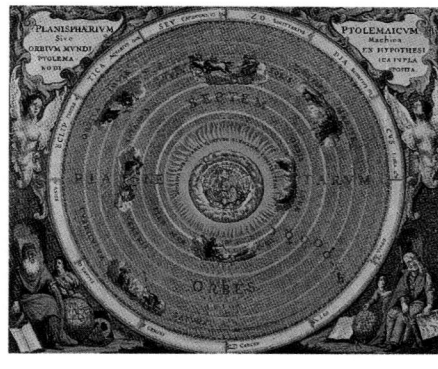

A Many old maps of the universe show the sun, the moon, and the planets orbiting Earth in perfect circles.

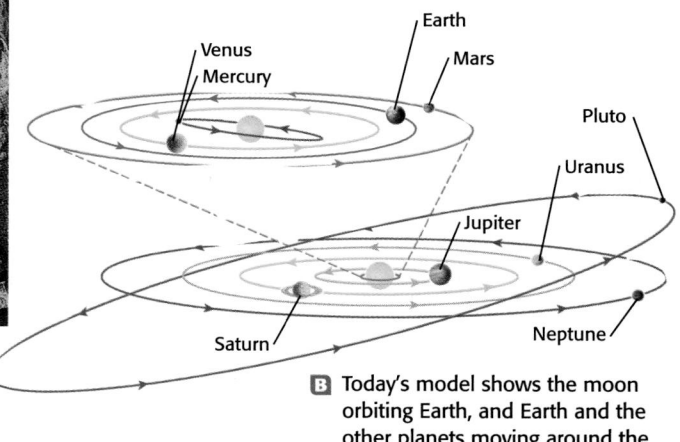

B Today's model shows the moon orbiting Earth, and Earth and the other planets moving around the sun in elliptical orbits.

Table 16-1 Properties of the Planets

Planet	Average surface temperature (°C)	Number of moons	Presence of rings	Atmosphere
Mercury	350	0	No	Essentially none
Venus	460	0	No	Thick: carbon dioxide, sulfuric acid
Earth	20	1	No	Nitrogen, oxygen
Mars	−23	2	No	Thin: carbon dioxide
Jupiter	−120	16	Yes	Hydrogen, helium, ammonia, methane
Saturn	−180	18	Yes	Hydrogen, helium, ammonia, methane
Uranus	−210	20	Yes	Hydrogen, helium, ammonia, methane
Neptune	−220	8	Yes	Hydrogen, helium, methane
Pluto	−230	1	No	Very thin: nitrogen and methane

Nine planets orbit the sun

After people started using telescopes to study the sky, three more planets were discovered: Uranus, Neptune, and Pluto. Pluto, which is small and very far away, was not discovered until 1930. Some facts about the planets are summarized in **Table 16-1.**

The **solar system** includes the sun, the nine planets, and all of the other objects orbiting the sun. These other objects include meteors, comets, and asteroids. Sometimes, one of these smaller objects strikes a planet, producing a crater.

The planets in our solar system are much smaller and much nearer than stars. As the planets move in elliptical orbits around the sun, their positions as seen against the backdrop of stars change. That is why they appear to wander through the sky.

Planets reflect sunlight

Planets do not give off their own light. They can be seen from Earth because the surfaces of the planets or clouds in their atmospheres reflect sunlight.

Besides the sun and the moon, the brightest object in the sky is Venus. It is the so-called "morning star" and "evening star" that can be seen near the sun at dawn and at dusk. Venus appears bright in the sky because it has a thick atmosphere that reflects sunlight very well.

▶ **solar system** the sun and all the objects that orbit around it

Did You Know?

Scientists now have evidence of planets orbiting other stars. However, because planets do not give off their own light, distant planets are hard to detect. So far, astronomers have only found distant planets that are larger than Jupiter. With improved telescopes, astronomers hope to someday find smaller planets that are more like Earth.

THE UNIVERSE **543**

Reading Hint Table 16-1, **Properties of the Planets,** will help students understand differences between the nine planets in the solar system.

Resources *Blackline Master 53* shows this visual.

Connection to SOCIAL STUDIES

The English names for the planets come from the names of Roman gods. Have students research the origins of the names of the planets, moons, and asteroids and share their results with the class. Are the names appropriate for each planet? Why or why not?

Historical Perspective

Italian astronomer Galileo Galilei was the first astronomer to work with a telescope. In the summer of 1609, Galileo made his first three-power telescope. He presented an eight-power telescope to the Venetian Senate later that summer and then created a twenty-power telescope that he used to observe the moon and the four largest moons of Jupiter.

At the time of Galileo's observations, Copernicus's sun-centered model of the universe was still not widely accepted; most people still used Ptolemy's Earth-centered model, which theorized that every object in the heavens orbits Earth. When Galileo saw four moons orbiting Jupiter, he realized that objects can orbit around other heavenly bodies as well. Galileo also observed that Venus has phases like the moon. Galileo's observations were of key importance in establishing that Earth and the other planets orbit the sun.

543

Teaching Tip

Circular Or Elliptical Orbit?
Your students may have difficulty distinguishing between a circular orbit and an elliptical orbit. Differentiate between the two by drawing both shapes on the board for your students.

SKILL BUILDER

Interpreting Visuals Have students examine **Figure 16-23.** If Venus is obscured by clouds, then how could this map be created? *(by using radar; radio waves can pass through the clouds, while visible light cannot.)* What do the colors on the map represent? *(Yellow and brown are higher elevations; blue and green are lower elevations.)*
  Prompt students to look for features on the surface of Venus, such as mountain ranges, lowland plains, and craters. *(The large brown areas are like continents; there are even higher areas on them that are mountain ranges. The large blue and green patches are comparable to Earth's oceans, but because they contain no liquid water, they are more like low plains. Some of the small circular features may be craters.)*

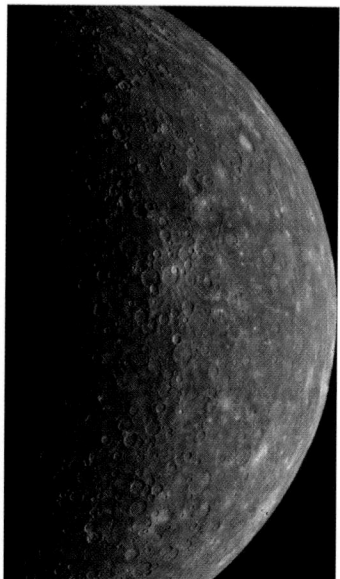

Figure 16-22
Mercury is pocked with craters.

The Inner Planets

The four inner planets—Mercury, Venus, Earth, and Mars—are relatively small and have solid, rocky surfaces. Using telescopes, orbiting satellites, and surface probes, scientists can study the geologic features of these planets.

Mercury has extreme temperatures

Much of our knowledge of Mercury comes from the *Mariner 10* fly-by mission in 1974. The photographs taken from *Mariner 10,* such as the one in **Figure 16-22,** showed for the first time that Mercury is pocked with craters, much like the moon.
  Mercury is so close to the sun that its surface has a temperature over 670 K (397°C), which is hot enough to melt a tin can. But on the dark side, the temperature drops to an extremely cold 103 K (–170°C). Mercury spins slowly on its axis, managing to get three spins (days) for every two orbits (years) around the sun.
  Mercury would not be a likely place to find life. In addition to having very extreme temperatures, it has hardly any atmosphere at all and no water.

Venus's thick clouds cause a greenhouse effect

On its way to Mercury, *Mariner 10* also took photos of the next planet out from the sun, Venus. The photos showed thick layers of clouds. Venus has a very thick atmosphere composed mostly of carbon dioxide. Radar maps, such as the one shown in **Figure 16-23,** indicate that Venus's surface has mountains and plains.
  Although Venus is about the same size as Earth, it does not provide an environment for life. Not only is Venus hot, but its atmosphere contains high levels of sulfuric acid, which is very corrosive. In addition, the atmospheric pressure at the surface is more than 90 times the pressure on Earth. Venus's thick atmosphere prevents the release of energy by radiation, creating a greenhouse effect that keeps the surface temperature of Venus over 700 K. For more on the greenhouse effect, see Section 18.1.

Figure 16-23
Although the surface of Venus is obscured by a thick atmosphere, maps of Venus can be made by using radar. On this map, yellow and brown represent higher ground, and blue and green represent lower ground.

DEMONSTRATION 3 TEACHING

The Reflection of Light from Venus

Time: Approximately 15 minutes
Materials: flashlight, 2 golf balls, black paint

Venus is bright because its atmosphere reflects a large amount of the sunlight that it receives. Use this demonstration to illustrate this fact.

Paint one golf ball black and leave the other white. Put the golf balls on a table, and turn out the classroom lights, making sure that the room is as dark as can be. Ask students if they can see the golf balls. The answer should be no; if they can see the balls, then the room is not dark enough. Next shine the light on the balls. The white golf ball is visible because it is reflecting the light from the flashlight to your eyes. The black ball is still not visible because it is not reflecting enough light. (This demonstration works only in a room that is very dark.)

Earth has ideal conditions for living creatures

Earth is the third planet out from the sun. Of all the planets, Earth is by far the most likely home for life as we know it. Earth is the only planet with large amounts of liquid water on its surface. It also has an atmosphere rich with oxygen, nitrogen, and carbon dioxide, and moderate temperatures that are stable around the globe. Earth and its atmosphere will be discussed further in Chapters 17 and 18.

Many missions have been sent to Mars

Although humans have yet to visit Mars, we have landed several probes on the surface. *Viking 1* and *Viking 2* both arrived at Mars in 1976, and each sent a lander to the surface. In 1997, the Pathfinder mission reached Mars and deployed a rover, the *Sojourner*, which freely explored the surface using a robotic navigation system.

Earlier orbiting missions had already detected some of Mars's unique features. The Martian volcano Olympus Mons, shown in **Figure 16-24,** is the largest mountain in the solar system. Its base is larger than the entire state of Louisiana, and it is almost three times the height of Mount Everest.

Figure 16-25 shows white regions around the poles of Mars. These are polar icecaps that contain at least some water. Features on other parts of the planet suggest that water used to flow across the surface as a liquid. Mars even has an atmosphere, but it is mostly carbon dioxide and much thinner than Earth's.

The asteroid belt divides the inner and outer planets

Between Mars and Jupiter lie hundreds of smaller rocky objects ranging in diameter from 3 km to 700 km. There are probably thousands of others too small to see from Earth. These objects are called **asteroids.**

Many of the largest asteroids remain between Mars and Jupiter, but some wander away from this region. A few climb high above the plane in which the planets move. Others pass closer to the sun, sometimes even crossing Earth's orbit. The odds of a large asteroid hitting Earth directly are fortunately very small.

Figure 16-24
The Martian volcano Olympus Mons is larger than the entire state of Louisiana.

Figure 16-25
This picture of Mars, taken by the Hubble Space Telescope, clearly shows a polar icecap.

▶ **asteroid** a small rocky object that orbits the sun, usually in a band between the orbits of Mars and Jupiter

THE UNIVERSE **545**

|SKILL BUILDER

Interpreting Visuals Have students examine **Figure 16-24.** What is the primary feature shown on the surface of Mars? *(a volcano, Olympus Mons)* The outline of what state is superimposed on the volcano? *(Louisiana)*

Additional Application

Mars Have students research the Viking mission and other missions to Mars. What have these missions discovered about Mars? What other planets have been explored by humans?

Connection to
LANGUAGE ARTS

In Antoine de Saint Exupery's story *The Little Prince,* the prince lives on a small asteroid. Read passages from the story, or have students read it on their own, and then discuss which factors in the story are scientifically accurate and which factors are not. *(For example, the prince could not really live on an asteroid because asteroids have no atmosphere. However, the low gravity on the asteroid is accurately portrayed.)*

Resources Assign students worksheet *16.1: Connection to Language Arts—Science Fiction and Fact* in the **Integration Enrichment Resources** ancillary.

The Solar System

READING SKILL BUILDER *Reading Organizer* Have students read the section on the outer planets and then organize what they learned in a chart. The heading on the left side of the chart should be *Similarities* and the heading on the right side should be *Differences*. Have students fill in their charts using the information about the outer planets from the text.

Did You Know?

The thickness of a planet's atmosphere is closely related to the planet's mass. Larger planets, such as the gas giants, have stronger gravitational influences, so they can hold light gases such as helium and hydrogen. Medium-sized planets, such as Earth and Venus, can hold heavier gases, such as nitrogen, oxygen, and carbon dioxide, but cannot hold lighter gases. Small planets such as Mercury and Pluto cannot sustain much of an atmosphere at all.

internetconnect

SC_**LINKS**_

NSTA

TOPIC: Planets
GO TO: www.scilinks.org
KEYWORD: HK1165

Figure 16-26

Ⓐ Jupiter is the largest planet in the solar system.

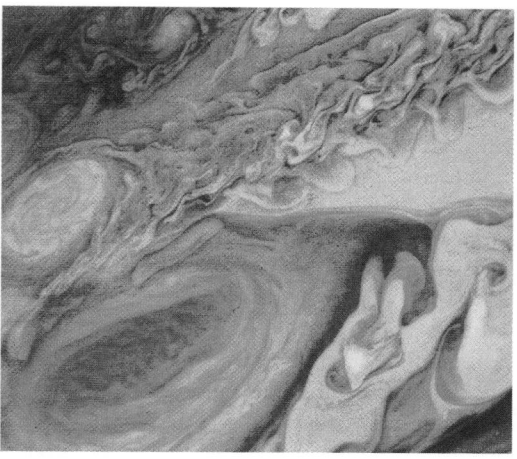

Ⓑ The Great Red Spot is a huge, hurricane-like storm in Jupiter's atmosphere.

The Outer Planets

The outer planets are Jupiter, Saturn, Uranus, Neptune, and Pluto. All of them except Pluto are much larger than the inner planets and have thick gaseous atmospheres. For this reason, they are called the *gas giants*.

Because the gas giants have no solid surface, a spaceship cannot land on one of them. However, the *Pioneer* (launched in 1972 and 1973), *Voyager* (launched in 1977), and *Galileo* (launched in 1989) spacecraft have flown to all of the outer planets except Pluto. *Galileo* even dropped a probe into the atmosphere of Jupiter in 1995.

Jupiter is the largest planet in the solar system

Jupiter, shown in **Figure 16-26A,** is the first planet beyond the asteroids. Jupiter is big enough to hold 1300 Earths. If it were only 80 times more massive than that, it would have sufficient pressure and temperature to sustain nuclear fusion, as a star does.

Images of Jupiter's atmosphere show swirling clouds of hydrogen, helium, methane, and ammonia. Complex features appear in Jupiter's atmosphere, including banded structures that appear to be jet streams and huge storms.

One of these storms, the Great Red Spot, shown in **Figure 16-26B,** is a huge hurricane about twice the diameter of Earth. The Great Red Spot has existed for hundreds of years. From year to year it changes slightly in size, shape, and color.

All of the gaseous outer planets have rings and moons

The astronomer Galileo was one of the first to use telescopes to look at the planets. Among his many discoveries, he found four moons orbiting Jupiter. These were the first moons to be seen orbiting a planet other than Earth. Any object orbiting a planet, whether natural or man-made, is called a satellite. The moons Galileo discovered are now known as the Galilean satellites.

Since the time of Galileo, astronomers have discovered 12 other moons orbiting Jupiter and 18 moons orbiting Saturn, the next planet beyond Jupiter. Several of these moons were discovered by the Voyager missions that passed through the outer solar system between 1979 and 1989.

In addition to its many moons, Saturn has a spectacular system of rings, shown in **Figure 16-27.** These rings are narrow bands of tiny particles of dust, rock, and ice. Competing gravitational forces from Saturn and its many moons hold the particles in place around the planet. Jupiter, Uranus, and Neptune also have rings, but they are much thinner and harder to detect than the rings of Saturn.

Uranus and Neptune are blue giants

Beyond Saturn lie the planets Uranus and Neptune, shown in **Figure 16-28.** These two planets are similar to each other in size and color. Both are smaller than Saturn and Jupiter, but are large enough to hold very thick, gaseous atmospheres. Their upper atmospheres contain a lot of methane, which gives both planets a bluish color. Uranus has 20 known moons, and Neptune has 8. Both planets have faint rings.

Figure 16-27
Saturn, shown here in a photograph taken by *Voyager 2,* is famous for its spectacular system of rings.

Figure 16-28
(A) Methane in its atmosphere gives Uranus a uniform blue color. (B) The Great Dark Spot is a huge storm in Neptune's blue atmosphere.

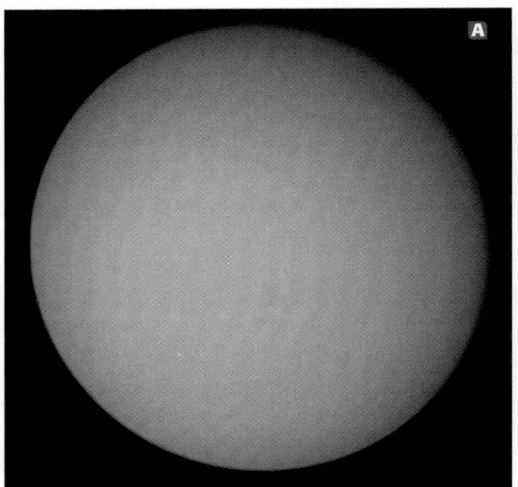
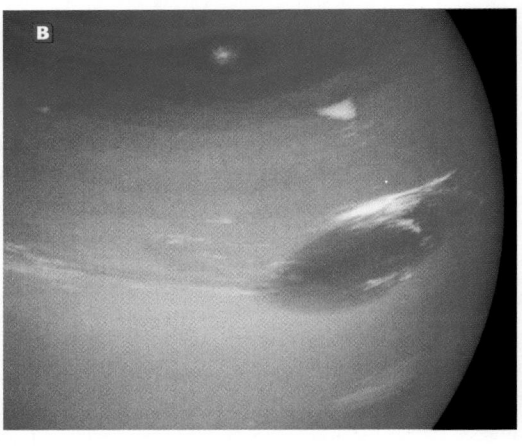

THE UNIVERSE **547**

Teaching Tip
Planets and Their Orbits
Have students come up with a phrase or saying that will help them remember the order of the planets from the sun. Each word in the phrase should start with the first letter of the planet.

Historical Perspective
Observers have known of the existence of Jupiter and Saturn for many centuries. The other outer planets were discovered much later.

Uranus was discovered in 1781 by an English music teacher named William Herschel. He originally named the planet *Georgium Sidus* (George's Star), in honor of King George III. The name Uranus was later officially chosen to continue the tradition of naming the planets after Roman gods.

Astronomers in the nineteenth century observed discrepancies in the orbit of Uranus that could not be explained by its attraction to the sun and to other known planets. They predicted that another large planet existed beyond Uranus. In 1846, that planet, Neptune, was discovered by the English astronomer John Adams and the French astronomer Joseph Leverrier.

The Solar System

Historical Perspective

Figure 16-29 shows Pluto with its moon, Charon. Because it is so small and so distant, Pluto was not discovered until 1930. Like Neptune, the existence of Pluto was predicted before the planet was actually observed.

Charon was discovered in 1978. Even with many powerful telescopes, Pluto and Charon cannot be seen separately. This image taken by the Hubble Space Telescope is one of the clearest ever obtained.

 **READING SKILL BUILDER** *Paired Summarizing* Pair students together and have them read the section on the formation of the solar system silently. Choose one of the pair to be the "reteller" and the other, the "listener." The reteller then summarizes the selection for the listener, who does not interrupt until the reteller has finished or unless there is a portion that requires clarification. The reteller may consult the text during his or her summary. The listener should then state any inaccuracies or omissions, and the two students should work together to refine the summary. Students should then alternate roles.

Figure 16-29
Pluto's moon, Charon, has a diameter almost half as large as Pluto. For that reason, some consider Pluto to be a double planet.

▶ **nebular model** a model that describes the sun and the solar system forming together out of a cloud of gas and dust

Did You Know ?

Because our solar system contains elements heavier than iron, at least some of the dust in the original nebular cloud must have been produced in a supernova some time in the past.

Pluto is an oddball planet

Pluto, shown in **Figure 16-29** with its moon Charon, is not like the other outer planets. It has only a thin, gaseous atmosphere, and a solid, icy surface. Pluto's orbit around the sun follows a long ellipse, and the plane of orbit is at an angle to the rest of the solar system. For these reasons, some scientists believe Pluto was captured by the gravity of the sun some time after the formation of the rest of the solar system. Pluto isn't always the farthest planet in the solar system; its orbit sometimes cuts inside the orbit of Neptune, as it was for a few years prior to 1999. The next time this will happen is in 2231.

Formation of the Solar System

According to geologic dating of rocks from Earth, the moon, and asteroids, the age of the solar system is around 4.6 billion years. The most widely accepted model of the formation of the solar system is the **nebular model**. In this model, the sun and the solar system condensed out of a nebula, a huge cloud of interstellar gas and dust.

The solar system may have formed from a rotating disk

According to the nebular model, the sun, like every star, formed from a cloud of gas and dust collapsing due to gravity. As this cloud collapsed, it formed into a flat, rotating disk. In the disk's center, the sun formed. Planets formed from the material farther out. This explains why all the planets lie in one plane and also why the planets orbit in the same direction that the sun rotates.

Planets formed by accretion of matter in the disk

The planets formed out of orbiting material mostly through the process of *accretion*. Accretion occurs when small particles collide and stick together to form larger masses.

Radiation from the newly born sun exerted pressure on the rest of the gas and dust in the disk. The lighter material was pushed farther away, where it combined to form the outer gas giant planets. Heavier rocky and metallic pieces that were left behind formed the solid inner planets. Even with the pressure, though, the force of gravity due to the sun was strong enough to keep most of the material in orbit.

The Moon

The moon is probably the most familiar object in the night sky. Like the planets, it shines because it reflects light from the sun. But the moon does not orbit the sun directly; it orbits our own planet Earth at a distance of 385 000 km.

The surface of the moon is covered with craters, mostly caused by asteroids crashing into the moon early in the history of the solar system. Larger dark patches on the moon's surface are seas of lava that flowed out of the moon's interior.

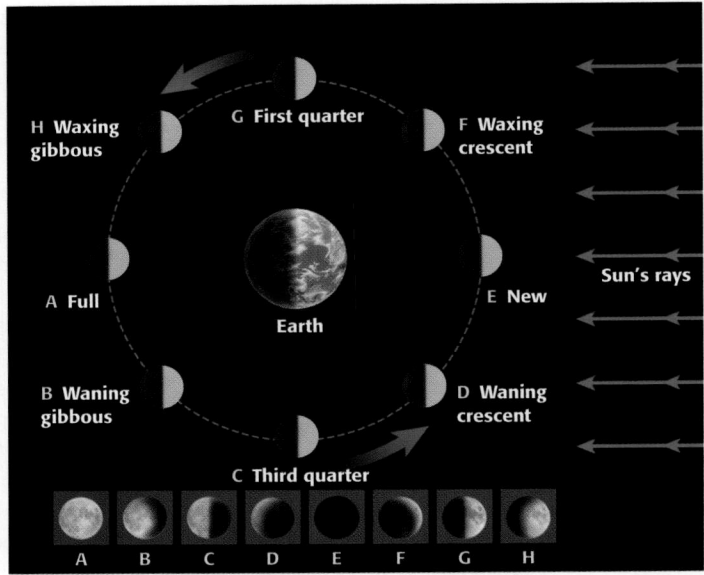

The moon has phases because it orbits Earth

As the moon orbits Earth, it appears to have different shapes. These are called **phases.** The phases of the moon are determined by the relative positions of Earth, the moon, and the sun, as shown in **Figure 16-30.**

At any given time, the sun illuminates half the moon's surface, just as at any time it is daytime on one half of Earth and nighttime on the other half. When the moon is *full*, the half that is lit is facing you. The observed time from one full moon to the next is 29.5 days.

When you see a *crescent* moon, you can see only a small portion of the lit side of the moon and a lot of the dark side. Between full and crescent moons are *quarter* moons, when you can see half of the lit side of the moon, and *gibbous* moons, when you see more than half of the lit side. Times when the moon's lit side is not visible are called *new* moons.

Eclipses occur when Earth, the moon, and the sun are in a line

While exploring Jamaica in 1504, Christopher Columbus impressed the native people he met by predicting an **eclipse.** He was able to do this by consulting a table of astronomical observations. Eclipses can be predicted because they happen only when Earth, the sun, and the moon are in a straight line. An eclipse occurs when one object moves into the shadow cast by another object.

Figure 16-30
As the moon changes position relative to Earth and the sun, it goes through different phases.

▶ **phases** the different apparent shapes of the moon or a planet due to the relative positions of the sun, Earth, and the moon or planet

▶ **eclipse** an event that occurs when one object passes into the shadow of another object

THE UNIVERSE **549**

|SKILL BUILDER

Interpreting Visuals Have students examine **Figure 16-30.** Follow the path of the moon counterclockwise, starting with the new moon. At each phase, refer students to the corresponding picture of the moon along the bottom of the figure. This shows how the moon would appear to an observer on Earth.

To reinforce understanding and for fun, you may ask students at each phase to describe or draw on the board what Earth would look like to an astronaut on the moon.

Resources *Teaching Transparency 52* shows this visual.

Teaching Tip

Solar Eclipse Tell students that even if they are wearing sunglasses, they should never look directly at the sun, even during a solar eclipse. Looking at the sun for even a short time can damage the eyes and even lead to blindness.

The solar viewer that students will construct in the end-of-chapter lab can be used for observing the sun indirectly. The solar viewer can be used to safely view a solar eclipse.

DEMONSTRATION 4 TEACHING

Phases of the Moon

Time: Approximately 15 minutes
Materials: lamp, a bright flashlight, round ball (plastic foam), 2 ft of string, tape, a meterstick

Attach one end of the string to the ball, and the other end to the meterstick. Turn out the lights in the room. Have one student hold the ball on the meterstick in the middle of the room and another student point the flashlight so that it illuminates one side of the ball.

Students should take turns slowly walking around the ball and observing the shape of the illuminated portion of the ball that they can see. Have students determine where they can see a crescent moon, a quarter moon, and a gibbous moon.

Ask students where they would have to stand to simulate a solar eclipse or a lunar eclipse.

The Solar System

Historical Perspective

Have students research some of the more recent solar and lunar eclipses. Where were they visible? When are the next eclipses predicted to occur, and what kind will they be?

SECTION 16.3 REVIEW

Check Your Understanding

1. Mercury, Venus, Earth, Mars, Jupiter, Saturn, Uranus, Neptune, Pluto
2. The surface of Venus is hotter than the surface of Mercury because Venus's atmosphere causes a greenhouse effect.
3. Some of the geologic features on Mars are volcanoes, mountain systems, canyons, and polar icecaps. (Volcanoes and polar icecaps were the two primary features described in the text.)
4. The inner planets are small and have solid, rocky surfaces. The outer planets, except for Pluto, are larger than the inner planets are and have thick gaseous atmospheres. They also have no solid surfaces.

Answers continue on p. 555B.

RESOURCE LINK
STUDY GUIDE

Assign students *Review Section 16.3 The Solar System.*

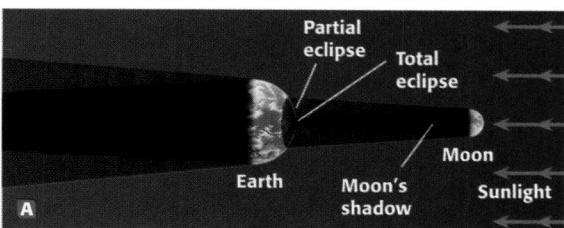

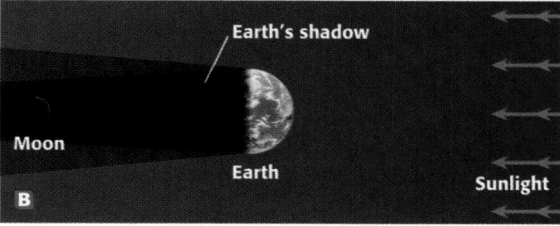

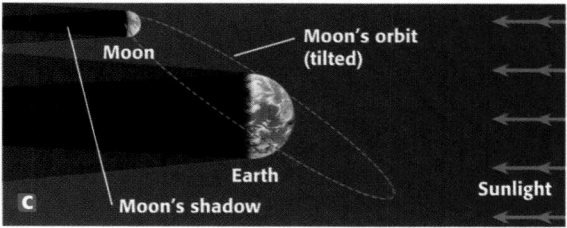

During a new moon, the moon may cast a shadow onto Earth, as shown in **Figure 16-31A.** Observers within that shadow on Earth see the sky turn dark as the moon blocks out the sun. This is called a solar eclipse.

On the other hand, when the moon is full, it may pass into the shadow of Earth, as shown in **Figure 16-31B.** Observers on Earth see the full moon become temporarily dark as it passes through Earth's shadow. This is called a lunar eclipse.

Because the moon's orbit is slightly tilted compared with Earth's orbit around the sun, the moon is usually slightly above or below the line between Earth and the sun, as shown in **Figure 16-31C.** For that reason, eclipses are relatively rare.

Figure 16-31
Eclipses occur when Earth, the sun, and the moon are in a line. (A) shows a solar eclipse, (B) shows a lunar eclipse, and in (C) there is no eclipse at all.

SECTION 16.3 REVIEW

SUMMARY

▶ The solar system consists of the sun, nine planets, and other objects orbiting the sun.

▶ The inner planets are small and rocky. The outer planets, except Pluto, are large and gaseous.

▶ The planets were formed out of the cloud from which the sun condensed.

▶ Eclipses and the phases of the moon depend on the relative positions of Earth, the moon, and the sun.

CHECK YOUR UNDERSTANDING

1. **List** the planets in order of their distance from the sun.
2. **Explain** why the surface of Venus is hotter than the surface of Mercury.
3. **Describe** some of the geologic features on Mars.
4. **Compare** the inner planets with the outer planets.
5. **Describe** the origin of the planets.
6. **Describe** the positions of the sun, the moon, and Earth during a new moon.
7. **Explain** what happens during a lunar eclipse. Why does an eclipse happen only during a full moon?
8. **Critical Thinking** If the moon is half-full as seen from Earth, what would Earth look like to a man on the moon?
9. **Creative Thinking** Some astronomers have found evidence for the formation of planets around other stars. Make a list of three characteristics these planets might need to support life.

550 CHAPTER 16

CHAPTER 16 — REVIEW

Chapter Highlights

Before you begin, review the summaries of the key ideas of each section, found on pages 534, 541, and 550. The key vocabulary terms are listed on pages 526, 535, and 542.

UNDERSTANDING CONCEPTS

1. The basic types of galaxies are _____.
   a. spiral, elliptical, and irregular
   b. barred, elliptical, and open
   c. spiral, quasar, and pulsar
   d. open, binary, and globular
2. Which of the following is a possible age of the universe, according to the big bang theory?
   a. 4.6 million years   c. 4.6 billion years
   b. 15 million years   d. 15 billion years
3. A pattern of stars as seen from Earth is called a _____.
   a. galaxy   c. Milky Way
   b. nebula   d. constellation
4. By studying starlight, astronomers may learn which of the following things about stars?
   a. the elements that compose the star
   b. the surface temperature of the star
   c. the speed of the star relative to Earth
   d. all of the above
5. The core of a star that remains after a supernova may be any of the following except _____.
   a. a black hole   c. a red giant
   b. a neutron star   d. a pulsar
6. The shape of the orbit of Earth is _____.
   a. a circle   c. an arc
   b. an ellipse   d. a sphere
7. The only outer planet that is not a gas giant is _____.
   a. Jupiter   c. Neptune
   b. Saturn   d. Pluto
8. According to radioisotope dating of rocks from the moon, Mars, and asteroids as well as here on Earth, what is the approximate age of the solar system?
   a. 4.6 million years
   b. 15 million years
   c. 4.6 billion years
   d. 15 billion years
9. The theory that the sun and the planets formed out of the same cloud of gas and dust is called the _____.
   a. big bang theory   c. planetary theory
   b. nebular theory   d. nuclear theory
10. A lunar eclipse can occur when the moon is _____.
    a. full   c. rising
    b. new   d. setting

Using Vocabulary

11. Arrange the following from largest to smallest: *cluster, galaxy, planet, solar system, supercluster, star.*
12. What type of *galaxy* is the Milky Way galaxy?
13. Using the terms *galaxy* and *red shift*, explain the primary evidence that the universe is expanding.
14. What is the *big bang theory*?
15. Write a paragraph explaining in your own words the origin of the sun and *solar system*. Use the following terms: *planet, accretion, nebular model.*   **WRITING SKILL**
16. List and explain several different possible ways a star's life could end. Use the following terms: *black hole, neutron star, supernova, white dwarf.*
17. Where are most *asteroids* located?
18. Name four different *phases* of the moon.
19. What conditions are necessary for a *solar eclipse* to occur?

THE UNIVERSE **551**

CHAPTER 16

REVIEW

UNDERSTANDING CONCEPTS

1. a
2. d
3. d
4. d
5. c
6. b
7. d
8. c
9. b
10. a

Using Vocabulary

11. supercluster, cluster, galaxy, solar system, star, planet
12. The Milky Way galaxy is a spiral galaxy.
13. A red shift is a shift in light from a star or galaxy toward the red end of the spectrum, indicating that the light source is moving away from the observer. Because almost all observed galaxies display a red shift, scientists have concluded that the universe is expanding.
14. The big bang theory proposes that the universe began with a gigantic explosion 10 billion–20 billion years ago.
15. The nebular model is a model that is used to explain the formation of the sun and the planets that make up the solar system. The planets formed out of orbiting material mostly through the process of accretion. The sun was formed as a cloud of gas and dust collapsed due to gravity.

RESOURCE LINK
STUDY GUIDE

Assign students *Mixed Review Chapter 16.*

551

CHAPTER 16 *REVIEW*

16. A star's life can end in many ways. For example, the sun will become a red giant before it dies. This means that when the fusion of hydrogen slows, the core of the sun will contract and cool, and the sun will become a white dwarf. The planets formed through the process of accretion, in which orbiting material slowly collected and stuck together, forming larger bodies. Stars larger than the sun will also experience the end of fusion, which will lead to a supernova. This is when a star collapses and explodes. If the core that remains after a supernova has a mass of 1.4 to about 3 times that of the sun, the remaining core will become a neutron star. If the remaining core is larger than three times the core of the sun, then the core will collapse and form a black hole, where nothing can escape from its gravity.

17. Most asteroids are located in a band between the orbits of Mars and Jupiter.

18. full, quarter, gibbous, new

19. The sun, Earth, and the moon must be in a straight line with the moon between Earth and the sun (a new moon).

BUILDING MATH SKILLS

See p. 555B for worked-out solutions.

20. Star 1 contains only hydrogen. Star 2 contains hydrogen and helium.

21. Mercury: 3.8 m/s²
Venus: 8.8 m/s²
Earth: 9.8 m/s²
Mars: 3.7 m/s²

BUILDING MATH SKILLS

20. Interpreting Graphics The spectra shown below were taken for hydrogen, helium, and lithium in a laboratory on Earth. The spectra labeled as *Star 1* and *Star 2* were taken from starlight. What elements are found in Star 1 and Star 2?

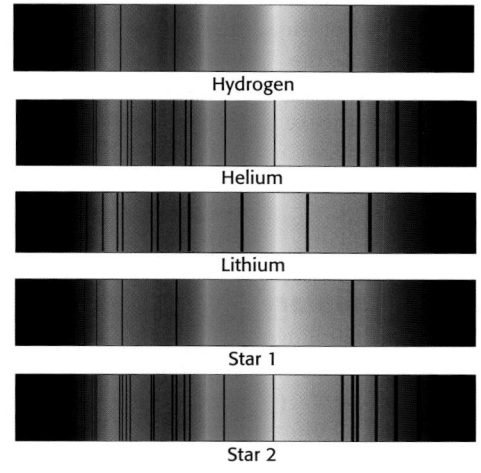

Hydrogen

Helium

Lithium

Star 1

Star 2

21. Applying Technology The free-fall acceleration, *g*, near the surface of a planet is given by the equation below.

$$g = \left(6.67 \times 10^{-11} \ \frac{\text{m}^3}{\text{kg} \cdot \text{s}^2}\right) \times \frac{(planet\ mass)}{(planet\ radius)^2}$$

Use this equation to create a spreadsheet that will calculate the free-fall acceleration near the surface of each of the planets in the table below.

Planet	Mass	Radius
Mercury	3.3×10^{23} kg	2.4×10^6 m
Venus	4.9×10^{24} kg	6.1×10^6 m
Earth	6.0×10^{24} kg	6.4×10^6 m
Mars	6.4×10^{23} kg	3.4×10^6 m

22. Applying Technology Add a column to the spreadsheet you created in item 21 that will show the weight of a 300 kg person on each of the inner planets. Use the weight equation from Chapter 8: *w = mg*. Which of the planets has gravity the most like Earth?

THINKING CRITICALLY

23. Applying Knowledge While looking through a telescope, you observe a galaxy that has mostly old, red stars, and no young, blue stars. The galaxy also does not appear to have very much gas or dust. What kind of galaxy are you probably looking at?

24. Evaluating Data If Hubble had observed that the spectral lines in light from every galaxy were shifted toward the blue end of the spectrum, what might he have concluded about the universe?

25. Understanding Systems What keeps a star from collapsing under its own weight?

26. Applying Knowledge Why will the sun never explode in a supernova?

27. Creative Thinking How can Venus be the brightest object in the sky, besides the sun and the moon, when it doesn't even produce any visible light of its own?

28. Understanding Systems You and a friend are looking at a crescent moon, and your friend comments that the phases of the moon are caused by Earth's shadow falling on the moon. How would you explain to your friend the true cause of the moon's phases?

29. Creative Thinking Name two reasons why Earth provides a better home for living creatures than would any of the other planets in the solar system.

DEVELOPING LIFE/WORK SKILLS

30. Interpreting and Communicating In your library or on the Internet, research the sizes of the planets and the sun and the distances between different objects in the solar system. Create a poster, booklet, computer presentation, or other presentation that can be used to teach a third-grade class about these distances.

31. Working Cooperatively Working with a team of at least four other students, make a list of your needs if you were planning the first human mission to Mars. Each team member should research and consider what the astronauts will need once they arrive on Mars for one of the following categories: food, shelter, clothing, air, and transportation. What ideas can your team come up with to meet these needs?

INTEGRATING CONCEPTS

32. Connection to Fine Arts In the years 1914 to 1916, the composer Gustav Holst created *The Planets*, a symphonic suite that portrays each of the planets according to its role in mythology. Listen to a recording of *The Planets*. Write a paragraph describing which parts of the music seem to match scientific facts about the planets and which parts do not.

WRITING SKILL

33. Connection to Fine Arts Holst composed *The Planets* before Pluto was discovered, so Neptune is the last planet he describes. Create your own work of art, such as a drawing, a computerized slideshow, or a brief musical theme, that portrays some of the scientific facts about the nature of Pluto.

34. Connection to Chemistry Based on the description in this chapter, how were hydrogen and helium first formed in the universe? What are the possible sources of elements from lithium to carbon? What are the possible sources of elements from carbon to iron? How could atoms larger than iron be formed?

35. Concept Mapping Copy the unfinished concept map below onto a sheet of paper. Complete the map by writing the correct word or phrase in the lettered boxes.

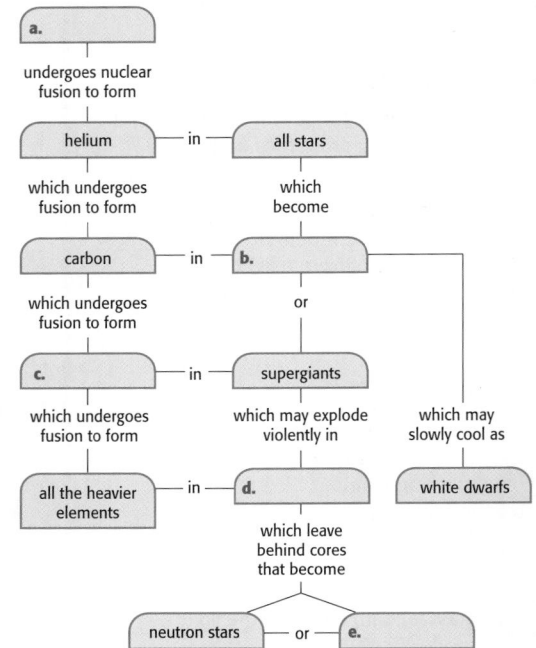

TOPIC: Formation of the elements
GO TO: www.scilinks.org
KEYWORD: HK1166

THE UNIVERSE **553**

22. Mercury: 1.1×10^3 N
Venus: 2.6×10^3 N
Earth: 2.9×10^3 N
Mars: 1.1×10^3 N

THINKING CRITICALLY

23. an elliptical galaxy
24. that the universe is shrinking
25. The radiation pressure from the nuclear fusion in the cores of stars prevents them from collapsing under their own weight.
26. The sun will never explode in a supernova because it is not big enough.
27. Venus is bright because it has a thick atmosphere that reflects large amounts of sunlight.
28. The moon's phases are caused by sunlight reflecting off the moon and toward Earth. The phases appear different as the relative positions of Earth, the moon, and the sun change.
29. the availability of oxygen and liquid water, moderate temperatures, a solid surface

DEVELOPING LIFE/ WORK SKILLS

30. Answers will vary.
31. Answers will vary.

Answers continue on p. 555B.

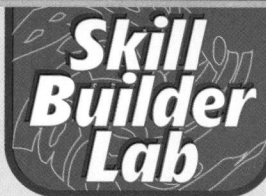

Skill Builder Lab

Estimating the Size and Power Output of the Sun

Introduction

For the first part of the lab, students measure the diameter of a projected image of the sun, and the distance to the image. Students then use these measurements and the known distance to the sun in an equation of equivalent ratios to calculate the diameter of the sun.

As light travels away from a light source, whether a light bulb or the sun, the energy in the light spreads out over a larger area. As a result, a nearby light bulb may seem to be as bright as the sun. For the second part of the lab, students will take two measurements, one using a light bulb and the other using light from the sun. Students then use these findings to estimate the sun's power output.

Objectives

Students will:

▶ **Use** appropriate lab safety precautions.

▶ **Construct** devices for indirectly observing and measuring properties of the sun.

▶ **Measure** the size of an image of the sun to calculate its size and power output.

Planning

Recommended Time: 1 lab period
Materials: *(for each lab group)*

▶ shoe box
▶ scissors
▶ aluminum foil
▶ pin
▶ masking tape
▶ index card
▶ Celsius thermometer
▶ very thin sheet metal (2 × 8 cm)
▶ black paint or magic marker
▶ glass jar with a hole in the lid
▶ modeling clay
▶ lamp with 100 W bulb
▶ meterstick

554

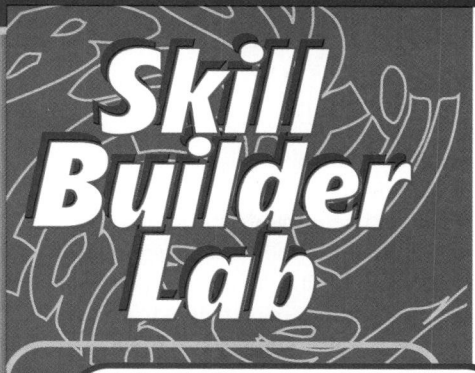

Skill Builder Lab

Introduction

The sun is 1.496×10^{11} m from Earth. How can you use this distance and a few simple measurements to find the size and power output of the sun?

Objectives

▶ **Construct** devices for observing and measuring properties of the sun.

▶ **Measure** the size of an image of the sun in a solar viewing device.

▶ **Measure** temperatures in sunlight and in light from a light bulb.

▶ **Calculate** the size of the sun and the power output of the sun.

Materials

shoe box and scissors
aluminum foil and pin
masking tape
index card
Celsius thermometer
very thin sheet metal (2 × 8 cm)
black paint or magic marker
glass jar with a hole in the lid
modeling clay
lamp with a 100 W bulb
meterstick

Safety Needs

safety goggles, gloves

Estimating the Size and Power Output of the Sun

▶ Preparing for Your Experiment

1. Construct a solar viewer in the following way.
   a. Cut a round hole in one end of the shoe box.
   b. Tape a piece of aluminum foil over the hole. Use the pin to make a tiny hole in the center of the foil.
   c. Tape the index card inside the shoebox on the end opposite the hole.
2. Construct a solar collector in the following way.
   a. Gently fit the sheet metal around the bulb of the thermometer. Bend the edges out so that they form "wings," as shown at right. Paint the wings black.
   SAFETY CAUTION Thermometers are fragile. Do not squeeze the bulb of the thermometer or let the thermometer strike any solid objects.
   b. Slide the top of the thermometer through the hole in the lid of the jar. Use modeling clay and masking tape to hold the thermometer in place.
   c. Place the lid on the jar. Adjust the thermometer so the metal wings are centered.
3. Place the lamp on one end of a table that is not in direct sunlight. Remove any shade or reflector from the lamp.

▶ Measurements with the Solar Viewer

4. Stand in direct sunlight, with your back to the sun, and position the solar viewer so that an image of the sun appears on the index card.
   SAFETY CAUTION Never look directly at the sun. Permanent eye damage or even blindness may result.
5. Carefully measure and record the diameter of the image of the sun. Also measure and record the distance from the image to the pinhole.

SOLUTIONS/MATERIAL PREPARATION

1. Poke holes in the jar lids using an ice pick or an awl, and cut the metal strips to size. Smooth any rough edges.
2. Shape the metal strips into the wings by bending the strips around a pencil. This will reduce the risk of students breaking a thermometer when constructing the collectors.
3. To save time and minimize risks, teachers may want to construct the collectors. A CBL probe thermometer can be used to remove the risk of breaking a glass thermometer.

REQUIRED PRECAUTIONS

▶ Read all safety precautions, and discuss them with your students.

▶ Safety goggles and a lab apron must be worn at all times.

▶ Long hair and loose clothing must be tied back.

▶ Gloves should be worn when working with sheet metal.

▶ Emphasize to students the danger of looking directly at the sun.

▶ Measurements with the Solar Collector

6. Place the solar collector in sunlight. Tilt the jar so that the sun shines directly on the metal wings. Watch the temperature reading rise until it reaches a maximum value. Record that value. Place the collector in the shade to cool.

7. Now place the solar collector about 30 cm from the lamp on the table. Tilt the jar so that the light shines directly on the metal wings. Watch the temperature reading rise until it reaches a stable value.

8. Move the collector toward the lamp in 2 cm increments. At each position, let the collector sit until the temperature reading stabilizes. When you find a point where the reading on the thermometer matches the reading you observed in step 6, measure and record the distance from the solar collector to the light bulb.

▶ Analyzing Your Results

1. The ratio of the sun's actual diameter to its distance from Earth is the same as the ratio of the diameter of the sun's image to the distance from the pinhole to the image.

$$\frac{diameter\ of\ the\ sun,\ S}{Earth - sun\ distance,\ D} = \frac{diameter\ of\ image,\ i}{pinhole - image\ distance,\ d}$$

Solving for the sun's diameter, S, gives the following equation.

$$S = \frac{D}{d} \times i.$$

Substitute your measured values, and $D = 1.5 \times 10^{11}$ m, into this equation to calculate the value of S. Remember to convert all distance measurements to units of meters.

2. The ratio of the power output of the sun to the sun's distance from Earth squared is the same as the ratio of the power output of the light bulb to the solar collector's distance from the bulb squared.

$$\frac{power\ of\ sun,\ P}{(earth - sun\ distance,\ D)^2} = \frac{power\ of\ light\ bulb,\ b}{(bulb - collector\ distance,\ d)^2}$$

Solving for the sun's power output, P, gives the following equation.

$$P = \frac{D^2}{d^2} \times b$$

Substitute your measured distance for d, the known wattage of the bulb for b, and $D = 1.5 \times 10^{11}$ m, into this equation to calculate the value of P. Remember to convert all distance measurements to units of meters. Your answer should be in watts.

▶ Defending Your Conclusions

3. How does your S compare with the accepted diameter of the sun, 1.392×10^9 m?

4. How does your P compare with the accepted power output of the sun, 3.83×10^{26} W?

Pre-Lab

Teaching Tips

If the lab is conducted indoors, turn off any artificial lights in the room while collecting data on the sun.

The solar viewer may also be used for observing solar eclipses.

If you are using a device other than the solar collector, ask the students to look at the device that they used to determine relative intensity. In what units does the device give data? What kind of energy is the light energy converted into by the device? What other kinds of devices could be used to perform this experiment?

To extend the discussion of the sun's characteristics, give the students the diameter of Earth as 1.2×10^4 km. Ask how many Earths, placed side-by-side, would fit on a line as long as the sun's diameter. *(116)* Also, the volume of a sphere with radius r is equal to $\frac{4}{3}\pi \bullet r^3$. How many Earths would fit inside a space with the same volume as the sun? *(1.5×10^6)*.

Continue on p. 555A.

RESOURCE LINK
DATASHEETS

Have students use *Datasheet 16.3: Skill Builder Lab—Estimating the Size and Power Output of the Sun* to record their results.

CONTINUATION OF ANSWERS

Skill Builder Lab from page 555

Estimating the Size and Power Output of the Sun

Procedure

▶ Preparing for Your Experiment

The first part of the experiment may be performed with an index card and a piece of paper. Poke a pinhole in the card, then have a student hold the card in the sun. Have a second student position the paper so that an image of the sun focuses on it. Have a third student measure the diameter of the image and the distance from the card to the paper.

▶ Measurements with the Solar Collector

Instead of constructing the solar collector, the second part of this lab may be performed with any device that measures a quantity dependent on light energy, e.g. Ward's 36 E 4408. The units of measurement are not important, because this measurement is only used to calibrate the distance from the sun to the distance from the light bulb.

Post Lab

▶ Disposal

Both the solar viewers and the solar collectors can be saved and reused when other classes perform the experiment.

▶ Analyzing Your Results

1. Answers will vary. Values should be relatively close to 1.4×10^9 m.
2. Answers will vary. Values should be relatively close to 3.8×10^{26} W.

▶ Defending Your Conclusions

3. Answers will vary based upon the value obtained in item 1.
4. Answers will vary based upon the value obtained in item 2.

Answers from page 534

SECTION 16.1 REVIEW

8. No, the Milky Way is not necessarily at the center of the universe. Observers in *any* galaxy would see all the other galaxies moving away from the others. On the surface of an inflating balloon, *every* dot moves away from the other dots.
9. If the universe were shrinking, every galaxy would appear to be moving toward Earth. (**Note:** Light from the galaxies would be shifted toward the blue end of the spectrum.)

Answers from page 541

SECTION 16.2 REVIEW

5. b. Stars that are larger than the sun do not become red giants but instead become supergiants. Supergiant stars do not stop with carbon fusion; they produce heavier elements until their cores become iron and fusion stops. Once fusion stops in a supergiant star, the core collapses and explodes in a supernova. The remaining core becomes a neutron star or a black hole.
6. (a) and (b)
7. Stars are not always shrinking; stars are driven by nuclear fusion reactions, and the energy that is released by those reactions balances the inward pull of gravity.

Answers from page 550

Answers from page 550

SECTION 16.3 REVIEW

5. The planets were formed out of the cloud from which the sun condensed.
6. The moon, the sun, and Earth are in a straight line or nearly in a straight line, with the moon between the sun and the Earth.
7. During a lunar eclipse, the Earth comes between the moon and the sun. An eclipse happens only during a full moon because that is the only time that Earth, the moon, and the sun are in the required position.
8. The Earth would look half full as well.
9. Answers may include liquid water, oxygen, sunlight, gravity, soil, and atmosphere.

Answers from page 552

BUILDING MATH SKILLS

21. $$\dfrac{\left(6.67 \times 10^{-11} \dfrac{m^3}{kg \bullet s^2}\right)(3.3 \times 10^{23} \text{ kg})}{(2.4 \times 10^6 \text{ m})^2} =$$

3.8 m/s^2; Mercury

$$\dfrac{\left(6.67 \times 10^{-11} \dfrac{m^3}{kg \bullet s^2}\right)(4.9 \times 10^{24} \text{ kg})}{(6.1 \times 10^6 \text{ m})^2} =$$

8.8 m/s^2; Venus

$$\dfrac{\left(6.67 \times 10^{-11} \dfrac{m^3}{kg \bullet s^2}\right)(6.0 \times 10^{24} \text{ kg})}{(6.4 \times 10^6 \text{ m})^2} =$$

9.8 m/s^2; Earth

$$\dfrac{\left(6.67 \times 10^{-11} \dfrac{m^3}{kg \bullet s^2}\right)(6.4 \times 10^{23} \text{ kg})}{(3.4 \times 10^6 \text{ m})^2} =$$

3.7 m/s^2; Mars

22. $w = mg$
Mercury: (300 kg)(3.8 m/s^2) = 1.1 $\times$ 10^3 N
Venus: (300 kg)(8.8 m/s^2) = 2.6 $\times$ 10^3 N
Earth: (300 kg)(9.8 m/s^2) = 2.9 $\times$ 10^3 N
Mars: (300 kg)(3.7 m/s^2) = 1.1 $\times$ 10^3 N

Answers from page 553

INTEGRATING CONCEPTS

32. Answers will vary.
33. Answers will vary.
34. According to the big bang theory, hydrogen and helium were formed when the universe expanded and cooled after the big bang. The possible sources of elements from lithium to carbon are red giants. Elements heavier than carbon up to iron, can be formed in supergiant stars. Atoms larger than iron can be formed if a supergiant produces more energy after its core becomes iron; it is possible for this to happen only when a dying supergiant explodes as a supernova.
35. a. hydrogen
    b. red giants
    c. iron
    d. supernovas
    e. black holes

Tailoring the Program to YOUR Classroom

CHAPTER 17

Planet Earth

Annotated Descriptions of the Correlated National Science Standards

The following descriptions summarize the National Science Standards that specially relate to Chapter 17. For the full text of the Standards, see p. 40T.

SECTION 17.1
Earth's Interior and Plate Tectonics
Life Science
LS 2a, 2b
Unifying Concepts and Processes
UCP 1, 2, 4, 5
Science as Inquiry
SAI 2

SECTION 17.2
Earthquakes and Volcanoes
Physical Science
PS 6a
Unifying Concepts and Processes
UCP 1, 4
Science as Inquiry
SAI 2
Science and Technology
ST 2
Science in Personal and Social Perspectives
SPSP 3

SECTION 17.3
Minerals and Rocks
Unifying Concepts and Processes
UCP 1, 4
Science as Inquiry
SAI 2

SECTION 17.4
Weathering and Erosion
Unifying Concepts and Processes
UCP 1, 4

Cross-Discipline Teaching RESOURCES

Cross-Discipline Teaching, ATE p. 556
Language Arts   Life Science
Mathematics

Integration Enrichment Resources
Physics, **PE** and **ATE** p. 563
    IE 17.1 *High Up in the Himalayas*
Social Studies, **PE** and **ATE** p. 574
    IE 17.2 *Plinian Eruptions*
Social Studies, **PE** and **ATE** p. 577
    IE 17.3 *Human Tools: From Stone to Iron*

Additional Worksheets
    IE 17.4 Chemistry
    IE 17.5 Environmental Science
    IE 17.6 Biology   IE 17.7 Language Arts
    IE 17.8 Biology

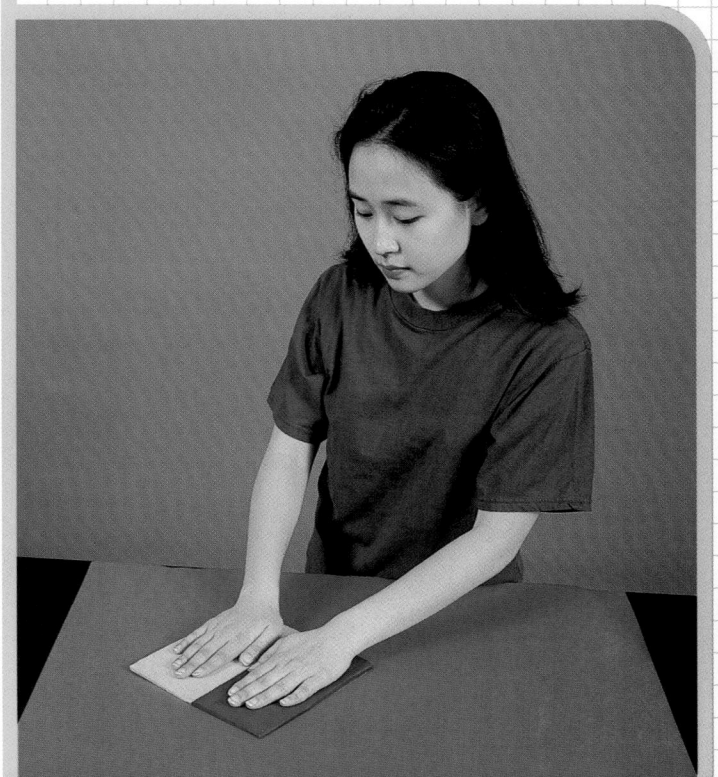

Use the Planning Guide on the next page to help you organize your lessons.

MATH AND COMPUTER RESOURCES

Chapter 17	Math Skills	Assess	Media/Computer Skills
Section 17.1			■ Section 17.1
Section 17.2		PE **Building Math Skills,** p. 590, item 19	■ Section 17.2 PE **Developing Life/Work Skills,** p. 591, item 28
Section 17.3			■ Section 17.3
Section 17.4			■ Section 17.4

PE Pupil's Edition   **ATE** Annotated Teacher's Edition   **MS** Math Skills   **BS** Basic Skills
IE Integration Enrichment   ■ Guided Reading Audio   **CRT** Critical Thinking

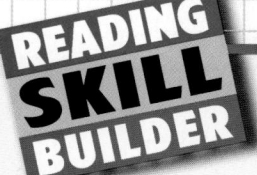

READING SKILL BUILDER

The following activities found in the Annotated Teacher's Edition provide techniques for developing useful reading strategies to increase your students' reading comprehension skills.

Section 17.1 **Brainstorming,** p. 556
Anticipation/Prediction, p. 560

Section 17.2 **Reading Aloud/Discussion,** p. 567

Section 17.3 **Reading Organizer,** p. 576
Brainstorming, p. 576

Section 17.4 **Reading Organizer,** p. 583

Smithsonian Institution®
Visit www.si.edu/hrw for additional online resources.

Spanish Resources

The following resources are made available for students who speak Spanish as their first language.

Spanish Resource Package Guided Reading Audio CD-ROM Chapter 17

Spanish Glossary Chapter 17

Planet Earth

CLASSROOM RESOURCES

	FOCUS	TEACH	HANDS-ON
Section 17.1: Earth's Interior and Plate Tectonics			
BLOCK 1 45 minutes	ATE **RSB** Brainstorming, 556 ATE Focus Activities 1, 2, p. 557 ATE **RSB** Anticipation, p. 560 ATE **Demo 1** Convection, p. 560 PE Earth's Interior; pp. 558–561 ★ Focus Transparency LT 55	ATE **Skill Builder** Interpreting Visuals, pp. 557, 559 TT 54 Tectonic Plates	
BLOCK 2 45 minutes	PE Plate Boundaries; Evidence for Plate Tectonics, pp. 562–566	ATE **Skill Builder** Vocabulary, p. 562 Interpreting Visuals, p. 562, p. 563 TT 55 Divergent Boundary TT 56 Convergent Boundary TT 57 Magnetic Bands	IE Worksheets 17.1, 17.8 PE Inquiry Lab *Can you model tectonic plate boundaries with clay?* p. 565 **DS** 17.1 LE 17 *Relating Convection to the Movement of Tectonic Plates* **DS** 17.3
Section 17.2: Earthquakes and Volcanoes			
BLOCK 3 45 minutes	ATE **RSB** Discussion, p. 567 ATE **Demo 2** Faults p. 567 ATE **Demo 3** Earthquake! p. 568 PE Earthquakes, pp. 567–572 ★ Focus Transparency LT 56	BLM 54 Epicenter and Focus TT 58 P and S Waves	IE Worksheet 17.5
BLOCK 4 45 minutes	PE Volcanoes, pp. 572–575 ATE **Demo 4** Eruption, p. 572	ATE **Skill Builder** Interpreting Diagrams, p. 573 **Skill Builder** Interpreting Visuals, p. 574 TT 59 Volcanoes	IE Worksheet 17.2
Section 17.3: Minerals and Rocks			
BLOCK 5 45 minutes	ATE **RSB** Reading Organizer, p. 576 ATE **RSB** Brainstorming, p. 576 ATE **Demo 5** Crystals, p. 576 ATE **Demo 6** Classifying Rocks, p. 579 PE Structure of Rocks, pp. 576–581 ★ Focus Transparency LT 57	ATE **Skill Builder** Interpreting Visuals, p. 576, p. 577, p. 580 TT 60 Rock Cycle	IE Worksheets 17.3, 17.4, 17.7
BLOCK 6 45 minutes	PE How Old Are Rocks? pp. 581–582	ATE **Skill Builder** Interpreting Visuals, p. 581	
Section 17.4: Weathering and Erosion			
BLOCK 7 45 minutes	ATE **RSB** Reading Organizer, p. 583 ATE **Demo 7** Weathering, p. 583 PE Weathering, pp. 583–585 ★ Focus Transparency LT 58	ATE **Skill Builder** Interpreting Visuals, p. 583, p. 584	IE Worksheet 17.6
BLOCK 8 45 minutes	ATE **Demo 8** Erosion, p. 586 PE Erosion, pp. 586–588	ATE **Skill Builder** Interpreting Visuals, p. 588	PE Skill Builder Lab *Analyzing Seismic Waves*, p. 592 **DS** 17.2

CLASSROOM RESOURCES

HOMEWORK	ASSESS
PE Section Review 1, p. 566 **Chapter 17 Review,** p. 589, items 11, 12	**SG** Chapter 17 Pretest
PE Section Review 2–7, p. 566 **Chapter 17 Review,** p. 589, items 1, 2	**SG** Section 17.1
PE Section Review 1, 4, p. 575 **Chapter 17 Review,** p. 589, items 3–5, 13, 14, 19	**ATE** *ALTERNATIVE ASSESSMENT,* Richter Scale, p. 571
PE Section Review 2, 3, 5–7, p. 575	**ATE** *ALTERNATIVE ASSESSMENT,* Volcano, p. 574 Plate Boundaries, p. 575 **SG** Section 17.2
PE Section Review 1, 3–5, p. 582 **Chapter 17 Review,** p. 589, items 6–8, 15, 16	
PE Section Review 2, 6, p. 582	**SG** Section 17.3
PE Section Review 1, 4, 5, p. 588 **Chapter 17 Review,** p. 589, items 9, 10	
PE Section Review 2, 3, 6, p. 588 **Chapter 17 Review,** p. 589, items 17, 18	**SG** Section 17.4

BLOCK 9

PE Chapter 17 Review
Thinking Critically, 20–24, p. 590
Developing Life/Work Skills, 25–28, p. 591
Integrating Concepts, 29–31, p. 591
SG Chapter 17 Mixed Review

BLOCK 10

Chapter Tests
Chapter 17 Test

One-Stop Planner CD–ROM **with Test Generator**
Chapter 17

Teaching Resources
Scoring Rubrics and assignment checklist.

 internet**connect**

SCILINKS
NSTA
**National Science Teachers
Association
Online Resources:
www.scilinks.org**
The following *sci*LINKS Internet resources can be found
in the student text for this chapter.

Page 557 **TOPIC:** Volcanoes **KEYWORD:** HK1704	**Page 581** **TOPIC:** Rock types **KEYWORD:** HK1705
Page 559 **TOPIC:** Earth's geologic layers **KEYWORD:** HK1701	**Page 587** **TOPIC:** Erosion **KEYWORD:** HK1706
Page 560 **TOPIC:** Plate tectonics **KEYWORD:** HK1702	**Page 591** **TOPIC:** Sonar **KEYWORD:** HK1707
Page 569 **TOPIC:** Earthquakes **KEYWORD:** HK1703	

CNN fyi.com   www.cnnfyi.com

Visit this site for coverage of current events and related
classroom resources.

PE Pupil's Edition   **ATE** Annotated Teacher's Edition
RSB Reading Skill Builder   **DS** Datasheets
IE Integrated Enrichment   **SG** Study Guide
LE Laboratory Experiments
TT Teaching Transparencies   **BLM** Blackline Masters
★ Lesson Focus Transparency

Planet Earth

Tapping Prior Knowledge

Tapping Prior Knowledge

Chapter 5
Chemical Reactions

Chapter 6
Acids, pH

Chapter 7
Radiation, radioactive dating

Chapter 11
Waves

Chapter 14
Magnetic fields

READING SKILL BUILDER *Brainstorming* Write on the chalkboard the words *crust, mantle,* and *core.* Ask students to hypothesize about what parts of the Earth those words refer to. Using Section 17.1, have the students draw a cross-section of the Earth and label which parts of the diagram they think the three vocabulary words apply to. After they read the section, have them go back and make any necessary corrections to their diagram.

Chapter Preview

556

RESOURCE LINK
STUDY GUIDE

Assign students *Pretest Chapter 17 Planet Earth* before beginning Section 17.1.

CROSS-DISCIPLINE TEACHING

Language Arts Have students read *Journey To the Center of the Earth,* by Jules Verne. After completing Chapter 17, ask students for relevant comments that show connections between the book and some of the concepts encountered in the chapter.

Mathematics Have students figure out the distance from the crust of the Earth to the core in km. Then have them convert that figure into miles. Ask students how long it would take to drive that distance at a rate of 89 km/h (55 mi/h).

Life Science Ask a biologist or paleontologist to visit your classroom and explain the fossil formation process, and the importance of fossil evidence in Wegener's theory of continental drift.

Focus ACTIVITY

Background Crater Lake, in Oregon, is the deepest lake in North America, measuring 589 m (1932 ft) at its deepest point. The lake is inside the collapsed center of a volcano called Mount Mazama.

So how did a volcano form a lake? As Mount Mazama erupted around 6800 years ago, the molten rock and volcanic ash that helped to support the cone of the volcano were ejected. The top then collapsed, creating a big hole. As the hole filled with rainwater and melted snow, Crater Lake was formed. A secondary eruption produced a small volcanic cone, which rose above the water's surface and became Wizard Island, the small island seen in the photo at left.

Activity 1 Imagine you are an early explorer who has just discovered Crater Lake. Examine the photos at left, and write two other possible explanations for how the lake may have formed. When you are finished, think of possible weaknesses in each of your explanations. Write these weaknesses down, and share your results with your class.

Activity 2 Mount Mazama exploded with a great deal of force. Go to the library and research Mount Mazama. How tall is Mount Mazama thought to have been before it erupted? How does that size compare with the size of other volcanoes in Oregon and Washington? How big was the eruption? How might the eruption have affected Earth's global climate?

🖪 internet**connect**

SC*LINKS*
NSTA

TOPIC: Volcanoes
GO TO: www.scilinks.org
KEYWORD: HK1704

Crater Lake, in Oregon, sits within the top of a collapsed volcano.

557

Focus ACTIVITY

Background Because of the constant movement of the Earth, landforms such as mountains, canyons, and in this instance, a volcano, have been transformed in different ways over time. It is important to make sure that students understand that the Earth has been and will continue to be in motion and that those motions can cause dramatic changes in the Earth's surface.

Activity 1 Responses will vary, but explanations about how the lake formed might include: the lake is a crater formed by the impact of a meteor, or Mount Mazuma was pushed up by colliding continental plates, and the top of the mountain became a lake by collecting rainwater.

Activity 2 Answers will vary depending on what sources of information are used.

SKILL BUILDER

Interpreting Visuals Have students look at the crater lake in the small photo. How is this crater different from the crater shown in the small photo in the opener for Chapter 16? *(This lake's crater was formed when the cone of a volcano collapsed. The crater on p. 525 was formed by a meteorite impact.)*

Earth's Interior and Plate Tectonics

Scheduling

Refer to pp. 556A–556D for lecture, classwork, and assignment options for Section 17.1.

★ **Lesson Focus**

Use transparency *LT 55* to prepare students for this section.

INTEGRATING

MATH Tell students to assume that the average thickness of the oceanic crust is about 5.5 km and the average thickness of the continental crust is about 35 km. Have the students calculate how much thicker the mantle is than the oceanic crust and how much thicker the mantle is than the continental crust. *(The mantle is about 530 times the thickness of the oceanic crust, 2900 km/5.5 km = 530; the mantle is about 83 times the thickness of the continental crust, 2900 km/35 km = 83)*

SKILL BUILDER

Interpreting Visuals

Have students look at **Figure 17-1.** Tell them that Earth's core contains about 33 percent of Earth's mass, the mantle contains 67 percent, and the crust contains less than 1 percent of Earth's mass. However, Earth's core is about 16 percent of Earth's volume while the mantle makes up about 84 percent of Earth's volume. What does this suggest about Earth's core? *(the core is much denser than the mantle)*

Earth's Interior and Plate Tectonics

▶ **KEY TERMS**

crust
mantle
core
lithosphere
plate tectonics
asthenosphere
magma
subduction
fault

OBJECTIVES

▶ Identify Earth's different geologic layers.
▶ Describe the movement of Earth's lithosphere using the theory of plate tectonics.
▶ Identify the three types of plate boundaries and the principal structures that form at each of these boundaries.
▶ Explain how the presence of magnetic bands on the ocean floor supports the theory of plate tectonics.

You know from experience that Earth's surface is solid. You walk on it every day. You may have even dug into it and found that it is often more solid once you dig and reach rock. However, Earth is not solid all the way to the center.

What Is Earth's Interior Like?

Figure 17-1 shows Earth's major compositional layers. We live on the topmost layer of Earth—the **crust.** Because the crust is relatively cool, it is made up of hard, solid rock. The crust beneath the ocean is called *oceanic crust* and has an average thickness of 4–7 km (2.5–4.3 mi). *Continental crust* is less dense and thicker, with an average thickness of about 20–40 km (12–25 mi). The continental crust is deepest beneath high mountains, where it reaches depths as great as 70 km.

Beneath the crust lies the **mantle,** a layer of rock that is denser than the crust. Almost 2900 km (1800 mi) thick, the mantle makes up about 80 percent of Earth's volume. Because humans have never drilled all the way to the mantle, we do not know for sure what it is like. However, geologic events, such as earthquakes and volcanoes, provide evidence of the mantle's consistency.

▶ **crust** the outermost and thinnest layer of Earth

▶ **mantle** the layer of rock between the Earth's crust and its core

Figure 17-1
Earth is composed of an inner core, an outer core, a mantle, and a crust.

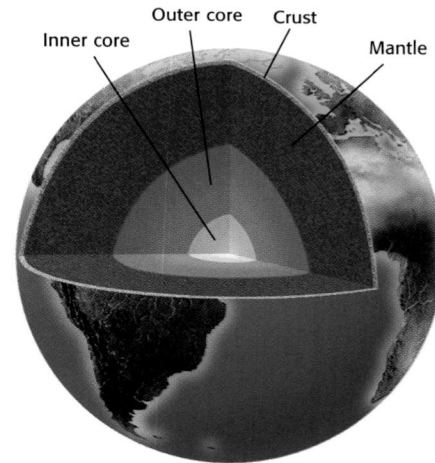

Inner core   Outer core   Crust   Mantle

558 CHAPTER 17

In the outer mantle, the rocks are mostly solid, as they are in the crust. The rocks in the inner portion of the mantle, however, are extremely hot and are said to be "plastic"—soft and easily deformed, like a stiff piece of gum.

The center of Earth, the **core,** is believed to be composed mainly of iron and nickel. It has two layers. The *inner core* is solid metal, and the *outer core*, which surrounds the inner core, is liquid metal.

Earth's interior gets warmer with depth

If you have ever been in a cave, you may have noticed that the temperature in the cave was cool. That's because the air and rocks beneath Earth's surface are shielded from the warming effects of the sun. However, if you were to travel far beneath the surface, such as into a deep mine, you would find that the temperature becomes uncomfortably hot. South African gold mines, for instance, reach depths of up to 3 km (2 mi), and their temperatures approach 50°C (120°F). The high temperatures in these mines are caused not by the sun but by energy that comes from Earth's interior.

Geologists believe the mantle is much hotter than the crust, as shown in **Figure 17-2.** These high temperatures cause the rocks in the mantle to behave plastically. This is the reason for the inner mantle's plastic, gumlike consistency.

The core is hotter still. On Earth's surface, the metals contained in the core would boil at the temperatures shown in **Figure 17-2.** Iron boils at 3000°C (5400°F), and nickel boils at 2900°C (5300°F). But in the outer core, these metals remain liquid because the pressure due to the weight of the mantle and crust is so great that the substances in the outer core are prevented from changing to their gaseous form. Similarly, pressure in the inner core is so great that the atoms are forced together as a solid.

Radioactive elements contribute to Earth's high internal temperature

Earth's interior contains radioactive isotopes. These radioactive isotopes (mainly those of uranium, thorium, and potassium) are quite rare. Their nuclei break up, releasing energy as they become smaller nuclei. Because Earth is so large, it contains enough atoms of these elements to produce a huge quantity of energy. This energy is one of the major factors contributing to Earth's high internal temperature.

▶ **core** the center of a planetary body, such as Earth

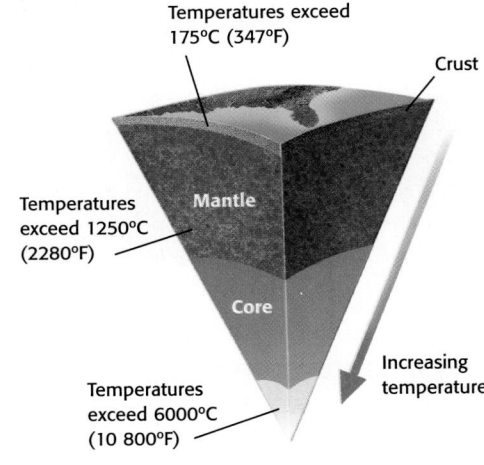

Temperatures exceed 175°C (347°F)

Crust

Mantle

Temperatures exceed 1250°C (2280°F)

Core

Increasing temperature

Temperatures exceed 6000°C (10 800°F)

Figure 17-2
Temperatures in Earth's interior increase with depth. Temperatures near the center of the core can be as hot as the surface of the sun.

internetconnect

SC*LINKS*
NSTA

TOPIC: Earth's geologic layers
GO TO: www.scilinks.org
KEYWORD: HK1701

PLANET EARTH **559**

Earth's Interior and Plate Tectonics

Teaching Tip

Earth's Layers The energy generated as heat in Earth's interior contributes to the process of dividing the Earth into layers with distinct characteristics. This heat has three main sources: the decay of radioactive elements, the processes by which different rock types are produced from magma, and the leftover energy from the accretion and compression of particles that coalesced to form Earth.

|SKILL BUILDER

Interpreting Visuals Have the students look at **Figure 17-2.** Tell them that Earth's inner core spins faster than the rest of the planet and that the outer core is an electrically conducting liquid thought to be continuously moved by convection. Explain to them that the conductivity of the outer core combined with the differential spin of the inner core produces powerful electric currents inside the Earth. Ask them to hypothesize about what phenomenon these currents might produce. (*Earth's magnetic field*)

LINKING
CHAPTERS

Have students review Chapter 7 for the definition of radioactivity.

Earth's Interior and Plate Tectonics

READING SKILL BUILDER *Anticipation/Prediction* Before the students read the section on plate tectonics, ask them if the continents have ever been in different positions than they are now. Write the words *Pangaea* and *continental drift* on the board, and ask students what these words might mean. Have them discuss opinions, and make a list of hypotheses for discussion after the section has been read.

Teaching Tip

Continental Drift Have students find South Africa and Argentina on a map, and ask students if any similarities or differences exist between the two countries. Let the students know that mineral deposits, particularly diamond deposits, are shared by both countries. Have students generate hypotheses as to how those two countries, which are separated by the Atlantic Ocean, have come to share these similar mineral deposits.

Additional Application

Biodiversity Before Pangaea broke up, dinosaurs roamed the entire continent and their populations were very widespread. As Pangaea began to break up, the populations of dinosaurs were fragmented and isolated on the new continents. The fossil record indicates that dinosaurs began to evolve divergently as a result. By the time dinosaurs became extinct, about 65 million years ago, there was great biological diversity among the dinosaurs. Have the students research the biodiversity among the dinosaurs and plants before and after Pangaea broke up.

560

Plate Tectonics

Figure 17-3
This map shows Pangaea as Alfred Wegener envisioned it.

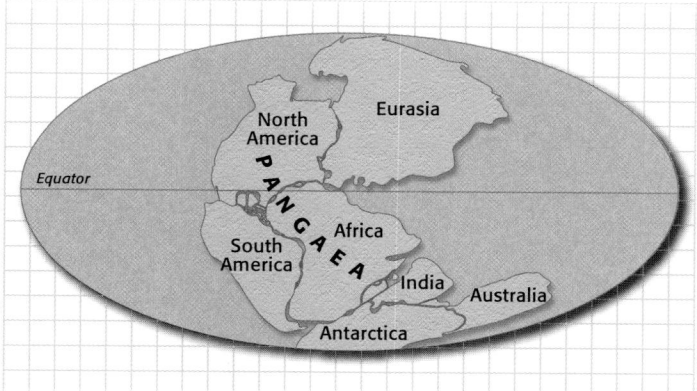

internetconnect

SC*LINKS*
NSTA

TOPIC: Plate tectonics
GO TO: www.scilinks.org
KEYWORD: HK1702

▶ **lithosphere** the thin outer shell of Earth, consisting of the crust and the rigid upper mantle

▶ **plate tectonics** the theory that Earth's surface is made up of large moving plates

In the early twentieth century, a German scientist named Alfred Wegener noticed that the eastern coast of South America and the western coast of Africa appeared to fit together like pieces of a puzzle. By studying world maps, Wegener found that several of the other continents' coastlines also seemed to fit together. Wegener pieced together parts of a map and joined all the continents together, forming a supercontinent that he called *Pangaea* (pan GEE uh). **Figure 17-3** is an illustration of what Wegener thought Pangaea might have looked like approximately 200 million years ago.

Using remains of ancient organisms, Wegener showed that 200 million years ago, the same kinds of animals lived on continents that are now oceans apart. He argued that the animals could not have evolved on separate continents. Therefore, there must have been some sort of physical connection between the continents.

The evidence was appealing, but scientists did not have an explanation of how continents could move. Wegener's theory was ignored until the mid-1960s, when structures on the ocean floor gave evidence of a mechanism for the movement of continents, or *continental drift.*

Earth has plates that move over the tar-like mantle

Earth's stiff outer shell, called the lithosphere, is approximately 100 km (60 mi) thick. The lithosphere consists of the crust and the rigid, upper portion of the mantle. The lithosphere is made of about seven large pieces (and several smaller pieces) called *tectonic plates.* These plates fit together like pieces of a puzzle and move in relation to one another. The theory describing the movement of plates is called plate tectonics.

Figure 17-4 shows the edges of Earth's tectonic plates. The arrows indicate the direction of each plate's movement. Note that plate boundaries do not always coincide with continental boundaries. Some plates move toward each other, some move away from each other, and still others move alongside each other.

DEMONSTRATION 1 TEACHING

Convection Currents

Time: Approximately 15 minutes
Materials: water, beaker, hot plate, several grains of rice, oven mitt

Step 1 Using a hot plate, boil 750 mL of water in a large beaker. When the water is boiling, use the oven mitt to position the beaker carefully and hold it so that only half of it is in contact with the hot plate.

Step 2 Drop several grains of rice in the water and observe the motion of the rice.

Analysis

Ask the students to describe the movement of the grains of rice. If students have trouble answering, guide them with the following questions:
• On what side of the beaker does the rice rise?
  (the hot side)

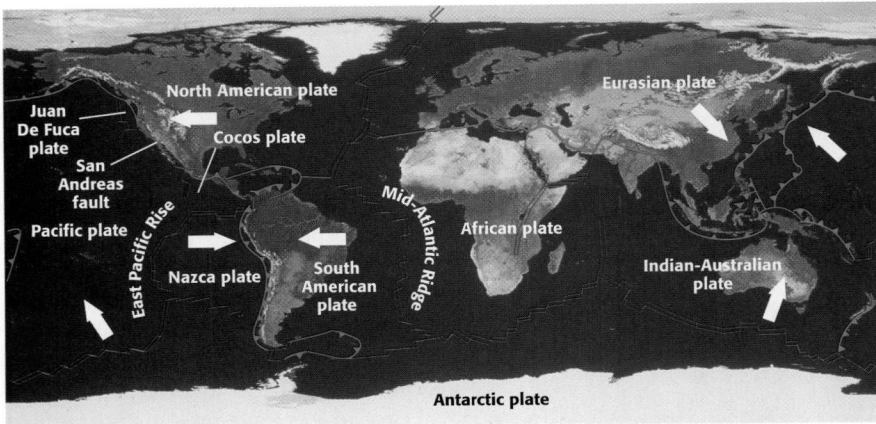

Plates move apart   Plates move together   Plates slide past each other

Tectonic plates move at speeds ranging from 1 to 16 cm (0.4 to 6.3 in.) per year. Although this speed may seem slow, tectonic plates have moved a considerable distance because they have been moving for hundreds of millions of years.

It is unknown exactly why tectonic plates move

One hypothesis suggests that plate movement results from convection currents in the asthenosphere, the hot, plastic portion of the mantle. As shown in **Figure 17-5,** the plates of the lithosphere "float" on top of the asthenosphere.

The soft rock in the asthenosphere might circulate by convection, similar to the way mushy oatmeal circulates as it boils. This slow movement of rock might push the plates of the lithosphere along. Some scientists believe that the plates are pieces of the lithosphere that are being moved around by convection currents. Other scientists believe that the forces generated by convection currents are not sufficient to move the plates. The origin of the forces that move the plates is not clear.

Figure 17-4
Earth's lithosphere is made up of several large tectonic plates. Plate boundaries are marked in red, and arrows indicate plate movement.

▶ **asthenosphere** the zone of the mantle beneath the lithosphere that consists of slowly flowing solid rock

Figure 17-5
According to one theory, convection currents are the mechanism that moves tectonic plates.

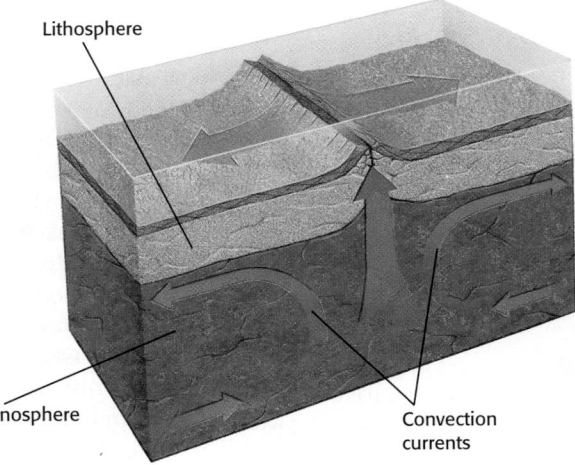

Lithosphere

Asthenosphere

Convection currents

INTEGRATING

MATH Have students calculate the number of years that it took New York and the west coast of Africa to reach their current locations, 6.76×10^8 cm apart, if the sea floor is spreading an average of 4 cm a year. *(about 169 million years, 6.76×10^8 cm/(4 cm/year) = 1.69×10^8 years; this is fairly close to the estimate based on geologic and fossil evidence of when the breakup of Pangaea began 180 million years ago.)*

RESOURCE LINK
LABORATORY MANUAL

Have students perform *Lab 17 Planet Earth: Relating Convection to the Movement of Tectonic Plates* in the lab ancillary.

DATASHEETS

Have students use *Datasheet 17.3* to record their results from the lab.

- On what side of the beaker does the rice drop? *(the cold side)*
- What is responsible for this rising and falling action? *(convection currents)*
- How does this demonstration relate to the movement of the slowly flowing solid rock in the asthenosphere? *(The rice follows the same path that the slowly flowing rock does, due to convection currents.)*

Earth's Interior and Plate Tectonics

SKILL BUILDER

Vocabulary Before reading the section on divergent and convergent plate boundaries, write the words *divergent* and *convergent* on the board, and ask students if they know what those words mean. Having students think about the prefixes *di-* and *con-* may give them clues as to what the words mean.

SKILL BUILDER

Interpreting Visuals Have students use **Figure 17-6** to explain the forces that pull rocks outward from mid-oceanic ridges. Guide their explanations by asking the following questions: Why does molten rock from the mantle come to the surface at the ridges? Why does the ocean floor spread apart at the ridges? Why is rock at the ridge "new" rock?

Be sure students understand that it was not until the 1950s, when researchers used sonar to study the ocean floor, that the mid-oceanic ridge was discovered. Stress that mid-oceanic ridges are not always in the middle of an ocean.

Resources Teaching Transparency 55 shows this visual.

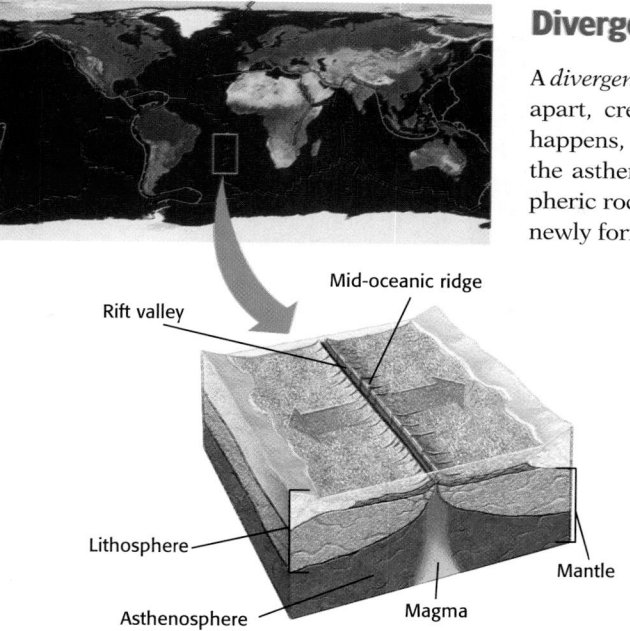

Figure 17-6
Tectonic plates move apart at divergent boundaries, forming rift valleys and mountain systems, such as this mid-oceanic ridge.

▶ **magma** molten rock within the Earth

▶ **subduction** the process in which a tectonic plate dives beneath another tectonic plate and into the asthenosphere

Divergent Plate Boundaries

A *divergent boundary* occurs where two plates move apart, creating a gap between them. When this happens, hot molten rock, or *magma*, rises from the asthenosphere and cools, forming new lithospheric rock. The two diverging plates then pull the newly formed lithosphere away from the gap.

Mid-oceanic ridges result from volcanic activity at a divergent boundary

Mid-oceanic ridges are mountain ranges that form at divergent boundaries in oceanic crust. **Figure 17-6** shows how a mid-oceanic ridge forms. As the plates move apart, magma rises from between the diverging plates and fills the gap. The result is new oceanic crust that forms a large central valley, called a *rift valley*, surrounded by high mountains, the mid-oceanic ridge.

Unlike most mountains on land, which are formed by the bending and folding of continental crust, mid-oceanic ridges are mountain ranges created by magma rising to Earth's surface and cooling. The most studied mid-oceanic ridge is called the Mid-Atlantic Ridge. This ridge runs roughly down the center of the Atlantic Ocean from the Arctic Ocean to an area off the southern tip of South America.

Convergent Plate Boundaries

Knowing that lithosphere is being created at mid-oceanic ridges, you may wonder why Earth isn't expanding. The reason is that while the new lithosphere is formed at divergent boundaries, the older lithosphere is destroyed at *convergent boundaries* as oceanic plates dive beneath continental or oceanic plates.

Oceanic plates dive beneath continental plates as they collide

The Andes Mountains, in South America, are formed along a convergent boundary between an oceanic plate and the South American continental plate. At this boundary, the oceanic plate, which is denser, dives beneath the continental plate and drags the oceanic crust along with it. This process is called *subduction*. As shown in **Figure 17-7,** ocean trenches, mountains, and volcanoes are formed at *subduction zones*.

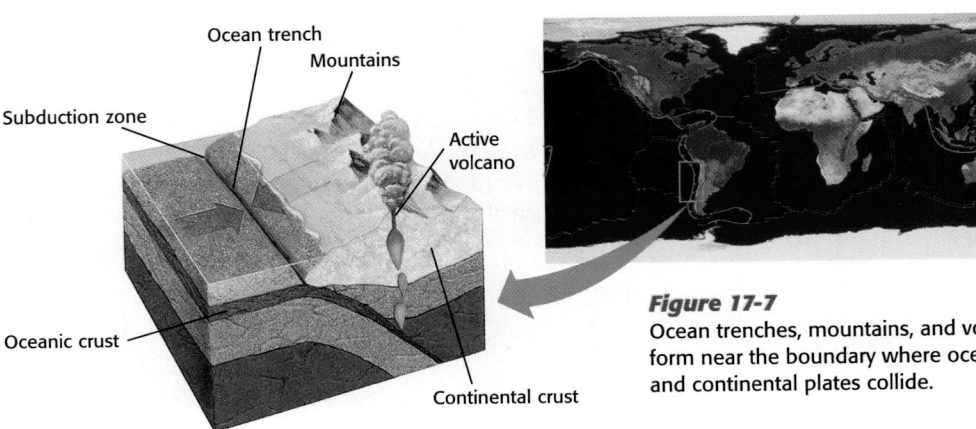

Figure 17-7
Ocean trenches, mountains, and volcanoes form near the boundary where oceanic and continental plates collide.

Ocean trenches form along the boundary between two oceanic plates or between an oceanic plate and a continental plate. These trenches can be very deep. The ocean floor is deepest at the Mariana Trench, in the Pacific Ocean. Located off the coast of Asia, the trench is more than 11 km (6.8 mi) beneath the ocean surface. The Peru-Chile Trench, on the eastern side of the Pacific Ocean off the coast of South America, is associated with the formation of the Andes Mountains. This trench is more than 7 km (4.3 mi) deep.

Oceanic crust melts when it subducts

Mountains form at the boundary between oceanic crust and continental crust because of what occurs deep below Earth's surface. In the subduction zone, when the oceanic plate dives into the hotter mantle, materials in the plate reach their boiling point and begin to melt, forming magma. Because this magma is less dense than the rock above it, it rises toward the surface. This rising magma pushes the continental crust upward, forming mountains. Subtler effects of heating by the magma cause the continental crust to swell and become less dense, adding height to the continental mountains.

Volcanic mountains also form at convergent boundaries. Magma rises to the surface and cools, forming new rock. These volcanoes are formed far inland from their associated oceanic trenches. Many volcanoes in the Andes Mountains, for instance, are more than 200 km (125 mi) from the Peru-Chile Trench.

Aconcagua (ah kawng KAH gwah), the tallest mountain in the Western Hemisphere, is a volcanic mountain in the Andes. At a height of 6959 m (22 831 ft), the peak of Aconcagua is more than 13.8 km (8.6 mi) above the bottom of the Peru-Chile Trench.

INTEGRATING

PHYSICS
As mentioned earlier in this chapter, Earth's crust is cooler than the layers below. As hot magma rises, it transfers energy to the atoms in the crust and causes them to vibrate more energetically. Because of this increased vibration, the atoms press one another outward and the crust expands and swells upward.

INTEGRATING

PHYSICS
Resources   Assign students worksheet *17.1: Integrating Physics—High Up in the Himalayas* from the **Integration Enrichment Resources** ancillary.

SKILL BUILDER

Interpreting Visuals   Have the students use **Figure 17-7** to explain how both mountains and volcanoes are formed at convergent boundaries. *(Mountains can be formed by buckling crust as two plates collide. Volcanoes are formed when subducting rock melts and rises back to the surface.)*

Resources   Teaching Transparency 56 shows this visual.

INTEGRATING

SPACE SCIENCE   Astronomers give extraterrestrial mountains the name "mons," while extraterrestrial mountain ranges are called either "montes," or "highlands." Encourage students to find out more about the formation of mountains on Mercury, Mars, Earth's moon, or one of the moons of Jupiter or Saturn. Have students compare the mountains they study with mountains on Earth in terms of their size and formation.

PLANET EARTH   **563**

Transform Fault Boundaries
Have students find out if there are any plate boundaries in their geographical area. What is a possible danger of living near a plate boundary? (Earthquakes occur at each type of plate boundary.)

Additional Application

Colliding Continental Plates

The Appalachian Mountains, like the Himalayas, were formed by colliding continental plates. About 390 million years ago, the landmasses that would become North America and Africa collided, buckling the crust between them to form the Appalachian Mountains. Then about 208 million years ago, North America and Africa began to break apart and a mid-ocean ridge formed between them. By 65 million years ago, the Appalachians were no longer at a plate boundary due to the production of new oceanic crust.

Have the students research a mountain range of their choice using the library and the Internet and prepare a short summary describing its formation.

RESOURCE LINK

IER

Assign students worksheet *17.8: Integrating Biology—Mountaineering: How Our Bodies Acclimatize* in the **Integration Enrichment Resources** ancillary.

Figure 17-8
The Himalayas are still growing today as the tectonic plate containing Asia and the plate containing India continue to collide.

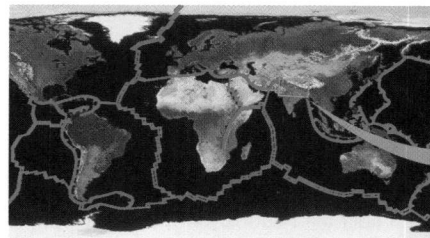

▶ **fault** a crack in the Earth created when rocks on either side of a break move

Colliding continental plates create mountains
The Himalayas, shown in **Figure 17-8,** are the tallest mountain range in the world. They formed during the collision between the tectonic plate containing India and the Eurasian plate.

The Himalayas are presently 320 km wide (about 200 mi) at their widest point. They continue to grow in both width and height as the two plates continue to collide. Mount Everest, the highest mountain in the world, is part of this range. Mount Everest's peak is 8850 m (29 034 ft) above sea level.

Transform Fault Boundaries

Plate movement can cause breaks in the lithosphere as well. Once a break occurs, rocks in the lithosphere continue to move, scraping past one another. The cracks in the Earth where the rocks move past one another are called faults.

Faults can occur in any area where forces in the lithosphere are great enough to break rock. When rocks move horizontally past each other at faults along plate boundaries, the boundary is called a *transform fault boundary*.

Figure 17-9 shows how plates move past each other at a transform fault boundary.

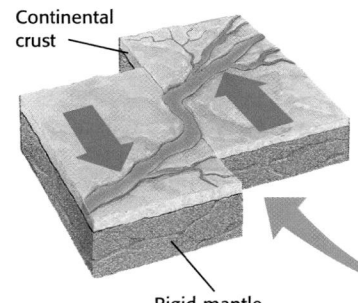

Continental crust

Rigid mantle

Figure 17-9
Plates scrape past each other at transform fault boundaries. The change in the course of the river results from plate movement.

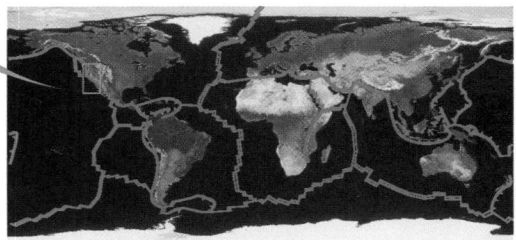

At transform fault boundaries, the great forces involved in plate movement tear at the Earth and cause earthquakes. You may have heard or read about some of the earthquakes along the San Andreas fault, which runs from Mexico through California and out to sea north of San Francisco. Transform fault boundaries occur in many places across Earth, including the ocean floor.

Evidence for Plate Tectonics

In the 1960s, evidence was discovered in the middle of the oceans that helped explain the mechanisms of plate tectonics. New technology provided images of "bands" of rock on the ocean floor with alternating magnetic polarities, like the bands illustrated in **Figure 17-10**. These bands differ from one another in the alignment of the magnetic minerals in the rocks they contain.

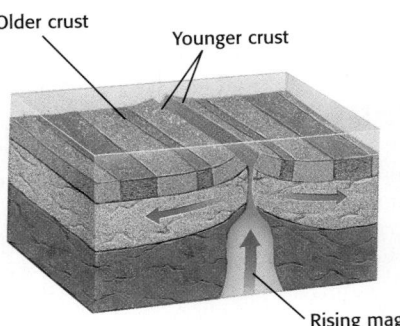

Older crust Younger crust

Rising magma

Figure 17-10
The stripes in the crust illustrate Earth's alternating magnetic field. Light stripes represent the ocean floor when Earth's magnetic polarity was oriented the same way it is today, while the darker stripes show reversed polarity.

Teaching Tip

Faults Transform plate boundaries are strike-slip faults. In a strike-slip fault, the fracture is vertical, or close to vertical, and rocks on opposite sides of the fault move horizontally past each other. The San Andreas fault is a strike-slip fault. Rocks can also move vertically at a fault. Vertical motion at a fault occurs at both convergent and divergent plate boundaries.

INTEGRATING

BIOLOGY Chemosynthetic bacteria abound at volcanic vents along the mid-ocean ridges. They are the foundation for a flourishing deep-sea floor community that includes tubeworms, giant mollusks, shrimp, crabs, and fish. Hot water circulating through fractures in the crust dissolves sulfur, minerals, and metals from the rock. This mineral-laden water rises to the surface of the sea floor and shoots through fractures in the rock, producing black smokers. Bacteria found at these vents produce energy from hydrogen sulfide. It was once thought that there is little or no life on the deep sea floor because sunlight cannot penetrate to such depths.

Inquiry Lab

Can you model tectonic plate boundaries with clay?

Materials
- ✔ ruler
- ✔ plastic knife
- ✔ paper
- ✔ lab apron
- ✔ scissors
- ✔ 2–3 lb modeling clay
- ✔ rolling pin or rod

Procedure

1. Use a ruler to draw two 10 × 20 cm rectangles on your paper, and cut them out.
2. Use a rolling pin to flatten two pieces of clay until they are each about 1 cm thick. Place a paper rectangle on each piece of clay. Using the plastic knife, trim each piece of clay along the edges to match the shape of the paper.
3. Flip the two clay rectangles so that the paper is at the bottom, and place them side by side on a flat surface, as shown at right. Slowly push the models toward each other until the edges of the clay make contact and begin to buckle and rise off the surface of the table.
4. Turn the models around so that the unbuckled edges are touching. Place one hand on each clay model. Slide one clay model toward you and the other model away from you. Apply only slight pressure toward the seam where the two pieces of clay touch.

Analysis

1. What type of plate boundary are you demonstrating with the model in step 3?
2. What type of plate boundary are you demonstrating in step 4?
3. How do the appearances of the facing edges of the models in the two processes compare? How do you think these processes might affect the appearance of Earth's surface?

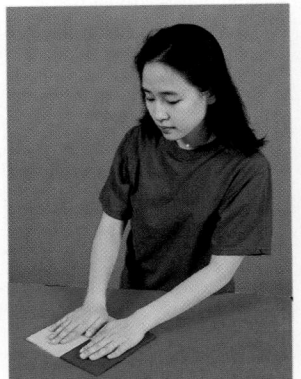

PLANET EARTH **565**

Inquiry Lab

Can you model tectonic plate boundaries with clay?

Analysis:
1. convergent plate boundary
2. transform fault plate boundary

3. Answers will vary but may include rough, wrinkled, and bumpy for step 3. Mountains, volcanoes, and trenches form at convergent plate boundaries. In contrast to the previous step, step 4 answers may include words like smoother, flatter, and less bumpy.

RESOURCE LINK

DATASHEETS

Have students use *Datasheet 17.1 Inquiry Lab: Can you model tectonic plate boundaries with clay?* to record their results.

Earth's Interior and Plate Tectonics

Teaching Tip

GPS Geophysicists use the Global Positioning System (GPS) to measure the rate of tectonic plate movement. Radio signals are continuously beamed from satellites to GPS ground stations, which record the exact distance between the satellites and the ground station. By calculating the time it takes for the GPS ground stations to move a given distance, scientists can measure the rate of motion of each tectonic plate.

SECTION 17.1 REVIEW

Check Your Understanding

1. The inner core remains a solid even though it is very hot; pressure due to the weight of the mantle and crust is so great that the atoms are forced together as a solid.

2. **a.** transform fault boundary
   b. convergent plate boundary
   c. divergent plate boundary

3. When two tectonic plates move away from each other, the gap is filled by hot molten rock (magma) that rises from the asthenosphere and cools. This cooled magma forms new lithospheric rock.

Answers continue on p. 593A.

RESOURCE LINK
STUDY GUIDE

Assign students *Review Section 17.1 Earth's Interior and Plate Tectonics.*

VOCABULARY *Skills Tip*

The word tectonic *originates from the Greek word* tektonikos, *meaning "construction." In everyday usage, the word* tectonics *relates to architecture.*

Magnetic alignment of oceanic rocks supports the plate tectonics theory

As hot, molten rock pours out onto the ocean floor, iron minerals, such as magnetite, align themselves parallel to Earth's magnetic field, just as compass needles do. After the rocks cool to about 550°C (1020°F), the alignment of these magnetic regions in the iron minerals becomes fixed. The result is a permanent record of Earth's magnetic field as it was just before the rock cooled.

So why are there differently oriented magnetic bands of rock? Earth's magnetic field has reversed direction many times during its history, with the north magnetic pole becoming the south magnetic pole and the south magnetic pole becoming the north magnetic pole. This occurs on average once every 200 000 years. This process is recorded in the rocks as bands. These magnetic bands are symmetrical on either side of the Mid-Atlantic Ridge. The rocks appear to be the youngest near the center of the ridge. The farther away from the ridge you go, the older the rocks appear. This suggests that the crust was moving away from the plate boundary.

SECTION 17.1 REVIEW

SUMMARY

▶ The layers of Earth are the crust, mantle, and core.

▶ Earth's outer layer (lithosphere) is broken into several pieces called tectonic plates. These plates ride on top of the soft mantle beneath them.

▶ Plates spread apart at divergent boundaries, collide at convergent boundaries, and slide past each other at transform fault boundaries. The entire landscape of the planet has been shaped by these processes.

▶ The alignment of iron minerals in oceanic rocks supports the theory of plate tectonics.

CHECK YOUR UNDERSTANDING

1. **Explain** why the inner core remains a solid even though it is very hot.

2. **Determine** what type of plate tectonic boundary each of the following describes:
   a. plates move alongside each other
   b. plates move toward each other
   c. plates move away from each other

3. **Describe** how the gap is filled when two tectonic plates move away from each other.

4. **Determine** whether each of the following is likely to occur at convergent or divergent boundaries:
   a. rift valley   **c.** mid-oceanic ridge
   b. continental mountains   **d.** ocean trench

5. **Explain** how magnetic bands provide evidence that tectonic plates are moving apart at mid-oceanic ridges.

6. **Predict** what type of plate boundary exists along the coastline near Japan's volcanic mountain ranges.

7. **Critical Thinking** The oldest continental rocks are 4 billion years old, whereas the oldest sea-floor rocks are 200 million years old. Explain the difference in these ages.

17.2

Earthquakes and Volcanoes

OBJECTIVES

▶ Identify the causes of earthquakes.
▶ Distinguish between S waves, P waves, and surface waves in earthquakes.
▶ Describe how earthquakes are measured and rated.
▶ Explain how and where volcanoes occur.
▶ Describe the different types of common volcanoes.

▶ KEY TERMS

focus
epicenter
P waves
S waves
surface waves
seismology
Richter scale
vent

Scheduling

Refer to pp. 556A–556D for lecture, classwork, and assignment options for Section 17.2.

★ **Lesson Focus**
Use transparency *LT 56* to prepare students for this section.

READING SKILL BUILDER *Reading Aloud/Discussion* Read the section titled What Are Earthquakes? aloud to your students. As you read, have students write down on self-adhesive notes those concepts and vocabulary words that they find challenging and difficult. After reading, have the students work together through discussion and note taking to clarify the confusing portions of the passage.

Imagine rubbing two rough-sided rocks back and forth against each other. The movement won't be smooth. Instead, the rocks will create a vibration that is transferred to your hands. The same thing happens when rocks slide past one another at a fault. The resulting vibrations are called earthquakes.

What Are Earthquakes?

Compare the occurrence of earthquakes, shown as yellow dots in **Figure 17-11,** with the plate boundaries, marked by red lines. Each yellow dot marks the occurrence of an earthquake sometime between 1985 and 1995. You can see that earthquakes occur mostly at the boundaries of tectonic plates, where the plates shift with respect to one another.

Figure 17-11
Each yellow dot in this illustration marks the occurrence of an earthquake sometime between 1985 and 1995.

MISCONCEPTION ALERT
Earthquakes
Earthquakes are not a rare phenomenon. In fact, more than 3 million earthquakes happen each year, about one every 10 s! Most earthquakes are too weak to be felt by humans. The Ring of Fire, a volcanic zone which lies along the plate boundaries surrounding the Pacific Ocean, is also the world's largest and most active earthquake zone.

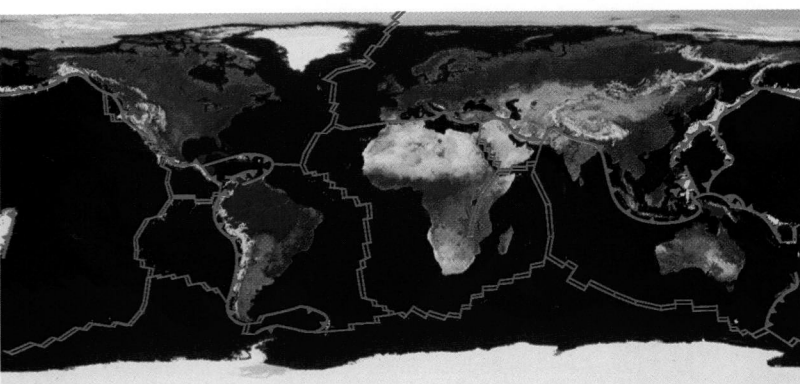

⊨⊨⊨⊨ Divergent boundary   ▲▲▲ Convergent boundary   —— Transform boundary

DEMONSTRATION 2 TEACHING

Faults and Earthquakes

Time: Approximately 10 minutes
Materials: 2 smooth wooden blocks
coarse sandpaper
glue

Step 1 Glue or staple coarse sandpaper onto one side of each block.

Step 2 Firmly hold the sandpaper-covered sides against each other while pushing them in opposite directions until there is a sudden movement.

Explain that this is how rock slides along a fault. As the rock slides, it releases energy that travels as seismic waves.

Earthquakes and Volcanoes

Additional Application

Tsunami Underwater earthquakes, if strong enough, can create a giant wave called a tsunami. Have students research the origin of the word *tsunami* and the damaging effects that tsunamis may have. Make sure students understand that the term *tidal wave* is invalid.

Teaching Tip

Waves Have students make a list of the characteristics of P waves, S waves, and surface waves. Lists should include the following:

- P waves travel the fastest.
- Surface waves travel the slowest.
- P waves can travel through solids, liquids, and gases.
- S waves can travel only through solids.
- P waves move rock back and forth between a squeezed and stretched position, while S waves move rock in a direction perpendicular to the direction of wave travel.
- Surface waves move points on Earth's surface in a vertical circle, like ocean waves move water particles.

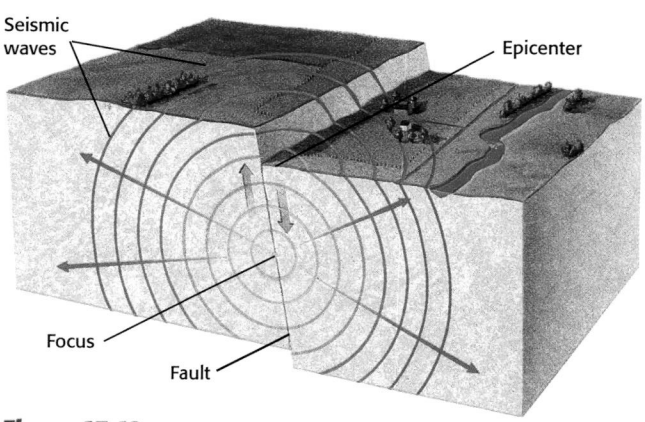

Figure 17-12
The epicenter of an earthquake is the point on the surface directly above the focus.

▶ **focus** the area along a fault at which slippage first occurs, initiating an earthquake

▶ **epicenter** the point on Earth's surface directly above the focus of an earthquake

▶ **P waves** primary waves; the longitudinal waves generated by an earthquake

Japan and California experience earthquakes often because they are situated at plate boundaries.

As plates move, the rocks along their edges experience immense pressure. Eventually, the stress becomes so great that it breaks these rocks along a fault line. As the rocks break, energy is released as *seismic waves*. As the seismic waves travel through and along the surface of Earth, they create the shaking effect that we experience during an earthquake.

The exact point inside Earth where the rocks first break, and thus where an earthquake originates, is called the **focus**. Earthquake waves travel in all directions from the focus, which is often located far below Earth's surface. The point on the surface immediately above the focus is called the **epicenter**, as shown in **Figure 17-12.** Because the epicenter is the point on Earth's surface that is closest to the focus, the damage there is usually greatest.

Energy from earthquakes is transferred through Earth by waves

The energy released by an earthquake is measured as shock waves. Earthquakes generate three types of waves. *Longitudinal waves* originate from an earthquake's focus. Longitudinal waves move faster through rock than other seismic waves. So they are the first waves to reach shock-wave recording stations. For this reason, longitudinal waves are also called *primary waves*, or **P waves.**

A longitudinal wave travels by compressing Earth's crust in front of it and stretching the crust in back of it. You can simulate longitudinal waves by compressing a portion of a spring and then releasing it, as shown in **Figure 17-13A.** Energy will travel through the coil as a longitudinal wave.

Figure 17-13

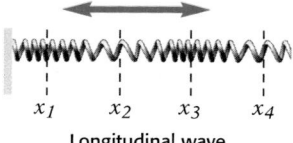

x_1 x_2 x_3 x_4

Longitudinal wave

A P waves are longitudinal waves, which can be modeled by compressing and releasing a spring.

Transverse wave

B S waves are transverse waves, which can be modeled by shaking a rope vertically.

DEMONSTRATION 3 TEACHING

Earthquake!

Time: Approximately 10 minutes
Materials: 2 or more different colors of clay

Shape the clay into flat sheets of varying thicknesses and stack the layers on top of each other. Make two separate stacks of clay to represent two different plates. Use the stacks of clay to demonstrate the motions of each type of boundary, and ask students to observe the effect of the motion on the stacks of clay—your tectonic plates. Tell

them that earthquakes at two types of boundaries are shallow and that earthquakes at the third type of boundary are usually deep. Ask students to hypothesize about which earthquakes occur at which boundaries. Then ask students to predict whether earthquakes at each type of boundary would be weak, moderate, or strong. *(transform boundary—moderate and shallow; divergent boundary—weak and shallow; convergent boundary—strong and deep)*

The second type of wave originating from an earthquake's focus is a *transverse wave*. Transverse waves move more slowly through Earth than longitudinal waves. Thus, these slower waves are called *secondary waves*, or **S waves**. The motion of a transverse wave is similar to that of the wave created when a rope is shaken up and down, as shown in **Figure 17-13B.**

Both P waves and S waves spread out from the focus in all directions, like light from a light bulb. In contrast, the third type of wave moves only across Earth's surface. These waves, called **surface waves,** are the result of Earth's entire mass shaking like a bell that has been rung. Earth's surface bends and reshapes as it shakes. The resulting rolling motion of Earth's surface is a combination of up-and-down motion and back-and-forth motion. In this type of wave, points on Earth's surface have a circular motion, like the movement of ocean waves far from shore.

Surface waves cause more destruction than either P waves or S waves. P waves and S waves shake buildings back and forth or up and down at relatively high frequencies. But the rolling action of surface waves, with their longer wavelengths, can cause buildings to collapse.

Seismology is the science of detecting and measuring earthquakes

Seismology is the study of earthquakes. Seismologists use sensitive machines called *seismographs* to record data about earthquakes, including P waves, S waves, and surface waves. **Figure 17-14** shows a simple seismograph. Remember learning about inertia and Newton's first law from Chapter 8? Seismographs use inertia to measure ground motion during an earthquake.

Examine the seismograph in **Figure 17-14.** A stationary pendulum hangs from a support fastened to Earth as a drum of paper turns slowly beneath the pendulum, which has a pen at its tip. When the Earth does not shake, the seismograph records an almost straight line because both Earth and the pendulum are relatively still. As Earth shakes, the base of the seismograph moves with Earth, but the pendulum remains stationary because it is protected from

▶ **S waves** secondary waves; the transverse waves generated by an earthquake

▶ **surface waves** a seismic wave that travels along Earth's surface

TOPIC: Earthquakes
GO TO: www.scilinks.org
KEYWORD: HK1703

▶ **seismology** the study of earthquakes and related phenomena

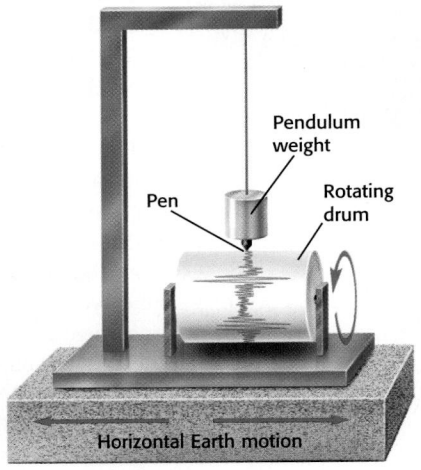

Figure 17-14
When the ground shakes, the pendulum on a seismograph remains relatively still while a rotating drum of paper at the seismograph's base records Earth's movement.

Pendulum weight

Pen

Rotating drum

Horizontal Earth motion

Earthquakes and Volcanoes

INTEGRATING

LIFE SCIENCE There are changes in Earth's crust that occur prior to an earthquake, such as magnetic field changes and the sinking, tilting, and bulging of the surface. These changes can be monitored by scientific instruments. Many studies have shown that eletromagnetic fields affect the behavior of living organisms. For example, migrating birds and fish navigate using magnetic fields, and fish and sharks utilize electroreceptors to detect objects around them. Have students conduct research to see if there is a relationship between animal behavior and earthquakes.

Multicultural Extension

References to observing animal behavior to predict earthquakes date back 3000 years in Chinese literature. This behavior includes dogs howling, chickens leaving their roosts, fish thrashing about in ponds, and snakes awakening from hibernation to leave their holes. The Chinese government still monitors animal behavior as part of an early warning system for earthquakes. On February 4, 1975, the Chinese government issued an earthquake warning in Liaoning province based on observations of animal behavior, and more than 3 million people were evacuated from their homes. That night a 7.3 magnitude earthquake occurred. Many buildings were destroyed, but only about 300 people were killed.

Earthquakes and Volcanoes

Historical Perspective

Have students study the more powerful earthquakes in history, researching aspects such as damage, intensity, depth of focus, type of fault, and geographical location. Examples of such earthquakes include the 1960 Chilean earthquake, the 1811–1812 New Madrid, Missouri earthquakes, and the 1923 Great Kanto earthquake, in Tokyo, Japan.

Teaching Tip

Discovering Earth's Layers

The speed of seismic waves increases sharply at the Moho, which is the boundary between the crust and mantle. The evidence for a liquid core is based on the shadow zones, the areas of Earth's surface where no direct seismic waves from a particular earthquake can be detected. In 1936, Inge Lehmann demonstrated that Earth's core had two parts—an outer, liquid part and an inner, solid part. She came up with the idea partly by calculating the time it took waves to pass through Earth's core. Her discovery was based on observations of the reflection and refraction of seismic waves generated by deep-focus earthquakes.

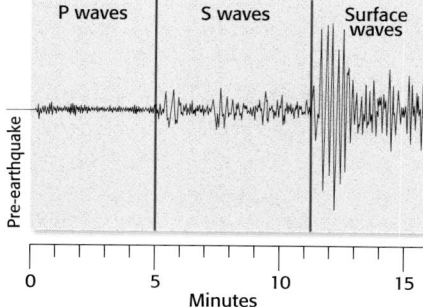

Figure 17-15
Each type of seismic wave leaves a unique zigzag pattern on a seismogram.

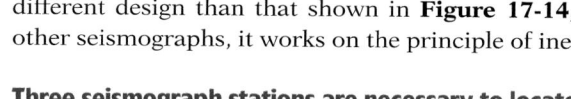
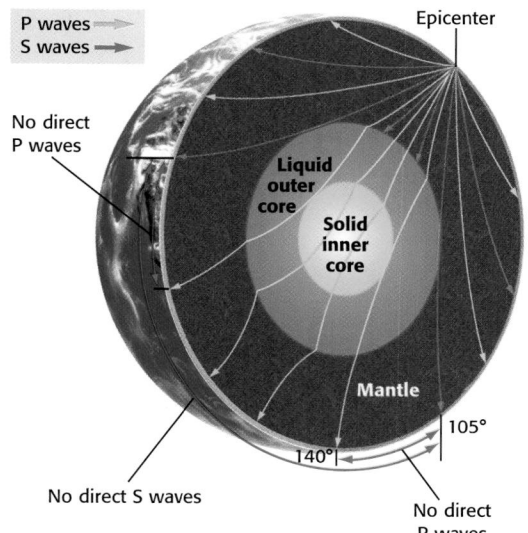

Figure 17-16
No direct S waves can be detected in locations more than 105° from the earthquake's epicenter. No direct P waves can be detected in locations between 105° and 140° from the earthquake's epicenter.

Earth's movement by the string. The pendulum draws zigzag lines on the paper that indicate an earthquake has occurred somewhere. Records of seismic activity are called *seismograms*.

There are more than 1000 seismograph stations across the world. At each station, three seismographs are used to measure different motions: north to south, east to west, and up and down. The north-to-south and east-to-west seismographs use a design similar to the seismograph in **Figure 17-14** but face perpendicular to each other. The up-and-down seismograph has a different design than that shown in **Figure 17-14,** but like the other seismographs, it works on the principle of inertia.

Three seismograph stations are necessary to locate the epicenter of an earthquake

As shown in **Figure 17-15,** P waves are the first to be recorded by seismographs, making a series of small, zigzag lines on the seismogram. S waves arrive later, appearing as larger, more ragged lines. Surface waves arrive last and make the largest lines. The difference in time between the arrival of P waves and the arrival of S waves enables seismologists to calculate the distance between the seismograph station and the earthquake's focus. By combining information from at least three different seismograph stations, seismologists can locate the focus and epicenter of an earthquake.

Geologists use seismographs to investigate Earth's interior

Seismologists have found that S waves do not reach seismographs on the side of Earth's core opposite the focus, as shown in **Figure 17-16.** This is evidence that part of the core is liquid because S waves, which are transverse waves, cannot travel through a liquid.

By comparing seismograms recorded during earthquakes, seismologists have noticed that the velocity of seismic waves varies depending on where they are measured. Waves change speed and direction whenever the density of the material they are traveling through changes. The differences in velocity suggest that Earth's interior consists of several layers of different densities. By comparing data, scientists have constructed the model of Earth's interior described in Section 17.1.

Table 17-1   Earthquake Magnitude, Effects, and Frequency

Magnitude	Characteristic effects of shallow earthquakes	Estimated number of earthquakes recorded each year
2.0 to 3.4	Not felt but recorded	More than 150 000
3.5 to 4.2	Felt by a few people in the affected area	30 000
4.3 to 4.8	Felt by most people in the affected area	4800
4.9 to 5.4	Felt by everyone in the affected area	1400
5.5 to 6.1	Moderate to slight damage	500
6.2 to 6.9	Widespread damage to most structures	100
7.0 to 7.3	Serious damage	15
7.4 to 7.9	Great damage	4
8.0 to 8.9	Very great damage	Occur infrequently
9.0	Would be felt in most parts of the Earth	Possible but never recorded
10.0	Would be felt all over the Earth	Possible but never recorded

The Richter scale is a measure of the magnitude of earthquakes

The **Richter scale** is a measure of the energy released at the focus of an earthquake. The magnitude of an earthquake is limited by the strength of the rocks of Earth's crust. The 1964 Alaskan earthquake, with a Richter magnitude of 8.4, is the largest earthquake of recent times. Each step on the Richter scale represents a 30-fold increase in the energy released. So an earthquake of magnitude 8 releases 30^4, or 810 000, times as much energy as one of magnitude 4! **Table 17-1** summarizes the effects and number of earthquakes with varying magnitudes. Notice that low magnitude earthquakes occur frequently.

The Richter scale cannot predict how severe an earthquake will be in terms of the damage it can cause. The amount of damage depends on several factors, such as the distance between populated areas and the epicenter and the type of construction used in buildings in those areas. The Armenian earthquake of 1988 and the San Francisco earthquake of 1989 both had a magnitude of 7 on the Richter scale. Yet the damage caused by each was very different. In Armenia, there was devastating property damage, and more than 25 000 people died. In contrast, 70 people died in San Francisco, and the only major damage was to an elevated freeway and some homes.

Why was there such a big difference between the effects of these two earthquakes? The depth of the focus of the earthquakes differed: the focus of the Armenian earthquake was 5 km down, but in San Francisco it was 19 km down. The deeper the focus, the less the effects will be felt at the surface.

▶ **Richter scale** scale that expresses the relative magnitude of an earthquake

Did You Know ?

The effect of an earthquake on Earth's surface is called the earthquake's intensity. The modified Mercalli scale is the most commonly used intensity scale. An earthquake is assigned a lower number if people felt the quake but it didn't cause much damage. Earthquakes that cause structural damage are assigned a higher number. The scale has been used to develop intensity maps for planners, building officials, and insurance companies.

MISCONCEPTION ALERT

Measuring Earthquakes Earthquakes can be measured by magnitude or intensity. An earthquake's magnitude is a quantitative measurement of its strength. The Richter scale is used to measure magnitude. Intensity is a qualitative measurement of an earthquake's effect on a particular area. The modified Mercalli Intensity scale is used to assess an earthquake's intensity. This scale incorporates observations of the earthquake's effects at a particular location. Although an earthquake may have different intensities at different locations, it has only one magnitude.

Additional Application

Earthquake Damage The best structures for resisting earthquake damage are wood-framed buildings because they are not very rigid and can flex quite a bit without collapsing. Structures built on waterlogged or unconsolidated sediment such as sand are more likely to suffer intense damage than are structures that are built on bedrock.

ALTERNATIVE ASSESSMENT

Richter Scale

Ask the students to answer the following question: If the amount of energy released by an earthquake with a magnitude of 2.0 on the Richter scale is n, what are the amounts of energy released by earthquakes with the following magnitudes in terms of n: 3.0, 4.0, 5.0, and 6.0? If necessary, give the hint that the energy released by an earthquake with a magnitude of 3.0 is $30n$. (energy released by magnitude 4.0 earthquake is about $900n$; energy released by magnitude 5.0 earthquake is about $27 000n$; energy released by magnitude 6.0 earthquake is about $810 000n$)

Earthquakes and Volcanoes

Connection to
SOCIAL STUDIES

Have students research several aspects of volcanic eruptions, including the name and date of the eruption, the type of volcano, the geographic location, and other disruption in the surrounding ecosystem.

Teaching Tip

Physics of Volcanic Eruptions   When temperature and pressure conditions allow, water and carbon dioxide dissolve in liquid magma.

When the water contained in magma changes from liquid to steam, its volume increases dramatically. This change causes pressure that creates a great deal of explosive force. Have students think of other examples in which water can be an explosive force, such as in a car's radiator, or in popcorn.

▶ **vent** an opening through which molten rock flows onto Earth's surface

Figure 17-17
Volcanoes build up into hills or mountains as lava and ash explode from openings in the Earth called vents.

Also, the physical properties of the rocks at the surface were different. The rocks in San Francisco are generally harder than those in Armenia. Softer rock breaks apart and changes position more easily than rigid rock, which is more likely to bend and return to its original position.

The difference in the amount of fatalities and damage between the two earthquakes was mainly due to the building construction in the two areas. California building codes require that buildings are able to withstand earthquakes of a certain magnitude. The buildings in Armenia were much less stable.

Volcanoes

As mentioned in Section 17.1, volcanoes can result from the movement of tectonic plates. A volcano is any opening in Earth's crust through which magma has reached Earth's surface. These openings are called **vents.**

Volcanoes often form hills or mountains as materials pour or explode from the vent, as shown in **Figure 17-17.** Volcanoes release molten rock, ash, and poisonous gases. All these products result from melting in the mantle or in the crust.

The type of eruption determines the volcano type

Volcanoes generally have one central vent, but they can also have several smaller vents. Magma from inside a volcano can reach Earth's surface through any of these vents. When magma reaches the surface, its physical behavior changes, and it is called *lava*.

Magma rich in iron and magnesium is very fluid and forms lava that tends to flow great distances. The eruptions are usually mild and can occur several times. The buildup of this kind of lava produces a gently sloping mountain, called a *shield volcano.* Shield volcanoes are some of the largest volcanoes. Mauna Loa, in Hawaii, is a shield volcano, as shown in **Figure 17-18A.** Mauna Loa's summit is more than 4000 m (13 000 ft) above sea level and more than 9020 m (29 500 ft) above the sea floor.

Composite volcanoes are made up of alternating layers of ash, cinders, and lava. Their magma is rich in silica and therefore is much thicker than the magma of a shield volcano. Gases are trapped in the magma, causing eruptions that alternate between flows and explosive activity that produces cinders and ash. Composite volcanoes are typically thousands of meters high, with much steeper slopes than shield volcanoes. Japan's Mount Fuji, shown in **Figure 17-18B,** is a composite volcano. Mount St. Helens, Mount Rainier, Mount Hood, and Mount Shasta, all in the northwestern United States, are also composite volcanoes.

DEMONSTRATION 4 TEACHING

Eruption Simulation

Time: Approximately 15 minutes
Materials: 10 mL of baking soda, 50 mL of vinegar, 200 mL beaker or measuring cup, bathroom tissue, large plate or pan, modeling clay, funnel, red food coloring, liquid dish soap, stirring stick

Step 1 Place 10 mL of baking soda in the center of a piece of bathroom tissue. Fold the corners of the tissue over the baking soda, and press the edges until the ends stay in place. Place the tissue packet in the middle of a large plate or pan.

Step 2 Put some modeling clay around the top edge of a funnel. Turn the funnel upside down over the tissue packet in the bottom of the pan. The clay should form a watertight seal between the base of the funnel and the plate or pan. Press down to make a tight seal.

Cinder cones are the smallest and most abundant volcanoes. When large amounts of gas are trapped in magma, violent eruptions occur—vast quantities of hot ash and lava are thrown from the vent. These particles then fall to the ground around the vent, forming the cone. Cinder cones tend to be active for only a short time and then become dormant. As shown in **Figure 17-18C,** Parícutin (pah REE koo teen), in west-central Mexico, is a famous cinder cone. Parícutin first erupted in 1943. After 2 years, the top of the volcano's cone had grown to a height of 450 m (1480 ft) above the base. The eruptions finally ended in 1952.

Volcanoes form not only on land but also under the oceans. In shallow water, volcanoes can erupt violently, forming clouds of ash and steam. An underwater volcano is called a *seamount.* Seamounts look much like composite volcanoes.

Types of Volcanoes

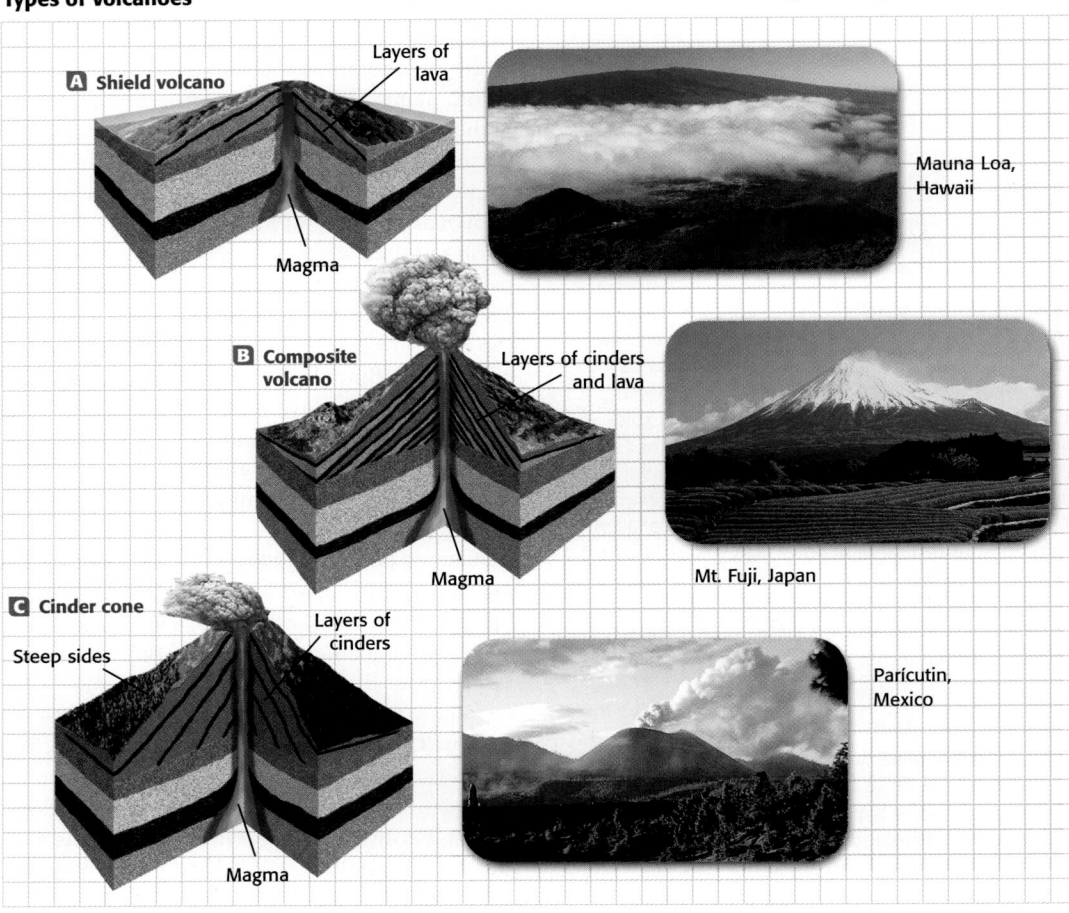

Figure 17-18
The type of volcano that forms depends largely on the makeup of the magma. Differences in the fluidity of the magma determine the type of eruption that occurs.

SKILL BUILDER

Interpreting Diagrams Ask students to define viscosity and describe a material that would have a high viscosity. *(a liquid's resistance to flow; honey, molasses, lava)* Then have students look at **Figure 17-18,** and ask them to explain each volcano's shape in terms of the viscosity of the magma that formed it. *(shield volcano: low viscosity; composite volcano: more viscosity; cinder cone: highly viscous)*

Resources Teaching Transparency 59 shows this visual.

Teaching Tip

Predicting Eruptions Geologists use sensitive instruments to monitor an active volcano to determine if magma is approaching the surface. Signs that a volcano is about to erupt include: increasing temperature of hot springs near the volcano, changes in the shape of the volcano or surrounding land, an increase in hot gas and ash from the vent, and small earthquakes around the volcano.

MISCONCEPTION

Eruptions **ALERT**
Although explosive volcanoes get the most attention, nonexplosive extrusions play a much more significant role in shaping our world. Much of the ocean floor is covered by lava from nonexplosive eruptions at the mid-oceanic ridges, and nonexplosive volcanoes formed many of the Pacific islands. In fact, there are 10 times as many active volcanoes at the bottom of the ocean as there are on land. The ocean floor, roughly three-fourths of Earth's surface, was produced primarily by volcanic activity.

Step 3 Add 50 mL of vinegar, two drops of red food coloring, and several drops of liquid dish soap to a 200 mL beaker or measuring cup, and stir.

Step 4 Carefully pour the liquid into the spout of the upturned funnel. Have your students predict how much time will elapse before the volcano erupts. Have one student record the time of the final eruption.

Analysis
1. Have students describe how the model volcano is similar to a real one. In what ways is it different?
2. Based on the predictions of the entire class, what can students conclude about the accuracy of predicting volcanic eruptions?

Earthquakes and Volcanoes

Connection to SOCIAL STUDIES

Making the Connection

1. Answers may vary, but should include the fact that gases and magma may have been building up for an extended amount of time before the eruption. Mount St. Helens is a composite volcano and has very thick magma with gases trapped in it.

2. Winds in the atmosphere were responsible for carrying ash from Washington to Montana.

Resources Assign students worksheet *17.2 Connection to Social Studies—Plinian Eruptions* in the **Integration Enrichment Resources** ancillary.

SKILL BUILDER

Interpreting Visuals Point out to students that most volcanic activity takes place on the ocean floor, where vast amounts of lava rise through rifts or volcanoes at diverging plate boundaries. Ask students to identify a spot where plates are diverging. (*the* Mid-*Atlantic Ridge*)

What landmass formed as a result of volcanic activity along this diverging plate boundary? (*the island of Iceland*)

Then remind students that Iceland is merely a visible part of the Mid-Atlantic Ridge. Also explain that volcanic eruptions along diverging tectonic plates are generally much less violent than volcanoes typical of convergent boundaries.

Figure 17-19
Seventy-five percent of the active volcanoes on Earth occur along the edges of the Pacific Ocean. Together these volcanoes form the Ring of Fire.

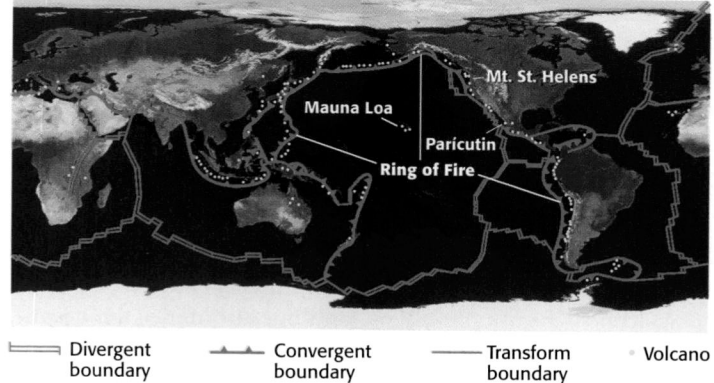

Mt. St. Helens
Mauna Loa
Paricutin
Ring of Fire

⊏⊐ Divergent boundary ⎯▲⎯ Convergent boundary ⎯⎯ Transform boundary · Volcano

Volcanoes occur at convergent plate boundaries surrounding the Pacific Ocean

Like earthquakes, volcanoes are linked to plate movement. Volcanoes are common all around the edges of the Pacific Ocean, where oceanic tectonic plates collide with continental plates. In fact, 75 percent of the active volcanoes on Earth are located in these areas. As seen in **Figure 17-19,** the volcanoes around the Pacific Ocean lie in a zone known as the Ring of Fire.

As a plate sinks at a convergent boundary, part of it melts and magma rises to the surface. The volcanoes that result form the edges of the Ring of Fire. These volcanoes tend to erupt cooler, less-fluid lava and clouds of ash and gases. The sticky lava makes it difficult for the gases to escape. Gas pressure builds up, causing explosive eruptions that often lead to loss of life and damage to property.

Volcanoes occur at divergent plate boundaries

As plates move apart at divergent boundaries, magma rises to fill in the gap. This magma creates the volcanic mountains that form the ridges around a central rift valley.

The volcanic island of Iceland, in the North Atlantic Ocean, is on the Mid-Atlantic Ridge. The island is continuously expanding from its center; the eastern and western sides of the island are growing outward in opposite directions. As a result, a great deal of geologic activity, such as volcanoes and hot springs, occurs on the island.

Connection to SOCIAL STUDIES

Mount St. Helens, in the Cascade Range in Washington, erupted explosively on May 18, 1980. Sixty people and thousands of animals were killed, and 10 million trees were blown down by the air blast created by the explosion. During the eruption, the north side of the mountain was blown away. Gas and ash were ejected upward, forming a column more than 19.2 km (11.9 mi) high. The ash was reported to have fallen as far east as central Montana.

Since the May 18 explosion, Mount St. Helens has had several minor eruptions. As a result, a small volcanic cone is now visible in the original volcano's crater.

Making the Connection

1. What might have caused the eruption of Mount St. Helens to be so explosive?
2. The force of the blast didn't push the ashes all the way to Montana. What other natural force might have transported the ashes that far?

ALTERNATIVE ASSESSMENT

Volcano

Have students draw a cross section of a volcano, showing what is within the volcano and in the ground underneath. The picture should include information which shows and details how the volcano was created, and the forces at work which lead to eruptions.

Volcanoes occur at hot spots

Some volcanoes occur in the middle of plates. They occur because mushroom-shaped trails of hot magma, called *mantle plumes*, rise from deep inside the mantle and erupt from volcanoes at *hot spots* at the surface.

When mantle plumes form below oceanic plates, lava and ash build up on the ocean floor. If the resulting volcanoes grow large enough, they break through the water's surface and become islands. As the oceanic plate continues moving, however, the mantle plume does not move along with it. The plume continues to rise under the moving oceanic plate, and a new volcano is formed at a different point. A "trail" in the form of a chain of extinct volcanic islands is left behind.

The Hawaiian Islands, which were formed by rising mantle plumes, lie in a line that roughly corresponds to the motion of the Pacific plate. The island of Hawaii is the most recently formed volcano in the chain, and it still contains the active volcano situated over the mantle plume.

SECTION 17.2 REVIEW

SUMMARY

▶ Earthquakes occur as a result of sudden movement within Earth's lithosphere.

▶ P waves are longitudinal waves, and they travel the fastest.

▶ S waves are transverse waves, and they travel more slowly.

▶ Surface waves travel the slowest. They result from Earth's vibrating like a bell.

▶ Volcanoes are formed when magma rises and penetrates the surface of Earth.

▶ The three types of volcanoes are shield volcanoes, cinder cones, and composite volcanoes.

CHECK YOUR UNDERSTANDING

1. **Identify** which type of seismic wave is described in each of the following:
   a. cannot travel through the core
   b. cause the most damage to buildings
   c. are the first waves to reach seismograph stations
2. **Select** which of the following describes a shield volcano:
   a. formed from violent eruptions
   b. has gently sloping sides
   c. formed from hot ash
   d. has steep sides
3. **Identify** whether volcanoes are likely to form at the following locations:
   a. hot spot
   b. transform fault boundary
   c. divergent plate boundary
   d. convergent boundary between continental and oceanic plates
4. **Differentiate** between the focus and the epicenter of an earthquake.
5. **Explain** how a mid-oceanic ridge is formed.
6. **Explain** why Iceland is a good place to use hydrothermal power, power produced from heated water.
7. **Critical Thinking** Are quiet eruptions or explosive eruptions more likely to increase the height of a volcano? Why?

Earthquakes and Volcanoes

MISCONCEPTION ALERT

Hot Spot Be sure students understand that a hot spot remains relatively stationary and that volcanic activity occurs as a tectonic plate moves over a hot spot. You might compare a hot spot to a candle flame and a tectonic plate to a piece of paper passing over the flame.

SECTION 17.2 REVIEW

Check Your Understanding

1. a. S waves
   b. surface waves
   c. P waves
2. (b)
3. a. yes
   b. no
   c. yes
   d. yes
4. The focus of an earthquake is the area along a fault where an earthquake originates, while the epicenter of an earthquake is the point on the surface of the Earth directly above the focus.
5. A mid-oceanic ridge is formed as plates move apart at divergent boundaries. Magma rises to fill the gap between the plates, and this magma creates the volcanic mountains that form ridges.

Answers continue on p. 593A.

ALTERNATIVE ASSESSMENT

Tectonic Plate Boundaries

Post a map of the world on the bulletin board that shows the location of tectonic plates. Pair students together, and have partners explain how tectonic plate boundaries and volcanoes are related. Each partner should evaluate the other's understanding by assessing their descriptions of converging and diverging tectonic plates, subduction, hot spots, and magma formation.

RESOURCE LINK
STUDY GUIDE

Assign students *Review Section 17.2 Earthquakes and Volcanoes.*

Minerals and Rocks

Scheduling

Refer to pp. 556A–556D for lecture, classwork, and assignment options for Section 17-3.

★ **Lesson Focus**
Use transparency *LT 57* to prepare students for this section.

READING SKILL BUILDER *Reading Organizer* Students should read the section titled Structure and Origins of Rocks and then create a table with the following headings: *Formation process, Texture, and Examples*. Have students fill in the table using information on the three different types of rocks that they have just read about.

READING SKILL BUILDER *Brainstorming* Discuss with students the definition of a mineral. Have them brainstorm a list of minerals. Have them use Section 17.3 and a geology field guide to confirm or deny the items on their lists. Make sure students list reasons as to why the item they listed is or is not a mineral.

SKILL BUILDER

Interpreting Visuals Have students examine **Figure 17-20** and describe all the characteristics of Devils Tower. Have students imagine that they are geologists exploring the tower. Have students write a short story, script, or poem describing the formation of Devils Tower based on their reading. Encourage students to speculate about the original height of the volcano and the history of rivers in the area.

▶ **KEY TERMS**
mineral
igneous rock
weathering
sedimentary rock
fossils
metamorphic rock

OBJECTIVES

▶ Identify the three types of rock.
▶ Explain the properties of each type of rock based on physical and chemical conditions under which the rock formed.
▶ Describe the rock cycle and how rocks change form.
▶ Explain how the relative and absolute ages of rocks are determined.

Devils Tower, in Wyoming, shown in **Figure 17-20,** rises 264 m (867 ft) above its base. According to an American Indian legend, the tower's jagged columns were formed by a giant bear scraping its claws across the rock. The tower is actually the solidified core of a volcano. Over millions of years, the surrounding softer rock was worn away by the Belle Fourche River finally exposing the core. Volcanic pipes, which are similar to volcanic cores, can be a source of diamonds. They contain solidified magma that extends from the mantle to Earth's surface.

▶ **mineral** a natural, inorganic solid with a definite chemical composition and a characteristic internal structure

Figure 17-20
Devils Tower, in northeastern Wyoming, is the solidified core of a volcano.

Structure and Origins of Rocks

All rocks are composed of **minerals.** Minerals are naturally occurring, nonliving substances found in Earth that have a composition that can be expressed by a chemical formula. Minerals also have a definite internal structure. Quartz, for example, is a mineral made of silicon dioxide, SiO_2. It is composed of crystals, as are most minerals. Coal, on the other hand, is not a mineral because it is formed from decomposed plant matter. *Granite* is not a mineral either; it is a rock composed of different minerals.

There are about 3500 known minerals in Earth's crust. However, no more than 20 of these are commonly found in rocks. Together, these 20 or so minerals make up more than 95 percent of all the rocks in Earth's crust. The nine most common of these *rock-forming minerals* are feldspar, pyroxene, mica, olivine, dolomite, quartz, amphibole, clay, and calcite.

Each combination of rock-forming minerals results in a rock with a unique set of properties. Rocks may be porous, granular, or smooth; they may be soft or hard and have different densities or colors. The appearance and characteristics of a rock reflect its mineral composition and the way it formed.

576 CHAPTER 17

DEMONSTRATION 5 TEACHING

Temperature Affects Crystal Growth

Time: Approximately 45 minutes
Materials: heat-resistant gloves, 400 mL beaker, hot plate, Celsius thermometer, magnesium sulfate (Epsom salts), hand lens, pointed laboratory scoop, medium test tube, distilled water, clock, aluminum foil, test-tube tongs

SAFETY CAUTION: *In step 3, be sure to direct the opening of the test tube away from you and the*

students. Always use the test-tube tongs to handle the hot test tube.

Step 1 Fill the beaker halfway with tap water and place it on the hot plate. The temperature of the water should be between 40°C and 50°C.

Step 2 Have students examine crystals of magnesium sulfate with a hand lens. Then fill the test tube about halfway with the magnesium sulfate and add an equal amount of distilled water. Use one finger to tap the test tube gently to mix it.

Figure 17-21

A Notice the coarse-grained texture of this sample of granite, an intrusive igneous rock.

B Obsidian, an extrusive igneous rock, cools much more quickly than granite.

Intrusive igneous rock

Extrusive igneous rock

Ask students to identify some of the differences between the intrusive igneous rock and the extrusive igneous rock seen in **Figure 17-21.**

Multicultural Extension

Obsidian is a smooth stone that was used by many Native Americans to make tools. Have students research other types of stones that were used by Native Americans. What were these tools used for, and what do these rocks imply about the environments that the Native Americans lived in?

Molten rock cools to form igneous rock

When molten rock cools and solidifies it forms **igneous rock.** Nearly all igneous rocks are made of crystals of various minerals, such as those shown in the granite in **Figure 17-21A.** As the rock cools, the minerals in the rock crystallize and grow. In general, the more quickly the rock cools, the less the crystals grow. For instance, obsidian, a smooth stone used by early American Indians to make tools, is similar to granite in composition, but it cools much more quickly. As a result, obsidian has either very small crystals or no crystals at all. **Figure 17-21B** shows a piece of obsidian.

Obsidian is categorized as an *extrusive* igneous rock because it cools on Earth's surface. *Basalt*, a fine-grained, dark-colored rock, is the most common extrusive igneous rock. Granite, on the other hand, is called an *intrusive* igneous rock because it forms from magma that cools while trapped beneath Earth's surface. Because the magma is insulated by the surrounding rocks, it takes a very long time to cool—sometimes millions of years. Because of this long cooling period, the crystals in intrusive igneous rocks are larger than those in extrusive igneous rocks. The crystals of granite, for example, are easy to see with the naked eye and are much lighter in color than those of basalt. Both rocks contain feldspar, but granite also has quartz, while basalt has pyroxene.

▶ **igneous rock** rock formed from cooled and hardened magma or lava

Connection to SOCIAL STUDIES

Throughout history, humans have used rocks and minerals to fashion tools. During the Stone Age, the Bronze Age, and the Iron Age people used stone, bronze, and iron, respectively, to make tools and weapons. The industrial revolution began when humans learned to burn coal to run machinery. After humans learned to extract oil from Earth's crust, gasoline-powered vehicles were invented, and we entered the automobile age.

Making the Connection

1. Research minerals that have been mined for their iron content. Where are the mines that were first used to harvest these minerals?
2. Scientists have divided the Stone Age into three phases—Paleolithic, Mesolithic, and Neolithic—on the basis of toolmaking techniques. Research these phases, and distinguish between the techniques used in each.

Connection to SOCIAL STUDIES

Making the Connection

1. Answers will vary according to the sources used.
2. Answers will vary.

Resources Assign students worksheet *17.3 Connection to Social Studies—Human Tools: From Stone to Iron* in the **Integration Enrichment Resources** ancillary.

PLANET EARTH **577**

Place the test tube in the beaker of hot water, and heat it for 3 minutes.

Step 3 Shape the aluminum foil into two small boatlike containers and label the boats.

Step 4 If all the magnesium sulfate is not dissolved after 3 minutes, tap the test tube again, and heat it for 3 more minutes.

Step 5 Place the first boat on the hot plate and turn the hot plate off. Place the second boat on

the table away from the hot plate.

Step 6 Using the test-tube tongs, remove the test tube from the beaker of water and evenly distribute the contents to each of the boats. Do not move or disturb the boats. Ask students how the temperature of the solution will affect the size of the crystals and the rate at which they form.

Step 7 Record the time it takes for the first crystals to appear. When the crystals form let the students use a hand lens to examine them.

Teaching Tip

Limestone and Fossils Limestone is about 95 percent calcite, or calcium carbonate. Many mollusks remove calcium and carbonate from sea water and combine them in special tissues that then harden to form a calcium carbonate shell. When the mollusk dies, its shell either dissolves back into the water or becomes part of the sediment on the bottom of the ocean. If the shell is part of deposited sediment, it may become a fossil. Have students research the Mazon Creek Deposits, in Kansas, or the Burgess Shale, in Canada, to learn more about these fossil beds.

Connection to FINE ARTS

One type of printing used to reproduce fine art is called lithography. Lithography uses a flat piece of fine-grained porous limestone. Interestingly, many important fossil beds were discovered while people quarried for lithographic limestone. The same qualities that make some limestone good for lithography also allow the preservation of extremely detailed fossils. Ask students to find out more about lithography and lithographic limestone beds around the world.

RESOURCE LINK
IER

Assign students worksheet *17.4: Integrating Chemistry—From Granite to Paper* in the **Integration Enrichment Resources** ancillary.

▶ **weathering** change in the physical form or chemical composition of rock materials exposed at Earth's surface

▶ **sedimentary rock** rock formed from compressed or cemented deposits of sediment

▶ **fossils** the traces or remains of a plant or an animal found in sedimentary rock

Remains of older rocks and organisms form sedimentary rocks

Even very hard rock with large crystals will break down over thousands of years. The process by which rocks are broken down is called **weathering.** Pieces of rock fall down hillsides due to gravity or get washed down by wind and rain. Rivers then carry the pieces down into deltas, lakes, or the sea. Waves beating against cliffs also knock pieces of rock away. The action of the waves and the movement of rivers and streams eventually break the pieces into pebbles, sand, and even smaller pieces. Weathering will be discussed further in Section 17-4.

As pieces of rock accumulate, they can form another type of rock—**sedimentary rock.** Think of sedimentary rocks as recycled rocks. The sediment they are made of contains fragments of older rocks and, in some cases, the remains of living organisms, called **fossils.**

There are two ways loose sediment can become rock. As sediment accumulates, the layers on the bottom get compressed from the weight of sediment above, forming rock. In the second way, other minerals dissolved in water seep between bits of rock and other material and "glue" them together. In **Figure 17-22A,** the pebbles and bits of rounded rock in the *conglomerate* are glued together with a brown material containing mostly quartz.

Sedimentary rocks are named according to the size of the fragments they contain. As mentioned, a rock made of pebbles is called a conglomerate. A rock made of sand is called *sandstone*. A rock made of fine mud is usually called *mudstone*, but if it is flaky and breaks easily into layers, it is called *shale*. Limestone, another kind of sedimentary rock, is made mostly of the fossils of organisms that lived in the water, as shown in **Figure 17-22B.** Sometimes the fossilized skeletons are so small or are broken up into such small fragments that they can't be seen with the naked eye. Places where limestone is found were once beneath the sea.

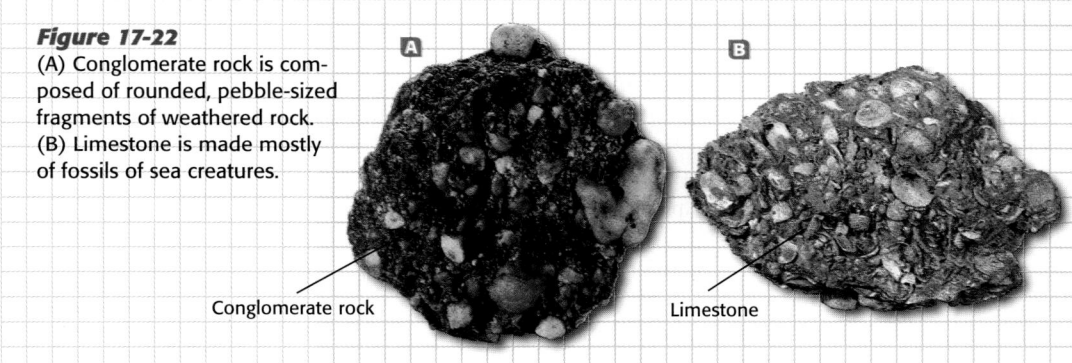

Figure 17-22
(A) Conglomerate rock is composed of rounded, pebble-sized fragments of weathered rock.
(B) Limestone is made mostly of fossils of sea creatures.

Conglomerate rock   Limestone

Rocks that undergo pressure and heating without melting form metamorphic rock

Heat and pressure within Earth cause changes in the texture and mineral content of rocks. These changes produce **metamorphic rocks.** The word *metamorphic* comes from the Greek word *metamorphosis*, which means "to change form."

Limestone, a sedimentary rock, will turn into *marble*, a metamorphic rock, under the effects of heat and pressure. Marble is a stone used in buildings, such as the Taj Mahal, in India. **Figure 17-23** is a photo of the marble exterior of the Taj Mahal. Notice the swirling, colored bands that make marble so attractive. These bands are the result of impurities that existed in the limestone before it was transformed into marble.

Rocks may be changed, or *metamorphosed*, in two ways: by heat alone or, more commonly, by a combination of heat and pressure. In both cases, the solid rock undergoes a chemical change over millions of years, without melting. As a result, new minerals form in the rocks. The texture of the rocks is changed too, and any fossils in sedimentary rocks are transformed and destroyed.

The most common types of metamorphic rock are formed by heat and pressure deep in the crust. *Slate* forms in this way. It metamorphoses from mudstone or shale, as shown in **Figure 17-24.** Slate is a hard rock that can be split very easily along planes in the rock, creating large, flat surfaces.

Figure 17-23
The Taj Mahal, in India, is made of marble, a metamorphic rock often used in buildings.

▶ **metamorphic rock** rock formed from other rocks as a result of heat, pressure, or chemical processes

Heat and pressure

Shale

Slate

Figure 17-24
Slate (B) is a metamorphic rock that is transformed under heat and pressure from the sedimentary rocks shale (A) or mudstone.

PLANET EARTH **579**

Teaching Tip

Foliated Versus Nonfoliated
Texture can be used to classify metamorphic rock. A metamorphic rock can be either *foliated* or *nonfoliated*. Foliated metamorphic rock consists of minerals that are aligned, while minerals in nonfoliated metamorphic rock are randomly oriented. Many metamorphic rocks break easily along planes because the minerals are aligned along those planes.

Did You Know ?

Ninety-five percent of the outer 10 km of Earth is igneous and metamorphic rock. Although sedimentary rock makes up less than 5 percent of Earth's crust, it is spread thinly over much of the planet's surface. Sedimentary rock covers 75 percent of Earth's continental surfaces.

Additional Application

Continental Rock Continental crust is much older than the surrounding oceanic crust. The core of a continent, called a craton, is generally composed of ancient, crystalline igneous and metamorphic rock. Cratons are relatively thick and make up the most stable part of continents. They range from 200 million to 3.9 billion years of age.

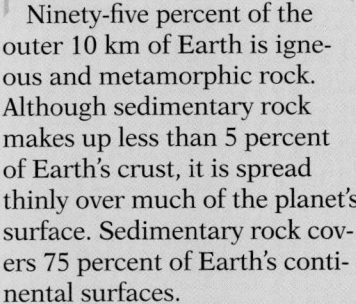

DEMONSTRATION 6 TEACHING

Classifying Rocks

Time: Approximately 25 minutes
Materials: magnifying glasses; several common examples of each type of rock: igneous rock—pumice, granite, obsidian, basalt, rhyolite; sedimentary rock—shale, limestone, coal, conglomerate, sandstone; and metamorphic rock—slate, marble, quartzite, gneiss, schist

Organize the rocks by rock type, and ask the class to describe how each type of rock forms. Invite the students to examine all the rocks with the magnifying glasses and to list some of their general characteristics. Then mix the rocks up. Put the students in small groups and give each group a chance to try to organize the rocks by rock type.

RESOURCE LINK

IER

Assign students worksheet *17.7: Connection to Language Arts—Names of Rocks* in the **Integration Enrichment Resources** ancillary.

Minerals and Rocks

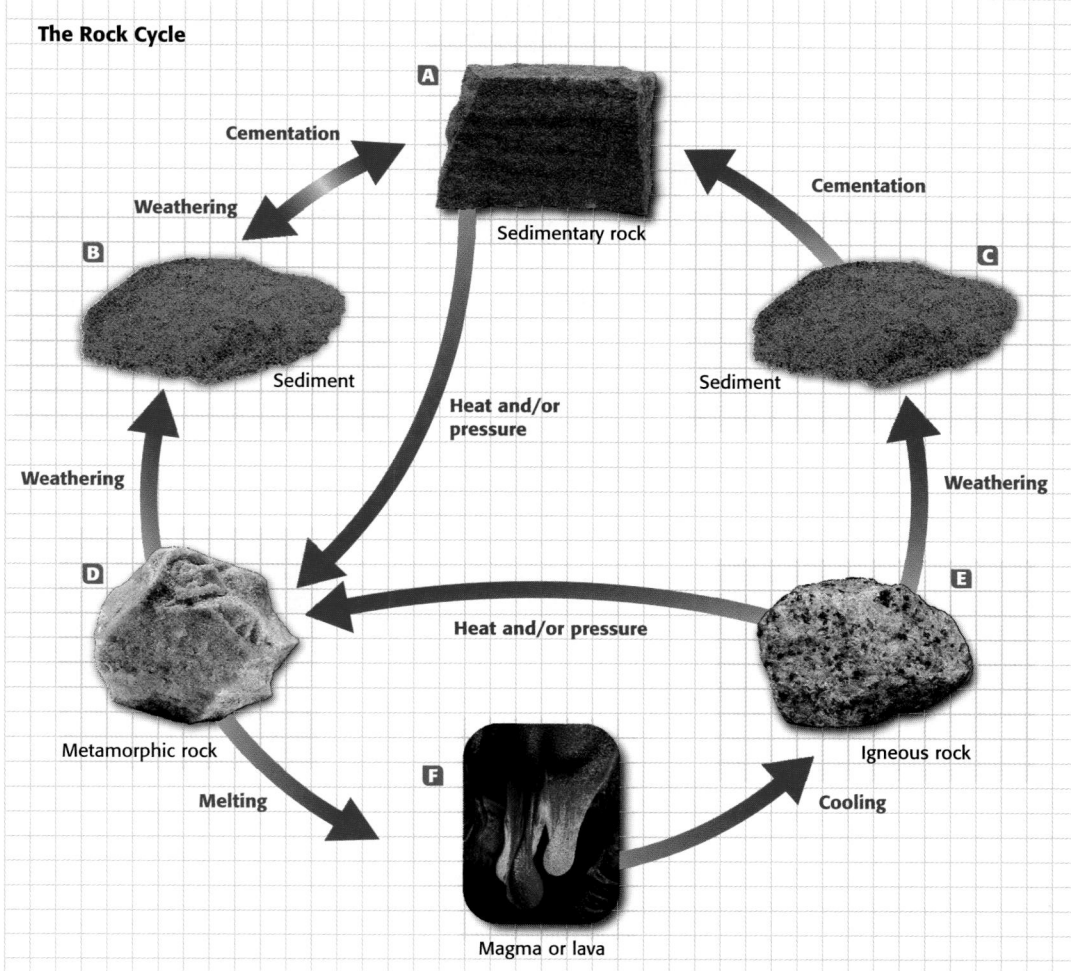

The Rock Cycle

Figure 17-25
The rock cycle illustrates the changes that sedimentary, igneous, and metamorphic rocks undergo.

Old rocks in the rock cycle form new rocks

So far, you have seen some examples of one type of rock becoming another. For instance, limestone exposed to heat and pressure becomes marble. Exposed rocks are weathered, forming sediments. These sediments may be cemented together to make sedimentary rock. The various types of rock are all a part of one rock system. The sequence of events in which rocks are weathered, melted, altered, and formed is described by the *rock cycle*.

Figure 17-25 illustrates the stages of the rock cycle. Regardless of which path is taken, rock formation occurs very slowly, often over tens of thousands to millions of years.

580 CHAPTER 17

As magma (F) cools underground, it forms igneous rock (E), such as granite. If the granite is heated and put under pressure, it may become metamorphic rock (D); if it is exposed to the sea, it may be fragmented by waves and become sand (C). The sand may be transported, deposited, and cemented to become the sedimentary rock (A) sandstone. As more time passes, several other layers of sediment are deposited above the sandstone. With enough heat and pressure, the sandstone becomes a metamorphic rock (D). This metamorphic rock (D) may then be forced deep within the Earth, where it melts, forming magma (F).

How Old Are Rocks?

Rocks form and change over millions of years. It is difficult to know the exact time when a rock formed. To determine the age of rocks on a geological time scale, several techniques have been developed.

The relative age of rocks can be determined using the principle of superposition

Think about your hamper of dirty clothes at home. If you don't disturb the stack of clothes in the hamper, you can tell the relative time the clothes were placed in the hamper. In other words, you may not know how long ago you placed a particular red shirt in the hamper, but you can tell that the shirts above the red shirt were placed there more recently. In a similar manner, the *relative age* of rocks can be determined using the *principle of superposition*. The principle of superposition states the following:

Assuming no change in the position of the rock layers, the oldest will be on the bottom, and the youngest will be on top.

The principle of superposition is useful in studying the sequence of life on Earth. For instance, the cliffside in **Figure 17-26** shows several sedimentary layers stacked on top of one another. The layers on the bottom are older than the layers above them.

Although the various layers of sedimentary rock are most visible in cliffsides and canyon walls, you would also find layering if you dug down anywhere there is sedimentary rock. By applying the principle of superposition, scientists know that fossils in the upper layers are the remains of animals that lived more recently than the animals that were fossilized in lower layers.

internetconnect

SC/LINKS
NSTA

TOPIC: Rock types
GO TO: www.scilinks.org
KEYWORD: HK1705

Figure 17-26
According to the principle of superposition, the layers of sedimentary rock on top are the most recent layers if the rocks have not been disturbed.

PLANET EARTH **581**

|SKILL BUILDER

Interpreting Visuals Have students analyze **Figure 17-26.** Make sure that students can see the different layers of sedimentary rock. Remind the students that rock layers do not have to be oriented parallel to the ground. Rock layers may be curved and folded due to compression stress, or angled with respect to the ground. Tell the students that the rocks that make up the walls of the Grand Canyon range from about 200 million years to almost 2 billion years old. Does the principle of superposition tell us that the rocks formed continuously over this time? *(No, it only states that the deepest rocks are the oldest and that the rocks are younger higher up in the canyon.)*

LINKING CHAPTERS

Review the concepts of radioactive decay and half-lives from chapter 7 with the students. Then give them the following problem: Potassium-40 decays to argon-40 with a half-life of 1.3 billion years. A sample of volcanic rock has been analyzed for potassium-40 to determine its absolute age. The rock contains 8.0×10^{-5} g potassium-40 and 2.4×10^{-4} g argon-40. How old is the rock? *(2.6 billion years old; the ratio of daughter isotope to parent isotope is 3:1 so the rock contains a mixture of 75 percent daughter isotope and 25 percent parent isotope. This means that the rock's age is two half-lives, or 2.6 billion years.)*

Ask students to explain which isotopes—those with long half-lives or short half-lives—should be used to date older rocks and younger rocks. *(Isotopes with long half-lives give accurate ages for older rocks. Isotopes with short half-lives give accurate ages for younger rocks.)*

Minerals and Rocks

SECTION 17.3 REVIEW

Check Your Understanding

1. "Fossils are found in sedimentary rock." It is also true to say, "Fossils are not found in igneous rock."

2. Because of the principle of superposition, geologists know that the oldest rocks will always be in the bottom layers and that the youngest rocks will be in the top layers.

3. a. igneous
   b. sedimentary
   c. metamorphic

4. A construction worker who uses a jackhammer on a rock does not produce a metamorphic rock because metamorphic rocks are formed when heat and pressure within the Earth cause changes in a rock's texture and mineral content.

5. An extrusive igneous rock might have a lot of holes in it due to the formation of gas bubbles. Igneous rocks are formed from cooled molten rock from a volcanic eruption. Gases trapped in the magma form bubbles in the molten rock because the pressure decreases when the volcano erupts.

6. In order to determine when these animals became extinct, a paleontologist should use absolute dating because the fossils are found in different layers at different depths.

RESOURCE LINK
STUDY GUIDE
Assign students *Review Section 17.3 Minerals and Rocks.*

582

Did You Know?

Radioactive dating is not always accurate. For instance, as heat and pressure are applied to a rock and water flows through it, soluble radioactive materials can escape from the minerals in the rock. Because there is no method for measuring how much radioactive material is lost, it is difficult to accurately date some older rocks that have been heated and put under pressure or that are partly weathered.

Radioactive dating can determine a more exact, or absolute, age of rocks

The chapter on nuclear changes showed that the nuclei of some isotopes decay, emitting energy at a fairly constant rate. These isotopes are said to be radioactive. The radioactive elements that make up minerals in rocks decay over billions of years. Physicists have determined the rate at which these elements decay, and geologists can use this data to determine the age of rocks. They measure both the amount of the original radioactive material left undecayed in the rock and the amount of the product of the radioactive material's decay. The amount of time that passed since the rock formed can be calculated from this ratio.

Many different isotopes can be analyzed when rocks are dated. Some of the most reliable are isotopes of potassium, argon, rubidium, strontium, uranium, and lead.

While the principle of superposition gives only the relative age of rocks, radioactive dating gives the *absolute age* of a rock.

SECTION 17.3 REVIEW

SUMMARY

▶ Igneous rocks are formed from cooling molten rock.

▶ Sedimentary rocks form by the deposition of pieces of other rocks and the remains of living organisms.

▶ Metamorphic rocks form after exposure to heat and/or pressure for an extended time.

▶ Rocks can change type, as described by the rock cycle.

▶ The relative age of rock can be determined using the principle of superposition. Unless the layers are disturbed, the layers on the bottom are the oldest.

▶ Radioactive dating is used to determine the absolute age of rocks.

CHECK YOUR UNDERSTANDING

1. **Modify** the following false statement to make it a true statement: Fossils are found in igneous rock.

2. **Explain** how the principle of superposition is used by geologists to compare the ages of rocks.

3. **Determine** the type of rock that will form in each of the following scenarios:
   a. Lava pours onto the ocean floor and cools.
   b. Minerals cement small pieces of sand together.
   c. Mudstone is subjected to great heat and pressure over a long period of time.

4. **Explain** why a construction worker who uses a jackhammer on a rock does not produce a metamorphic rock.

5. **Identify** what type of rock might have a lot of holes in it due to the formation of gas bubbles. Explain your answer.

6. **Creative Thinking** A paleontologist who is researching extinctions notices that certain fossils are never found above a layer of sediment containing the radioactive isotope rubidium-87 or below another layer containing the same isotope. To determine when these animals became extinct, should the paleontologist use relative dating, absolute dating, or a combination of the two? Explain your answer.

Weathering and Erosion

OBJECTIVES

▶ Identify the causes of rock shaping due to weathering and erosion.
▶ Explain how chemical weathering can form underground caves in limestone.
▶ Describe how acid rain affects the landscape.

▶ **KEY TERMS**
erosion
deposition
acid rain

Scheduling

Refer to pp. 556A–556D for lecture, classwork, and assignment options for Section 17.4.

★ **Lesson Focus**
Use transparency *LT 58* to prepare students for this section.

Compared to the destructive power of an earthquake or a volcano, the force exerted by a river on Earth's surface may seem trivial. But, over time, forces such as water and wind can make vast changes in the landscape. Parunaweep Canyon, in southern Utah, shown in **Figure 17-27,** is one of the most magnificent examples of how water can shape Earth's rocky surface.

Physical Weathering

There are two types of weathering processes: physical and chemical. Physical, or mechanical, weathering breaks rocks into smaller pieces but does not alter the rocks' chemical composition. Chemical weathering breaks down rock by changing its chemical composition.

Ice can break rocks

Ice can play a part in the physical or mechanical weathering of rock. A common kind of mechanical weathering is called *frost wedging.* This occurs when water seeps into cracks or joints in rock and then freezes. When the water freezes, its volume increases by about 10 percent, pushing the rock apart. Every time the ice thaws and refreezes, it wedges farther into the rock, and the crack in the rock widens and deepens. This process eventually breaks off pieces of the rock or splits the rock apart.

Plants can also break rocks

The roots of plants can also act as wedges as the roots grow into cracks in the rocks. As the plant grows, the roots exert a constant pressure on the rock. The crack continues to deepen and widen, eventually causing a piece of the rock to break off.

Figure 17-27
Parunaweep Canyon, in Zion National Park, Utah, is a striking example of the effect of water on Earth's surface.

READING SKILL BUILDER *Reading Organizer* Students should read the section titled Weathering, and then create a table with the following headings: *Description of process, Agents of weathering,* and *Examples.* Have students fill in the table using information from the text on the two different types of weathering (physical and chemical).

SKILL BUILDER

Interpreting Visuals Have students examine **Figure 17-27,** and ask them to describe what they see. Encourage students to hypothesize about what forces may have caused the canyon to look the way it does.

PLANET EARTH **583**

DEMONSTRATION 7 TEACHING

Physical Weathering

Time: Approximately 10 minutes over two class periods
Materials: a small plastic container (Do not use glass!), small pebbles, water, a freezer

To demonstrate the role that ice plays in physical weathering, place some small pebbles in the bottom of a plastic container. Fill the container with water, secure the lid in place, and put the container in a freezer overnight. As you are filling the container, have students generate hypotheses as to what will happen to the water and pebbles as they freeze overnight.

RESOURCE LINK

IER

Assign students worksheet *17.6: Integrating Biology— Living Sources of Weathering* in the **Integration Enrichment Resources** ancillary.

Oxidation And Rusting Tell your students that rusting is an example of oxidation. Challenge your students to think of common items around their house that might be subject to oxidation. What do they all have in common?

SKILL BUILDER

Interpreting Visuals Have the students look at **Figure 17-29** and identify the features along the ceiling of the cave. Ask them how they think the stalactites could have formed if limestone was dissolved away by acidic rainwater to form the cave. These stalactites are made of a type of limestone called *dripstone*. Water and dissolved limestone can drip downward from cracks in a cave's ceiling, leaving behind calcite deposits that form the stalactite. At the same time, water drops that fall to the cave's floor build the stalagmites.

Figure 17-28
Red sedimentary layers in Badlands National Park contain iron that has reacted with oxygen to form hematite.

Figure 17-29
Carbonic acid dissolved the calcite in the sedimentary rock limestone to produce this underground cavern.

Chemical Weathering

As shown in **Figure 17-28,** many of the sedimentary layers in Badlands National Park, in South Dakota, appear red because they contain hematite. Hematite, Fe_2O_3, is one of the most common minerals on the surface of Earth. Hematite is formed as iron reacts with oxygen in an oxidation reaction. This is an example of *chemical weathering.*

You studied the process of oxidation in Section 5.2. As exemplified by the hematite, when certain elements, especially metals, react with oxygen, they become oxides and their properties change. When these elements are in minerals, oxidation can cause the mineral to decompose or form new minerals. As a result, both the chemical composition and the physical appearance of the rock change.

The results of chemical weathering are not as easy to see as those of physical weathering, but chemical weathering can have a great effect on the landscape over millions of years.

Carbon dioxide dissolved in water can cause chemical weathering

Another common type of chemical weathering occurs when carbon dioxide from the air dissolves in rainwater. The result is water that contains carbonic acid, H_2CO_3. Although carbonic acid is a weak acid, it reacts with some minerals. As the slightly acidic water seeps into the ground, it can weather rock underground.

For example, calcite, the major mineral in the sedimentary rock limestone, reacts with carbonic acid in water to form calcium bicarbonate. Because the calcium bicarbonate is dissolved in water, the decomposed rock is carried away in the water, leaving underground pockets filled with air or water. The cave shown in **Figure 17-29** resulted from the weathering action of carbonic acid on calcite in underground layers of limestone.

Acid rain can slowly dissolve minerals

In most areas, natural rain has a slightly acidic pH, around 5.7, because it contains carbonic acid. As humans have burned increasing amounts of fossil fuels to run car engines, power stations, and factories, the amount of acid in rain has greatly increased. For instance, because of air pollution, the pH value of rainwater in United States cities between 1940 and 1990 averaged between 4 and 5. In some individual cases, the pH dropped below 4, to levels nearly as acidic as vinegar.

Acid rain causes damage to both living organisms and inorganic matter. In Europe, acid rain may have contributed to the death of pine trees, particularly in Germany. Acid rain can erode metal and rock, such as the statue in Brooklyn, New York, shown in **Figure 17-30.** Marble and limestone dissolve relatively rapidly even in weak acid.

How does pollution contribute to acid rain? When fossil fuels, such as coal, oil, and gasoline, are burned, they release gases, including small amounts of sulfur dioxide from the sulfur in the fuel, and nitrogen oxides from nitrogen in the air. After these gases are released, they may react with water in the air and clouds to form nitric acid, or nitrous acid, and sulfuric acid.

In the United States, the release of chemicals that cause acid rain is declining. In 1990, the Acid Rain Control Program was added to the Clean Air Act of 1970. According to the program, power plants and factories were given 10 years to decrease the release of sulfur dioxide to about half the amount they emitted in 1980. The acidity of rain has been greatly reduced since power plants have installed *scrubbers* that remove the sulfur oxide gases.

▶ **acid rain** precipitation that has an unusually high concentration of sulfuric or nitric acids resulting from chemical pollution of the air

Figure 17-30
Acid rain weathers stone structures, such as this marble statue in Brooklyn, New York.

Weathering

LINKING CHAPTERS

Review Chapter 6 on chemical reactions and acids. Calcite (calcium carbonate, $CaCO_3$) slowly dissolves in rain water, which contains some dissolved CO_2, to form calcium hydrogen carbonate, $Ca(HCO_3)_2$, in three steps. $CO_2 + H_2O \rightarrow H_2CO_3$ Some of the carbonic acid ionizes in the rain water. $H_2CO_3 + H_2O \rightarrow H_3O^+ + HCO_3^-$ Calcite dissolves in the carbonic acid solution. $CaCO_3 + H_3O^+ \rightarrow Ca^{2+} + HCO_3^- + H_2O$ This reaction is reversible. Some of the dissolved calcium hydrogen carbonate decomposes very slowly over many years to form solid calcium carbonate (calcite), which makes the stalactites and stalagmites found in limestone caves. Therefore, in limestone country, water contains dissolved calcium hydrogen carbonate, which makes the water "hard."

PLANET EARTH **585**

Weathering

Erosion and De-position When water flows down a river channel, it does not flow straight down the channel. Water flowing in a river or stream channel moves in a helical or corkscrew motion. This motion causes erosion on the bank where the water is rising and causes deposition on the bank where the water is falling. The helical flow of water helps explain the formation of bends or meanders in the channel.

Teaching Tip

River Erosion A river or stream can carry particles in three ways. A river can bounce large materials such as pebbles and boulders along the riverbed. Small rocks and soil can be carried in suspension. This suspended material makes a river look muddy. When the current slows to a point where the particles can no longer be carried in suspension, the rocks and soil are deposited. Some materials, such as sodium and calcium, are carried in solution. Ask students how erosion and deposition might be related to the rate of flow of the river. What would happen to the different materials carried by a river if the river slowed down? *(The small rocks and soil suspended in the river would be deposited. The large materials moved along the bed would also be slowed or stopped.)*

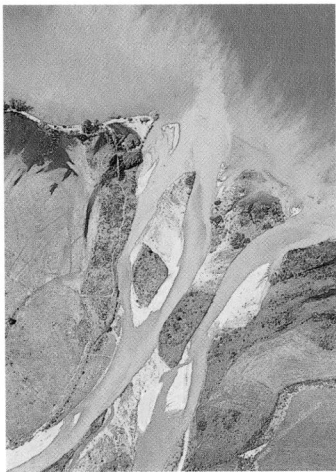

Figure 17-31
Deltas, such as this one in New Zealand, are formed by deposition.

▶ **erosion** the process by which rock and/or the products of weathering are removed

▶ **deposition** process in which sediment is laid down

Erosion

Erosion is the removal and transportation of weathered and non-weathered materials by running water, wind, waves, ice, underground water, and gravity.

Water erosion shapes Earth's surface

Water is by far the most effective physical weathering agent. Have you ever seen a brown or murky river? Muddy rivers carry sediment in their water. As this sediment moves along with the water, it scrapes and scratches rocks and soil on the riverbanks and along the river bottom. As the water continues to scour out new places on the surface, it carries the new sediment away. This process of loosening and moving sediments is known as **erosion.**

There is a direct relationship between the velocity of the water and the size and amount of sediment it can carry. Quickly moving rivers can carry away a lot of sediment, and create extraordinary canyons.

As a river or stream becomes wider or deepens, the water flows more slowly and therefore cannot carry as much sediment. As a result, sediment is deposited on the floor of these calmer portions of the river or stream. The process of depositing sediment is called **deposition.** Rivers eventually flow into large bodies of water, such as seas and oceans, where the sediment in the water is deposited along the continental shores. As rivers widen and slow at the continental boundary, large deposits of sediment are laid down. These areas, called deltas, often have rich, fertile soils, making them excellent agricultural areas. **Figure 17-31** shows the Greenstone River delta, in New Zealand.

The oceans also have a dramatic effect on Earth's landscape. Underwater, currents carry vast amounts of sediment across the ocean floor much like rivers do on land. On seashores, the waves crash onto land, creating tall cliffs and jagged coastlines. The Cliffs of Moher, in Western Ireland, shown in **Figure 17-32,** reach heights of 204 m (669 ft) above the water. The cliffs were formed partially by the force of waves in the Atlantic Ocean eroding the rocky shale and sandstone coast.

Figure 17-32
The action of waves slowly tearing away at the rocky coast formed the Cliffs of Moher.

DEMONSTRATION 8 TEACHING

Erosion

Time: Approximately 15 minutes
Materials: erosion tray (or a rain gutter or baking pan), soil or sand, pebbles in a layer on the bottom of the erosion tray, water

Put pebbles in a layer on the bottom of the erosion tray and a layer of soil or sand on top. Tilt one end of the tray upward by placing some books underneath one end. Slowly drip water over the top of the tray. Have students observe the action and flow of the water as it cuts a path and carries soil to the bottom of the tray. Ask the students to relate what they have seen in the demonstration to the words *erosion* and *deposition.* Ask students to hypothesize about results if the tray is tilted further upward or is placed on a level surface.

Figure 17-33
(A) Tustamena Glacier, in Alaska, has slowly pushed its way through these mountains.
(B) Glaciers are capable of carving out large U-shaped valleys, such as this valley in Alaska.

Glaciers erode mountains

Large masses of ice, such as the glacier shown in **Figure 17-33A,** can exert tremendous forces on rocks. The constantly moving ice mass carves the surface it rests on, often creating U-shaped valleys, such as the one shown in **Figure 17-33B.** The weight of the ice and the forward movement of the glacier cause the mass to act like a huge scouring pad. Immense boulders that are carried by the ice scrape across other rocks, grinding them to a fine powder. Glacial meltwater streams carry the fine sediment away from the glacier and deposit it along the banks and floors of streams or at the bottom of glacier-formed lakes.

Wind can also shape the landscape

Just as water or glaciers can carry rocks along, scraping other rocks as they pass, wind can also weather the Earth's surfaces. Have you ever been in a dust storm and felt your skin "burn" from the swirling dust? This happens because fast-moving wind can carry sediment, just as water can. Wind that carries sediment creates a sandblaster effect, smoothing Earth's surface and eroding the landscape.

The sandstone arches of Arches National Park, in Utah, are formed partly by wind erosion. Look at **Figure 17-34.** Can you guess how these arches might have formed? Geologists have struggled to find a good explanation for the formation of arches.

The land in and around Arches National Park is part of the Colorado Plateau, an area that was under a saltwater sea more than 300 million years ago. As this sea evaporated, it deposited a thick layer of salt that has since been covered by many layers of sedimentary rock. The salt layer deforms more easily than rock layers. As the salt layers warped and deformed over the years, they created surface depressions and bulges. Arches formed where the overlying sedimentary rocks were pushed upward by the salt.

> **internet connect**
>
> SC/LINKS
> NSTA
>
> **TOPIC:** Erosion
> **GO TO:** www.scilinks.org
> **KEYWORD:** HK1706

Figure 17-34
This sandstone arch in Arches National Park, in Utah, was created as high-speed winds weathered the terrain.

Teaching Tip

Glacier Movement Tell students that 14 000 years ago, much of North America was covered in a thick layer of ice (as much as 4000 m thick) called a continental glacier, which moved as far as southern Illinois. The weight of the ice pushed the North American continent down by almost 400 m. Since the ice sheet melted about 10 000 years ago, the continent has risen over 300 m and is still rising at a rate of about 2 cm per year. This is known as postglacial rebound. Have students discuss geologic features in your area that might have been affected by glacial advance and retreat.

Multicultural Extension

The Taka Makan Desert in China's arid northwest is so inhospitable that its name in the local language means "Go in, and you don't come out." The desert is covered with treacherous dunes of fine, dry sand. Buried under those dunes are the remains of cities that prospered along the ancient Silk Road. The Silk Road was a trade route that connected China to civilizations in the West. NASA's Spacedome Imaging Radar (SIR-C), which flew on space shuttles twice in 1994, is being used to examine the desert. The radar-imaging technology has already helped archaeologists locate some cities and promises to help them find other ruins.

Weathering

|SKILL BUILDER

Interpreting Visuals Have the students study **Figure 17-35.** Then ask them to work in pairs to describe how sandstone arches form. Encourage them to draw diagrams and to describe the physical weathering and erosion processes that are involved. They should also discuss how the composition of the rock affects the rate of erosion. Ask them to identify the physical forces involved. *(gravity and friction)*

SECTION 17.4 REVIEW

Check Your Understanding

1. Two agents of physical weathering that might occur in the mountains in northern Montana are ice and plants.

2. After the narrow, free-standing rocks (fins) are formed, exposure to the wind leaves them vulnerable to erosion. As the wind wears away at the cement that holds the sediments together, large pieces of rock fall away, while others are more sturdy and form balanced arches.

3. **a.** chemical weathering
   b. physical weathering
   c. erosion
   d. chemical weathering

4. The statement is incorrect because in most areas, natural rain has a slightly acidic pH of around 5.7.

Answers continue on p. 593A.

RESOURCE LINK
STUDY GUIDE

Assign students *Review Section 17.4 Weathering and Erosion.*

Figure 17-35
Fins are formed when sandstone is pushed upward, and cracks are slowly eroded. Wind, water, and ice erode the fins until they collapse or form arches.

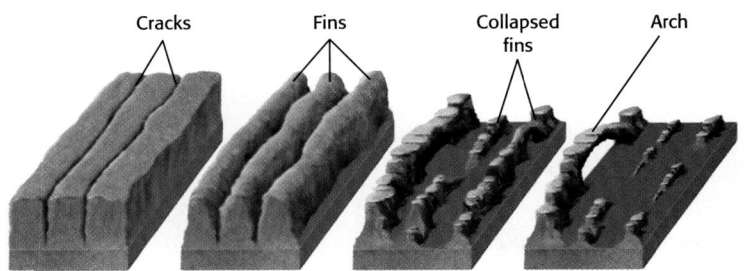

Cracks   Fins   Collapsed fins   Arch

Figure 17-35 shows how one theory explains the formation of arches. As land is pushed upward in places, small surface cracks form. These cracks are eroded by water, ice, and wind until narrow free-standing rock formations, called *fins*, are formed. When these fins are exposed along their sides, the wind wears away at the cement that holds the sediment together, causing large pieces of the rock to fall away. Some fins collapse completely; others that are more sturdy and balanced form arches.

SECTION 17.4 REVIEW

SUMMARY

▶ Physical weathering breaks down rock by water erosion, ice wedging, wind abrasion, glacial abrasion, and many other physical forces.

▶ In chemical weathering, rock is altered as minerals in rock react chemically and break down.

▶ Carbonic acid acts as a chemical weathering agent and is responsible for the formation of underground limestone caves.

▶ Acid rain can weather rock and harm living organisms. It is the byproduct of fossil-fuel emissions reacting with water in the atmosphere.

CHECK YOUR UNDERSTANDING

1. **List** two agents of physical weathering that might occur in the mountains in northern Montana.

2. **Explain** how the wind may be involved in the formation of sandstone arches.

3. **Distinguish** between physical weathering, chemical weathering, and erosion in the following examples:
   a. Rock changes color as it is oxidized.
   b. Rock shatters as it freezes.
   c. Wind erodes the sides of the Egyptian pyramids in Giza.
   d. An underground cavern is formed as water drips in from the Earth's surface.

4. **Explain** why the following statement is incorrect: Acid rain is any rain that has a pH less than 7.

5. **Predict** which will experience more weathering, a rock in the Sonora Desert, in Southern Arizona, or a rock on a beach in North Carolina.

6. **Creative Thinking** On many coastlines, erosion is wearing the beach away and threatening to destroy homes. How would you prevent this destruction?

Chapter Highlights

Before you begin, review the summaries of the key ideas of each section, found on pages 566, 575, 582, and 588. The key vocabulary terms are listed on pages 558, 567, 576, and 583.

UNDERSTANDING CONCEPTS

1. The layer of tar-like mantle under the tectonic plates is called the _____.
   a. lithosphere
   b. oceanic crust
   c. asthenosphere
   d. tectonic plate boundary
2. Two tectonic plates moving away from each other form a(n) _____.
   a. transform fault boundary
   b. convergent boundary
   c. ocean trench
   d. divergent boundary
3. Vibrations in Earth caused by sudden movements of rock are called _____.
   a. epicenters
   b. earthquakes
   c. faults
   d. volcanoes
4. Using the difference in the time it takes for P waves and S waves to arrive at three different seismograph stations, seismologists can find an earthquake's _____.
   a. epicenter
   b. surface waves
   c. fault zone
   d. intensity
5. The Richter scale expresses an earthquake's _____.
   a. intensity
   b. location
   c. duration
   d. magnitude
6. High pressure and high temperature cause igneous rocks to become _____.
   a. sedimentary rocks
   b. limestone
   c. metamorphic rocks
   d. clay

7. The sequence of events in which rocks change from one type to another and back again is described by _____.
   a. a rock family
   b. the rock cycle
   c. metamorphism
   d. deposition
8. _____ rock is formed from magma.
   a. Igneous
   b. Metamorphic
   c. Sedimentary
   d. Schist
9. A common kind of mechanical weathering is called _____.
   a. oxidation
   b. carbonation
   c. ice wedging
   d. leaching
10. Acid rain results from pollutants reacting with water in the air to form_____.
   a. sulfuric acid
   b. carbon dioxide
   c. ice crystals
   d. carbonic acid

Using Vocabulary

11. Using the terms *crust*, *mantle*, and *core*, describe Earth's internal structure.
12. What is the name of the thin outer shell of Earth consisting of the *crust* and the rigid upper *mantle*?
13. What is the name of the field of study concerning earthquakes?
14. Use the terms *focus*, *epicenter*, *P waves*, *S waves*, and *surface waves* to describe what happens during an earthquake.
15. What type of rock is formed when small rock fragments are cemented together?
16. In what type of rock—*igneous, sedimentary,* or *metamorphic*—are you most likely to find a fossil?
17. What is the name of the process of breaking down rock?
18. Explain how deltas form at the continental boundary using the terms *erosion* and *deposition*.

PLANET EARTH **589**

UNDERSTANDING CONCEPTS

1. c   6. c
2. d   7. b
3. b   8. a
4. a   9. c
5. d   10. a

Using Vocabulary

11. The crust is the Earth's topmost layer, the mantle lies beneath the crust, and the core is the center of the Earth. There is a liquid outer core and a solid inner core.
12. lithosphere
13. seismology
14. The point inside the Earth where an earthquake originates is called the focus. The epicenter is the point on the surface of the Earth immediately above the focus. An earthquake releases energy through three types of waves. The first is a P wave, which is the first to reach seismology recording stations. The second type of wave originating from an earthquake's focus is an S wave, which travels at a slower rate than a P wave. Finally, surface waves move across the surface of the Earth, causing the most destruction.

RESOURCE LINK
STUDY GUIDE
Assign students *Mixed Review Chapter 17.*

15. sedimentary

16. sedimentary

17. weathering

18. Erosion is the process of loosening and moving sediments. Rivers carry these loose sediments, and as a river widens and slows at the continental boundary, it deposits these sediments onto the shores. This is called deposition, and these areas are called deltas.

BUILDING MATH SKILLS

19. a. about 3200 km

b. about 6.5 min after the earthquake started

c. about 11 min after the earthquake started

d. about 4.5 min

THINKING CRITICALLY

20. because humans have never drilled all the way to the core

21. Because sediment is looser and not as compact or sturdy as granite, a building in a valley of sediment is more likely to be damaged by an earthquake.

22. Over time these rocks have been transformed by heat and pressure within the Earth, and currently they have different textures and mineral content than they did in the past. The layer of rock may have been pushed upward by tectonic movement and then exposed by weathering and erosion.

23. The rock is between 120 to 130 million years old.

BUILDING MATH SKILLS

19. Graphing Examine the graph in the figure below, and answer the questions that follow.

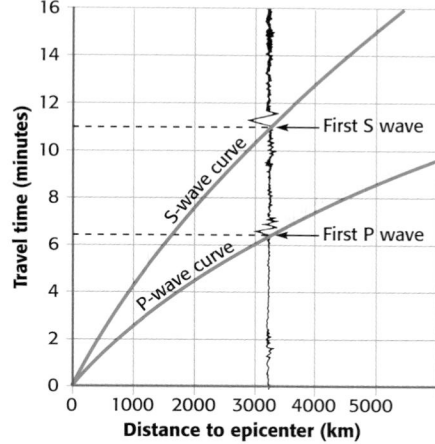

a. Approximately how far, in kilometers, was the epicenter of the earthquake from the seismograph that recorded the seismogram shown here?

b. When did the first P wave reach the seismograph?

c. When did the first S wave reach the seismograph?

d. What is the difference in travel time between the two waves?

THINKING CRITICALLY

20. Critical Thinking Why are mathematics and theory the only practical ways to determine the temperature of Earth's core?

21. Applying Knowledge Is a tall building more likely to be damaged by an earthquake if it is on a mountain of granite or in a valley of sediment? Explain.

---

22. Applying Knowledge You and your classmates are on a field trip to the top of a mountain. Your teacher tells you that the rocks are metamorphic. What can you tell your classmates about the geologic history of the area?

23. Problem Solving Imagine you are on a dinosaur dig and your team finds two sets of dinosaur bones entwined as if they died while engaged in battle. You know one of the dinosaurs lived 180 million to 120 million years ago and the other lived 130 million to 115 million years ago. What can you say about the age of the rock the dinosaur fossils were found in?

24. Interpreting Diagrams The figure below shows a cross-sectional diagram of a portion of a plate boundary. It shows plates, the ocean, mountains, and rivers. The mouths of the rivers reach the shore, where they deposit sediments. Using the diagram, answer the following questions:

a. What type of plate boundary is shown? How do you know?

b. What type of physical weathering processes are probably acting on the mountains?

c. What type of land-shaping processes are occurring on and near the beach?

d. What forces might have formed this coastal mountain range?

DEVELOPING LIFE/WORK SKILLS

25. Interpreting Graphics Use a map of the United States to plan a car trip to study the geology of three national parks. How many miles will you have to drive roundtrip? How many days will you stay in each park? How long will the trip take?

26. Making Decisions Pretend you are the superintendent of the Washington State Police Department. Seismologists in the area of Mount St. Helens predict that the volcano will erupt in 1 week. Write a report describing the evacuation procedures. In your report, describe the area you will evacuate and a plan for how people will be contacted.

WRITING SKILL

27. Applying Technology Sonar is the best method for identifying features under water. Sound waves are emitted from one device, and the time it takes for the wave to bounce off an object and return is calculated by another. This information is used to determine how far away a feature is. Draw a graph that could be made by a ship's sonar device as it tracks the ocean bottom from the shoreline to a deep ocean trench and farther out to sea.

28. Applying Technology Use a computer drawing program to create cutaway diagrams of a fault before, during, and after an earthquake.

COMPUTER SKILL

INTEGRATING CONCEPTS

29. Connection to Biology Charles Darwin, known for his theory of evolution by natural selection, was the first to explain how *atolls* (AT ahls) form. What are atolls? What was his explanation?

30. Concept Mapping Copy the unfinished concept map below onto a sheet of paper. Complete the map by writing the correct word or phrase in the lettered boxes.

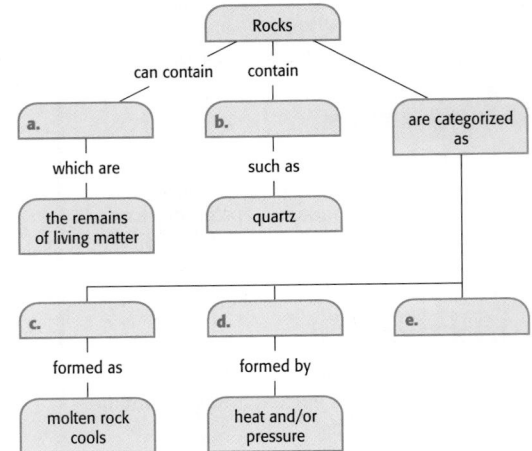

31. Connection to Social Studies The Grand Canyon is one of the most geologically informative and beautiful sites in the United States. Read about the people who have lived along the Colorado River and in the Grand Canyon. How do we know Paleo-Indians lived there? Who were the Anasazi? Who was John Wesley Powell? What role did the Mormon settlers play in the canyon's history? What is special about the region today? Write a one-page essay about the history of these people and this region.

WRITING SKILL

internet connect

SC*LINKS* NSTA
TOPIC: Sonar
GO TO: www.scilinks.org
KEYWORD: HK1707

24. a. convergent plate boundary; an oceanic plate is subducting under a continental plate forming an ocean trench and mountains
b. frost wedging and physical weathering due to plant growth
c. erosion and deposition
d. Answers may vary. The continental crust may have buckled to the force of the collision between the plates. Magma produced during subduction of the oceanic plate may have risen to the surface to form a volcanic mountain range.
25. Answers will vary.
26. Answers will vary.
27. Check students' drawings for accuracy.
28. Check students' drawings for accuracy.
29. Atolls are rings of coral reefs that form on the top of underwater volcanic islands. Darwin correctly theorized that atolls form as volcanic islands slowly subside over time.
30. a. fossils
b. minerals
c. igneous
d. metamorphic
e. sedimentary

Answers continue on p. 593B.

Skill Builder Lab

Analyzing Seismic Waves

Introduction

The most common method which seismologists use to find an earthquake's epicenter is the S-P-time method. When using this method, seismologists begin by collecting several seismograms of the same earthquake from different locations. Seismologists then place the seismograms on the distance-time graph so the first P wave lines up with the P-wave curve and the first S wave lines up with the S-wave curve. Seismologists can then see how far away from each station the earthquake is by reading the distance axis. After the distances are found, seismologists can find the earthquake's epicenter.

Objectives

Students will:

▶ **Use** appropriate lab safety procedures.

▶ **Calculate** the distance from an earthquake's epicenter to surrounding seismographs.

▶ **Find** the location of the earthquake's epicenter.

Planning

Recommended time: 1 lab period
Materials: *(for each lab group)*

▶ drawing compass

▶ ruler

▶ calculator

▶ map of the western United States

Skill Builder Lab

Introduction

During an earthquake, seismic waves travel through Earth in all directions from the earthquake's epicenter. How can you find the location of the epicenter by studying seismic waves?

Objectives

▶ **Calculate** the distance from an earthquake's epicenter to surrounding seismographs.

▶ **Find** the location of the earthquake's epicenter.

Materials

drawing compass
ruler
calculator
map of the western United States

REQUIRED PRECAUTIONS

▶ Read all safety precautions and discuss them with your students.

▶ Safety goggles and a lab apron must be worn at all times.

▶ Long hair and loose clothing must be tied back.

Analyzing Seismic Waves

▶ Preparing for Your Experiment

1. In this lab, you will examine seismograms showing two kinds of seismic waves: primary waves (P waves) and secondary waves (S waves).

2. P waves have an average speed of 6.1 km/s. S waves have an average speed of 4.1 km/s.
   a. How long does it take P waves to travel 100 km?
   b. How long does it take S waves to travel 100 km?
   (**Hint:** You will need to use the speed equation from Section 8.1, and rearrange it to solve for time.)

3. Because S waves travel more slowly than P waves, S waves will reach a seismograph after P waves arrive. This difference in arrival times is known as the *lag time*.

4. Use the time intervals found in step 2 to calculate the lag time you would expect from a seismograph located exactly 100 km from the epicenter of an earthquake.

▶ Measuring the Lag Time from Seismographic Records

5. On a blank sheet of paper, prepare a table like the one shown below.

City	Lag time (s)	Distance from city to epicenter (km)
Austin, TX		
Portland, OR		
Bismarck, ND		

6. The illustration at the top of the next page shows the records produced by seismographs in three cities following an earthquake.

7. Using the time scale at the bottom of the illustration, measure the lag time for each city. Be sure to measure from the start of the P wave to the start of the S wave. Enter your measurements in your table.

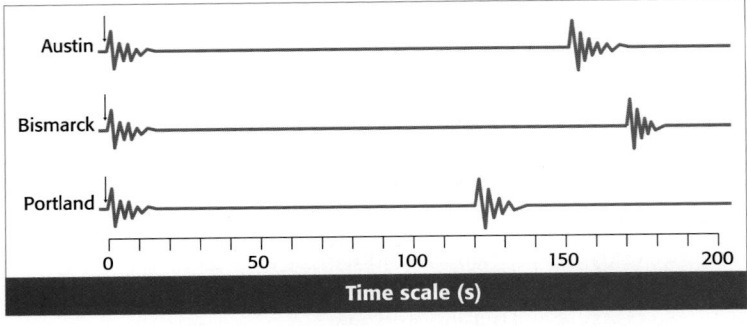

8. Using the lag time you found in step 4 and the formula below, calculate the distance from each city to the epicenter of the earthquake. Enter your results in your table.

$$distance = (measured\ lag\ time \div lag\ time\ for\ 100\ km) \times 100\ km$$

▶ Analyzing Your Results

1. Copy the map at the bottom of this page on a blank sheet of paper. Using the scale below your map, adjust the drawing compass so that it will draw a circle whose radius equals the distance from the epicenter of the earthquake to Austin. Then put the point of the compass on Austin, and draw a circle on your map. How is the location of the epicenter related to the circle?
2. Repeat the process in item 1 using the distance from Portland to the epicenter. This time put the point of the compass on Portland, and draw the circle. Where do the two circles intersect? The epicenter is one of these two sites.
3. **Reaching Conclusions** Repeat the process once more for Bismarck, and find that city's distance from the epicenter. The epicenter is located at the site where all three circles intersect. What city is closest to that site?

▶ Defending Your Conclusions

4. Why is it necessary to use seismographs in three different locations to find the epicenter of an earthquake?
5. Would it be possible to use this method for locating an earthquake's epicenter if earthquakes produced only one kind of seismic wave? Explain your answer.
6. Someone tells you that the best way to determine the epicenter is to find a seismograph where the P and S waves occur at the same time. What is wrong with this reasoning?

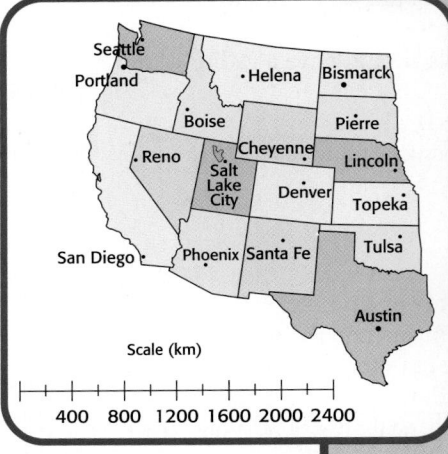

Scale (km)

400 800 1200 1600 2000 2400

PLANET EARTH **593**

Pre-Lab

None

Procedure

▶ Preparing for Your Experiment

2. **a.** For the P waves:

$$speed = \frac{distance}{time}$$

$$time = \frac{distance}{speed}$$

$$t = \frac{100\ km}{6.1\ km/s} = 16\ s$$

2. **b.** For the S waves:

$$speed = \frac{distance}{time}$$

$$time = \frac{distance}{speed}$$

$$t = \frac{100\ km}{4.1\ km/s} = 24\ s$$

4. $lag\ time = time_{Swave} - time_{Pwave}$

Substituting the time each wave takes to travel 100 km from step 2:

$lag\ time = 24\ s - 16\ s = 8\ s$

▶ Measuring the Lag Time from Seismographic Records

7. See Data Table 1 below.
8. Austin:

$distance = (measured\ lag\ time/lag\ time\ for\ 100\ km) \times 100\ km$

$d = (150\ s/8\ s) \times 100\ km$

$d = 1875\ km$

Continue on p. 593A.

Data Table 1 Measuring the Lag Time from Seismographic Records

City	Lag time (s)	Distance from city to epicenter (km)
Austin, TX	150	1875
Portland, OR	120	1500
Bismarck, ND	170	2125

RESOURCE LINK
DATASHEETS

Have students use *Datasheet 17.2: Skill Builder Lab—Analyzing Seismic Waves* to record their results.

CONTINUATION OF ANSWERS

Skill Builder Lab from page 593

Analyzing Seismic Waves

Procedure

▶**Measuring the Lag Time from Seismographic Records**

8. Bismarck:
$d = (170 \text{ s}/8 \text{ s}) \times 100 \text{ km} = 2125 \text{ km}$

Portland:
$d = (120 \text{ s}/8 \text{ s}) \times 100 \text{ km} = 1500 \text{ km}$

Post-Lab

▶**Disposal**

None required

▶**Analyzing Your Results**

1. The circle centered on Austin, TX should have a radius of 1875 km. The epicenter of the earthquake will be somewhere on the circumference of the circle.
2. The circle centered on Portland, OR should have a radius of 1500 km.
3. The circle centered on Bismarck, ND should have a radius of 2125 km. The circles intersect at San Diego, CA or Tijuana, Mexico.

▶**Defending Your Conclusions**

4. The three circles can intersect at only one point.
5. This technique would not work if an earthquake produced only one kind of wave, because the lag time between P waves and S waves is necessary to determine the location of the epicenter by triangulation. There will always be a lag time between P waves and S waves because they travel at different speeds.
6. If the P waves and S waves arrived at the same time, the lag time between them would be 0 s. A lag time is needed to locate the earthquake's epicenter.

Answers from page 566

SECTION 17.1 REVIEW

4. a. divergent plate boundary
   b. convergent plate boundary
   c. divergent plate boundary
   d. convergent plate boundary
5. During the Earth's history, Earth's magnetic field has reversed directions many times, meaning that the north magnetic pole has become the south magnetic pole and the south magnetic pole has become the north magnetic pole. This process of switching poles is recorded in rocks as the iron in the rocks cooled and became magnetically fixed. These magnetic bands are symmetrical on either side of the Mid-Atlantic Ridge, with the rocks nearest the center of the ridge being the youngest, and the rocks farthest away from the ridge being the oldest.
6. A convergent plate boundary exists along the coastline near Japan's volcanic mountain ranges because convergent plate boundaries form volcanic mountains.
7. There is a difference in the age of continental rocks and sea floor rocks because crust on the sea floor is created and destroyed at a faster rate than crust on land.

Answers from page 575

SECTION 17.2 REVIEW

6. Iceland is a volcanic island on a mid-oceanic ridge. It is an excellent place to use hydrothermal power because of the heat that results from the large amount of geologic activity that occurs on the island.
7. Accept both answers. Students should support their choice with reasoning based on the chapter material. Answers may include that explosive eruptions tend to produce volcanoes with steeper slopes, and so they will build more height than quiet eruptions. However, explosive eruptions are more likely to destroy the build-up of materials around the vent of a volcano, preventing an increase in height. Over time, quiet eruptions can build tall volcanoes with gently sloped sides.

Answers from page 588

SECTION 17.4 REVIEW

5. A rock on a beach in North Carolina will experience more weathering because it is exposed to more physical and chemical weathering agents—water, wind, sea water.
6. Answers will vary but may include ideas like: jetties, groins, sea walls, beach nourishment (bringing sand from other places and pumping it onto the beach), and moving homes away from the water.

Answers from page 591

31. Students' answers may vary. Paleo-Indians lived in the region about 9000 to 11 000 years ago. They left pictographs and rock paintings. The Anasazi (circa AD 100–AD 1300) were a Native American agricultural people of the southwestern U.S. who lived in adobe villages and great cliff dwellings. They are the predecessors of the Pueblo Indians. John Wesley Powell (1834–1902) was an American geologist and anthropologist who studied the Rocky Mountains, the canyons of the Green and Colorado rivers (including the Grand Canyon), and Native American languages. He was the first United States explorer to map the Colorado river. The Mormons were some of the first United States settlers in the region and continue to live there today. Today, the Havasupai live in villages and farm on the floor of the Grand Canyon.

CareerLink

CareerLink

Paleontologist

LINKING CHAPTERS

The recent history of our planet has been greatly affected by the presence of life, as will be described in the section about Earth's early atmosphere in Chapter 18. At the same time, paleontologists like Dr. Vermeij need to know a lot about Earth's history and the nature of geologic changes on Earth, as described in Chapter 17, to be able to understand the significance of their finds.

SKILL BUILDER

Vocabulary The word *paleontology* comes from three different root words. The Greek word *palaios* means "ancient", and the Greek words *ontos* and *logos* mean "being" and "word," respectively. Thus, paleontology is the study of ancient beings.

Paleontologists are life's historians. They study fossils and other evidence to understand how and why life has changed during Earth's history. Most paleontologists work for universities, government agencies, or private industry. To learn more about paleontology as a career, read this interview with paleontologist Geerat Vermeij, who works in the Department of Geology at the University of California, Davis.

"I think one needs to be able to recognize puzzles and then think about ways of solving them."

Vermeij is a world-renowned expert on living and fossil mollusks, but he has never seen one. Born blind, he has learned to scrutinize specimens with his hands.

 Describe your work as a paleontologist.

I study the history of life and how life has changed from its beginning to today. I'm interested in long-term trends and long-term patterns. My work involves everything from field studies of how living organisms live and work to a lot of work in museum collections. I work especially on shell-bearing mollusks, but I have thought about and written about all of life.

 What questions are you particularly interested in?

How enemies have influenced the evolution of plants and animals. I study arms races (evolutionary competitions) over geological time. And I study how the physical history of Earth has affected evolution.

 What is your favorite part of your work?

That's hard to say. I enjoy doing the research and writing. I'd say it was a combination of working with specimens, reading for background, and writing (scientific) papers and popular books. I have written four books.

 What qualities make a good paleontologist?

First and foremost, hard work. The second thing is you need to know a lot. You have to have a lot of information at hand to put what you observe into context. And you need to be a good observer.

 What skills does a paleontologist need?

To me, the curiosity to learn a lot is essential. You have to have the ability to understand and do science and to communicate it.

Paleontologist

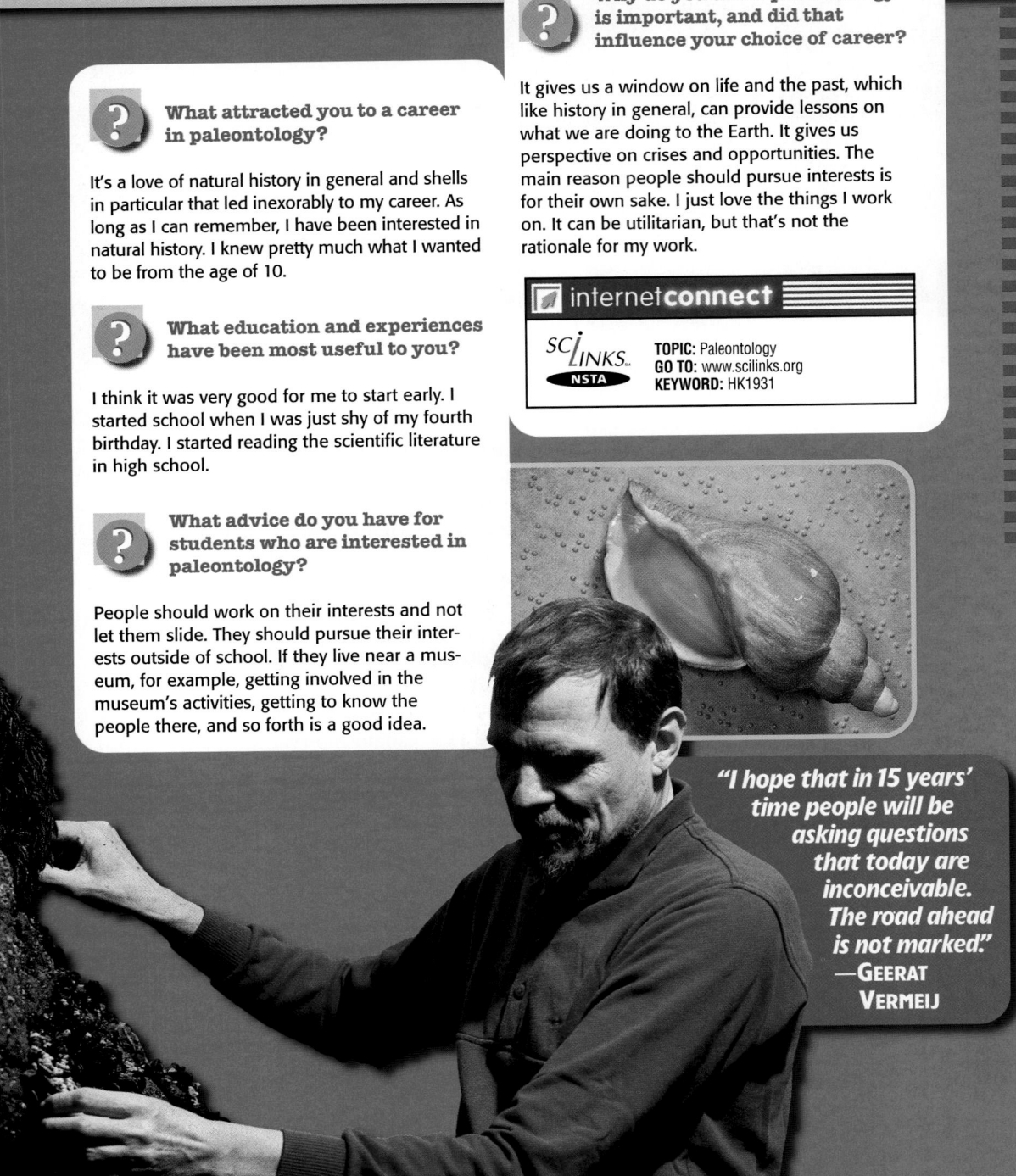

? What attracted you to a career in paleontology?

It's a love of natural history in general and shells in particular that led inexorably to my career. As long as I can remember, I have been interested in natural history. I knew pretty much what I wanted to be from the age of 10.

? What education and experiences have been most useful to you?

I think it was very good for me to start early. I started school when I was just shy of my fourth birthday. I started reading the scientific literature in high school.

? What advice do you have for students who are interested in paleontology?

People should work on their interests and not let them slide. They should pursue their interests outside of school. If they live near a museum, for example, getting involved in the museum's activities, getting to know the people there, and so forth is a good idea.

? Why do you think paleontology is important, and did that influence your choice of career?

It gives us a window on life and the past, which like history in general, can provide lessons on what we are doing to the Earth. It gives us perspective on crises and opportunities. The main reason people should pursue interests is for their own sake. I just love the things I work on. It can be utilitarian, but that's not the rationale for my work.

internet connect

SC/LINKS.
NSTA

TOPIC: Paleontology
GO TO: www.scilinks.org
KEYWORD: HK1931

"I hope that in 15 years' time people will be asking questions that today are inconceivable. The road ahead is not marked."
—GEERAT VERMEIJ

Connection to LANGUAGE ARTS

In September of 1996, W. H. Freeman and Company published Vermeij's memoirs, entitled *Privileged Hands: A Scientific Life*.

In it, Vermeij describes the current state of evolutionary theory and discusses his contributions through his study of marine mollusks. He also explores what it is like to work in science as a career, how discoveries are made, and what it is like to visit places from Baja California to New Zealand in search of scientific facts about living things.

Vermeij has also written a book entitled *A Natural History of Shells*.

CHAPTER 18

The Atmosphere

Annotated Descriptions of the Correlated National Science Standards

The following descriptions summarize the National Science Standards that specially relate to Chapter 18. For the full text of the Standards, see p. 40T.

SECTION 18.1
Characteristics of the Atmosphere

Earth and Space Science
ES 1a, 3d
Unifying Concepts and Processes
UCP 1, 2, 3
Science as Inquiry
SAI 1, 2
Science and Technology
ST 1
History and Nature of Science
HNS 1, 3
Science in Personal and Social Perspectives
SPSP 1, 2, 4, 5

SECTION 18.2
Water and Wind

Earth and Space Science
ES 1c, 2a, 2b
Unifying Concepts and Processes
UCP 1, 3
Science as Inquiry
SAI 1, 2
Science and Technology
ST 1, 2
Science in Personal and Social Perspectives
SPSP 1, 2, 3

SECTION 18.3
Weather and Climate

Earth and Space Science
ES 1d, 3c
Unifying Concepts and Processes
UCP 1, 3
Science as Inquiry
SAI 1
History and Nature of Science
HNS 1
Science in Personal and Social Perspectives
SPSP 1, 5

Cross-Discipline Teaching RESOURCES

Cross-Discipline Teaching, ATE p. 596
Life Science   Language Arts
Fine Arts   Chemistry

Integration Enrichment Resources
Health, **PE** and **ATE** p. 610
    IE 18.1 *Why Your Ears Pop*
Real World Applications, **PE** and **ATE** p. 615
    IE 18.2 *Understanding Thunderstorms*
Physics, **PE** and **ATE** p. 619
    IE 18.3 *Adobe*

Additional Integration Enrichment Worksheets
    IE 18.4 Physics
    IE 18.5 Language Arts
    IE 18.6 Chemistry
    IE 18.7 Technology

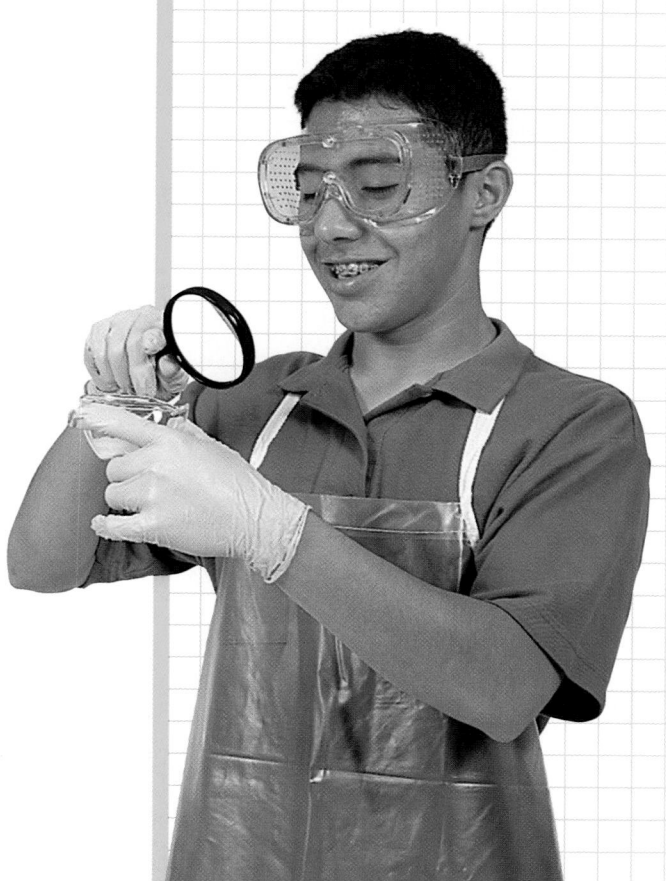

Use the Planning Guide on the next page to help you organize your lessons.

MATH AND COMPUTER RESOURCES

Chapter 18	Math Skills	Assess	Media/Computer Skills
Section 18.1	**BS** **Worksheet 1.7:** Classifying Items		■ Section 18.1
Section 18.2			■ Section 18.2
Section 18.3		**PE** **Building Math Skills,** p. 622, item 18	■ Section 18.3 **PE** **Thinking Critically,** p. 622, item 27

PE Pupil's Edition   **ATE** Annotated Teacher's Edition   **MS** Math Skills   **BS** Basic Skills
IE Integration Enrichment   ■ Guided Reading Audio   **CRT** Critical Thinking

READING SKILL BUILDER

The following activities found in the Annotated Teacher's Edition provide techniques for developing useful reading strategies to increase your students' reading comprehension skills.

Section 18.1 **K-W-L,** p. 596, 602
Brainstorming, p. 598, 605
Reading Organizer, p. 601

Section 18.2 **Summarizing,** p. 606, 611

Section 18.3 **Reading Organizer,** p. 613

Smithsonian Institution®

Visit www.si.edu/hrw for additional online resources.

Spanish Resources

The following resources are made available for students who speak Spanish as their first language.

Spanish Resources
Guided Reading Audio CD-ROM
Chapter 18

Spanish Glossary
Chapter 18

CHAPTER 18 PLANNING GUIDE

The Atmosphere

CLASSROOM RESOURCES

	FOCUS	TEACH	HANDS-ON
Section 18.1: Characteristics of the Atmosphere			
BLOCK 1 45 minutes	**ATE RSB** K-W-L, p. 596 **ATE** Focus Activities 1, 2, p. 597 **ATE RSB** Brainstorming, p. 598 **ATE Demo 1** Temperature Inversion, p. 599 **ATE RSB** Reading Organizer, p. 601 **PE** Layers of the Atmosphere, pp. 598–602 ★ Focus Transparency LT 59	**ATE Skill Builder** Interpreting Visuals, p. 598, p. 601 **BLM** 55 Oxygen and Ozone	**IE** Worksheet 18.5
BLOCK 2 45 minutes	**ATE RSB** K-W-L, p. 602 **ATE RSB** Brainstorming, p. 605 **PE** Changes in the Earth's Atmosphere, pp. 602–605	**ATE Skill Builder** Interpreting Visuals, p. 603 **TT** 61 Greenhouse Effect	
Section 18.2: Water and Wind			
BLOCK 3 45 minutes	**ATE RSB** Summarizing, p. 606 **ATE Demo 2** Water Is in the Air, p. 606 **ATE Demo 3** Transpiration, p. 607 **ATE Demo 4** How to Make a Cloud, p. 608 **PE** The Water Cycle, pp. 606–609 ★ Focus Transparency LT 60	**TT** 62 Water Cycle **BLM** 56 Humidity **TT** 63 Cloud Types	**PE** Quick Activity *Measuring Rainfall*, p. 609 **DS** 18.1 **IE** Worksheet 18.6
BLOCK 4 45 minutes	**ATE Demo 5** Windsocks, p. 610 **ATE RSB** Summarizing, p. 611 **PE** Air Pressure; Wind, pp. 609–612	**BLM** 57 Barometer	**IE** Worksheet 18.1 **LE** 18 *Predicting Coastal Winds* **DS** 18.3
Section 18.3: Weather and Climate			
BLOCK 5 45 minutes	**ATE RSB** Reading Organizer, p. 613 **ATE Demo 6** A Cold Front Meets a Warm Front, p. 613 **PE** Fronts and Severe Weather, pp. 613–616 ★ Focus Transparency LT 61	**ATE Skill Builder** Interpreting Visuals, pp. 613–615 **TT** 64 Hurricane	**PE** Real World Applications *Calculating the Distance to a Thunderstorm*, p. 615 **IE** Worksheet 18.2
BLOCK 6 45 minutes	**PE** Weather Maps; Climate, pp. 617–620	**ATE Skill Builder** Interpreting Visuals, p. 619 **BLM** 58 Climatograph	**IE** Worksheets 18.3, 18.4, 18.7 **PE** Design Your Own Lab *Measuring Temperature Effects*, p. 624 **DS** 18.2

CLASSROOM RESOURCES

HOMEWORK	ASSESS
PE Section Review 1, 2, 6, 7, p. 605 **Chapter 18 Review,** p. 621, items 1, 14	**SG** Chapter 18 Pretest
PE Section Review 3–5, p. 605 **Chapter 18 Review,** p. 621, items 2, 4, 5, 13	**SG** Section 18.1
PE Section Review 1, 3, 4, 6, p. 612 **Chapter 18 Review,** p. 621, items 3, 6, 7, 9, 15, 16	
PE Section Review 2, 5, 7, p. 612 **Chapter 18 Review,** p. 621, item 8	**SG** Section 18.2
PE Section Review 2, 4, 5, p. 620 **Chapter 18 Review,** p. 621, items 11, 12, 17	**ATE** *ALTERNATIVE ASSESSMENT,* Fronts, p. 614
PE Section Review 1, 3, 6, 7, p. 620 **Chapter 18 Review,** p. 621, items 10, 18	**SG** Section 18.3

REVIEW AND ASSESS

BLOCK 7

PE Chapter 18 Review
 Thinking Critically 19–28, pp. 622, 623
 Developing Life/Work Skills 29–31, p. 623
 Integrating Concepts 32–34, p. 623
SG Chapter 18 Mixed Review

BLOCK 8

Chapter Tests
 Holt Science Spectrum: A Physical Approach
 Chapter 18 Test

One-Stop Planner CD–ROM with Test Generator
Holt Science Spectrum Test Generator
 FOR MACINTOSH AND WINDOWS
 Chapter 18

Teaching Resources
 Scoring Rubrics and assignment evaluation
 checklist.

 internet**connect**

SCiLINKS **NSTA**
National Science Teachers
Association
Online Resources:
www.scilinks.org
The following *sci*LINKS Internet resources can be found
in the student text for this chapter.

Page 597 **TOPIC:** Visible light **KEYWORD:** HK1801	**Page 606** **TOPIC:** Water cycle **KEYWORD:** HK1804
Page 599 **TOPIC:** Layers of the atmosphere **KEYWORD:** HK1802	**Page 613** **TOPIC:** Severe weather **KEYWORD:** HK1805
Page 603 **TOPIC:** Ozone depletion **KEYWORD:** HK1803	**Page 623** **TOPIC:** Weather maps **KEYWORD:** HK1806

CNNfyi.com   www.cnnfyi.com

Visit this site for coverage of current events and related
classroom resources.

PE Pupil's Edition   **ATE** Annotated Teacher's Edition
RSB Reading Skill Builder   **DS** Datasheets
IE Integrated Enrichment   **SG** Study Guide
LE Laboratory Experiments
TT Teaching Transparencies   **BLM** Blackline Masters
★ Lesson Focus Transparency

The Atmosphere

596

Tapping Prior Knowledge

Be sure students understand the following concepts:

Chapter 2
Properties of matter

Chapter 4
Compounds and molecules

Chapter 12
Reflection and color

Chapter 16
The solar system

READING SKILL BUILDER *K-W-L* Write the word *atmosphere* on the board. Have the students list what they know or think they know about the atmosphere on a separate sheet of paper. Also have them list any questions they have about the atmosphere. Students should refer back to their list after reading the chapter. Clarify any concepts that students have trouble understanding. For an extension activity, collect the students' lists and choose one or two questions for students to do additional research on.

RESOURCE LINK
STUDY GUIDE

Assign students *Pretest Chapter 18 The Atmosphere* before beginning Chapter 18.

CROSS-DISCIPLINE TEACHING

Life Science Ask a biology teacher to visit your classroom and explain some of the respiratory conditions, such as asthma, bronchitis, and emphysema that can result from breathing air with pollutants in it. Have your students research the harmful effects air pollutants have on other organisms.

Fine Arts Have students make paintings or drawings of Earth as it might look if there were no atmosphere.

Language Arts Have students write a short story, poem, or script that describes an imaginary trip through the atmosphere from the ground to outer space. Students should include characteristics of the various layers of the atmosphere.

Chemistry Have students look at **Figure 18-2.** Tell them that the polluted air trapped in the Los Angeles Basin is called smog. Ask a chemistry teacher to visit your classroom and explain the principles behind the formation of smog.

Focus ACTIVITY

Background Like many other weather phenomena, rainbows are caused by water in Earth's atmosphere. Rainbows are visible when the air is filled with water droplets and the viewer is positioned between the sun and the droplets. Sunlight striking the droplets passes through their front surface and is partially reflected back toward the viewer from the back of the droplet.

But why do we see the rainbow of colors? A rainbow occurs when sunlight is bent as it passes from air to water and back to air again. The degree to which the light bends depends on the frequency of the light. In this way, observers see only the frequency (the color) that is directed toward them from each droplet.

Activity 1 Look at the two rainbows in the smaller photo at left. One of these rainbows, called a secondary rainbow, results when light is reflected a second time in the raindrops. The second reflection causes the order of the colors to be reversed. Compare the order of the colors in the two rainbows with that of the rainbow in the photo of the irrigation trucks. Can you tell which rainbow is the secondary rainbow? How?

Activity 2 Rainbows are most commonly seen as arches because the ends of the rainbow disappear at the horizon. But if an observer is at an elevated vantage point, such as on an airplane or at the rim of a canyon, a complete circular rainbow can be seen.

You can create a circular rainbow in your yard. On a warm, clear day when the sun is overhead, turn on a water hose and spray water into the air above you. If the mist is fine enough, you should be able to create a rainbow encircling your body.

Rainbows can be seen when the air is filled with water droplets and the observer is positioned between the sun and the droplets.

internet**connect**

SCI**LINKS**
NSTA

TOPIC: Visible light
GO TO: www.scilinks.org
KEYWORD: HK1801

597

Focus ACTIVITY

Background Ask your students if they know why and how rainbows occur. Have them hypothesize reasons why rainbows form.

Rainbows are produced by the reflection and refraction of sunlight on raindrops. The raindrops act as mirrors or prisms that cause the sunlight to separate into a spectrum of visible colors. Only one color can be produced from a single raindrop at a time. The highest raindrops produce a red color, and the lowest raindrops produce a violet color. Orange, yellow, green, blue, and indigo complete the middle spectrum of the rainbow.

When sunlight is reflected twice in a raindrop, a secondary rainbow that is much dimmer than the first may be produced.

Activity 1 The first rainbow shown in the photo is actually the secondary rainbow. When light from the sun is reflected twice in the same set of raindrops, two rainbows are produced. The primary rainbow is more intense in color than the dimmer secondary rainbow.

Activity 2 If your school has access to a water hose, you may want to demonstrate this activity before instructing your students to perform it. Make sure the sun is positioned behind you before spraying the water in front and over your head.

Characteristics of the Atmosphere

Characteristics of the Atmosphere

▶ **KEY TERMS**
troposphere
temperature inversion
stratosphere
ozone
mesosphere
thermosphere
greenhouse effect

OBJECTIVES
▶ Identify the primary layers of the atmosphere.
▶ Describe how the atmosphere has evolved over time.
▶ Describe how the oxygen–carbon dioxide cycle works, and explain its importance to living organisms.
▶ Discuss the recent changes in Earth's atmosphere.

I f you were to see Earth's atmosphere from space, it would look like a thin blue halo of light around the Earth. This fragile envelope provides the air we breathe, regulates global temperature, and filters out dangerous solar radiation.

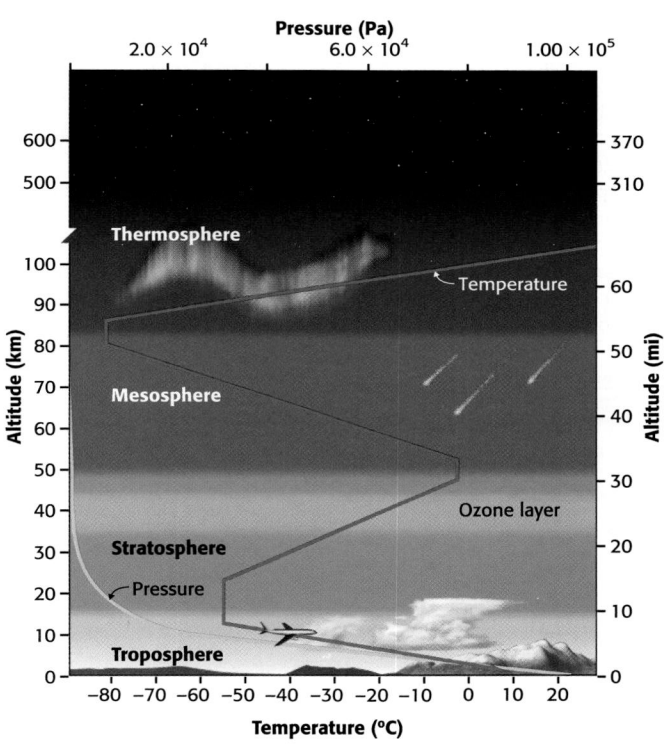

Pressure (Pa)

Layers of the Atmosphere

Without the atmosphere, you would have no oxygen to breathe. The atmosphere, however, does not contain oxygen alone. Earth's atmosphere consists of a variety of gases. The two main gases in the atmosphere are nitrogen (about 78 percent) and oxygen (about 21 percent). The remaining elements exist only in very small amounts and are called *trace gases*.

The atmosphere has several layers. These layers differ in temperature, density, and amount of certain gases present. **Figure 18-1** shows the order and relative sizes of Earth's atmospheric layers.

Figure 18-1
The layers of the atmosphere are marked by changes in temperature and pressure. The red line indicates temperature, and the yellow line indicates pressure in pascals.

Almost all weather occurs in the troposphere

You live in the layer closest to Earth's surface. This layer is called the troposphere. Clouds, wind, rain, and snow occur mostly in the troposphere.

The troposphere is the densest of the atmospheric layers. To understand why, consider the weight of all the other gas layers pressing down on the gases in the troposphere. The weight causes the gas molecules to squeeze together into a smaller volume. The result is a greater density than exists in higher layers of the atmosphere.

The troposphere gets cooler with increasing altitude

If you were to climb a mountain, you would notice that the air is much colder at the top of the mountain than it is at the base. The air closest to the mountain's base is warmed by the ground and oceans, which absorb solar energy during the day and heat the atmosphere by radiation and conduction. Air at higher altitudes is less dense and is not as close to those sources of heat. As you travel higher into the troposphere, the temperature decreases by about 6°C for every kilometer of altitude.

At the top of the troposphere, the temperature stops decreasing. The boundary where this occurs is called the *tropopause*. The altitude of the tropopause is different at different places on Earth. At the poles, it occurs at about 8 km (5 mi). Near the equator, it rises to nearly 18 km (11 mi).

Cold air can become trapped beneath warm air

Although the troposphere is generally warmer close to Earth's surface, cool air sometimes gets trapped beneath the warm air. This is called a temperature inversion.

When a temperature inversion occurs, the air sometimes becomes thick with pollution. This is true especially in areas surrounded by mountains, which prevent the cooler, polluted air from escaping. The Los Angeles Basin, in California, for instance, is often filled with a brown haze of pollution, as shown in **Figure 18-2.** Cool air from the Pacific Ocean blows into the basin, becomes trapped by the overriding warm air, and fills with pollutants.

Figure 18-2
A temperature inversion traps polluted air in the Los Angeles Basin, in California.

> **troposphere** the atmospheric layer closest to Earth's surface where nearly all weather occurs

VOCABULARY *Skills Tip*
The names of all of Earth's atmospheric layers end in the root word sphere, *implying their spherical shape.*

internet connect

SCI*LINKS*
NSTA

TOPIC: Layers of the atmosphere
GO TO: www.scilinks.org
KEYWORD: HK1802

> **temperature inversion** the atmospheric condition in which warm air traps cooler air near Earth's surface

THE ATMOSPHERE **599**

Teaching Tip

The Tropopause The troposphere is the layer where the weather we experience occurs. This is because the troposphere contains the most water vapor and is heated from below by contact with the ground and oceans. The tropopause, or boundary between the troposphere and the stratosphere, is highest at the equator (about 16 km or 10 mi) and lowest at the poles (about 10 km or 6 mi) Students have probably seen evidence of the tropopause without realizing it. The flattened anvil-shaped top of large thunderheads results when a cloud rises so high that it reaches the tropopause. At the tropopause, clouds encounter the fierce winds of the stratosphere, which shear off the top of the clouds.

Teaching Tip

Clouds Tell students that clouds at the bottom of the troposphere are made of drops of water, while clouds at the top of the troposphere are made of ice crystals. Ask students to explain why this is. (*The temperature decreases higher in the atmosphere.*)

REAL WORLD APPLICATIONS

Pressure Altimeter A pressure altimeter uses atmospheric pressure as an indicator of altitude. Airplane pilots use this device to track the changing conditions of Earth's atmosphere. Yet because standard air pressure at a specific elevation may vary from the actual air pressure, pilots must adjust their altimeter before and during flights.

599

DEMONSTRATION 1 TEACHING

Temperature Inversion

Time: Approximately 10 minutes
Materials: 2 glass beakers, hot tap water, cold tap water, food coloring, a spoon

Fill one of the beakers halfway with cold water. Fill the other beaker with hot water, and stir two drops of food coloring in it. Slowly and carefully use the spoon to layer the colored warm water on top of the cold water. Ask students to relate this demonstration to what occurs in Earth's atmosphere when cool air gets trapped beneath a layer of warm air in the troposphere. (*A temperature inversion results.*) Alternatively, you can set this up as a lab, give students the materials, and challenge them to demonstrate a temperature inversion without any other guidance.

Characteristics of the Atmosphere

Teaching Tip

The Troposphere and Stratosphere Earth's diameter is 12 756 km (7911 mi), and the troposphere and stratosphere extend about 50 km (about 30 mi) from the surface. To give your students a visual image of how thin these layers are, have them go to a paved area of the school's parking area. Using colored chalk, draw a circle with a diameter of 4 m (about 13 ft) to represent Earth. This is easy if you tie the chalk to a string 2 m (about 6.5 ft) long and have one person hold the end of the string on the ground while another person moves around drawing the circle.

Calculate how thick the combined troposphere and stratosphere need to be on your drawing to be in proportion to your "Earth." Then use white chalk to draw another circle around the first one to represent these two layers. Ask your students if the layers are thinner than they thought.

Figure 18-3
A heated cabin in this aircraft allows its pilot to do high-altitude atmospheric research, such as collecting air and particle samples after a volcanic eruption.

▶ **stratosphere** the layer of the atmosphere that extends upward from the troposphere to an altitude of 50 km; contains the ozone layer

▶ **ozone** the form of atmospheric oxygen that has three atoms per molecule

As long as the temperature difference remains unchanged, the trapped pollutants cannot escape. A person breathing these toxins can become ill. While these conditions exist, it is not healthy for people to exercise too much because they inhale a greater amount of pollutants as they breathe heavily.

The stratosphere gets *warmer* with increasing altitude

In 1892, unmanned balloons were built that could record temperatures in the **stratosphere**, the layer above the tropopause. Later, humans further explored this cold, oxygen-deficient layer by using balloons and airplanes with enclosed, heated cabins. The WB-57F in **Figure 18-3** is just such an aircraft. These explorers found that the temperature in the lower stratosphere remains fairly constant, staying around –55°C (–67°F) from near the tropopause to an altitude of about 25 km (about 16 mi). At 25 km, the temperature begins to increase with altitude until it reaches about 0°C (32°F).

The stratosphere extends upward to about 50 km (31 mi). In addition to getting slightly warmer instead of cooler, the stratosphere differs from the troposphere in composition, weather, and density.

Unlike the troposphere, the stratosphere has very little water vapor—the gaseous form of water. Because of this lack of water vapor, the stratosphere is relatively calm and contains few clouds and no storms.

The increase in temperature in the upper stratosphere occurs in the atmospheric layer known as the *ozone layer*. The ozone layer is warmer because it contains a form of oxygen called **ozone** that absorbs solar radiation. Whereas the oxygen we breathe is a molecule that consists of two oxygen atoms, ozone molecules have three oxygen atoms, as shown in **Figure 18-4.** Ozone is important because it absorbs much of the sun's ultraviolet radiation. The ozone layer shields life on Earth's surface from ultraviolet-radiation damage. Ozone will be discussed later in this section.

Figure 18-4

A Oxygen molecules have two atoms of oxygen.

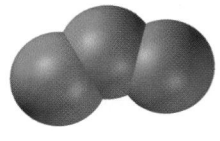

B Ozone molecules have three atoms of oxygen.

600 CHAPTER 18

RESOURCE LINK
IER

Assign students worksheet *18.5 Connection to Language Arts—The Layers of the Atmosphere* in the **Integration Enrichment Resources** ancillary.

The mesosphere and thermosphere exhibit extremes of temperature

Temperature begins to fall again in the mesosphere. As in the troposphere, temperatures in the mesosphere, 50–80 km (31–50 mi) above Earth's surface, decrease with increasing altitude. Near the top of this layer, temperatures fall to below –80°C (–112°F), the coldest temperature in Earth's atmosphere.

Beyond the mesosphere, temperatures begin to rise again. This layer, at an altitude of about 80–480 km (50–298 mi), is called the thermosphere. The main gases are still nitrogen and oxygen, but the molecules are very far apart. This may lead you to think that the thermosphere is very cold, but it is actually very hot. Temperatures in this layer average around 980°C (1796°F) because the small amount of molecular oxygen in the thermosphere heats up as it absorbs intense solar radiation.

The outermost portion of the thermosphere, at about 480 km, is known as the *exosphere*. In the exosphere, some gases escape from the gravitational pull of Earth and exit into space. In addition, gases in space are captured by Earth's gravity and added to Earth's atmosphere.

The ionosphere is used in radio communication

When solar energy is absorbed in the lower thermosphere and upper mesosphere, electrically charged ions are formed. The area where this occurs is sometimes called the *ionosphere*.

Electrons in the ionosphere reflect radio waves, as shown in **Figure 18-5,** allowing them to be received over long distances. Without the ionosphere, most radio signals would travel directly into space, and only locations very close to a transmitter could receive the signals.

Because these ions require solar radiation in order to form, their number in the lower layers of the ionosphere decreases at night. This means the radio waves can travel higher into the atmosphere before being reflected. As a result, the radio waves return to Earth's surface farther from their source than they do in the daytime, as shown at right.

 **mesosphere** the coldest layer of the atmosphere; located above the stratosphere

 **thermosphere** the atmospheric layer above the mesosphere

Figure 18-5
Radio waves can be received from far away because they are reflected by the ionosphere. At night, when ion density decreases in the lower atmosphere, transmissions can be received farther away.

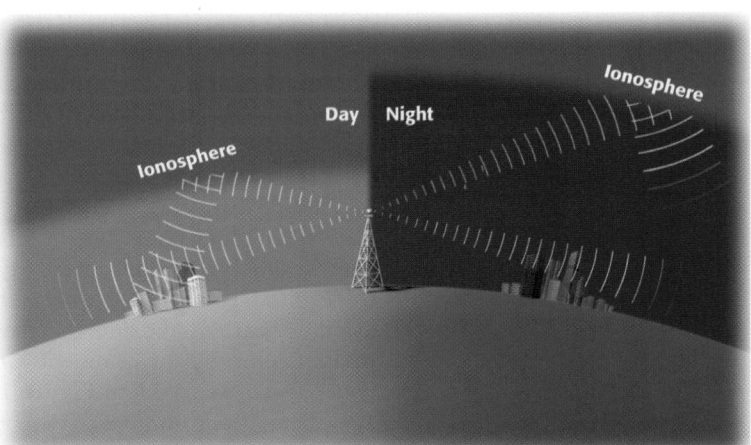

THE ATMOSPHERE **601**

Characteristics of the Atmosphere

Additional Application
Divisions of the Atmosphere
The atmosphere is made up of two divisions. The upper division, called the heterosphere, consists of the thermosphere and ionosphere layers. The lower portion, called the homosphere, consists of the troposphere, stratosphere, and mesosphere layers.

READING SKILL BUILDER *Reading Organizer* Have students create a table like the one shown below. Once the table is set up, have students fill the table with appropriate information from **Figure 18-1** and from the student text.

Layers of the Atmosphere

	Troposphere	Stratosphere	Mesosphere	Thermosphere
Height	*8–18 km*	*about 50 km*	*50–80 km*	*80–480 km*
Temperature	*−55°C–10°C*	*−55°C–0°C*	*–80°C–0°C*	*average = 980°C*
Pressure	$2.0 \times 10^4 - 1.0 \times 10^5 Pa$	$< 2.0 \times 10^4 Pa$	$< 2.0 \times 10^4 Pa$	$< 2.0 \times 10^4 Pa$

Characteristics of the Atmosphere

Connection to
LANGUAGE ARTS

Aurora was the Roman goddess of dawn, and *borealis* is the Latin word for "northern." Aurora borealis refers to the Northern Lights, which are visible only in the Northern Hemisphere. Similarly, *australis* is the Latin word for "southern," and the aurora australis is visible only in the Southern Hemisphere.

READING SKILL BUILDER   *K-W-L*   Write the word *outgassing* on the board. Have students list all the words, phrases, and ideas that they associate with the term. Begin a discussion in which students inquire about clarification of the listed ideas. Form a definition of outgassing and its role in the creation of an atmosphere of gases.

INTEGRATING

CHEMISTRY   Photosynthetic plants use carbon dioxide, water, and light energy, and they produce carbohydrates and oxygen. Write the following photosynthesis reaction on the board, and have students balance the equation.

$$CO_2 + H_2O + \text{light energy} \rightarrow$$
$$C_6H_{12}O_6 + O_2$$

Figure 18-6
Auroras, such as this one seen above mountains in Alaska, occur in the ionosphere.

Figure 18-7

A Early in Earth's existence, the atmosphere was filled with mostly carbon dioxide, nitrogen, and a few other trace gases.

B Once plants evolved, they converted much of the planet's carbon dioxide into oxygen.

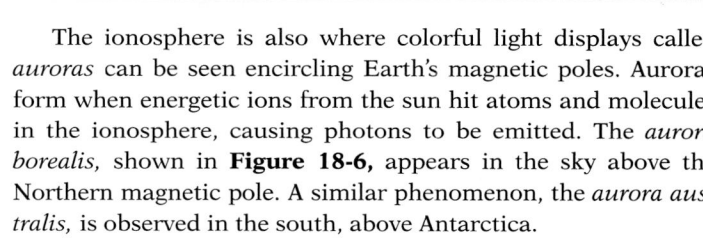

The ionosphere is also where colorful light displays called *auroras* can be seen encircling Earth's magnetic poles. Auroras form when energetic ions from the sun hit atoms and molecules in the ionosphere, causing photons to be emitted. The *aurora borealis*, shown in **Figure 18-6,** appears in the sky above the Northern magnetic pole. A similar phenomenon, the *aurora australis*, is observed in the south, above Antarctica.

Changes in the Earth's Atmosphere

When Earth began to solidify about 4.4 billion years ago, volcanic eruptions released a variety of gases. This process, called *outgassing*, created an atmosphere of gases, some of which would be poisonous to us today. As shown in **Figure 18-7A,** some of these gases included hydrogen, H_2, water vapor, H_2O, ammonia, NH_3, methane, CH_4, carbon monoxide, CO, carbon dioxide, CO_2, and nitrogen, N_2.

Photosynthetic plants contribute oxygen to the atmosphere

Amazingly, life-forms evolved that were comfortable in this early atmosphere. Bacteria and other single-celled organisms lived in the oceans. Around 2.5 billion years ago, some cells evolved a method of capturing energy from the sun and converting it to sugar that could be used as a food source. This process, called *photosynthesis*, also produced oxygen as a byproduct. Because these organisms needed only sunlight, water, and the readily available carbon dioxide for their survival, they thrived and multiplied in this environment. Gradually, the atmosphere filled with oxygen, as shown in **Figure 18-7B.** About 350 million years ago, the concentration of oxygen reached a level similar to what it is today.

Animals produce carbon dioxide necessary for photosynthesis

As *aerobic*, oxygen-breathing organisms evolved, they joined plants in a balance that led to our present atmosphere. The steps of the oxygen–carbon dioxide cycle describe this balance. These steps are summarized in **Figure 18-8.**

Figure 18-8 is a simple depiction of a series of chemical reactions. Basically, plants need carbon dioxide, CO_2, for photosynthesis and food production. Oxygen, O_2, is then released as a waste product of photosynthesis. Animals breathe oxygen during a process called *respiration* and release carbon dioxide as waste. The carbon dioxide they exhale is then used by plants and other photosynthetic organisms, and the process is repeated.

Man-made chemicals can deplete the ozone layer

Recall that the upper stratosphere contains ozone molecules in a layer called the ozone layer. Ozone is formed when the sun's dangerous ultraviolet rays strike molecules of O_2. The energy splits the molecules, and the single atoms of oxygen bond with other O_2 molecules to make O_3, ozone. These O_3 molecules in turn absorb much of the sun's damaging ultraviolet radiation.

If the ozone layer didn't exist, ultraviolet rays would cause serious damage to the DNA in the cells of living things. Thus, scientists were concerned when they found lower than expected concentrations of ozone in the stratosphere in 1985.

Low ozone concentrations are caused in part by chemicals known as chlorofluorocarbons, or CFCs. These gases were widely used in the first 80 years of the twentieth century as refrigerants and as propellants in spray cans. Even though the atmosphere is only 0.004 to 0.03% CFCs, a single molecule can react with and destroy many ozone molecules.

VOCABULARY *Skills Tip*

The word ozone *comes from the Greek word* ozein, *which means "to smell." Ozone gas has a strong odor. You may have smelled ozone after a thunderstorm when atmospheric oxygen was converted to ozone by the electrical energy of lightning.*

internetconnect

SC/LINKS.
NSTA

TOPIC: Ozone depletion
GO TO: www.scilinks.org
KEYWORD: HK1803

Figure 18-8
In the oxygen–carbon dioxide cycle, plants produce oxygen, which is used by animals for respiration. Animals produce carbon dioxide, which is used by plants for photosynthesis.

THE ATMOSPHERE **603**

Characteristics of the Atmosphere

MISCONCEPTION
Ozone Layer **ALERT**
Many students may have heard about the ozone layer, probably in connection to ozone depletion. Stress to students that the ozone layer, found on the stratosphere, protects us from harmful ultraviolet radiation. Ozone, as a result of human activities, can also form in the lower troposphere. In this layer, ozone is a pollutant and can be harmful to people.

SKILL BUILDER

Interpreting Visuals Have students examine **Figure 18-8,** and briefly discuss the steps of the oxygen–carbon dioxide cycle. Have students write a brief paragraph explaining the roles that plants and animals play in the cycle.

Did You Know ?

In addition to the ozone layer, there is a magnetic field around Earth that also protects us from harmful radiation. High-energy particles and rays are caught in the Van Allen Belt that surrounds our planet and deflects the particles from our planet's surface. There is geological evidence that this magnetic field is disrupted occasionally, which results in dangerous particles and rays hitting unprotected organisms.

Characteristics of the Atmosphere

Teaching Tip

CFC Molecules Inform students that CFC molecules remain active in the stratosphere for decades. CFCs released thirty years ago are still destroying ozone today, so it will be many years before the ozone layer recovers.

REAL WORLD APPLICATIONS • • • • • • • • • • • • • • •

CFCs People who work with chlorofluorocarbons, such as air conditioner repair personnel, must be trained and licensed in the proper handling of CFCs. Strict guidelines must be followed. Invite someone who repairs air conditioners to be a guest lecturer in your class. Have the person explain how the handling of CFCs has changed in recent years.

• •

SKILL BUILDER

Interpreting Visuals Have students examine **Figure 18-9.** Ask students to come up with solutions that might slow global warming.

Resources Teaching Transparency 6 shows this visual.

Persuaded by the evidence that there is a connection between CFCs and deterioration of the ozone layer, most industrialized countries stopped production of CFCs on January 1, 1996. The international bans have drastically decreased the amount of CFCs entering the stratosphere. Time is now the important factor in finding out if ozone concentrations will begin to rise again.

The greenhouse effect keeps Earth warm

Have you ever been in a greenhouse on a cold day? It is surprisingly warm inside compared with the outside. Although some greenhouses are heated by a furnace or other heating system, much of the warmth results from the sun's energy entering and becoming trapped inside the glass or plastic walls of the greenhouse.

Unlike a greenhouse, Earth's atmosphere has no walls, but certain atmospheric gases keep Earth much warmer than it would be without an atmosphere. As shown in **Figure 18-9,** energy that is released from the sun as radiation and reaches Earth's surface is absorbed. Then some of this energy is transferred back toward space as radiation. Carbon dioxide, water vapor, and other gases absorb some of this energy. Absorbing this energy makes the atmosphere warmer. The warm atmosphere in turn releases some of this energy in the form of radiation, some of which is directed back toward Earth's surface. This effect is called the greenhouse effect.

▶ **greenhouse effect** the process by which the atmosphere traps some of the energy from the sun in the troposphere

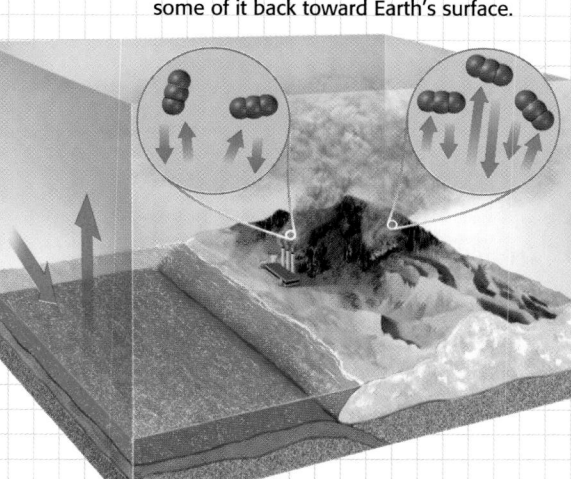

Figure 18-9 The greenhouse effect is a process in which atmospheric gases trap some of the energy from the sun in the troposphere.

A Solar radiation warms Earth's surface and is radiated back into the atmosphere as heat radiation.

B Greenhouse gases, such as CO_2 and H_2O, receive this heat radiation and radiate some of it back toward Earth's surface.

C CO_2 is added to the air in the burning of fossil fuels and in forest fires, possibly causing global warming.

Increased levels of carbon dioxide may lead to global warming

Without the greenhouse effect, Earth would have a colder average temperature than it does. But too much of the greenhouse effect can cause problems. If too much heat is trapped, the global temperature will rise. This *global warming* could cause the icecaps to melt, ocean levels to rise, and droughts to occur in some areas.

Carbon dioxide occurs naturally and is necessary for plant photosynthesis. In the last 100 years, the burning of coal, oil, and gas for power plants, machinery, and cars has added excess carbon dioxide to the air. Recently, scientists have hypothesized that this increase to the amount of carbon dioxide is the reason the troposphere's average temperature has risen 0.5°C in the past 100 years. Whether carbon dioxide is responsible for global warming and what to do about it continues to be debated around the world.

SECTION 18.1 REVIEW

SUMMARY

- The layers of Earth's atmosphere are the troposphere, stratosphere, mesosphere, and thermosphere.

- The oxygen–carbon dioxide cycle produces the oxygen we breathe. Plants release oxygen. Animals breathe this oxygen and release carbon dioxide, which is used by plants.

- The ozone layer protects life on Earth by absorbing much of the ultraviolet radiation entering Earth's atmosphere.

- CFCs are linked to the deterioration of the ozone layer. For this reason, their use has been banned in most countries.

- The addition of CO_2 to the atmosphere by the burning of fossil fuels may cause global warming. This issue continues to be debated.

CHECK YOUR UNDERSTANDING

1. **Identify** the two atmospheric layers that contain air as warm as 25°C.
2. **Identify** which of the following gases is most abundant in Earth's atmosphere today.
   a. argon
   c. oxygen
   b. nitrogen
   d. carbon dioxide
3. **Compare** Earth's early atmosphere with its present atmosphere.
4. **Arrange** the steps of the oxygen–carbon dioxide cycle in the correct order:
   a. animals breathe oxygen
   b. plants produce oxygen
   c. plants use carbon dioxide
   d. animals exhale carbon dioxide
5. **Explain** why the following statement is incorrect:
   Global warming could cause oceans to rise, so the greenhouse effect must be eliminated completely.
6. **Predict** how much colder it is at the top of Mount Everest, which is almost 9 km above sea level, than it is at the Indian coastline. Consider only the difference in altitude. (**Hint:** The temperature in the troposphere decreases by 6°C/km.)
7. **Critical Thinking** In 1982, Larry Walters rose to an altitude of approximately 4900 m (just over 3 mi) on a lawn chair attached to 45 helium-filled weather balloons. Give two reasons why Walters's efforts were dangerous.

THE ATMOSPHERE **605**

Characteristics of the Atmosphere

 **READING SKILL BUILDER** *Brainstorming* Write some of the effects of global warming on the board. Ask students to brainstorm possible effects of global warming. *(Answers might include extinction of animals, flooding, change in weather patterns, relocation of people, etc.)* Have students propose solutions to reduce the effects of global warming.

SECTION 18.1 REVIEW

Check Your Understanding

1. troposphere and thermosphere
2. b
3. Earth's early atmosphere was composed of many gases that would be poisonous to us today. As lifeforms evolved and began to photosynthesize, oxygen was produced. Once animals adapted to breathing oxygen, they began to give off carbon dioxide, balancing the production of oxygen.
4. b, a, d, c
5. If we were to eliminate the greenhouse effect completely, the world's climate would become too cold for humans to survive.
6. About 54°C colder
7. The oxygen content of the air is considerably lower at that high altitude, and the temperature is extremely cold.

RESOURCE LINK
STUDY GUIDE

Assign students *Review Section 18.1 Characteristics of the Atmosphere* before beginning Section 18.2.

Scheduling

Refer to pp. 596A–596D for lecture, classwork, and assignment options for Section 18.2.

★ **Lesson Focus**
Use transparency *LT 60* to prepare students for this section.

READING SKILL BUILDER *Summarizing* Have students read a passage, then ask for volunteers to summarize it for the class. After the summary is completed, have members of the class ask for clarification of parts of the summary. All students may consult the text during the clarification process.

MISCONCEPTION ALERT
Water Vapor Versus Water Droplets Stress to students that water vapor is invisible because it is a gas. Water droplets are condensed water vapor.

18.2

Water and Wind

▶ **KEY TERMS**
water cycle
transpiration
precipitation
humidity
relative humidity
dew point
barometric pressure
Coriolis effect

internetconnect

SCI*LINKS*
NSTA

TOPIC: Water cycle
GO TO: www.scilinks.org
KEYWORD: HK1804

▶ **water cycle** the continuous movement of water from the atmosphere to Earth and back

OBJECTIVES

▶ Describe the three phases of the water cycle.
▶ Explain how temperature and humidity are related.
▶ Identify various cloud types by their appearance and the altitudes at which they typically occur.
▶ Use the concept of pressure gradients to explain how winds are created, and explain how Earth's rotation affects their direction.

You come in contact with water throughout every day, not just when you drink it or when you shower or wash your hands. You experience water in the air because water exists as an invisible gas in the air. It also exists in air as a liquid, suspended in the atmosphere as clouds or fog, or falling as rain or snow. All of this water in the atmosphere affects the weather on Earth.

The Water Cycle

Water is continuously being moved through the troposphere in a process described by the water cycle. **Figure 18-10** shows the main processes that take place in the water cycle.

The major part of the water cycle occurs between the oceans and the continents. Solar energy strikes ocean water, causing water molecules to escape from the liquid and rise as gaseous water vapor. This process, as defined in Chapter 2, is known as evaporation.

Precipitation
Condensation
Transpiration
Evaporation
Ground water

Figure 18-10
Evaporation, transpiration, condensation, and precipitation make up the continuous process called the water cycle.

606 CHAPTER 18

DEMONSTRATION 2 TEACHING

Water Is in the Air

Time: Approximately 10 minutes
Materials: glass container
ice water
food coloring

Step 1 Fill the glass container with ice water.

Step 2 Add a few drops of food coloring to the water to distinguish it from liquid water that condenses on the glass surface.

Step 3 Allow the glass to sit for a few minutes. Have students describe what they observe, and explain how this demonstration proves that water is in the air.
• Does the water seep through the glass?
• Does the water come from the air?
• Why don't the water beads form on the warm container?

On the continents, some evaporation occurs as sunlight strikes water in lakes, rivers, and the soil. But much of the addition of water from land to the air occurs through transpiration. In the process of transpiration, plants lose moisture through small pores in their leaves. While this may seem insignificant, the addition of water vapor to the atmosphere through transpiration can be large. For example, 1 km² of corn typically transpires 3 400 000 L (900 000 gal) of water per day.

In the atmosphere, water vapor rises with warm air until the air is cool enough to condense the vapor into tiny droplets of liquid water. We observe these droplets as clouds. As these clouds cool and condense more vapor, they often release their moisture content in the form of precipitation. The most familiar kinds of precipitation are rain, snow, hail, and sleet. Precipitation can occur over land or water.

When precipitation falls on land, it flows across the surface until it evaporates, flows into a larger body of water, or is absorbed into the ground. *Ground water*, water that is absorbed into the ground, eventually reaches the oceans and evaporates to begin the cycle again.

Air contains varying quantities of water vapor

You have probably noticed that the air doesn't always feel the same. Sometimes it is thick and moist, while at other times it seems crisp and dry. Because the air around you contains various amounts of water vapor, you experience the effects of changing humidity, the quantity of moisture in the atmosphere.

Relative humidity is the actual quantity of water vapor present in the air compared with the maximum quantity of water vapor that can be present at that particular temperature. In weather forecasts, the relative humidity is usually given as a percentage. A relative humidity of 85 percent means that the air contains 85 percent of the water that it can contain at that temperature. A relative humidity of 100 percent means the air contains as much water vapor as is possible at that temperature. Air that has a relative humidity of 100 percent is said to be *saturated*.

Warmer temperatures evaporate more water

As illustrated in **Figure 18-11,** the temperature of the air determines the air's maximum water vapor content. At warm temperatures, molecules move very quickly and are farther apart. Thus, the water is more likely to exist as a gas. As the temperature decreases, the water molecules slow down. At these slower speeds, the attractive forces between water molecules have a greater effect, and the molecules condense into a liquid.

▶ **transpiration** the evaporation of water through pores in a plant's leaves

▶ **precipitation** any form of water that falls back to Earth's surface from clouds; includes rain, snow, sleet, and hail

▶ **humidity** the quantity of water vapor in the atmosphere

▶ **relative humidity** ratio of the quantity of water vapor in the air to the maximum quantity of water vapor that can be present at that temperature

Figure 18-11
Warm temperatures evaporate more water than cold temperatures do.

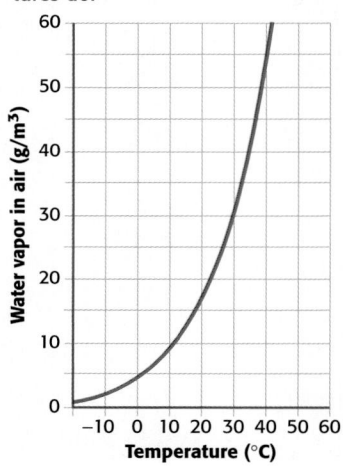

THE ATMOSPHERE **607**

Section 18.2

Water and Wind

INTEGRATING

LIFE SCIENCE When the air is humid, hair becomes frizzy. Hair is made of a protein called keratin. Each hair fiber has a scaly outer cuticle, which you can feel by running your fingers up and down a single hair. The scales allow moisture to enter the inner part of the hair fiber.

When the air is humid, hair absorbs moisture and becomes longer, which makes it frizzy. Hair dries out and becomes shorter when the air is dry. Humidity can cause hair length to change by as much as 2.5 percent. A device called a hair hygrometer can very accurately measure changes in humidity.

Multicultural Extension

Before modern weather instruments were invented, natives on the Chiloé Islands, off the coast of Chile, used shells of the crab *Lithodes antarcticus* to measure relative humidity. A dry shell, normally light gray in color, shows red patches when humidity increases. The shell will become completely red if the humidity continues to rise, as it does during the rainy season.

REAL WORLD APPLICATIONS

Relative Humidity What is the relative humidity today? Have students find out the day's relative humidity by reading the weather section of a newspaper or watching a weather forecast on television.

DEMONSTRATION 3 TEACHING

Transpiration

Time: Approximately 20 minutes (3–4 days to complete)

Materials: plastic bag
rubber band
healthy plant with large leaves

Ask students how they might capture some of the moisture that passes through a plant's pores during transpiration. Allow students to discuss ideas among themselves. If students have trouble coming up with an answer, take a plastic bag and tie it around a large leaf of a healthy plant. Allow the plant to photosynthesize for several days, and watch the moisture appear in the bag eventually.

Condensation Have students breathe onto a mirror and observe the results. The resulting "fog" is actually condensed water droplets. The air you breathe on the mirror is moist; it has water vapor from your mouth in it. As your breath makes contact with the colder mirror, the coolness of the mirror makes the water vapor in your breath condense into water droplets. Relate this activity to the formation of clouds.

Additional Application

Condensation Ask students why they are able to "see their breath" on a cold day but can't on a warm day? (*Water vapor in their breath condenses when it hits the cold air. This does not happen in warm air because condensation only occurs in cold temperatures.*)

Teaching Tip

Cooling Process On a windy day, why might you shiver when you get out of a swimming pool? (*As you get out of the pool, the wind blowing over you is evaporating the water on your body, and because evaporation is a cooling process, it chills you slightly.*)

▶ **dew point** the temperature at which water vapor molecules start to form liquid water

Figure 18-12
Clouds are classified by their form and the altitude at which they occur.

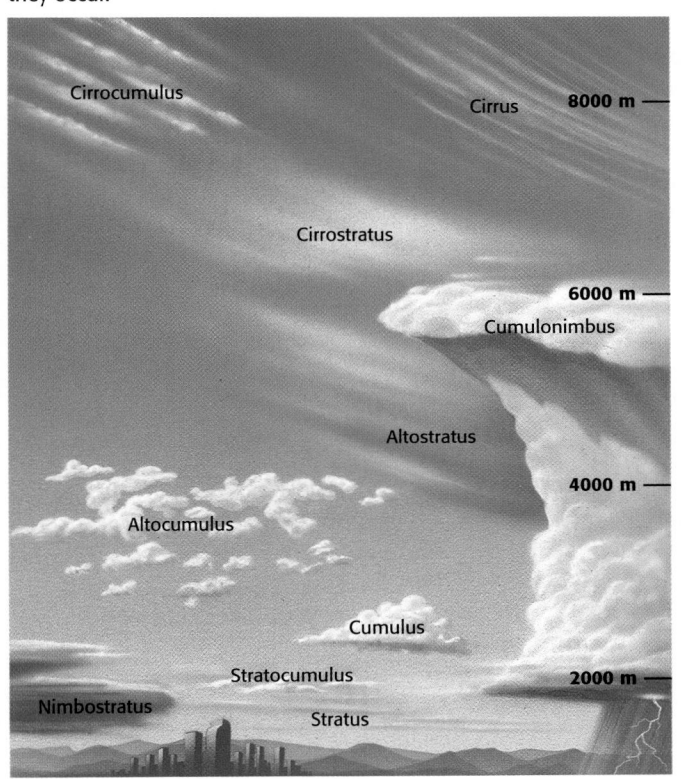

The exact temperature at which water vapor molecules move slowly enough to form liquid water is called the **dew point.** Dew point also depends on the humidity. When the humidity is high, there are more molecules of water vapor in the air and it is easier for them to form liquid water. So the higher the humidity is, the higher the dew point is. In fact, we can measure humidity by finding the dew point.

You may have seen drops of water, or condensation, on a glass of ice water. The cold surface of the glass provides a place where the dew point is reached, and water shifts from gas to liquid.

Clouds form as warm, moist air rises

You may know from walking through fog—a low-lying cloud—that clouds are wet. Clouds are formed when warm air rises and water vapor condenses into tiny droplets of liquid as it cools. This process usually occurs in the troposphere. Clouds are made up of tiny droplets of liquid water and, at higher altitudes, small ice crystals. Depending on where clouds form, they can have many different shapes and characteristics.

Cloud names describe their shape and altitude

Figure 18-12 shows the different kinds of clouds that can occur. Cloud names describe both their appearance and the altitude at which they occur.

There are three main types of clouds: *cirrus, stratus,* and *cumulus.* Cirrus clouds are thin and wispy, and they occur at high altitudes—between 6 km and 11 km (3.7–6.8 mi) above Earth. Stratus clouds are sheetlike and layered. These clouds typically form at lower altitudes—between Earth's surface and about 6 km. Cumulus clouds are white and fluffy with somewhat flat bottoms. The flat base is the point at which rising air begins to condense. Cumulus clouds form at various altitudes—anywhere from about 500 m to about 12 km (1641 ft–7.5 mi) above the Earth.

DEMONSTRATION 4 TEACHING

How to Make a Cloud

Time: Approximately 20 minutes
Materials: 2 L soda bottle
            matches
            water

Step 1 Pour a small amount of water into the bottle.

Step 2 Light one of the matches and hold it in the bottle, so that smoke enters the bottle. The object

is to capture as much smoke in the bottle as possible.

Step 3 Put the lid on the bottle, shake it up (to moisten the air), and then squeeze the bottle and release it quickly. Observe the results. If the cloud is difficult to see, turn off the classroom lights and have a student shine a flashlight at the bottle, so the beam of light is passing through the bottle.

The names of other clouds, as shown in **Figure 18-12,** are combinations of the three root words *cirrus, stratus,* and *cumulus.* These names reflect the combined characteristics of each cloud type. *Cirrostratus* clouds, for instance, are high, layered clouds that form a thin white veil over the sky. *Altostratus* and *altocumulus* clouds are simply stratus and cumulus clouds that occur at middle altitudes. When a cloud name includes the root *nimbo* or *nimbus*—as in *cumulonimbus* and *nimbostratus*—the cloud is the type that produces precipitation. Cumulonimbus clouds are the towering rain clouds that often produce thunderstorms. Nimbostratus clouds are large, featureless gray clouds that often shadow the sky and produce steady precipitation.

You may have seen a halo around the sun or moon. This halo results from the refraction of light as it passes through ice crystals in cirrostratus clouds. Sometimes the presence of a halo is the only way to tell that a very thin, transparent layer of cirrostratus clouds is present.

Air Pressure

The term **barometric pressure** is often used in weather reports in the newspaper and on television. The barometric pressure, also called *atmospheric pressure* or *air pressure,* is the pressure that results from the weight of a column of air extending from the top of the thermosphere to the point of measurement.

Air pressure is measured using a barometer

Both *barometers* shown in **Figure 18-13** are used to measure air pressure. On the left is a photo of a *mercury barometer,* and the photo on the right shows an *aneroid barometer.* Although aneroid barometers are more portable than mercury barometers, mercury barometers are more accurate.

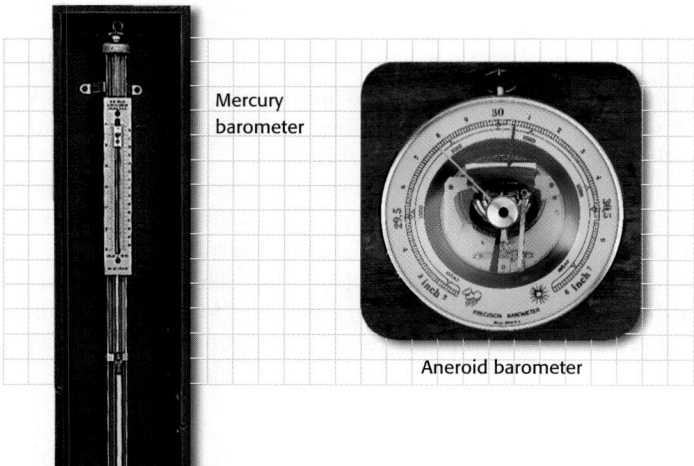
Mercury barometer

Aneroid barometer

Quick ACTIVITY

Measuring Rainfall
1. Set an empty soup can outside in the open, away from any source of runoff. At the same time each day, use a metric ruler to measure the amount of rain or other precipitation that has accumulated in the can.
2. Record your measurements. Keep a record of the precipitation in your area for a week.
3. Listen to or read local weather reports to see if your measurements are close to those given in the reports.

▶ **barometric pressure** the pressure due to the weight of the atmosphere; also called *air pressure* or *atmospheric pressure*

Figure 18-13
Mercury barometers are more accurate than aneroid barometers.

Additional Application

Air Pressure and Barometers Show students a barometer, and tell them that barometers are still widely used in weather forecasting. A low pressure reading on a barometer usually indicates stormy weather while a high pressure reading usually indicates clear weather. Show students how to read a barometer and how to use the movable pointer to track whether air pressure is increasing or decreasing.

Quick ACTIVITY

Measuring Rainfall If you live in a different area than your students, you may want to take a precipitation measurement and compare your results with those of your students. Account for any differences you find.

Resources Have students use Datasheet 18.1 to record their results.

THE ATMOSPHERE **609**

Squeezing the bottle increases the temperature of the air, enabling it to hold more moisture. Releasing the bottle reduces the temperature and promotes condensation of the water vapor. Clouds need condensation nuclei, or small bits of dust or dirt, to condense around. In this case, the smoke from the match served as the condensation nuclei.

INTEGRATING

BIOLOGY Middle ear barotrauma is an earache caused by a difference in pressure between the air and a person's middle ear. Although airplane cabins are pressurized, passengers still feel the pressure decrease as the plane climbs and increase as the plane descends.

The trauma occurs when the Eustachian tube, a passageway between the middle ear and the throat, fails to open wide enough to equalize the pressure. Chewing gum, yawning, or swallowing often alleviates the condition.

Additional Application

How Does Pressure Affect Air? Blow up a balloon and then release it. Have the students watch the balloon travel around the room. Ask them to explain what made the balloon move from one place to another. *(By blowing air into the balloon and forcing the air into a small space, you put that air under high pressure. The air outside the balloon is at a lower pressure. When you released the balloon, the high pressure air escaped to the low pressure air outside. As the high-pressure air escaped, it pushed the balloon away.)*

Have your students relate this demonstration to the formation of winds.

RESOURCE LINK

IER

Assign students worksheet *18.1 Integrating Health—Why Your Ears Pop* in the **Integration Enrichment Resources** ancillary.

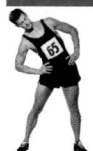

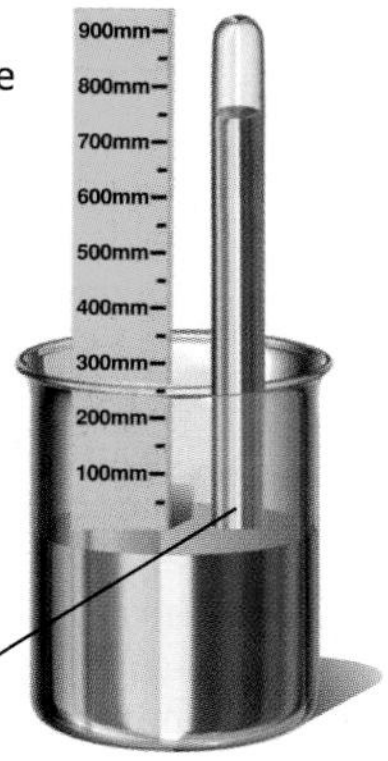
900mm
800mm
700mm
600mm
500mm
400mm
300mm
200mm
100mm
Mercury

Figure 18-14 The height of the mercury in the tube of a mercury barometer indicates the barometric pressure in millimeters.

Figure 18-14 is an illustration of how a simple mercury barometer works. The mercury barometer contains a long tube that is open at one end and closed at the other. The tube is filled with mercury and then inverted into a small container of mercury. Once in place, some but not all of the mercury spills out of the tube and into the container. The atmosphere exerts a pressure on the mercury in the container, holding some of the mercury in the tube to some height above the mercury in the container. Any change in the height of the column of mercury means that the atmosphere's pressure has changed.

At sea level, the barometric pressure of air at 0°C is around 760 mm of mercury. This amount of pressure is defined as 1 atmosphere (1 atm) of pressure. The SI unit for pressure is the pascal (Pa), which is equivalent to one newton per square meter.

Aneroid barometers are more commonly used. The word *aneroid* means "without liquid." This type of barometer contains a sealed metal chamber from which part of the air has been removed. When the air pressure changes, the chamber expands or contracts, moving a needle on a dial.

INTEGRATING

HEALTH

Just as air exerts pressure on the objects around it, blood in your body exerts pressure against the walls of your arteries. To measure a person's blood pressure, a cuff is wrapped around the upper arm and a stethoscope is placed over the arteries of the forearm. Air is pumped into the cuff until the pressure exerted by the cuff stops the flow of blood.

The doctor or nurse then listens to the person's pulse as air is let out slowly until the pressure in the cuff is less than the blood pressure when the heart contracts. This pressure is called the *systolic* pressure.

More air is released until the pulsing of the heart is no longer audible. The pressure at this point, called the *diastolic* pressure, is the blood pressure when the heart relaxes.

Wind

Have you ever seen a movie in which an airplane window gets broken? When the window breaks, all the loose objects in the plane are pushed out the window. Although it is unlikely that an airplane window would actually break, the portrayal of objects flying out the window is correct.

Differences in pressure create winds

Commercial airplanes fly very high in the troposphere, between 10 km and 13 km above Earth. At this altitude, the air is not very dense and the atmospheric pressure is very low. The pressure inside the airplane, however, is relatively high—similar to the air pressure at Earth's surface.

If an airplane window were to break, the densely packed air in the plane's cabin would spread out into the less densely packed air outside the cabin. The airflow produced in this situation would push loose objects out the window.

Just as a difference in air pressure would create airflow from inside the airplane to the outside, differences in pressure in the atmosphere can cause wind. When air pressure varies from one place to another, a *pressure gradient* exists. The air in a pressure gradient moves from areas of high pressure to areas of low pressure. This movement of air from a high-pressure area to a low-pressure area is called wind.

DEMONSTRATION 5 SCIENCE AND THE CONSUMER

Windsocks

Time: Approximately 40 minutes

Materials: old bed sheet
pillow cases or fabric remnants
scissors
stapler
dowels (1 m long)
wire, wire cutters

SAFETY CAUTION: *Be careful when handling wire pieces because the ends may be sharp.*

Step 1 Cut the wire into pieces long enough to bend into a 20 cm diameter circle and still wrap the ends around one end of the dowel.

Step 2 Draw a square with 63 cm sides on the fabric.

Step 3 Draw a line from each lower corner to the midpoint of the top, forming a large triangle.

Earth's rotation affects the direction of winds

The direction in which wind moves is influenced by Earth's rotation. The effect of Earth's rotation on the direction of wind is described by the **Coriolis effect.**

To understand how the Coriolis effect works, you must first understand that points at different latitudes on Earth move at different speeds as the Earth rotates. Consider two houses at different latitudes. A house located on the equator travels faster than a house located near one of the poles. Can you see why this must be true? Earth goes through one full rotation in 24 hours. During this time, the house at the equator must travel the distance of Earth's circumference. Closer to the poles, a circle of latitude is smaller. Therefore, the house closer to the pole moves through a shorter distance in the same amount of time. Thus, this house moves more slowly.

Now imagine a cannonball in a cannon at the equator. The cannonball is moving along with Earth as it rotates. The cannonball's speed at this time is a little greater than 1610 km/h (1000 mi/h) to the east—the speed at which all points on the equator move because of Earth's rotation. When the cannonball is fired to the north, it continues to move east at about 1610 km/hr. As the cannonball moves farther north, however, the Earth beneath the cannonball is moving more slowly. The result is a flight path like the one depicted in **Figure 18-15.** The cannonball's path appears to curve eastward relative to the Earth below.

The movement of winds is analogous to the cannonball's movement. When moving north in the Northern Hemisphere, winds curve to the right. Conversely, winds moving south from the equator curve to the left.

Now consider air moving south from the North Pole. In this case, the wind would lag behind the rotation of Earth and travel west, or to the right, relative to the ground below, because it has a slower speed than the spinning Earth. Similarly, wind moving north from the South Pole would travel west, or to the left, in respect to the ground beneath it because of its slower speed.

In summary, *winds in the Northern Hemisphere curve clockwise, and winds in the Southern Hemisphere curve counterclockwise.* The resulting circulation patterns are so regular that meteorologists have named them. **Figure 18-16** shows the directions and names of the global wind patterns.

▶ **Coriolis effect** the change in the direction of an object's path due to Earth's rotation

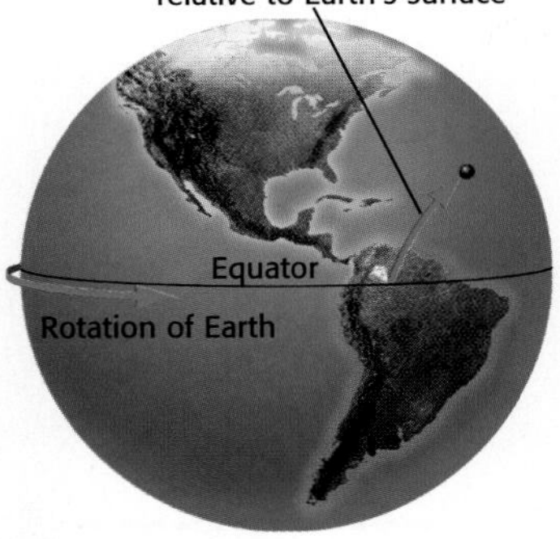

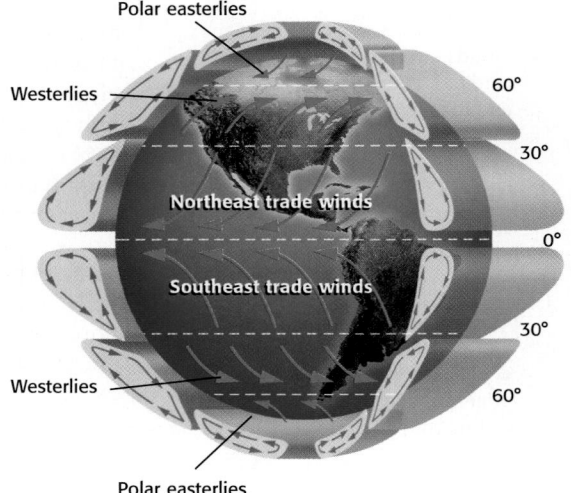

Path of cannonball relative to Earth's surface

Equator

Rotation of Earth

Figure 18-15
Because of Earth's rotation, a cannonball fired directly north from the equator will curve to the east relative to Earth's surface.

Figure 18-16
Both the Northern Hemisphere and the Southern Hemisphere have three wind belts.

Polar easterlies

Westerlies

Northeast trade winds

Southeast trade winds

Westerlies

Polar easterlies

60°

30°

0°

30°

60°

THE ATMOSPHERE **611**

Section 18.2

Water and Wind

READING SKILL BUILDER *Summarizing* Have students read the passage on the Coriolis effect, then ask for a volunteer to summarize the passage. Allow students to ask for clarification and to consult their text.

Did You Know ?

For the same reason that winds are deflected clockwise in the Northern Hemisphere and counterclockwise in the Southern Hemisphere, ocean currents are deflected in the same directions.

Connection to SOCIAL STUDIES

Have students research how sailing ships took advantage of trade winds and ocean currents.

RESOURCE LINK
LABORATORY MANUAL

Have students perform *Lab 18 The Atmosphere: Predicting Coastal Winds* in the lab ancillary. Have students use Datasheet 18.3 to record their results.

Step 4 Cut out this triangle with scissors. Fold the triangle so the sides meet and overlap about 1 cm.

Step 5 Staple the edges together, and cut off the tip of the triangle.

Step 6 Bend the wire into a 20 cm diameter circle, and wrap the extra wire around the end of the dowel.

Step 7 Roll the bottom edge of the windsock around the wire and staple it.

Step 8 Once you have a finished windsock, take your students outside and use a directional compass to determine the direction of the wind.

Water and Wind

Have students research some of the names that have been given to winds in various parts of the world. Why do these winds have the names they do? How do these winds affect parts of the world? *(Winds to research include but are not limited to: monsoons, jet streams, williwaws, Pineapple Express, Chinooks, mistrals, and Santa Ana.)*

SECTION 18.2 REVIEW

Check Your Understanding

1. c
2. eastward
3. Humidity is the quantity of water vapor (moisture) in the air, while relative humidity is the quantity of water vapor in the air compared with the maximum quantity of water vapor that can be present at a given temperature.
4. b
5. c
6. The Texas coast on a warm day would be more humid because along the coastline there is water that can evaporate into the air, unlike in the Sahara Desert.
7. The air is under less pressure where it is less densely packed, inside your lungs.

RESOURCE LINK
STUDY GUIDE

Assign students *Review Section 18.2 Water and Wind* before beginning Section 18.3.

Global wind patterns form circulation cells

Note that the wind patterns shown in **Figure 18-16** move in vertical loops. Because temperatures at the equator tend to be warmer than at other latitudes, the air there rises and creates a low-pressure belt. As this warm air rises, it moves toward the poles.

In the Northern Hemisphere, much of the northward-moving air sinks at about 30° latitude, forming a high pressure area near Earth's surface. Flowing from a high-pressure area to a low-pressure area, air flows both north and south. At about 60° latitude, air flowing along the surface from the polar high and the high pressure band at 30° converge. As these air masses converge, air rises, forming a low-pressure belt.

A similar circulation pattern, in which rising warm air is coupled with sinking cold air, occurs in the Southern Hemisphere. Thus, air in each of the hemispheres completes three loops, called *cells*.

SECTION 18.2 REVIEW

SUMMARY

▶ In the water cycle, water from oceans and lakes evaporates and rises in the atmosphere. After it cools and condenses, the water falls back to Earth as precipitation.

▶ Warm air can contain more water vapor than cold air.

▶ Clouds are classified according to their appearance and the altitude at which they occur. **Figure 18-12** summarizes the various types of clouds.

▶ Wind is caused by the air in a pressure gradient moving from a high-pressure area to a low-pressure area.

▶ Earth's rotation affects the direction of winds. This phenomenon is described by the Coriolis effect.

CHECK YOUR UNDERSTANDING

1. **Identify** which one of the following processes is not a step in the water cycle:
   a. evaporation   c. photosynthesis
   b. condensation   d. precipitation
2. **Determine** whether wind moving north from the equator will curve eastward or westward due to the Coriolis effect.
3. **Distinguish** between humidity and relative humidity.
4. **Select** which one of the following describes a cumulus cloud:
   a. sheetlike
   b. fluffy, white, and flat-bottomed
   c. wispy and feathery
   d. high altitude
5. **Identify** which one of the following statements describes a mercury barometer:
   a. less accurate than an aneroid barometer
   b. contains a chamber that has a lot of water inside
   c. the height of the mercury in the tube indicates the barometric pressure
   d. more commonly used than aneroid barometers
6. **Predict** which of the following would be a more humid area: the Sahara Desert on a cold night or the Texas coast on a warm day.
7. **Critical Thinking** Which has a lower pressure, the air in your lungs as you inhale or the air outside your body?

Weather and Climate

OBJECTIVES

▶ Describe the formation of cold fronts and warm fronts.
▶ Describe various severe weather situations, including thunderstorms, tornadoes, and hurricanes.
▶ Analyze weather maps.
▶ Distinguish between climate and weather.
▶ Identify factors that affect Earth's climate or that have changed it over time.

▶ KEY TERMS

air mass
front
isobar
climate
topography

Scheduling
Refer to pp. 596A–596D for lecture, classwork, and assignment options for Section 18.3

★ **Lesson Focus**
Use transparency *LT 61* to prepare students for this section.

READING SKILL BUILDER *Reading Organizer* Have students read the section on fronts. Each student should construct a table with the following column headings: *Warm front, Cold front,* and *Stationary front.* Have them create two rows with these headings: *Associated weather, Associated clouds,* and *Diagram.* Students should use information from the text to fill in their table.

SKILL BUILDER

Interpreting Visuals Have students examine **Figure 18-17,** and use it to describe what happens with a warm front. What kinds of clouds are associated with warm fronts? *(cirrus, cirrostratus, altostratus, and nimbostratus)* What kind of weather is associated with warm fronts? *(clouds, rain, sometimes snow)*

ow is a weather forecast made? *Meteorologists,* people who study weather, gather data about weather conditions in different areas. By using maps, meteorologists can try to predict weather by tracking the movement of warmer or cooler air pockets called **air masses.** Interactions between air masses have predictable effects on the weather in a given location.

internetconnect

SCI LINKS
NSTA

TOPIC: Severe weather
GO TO: www.scilinks.org
KEYWORD: HK1805

Fronts and Severe Weather

You have probably heard about *cold fronts* moving down from the northwest and *warm fronts* moving in from the southeast. A **front** is the place where a cold air mass and a warm air mass meet. Clouds, rain, and sometimes snow can occur at fronts. When fronts move through an area, the result is usually precipitation and a change in wind direction and temperature.

In a warm front, a mass of warm air moves toward and over a slower mass of cold air, as shown in **Figure 18-17.** As the warm air is pushed up over the cool air, it cools and forms clouds.

▶ **air mass** a large body of air with uniform temperature and moisture content

▶ **front** the boundary between air masses of different densities

Figure 18-17
In a warm front, a warm air mass moves above a slower cold air mass.

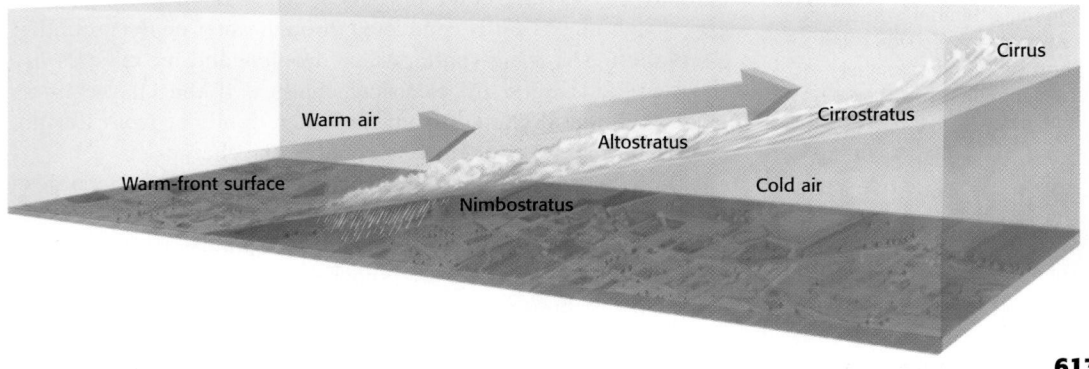

613

DEMONSTRATION 6 TEACHING

A Cold Front Meets a Warm Front

Time: Approximately 10 minutes
Materials: cold water
warm water dyed with food coloring
a transparent container

Fill the container with the warm, dyed water. Next, slowly pour a small amount of the cold water down the side the container. Have your students comment on the results and apply them to cold and warm fronts. *(The cold water represents a cold front. When these types of fronts meet, the cold air slides under the warm front and pushes it up because the cold air is denser.)*

Interpreting Visuals Have students examine **Figure 18-18,** and use it to describe what happens with a cold front. What kinds of clouds are associated with cold fronts? *(cumulonimbus)* What kind of weather is associated with cold fronts? *(high winds, thunderstorms, and sometimes tornadoes)*

Teaching Tip

Coriolis Effect Make sure students understand that the two air masses that move side by side along a stationary front move in opposite directions. The winds blow in opposite directions as a result of the Coriolis effect.

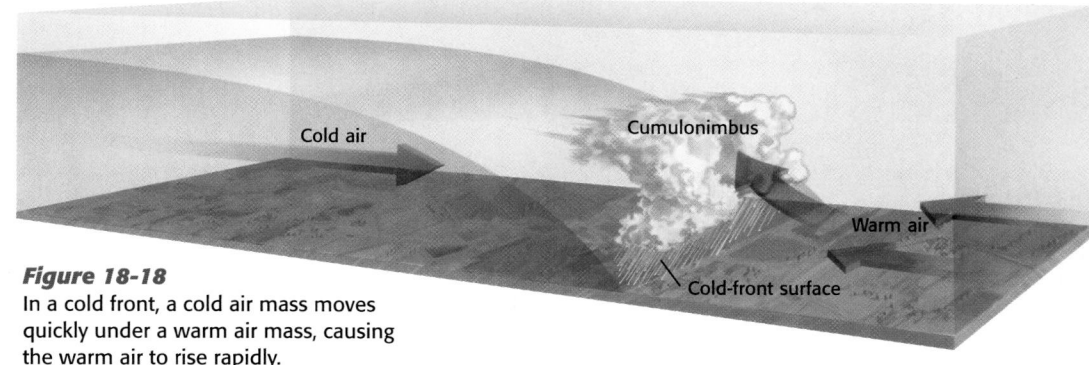

Figure 18-18
In a cold front, a cold air mass moves quickly under a warm air mass, causing the warm air to rise rapidly.

Cirrus and cirrostratus clouds can be seen high in the sky as a warm front approaches. As time passes, lower-lying clouds move overhead. Often, nimbostratus clouds release steady rain or snow for one to two days.

With a cold front, the forward edge of a mass of cold air moves under a slower mass of warm air and pushes it up, as shown in **Figure 18-18.** Note that the front edge of the cold front is steeper than that of the warm front shown in **Figure 18-17.** Because of this steep edge, warm air rises quickly, forming cumulonimbus clouds. High winds, thunderstorms, and sometimes tornadoes accompany this type of front.

A *stationary front* occurs when two air masses meet but neither is displaced. Instead, the air masses move side by side along the front. The weather conditions near a stationary front are similar to those near a warm front.

Did You Know ?

If you count 10 s or less between seeing a lightning strike and hearing its corresponding thunder, you should seek protective cover. This short count indicates that the lightning is less than 2 mi away.

Lightning is a discharge of atmospheric electrical energy

Lightning is a dangerous element of nature that occurs in the atmosphere during a thunderstorm. Thunderstorms can be very exciting to watch and listen to, but they can also be very dangerous if lightning strikes the ground somewhere near you. The electrical energy of lightning is easily conducted through water on the ground.

Lightning is a big spark. Water droplets and ice crystals in thunderclouds build up electrical charges. If the charge in a cloud is different enough from the other clouds or from Earth, sparks jump between the two to equalize the charge.

Thunder is the noise that is made when electrical charges move through the air as lightning. When lightning occurs, it superheats the air. As the air is heated, it expands faster than the speed of sound. We hear the shockwave created by this rapid expansion as thunder.

ALTERNATIVE ASSESSMENT

Fronts

After performing Demonstration 6 on page 613, ask students if an airline pilot should avoid flying into an area where two different fronts are meeting. Have students explain their answers.

...REAL WORLD APPLICATIONS

Calculating the Distance to a Thunderstorm How can you tell if lightning is close or far away? The distance can be determined by counting the seconds between the lightning flash and the sound of thunder. This time lag occurs because light travels so fast it reaches you almost immediately, whereas sound travels more slowly and takes longer to reach you. Count the seconds between the flash of lightning and the sound of thunder, and use the following calculation:

time (s)/3 = distance (km)
time (s)/5 = distance (mi)

Applying Information
1. You see lightning in the distance and begin counting in seconds. When you reach the count of 3, you hear thunder. How far away, in kilometers, was the lightning when it struck?
2. At 3:37:45 P.M., you see lightning strike. You hear the

associated thunder at 3:38:03 P.M. How many miles away did the lightning strike?

Tornadoes are funnels of high-speed wind

Figure 18-19 is a photo of a tornado. Tornadoes are high-speed, rotating winds that extend downward from thunderclouds. Tornadic winds are the most violent winds to occur on Earth. Wind speeds in the most violent tornadoes are thought to be as great as 500 km/h (about 310 mi/h).

Tornadoes occur most commonly in the United States, especially in the Midwest and in states along the Gulf of Mexico. They tend to occur during spring and early summer.

In the United States, tornadoes typically form along a front between cool, dry air from the north and warm, humid air from the Gulf of Mexico. As warm, humid air rises, more warm air rushes in to replace it. This warm air sometimes begins to rotate as it rises and can become a strong rotating thunderstorm that can spawn a tornado.

Typically a tornado begins as a tapered column of water droplets, called a *funnel cloud*, that reaches down from dark storm clouds with heavy rain and lightning. As the funnel reaches the ground, it begins sucking objects upward as air rises through its center. The rotating winds on the outer edge of a tornado can tear apart homes and trees.

Tornadoes are too fast and unpredictable to attempt to outrun, even if you are in a car. If you see a tornado approaching, move to a storm cellar or basement. The forces caused by tornadic winds can easily lift trailer homes and destroy houses. If a cellar is not available, lie flat under a table at the center of a room with few windows. If you are outside, lie in a ditch or low-lying area, and cover your head with your hands.

Figure 18-19
Tornadoes, such as this one that occurred in Pampa, Texas, in 1995, can be seen as rapidly spinning funnel clouds.

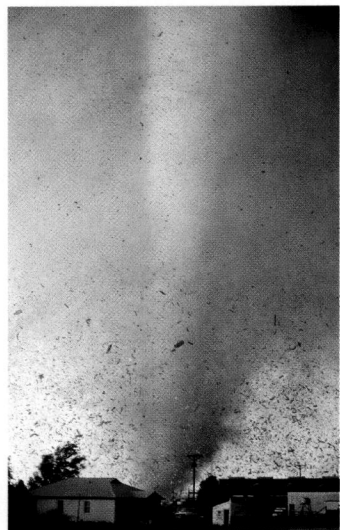

THE ATMOSPHERE **615**

REAL WORLD APPLICATIONS

Applying Information

1. 1 km
2. $\frac{58}{5}$ = 12 mi

Resources Assign students worksheet *18.2: Real World Applications—Understanding Thunderstorms* in the **Integration Enrichment Resources** ancillary.

SKILL BUILDER

Interpreting Visuals Have students examine the tornado pictured in **Figure 18-19.** Ask them to write a creative story about an object that becomes trapped in a tornado. Be sure that their stories have some of the scientific elements in them that are described in the text.

Teaching Tip

Creating a Tornado Use this demonstration to model a tornado vortex. You will need a clean, empty jar with its lid, water, food coloring, a teaspoon of liquid dishwashing detergent, and a teaspoon of vinegar. Fill the jar about three-quarters full of water. Add a few drops of food coloring, the soap, and the vinegar to the water. Cap the jar tightly and shake it vigorously. Once the solution is mixed, give the jar a quick twist with a flick of the wrist. Students will observe that a vortex forms.

Historical Perspective

Hurricanes played a significant role in early colonial history. In 1609, a fleet of ships with settlers from England bound for Virginia was blown off course by a hurricane. Some of the ships landed in Bermuda, and the settlers started the first European colony there.

INTEGRATING

ASTRONOMY   Wind speeds on Jupiter reach up to 540 km/h. Storms last for decades, and one—the Great Red Spot of Jupiter—has been swirling around since it was first discovered in 1664. The Great Red Spot has a diameter of more than one and a half times that of the Earth. It is like a hurricane that has lasted more than 300 years.

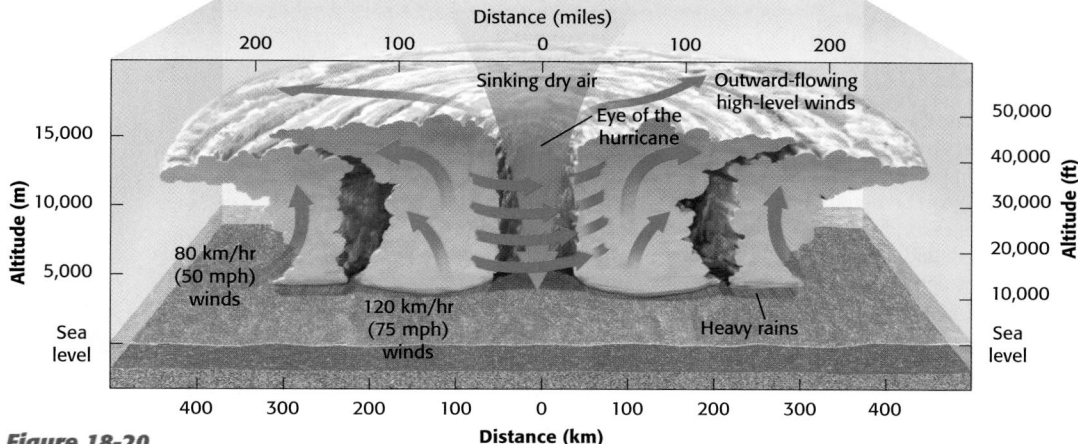

Figure 18-20
Hurricanes are nearly circular in shape and rotate around a center called the eye.

Hurricanes are large storm systems

Hurricanes are similar to thunderstorms but are much larger. Whereas these storms are called hurricanes in North America and the Caribbean, they are called *cyclones* in the Indian Ocean and *typhoons* in the western Pacific.

In the Northern Hemisphere, hurricanes occur in late summer and early fall, when the ocean temperatures are warmest. As the warm ocean water evaporates and the water vapor rises, intense low-pressure areas called *tropical depressions* form. As these tropical depressions build strength, they can become hurricanes. As shown in **Figure 18-20,** hurricanes are large circulating masses of clouds, wind, and rain with average diameters of about 600 km (373 mi).

Hurricanes are powered by the energy released as water vapor condenses to form clouds. As this condensation releases energy, the air heats and expands, and the pressure inside the clouds decreases. Warm, moist air continues to rise toward the low pressure area and condenses, releasing more energy. This rising air creates fierce winds, shown by the red arrows in **Figure 18-20,** that swirl upward around the eye of the storm. When the storm moves over land or cool water, it gradually weakens.

Although hurricanes move fairly slowly, they are extremely powerful. To be classified as a hurricane, winds in a storm must reach speeds greater than 118 km/h (73 mi/h). Winds in intense hurricanes can reach speeds greater than 250 km/h (155 mi/h).

The eye of the hurricane is very calm and free of clouds, as shown on **Figure 18-20.** This can be very dangerous because people often believe the storm has passed and leave the protective cover of their homes only to be caught in the storm again.

Weather Maps

Meteorologists use weather maps like the one shown in **Figure 18-21** when they are preparing forecasts. These maps use different symbols, such as the ones shown in Appendix B, to show weather conditions such as precipitation, wind speed, and cloud coverage. On the wind-speed symbol, wind direction is indicated by the direction from which the line comes into the circle.

Lines called **isobars** show points of equal barometric pressure. When isobars are close together, the wind is stronger. The number that appears on the isobar denotes the barometric pressure at points along the line.

Look at the wind directions in **Figure 18-21.** You might expect that winds would always blow perpendicular to isobars, from high-pressure areas to low-pressure areas. Instead, the map shows that winds near Earth's surface are directed slightly across isobars toward areas of lower pressure. This is because the direction of the wind is changed by the Coriolis effect. Because of the combined effects of force, the Coriolis effect, and friction, near-surface winds in the Northern Hemisphere generally travel across the isobars with higher pressure areas on the right.

When isobars form a closed loop, the center of the loop is called a *pressure center*. Low pressure centers (L) are areas where the air pressure is generally lower than the surrounding areas. These *lows* are usually accompanied by clouds and precipitation. High pressure centers (H), on the other hand, usually mark regions of fair weather.

Climate

Weather is something that changes day to day, moment to moment. Climate, on the other hand, does not change as readily. Climate is the *average* weather of a region, often measured over many years. Just as a student may receive several grades above 90 percent but still have an 85 percent average, the weather in a region may be cold and overcast on some days but still have a warm and sunny climate overall.

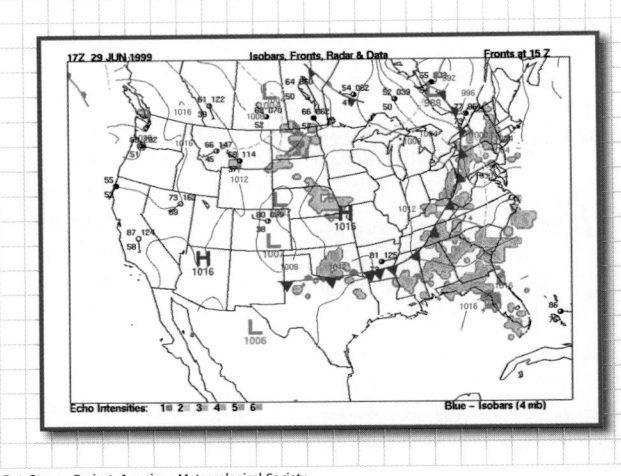

DataStreme Project, American Meteorological Society

Figure 18-21
A typical weather map shows isobars, highs and lows, fronts, wind direction and speed, temperature, and precipitation.

▶ **isobar** a line drawn on a weather map connecting points of equal barometric or atmospheric pressure

▶ **climate** the general weather conditions over many years

THE ATMOSPHERE **617**

Teaching Tip

Weather Prediction
Throughout history, people have predicted approaching weather by interpreting natural signs. Animals and plants are usually more sensitive to changes in the atmosphere—such as changes in air pressure, humidity, and temperature—than are humans.

Have students research natural signs for predicting weather and write a short report. Also have students answer the following question: If you did not have access to the weather forecast on the news, radio, or television, how would you forecast the weather? Students should include their answer in their reports.

APPLICATIONS ·····················

Weather Obtain the weather section of the local newspaper. Challenge students to decipher the weather map with the help of the key. Ask them to describe all aspects of the weather for various geographical points across the country.

Resources Assign students worksheet *18.7: Integrating Technology—Doppler Weather Radar* in the **Integration Enrichment Resources** ancillary.

·······························

Weather and Climate

Weather and climate have inspired many rhymes, greetings, sayings, and other folklore. For example, in the hot, wet climate of Venezuela, indigenous people sometimes greet each other by saying, "How have the mosquitoes used you?" Russia's cold climate inspired the saying, "There's no bad weather, only bad clothing."

Invite students to interview friends and relatives or research weather and climate folklore in another country. Have them share their findings with the class.

Figure 18-22
When Earth's equator faces the sun directly, the solar energy is more concentrated than it is closer to the poles.

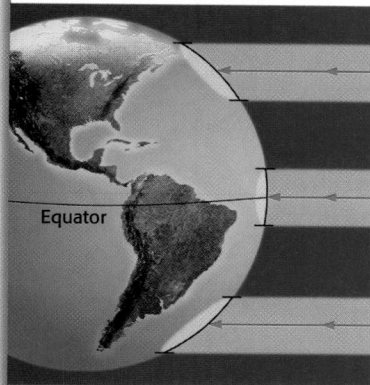

Equator

Figure 18-23
This illustration (not to scale) shows that Earth's axis is tilted 23.5° from the perpendicular to the orbital plane. The direction of tilt of Earth's axis remains the same throughout Earth's orbit.

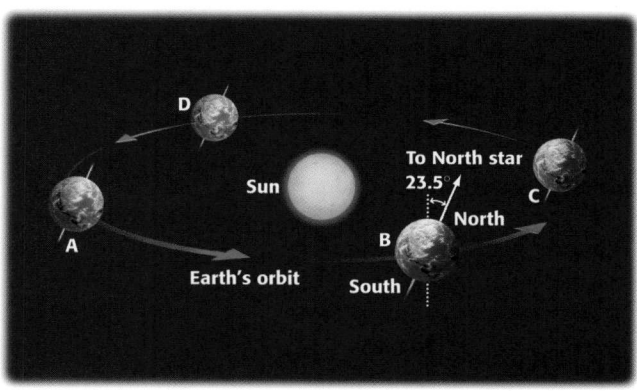

Temperatures tend to be higher close to the equator

Imagine sunlight striking Earth, as shown in **Figure 18-22.** Rays striking farther from the equator spread out over a greater area of Earth's surface and therefore are less concentrated than rays that strike Earth at the equator. At the poles, rays pass parallel to Earth's surface and do not warm the atmosphere as much. Hence, the poles are very cold.

Earth is not always oriented so that the equator is perpendicular to incoming solar radiation. However, the equator is closer to perpendicular to the incoming sunlight throughout the year than are areas closer to the poles. Because of this, countries and islands close to the equator usually have warmer climates.

Earth's tilt and rotation account for our seasons

Another major factor that affects climate is the cycling of our seasons. In summer months, the sun appears high in the sky and the days are longer and warmer. But in winter months, the sun does not appear very high, and the days are shorter and colder.

Why do we experience these differing conditions on such a regular basis? Having read in the chapter on the universe that Earth's orbit is an ellipse, you might expect that summertime corresponds with the times of year when the Earth is closest to the sun. This is not true. In fact, Earth is farthest from the sun on July 4 and closest to the sun on about January 3. Earth's seasons are actually caused by the tilt of Earth on its axis.

As shown in **Figure 18-23,** Earth's axis is tilted 23.5° from the perpendicular to the plane of the planet's orbit about the sun. Although there can be tiny changes in the amount of tilt, Earth maintains this orientation as it orbits the sun. Because of this tilted orientation, the sun seems to rise to different heights in the sky at different times of the year.

When the North Pole is tilted toward the sun, as it is in position A in **Figure 18-23,** the sun rises higher in the Northern Hemisphere than when the North Pole is pointed away from the sun. When this occurs, the days in the Northern Hemisphere become longer and the temperature increases. This is summer in the Northern Hemisphere and winter in the Southern Hemisphere. The longest day of the year in the Northern Hemisphere, the *summer solstice,* occurs on approximately June 21.

When the South Pole is tilted toward the sun, as it is in position C in **Figure 18-23,** the sun rises higher in the Southern Hemisphere than when the South Pole is pointed away from the sun. In other words, it is summer in the Southern Hemisphere and winter in the Northern Hemisphere. The shortest day of the year in the Northern Hemisphere occurs on December 21. This day is called the *winter solstice*.

At positions B and D, Earth's axis is tilted neither away from nor toward the sun. When this occurs, day and night are of equal length all over the Earth. The day on which this happens is called an *equinox*. Position D corresponds to the *vernal* (spring) *equinox* in the Northern Hemisphere and occurs around March 21. Position B, on the other hand, occurs on about September 22 and is called the *autumnal* (fall) *equinox* in the Northern Hemisphere.

Earth's surface features affect climate

The rise and fall of a land surface is called topography. The hills, mountains, valleys, and wide stretches of flat surface in Earth's topography all affect the climate of a region.

Mountains can have a profound effect on the climate of an area. Tall mountains force air to rise over them. As the air rises, it cools, and clouds form. When mountains are near oceans, as shown in **Figure 18-24,** the rising air is usually so humid that the resulting clouds cannot hold all of the condensed water vapor, and precipitation results. This rain or snow is dropped over the mountains. On the other side of the mountain range, this cool, dry air warms as it descends. The deserts that form on this side of the mountain are said to lie in a rain shadow.

Broad flat surfaces, such as the Great Plains of North America, do not stop wind flow very well. Winds can come from several directions and merge on the plains. During certain seasons, this mixing of wind produces thunderstorms and even tornadoes.

Warm air cools as it rises.

Cool air warms as it descends.

Figure 18-24
Air passing over a mountain range loses its moisture as it rises and cools. This dense, dry air warms as it descends the other side of the mountain.

THE ATMOSPHERE **619**

INTEGRATING

PHYSICS

Large bodies of water regulate local climates because water has a high specific heat. For instance, even though Minneapolis, Minnesota, in the Midwest, and Portland, Oregon, along the Pacific Coast, are at about the same latitude, they have very different climates. The difference is caused by the Pacific Ocean. During winter months, the ocean does not get as cold as the surrounding air. As a result, Pacific winds warm the Oregon coastline. Meanwhile, Minneapolis has no large body of water to regulate its temperature.

In summertime, the Pacific Ocean does not get as warm as the surrounding air, and Pacific winds cool Portland. Minneapolis does not receive cool ocean breezes during the summertime.

▶ **topography** the surface features of Earth

INTEGRATING

PHYSICS
Resources Assign students worksheet *18.3: Integrating Physics—Adobe* in the **Integration Enrichment Resources** ancillary

Additional Application
Topography Remind students that topography is an important factor in the formation of a temperature inversion in areas like the Los Angeles Basin, as explained on p. 599. In this way, topography can affect air quality as well as climate.

SKILL BUILDER
Interpreting Visuals Have students examine **Figure 18-24** and explain all aspects of the diagram. Make sure they incorporate the words *evaporation* and *condensation* in their explanations.

RESOURCE LINK
IER
Assign students worksheet *18.4: Integrating Physics—The Tropopause* in the **Integration Enrichment Resources** ancillary.

Weather and Climate

SECTION 18.3 REVIEW

Check Your Understanding

1. c
2. Lightning is a large spark that results from the buildup of electrical charges in the atmosphere, and thunder is the noise that results from the shock wave that is produced when electrical charges move through the air as lightning.
3. c
4. **a.** warm front
   b. cold front
   c. cold front
   d. warm front
5. A tornado is more likely to form along a cold front.
6. Wind speed will be greater when isobar lines are closer together.
7. You would recommend planting grapes on the California coast because large bodies of water can regulate local climates. Plains do not stop wind flow, which can result in severe weather.

Global climate changes over time

From the warm, lifeless early atmosphere to the many ice ages characterized by glaciers covering much of the continents, Earth's global climate has varied greatly over time. Many factors, such as the changes in the position of the continents and slight changes in Earth's tilt, have produced these climatic variations.

If the greenhouse effect increases because of increased carbon dioxide in the atmosphere, temperatures could rise. Volcanic eruptions can produce gases that condense in the atmosphere and reflect solar energy, causing cooling. Because of all the factors that determine global climate, Earth's climate is likely to continue to change over the millennia to come.

SECTION 18.3 REVIEW

SUMMARY

▶ A warm front forms as a warm air mass moves over a slower cold air mass. A cold front forms as a cold air mass moves under a slower warm air mass.

▶ Lightning is a discharge of atmospheric electrical energy.

▶ Tornadoes are high-speed rotating winds that form as air begins to rotate around quickly rising warm air.

▶ Hurricanes are large storm systems that are characterized by high-speed winds and very low pressures.

▶ Symbols on weather maps explain a variety of weather conditions.

▶ Climate is the average weather of a region over a length of time, usually many years.

▶ Some factors that affect climate are latitude, seasons, and topography.

CHECK YOUR UNDERSTANDING

1. **Identify** which of the following is NOT a factor of global climate change:
   a. slight changes in Earth's tilt
   b. movement of continents
   c. reversing of the magnetic poles
   d. increase or decrease of solar energy
2. **Distinguish** between thunder and lightning.
3. **Identify** which of the following probably would not have an effect on the climate of a region:
   a. the region is next to a mountain range
   b. the region is on the equator
   c. a thunderstorm just blew through the region
   d. the region is next to the Atlantic Ocean
4. **Determine** whether each of the following statements describes a warm front or a cold front:
   a. A warm air mass moves above a slower cold air mass.
   b. It is characterized by high winds and thunderstorms.
   c. A cold air mass moves quickly under a slower-moving warm air mass.
   d. It is characterized by steady rain.
5. **Determine** whether a tornado is more likely to form along a cold front or a warm front.
6. **Predict** whether wind speed will be greater when isobar lines on a weather map are closer together or farther apart.
7. **Critical Thinking** Grapes grow well in areas where the climate is generally mild. Would you recommend planting grapes on the California coast or on the plains of North Dakota? Explain your answer.

620 CHAPTER 18

RESOURCE LINK
STUDY GUIDE

Assign students *Review Section 18.3 Weather and Climate*

Chapter Highlights

Before you begin, review the summaries of the key ideas of each section, found on pages 605, 612, and 620. The key vocabulary terms are listed on pages 598, 606, and 613.

UNDERSTANDING CONCEPTS

1. Around Los Angeles, frequent temperature inversions are the result of cool, polluted air being trapped by _____.
   a. acid rain
   b. a layer of warmer air
   c. a thunderstorm
   d. the ocean
2. The _____ is the process in which the atmosphere traps warming solar energy near Earth's surface.
   a. summer solstice   c. greenhouse effect
   b. Coriolis effect   d. water cycle
3. Almost all the water vapor in the atmosphere is in the _____.
   a. exosphere   c. stratopause
   b. ionosphere   d. troposphere
4. The addition of _____ to the atmosphere by the burning of fossil fuels for cars, machinery, and power plants may lead to global warming.
   a. gasoline   c. oxygen
   b. CFCs   d. carbon dioxide
5. CFCs, chemicals that are used as refrigerants and propellants in spray cans, are partly to blame for the reduction of _____ in the stratosphere.
   a. carbon dioxide   c. ozone
   b. oxygen   d. clouds
6. Clouds form when water vapor in the air condenses as _____.
   a. the air is heated   c. snow falls
   b. the air is cooled   d. snow forms

7. When air temperature drops, the air's ability to contain water vapor is _____.
   a. slightly higher   c. about the same
   b. much higher   d. lower
8. Winds in the Northern Hemisphere curve clockwise because of _____.
   a. isobars   c. the Coriolis effect
   b. climate   d. CFCs
9. Cumulonimbus and nimbostratus clouds both _____.
   a. appear white and fluffy
   b. produce precipitation
   c. occur at high altitudes
   d. look thin and wispy
10. _____ are lines on a weather map that connect points of equal pressure.
   a. Isobars   c. Highs
   b. Isotherms   d. Lows
11. When a moving warm air mass encounters a mountain range, it _____.
   a. stops moving   c. rises and cools
   b. slows and sinks   d. reverses direction
12. If you hear on the radio that a tornado is approaching, you should _____.
   a. head to high ground
   b. attempt to drive away from the tornado
   c. sit in the center of a basement
   d. hold onto a solid object, such as a tree

Using Vocabulary

13. Explain how carbon dioxide in the atmosphere relates to the *greenhouse effect*.
14. How is *ozone* formed?
15. Describe the *water cycle* using the terms *precipitation, condensation, transpiration,* and *evaporation*.
16. Using the terms *humidity* and *dew point*, explain why you might find small droplets of water on your lawn in the morning.
17. Describe the formation of a warm *front*.

THE ATMOSPHERE **621**

UNDERSTANDING CONCEPTS

1. b   8. c
2. c   9. b
3. d   10. a
4. d   11. c
5. c   12. c
6. b
7. d

Using Vocabulary
13. Carbon dioxide is a greenhouse gas, and it helps to trap solar energy within the Earth's atmosphere. High levels of carbon dioxide may trap too much heat, leading to increased global temperatures.
14. Ozone is formed when the sun's ultraviolet rays strike molecules of O_2. The energy splits the molecules, and then the single atoms of oxygen bond with other O_2 molecules to make ozone.
15. Evaporation occurs as sunlight strikes water in lakes, rivers, oceans, and soil. The water that evaporates goes into the atmosphere. Transpiration, in which plants lose moisture through their pores, also adds water to the atmosphere. As the temperature cools, the moisture in the air condenses and eventually precipitates back to the Earth in the form of rain, snow, or sleet.

RESOURCE LINK
STUDY GUIDE
Assign students *Mixed Review Chapter 18.*

16. Humidity is the amount of moisture in the air. As the temperature drops overnight, the moisture in the air will condense on a surface—in this case, the lawn. The temperature at which the moisture in the air condenses and forms water droplets is known as the dew point.

17. A warm air mass moves above a slower cold air mass.

BUILDING MATH SKILLS

18. a. 22°C
b. 3 in.
c. 26 in.

THINKING CRITICALLY

19. The peaks are covered with snow because they are tall, and temperatures are cold at high altitudes in the troposphere.

20. The CFC ban helps the stratosphere because that is where ozone is, and CFCs destroy ozone.

21. Answers will vary but might include: having to move, different climate and weather patterns, increased severity of storms.

22. Knowledge of the wind belts would help an explorer chart the quickest route between Spain and South America.

23. The body of air with a relative humidity of 97 percent would be closer to its dew point because the water vapor in the more humid air will condense at a warmer temperature than the less humid air sample would.

BUILDING MATH SKILLS

18. Climatography Visual aids called climatographs are used to display information about the climate of a specific region. Using the climatograph for Moscow, Idaho, in the figure below, answer the following questions:

a. What was the average temperature in Moscow during August?

b. What was the total precipitation in the Moscow area for the month of January?

c. What was the approximate total precipitation for the year?

Climatograph for Moscow, Idaho

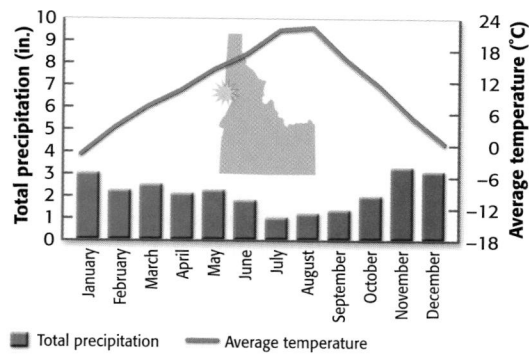

■ Total precipitation ── Average temperature

THINKING CRITICALLY

19. Critical Thinking How would you explain why some of the mountain peaks located near the equator are covered with snow?

20. Applying Knowledge All use of CFCs has been banned in the United States for environmental reasons. Which one of the four layers of the atmosphere does this ban help protect? Explain your answer.

21. Creative Thinking Describe how your life would be changed if global temperatures were to increase by several degrees.

---

22. Creative Thinking In what ways would a knowledge of the global wind belts have helped a sixteenth-century explorer sailing between Spain and the northern part of South America?

23. Applying Knowledge One body of air has a relative humidity of 97 percent. Another has a relative humidity of 44 percent. If they are at the same temperature, which body of air is closer to its dew point? Explain your answer.

24. Making Comparisons Where would the air contain the most moisture, over Panama or over Antarctica? Explain your answer.

25. Critical Thinking Is it safe to be on the street in an automobile during a tornado? Explain your answer.

26. Interpreting Graphics Using the weather map shown in **Figure 18-25,** predict which way the winds will blow across the state of California.

27. Acquiring and Evaluating Data Find out the local high and low temperatures for each day of a recent 2 week period. Using a computer spreadsheet program, graph these temperatures and find the average high and low for this period.

COMPUTER SKILL

Figure 18-25

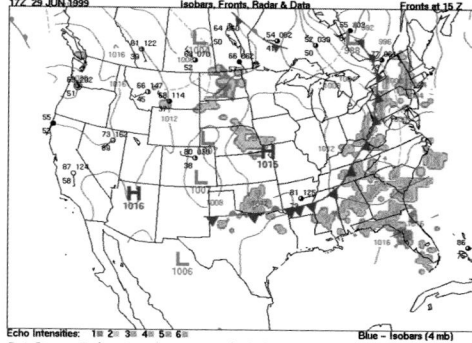

DataStreme Project, American Meteorological Society

---

28. Creative Thinking Predict how the strength of a Northern Hemisphere hurricane will change as it moves northward in the Atlantic Ocean, and explain why.

DEVELOPING LIFE/WORK SKILLS

29. Allocating Resources You are planning an expedition to Mount Everest, the tallest mountain in the world. Identify which four of the following items you will need the most, and explain why.
a. inflatable raft
b. insulated clothes
c. life vest
d. television
e. oxygen equipment
f. fire-starting equipment
g. raincoat

30. Applying Technology Satellites are used to observe weather and climate around the world. Research the use of weather satellites, and write a short paragraph describing how satellites help predict the weather and climate.

WRITING SKILL

31. Working Cooperatively Obtain a week's worth of local or national weather maps from the paper or the Internet. In a small group, prepare a weather forecast. Interpret the daily weather, and follow any trends. Explain the high and low pressure areas and the resulting fronts, any precipitation, and average temperatures. Have a volunteer from your group present the forecast to the class.

internet**connect**

SCLINKS
NSTA
TOPIC: Weather maps
GO TO: www.scilinks.org
KEYWORD: HK1806

INTEGRATING CONCEPTS

32. Concept Mapping Copy the unfinished concept map below onto a sheet of paper. Complete the map by writing the correct word or phrase in the lettered boxes.

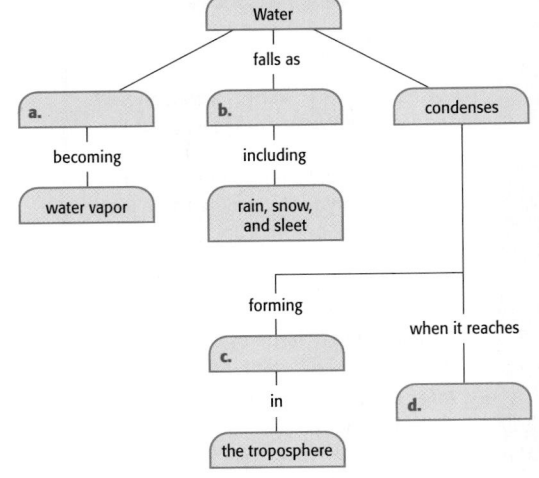

33. Connection to Chemistry Research the effects of the gas methane on the atmosphere. How is methane produced? What are some of the sources of methane in the atmosphere? What is methane's effect on the greenhouse effect? Can we eliminate methane from the atmosphere?

34. Connection to Social Studies Early explorers often ventured to find resources and wealth, but they brought back more than that. They made and improved maps. They also kept journals of weather and climates of new lands. Research a famous explorer, and describe the contributions to understanding weather or climate made by the explorer. What instruments did the explorer use to make measurements?

THE ATMOSPHERE   **623**

24. Air over Panama would contain the most moisture because it is warm, and warmer temperatures can produce more water vapor.
25. No, because a tornado contains winds strong enough to destroy the car.
26. Winds will blow from south to north, toward areas of lower pressure.
27. Answers will vary depending on the weather.
28. The hurricane will become weaker as it moves northward over cooler waters, because less water vapor is present at lower temperatures.

DEVELOPING LIFE/WORK SKILLS

29. b. because the temperature at high altitudes is cold
e. because the levels of oxygen in the air decrease with altitude
f. because a fire can be used for warmth (Is there enough oxygen to light a fire at such a high altitude?)
g. because a raincoat can provide you with waterproof protection from rain, snow and sleet
30. Answers will vary depending upon the source used.
31. Answers will vary depending upon the weather.

Answers continue on p. 625A.

Design Your Own
Lab

Measuring Temperature Effects

Introduction

Have the students review density in Section 2.3. Boyle's law, $PV = k$, shows the inverse relationship between the pressure and the volume of a gas. Charles's law, $V = kT$, shows the direct relationship between the temperature and the volume of a gas. The combined gas law, $\frac{PV}{T} = k$, expresses Boyle's law and Charles's law in one equation. Although students may not know these relationships by name, their observation of the world around them probably has given them some familiarity with these concepts.

Objectives

Students will:

▶ **Use** appropriate lab safety procedures.

▶ **Measure** the volume of a constant mass of air at different temperatures.

▶ **Infer** changes in buoyancy and density from changes in volume.

Planning

Recommended Time: 1 lab period
Materials: (for each lab group)
400 mL beaker
60 mL disposable syringe
glycerin
petroleum jelly
hot and cold tap water
ice
thermometer

Design Your Own
Lab

Introduction

Air rises or sinks in Earth's atmosphere due to differences in buoyancy related to changes in the density of air that are caused by differences in temperature. How can you determine the effect of temperature on the buoyancy of air?

Objectives

▶ **Measure** the volume of a constant mass of air at different temperatures.

▶ **Infer** changes in buoyancy and density from changes in volume.

Materials

400 mL beaker
60 mL disposable syringe
glycerin
petroleum jelly
hot and cold tap water
ice
thermometer

Safety Needs

safety goggles

REQUIRED PRECAUTIONS

▶ Read all safety cautions and discuss them with your students. Safety goggles must be worn at all times.

▶ Do not allow students to point syringes at one another or to play with the syringes in any way.

▶ Use hot water with caution, in some schools the water may be hot enough to cause burns.

▶ Caution the students not to depress the syringe plunger with excessive force. The syringe can break.

Measuring Temperature Effects

▶ Preparing for Your Experiment

1. On a blank sheet of paper, prepare a table like the one shown below.

Temp. (°C)	Pull volume (mL)	Push volume (mL)	Average volume (mL)

2. Measure the air temperature in the room, and record the temperature in your data table.

3. Remove the cap from the tip of the syringe, and move the plunger. If the plunger does not move smoothly and easily, lubricate the inside wall of the syringe with a few drops of glycerin.

4. Adjust the position of the plunger until the syringe is about two-thirds full of air. Add a dab of petroleum jelly to the tip of the syringe, and replace the cap.

▶ Measuring the Volume of Air

5. Gently pull on the plunger, and then release it. When the plunger stops, read the volume of air inside the syringe. Record the volume in your data table in the column labeled "Pull volume."

6. With your finger on the cap, gently push on the plunger and then release it. When the plunger stops, read the volume of air inside the syringe. Record the volume in your data table in the column labeled "Push volume." **SAFETY CAUTION** Do not point the syringe at anyone while you push on the plunger. Wear safety goggles.

▶ Designing Your Experiment

7. With your lab partners, decide how you will use the materials available in the lab to determine the effect of temperature on air density. Test at least two temperatures below room temperature and two temperatures above room temperature. It is important that the mass of air inside the syringe does not change during your experiment. How can you ensure that the mass of air remains constant?

8. In your lab report, list each step you will perform in your experiment.

9. Before you carry out your experiment, your teacher must approve your plan.

▶ Performing Your Experiment

10. After your teacher approves your plan, carry out your experiment.

11. Record your results in your data table.
SAFETY CAUTION Use care when working with hot water; it can cause severe burns.

▶ Analyzing Your Results

1. At each temperature you tested, calculate the average volume by adding the pull volume and push volume and dividing the sum by 2. Record the result in your data table.

2. Plot your data in your lab report in the form of a graph set up like the one at right. Draw a straight line on the graph that fits the data points best.

3. Reaching Conclusions How does the volume of a constant mass of air change as the temperature of the air increases? For the mass of air you used in your experiment, how much would the volume change if the temperature increased from 10°C to 60°C?

4. Reaching Conclusions Recall that the density of a substance equals the substance's mass divided by its volume. Do your results indicate that the density of air increases or decreases as the temperature of the air increases? Explain.

5. Reaching Conclusions Based on your results, would a body of air become more or less buoyant as it becomes colder than the surrounding air? (Hint: See Section 2.3)

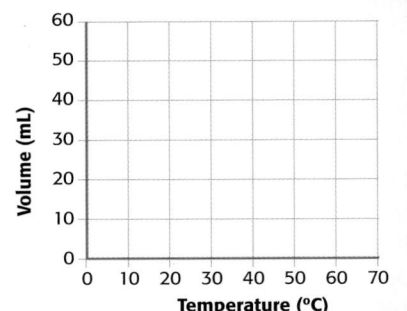

▶ Defending Your Conclusions

6. Suppose someone tells you that your conclusions are invalid because some of your data points lie above or below the best-fit line you drew. How could you show that your conclusions are valid?

Pre-Lab

Teaching Tips

Review the density equation, $D = \frac{m}{V}$ and the rearrangement to $V = \frac{m}{D}$. Ask students what changes they would expect in the density of the air if a known mass occupied a larger volume? *(the density would be less)* a smaller volume? *(the density would be greater)* Ask students what would happen if a balloon is placed in a freezer *(volume would decrease, density would increase)* or in a warm oven *(volume would increase, density would decrease)*.

Procedure

▶ Designing Your Experiment

To test temperatures below room temperature, students should add ice to a beaker of cold tap water. To test temperatures above room temperature, students should use a beaker of hot tap water. In all tests, students should place the syringe in the beaker such that the air in the syringe is completely submerged. After five minutes, students should measure the temperature of the water in the beaker and find the volume of air in the syringe using the pull and push method. To keep the mass of air in the syringe constant, students must leave the cap on the tip of the syringe and must not remove the plunger from the syringe.

Continue on p. 625A.

RESOURCE LINK
DATASHEETS

Have students use *Datasheet 18.2 Design Your Own Lab—Measuring Temperature Effects* to record their results.

Sample Data Table			
Temperature (°C)	**Pull volume (mL)**	**Push volume (mL)**	**Average volume (mL)**
28	42.5	38.5	40.5
25	42.5	38.5	40.5
6	41.0	39.0	40.0
46	44.5	39.5	42.5
92	47.5	42.5	45.0

Design Your Own Lab from page 625

Measuring Temperature Effects

Post-Lab

▶ Disposal

The syringes should be disposed of in a separate disposal container.

▶ Analyzing Your Results

1. Answers will vary.

2. The best-fit line through the data points should have a positive slope.

3. The volume increases linearly with temperature. Using their own graph, students should read up from the 10°C and 60°C marks on the temperature axis to the best-fit line, and then read over to the corresponding values on the volume axis. Subtracting these two volume values gives the expected volume change. Students may have to extrapolate their best-fit line above and below their data points to find the answer.

4. Density decreases as temperature increases. Density = mass/volume, and volume increases with temperature. When volume increases, mass/volume decreases. Therefore, density decreases.

5. A body of air would become less bouyant as it cools. The density of the colder air would be greater than the density of the surrounding, warmer air.

▶ Defending Your Conclusions

6. Students could combine results from all of their classmates and show that their own results are corroborated by the combined results.

Answers from page 623

32. a. evaporates
   b. precipitation
   c. clouds
   d. the dew point

33. Methane is the main component of natural gas. It is produced by the decomposition of plants. Some sources are ruminant animals, swamps, and wetlands. Methane is a greenhouse gas that may promote global warming. No, we cannot eliminate it from the atmosphere.

34. Answers will vary.

Should Laws Require Zero-Emission Cars?

> ## Your Turn

1. Critiquing Viewpoints

Students' analyses of a single argument's weak points may vary. Be sure that student responses clearly identify a weakness and respond in some way that provides support. Possible responses for each of the viewpoints in the feature are listed below. (Note that students should analyze only *one of the following*.)

Sheneah T.: The technology has not advanced far enough yet, so requiring it now is a bad idea.

But the requirement might spur companies to develop the technology.

Megan B.: Requiring more expensive cars by law may not be fair to those who will now be unable to afford a car.

But the decreases in air pollution that will result will benefit all of society in many ways.

Kathryn W.: We can't go back in time to fix the problem, so we should act now.

But if we act too soon, when the right technology is not available and not all of the information is in, we may create an even greater problem in the future.

Margo K.: People don't always act on good ideas.

But it may not be right to force them to act by law.

---

viewpoints

Should Laws Require Zero-Emission Cars?

California law requires that by the year 2004, 10 percent of all cars sold in the state be zero-emission vehicles that produce no pollution as they are operated. Automobile companies are scrambling to develop electric cars and other technologies to meet this deadline.

Often these cars are substantially more expensive than gasoline-burning models. Is the pollution situation so desperate that this is necessary? Or is this a case of laws interfering with the car market?

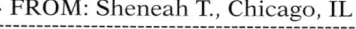

> FROM: Sheneah T., Chicago, IL
>
> ---
>
> As technology advances, we will be able to make better cars that won't depend on gas as much. If we were to cut down on the amount of pollution, this would make our environment better to live in. This goes back to an issue of public health. If cars emit less pollution, we would have fewer cases of respiratory disorders and a much cleaner environment.

Require These Cars Now

> FROM: Megan B., Houston, TX
>
> ---
>
> A law requiring zero-emission vehicles after the year 2003 is probably the best way to prevent air pollution. The various ways companies are changing cars to be more environmentally safe just isn't cutting it. Why do we spend tens of thousands of dollars for fun but not to help save the world?

> FROM: Kathryn W., Rochester, MN
>
> ---
>
> I think the government should definitely get involved in these issues. The laws can be changed later, if needed, but we can't go back in time and fix the problem.

Marianne C.: Planting trees or carpooling may not be enough to undo the damage of many years.

But it is better for people to voluntarily choose what they want to do than to force them to do something by law.

Amar T.: Damage being done to the environment should outweigh car performance issues.

But if the new cars do not compete well with the old ones, they are unlikely to be widely adopted.

2. Critiquing Viewpoints

Students' analyses of strong points in opposing arguments may vary. Be sure that student responses clearly identify the strong points and respond in some way that provides support for the opposite point of view. Possible responses for each of the viewpoints in the feature are listed below. (Note that students should analyze only *one of the following*.)

Sheneah T.: This is a public issue that affects both individual health and the environment.

But requiring something by law when there's no technology in place is not a good thing.

Megan B.: A long-term view is better than a short-term, fun-centered view when it comes to environmental impacts.

But is it right to require people to choose something that will benefit the environment, if it is at great personal economic cost?

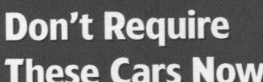

> FROM: Margo K., Coral Springs, FL

Although zero-emission vehicles are better for the environment, there are many expenses that come along with them. I disagree with the law because of the cost of the new vehicles. Rather than making zero-emission vehicles mandatory, if the idea is spread, people will act upon it.

Don't Require These Cars Now

> FROM: Marianne C., Bowling Green, KY

Not everyone will be able to afford these expensive cars. I don't think people should be obligated to buy cars to save the planet. People should do other things instead, like planting trees or carpooling.

> FROM: Amar T., Palos Park, IL

From a car enthusiast's point of view, I feel that no state should make zero-emission cars mandatory for three main reasons: First, at this time zero-emission cars do not perform as well as cars with an internal-combustion engine. Second, zero-emission cars, like electrical cars, have small cruising ranges, and their fuel cells take up too much space. Finally, they are more expensive than gasoline-burning cars.

> Your Turn

1. **Critiquing Viewpoints** Select one of the statements on this page that you *agree* with. Identify and explain at least one weak point in the statement. What would you say to respond to someone who brought up this weak point as a reason you were wrong?

2. **Critiquing Viewpoints** Select one of the statements on this page that you *disagree* with. Identify and explain at least one strong point in the statement. What would you say to respond to someone who brought up this point as a reason they were right?

3. **Interpreting and Communicating** Imagine that you work for an advertising firm that has been hired to promote a car manufacturer's new zero-emission vehicle. The new car costs more than a regular car. Create an advertisement or brochure for the car that tries to persuade people to buy the new car.

4. **Understanding Systems** Other critics of such laws point out that zero-emission cars do not end the pollution entirely. Some toxic waste is made when these cars are manufactured. Write a paragraph in which you outline a method for deciding whether the pollution emitted by a regular car is worse for the environment than the waste made in making a zero-emission vehicle.

internet connect

go.hrw.com

TOPIC: Zero-emission vehicles
GO TO: go.hrw.com
KEYWORD: HK1Zero-emission

Should zero-emission vehicles be required? Why or why not? Share your views on this issue and find out what others think about it at the HRW Web site.

627

Kathryn W.: Better to make the law now and decide you don't need it later than to wait until it's too late.

But the government rarely revises laws to loosen restrictions.

Margo K.: New technologies are often very costly.

But if people don't have a reason to adopt them, the new technologies will fail.

Marianne C.: There are many voluntary measures that can be taken to improve the environment.

But too many people don't take these measures.

Amar T.: Improvements are needed before the new technologies will be effective enough for common use.

But laws should plan for the future rather than being focused solely on the present.

3. Interpreting and Communicating
Student answers will vary. Evaluate students' advertisements or brochures for the more expensive, but environmentally friendly cars using a scale of 1–5 points for each of the following: organization, clarity and factuality, persuasiveness, creativity, and effort. (25 total possible points)

4. Understanding Systems
Student answers will vary. Evaluate students' paragraphs explaining their method for evaluating environmental impacts using a scale of 1–5 points for each of the following: practicality, thoroughness, probable ease of use, creativity, and effort. (25 total possible points)

internet connect

The HRW Web site has more opinions from other students and also provides an opportunity for your students to contribute their points of view. Every few months, more opinions will be added from the ones submitted. Student opinions that are posted will be identified only by the student's first name, last initial, and city to protect his or her privacy.

CHAPTER 19

Using Natural Resources

Annotated Descriptions of the Correlated National Science Standards

The following descriptions summarize the National Science Standards that specially relate to Chapter 19. For the full text of the Standards, see p. 40T.

SECTION 19.1
Organisms and Their Environment
Life Science
LS 4c–4e, 5b
Earth Science
ES 1d
Unifying Concepts and Processes
UCP 1, 5
Science as Inquiry
SAI 1
History and Nature of Science
HNS 1
Science in Personal and Social Perspectives
SPSP 3

SECTION 19.2
Energy and Resources
Physical Science
PS 3b
Earth and Space Science
ES 1a
Unifying Concepts and Processes
UCP 2
Science as Inquiry
SAI 1
Science in Personal and Social Perspectives
SPSP 3, 4

SECTION 19.3
Integrating Technology and Society—Pollution and Recycling
Life Science
LS 5e
Science and Technology
ST 2
Science in Personal and Social Perspectives
SPSP 4, 5

Cross-Discipline Teaching RESOURCES

Cross-Discipline Teaching, ATE p. 628
Social Studies
Life Science

Integration Enrichment Resources
Social Studies, **PE** and **ATE** p. 642
   IE 19.1 *TVA: Finding Solutions*
Science and the Consumer, **PE** and **ATE** p. 646
   IE 19.2 *Solar Energy*
Biology, **PE** and **ATE** p. 654
   IE 19.3 *Composting*
Science and the Consumer, **PE** and **ATE** p. 655
   IE 19.4 *Recycling Plastics*

Additional Worksheets
   IE 19.5 Language Arts
   IE 19.6 Chemistry   **IE 19.7** Physics

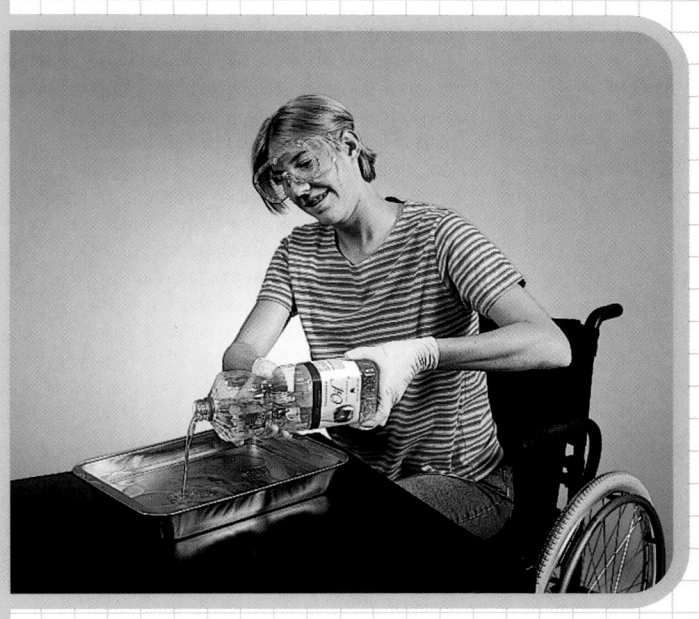

Use the Planning Guide on the next page to help you organize your lessons.

MATH AND COMPUTER RESOURCES

Chapter 19	Math Skills	Assess	Media/Computer Skills
Section 19.1		PE **Building Math Skills,** p. 657, item 15	■ Section 19.1
Section 19.2		CRT Worksheet 11 CRT Worksheet 15	■ Section 19.2 CNN Presents **Physical Science** Segment 11 Energy-Saving House CNN Presents **Chemistry Connections** Segment 15 Coal-Oil Technology PE **Developing Life/Work Skills,** p. 658, item 21
Section 19.3		PE **Building Math Skills,** p. 658, item 16	■ Section 19.3 CNN Presents **Chemistry Connections** Segment 29 Electric Car PE **Developing Life/Work Skills,** p. 658, item 19

PE Pupil's Edition   ATE Annotated Teacher's Edition   MS Math Skills   BS Basic Skills
IE Integration Enrichment   ■ Guided Reading Audio   CRT Critical Thinking

READING SKILL BUILDER

The following activities found in the Annotated Teacher's Edition provide techniques for developing useful reading strategies to increase your students' reading comprehension skills.

Section 19.1 **Brainstorming,** p. 628
K-W-L, p. 630
L.I.N.K., p. 633
Reading Organizer, p. 634, 636

Section 19.2 **Anticipation,** p. 638
Brainstorming, p. 639
Reading Organizer, p. 641
Paired Reading, p. 644

Section 19.3 **K-W-L,** p. 647
L.I.N.K., p. 650
Reading Organizer, p. 652
K-W-L, p. 654

Smithsonian Institution®
Visit www.si.edu/hrw for additional online resources.

Spanish Resources

The following resources are made available for students who speak Spanish as their first language.

Spanish Resources Guided Reading Audio CD-ROM Chapter 19

Spanish Glossary Chapter 19

Using Natural Resources

CLASSROOM RESOURCES

FOCUS	TEACH	HANDS-ON

Section 19.1: Organisms and Their Environment

BLOCK 1
45 minutes

FOCUS	TEACH	HANDS-ON
ATE **RSB** Brainstorming, p. 628 ATE **Focus** Activities 1and 2, p. 629 ATE **RSB** K-W-L, p. 630 ATE **RSB** L.I.N.K., p. 633 ATE **Demo 1** Ecosystem, p. 630 PE Ecosystems, pp. 630-634 ★ Focus Transparency LT 62	ATE **Skill Builder** Interpreting Visuals, pp. 629, 630, 631, 632 Vocabulary, p. 633 BLM 59 Population Graph TT 65 Desert Ecosystem TT 66 Ecosystem Structure	

BLOCK 2
45 minutes

FOCUS	TEACH	HANDS-ON
ATE **RSB** Reading Organizer, p. 634, 636 PE Evaluating Changes in Ecosystems, pp. 634-637	ATE **Skill Builder** Interpreting Visuals, pp. 634, 636	PE Inquiry Lab *Why do seasons occur?* p. 635 **DS** 19.1

Section 19.2: Energy and Resources

BLOCK 3
45 minutes

FOCUS	TEACH	HANDS-ON
ATE **RSB** Anticipation, p. 638 ATE **RSB** Brainstorming, p. 639 PE The Search for Resources, pp. 638-640 ★ Focus Transparency LT 63	ATE **Skill Builder** Interpreting Visuals, p. 638 BLM 60 Energy Use BLM 61 World Energy Sources TT 67 Carbon Cycle TT 68 Making Oil	

BLOCK 4
45 minutes

FOCUS	TEACH	HANDS-ON
ATE **RSB** Reading Organizer, p. 641 ATE **RSB** Paired Reading, p. 644 PE Alternative Sources of Energy; The Efficiency of Energy Conversion, pp. 641-645	TT 69 Solar Cell Diagram	IE Worksheet 19.1 PE Science and the Consumer *Sun-Warmed Houses*, p. 646 IE Worksheets 19.2, 19.5, 19.7 LE 19 *Investigating the Effects of Acid Rain* **DS** 19.6

Section 19.3: Pollution and Recycling

BLOCK 5
45 minutes

FOCUS	TEACH	HANDS-ON
ATE **RSB** K-W-L, p. 647 ATE **RSB** L.I.N.K., p. 650 ATE **Demo 2** Carbon Dioxide Analysis, p. 650 PE What Causes Pollution? pp. 647-651 ★ Focus Transparency LT 64	ATE **Skill Builder** Interpreting Tables, p. 648 Interpreting Visuals, pp. 649, 650 Vocabulary, p. 649 BLM 62 Air Pollutants BLM 63 Air Pollution Graphs BLM 64 Carbon dioxide Graph	PE Quick Activity *The Effects of Acid Rain*, p. 650 **DS** 19.2 PE Quick Activity *Observing Air Pollution*, p. 651 **DS** 19.3

BLOCK 6
45 minutes

FOCUS	TEACH	HANDS-ON
ATE **RSB** Reading Organizer, p. 652 ATE **RSB** K-W-L, p. 654 PE Water Pollution; Pollution on Land; Reducing Pollution, pp. 651-656		PE Inquiry Lab *How can oil spills be cleaned up?* p. 653 **DS** 19.4 IE Worksheet 19.3 PE Science and the Consumer *Recycling Codes*, p. 655 IE Worksheets 19.4, 19.6 PE Skill Builder Lab *Changing the Form of a Fuel*, p. 660 **DS** 19.5

CLASSROOM RESOURCES

HOMEWORK	ASSESS
PE Section Review 1–4, p. 637 **Chapter 19 Review,** p. 657, item 2	**SG** Chapter 19 Pretest
PE Section Review 5–8, p. 637 **Chapter 19 Review,** p. 657, items 12, 15	**SG** Section 19.1
PE Section Review 1–3, p. 645 **Chapter 19 Review,** p. 657, item 14	
PE Section Review 4–7, p. 645 **Chapter 19 Review,** p. 657, items 1, 5–7, 10, 20, 23	**SG** Section 19.2
PE Section Review 2, 3, 6, p. 656 **Chapter 19 Review,** p. 657, items 3, 4, 11, 13	
PE Section Review 1, 4, 5, 7, p. 656 **Chapter 19 Review,** p. 657 items 8, 9, 16	**ATE** *ALTERNATIVE ASSESSMENT,* Aquatic Plants and Fertilizers, p. 652 **SG** Section 19.3

BLOCK 7

PE Chapter 19 Review
   Thinking Critically 17, 18, p. 658
   Developing Life/Work Skills 19–27, pp. 658–659
   Integrating Concepts 28–32, p. 659
SG Chapter 19 Mixed Review

BLOCK 8

Chapter Tests
   Chapter 19 Test

One-Stop Planner CD–ROM **with Test Generator**
   Chapter 19

Teaching Resources
   Scoring Rubrics and assignment checklist.

internetconnect

SCI LINKS **NSTA**

National Science Teachers
Association
Online Resources:
www.scilinks.org

The following *sci*LINKS Internet resources can be found
in the student text for this chapter.

Page 629 **TOPIC:** Solar energy **KEYWORD:** HK1901	**Page 646** **TOPIC:** Solar heated homes **KEYWORD:** HK1900
Page 630 **TOPIC:** Ecosystem factors **KEYWORD:** HK1902	**Page 649** **TOPIC:** Pollution **KEYWORD:** HK1907

Page 631
TOPIC: Populations and
    communities
KEYWORD: HK1903
	Page 652
	TOPIC: Solutions to
	    pollution problems
	KEYWORD: HK1908

Page 636 **TOPIC:** Changes in ecosystems **KEYWORD:** HK1904	**Page 659** **TOPIC:** Global warming **KEYWORD:** HK1909
Page 641 **TOPIC:** Alternative energy sources **KEYWORD:** HK1906	

CNNfyi.com   www.cnnfyi.com

Visit this site for coverage of current events and related
classroom resources.

PE Pupil's Edition   **ATE** Annotated Teacher's Edition
RSB Reading Skill Builder   **DS** Datasheets
IE Integrated Enrichment   **SG** Study Guide
LE Laboratory Experiments
TT Teaching Transparencies   **BLM** Blackline Masters
★ Lesson Focus Transparency

Using Natural Resources

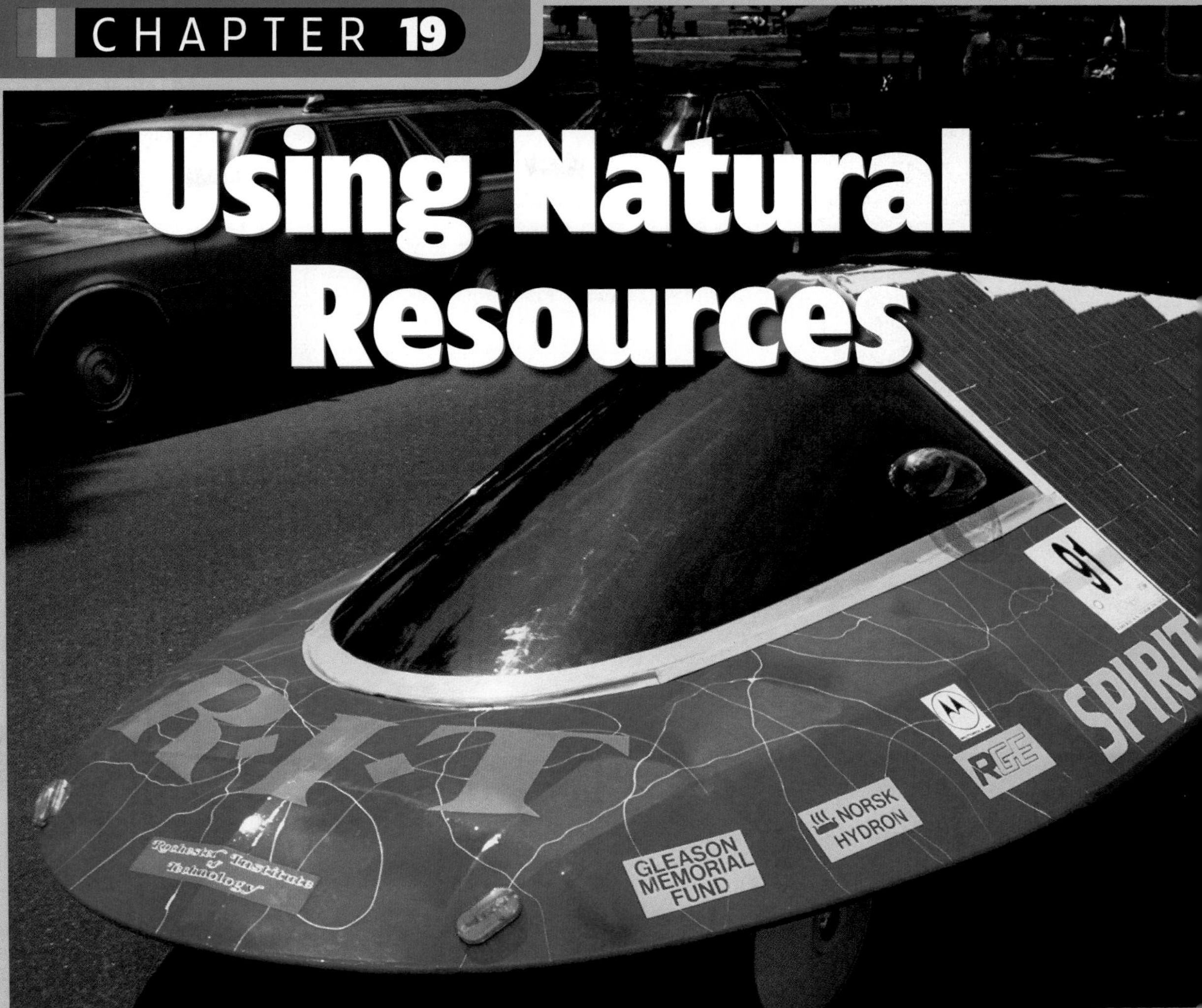

Tapping Prior Knowledge

Be sure students understand the following concepts:

Chapter 6
Solutions, acids, bases, and pH

Chapter 9
Work and energy

Chapter 10
Heat, temperature, and energy transfer

Chapter 16
The solar system

Chapter 17
Planet Earth, Earth's interior, and plate tectonics

Chapter 18
Weather, climate, and characteristics of the atmosphere

 **READING SKILL BUILDER** **Brainstorming** Write the words *ecosystem* and *community* on the board. Ask students to come up with words and phrases that relate to the concepts and definitions of ecosystem and community. Have two students record the responses on the board under each word. Encourage students to use the section objectives and the figures on pp. 630–631 to develop definitions of the words and to understand how they relate to each other. Have the students use their new knowledge to illustrate how their school is like an ecosystem with different communities of people in it.

Chapter Preview

CROSS-DISCIPLINE TEACHING

Social Studies During the section on succession, have students conduct research to find out how their local ecosystem has changed over time. What did their ecosystem look like 50 years ago? 100 years ago? How have the living and nonliving elements of the ecosystem changed? What impact have humans had on the ecosystem, and have they been positive or negative? How have natural forces changed the ecosystem?

Life Science Have a biology teacher visit your class to characterize the local ecosystem based on the native flora and fauna.

Focus ACTIVITY

Background The engines are started. The drivers check their gauges one last time. The flag rises, then falls. They're off!

Is this a typical race? Not quite. These race cars are powered by solar energy. Not a drop of gasoline is needed to make them run. Teams of college students designed and built the cars to compete in an annual event called Sunrayce.

Sunrayce began in 1990, and its goal is to raise awareness of alternative energy sources, such as the sun. Each summer, students travel more than 2093 km (1300 mi) across the United States in these solar-powered cars.

Solar-powered cars must be lightweight and efficient. Although the average race speed is about 35 mi/h, the cars can reach top speeds of 65 mi/h. Each car is fueled by solar cells. These cells, which are made of thin layers of silicon, capture the sun's energy and store it in batteries.

Activity 1 Obtain a solar cell from an electronics store or your school's science lab. Using the solar cell, a low-wattage light bulb, and two pieces of insulated electrical wire, create a current in the cell and the bulb. Place the end of one wire on the metal bottom of the bulb and the end of the other wire on the side of the bulb. Place the other ends of both wires on the solar cell. In your own words, describe the movement of charges between the cell and the bulb.

Activity 2 Make a list of the energy sources you use at home. Find out from your parents which source of energy costs the most per month. Make a pie chart showing your results. Call your local power company to find out what type of resource is used to generate electrical power.

internet connect

SCLINKS.
NSTA

TOPIC: Solar energy
GO TO: www.scilinks.org
KEYWORD: HK1901

Sunrayce is held each year to raise awareness of alternative energy sources. Drivers travel more than 2093 km across the United States using solar-powered cars.

629

Focus ACTIVITY

Background Solar-powered cars use light to create electrical energy, which in turn provides power. Although electric vehicles, or EVs may seem futuristic, they are already in use in California and Arizona. One example is the EVI, an EV that can travel between 80 km and 145 km on a single charge. The EVI's rechargeable battery contains slightly more than two-dozen 12 V modules capable of holding more than 16 k•Wh of energy.

Activity 1 Electrons will flow through the insulated wire from negative to positive until the materials in the solar cell are electrically neutral.

Activity 2 Answers will vary depending on the student. After students make their lists, have them classify their answers according to how the energy was produced.

SKILL BUILDER

Interpreting Visuals Have students examine the photographs to the left and ask them to think of other alternative energy sources that could possibly be used to power a car.

RESOURCE LINK
STUDY GUIDE

Have students do *Pretest Chapter 19 Using Natural Resources* before beginning section 19.1.

Organisms and Their Environment

Scheduling

Refer to pp. 628A–628D for lecture, classwork, and assignment options for Section 19.1.

★ **Lesson Focus**
Use transparency *LT 62* to prepare students for this section.

**READING SKILL BUILDER** *K-W-L* Have students list what they know about ecosystems, communities, and changes in ecosystems. After students read the relevant sections, encourage them to look at their lists and write down what they have learned about the subject, including any new questions that they may have. Have volunteers share their lists and questions with the class.

|SKILL BUILDER

Interpreting Visuals Have students look at the desert ecosystem in **Figure 19-1.** Have them list both the living and nonliving elements of this desert ecosystem. Discuss how different desert ecosystems will have different living and nonliving elements in them. Ask students to use their classroom and school as examples of ecosystems, and to name the living and nonliving elements in them.

Resources Teaching Transparency 65 shows this visual.

630

▶ **KEY TERMS**
ecosystem
community
succession
hydroelectric power

internetconnect

SC*LINKS*
NSTA

TOPIC: Ecosystem factors
GO TO: www.scilinks.org
KEYWORD: HK1902

▶ **ecosystem** all of the living and nonliving elements in a particular place

▶ **OBJECTIVES**

▶ Explain the structure of an ecosystem.
▶ Describe the effects one species can have on an ecosystem.
▶ Discuss two ways natural forces can change ecosystems.
▶ Discuss two ways humans can change ecosystems.

S hould money be spent drilling for oil in the wilderness of Alaska, or would the money be better spent promoting solar power? Should a nearby swamp be drained to provide parking for a mall in your town, or is the swamp best left alone? No matter how you feel about these issues, you need to know how they will change the world around you.

We humans, like all other living things, fill our needs by using natural resources. These resources are taken from the world around us. Every action taken, whether it is someone draining a swamp or a bird catching prey, affects all the other living things in the ecosystem, as shown in **Figure 19-1.**

To evaluate the effects of your decisions on the issues that cause change in your environment, you must first understand how the many parts of an ecosystem relate to one another.

Figure 19-1
Each living and nonliving element in this desert ecosystem directly affects the other.

630 CHAPTER 19

DEMONSTRATION 1 TEACHING

What Is an Example of an Ecosystem?

Time: Approximately 10 minutes
Materials: aquarium or terrarium with assorted flora and fauna

(If you are not able to obtain an aquarium, simply collect some leaves and insects from outside and place them in a bowl covered with plastic wrap with air holes.)

Show the students the aquarium with plants and fish or a terrarium with plants and insects. Have students examine all aspects of the system closely.

Analysis

1. Is this an example of an ecosystem? Why or why not? *(Yes, because it is a distinct area where living and nonliving elements are interacting.)*

What Is an Ecosystem?

Consider a squirrel in a city park. The squirrel gathers and stores food. It lives in a tree and drinks water from a sun-dappled pond. The soil, trees, sunshine, and water are natural resources found within the city park. The city park itself is an ecosystem.

Living elements in an ecosystem can include plants, animals, and people. Nonliving elements include sunlight, air, soil, water, and temperature. The different elements within a desert ecosystem are shown in **Figure 19-1**. The cactuses, sagebrush, lizards, snakes, scorpions, and birds interact with one another and with their surroundings to make a stable, balanced ecosystem.

All ecosystems are not the same size

Ecosystems can be large or small. The entire planet is one big ecosystem containing all the living and nonliving things on Earth—the land and water, the organisms, and the atmosphere. A shallow forest pool no bigger than a rain puddle is also an example of an ecosystem. This ecosystem is made up of water, mud, bacteria, mosquitoes, air, and larvae all living together.

Living things are adapted to their ecosystem

Living things are found almost everywhere: on land, in the air, and in water. Each organism has adapted to factors in its environment, such as temperature, humidity, and the other living things around it. These factors determine where a particular organism lives. For instance, polar bears are adapted to cold, wet places, and camels are adapted to hot, dry places. Neither animal could survive in the other's environment.

Ecosystems are divided into communities

Groups of animals and plants that are adapted to similar conditions form a community. There can be several communities within an ecosystem. For example, the animals and plants of the tundra make up one community. The seals, fish, and algae of the nearby ocean make up another. Polar bears belong to *both* communities. **Figure 19-2** shows the different divisions within an ecosystem.

internet connect

SCI LINKS
NSTA

TOPIC: Populations and communities
GO TO: www.scilinks.org
KEYWORD: HK1903

▶ **community** all of the animals and plants living in one area within an ecosystem

Figure 19-2
Ecosystems are made up of communities that contain different populations of organisms.

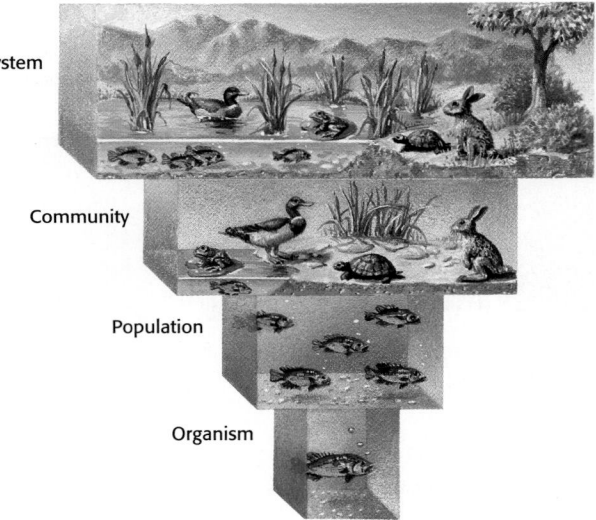

Ecosystem

Community

Population

Organism

USING NATURAL RESOURCES **631**

Section 19.1

Organisms and Their Environment

SKILL BUILDER

Interpreting Visuals Have students look at **Figure 19-2**. What do they notice about the levels of the inverted pyramid? *(The levels are more complex the higher you go. There are greater numbers of living and nonliving elements in each level of organization.)*

Resources *Teaching Transparency 66 shows this visual.*

Teaching Tip

Community Take your class outside on the school grounds for a mini field trip. Tell them that the objective of the trip is to find as many communities of organisms as possible. As students identify these communities, have them list the living and nonliving elements of the environments where the communities are found. Are more communities found where there are more living or nonliving elements interacting?

Connection to ECOLOGY

Habitat loss as a result of human activities (destruction of forests, draining of wetlands, pollution) is one of the leading reasons why ecosystems are becoming unbalanced around the world today. Have students research how habitat loss has caused changes in their environment.

2. Ask students to list the living and nonliving elements of these ecosystems. *(Fish, plants, insects, sunlight, air, water, etc.)*

3. Ask students how the nonliving and living elements are interacting together. *(Plants are using sunlight, animals are drinking water.)*

4. Ask the students to list the communities of each of those ecosystems. *(Fish, plants, insects.)*

5. Ask the students: Could this ecosystem be considered part of a larger ecosystem? *(Yes, the classroom ecosystem or the school ecosystem.)*

Organisms and Their Environment

Figure 19-3
The living and nonliving elements of this aquarium ecosystem help to keep it balanced.

Changes in Ecosystems

Sunlight, water, air, soil, animals, plants— the elements that make up an ecosystem are numerous. Each element is balanced with the others so that the ecosystem can be maintained over a long period of time.

Look at the aquarium shown in **Figure 19-3.** The amount of salt in the water and the temperature of the water are at the right levels. The fish, snails, and plants all have sufficient space and food. In short, there are enough resources for every living thing in the aquarium ecosystem. The ecosystem is balanced.

Balanced ecosystems remain stable

When an ecosystem is balanced, the population sizes of the different species do not change relative to one another. Overall, there is a natural balance between those that eat and those that are eaten. Other factors, such as disease or food shortage, prevent populations from growing too much. If the balance within an ecosystem is disturbed, change results.

The graph in **Figure 19-4** is based on a Canadian study of the snowshoe hare and its predator, the lynx. What happened to the lynx population when there where fewer snowshoe hares?

When the prey population of a particular place decreases, there is less food for the predators. As a result, some of the predators die. On the other hand, if the prey population increases, more predators may move into the area. A variety of factors, including population change, can affect the balance in an ecosystem. What happens when one factor changes?

Figure 19-4
The population of snowshoe hares directly affects the population of lynxes.

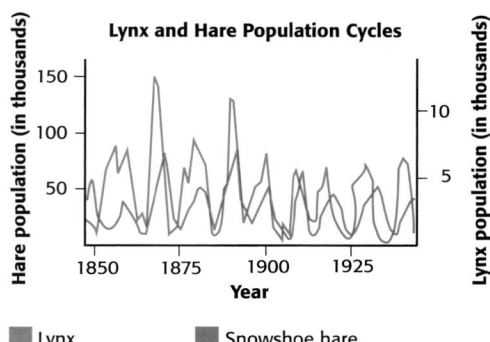

632 CHAPTER 19

DEMONSTRATION 2   TEACHING

The Effects of Temperature Changes

Time: Approximately 30 minutes
Materials: paramecium culture, 12 cm *v*-shaped glass tubing, 2 corks, 200 mL beaker, hot plate, 100 mL of tap water, thermometer

Ask students to determine whether organisms change in response to temperature changes.

Step 1 Fill the beaker with 100 mL of tap water. Place the beaker on the hot plate. When the water begins to boil, turn the hot plate off. Allow the water to cool to about 68°C.

Step 2 Place a paramecium culture in 12 cm *v*-shaped glass tubing that can be corked at both ends.

Step 3 Gently place one end of the glass tubing in a beaker of very hot tap water (68°C) and the other end in ice water. Have a student volunteer determine the temperature range using a thermometer.

A change in one feature can affect the whole system

Throughout the 1990s, researchers have been closely watching a piece of land in Central America that was once a tropical rain forest. After the trees were logged, a species of wild pig vanished from the forest because the pigs no longer had enough food and shelter. Three species of frogs disappeared soon thereafter. Was this related to the loss of the wild pigs?

The pigs wallowed in mud, forming puddles that the frogs used for breeding. Without the pigs, there were no puddles, and the frogs had to find another place to breed. In this way, a change in one factor of an ecosystem can affect all the living and nonliving elements within the system.

The key to understanding ecosystems can be summed up in one word: *interrelatedness*. The elements that make up an ecosystem function together to keep the entire system stable. If something changes, time and natural forces often work to return the ecosystem to its undisturbed state.

Ecosystems tend to gradually return to their original conditions

Yellowstone National Park is one of the largest tourist attractions in the United States. The park, located in northwestern Wyoming and southern Montana, covers about 2.2 million acres (3,472 square miles) of land and is know for its active geysers and hot springs.

But during the summer of 1988, large areas of the park were burned to the ground by fires, as shown in **Figure 19-5A.** The fires, which were started by lightning and careless human activity, spread quickly through the open forest during this particularly dry summer, and left nearly a third of the park blackened with ash. Firefighters and Army and Marine troops worked continuously to put the fires out but were unsuccessful. In early September, rain and snow finally put the fires out.

The following spring, the appearance of the "dead" forest began to change. Large numbers of small, green plants began to flourish and replace areas that had been covered with fallen trees. Year after year, gradual developments took place in the recovering area, as shown in **Figure 19-5B.**

Figure 19-5
(A) During the summer of 1988, Yellowstone National Park was plagued with a series of uncontrollable fires. (B) The following spring, new plant life flourished in the recovering park.

Ⓐ

Ⓑ

USING NATURAL RESOURCES **633**

READING SKILL BUILDER *L.I.N.K.* Write the word *interrelatedness* on the board, and have students brainstorm all the words, phrases, and ideas that they associate with the word. List student contributions on the board and begin a discussion in which students seek clarification of the listed ideas. At the end of the discussion, have students make notes of everything they remember from the discussion. Encourage students to look over their notes to see what they know about the topic based on experience and the discussion.

SKILL BUILDER

Vocabulary Point out that the word *succession* is often used in conjunction with discussing an orderly progression of events. To succeed means to come after.

Historical Perspective

Mount Saint Helens is a volcano in Washington State. In May of 1980, the volcano erupted, spewing hot ash and rocks into the air. The hot ash and rocks started forest fires, and melted snow which resulted in flooding and mud slides. Millions of trees were destroyed, along with crops and wildlife. The eruption is an example of a long-term disruption of a balanced ecosystem.

Extension Challenge students to research the condition of Mount Saint Helens before the eruption and to characterize the process of succession that occurred after the eruption. What species moved in first? Is the ecosystem still recovering from the disturbance?

Step 4 Wait 5-10 minutes and then allow students to observe any differences in the response of the paramecia to their environments using a dissecting scope or magnifying glass. Have students also note the number of paramecia that congregate in the hot and cold ends of the tubing as opposed to the middle of the tubing.

Analysis

1. Ask students what temperature they think paramecia prefer. *(They prefer the temperature in the middle of the tube.)*
2. Ask students where paramecia live in nature. *(They live in every area on Earth except the polar regions and thermal hot spots.)*

Organisms and Their Environment

Figure 19-6
Different views of Glacier Bay, Alaska, show the types of change that took place over 200 years, as glaciers receded.

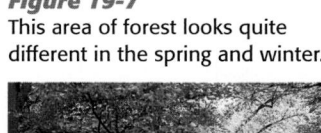 **succession** the gradual repopulating of a community by different species over a period of time

In time, a complex ecosystem will develop. This process, shown in **Figure 19-6,** is known as succession. The end product is a stable but complicated community where birth, death, growth, and decay take place at a steady rate. This will keep the ecosystem stable if no major disruptions occur.

Evaluating Changes in Ecosystems

Ecosystems undergo both short-term and long-term changes. Short-term changes are usually easily reversed, but long-term changes can take many years to be reversed.

Short-term ecosystem changes

During autumn, many trees and shrubs lose their leaves. In the winter, many birds migrate to warmer places. Other animals hibernate by lowering their metabolism. These animals can sleep through the winter in snug burrows or caves. In spring, the migrating birds return, animals come out of hibernation, buds open, and seeds begin to sprout. As **Figure 19-7** shows, the same ecosystem can appear quite different during different times of the year.

Figure 19-7
This area of forest looks quite different in the spring and winter.

Long-term ecosystem changes

As you have learned, long-term changes in ecosystems can be caused by events such as volcanic eruptions. At other times, many factors act together to cause change. In these cases, it may be hard to know how much each factor adds to the change. An example is the many causes of global temperature change.

Climatic changes affect ecosystems

In your lifetime, the climate where you live probably hasn't changed much. Some years may be colder than others, but average monthly temperatures do not vary greatly from year to year. Throughout Earth's geologic history, there have been periods known as ice ages, when icy glaciers covered much of the continents. **Figure 19-8** shows the size of the glacier that covered much of North America during the last ice age. This period ended roughly 11 500 years ago.

During ice ages, temperatures are much colder than usual. These cold spells alternate with warmer, or interglacial, periods. Scientists hypothesize that ice ages are caused by a variety of factors, including the tilt of Earth's axis, continental drift, and the Earth's orbit around the sun.

The combined effect of these changes in Earth's position in space is difficult to predict. One thing we do know is that these changes cause temperature differences in ecosystems.

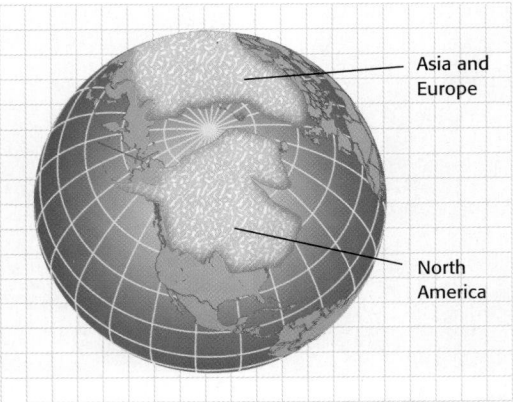

Asia and Europe

North America

Figure 19-8
Icy glaciers covered much of North America and parts of Europe and Asia during the last ice age.

Inquiry Lab

Why do seasons occur?

Materials ✔ globe   ✔ unshaded lamp

Procedure
1. Place the lamp on a table, and turn the lamp on.
2. Stand about 2 m from the table, and hold the globe at arm's length, pointing it toward the lamp.
3. Tilt the globe slightly so that the bottom half—the Southern Hemisphere—is illuminated by the lamp.
4. Keeping the axis of the Earth's rotation pointing in the same direction, walk halfway around the table.

Analysis
1. What part of the globe is lit by the lamp's light now? What season does this represent in this part of Earth?
2. Would there be any seasonal changes if the Earth's axis were not tilted? Explain your answer.
3. In addition to experiencing seasonal changes, ecosystems also experience short-term changes as day changes into night. What movement of Earth causes night and day to occur?

Inquiry Lab

Why do seasons occur?
During spring and summer in the Northern Hemisphere, the Northern Hemisphere tilts toward the sun and receives concentrated, direct sunlight. The Southern Hemisphere tilts away from the sun and receives less concentrated sunlight. The opposite is true for both hemispheres during fall and winter.

Analysis
1. the Northern Hemisphere; summer.
2. No, because there would be no variation in the amount of sunlight the Earth receives.
3. the rotation of the Earth on its own axis

Organisms and Their Environment

MISCONCEPTION ALERT

Long-Term Ecosystem Change
Alert your students to the fact that long-term ecosystem changes are not limited to only destructive events such as volcanic eruptions. The construction of roads, shopping malls, and other human-related activities can be classified as long-term ecosystem changes as well.

REAL WORLD APPLICATIONS

Climate Change and Disease
Ecologists are working with climatologists to investigate the relationship between climatic changes and the outbreak of disease.

In 1993, a virus began killing young people in the southwestern United States. An unusually mild winter and a wet spring caused piñon trees to bloom vigorously, providing virus-carrying mice with a plentiful supply of pine nuts. The mice population increased tenfold. The mice found their way into people's homes and spread the virus to humans. Half the people infected with the virus died.

Researchers are carefully monitoring mice and other disease carriers in an effort to predict if, when, and where the next outbreak of disease might occur.

RESOURCE LINK
DATASHEETS

Have students use *Datasheet 19.1 Inquiry Lab: Why do seasons occur?* to record their results.

Organisms and Their Environment

Figure 19-9
Clearing trees, driving cars, constructing buildings, and farming are just a few human activities that cause changes in ecosystems.

internetconnect

SCiLINKS
NSTA

TOPIC: Changes in ecosystems
GO TO: www.scilinks.org
KEYWORD: HK1904

▶ **hydroelectric power**
the energy of moving water converted to electricity

Changes can be caused by human activity

Physical factors are not the only things that cause changes in ecosystems. People also alter the environment in a variety of ways, as shown in **Figure 19-9.** Activities such as driving cars, growing crops, and constructing roads and buildings change the environment.

All of those activities have some benefits, but they also cause some problems. The benefits of some human activities, such as building dams, are numerous. For instance, the El Chocon Cerros Colorados project brought much-needed flood control to the foothills of the Andes Mountains in Argentina. Formerly, the rivers that flowed down from the mountains flooded twice each year. At other times the region was too dry to grow crops. The construction of a system of dams stopped this cycle. Excess water is now stored in large reservoirs behind the dams. This water is used for irrigation. This allows farmers to grow crops year-round. In addition, the dam is used to generate **hydroelectric power** for much of the country. This energy resource will be discussed further in Section 19-2.

Such large dams, however, can cause problems. Without the floods, rivers no longer deposit rich soil, so farmers use chemical fertilizers on their crops instead. Runoff from these fertilizers can contaminate ground water and streams, making water supplies unsafe for humans and other living things.

Many of the adverse effects of dams constructed before the 1970s were not foreseen by their developers. Today scientists and engineers have a better understanding of how ecosystems work. Often, major projects such as constructing a dam must undergo an environmental analysis before construction begins. If the project is likely to destroy an entire ecosystem, it may have to be redesigned, relocated, or canceled altogether.

636 CHAPTER 19

Changes can be caused by introduction of nonnative species

Some species move from one ecosystem to another on their own. Animals may migrate to new areas, and seeds can be carried by wind or water to different places. Even humans can influence the spread of nonnative species to other ecosystems, sometimes accidentally and sometimes on purpose.

Starlings, for instance, were purposely brought to the United States. In the 1800s, a few dozen European starlings were released in New York City. The birds rapidly multiplied, and today there are millions of them across the United States.

Both starlings and native North American bluebirds nest in holes in tree trunks and fence posts, as shown in **Figure 19-10.** As a result, the two species compete for shelter. The bluebirds nearly lost the battle. Concerned citizens launched a multistate effort to build and distribute bird boxes. These boxes, specially designed with small entrances, provided nesting places for the bluebirds and kept the larger starlings out.

There are other ways to introduce organisms to an ecosystem. For instance, small insects can be carried across borders accidentally. Often they are hidden in crates of fruit and vegetables.

In its new environment, the nonnative species may have no natural enemies to keep its numbers in check. As a result, its members can quickly multiply and take over an ecosystem. The new competing species may wipe out an existing native species and cause change in the ecosystem.

Figure 19-10
Starlings compete with bluebirds for nesting sites in the holes of tree trunks or fence posts.

SECTION 19.1 REVIEW

SUMMARY

▶ Living and nonliving elements form an ecosystem.

▶ The elements of an ecosystem work together to maintain a balance.

▶ One change can affect the entire ecosystem.

▶ A disturbed ecosystem may gradually return to its original state.

▶ Ecosystem changes can be short-term or long-term.

CHECK YOUR UNDERSTANDING

1. **List** two factors that keep populations stable.
2. **Analyze** the following statement: An ecosystem is like a fine-tuned car.
3. **Describe** how the loss of one species in a pond can affect other species.
4. **Define** *succession*.
5. **Predict** how a thunderstorm could lead to a long-term change in an ecosystem.
6. **List** two changes in the Earth's position in space that can affect climatic change in ecosystems.
7. **Critical Thinking** Describe a common human activity that can disrupt an ecosystem. Propose a solution to the problem.
8. **Critical Thinking** List several ways nonnative plants may be introduced to an environment.

USING NATURAL RESOURCES **637**

Scheduling

Refer to pp. 628A–628D for lecture, classwork, and assignment options for Section 19.2.

★ **Lesson Focus**
Use transparency *LT 63* to prepare students for this section.

READING SKILL BUILDER *Anticipation* Write the following questions on the board:

- How do living things (plants, animals, and people) use energy?

- Where does this energy come from?

Group the students in pairs and have them provide answers to these questions. Encourage students to read the section and then discuss whether their answers changed or remained the same. Have students cite passages in the text that account for the change in or reinforcement of their original answers.

SKILL BUILDER

Interpreting Visuals Have students examine **Figure 19-11.** Ask students what the similarities and differences are concerning how energy is used worldwide and how it is used in the United States.

Resources Blackline Master 60 shows this visual.

Energy and Resources

▶ **KEY TERMS**
fossil fuels
nonrenewable resources
renewable resources
geothermal energy

OBJECTIVES

▶ Identify different sources of energy used by living things, and trace each source back to the sun.
▶ Describe the advantages and disadvantages of several energy sources.
▶ Describe the types of conversion processes necessary for different energy sources to produce electricity.
▶ Identify how efficient different conversion processes are.

How Energy Is Used Worldwide

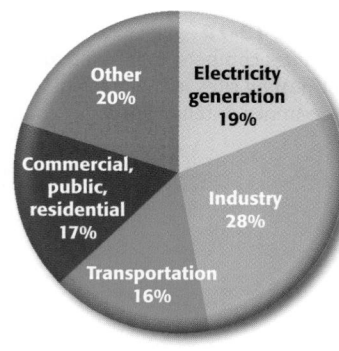

How Energy Is Used in the United States

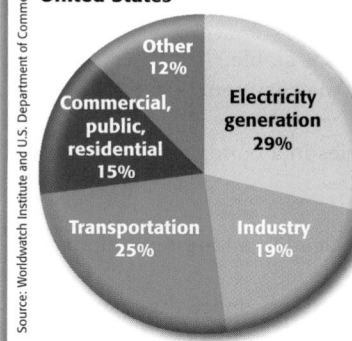

Source: Worldwatch Institute and U.S. Department of Commerce

Figure 19-11
These pie charts show how energy use in the United States compares with energy use worldwide, including the United States.

How much energy do you use in a day, a week, or a month? You probably use more than you think. Energy is needed to light streets and homes, heat water and buildings, cook food, power vehicles, and run appliances. Energy is also needed to make the products you use every day. Where does all this energy come from?

The Search for Resources

You have already learned that we rely on natural resources to meet our basic needs for food and shelter. We also depend on natural resources to provide the energy and raw materials needed at home, at work, and for growing food. **Figure 19-11** compares the patterns of energy use in the United States with the patterns of energy use worldwide.

The sun is the source of energy

Almost all of this energy comes from the sun. The sun sends out energy as radiation of various wavelengths. Living things use this energy in many different ways.

Plants change energy from the sun into chemical energy

Plants use some of the energy from sunlight to change the simple molecules of carbon dioxide and water into oxygen and more complex molecules of simple sugars. This process is called photosynthesis. It allows plants to change the sun's energy into stored chemical energy.

Some animals eat plants to obtain energy. Through a series of chemical reactions, the animals are able to convert the sugars in plants back to carbon dioxide and water. This process, which also

produces energy, is known as cellular respiration. This cycle of energy transfer repeats itself continuously in nature. **Figure 19-12,** at right, shows both animals and plants undergoing cellular respiration.

Fossil fuels form deep underground

Living things cannot decompose and release their stored energy without air. For example, microscopic plants and animals living in the ocean die and are buried under layers of sediment where they are not in contact with air. Without air, the organic chemicals in the remains of the living things cannot combine with oxygen and change back to carbon dioxide and water. Instead, pressure and heat from the settled rock above the remains cause different chemical reactions. These reactions turn the organic chemicals into substances that contain mainly carbon and hydrogen, as shown in **Figure 19-13.** These substances are known as **fossil fuels.**

Fossil fuels can be solids, liquids, or gases

Although substances such as natural gas and coal seem very different, they have one thing in common—they are made of carbon and carbon-containing molecules.

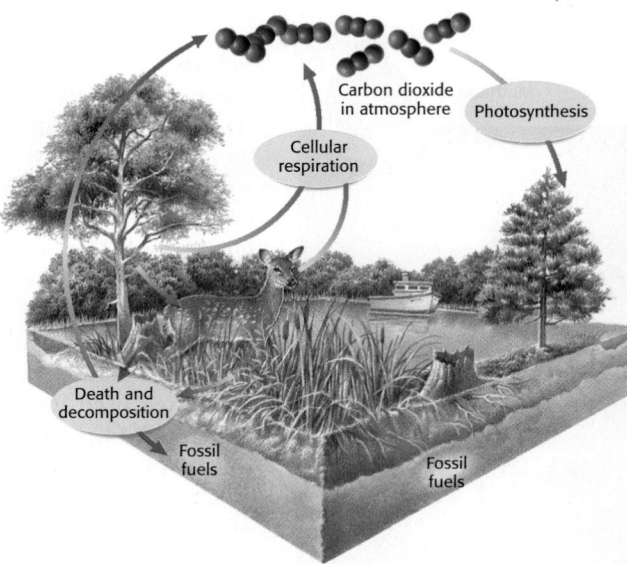

Figure 19-12
Carbon dioxide is a product of cellular respiration.

▶ **fossil fuels** any fuels formed from the remains of ancient plant and animal life

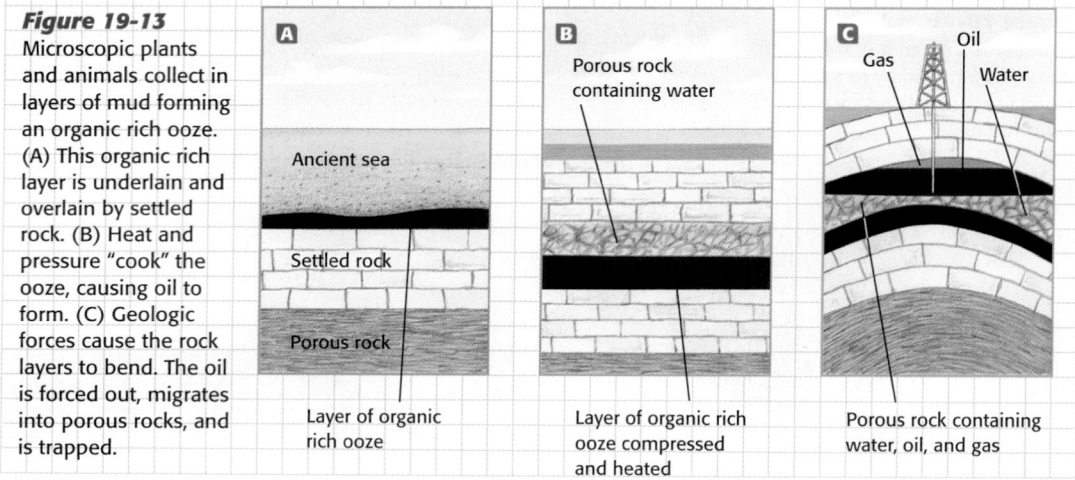

Figure 19-13
Microscopic plants and animals collect in layers of mud forming an organic rich ooze. (A) This organic rich layer is underlain and overlain by settled rock. (B) Heat and pressure "cook" the ooze, causing oil to form. (C) Geologic forces cause the rock layers to bend. The oil is forced out, migrates into porous rocks, and is trapped.

A
Ancient sea
Settled rock
Porous rock
Layer of organic rich ooze

B
Porous rock containing water
Layer of organic rich ooze compressed and heated

C
Gas
Oil
Water
Porous rock containing water, oil, and gas

READING SKILL BUILDER *Brainstorming* Write the phrase *fossil fuels* on the chalkboard, and have students come up with words that relate to the phrase. Encourage students to devise a hypothesis about the definition of the phrase based on their combined thoughts.

Teaching Tip

Photosynthesis To demonstrate how plants change energy from the sun into chemical energy (by photosynthesis), lead your students to a patch of grass outside. Place a small waterproof container (plastic bowl or a shoe box covered with plastic wrap) over some of the grass, so that it is deprived of sunlight. Adjacent to the covered grass make sure there is a patch that will receive sunlight. Ask students to record their hypotheses about what the two patches will look like over the course of several days or a weekend. After a few days have passed, go back to the patches of grass and have students make observations.

Energy and Resources

Teaching Tip

Air Pollutants Fumes from the burning of fossil fuels contain tiny particles of pollutants that circulate throughout the air that we breathe. Ask students if they can propose a hypothesis for a method of trapping some of these tiny air pollutants. *(Answers will vary.)*

For a demonstration, take pieces of plastic and smear petroleum jelly on them. Place the plastic pieces in various locations around the school and collect them in a week. Look for any particulates or debris that may have collected on the jelly, and discuss the results with your students.

Dependence on Cars For one week, have students keep track of how many miles they travel by car. At the end of the week, have them graph their travel data. Have each student assume that the vehicle(s) they traveled in used 1 gal of gasoline per 25 mi traveled. Have each student divide the distance traveled by 25 to determine how many gallons of fuel were used during the week. Students can then analyze the data and make comparisons with their classmates. Are there any alternatives that students can think of that will reduce their dependence on cars?

Methane

Figure 19-14
Natural gas can provide the energy needed to prepare food.

▶ **nonrenewable resources** any resources that are used faster than they can be replaced

Figure 19-15
Although 86 percent of the world's energy is supplied by fossil fuels, oil and natural-gas reserves will soon run out.

Some fossil fuels are mixtures of liquids and gases. These fuels can leak out of porous rocks where they formed into rocks above. Porous rocks contain holes inside them and serve as reservoirs for the liquid oil and natural gas. Wells must be drilled into these porous rocks to reach the fossil fuels.

Oil is a mixture of many different substances. It comes out of the ground as a tarlike black liquid. It is useful for many things, but it must be purified and separated before it can be used. Refineries separate oil into gasoline, kerosene, diesel fuel, and other products.

Natural gas is made mostly of methane, CH_4. Methane is a colorless, odorless, poisonous gas that burns with a clean flame. It is often used for heating homes and cooking, as shown in **Figure 19-14.** In the United States, natural gas makes up 22 percent of the fossil fuels used.

Coal is a solid fossil fuel composed mainly of carbon. Unlike oil and natural gas, which formed in shallow oceans, coal formed in ancient swamps when the remains of large, fernlike plants were buried under layers of sediment.

The supply of fossil fuels is limited

When fossil fuels are burned, they form carbon dioxide and water and release energy. This energy is the energy of the sun that was trapped in plants hundreds of millions of years ago. Because fossil fuels take so long to form, they are considered **nonrenewable resources.** They are being used much faster than natural processes can replace them.

Figure 19-15A shows that the vast majority of the world's energy needs are met by the burning of fossil fuels. **Figure 19-15B** shows the estimated reserves of the world's supply of fossil fuels. If oil and natural gas use continue at current rates, the reserves may run out while you are still alive. What alternative sources of energy will provide the energy needed for everyday activities?

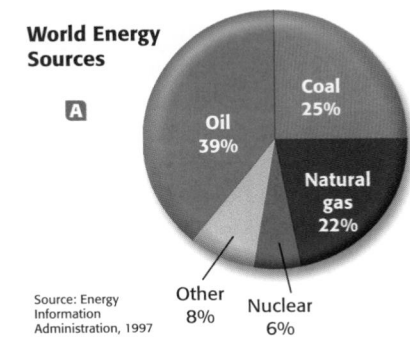

World Energy Sources

A

Coal 25%

Oil 39%

Natural gas 22%

Other 8%

Nuclear 6%

Source: Energy Information Administration, 1997

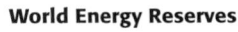

World Energy Reserves

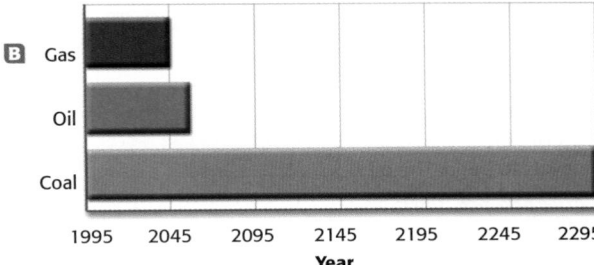

B Gas

Oil

Coal

1995 2045 2095 2145 2195 2245 2295

Year

Alternative Sources of Energy

Fossils fuels are not the only energy source around. We can harness energy from the sun, wind, water, and Earth. We can even obtain energy from atoms. The more these alternative sources of energy are used, the less we will rely on fossil fuels.

Another advantage of using alternative sources of energy is that many are **renewable resources.** This means they can be replaced by natural processes in a relatively short amount of time.

Solar power plants and solar cells can make electricity from sunlight

Every day, the sun makes more energy than is used to supply electricity to the United States for a year. But harnessing the sun's energy to supply electricity is not simple. Some parts of Earth do not get as much sunlight as other parts. Even when there is enough sunlight, tools are needed to convert the sun's energy and change it into a useful form.

In the 1990s, the first solar power plant capable of storing energy as heat was opened in the Mojave Desert, in California. This power plant, shown in **Figure 19-16,** stores the sun's heat and uses it for energy.

Another tool used to harness the sun's energy is a solar cell, shown in **Figure 19-17.** Solar cells are able to produce electricity from sunlight. But their use is limited due to high installation cost and a low output of energy.

The energy in wind can be used by windmills

Energy from the sun is a contributing factor in the production of another renewable energy resource—wind energy. Wind energy actually comes from the sun. Different places on Earth receive different amounts of sunlight, which causes variations in temperature. These temperature differences cause the movement of air, known as wind.

Wind is one of the oldest sources of renewable energy used by humans. It has been used to sail ships for thousands of years. As with other sources of energy, the use of wind energy has advantages and disadvantages. It can be unreliable. Even in exceptionally windy areas, wind doesn't blow steadily all the time. This can cause differences in the amount of power generated. However, the use of windmills is becoming increasingly popular in some areas because of their low cost.

internetconnect

SC*LINKS*
NSTA

TOPIC: Alternative energy sources
GO TO: www.scilinks.org
KEYWORD: HK1906

▶ **renewable resources**
any resources that can be continually replaced

Figure 19-16
Mojave Desert, in California, is home to the first solar-power plant capable of storing heat.

Figure 19-17
Solar cells convert sunlight into electricity.

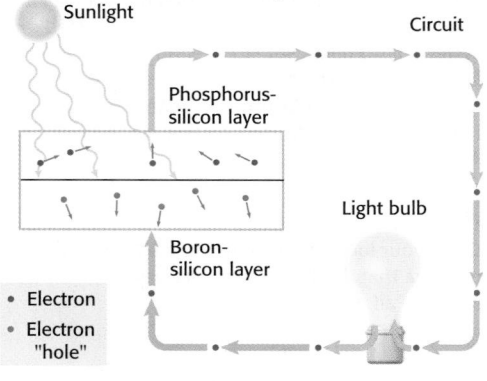

- Electron
- Electron "hole"

Alternative Energy Resources

Type/Source	Advantage	Disadvantage
Solar power/sun	Clean	High installation cost
Wind	Inexpensive	Unreliable
Hydroelectric/water	Renewable	May harm environment
Geothermal/Earth	Convenient in some areas	Limited by location

Energy and Resources

READING SKILL BUILDER *Reading Organizer* Have students read the section on the different types of energy sources, and have them organize the information in a table like the one shown below. Have students fill in the table with the appropriate information from Section 19.2 and share their information with the class.

Teaching Tip

Solar Heating Have your students determine what materials are best for a solar heating system by gathering items made of different materials, such as aluminum, steel, copper, stone, wood, plastic, and glass. Tape a thermometer to the back of each item, and place the items outside in the sunlight. After 30 minutes, have your students record the temperature of each item. (CAUTION: *Be sure to warn students about touching very hot materials.*)

Have your students make a list of the results, showing the hottest materials at the top of the list and the coolest at the bottom. Which material would work best in a solar heater?

RESOURCE LINK
IER

Assign students worksheet *19.7 Integrating Physics—Solar Cells* in the **Integration Enrichment Resources** ancillary.

Energy and Resources

Figure 19-18
The spinning blades of a windmill are connected to a generator. The faster the blades spin, the more electricity that is produced.

▶ **geothermal energy** the energy drawn from heated water within Earth's crust

Connection to SOCIAL STUDIES

To aid the nation's economic recovery following the Great Depression, President Franklin D. Roosevelt proposed a series of projects aimed at increasing employment and serving the public good. One such project was the Tennessee Valley Authority (TVA), a connected system of 40 dams spread over an area of 106 000 km². The TVA system still provides electricity to homes, farms, and factories in Tennessee, Kentucky, Virginia, North Carolina, Georgia, Alabama, and Mississippi.

Making the Connection

Go to your local library and find a map showing the area that the TVA covers. Draw your own map showing all 40 dams.

Windmills have been in use since about A.D. 600. Today, large windmills are set up in wind farms, like the one shown in **Figure 19-18,** to generate electrical power.

Moving water produces energy
Falling water releases a lot of energy. But even the energy produced from water depends on sunlight. For example, the water in oceans evaporates as sunlight transfers energy by heat. This water rises into the atmosphere, falls back down later as rain or snow, and flows downhill into creeks and rivers. Once the water is in the creeks and rivers, it flows back to the ocean, and the cycle begins again.

In some power plants, dams are built on fast-moving rivers to create large holding places for water. **Figure 19-19,** on page 643, illustrates how the stored water pours through turbines, making them spin. The turbines are connected to generators that produce hydroelectric power, another type of renewable resource.

Dams have already been built on most of the world's big rivers, so the potential for increasing the use of this energy source is limited.

Geothermal energy taps Earth's warmth
Another type of renewable energy resource can be found under Earth's crust. Underground reservoirs of steam or hot water produce **geothermal energy**. These holding pools usually lie near beds of molten magma, which heat the steam or water. Wells are drilled into the reservoirs, and the steam or hot water rises to the surface, where it is used to turn turbines to generate electrical power.

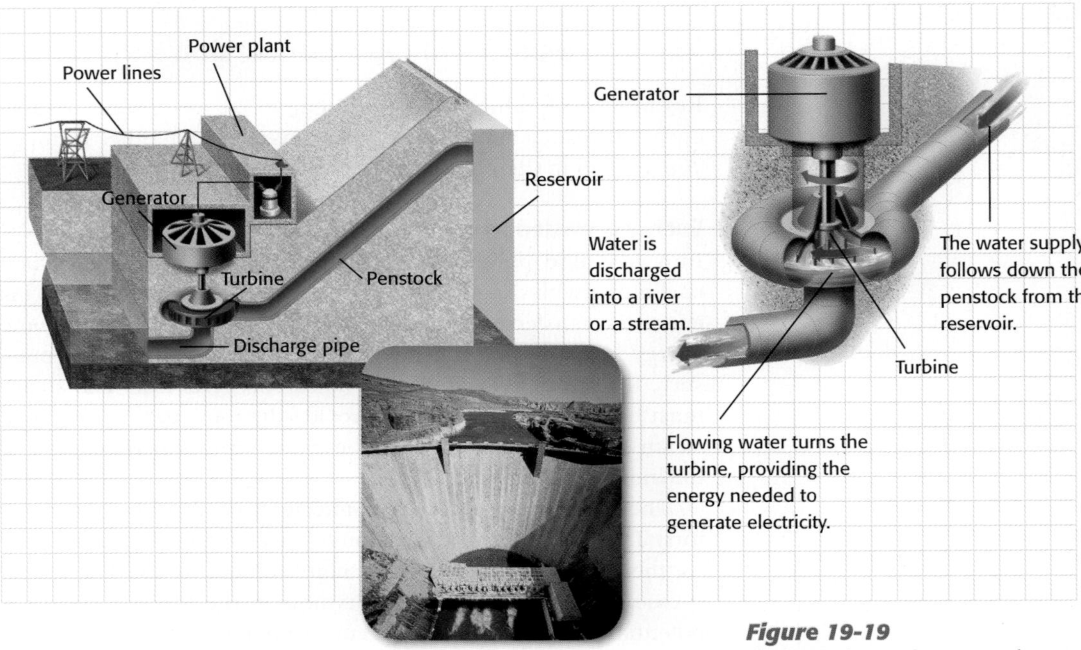

Power lines
Power plant
Generator
Turbine
Penstock
Discharge pipe
Generator
Reservoir
Water is discharged into a river or a stream.
The water supply follows down the penstock from the reservoir.
Turbine
Flowing water turns the turbine, providing the energy needed to generate electricity.

Figure 19-19
The incoming water causes the turbines in a dam to turn. The turbines run a generator that produces electricity.

Geothermal energy is a major source of electricity in volcanically active areas such as New Zealand, Iceland, and parts of California. Geothermal plants, such as the one shown in **Figure 19-20,** are common in these places. This type of energy works best when the beds of melted rock lie very close to the Earth's surface. However, not many areas have magma beds close to the surface, so widespread use of this resource is unlikely.

Atoms produce nuclear energy

In Chapter 7, you learned that atomic reactions produce a type of alternative energy resource called nuclear energy. Chain reactions involving nuclear fission produce a great deal of energy. This energy can be transferred as heat to water in a nuclear reactor. The heated water or steam can then be used to turn a turbine and generate electricity.

There are some disadvantages to harnessing nuclear energy, including the radioactive waste produced. For this reason, nuclear energy has seen limited use in the United States. It currently provides only 8 percent of our energy. Scientists working with nuclear fusion hope that it will someday be a more useful and renewable resource. But so far, more energy is needed to sustain a fusion reaction than is produced by the reaction.

Figure 19-20
This geothermal plant in New Zealand produces electricity.

USING NATURAL RESOURCES **643**

LINKING
CHAPTERS
Review nuclear fission reactions discussed in Chapter 7.

Teaching Tip

Nuclear Power Plants
Nuclear power plants use heat from nuclear reactors to produce electrical energy. These power plants have five main components: shielding, fuel, control rods, a moderator, and coolant. Shielding is a radiation-absorbing material that is used to decrease radiation exposure from nuclear reactors. Control rods are neutron-absorbing rods that help control the reaction by limiting the number of free neutrons. A moderator is used to slow down the fast neutrons produced by fission.

Additional Applications

Safety Concerns Current problems with nuclear power plant development include environmental requirements, safety of operation, plant construction costs, and storage of spent fuel.

The fission reaction creates radioactive products, many of which are very dangerous. If the reaction gets out of control, the enormous heat it generates may destroy the reactor building and spew the radioactive products into the air.

Energy and Resources

READING SKILL BUILDER *Paired Reading* Have students silently read the passage on the efficiency of energy conversion and have them mark on self-adhesive notes those sections that are not understood. Be sure that students study **Figure 19-21** in order to clarify the relevant passages. Pair students together before or after the reading, and have them discuss the passages they found difficult.

The Efficiency of Energy Conversion

Regardless of which energy resource we use, some usable energy is lost each time energy is converted to another form, as you learned in Chapter 9.

Energy is wasted when input is greater than output

In a coal-fired power plant, chemical energy is released when coal burns with oxygen in the air in a combustion reaction. This energy is transferred by heat to water, which forms steam. Some energy is lost in this conversion. In order to obtain a high pressure, the steam is heated, and more energy is lost. The steam must be at a high pressure to provide the force to turn the huge steam turbines. This changes the energy into kinetic energy of the moving turbines.

The spinning turbines are connected to coils of large generators. These coils carry current and act as large electromagnets. As they spin, they generate a high voltage in the fixed coils surrounding them. The energy is now in the form of electrical potential energy. This causes a current that carries the electricity to local consumers through a cable. **Figure 19-21** shows how electricity is produced in a typical power station.

Figure 19-21
This power plant converts coal into electrical energy.

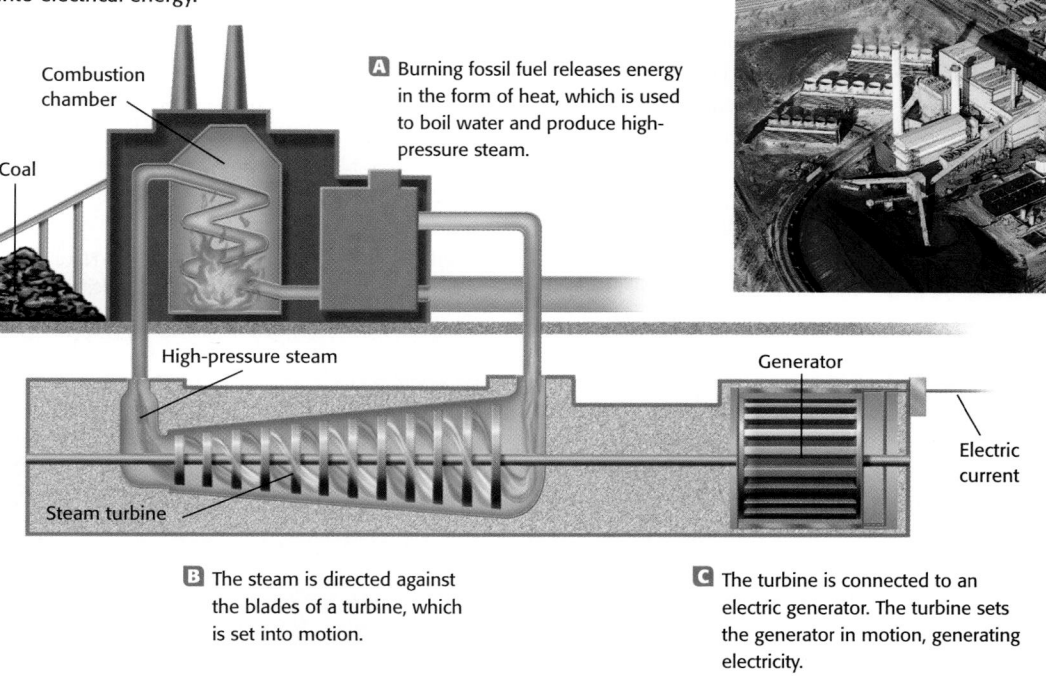

Combustion chamber

Coal

A Burning fossil fuel releases energy in the form of heat, which is used to boil water and produce high-pressure steam.

High-pressure steam

Generator

Electric current

Steam turbine

B The steam is directed against the blades of a turbine, which is set into motion.

C The turbine is connected to an electric generator. The turbine sets the generator in motion, generating electricity.

644 CHAPTER 19

RESOURCE LINK
IER

Assign students worksheet *19.5 Connection to Language Arts—The Meaning of Efficiency* in the **Integration Enrichment Resources** ancillary.

A large power station might be rated at 1000 MW. This means that it delivers 1 billion joules of energy every second. But three times the amount of fuel, equal to 3 billion joules of energy, is needed because two-thirds of the energy input is wasted. Most power stations that use fossil fuels for energy are only 30 to 40 percent efficient.

Wasted energy can be used

Wasted energy occurs in the production of all energy sources. Nuclear power stations are roughly as efficient, or inefficient, as fossil-fuel power plants. Even wind-powered plants have some inefficiency because of the energy conversions involved.

There are ways to make use of some of this wasted energy. For example, although the water from power stations is not hot enough to make electricity, it can be used to heat homes. In Germany, most towns have their own small power station. Rather than dump the warm water into a river, it is piped to people's homes to keep them heated. These are called combined heat and power schemes. They reduce wasted energy and make electricity less expensive.

SECTION 19.2 REVIEW

SUMMARY

▶ Most of the energy used in the world comes from fossil fuels, which are nonrenewable resources.

▶ Energy from the sun produces solar energy and wind energy.

▶ Hydroelectric power can be generated from large reservoirs of water.

▶ Geothermal energy is generated from underground reservoirs in volcanically active areas.

▶ The use of nuclear energy is limited.

▶ Energy is lost each time it is converted to another form.

CHECK YOUR UNDERSTANDING

1. **List** five ways that you use electricity during lunch.
2. **Describe** the cycle of energy transfer among organisms.
3. **Compare** the amount of energy used in the United States with the amount used worldwide. Write a paragraph explaining the social and economic reasons for the difference.
4. **Explain** in a paragraph the energy conversions that occur when a drop of rain falls on a mountain, rolls downhill, passes through a hydroelectric plant, and turns a turbine to generate electricity.
5. **Describe** some advantages and disadvantages of solar energy.
6. **Predict** which of the following will be more efficient in terms of capturing the most energy. Justify your answer.
   a. burning paper to boil water to make steam to turn a turbine
   b. using wind to generate electricity
7. **Critical Thinking** A classmate says that geothermal power is perfectly efficient because it never runs out. What's wrong with this reasoning?

Energy and Resources

SECTION 19.2 REVIEW

Check Your Understanding

1. to boil water, to keep your drink cold, to turn the lights on in the kitchen, to open cans (electric can opener), to dispose of waste (garbage disposal)

2. The sun sends out energy as radiation, and this energy is used by animals and plants. Plants use this energy to make oxygen and simple sugars, and animals eat plants and other animals to get energy for themselves.

3. The amount of energy used in the United States is much higher than in other places in the world. This is due to the fact that the United States is quite affluent compared to many other countries. This affluent lifestyle that many Americans enjoy contributes to high amounts of energy consumption.

4. As rain rolls downhill, its kinetic energy increases, and as the rain moves through turbines in a hydroelectric plant, it makes the turbines spin. The turbines are connected to generators that produce hydroelectric power.

Answers continue on p. 661A.

RESOURCE LINK
STUDY GUIDE

Assign students *Review Section 19.2 Energy and Resources.*

Sun-Warmed Houses Many specially designed homes in Colorado are able to receive the majority of their heat from the sun. But in Canada and Alaska, where the climate is similar to the climate in Colorado, solar heating systems are often inadequate. Talk to your students about latitude and longitude and offer an explanation for why this occurs.

Your Choice
1. Answers will vary.
2. overheating during hot days; people can solve those problems with windows designed to release heat.

Sun-Warmed Houses

Specially designed houses make use of the sun's heat in two different ways—passive solar heating and active solar heating.

How Does Passive Solar Heating Work?

In passive solar heating, no special devices are used. The house is simply built to take advantage of the sun's energy. For example, passive solar houses have large windows that face south, enabling them to receive a lot of sunlight throughout the day. Many have glass-enclosed fronts called sunspaces, which work to trap solar energy like glass in a greenhouse. During the winter, the energy that enters the sunspace keeps the room comfortably warm during the day. The floor is made of special tiles that absorb heat and then radiate it out into the room throughout the evening.

How Is Energy Conserved in Passive Solar Heating?

The rest of the house still has to be heated in winter, but heating costs are generally much lower than they ordinarily would be. Some of the energy that would normally escape through an outside wall is kept inside because the sunspace acts as a good insulator.

Homes that take advantage of solar heating generally have lower electric bills.

On the north side of passive solar houses, there are only small windows in order to reduce energy loss. Also, the walls are built to be good insulators. Once the house is warm, its walls and furnishings act as a large "heat store," keeping the warmth inside.

How Does Active Solar Heating Work?

In active solar heating, houses use solar heaters—active solar-energy devices—to heat water or air. In solar heaters, a flat-plate collector is placed on the roof to gather sunlight. The collector is a flat box covered with glass or plastic. The bottom of the box is often painted black because dark colors absorb radiation better than light colors do. The collector gathers and traps heat, warming the air or water inside. The heated air or water flows into an insulated storage tank. Electric pumps or fans circulate the heated air or water throughout the house. Because they can store solar energy, active solar heating systems work 24 hours a day. However, during long periods of cloudy days, backup heating systems are necessary.

1. **Making Decisions** A house that uses fossil fuels for energy might cost its owners $2000 in heating expenses during the winter. An energy-efficient house could reduce this cost by 50 percent, but it might cost $10 000 more to build. Do you think the energy savings are worth the added construction cost? Explain your reasoning.
2. **Critical Thinking** What problem might people who live in houses with sunspaces have in the summer? How could they solve this problem?

internetconnect

SCLINKS
NSTA
TOPIC: Solar heated homes
GO TO: www.scilinks.org
KEYWORD: HK1932

RESOURCE LINK

IER

Assign students worksheet *19.2 Science and the Consumer—Solar Energy* in the **Integration Enrichment Resources** ancillary.

19.3

Pollution and Recycling

INTEGRATING TECHNOLOGY and Society

OBJECTIVES

▶ Compare the economic and environmental impacts of using various energy sources.
▶ Identify several pollutants caused by fossil fuel use.
▶ Describe types of pollution in air, in water, and on land.
▶ Identify ways to reduce, reuse, and recycle.

▶ **KEY TERMS**
pollution
global warming
eutrophication
recycling

Scheduling

Refer to pp. 628A–628D for lecture, classwork, and assignment options for Section 19.3.

★ **Lesson Focus**
Use transparency *LT 64* to prepare students for this section.

READING SKILL BUILDER   *K-W-L*   Have students list what they know or what they think they know about the topic of pollution. After they have read the relevant portions of the text and studied the topic, have them look at their lists and write down what they have learned about the subject. Also have them write down any new questions they may have after reading the section.

T hink about the items in your classroom. You can probably identify ordinary items such as desks, lights, chalk, paper, pencils, backpacks, books, doors, and windows. Your classroom contains many products, all made from natural resources.

Making each product required energy. And the manufacture of nearly all of the products caused some kind of **pollution**. Whenever natural resources generate energy or become products, other things are usually made in the process. If these things are not used, they may be thrown out and cause pollution. Pollution is the contamination of the air, the water, or the soil, as shown in **Figure 19-22**.

▶ **pollution** the contamination of the air, water, or soil

What Causes Pollution?

When you think of pollution, you may think of litter, such as that cluttering the water in **Figure 19-22A**. Or you may think of smog, the clouds of dust, smoke, and chemicals shown in **Figure 19-22B**.

Pollution can be as invisible as a colorless, odorless gas or as obvious as bad-smelling trash left by the side of the road. Most forms of pollution have several common features. Understanding these features will help you make better choices.

Figure 19-22
(A) Trash polluted the water off the coast of Oahu, Hawaii.
(B) Contaminants polluted the air in Mexico City.

USING NATURAL RESOURCES   **647**

RESOURCE LINK
LABORATORY MANUAL

Have students perform *Lab 19 Using Natural Resources: Investigating the Effects of Acid Rain* in the lab ancillary.

DATASHEETS

Have students use *Datasheet 19.6* to record their results.

Pollution and Recycling

SKILL BUILDER

Interpreting Tables Have students study **Table 19-1, Air Pollutants.** Students should compare and contrast the different pollutants, their descriptions, primary sources, and effects. Lead students in a discussion about some of the similarities and differences among pollutants.

Resources Blackline Master 62 shows this table.

REAL WORLD APPLICATIONS •••••••••••••••••

Carbon Monoxide Carbon monoxide is a difficult pollutant to detect because it is odorless and colorless. Ask students if they have carbon monoxide detectors in their homes. Bring a detector in to show your students, and explain the benefits of having one.

•••••••••••••••••••••••••••••••••

Table 19-1 **Air Pollutants**

Pollutant	Description	Primary Sources	Effects
Carbon monoxide	CO is an odorless, colorless, poisonous gas.	It is produced by the incomplete burning of fossil fuels. Cars, trucks, buses, small engines, and some industrial processes are the major sources of CO.	◆ Interferes with the blood's ability to carry oxygen ◆ Slows reflexes and causes drowsiness ◆ Can cause death in high concentrations ◆ Can cause headaches and stress on the heart ◆ Can hamper the growth and development of the fetus
Nitrogen oxides (NO_x)	When combustion (burning) temperatures are greater than 538°C (1000°F), nitrogen and oxygen combine to form nitrogen oxides.	NO_x compounds come from the burning of fuels in vehicles, power plants, and industrial boilers.	◆ Can make the body vulnerable to respiratory infection, lung disease, and possibly cancer ◆ Contribute to the brownish haze often seen over congested areas and to acid rain ◆ Can cause metal corrosion and the fading and deterioration of fabrics
Sulfur dioxide (SO_2)	SO_2 is produced by chemical interactions between sulfur and oxygen.	SO_2 comes from the burning of fossil fuels. It is released from petroleum refineries, smelters, paper mills, chemical plants, and coal-burning power plants.	◆ Contributes to acid rain ◆ Can harm plant life and irritate the respiratory systems of humans and animals
Volatile organic compounds (VOCs)	VOCs are organic chemicals that vaporize readily and produce toxic fumes. Some examples are gasoline, paint thinner, and lighter fluid.	Cars are a major source of VOCs. They also come from solvents, paints, glues, and burning fuels.	◆ Contribute to the formation of smog ◆ Cause serious health problems, such as cancer ◆ May harm plants
Particulate matter (particulates or PM)	Particulates are tiny particles of liquid or solid matter. Some examples are smoke, dust, and acid droplets.	Construction, agriculture, forestry, and fires produce particulates. Industrial processes and motor vehicles that burn fossil fuels also produce particulates.	◆ Form clouds that reduce visibility and cause a variety of respiratory problems ◆ Linked to cancer ◆ Corrode metals, erode buildings and sculptures, and soil fabrics

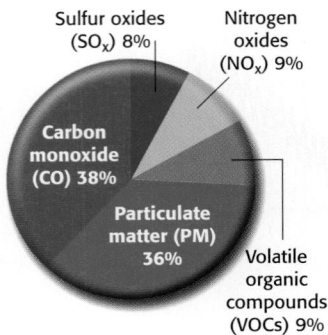

Sulfur oxides (SO$_x$) 8%

Nitrogen oxides (NO$_x$) 9%

Carbon monoxide (CO) 38%

Particulate matter (PM) 36%

Volatile organic compounds (VOCs) 9%

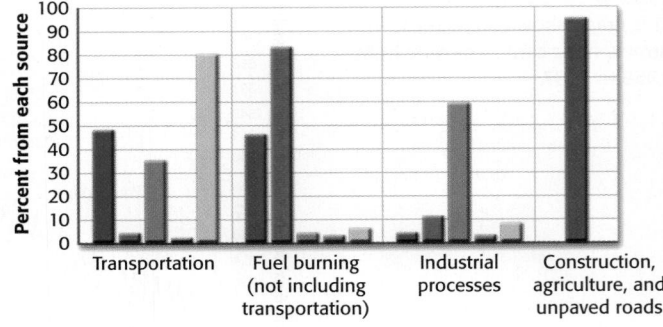

Figure 19-23
Carbon monoxide, produced mainly from the burning of fossil fuels, is the major air pollutant in the United States.

Some pollution has natural causes

Pollution can be caused by natural processes. For example, following an explosive volcanic eruption, dust and ash can be spread throughout the air. This can make it hard for some people to breathe. The dust and ash can also cover leaves of trees and plants, preventing them from absorbing sunlight.

Manmade pollution is more common

Most pollution is caused by human activities. As you learned in Chapter 5, many chemical reactions can be used to make new materials or to release energy. But most chemical reactions produce two or more products. If the other products are not used properly, they can add to the pollution problem.

Air pollution

Air pollution comes in many forms, from individual molecules to clumps of dust and other matter, called particulates. **Figure 19-23** shows major air pollutants and sources of air pollutants in the United States. **Table 19-1,** on page 648, describes these different forms of pollution.

Combustion of fuels produces most air pollution

As you have learned, most of the energy we use to drive cars, heat and light buildings, and power machinery comes from the burning of fossil fuels. The burning process is known as combustion.

During combustion, the fuel, which contains carbon and hydrogen, reacts with oxygen to release energy. Along with this desirable product, two other products are formed: carbon dioxide gas and water vapor. These combustion products escape into the air as invisible gases. The reaction for burning methane from natural gas is shown below.

$$CH_4 + 2O_2 \longrightarrow CO_2 + 2H_2O$$

USING NATURAL RESOURCES **649**

internet**connect**

SC*I*LINKS
NSTA

TOPIC: Pollution
GO TO: www.scilinks.org
KEYWORD: HK1907

Pollution and Recycling

|SKILL|BUILDER

Interpreting Visuals Have students look at **Figure 19-23.** Carbon monoxide is the major air pollutant in the United States. According to the pie chart, which pollutant is present in the smallest percentage? *(sulfur oxides)* See if students can remember some of the sources of carbon monoxide. *(combustion of fossil fuels; cars, trucks, buses, and small engines)* Ask students why carbon monoxide is the most prevalent air pollutant in the United States. *(Most of the energy we use comes from the combustion of fossil fuels, and our country is dependent on the use of cars and other vehicles.)*

Resources Blackline Master 63 shows this visual.

|SKILL|BUILDER

Vocabulary Bits of dust and other solids are called particulate matter. Ask students what other word is related to the word *particulate*. *(particle)* Ask students to define the word *particle* and to apply its meaning to the word *particulate.*

Teaching Tip

Fossil Fuel Dependence To illustrate our dependence on vehicles that require fossil fuels for energy, have students keep track of their activities that involve using a motorized vehicle for one week. At the end of the week, have students present their results. Have students think of ways in which they can reduce their dependence on fossil fuels for transportation.

 SKILL BUILDER

Interpreting Visuals Have students examine **Figure 19-24.** Levels of carbon dioxide in the atmosphere have been increasing for several decades, and they will not drop any time soon. Ask students for hypotheses about future levels of carbon dioxide in the atmosphere; have them justify their answers. *(Levels will continue to rise because of increasing numbers of people on the planet.)*

READING SKILL BUILDER

L.I.N.K. Write the phrase *global warming* on the board, and have students list all words, phrases, and ideas that they associate with the phrase. Begin a discussion in which students inquire about the listed ideas. At the end of the discussion, have students make notes of everything they remember from the discussion, then have them look over their notes to see what they know about the topic based on experience and the discussion.

Quick ACTIVITY

Modeling Acid Rain

Point out to students that vinegar is 10–100 times more acidic than most acid rain. It is used to show a measurable effect within a class period. In highly industrialized regions, acid rain can be extreme. The northeastern United States sometimes gets "soda-pop" rain with a pH near 4.0, similar to the pH of soft drinks.

RESOURCE LINK
DATASHEETS

Have students use *Datasheet 19.2: Quick Activity—The Effects of Acid Rain* to record their results.

650

Figure 19-24
This graph shows an increase in atmospheric carbon dioxide from 1958 to 1997.

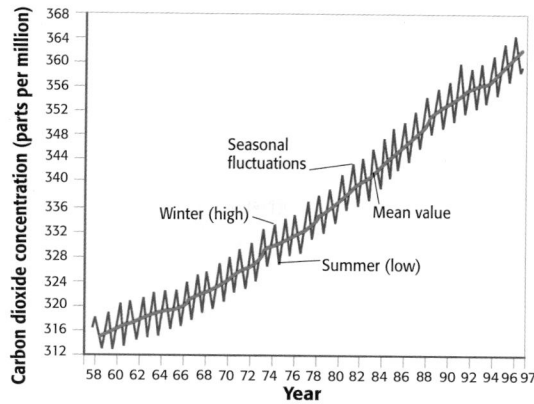

▶ **global warming**
an increase in Earth's temperature due to an increase in greenhouse gases

Quick ACTIVITY

Modeling Acid Rain
1. Place a few small pieces of marble on a balance. Measure the initial mass, and record it in your lab notebook. Place the small pieces of marble in an empty beaker.
2. Repeat step 1 with limestone, granite, and concrete.
3. Pour 50 mL of vinegar into each beaker of rocks. Observe and listen to the reactions in all four beakers. After 10 min, dispose of the vinegar as directed by your teacher. (Note: vinegar is more acidic than most acid rain.)
4. Dry the rocks with a towel. Measure the final mass and record your results. Calculate and record the percentage of rock lost.

650 CHAPTER 19

Carbon dioxide is a greenhouse gas

Carbon dioxide is found naturally in Earth's atmosphere. It is one of the greenhouse gases, which help keep temperatures on Earth balanced. Just as the glass of a greenhouse garden traps radiation that keeps the inside warm, greenhouse gases in the atmosphere trap radiation that keeps Earth warm. Without the greenhouse effect, temperatures on Earth would be roughly 33°C lower.

Humans release about 5 billion metric tons of carbon dioxide into the air every year. **Figure 19-24** shows how the amount of atmospheric carbon dioxide has changed since 1958. Some scientists hypothesize that by 2020 the amount of carbon dioxide in the atmosphere will be twice its present level. Some records indicate that the average temperature of Earth is already showing a small increase. In the past 100 years, the average temperature in the United States has increased by about 2°C. It is estimated that if the level of atmospheric carbon dioxide doubles, global temperatures might increase by about 3°C. This global warming may not sound like a lot, but it could drastically affect Earth's climate. Weather patterns could change, bringing droughts to some areas and floods to others. Other scientists point out that ice ages and warming periods occured in the past without large human sources of CO_2.

Combustion releases other pollutants

The burning of fossil fuels in vehicles, power stations, and factories releases more than carbon dioxide into the air. It also releases sulfur dioxide and nitrogen dioxide. Once these gases are released into the air, they react with other atmospheric gases and with water. Chemical reactions like these can make rain, sleet, or snow acidic. Normal rain is slightly acidic, with a pH of roughly 5.6. Acid rain typically has a pH of between 4 and 5. In extreme cases in the 1970s, polluted rainfall was as acidic as vinegar.

DEMONSTRATION 3 TEACHING

Carbon Dioxide Analysis

Time: Approximately 15 minutes
Materials: bromothymol blue, balloons (2), twist ties (4), straws (2), beakers (2)

Bromothymol blue (BTB) is a solution that changes color in the presence of carbon dioxide. Hence, it is known as an indicator. You can compare the amounts of carbon dioxide present in two different samples of gas by introducing the gas into the BTB and comparing the resulting colors. The first sample of gas should be obtained from the tailpipe of a car. Turn your car's engine on. Put a balloon around the small end of a funnel, and place the funnel over the tailpipe. (Make sure that the students are observing from a safe distance where they cannot breathe in any fumes.)

When acid rain falls into streams and lakes, it makes them acidic. This can harm or even kill aquatic life. Acid rain can also make soil more acidic, leaching out nutrients and damaging large areas of forests. In addition, it can corrode metals and damage buildings by eroding stonework.

Air pollution can cause breathing problems

When nitrogen oxide compounds in car exhaust react with sunlight, they can produce a cloud of chemicals called photochemical smog. The result is a brown haze that can make eyes sting and cause severe headaches and breathing difficulties.

Ozone is one of the harmful chemicals in photochemical smog. High up in the atmosphere, ozone blocks harmful ultraviolet radiation. Close to Earth's surface, however, ozone is a pollutant. It can cause problems for people who suffer from asthma or other conditions affecting the throat and lungs.

Photochemical smog is most common in sunny, densely populated cities, such as Los Angeles and Tokyo. In Tokyo, many people wear masks to protect themselves from the polluted air, and companies supply fresh-air dispensers to their employees. The smog also damages plants. Decreased yields of citrus fruits, such as oranges and lemons, may be linked to photochemical smog in areas not far from Los Angeles. To combat the problem, many cities have made concerted efforts to expand public transportation systems and to encourage people to carpool. These efforts help reduce the number of vehicles on the road and thus the amount of pollutants released into the air.

Water Pollution

All living things need water to survive. In fact, the bodies of most organisms, including humans, are made up mostly of water. Many people believe that water is our most valuable natural resource. Unpolluted water is even more important to aquatic organisms, which spend all their life in a liquid environment.

On July 6, 1988, a load of aluminum sulfate was accidentally tipped into the water supply in Camelford, England. Before the mistake was discovered, people became ill.

Accidents are responsible for some water pollution but not all. Most water pollution can be traced to industrial waste, agricultural fertilizers, and everyday human activities. A bucket of dirty, soapy water dumped down a kitchen drain can eventually make its way into the water supply. Flushing toilets, washing cars, and pouring chemicals down drains are actions that can contribute to water pollution.

Quick ACTIVITY

Observing Air Pollution

1. Cut off a piece of masking tape about 8 cm long.
2. Place the sticky side of the tape against an outside wall, and press gently.
3. Remove the tape, and hold it against a sheet of white paper.
4. Did the tape pick up dust? If so, what might be the source of the dust?
5. Repeat the experiment on other walls in different places, and compare the amounts of dust observed.
6. Suggest reasons why some walls appear to have more dirt than others.

Pollution and Recycling

Connection to HEALTH

Smog and ozone are air pollutants that make it difficult to breathe. People with respiratory problems such as asthma and bronchitis are severely affected by air pollution. Have students research several respiratory-system conditions and explain how these conditions are affected by air pollution.

Quick ACTIVITY

Observing Air Pollution
Before conducting this Quick Activity, brainstorm with your students:

- Where around the school grounds might we find the greatest amount of air pollutants?

- What causes the air pollution?

Have them work in areas where the differences in results will be greatest. (near a bus stop, near a chalkboard, inside an office with an air conditioner, etc.)

Resources Have students use *Datasheet 19.3 Quick Activity: Observing Air Pollution* to record their results.

Let the balloon fill, and then close it with a twist tie. For the next sample of gas, have a student exhale into another balloon. Close the balloon with a twist tie.

Insert a straw into the mouth of one of the balloons, and use another twist tie to tighten the balloon around the straw. Repeat this procedure with the other balloon. (When the first twist tie is removed, the gas should come out of the straw.) Put 100 mL of BTB into two small beakers, and slowly introduce the samples of gas into each beaker. BTB turns yellow in the presence of carbon dioxide, so the sample that is more yellow contains a higher concentration of carbon dioxide.

Pollution and Recycling

▶ **eutrophication** an increase in the amount of nutrients, such as nitrates, in an environment

internet connect

SCLINKS NSTA

TOPIC: Solutions to pollution problems
GO TO: www.scilinks.org
KEYWORD: HK1908

In many countries, water is cleaned at water-purification plants before it is piped to consumers. But because many chemicals dissolve easily in water, it's difficult to remove all of the impurities from the water.

Pesticides and fertilizers often end up polluting water

Some modern farms use chemical fertilizers to increase crop yields. These fertilizers can get washed away by rain and end up in streams, rivers, lakes, or ponds. The fertilizers may contain nitrate ions, which encourage the growth of bacteria and algae.

Fed on the nitrates, the bacteria and algae grow so fast that they use up most of the oxygen in the water. The result is an algal bloom, such as the one shown in **Figure 19-25.** Fish and other aquatic wildlife suffer from the reduced oxygen and die. This process, known as **eutrophication,** is made worse if hot water from power stations or factories is discharged into the river or lake. The extra warmth makes the bacteria and algae multiply even faster.

Animals on land can be affected by another group of chemicals that eventually make their way into bodies of water. These chemicals, called pesticides, are used to control crop-damaging pests.

Like fertilizers, pesticides can be washed by rain into streams, rivers, lakes, or ponds. There they are ingested by fish and other aquatic animals. As larger animals eat the fish, the chemicals are passed along the food chain. In the 1970s, a pesticide called DDT was widely used to control mosquitoes and other insects, leading to the eradication of malaria in the United States. DDT caused the eggs of fish-eating pelicans and other fish-eating birds to become thin and fragile. The pelicans nearly became extinct before the use of DDT was banned in the United States.

Figure 19-25
This algal bloom is the result of an abundance of nitrates in the water.

ALTERNATIVE ASSESSMENT

Aquatic Plants and Fertilizers

Materials: *Elodea* (or a similar aquatic plant), two small aquaria (or plastic containers), pond water, fertilizer

Ask your students to predict what will happen if you take two equivalent samples of *Elodea* and expose them to similar amounts of sunlight, but give only one of the samples a daily amount of fertilizer. Ask students for hypotheses, and then conduct the experiment, comparing the results at the end of a week.

Challenge students to design an experiment to test the hypothesis: What effect does warm water have on *Elodea*? (Maintain one container at room temperature and the other at an elevated temperature. Compare the results at the end of the week or keep the experiment running longer to see more definitive results.)

Inquiry Lab

How can oil spills be cleaned up?

Materials
- ✔ cooking oil
- ✔ cold water
- ✔ cleaning materials
- ✔ rectangular baking pan

Procedure

1. Fill the pan halfway with cold water.
2. Pour a small amount of cooking oil into the water.
3. Try to clean up the "oil spill" using at least four different cleaning materials.

Analysis

1. Evaluate the effectiveness of each material. Which worked best? Explain why.
2. Did any of the materials "pollute" the water with particles or residue? How might you clean up this pollution?

Pollution on Land

Pollution that affects our land has many sources. In some cases, the source is obvious, as when trash is dumped illegally by a roadside. In other cases, the source is not so obvious. For example, dirt near many highways contains an unusually high amount of lead. This lead originally came from car exhaust. The lead was part of a compound added to gasoline to help car engines run more smoothly. This type of gasoline was banned in the 1970s, but there are still greater amounts of lead in soil near busy highways.

Contaminants in soil are hard to remove

A common type of land-based pollution occurs when hazardous chemicals soak into the soil. For example, in 1983, the entire town of Times Beach, Missouri, was bought by the U.S. Environmental Protection Agency. The town's soil was contaminated by a highly toxic chemical compound called dioxin.

Exposure to dioxin, a chemical produced in the paper-making process, had been linked to an increased risk of cancer. The soil in the town had become contaminated because the waste oil used to keep the dust on the town's roads down contained small amounts of dioxin. After the roads were repeatedly sprayed over several years, the dioxin levels became very high. This resulted in the deaths of some livestock and other animals and it also adversely affected the health of some of the town's residents.

Dioxin, like many land-based pollutants, does not dissolve well in water. It does not break down easily. It is therefore very difficult to remove it from the soil. The EPA bought the town because it was less expensive than cleaning the entire town's soil.

USING NATURAL RESOURCES **653**

Inquiry Lab

How can oil spills be cleaned up? Students may benefit from wearing plastic gloves if they are available. This should prevent the classroom and materials from getting too oily. Ask students what other materials might be tested to help clean up the spill.

REAL WORLD APPLICATIONS ················

Oil Spill The *Exxon Valdez* was an oil tanker that ran aground in 1986, spilling millions of gallons of oil into Prince William Sound, Alaska. Challenge students to find out what resources were used to clean up the oil from the *Exxon Valdez* and what damage was done to the surrounding environment by the spill.

·······································

RESOURCE LINK

IER

Assign students worksheet *19.6: Integrating Chemistry—Pesticides* in the **Integration Enrichment Resources** ancillary.

DATASHEETS

Have students use *Datasheet 19.4: Inquiry Lab—How can oil spills be cleaned up?* to record their results.

Pollution and Recycling

Figure 19-26
Many landfills are closing because of a lack of space.

INTEGRATING

BIOLOGY
When trash is buried at a landfill, microorganisms called aerobes use oxygen in the dirt to slowly decompose food, paper, and other biodegradable garbage. This process causes soil temperatures to rise, killing off the aerobes.

Anaerobes, microorganisms that thrive in oxygen-free environments, continue the long task of decomposing the refuse. But generally, anaerobes break down trash even more slowly than aerobes do. Non-biodegradable trash, such as plastics, glass, and metals, stays essentially intact in landfills.

654 CHAPTER 19

Landfill space is running out

Even when trash is taken to a landfill, like the one shown in **Figure 19-26,** and disposed of legally, it can still cause pollution. Each time an item is placed in a landfill, there is less space remaining for other materials. In some regions of the United States, landfills are closing because they are full. Few new landfills are opening.

Currently, each person in the United States throws away almost a half ton of garbage every year. If current trends continue, parts of the United States will soon run out of landfill space.

Reducing Pollution

The are many ways to reduce or limit pollution. Government regulation is one way. In the United States there are several laws that encourage clean water supplies and discourage the pollution of air, soil, and water. Countries may also work together to combat the problem. For instance, in December 1997, international representatives met in Kyoto, Japan, to negotiate an agreement to reduce greenhouse-gas emissions.

Choosing alternatives often involves trade-offs

Even greater improvements in the pollution problem come when individuals, communities, and companies make careful choices. For example, to reduce the air pollution caused by the burning of fossil fuels, people can switch to alternative energy sources. Individuals can make a difference by conserving energy. However, even nonpolluting sources of energy, such as wind, solar, and hydroelectric power, require large amounts of land and are potentially disruptive to ecosystems.

Small-scale sources of energy, such as disposable batteries, have an environmental impact too. These batteries contain mercury and other potentially toxic chemicals. In the United States alone, more than 2 billion disposable batteries are discarded every year. The toxic chemicals can leak into the ground, polluting water supplies and soil.

Reducing the use of energy and products can cut down on pollution

Because of the trade-offs involved, many people believe that the best solution to the problem of pollution is to reduce our overall consumption of energy and material goods. If less energy is used, less pollution is generated. Turning off lights and lowering thermostats are two simple ways to conserve energy. Carpooling is another way to conserve energy.

Recycling Codes: How Are Plastics Sorted?

More than half of the states in the United States have enacted laws that require plastic products to be labeled with numerical codes that identify the type of plastic used in them. These codes are shown in the table below. Used plastic products can be sorted by these codes and properly recycled or processed. Only codes 1 and 2 are widely accepted for recycling. Codes 3 and 6 are rarely recycled. Knowing what the numerical codes mean will give you an idea of how successfully a given plastic product can be recycled. This may affect your decision to buy or not buy particular items.

1. **Making Decisions** Find out what types of plastic are recycled in your area.
2. **Critical Thinking** Do you think recycling should be mandatory? Explain your views on the topic of recycling.

internetconnect

SC*LINKS*
NSTA

TOPIC: Recycling plastics
GO TO: www.scilinks.org
KEYWORD: HK1910

Recycling Codes for Plastic Products

Recycling code	Type of plastic	Physical properties	Example	Uses for recycled products
1	Polyethylene terephthalate (PET)	Tough, rigid; can be a fiber or a plastic; solvent resistant; sinks in water	Soda bottles, clothing, electrical insulation, automobile parts	Backpacks, sleeping bags, carpet, new bottles, clothing
2	High density polyethylene (HDPE)	Rough surface; stiff plastic; resistant to cracking	Milk containers, bleach bottles, toys, grocery bags	Furniture, toys, trash cans, picnic tables, park benches, fences
3	Polyvinyl chloride (PVC)	Elastomer or flexible plastic; tough; poor crystallization; unstable to light or heat; sinks in H_2O	Pipe, vinyl siding, automobile parts, clear bottles for cooking oil	Toys, playground equipment
4	Low density polyethylene (LDPE)	Moderately crystalline, flexible plastic; solvent resistant; floats on water	Trash bags, dry-cleaning bags, frozen-food packaging, meat packaging	Trash cans, trash bags, compost containers
5	Polypropylene (PP)	Rigid, very strong; fiber or flexible plastic; lightweight; heat- and stress-resistant	Heat-proof containers, rope, appliance parts, outdoor carpet, luggage, diapers, automobile parts	Brooms, brushes, ice scrapers, battery cable, insulation, rope
6	Polystyrene (P/S, PS)	Somewhat brittle, rigid plastic; resistant to acids and bases but not to organic solvents; sinks in water, unless it is a foam	Fast-food containers, toys, videotape reels, electrical insulation, plastic utensils, disposable drinking cups, CD jewel cases	Insulated clothing, egg cartons, thermal insulation

Recycling Codes Bring in different examples of plastics to display to your class, or ask your class to do the same. Ask your students to come up with hypotheses as to why Plastic Codes 3 and 6 are rarely recycled. *(too rigid to break down, too expensive.)*

To demonstrate how pervasive plastics are in our lives, ask students to make a list of all of the different types of plastics (and their codes) that are in their homes.

Your Choice
1. Answers will vary.
2. Accept all well thought-out responses.

Resources Assign students worksheet *19.4: Science and the Consumer—Recycling Plastics* in the **Integration Enrichment Resources** ancillary.

Pollution and Recycling

SECTION 19.3 REVIEW

Check Your Understanding

1. using pesticides and fertilizers on the lawn or garden

2. The greenhouse effect is the natural warming of the Earth by greenhouse gases, while global warming is an increase in the Earth's temperature due to an increase in greenhouse gases.

3. Photochemical smog results from car exhaust. If you are riding a bike, then you are not producing any exhaust that can lead to the formation of photochemical smog.

4. Eutrophication is an increased amount of nutrients in an aquatic environment. It occurs when excess fertilizers are washed into streams, rivers, lakes, or ponds.

Answers continue on p. 661B.

Figure 19-27
This recycling plant in New York City helps reduce the amount of waste going into landfills.

▶ **recycling** the process of breaking down discarded material for reuse in other products

Some people conserve water by reusing rinse water from dishes and laundry to water gardens and lawns. This way, they use less water, so less energy is required to purify it and pump it to them. In addition, the water they use does not enter the sewer system. This reduces the amount of energy used by the water-treatment plant.

Recycling is the final way to prevent pollution
After you have tried to reduce how much you use and are successfully reusing it as much as possible, there's still one more thing you can do. When something is worn out and is no longer useful, instead of throwing it away, you can try **recycling**.

Recycling allows materials to be used again to make other products rather than being thrown away. **Figure 19-27** shows a recycling plant in New York City. Such plants commonly recycle paper products such as cardboard and newspapers; metal products such as copper, aluminum, and tin; and plastics such as detergent bottles and shopping bags.

Recycling these materials can make a huge difference in the amount of waste that ends up in a landfill. Paper products alone take up 41 percent of landfill space. Yet we currently recycle less than 30 percent of our paper.

SECTION 19.3 REVIEW

SUMMARY

▶ Pollution can be caused by natural events and by human activities.

▶ Acid rain is caused when sulfur dioxide and nitrogen oxides react with moisture and other gases in the air.

▶ Government regulation and recycling can lessen the pollution of air, water, and soil.

CHECK YOUR UNDERSTANDING

1. **List** an activity related to home, work, and growing food that can lead to water pollution.
2. **Distinguish** between the greenhouse effect and global warming.
3. **Explain** how riding a bike can reduce photochemical smog.
4. **Define** *eutrophication.* Explain how it occurs.
5. **Name** an alternative energy source, and describe one benefit and one drawback.
6. **Analyze** all of the possible polluting steps in the making of a pencil. Write a paragraph describing each step. **WRITING SKILL**
7. **Critical Thinking** Do you think recycling should be mandatory? Explain your reasoning.

656 CHAPTER 19

Chapter Highlights

Before you begin, review the summaries of the key ideas of each section, found on pages 637, 645, and 656. The key vocabulary terms are listed on pages 630, 638, and 647.

UNDERSTANDING CONCEPTS

1. Hydroelectric power is a(n) _____ energy source.
   a. nonrenewable
   b. renewable
   c. small-scale
   d. atomic

2. An aquarium ecosystem is made up of _____.
   a. cactuses, sagebrush, lizards, snakes, scorpions, and birds
   b. grassland, termites, wild dogs, hyenas, and antelopes
   c. water, fish, glass, and water plants
   d. musk oxen, opposite-leaved saxifrage, wolves, and brown bears

3. When fossil fuels are burned, they form carbon dioxide and _____.
   a. water
   b. oxygen
   c. hydrocarbons
   d. carbohydrates

4. The Earth's temperature is kept slightly warmer by _____.
   a. the surface of Earth
   b. the greenhouse effect
   c. the ozone layer
   d. wind

5. In power stations, _____ of the energy input is wasted.
   a. one-third
   b. one-half
   c. two-thirds
   d. all

6. Geothermal energy is produced by _____.
   a. wind
   b. underground reservoirs of steam or hot water
   c. fast-moving water
   d. solar radiation

7. Usable energy is lost each time energy is _____.
   a. gained
   b. released
   c. converted
   d. transferred

8. Which of the following is not true of recycling?
   a. Recycling does not affect the amount of waste that ends up in a landfill.
   b. Recycling reduces litter.
   c. Recycling reduces energy usage.
   d. Recycled materials can be used to make other products.

9. What causes an algal bloom?
   a. CFCs
   b. global warming
   c. eutrophication
   d. recycling

Using Vocabulary

10. Compare *hydroelectric power* with *geothermal energy*. List advantages and disadvantages of each.

11. Driving cars releases pollutants into the atmosphere. State how these pollutants can lead to *acid rain*.

12. A forest *ecosystem* is wiped out by disease. Using the concept of *succession*, explain how the forest might recover.

13. Most energy on Earth comes from the sun. Analyze how the burning of *fossil fuels* releases stored energy from the sun.

14. Is land a *renewable* or *nonrenewable* resource? Explain your reasoning.

BUILDING MATH SKILLS

15. **Estimating** The world population in 1999 was approximately 5.8 billion. That number is expected to double in 40 years. Assuming a steady growth rate, estimate the world population in the years 2019, 2039, 2059, and 2079. Write a paragraph explaining how population changes might affect an ecosystem.

UNDERSTANDING CONCEPTS

1. b	**6.** b
2. c	**7.** c
3. a	**8.** a
4. b	**9.** c
5. c	

Using Vocabulary

10. Hydroelectric power means generating energy from water, which is a renewable resource. These generators must be built on large rivers, and most of the world's large rivers have been dammed already. Geothermal energy is energy derived from heated water within the Earth's crust. It is renewable as well but quite expensive, and is only practical in a few places around the world.

11. The pollutants that come from driving cars are carbon dioxide, sulfur dioxide, and nitrogen dioxide. Sulfur dioxide and nitrogen dioxide can combine with other atmospheric gases to form acid rain.

RESOURCE LINK
STUDY GUIDE

Assign students *Mixed Review Chapter 19.*

12. The forest will recover as pioneer organisms move into the area. Hardy plants that can live in sub-optimum conditions will move in and establish themselves, which will lead to other communities eventually moving in as habitats return.

13. Fossil fuels are fuels that have formed from the re-mains of ancient plant and animal life. When those animals and plants were living, they needed energy to live, either by absorbing sunlight or by eating plants and other animals. The stored en-ergy in these plants and animals did not have the chance to release while the organisms were alive. The burning of fossil fuels is actually the release of stored energy from the sun stored in the remains of ancient plant and ani-mal life.

14. Land can be thought of as both a renewable and nonrenewable resource, depending on the prac-tices that go on with the land. Land is a renewable resource because if it is cared for and pollutants do not destroy it, the land can be used for genera-tions without diminishing returns. Land can also be thought of as a nonrenew-able resource because it is not in perpetual supply. As people build on, excavate, and pollute land, these actions render it useless for future generations.

16. Calculating Each person in the United States produces roughly 2 kg (4.4 lb) of garbage per day. How long would it take you to fill a dump truck with a 16 000 lb capacity? If each person recycled one-half of his or her trash, how much less garbage would each person produce in one year?

THINKING CRITICALLY

17. Creative Thinking Green plants use sunlight to convert carbon dioxide and water into food in the process of photosynthesis. Explain how large-scale deforestation might affect global climate.

18. Applying Knowledge A factory is situated along the banks of a river. A large city is located farther upstream. On the outskirts of the city, farm-ers grow corn and wheat. **WRITING SKILL** Researchers are finding dead fish in the river. Write several paragraphs explaining the steps you would take to determine the cause.

DEVELOPING LIFE/WORK SKILLS

19. Teaching Others Using a desktop-publishing program, **COMPUTER SKILL** work in groups of three or four students to design a brochure to encourage recycling or energy conservation at your **WRITING SKILL** school. As a group, decide beforehand who your audience will be—do you want to reach younger students, your peers, or the school admin-istration? List the benefits and possible drawbacks in your brochure. Explain how costs can be reduced without hindering the school's operation.

20. Applying Technology Research recent developments and advancements in solar-power **WRITING SKILL** technology. Then write a brief report analyzing the feasibility of the technology. Share your results with the class.

21. Allocating Resources Three people live in the same neighborhood and work at the same office. One person spends $20 per week, one spends $25 per week, and one spends $30 **COMPUTER SKILL** per week for gasoline and parking. They work 51 weeks per year. If they formed a car pool, how much could each person save annually? Using a spreadsheet program, create a spreadsheet that will calculate how much each person would save in 5 years. (**Hint:** Assume that each person drives a total of 17 weeks.)

22. Interpreting and Communicating Visit a local senior center and interview elderly people who have grown up in your area. Ask them to de-scribe the natural habitats in **WRITING SKILL** and around your area as they were 50 years ago. Compare their de-scriptions with your observations of how your area's environment looks now. Then write a brief paragraph describing the changes that have occurred. Share your interview with your class.

23. Improving Systems Use an atlas to find out the main sources of energy in your state. Based on the information in the atlas, identify alternative energy sources that might be used in different areas. For instance, are some places suitable for wind, hydroelectric, or solar power? Develop an alternative energy plan for your state.

24. Acquiring and Evaluating Data Call your local recycling company and find out where and how recycled materials are processed and reused. Also research how much money your city saves or spends by using recycled materials.

25. Acquiring and Evaluating Data Using an almanac, determine which five states have the most hazardous-waste sites and which five states have the fewest sites. What factors do you think might account for the number of hazardous-waste sites located in a state?

26. Acquiring and Evaluating Data Go to your local library and research any nonnative species that have been introduced into your area. What positive and negative effects have resulted from their arrival?

27. Acquiring and Evaluating Data Research the 1986 Safe Drinking Water Act and the 1987 Clean Water Act. What incentives are in place to encourage clean water supplies?

INTEGRATING CONCEPTS

28. Connection to Health Sunscreens, which protect people from ultraviolet rays, have different sun protection factors (SPFs). For someone who burns after 10 minutes in the sun, a sunscreen with an SPF of 8 would give that person 80 minutes of protection. If the same person wanted to stay in the sun for 2.5 hours without reapplying sunscreen, what SPF should he or she use?

29. Connection to Social Studies Research a particular region of the world other than the area where you live. Find out which energy resource is used to meet the energy needs of this particular region.

30. Mapping Concepts Copy the unfinished concept map below onto a sheet of paper. Complete the map by writing the correct word or phrase in the lettered boxes.

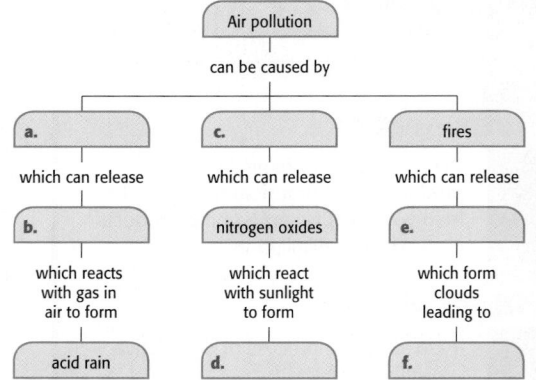

31. Connection to Social Studies One of the purported causes of global warming is the burning of fossil fuels. As a group, discuss how building energy-efficient houses might help counteract this effect. What incentives would you suggest to encourage people to make their homes more efficient? How would you judge if they're worth the cost?

32. Connection to History Human-caused environmental pollution has occurred throughout history. Research a historical example of environmental pollution, and write a short essay about it. Also research and include information about a historic conservation effort.

WRITING SKILL

internet**connect**

SC**LINKS**
NSTA
TOPIC: Global warming
GO TO: www.scilinks.org
KEYWORD: HK1909

USING NATURAL RESOURCES **659**

BUILDING MATH SKILLS

15. Answers may vary. One set of reasonable estimates follows.
2019: 9 billion
2039: 12 billion
2059: 18 billion
2079: 23 billion

16. 3636 days; you would produce 1606 lbs per year—but only 803 lbs per year if you recycled one-half of the trash.

$$\frac{16\ 000\ lb}{4.4\ lb/day} = 3636\ days$$

365 days × 4.4 lb/day = 1606 lb

$$\frac{1606\ lb}{2} = 803\ lb$$

THINKING CRITICALLY

17. Answers will vary. Cutting down trees could lead to an increase in the amount of carbon dioxide in the atmosphere. Carbon dioxide is a greenhouse gas that may contribute to global warming.

18. Have students make a sketch of the problem to help them visualize the scenario. Students would want to know the following: Are fertilizers and pesticides used on the farm? Is the factory releasing pollution into the river? Is eutrophication a problem in the river?

DEVELOPING LIFE/WORK SKILLS

19. Student brochures will vary. Good brochures should give logical and persuasive arguments.

20. Answers will vary. Good reports should explain both pros and cons of technology using solar power.

Answers continue on p. 661B.

Skill Builder Lab

Changing the Form of a Fuel

Introduction

Processing materials to make more efficient fuels or to make energy sources easier to transport and store are some of the common reasons why natural materials are converted from one form into another. In some cases, changing the form of a fuel removes pollutants at the point of origin for more effective pollution minimization. In this experiment, students will destructively distill wood to produce gases, liquids, and a solid fuel.

Objectives

Students will

▶ **Use** appropriate lab safety procedures.

▶ **Observe** the process of destructive distillation.

▶ **Analyze** the amounts of products produced, and try to identify the products.

Planning

Recommended Time: 1 lab period
Materials: *(for each lab group)*

▶ 2 test tubes
▶ one-hole stopper
▶ two-hole stopper
▶ bent glass tubing with fire-polished ends
▶ 20-cm long rubber tubing
▶ gas burner
▶ glycerin
▶ ringstand and 2 buret clamps
▶ 2 widemouth bottles
▶ 2 glass plates, 7 x 7 cm square
▶ gas-collecting trough
▶ pieces of wood splints
▶ graduated cylinder
▶ balance

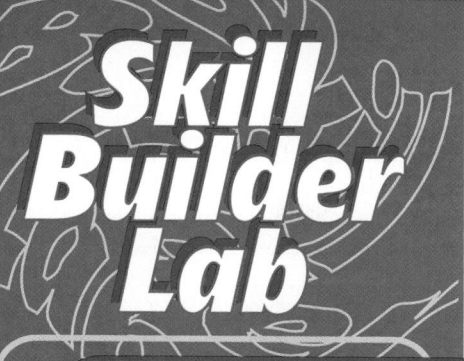

Skill Builder Lab

Introduction

Can you use your familiarity with products used in or near the home to help you identify some of the products of destructive distillation?

Objectives

▶ **Observe** the process of destructive distillation.

▶ **Analyze** the amounts of products produced, and try to identify the products.

Materials

2 test tubes
one-hole stopper
two-hole stopper
bent glass tubing with fire-polished ends
20-cm long rubber tubing
gas burner
ringstand and 2 buret clamps
2 widemouth bottles
2 glass plates, 7 × 7 cm square
gas-collecting trough
pieces of wood splints
graduated cylinder
balance

Safety Needs

safety goggles
protective gloves
laboratory apron
tongs

Changing the Form of a Fuel

▶ Preparing for Your Experiment

Destructive distillation is the process of heating a material such as wood or coal in the absence of air. The material that is driven off as a gas is called volatile matter. When cooled, some of the matter remains as a gas. Much of the matter condenses to form a mixture of liquids. These liquids can be distilled to yield a number of different products. In this investigation, you (or your teacher) will heat wood to temperatures high enough to cause the wood to break down into different components, which you will try to identify.

1. On a clean sheet of paper, make a table like the one shown below.
2. Label your glassware as shown in the illustration on page 661.
3. Determine the mass of test tube A. Record the value in your table.
4. Determine the volume of gas bottles 1 and 2. Record the values in your table.
5. Determine the volume of test tube B. Record the value in your table. Dry test tube B before setting up your equipment.

Data Table	
Mass of test tube A (g)	
Mass of test tube A with wood (g)	
Mass of wood (g)	
Mass of test tube A with solid residue (g)	
Mass of solid residue (g)	
Volume of gas bottle 1 (mL)	
Volume of gas bottle 2 (mL)	
Volume of gas produced (mL)	
Volume of test tube B (mL)	
Volume of liquid produced (mL)	

SOLUTION/MATERIAL PREPARATION

Fresh wood splints made of pine will produce more condensate than dry wood splints will produce. Wood splints should be cut or broken to a length no more than half of the length of the test tubes used in the distillation to keep students from heating too close to the rubber stopper. Inserting the glass tubing through the rubber stoppers prior to the lab will minimize the risk that a student will force the tubing, break it, and be cut. Because the destructive distillation leaves residues that are difficult to remove, the test tubes used may need to be replaced after the lab. The volumes of the gas bottles and test tubes can be measured by filling them with water, then pouring this water into a graduated cylinder and reading the level.

▶ Destructive Distillation of Wood

SAFETY CAUTION Wear protective gloves when inserting the glass tubing through the stoppers. Rub glycerin on the tubing and the inside of the stopper holes before pushing the tubing through the stoppers. Rotate the tubing slowly, and push gently. If you have difficulty, ask your teacher for help.

6. Set up the equipment as illustrated below.
7. The gas bottle in the pan should be completely filled with water. Insert the delivery tube into the gas bottle.

SAFETY CAUTION Protect clothing, hair, and eyes when using a gas burner. The gases formed in the destructive distillation of wood are combustible.

8. Fill test tube A about two-thirds full with pieces of wood splints. Determine the mass of the test tube and the wood. Record the value in your table. Stopper the test tube, connect it, and heat the test tube. Move the gas burner frequently so that the entire mass of the wood heats equally.
9. When all the water is driven from the gas bottle, place a glass plate over the mouth of the bottle, and remove the bottle from the pan. Set the gas bottle upright on the table, leaving it covered with the glass plate.
10. Place another water-filled bottle in the pan as before, and reinsert the gas delivery tube. Keep heating until the gas stops coming from test tube A.

▶ Analyzing Your Results

1. How much gas was produced? How much gas was produced for 1 g of wood?
2. What happens when a burning splint is thrust into the gas?
3. Describe the contents of test tube B. How much liquid was produced for 1 g of wood?
4. What does the solid material remaining in test tube A look like?
5. How much solid material was left? How much solid material is that for 1 g of wood?
6. Using insulated tongs, hold a piece of the solid material in the gas burner flame. How does it burn?

Test Tube A
Test Tube B
Gas Bottle 1

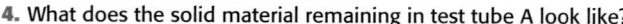

▶ Defending Your Conclusions

7. Why would you expect charcoal to give off little or no flame when it is burned?
8. Why is this type of distillation called destructive?
9. What do you think the liquids can be used for?

Procedure
Teaching Tips

Have the students account for "lost" material based on the masses of the solid residue and the liquid in test tube B. To reduce the number of test tubes that may be discarded, students can work in groups of two or three. The distillation can be conducted as a demonstration with discussions of the principles of distillation and condensation as well as discussions of resource use and clean fuel production.

Post Lab

▶**Disposal**

The charcoal can be discarded in any sanitary landfill. The liquids can be rinsed down the drain with water.

▶**Analyzing Your Results**

1. The volume of gas produced will depend on the wood used. The volume of gas collected will vary greatly depending on the skill of the student collecting the gas. For each gram of wood, collection of more than 100 mL of gas is not uncommon.

Continue on p. 661A.

RESOURCE LINK
DATASHEETS

Have students use *Datasheet 19.5: Skill Builder Lab—Changing the Form of a Fuel* to record their results.

REQUIRED PRECAUTIONS

▶ Safety goggles, protective gloves, and a laboratory apron should be worn at all times.
▶ Tongs must be used for hot test tubes.
▶ Buret clamps with protective rubber tips should be used if possible.
▶ Do not allow students to insert glass tubing through the rubber stopper by putting a hand behind the stopper and pushing the glass tube toward the hand.

▶ Inspect the distillation setup to make sure that the system is not plugged and that the tubing cannot become kinked and allow pressure to build in the system.
▶ Make sure that loose hair and loose clothing are tied back and that no jewelry is worn during the distillation.
▶ Review safety precautions about fire and burn procedures, and caution students about the hazards of using an open flame.

CONTINUATION OF ANSWERS

Skill Builder Lab from page 661

Changing the Form of a Fuel

▶**Analyzing Your Results**

2. The burning splint test can produce ambiguous results. A burning splint may be extinguished, suggesting the presence of CO_2. However, it may be possible that methane is present, resulting in a sudden burst of light. To test for methane, students can remove the rubber tubing and try to light the gas coming out of the glass tubing with a match or a burning splint.

3. The liquid in test tube B is brownish and watery. After a few minutes, the liquid may form two layers, one brown and one colorless. For each gram of wood, about 0.5 mL of liquid will be produced.

4. The material in test tube A is black and fragile. Students may recognize that the material is similar to common charcoal.

5. For each gram of wood, about 0.25 g of solid residue will be produced.

6. The solid material burns with a red glow.

▶**Defending Your Conclusions**

7. Most of the original material in the wood has been changed into gases and liquids.

8. The wood cannot return to its original form.

9. The liquids in test tube B could be used as a stain. Some of the liquid in test tube B could be used as a liquid fuel.

Sample Data			
Mass of test tube A with wood (g)	30.88	Volume of gas bottle 1 (mL)	515
Mass of test tube A (g)	23.60	Volume of gas bottle 2 (mL)	512
Mass of wood (g)	7.28	Volume of gas produced (mL)	903
Mass of test tube A with solid residue (g)	25.25	Volume of test tube B (mL)	36
Mass of solid residue (g)	1.65	Volume of liquid produced (mL)	4.08

Answers from page 645

SECTION 19.2 REVIEW

5. advantage: solar energy is a nonpolluting renewable energy resource; disadvantages: solar energy is expensive, and some parts of Earth receive more sunlight than others.

6. Using wind to generate electricity will be more efficient because there are fewer steps involved in the electricity production process; hence, there are fewer places for energy to be lost to the system.

7. Geothermal power is difficult for humans to access. To harness the power, the geothermal sites must be close to the Earth's surface, and there are only a few such spots across the Earth. Also, volcanic activity does not always last forever.

Answers from page 656

5. A benefit of solar power is that it does not directly produce pollutants. A drawback to solar power is that harnessing it requires large amounts of land and establishing that land may disrupt ecosystems.
6. The resources (wood, graphite, paint, rubber, and metal) must be obtained, shaped, and refined in the proper fashion.
7. Answers will vary.

Answers from page 659

DEVELOPING LIFE/
WORK SKILLS

21. The average annual cost of parking and gas is $1,275. Divided by three, the cost for each driver would be $425. Person A ($20 per week) would save $595 a year, Person B ($25 per week) would save $850 a year, and Person C ($30 per week) would save $1,105 a year. Students' methods and spreadsheets will vary. Another possible method of calculation shows that Person A would save $680 a year, Person B would save $850 a year, and Person C would save $1,020 a year.
22. Answers will vary.
23. Answers will vary depending on location.
24. Answers will vary depending on location.
25. Population and types of businesses in the state will influence the number of hazardous waste sites in a state.
26. Answers will vary depending on location.
27. Incentives put in place to encourage clean water supplies include financial resources to clean up rivers and wells, legal support for citizens wanting to sue polluters, and governmental agencies responsible for regulation.

INTEGRATING
CONCEPTS

28. SPF 15
29. Answers will vary.
30. a. combustion of fossil fuels
    b. sulfur dioxide and/or nitrogen dioxide
    c. car exhaust
    d. photochemical smog
    e. particulates
    f. a reduction in visibility and/or respiratory problems
31. An energy-efficient house conserves energy. As more energy is conserved, fewer fossil fuels are used and fewer amounts of greenhouse gases are emitted into the atmosphere. Incentives might include tax cuts and no- or low-interest loans from government or local utilities. Students should indicate which criteria would be used to judge whether such a program is feasible.
32. Students' research should be thorough and concise.

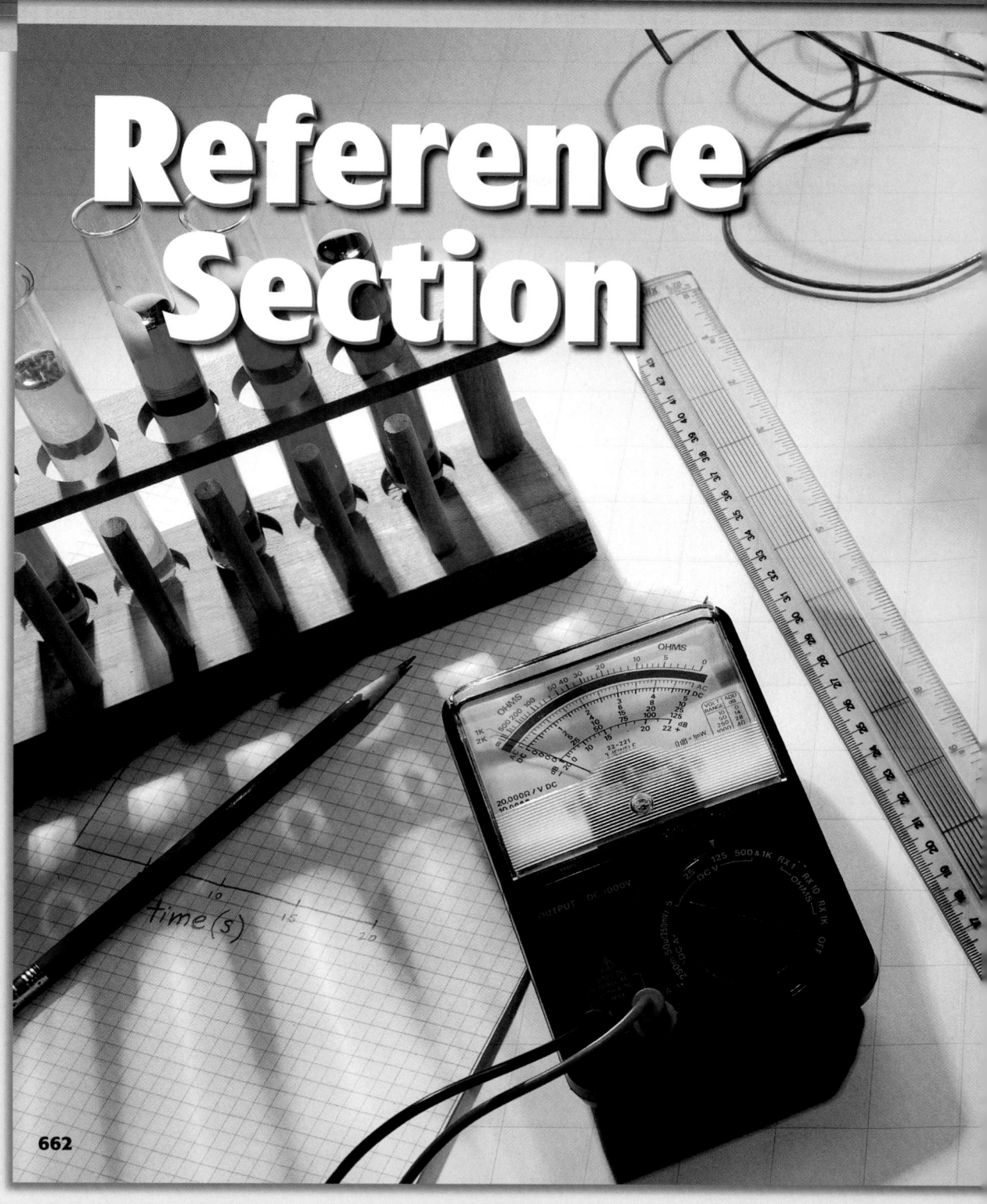

Reference Section

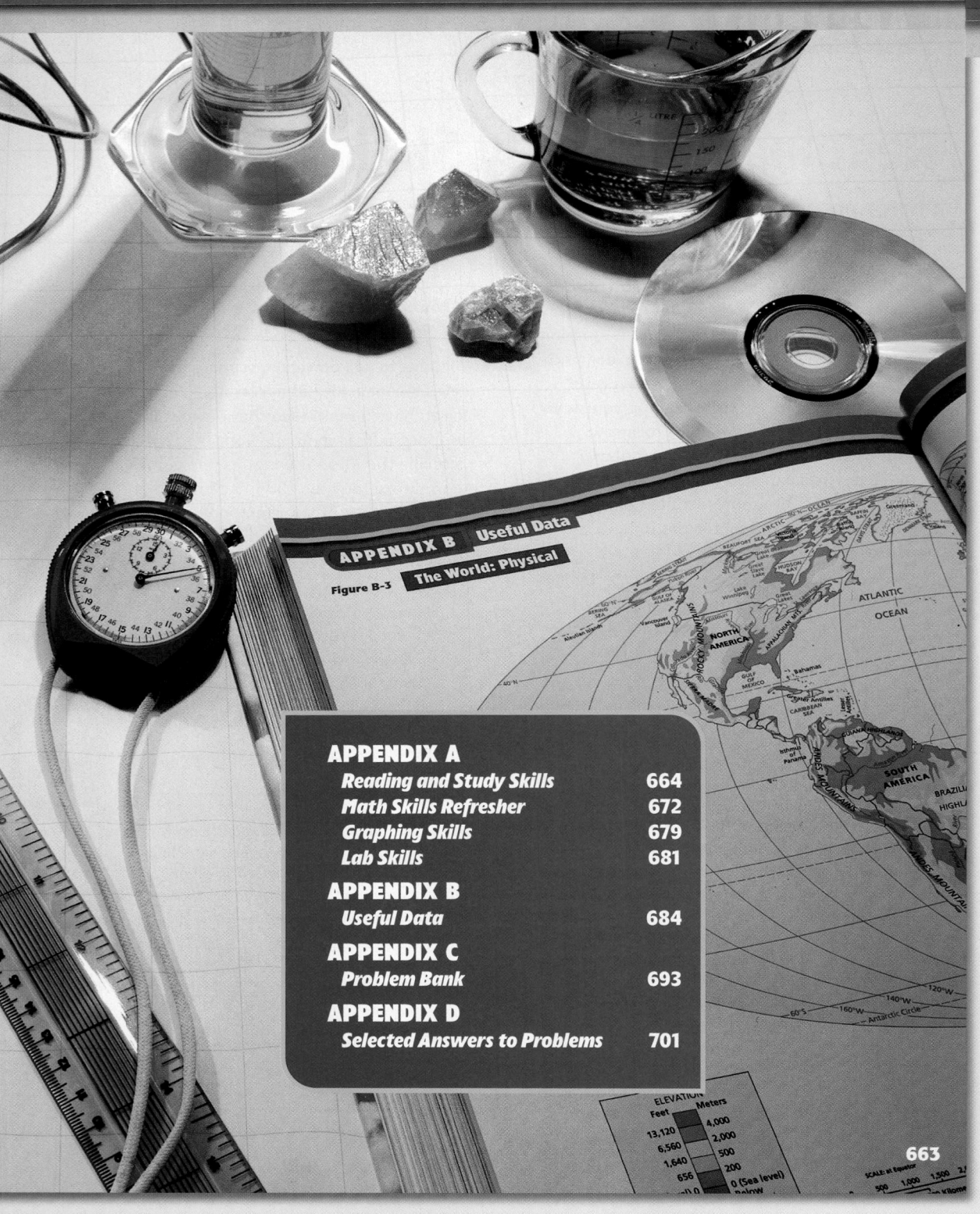

APPENDIX B   Useful Data

Figure B-3   The World: Physical

ELEVATION
Feet | Meters
13,120 | 4,000
6,560 | 2,000
1,640 | 500
656 | 200
0 | 0 (Sea level)
below

SCALE: at Equator
500   1,000   1,500   2,0

663

Power Notes

Teaching Tip

Many students have not developed note-taking skills in earlier grades. At first, they may try to simply write down everything you say. Introducing them to strategies like Power Notes will help them learn to organize the information provided in class.

Practice Answers

1. Power 1: Ionization
  Power 2: Electron lost
    Power 3: Cation
    Power 3: Positive
      charge
  Power 2: Electron gained
    Power 3: Anion
    Power 3: Negative
      charge

Reading and Study Skills

Power notes

Power notes help you organize the concepts you are studying by distinguishing main ideas from details and providing a framework of important concepts. Power notes are easier to use than outlines because their structure is simpler. You assign a power of *1* to each main idea and a *2, 3,* or *4* to each detail. You can use power notes to organize ideas while reading your text or to reorganize your class notes to study.

Start with a few boldfaced vocabulary terms. Later you can strengthen your notes by expanding these into more-detailed phrases. Use the following general format to help you structure your power notes.

  Power 1 Main idea
    Power 2 Detail or support for power 1
      Power 3 Detail or support for power 2
        Power 4 Detail or support for
          power 3

1. Pick a Power 1 word.
  We'll use the term *atom* found in Section 3.1 of your textbook.
  Power 1 Atom

2. Using the text, select some Power 2 words to support your Power 1 word.
  We'll use the terms *nucleus* and *electron cloud,* which are two parts of an atom.
  Power 1 Atom
    Power 2 Nucleus
    Power 2 Electron Cloud

3. Select some Power 3 words to support your Power 2 words.
  We'll use the terms *positive charge* and *negative charge,* two terms that describe the Power 2 words.

  Power 1 Atom
    Power 2 Nucleus
      Power 3 Positive charge
    Power 2 Electron cloud
      Power 3 Negative charge

4. Continue to add powers to support and detail the main idea as necessary.
  If you have a main idea that needs a lot of support, add as many powers as needed to describe the idea. You can use power notes to organize the material in an entire section or chapter of your textbook to study for classroom quizzes and tests.

  Power 1 Atom
    Power 2 Nucleus
      Power 3 Positive charge
      Power 3 Protons
        Power 4 Positive charge
      Power 3 Neutrons
        Power 4 No charge
    Power 2 Electron cloud
      Power 3 Negative charge

Practice

1. Use Chapter 3 of your text and the power notes structure below to organize the following terms: *electron lost, electron gained, ionization, anion, cation, negative charge,* and *positive charge.*

  Power 1 _____
    Power 2 _____
      Power 3 _____
      Power 3 _____
    Power 2 _____
      Power 3 _____
      Power 3 _____

Pattern puzzles

You can use pattern puzzles to help you remember information in the correct order. Pattern puzzles are not just a tool for memorization. They can also help you better understand a variety of scientific processes, from the steps in solving a mathematical conversion to the procedure for writing a lab report.

1. Write down the steps of a process in your own words.

We'll use the Math Skills feature on converting amount to mass from Section 3.4. On a sheet of notebook paper, write down one step per line, and do not number the steps. Also, do not copy the process straight from your text. Writing the steps in your own words helps you check your understanding of the process. You may want to divide the longer steps into two or three shorter steps.

- List the given and unknown information.

- Look at the periodic table to determine the molar mass of the substance.

- Write the correct conversion factor to convert moles to grams.

- Multiply the amount of substance by the conversion factor.

- Solve the equation and check your answer.

2. Cut the sheet of paper into strips with only one step per strip of paper.

Shuffle the strips of paper so that they are out of sequence.

- Look at the periodic table to determine the molar mass of the substance.

- Solve the equation and check your answer.

- List the given and unknown information.

- Multiply the amount of substance by the conversion factor.

- Write the correct conversion factor to convert moles to grams.

Pattern Puzzles

Teaching Tip

Pattern puzzles are an excellent strategy for reinforcing information that belongs in a specific order. Examples of the kinds of information that can be studied in this way include lab procedures, problem-solving steps, and historical developments of scientific models.

Pattern Puzzles

Practice Answers

1. Choose a multiple-step process from your text.
Write down the steps of the process in your own words.
Cut the paper into strips so that there is one sentence per strip.
Shuffle the strips of paper.
Place the strips in their proper sequence.
Using your text, confirm the order of the process.

3. Place the strips in their proper sequence.
   Confirm the order of the process by checking your text or your class notes.

- List the given and unknown information.
- Look at the periodic table to determine the molar mass of the substance.
- Write the correct conversion factor to convert moles to grams.
- Multiply the amount of substance by the conversion factor.
- Solve the equation and check your answer.

Pattern puzzles can be used to help you prepare for a laboratory experiment. That way it will be easier for you to remember what you need to do when you get into the lab, especially if your teacher gives pre-lab quizzes.

You'll want to use pattern puzzles if your teacher is planning a lab practical exam to test whether you know how to operate laboratory equipment. That way you can study and prepare for such a test even though you don't have a complete set of lab equipment at home.

Pattern puzzles work very well with problem-solving. If you work a pattern puzzle for a given problem type several times first, you will find it much easier to work on the different practice problems assigned in your homework.

Pattern puzzles are especially helpful when you are studying for tests. It is a good idea to make the puzzles on a regular basis so that when test time comes you won't be rushing to make them. Bind each puzzle using paper clips, or store the puzzles in individual envelopes. Before tests, use your puzzles to practice and to review.

Pattern puzzles are also a good way to study with others. You and a classmate can take turns creating your own pattern puzzles and putting each other's puzzles in the correct sequence. Studying with a classmate in this way will help make studying fun and allow you and your classmate to help each other.

Practice

1. Write the following sentences describing the process of making pattern puzzles in the correct order.

   Place the strips in their proper sequence.

   Write down the steps of the process in your own words.

   Shuffle the strips of paper.

   Choose a multiple-step process from your text.

   Using your text, confirm the order of the process.

   Cut the paper into strips so that there is one step per strip.

KWL notes

The KWL strategy is an exciting and helpful way to learn. It is somewhat different from the other learning strategies you have seen in this appendix. This strategy stands for "what I **K**now—what I **W**ant to know—what I **L**earned." KWL differs in that it prompts you to brainstorm about the subject matter before you read the assigned pages. This strategy helps you relate your new ideas and concepts with those you have already learned. This allows you to understand and apply new knowledge more easily. The objectives at the beginning of each section in your text are ideal for using the KWL strategy. Just read and follow the instructions in the example below.

1. **Read the section objectives.**

   You may also want to scan headings, bold-face terms, and illustrations in the section. We'll use a few of the objectives from Section 2.1.

   ▶ Explain the relationship between matter, atoms, and elements.

   ▶ Distinguish between elements and compounds.

   ▶ Categorize materials as pure substances or mixtures.

2. **Divide a sheet of paper into three columns, and label the columns "What I know," "What I want to know," and "What I learned."**

3. **Brainstorm about what you know about the information in the objectives, and write these ideas in the first column.**

   It is not necessary to write complete sentences. What's most important is to get as many ideas out as possible. In this way, you will already be thinking about the topic being covered. That will help you learn new information, because it will be easier for you to link it to recently-remembered knowledge.

4. **Think about what you want to know about the information in the objectives, and write these ideas in the second column.**

   You should want to know the information you will be tested over, so include information from both the section objectives and any other objectives your teacher has given you.

5. **While reading the section, or after you have read it, use the third column to write down what you learned.**

   While reading, pay close attention to any information about the topics you wrote in the "What I want to know" column. If you do not find all of the answers you are looking for, you may need to reread the section or find a second source for the information. Be sure to ask your teacher if you still cannot find the information after reading the section a second time.

What I know	What I want to know	What I learned

KWL Notes

Teaching Tip

The KWL strategy provides a structure that helps students focus on what they should be learning as they read the textbook. As such, it works well with students at all ability levels.

APPENDIX A

Study Skills

KWL Notes

What I know	What I want to know	What I learned
▶ atoms are very small particles ▶ oxygen is an element ▶ elements are listed on the periodic table	▶ Explain the relationship between matter, atoms, and elements.	▶ matter is anything that occupies space ▶ atoms are the smallest particles with properties of an element ▶ elements cannot be broken down into simpler substances with the same properties ▶ atoms and elements are matter
▶ compounds are made of elements	▶ Distinguish between elements and compounds.	▶ elements combine chemically to make compounds ▶ compounds can be broken down into elements
▶ mixtures are combinations of more than one substance ▶ pure substances have only one component	▶ Categorize materials as pure substances or mixtures.	▶ pure substances have fixed compositions and definite properties ▶ mixtures are combinations of more than one pure substance ▶ elements and compounds are pure substances ▶ grape juice is a mixture

Practice Answers

1. a. As written, this was a misconception according to row 2 of "What I learned" of the notes. Elements must be chemically combined to make a compound, not just physically combined.

b. As written, this was a misconception. According to "What I learned" in rows 1 and 2 of the notes, a compound can be broken down into elements but diamond cannot. Diamond is a form of the element carbon because it contains only one type of atom.

c. This is another misconception. According to row 1 of "What I learned," elements contain only one type of atom. Sodium chloride is a compound made up of two elements, sodium and chlorine.

d. This is another misconception. Lemonade contains many substances. It is a mixture, just as grape juice is a mixture.

6. It is also important to review your brainstormed ideas when you have completed reading the section.

Compare your ideas in the first column with the information you wrote down in the third column. If you find that some of your brainstormed ideas are incorrect, cross them out. It is extremely important to identify and correct any misconceptions you had before you begin studying for your test.

Your completed KWL notes can make learning science much easier. First of all, this system of note-taking makes gaps in your knowledge easier to spot. That way you can focus on looking for the content you need easier, whether you look in the textbook or ask your teacher.

If you've identified the objectives clearly, the ideas you are studying the most are the ones that will matter most.

Practice

1. Use column 3 from the table above to identify and correct any misconceptions in the following brainstorm list.

a. Physically mixing elements will form a compound.

b. Diamond is a compound.

c. Sodium chloride is an element.

d. Lemonade is a pure substance.

Two-column notes

Two-column notes can be used to learn and review definitions of vocabulary terms or details of specific concepts. The two-column-note strategy is simple: write the term, main idea, or concept in the left-hand column. Then write the definition, example, or detail on the right.

One strategy for using two-column notes is to organize main ideas and their details. The main ideas from your reading are written in the left-hand column of your paper and can be written as questions, key words, or a combination of both. Key words can include boldface terms as well as any other terms you may have trouble remembering. Questions may include those the author has asked or any questions your teacher may have asked during class. Details describing these main ideas are then written in the right-hand column of your paper.

1. Identify the main ideas.
The main ideas for each chapter are listed in the section objectives. However, you decide which ideas to include in your notes. The table below shows some of the main ideas from the objectives in Section 1.1.

2. Divide a blank sheet of paper into two columns, and write the main ideas in the left-hand column.
Do not copy ideas from the book or waste time writing in complete sentences. Summarize your ideas using quick phrases that are easy to understand and remember. Decide how many details you need for each main idea, and include that number to help you to focus on the necessary information.

3. Write the detail notes in the right-hand column.
Be sure you list as many details as you designated in the main-idea column.

The two-column method of review is perfect for preparing for quizzes or tests. Just cover the information in the right-hand column with a sheet of paper, and after reciting what you know, uncover the notes to check your answers.

Practice

1. Make your own two-column notes using the periodic table in Chapter 3. Include in the details the symbol and the atomic number of each of the following elements.

a. neon	**c.** calcium	**e.** oxygen
b. lead	**d.** copper	**f.** sodium

Main idea	Detail notes	
▶ Scientific theory (4 characteristic properties)	▶ tested experimentally ▶ possible explanation	▶ explains natural event ▶ used to predict
▶ Scientific law (3 characteristic properties)	▶ tested experimentally ▶ summary of an observation	▶ can be disproved
▶ Models (4 characteristic properties)	▶ represents an object or event ▶ physical	▶ computer ▶ mathematical

KWL Notes
Teaching Tip
Two-column notes help students build analysis skills, because it requires them to distinguish between main ideas and details. Often, students are so overwhelmed by new information in science classes that they do not remember to make the distinction.

Practice Answers

1.

Main idea	Detail notes
a. neon	• Ne • 10
b. lead	• Pb • 82
c. calcium	• Ca • 20
d. copper	• Cu • 29
e. oxygen	• O • 8
f. sodium	• Na • 11

Concept Maps

Teaching Tip

At first, students may not like to make concept maps because they are not as structured as other forms of note-taking. However, this freedom to create one's own method of organizing information usually wins students over.

At first, you may want to use concept maps as a review activity. Making the concept map in preparation for studying is actually a good way to reinforce the concepts of a lesson or chapter.

Concept maps

Making concept maps can help you decide what material in a chapter is important and how best to learn that material. A concept map presents key ideas, meanings, and relationships for the concepts being studied. It can be thought of as a visual road map of the chapter.

Concept maps can begin with vocabulary terms. Vocabulary terms are generally labels for concepts, and concepts are generally nouns. Concepts are linked using linking words to form propositions. A proposition is a phrase that gives meaning to the concept. For example, "matter is changed by energy" is a proposition.

1. **List all the important concepts.**
   We'll use some of the terms in Section 2.3.
   energy   chemical change
   chemical property   physical change
   physical property   reactivity
   density

2. **Select a main concept for the map.**
   We will use *matter* as the main concept for this map.

3. **Build the map by placing the concepts according to their importance under the main concept, *matter*.**
   One way of arranging the concepts is shown in **Map A.**

4. **Add linking words to give meaning to the arrangement of the concepts.**
   When adding the links, be sure that each proposition makes sense. To distinguish concepts from links, place your concepts in circles, ovals, or rectangles. Then add cross-links with lines connecting concepts across the map. **Map B** on the next page is a finished map covering the main ideas found in the vocabulary list in Step 1.

Map A

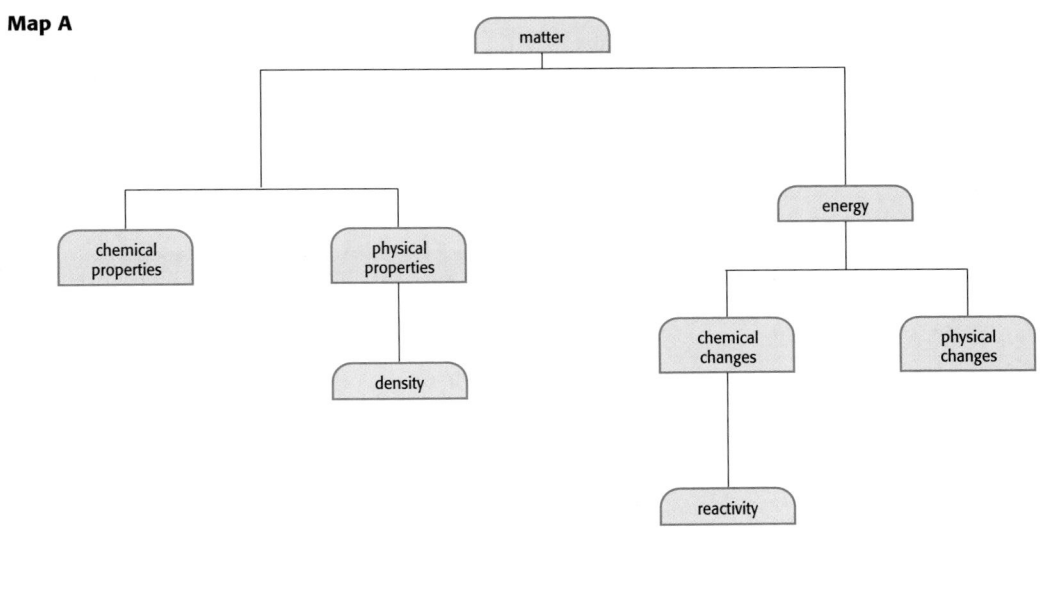

Practice mapping by making concept maps about topics you know. For example, if you know a lot about a particular sport, such as basketball, you can use that topic to make a practice map. By perfecting your skills with information that you know very well, you will begin to feel more confident about making maps from the information in a chapter.

Making maps might seem difficult at first, but the process gets you to think about the meanings and relationships among concepts. If you do not understand those relationships, you can get help early on.

In addition, many people find it easier to study by looking at a concept map, rather than flipping through a chapter full of text because concept mapping is a visual way to organize the information in a chapter. Not only does it isolate the key concepts in a chapter, it also makes the relationships and linkages among those ideas easy to see and understand.

One useful strategy is to trade concept maps with a classmate. Everybody organizes information slightly differently, and something they may have done may help you understand the content better.

Remember, although concept mapping may take a little extra time, the time you spend mapping will pay off when it is time to review for a test or final exam.

Concept Maps

Practice

1. Classify each of the following as either a concept or linking word(s).

   a. compound   e. element
   b. is classified as   f. reacts with
   c. forms   g. pure substance
   d. is described by   h. defines

2. Write three propositions from the information in **Map B.**

Practice Answers

1. *a.* concept
   b. linking words
   c. linking word
   d. linking words
   e. concept
   f. linking words
   g. concept
   h. linking word
2. Answers will vary. Check student responses against Map B, shown on this page. Some possible responses are the following.

   Matter is described by chemical properties, which describe reactivity.

   Matter is also described by physical properties such as density.

   Matter is changed by energy, which causes chemical and physical changes.

Map B

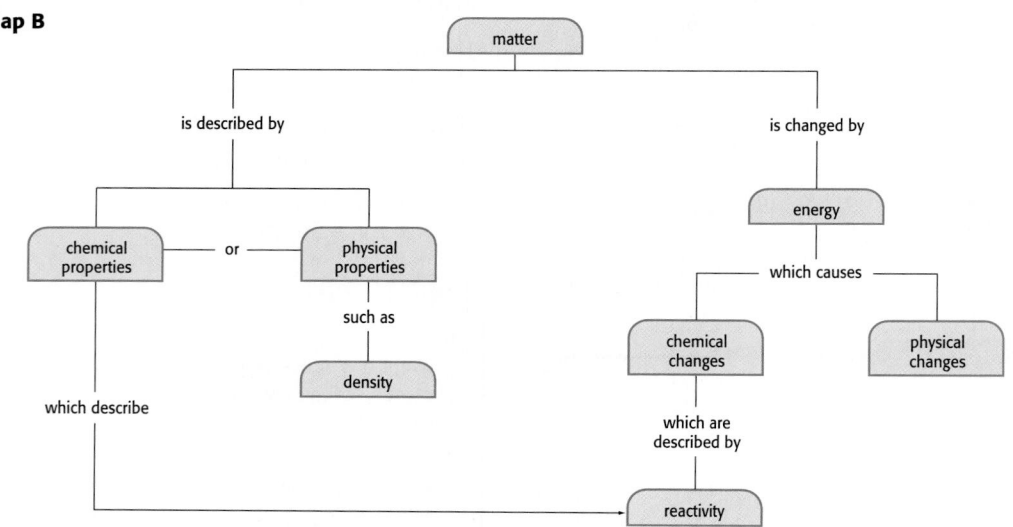

Fractions

Practice Answers

1. **a.** $\dfrac{29}{24}$ or $1\dfrac{5}{24}$

b. $\dfrac{7}{24}$

c. $\dfrac{21}{8}$ or $2\dfrac{5}{8}$

d. $\dfrac{13}{24}$

Percentages

Practice Answers

1. 88.84%
2. saturated fat: 21%
unsaturated fats: 79%

Math Skills Refresher

Fractions

Fractions represent numbers that are less than one. In other words, fractions are a way of numerically representing a part of a whole. For example, if you have a pizza with 8 slices, and you eat 2 of the slices, you have 6 out of the 8 slices, or $\dfrac{6}{8}$, of the pizza left. The top number in the fraction is called the numerator. The bottom number is the denominator.

There are special rules for adding, subtracting, multiplying, and dividing fractions. These rules are summarized in **Table A-1.**

Table A-1   Basic Operations for Fractions

	Rule and example
Multiplication	$\left(\dfrac{a}{b}\right)\left(\dfrac{c}{d}\right)=\dfrac{ac}{bd}$ $\left(\dfrac{2}{3}\right)\left(\dfrac{4}{5}\right)=\dfrac{8}{15}$
Division	$\dfrac{a}{b}\div\dfrac{c}{d}=\dfrac{\left(\dfrac{a}{b}\right)}{\left(\dfrac{c}{d}\right)}=\dfrac{ad}{bc}$ $\dfrac{2}{3}\div\dfrac{4}{5}=\dfrac{\left(\dfrac{2}{3}\right)}{\left(\dfrac{4}{5}\right)}=\dfrac{(2)(5)}{(3)(4)}=\dfrac{10}{12}$
Addition and subtraction	$\dfrac{a}{b}\pm\dfrac{c}{d}=\dfrac{ad\pm bc}{bd}$ $\dfrac{2}{3}-\dfrac{4}{5}=\dfrac{(2)(5)-(3)(4)}{(3)(5)}=-\dfrac{2}{15}$

Practice

1. Perform the following calculations:

a. $\dfrac{7}{8}+\dfrac{1}{3}=$ **c.** $\dfrac{7}{8}\div\dfrac{1}{3}=$

b. $\dfrac{7}{8}\times\dfrac{1}{3}=$ **d.** $\dfrac{7}{8}-\dfrac{1}{3}=$

Percentages

Percentages are no different from other fractions, except that in a percentage, the whole (or the number in the denominator) is considered to be 100. Any percentage, $x\%$, can be read as x out of 100. For example, if you have completed 50% of an assignment, you have completed $\dfrac{50}{100}$ or $\dfrac{1}{2}$ of the assignment.

Percentages can be calculated by dividing the part by the whole. When your calculator solves a division problem that is less than 1, it gives you a decimal value instead of a fraction. For example, 0.45 can be written as the fraction $\dfrac{45}{100}$. This is equal to 45%. An easy way to calculate percentages is to divide the part by the whole, then multiply by 100. This multiplication moves the decimal point two positions to the right, giving you the number that would be over 100 in a fraction. Try this example.

You scored 73 out of 92 problems on your last exam. What was your percentage score?

First divide the part by the whole to get a decimal value: $\dfrac{73}{92}$. Note that 0.7935 is equal to $\dfrac{79.35}{100}$

Then multiply by 100 to yield the percentage: $0.7935\times100=79.35\%$.

Practice

1. Oxygen in water has a mass of 16.00 g. The water has a total mass of 18.01 g. What percentage of the mass of water is made up of oxygen?

2. A candy bar contains 14 g of fat. The total fat contains 3.0 g of saturated fat and 11 g of unsaturated fats. What are the percentages of saturated and unsaturated fat in the candy bar?

672 **APPENDIX A**

Exponents

An exponent is a number that is superscripted to the right of another number. The best way to explain how an exponent works is with an example. In the value 5^4, 4 is the exponent on 5. The number with its exponent means that 5 is multiplied by itself 4 times.

$$5^4 = 5 \times 5 \times 5 \times 5 = 625$$

You will frequently hear exponents referred to as powers. Using this terminology, the above equation could be read as *five to the fourth power equals 625*. Keep in mind that any number raised to the zero power is equal to one. Also, any number raised to the first power is equal to itself: $5^1 = 5$.

Just as there are special rules for dealing with fractions, there are special rules for dealing with exponents. These rules are summarized in **Table A-2.**

You probably recognize the symbol for a square root, $\sqrt{\ }$. This means that a number times itself equals the value inside the square root. It is also possible to have roots other than the square root. For example, $\sqrt[3]{x}$ means that some number, n, times itself three times equals the number x, or $n \times n \times n = x$. We can turn our example of $5^4 = 625$ around to solve for the fourth root of 625.

$$\sqrt[4]{625} = 5$$

Taking the nth root of a number is the same as raising that number to the power of $1/n$. Therefore, $\sqrt[4]{625} = 625^{1/4}$.

A scientific calculator is a must for solving most problems involving exponents and roots. Many calculators have dedicated keys for squares and square roots. But what about different powers, such as cubes and cube roots? Most scientific calculators have a key shaped like a caret, ^. If you type in "5^4," when you hit the equals sign or the enter key, the calculator will determine that $5^4 = 625$, and display that answer.

For roots, you enter the decimal equivalent of the fractional exponent. For example, to solve the problem of the fourth root of 625, instead of entering one-fourth as the exponent, enter "625^0.25," because 0.25 is equal to one-fourth.

Practice

1. Perform the following calculations:

a. $9^1 =$

b. $(3^3)^5 =$

c. $\dfrac{2^8}{2^2} =$

d. $(14^2)(14^3) =$

e. $11^0 =$

f. $6^{1/6} =$

Table A-2   Rules for dealing with exponents

	Rule	Example
Zero power	$x^0 = 1$	$7^0 = 1$
First power	$x^1 = x$	$6^1 = 6$
Multiplication	$(x^n)(x^m) = x^{(n+m)}$	$(x^2)(x^4) = x^{(2+4)} = x^6$
Division	$\dfrac{x^n}{x^m} = x^{(n-m)}$	$\dfrac{x^8}{x^2} = x^{(8-2)} = x^6$
Exponents that are fractions	$x^{1/n} = \sqrt[n]{x}$	$4^{1/3} = \sqrt[3]{4} = 1.5874$
Exponents raised to a power	$(x^n)^m = x^{nm}$	$(5^2)^3 = 5^6 = 15\ 625$

Exponents

1. a. $9^1 = 9$
   b. $(3^3)^5 = 3^{15} = 14\ 348\ 907$
   c. $\dfrac{2^8}{2^2} = 2^{(8-2)} = 2^6 = 64$
   d. $(14^2)(14^3) = 14^{(2+3)} = 14^5 = 537\ 824$
   e. $11^0 = 1$
   f. $6^{1/6} = \sqrt[6]{6} = 1.348$

Order of Operations

Practice Answers

1. $2^3 \div 2 + 4 \times (9 - 2^2) =$
$8 \div 2 + 4 \times (9 - 4) =$
$8 \div 2 + 4 \times 5 =$
$4 + 20 = 24$

2. $\dfrac{2 \times (6 - 3) + 8}{4 \times 2 - 6} =$
$\dfrac{2 \times 3 + 8}{4 \times 2 - 6} =$
$\dfrac{6 + 8}{8 - 6} =$
$\dfrac{14}{2} = 7$

Geometry

Practice Answers

1. $r = \dfrac{14 \text{ cm}}{2} = 7$ cm
$volume = \pi r^2 h =$
$\pi(7 \text{ cm})^2 (8 \text{ cm}) =$
$volume = 1232 \text{ cm}^3$
2. $surface\ area = 2(lh + lw + hw) = 2[(4 \text{ cm})^2 + (4 \text{ cm})^2 + (4 \text{ cm})^2]$
$surface\ area = 96 \text{ cm}^2$
3. $volume\ of\ a\ sphere =$
$\dfrac{4}{3}\pi r^3 = 76 \text{ cm}^3$
$r^3 = 18 \text{ cm}^3$
$r = 2.6$ cm
$diameter = r \times 2 = 5.2$ cm
The box must be at least 5.2 cm in each dimension in order for the sphere to fit. The box has one dimension that is too small. Therefore, the sphere will not fit.

Order of operations

Use this phrase to remember the correct order for long mathematical problems: *Please Excuse My Dear Aunt Sally.* This phrase stands for *Parentheses, Exponents, Multiplication, Division, Addition, Subtraction.* These rules can be summarized in **Table A-3**.

Table A-3 **Order of Operations**

Step	Operation
1	Simplify groups inside parentheses. Start with the innermost group and work out.
2	Simplify all exponents.
3	Perform multiplication and division in order from left to right.
4	Perform addition and subtraction in order from left to right.

Look at the following example:
$$4^3 + 2 \times [8 - (3 - 1)] = ?$$
First simplify the operations inside parentheses. Begin with the innermost parentheses:
$$(3 - 1) = 2$$
$$4^3 + 2 \times [8 - 2] = ?$$
Then move on to the next-outer parentheses:
$$[8 - 2] = 6$$
$$4^3 + 2 \times 6 = ?$$
Now, simplify all exponents:
$$4^3 = 64$$
$$64 + 2 \times 6 = ?$$
The next step is to perform multiplication:
$$2 \times 6 = 12$$
$$64 + 12 = ?$$
Finally, solve the addition problem:
$$64 + 12 = 76$$

Practice

1. $2^3 \div 2 + 4 \times (9 - 2^2) =$

2. $\dfrac{2 \times (6 - 3) + 8}{4 \times 2 - 6} =$

Geometry

Quite often, a useful way to model the objects and substances studied in science is to consider them in terms of their shapes. For example, many of the properties of a wheel can be understood by pretending that the wheel is a perfect circle.

For this reason, being able to calculate the area or the volume of certain shapes is a useful skill in science. **Table A-4** provides equations for the area and volume of several geometric shapes.

Table A-4 **Geometric Areas and Volumes**

Geometric Shape		Useful Equations
Rectangle		Area $= lw$
Circle		Area $= \pi r^2$ Circumference $= 2\pi r$
Triangle		Area $= \dfrac{1}{2}bh$
Sphere		Surface area $= 4\pi r^2$ volume $= \dfrac{4}{3}\pi r^3$
Cylinder		Volume $= \pi r^2 h$
Rectangular box		Surface area $= 2(lh + lw + hw)$ volume $= lwh$

Practice

1. What is the volume of a cylinder with a diameter of 14 cm and a height of 8 cm?

2. Calculate the surface area of a 4 cm cube.

3. Will a sphere with a volume of 76 cm³ fit in a rectangular box that is 7 cm × 4 cm × 10 cm?

Algebraic rearrangements

Algebraic equations contain *constants* and *variables*. Constants are simply numbers, such as 2, 5, and 7. Variables are represented by letters such as x, y, z, a, b, and c. Variables are unspecified quantities and are also called the unknowns.

Often, you will need to determine the value of a variable, but all you will be given will be an equation expressed in terms of algebraic expressions instead of a simple equation expressed in numbers only.

An algebraic expression contains one or more of the four basic mathematical operations: addition, subtraction, multiplication, and division. Constants, variables, or terms made up of both constants and variables can be involved in the basic operations.

The key to figuring out the value of a variable in an algebraic equation is that the quantity described on one side of the equals sign is equal to the quantity described on the other side of the equals sign.

If you are trying to determine the value of a variable in an algebraic expression, you would like to be able to rewrite the equation as a simple one that tells you exactly what x (or some other variable) equals.

But how do you get from a more complicated equation to a simple one?

Again, the key lies in the fact that both sides of the equation are equal. That means if you do the same operation on either side of the equation, the results will still be equal.

Look at the following simple problem:

$$8x = 32$$

If we wish to solve for x, we can multiply or divide each side of the equation by the same factor. You can add, subtract, multiply, or divide anything to or from one side of an equation as long as you do the same thing to the other side of the equation. In this case, if we divide both sides by 8, we have:

$$\frac{8x}{8} = \frac{32}{8}$$

The 8s on the left side of the equation cancel each other out, and the fraction $\frac{32}{8}$ can be reduced to give the whole number, 4. Therefore, $x = 4$.

Next consider the following equation:

$$x + 2 = 8$$

Remember, we can add or subtract the same quantity from each side. If we subtract 2 from each side, we get

$$x + 2 - 2 = 8 - 2$$
$$x + 0 = 6$$
$$x = 6$$

Now consider one more equation:

$$\frac{x}{5} = 9$$

If we multiply each side by 5, the 5 originally on the left side of the equation cancels out. We are left with x on the left by itself and 45 on the right:

$$x = 45$$

In all cases, *whatever operation is performed on the left side of the equals sign must also be performed on the right side.*

Practice

1. Rearrange each of the following equations to give the value of the variable indicated with a letter.

   a. $8x - 32 = 128$

   b. $6 - 5(4a + 3) = 26$

   c. $-3(y - 2) + 4 = 29$

   d. $-2(3m + 5) = 14$

   e. $\left[8\dfrac{(8 + 2z)}{32}\right] + 2 = 5$

   f. $\dfrac{(6b + 3)}{3} - 9 = 2$

Practice Answers

1. a. $8x - 32 = 128$
   $8x - 32 + 32 = 128 + 32$
   $8x = 160$
   $x = \dfrac{160}{8} = 20$

   b. $6 - 5 \times (4a + 3) = 26$
   $6 - 6 - 5 \times (4a + 3) = 26 - 6$
   $-5 \times (4a + 3) = 20$
   $\dfrac{-5 \times (4a + 3)}{-5} = \dfrac{20}{-5}$
   $4a + 3 = -4$
   $4a + 3 - 3 = -4 - 3$
   $4a = -7$
   $a = -1.75$

   c. $-3 \times (y - 2) + 4 = 29$
   $-3 \times (y - 2) + 4 - 4 = 29 - 4$
   $-3 \times (y - 2) = 25$
   $\dfrac{-3 \times (y - 2)}{-3} = \dfrac{25}{-3}$
   $y - 2 = -8.3$
   $y - 2 + 2 = -8.3 + 2$
   $y = -6.3$

   d. $-2 \times (3m + 5) = 14$
   $\dfrac{-2 \times (3m + 5)}{-2} = \dfrac{14}{-2}$
   $(3m + 5) = -7$
   $3m + 5 - 5 = -7 - 5$
   $3m = -12$
   $m = -4$

   e. $\left[8\dfrac{(8 + 2z)}{32}\right] + 2 = 5$
   $\left[8\dfrac{(8 + 2z)}{32}\right] + 2 - 2 = 5 - 2$
   $8\dfrac{(8 + 2z)}{32} = 3$
   $8\dfrac{(8 + 2z)}{32} \times 32 = 3 \times 32$
   $8(8 + 2z) = 96$
   $\dfrac{8(8 + 2z)}{8} = \dfrac{96}{8}$
   $8 + 2z = 12$
   $8 - 8 + 2z = 12 - 8$
   $2z = 4$
   $z = 2$

   f. $\dfrac{(6b + 3)}{3} - 9 = 2$
   $\dfrac{(6b + 3)}{3} - 9 + 9 = 2 + 9$
   $\dfrac{(6b + 3)}{3} = 11$
   $\dfrac{(6b + 3)}{3} \times 3 = 11 \times 3$
   $6b + 3 = 33$
   $6b + 3 - 3 = 33 - 3$
   $6b = 30$
   $b = 5$

Scientific Notation

Practice Answers

1.
  a. 1.23×10^{7} m/s
  b. 4.5×10^{-12} kg
  c. 6.53×10^{-5} m
  d. 5.5432×10^{13} s
  e. 2.7315×10^{2} K
  f. 6.2714×10^{-4} kg

Scientific notation

Many quantities that scientists deal with have very large or very small values. For example, about 3 000 000 000 000 000 000 electrons' worth of charge pass through a standard light bulb in one second, and the ink required to make the dot over an *i* in this textbook has a mass of about 0.000 000 001 kg.

Obviously, it is very cumbersome to read, write, and keep track of numbers like these. We avoid this problem by using a method dealing with powers of the number 10.

Study the positive powers of ten shown on page 22 in Chapter 1. You should be able to check those numbers on your own using what you know about exponents. The number of zeros corresponds to the exponent on 10. The number for 10^{4} is 10 000; it has 4 zeros.

But how can we use the powers of 10 to simplify large numbers such as the number of electron-sized charges passing through a light bulb? This large number is equal to $3 \times 1\ 000\ 000\ 000\ 000\ 000\ 000$. The factor of 10 has 18 zeros. Therefore, it can be rewritten as 10^{18}. This means that 3 000 000 000 000 000 000 can be expressed as 3×10^{18}.

That explains how to simplify really large numbers, but what about really small numbers, like 0.000 000 001 kg? Negative exponents can be used to simplify numbers that are less than 1.

Study the negative powers of 10 on page 22 of Chapter 1. In these cases, the exponent on 10 equals the number of decimal places you must move the decimal point to the right so that there is one digit just to the left of the decimal point. Using the mass of the ink in the dot on an *i*, the decimal point has to be moved 9 decimal places to the right for the numeral 1 to be just to the left of the decimal point. The mass of the ink, 0.000 000 001 kg, can be rewritten as 1×10^{-9} kg.

Numbers that are expressed as some power of 10 multiplied by another number with only one digit to the left of the decimal point are said to be written in scientific notation. For example, 5943 000 000 is 5.943×10^{9} when expressed in scientific notation. The number 0.000 0832 is 8.32×10^{-5} when expressed in scientific notation.

When a number is expressed in scientific notation, it is easy to determine the order of magnitude of the number. The order of magnitude is the power of ten that the number would be rounded to. For example, in the number 5.943×10^{9}, the order of magnitude is 10^{10}, because 5.943 rounds to another 10, and 10 times 10^{9} is 10^{10}. For numbers less than 5, the order of magnitude is just the power of ten when the number is written in scientific notation.

The order of magnitude can be used to help quickly estimate your answers. Simply perform the operations required, but instead of using numbers, use the orders of magnitude. Your final answer should be within two orders of magnitude of your estimate.

Practice

1. Rewrite the following values using scientific notation:
  a. 12 300 000 m/s
  b. 0.000 000 000 0045 kg
  c. 0.00 006 53 m
  d. 55 432 000 000 000 s
  e. 273.15 K
  f. 0.000 627 14 kg

SI

One of the most important parts of scientific research is being able to communicate your findings to other scientists. Today, scientists need to be able to communicate with other scientists all around the world. If you do an experiment in which all of your measurements are in pounds, and you want to compare your results to a French scientist whose measurements are in grams, you will need to convert all of your measurements. For this reason, *Le Système International d'Unités,* or SI system was devised in 1960.

You are probably accustomed to measuring distance in inches, feet, and miles. Most of the world, however, measures distance in centimeters (abbreviated cm), meters (abbreviated m), and kilometers (abbreviated km). The meter is the official SI unit for measuring distance.

Notice that centi*meter* and kilo*meter* each contain the word *meter.* When dealing with SI units, you frequently use the base unit, in this case the meter, and add a prefix to indicate that the quantity you are measuring is a multiple of that unit. Most SI prefixes indicate multiples of 10. For example, the centimeter is 1/100 of a meter. Any SI unit with the prefix

Table A-5 **Some SI Units**

Quantity	Unit name	Abbreviation
Length	meter	m
Mass	kilogram	kg
Time	second	s
Temperature	kelvin	K
Amount of substance	mole	mol
Electric current	ampere	A
Pressure	pascal	Pa
Volume	meters^3	m^3

Table A-6 **Some SI Prefixes**

Prefix	Abbreviation	Exponential factor
Giga-	G	10^9
Mega-	M	10^6
Kilo-	k	10^3
Hecto-	h	10^2
Deka-	da	10^1
Deci-	d	10^{-1}
Centi-	c	10^{-2}
Milli-	m	10^{-3}
Micro-	μ	10^{-6}
Nano-	n	10^{-9}
Pico-	p	10^{-12}
Femto-	f	10^{-15}

centi- will be 1/100 of the base unit. A centigram is 1/100 of a gram.

What about the *kilo*meter? The prefix *kilo-* indicates that the unit is 1000 times the base unit. A kilometer is equal to 1000 meters. Multiples of 10 make dealing with SI values much easier than values such as feet or gallons. If you wish to convert from feet to miles, you must remember the conversion factor 1.893939×10^{-4} miles/foot. If you wish to convert from kilometers to meters, you need only look at the prefix to know that you will multiply by 1000.

Table A-5 lists the SI units. **Table A-6** gives the possible prefixes and their meaning. When working with a prefix, simply take the unit abbreviation and add the prefix abbreviation to the front of the unit. For example, the abbreviation for kilometer is written km.

Practice

1. Convert each value to the requested units.
   a. 0.035 m to decimeters
   b. 5.24 m^3 to centimeters^3
   c. 13450 g to kilograms

SI

Practice Answers

1. a. 0.35 dm
   b. 5.24×10^6 cm^3
   c. 13.45 kg

Study Skills

Significant Figures

Practice Answers

1. **a.** 4
   b. 5
   c. 4
   d. 3
2. **a.** 0.004 dm + 0.12508 dm
   = 0.12908 dm =
   0.129 dm
   b. $\dfrac{340 \text{ m}}{0.1257 \text{ s}}$ =
   2704.852824 m/s =
   2700 m/s
   c. 40.1 kg × 0.2453 m² =
   9.83653 kg•m² =
   9.84 kg•m²
   d. 1.03 g − 0.0456 g =
   0.9844 g = 0.98 g

Significant figures

The following list can be used to review how to determine the number of significant figures in a reported value. After you have reviewed the rules, use **Table A-7** to check your understanding of the rules. Cover up the second column of the table, and try to determine how many significant figures each number has. If you get confused, refer to the rule given.

Table A-7 Significant Figures

Measurement	Number of significant figures	Rule
12 345	5	1
2400 cm	2	3
305 kg	3	2
2350. cm	4	4
234.005 K	6	2
12.340	5	6
0.001	1	5
0.002 450	4	5 and 6

Rules for Determining the Number of Significant Figures in a Measurement:

1. All nonzero digits are significant. **Example:** 1246 has four significant figures (shown in red).
2. Any zeros between significant digits are also significant. 1206 has four significant figures.
3. If the value does not contain a decimal point, any zeros to the right of a nonzero digit are not significant. 1200 has only two significant figures.
4. Any zeros to the right of a significant digit and to the left of a decimal point are significant. 1200. has four significant figures.
5. If a value has no significant digits to the left of a decimal point, any zeros to the right of the decimal point, and to the left of a significant digit, are not significant. **Example:** 0.0012 has only two significant figures.
6. If a measurement is reported that ends with zeros to the right of a decimal point, those zeros are significant. **Example:** 0.1200 has four significant figures.

If you are adding or subtracting two measurements, your answer can only have as many decimal positions as the value with the least number of decimal places. The final answer in the following problem has five significant figures. It has been rounded to two decimal places because 0.04 g only has two decimal places.

$$\begin{array}{r} 134.050 \text{ g} \\ -\ 0.04 \text{ g} \\ \hline 134.01 \text{ g} \end{array}$$

When multiplying or dividing measurements, your final answer can only have as many significant figures as the value with the least number of significant figures. Examine the following multiplication problem.

$$\begin{array}{r} 12.0 \text{ cm}^2 \\ \times\ 0.04 \text{ cm} \\ \hline 0.5 \text{ cm}^3 \end{array}$$

The final answer has been rounded to one significant figure because 0.04 cm has only one. When performing both types of operations (addition/subtraction vs. multiplication/division), complete one type, round, perform the other type, and round the result.

Practice

1. Determine the number of significant figures in each of the following measurements:
   a. 65.04 mL   **c.** 0.007 504 kg
   b. 564.00 m   **d.** 1210 K
2. Perform each of the following calculations, and report your answer with the correct number of significant figures and units:
   a. 0.004 dm + 0.125 08 dm
   b. 340 m ÷ 0.1257 s
   c. 40.1 kg × 0.2453 m²
   d. 1.03 g − 0.0456 g

Graphing Skills

Line graphs

In laboratory experiments, you will usually be controlling one variable and seeing how it affects another variable. Line graphs can show these relations clearly. For example, you might perform an experiment in which you measure the growth of a plant over time to determine the rate of the plant's growth. In this experiment, you are controlling the time intervals at which the plant height is measured. Therefore, time is called the *independent variable*. The height of the plant is the *dependent variable*. **Table A-8** gives some sample data for an experiment to measure the rate of plant growth.

The independent variable is plotted on the *x*-axis. This axis will be labeled *Time (days)*, and will have a range from 0 days to 35 days. Be sure to properly label each axis including the units on the values.

The dependent variable is plotted on the *y*-axis. This axis will be labeled *Plant Height (cm)* and will have a range from 0 cm to 5 cm.

Figure A-1

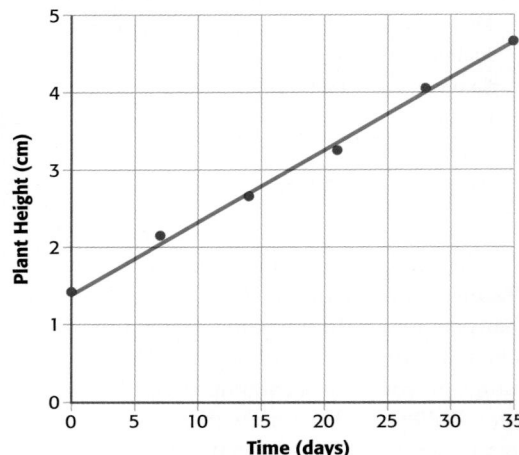

Think of your graph as a grid with lines running horizontally from the *y*-axis, and vertically from the *x*-axis. To plot a point, find the *x* (in this example time) value on the *x* axis. Follow the vertical line from the *x* axis until it intersects the horizontal line from the *y*-axis at the corresponding *y* (in this case, height) value. At the intersection of these two lines, place your point. **Figure A-1** shows what a line graph of the data in **Table A-8** might look like.

Bar graphs

Bar graphs are useful for comparing different data values. If you wanted to compare the sizes of the planets in our solar system, you might use a bar graph. **Table A-9** on the next page gives the necessary data for such a graph.

Table A-8 **Experimental Data for Plant Growth versus Time**

Time (days)	Plant height (cm)
0	1.43
7	2.16
14	2.67
21	3.25
28	4.04
35	4.67

Graphing Skills
Teaching Tip

Be sure students understand that not all graphs are alike. Each type of graph showcases a certain aspect of a data set. A line graph reveals trends over constant ranges. Bar graphs work better for data that is organized by category. Pie charts easily show proportions making up a whole.

Graphing Skills

Table A-9 Radii of the Planets in Our Solar System

Planet	Radius (km)
Mercury	2 439
Venus	6 052
Earth	6 378
Mars	3 393
Jupiter	71 398
Saturn	60 000
Uranus	25 400
Neptune	24 300
Pluto	1 500

Figure A-2

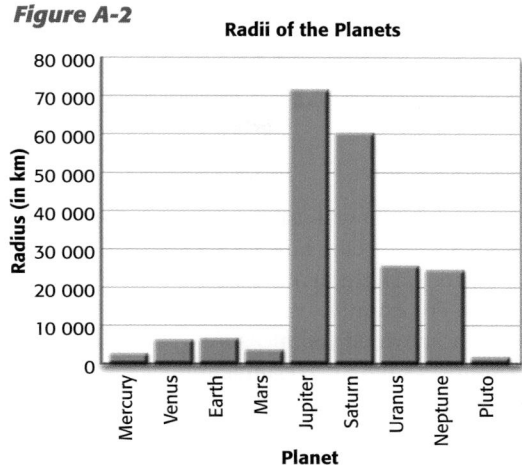

To create a bar graph from the data in **Table A-9,** begin on the *x*-axis by labeling nine bar positions with the names of the nine planets. Label the *y*-axis *Radius (km).* Be sure the range on your *y*-axis encompasses 1500 km and 71 398 km. Then draw the bars for each planet with a bar height that matches the radius value for that planet on the *y*-axis, as shown in **Figure A-2.**

Pie charts

Pie charts are an easy way to visualize how many parts make up a whole. Frequently, pie charts are made from percentage data. For example, you could create a pie graph showing the elemental composition of Earth's crust. Data for this sample pie chart can be found in **Table A-10.**

To create a pie chart from the data in **Table A-10,** begin by drawing a circle. Then imagine dividing the circle into 100 equal sections. Shade in 46 consecutive sections, and label that region *Oxygen.* Continue in the same manner with other colors until

the entire pie chart has been filled in, and each element has a corresponding region on the chart as shown in **Figure A-3.**

Figure A-3

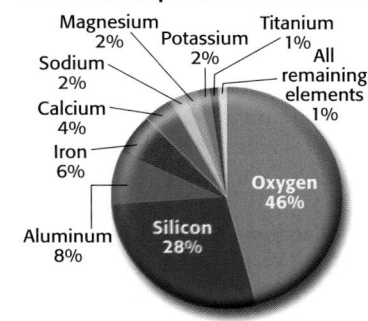

Table A-10 Elemental Composition of Earth's Crust

Element	Percentage of Earth's Crust	Element	Percentage of Earth's Crust
Oxygen	46%	Sodium	2%
Silicon	28%	Magnesium	2%
Aluminum	8%	Potassium	2%
Iron	6%	Titanium	1%
Calcium	4%	All remaining elements	1%

Lab Skills

Making Measurements in the Laboratory

Reading a balance for mass

When a balance is required for determining mass, you will probably use a centigram balance like the one shown in **Figure A-4.** The centigram balance is sensitive to 0.01 g. This means that your mass readings should all be recorded to the nearest 0.01 g.

Before using the balance, always check to see if the pointer is resting at zero. If the pointer is not at zero, check the riders. If all the riders are at zero, turn the zero adjust knob until the pointer rests at zero. The zero adjust knob is usually located at the far left end of the balance beam, as shown in **Figure A-4.** Note: The balance will not adjust to zero if the movable pan has been removed.

Figure A-4

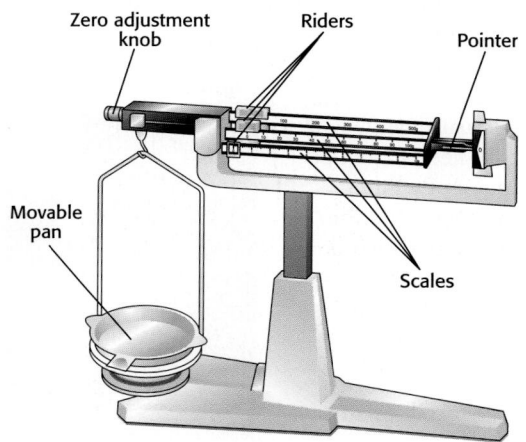

In many experiments, you will be asked to obtain a specified mass of a solid. When measuring the mass of a chemical, place a piece of weighing paper on the movable pan. **Never place chemicals or hot objects directly on the pan.** They can permanently damage the surface of the pan and affect the accuracy of later measurements.

Determine the mass of the paper by adjusting the riders on the various scales. Record the mass of the weighing paper to the nearest 0.01 g. Then add the mass you wish to obtain by sliding the appropriate riders on the scales. For example, if your weighing paper has a mass of 0.15 g, the balance reads 0.15 g. To measure 13 g of a solid, you then need to add 13 g to this mass. Do this by sliding the 10-gram rider to 10 and the 1-gram rider to 3. The balance is no longer balanced.

Slowly add the solid onto the weighing paper until the balance is once again balanced. Do not waste time trying to obtain *exactly* 13.00 g of a solid. Instead, read the mass when the pointer swings close to zero. Remember, you must read the final mass on the balance and subtract the mass of the weighing paper (0.15 g) from this final mass to determine the solid's mass to two decimal places, as is appropriate for measurements made using a centigram balance.

Lab Skills

Teaching Tip

It is not practical to show every possible balance configuration in the textbook. If your balances are significantly different from the one shown in **Figure A-4,** be sure to make clear to students what the differences are.

Lab Skills

Teaching Tip

Because of the hazards due to spills, many school districts are eliminating use of mercury thermometers. While red alcohol thermometers are not quite as precise, the slight variation encountered is usually not significant for the high school science lab.

Interpreting Visuals

The meniscus shown is actually from a titration buret, rather than a graduated cylinder. While the titration buret is numbered from the top down, a graduated cylinder is numbered from the bottom up. With either instrument, though, the meniscus is interpreted the same way. The measurement is taken at the lowest point of the water's surface, near the center of the vessel.

Measuring temperature with a thermometer

A thermometer is used to measure temperature. Examine your thermometer and the temperature range for the Celsius temperature scale. You will probably be using an alcohol thermometer in your laboratory. However, you may also use a digital thermometer.

Mercury thermometers are hazardous and probably will not be available in your school laboratory, although you may still have a mercury fever thermometer at home. **If a mercury thermometer should ever break, immediately notify your teacher or parent. Your teacher or parent will clean up the spill. Do not touch the mercury.**

Alcohol thermometers, like mercury thermometers, have a column of liquid that rises in a glass cylinder depending on the temperature at the tip of the thermometer. One caution concerning alcohol thermometers is that they can burst at very high temperatures. Never let the thermometer be exposed to temperatures above its range.

When working with any thermometer, it is especially important to pay close attention to the precision of the instrument. Most alcohol thermometers are marked in intervals of 1°C. The intervals are usually so close together that it is impossible to estimate temperature values measured with such a thermometer to any more precision than a half a degree, 0.5°C. Thus, if you are using this type of thermometer, it would be impossible to actually measure a temperature like 25.15°C.

It is also very important to keep your eye at about the same level as the colored fluid in the thermometer. If you are looking at the thermometer from below, the reading you see will appear a degree or two lower than it really is. Similarly, if you look at the thermometer from above, the reading will seem to be a degree or two higher than it really is.

Reading a graduated cylinder for volume

Many different types of laboratory glassware, from beakers to flasks, contain markings indicating approximate volume in milliliters. However, these markings are merely approximate, and they were not consistently checked when the piece of glassware was made.

For truly accurate volume measurements, you should use a graduated cylinder, or a buret, like the one shown in **Figure A-5.** When a graduated cylinder or a buret is made, its accuracy is checked and rechecked. You will also notice that graduated cylinders and burets are marked in smaller increments than are beakers (usually individual milliliters, although some are even more precise).

Most liquids have a concave surface that forms in a buret or a graduated cylinder. This concave surface is called a meniscus. When measuring the volume of a liquid, you must consider the meniscus, like the one shown in the buret in **Figure A-5.** Always measure the volume from the bottom of the meniscus. The markings on a graduated cylinder or a buret are designed to take into account the water that extends up along the walls slightly above the marking lines.

It may be difficult to read a volume measurement, so if you need to, hold a piece of white paper behind the graduated cylinder or buret. This should make the meniscus level easier to see.

Figure A-5

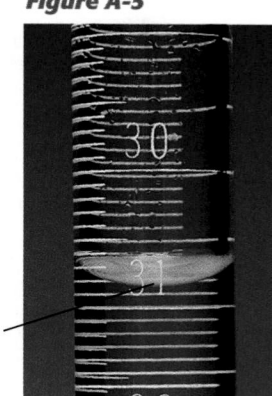

Meniscus, 30.84 mL

How to Write a Laboratory Report

In many of the laboratory investigations that you will be doing, you will be trying to support a hypothesis or answer a question by performing experiments following the scientific method. You will frequently be asked to summarize your experiments in a laboratory report. Laboratory reports should contain the following parts:

Title

This is the name of the experiment you are doing. If you are performing an experiment from this book, the title will be the same as the title of the experiment.

Hypothesis

The hypothesis is what you think will happen during the investigation. It is often written as an "If . . . then" statement. When you conduct your experiment, you will be changing one condition, or variable, and observing and measuring the effect of this change. The condition that you are changing is called the *independent* variable and should follow the "If . . ." statement. The effect that you expect to observe is called the *dependent* variable and should follow the ". . . then" statement. For example, look at the following hypothesis:

> *If salamanders are reared in acidic water, then more of the salamanders will develop abnormally.*

"If salamanders are reared in acidic water" is the independent variable—salamanders normally live in nearly neutral water and you are changing this to acidic water. "Then more of the salamanders will develop abnormally" is the dependent variable—this is the change that you expect to observe and measure.

Materials

List all of the equipment and other supplies you will need to complete the experiment. If the investigation is taken from this book, the materials are listed for you, but you will need to recopy them into your lab report. It is important that your lab report be complete enough so that someone else can repeat your experiment to test your results.

Procedure

The procedure is a step-by-step explanation of exactly what you did in the experiment. Investigations in this book will have the procedure carefully written out for you, but you must write the procedure in your lab report EXACTLY as you performed it. This will not necessarily be an exact copy of the procedure written in the book.

Data

Your data are your observations. They are often recorded in the form of tables, graphs, and drawings.

Analyses and Conclusions

This part of the report explains what you have learned. You should evaluate your hypothesis and explain any errors you might have made in the investigation. Keep in mind that not all of your hypotheses will be correct. Sometimes you will disprove your original hypothesis rather than prove it. You simply need to explain why things did not work out the way you thought they would. The labs included in this book will have questions to guide you as you analyze your data. You should use these questions as a basis for your conclusions.

Lab Skills

Teaching Tip

While instructions for the traditional lab report are given here, this is not necessary for most labs. The decision whether to require full-fledged traditional lab reports is best left up to the teacher.

The *Holt Science Spectrum* package includes a system of *Datasheets*, which provide blank data tables, spaces for graphs, and room for answering the in-lab questions. These *Datasheets* are available as a booklet and also can be found on the *One-Stop Planner CD-ROM with Test Generator*.

Resources Blackline Master 74 shows **Table B-1.** Blackline Master 75 shows **Table B-2.**

Table B-1 **Densities of Various Materials**

Material	Density (g/cm³)	Material	Density (g/cm³)
Air, dry	1.293×10^{-3}	Iron	7.86
Aluminum	2.70	Jupiter	1.33*
Bone	1.7–2.0	Lead	11.3
Butter	0.86–0.87	Mars	3.94*
Carbon (diamond)	3.5155	Mercury (Hg)	13.5336
Carbon (graphite)	2.2670	Paper	0.7–1.15
Copper	8.96	Rock salt	2.18
Cork	0.22–0.26	Saturn	0.70*
Earth	5.515*	Silver	10.5
Earth's moon	3.34*	Sugar	1.59
Ethanol	0.7893	Sodium	0.97
Gold	19.3	Stainless steel	8.02
Helium	1.78×10^{-4}	Steel	7.8
Ice	0.917	Water (at 25°C)	0.997 05

* Astronomical values are for mean density

Table B-2 **International Morse Code**

Letter	Code	Letter	Code	Number	Code	Symbol	Code
A	• —	N	— •	0	— — — — —	Period	• — • — • —
B	— • • •	O	— — —	1	• — — — —	Comma	— — • • — —
C	— • — •	P	• — — •	2	• • — — —	Interrogation	• • — — • •
D	— • •	Q	— — • —	3	• • • — —	Colon	— — — • • •
E	•	R	• — •	4	• • • • —	Semicolon	— • — • — •
F	• • — •	S	• • •	5	• • • • •	Hyphen	— • • • • —
G	— — •	T	—	6	— • • • •	Slash	— • • — •
H	• • • •	U	• • —	7	— — • • •	Quotation marks	• — • • — •
I	• •	V	• • • —	8	— — — • •		
J	• — — —	W	• — —	9	— — — — •		
K	— • —	X	— • • —				
L	• — • •	Y	— • — —				
M	— —	Z	— — • •				

Table B-3 Specific Heats

Material	c (J/kg·K)	Material	c (J/kg·K)
Acetic acid (CH_3COOH)	2070	Lead (Pb)	129
Air	1007	Magnetite (Fe_3O_4)	619
Aluminum (Al)	897	Methane (CH_4)	2200
Calcium (Ca)	647	Mercury (Hg)	140
Calcium carbonate ($CaCO_3$)	818	Neon (Ne)	1030
Carbon (C, graphite)	709	Nickel (Ni)	444
Carbon (C, diamond)	487	Nitrogen (N_2)	1040
Carbon dioxide (CO_2)	843	Oxygen (O_2)	918
Copper (Cu)	385	Platinum (Pt)	133
Ethanol (CH_3CH_2OH)	2440	Silver (Ag)	234
Gold (Au)	129	Sodium (Na)	1228
Helium (He)	5193	Sodium chloride (NaCl)	864
Hematite (Fe_2O_3)	650	Tin (Sn)	228
Hydrogen (H_2)	14 304	Tungsten (W)	132
Hydrogen peroxide (H_2O_2)	2620	Water (H_2O)	4186
Iron (Fe)	449	Zinc (Zn)	388

Values at 25°C and 1 atm pressure

Figure B-1 Electromagnetic Spectrum

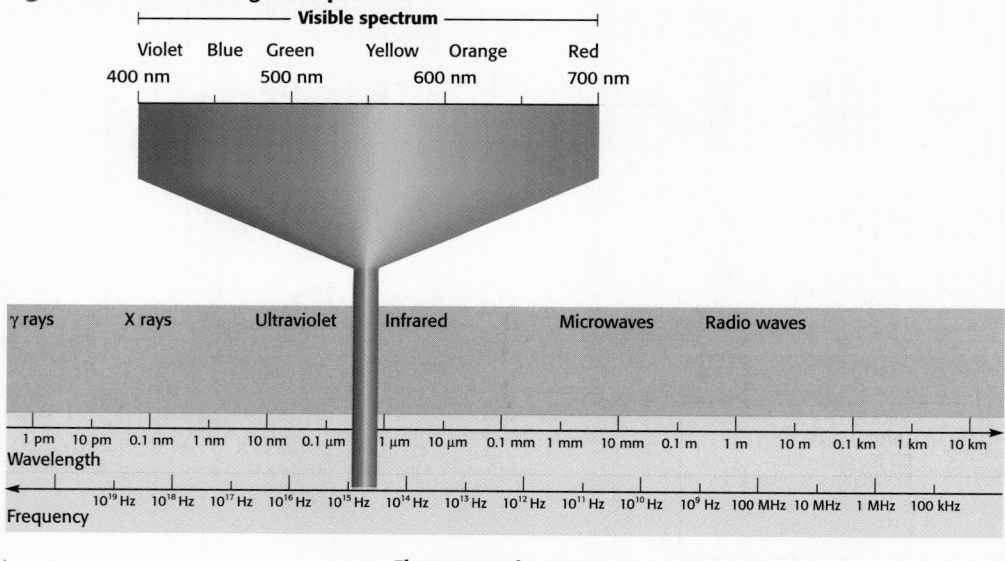

Resources Blackline Master 76 shows **Table B-3.** Teaching Transparency 84 shows **Figure B-1.**

APPENDIX B   Useful Data

Figure B-2   **Periodic Table of the Elements**

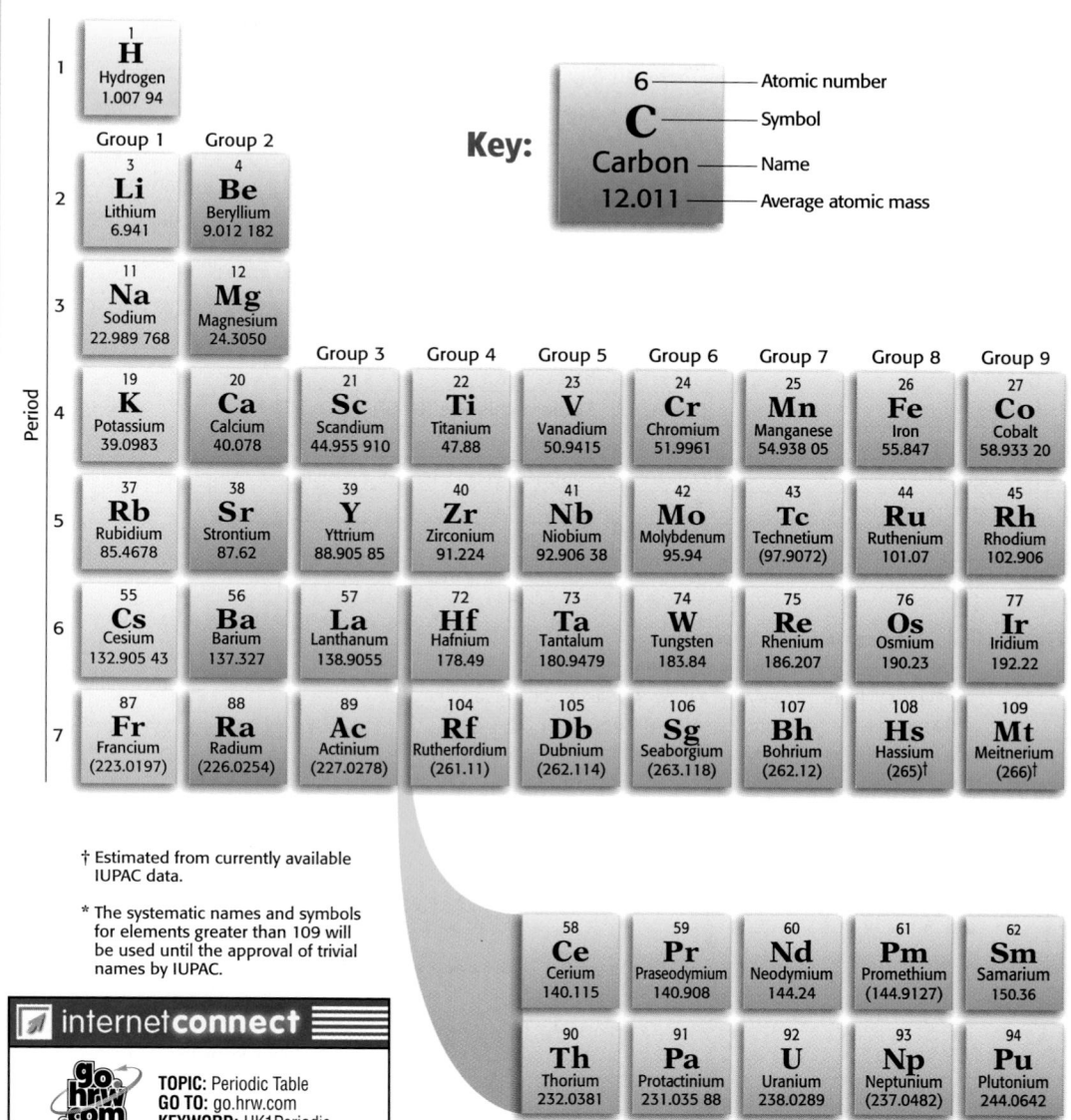

Key:

6 — Atomic number
C — Symbol
Carbon — Name
12.011 — Average atomic mass

† Estimated from currently available
IUPAC data.

* The systematic names and symbols
for elements greater than 109 will
be used until the approval of trivial
names by IUPAC.

internet connect

go.hrw.com

TOPIC: Periodic Table
GO TO: go.hrw.com
KEYWORD: HK1Periodic

Visit the HRW Web site to see the most
recent version of the periodic table.

Metals
- Alkali metals
- Alkaline-earth metals
- Transition metals
- Other metals

Nonmetals
- Hydrogen
- Semiconductors
- Halogens
- Noble gases
- Other nonmetals

					Group 13	Group 14	Group 15	Group 16	Group 17	Group 18
										2 **He** Helium 4.002 602
					5 **B** Boron 10.811	6 **C** Carbon 12.011	7 **N** Nitrogen 14.006 74	8 **O** Oxygen 15.9994	9 **F** Fluorine 18.998 4032	10 **Ne** Neon 20.1797
		Group 10	Group 11	Group 12	13 **Al** Aluminum 26.981 539	14 **Si** Silicon 28.0855	15 **P** Phosphorus 30.9738	16 **S** Sulfur 32.066	17 **Cl** Chlorine 35.4527	18 **Ar** Argon 39.948
		28 **Ni** Nickel 58.6934	29 **Cu** Copper 63.546	30 **Zn** Zinc 65.39	31 **Ga** Gallium 69.723	32 **Ge** Germanium 72.61	33 **As** Arsenic 74.921 59	34 **Se** Selenium 78.96	35 **Br** Bromine 79.904	36 **Kr** Krypton 83.80
		46 **Pd** Palladium 106.42	47 **Ag** Silver 107.8682	48 **Cd** Cadmium 112.411	49 **In** Indium 114.818	50 **Sn** Tin 118.710	51 **Sb** Antimony 121.757	52 **Te** Tellurium 127.60	53 **I** Iodine 126.904	54 **Xe** Xenon 131.29
		78 **Pt** Platinum 195.08	79 **Au** Gold 196.966 54	80 **Hg** Mercury 200.59	81 **Tl** Thallium 204.3833	82 **Pb** Lead 207.2	83 **Bi** Bismuth 208.980 37	84 **Po** Polonium (208.9824)	85 **At** Astatine (209.9871)	86 **Rn** Radon (222.0176)
		110 **Uun*** Ununnilium (269)†	111 **Uuu*** Unununium (272)†	112 **Uub*** Ununbium (277)†		114 **Uuq*** Ununquadium (285)†		116 **Uuh*** Ununhexium (289)†		118 **Uuo*** Ununoctium (293)†

63 **Eu** Europium 151.966	64 **Gd** Gadolinium 157.25	65 **Tb** Terbium 158.925 34	66 **Dy** Dysprosium 162.50	67 **Ho** Holmium 164.930	68 **Er** Erbium 167.26	69 **Tm** Thulium 168.934 21	70 **Yb** Ytterbium 173.04	71 **Lu** Lutetium 174.967
95 **Am** Americium (243.0614)	96 **Cm** Curium (247.0703)	97 **Bk** Berkelium (247.0703)	98 **Cf** Californium (251.0796)	99 **Es** Einsteinium (252.083)	100 **Fm** Fermium (257.0951)	101 **Md** Mendelevium (258.10)	102 **No** Nobelium (259.1009)	103 **Lr** Lawrencium (262.11)

The atomic masses listed in this table reflect the precision of current measurements. (Values listed in parentheses are those of the element's most stable or most common isotope.) In calculations throughout the text, however, atomic masses have been rounded to two places to the right of the decimal.

Figure B-3   **The World: Physical**

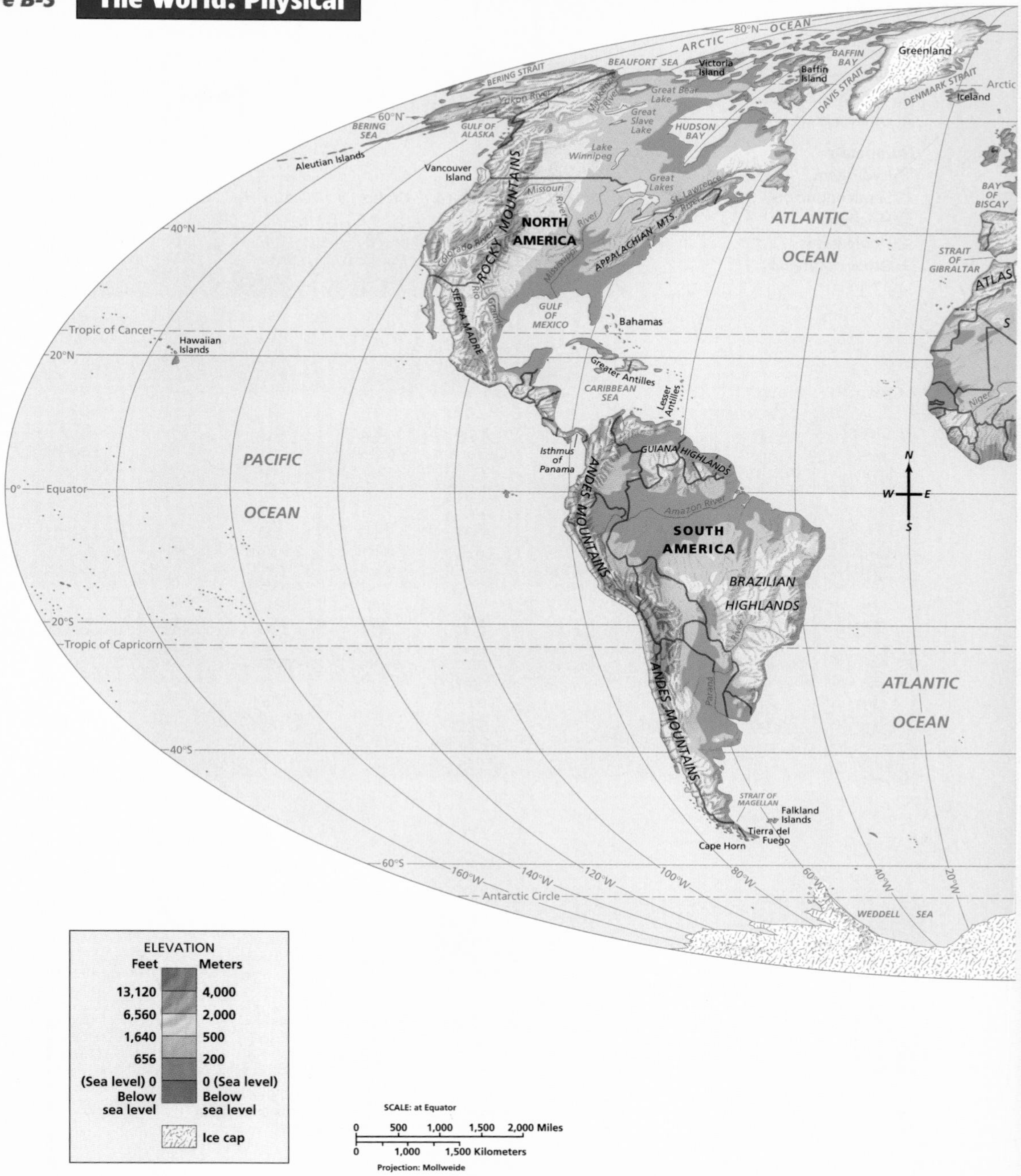

ELEVATION

Feet		Meters
13,120		4,000
6,560		2,000
1,640		500
656		200
(Sea level) 0		0 (Sea level)
Below sea level		Below sea level
	Ice cap	

SCALE: at Equator

0   500   1,000   1,500   2,000 Miles

0   1,000   1,500 Kilometers

Projection: Mollweide

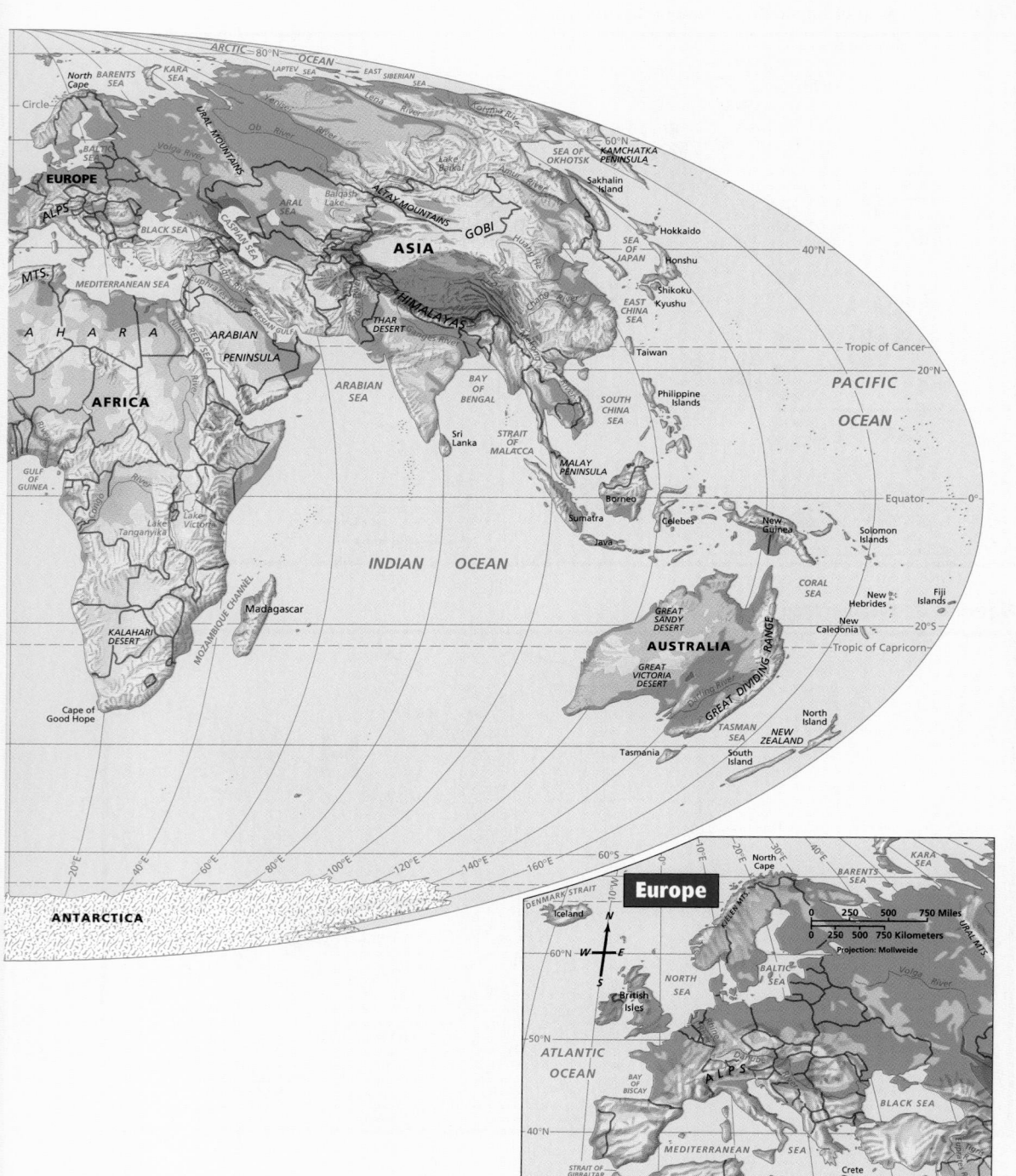

Figure B-4 Map of United States Natural Resources

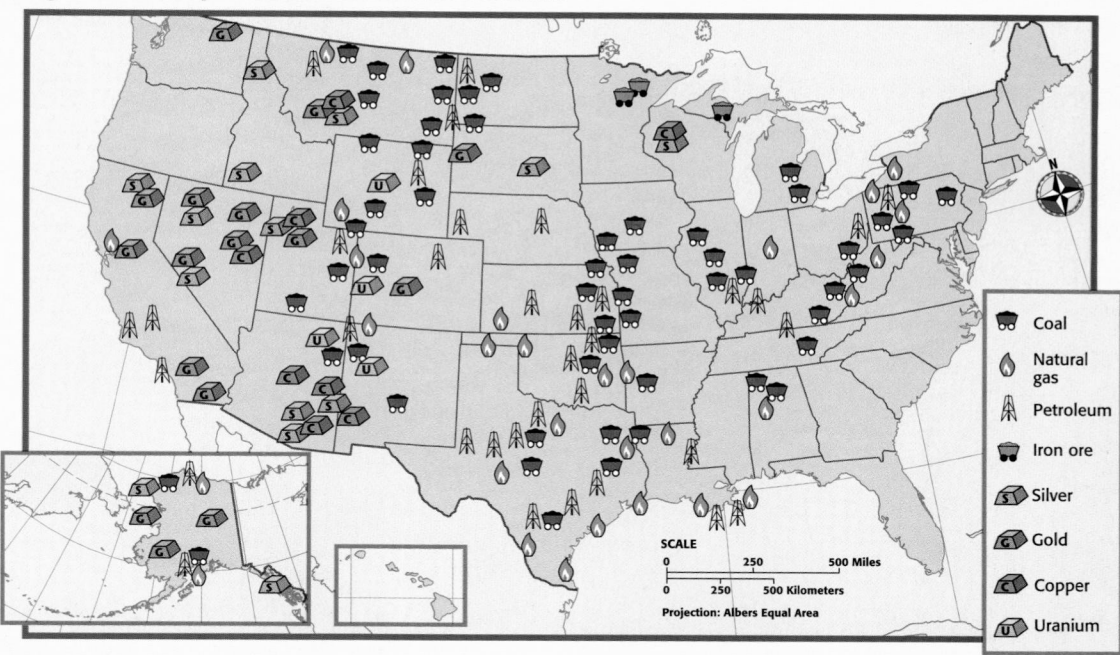

- Coal
- Natural gas
- Petroleum
- Iron ore
- S Silver
- G Gold
- C Copper
- U Uranium

SCALE

0 · 250 · 500 Miles

0 · 250 · 500 Kilometers

Projection: Albers Equal Area

Figure B-5 Weather Map

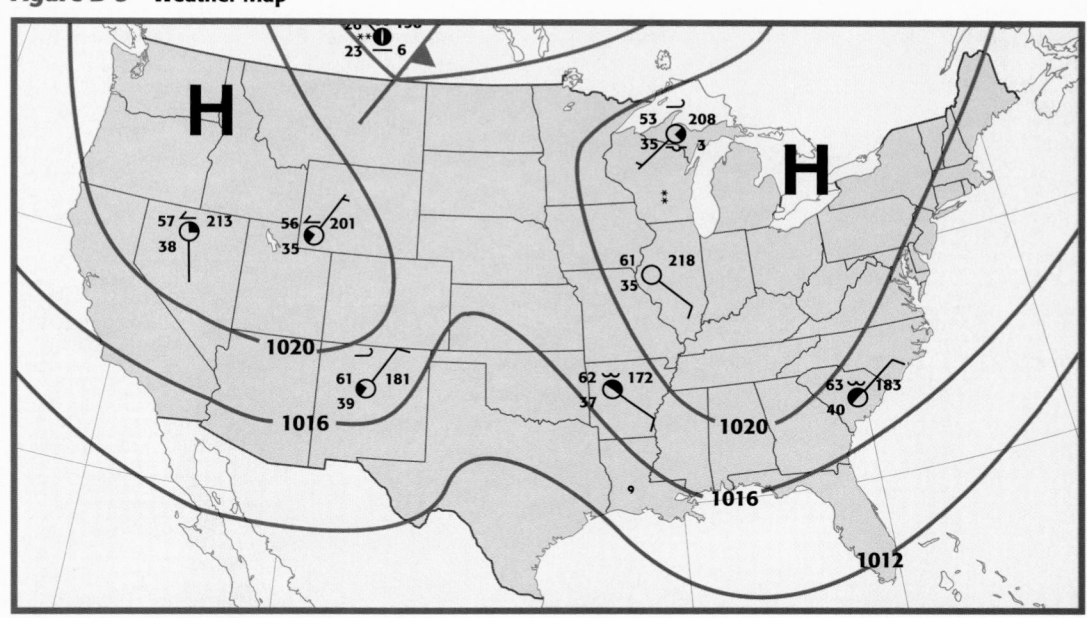

Table B-4 **International Weather Symbols**

Current Weather

Hail	⊖	Light drizzle	⍤	Light rain	•	Light snow	✳
Freezing rain	∿•	Steady, light drizzle	⍤⍤	Steady, light rain	••	Steady, light snow	✳ ✳
Smoke	⌇	Intermittent, moderate drizzle	⍤⍤	Intermittent, moderate rain	•/•	Intermittent, moderate snow	✳/✳
Tornado	)(	Steady, moderate drizzle	⍤⍤⍤	Steady, moderate rain	•• /•	Steady, moderate snow	✳/✳✳
Dust storms	⤳	Intermittent, heavy drizzle	⍤/⍤	Intermittent, heavy rain	•/•	Intermittent, heavy snow	✳/✳
Fog	≡	Steady, heavy drizzle	⍤⍤/⍤	Steady, heavy rain	•∘•	Steady, heavy snow	✳/✳✳
Thunder-storm	⫪						
Lightning	<						
Hurricane	৶						

Sky Coverage

No clouds	○	Two- to three-tenths covered	◔	Half covered	◑	Nine-tenths covered	◕
One-tenth Coverage	⊘	Four-tenths covered	◔	Six-tenths covered	◑	Completely overcast	●

Clouds

Low		Stratus	—	Cumulus	◠	Cumulonimbus calvus	⌂
		Stratocumulus	⌣	Cumulus congestus	◠	Cumulonimbus with anvil	⊠
Middle		Altostratus	∠	Altocumulus	⌣	Altocumulus castellanus	M
High		Cirrus	⌐	Cirrostratus	2	Cirrocumulus	⌇

Wind Speed (in km/h)

Calm	◎	4–13	⌐	24–33	⌐⌐
1–3	—	14–23	⌐	34–40	⌐⌐⌐

Resources Blackline Masters
77 and 78 show **Table B-4.**

Resources Teaching Transparencies 85 and 86 show **Figure B-6.**

Figure B-6   **Sky Map for the Northern Hemisphere, Winter**

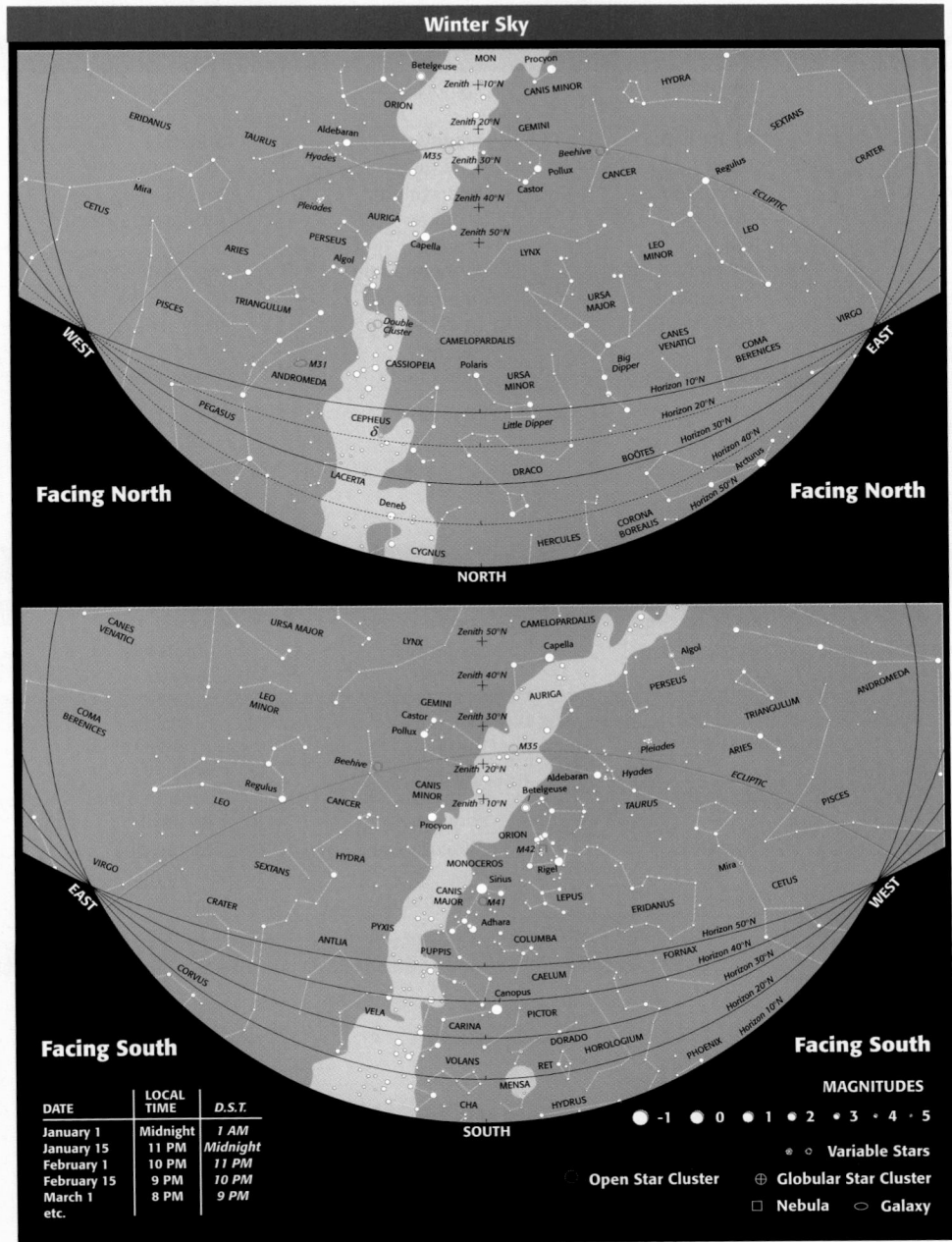

DATE	LOCAL TIME	D.S.T.
January 1	Midnight	1 AM
January 15	11 PM	Midnight
February 1	10 PM	11 PM
February 15	9 PM	10 PM
March 1	8 PM	9 PM
etc.		

Conversions

1. Earth's moon has a radius of 1738 km. Write this measurement in megameters.
2. Convert each of the following values as indicated:
   a. 113 g to milligrams
   b. 700 pm to nanometers
   c. 101.1 kPa to pascals
   d. 13 MA to amperes
3. Maryland has 49 890 m of coastline. What is this length in centimeters?
4. In 1997 Andy Green, a Royal Air Force pilot, broke the land speed record in Black Rock Desert, Nevada. His car averaged 341.11 m/s. The speed of sound in Black Rock at the time that he broke the record was determined to be 0.33584 km/s. Did Andy Green break the sound barrier?
5. The mass of the planet Pluto is 15 000 000 000 000 000 000 000 kg. What is the mass of Pluto in gigagrams?

Writing Scientific Notation

6. Express each of the following values in scientific notation:
   a. 110.45 m   c. 132 948 kg
   b. 0.000 003 45 s   d. 0.034 3900 cm
7. In 1998, the population of the U.S. was about 270 000 000 people. Write the estimated population in scientific notation.
8. In 1997, 70 294 601 airplanes either took off or landed at Chicago's O'Hare airport. What is the number of arrivals and departures at O'Hare given in scientific notation?
9. The planet Saturn has a mass of 568 500 000 000 000 000 000 000 000 kg. Express the mass of Saturn in scientific notation.
10. Approximately four-and-a-half million automobiles were imported into the United States last year. Write this number in scientific notation.

Using Scientific Notation

11. Perform the following calculations involving numbers that have been written in scientific notation:
    a. $3.02 \times 10^{-3} + 4.11 \times 10^{-2}$
    b. $(6.022 \times 10^{23}) \div (1.04 \times 10^{4})$
    c. $(1.00 \times 10^{2}) \times (3.01 \times 10^{3})$
    d. $6.626 \times 10^{34} - 5.442 \times 10^{32}$
12. Mount Everest, the tallest mountain on Earth, is 8.850×10^{3} m high. The Mariana Trench is the deepest point of any ocean on Earth. It is 1.0924×10^{4} m deep. What is the vertical distance from the highest mountain on Earth to the deepest ocean trench on Earth?
13. In 1950 Americans consumed nearly 1.4048×10^{9} kg of poultry. In 1997, Americans consumed 1.2369×10^{10} kg of poultry. By what factor did America's poultry consumption increase between 1950 and 1997?
14. The following data were obtained for the number of immigrants admitted to the U.S. in major Texas cities in 1996. What is the total number of immigrants admitted in these Texas cities for that year?

City	Number of immigrants admitted
Houston	2.1387×10^{4}
Dallas	1.5915×10^{4}
El Paso	8.701×10^{3}
Ft. Worth/ Arlington	6.274×10^{3}

15. The surface area of the Pacific Ocean is 1.66×10^{14} m². The average depth of the Pacific Ocean is 3.9395×10^{3} m. If you could calculate the volume of the Pacific by simply multiplying the surface area by the average depth, what would the volume of the Pacific Ocean be?

Problem Bank Solutions

Conversions

1. 1.738 Mm
2. a. $113 \text{ g} \times \dfrac{1000 \text{ mg}}{1 \text{ g}} =$ 113 000 mg
   b. $700 \text{ pm} \times \dfrac{10^{-12} \text{ m}}{1 \text{ pm}} \times \dfrac{1 \text{ nm}}{10^{-9} \text{ m}} = 0.7$ nm
   c. $101.1 \text{ kPa} \times \dfrac{1000 \text{ Pa}}{1 \text{ kPa}} =$ 101 100 Pa
   d. $13 \text{ MA} \times \dfrac{10^{6} \text{ A}}{1 \text{ MA}} =$ 13 000 000 A
3. 4989 000 cm
4. 341.11 m/s>335.84 m/s
   Yes, he did break the sound barrier.
5. 15 000 000 000 000 000 Gg

Writing Scientific Notation

6. a. 1.1045×10^{2} m
   b. 3.45×10^{-6} s
   c. $1.329 48 \times 10^{5}$ kg
   d. $3.439 00 \times 10^{-2}$ cm
7. 2.7×10^{8} people
8. $7.029 4601 \times 10^{7}$ airplanes
9. 5.685×10^{26} kg
10. 4.5×10^{6} automobiles

Using Scientific Notation

11. a. 4.41×10^{-2}
    b. 5.79×10^{19}
    c. 3.01×10^{5}
    d. 6.572×10^{34}
12. $(8.850 \times 10^{3} \text{ m}) + (1.0924 \times 10^{4} \text{ m}) = (0.8850 \times 10^{4} \text{ m}) + (1.0924 \times 10^{4} \text{ m}) = 1.9774 \times 10^{4}$ m
13. by 8.8048 times
14. 5.2277×10^{4} immigrants
15. 6.54×10^{17} m³

Problem Bank Solutions

Significant Figures

16. a. 4
b. 4
c. 4
d. 4

17. a. 0.0147 g
b. 27.15 cm
c. 4.48 L

18. a. $\dfrac{129\ g}{29.20\ cm^3}$
= 4.417 808 219 g/cm³
= 4.42 g/cm³

b. 120 mm × 355 mm × 12.1 mm =
5.1546 × 10⁵ mm³ =
5.2 × 10⁵ mm³

c.
$\dfrac{45.4\ g}{0.012\ cm \times 0.444\ cm \times 0.221\ cm}$
= 3.855 665 62 × 10⁴ g/cm³ =
3.9 × 10⁴ g/cm³

19. (32.1 cm)³ = 3.31 × 10⁴ cm³
20. a. 1.23 cm³ − 0.044 cm³ = 1.19 cm³
b. 89.00 kg − 0.1 kg = 88.9 kg
c. 780 mm − 64 mm = 716 mm

Density

21. 140 cm³ × 1.59 g/cm³ = 220 g
22. density = $\dfrac{people}{area}$ =
$\dfrac{4.64 \times 10^8\ people}{2.4346 \times 10^{13}\ m^2}$ =
1.91 × 10⁻⁵ people/m²
23. 55.2 g − 33.4 g = 21.8 g
24. m = 0.45 g + (1.78 × 10⁻³ m³)
(0.178 kg/m³) =
7.7 × 10⁻⁴ kg *or* 0.77 g
25. $\dfrac{0.996\ g}{0.44\ cm^3}$ = 2.3 g/cm³

Conversion Factors

26. a. $\dfrac{2000\ sheets}{4\ reams} = \dfrac{500\ sheets}{1\ ream}$
b. $\dfrac{170\ g\ Ga}{2.5\ mol\ Ga} = \dfrac{68\ g\ Ga}{1\ mol\ Ga}$
c. $\dfrac{0.997\ g\ H_2O}{1.00\ cm^3\ H_2O}$
d. $\dfrac{2.24 \times 10^{10}\ mol\ Ag}{1.35 \times 10^{34}\ atoms\ Ag}$ =
$\dfrac{1\ mol\ Ag}{6.03 \times 10^{23}\ atoms\ Ag}$

27. $\dfrac{4.184\ kJ}{1\ Calorie}$ × 150 Calories =
6.3 × 10² kJ = 6.3 × 10⁵ J

Significant Figures

16. Determine the number of significant figures in each of the following values:
  a. 0.026 48 kg   **c.** 1 625 000 J
  b. 47.10 g   **d.** 29.02 cm

17. Solve the following addition problems, and round each answer to the correct number of significant figures:
  a. 0.00241 g + 0.0123 g
  b. 24.10 cm + 3.050 cm
  c. 0.367 L + 2.51 L + 1.6004 L

18. Solve the following multiplication or division problems, and round each answer to the correct number of significant figures:
  a. 129 g ÷ 29.20 cm³
  b. 120 mm × 355 mm × 12.1 mm
  c. 45.4 g ÷ (0.012 cm × 0.444 cm × 0.221 cm)

19. Determine the volume of a cube with a width of 32.1 cm. Round your answer to the correct number of significant figures.

20. Solve the following subtraction problems, and round each answer to the correct number of significant figures:
  a. 1.23 cm³ − 0.044 cm³
  b. 89.00 kg − 0.1 kg
  c. 780 mm − 64 mm

Density

21. Sugar has a density of 1.59 g/cm³. What mass of sugar fits into a 140 cm³ bowl?

22. The continent of North America has an area of 2.4346 × 10¹³ m². North America has a population of 4.64 × 10⁸ people. What is the population density of North America?

23. The average density of Earth is 5.515 g/cm³. The average density of Earth's moon is 3.34 g/cm³. What is the difference in mass between 10.0 cm³ of Earth and 10.0 cm³ of Earth's moon?

---

24. A rubber balloon has a mass of 0.45 g, and can hold 1.78 × 10⁻³ m³ of helium. If the density of helium is 0.178 kg/m³, what is the balloon's total mass?

25. What is the density of a 0.996 g piece of graphite with a volume of 0.44 cm³?

Conversion Factors

26. Give the correct factor to convert between each of the following values:
  a. 4 reams of paper → 2000 sheets of paper
  b. 2.5 mol of gallium, Ga → 170 g of Ga
  c. 1.00 cm³ of water → 0.997 g of water
  d. 1.35 × 10³⁴ atoms of silver, Ag → 2.24 × 10¹⁰ mol of silver

27. A Calorie, as reported on nutritional labels, is equal to 4.184 kJ. A carbonated beverage contains about 150 Calories. What is the energy content in joules?

28. a. The density of gold is 19.3 g/cm³. What is the mass of a bar of gold with dimensions of 10.0 cm × 26.0 cm × 8.0 cm?
  b. Gold is priced by the ounce. One gram is equal to 0.0353 oz. If the price of gold is $253.50 per ounce, what is the value of the bar described in part (a)?

29. How many atoms of copper are there in a piece of copper tube that contains 34.5 mol of copper, Cu? (**Hint:** There are 6.02 × 10²³ atoms in one mole.)

30. In February of 1962 John Glenn orbited Earth three times in 4 hours and 55 minutes. How long did it take him to make one revolution around Earth? In June of 1983 Sally Ride became the first U.S. woman in space. Her mission lasted 146 hours, 24 minutes. If each revolution of Sally Ride's mission took the same amount of time as each revolution of John Glenn's mission, how many times did Ride orbit around Earth?

---

28. a. m = dV =
19.3 g/cm³ (10.0 cm × 26.0 cm × 8.0 cm) =
4.0 × 10⁴ g
b. (4.0 × 10⁴ g) ×
$\dfrac{0.0353\ oz}{1\ g} \times \dfrac{\$253.50}{1\ oz}$ =
$3.6 × 10⁵

29. 34.5 mol Cu ×
$\left(\dfrac{6.02 \times 10^{23}\ atoms\ Cu}{1\ mol\ Cu}\right)$ =
2.08 × 10²⁵ atoms Cu

30. 295 min ÷ 3 rev =
98.3 min/rev for John Glenn
$\dfrac{\left(146\ h \times \dfrac{60\ min}{1\ h}\right) + 24\ min}{98.3\ min/rev}$ =
89.4 rev for Sally Ride

Converting Amount to Mass

31. Determine the mass in grams of each of the following:
   a. 67.9 mol of silicon, Si
   b. 1.45×10^{-4} mol of cadmium, Cd
   c. 0.045 mol of gold, Au
   d. 3.900 mol of tungsten, W

32. Fullerenes, also known as buckyballs, are a form of elemental carbon. One variety of fullerene has 60 carbon atoms in each molecule. What is the molar mass of 1 mol of this 60-carbon atom molecule? What is the mass of 5.23×10^{-2} mol of this fullerene?

33. An experiment requires 2.0 mol of cadmium, Cd, and 2.0 mol of sulfur, S. What mass of each element is required?

34. If there are 6.02×10^{27} mol of iron, Fe, in a portion of Earth's crust, what is the mass of iron present?

35. a. A certain molecule of polyester contains one-hundred thousand carbon atoms. What is the mass of carbon in 1 mol of this polyester?
   b. The same polyester molecule contains forty-thousand oxygen atoms. What is the mass of oxygen in 1 mol?

Converting Mass to Amount

36. Imagine that you find a jar full of diamonds. You measure the mass of the diamonds and find that they have a mass of 45.4 g. Determine the amount of carbon in the diamonds.

37. A tungsten, W, filament in a light bulb has a mass of 2.0 mg. Calculate the amount of tungsten in this filament.

38. One liter of sea water contains 1.05×10^4 mg of sodium. How much sodium is in one liter of sea water?

39. Every kilogram of Earth's crust contains 282 g of silicon. How many moles of silicon are present in 2 kg of Earth's crust?

40. Chlorine rarely occurs in nature as Cl atoms. It usually occurs as gaseous Cl_2 molecules, molecules made up of two chlorine atoms joined together. What is the molar mass of gaseous Cl_2? Calculate the amount of chlorine molecules found in 4.30 g of chlorine gas.

Writing Ionic Formulas

41. Write the ionic formula for the salt made from potassium and bromine.

42. Calcium chloride is used by the canning industry to make the skin of fruit such as tomatoes more firm. What is the ionic formula for calcium chloride?

43. Write the ionic formulas formed by each of the following pairs:
   a. lithium and oxygen
   b. magnesium and oxygen
   c. sodium and chlorine
   d. magnesium and nitrogen

44. The active ingredient in most toothpastes is sodium fluoride. Write the ionic formula for this cavity-fighting compound.

45. What is the formula for the ionic compound formed from strontium and iodine?

Balancing Chemical Equations

46. Hydrogen peroxide decomposes to form water and oxygen. Balance the equation for the decomposition of hydrogen peroxide.
$$H_2O_2 \rightarrow H_2O + O_2$$

47. Iron is often produced from iron ore by treating it with carbon monoxide in a blast furnace. Balance the equation for the production of iron.
$$Fe_2O_3 + CO \rightarrow Fe + CO_2$$

APPENDIX C
Problem Bank

Problem Bank Solutions

Converting Amount to Mass

31. a. $67.9 \text{ mol Si} \times \dfrac{28.09 \text{ g Si}}{1 \text{ mol Si}} =$
1.91×10^3 g Si
   b. $1.45 \times 10^{-4} \text{ mol Cd} \times$
$\dfrac{112.41 \text{ g Cd}}{1 \text{ mol Cd}} =$
1.63×10^{-2} g Cd
   c. $0.045 \text{ mol Au} \times$
$\dfrac{196.97 \text{ g Au}}{1 \text{ mol Au}} =$
8.9 g Au
   d. $3.900 \text{ mol W} \times \dfrac{183.84 \text{ g W}}{1 \text{ mol W}} =$
7.170×10^2 g W

32. $60 \times \dfrac{12.01 \text{ g C}}{1 \text{ mol C}} =$
720.6 g/mol C_{60}
$5.23 \times 10^{-2} \text{ mol } C_{60} \times$
$\dfrac{720.6 \text{ g } C_{60}}{1 \text{ mol } C_{60}} =$
37.7 g C_{60}

33. $2.0 \text{ mol Cd} \times \dfrac{112.41 \text{ g Cd}}{1 \text{ mol Cd}} =$
220 g Cd
$2.0 \text{ mol S} \times \dfrac{32.07 \text{ g S}}{1 \text{ mol S}} = 64$ g S

34. $6.02 \times 10^{27} \text{ mol Fe} \times$
$\dfrac{55.85 \text{ g Fe}}{1 \text{ mol Fe}} =$
3.36×10^{29} g Fe

35. a. 1 mol polyester $\times$
$\dfrac{6.02 \times 10^{23} \text{ molecules}}{1 \text{ mol}} \times$
$\dfrac{10^5 \text{ atoms C}}{1 \text{ molecule polyester}} \times$
$\dfrac{12.01 \text{ g C}}{6.02 \times 10^{23} \text{ atoms C}} = 1 \times 10^6$ g C

   b. 1 mol polyester $\times$
$\dfrac{6.02 \times 10^{23} \text{ molecules}}{1 \text{ mol}} \times$
$\dfrac{4 \times 10^3 \text{ atoms O}}{1 \text{ molecule polyester}} \times$
$\dfrac{16.00 \text{ g O}}{6.02 \times 10^{23} \text{ atoms O}} = 6 \times 10^3$ g O

Converting Mass to Amount

36. $45.4 \text{ g C} \times \dfrac{1 \text{ mol C}}{12.01 \text{ g C}} =$
3.78 mol C

37. $2.0 \times 10^{-3} \text{ g W} \times \dfrac{1 \text{ mol W}}{183.84 \text{ g W}} =$
1.1×10^{-5} mol W

38. $1.05 \times 10^1 \text{ g Na} \times$
$\dfrac{1 \text{ mol Na}}{22.99 \text{ g Na}} =$
0.457 mol Na

39. $2 \text{ kg crust} \times \dfrac{282 \text{ g Si}}{1 \text{ kg crust}} \times$
$\dfrac{1 \text{ mol Si}}{28.09 \text{ g Si}} =$
20 mol Si

40. $\dfrac{2 \text{ mol Cl}}{1 \text{ mol } Cl_2} \times \dfrac{35.45 \text{ g Cl}}{1 \text{ mol Cl}} =$
70.90 g/mol Cl_2
$4.30 \text{ g } Cl_2 \times \dfrac{1 \text{ mol } Cl_2}{70.90 \text{ g } Cl_2} =$
6.06×10^{-2} mol Cl_2

Writing Ionic Formulas

41. KBr
42. $CaCl_2$
43. a. Li_2O
   b. MgO
   c. NaCl
   d. Mg_3N_2
44. NaF
45. SrI_2

Balancing Chemical Equations

46. $2H_2O_2 \rightarrow 2H_2O + O_2$
47. $Fe_2O_3 + 3CO \rightarrow 2Fe + 3CO_2$

Problem Bank

Problem Bank Solutions

48. $Na_2S + Zn(NO_3)_2 \rightarrow ZnS + 2NaNO_3$

49. $2C_{14}H_{30} + 43O_2 \rightarrow 30H_2O + 28CO_2$

50. $6CO_2 + 6H_2O \rightarrow C_6H_{12}O_6 + 6O_2$

Nuclear Decay

51. a. $^{40}_{19}K \rightarrow ^{40}_{20}Ca + ^{0}_{-1}e$

b. $^{40}_{19}K \rightarrow ^{40}_{18}Ar + ^{0}_{1}e$

52. nitrogen

53. $^{26}_{13}Al \rightarrow ^{26}_{12}Mg + ^{0}_{1}e$

54. thorium

55. $^{222}_{86}Rn \rightarrow ^{218}_{84}Po + ^{4}_{2}He$

Half-life

56. $\dfrac{4.2 \times 10^{10}\ y}{1.4 \times 10^{10}\ y} = 3$ half-lives

$50.0\ g \times \dfrac{1}{2} \times \dfrac{1}{2} \times \dfrac{1}{2} = 6.25\ g$ Th

57. $\dfrac{8.00 \times 10^3\ y}{1.60 \times 10^3\ y} = 5$ half-lives

$0.25\ g \times \dfrac{1}{2} \times \dfrac{1}{2} \times \dfrac{1}{2} \times \dfrac{1}{2} \times \dfrac{1}{2} = 7.8 \times 10^{-3}\ g$ Ra

58. $\dfrac{1}{16} = \dfrac{1}{2} \times \dfrac{1}{2} \times \dfrac{1}{2} \times \dfrac{1}{2} = 4$ half-lives

4×8.04 days $= 32.2$ days

59. $\dfrac{1}{8} = \dfrac{1}{2} \times \dfrac{1}{2} \times \dfrac{1}{2} = 3$ half-lives

$\dfrac{12\ \text{years}}{3} = 4$ years

60. $\dfrac{52.35\ \text{min}}{10.47\ \text{min}} = 5$ half-lives

$\dfrac{1}{2} \times \dfrac{1}{2} \times \dfrac{1}{2} \times \dfrac{1}{2} \times \dfrac{1}{2} = \dfrac{1}{32}$

Velocity

61. $\dfrac{50.0\ m}{26.55\ s} = 1.88$ m/s straight ahead

62. $v = 0$ m/s (velocity is change in position over time, but at the end there was no change in position)

63. $4500.\ m \times \dfrac{1\ s}{341.11\ m} = 13.19$ s

---

48. Zinc sulfide can be used as a white pigment. Balance the following equation for synthesizing zinc sulfide.

$$Na_2S + Zn(NO_3)_2 \rightarrow ZnS + NaNO_3$$

49. Kerosene, $C_{14}H_{30}$, is often used as a heating fuel or a jet fuel. When kerosene burns in oxygen, O_2, it produces carbon dioxide, CO_2, and water, H_2O. Write the balanced chemical equation for the reaction of kerosene and oxygen.

50. When plants undergo photosynthesis, they convert carbon dioxide and water to glucose and oxygen. This process helps remove carbon dioxide from the atmosphere. Balance the following equation for the production of glucose and oxygen from carbon dioxide and water.

$$CO_2 + H_2O \rightarrow C_6H_{12}O_6 + O_2$$

Nuclear Decay

51. Potassium undergoes nuclear decay by β-emission and positron emission. Complete the following equations for the nuclear decay of potassium.

a. $^{40}_{19}K \longrightarrow ^{40}_{20}\underline{\quad} + ^{0}_{-1}e$

b. $^{40}_{19}K \longrightarrow ^{40}_{18}\underline{\quad} + ^{0}_{1}e$

52. Carbon-14 decays by β-emission. What element is formed when carbon loses a β-particle?

53. Aluminum can undergo decay by positron emission. Complete the following equation for the decay of aluminum into magnesium.

$$^{26}_{13}Al \longrightarrow ^{26}_{12}Mg + \underline{\quad}e$$

54. Uranium-238 decays by α-emission. What element is formed when a uranium atom loses an α-particle?

---

55. Complete the following equation for the decay of radon-222.

$$^{222}_{86}Rn \longrightarrow ^{218}_{84}\underline{\quad} + ^{4}_{2}He$$

Half-life

56. The half-life of thorium-232, $^{232}_{90}Th$, is 1.4×10^{10} years. How much of a 50.0 g sample of thorium-232 will remain as thorium after 4.2×10^{10} years?

57. Radium, used in radiation treatment for cancer, has a half-life of 1.60×10^3 years. If you begin with a 0.25 g sample, what mass of radium will remain after 8.00×10^3 years?

58. The half-life of iodine-131 is 8.04 days. How long will it take for the mass of iodine present to drop to 1/16?

59. What is the half-life of an element if 1/8 of a sample remains after 12 years?

60. The half-life of cobalt-60 is 10.47 minutes. What fraction of a sample will remain after 52.35 minutes?

Velocity

61. Amy Van Dyken broke the world record for a 50.0 m swim using the butterfly stroke in 1996. She swam 50.0 m in 26.55 seconds. What was her average velocity assuming that she swam the 50.0 m in a perfectly straight line?

62. If Amy Van Dyken swam her record-breaking 50 m by swimming to one end of the pool, then turning around and swimming back to her starting position, what would her average velocity be?

63. When Andy Green broke the land speed record, his vehicle was traveling across a flat portion of the desert with a forward velocity of 341.11 m/s. How long would it take him at that velocity to travel 4.500 km?

64. If a car moves along a perfectly straight road at 24 m/s, how far will the car go in 35 minutes?

65. If you travel southeast from one city to another city that is 314 km away, and the trip takes you 4.00 hours, what is your average velocity?

Momentum

66. a. A 703 kg car is traveling with a forward velocity of 20.1 m/s. What is the momentum of the car?
   b. If a 315 kg trailer is attached to the car, what is the new combined momentum?

67. You are traveling west on your bicycle at 4.2 m/s, and you and your bike have a combined mass of 75 kg. What is the momentum of you and your bicycle?

68. A runner, who has a mass of 52 kg, has a momentum of 218 kg · m/s along a trail. What is the runner's velocity?

69. A commercial airplane travels north at a speed of 234 m/s. The plane seats 253 people. If the average person on the plane has a mass of 68 kg, what is the momentum of the passengers on the plane?

70. A bowling ball has a mass of 5.44 kg. It is moving down the lane at 2.1 m/s when it strikes the pins. What is the momentum with which the ball hits the pins?

Acceleration

71. While driving at an average velocity of 15.6 m/s down the road, a driver slams on the brakes to avoid hitting a squirrel. The car stops completely in 4.2 s. What is the average acceleration of the car?

72. A sports car is advertised as being able to go from 0 to 60 mi/h straight ahead in 6.00 s. If 60 mi/h is equal to 27 m/s, what is the sports car's average acceleration?

73. If a bicycle has an average acceleration of −0.44 m/s², and its initial forward velocity is 8.2 m/s, how long will it take the cyclist to bring the bicycle to a complete stop?

74. An airliner has an airborne velocity of 232 m/s toward Chicago. What is the plane's average acceleration if it takes the plane 15 minutes to reach its air-borne velocity?

75. A school bus can accelerate from a complete stop at 1.3 m/s². How long will it take the bus to reach a speed of 12.1 m/s?

Newton's Second Law

76. A peach falls from a tree with an acceleration of 9.8 m/s² downward. The peach has a mass of 7.4 g. With what force does the peach strike the ground?

77. A group of people push a car from a resting position forward with a force of 1.99×10^3 N. The car and its driver have a mass of 831 kg. What is the acceleration of the car?

78. If the space shuttle accelerates upward at 35 m/s², what force will a 59 kg astronaut experience?

79. A soccer ball is kicked with a force of 15.2 N. The soccer ball has a mass of 2.45 kg. What is the ball's acceleration?

80. A person steps off a diving board and falls into a pool with an acceleration of 9.8 m/s², which causes the person to hit the water with a force of 637 N. What is the mass of the person?

Work

81. A car breaks down 2.1 m from the shoulder of the road. 1.99×10^3 N of force is used to push the car off the road. How much work has been done on the car?

Problem Bank Solutions

64. $35 \text{ min} \times \dfrac{60 \text{ s}}{1 \text{ min}} \times \dfrac{24 \text{ m}}{1 \text{ s}} = 5.0 \times 10^4$ m

65. $\dfrac{314 \text{ km}}{4.00 \text{ h}} = 78.5$ km/h southeast

Momentum

66. a. $p = mv =$
   $(703 \text{ kg})(20.1 \text{ m/s}) =$
   1.41×10^4 kg•m/s forward
   b. $p = mv =$
   $(703 \text{ kg} + 315 \text{ kg})(20.1 \text{ m/s})$
   $= 2.05 \times 10^4$ kg•m/s forward

67. $p = mv = (75 \text{ kg})(4.2 \text{ m/s}) =$
   320 kg•m/s west

68. $\dfrac{218 \text{ kg•m/s}}{52 \text{ kg}} = 4.2$ m/s along the trail

69. $253 \text{ people} \times \dfrac{68 \text{ kg}}{1 \text{ person}} \times$
   $234 \text{ m/s} = 4.0 \times 10^6$ kg•m/s north

70. $5.44 \text{ kg} \times 2.1 \text{ m/s} = 11$ kg•m/s down the lane

Acceleration

71. $a = \dfrac{\Delta v}{t} = \dfrac{0 \text{ m/s} - 15.6 \text{ m/s}}{4.2 \text{ s}} =$
   -3.7 m/s²

72. $a = \dfrac{\Delta v}{t} = \dfrac{27 \text{ m/s} - 0 \text{ m/s}}{6.00 \text{ s}} =$
   4.5 m/s²

73. $\dfrac{-8.2 \text{ m/s}}{-0.44 \text{ m/s}^2} = 19$ s

74. $\dfrac{232 \text{ m/s}}{15 \text{ min} \times \dfrac{60 \text{ s}}{1 \text{ min}}} = 0.26$ m/s²

75. $\dfrac{12.1 \text{ m/s}}{1.3 \text{ m/s}^2} = 9.3$ s

Newton's Second Law

76. $F = ma =$
   $(7.4 \times 10^{-3} \text{ kg})(9.8 \text{ m/s}^2) =$
   7.3×10^{-2} N

77. $\dfrac{1.99 \times 10^3 \text{ N}}{831 \text{ kg}} = 2.39$ m/s²

78. $59 \text{ kg} \times 35 \text{ m/s}^2 = 2.1 \times 10^3$ N

79. $\dfrac{15.2 \text{ N}}{2.45 \text{ kg}} = 6.20$ m/s²

80. $\dfrac{637 \text{ N}}{9.8 \text{ m/s}^2} = 65$ kg

Work

81. $(1.99 \times 10^3 \text{ N})(2.1 \text{ m}) =$
   4.2×10^3 J

APPENDIX C

Problem Bank

Problem Bank Solutions

82. $\dfrac{157 \text{ J}}{5.3 \text{ m}} = 3.0 \times 10^1 \text{ N}$

83. $(0.667 \text{ m})(3.2 \text{ kg})(3.2 \text{ m/s}^2) = 6.8 \text{ J}$

84. $\dfrac{1.56 \text{ J}}{(1.54 \text{ m/s}^2)(0.78 \text{ m})} = 1.3 \text{ kg}$

85. $\dfrac{686 \text{ J}}{(227 \text{ kg})(2.4 \text{ m})} = 1.3 \text{ m/s}^2$

Power

86. $P = \dfrac{W}{t} = \dfrac{686 \text{ J}}{3.1 \text{ s}} = 2.2 \times 10^2 \text{ W}$

87. $(60 \text{ W})(8 \text{ h})\left(\dfrac{60 \text{ min}}{1 \text{ h}}\right)\left(\dfrac{60 \text{ s}}{1 \text{ min}}\right) = 2 \times 10^6 \text{ J}$

88. $1.02 \times 10^{11} \text{ W}\left(\dfrac{24 \text{ h}}{1 \text{ day}}\right)$
$\left(\dfrac{60 \text{ min}}{1 \text{ h}}\right)\left(\dfrac{60 \text{ s}}{1 \text{ min}}\right) =$
$8.81 \times 10^{15} \text{ J} = 8.81 \times 10^9 \text{ MJ}$

89. $\dfrac{8.75 \times 10^3 \text{ J}}{350 \text{ W}} = 25 \text{ s}$

90. $\dfrac{(157 \text{ N})(2.3 \text{ km})\left(\dfrac{1000 \text{ m}}{1 \text{ km}}\right)}{20 \text{ min}\left(\dfrac{60 \text{ s}}{1 \text{ min}}\right)} =$

$3.0 \times 10^2 \text{ W per horse}$
$9.0 \times 10^2 \text{ W total}$

Mechanical Advantage

91. $\dfrac{1549 \text{ N}}{446 \text{ N}} = 3.47$

92. *input force =*
$\dfrac{output\ force}{mechanical\ advantage} =$
$\dfrac{660 \text{ N}}{6} = 110 \text{ N}$

93. $(8650 \text{ N})(27) = 2.3 \times 10^5 \text{ N}$

94. *mechanical advantage*
$\dfrac{87 \text{ cm}}{92 \text{ cm}} = 0.95$
If the knob were moved closer to the hinge, the mechanical advantage would be less.

95. $MA = \dfrac{d_{in}}{d_{out}} =$
$\dfrac{2\pi(8.0 \times 10^{-2} \text{ m})750}{1.6 \times 10^3 \text{ m}} = 0.24$

Gravitational Potential Energy

96. $PE = mgh =$
$(0.14 \text{ kg})(9.8 \text{ m/s}^2)(3.5 \text{ m}) =$
4.8 J

97. $\dfrac{6.6 \times 10^6 \text{ J}}{(74 \text{ kg})(9.8 \text{ m/s}^2)} = 9.1 \times 10^3 \text{ m}$

82. Pulling a boat forward into a docking slip requires 157 J of work. The boat must be pulled a total distance of 5.3 m. What is the force with which the boat is pulled?

83. A box with a mass of 3.2 kg is pushed 0.667 m across a floor with an acceleration of 3.2 m/s². How much work is done on the box?

84. You need to pick up a book off the floor and place it on a table top that is 0.78 m above the ground. You expend 1.56 J of energy to lift the book. The book has an acceleration of 1.54 m/s². What is the book's mass?

85. A weight lifter raises a 227 kg weight above his head. The weight reaches a height of 2.4 m. The lifter expends 686 J of energy lifting the weight. What is the acceleration of the weight?

Power

86. A weight lifter does 686 J of work on a weight that he lifts in 3.1 seconds. What is the power with which he lifts the weight?

87. How much energy is wasted by a 60 W bulb if the bulb is left on over an 8 hour night?

88. A nuclear reactor is designed with a capacity of 1.02×10^8 kW. How much energy, in megajoules, should the reactor be able to produce in a day?

89. An electric mixer uses 350 W. If 8.75×10^3 J of work are done by the mixer, how long has the mixer run?

90. A team of three horses are hitched to a wagon. Each horse pulls with a force of 157 N. The cart travels a distance of 2.3 km in 20 minutes. Calculate the power delivered by the horses.

Mechanical Advantage

91. A roofer needs to get a stack of shingles onto a roof. Pulling the shingles up manually uses 1549 N of force. The roofer decides that it would be easier to use a system of pulleys to raise the shingles. Using the pulleys, 446 N are required to lift the shingles. What is the mechanical advantage of the system of pulleys?

92. A dam used to make hydroelectric power opens and closes its gates with a lever. The gate weighs 660 N. The lever has a mechanical advantage of 6. Calculate the input force on the lever needed to move the gate.

93. A crane uses a system of pulleys with a mechanical advantage of 27. An input force of 8650 N is used by the crane to lift a pile of steel girders. What is the weight of the girders?

94. A door that is 92 cm wide has a door knob that is 87 cm from the door hinge. What is the mechanical advantage of the door? Would the mechanical advantage be greater or less if the knob were moved 10 cm closer to the hinge?

95. A student pedals a bicycle to school. The gear on the bicycle has a radius of 8.0 cm. The student travels 1.6 km to school. During the journey, the pedals make 750 revolutions. What is the mechanical advantage of the bicycle?

Gravitational Potential Energy

96. A pear is hanging from a pear tree. The pear is 3.5 m above the ground and has a mass of 0.14 kg. What is the pear's gravitational potential energy?

97. A person in an airplane has a mass of 74 kg and has 6.6 MJ of gravitational potential energy. What is the altitude of the plane?

98. A high jumper jumps 2.04 m. If the jumper has a mass of 67 kg, what is his gravitational potential energy at the highest point in the jump?

99. A cat sits on the top of a fence that is 2.0 m high. The cat has a gravitational potential energy of 88.9 J. What is the mass of the cat?

100. A frog with a mass of 0.23 kg hops up in the air. At the highest point in the hop, the frog has a gravitational potential energy of 0.744 J. How high can it hop?

Kinetic Energy

101. A sprinter runs at a forward velocity of 10.9 m/s. If the sprinter has a mass of 72.5 kg, what is the sprinter's kinetic energy?

102. A car having a mass of 654 kg has a kinetic energy of 73.4 kJ. What is the car's speed?

103. A tennis ball with a mass of 51 g has a velocity of 9.7 m/s upward. What is the kinetic energy of the tennis ball?

104. A rock is rolling down a hill with a speed of 4.67 m/s. It has a kinetic energy of 18.9 kJ. What is the mass of the rock?

105. Calculate the kinetic energy of an airliner with a mass of 7.6×10^4 kg that is flying at a speed of 524 km/h.

Efficiency

106. If a cyclist has 26.7% efficiency, how much energy is lost if 40.5 kJ of energy are put in by the cyclist?

107. What is the efficiency of a machine if 55.3 J of work are done on the machine, but only 14.3 J of work are done by the machine?

108. A microwave oven uses 89 kJ of energy in one minute. The microwave has an output of 54 kJ per minute. What is the efficiency of the microwave?

109. A coal-burning power plant has an efficiency of 42%. If 4.99 MJ of energy are used by the power plant, how much useful energy is generated by the power plant?

110. A swimmer does 45 kJ of work while swimming. If the swimmer is wasting 42 kJ of energy while swimming, what is the efficiency for the activity?

Temperature Conversions

111. A normal body temperature is 98.6°F. What is this temperature in degrees Celsius?

112. Convert the following temperatures to the Kelvin scale.
   a. 214°F   **c.** 27°C
   b. 100.°C   **d.** 32°F

113. What are the freezing point and boiling point of water in the Celsius, Fahrenheit, and Kelvin scales?

114. What is absolute zero in the Celsius scale?

115. If it is 315 K outside, is it hot or cold?

Specific Heat

Use the values in **Table B-3** for specific heat.

116. How much energy is required to raise the temperature of 5.0 g of silver from 298 K to 334 K?

117. A burner transfers 45 J of energy to a small beaker with 5.3 g of water. If the water was initially 27°C, what is the final temperature of the water?

118. A piece of aluminum foil is left on a burner until the temperature of the foil has risen from 27°C to 98°C. The foil absorbs 344 J of energy from the burner. What is the mass of the foil?

119. If a piece of graphite and a diamond both have the same mass, and are placed on the same burner, which will become hot faster? Why?

Problem Bank Solutions

98. $PE =$
$(67 \text{ kg})(9.80 \text{ m/s}^2)(2.04 \text{ m})$
$= 1.3 \times 10^3$ J

99. $\dfrac{88.9 \text{ J}}{(2.0 \text{ m})(9.80 \text{ m/s}^2)} = 4.5$ kg

100. $\dfrac{0.744 \text{ J}}{(0.23 \text{ kg})(9.80 \text{ m/s}^2)} = 0.33$ m

Kinetic Energy

101. $\dfrac{1}{2}(72.5 \text{ kg})(10.9 \text{ m/s})^2 =$
4.31×10^3 J

102. $v = \sqrt{\dfrac{2KE}{m}} =$
$\sqrt{\dfrac{2(7.34 \times 10^4 \text{ J})}{654 \text{ kg}}} = 15.0$ m/s

103. $\dfrac{1}{2}(0.051 \text{ kg})(9.7 \text{ m/s})^2 = 2.4$ J

104. $m = \dfrac{2(1.89 \times 10^4 \text{ J})}{(4.67 \text{ m/s})^2} =$
1.73×10^3 kg

105. $(524 \text{ km/h})(1000 \text{ m/km})$
$\left(\dfrac{1 \text{ h}}{60 \text{ min}}\right)\left(\dfrac{1 \text{ min}}{60 \text{ s}}\right) = 146$ m/s
$\dfrac{1}{2}(7.6 \times 10^4 \text{ kg})(146 \text{ m/s})^2$
$= 8.1 \times 10^8$ J

Efficiency

106. $energy\ lost = energy\ input \times$
$\left(\dfrac{100 - efficiency}{100}\right) =$
$40.5 \text{ kJ} \times \left(\dfrac{100 - 26.7}{100}\right) =$
29.7 kJ

107. $\dfrac{14.3 \text{ J}}{55.3 \text{ J}}(100) = 25.9\%$

108. $efficiency = \dfrac{54 \text{ kJ}}{89 \text{ kJ}}(100) = 61\%$

109. $4.99 \text{ MJ}\left(\dfrac{42}{100}\right) = 2.1$ MJ

110. $efficiency =$
$\dfrac{45 \text{ kJ} - 42 \text{ kJ}}{45 \text{ kJ}}(100) = 7\%$

Temperature Conversions

111. $\dfrac{5}{9}(98.6°F - 32.0) = 37.0°C$

112. **a.** $T = \dfrac{5}{9}(214°F - 32.0) + 273 =$
374 K
   b. $T = 100.°C + 273 = 373$ K
   c. $T = 27°C + 273 = 3.00 \times$
10^2 K
   d. $\dfrac{5}{9}(32°F - 32.0) + 273 =$
273 K

113. 0°C, 100°C, 32°F, 212°F,
273 K, 373 K

114. $t = 0 \text{ K} - 273 = -273°C$

115. 315 K − 273 = 42°C
As human body temperature is 37°C, this is hot.

Specific Heat

116. $energy = mc\Delta t = (5.0 \text{ g Ag})$
$(1 \text{ kg/1000 g})(234 \text{ J/kg•K})$
$(334 \text{ K} - 298 \text{ K}) = 42$ J

117. $\Delta t = \dfrac{energy}{mc} =$
$\dfrac{45 \text{ J}}{(5.3 \text{ g})\left(\dfrac{1 \text{ kg}}{1000 \text{ g}}\right)(4186 \text{ J/kg•K})} =$
$2.0°$ C

$t_f = 27°C + \Delta t = 29°C$

118. $m = \dfrac{energy}{c\ \Delta t} =$
$\dfrac{344 \text{ J}}{(897 \text{ J/kg•K})(98°C - 27°C)} =$
5.4×10^{-3} kg

119. Because **diamond** has a lower specific heat (487 J/kg•K) than graphite (709 J/kg•K), it will heat up faster.

APPENDIX C

Problem Bank

Problem Bank Solutions

120. $energy = mc\Delta t =$
(34 kg)(650 J/kg•K)(153°C) =
3.4×10^6 J

Wave Speed

121. $\dfrac{698 \times 10^{-9} \text{ m}}{3.0 \times 10^8 \text{ m/s}} = 2.3 \times 10^{-3}$ ps

122. $v = \dfrac{92 \text{ m}}{2.7 \times 10^{-1} \text{ s}} = 3.4 \times 10^2$ m/s

123. (1.3 m/s)(1.2 s) = 1.6 m

124. $t = \dfrac{7.78 \times 10^{11} \text{ m}}{3.0 \times 10^8 \text{ m/s}} = 2.6 \times 10^3$ s

125. $\dfrac{3.0 \times 10^8 \text{ m/s}}{5.08 \times 10^{-7} \text{ m}} = 5.9 \times 10^{14}$ Hz

Resistance

126. $R = \dfrac{V}{I} = \dfrac{6.0 \text{ V}}{1.4 \text{ A}} = 4.3\ \Omega$

127. $\dfrac{120 \text{ V}}{12.0 \text{ A}} = 10.\ \Omega$

128. $V = (7.78 \times 10^{-3} \text{ A})(1150\ \Omega) =$ 8.95 V

129. $\dfrac{120 \text{ V}}{9.17 \text{ A}} = 13\ \Omega$

130. $R = \dfrac{240 \text{ V}}{30 \text{ A}} = 8\ \Omega$

Electric Power

131. (3.0 V)(0.50 A) = 1.5 W

132. $I = \dfrac{P}{V} = \dfrac{60 \text{ W}}{120 \text{ V}} = 0.5$ A

133. $\dfrac{1200 \text{ W}}{120 \text{ V}} = 1.0 \times 10^1$ A in the United States

$\dfrac{120 \text{ V}}{1.0 \times 10^1 \text{ A}} = 12\ \Omega$

$\dfrac{240 \text{ V}}{12\ \Omega} = 2.0 \times 10^1$ A in Europe

(240 V)(2.0 × 10¹ A) = 4800 W in Europe

The hair dryer becomes hot in Europe because it is dissipating four times as much power as it does when used in the United States.

134. $\dfrac{43 \text{ W}}{12 \text{ V}} = 3.6$ A

135. (12.3 A)(120 V) = 1.5×10^3 W

---

120. The iron ore hematite is heated until its temperature has risen by 153°C. If the piece of hematite has a mass of 34 kg, how much energy was required to raise the temperature this much?

Wave Speed

121. The speed of light in a vacuum is 3.0×10^8 m/s. A red laser beam has a wavelength of 698 nm. How long, in picoseconds, will it take for one wavelength of the laser light to pass by a fixed point?

122. Two people are standing on opposite ends of a field. The field is 92 m long. One person speaks. It takes 270 ms for the person across the field to hear the sound. What is the speed of sound in the field?

123. A water wave has a speed of 1.3 m/s. A person sitting on a pier observes that it takes 1.2 s for a full wavelength to pass the edge of the pier. What is the wavelength of the water wave?

124. Jupiter is 7.78×10^8 km from the sun. How long does it take the sun's light to reach Jupiter?

125. A green laser has a wavelength of 508 nm. What is the frequency of this laser light?

Resistance

126. What is the resistance of a wire that has a current of 1.4 A in it when it is connected to a 6.0 V battery?

127. An electric space heater is plugged into a 120 V outlet. A current of 12.0 A is in the coils in the space heater. What is the resistance of the coils?

128. A graphing calculator needs 7.78×10^{-3} A to function. The resistance in the calculator is 1150 Ω. What is the voltage required to operate the calculator?

129. A steam iron has a current of 9.17 A when plugged into a 120 V outlet. What is the resistance in the steam iron?

130. An electric clothes dryer requires a potential difference of 240 V. The power cord that runs between the electrical outlet and the dryer supports a current of 30 A. What is the resistance in this power cord?

Electric Power

131. A flashlight has a potential difference of 3.0 V. The bulb has a current of 0.50 A. What is the electric power used by the flashlight?

132. What is the current in a 60 W light bulb when it is plugged into a 120 V outlet?

133. A student takes her hair dryer to Europe. In the United States, her hair dryer uses 1200 W of power when connected to a 120 V outlet. In Europe, the outlet has a potential difference of 240 V. When she uses her hair dryer in Europe, she notices that it gets very hot, and starts to smell as though it is burning. Determine the current in the hair dryer in the United States. Then calculate the resistance in the hair dryer. Calculate the current and the power in the hair dryer in Europe to explain why the hair dryer heats up when plugged into the European outlet.

134. A portable stereo requires a 12 V battery. It uses 43 W of power. Calculate the current in the stereo.

135. A microwave oven has a current of 12.3 A when operated using a 120 V power source. How much power does the microwave consume?

Selected Answers to Problems

These answers can help you determine whether or not you're on the right track as you work through the practice problems, the section reviews, and the chapter reviews.

Chapter 1

Practice, page 17
Conversions

2. $3.5 \text{ s} \times \dfrac{1000 \text{ ms}}{1 \text{ s}} = 3500 \text{ ms}$

4. 0.0025 kg
6. 2.8 mol
8. 3000 ng

Practice, page 23
Writing Scientific Notation

2. a. 4500 g
   b. 0.006 05 m
   c. 3115 000 km
   d. 0.000 000 0199 cm

Practice, page 24
Using Scientific Notation

2. a. 4.8×10^2 L/s
   b. 6.9 g/cm^3
   c. $5.5 \times 10^5 \text{ cm}^2$
   d. 0.83 cm^3

Practice, page 25
Significant Figures

2. $3.02 \text{ cm} \times 6.3 \text{ cm} \times 8.225 \text{ cm} = 156.\overline{488\ 85} \text{ cm}^3 = 160 \text{ cm}^3$
4. $3.244 \text{ m} \div 1.4 \text{ s} = 2.3\overline{17\ 142\ 857} \text{ m/s} = 2.3 \text{ m/s}$

Section 1.3 Review, page 26
Math Skills

6. a. $3.16 \times 10^3 \text{ m} \times 2.91 \times 10^4 \text{ m} = 9.20 \times 10^7 \text{ m}^2$
   b. $9.66 \times 10^{-5} \text{ cm}^2$
   c. 6.70 g/cm^3

Chapter 1 Review, page 28
Building Math Skills

16. a. 2.6×10^{14}
    b. 6.42×10^{-7}
    c. $3.4 \times 10^8 \text{ cm}^2$
    d. $3.3 \times 10^{-3} \text{ kg/cm}^3$

Chapter 2

Practice, page 56
Density

2. $D = \dfrac{m}{V} = \dfrac{163 \text{ g}}{50.0 \text{ cm}^3} = 3.26 \text{ g/cm}^3$

4. $D = 11 \text{ g/cm}^3$
   The metal is probably lead.
6. $m = 500 \text{ g}$
8. $V = 36 \text{ cm}^3$

Chapter 2 Review, page 62
Building Math Skills

16. $D = \dfrac{m}{V} = \dfrac{67.5 \text{ g}}{15 \text{ cm}^3} = 4.5 \text{ g/cm}^3$

18. $D = 0.77 \text{ g/cm}^3$
    The substance is less dense than water (1.00 g/cm^3), so it will float.
20. $m = 1.5 \times 10^5 \text{ g}$

Chapter 3

Practice, page 98
Conversion Factors

2. $50 \text{ eggs} \times \dfrac{1 \text{ dozen}}{12 \text{ eggs}} = 4.2 \text{ dozen eggs}$
   You must buy 5 dozen eggs.
   $5 \text{ dozen} \times \dfrac{12 \text{ eggs}}{1 \text{ dozen}} = 60 \text{ eggs}$
   $60 \text{ eggs} - 50 \text{ eggs} = 10 \text{ eggs left over}$

Practice, page 99
Converting Amount to Mass

2. $1.80 \text{ mol Ca} \times \dfrac{40.08 \text{ g Ca}}{1 \text{ mol Ca}} = 72.1 \text{ g Ca}$

4. 203 g Cu

Section 3.4 Review, page 100
Math Skills

6. $0.48 \text{ mol Pt} \times \dfrac{195.08 \text{ g Pt}}{1 \text{ mol Pt}} = 94 \text{ g Pt}$

8. 0.39 mol Si

Chapter 3 Review, page 102
Building Math Skills

18. $0.54 \text{ g He} \times \dfrac{1 \text{ mol He}}{4.00 \text{ g He}} = 0.14 \text{ mol He}$

20. 407 g Al

Chapter 4

Practice, page 125
Writing Ionic Formulas

2. $BeCl_2$
4. $Co(OH)_3$

Section 4.3 Review, page 128
Math Skills

6. Cd^{2+}
   Because each CN^- has a charge of 1–, the other ion must be Cd^{2+} for a neutral compound to form.

Chapter 4 Review, page 138
Building Math Skills

18. a. $Sr(NO_3)_2$
    b. NaCN
    c. $Cr(OH)_3$

Chapter 5
Practice, page 166
Balancing Chemical Equations

2. $Na_2S + 2AgNO_3 \longrightarrow 2NaNO_3 + Ag_2S$
4. $H_2S + 2O_2 \longrightarrow H_2SO_4$

Section 5.3 Review, page 168

2. a. $KOH + HCl \longrightarrow KCl + H_2O$
   b. $Pb(NO_3)_2 + 2KI \longrightarrow 2KNO_3 + PbI_2$

Chapter 5 Review, page 178
Building Math Skills

16. $2HgO \longrightarrow 2Hg + O_2$
18. $\dfrac{1 \text{ mol } C_{12}H_{22}O_{11}}{12 \text{ mol } O_2}, \dfrac{1 \text{ mol } C_{12}H_{22}O_{11}}{12 \text{ mol } CO_2}, \dfrac{1 \text{ mol } C_{12}H_{22}O_{11}}{11 \text{ mol } H_2O},$
    $\dfrac{12 \text{ mol } O_2}{12 \text{ mol } CO_2}, \dfrac{12 \text{ mol } O_2}{11 \text{ mol } H_2O}, \dfrac{12 \text{ mol } CO_2}{11 \text{ mol } H_2O}$
20. $Zn + 2HCl \longrightarrow ZnCl_2 + H_2$

Chapter 6
none

Chapter 7
Practice, page 225
Nuclear Decay

2. $^{225}_{89}Ac \longrightarrow {}^{221}_{87}Fr + {}^{4}_{2}He$, alpha decay
4. $^{212}_{83}Bi \longrightarrow {}^{208}_{81}Tl + {}^{4}_{2}He$, alpha decay

Practice, page 228
Half-Life

2. $1 - \dfrac{15}{16} = \dfrac{1}{16} = \dfrac{1}{2} \times \dfrac{1}{2} \times \dfrac{1}{2} \times \dfrac{1}{2}$; four half-lives
   $4 \times 3.82 \text{ days} = 15.3 \text{ days}$
4. 29.1 years

Section 7.1 Review, page 228
Math Skills

4. $^{212}_{86}Rn \longrightarrow {}^{208}_{84}Po + {}^{4}_{2}He$
6. $1 - \dfrac{3}{4} = \dfrac{1}{4} = \dfrac{1}{2} \times \dfrac{1}{2}$; two half-lives
   $2 \times 32.2 \text{ min} = 64.4 \text{ min}$
8. 2.29×10^4 years

Chapter 7 Review, page 242
Building Math Skills

18. a. $^{212}_{83}Bi \longrightarrow {}^{208}_{81}Tl + {}^{4}_{2}He$
       $^{208}_{81}Tl \longrightarrow {}^{208}_{82}Pb + {}^{0}_{-1}e$
    b. $^{212}_{83}Bi \longrightarrow {}^{212}_{84}Po + {}^{0}_{-1}e$
       $^{212}_{84}Po \longrightarrow {}^{208}_{82}Pb + {}^{4}_{2}He$
20. $^{149}_{62}Sm \longrightarrow {}^{145}_{60}Nd + {}^{4}_{2}He$
22. $15.2 \text{ days} \times \dfrac{1 \text{ half-life}}{3.82 \text{ days}} = 3.98 \text{ half-lives}$
    $\dfrac{1}{2} \times \dfrac{1}{2} \times \dfrac{1}{2} \times \dfrac{1}{2} = \dfrac{1}{16}$
    $\dfrac{1}{16} \times 4.38 \ \mu g = 0.274 \ \mu g$

Chapter 8
Practice, page 255
Velocity

2. $v = \dfrac{d}{t} = \dfrac{38 \text{ m}}{1.7 \text{ s}} = 22$ m/s to first base
4. $t = \dfrac{d}{v} = \dfrac{2.6 \text{ km} \times \left(\dfrac{1000 \text{ m}}{1 \text{ km}}\right)}{28 \text{ m/s}} = 93$ s

Practice, page 257
Momentum

1. a. $p = mv = (75 \text{ kg})(16 \text{ m/s}) = 1200$ kg•m/s forward
   b. $p = 2.19 \times 10^3$ kg•m/s north
   c. $p = 360$ kg•m/s eastward

Section 8.1 Review, page 258
Math Skills

8. $v = \dfrac{d}{t} = \dfrac{149 \text{ m}}{16.8 \text{ s}} = 8.87$ m/s north

Practice, page 260
Acceleration

2. $a = \dfrac{\Delta v}{t} = \dfrac{0.80 \text{ m/s} - 0.50 \text{ m/s}}{4.0 \text{ s}} = 0.075$ m/s² toward shore
4. $t = 0.85$ s

Section 8.2 Review, page 267
Math Skills

8. $\Delta v = at = (4.0 \text{ m/s}^2)(3.0 \text{ s}) = 12$ m/s
   The cyclist at a constant velocity of 15 m/s is faster after 3.0 s.

Practice, page 270
Newton's Second Law

2. $m = \dfrac{F}{a} = \dfrac{1.4 \text{ N}}{9.8 \text{ m/s}^2} = 0.14$ kg

Section 8.3 Review, page 274
Math Skills

6. $w = mg = (5.0 \text{ kg})(9.8 \text{ m/s}^2) = 49$ N

Chapter 8 Review, page 276
Building Math Skills

16. $v = \dfrac{d}{t} = \dfrac{72 \text{ m}}{45 \text{ s}} = 1.6$ m/s eastward
18. $p = mv = (85 \text{ kg})(2.65 \text{ m/s}) = 230$ kg•m/s north
20. $a = \dfrac{\Delta v}{t} = \dfrac{5.5 \text{ m/s} - 14.0 \text{ m/s}}{6.0 \text{ s}} = -1.4$ m/s² east = 1.4 m/s² west
22. $F = ma = (5.5 \text{ kg})(4.2 \text{ m/s}^2) = 23$ N right
24. $a = \dfrac{F}{m} = \dfrac{37 \text{ N}}{925 \text{ kg}} = 4.0 \times 10^{-2}$ m/s² away from the stop sign

Chapter 9
Practice, page 285
Work

2. $W = F \times d = (1 \text{ N})(1 \text{ m}) = 1$ J
4. $W = 30 \ (F \times d) = 30(165 \text{ N})(0.800 \text{ m}) = 3.96 \times 10^3$ J

Practice, page 287
Power

2. $P = \dfrac{W}{t} = \dfrac{9 \times 10^8 \text{ J}}{1 \text{ s}} = 9 \times 10^8 \text{ W} = 900 \text{ MW}$

4. **a.** $P = \dfrac{W}{t} = \dfrac{F \times d}{t} = \dfrac{(60.0 \text{ N}) \times (12.0 \text{ m})}{20.0 \text{ s}} = 36.0 \text{ W}$

   b. $P = \dfrac{W}{t} = \dfrac{F \times d}{t} = \dfrac{(300 \text{ N}) \times (1 \text{ m})}{3 \text{ s}} = 100 \text{ W}$

Practice, page 290
Mechanical Advantage

2. $mechanical\ advantage = \dfrac{output\ force}{input\ force} = \dfrac{9900 \text{ N}}{150 \text{ N}} = 66$

4. $output\ force = (mechanical\ advantage)\ (input\ force) =$
   $(15 \text{ N})(5.2) = 78 \text{ N}$

Section 9.1 Review, page 290
Math Skills

6. $mechanical\ advantage = \dfrac{output\ force}{input\ force} = \dfrac{132 \text{ N}}{55.0 \text{ N}} = 2.40$

8. $P = \dfrac{W}{t} = \dfrac{1.0 \times 10^6 \text{ J}}{50.0 \text{ s}} = 2.0 \times 10^4 \text{ W}$

   $2.0 \times 10^4 \text{ W} \times \dfrac{1 \text{ hp}}{746 \text{ W}} = 27 \text{ hp}$

Practice, page 299
Gravitational Potential Energy

2. $PE = mgh = (6.3 \times 10^{12} \text{ N})(220 \text{ m}) = 1.4 \times 10^{15} \text{ J}$
4. $m = 58 \text{ kg}$

Practice, page 301
Kinetic Energy

2. $v = \sqrt{\dfrac{2KE}{m}} = \sqrt{\dfrac{2(190 \text{ J})}{35 \text{ kg}}} = 3.3 \text{ m/s}$

Section 9.3 Review, page 305
Math Skills

8. $KE = \dfrac{1}{2}mv^2 = \dfrac{1}{2}(0.02 \text{ kg})(300 \text{ m/s})^2 = 900 \text{ J}$

Practice, page 313
Efficiency

2. $work\ input = \dfrac{useful\ work\ output}{efficiency} = \dfrac{1200 \text{ J}}{0.25} = 4800 \text{ J}$

Section 9.4 Review, page 314
Math Skills

8. **a.** $useful\ work\ output = work\ input \times efficiency =$
   $(6500 \text{ J})(0.12) = 780 \text{ J}$

   b. $P = \dfrac{W}{t} = \dfrac{780 \text{ J}}{1 \text{ s}} = 780 \text{ W}$

Chapter 9 Review, page 316
Building Math Skills

16. **a.** $W = F \times d = (425 \text{ N})(2.0 \text{ m}) = 850 \text{ J}$

    b. $P = \dfrac{W}{t} = \dfrac{850 \text{ J}}{5.0 \text{ s}} = 170 \text{ W}$

    c. $mechanical\ advantage = \dfrac{output\ force}{input\ force} = \dfrac{1700 \text{ N}}{425 \text{ N}} = 4.0$

18. **a.** $PE = mgh = (2.0 \text{ kg})(9.8 \text{ m/s}^2)(12 \text{ m}) = 2.4 \times 10^2 \text{ J}$
    b. $KE\ at\ end = PE\ at\ beginning = 2.4 \times 10^2 \text{ J}$

    c. $v = \sqrt{\dfrac{2KE}{m}} = \sqrt{\dfrac{2(2.4 \times 10^2 \text{ J})}{2.0 \text{ kg}}} = 15 \text{ m/s}$

    d. The kinetic energy is changed into sound, heat, and light energy after the rock hits the beach.

Chapter 10
Practice, page 328
Temperature Scale Conversion

2. $T_F = \dfrac{9}{5}t + 32.0 = \dfrac{9}{5}(21°C) + 32.0 = 70°F$

   $T = t + 273 = 21°C + 273 = 294 \text{ K}$
   $t = T - 273 = 388 \text{ K} - 273 = 115°C$

   $T_F = \dfrac{9}{5}t + 32.0 = \dfrac{9}{5}(115°C) + 32.0 = 239°F$

   $T_F = \dfrac{9}{5}t + 32.0 = \dfrac{9}{5}(-200.°C) + 32.0 = -328°F$

   $T = t + 273 = -200.0°C + 273 = 73 \text{ K}$

   $t = \dfrac{5}{9}(T_F - 32.0) = \dfrac{5}{9}(110.°F - 32.0) = 43°C$

   $T = t + 273 = 43°C + 273 = 316 \text{ K}$

4. **c.**

Section 10.1 Review, page 330
Math Skills

6. $T_F = \dfrac{9}{5}t + 32.0 = \dfrac{9}{5}(20.°C) + 32.0 = 68°F$

   $T = t + 273 = 20°C + 273 = 293 \text{ K}$

Practice, page 338
Specific Heat

2. $energy = mc\Delta t = (0.225 \text{ kg})(4186 \text{ J/kg} \bullet \text{K})(35°C - 5°C) =$
   $2.8 \times 10^4 \text{ J}$

4. $t = 25°C + \Delta t = 145°C$
6. $c = 480 \text{ J/kg} \bullet \text{K}$

Section 10.2 Review, page 338
Math Skills

6. $c = \dfrac{energy}{m\Delta t} = \dfrac{3250 \text{ J}}{(1.32 \text{ kg})(292 \text{ K} - 273 \text{ K})} = 130 \text{ J/kg} \bullet \text{K}$
   The metal is likely to be lead.

Chapter 10 Review, page 348
Building Math Skills

20. $t = T - 273 = 3 \text{ K} - 273 = -270°C$
    $T_F = \dfrac{9}{5}t + 32.0 = \dfrac{9}{5}(-270°C) + 32.0 = -454°F$

22. $energy = mc\Delta t = (0.55 \text{ kg})(385 \text{ J/kg} \bullet \text{K})(45°C - 24°C) =$
    4400 J

Chapter 11
Practice, page 370
Wave Speed

2. $v = f \times \lambda = (9.45 \times 10^7 \text{ Hz})(3.17 \text{ m}) = 3.00 \times 10^8 \text{ m/s}$
4. $\lambda = 1.5 \text{ m}$

Section 11.2 Review, page 373
Math Skills

8. $\lambda = 0.77 \text{ m}$

Chapter 11 Review, page 382
Building Math Skills
18. a. 9 cm
   b. 20 cm
   c. $v = f \times \lambda = (25.0 \text{ Hz})(20 \text{ cm})\left(\dfrac{1 \text{ m}}{100 \text{ cm}}\right) = 5 \text{ m/s}$
   d. $T = \dfrac{1}{f} = \dfrac{1}{25.0 \text{ Hz}} = 0.04 \text{ s}$
20. $v = 24 \text{ m/s}$
22. f range $= 1 \times 10^9 \text{ Hz}$ to $3 \times 10^{11} \text{ Hz}$

Chapter 12
none

Chapter 13
Practice, page 443
Resistance
2. $R = \dfrac{V}{I} = \dfrac{120 \text{ V}}{0.50 \text{ A}} = 240 \text{ }\Omega$
4. $I = 0.43 \text{ A}$

Section 13.2 Review, page 445
Math Skills
8. $I = 0.5 \text{ A}$

Practice, page 451
Electric Power
2. $P = IV = (2.6 \times 10^{-3} \text{ A})(6.0 \text{ V}) = 1.6 \times 10^{-2} \text{ W}$
4. $I = 0.62 \text{ A}$

Section 13.3 Review, page 452
Math Skills
8. $I = 0.3 \text{ A}$ for the 40 watt bulb
   $I = 0.62 \text{ A}$ for the 75 watt bulb

Chapter 13 Review, page 454
Building Math Skills
14. $R = \dfrac{V}{I} = \dfrac{12 \text{ V}}{0.30 \text{ A}} = 4.0 \times 10^1 \text{ }\Omega$
16. $I = 0.12 \text{ A}$
18. $I = \dfrac{P}{V} = \dfrac{2.4 \text{ W}}{1.5 \text{ V}} = 1.6 \text{ A}$

Chapters 14, 15, 16, 17, 18, 19
none

Appendix C Problem Bank, pages 693–700
Conversions
2. a. $113 \text{ g} \times \dfrac{1000 \text{ mg}}{1 \text{ g}} = 113\ 000 \text{ mg}$
   b. $700 \text{ pm} \times \dfrac{10^{-12} \text{ m}}{1 \text{ pm}} \times \dfrac{1 \text{ nm}}{10^{-9} \text{ m}} = 0.7 \text{ nm}$
   c. $101.1 \text{ kPa} \times \dfrac{1000 \text{ Pa}}{1 \text{ kPa}} = 101\ 100 \text{ Pa}$
   d. $13 \text{ MA} \times \dfrac{10^6 \text{ A}}{1 \text{ MA}} = 13\ 000\ 000 \text{ A}$

4. $341.11 \text{ m/s} > 335.84 \text{ m/s}$
   Yes, he did break the sound barrier.

Writing Scientific Notation
6. a. $1.1045 \times 10^2 \text{ m}$
   b. $3.45 \times 10^{-6} \text{ s}$
   c. $1.329\ 48 \times 10^5 \text{ kg}$
   d. $3.439\ 00 \times 10^{-2} \text{ cm}$
8. $7.029\ 4601 \times 10^7$ airplanes
10. 4.5×10^6 automobiles

Using Scientific Notation
12. $(8.850 \times 10^3 \text{ m}) + (1.0924 \times 10^4 \text{ m}) =$
    $(0.8850 \times 10^4 \text{ m}) + (1.0924 \times 10^4 \text{ m}) = 1.9774 \times 10^4 \text{ m}$
14. 5.2277×10^4 immigrants

Significant Figures
16. a. 4
    b. 4
    c. 4
    d. 4
18. a. $\dfrac{129 \text{ g}}{29.20 \text{ cm}^3} = 4.417\ 808\ 219 \text{ g/cm}^3 = 4.42 \text{ g/cm}^3$
    b. $120 \text{ mm} \times 355 \text{ mm} \times 12.1 \text{ mm} =$
       $5.1546 \times 10^5 \text{ mm}^3 = 5.2 \times 10^5 \text{ mm}^3$
    c. $\dfrac{45.4 \text{ g}}{0.012 \text{ cm} \times 0.444 \text{ cm} \times 0.221 \text{ cm}} =$
       $3.855\ 665\ 62 \times 10^4 \text{ g/cm}^3 = 3.9 \times 10^4 \text{ g/cm}^3$
20. a. $1.23 \text{ cm}^3 - 0.044 \text{ cm}^3 = 1.19 \text{ cm}^3$
    b. $89.00 \text{ kg} - 0.1 \text{ kg} = 88.9 \text{ kg}$
    c. $780 \text{ mm} - 64 \text{ mm} = 716 \text{ mm}$

Density
22. $density = \dfrac{people}{area} = \dfrac{4.64 \times 10^8 \text{ people}}{2.4346 \times 10^{13} \text{ m}^2} =$
    $1.91 \times 10^{-5} \text{ people/m}^2$
24. $m = 0.45 \text{ g} + (1.78 \times 10^{-3} \text{ m}^3)(0.178 \text{ kg/m}^3) =$
    $7.7 \times 10^{-4} \text{ kg } or \text{ 0.77 g}$

Conversion Factors
26. a. $\dfrac{2000 \text{ sheets}}{4 \text{ reams}}$
    b. $\dfrac{170 \text{ g Ga}}{2.5 \text{ mol Ga}}$
    c. $\dfrac{0.997 \text{ g H}_2\text{O}}{1.00 \text{ cm}^3 \text{ H}_2\text{O}}$
    d. $\dfrac{2.24 \times 10^{16} \text{ mol Ag}}{1.35 \times 10^{34} \text{ atoms Ag}}$
28. a. $19.3 \text{ g/cm}^3 \times (10.0 \text{ cm} \times 26.0 \text{ cm} \times 8.0 \text{ cm}) = 4.0 \times 10^4 \text{ g}$
    b. $(4.0 \times 10^4 \text{ g}) \times \dfrac{0.0353 \text{ oz}}{1 \text{ g}} \times \dfrac{\$253.50}{1 \text{ oz}} = \$3.6 \times 10^5$
30. 98.3 min/rev for John Glenn
    $\dfrac{\left(146 \text{ h} \times \dfrac{60 \text{ min}}{1 \text{ h}}\right) + 24 \text{ min}}{98.3 \text{ min/rev}} = 89.4 \text{ rev for Sally Ride}$

Converting Amount to Mass
32. $60 \times \dfrac{12.01 \text{ g C}}{1 \text{ mol C}} = 720.6 \text{ g/mol C}_{60}$

$$5.23 \times 10^{-2} \text{ mol } C_{60} \times \frac{720.6 \text{ g } C_{60}}{1 \text{ mol } C_{60}} = 37.7 \text{ g } C_{60}$$

34. 3.36×10^{29} g Fe

Converting Mass to Amount

36. $45.4 \text{ g C} \times \dfrac{1 \text{ mol C}}{12.01 \text{ g C}} = 3.78 \text{ mol C}$

38. 0.457 mol Na
40. 70.90 g/mol Cl_2
6.06×10^{-2} mol Cl_2

Writing Ionic Formulas
42. $CaCl_2$
44. NaF

Balancing Chemical Equations
46. $2H_2O_2 \longrightarrow 2H_2O + O_2$
48. $Na_2S + Zn(NO_3)_2 \longrightarrow ZnS + 2NaNO_3$
50. $6CO_2 + 6H_2O \longrightarrow C_6H_{12}O_6 + 6O_2$

Nuclear Decay
52. $^{14}_{6}C \longrightarrow ^{14}_{7}N + ^{0}_{-1}e$; nitrogen
54. $^{238}_{92}U \longrightarrow ^{234}_{90}Th + ^{4}_{2}He$; thorium

Half-life
56. $\dfrac{4.2 \times 10^{10} \text{ y}}{1.4 \times 10^{10} \text{ y}} = 3$ half-lives

$50.0 \text{ g} \times \dfrac{1}{2} \times \dfrac{1}{2} \times \dfrac{1}{2} = 6.25$ g Th

58. 32.2 days
60. 1/32

Velocity
62. $v = 0$ m/s (velocity is change in position over time, but at the end there was no change in position)
64. $d = vt = 35 \text{ min} \times \dfrac{60 \text{ s}}{1 \text{ min}} \times \dfrac{24 \text{ m}}{1 \text{ s}} = 5.0 \times 10^4$ m

Momentum
66. a. $p = mv = (703 \text{ kg})(20.1 \text{ m/s}) = 1.41 \times 10^4$ kg•m/s forward
b. $p = mv = (703 \text{ kg} + 315 \text{ kg})(20.1 \text{ m/s}) = 2.05 \times 10^4$ kg•m/s forward
68. $v = 4.2$ m/s along a trail
70. $p = 11$ kg•m/s down the lane

Acceleration
72. $a = \dfrac{\Delta v}{t} = \dfrac{27 \text{ m/s} - 0 \text{ m/s}}{6.00 \text{ s}} = 4.5 \text{ m/s}^2$
74. $a = 0.26 \text{ m/s}^2$ toward Chicago

Newton's Second Law
76. $F = ma = (7.4 \times 10^{-3} \text{ kg})(9.8 \text{ m/s}^2) = 7.3 \times 10^{-2}$ N
78. $F = 2.1 \times 10^3$ N
80. $m = 65$ kg

Work
82. $F = \dfrac{W}{d} = \dfrac{157 \text{ J}}{5.3 \text{ m}} = 3.0 \times 10^1$ N
84. $m = 1.3$ kg

Power
86. $P = \dfrac{W}{t} = \dfrac{686 \text{ J}}{3.1 \text{ s}} = 2.2 \times 10^2$ W
88. $W = 8.81 \times 10^9$ MJ

90. $P = 9.0 \times 10^2$ W

Mechanical Advantage
92. $input \ force = \dfrac{output \ force}{mechanical \ advantage} = \dfrac{660 \text{ N}}{6} = 110$ N
94. mechanical advantage = 0.95
If the knob were moved closer to the hinge, the mechanical advantage would be less.

Gravitational Potential Energy
96. $PE = mgh = (0.14 \text{ kg})(9.81 \text{ m/s}^2)(3.5 \text{ m}) = 4.8$ J
98. $PE = 1.3 \times 10^3$ J
100. $h = 0.33$ m

Kinetic Energy
102. $v = \sqrt{\dfrac{2KE}{m}} = \sqrt{\dfrac{2(7.34 \times 10^4 \text{ J})}{654 \text{ kg}}} = 15.0$ m/s
104. $m = 1.73 \times 10^3$ kg

Efficiency
106. $energy \ lost = energy \ input \times \left(\dfrac{100 - efficiency}{100}\right) =$
$40.5 \text{ kJ} \times \left(\dfrac{100 - 26.7}{100}\right) = 29.7$ kJ

108. efficiency = 61%
110. efficiency = 6.7%

Temperature Conversions
112. a. $T = t + 273 = \dfrac{5}{9}(T_F - 32.0) + 273 =$
$\dfrac{5}{9}(214°F - 32.0) + 273 = 374$ K
b. $T = t + 273 = 100.°C + 273 = 373$ K
c. $T = t + 273 = 27°C + 273 = 3.00 \times 10^2$ K
d. $T = t + 273 = \dfrac{5}{9}(T_F - 32.0) + 273 =$
$\dfrac{5}{9}(32°F - 32.0) + 273 = 273$ K

114. $t = T - 273 = 0 \text{ K} - 273 = -273°C$

Specific Heat
116. $energy = mc\Delta t =$
$(5.0 \text{ g Ag})(1 \text{ kg}/1000 \text{ g})(235 \text{ J/kg•K})(334 \text{ K} - 298 \text{ K}) = 42$ J
118. $m = 5.4 \times 10^{-3}$ kg
120. $energy = 3.4 \times 10^6$ J

Wave Speed
122. $v = \dfrac{92 \text{ m}}{2.7 \times 10^{-1} \text{ s}} = 3.4 \times 10^2$ m/s
124. $t = 2.6 \times 10^3$ s

Resistance
126. $R = \dfrac{V}{I} = \dfrac{6.0 \text{ V}}{1.4 \text{ A}} = 4.3 \ \Omega$
128. $V = 8.95$ V
130. $R = 8 \ \Omega$

Electric Power
132. $I = \dfrac{P}{V} = \dfrac{60 \text{ W}}{120 \text{ V}} = 0.5$ A
134. $I = 3.6$ A

Glossary

Key to Phonetic Spellings

Sound symbol	Key word(s)	Phonetic spelling	Sound symbol	Key word(s)	Phonetic spelling
a	map	MAP	uhr	paper fern	PAY puhr FUHRN
ay	face day	FAYS DAY	yoo	yule globule	YOOL GLAHB yool
ah	father cot	FAH thuhr KAHT	yu	cure	KYUR
aw	caught law	KAWT LAW	y	yes	YES
ee	eat ski	EET SKEE	g	get	GET
e	wet rare	WET RER	j	jig	JIG
oy	boy foil	BOY FOYL	k	card kite	KARD KIET
ow	out now	OWT NOW	s	cell kiss	SEL KIS
oo	shoot suit	SHOOT SOOT	ch	chin	CHIN
u	book put	BUK PUT	sh	shell	SHEL
uh	sun cut	SUHN KUHT	th	thin	THIN
i	lip	LIP	zh	azure	AZH uhr
ie	tide sigh	TIED SIE	ng	bring	BRING
oh	over coat overcoat	OH vuhr KOHT OH vuhr KOHT	nj	change	CHAYNJ
			z	is	IZ

CAPS = primary stress; SMALL CAPS = secondary stress; lowercase = unstressed

---

absolute zero (AB suh LOOT ZIR oh) the temperature at which an object's energy is minimal (327)

acceleration (ak SEL uhr AY shuhn) the change in velocity divided by the time interval in which the change occurred (259)

accuracy (AK yur uh see) the extent to which a measurement approaches the true value (25)

acid (AS id) a substance that donates protons, H^+, to form hydronium ions, H_3O^+, when dissolved in water (199)

acid rain (AS id RAYN) any precipitation that has an unusually high concentration of sulfuric or nitric acids resulting from chemical pollution of the air (585)

air mass (ER MAS) a large body of air with uniform temperature and moisture content (613)

alkali metals (AL kuh LIE MET uhls) the highly reactive metallic elements located in Group 1 of the periodic table (87)

alkaline-earth metals (AL kuh LIN UHRTH MET uhls) the reactive metallic elements located in Group 2 of the periodic table (88)

alpha particle (AL fuh PAHRT i kuhl) a positively charged particle, emitted by some radioactive nuclei, that consists of two protons and two neutrons (221)

alternating current (AWL tuhr NAYT ing KUHR uhnt) an electric current that changes direction at regular intervals; also called AC (476)

amino acid (uh MEE noh AS id) any one of 20 different naturally occurring organic molecules that combine to form proteins (134)

amplitude (AM pluh TOOD) the greatest distance that particles in a medium move from their normal position when a wave passes by (366)

analog signal (AN uh LAWG SIG nuhl) a signal corresponding to a quantity whose values can change continuously (491)

anion (AN IE ahn) an ion with a negative charge (81)

antacid (ANT AS id) a weak base that neutralizes excess stomach acid (210)

asteroid (AS tuhr OYD) a small rocky object that orbits the sun, usually in a band between the orbits of Mars and Jupiter (545)

asthenosphere (as THEN uh SFIR) the zone of the mantle beneath the lithosphere that consists of slowly flowing solid rock (561)

atmospheric transmission (AT muhs FIR ik trans MISH uhn) the transmission of a signal using electromagnetic waves (498)

atom (AT uhm) the smallest particle that has the properties of an element (39)

atomic mass unit (amu) (uh TAHM ik MAS YOON it) a quantity equal to one-twelfth the mass of a carbon-12 atom (84)

atomic number (uh TAHM ik NUHM buhr) the number of protons in the nucleus of an atom (82)

average atomic mass (AV uhr ij uh TAHM ik MAS) the weighted average of the masses of all naturally occurring isotopes of an element (84)

Avogadro's constant (AH voh GAH drohz KAHN stuhnt) the number of particles in 1 mol; equals 6.022×10^{23}/mol (96)

background radiation (BAK grownd RAY dee AY shuhn) the nuclear radiation that arises naturally from cosmic rays and from radioactive isotopes in the soil and air (235)

balanced forces (BAL uhnst FOHR sez) the forces acting on an object that combine to produce a net force that is equal to zero (263)

barometric pressure (BAR uh ME trik PRESH uhr) the pressure due to the weight of the atmosphere; also called *air pressure* or *atmospheric pressure* (609)

base (BAYS) a substance that either contains hydroxide ions, OH⁻, or reacts with water to form hydroxide ions (201)

beta particle (BAYT uh PAHRT i kuhl) an electron emitted during the radioactive decay of a neutron in an unstable nucleus (221)

big bang theory (BIG BANG THEE uh ree) a scientific theory that states that the universe began 10 billion to 20 billion years ago in an enormous explosion (532)

biochemical compound (BIE oh KEM i kuhl KAHM pownd) any organic compound that has an important role in living things (134)

black hole (BLAK HOHL) an object so massive and dense that not even light can escape its gravity (541)

bleach (BLEECH) a basic solution that can either be used as a disinfectant or to remove colors and stains (209)

boiling point (BOYL ing POYNT) the temperature at which a liquid becomes a gas below the surface (54)

bond angle (BAHND AYN guhl) the angle formed by two bonds to the same atom (110)

bond length (BAHND LENGKTH) the average distance between the nuclei of two bonded atoms (110)

buoyancy (BOY uhn see) the force with which a more dense fluid pushes a less dense substance upward (57)

carbohydrate (CAHR boh HIE drayt) any organic compound that is made of carbon, hydrogen, and oxygen and that provides nutrients to the cells of living things (134)

Glossary

carrier (CAR ee uhr) a continuous wave that can be modulated to send a signal (500)

catalyst (CAT uh list) a substance that changes the rate of chemical reactions without being consumed (171)

cathode ray tube (CATH OHD RAY TOOB) a tube that uses an electron beam to create a display on a phosphorescent screen (502)

cation (CAT IE ahn) an ion with a positive charge (81)

cell (SEL) a device that is a source of electric current because of a potential difference, or voltage, between the terminals (438)

chemical bond (KEM i kuhl BAHND) the attractive force that holds atoms or ions together (109)

chemical change (KEM i kuhl CHAYNJ) a change that occurs when a substance changes composition by forming one or more new substances (58)

chemical energy (KEM i kuhl EN uhr jee) the energy stored within atoms and molecules that can be released when a substance reacts (151)

chemical equation (KEM i kuhl ee KWAY zhuhn) an equation that uses chemical formulas and symbols to show the reactants and products in a chemical reaction (161)

chemical formula (KEM i kuhl FOHR myoo luh) the chemical symbols and numbers indicating the atoms contained in the basic unit of a substance (41)

chemical property (KEM i kuhl PRAHP uhr tee) the way a substance reacts with others to form new substances with different properties (53)

chemical structure (KEM i kuhl STRUHK chuhr) the arrangement of bonded atoms or ions within a substance (110)

chemistry (KEM is tree) the study of matter and how it changes (38)

circuit breaker (SUHR kit BRAYK uhr) a device that protects a circuit from current overloads (452)

climate (KLIE muht) the general weather conditions over many years (617)

cluster (KLUHS tuhr) a group of galaxies bound by gravity (530)

code (KOHD) a set of rules used to interpret signals that convey information (489)

colloid (KAHL OYD) a mixture of very tiny particles of pure substances that are dispersed in another substance but do not settle out of the substance (187)

combustion reaction (kuhm BUHST shuhn ree AK shuhn) a reaction in which a compound and oxygen burn (155)

community (kuh MYOO nuh tee) all of the animals and plants living in one area in an ecosystem (631)

compound (KAHM pownd) a substance made of atoms of more than one element bound together (39)

compound machine (KAHM pownd muh SHEEN) a machine made of more than one simple machine (296)

computer (kum PYOOT uhr) an electronic device that can accept data and instructions, follow the instructions, and output the results (506)

concentration (KAHN suhn TRAY shuhn) the quantity of solute dissolved in a given quantity of solution (196)

condensation (KAHN duhn SAY shuhn) the change of a substance from a gas to a liquid (49)

conduction (kuhn DUK shuhn) the transfer of energy as heat between particles as they collide within a substance or between two objects in contact (332)

conductor (kuhn DUK tuhr) a material through which energy can be easily transferred as heat (334); a material that transfers charge easily (432)

constellation (KAHN stuh LAY shuhn) a group of stars appearing in a pattern as seen from Earth (535)

constructive interference (kuhn STRUHK tiv IN tuhr FIR uhns) any interference in which waves combine so that the resulting wave is bigger than the original waves (377)

convection (kuhn VEK shuhn) the transfer of energy by the movement of fluids with different temperatures (332)

convection current (kuhn VEK shuhn KUHR uhnt) the flow of a fluid due to heated expansion followed by cooling and contraction (333)

conversion factor (kuhn VUHR zhuhn FAK tuhr) a ratio equal to one that expresses the same quantity in two different ways (97)

cooling system (KOOL ing SIS tuhm) a device that transfers energy as heat out of an object to lower its temperature (343)

core (KOHR) the center of a planetary body, such as Earth (559)

Coriolis effect (KOHR ee OH lis e FEKT) the change in the direction of an object's path due to Earth's rotation (611)

covalent bond (KOH VAY luhnt BAHND) a bond formed when atoms share one or more pairs of electrons (119)

crest (KREST) the highest point of a transverse wave (366)

critical mass (KRIT i kuhl MAS) the minimum mass of a fissionable isotope in which a nuclear chain reaction can occur (233)

critical thinking (KRIT i kuhl THINGK ing) the application of logic and reason to observations and conclusions (12)

crust (KRUHST) the outermost and thinnest layer of Earth (558)

current (KUHR uhnt) the rate that electric charges move through a conductor (439)

D

decomposition reaction (DEE kahm puh ZISH uhn ree AK shuhn) a reaction in which one compound breaks into at least two products (155)

density (DEN suh tee) the mass per unit volume of a substance (55)

deposition (DE puh ZISH uhn) the process in which sediment is laid down (586)

destructive interference (di STRUK tiv IN tuhr FIR uhns) any interference in which waves combine so that the resulting wave is smaller than the largest of the original waves (377)

detergent (dee TUHR jent) a nonsoap water-soluble cleaner that can emulsify dirt and oil (208)

dew point (DOO POYNT) the temperature at which water vapor molecules start to form liquid water (608)

diffraction (di FRAK shuhn) the bending of a wave as it passes an edge or an opening (375)

digital signal (DIJ i tuhl SIG nuhl) a signal that can be represented as a sequence of discrete values (491)

disinfectant (DIS in FEK tuhnt) a substance that kills harmful bacteria or viruses (209)

dispersion (di SPUHR zhuhn) an effect in which white light separates into component colors (417)

domain (doh MAYN) a microscopic magnetic region composed of a group of atoms whose magnetic fields are aligned in a common direction (471)

Doppler effect (DAHP luhr e FEKT) an observed change in the frequency of a wave when the source or observer is moving (373)

double-displacement reaction (DUHB uhl dis PLAYS muhnt ree AK shuhn) a reaction in which a gas, a solid precipitate, or a molecular compound is formed from the apparent exchange of ions between two compounds (158)

E

eclipse (i KLIPS) an event that occurs when one object passes into the shadow of another object (549)

ecosystem (EK oh SIS tuhm) all of the living and nonliving elements in a particular place (630)

efficiency (e FISH uhn see) a quantity, usually expressed as a percentage, that measures the ratio of useful work output to work input (312)

electric charge (ee LEK trik chahrj) an electrical property of matter that creates a force between objects (430)

electric circuit (ee LEK trik SUHR kit) an electrical device connected so that it provides one or more complete paths for the movement of charges (446)

electric field (ee LEK trik FEELD) the region around a charged object in which other charged objects experience an electric force (435)

electric force (ee LEK trik FOHRS) the force of attraction or repulsion between objects due to charge (434)

electric motor (ee LEK trik MOHT uhr) a device that converts electrical energy to mechanical energy (472)

electrical energy (ee LEK tri kuhl EN uhr jee) the energy associated with electrical charges, whether moving or at rest (450)

electrical potential energy (ee LEK tri kuhl poh TEN shuhl EN uhr jee) the potential energy of a charged object due to its position in an electric field (437)

electrolysis (EE lek TRAHL i sis) the decomposition of a compound by an electric current (155)

electromagnet (ee LEK troh MAG nit) a strong magnet created when an iron core is inserted into the center of a current-carrying solenoid (470)

electromagnetic induction (ee LEK troh mag NET ik in DUHK shuhn) the production of a current in a circuit by a change in the strength, position, or orientation of an external magnetic field (474)

electromagnetic wave (ee LEK troh mag NET ik WAYV) a wave that is caused by a disturbance in electric and magnetic fields and that does not require a medium; also called a light wave (357)

electron (ee LEK trahn) a tiny negatively charged subatomic particle moving around outside the nucleus of an atom (72)

element (EL uh muhnt) a substance that cannot be broken down into simpler substances (39)

empirical formula (em PIR i kuhl FOHR myoo luh) the simplest chemical formula of a compound that tells the smallest whole-number ratio of atoms in the compound (126)

emulsion (ee MUHL shuhn) any mixture of immiscible liquids in which the liquids are spread throughout one another (188)

endothermic reaction (EN doh THUHR mik ree AK shuhn) a reaction in which energy is transferred to the reactants from the surroundings usually as heat (151)

energy (EN uhr jee) the ability to change or move matter (48)

energy level (EN uhr jee LEV uhl) any of the possible energies an electron may have in an atom (73)

enzyme (EN ziem) a protein that speeds up a specific biochemical reaction (171)

epicenter (EP i SEN tuhr) the point on Earth's surface directly above the focus of an earthquake (568)

equilibrium (EE kwi LIB ree uhm) the state in which a chemical reaction and its reverse occur at the same time and at the same rate (174)

erosion (ee ROH zhuhn) the process by which rock and/or the products of weathering are removed (586)

eutrophication (yoo TRAHF i KAY shuhn) an increase in the amount of nutrients, such as nitrates, in an environment (652)

evaporation (ee VAP uh RAY shuhn) the change of a substance from a liquid to a gas (49)

exothermic reaction (EK soh THUHR mik ree AK shuhn) a reaction that transfers energy from the reactants to the surroundings usually as heat (151)

F

fault (FAWLT) a crack in Earth created when rocks on either side of a break move (564)

fission (FISH uhn) the process by which a nucleus splits into two or more smaller fragments, releasing neutrons and energy (231)

focus (FOH kuhs) the area along a fault at which slippage first occurs, initiating an earthquake (568)

force (FOHRS) the cause of an acceleration, or change in an object's velocity (262)

fossil fuels (FAHS uhl FYOO uhlz) any fuels formed from the remains of ancient plant and animal life (639)

fossils (FAHS uhlz) the traces or remains of a plant or an animal found in sedimentary rock (578)

free fall (FREE FAWL) the motion of a body when only the force of gravity is acting on it (271)

frequency (FREE kwuhn see) the number of vibrations that occur in a 1 s time interval (367)

friction (FRIK shuhn) the force between two objects in contact that opposes the motion of either object (265)

front (FRUHNT) the boundary between air masses of different densities (613)

fuse (FYOOZ) an electrical device containing a metal strip that melts when current in the circuit becomes too great (452)

fusion (FYOO zhuhn) the process in which light nuclei combine at extremely high temperatures, forming heavier nuclei and releasing energy (234)

G

galaxy (GAL uhk see) a collection of millions or billions of stars bound together by gravity (527)

galvanometer (GAL vuh NAH muht uhr) an instrument that measures the amount of current in a circuit (471)

gamma ray (GAM uh RAY) the high-energy electromagnetic radiation emitted by a nucleus during radioactive decay (222)

generator (JEN uhr AYT uhr) a device that uses electromagnetic induction to convert mechanical energy to electrical energy (476)

geothermal energy (JEE oh THUHR muhl EN uhr jee) the energy drawn from heated water within Earth's crust (642)

global warming (GLOH buhl WAHRM ing) an increase in Earth's temperature due to an increase in greenhouse gases (650)

gravity (GRAV i tee) the attraction between two particles of matter due to their mass (266)

greenhouse effect (GREEN HOWS e FEKT) the process by which the atmosphere traps some of the energy from the sun in the troposphere (604)

group (GROOP) a vertical column of elements in the periodic table; also called a family (80)

H

half-life (HAF LIEF) the time required for half a sample of radioactive nuclei to decay (225)

halogens (HAL oh juhnz) the highly reactive elements located in Group 17 of the periodic table (92)

hardware (HAHRD WER) the equipment that makes up a computer system (510)

heat (HEET) the transfer of energy from the particles of one object to those of another object due to a temperature difference (330)

heating system (HEET ing SIS tuhm) a device that transfers energy as heat to a substance to raise the temperature of the substance (340)

humidity (hyoo MID uh tee) the quantity of water vapor in the atmosphere (607)

hydroelectric power (HIE DROH ee LEK trik POW uhr) the energy of moving water converted to electricity (636)

I

igneous rock (IG nee uhs RAHK) any rock formed from cooled and hardened magma or lava (577)

immiscible (im MIS uh buhl) describes two or more liquids that do not mix into each other (42)

indicator (IN di KAYT uhr) a compound that can reversibly change color in a solution, depending on the concentration of H_3O^+ ions (199)

inertia (in UHR shuh) the tendency of an object to remain at rest or in motion with a constant velocity (269)

infrasound (IN fruh sownd) any sound consisting of waves with frequencies lower than 20 Hz (393)

insulator (IN suh LAYT uhr) a material that is a poor energy conductor (335); a material that does not transfer charge easily (432)

intensity (in TEN suh tee) the rate at which light or any other form of energy flows through a given area of space (402)

interference (IN tuhr FIR uhns) the combination of two or more waves that exist in the same place at the same time (376)

Internet (IN tuhr NET) a large computer network that connects many local and smaller networks (513)

interstellar matter (IN tuhr STEL uhr MA tuhr) the gas and dust between the stars in a galaxy (528)

ion (IE ahn) an atom or group of atoms that has lost or gained one or more electrons and therefore has a net electric charge (81)

ionic bond (ie AHN ik BAHND) a bond formed by the attraction between oppositely charged ions (116)

ionization (IE uhn i ZAY shuhn) the process of adding electrons to or removing electrons from an atom or group of atoms (81)

isobar (IE soh BAHR) a line drawn on a weather map connecting points of equal barometric or atmospheric pressure (617)

isotopes (IE suh TOHPS) any atoms having the same number of protons but different numbers of neutrons (83)

K

kinetic energy (ki NET ik EN uhr jee) the energy of a moving object due to its motion (300)

L

length (LENGTH) the straight-line distance between any two points (18)

lens (LENZ) a transparent object that refracts light rays, causing them to converge or diverge to create an image (415)

light ray (LIET RAY) a model of light that represents light traveling through space in an imaginary straight line (406)

light-year (LIET YIR) a unit of distance equal to the distance light travels in one year; 1 ly = 9.5×10^{15} m (527)

lithosphere (LITH oh SFIR) the thin outer shell of Earth, consisting of the crust and the rigid upper mantle (560)

longitudinal wave (LAHN juh TOOD uhn uhl WAYV) a wave that causes the particles of the medium to vibrate parallel to the direction the wave travels (363)

M

magma (MAG muh) the molten rock within Earth (562)

magnetic field (mag NET ik FEELD) a region where a magnetic force can be detected (465)

magnetic pole (mag NET ik POHL) an area of a magnet where the magnetic force appears to be the strongest (464)

magnification (MAG nuh fi KAY shuhn) a change in the size of an image compared with the size of an object (415)

mantle (MAN tuhl) the layer of rock between Earth's crust and its core (558)

mass (MAS) a measure of the quantity of matter in an object (18)

mass number (MAS NUHM buhr) the total number of protons and neutrons in the nucleus of an atom (82)

matter (MAT uhr) anything that has mass and occupies space (38)

mechanical advantage (muh KAN i kuhl ad VANT ij) a quantity that measures how much a machine multiplies force or distance (289)

mechanical energy (muh KAN i kuhl EN uhr jee) the sum of the kinetic and potential energy of large-scale objects in a system (302)

mechanical wave (muh KAN i kuhl WAYV) a wave that requires a medium through which to travel (357)

medium (MEE dee uhm) the matter through which a wave travels (357)

melting point (MELT ing POYNT) the temperature at which a solid becomes a liquid (54)

mesosphere (MES oh SFIR) the coldest layer of the atmosphere; located above the stratosphere (601)

metallic bond (muh TAL ik BAHND) a bond formed by the attraction between positively charged metal ions and the electrons around them (118)

metals (MET uhls) the elements that are good conductors of heat and electricity (87)

metamorphic rock (MET uh MOHR fik RAHK) any rock formed from other rocks as a result of heat, pressure, or chemical processes (579)

mineral (MIN uhr uhl) a natural, inorganic solid with a definite chemical composition and a characteristic internal structure (576)

miscible (MIS uh buhl) describes two or more liquids that are able to dissolve into each other in various proportions (42)

mixture (MIKS chuhr) a combination of more than one pure substance (41)

modulate (MAHJ uh LAYT) the process of changing a wave's amplitude or frequency in order to send a signal (500)

molar mass (MOH luhr MAS) the mass in grams of 1 mol of a substance (96)

molarity (moh LER i tee) a concentration unit of a solution that expresses moles of solute dissolved per liter of solution (198)

mole (MOHL) the SI base unit that describes the amount of a substance (96)

mole ratio (MOHL RAY shee OH) the smallest relative number of moles of the substances involved in a reaction (168)

molecular formula (moh LEK yoo luhr FOHR myoo luh) a chemical formula that reports the actual numbers of atoms in one molecule of a compound (128)

molecule (MAHL i KYOOL) the smallest unit of a substance that exhibits all of the properties characteristic of that substance (40)

momentum (moh MEN tuhm) a quantity defined as the product of an object's mass and velocity (256)

N

nebular model (NEB yuh luhr MAHD uhl) a model that describes the sun and the solar system forming together out of a cloud of gas and dust (548)

neutralization reaction (NOO truhl i ZAY shuhn ree AK shuhn) a reaction in which hydronium ions from an acid and hydroxide ions from a base react to produce water molecules (204)

neutron (NOO trahn) a neutral subatomic particle in the nucleus of an atom (72)

neutron emission (NOO trahn ee MISH uhn) the release of a high-energy neutron by some neutron-rich nuclei during radioactive decay (222)

neutron star (NOO trahn STAHR) a dead star with the density of atomic nuclei (541)

noble gases (NOH buhl GAS iz) the unreactive gaseous elements located in Group 18 of the periodic table (93)

nonmetals (NAHN MET uhlz) the elements that are usually poor conductors of heat and electricity (87)

nonrenewable resources (NAHN ri NOO uh buhl REE sohrs uz) any resources that are used faster than they can be replaced (640)

nuclear chain reaction (NOO klee uhr CHAYN ree AK shuhn) a series of fission processes in which the neutrons emitted by a dividing nucleus cause the division of other nuclei (232)

nuclear radiation (NOO klee uhr RAY dee AY shuhn) the charged particles or energy emitted by an unstable nucleus (220)

nucleus (NOO klee uhs) the center of an atom; made up of protons and neutrons (72)

O

operating system (AHP uhr AYT ing SIS tuhm) the software that controls a computer's activities (510)

optical fiber (AHP ti kuhl FIE buhr) a hair-thin, transparent strand of glass or plastic that transmits signals using pulses of light (493)

orbital (OHR bit uhl) a region in an atom where there is a high probability of finding electrons (75)

organic compound (ohr GAN ik KAHM pownd) any covalently bonded compound that contains carbon (129)

ozone (OH ZOHN) the form of atmospheric oxygen that has three atoms per molecule (600)

P

P waves (PEE WAYVZ) primary waves; the longitudinal waves generated by an earthquake (568)

parallel (PAR uh LEL) describes components in a circuit that are connected across common points, providing two or more separate conducting paths (449)

period (PIR ee uhd) a horizontal row of elements in the periodic table (80); the time required for one full wavelength to pass a certain point (367)

periodic law (PIR ee AHD ik LAW) the properties of elements tend to repeat in a regular pattern when elements are arranged in order of increasing atomic number (77)

pH (pee AYCH) a measure of the hydronium ion concentration in a solution (202)

phases (FAYZ iz) the different apparent shapes of the moon or a planet due to the relative positions of the sun, Earth, and the moon or planet (549)

photon (FOH tahn) a particle of light (400)

physical change (FIZ i kuhl CHAYNJ) a change that occurs in the physical form or properties of a substance that occurs without a change in composition (59)

physical property (FIZ i kuhl PRAHP uhr tee) a characteristic of a substance that can be observed or measured without changing the composition of the substance (54)

physical transmission (FIZ i kuhl trans MISH uhn) the transmission of a signal using wires, cables, or optical fibers (498)

pitch (PICH) the perceived highness or lowness of a sound, depending on the frequency of sound waves (392)

pixel (PIKS uhl) the smallest element of a display image (503)

planet (PLAN it) any of the nine primary bodies orbiting the sun; a similar body orbiting another star (542)

plate tectonics (PLAYT tek TAHN iks) the theory that Earth's surface is made up of large moving plates (560)

pollution (puh LOO shuhn) the contamination of the air, water, or soil (647)

polyatomic ion (PAHL ee uh TAHM ik IE ahn) an ion made of two or more atoms that are covalently bonded and that act like a single ion (120)

polymer (PAHL i MUHR) a large organic molecule made of many smaller bonded units (133)

potential difference (poh TEN shuhl DIF uhr uhns) the change in the electrical potential energy per unit charge (438)

potential energy (poh TEN shuhl EN uhr jee) the stored energy resulting from the relative positions of objects in a system (298)

power (POW uhr) a quantity that measures the rate at which work is done (286)

precipitation (pree SIP uh TAY shuhn) any form of water that falls back to Earth's surface from clouds; includes rain, snow, sleet, and hail (607)

precision (pree SIZH uhn) the degree of exactness of a measurement (24)

pressure (PRESH uhr) the force exerted per unit area of a surface (47)

prism (PRIZ uhm) a transparent block with a triangular cross section (417)

product (PRAHD uhkt) a substance that is the result of a chemical change (149)

protein (PROH teen) a biological polymer made of bonded amino acids (134)

proton (PROH tahn) a positively charged subatomic particle in the nucleus of an atom (72)

pure substance (PYUR SUB stuhns) any matter that has a fixed composition and definite properties (41)

R

radar (RAY DAHR) a system that uses reflected radio waves to determine the distance to and location of objects (404)

radiation (RAY dee AY shuhn) the transfer of energy by electromagnetic waves (333)

radicals (RAD ik uhls) the fragments of molecules that have at least one electron available for bonding (159)

radioactive tracer (RAY dee oh AK tiv TRAYS uhr) a radioactive material added to a substance so that the substance's location can later be detected (238)

radioactivity (RAY dee oh ak TIV uh tee) a process by which an unstable nucleus emits one or more particles or energy (220)

random-access memory (RAN duhm AK SES MEM uh ree) a storage device that allows any stored data to be read in the same access time (509)

reactant (REE AK tuhnt) a substance that undergoes a chemical change (149)

reactivity (REE ak TIV i tee) the ability of a substance to combine chemically with another substance (54)

read-only memory (REED OHN lee MEM uh ree) a memory device containing data that cannot be changed (510)

real image (REEL IM ij) an image of an object formed by many light rays coming together in a specific location (409)

recycling (ree SIE kuhl ing) the process of breaking down discarded material for re-use in other products (656)

red giant (RED JIE uhnt) a large, reddish star late in its life cycle that fuses helium into carbon or oxygen (540)

red shift (RED SHIFT) a shift toward the red end of the spectrum in the observed spectral lines of stars or galaxies (531)

reduction/oxidation (redox) reaction (ri DUK shuhn AHKS i DAY shuhn (REE DAHKS) ree AK shuhn) a reaction that occurs when electrons are transferred from one reactant to another (159)

reflection (ri FLEK shuhn) the bouncing back of a wave as it meets a surface or boundary (374)

refraction (ri FRAK shuhn) the bending of waves as they pass from one medium to another (376)

refrigerant (ri FRIJ uhr uhnt) a substance used in cooling systems that transfers large amounts of energy as it changes state (344)

relative humidity (REL uh tiv hyoo MID uh tee) the ratio of the quantity of water vapor in the air to the maximum quantity of water vapor that can be present at that temperature (607)

renewable resources (ri NOO uh buhl REE sohrs uhz) any resources that can be continually replaced (641)

resistance (ri ZIS tuhns) the ratio of the voltage across a conductor to the current it carries (441)

resonance (REZ uh nuhns) an effect in which the vibration of one object causes the vibration of another object at a natural frequency (395)

Richter scale (RIK tuhr SKAYL) a scale that expresses the relative magnitude of an earthquake (571)

S

S waves (ES WAYVZ) secondary waves; the transverse waves generated by an earthquake (569)

salt (SAWLT) an ionic compound composed of cations bonded to anions, other than oxide or hydroxide anions (205)

saturated solution (SACH uh RAYT id suh LOO shuhn) a solution that cannot dissolve any more solute at the given conditions (196)

schematic diagram (skee MAT ik DIE uh GRAM) a graphic representation of an electric circuit or apparatus, with standard symbols for the electrical devices (447)

science (SIE uhns) a system of knowledge based on facts or principles (6)

scientific law (SIE uhn TIF ik LAW) a summary of an observed natural event (8)

scientific method (SIE uhn TIF ik METH uhd) a series of logical steps to follow in order to solve problems (13)

scientific notation (SIE uhn TIF ik noh TAY shuhn) a value written as a simple number multiplied by a power of 10 (22)

scientific theory (SIE uhn TIF ik THEE uh ree) a tested, possible explanation of a natural event (8)

sedimentary rock (SED uh MEN tuh ree RAHK) any rock formed from compressed or cemented deposits of sediment (578)

seismology (siez MAHL uh gee) the study of earthquakes and related phenomena (569)

semiconductors (SEM i kuhn DUHK tuhrz) the elements that are intermediate conductors of heat and electricity (87)

series (SIR eez) describes a circuit or portion of a circuit that provides a single conducting path (449)

signal (SIG nuhl) a sign that represents information, such as a command, a direction, or a warning (488)

significant figures (sig NIF uh kuhnt FIG yurz) the digits in a measurement that are known with certainty (24)

simple machine (SIM puhl muh SHEEN) any one of the six basic types of machines of which all other machines are composed (291)

single-displacement reaction (SING guhl dis PLAYS muhnt ree AK shuhn) a reaction in which atoms of one element take the place of atoms of another element in a compound (157)

soap (SOHP) a cleaner that dissolves in both water and oil (207)

software (SAWFT WER) the instructions, data, and programming that enables a computer system to work (510)

solar system (SOH luhr SIS tuhm) the sun and all the objects that orbit around it (543)

solenoid (SOH luh noyd) a long, wound coil of insulated wire (469)

solubility (SAHL yoo BIL uh tee) the greatest quantity of a solute that will dissolve in a given quantity of solvent to produce a saturated solution (197)

solute (SAHL YOOT) the substance that dissolves in a solution (190)

solution (suh LOO shuhn) a homogeneous mixture of two or more substances uniformly spread throughout a single phase (190)

solvent (SAHL vuhnt) the substance that dissolves the solute to make a solution (190)

sonar (SOH NAHR) a system that uses reflected sound waves to determine the distance to, and location of, objects (397)

specific heat (spuh SIF ik HEET) the amount of energy transferred as heat that will raise the temperature of 1 kg of a substance by 1 K (336)

speed (SPEED) the distance traveled divided by the time interval during which the motion occurred (252)

standing wave (STAN ding WAYV) a wave form caused by interference that appears not to move along the medium and that shows some regions of no vibration (nodes) and other regions of maximum vibration (antinodes) (379)

star (STAHR) a huge ball of hot gas that emits light (527)

stratosphere (STRAT uh SFIR) the layer of the atmosphere that extends upward from the troposphere to an altitude of 50 km; contains the ozone layer (600)

strong nuclear force (STRAWNG NOO klee uhr FOHRS) the force that binds protons and neutrons together in a nucleus (230)

subduction (suhb DUHK shuhn) the process in which a tectonic plate dives beneath another tectonic plate and into the asthenosphere (562)

sublimation (SUHB luh MAY shuhn) the change of a substance from a solid to a gas (50)

substrate (SUHB STRAYT) the specific substance affected by an enzyme (172)

succession (suhk SESH uhn) the gradual repopulating of a community by different species over a period of time (634)

supergiant (SOO puhr JI uhnt) an extremely large star that creates elements as heavy as iron (540)

supernova (SOO puhr NOH vuh) a powerful explosion that occurs when a massive star dies (540)

supersaturated solution (SOO puhr SACH uh RAYT uhd suh LOO shuhn) a solution holding more dissolved solute than is specified by its solubility at a given temperature (197)

surface waves (SUHR fis WAYVZ) the seismic waves that travel along Earth's surface (569)

suspension (suh SPEN shuhn) a mixture that looks uniform when stirred or shaken that separates into different layers when it is no longer agitated (186)

synthesis reaction (SIN thuh sis ree AK shuhn) a reaction of at least two substances that forms a new, more complex compound (154)

T

technology (tek NAHL uh gee) the application of science to meet human needs (7)

telecommunication (TEL i kuh MYOO ni KAY shuhn) a communication method using electromagnetic means (490)

Glossary

temperature (TEM puhr uh chuhr) a measure of the average kinetic energy of all the particles within an object (324)

temperature inversion (TEM puhr uh chuhr in VUHR zhuhn) the atmospheric condition in which warm air traps cooler air near Earth's surface (599)

terminal velocity (TUHR muh nuhl vuh LAHS uh tee) the maximum velocity reached by a falling object, occurring when resistance of the medium is equal to the force due to gravity (272)

thermometer (thuhr MAHM uht uhr) a device that measures temperature (325)

thermosphere (THURM oh SFIR) the atmospheric layer above the mesosphere (601)

topography (tuh PAHG ruh fee) the surface features of Earth (619)

total internal reflection (TOHT uhl in TUHR nuhl ri FLEK shuhn) the compete reflection of light at the boundary between two transparent mediums when the angle of incidence exceeds the critical angle (414)

transformer (trans FOHRM uhr) a device that can change one alternating-current voltage to a different alternating-current voltage (479)

transition metals (tran ZISH uhn MET uhls) the metallic elements located in Groups 3–12 of the periodic table (89)

transpiration (TRAN spuh RAY shuhn) the evaporation of water through pores in a plant's leaves (607)

transverse wave (TRANS VUHRS WAYV) a wave that causes the particles of the medium to vibrate perpendicularly to the direction the wave travels (363)

troposphere (TRO poh SFIR) the atmospheric layer closest to Earth's surface where nearly all weather occurs (599)

trough (TRAWF) the lowest point of a transverse wave (366)

U

ultrasound (UHL truh SOWND) any sound consisting of waves with frequencies higher than 20 000 Hz (393)

unbalanced forces (UHN BAL uhnst FOHR sez) the forces acting on an object that combine to produce a net nonzero force (263)

universe (YOON uh VUHRS) the sum of all matter and energy that exists, that ever has existed, and that ever will exist (526)

unsaturated solution (UHN SACH uh RAYT uhd suh LOO shuhn) a solution that is able to dissolve more solute (196)

V

valence electron (VAY luhns ee LEK trahn) an electron in the outermost energy level of an atom (76)

variable (VER ee uh buhl) anything that can change in an experiment (13)

velocity (vuh LAHS uh tee) a quantity describing both speed and direction (254)

vent (VENT) an opening through which molten rock flows onto Earth's surface (572)

virtual image (VUHR choo uhl IM ij) an image that forms at a point from which light rays appear to come but do not actually come (408)

viscosity (vis KAHS uh tee) the resistance of a fluid to flow (48)

volume (VAHL yoom) a measure of space, such as the capacity of a container (18)

W

water cycle (WAH tuhr SIE kuhl) the continuous movement of water from the atmosphere to Earth and back (606)

wave (WAYV) a disturbance that transmits energy through matter or space (356)

wave speed (WAYV SPEED) the speed at which a wave passes through a medium (369)

wavelength (WAYV LENGTH) the distance between any two successive identical parts of a wave (366)

weathering (WETH uhr ing) the change in the physical form or chemical composition of rock materials exposed at Earth's surface (578)

weight (WAYT) the force with which gravity pulls on a quantity of matter (18)

white dwarf (HWIET DWOHRF) a small, very dense star that remains after fusion in a red giant stops (540)

work (WUHRK) quantity of energy transferred by a force when it is applied to a body and causes that body to move in the direction of the force (284)

Art Credits

Page iii, Kristy Sprott; vi-vii, Kristy Sprott; ix(t), Kristy Sprott; ix(b), Uhl Studios Inc.; x, Stephen Durke/Washington-Artists' Represents; xiii, Uhl Studios Inc.; xiv, Uhl Studios Inc. Chapter 1: Page 6, Leslie Kell; 10, Kristy Sprott; 13, Leslie Kell; 18, Uhl Studios Inc.; 21, Leslie Kell; 28, Leslie Kell. Chapter 2: Page 40, Kristy Sprott; 42, Kristy Sprott; 47, Stephen Durke/Washington-Artists' Represents; 48, Kristy Sprott; 49, Leslie Kell; 51, Uhl Studios Inc.; 59, Kristy Sprott; 60, Kristy Sprott; 61, Uhl Studios Inc.; 63, Leslie Kell. Chapter 3: Page 71, Kristy Sprott; 72, Kristy Sprott; 73, Uhl Studios Inc.; 75, J/B Woolsey Associates; 76, Kristy Sprott; 78-83, Kristy Sprott; 86-89, Kristy Sprott; 91-93, Kristy Sprott; 96, Kristy Sprott; 99, Leslie Kell; 102, Kristy Sprott. Chapter 4: Page 109, Kristy Sprott; 111(t), Kristy Sprott; 111(b), J/B Woolsey Associates; 112, Kristy Sprott; 114, Kristy Sprott; 116-121, Kristy Sprott; 127(t), Leslie Kell; 127(br), Kristy Sprott; 129-133, Kristy Sprott; 135, Kristy Sprott; 136, Morgan-Cain & Associates. Chapter 5: Page 149-150, Kristy Sprott; 151, Uhl Studios Inc.; 152, Kristy Sprott; 154-158, Kristy Sprott; 161, Kristy Sprott; 163, Kristy Sprott; 167, Kristy Sprott; 169, Kristy Sprott; 173, Kristy Sprott; 179, Kristy Sprott. Chapter 6: Page 187, Kristy Sprott; 189, Kristy Sprott; 193-196, Kristy Sprott; 200, Kristy Sprott; 202, Kristy Sprott. Chapter 7: Page 220, Kristy Sprott; 221, Kristy Sprott; 224-225, Kristy Sprott; 231, Kristy Sprott; 232, Kristy Sprott; 237, Kristy Sprott; 239, Uhl Studios Inc. Chapter 8: Page 265, Uhl Studios Inc.; 267, Uhl Studios Inc.; 273, Uhl Studios Inc.; 274, Uhl Studios Inc.; 276, Uhl Studios Inc. Chapter 9: Page 292-294, Stephen Durke/Washington-Artists' Represents; 302, Stephen Durke/Washington-Artists' Represents; 311, Uhl Studios Inc. Chapter 10: Page 327, Uhl Studios Inc.; 329, Uhl Studios Inc.; 332, Stephen Durke/Washington-Artists' Represents; 339(br), Uhl Studios Inc.; 339(cr), Kristy Sprott; 341-342, Uhl Studios Inc.; 344-345, Uhl Studios Inc.; 348, Uhl Studios Inc. Chapter 11: Page 359, Uhl Studios Inc.; 361, Uhl Studios Inc.; 364, Uhl Studios Inc.; 365, Mark Schroeder; 367, Uhl Studios Inc.; 372, Uhl Studios Inc.; 374, Mark Schroeder; 377, Uhl Studios Inc. Chapter 12: Page 390, Uhl Studios Inc.; 393, Leslie Kell; 396, Keith Kasnot; 400, Uhl Studios Inc.; 401, Leslie Kell; 402, Boston Graphics; 412, Uhl Studios Inc.; 416(tl), Morgan-Cain & Associates; 416(bl), Keith Kasnot; 422, Uhl Studios Inc.; 423, Uhl Studios Inc. Chapter 13: Page 432, Uhl Studios Inc.; 433 (tr) (tl) (b), Kristy Sprott; 433, Uhl Studios Inc.; 434-437, Kristy Sprott; 441(t), Stephen Durke/Washington-Artists' Represents; 441(b) Boston Graphics; 444, Stephen Durke/Washington-Artists' Represents. Chapter 14: Page 462, Uhl Studios Inc.; 465, Uhl Studios Inc.; 466, Stephen Durke/Washington-Artists' Represents; 469(tr), Mark Persyn; 469(b), Boston Graphics; 470, Uhl Studios Inc.; 471, Stephen Durke/Washington-Artists' Represents; 472, Uhl Studios Inc.; 473-474, Stephen Durke/Washington-Artists' Represents; 476 (tr), Kristy Sprott; 476 (b), Stephen Durke/Washington-Artists' Represents; 477-478, Kristy Sprott; 479, Stephen Durke/Washington-Artists' Represents; 482, Stephen Durke/ Washington-Artists' Represents; 484, Uhl Studios Inc. Chapter 15: Page 492, Uhl Studios Inc.; 494, Uhl Studios Inc.; 496-497, Uhl Studios Inc.; 499, Uhl Studios Inc.; 500, Uhl Studios Inc.; 502, Uhl Studios Inc.; 503, Uhl Studios Inc.; 507, Uhl Studios Inc.; 512, Leslie Kell; 515, Uhl Studios Inc.; 516, Uhl Studios Inc.; 519, Uhl Studios Inc. Chapter 16: Page 527, Uhl Studios Inc.; 529, Uhl Studios Inc.; 533, Uhl Studios Inc.; 538, Tony Randazzo/American Artist's Rep., Inc.; 540, Uhl Studios Inc.; 542, Uhl Studios Inc.; 549-550, Uhl Studios Inc. Chapter 17: Page 558-560, Ortelius Design; 561-565, Uhl Studios Inc.; 568-570, Uhl Studios Inc.; 573, Uhl Studios Inc.; 588, Uhl Studios Inc.; 590, Uhl Studios Inc.; 593, Doug Walston. Chapter 18:

Page 600, Kristy Sprott; 601, Uhl Studios Inc.; 602, Uhl Studios Inc.; 604, Uhl Studios Inc.; 606, Uhl Studios Inc.; 608, Uhl Studios Inc.; 610, Stephen Durke/Washington-Artists' Represents; 611, Uhl Studios Inc.; 613, Craig Attebery/Jeff Lavaty Artist Agent; 614, Craig Attebery/Jeff Lavaty Artist Agent; 616, Uhl Studios Inc.; 618-619, Uhl Studios Inc.; 622, Leslie Kell. Chapter 19: Page 630, Robert Hynes; 631, Robert Hynes; 635, Ortelius Design; 638, Leslie Kell; 639, Robert Hynes; 640,(tl) Kristy Sprott; 640(bl), Leslie Kell; 640(br), Leslie Kell; 641, Stephen Durke/Washington-Artists' Represents; 643-644, Uhl Studios Inc.; 649, Uhl Studios Inc.; 649(l), Leslie Kell; 649(r), Leslie Kell; 655, Uhl Studios Inc.; 661, Uhl Studios Inc.; Page 680, Leslie Kell; 681, Thomas Gagliano; 686-687, Kristy Sprott; 688-690, MapQuest.com, Inc.

Photo Credits

Images by Sam Dudgeon/HRW Photo: vi(cl); 1(br); 31; 32(cr); 40(tc); 42(bl); 45(br); 60(tl); 95(all); 96(bc); 97(all); 98(all); 108(br); 109(tl,tr); 113; 117; 118(all); 132(t); 133; 162; 173(bl,cr); 269(tr); 287; 292(cr); 311; 324(bc); 325(br,tc); 334; 335(br,tc); 349; 394(c); 411(tr); 446; 447(all); 448(cl); 449(all); 458; 459(all); 485; 486-487(inset); 565; 579(bc); 580(tc); 662-663

Unless otherwise noted all other photographs by Peter Van Steen/HRW

Page iii(br), David Malin/Anglo-Australian Observatory; v(br), Visuals Unlimited/Glen M. Oliver; vi(bl), Michael Keller/The Stock Market; viii(tl), Sergio Purtell/Foca/HRW; x(bl), Courtesy Martha McCaslin/US Army; xi, Rich Iwasaki/Allstock/PNI; xiii(cr), Celestial Image Picture Co./Science Photo Library/Photo Researchers, Inc.; xiv(cl), Richard Thom/Visuals Unlimited; xiv(bl), Mark Richards/PhotoEdit; xiv(bc), Myrleen Ferguson/ PhotoEdit; xiv(br), Peter Dean/Grant Heilman Photography; xvii(br), Nicholas Pinturas/Tony Stone Images; xviii(tl), Andy Christiansen/HRW; 2(all), Roger Ressmeyer/Corbis; 2-3(inset), Corbis-Bettmann; 4(bl), Hulton Getty/Liaison Agency; 4(br), Phil Degginger/ Color-Pic, Inc.; 5, ©2001 PhotoDisc, Inc.; 6, AIP Emilio Segrè Visual Archives; 7(br), Corbis/Bettmann; 7(bl), Sheila Terry/SPL/Photo Researchers, Inc.; 7(bc), SuperStock; 7(tr), Leonard Lessin/Peter Arnold,Inc.; 10(tl), Kristian Hilsen/Tony Stone Images; 10(c, bc), BMW of North America, Inc.; 11, Chris Johns/Tony Stone Images; 14(b), SPL/ Photo Researchers, Inc.; 14(tl), 15(tl), Roger Ressmeyer/Corbis; 15(tr), Celestial Image Co./SPL/ Photo Researchers, Inc.; 18-19 (nickles), EyeWire, Inc, (tape measure,CD) ©2001 Photodisc, Inc.; (triple beam) Sam Dudgeon/HRW; (wristwatch), Michelle Bridwell/Frontera Fotos/HRW; 34-35(all), Alfred Pasieka/Photo Researchers, Inc.; 36(all), Theresa Batty/Dale Chihuly Studio; 36-37(c), Russell Johnson/ Dale Chihuly Studio; 38, James L. Amos/Peter Arnold, Inc.; 39(tr), IBM Corporation/Research Division/Almaden Research Center; 39(bl), Tom Van Sant/The Geosphere Project/The Stock Market; 39(br), ©2001 PhotoDisc, Inc.; 40(tr), Ken Eward/Science Source/ Photo Researchers, Inc.; 41, ©2001 PhotoDisc, Inc.; 42(br), Sergio Purtell/Foca/ HRW; 45(br), Bruce Byers/FPG; 46(tl,tc,tr), Sergio Purtell /Foca/HRW; 47, Andrew Syred/Tony Stone Images; 48, John Langford/HRW; 49(cl), Steve Joester/ FPG; 49(c), Michael Keller/The Stock Market; 49(tr), E. R. Degginger/ Color-Pic, Inc.; 50(b), Uniphoto Picture Agency; 50(tl), Charles D. Winters; 53, Robert Essel/The Stock Market; 55, Comstock; 57, Roine Magnusson/Tony Stone Images; 58, Corbis/Philadelphia Museum of Art; 59, Tom Pantages Photography; 61(tl), Charles D. Winters/ Photo Researchers, Inc.; 61(br), Charles D. Winters; 66(c,tc), Victoria Smith/ HRW; 67, Daniel Schaefer/ HRW; 68(all), Pete Saloutos/The Stock Market; 69, George Goodwin/The Picture Cube/Index Stock; 70(bl),

The Periodic Table of the Elements

Key:

6	Atomic number
C	Symbol
Carbon	Name
12.011	Average atomic mass

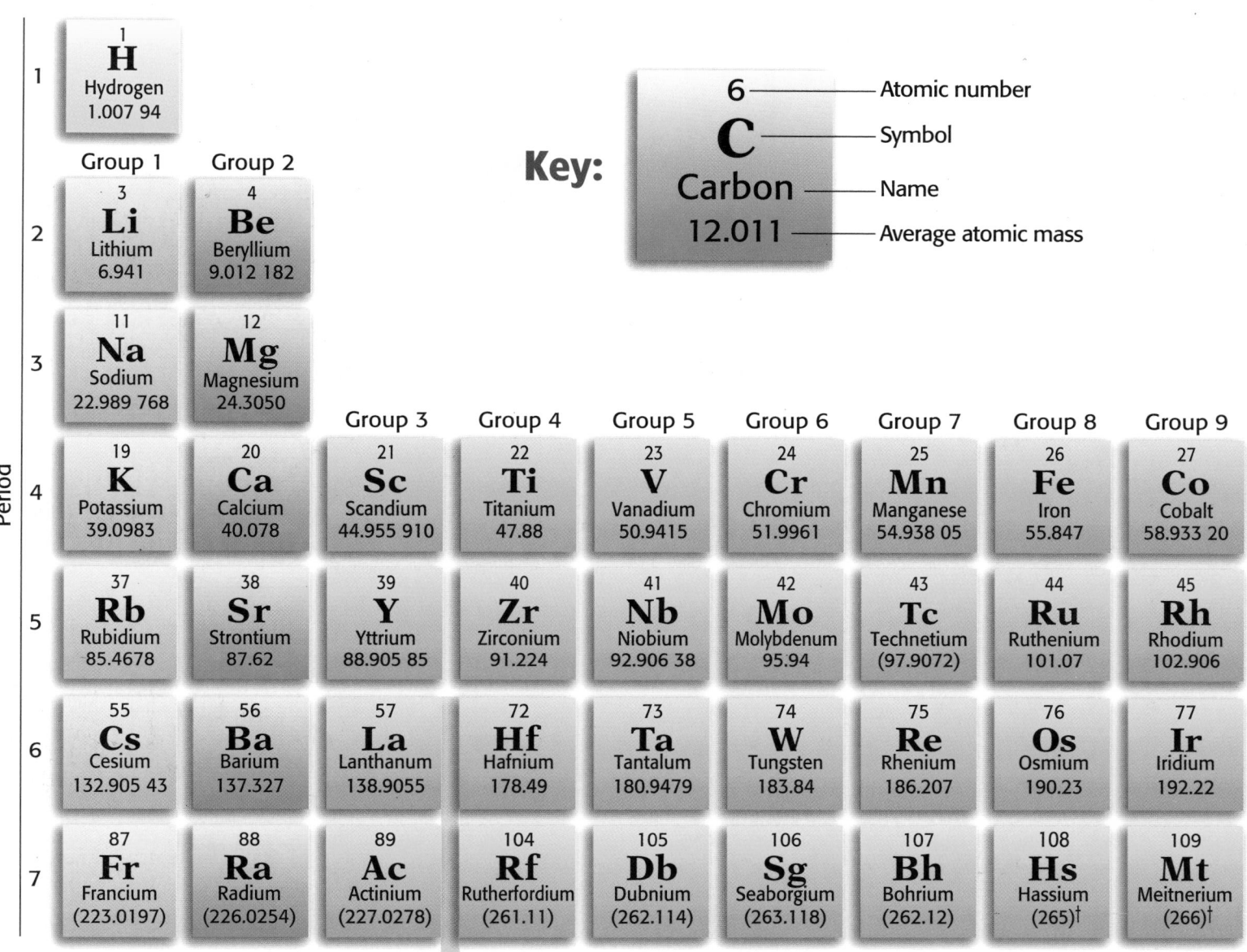

Period	Group 1	Group 2	Group 3	Group 4	Group 5	Group 6	Group 7	Group 8	Group 9
1	1 **H** Hydrogen 1.007 94								
2	3 **Li** Lithium 6.941	4 **Be** Beryllium 9.012 182							
3	11 **Na** Sodium 22.989 768	12 **Mg** Magnesium 24.3050							
4	19 **K** Potassium 39.0983	20 **Ca** Calcium 40.078	21 **Sc** Scandium 44.955 910	22 **Ti** Titanium 47.88	23 **V** Vanadium 50.9415	24 **Cr** Chromium 51.9961	25 **Mn** Manganese 54.938 05	26 **Fe** Iron 55.847	27 **Co** Cobalt 58.933 20
5	37 **Rb** Rubidium 85.4678	38 **Sr** Strontium 87.62	39 **Y** Yttrium 88.905 85	40 **Zr** Zirconium 91.224	41 **Nb** Niobium 92.906 38	42 **Mo** Molybdenum 95.94	43 **Tc** Technetium (97.9072)	44 **Ru** Ruthenium 101.07	45 **Rh** Rhodium 102.906
6	55 **Cs** Cesium 132.905 43	56 **Ba** Barium 137.327	57 **La** Lanthanum 138.9055	72 **Hf** Hafnium 178.49	73 **Ta** Tantalum 180.9479	74 **W** Tungsten 183.84	75 **Re** Rhenium 186.207	76 **Os** Osmium 190.23	77 **Ir** Iridium 192.22
7	87 **Fr** Francium (223.0197)	88 **Ra** Radium (226.0254)	89 **Ac** Actinium (227.0278)	104 **Rf** Rutherfordium (261.11)	105 **Db** Dubnium (262.114)	106 **Sg** Seaborgium (263.118)	107 **Bh** Bohrium (262.12)	108 **Hs** Hassium (265)†	109 **Mt** Meitnerium (266)†

Estimated from currently available IUPAC data.

* The systematic names and symbols for elements greater than 109 will be used until the approval of trivial names by IUPAC.

58 **Ce** Cerium 140.115	59 **Pr** Praseodymium 140.908	60 **Nd** Neodymium 144.24	61 **Pm** Promethium (144.9127)	62 **Sm** Samarium 150.36
90 **Th** Thorium 232.0381	91 **Pa** Protactinium 231.035 88	92 **U** Uranium 238.0289	93 **Np** Neptunium (237.0482)	94 **Pu** Plutonium 244.0642

For Malachi, Flynn,
and Seamus ~ C.W.

For Ian ~ C.T.

National Monuments of the USA © 2023 Quarto Publishing plc.
Text © 2023 Cameron Walker.
Illustrations © 2023 Chris Turnham.

First published in 2023 by Wide Eyed Editions, an imprint of The Quarto Group.
100 Cummings Center, Suite 265D, Beverly, MA 01915, USA.
T +1 978-282-9590 **www.Quarto.com**

A CIP record for this book is available from the Library of Congress.

ISBN 978-0-7112-6549-3

The illustrations were created digitally
Set in Pistacho and School Hand

Published by Debbie Foy
Designed by Myrto Dimitrakoulia
Edited by Hattie Grylls
Production by Dawn Cameron

Manufactured in Guangdong, China CC092023

9 8 7 6 5 4 3 2